Adobe® Acrobat® 9 PDF Bible

Ted Padova

WILEY

Wiley Publishing, Inc.

Adobe® Acrobat® 9 PDF Bible

Published by
Wiley Publishing, Inc.
10475 Crosspoint Boulevard
Indianapolis, IN 46256
www.wiley.com

Copyright © 2009 by Wiley Publishing, Inc., Indianapolis, Indiana

Published by Wiley Publishing, Inc., Indianapolis, Indiana

Published simultaneously in Canada

ISBN: 978-0-470-37919-6

Manufactured in the United States of America

10 9 8 7 6 5 4 3 2 1

For general information on our other products and services or to obtain technical support, please contact our Customer Care Department within the U.S. at (800) 762-2974, outside the U.S. at (317) 572-3993 or fax (317) 572-4002.

Library of Congress Control Number: 2008936639

About the Author

Ted Padova is the former chief executive officer and managing partner of The Image Source Digital Imaging and Photo Finishing Centers of Ventura and Thousand Oaks, California. He has been involved in digital imaging since founding a service bureau in 1990. He retired from his company in 2005 and now spends his time writing and speaking on Acrobat and PDF.

For more than 17 years, Ted has taught university and higher education classes in graphic design applications and digital prepress at the University of California, Santa Barbara, and the University of California at Los Angeles. He has been, and continues to be, a conference speaker nationally and internationally at PDF conferences.

Currently he lives in the Philippines where he serves as President/CEO of his company ApoVisions, Inc. — a company working with third world nations on developing electronic document workflows and PDF forms routing.

Ted has written more than 30 computer books and is one of the world's leading authors on Adobe Acrobat. He has written books on Adobe Acrobat, Adobe Photoshop, Adobe Photoshop Elements, Adobe Reader, Microsoft PowerPoint, and Adobe Illustrator. Recent books published by John Wiley and Sons include *Adobe Acrobat PDF Bible (versions 4, 5, 6, 7, and 8), Adobe Creative Suite Bible (versions CS, CS2, CS3, and CS4), Color Correction for Digital Photographers Only, Color Correction for Digital Photographers For Dummies, Microsoft PowerPoint 2007 For Dummies — Just the Steps, Creating Adobe Acrobat PDF Forms, Teach Yourself Visually Acrobat 5,* and *Adobe Acrobat 6.0 Complete Course*. He also co-authored *Adobe Illustrator Master Class — Illustrator Illuminated* and wrote *Adobe Reader Revealed* for Peachpit/Adobe Press.

For Arnie.

Credits

Associate Acquisitions Editor
Aaron Black

Project Editor
Jade L. Williams

Technical Editor
Lori DeFurio

Copy Editor
Scott Tullis

Editorial Manager
Robyn Siesky

Business Manager
Amy Knies

Sr. Marketing Manager
Sandy Smith

Vice President and Executive Group Publisher
Richard Swadley

Vice President and Executive Publisher
Bob Ipsen

Vice President and Publisher
Barry Pruett

Project Coordinator
Katherine Key

Graphics and Production Specialists
Stacie Brooks
Carrie A. Cesavice
Joyce Haughey
Ronald Terry
Tobin Wilkerson

Quality Control Technician
Melanie Hoffman

Proofreading and Indexing
Christopher M. Jones
Christine Spina Karpeles

Media Development Project Manager
Laura Moss

Media Development Assistant Project Manager
Jenny Swisher

Media Development Associate Producer
Kit Malone

Contents

Contents

Contents

Contents

Part III: Editing PDFs   357

Chapter 11: Exporting PDF Content 359

Chapter 12: Combining, Packaging, and Attaching PDFs 375

Contents

Contents

Contents

Contents

Contents

Part VI: Acrobat PDF Forms   1045

Chapter 33: Using Adobe LiveCycle Designer ES (Windows Only) 1047

Contents

Adobe Acrobat 8 PDF Bible is written for a cross-platform audience. Users of Microsoft Windows 2000 with Service Pack 2, Windows XP Professional or Home Edition, Windows Vista Professional and Home Editions, Tablet PC Edition, and Apple Macintosh computers running OS X v10.2.8, 10.3, 10.5 and later will find references to these operating systems.

About This Book

Most of the chapters in this book include screenshots from Acrobat running under Windows. The user interface is closely matched between Windows and the Macintosh; therefore, Macintosh users will find the same options in dialog boxes and menu commands as found in the screenshots taken on a Windows machine. Where significant differences do occur, you'll find additional screenshots taken on a Macintosh to distinguish the differences.

How to read this book

I have to admit this publication is not a page turner that leaves you grasping for more time to finish up a chapter before retiring at night. After all, it's a computer book and inasmuch as my editors at Wiley always strive to get me to add a little *drama* to the text, few people will pick up this *Bible* and read it cover to cover. This book should be thought of more as a reference where you can jump to an area and read over the contents to help simplify your work sessions in Acrobat Standard (available only on Windows in versions 9.0), Acrobat Professional version 9.0 (both Windows and Macintosh), and Acrobat Professional Extended 9.0 (Windows only).

Because Acrobat is such a behemoth program and can do so many things for almost any kind of work activity, most people won't use every feature the program provides. You may be interested in converting files to PDF and setting up reviews, or you may devote more attention to the area of prepress and printing, or perhaps it's accessibility or PDF forms that's part of your work. Therefore, you may ignore some chapters and just want to jump to the area that interests you most.

Regardless of where you are in Acrobat experience, you should be able to gain much insight and skill at using the new version of Acrobat by studying in detail those areas that interest you most. However, don't completely ignore chapters that cover features you think you won't use. You can find many related concepts falling under headings that are not exclusively related to the general topic for each chapter. For example, you may not be interested in creating accessible PDFs for screen readers. However, the Accessibility chapter also includes coverage of document structures and tagging, which will be important if you need to get the content of a PDF back out to an authoring application.

Because many chapters may include features that relate to the work you want to perform, studying over the most important features of interest to you and skimming over those chapters that appear to be less beneficial for you works best.

To begin, I recommend you look closely at the section in the Introduction where I give you my top 9 reasons for upgrading to Acrobat 9.0. No matter where you are in Acrobat skill, be certain to understand PDF navigation, — especially navigating the new PDF Portfolio documents that I cover in Chapter 12. Look closely at the Help documents and the Help features in Acrobat 9.0 that I cover in Chapter 3. Pay particular attention to Chapters 3, 12, 14, 17, 21, 23, 28, 29, and 32, and 35. If you've read the *Adobe Acrobat 8 PDF Bible*, these chapters contain much new material in this revision of the book. In many other chapters of the book, the text has been completely updated and revised. Some chapters have been rewritten to cover more depth in specific areas. For example, Chapter 29 on Using Acrobat.com is a complete overhaul of this chapter and covers all the great new features you have for holding online meetings and sharing files on Acrobat.com.

Throughout the book are sections called "Steps." If you find the contents of a given series of steps interesting, follow the steps to see whether you can replicate what is covered in that section. In this book, I've made an effort to expand steps greatly to provide you some tutorial assistance in understanding many concepts.

Icons

The use of icons throughout the book offers you an at-a-glance hint of what content is being addressed. You can jump to this text to get extra information, be warned of a potential problem, or amplify the concept being addressed in the text. In this book you'll find icons for the following:

CAUTION A Caution icon alerts you to a potential problem in using Acrobat, any tools or menus, or any supporting application that may be the origination of a document to be converted to PDF. Pay close attention to these caution messages to avoid potential problems.

CROSS-REF The Cross-Ref icon indicates a cross-reference to another area in the book or to the CD-ROM where more information can be found on a topic. It is almost impossible to walk you through Acrobat in a linear fashion because it has so many interrelated features. Covering all aspects of a single feature in a contiguous section of the book just doesn't work. Therefore some common features for a command, a tool, an action, or task may be spread out and discussed in different chapters. When the information is divided between different sections of the book, you'll find a Cross-Reference icon that cross-references the current passage to another part of the book covering related information.

NEW FEATURE An icon appears throughout the book where a new feature in Acrobat 9 has been added to the program. Pay special attention to these icons to learn more about what has been added to Acrobat 9, Adobe Reader 9, and Adobe LiveCycle Designer 8.2.

NOTE A Note icon signifies a message that may add more clarity to a text passage or help you deal with a feature more effectively.

ON the CD-ROM There has been so much added to Acrobat 9, I ran out of pages. Chapter 36 had to be placed on the book's CD-ROM. Where you see this icon referencing Chapter 36, look on the CD-ROM of the chapter.

PDF WORKFLOW Where workflow solutions are particularly applicable, you'll see an icon indicating that the text describes tasks or features that apply to workgroups and workflows. This icon will be an important signal for people in large businesses, government, and education where large workgroups with common tasks exist.

PREPRESS Much support is offered in version 9.0 for the prepress and printing market. If you're a design professional, service bureau, or print shop, take note of these messages for information related to prepress and printing.

TIP Tips are handy shortcuts. They help you to more quickly produce results or work through a series of steps to complete a task. Some tips provide you with information that may not be documented in the Help files accompanying Acrobat Professional.

The book's contents

This book is about Adobe Acrobat Standard (on Windows), Adobe Acrobat Professional on Windows and the Macintosh, and Adobe Acrobat Professional Extended (formerly Adobe Acrobat 3D) on Windows. All the content in the book applies to Acrobat Standard, unless you see a reference that a specific section applies only to Acrobat Professional or Professional Extended. Acrobat Professional features are clearly marked throughout the book so you know when Acrobat Standard doesn't support a particular feature. In many instances I refer to Acrobat Professional to include both Professional and Professional Extended. When a feature is unique to Acrobat Professional Extended, you'll find a specific mention of this difference.

Just about everything that you can do with Adobe Acrobat is contained in the chapters ahead. This book is *not* about Adobe LiveCycle Designer, Acrobat PDF Forms, collaboration, PDF creation, Acrobat JavaScript, or some other aspect of Acrobat exclusively. Some Acrobat features can take a book this size alone to cover in their entirety. What this book does for you is provide you some exposure and understanding for *all* that Acrobat can do. You'll find chapters on Adobe LiveCycle Designer and Acrobat JavaScript, several chapters on PDF creation, and chapters on collaboration. However, any one of these areas is not exclusive to the content of the book.

I've made an effort to address many different uses for all types of users. This book covers Acrobat features and how to work with Adobe Acrobat Professional, Adobe Acrobat Professional Extended, Adobe Acrobat Standard, Adobe Reader, and companion products. Individual industries such as office occupations, digital prepress, engineering, enterprise workflows, and multimedia and Web publishing are covered. Regardless of what you do, you should be able to find some solutions for your particular kind of work. Whether you are an accounting clerk, a real estate salesperson, a digital prepress technician, an engineer, a Web designer, or a hobbyist who likes to archive information from Web sites, there's a reference to your needs and Acrobat will provide a solution.

To simplify your journey through the new release, the book is broken up into six separate parts. A total of 36 chapters address Acrobat features and some individual purposes for using the software. The six parts include the following:

Part I: Welcome to Adobe Acrobat. To start off, I offer some discussion on the PDF format and its new revision. Acrobat 9.0 has many new features — approximately 350 new additions have been added to the product(s). I cover tools, menus, and palettes to help you understand many Acrobat 9.0 features. This section covers the distinctions between different viewer types, navigating through PDFs, and using the Find tool and the Search panel to search PDF files.

Part II: Converting Documents to PDF. There are many different ways to create a PDF document and all these methods are thoroughly covered in Part II. I begin by discussing the ease of creating simple PDF files that might be used by office workers and travel through to much more sophisticated PDF file creation for more demanding environments. One chapter is devoted entirely to Microsoft Office applications. In addition, I discuss how many application software developers are supporting PDFs through direct exports from their programs. I discuss the Adobe Creative Suite and how you can integrate PDF with the CS applications. The advantages and disadvantages of using all these methods are also discussed.

Part III: Editing PDFs. This section covers editing, modifying, and enhancing PDF files for many different purposes. Also covered are how to modify content and how to flow content between Acrobat and authoring programs. New features for combining files into single PDFs, creating the new Acrobat 9 PDF Portfolios, and redacting PDFs are added in this section. I also discuss scanning in Acrobat and converting scans to text with Optical Character Recognition (OCR) using many new impressive features added in Acrobat 9.0. You'll find much new material in Chapter 17 where I talk about scanning and OCR conversion. Document repurposing is covered in this section for users who want to modify files for different output mediums. Another chapter on all the enabling features available in Acrobat Standard and the Acrobat Professional products is included in this section.

Part IV: PDF Interactivity. Part IV covers interactivity with PDF documents for workgroups through the use of Review and Comment tools, shared reviews, adding interactive elements such as multimedia, and links and buttons. I address the layer features in Acrobat Professional and include a chapter devoted to making PDF documents accessible. Much new material has been added to Chapter 23 where I talk about multimedia and all the new support for Adobe Flash files.

Part V: PDF Publishing. This section covers distribution of PDF files in some of the more common means available today. I begin with security and authentication as your first step in document distribution and then move on to PDF workflows. I discuss creating PDFs for different kinds of distribution, such as presentations, and offer complete coverage of all the printing and prepress features. You'll find new material in Chapter 28 where I cover using Adobe Presenter in Acrobat Professional Extended with Microsoft PowerPoint. I also offer information about eBooks in Part V. Hosting your PDFs on the Web and sending them via e-mail are also covered in this section. A complete rewrite of Chapter 29 was needed for this version where I cover sharing files online with Acrobat.com and all the features you have available to you with this new Acrobat 9.0 addition. This section concludes with desktop color printing and commercial printing. Most of the new features for print production professionals are addressed in the last chapter in this section.

Part VI: Acrobat PDF and LiveCycle Designer Forms. This section covers PDF forms and handling form data. For Windows users, I cover using Adobe LiveCycle Designer 8.2 in detail. All new features for creating forms using the new Forms Edit mode are now also available to Acrobat Standard users. These forms are covered in this section. Distributing forms via Acrobat.com, collecting form data, and running form field recognition are included in this section.

Staying Connected

It seems like new products and new upgrades are distributed about every five minutes. If you purchase a software product, you can often find an updated revision soon after. Manufacturers rely more and more on Internet distribution and less on postal delivery. You should plan on making routine visits to Adobe's Web site and the Web sites of third-party product manufacturers. Any software vendor that has a Web site will offer a product revision for download or offer you details on acquiring the update.

Internet connection

With newer releases of computer software, an Internet connection is now essential. Programs, including Acrobat, prompt you routinely to check for updates over the Internet. To optimize your performance with Acrobat, you should run the software on a computer that has an Internet connection.

Registration

Regardless of whether you purchase Acrobat Professional Extended, Acrobat Professional, Acrobat Standard, or download the free Adobe Reader software, Adobe Systems has made it possible to register the product. You can register on the World Wide Web or mail a registration form to Adobe. If you develop PDF documents for distribution, Adobe likes to keep track of this information. You will find great advantage in being a registered user. First, update information will be sent to you, so you'll know when a product revision occurs. Second, information can be distributed to help you achieve the most out of using Acrobat. Who knows — some day you may be asked to provide samples of your work that might get you a hit from Adobe's Web site. By all means, complete the registration. It will be to your benefit.

Web sites to contact

Obviously, the first Web site to frequent is Adobe's Web site. When Acrobat and the Acrobat plug-ins are revised, downloads for updates will become available. You can also find tips, information, and problem solutions. Visit Adobe's Web site at www.adobe.com. Also make use of the Help ➪ Adobe Expert Support menu command in all Acrobat viewers. This command opens a Web page where you can order technical support for a nominal fee. For acquiring plug-ins for Acrobat visit the Adobe Store where you can find a comprehensive list of plug-ins and demonstration software that works with Acrobat. Visit the Adobe Store at: www.store.adobe.com/store.

Preface

A wealth of information is available on the Acrobat Users Community Web site at `www.acrobat users.com`. Here you can find tips, techniques, blogs hosted by some of the world's leading Acrobat professionals, and support for starting and maintaining a local Acrobat User Group. Be certain to routinely check Acrobat Users for up-to-date information and assistance. You can e-mail leading professionals who can help you solve problems.

Acrobat tips are available on many Web sites — all you need to do is search the Internet for Acrobat information. An excellent source for information as well as a comprehensive collection of third-party plug-ins is Planet PDF. You can visit them at `www.planetpdf.com`.

More Acrobat plug-ins can be found on the Plugin World Web site. Log on to `http://acrobat. pluginsworld.com/-`Web site for a vast list of Acrobat plug-ins and demo software.

Another source of information, articles, tips, Acrobat and PDF information can be found at `www. pdfZone.com`. Visit the pdfZone Web site for up-to-date articles and interviews with industry leaders.

If learning more about Acrobat is your interest, you can find regional conferences sponsored by Mogo Media. If you want to meet and discuss PDF issues with some of the world's experts, look for a conference in your area. You can find information at `http://www.mogo-media.com/`.

If JavaScript is what you want to learn, you can find a wealth of information on Thom Parker's Acrobat Users blog site. Log on to `www.acrobatusers.com/tech_corners/javascript_ corner/` to see Thom's JavaScript Corner that contains a number of blog posts on using Acrobat JavaScript. Thom also hosts the `www.pdfscripting.com` web site where you'll find hours and hours of video tutorials, easy copy/paste JavaScripts, a generous library of PDF example forms, automation tools, and the most comprehensive single source of information on using Acrobat JavaScript. When I'm in trouble with getting my code debugged, Thom is always the one person who bails me out and helps me correct my errors.

A new conference has popped up in the midwestern part of the USA in Minneapolis/St. Paul. To find out more about the Acrobat Central Conference log on to `www.pdfcentralconference.com`.

The Open Publish conference in Sydney, Australia, is an annual conference for design and creative professionals. This organization hosts many PDF-related seminars and workshops annually. Find out more at `www.openpublish.com.au`.

In Japan try out the PDF Conference held in Tokyo. Visit `www.pdfconf.gr.jp` for more information.

Whatever you may desire is usually found on some Web site. New sites are developed continually so be certain to make frequent searches.

Contacting Me

If, after reviewing this publication, you feel some important information was overlooked or you have any questions concerning Acrobat, you can contact me and let me know your views, opinions, hoorahs, or complaints, or provide information that might get included in the next revision. (If it's good enough, you might even get a credit line in the acknowledgments!) By all means, send me a note. Send your e-mail inquiries to ted@west.net.

Chances are that if you have a problem or question about Acrobat, you're not alone and many others might be interested in your question and a response to the question. Send your questions directly to my blog on Acrobat Users at www.acrobatusers.com/blogs/tedpadova. You can also visit the Acrobat Users Forum at: http://www.acrobatusers.com/forums/ aucbb/. In addition to my blog, some very talented friends who know so much more than I do also host blogs on Acrobat Users. Visit www.acrobatusers.com/blogs to see a complete list of the blog hosts.

If you happen to have some problems with Acrobat, keep in mind that I didn't engineer the program. Inquiries for technical support should be directed to the software developer(s) of any products you use. This is one more good reason to complete your registration form.

There you have it — a short description of what follows. Don't wait. Turn the page and learn how Acrobat can help you gain more productivity with its amazing new features.

Acknowledgments

I would like to acknowledge some of the people who have contributed in one way or another to make this edition possible. Barry Pruett, Publisher at Wiley, who filled in the role of Acquisitions Editor, was very helpful to me for getting this version completed. In addition, I find Barry continually interested in bringing new ideas to publishing that ultimately help the readers of Wiley publications. Barry's support and enthusiasm for exploring new concepts and ideas are what make some of the content you find on the book's CD-ROM a reality. A special thank you goes to my project editor, Jade Williams, who nicely coordinated the project and kept things moving in a timely manner; copy editor, Scott Tullis; and editorial manager, Robyn Siesky; as well as the rest of the Wiley crew who participated in the project.

Once again I'm so fortunate to have my favorite Technical Editor, Lori DeFurio back on this project. Lori is perhaps the single best advocate for Acrobat and PDF, promoter, and solutions provider to people worldwide than any other individual on the planet. With an incredibly demanding schedule that takes her to all corners of the earth, Lori finds time to review more than a thousand pages of text and can find things as small as a period out of place in a manuscript. As Adobe's premiere Acrobat and PDF authority, her technical expertise in reviewing this book was invaluable to me. Lori is always my first contact when I don't understand something about Acrobat. This is the sixth book Lori and I have worked on together and my Acrobat books are always that much better because of Lori's contributions.

A close second to Lori is Ali Hanyaloglu of Adobe Systems. Ali equally travels to many places evangelizing Acrobat and PDF and assisting users on a daily basis. Ali is such a great support to me and his assistance was instrumental for getting this work completed.

Much appreciation and thanks also go to my good friend and colleague Leonard Rosenthal of Adobe Systems, who was a great help in walking me through new features and took time out of his busy schedule to review some of the content in this work. A special thank you is extended to another good friend and colleague, Thom Parker of Windjack Solutions (www.windjack.com), who graciously helped me with questions related to Acrobat JavaScript. Whenever I have a question regarding JavaScript, Thom is my first and only contact.

I feel very fortunate in having so much support from many people at Adobe Systems who were continually available for comments, suggestions, and favors over a four-month period of time while Acrobat 9.0 was in development. The energy and enthusiasm of the engineering and marketing teams throughout the development period made it evident that this is a group of people with passion and excitement for their work. A hearty thank you is extended to Rick Brown, senior Acrobat Product Manager (and Chief Acrobatist), for his support, telephone conversations, and

Acknowledgments

offering a quote you see appearing on the cover of the book. I so much appreciate all the assistance Rick provides me, and the contact I have with him throughout the lifecycle of a product version. If there's a glue that keeps the development team together through the rigorous schedule to make the deadlines, it's Rick Brown.

Other Adobe employees who were very helpful include David Stromfeld, Product Manager, who spent time with me in a number of phone conversations and e-mails; Greg Pisocky for adding some pointers on Acrobat and accessibility; Randy Swineford, for a number of assists in getting familiar with new features; Joel Geraci for his advice and help with Adobe Flex and Adobe Flash; Chris French for help with many of the new multimedia features; Amy Wang who went above and beyond the call of duty by assisting me countless times on working through the new features for shared reviews and distributing forms — if it wasn't for Amy, you wouldn't be reading this book now; Gladys Liu and Tae-Ho Kim for help with some of the color management and printing issues; Ashu Mittal for constant assistance for getting things going with Acrobat and Adobe Reader 9 and so many debugging issues; and many other Adobe employees in the engineering and marketing divisions who graciously offered feedback and advice during the development of the Acrobat 9 family of products.

Another Adobe employee so helpful in the area of the new PDF Ads for Yahoo! was Cynthia Tillo. Cynthia's support and assistance in getting me started with Yahoo! Ads was invaluable and when she needed some additional assistance Mike McCullough of Yahoo! jumped in. Thank you, Mike, for your help.

I'd also like to thank Kurt Foss, editor of Acrobat Users Community; Stephanie Baartz-Bowman and Lori Kassuba of Adobe Systems; my colleagues on Acrobat Users, Carl Young, Jo Lou Young, Duff Johnson, Dimitri Munkirs, Douglas Hanna, and Patty-Bing-You for much support in keeping up-to-date information available on the Acrobat Users Community Web site and for their willingness to help when I needed it. And in my local Davao City Philippines Acrobat User Group, Chris Cubos, Blogie Robillo, and MiGs for all their generous assistance in helping organize Acrobat users in our area.

Additionally, I'd like to thank another friend and colleague, Robert Connolly of pdfPictures.com, and his client Aruba Bonbini for permissions to include the Aruba Bonbini eBrochure on the book's CD-ROM. And again, I would like to thank my good friend Lisle Gates for permitting me to use his photos in several layouts.

Last, but certainly one of the most valuable, I'd like to thank the many readers of my previous works who through the years have sent me direct mails with questions, kudos, and helpful remarks that has helped me refine this work. My labors as an author, alone behind a computer writing daily, is really very dull during the project period. What makes it all worthwhile is hearing from people about real world applications for Acrobat and interacting with all of you — that's the real treasure and the reward for me spending every waking moment putting this thing together over a 3 to 4 month period of time.

Introduction

This book is the sixth edition of the *Acrobat PDF Bible*. As a result of feedback from many users, this edition is an effort to include coverage of some topics missed in the last version and to add additional material where users asked for more detail. As you will see by browsing the contents of the book or launching the new version of all the Acrobat viewers, including Adobe Reader, Adobe Acrobat Standard (Windows only), Adobe Acrobat Professional, and Adobe Acrobat Extended (Windows only) there are many changes in the programs. As such, I've made an effort to cover as much of the new version as is possible in this single, comprehensive book.

What Is Adobe Acrobat?

We've come a long way in Acrobat evolution, and those users of Adobe Acrobat are familiar with the distinctions between the Adobe Reader software and Adobe Acrobat (either Standard or Professional). However, among the many users of Adobe Reader, there still exists some confusion about what Reader can and cannot do. When acquiring Adobe Reader, many folks think the viewing of PDF documents with Adobe Reader is the extent of Acrobat. Now in version 9, Adobe Reader can do much more in terms of editing PDF documents. In addition to editing features, Acrobat Standard 9.0 now includes the much desired options for forms authoring and enabling PDFs with special features for Adobe Reader users for saving form data and adding digital signatures.

For those who don't know the difference, I explain in Chapter 2 that Adobe Reader is only one small component of Acrobat. Other programs included in the suite of Acrobat software provide you with tools for creating, editing, viewing, navigating, and searching Portable Document Format (PDF) information. Regardless of your familiarity with previous versions of Acrobat, you should carefully review Chapter 2. In Chapter 4, you'll find some details on all the new features added to Adobe Reader and how you can add to PDF documents some new Reader Extensions that enable the Adobe Reader user much more functionality than was available in all versions prior to version 9.

Acrobat has evolved with many different changes both to the features it offers you and often to the names associated with the various components. In earlier versions of Acrobat, names such as Acrobat Professional, Acrobat Exchange, and then simply Acrobat were used to refer to the authoring application. Version 9.0 of Adobe Acrobat, fortunately, continues with the same product names as found in Acrobat 8 with one exception. Acrobat 3D has been rebranded and is now introduced as Acrobat Professional Extended. The high-end performance application is referred to as Adobe Acrobat Professional that operates on Windows and Macintosh and Acrobat Professional Extended available on Windows only. In release 9, as was the case in versions 7 and 8, there is also a lighter Acrobat version of Acrobat called Acrobat Standard. As was the case in Acrobat 8, Acrobat Standard is available on Windows only. Now in version 9 of Acrobat, Acrobat Standard has been overhauled and now offers much more functionality — especially in the area of forms authoring, This program has all the features you find available in Acrobat Professional with the exception of high-end printing and pre-press, enabling documents with Adobe Reader extensions for commenting, and some differences in tools and menu commands. However, the degree of differences between Acrobat Professional and Acrobat Standard in version 9 has narrowed and you'll find you can do much more with Standard than with earlier versions. As you follow the pages in this book, you can apply most of what is contained herein to either Acrobat Standard or the Acrobat Professional products.

Nomenclature

The official name for the new release of the high-end Acrobat product is Adobe® Acrobat® 9.0 Professional and Adobe® Acrobat® 9.0 Professional Extended. You'll notice the registered marks appearing in the name. For the sake of ease and clarity, as you read through the book and see a reference to Acrobat, Adobe Acrobat, Acrobat Professional (also called Acrobat Pro) and Acrobat Professional Extended (also called Acrobat Pro Extended), please realize that the reference is to Adobe Acrobat Professional or Adobe Acrobat Professional Extended. For purposes of clarity, when I refer to Acrobat Professional, I'll be talking about both Acrobat Professional and Acrobat Professional Extended. For the other authoring application, the official name is Adobe® Acrobat® Standard. When referring to this product I may use terms such as Acrobat Standard or simply Standard. Where it makes sense I'll say it like it is supposed to be used; otherwise, I'll use an abbreviated name.

The free downloadable software is Adobe Reader. Again, for the purposes of communication and ease, I may refer to Adobe Reader simply as Reader. Please realize, however, that the official name should prevail when you communicate in writing about these products.

For Windows users, Acrobat 9.0 Professional and Adobe Acrobat 9.0 Professional Extended also ship with Adobe® LiveCycle® Designer 8.2. You may find references to this product stated as LiveCycle Designer, Designer, or LCD. All of these references are made to the Adobe LiveCycle Designer product used for authoring dynamic XML-based forms.

Why is this important? Adobe Systems, Inc., has spent much time, labor, and money on developing branding for their products. With the different changes to product names and the different components of the software, some people using the products don't completely understand the differences or where the product came from. An Adobe Reader installer can appear on CD-ROMs distributed legitimately by users, and some end users may not know that it is a product available for upgrading at the Adobe Systems, Inc., Web site. Therefore, using the formal name can help users understand a little bit more about the software.

And there's a very good reason for helping Adobe Systems with the recognition and marketing of its products. If the product doesn't do well in the marketplace, you might one day see it disappear. You won't want that to happen because when you start working with the new release, you'll easily see many great new features and much more polish added to the programs. Adobe Systems has done well in bringing the entire Acrobat family of products to maturity and I'm certain you'll find many more new uses for Acrobat.

Above all, realize that *Adobe* is not a product. Adobe or Adobe Systems is a company. Making a reference to Adobe when you mean Acrobat or Adobe Reader is improper and promotes confusion. When referring to the products, be certain to include Acrobat, Standard, or Reader.

Adobe Systems and the Acrobat mission

Adobe Systems, Inc. began as a company serving the graphic design and imaging markets. With the release of PostScript, its first product, much development in the early years of its history was devoted to imaging programs, font libraries, and tools to help service graphic design professionals. When you speak to graphic designers and advertising people, they connect Adobe Systems with products such as Adobe Photoshop, Adobe Illustrator, Adobe InDesign, Adobe Premiere, and so on. With some of these flagship programs having long histories and large installed user bases, some people may think that a product such as Adobe Acrobat takes a back seat to the high-end graphics and multimedia programs.

Where does Acrobat fit into Adobe's mission and view of its product line? Adobe former Chairman and CEO Bruce Chizen was quoted as saying that he expected the Acrobat family of products to weather economic storms in the software market. Acrobat is Adobe's fastest-growing product, experiencing between 40 to 60 percent growth in year-over-year sales. Chizen also stated that more than 60 percent of Adobe's worldwide sales and marketing personnel are devoted to Acrobat-related products from the Acrobat 5 life cycle to the present.

Adobe sees Acrobat as an integral part of its future and is investing much energy into Acrobat's growth. With more than 750,000,000 installed users of the Adobe Reader software, Acrobat and the PDF file format are among the most popular software products available today.

Acrobat has become a standard in many different industries. In the publishing market many large newspaper chains, publishing houses, and book and magazine publishers have standardized on the PDF format for printing and prepress. The prepress industry has long adopted PDF as a standard for commercial and quick-print houses. Almost every software manufacturer includes last-minute notes, user manuals, and supporting information in PDF format on CD-ROM installer disks. The U.S. federal, state, and city governments and the U.S. government contractor organizations have standardized on PDF for everything from forms, applications, notices, and official documents to intra-office document exchanges. Also, PDF itself has become an international standard adopted by the International Standards Organization (ISO).

With the introduction of the Acrobat 6 product line, Adobe Systems expanded existing markets and targeted new markets. The features in Acrobat 6 and 7 Professional appealed to all kinds of engineering professionals. With the support for layers and direct exports from programs such as Microsoft Visio and Autodesk AutoCAD, engineers, planners, and architects welcomed the new additions to Acrobat. In Acrobat 8, users of Acrobat Professional could convert AutoCAD .dwg drawings to PDF complete with layers and comments without having AutoCAD installed on a computer. Enterprises, in which document flows include different workgroups for almost any industry, welcomed additions to the comment and review tools in Acrobat Professional 8.0. Additional enabling usage rights for Adobe Reader users were introduced in Acrobat 8. The already standardized prepress market applauded new features for printing to high-end imaging devices without the use of third-party plug-ins. In Acrobat 9 you find all the great features of Acrobat 8 now being introduced with online support services and real-time collaboration. You find much integration with Adobe Flash and many beefed up features that were introduced with Acrobat 8.0.

PDF workflows

A workflow can mean different things to different people. One of the nice aspects of working with Acrobat is the development of a workflow environment. Quite simply, workflow solutions are intended to get out of a computer what the computer was designed for: productivity in a more automated and efficient fashion. Editing page by page and running manual tasks to change or modify documents could hardly be called workflow solutions. Workflows enable office or production workers a means of automating common tasks for maximum efficiency. Batch processing documents, running them through automated steps, and routing files through computer-assisted delivery systems are among workflow solutions.

Acrobat provides workflow solutions in almost every industry and new features added to Acrobat 9 add some polish to an already great product. But the real advance in workflow activity is the introduction of Acrobat.com. Now, instead of having documents flow across wide area networks, people can collaborate in real-time online events without configuring servers. The introduction of Acrobat.com will not only ease a tremendous financial burden saving companies huge expenses for employee travel, but increase productivity in workflows through dynamic interaction.

New Features in Adobe Acrobat Professional

The changes to Acrobat in version 9.0 represent many more expanded and new features to an already impressive product. Just about everything you could do in the last version is still available in version 9.0, but there have been many additions to existing features and some new options for a variety of Acrobat uses.

More than 350 new features have been added to Acrobat 9.0. Listing all the new features here is not possible. However, in each chapter I've added a special icon to point out new features that will help you familiarize yourself with changes in the product and discover what's new.

Rather than list all the new features, let me cover some of the more impressive new additions to Acrobat and point out some of my favorites. Here's a list of my top 9 reasons to upgrade to Acrobat 9.0:

- **Acrobat.com.** I rank Acrobat.com and all the things you can do with this new online service as the best new feature Adobe has added to any of its products in the past two decades. With Acrobat.com you have a free online service and online library. You can upload files, share files, engage in review sessions, hold online meetings in real-time, distribute forms, collect form data, and more. The service is free to users of the Adobe

Reader and all Acrobat software. Chapter 29 has been completely rewritten to explain all the features you have with Acrobat.com and how to engage in online meetings.

- **PDF Portfolios.** In Acrobat 8 we were introduced to PDF Packages. PDF Packages have given way to PDF Portfolios. A PDF Portfolio provides you an opportunity to add a number of different files (any file type) to the portfolio. You have options for creating the design and visual look, adding Adobe Flash animation to a Welcome page, and display your collected files in a neat new interface that is attractive and powerful for users to browse the content. Look to Chapter 12 that has been completely revised to cover all the new PDF Portfolio features.

- **Shared Reviews.** Real-time collaboration on a server that you don't have to configure makes shared reviews a quantum leap in Acrobat development. Now together with Acrobat.com you don't have to worry about talking to your IT department to configure a server. It's all handled for you by Adobe and it's a free service as you discover in Chapter 21.

- **Forms Authoring in Acrobat Standard.** Acrobat Standard has become more powerful with the introduction of forms authoring support. In Acrobat Standard you can now create PDF forms, distribute forms, collect form data, and track forms on Acrobat.com. All of what I talk about in Chapter 34 now applies to users of Acrobat Standard.

- **Flash Integration.** Adobe Flash is all over Acrobat and PDF. You no longer need to use a Flash Player plug-in with the Acrobat viewers. Adobe Flash Player is hard coded in all version 9.0 viewers. You can convert Adobe Flash .swf and .flv files directly to PDF. When working with Acrobat.com, you're working within an Adobe Flash interface. You can add Adobe Flash animation to PDF Portfolios. For more information on using Adobe Flash with PDF, see Chapters 7, 12, 23, 28, and 29.

- **Scanning and OCR.** Much new improvement has been added to scanning and recognizing text using OCR. Clearscan technology is supported with Acrobat.scan and support for Windows Imaging Architecture (WIA) scanners (Windows only). If you're looking for suspect words after converting an image scan with OCR, don't expect to find many suspect words with the new improvements to scanning and OCR as I explain in Chapter 17.

- **Adobe Presenter.** If you're an Acrobat Professional Extended and Microsoft PowerPoint user (Windows only), you get Adobe Presenter on your installer CD-ROM. Adobe Presenter is a PowerPoint add-on that enables you to export your slide presentations with animation and export directly to an Adobe Flash interface. You'll be amazed at the new developments you have available for creating dynamic presentations, as you'll see in Chapter 23.

- **Commercial Printing Support.** Several new additions appear with the Print Production tools in Acrobat Professional products. You can use the Preflight tool to create new Adobe PDF Layers, use the new Object Inspector tool, and find a huge range of new options for converting color. Look at Chapters 24 and 32 for more information.

- **Adobe Reader.** Adobe Reader 9.0 has become a much more useful tool and you'll want to encourage all people not using one of the commercial Acrobat products to upgrade to Adobe Reader 9.0. With Reader 9 you can start a meeting on Acrobat.com, participate in real-time conferencing and reviews, and create PDFs online dynamically as you wait for the conversion. Adobe Reader has much more as I explain in Chapter 4.

In addition to the top 9, you'll find new enhancements and improvements in areas such as PDF creation, combining files into single PDF documents, redaction, batch processing, comparing documents, exporting PDF content, splitting files, forms distribution and tracking forms and reviews, LiveCycle Designer forms creation, converting Web pages to PDF, adding Flash widgets, and more.

You'll find detailed descriptions of all the new features in the chapters ahead.

Part I

Welcome to Adobe Acrobat

This section begins with an overview of the Acrobat user interface and familiarizes you with tools, menus, and panels. In Chapter 2 you find a detailed description for the Acrobat viewers and how they are distinguished from each other. Chapter 3 follows with opening and managing PDF documents in Acrobat viewers, followed by Chapter 4 where I cover all the features you find in the Adobe Reader software. In Chapter 5 you'll find everything you need to know about viewing and navigating PDF files in Acrobat viewers. This section ends with searching PDF files using the impressive search features you find in all Acrobat viewers.

Chapter 1

Getting to Know Adobe Acrobat

To start off this large book on Adobe Acrobat, let's first take a look at what Acrobat is and what PDF is, and let's try to get a grasp on some of the many options you have for working with PDF files in Acrobat.

What Is Adobe Acrobat?

Assuming you know little about Adobe Acrobat, I start with a brief description of what Acrobat is and what it is not. As I explain to people who ask about the product, I usually define it as the most misunderstood application available today. Most of us are familiar with the Adobe Reader software, which is a product from Adobe Systems Incorporated that you can download free from the Adobe Web site (`www.adobe.com/acrobat/readermain.html`). You can also acquire the Adobe Reader from all the installation CD-ROMs for other Adobe software. You can even acquire Adobe Reader from other sources, as long as the Adobe licensing requirements are distributed with the installer program. The Adobe Reader, however, is *not* Adobe Acrobat. Adobe Reader is a component of a much larger product family that has evolved through several iterations over more than a decade.

You're probably a little more sophisticated and realize there is a major difference between these applications, and you may wonder why I even spend any time discussing the difference between Acrobat and Adobe Reader. Unfortunately, many people still believe that Adobe Acrobat is the free Adobe Reader program.

To add a little more confusion, Adobe continues to market several Acrobat products in the Acrobat family. While Adobe Reader remains a free download from Adobe Systems, there are three additional commercial viewers —

IN THIS CHAPTER

About Adobe Acrobat

Understanding PDF

Understanding PDF standards

Taking a look at the new user interface

Looking at the Acrobat workplace

About Preferences

Acrobat Standard on Windows only), Acrobat Pro (on Windows and Macintosh), and Acrobat Pro Extended (includes functionality of the former Acrobat 3D and on Windows only). With the release of Acrobat 9, Acrobat Standard on Windows has been improved and offers many new features formerly reserved for the Acrobat Pro product. As I talk about Adobe Acrobat in this chapter and throughout the book, I'm referring to Acrobat Pro for both Windows and Macintosh, Acrobat Pro Extended for Windows, and Acrobat Standard for Windows users only. Where the programs differ in features, I point them out. I also mention when a feature is only available in Acrobat Pro or Acrobat Pro Extended.

NOTE   **There are distinctions between the Acrobat Standard product (Windows) and the Acrobat Pro and Acrobat Pro Extended (Windows) products in terms of tools, commands, and features. Most editing tasks can be handled in all viewers; however, Acrobat Pro does provide more editing features than Acrobat Standard, and Acrobat Pro Extended provides more features than Acrobat Pro. Throughout this book I delineate the differences and point out when a feature is unique to a given viewer.**

Adobe Acrobat (Standard, Pro, or Pro Extended) in version 9 is the upgrade from Adobe Acrobat 8 (Standard, Professional, and/or Acrobat 3D) and all viewers are the subject of the remaining chapters of this book. Acrobat is the authoring application that provides you tools and commands for a host of features outlined in the following chapters. If you haven't yet purchased a copy of Acrobat, either the Standard version (Windows only), the Pro version (Windows and Macintosh), or the Pro Extended version (Windows), you might want to look over Chapter 2 and observe some of the comparisons between the viewers. If fewer tools and features suit your purpose, you might find the Standard version satisfactory — but remember, Acrobat Standard is available only on Windows in versions 8 and 9. Although some of the features differ between the viewers, they both provide many features for editing, enhancing, printing, and working with PDF documents.

NOTE   **For the purposes of clarity, henceforth I'll refer to Acrobat when features are common to all viewers. I'll make specific mention of one of the Acrobat products when a particular feature is unique to a given viewer. For a quick comparison of the viewers and related features, be sure to look over Chapter 2.**

Acrobat is an authoring application, but it has one little feature that distinguishes it from almost any other authoring program. Rather than starting from scratch and creating a new document in Acrobat, your workflow usually involves converting a document, created in just about any program, to a Portable Document Format (PDF) file. Once converted to PDF you use Acrobat to edit and refine the document, add bells and whistles and interactivity, or prepare it for professional printing. In addition to the Acrobat program, Acrobat Pro ships with companion programs such as Adobe Acrobat Distiller, Adobe Acrobat Catalog, and Adobe LiveCycle Designer (Windows only). Acrobat Professional Extended ships with all the Acrobat Pro components and Adobe Presenter and Adobe 3D Reveiwer, Acrobat Standard ships only with Acrobat Distiller. These companion products are used to convert PostScript files to PDF, create search indexes, and author XML-based forms.

CROSS-REF For information related to Acrobat Distiller see Chapter 10. For more information on Acrobat Catalog, see Chapter 6. For more information related to LiveCycle Designer, see Chapter 35.

Acrobat solutions are greatly extended with other supporting programs from Adobe Systems and many different third-party vendors. If Acrobat can't do the job, chances are you can find a plug-in or companion program to handle all you want to do with a PDF file.

CROSS-REF For information related to Acrobat plug-ins and companion products see Chapter 2.

What Is PDF?

PDF, short for *Portable Document Format*, was developed by Adobe Systems as a unique format to be viewed through Acrobat viewers. As the name implies, it is portable, which means the file you create on one computer can be viewed with an Acrobat viewer on other computers, handheld devices, and on other platforms. For example, you can create a page layout on a Macintosh computer and convert it to a PDF file. After the conversion, this PDF document can be viewed on a Linux or Windows machine.

Multiplatform compliance (to enable the exchange of files across different computers, for example) is one of the great values of PDF documents.

So what's special about PDF and its multiplatform compliance? It's not so much an issue of viewing a page on one computer created from another computer that is impressive about PDF. After all, such popular programs as Microsoft Excel, Microsoft Word, Adobe Photoshop, Adobe InDesign, Adobe FrameMaker, and Adobe Illustrator all have counterparts for multiplatform usage. You can create a layout on one computer system and view the file on another system with the same software installed. For example, if you have Adobe InDesign installed on a Macintosh computer and you create an InDesign document, that same file can be viewed on a PC with InDesign running under Windows.

In a perfect world, you may think the capability to view documents across platforms is not so special. Document viewing, however, is secondary to document integrity. The preservation of the contents of a page is what makes the PDF so extraordinary. To illustrate, suppose you have an InDesign document created in Windows using fonts generic to Windows applications. After it's converted to PDF, the document, complete with graphics and fonts intact, can be displayed and printed on other computer platforms. And the other computer platforms don't need the fonts, graphics, or the original authoring application to print the file with complete integrity.

This level of document integrity can come in handy in business environments, where software purchases often reach quantum costs. PDF documents eliminate the need to install all applications used within a particular company on all the computers in that company. For example, art department employees can use a layout application to create display ads and then convert them to PDF so that other departments can use the free Adobe Reader software to view and print those ads for approval.

The benefits of PDF viewing were initially recognized by workgroups in local office environments for electronic paper exchanges. Today users have much more opportunity for global exchange of documents in many different ways. As you look at Acrobat and discover some of the features available for document comment and markup, comparing documents, support for layered files (which adds much more functionality to Adobe Reader), and preparing PDFs for screen readers, you'll see how Acrobat and the PDF have evolved with new technologies.

CROSS-REF   **The term "screen reader" is used extensively throughout this book. When you see a reference to "screen reader," I'm referring to either a hardware device or special software (JAWS, Kurzweil, and so on) used to convert visual information to audio format. For more information on screen readers and making documents accessible to the readers, see Chapter 25.**

Document repurposing

The computer revolution has left extraordinary volumes of data that were originally designed to be printed on paper on computer systems. Going all the way back to UNIVAC, the number crunching was handled by the computer and the expression was the printed piece. Today, forms of expression have evolved to many different media. No longer do people want to confine themselves to printed material. Now, in addition to publishing information on paper, we use CD-ROMs, the Internet, file exchanges, and meeting sessions via the Internet between computers. Sometimes we use motion video, television, and satellite broadcasts. As high-speed access evolves, we'll see much larger bandwidths, so real-time communication will eventually become commonplace.

Technology will advance, bringing many improvements to bandwidth, performance, and speed. To enable the public to access the mountains of digital data held on computer systems in a true information superhighway world, files need to be converted to a common format. A common file format would also enable new documents to be more easily *repurposed*, to exploit the many forms of communication that we use today and expect to use tomorrow.

Acrobat Pro has many tools for helping users repurpose documents. Tools for repairing problem files, downsizing file sizes, porting files to a range of different devices, and eliminating unnecessary data are part of the many features found in Acrobat Pro. In addition, the PDF/A format introduced in Acrobat 8 is designed specifically for archiving documents. A standards committee has developed this format so documents viewed on computer systems 100 years from now will be compatible with future operating systems.

PDF and Adobe PostScript

The de facto standard for nearly all printing in the graphics industry has been Adobe PostScript. While PostScript is still the dominant printing language, this will slowly change because Adobe has announced in 2006 support for PDF as the new print standard.

Okay, so how does PostScript relate to PDF? In the initial release of Acrobat, all PDF conversion began with a file that was created as a PostScript file. Users selected the Print command in an authoring program and printed the file to disk — thus creating a PostScript file. This file was then opened in the Acrobat Distiller program and Distiller converted the PostScript to a PDF.

Distiller is still a part of Acrobat. In some cases, creating a PDF from a PostScript file rather than through any of the many other means available may be preferable. It could be that you have a problem with exporting to PDF from a program, such as fonts not appearing embedded, or you may need to create a PDF for a special purpose such as printing and prepress. In such circumstances using Acrobat Distiller may be your best solution for generating a PDF document to properly suit the purpose.

CROSS-REF For information related to printing PostScript files and using Acrobat Distiller see Chapter 10.

Printing to PostScript and opening PostScript files in Distiller is used much less today because now so many programs support PDF creation through one-button clicks or using the Save As command. However, many of these one-button clicks still use the Distiller application in the background to create the PDF file. You may not see Distiller launched when PDFs are created in the background, but the program is working away to convert your authoring application document to a PDF file.

PostScript can be a problem solver for you, and you may have an occasional need to use it even if your workflow does not require its use all the time. The more you know about PostScript and Acrobat Distiller, the more often you might be able to rescue problem files that don't seem to properly convert to PDF.

PDF versions

Acrobat is now in version 9. The version number indicates the number of releases of the product. PDF is a file format and with it you'll also find a version number — that is, up until version 9 of Acrobat. The PDF version in versions prior to 9 related to the specifications of the file format; for the end user it's usually not so important to understand all the specifications as much as it is to know what it does for you or what you can expect from it. If you create PDF documents for users of older Acrobat viewers and use the newer PDF format, your users may not be able to view your PDF files. Conversely, creating PDF files with the older version might prohibit you from using some newer features in the recent release.

PDF versions are typically referred to as Acrobat Compatibility. A PDF version 1.7 file, for example, is an Acrobat 8–compatible file. To understand how the PDF version relates to the Acrobat version, simply add the digits of the PDF version together. For example, PDF version 1.4 is Acrobat 5 compatible (1 + 4 = 5). PDF version 1.5 is Acrobat 6 compatible, and so on.

Now in version 9 however, PDF has lost its version number — the reason being, Adobe no longer owns the PDF specification. PDF has become an adopted standard by the International Organization for Standardization (ISO). Since the ISO committee sets the standard, it's taken out of the hands of Adobe and no longer carries a version number.

Each release of Acrobat provides support for additional features in PDF documents. It's not as important to know all the features enabled by one version as it is to know which Acrobat compatibility you need to use. For example, to optimize a PDF file for printing, you may need to use PDF version 1.3 or Acrobat 4 compatibility. Or, if you want to embed movie files in a PDF, then you need to use an Acrobat 6–compatible file. Or, you may want to add password security to a PDF that requires a newer Acrobat viewer to open a file using a password.

Whereas you previously may have thought of PDF version files, you now need to think in terms of Acrobat version compatibility. The PDF specification is handled by ISO, but the Acrobat compatibility is handled by Adobe Systems. ISO 32000 is the ISO specification for the current PDF version.

Understanding PDF Standards

PDF has been adopted as a standard file format in many industries, including engineering, legal, manufacturing, and prepress and printing. Even the United States Federal Government has embraced PDF as a standard file format.

So what are *standards*? Without regulation and approved standards, the computer industry would be chaotic. Fortunately, the International Organization for Standardization (ISO) develops and approves standards for the technical industry. This international committee, an entity apart from Adobe Systems, has approved and developed substandards of the PDF format.

The PDF standards available now include the following:

- **PDF/X.** This standard is a subset of the PDF format used in the printing industry. PDFs meeting PDF/X compliance are typically reliable and, theoretically, can be accurately printed on almost any kind of PostScript device.
- **PDF/E.** This standard is a subset of the PDF format designed for engineers to insure that industrial designs and drawings comply with a PDF standard.
- **PDF/A.** This standard is a subset of the PDF format used for archiving documents. The standards committee wants to insure that the files you create today and save as PDF can be viewed by computers many years in the future. To do so, the PDFs you create for archival purposes can be saved as PDF/A documents.

■ **PDF/UA.** Although, as of this writing, this subset of the PDF format is in an early draft stage, you may be hearing more about it in the near future — about one to two years from this writing. The goal of this proposed new standard is to provide universal access (UA) to all users including those persons working with assistive devices (see Chapter 25 for more on PDFs and assistive devices). The proposed new format is in the hands of the AIIMS Standards Board Committee that also proposed the PDF/X and PDF/A standards and submitted them to the ISO. People interested in participating on the committee can find more information at `www.aiim.org/standards.asp?ID=27861`.

Acrobat Environment

Acrobat provides you with features such as menu commands, toolbars, and palettes to accomplish work for whatever goal you hope to achieve with PDF documents. When you launch the program you see many of these features in the Acrobat window. Just so you know what is being referred to when I discuss accessing a feature in Acrobat, take a look at Figure 1.1 to understand the names used to describe the various areas of the new Acrobat workplace.

A **Title bar.** By default, the name of the file you open appears in the title bar. The title appearing in the title bar can change according to an option for displaying the Document Title in the Initial View properties.

CROSS-REF For information related to Initial View and displaying Document Titles, see Chapter 5.

Note that the left side of Figure 1.1 shows a PDF document opened in Form Edit mode while the right side of the figure is a PDF file opened in Viewer mode. See item J for more on Form Edit mode.

B **Menu bar.** The menu bar (Viewer mode) contains all the top-level menu commands. Many of these menu choices are also available from various actions associated with links and form fields when you choose the Execute a menu item command in the Actions Properties dialog box for links, form fields, and other features that permit associating an action with a command. When viewing files showing toolbars and menus for each open document, the Acrobat window appears as shown in Figure 1.1 on the right side of the figure. This view can be toggled off in a preference setting.

CROSS-REF For information related to link actions and the Execute a menu item command action type, see Chapter 22. For more information on actions with form fields, see Part VI. For making preference choices for viewing PDFs, see "Customizing the Acrobat workplace" later in this chapter.

The Acrobat Pro Extended workplace contains menus, toolbars, and palettes.

C   **Toolbars.** A number of individual toolbars are nested below the menu bar in the Toolbar Well. When preferences are set to view toolbars attached to each open document, you'll see multiple sets of toolbars. Toolbars are marked with a vertical separator bar at the left side of the toolbar. This bar can be selected and dragged to move it out of the Toolbar Well.

CROSS-REF   For information related to working with toolbars, see the "Tools, task buttons and toolbars" section later in this chapter.

D   **Floating toolbar.** Toolbars can be opened by accessing the More Tools window and selecting a toolbar name. When a toolbar is opened, it appears as a floating toolbar. Floating toolbars can be *docked* in the Toolbar Well.

E   **Navigation pane buttons.** Individual panel buttons appear on the left side of the Navigation pane. Click one of these buttons to open the Navigation pane where you find menu commands from an Options pull-down menu or a context menu opened in the Navigation pane.

F   Pages panel. When you open the Pages panel, you'll see thumbnail images of each page in your document and you'll find many page-editing features available to you from the Pages panel pull-down menu.

CROSS-REF For information related to using the many options available in the Pages panel, see Chapter 16.

CROSS-REF To learn how to use the Comments panel options, see Chapter 20.

G   Navigation pane. The Navigation pane can be expanded or collapsed. The view in Figure 1.1 is an expanded view where the Pages panel is the active panel. To open the Navigation pane you can click a panel button to display the respective information associated with that panel in the expanded panel window. Clicking again on the panel collapses the view. You can also use the keyboard shortcut F4 to expand and collapse the Navigation pane.

H   Document pane. The Document pane is the container for PDF files you see in Acrobat. When no file is open, the Document pane is empty. When you open a PDF document, the document appears in the Document pane.

I   Toolbar. Tools that are used in Form Editing Mode.

J   Form Editing Mode. From a menu command in the Forms menu, you can open the Form Editing Mode. Form Editing Mode is a new user interface introduced with Acrobat 9 and is specifically designed for creating Acrobat PDF forms. This mode is available in Acrobat Standard (Windows), Acrobat Pro (Windows and Macintosh), and Acrobat Pro Extended (Windows). To exit Forms Edit mode and return to the Viewer mode shown on the right side of Figure 1.1, click the Close Form Editing button.

K   Fields panel. The Fields panel is used for editing fields and only appears when you enter Form Editing Mode.

L   PDF Form. A form appears in the Form Editing Mode Document pane when editing a form in Form Editing Mode.

CROSS-REF For more information on Form Editing Mode and creating PDF forms, see Chapter 34.

For more detail on specific menu commands, tools, and palettes, see the related chapters to discover the different options available to you. All of the items discussed here are explained in more depth in subsequent chapters.

Menus

As with any program operating on a computer system that supports a Windows type of environment, you'll notice menu commands at the top level of the Acrobat window. Users of previous versions will notice that Acrobat 9 features a editing mode that contains tools specific to creating PDF forms. If at first glance you don't see an option you used in Acrobat 8, poke around the menus.

None of the Acrobat 8 features have been eliminated; they may just be in a different place or referred to by a different name.

File menu

The File menu is where you open and close documents, create PDF files, import and export certain data, access print commands, and find some other nifty new additions in Acrobat such as the new Acrobat 9 PDF Portfolios and collaboration features. The Mac and Windows operating systems display recent files in different menus. On the Mac in OS X you'll find recently viewed documents by choosing File ⇨ Open Recent File. This command opens a submenu where you can access recent documents. On Windows, a list of the recently viewed documents is located at the bottom of the File menu, as shown in Figure 1.2.

CROSS-REF   Note that the Start Meeting command that appeared in Acrobat 8 has been removed in Acrobat 9. A new Share Screen command is contained in the Collaborate submenu as I explain in Chapter 29.

FIGURE 1.2

Recently opened files in Windows appear at the bottom of the File menu. Macintosh users can display a list of recently viewed files by choosing File ⇨ Open Recent File.

Edit menu

As shown in Figure 1.3, the traditional Cut, Copy, and Paste commands are located in the Edit menu along with other familiar commands from Acrobat 8. There are no changes to the Edit menu from Acrobat 8.

FIGURE 1.3

The Edit menu contains the same commands found in Acrobat 7.

View menu

The View menu (see Figure 1.4) contains all the commands you'll use for viewing PDF documents. An addition to the View menu is the Cursor Coordinates command. This command displays a tiny window showing the coordinates of the cursor as you move it around the Document pane. The display units are controlled by opening the Preferences (Ctrl/⌘+K) and changing the Units preferences.

Document menu

The Document menu (see Figure 1.5) contains a collection of commands specific to document handling. Options in the Document menu have a few changes in Acrobat 9 compared to the options in Acrobat 8. Notice a new command — Split Document. This new command now enables you to split PDF files by number of pages, file size, and top-level bookmarks. Although the Paper Capture command hasn't changed submenu commands, the new Clear Scan features in Acrobat 9 greatly improve scanning and OCR conversion. Notice the Compare Documents command, which was formerly in the Advanced menu in earlier Acrobat viewers, has now been moved to the Document menu.

CROSS-REF For information related to splitting documents see Chapter 16. For more information on scanning documents, see Chapter 17. For more information on comparing documents, see Chapter 20.

FIGURE 1.4

The View menu contains commands for viewing PDF documents and navigating through pages and different PDF files.

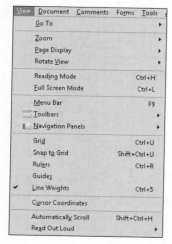

FIGURE 1.5

The Document menu contains commands for editing documents.

Comments menu

There's not so much change you'll find in the Comments menu in Acrobat 9, but selecting several different commands opens up windows and dialog boxes with some very impressive new features in Acrobat 9 (see Figure 1.6). For example, sending files for shared reviews opens a new wizard where you can choose to share reviews on Acrobat.com.

CROSS-REF   For details on working with Acrobat.com look over Chapters 4, 21, and 29.

FIGURE 1.6

The Comments menu.

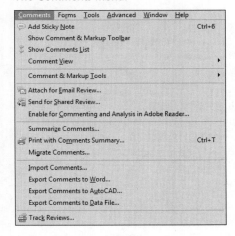

Forms menu

Perhaps the biggest change you'll find in Acrobat 9 is the many new features related to creating Acrobat PDF forms (see Figure 1.7). A huge departure from earlier Acrobat features is that all the form-editing options that were reserved for Acrobat Pro viewers are now included in Acrobat Standard on Windows. In addition, the way you create forms has greatly changed in Acrobat 9. Notice the two new menu commands at the top of the menu. Choosing either command opens a new user interface called Form Editing Mode where PDF forms are authored. In addition, you'll find a command that enables you to integrate PDF form data with the QuickBooks accounting software.

NEW FEATURE   Form Editing Mode is a new feature in Acrobat 9 where all your form authoring is performed in a new user interface.

FIGURE 1.7

The Forms menu contains commands specifically for working with forms and provides a gateway to open the Form Editing Mode.

CROSS-REF **For working with Acrobat PDF forms, see Chapters 33 and 34. For understanding more about Adobe Designer and XML forms (Windows only), see Chapter 35.**

Tools menu

Several changes appear in the Tools menu shown in Figure 1.8. Notice that the Forms command that opened the Forms toolbar in Acrobat 8 has been removed in Acrobat 9. There is no Forms toolbar in Acrobat 9 since forms editing takes place in Forms Edit mode where you'll find access to all the forms tools. The Measuring toolbar and the Object tool formerly found in the Acrobat 8 Tools menu have been eliminated and replaced by the Analysis toolbar. In Acrobat 9 you'll find the new Multimedia toolbar accessed by selecting Multimedia in the Tools menu.

FIGURE 1.8

The Tools menu contains a collection of tools accessed from submenus. Select a tool group from the menu options to open a submenu.

CROSS-REF **For more information on using the Multimedia tools, see Chapters 7 and 23.**

Advanced menu

The Advanced menu (see Figure 1.9) contains a collection of menu commands considered to be advanced Acrobat features. Several of these tools are not available to users of Acrobat Standard such as Batch Processing, the Redaction tools, access to Acrobat Catalog, Print Production,

Document Processing, PDF Optimizer, and Preflight some accessibility options are different in Standard. A few changes have been made in this menu in Acrobat 9. You'll notice a slight rearrangement of the commands with Accessibility now appearing at the top of the menu and the disappearance of the Compare Documents command that has been moved to the Document menu.

FIGURE 1.9

The Advanced menu offers menu commands related to advanced editing features.

CROSS-REF For information related to batch processing, see Chapters 18 and 36 (on the CD-ROM). For information on using Acrobat Catalog, see Chapter 6. For information on using all the security commands see Chapter 26.

Window menu

The Window menu (see Figure 1.10) provides menu commands to assist you in viewing documents. No changes appear in the Window menu in Acrobat 9 compared to earlier viewers.

FIGURE 1.10

The Window menu handles all the window views such as tiling, cascading, and splitting windows.

 For information related to window views and the split window views, see Chapter 5.

Help menu

The traditional help files added to your Acrobat folder at installation are found in the Help menu (see Figure 1.11). Various online help support is also located in this menu. You'll notice the rearrangement of help items in Acrobat 9 and the elimination of the Getting Started menu choice.

 CROSS-REF For information related to Help documents and Help menus, see Chapter 3.

Submenus

An extensive number of submenus appear in menus contained in the top-level menu bar and from many different tools contained in toolbars. Note that on individual toolbars you see a down-pointing arrow. Clicking the arrow opens a menu; some menus contain submenus. A submenu is denoted in Acrobat by a right-pointing arrow on the right side of a given menu command as shown in Figure 1.12. Select a command with one of these arrows adjacent to the command name and a submenu opens. In a few cases, you can find nested submenus where another right-pointing arrow may be visible in a submenu. If you want to access the second submenu, move the cursor to the menu option containing a right-pointing arrow. To make a selection from a sub-menu command, move the cursor to the desired menu command. When the menu command highlights, click the mouse button to execute the command.

FIGURE 1.11

The Help menu gives you access to Help information on selected topics as well as access to the complete Acrobat Help document.

Context menus

Wherever you are in the Acrobat window — the toolbars, panels, Document pane, or the various editing modes — you can gain quick access to menu items related to your task by opening a context menu. Context menus pop up in an area where you either click the right button on the mouse or use an appropriate key modifier. In Windows, right-click the mouse button to open a context menu. On a Macintosh, when not using a two-button mouse, press the Control key and click the mouse button. Context menu options relate to the particular tool you have selected from a toolbar. Selecting different tools provides you with different menu commands. In Figure 1.13 I opened a context menu with the Marquee Zoom tool selected.

FIGURE 1.12

To access a submenu, move the cursor to the command containing a right-pointing arrow and slide the cursor over to the submenu options. Click the desired command in the submenu to execute the command.

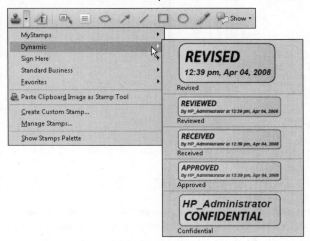

FIGURE 1.13

With the Marquee Zoom tool selected, right-clicking (Windows) or Control+clicking (Macintosh) the mouse button opens a context menu. From the menu, scroll the list and select the desired menu command.

If you change tools in a toolbar and open a context menu, the menu options change to reflect choices with that particular tool. Likewise, a context menu opened on a panel offers menu options respective to the panel, as shown in Figure 1.14.

FIGURE 1.14

When a panel is open in the Navigation pane and you open a context menu, the menu options reflect tasks you can perform respective to the panel.

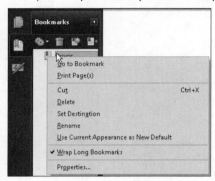

TIP Opening a context menu on one of the icons in the Navigation pane opens a menu where you can add or remove panels from the pane. Additionally, you can hide the Navigation panel icons by opening a context menu in the Navigation pane and select Hide Navigation Pane Buttons. To bring back the Navigation Pane Buttons, press F4 on your keyboard or select View ➪ Navigation Panels ➪ Show Navigation Pane.

Context menus are a great benefit during your Acrobat sessions and using them helps you work much faster. Throughout this book I often make references to the different choices you have in selecting a tool or command. In most incidences, you find mention of context menus. Be certain you know how to open a context menu in Acrobat on your computer. For the remainder of this book, I'll mention opening context menus without walking through the steps for how to open the menu.

Keyboard shortcuts

Pressing one or more keys on your keyboard can also open menus and invoke different commands. When you become familiar with keyboard shortcuts that perform the same function as when using a menu or context menu, you'll find yourself favoring this method for making different menu selections or grabbing a tool from a toolbar. Fortunately, you can learn as you work when it comes to memorizing keyboard shortcuts. As I'm certain you know, several shortcut combinations are noted in menu commands. You can learn these shortcuts when you frequently use a particular command. However, the keyboard shortcuts you see in the menu commands are just a fraction of what is available in Acrobat for quick access to commands and tools. For a complete list of all keyboard shortcuts, look over the Acrobat Help document you open by selecting Help ➪ Adobe Acrobat 9.0 (Standard, Pro, or Pro Extended) Help or pressing the F1 key.

NOTE Pressing a single key to access a tool requires you to have your Preferences set to accept single keystroke shortcuts. See the steps for "Setting up the Acrobat environment" later in this chapter for the proper Preferences settings.

Tools, task buttons, and toolbars

Tools are grouped together in separate toolbars in the Toolbar Well below the menu bar. The default view when you launch Acrobat contains several toolbars visible in the Toolbar Well. You can remove various toolbars from the Well, move them around the Acrobat window, close them, and add different toolbars to the Toolbar Well.

In addition to loading and unloading toolbars, you can also add or remove individual tools from any toolbar. Before you learn how to add and remove individual tools, let's first take a look at the Toolbar Well.

The Toolbar Well, where the toolbars are contained, is collapsed and expanded according to the number of toolbars you add to it. When a toolbar is contained within the Toolbar Well, it is said to be *docked*. When a toolbar is dragged away from the Toolbar Well and rests atop the Acrobat window, it is said to be *undocked* and appears as a *floating* toolbar.

Task buttons

One of the many different toolbars in Acrobat is called the Tasks toolbar. This toolbar houses various Task buttons. In Figure 1.15 the tasks toolbar is shown with the label descriptions to describe each tool's purpose. Task buttons differ a little from other tools in that they all support pull-down menus where menu commands related to specific tasks are addressed.

FIGURE 1.15

The Tasks toolbar contains several Task buttons all containing pull-down menus.

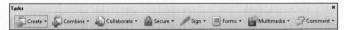

The Tasks toolbar features commands for creating PDFs, combining files, working with reviews and online collaboration, securing PDFs, digitally signing PDFs, working with forms, working with multimedia, and working with comments.

Loading and unloading tools

The default tools you see in the Toolbar Well when you first open Acrobat are but a mere fraction of all the tools available to you. Fortunately in Acrobat, a nifty window is available to help you easily manage tools.

It's important to realize that you have toolbars and tools. Tools appear as individual icons contained in a given toolbar. You can choose to show only one tool in a toolbar or all the tools that belong to a given toolbar and anything in between. The tools within toolbars can be added and deleted from the parent toolbar.

If you're familiar with earlier versions of Acrobat and you don't find tools loaded in the various toolbars, your first stop is to open the More Tools menu at the top right corner of your screen. Select More Tools from a context menu opened on the Toolbar Well and the More Tools window opens as shown in Figure 1.16.

FIGURE 1.16

Open the More Tools window to show/hide tools in toolbars.

Place a check mark beside any tool to be shown in a toolbar docked in the Toolbar Well or opened as a floating toolbar. Figure 1.16 shows you a small portion of available tools that appear in a scrollable window.

NOTE Toolbars themselves can be shown or hidden using the More Tools window. If you remove a check mark adjacent to a toolbar name to hide the toolbar, the toolbar and all the tools are hidden, even if the individual tools are all checked.

Yet another way to add and remove tools to and from toolbars is to simply open a context menu on a toolbar. Right-click (Windows) or Control+click (Macintosh) on a toolbar either docked in the Toolbar Well or as a floating toolbar and a pop-up menu provides options for adding or removing tools to/from that toolbar group.

In Figure 1.17 a context menu is opened on the Edit toolbar. When Show/Hide Tools is selected a submenu displays all toolbars. Select an item unchecked to open the respective toolbar, or select a checked toolbar to remove/hide it. Note that hiding a toolbar is temporary and only hides the toolbar from view in the Toolbar Well.

Open a context menu on a toolbar and select Show/Hide Toolbars to open a submenu where all toolbars can be opened or temporarily closed.

The Show/Hide menu command in the context menu shown in Figure 1.18 provides the same commands you have available in the View ➪ Toolbars submenu. Either of these menus provides you a quick and easy way to show and hide toolbars.

 TIP   If you want all tools within a given toolbar to be shown, select Show All Tools in the context menu.

The last menu item in the context menu shown in Figure 1.18 is used to open the More Tools window where you can add/remove tools among all toolbars.

Default toolbars

When you launch Acrobat for the first time or you set the toolbars to the default view, six different toolbars are docked in the Toolbar Well, including the Tasks toolbar discussed earlier in this section. The remaining default toolbars include:

■ **File toolbar.** These tools are used for general document handling. The default File tools activate commands for Open, Save, Print, and Email and Upload. When all the tools are loaded in the File toolbar the Create PDF from web page and Attach a File tools are added to the toolbar. In Figure 1.19 the File toolbar appears with all the File tools in view.

The File toolbar contains tools for document handling, such as opening PDF documents, saving documents, and printing files.

■ **Page Navigation toolbar.** The default tools in the Page Navigation toolbar shown on the left in Figure 1.19 contain tools for moving back and forth between PDF document pages. The numbers indicate what page you are currently viewing out of the total number of pages in the document. When the toolbar is expanded to show all tools as you see in Figure 1.19, the First Page, Previous Page, Next Page, Last Page, Previous View, and Next View tools are shown.

The Page Navigation toolbar, as the name implies, contains tools for navigating document pages.

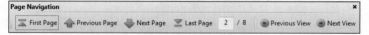

■ **Page Display toolbar.** The Page Display toolbar is the home of many different tools used for page viewing, but only two of the tools appear in the default toolbar. When you first open Acrobat, you see the Scrolling Pages and One Full Page tool. After expanding the toolbar to show all tools as shown in Figure 1.20, the Single Page Continuous, Single Page, Two-Up, Two-Up Continuous, Full Screen Mode, Rotate Counterclockwise, Rotate Clockwise, and Line Weights tools are shown.

The Page Display toolbar contains many tools used for page viewing.

■ **Select & Zoom toolbar.** The tools in this group are used to select text/images, move the page in the Document pane, and zoom in and out of pages in the Document pane. Figure 1.21 shows the Select tool followed by the Hand tool and then the Dynamic Zoom tool, the Zoom Out, Zoom In, Zoom Value tools, Actual Size, Fit Width, Fit Page, Pan & Zoom Window, Loupe tool, and Snapshot.

FIGURE 1.21

Select & Zoom tools are used to select text/images, move a document around the Document pane, copy selections, and view the document page using a number of different zoom tools.

■ **Find toolbar.** Of all the default toolbars, the Find toolbar shown in Figure 1.22 is the only one that does not have additional tools that can be added to the toolbar. However, a pull-down menu exists for making choices to refine your search for words in an open PDF document.

 For more information on searching PDFs, see Chapter 6.

FIGURE 1.22

The Find toolbar is used for searching words in a PDF document.

Managing default toolbars

In addition to loading and unloading tools within toolbars, the toolbars can be moved, docked, and undocked from the Toolbar Well. Here's a list of some of the things you can do with the default toolbars and any other toolbars you decide to view:

■ **Undocking toolbars.** Toolbars can be relocated from within the Toolbar Well to another area within the Acrobat window. For example, you might find it more convenient to move a toolbar you frequently access during an editing session so it is positioned at the right side of the Document pane. If so, just place the cursor on top of the vertical separator bar adjacent to the first tool in a toolbar and drag it away from the Toolbar Well. This vertical line is the *hot spot* used to select the toolbar instead of a tool in the group. Clicking anywhere else in the toolbar selects a tool.

- **Docking toolbars.** To dock a toolbar back in the Toolbar Well once removed, drag the toolbar, again by the vertical separator bar adjacent to the first tool, on top of the Toolbar Well. The toolbar snaps to an available position in the Well. If you drop the toolbar between two other toolbars, the toolbar you relocate back to the Toolbar Well snaps in position between the two docked toolbars.

  Toolbars can also be docked vertically on the left and right sides of the Document pane and at the bottom of the Acrobat window below the status bar. For example, if you drag a toolbar to the left of the Navigation pane and release the mouse button, the toolbar snaps to a docking station and the tools display vertically. In Figure 1.23 you can see toolbars docked on the left (A), and right (B), with one floating toolbar (C) in the Document pane.

- **Resetting toolbars:** You can position toolbars around the Acrobat window and return them to the default positions with one menu command. This is particularly helpful if multiple users work on a single computer or you frequently change editing tasks that require using different tools during different editing sessions. In many cases it's easier to reset toolbars to the original default view than open tools needed for a specific editing task. To set toolbars to their defaults, open a context menu from any toolbar or in the Toolbar Well by right-clicking (Control+clicking on Macintosh), and select the menu item Reset Toolbars as shown in Figure 1.24. Alternately, you can press Alt/Option+F8.

FIGURE 1.23

Toolbars can be docked on all four sides of the Acrobat window and undocked from the Toolbar Well where they appear as floating toolbars.

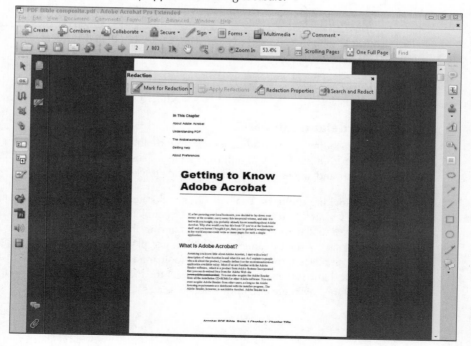

FIGURE 1.24

To return toolbars back to the default view, open a context menu from any toolbar or in the Toolbar Well and select Reset Toolbars.

- **Hiding all toolbars.** Toolbars can be hidden from view to offer you more room when editing a PDF document or browsing the contents of PDFs. To hide the toolbars from view, open a context menu from the Toolbar Well and choose Hide Toolbars. When toolbars are hidden you won't have access to a context menu to get the toolbars back in view. Instead, choose View ⇨ Toolbars ⇨ Show Toolbars to make all toolbars reappear. (Note that using this menu command also hides toolbars.)

- **Hiding a single toolbar.** You can hide a toolbar after it has been undocked from the Toolbar Well. Click the X in the top right corner of the toolbar (Windows) or the small circle on the top left side of the toolbar (Macintosh) to close it, and it disappears from view. From a context menu opened on any toolbar or the Toolbar Well, you can open the toolbar and display it in the Acrobat window again. Toolbars can also be hidden by using the More Tools window, opening a context menu on the Toolbar Well and selecting a toolbar with a check mark to hide it, and selecting toolbars in the View ⇨ Toolbars submenu.

- **Locking toolbars.** The vertical separator bar used to move toolbars disappears when you select Lock Toolbars from a context menu. The toolbars cannot be inadvertently moved after you lock them. To unlock the toolbars, open a context menu and select Lock Toolbars again. The check mark alongside the menu command becomes unchecked and the toolbars are unlocked in the Toolbar Well. If the toolbars are locked and you drag an undocked toolbar on top of the Toolbar Well, it won't dock. You need to first unlock the toolbars before you can redock them. Additionally, you need to unlock toolbars in order to use the Reset Toolbars command in a Toolbar Well context menu to return tools and toolbars back to the default position.

NOTE You can also lock toolbars that are undocked outside of the Toolbar Well. The separator bar on the toolbar disappears on floating toolbars the same as it does for toolbars docked in the Toolbar Well. However, locking undocked toolbars does not prevent you from moving them around the Acrobat window. You can click and drag the title bar for any undocked toolbar and move it to another location.

- **Setting new toolbar defaults.** If you decide to reposition your toolbars and want to keep them fixed as new defaults, Acrobat can do so for you automatically. Move the toolbars to the desired locations and go about your work. When you quit Acrobat and reopen the program, the toolbar positions remain as you last arranged them. Unfortunately, Acrobat does not have a Save Workspace command like you find in several Adobe Creative Suite applications.

TIP If you are unfamiliar with many Acrobat tools, you can change the tool labels to show you a more descriptive label for each tool that offers you a hint of what the tool does. To show more descriptive labels, open a context menu on the Acrobat Toolbar Well and choose Show Button Labels ⇨ All Labels. The toolbars expand and show a text description for each tool's name. Keep this option active until you are familiar with the tool names.

Understanding advanced toolbars

The default toolbars represent a fraction of the tools available to you in Acrobat. Many of the other toolbars remain hidden from view. The reason for this is obvious when you load all the toolbars in the Toolbar Well. You lose a lot of viewing real estate when all toolbars are docked in the Toolbar Well. Unless you have a large display monitor or a second monitor, working on a file in the Document pane when all toolbars are in view gives little room to see document pages. Fortunately, by managing the toolbars you can elect to show only the tools you want to work with and you can move them around the Acrobat window, allowing for the best view.

You open toolbars from menu commands in the Tools menu or by opening a context menu on the Toolbar Well. If you're a seasoned Acrobat user, your first encounter with Acrobat viewers 6 and above might be a bit frustrating if you don't know how to access the tools you want to use. "Where is that Form tool?" you may ask. Don't worry; it's there. You just have to poke around and search for it or, better yet, look over the following descriptions to understand more about how these other tools are grouped into separate toolbars.

Opening advanced toolbars

For the purpose of discussion, I'll refer to the non-default toolbars as advanced toolbars. Acrobat does not refer to all these tools as advanced tools. Some of the tools labeled in the menu commands are not referred to as advanced tools. For clarity in this chapter, though, consider all the following toolbars as advanced toolbars.

You can use three methods for displaying toolbars not visible when you open Acrobat. You can open the View ⇨ Toolbars menu where you find a list of tools in submenus. Select a submenu item to open a toolbar as a floating toolbar in the Acrobat window. Another method is to open a context menu on the Toolbar Well and open toolbars from commands in the menu. A third option, and one that provides more options for viewing all tools and toolbars in a single window, is to use the

More Tools menu command when you open a context menu on the Toolbar Well. As a matter of routine, you should use this option when preparing an Acrobat session that requires you to use several tools and toolbars. All tools except the Form tools Pro are accessible from the context menu.

Analysis toolbar

In Acrobat 8 you had the Measuring toolbar and the Object Data tool opening in two separate tool-bars. These two toolbars have been added to a new toolbar in Acrobat 9 shown in Figure 1.25. In addition to these tools you find the Geospatial Location tool and the Geospatial Registration tool (Acrobat Professional Extended only) that enable you to view geospatial data on maps.

FIGURE 1.25

The Analysis toolbar combines the Measuring tools and the Object Data tool with the new Geospatial tools added in Acrobat Professional Extended.

Advanced Editing toolbar

The Advanced Editing toolbar shown in Figure 1.26 is one you'll use in just about all Acrobat edit-ing sessions. Tools include the Select Object tool that is used to select content you add in Acrobat such as comment markups and form fields. The Article tool is used to create article threads; the Crop and Link tools follow. The TouchUp Text tool is used to edit text on a page, the TouchUp Reading Order is used with accessibility editing, and the last tool is the TouchUp Object tool that is used to select objects such as vector objects and images.

NEW FEATURE You'll notice that the Advanced Editing toolbar does not contain the Movie tool and the Sound tool. These tools have been moved to the new Multimedia toolbar in Acrobat 9. Also notice you have the Button tool in the Advanced Editing toolbar but no access to the other form tools. See "What happened to the Forms tools?" later in this chapter.

CROSS-REF For more information about PDF editing using the Advanced Editing tools, see the chapters in Part III. To learn more about the Link tool, see Chapter 22. To learn how to use the TouchUp Reading Order tool that follows the TouchUp Text tool, see Chapter 25.

FIGURE 1.26

The Advanced Editing toolbar contains a miscellaneous group of tools used for many different editing functions.

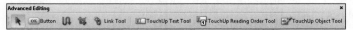

Comment & Markup toolbar

When you open either the View➪Toolbars submenu menus or a context menu on the Toolbar Well, the first menu option after the default Advanced Editing toolbar is the Comment & Markup toolbar. Additionally, you can open the Comment & Markup toolbar from the Comment task button pull-down menu and a menu command in the Comments menu. Select the menu option and the Comment & Markup tools open in their own toolbar. Open a context menu on the toolbar and select Show All Commenting Tools. The toolbar appears as you see in Figure 1.27 when all tools are loaded.

FIGURE 1.27

Open the Comment & Markup toolbar and open a context menu on a tool and select Show All Tools to see all the comment and markup tools.

 When you select the Comment & Markup tools from the More Tools window and check the boxes for all tools, all the tools are loaded *except* the Paste a copied image as stamp tool. To show the tool in the Comment & Markup toolbar, open the Comment & Markup toolbar and open a context menu on any tool in the toolbar. Select Show All Tools and the Paste a copied image as stamp tool is added to the toolbar.

CROSS-REF For more information on using all the Comment & Markup tools, see Chapter 20.

Edit toolbar

The Edit toolbar is the home of a miscellaneous group of editing tools, such as spell-checking, copy, undo, and redo. (See Figure 1.28.)

FIGURE 1.28

The Edit toolbar contains a miscellaneous selection of tools used for spell-checking and editing.

Multimedia toolbar

The Multimedia toolbar combines the Movie, Sound, and 3D tools found in the Advanced Editing toolbar in earlier versions of Acrobat along with the new Flash tool. Note that the Movie tool has been renamed as the Video tool (See Figure 1.29).

CROSS-REF For more information about using the Multimedia tools, see Chapter 23.

FIGURE 1.29

The Multimedia toolbar offer options for adding media to PDF documents.

Print Production toolbar

The Print Production toolbar (see Figure 1.30) enable you to make adjustments on the PDF or alter the content. This toolbar contains tools for assigning traps, preflighting, converting colors, assigning color profiles, adding crop marks, cropping pages, fixing hairlines, transparency flattening, and assigning Job Definitions.

FIGURE 1.30

Use the Print Production tools to open dialog boxes where you can preview and change PDF documents to accommodate prepress and commercial printing.

CROSS-REF For more information on using Print Production tools and preparing files for commercial printing, see Chapter 32.

Redaction toolbar

The Redaction tools are particularly helpful for users who need to remove text content from documents to protect sensitive data such as the names of minors, personal privacy information, and data breeching security policies. When you open the Redaction toolbar you'll see four tools to help you redact PDF documents as shown in Figure 1.31.

FIGURE 1.31

Redaction tools are used to remove sensitive information from PDF documents.

CROSS-REF For a complete explanation of redaction and using the Redaction tools, see Chapter 14.

Typewriter toolbar

The Typewriter tool was added to all Acrobat viewers in a maintenance upgrade during the Acrobat 7 life cycle. This toolbar, shown in Figure 1.32, contains tools for typing text on PDF documents. It's particularly helpful when filling out PDF forms that don't have form fields. Notice the new additions in Acrobat 9 for changing fonts, font colors, and font point sizes.

FIGURE 1.32

New additions to the Typewriter tool include changing fonts, font colors, and font point sizes.

CROSS-REF   For more information on using the Typewriter tools, see Chapter 33.

Properties Bar

You use the Properties Bar (see Figure 1.33) in conjunction with several different tools. After you create comments, links, buttons, and similar content in a PDF document, the selected comment, link, button, and so on displays current properties such as colors, fonts, and line weights in the Properties Bar. You can make changes in the Properties Bar without visiting the Properties dialog box. You can quickly open the Properties Bar with a keyboard shortcut (Ctrl/⌘+E) or via a context menu opened on the Toolbar Well.

FIGURE 1.33

The Properties Bar offers a quick solution for editing item properties without the need for opening dialog boxes.

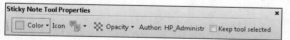

What happened to the Forms tools?

Don't be alarmed when you first open Acrobat 9 and look for the Forms toolbar. The form tools are all available to you but they don't appear in the current viewer mode when you open a PDF document. You need to change modes to the new Acrobat 9 Form Editing Mode.

NEW FEATURE   Choose Forms ➪ Start Form Wizard or Add or Edit Fields and you'll change the interface mode to Form Editing Mode. Instead of a toolbar housing the Form tools, you'll find all the same form tools available to you under the Add New Field pull-down menu as shown in Figure 1.34.

FIGURE 1.34

Enter Form Editing Mode and choose a form tool from the Add New Field pull-down menu.

Form Editing Mode does have a toolbar; however, the Form Editing Mode toolbar is not one that you can undock from the area reserved for toolbars. Toolbars are fixed to a location similar to the Acrobat Toolbar Well in Form Editing Mode appearing at the top of the window. If you want the individual tools to appear without having to open the Add New Field menu, open the menu and choose Show Tools on Toolbar. The individual form tools are displayed on the Form Edit toolbar as shown in Figure 1.35.

FIGURE 1.35

Open the Add New Field pull-down menu and choose Show Forms Toolbar to display the individual form tools in the Form Edit toolbar.

Customizing the Acrobat workplace

Whether you're an Acrobat pro or a new Acrobat user, seeing all those toolbars loaded and scattered across the Toolbar Well for the first time can be very intimidating. As you poke around and possibly feel a little frustration when trying to identify the right tool icon to select the right tool for the task at hand, please realize that Acrobat is a multifaceted program serving a huge array of needs for different users. Not all the tools and features are designed for use in a single Acrobat session. You may be a PDF forms author with a need only for Basic tools, Navigation tools, Edit tools, and who switches over to Form Editing Mode. In another session you may be a reviewer and only have need for the Comment and Markup tools. You might be an eBook author and need to work with many features for creating and viewing eBooks, or you might want to edit PDF pages and post modified PDFs on your Web site.

When learning all the tools and commands contained in Acrobat, be certain to look over all the chapters where tools are discussed. Learn how to access toolbars and organize them in the Toolbar Well. When you begin a new Acrobat session, set up your environment so you can easily select a tool from toolbars you dock in the Toolbar Well.

As a starting point, you can configure Acrobat to provide you with immediate feedback related to tools selection and keyboard shortcuts. As you first start using Acrobat, follow the steps in the next section to help you customize your environment for more efficient editing and less frustration. In this example, an environment for engaging in a commenting session is used. You can change the toolbars to meet needs in PDF editing or PDF creation, or add tools for some other kind of work you do.

STEPS: Setting up the Acrobat environment

1. **Return to toolbar defaults.** Open Acrobat. Position the cursor on any area in the Toolbar Well and right-click to open a context menu (Control+click for Macintosh) and select Reset Toolbars.

2. **Open the More Tools window.** From a context menu opened from the Toolbar Well, select More Tools to open the More Tools window.

3. **Add the tools you intend to use to the Comment & Markup toolbar.** This is a personal choice. Look over all the Comment & Markup tools and check just those tools you intend to use. Be certain to check the box for the Comment & Markup toolbar so the toolbar shows up when you leave the More Tools window. (See Figure 1.36.)

FIGURE 1.36

The More Tools window

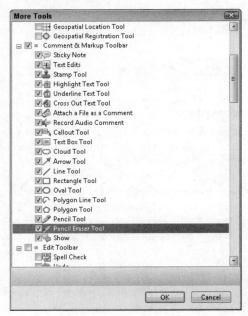

4. **Add some Edit tools.** While still in the More Tools window, scroll to the Advanced Editing toolbar. One tool you'll use frequently in almost all editing sessions is the Select Object tool (denoted with an arrowhead icon). Click the check box for this tool. Other tools won't be used under most circumstances such as the Article tool, Link tool, and so on. Uncheck all the tools you anticipate not using.

5. **Add the Spell Check tool.** Scroll to the Edit toolbar and check the Edit toolbar.

6. **Exit the More Tools window.** When certain about the tools you think you'll use in a given editing session, click OK and all the toolbars open as floating toolbars.

7. **Open the Properties Bar.** Again open a context menu on the Toolbar Well and select Properties Bar from the menu options. Note that this tool is not available in the More Tools window and needs to be opened from a context menu or the View ⇨ Toolbars submenu.

8. **Dock the toolbars.** After opening all the toolbars you want to use for a given editing session return to the Toolbar Well context menu and select Dock Toolbars. This command moves all the toolbars to the Toolbar Well, as shown in Figure 1.37.

FIGURE 1.37

Toolbars docked in the Toolbar Well include the A) File toolbar, B) Select & Zoom toolbar, C) Advanced Editing toolbar, D) Edit toolbar, E) Comment & Markup toolbar, and F) the Properties Bar.

Tooltips

When you select All Labels from a context menu or preference setting, you see tool descriptions on many tools. However, not all tools describe the tool with a label. For example, look at the Zoom In tool (the plus symbol). It should be apparent to you what the tool does by viewing the icon in the toolbar. Other tools' functions, however, may not be so apparent from viewing the tool icons. Fortunately, you have some extra help in the form of tooltips. To view a tooltip, place the cursor over a tool in the Toolbar Well or on a floating toolbar, and pause a moment before selecting the tool. A tooltip appears inside a yellow box directly below the cursor with a label describing the tool. In Figure 1.38 you can see the tooltip that appears when the cursor is placed over the Sticky Note tool. As you move the cursor over different tools, the tooltips change to reflect the description of the targeted tool.

FIGURE 1.38

Place the cursor over a tool and pause a moment before selecting the tool. A tooltip describing the tool opens below the mouse cursor.

As you become familiar with the tools, you can return to the context menu opened from the Toolbar Well and choose Button Labels ➪ No Labels. When No Labels is active, your toolbars shrink and offer you more room in the Toolbar Well.

Panels

Other tools available to you in all Acrobat viewers are *panels*. Panels are similar to toolbars in that they can be docked to a docking station called the Navigation pane; they can be undocked and floated around the Acrobat window; they can contain pull-down menus for selecting more options; a series of default panels appears docked in the Navigation pane; and you can open additional panels from menu commands.

A couple distinctions between toolbars and panels are that panels can be placeholders for information, and tools can appear inside a panel. Whereas tools are used in the Document pane, many panel operations take place directly in the panel. Toolbars remain relatively fixed in size, but panels can be sized and stretched along the Acrobat window to provide you with more room to work within the panel or view the information contained within the panel. In addition, some panels contain their own tools where edits can be made in the panel and dynamically reflected on the document page. Panels help you organize content, view specific content across many pages, and provide some tools for global editing of PDF files.

Default panels

As with toolbars, Acrobat displays a series of panels docked in a well when you first launch the program. Panels are contained in the Navigation pane along the left side of the Acrobat window. By default, the Navigation pane is collapsed; however, you can save PDF documents in such a manner where a panel expands when a file is opened in any Acrobat viewer. These settings are document-specific and can be toggled on or off for individual PDF documents.

CROSS-REF For more information about setting opening views for panel displays, see Chapter 4.

Pages

Acrobat users have been familiar with the thumbnail view of each page since the early days of Acrobat. A mini view of each page in the active PDF document is displayed in the Pages pane, as shown in Figure 1.39. The Pages pane offers you menu options for arranging, deleting, inserting, and editing pages in a number of ways. You can zoom in to the thumbnail views as large as or even larger than a page viewed in the Document pane.

FIGURE 1.39

Thumbnails are found in the Pages panel in all Acrobat viewers. The thumbnail view of document pages can be sized larger and smaller using context menu commands.

CROSS-REF For a complete description of working with pages (thumbnails), see Chapter 16.

Bookmarks

 The second default panel in the Navigation pane is the Bookmark panel. You can save PDF documents in a manner where the bookmarks are visible when the file opens in Acrobat. Bookmarks are visible in an open Navigation pane, as shown in Figure 1.40. You can open and close the Navigation pane by pressing F4. You can also grab the vertical separator bar at the right edge of the Navigation pane and move it left and right to size the pane.

Bookmarks are navigation buttons that can launch a page, a view, or one of many different Action types similar to link and button actions. Anyone familiar with Acrobat already knows much about bookmarks and how to navigate pages by clicking individual bookmarks in the panel.

FIGURE 1.40

Bookmarks can be displayed in the Navigation pane when a file opens.

CROSS-REF   To learn how to create and manage bookmarks and add actions, see Chapter 17.

Signatures

 Digital signatures help you manage signed documents; the Signatures panel enables you to perform tasks such as displaying signatures in the Signature pane, verifying signatures, clearing them, deleting them, and so on. All these editing tasks with signatures are still available in Acrobat Professional and Acrobat Standard as is signature validation, which is also available in all Acrobat viewers.

CROSS-REF   For a complete description of creating and managing digital signatures, see Chapter 26.

Attachments

 The Attachments pane (see Figure 1.41) in all Acrobat viewers is used to display, manage, and extract file attachments. You can attach files in Acrobat and extract file attachments using all Acrobat viewers including Adobe Reader.

FIGURE 1.41

The Attachments panel provides options for managing file attachments. Attachments can be extracted from within Adobe Reader.

CROSS-REF For a complete description of adding file attachments to PDF documents, see Chapter 15. For more on extracting attachments from within Adobe Reader, see Chapter 3.

Comments

The Comments panel shows you comments in an expanded horizontal view, just like the Attachments panel. When you click the Comments panel, you'll notice a number of pull-down menus (signified by down-pointing arrows at the top of the pane), a list of comments that can be expanded and collapsed, and a host of tools within the panel, as shown in Figure 1.42.

FIGURE 1.42

The Comments panel

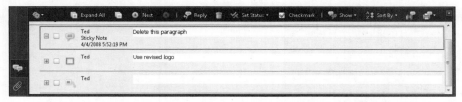

CROSS-REF For a complete description of creating and managing comments, see Chapters 20 and 21.

Hidden panels

As with toolbars, you can choose to view additional panels through menu commands. You can choose to display a number of other panels in the Acrobat window and dock them in the Navigation pane. To open a hidden panel, choose View ➪ Navigation Panels. From the submenu, you'll find all the panels available. In Figure 1.43, the list shows Navigation panels available in Acrobat Pro Extended.

Another way to access the Navigation panels is through a context menu. Right-click (Windows) or Control+click (Macintosh) on the Navigation pane and a menu shows all the Navigation panels. In order to see the panels, you must first open them from the Navigation Panels submenu and dock them in the Navigation pane. Opening a context menu offers an additional menu command for Show/Hide Navigation Panel Buttons as shown in Figure 1.44.

The list includes the default panels. If you select a default panel, the Navigation pane opens and the panel is selected. When you select a hidden panel — in other words, a panel other than those docked in the Navigation pane when you first launch Acrobat — the panel opens in the Acrobat window as a floating panel with one or more panels contained in the window. Drag a panel to the Navigation pane and it docks and then becomes visible in a context menu opened from the Navigation pane.

FIGURE 1.43

Open the Navigation Panels menu and a submenu displays all Navigation panels.

FIGURE 1.44

Once Navigation panels have been docked in the Navigation pane, they appear in a context menu opened from the Navigation pane.

Articles

The first of the hidden panels listed in the Navigation Panels submenu is Articles. Choose View ➪ Navigation Panels ➪ Articles to open a floating panel. Articles enable you to create article threads to help users follow passages of text in a logical reading order. You won't find any new features added to the Article tool since Acrobat 5.

CROSS-REF   For information on creating article threads and managing them, see Chapter 5.

Content

A panel designed for managing the structural content of PDF documents is found in the Content panel. When you choose View ➪ Navigation Panels ➪ Content, the Content panel opens in a floating panel as shown in Figure 1.45. Content features help you reflow tagged PDF files and manipulate the structure of tagged documents.

FIGURE 1.45

The Content panel opens in a floating panel where the structural content of the open file is reported.

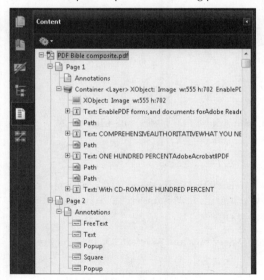

CROSS-REF   For information on working with the Content panel and tagged PDF documents, see Chapter 25.

Destinations

 Destinations work similarly to bookmarks, in that specific views are captured and listed in the panel. Clicking a destination opens the associated page in the Document pane, whereas clicking a bookmark opens the associated view (page and zoom).

 CROSS-REF For information on creating destinations and managing them, see Chapter 22.

Layers

 If you create documents containing Adobe PDF layers, the Layers panel permits you to toggle layer views and work with layer properties. In Figure 1.46, the Layers panel is open showing visible and hidden layers.

FIGURE 1.46

The Layers panel enables you to manage layer visibility.

CROSS-REF To understand more about working with Adobe PDF layers, see Chapter 24.

Model Tree

 The Model Tree panel lets you examine information related to 3D drawings. You can review assets, hide and show drawing parts, toggle views, review comments, and more on 3D drawings. In Figure 1.47 you can see the model tree shown for a 3D image.

CROSS-REF For more information about viewing 3D drawings and Acrobat 3D, see Chapter 2.

Order

You use the Order panel to manage reading order of documents. This panel also relates to document accessibility, like the options available in the Tags panel. The Order panel enables you to add tags to a document, clear tags, and reorder a page's contents to change a reading order that might be read aloud by a screen reader.

FIGURE 1.47

The Model Tree panel is designed to work with 3D drawings.

 CROSS-REF For information on working with the Order panel, understanding screen readers, and document accessibility, see Chapter 25.

Tags

Tagged PDF files provide more editing capability with PDF documents, and the files can be made accessible to adaptive devices such as screen readers. For adding, editing, and annotating tags in PDF documents, use the Tags panel. Together with the Content panel options, you have much control over document accessibility.

CROSS-REF To understand accessibility and the advantages of creating tagged PDF documents, see Chapter 25.

Panel menus

Each of the panels contains its own pull-down menu. When a panel is open in the Navigation pane or in a floating window, select the Options down-pointing arrow to open a pull-down menu, as shown in Figure 1.48. Menu commands found in panels may or may not be available from the top-level menu bar. Additionally, some panels, like the Attachments and Comments panels, offer you several pull-down menus.

FIGURE 1.48

Panel Options menus provide menu commands specific to each panel function.

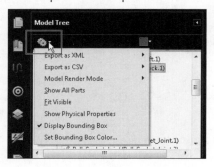

Context menus

Context menus can display different options for panel choices depending on where you open a context menu. If you move the cursor to an empty area when all text and objects in a panel are deselected and open a context menu, the menu options may be different than when you select text or an object in a panel. However, this is not always the case, because a few panels provide you with the same options regardless of whether something is selected or not. In Figure 1.49 a context menu is opened within the Bookmarks panel. In this case you need to open the menu on a bookmark name. If you attempt to open a context menu in an empty area in the pane, no menu opens.

FIGURE 1.49

A context menu opened on a bookmark.

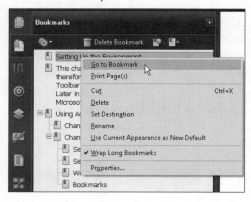

Understanding Preferences

Preferences enable you to customize your work sessions in Acrobat. You can access a Preferences dialog box from within any Acrobat viewer and from within a Web browser when viewing PDFs as inline views. A huge number of preferences exist that all relate to specific tool groups or task categories, and it would not make as much sense to cover them here in the opening chapter as it would within chapters related to using tools and methods influenced by preference choices.

Some general things you should know about preferences is that they are contained in a dialog box as shown in Figure 1.50. You make a topic selection in the list on the left side of the dialog box and the related preferences are shown to the right side of the list. You make choices for preferences by selecting check boxes or making menu selections from pull-down menus. When you complete making your preference choices, click OK at the bottom of the dialog box.

Almost all the preferences you change in the Preferences dialog box are dynamic, which means you don't need to quit Acrobat and relaunch the program for a preference choice to take effect. Preferences remain in effect until you change them again. If you quit Acrobat and relaunch the program, the preferences you last made are honored by Acrobat. However, if for some reason the program crashes and you don't shut it down properly, any new preference changes will not be recognized when the program is launched again.

FIGURE 1.50

Press Ctrl/⌘+K to open the Preferences dialog box. Click a category on the left and the choices are reflected to the left of the categories list.

If you find some operation in Acrobat not working as you think it should, first take a look at the Preferences dialog box. In many cases you'll find a check box or menu command not enabled to permit you to perform a task. As you become familiar with specific tool groups and menu commands, make a habit of routinely visiting the Preferences dialog box so you understand all the toggles and switches that affect tool and viewing behavior.

Summary

This chapter offers you a general introduction for working in Acrobat Standard Acrobat Pro and Acrobat Pro Extended and helps you understand the environment, the user interface, and some of the many new features added to the commercial Acrobat products. At the very least, you should know how to go about finding help when you first start working in the program. Some of the more important points discussed in this chapter include the following:

- Adobe Acrobat is a multifaceted program designed to provide solutions for many different business professionals. Several types of Acrobat viewers exist, ranging in features to suit different user needs. The most sophisticated of the three viewers is Acrobat Pro Extended (Windows), now in version 9. Acrobat Standard (Windows only) offers fewer tools and menu commands than Acrobat Pro (Windows and Macintosh).

- PDF, short for Portable Document Format, was developed by Adobe Systems and was designed to exchange documents between computers and across computer platforms while maintaining file integrity.

- The PDF language format has changed version numbers along with the Acrobat viewers. Beginning in Acrobat 9, the PDF specification is no longer owned by Adobe. The International Organization for Standards now regulates the PDF specification.

- Tasks are performed through the use of menus, tools, and panels that can be accessed through mouse selections and keyboard shortcuts.

- The extensive list of tools appears in an abbreviated form when you open Acrobat and view the default toolbars. You can open additional toolbars from menu commands or the new More Tools window. You can dock toolbars in the Toolbar Well or float them around the Acrobat window.

- Panels are similar to toolbars in that they can be docked and undocked from a well called the Navigation pane. Panels contain pull-down menus, and some panels contain tools.

- You can customize the Acrobat workplace to suit your work style through the use of different preference choices. When preferences, panels, and toolbars are changed from their default views, the new views are saved when you quit your Acrobat session. They remain unchanged until you change them again or reset them to defaults.

- Preferences are settings that apply globally to Acrobat and influence the behavior of tools and menu commands.

Chapter 2

Using Acrobat Viewers

IN THIS CHAPTER

Understanding the differences among the Acrobat viewers

Understanding the Acrobat Product Line

Using Acrobat plug-ins

In Chapter 1 you got a feel for some of the tools and menu commands provided in Acrobat Standard and Acrobat Pro, and Acrobat Pro Extended. If you're a PDF author and you use Acrobat Standard or Pro, or Pro Extended, knowing the capabilities of one viewer versus another is important for both job efficiency and productivity, as well as usefulness to the end user. You may want to add multimedia to a PDF document. Therefore, you need to know what authoring tool is needed to import video and sound. You may be sending out a document for review and want to solicit comments. Therefore, you need to know what viewer a user needs to send comments back to you.

At times you may find that none of the Acrobat products can help you do some editing tasks needed in your workflow. Fortunately, you have options for acquiring Acrobat plug-ins developed by third-party manufacturers that add much more functionality to the Acrobat tools and menu commands.

Many of the chapters ahead give you an idea of the distinctions between Acrobat Standard and Acrobat Pro, and Acrobat Pro Extended and the tools accessible from one viewer versus the other. This chapter introduces you to the Acrobat viewers, points out some differences among them, and shows you how to use Acrobat plug-ins when you need more features than the viewers provide.

Viewer Distinctions

Adobe Reader, Acrobat Standard (Windows only in version 8 and 9), Acrobat Pro, and Acrobat Pro Extended (Windows only) are designed to serve different users with different purposes. It should be obvious to you that

Adobe Reader, as a free download from Adobe's Web site, is much more limited in features and performance than the products you purchase.

For a general overview, take a look at the following descriptions of the Acrobat products.

Adobe Reader

Adobe Reader is available for download from Adobe's Web site free of charge. The Adobe Reader software is distributed for the purpose of viewing, printing, and searching, on PDF files created by users of Acrobat Standard, Acrobat Pro, or Acrobat Pro Extended. Additionally, Adobe Reader is used for filling in forms on PDFs created with Acrobat Standard (new in Acrobat 9), Acrobat Pro, and Acrobat Pro Extended. The major features of Adobe Reader include:

- **Viewing and printing.** These features are common across all Acrobat viewers. You can view, navigate, and print PDF documents with Adobe Reader.

- **Forms completion and submission.** Adobe Reader enables you to complete forms but not save the form field data unless the forms carry special usage rights for Adobe Reader users. Forms are submitted through the use of buttons created on forms for emailing or submitting data to Web servers.

CROSS-REF For more information on enabling PDFs with usage rights, see Chapter 19.

- **Comment and Review.** PDFs can be enabled with usage rights for commenting and review in Acrobat Pro, and Acrobat Pro Extended. Once enabled, Reader users can participate in a review workflow and save PDFs locally with comments and markups.

- Adobe LiveCycle **Reader Extensions ES.** If an organization uses the Adobe LiveCycle Reader Extensions ES product available from Adobe Systems to enhance PDF files, Adobe Reader users can digitally sign documents and save form data.

   A distinction exists between enabling PDFs with usage rights from within Acrobat Standard, Acrobat Pro, and Acrobat Pro Extended and using the Adobe LiveCycle Reader Extensions ES. Licensing restrictions do apply when enabling documents and you should be aware of these restrictions. See Chapter 19 for all you need to know about enabling PDFs and licensing restrictions.

In addition to the preceding, Adobe Reader provides support for eBook services and searching PDF documents, as well as extended support for working with accessible documents.

CROSS-REF For more information on using tools in Adobe Reader, see Chapter 4.

Acrobat Elements

What happened to Acrobat Elements? In a word, it's gone. You won't find the low cost PDF creation tool shipped with Acrobat 9.

Acrobat Standard versus Acrobat Pro Products

Acrobat Standard is available only on Windows in version 8 and 9 of Acrobat. The Macintosh version was discontinued when Acrobat 8 was released. Adobe Systems is a company that tries hard to respond to user needs, but there are limitations. If a product does not support the development costs, then it is likely to be discontinued. This is the case with Acrobat Standard on the Macintosh. Many users of Acrobat on the Mac acquire Acrobat Pro in a bundled purchase with the Adobe Creative Suite. Independent sales of Acrobat Standard were minimal on the Mac during the Acrobat 7 life cycle. Therefore, Adobe could not justify the development costs for continuing the product. On Windows, sales of Acrobat Standard were much greater, and therefore you see Acrobat Standard still available.

Acrobat Standard is the lightweight of the authoring programs. However, Acrobat Standard still offers many tools for PDF creation and authoring. Without going into every tool that differs between Acrobat Standard and Acrobat Pro, the major differences include the following limitations:

NEW FEATURE   **Acrobat 9 Standard now supports creating Acrobat PDF forms.**

- **Form field authoring.** The Forms toolbar has been added to Acrobat Standard. This is a major upgrade for Acrobat Standard users. You can create PDF forms with field objects, add JavaScripts, distribute forms, and collect form data. Acrobat Standard also supports enabling forms for Adobe Reader users.

CROSS-REF   **For information on writing JavaScripts, see Chapter 36 (on the CD-ROM).**

- **Professional printing.** Acrobat Standard does not provide options for soft proofing color, pre-flighting jobs, or commercial printing using such features as color separations, frequency control, transparency flattening, and so on. All these print controls are contained only in Acrobat Pro.

CROSS-REF   **For information on preflighting, soft proofing color, and commercial printing, see Chapter 32.**

- **Adding Adobe Reader usage rights.** You can add usage rights that enable Adobe Reader users to extract file attachments from PDF documents, and in Acrobat 9 Standard, add usage rights for Reader users to save form field data and add digital signatures.

CROSS-REF   **For information on adding usage rights for Adobe Reader users, see Chapter 19.**

- **Redaction.** The tools for redacting documents are not available to Acrobat Standard users.

CROSS-REF   **For information on using the Redaction tools and redacting documents, see Chapter 14.**

- **Batch processing.** Acrobat Standard does not support batch processing and running batch commands.

CROSS-REF For information on creating batch sequences, see Chapter 18.

- **Creating index files.** Acrobat Catalog is not part of Acrobat Standard. You can create index files only with the Acrobat Pro products through a menu command that launches Acrobat Catalog.

CROSS-REF For information on creating index files, see Chapter 6.

- **Creating PDFs.** Acrobat Standard offers support for an impressive range of file types that can be converted to PDF. However, Acrobat Standard doesn't support creating PDFs from certain file types such as AutoCAD, Microsoft Visio, and Microsoft Project. Acrobat Standard does use Acrobat Distiller, but the Acrobat Standard Distiller does not support PDF/X, PDF/E, and PDF/A compliance. Additionally, Acrobat Standard does not support Adobe Presenter features.

CROSS-REF For information on using Acrobat Distiller, see Chapter 10. For information on PDF/A and PDF/X, see Chapters 10 and 32.

- **Engineering tools.** Acrobat Standard does not support some features used by engineers and technical illustrators, such as merging and flattening layers.

CROSS-REF For information on using the measuring tools and working with layers, see Chapter 24.

The preceding items are some of the major differences between Acrobat Standard and the Acrobat Pro viewers. You will discover subtle differences as you work with the programs. For example, Acrobat Standard doesn't support comparing documents, migrating comments, Bates numbering, show and snap to grids, converting .dwg and .indd files, does not contain the PDF Optimizer for repurposing files, and so on.

If your mission is to recommend the product for purchase or make the decision for your own use, be aware of the three primary distinctions between the products: Acrobat Standard does not support professional printing, engineering tools, or adding Adobe Reader usage rights for review and comment and forms data saving and digital signatures. If your work is in one of these areas, you need to purchase Acrobat Pro.

Acrobat Pro Extended

Acrobat Pro Extended is a commercial Acrobat product with all the features of Acrobat Pro plus several other features making it the high end Acrobat performance tool. Acrobat Pro Extended has all the features previously found in the former Acrobat 3D product as well as more robust features for both technical people and knowledge workers. Included with Acrobat Pro Extended you find support for CAD drawing conversions from a huge range of file formats, the Adobe Presenter application for use with Microsoft PowerPoint, the ability to transcoded video files to Adobe Flash format, and special tools for adding geospatial data on maps.

CROSS-REF For more information on Adobe Presenter, see Chapter 28. For more information on transcoding video files, see Chapter 23.

- **File conversion.** Acrobat Pro Extended supports 3D drawing translations from all major 3D drawing programs including AutoCAD. These drawings can be imported directly into Acrobat Pro Extended where comments, reviews, and markups can be applied and then shared with anyone using the free Adobe Reader.

- **Capture 3D files.** Acrobat Pro Extended includes Acrobat Pro Extended Capture so that you can convert any 3D drawing to PDF for use in Acrobat Pro Extended.

- **Optimize, enhance, and animate.** Features in Acrobat Pro Extended enable you to optimize drawings for faster display. You can add multiple views, materials, textures, multiple types of lighting, and create animations such as exploded views and more.

- **File compression.** 3D drawing files can be optimized for smaller file sizes.

- **3D drawing creation.** You can create simple 3D drawings directly in Acrobat Pro Extended.

- **Photorealistic rendering.** You can render photorealistic images and create 2D raster and vector images.

- **Adobe Presenter.** Together with Microsoft PowerPoint, Adobe Presenter is used to preserve PowerPoint animations and export to a Flash file contained within a PDF document.

- **PDFMapping.** You can add geospatial data to maps such as longitude and latitude coordinates.

- **Transcoding any video/audio formats to FLV/SWF.** Video formats can be transcoded to Adobe Flash files.

There's much more to Acrobat Pro Extended. If you're an engineer or technical artist working with CAD applications, you might want to check out some of the benefits of working with Acrobat Pro Extended. This book does not cover all Acrobat Pro Extended features in the chapters ahead. To learn more about Acrobat Pro Extended, take a look at the Acrobat Pro Extended Corner on the Adobe Acrobat User Community Web site at www.acrobatusers.com/go/3D.

Acrobat Pro versus Acrobat Pro Extended

Acrobat Pro Extended takes advantage of some impressive new features Adobe made available in Acrobat 9. In addition to all the 3D features available in Acrobat Pro Extended that aren't available in Acrobat Pro, you also find some nonrelated 3D features that have been added to Acrobat Pro Extended in version 9 that include:

- **Video to Flash Conversion.** In Acrobat Pro Extended you can convert various video formats to FLV. Connecting to Flash Widgets and frame accurate commenting is supported on Flash video content.

CROSS-REF For information on video to Flash conversions, see Chapter 23.

- **Support for Adobe Presenter Features.** Adobe Presenter is a plug-in for Microsoft PowerPoint that enables you to create rich, interactive presentations from PowerPoint files.

CROSS-REF For information on Adobe Presenter and PDF presentations, see Chapter 28.

- **PDF Mapping.** Authoring PDF mapping features such as integration of geospatial data and collaboration is supported in Acrobat Pro Extended.

CROSS-REF For information on PDF mapping, see Chapter 20.

- **3D Support.** Expanded support for architectural and manufacturing engineers.

Adobe's Acrobat Product Line Strategy

In case you're confused about where the new Acrobat Pro Extended product fits in Adobe's Acrobat product lineup, let's take a quick look at the marketing strategy for the Acrobat products. In earlier versions of Acrobat you found Acrobat 3D, which was a product marketed to a vertical market audience of engineers and manufacturing professionals. Acrobat 3D contained all the features of Acrobat Pro with the addition of the 3D features that were primarily used by engineers. Adobe marketing was focused on delivering this product to engineering and manufacturing professionals.

In version 9 of Acrobat we have Adobe Acrobat Pro Extended, and we find the inclusion of new features such as video to flash conversion and support for Adobe Presenter, which aren't features related specifically to engineers. Therefore, you may be wondering why these types of features are added to a product that's targeted at the engineering market.

In short, Adobe is positioning Acrobat ProExtended to a horizontal audience. The 3D features remain in Acrobat Pro Extended with the expansion of additional features that will appeal to PDF authors in many other disciplines. Think of Acrobat Pro Extended much as you would view Adobe Photoshop Extended in the Photoshop line of products.

What Acrobat product you choose depends on your PDF creation needs and your budget. Acrobat Standard is the low-cost PDF authoring application on Windows only that now includes forms authoring and enabling features for Adobe Reader users. It doesn't have many vertical applications features for industries such as printing, law, and engineering but might be just the ticket for general business office workers, which is the market Adobe hopes to capture with this product.

Acrobat Pro is the midpoint for PDF authors. You find all the features of Acrobat Standard plus some vertical applications for the print industry and law. Unless you have a need for engineering tools such as CAD and map conversions but want more features than Acrobat Standard, this product might be your best option.

Acrobat Pro Extended is the high-end performer that includes all features of Acrobat Pro plus all the vertical applications including engineering. Additionally, it also includes some impressive new features for rich media including transcoding video files to Adobe Flash format, the addition of Adobe Presenter, and a wonderful set of tools designed for cartographers. If the high end is your desire, then Acrobat Pro Extended is your product.

Using Plug-ins

All Acrobat viewers support a plug-in architecture. Plug-ins are installed during your Acrobat installation and loaded when you launch Acrobat. Many of the features you find when exercising commands and using tools are made possible by the use of plug-ins. To view the current plug-ins loaded with the viewer you use, choose Help ⇨ About Adobe Plug-ins. The About Adobe Plug-Ins dialog box opens as shown in Figure 2.1.

FIGURE 2.1

The About Adobe Plug-Ins dialog box lists all the plug-ins accessible to your viewer.

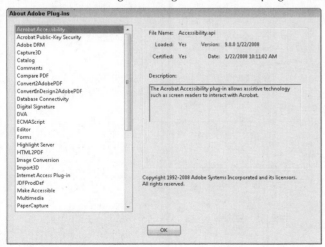

The list in the left side of the dialog box lists the names of the installed plug-ins. Click a name to see a description for the plug-in, including whether the plug-in is certified, the version number, creation date, text description, and dependencies. To examine different plug-ins, select them in the left pane and view the description on the right side of the dialog box.

Acrobat plug-ins are created by Adobe Systems and third-party developers. All plug-ins from Adobe Systems are *certified* plug-ins. No third-party plug-ins are certified. Some features in Acrobat require that only certified plug-ins be loaded before the feature is enabled. Working with eBooks is one example where only certified plug-ins can be used.

NOTE Any time a document has Adobe DRM (Digital Rights Management) protection such as eBooks and/or documents protected with the Adobe LiveCycle Rights Management ES Server, the viewer is launched in *certified plug-in mode*. This mode loads only Adobe plug-ins and disables all third-party plug-ins.

In order to instruct your Acrobat viewer to open with only certified plug-ins, open the Preferences dialog box by choosing Edit ➪ Preferences. Click General in the left pane and select the Use only certified plug-ins check box, as shown in Figure 2.2. When you quit your Acrobat viewer and relaunch the program, only certified plug-ins will load.

FIGURE 2.2

Select Use only certified plug-ins to allow only certified plug-ins to load upon opening.

Plug-ins developed by third-party developers can also be loaded. The list of available resources for adding to Acrobat functionality in the form of add-ons and plug-ins is almost limitless. As you review all the chapters in this book and find that something you want to accomplish in your work-flow is not covered, look for a plug-in developed by a third-party developer. Chances are that you can find a product well suited to do the job.

Plug-ins for Acrobat are far too numerous to mention in this book. For a single source where you can view a list of plug-ins, download demonstration copies, and make purchases, visit Acrobat Plug-ins World (`http://acrobat.pluginsworld.com`), the Planet PDF store at `www.pdfstore.com`, the Adobe Store at `www.adobe.com` and click on the Store link, or The PowerXChange at `www.thepowerxchange.com`. On several Web sites you'll find product descriptions and workflow solutions for almost any third-party product designed to work with Acrobat. When you visit one of the Web sites and review the products, be certain the product you purchase is upgraded to work with Acrobat 9.0 and the viewer you use. All products are listed with links to the manufacturer's Web sites, so you can find information on product descriptions, version numbers, and compatibility issues.

Installing plug-ins

Most plug-ins you acquire from third-party developers are accompanied by an installer program. Installing plug-ins is easy. Open the folder for a plug-in you download from a Web site and double-click the installer icon. The installer routine finds the plug-ins folder inside your Acrobat folder and the plug-in is loaded when you launch Acrobat.

If a plug-in is not accompanied by an installer program, you need to manually add the plug-in to your Acrobat plug-ins folder. On Windows, open the Program Files\Adobe\Acrobat 9.0\Acrobat\ plug_ins folder. Copy the plug-in you want to install to this folder.

On the Macintosh, open your Applications folder. Open the Acrobat 9 Pro folder from within the Applications folder. Press and hold the Control key and click the program icon (Adobe Acrobat 9 Pro) to open a context menu, as shown in Figure 2.3. From the menu items, click Show Package Contents.

When you open the Package Contents, the Contents folder appears in a single window. Double-click the folder to open it. Several folders appear within the Contents folder, one of which is named Plug-ins. Open this folder and copy your plug-in to it.

FIGURE 2.3

Open the Package Contents on the Macintosh to gain access to the Plug-ins folder.

Uninstalling plug-ins

If your plug-in is not accompanied by an uninstaller program, you need to either disable the plug-in or physically remove it from the Acrobat plug-ins folder. A temporary solution is to disable third-party plug-ins by opening the Preferences dialog box, clicking on Startup, and selecting the check box for Use only certified plug-ins, as shown earlier in Figure 2.2.

To permanently remove a plug-in, open the plug-ins folder as described in the previous section, "Installing plug-ins," and drag the plug-in out of the Acrobat plug-ins folder.

CAUTION   Some plug-ins are installed in their own folder. To remove a plug-in, drag the folder where the plug-in is installed out of the Acrobat plug-ins folder. Be certain not to remove the Acrobat plug-ins folder from within the Acrobat folder. Doing so disables all tools and menu commands using plug-ins.

Resolving plug-in conflicts

At times you may find a plug-in conflict among several third-party products or a plug-in that may have a bug. If your Acrobat functionality is impaired and you can't launch the program, hold down the Shift key while double-clicking the program icon to launch your viewer. All plug-ins are disabled when you use the modifier key. Open the Preferences dialog box again and select the Use only certified plug-ins check box. Quit and relaunch the program, and the offending plug-in is eliminated during startup.

If a plug-in is creating a problem, you may need to use a process of elimination to figure out which one it is by opening your plug-ins folder and removing all plug-ins. Then add several plug-ins at a time back to the plug-ins folder and launch your viewer. Keep adding plug-ins back into the plug-ins folder until you discover the plug-in that produces the error.

Working with plug-ins

There are many different plug-ins that provide you more features when working with Adobe Acrobat and Adobe Reader than can be covered in this book. To pick one out among the many is a hard choice. For your own workflow, visit the Planet PDF Store, Adobe Store, Acrobat plug-ins World, the PowerXChange, or the Acrobat User Community and explore various plug-ins available for download. Try to find a plug-in that offers at least a demo trial period and download it.

Almost all plug-ins come with a ReadMe file or user manual. Before installing a plug-in, be certain to review the installation recommendations by the developer. Install the plug-in and give it a try.

Summary

- The four Acrobat viewers include Adobe Reader, Acrobat Standard, Acrobat Pro, and Acrobat Pro Extended. All of these applications can create Adobe PDFs (with the exception of Adobe Reader).

- Adobe Reader is a free download from Adobe's Web site. All other products require purchase.

- Acrobat Standard offers fewer features than Acrobat Pro and is available in version 8 and 9 on Windows only. The primary limitations with Acrobat Standard are no commercial printing and engineering tools. These features are only available in Acrobat Pro and Acrobat Pro Extended.

- Acrobat ProExtended includes the functionality of Acrobat 3D version 8 that has been rebranded in version 9 and adds support for PDF Portfolio Templates and converting media files to the FLV (Flash Video) format, in addition to all the 3D features that were available in Acrobat 8.

- Acrobat plug-ins are additions to Acrobat that offer features and tools for adding more functionality to Acrobat viewers. Plug-ins are installed with Acrobat from sources developed by Adobe Systems.

- Plug-ins are available from third-party software manufacturers. A complete list of plug-ins and demonstration products is available at the Planet PDF Store, the Adobe Store, Acrobat Plug-ins World, and The PowerXChange.

Chapter 3

Using Help and Resources

I n Chapter 1, I talked about getting help in Adobe Acrobat using some different help menu commands. There's much more to getting help in Acrobat than I covered in Chapter 1. Therefore, a separate chapter detailing the specifics of various help options seems appropriate.

In addition to help documents, there are a number of resources installed in folders that you might want to become familiar with. Many resource files can be edited to customize your PDF creation and editing.

In this chapter, I talk about some of the help documents, Web links, and resources you have with Adobe Acrobat when you start up the program and when you begin to work on some different editing tasks.

IN THIS CHAPTER

Getting help

Using resource documents

Accessing Help

You can see the number of different commands and tools available in Acrobat is extraordinary — and you haven't yet looked at all the submenu options or different preference options accessed from the top-level menu bar. With all these features available to you, your initial Acrobat sessions can sometimes be overwhelming. Fortunately, the great engineers and program designers at Adobe Systems thought about you and they decided to provide some help.

Help with learning more about Acrobat comes in several forms, and you can choose from several help methods to find the one that works well in your workflow. This section covers different options for getting help in an Acrobat session.

Using Acrobat help

Acrobat doesn't ship with a user guide. When you open the box, the material of value is the CD-ROM and your serial number. When it comes to documentation, you first need to install Acrobat, and then use the Help menu to find information that will help you learn menu commands, features, and methods for working with the program.

Your first stop in the Help menu is the Adobe Acrobat (Standard, Pro, or Pro Extended) Help. Choose this command or press the F1 key on your keyboard and you open the Acrobat 9 Help Guide shown in Figure 3.1.

FIGURE 3.1

Choose Help ➪ Complete Adobe Acrobat (Standard, Pro, or Pro Extended) Help.

Navigation Pane   Topic Pane

The Help Guide opens in your default Web browser. From within the Help Guide you have several options for finding help relative to the task at hand.

Contents tab

By default the Adobe Help Viewer document opens with the Contents tab exposed as shown in Figure 3.1. In the Navigation pane you'll find a table of contents for the document, shown in a very similar manner to the way bookmarks are listed in a PDF document. Click one of the bookmark topics listed in the Contents tab to see the respective bookmarked page in the Topics pane.

Search tab

You can use the Search tab to find any word(s) in the help document. Click the Search button and the Navigation pane changes to display a field box where you type your search criteria as shown in Figure 3.2. Type one or more words in the field box and click Search. The results then appear in the Search tab. All text appearing in blue is linked to the page that opens in the Topic pane.

FIGURE 3.2

Click Search and type the search criteria in the text box.

Navigating topics

When you browse topics in the Topics pane, two buttons appear at the top of the pane. Click the Previous or Next button shown in Figure 3.3 to move back or forward in the help document.

FIGURE 3.3

Click Previous or Next to scroll back and forth through the help document.

Printing topics

You can choose File ⇨ Print in your Web browser to print a page; however, a much better alternative is to convert a page to a PDF document. From there, you can keep an electronic file stored on your hard drive or print the PDF document at a later time.

To convert a page to a PDF document in Microsoft Internet Explorer, select all the content on a page in the Topics pane you want to convert to PDF and open a context menu. From the menu commands choose Convert to Adobe PDF as shown in Figure 3.4. The selected area in the Topics pane is then converted to a PDF file.

FIGURE 3.4

Select the content you want to archive and choose Convert to Adobe PDF from a context menu.

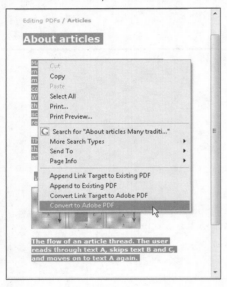

NOTE If using a web browser other than Microsoft Internet Explorer, you have to convert the entire page to PDF. On the Macintosh choose File ⇨ Print, and print to PDF. You have no options for converting a selection to PDF on the Mac with any web browser.

Setting zoom views

The lower right corner of the Topics pane displays your current zoom view. If you want to zoom in or out of the help document, click the Down Arrow to open a pop-up menu (refer to Figure 3.4). You can choose from preset zoom levels or choose Custom to add a custom zoom. You can also use the keyboard shortcuts Ctrl/⌘++ and Ctrl/⌘+- to zoom in and out of the help document.

Using Adobe LiveCycle Designer help

Adobe LiveCycle Designer is a separate executable program available to Acrobat Pro and Acrobat Pro Extended users on Windows only. Designer is used for creating dynamic XML forms. Designer also has a help document to assist you in learning the program. To access the Help file, select Help ⇨ Adobe LiveCycle Designer Help or press the F1 key. The help document shown in Figure 3.5 opens.

FIGURE 3.5

Press the F1 key in Adobe LiveCycle Designer ES to open the help document.

Contents

Like the Adobe Acrobat help document you find a Contents tab in the Navigation pane. The contents are also listed in a hierarchical tree. Click the plus buttons to expand the contents as shown in Figure 3.6. Subsequently, click on any item listed in the Contents list and the topics pane opens the respective link.

FIGURE 3.6

Contents are listed in a hierarchical tree similar to the Acrobat help document.

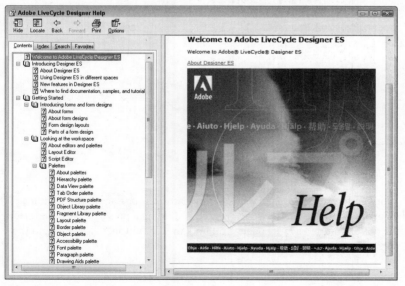

Index

The Designer help document contains an alpha index. Click the Index tab and the list is exposed. You can scroll the list to find indexed items linked to pages in the Topics pane.

Search

Designer provides you a more impressive search feature than you find with the Acrobat help guide. Click the Search tab and type the search criteria in the text box at the top of the Search pane. Click the Display button and your searched word(s) is listed on the page with the first occurrence of the search criteria. Each found word is highlighted by default as you see in Figure 3.7. To find additional pages with search results, click the arrow icons at the top of the Topics pane.

FIGURE 3.7

All occurrences of searched words are highlighted.

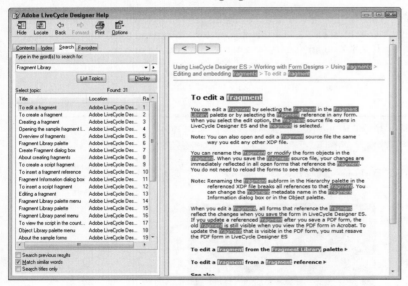

Favorites

The Favorites pane enables you to store searched items or any particular passage you find in the Topics pane. Click the Favorites tab after performing a search or finding a passage you want to add to a Favorites list. At the bottom of the Favorites pane you find an Add button. Click Add and the item is listed in the topics list window.

Button tools

At the top of the Contents pane you find some tools. The tools include:

- **Hide.** Click Hide and the Contents pane hides from view, offering you more room to view the topics pane. When you click Hide the button changes to Show. Click Show and you reopen the Contents pane.

- **Locate.** Click Locate and the selected item in the Contents pane opens the respective item in the topics pane.

- **Back/Forward.** Click the arrows to move back and forward in the document.

- **Print.** Click the Print button and a dialog box opens, prompting you to choose printing a topic or printing the selected heading and all related topics.

- **Options.** The pull-down menu provides several menu commands similar to the tool options, and additionally offers you a choice for turning the highlighting off. You can eliminate the highlights when searching for items using the Search pane.

> **TIP** In addition to the tools, you can also open a context menu in the Contents pane and choose to expand all topics by selecting the Open All menu item or collapse all items by selecting the Close All menu item.

Online help for Adobe Acrobat

In addition to the help file that covers working in Acrobat, some additional help and information is available online. Choose Help ➪ Online Support and the submenu displays three online help resources. The resources include:

- **Knowledge Base.** Choose Help ➪ Online Support ➪ Knowledge Base and the Acrobat Support Center Web page opens in your default Web browser. On this site you'll find help documents, error and troubleshooting messages, and general information related to performance problems.

- **Adobe Support Programs.** Choose Help ➪ Online Support ➪ Adobe Support Programs and the Support plans Web page opens. On this site you'll find information related to subscribing to support programs where you can call Adobe Technical Support for help diagnosing problems. A PDF document is available for download that details the specifics related to various support plans provided by Adobe.

- **Accessibility Resource Center.** Help ➪ Online Support ➪ Accessibility to open the Accessibility Resource Center Web site. Here you'll find information related to creating accessible documents.

On the various Web sites you'll also find menus that guide you to other support assistance. You can open the Support menus and find links to customer service, books, training and certification, updates, and more.

Online help for Adobe LiveCycle Designer

Under the Designer Help menu you'll find a link to another Web site dealing with LiveCycle Designer issues. Choose Help ➪ Adobe LiveCycle Development Center and the LiveCycle Development Center Web site opens. Here you'll find some valuable examples for creating dynamic XML forms in LiveCycle Designer.

The online tutorials and PDF documents available for download are valuable resources for anyone wanting to learn more about creating forms in LiveCycle Designer.

Acrobat User Community

Adobe Systems sponsors a user group forum and supports the development of user groups internationally. Some of the world's leading experts on Acrobat participate through providing tips, articles, and hosting blog sessions. You can find some of the most up-to-date information at `www.acrobat users.com`. Open the Adobe Acrobat User Community Web page and the opening page appears as shown in Figure 3.8. Here you'll find an easy to use Web site filled with many tips and solutions.

If you're interested in learning more about Acrobat, you may find a user group close to your home. If not, you can become one of the many people who start a local user group. You'll find great support from Adobe if you want to start a group. To learn more about the location of user groups and how to go about starting one, search the Adobe Acrobat User Community Web site.

FIGURE 3.8

Log on to www.acrobatusers.com to find up-to-date information on Acrobat and PDF.

Using Resources

When you install Acrobat there are a number of files stored in various folders that are used for templates and different resources that assist you in your PDF creation and document editing. Some of these files can be modified and customized to suit your personal PDF creation needs.

Modifying the coversheet

Users of Acrobat 8 will remember the coversheet that appeared in PDF Packages. The `coversheet.pdf` file was installed with your Acrobat installation. You could modify this file to create a custom coversheet with data relevant to you or your company.

NEW FEATURE In Acrobat 9 PDF Packages have given way to the new PDF Portfolios. PDF Portfolios enable you to create your own personal customized coversheets using several template configurations provided by Adobe, and new templates using Adobe Flex.

Since PDF Portfolios can only be viewed with the coversheet templates used in Acrobat 9, Adobe created a new coversheet that only opens when viewing PDF Portfolios in versions of Acrobat and Adobe Reader earlier than version 9. When Acrobat 7 or 8 users open a PDF Portfolio, the coversheet they see is shown in Figure 3.9.

FIGURE 3.9

PDF Portfolios display a coversheet created by Adobe when the Portfolios are viewed in Acrobat viewers earlier than version 9.

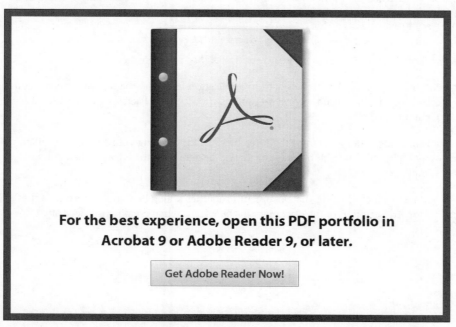

For the best experience, open this PDF portfolio in Acrobat 9 or Adobe Reader 9, or later.

Get Adobe Reader Now!

The coversheet shown in Figure 3.9 is a PDF document that resides in the folder:

- `Acrobat 9.0/Acrobat/DocSettings/CombineFiles/ENU/coversheet.pdf` (Windows)

- `Applications/Acrobat 9 Pro/Adobe Acrobat Pro/Contents/Mac OS/ DocSettings/CombineFiles/ENU/coversheet.pdf` (Macintosh)

Note that the ENU folder is for English language installations of Acrobat. Also note that Mac users need to open the Acrobat 9 Pro folder and open a context menu on the Acrobat 9 Pro application file. From the context menu commands choose Show Package Contents to display the Contents folder.

You can replace the file contained in the ENU folder with your own design. Just be certain to name the file `coversheet.pdf`.

CROSS-REF For more information about creating custom coversheets for PDF Portfolios, see Chapter 12.

Modifying DocTemplates

Doc Templates are used with Security Envelopes. When you choose Create Security Envelope from the Secure Task button pull-down menu, a wizard opens where you can choose from three templates installed with your Acrobat installation. The template1.pdf file is shown in Figure 3.10.

The Security Envelope templates have several form fields that you can modify in Acrobat, or you can create new templates and add them to the folder Acrobat searches the DocTemplates folder for when creating a security envelope. The DocTemplates folder is located at:

- `Acrobat 9.0/Acrobat/DocTemplates/ENU/` (Windows)

- `Acrobat 9 Pro/Contents/Resources/en.lproj/DocTemplates`

Note that you need to open the Adobe Acrobat Pro application folder on the Mac and open a context menu on the program icon. From the menu options choose Show Package Contents to gain access to the Contents folder.

Inside the DocTemplates folder you'll find the three files installed during your Acrobat installation. You can copy any file to this folder and the template will be shown in the wizard when you create a Security Envelope.

Be certain to add a Document Title in the Document Properties dialog box. The wizard uses the Document Title for a description of the document in the wizard when creating the Security Envelope.

FIGURE 3.10

template1.pdf is one of three templates installed with Acrobat for use with security envelopes.

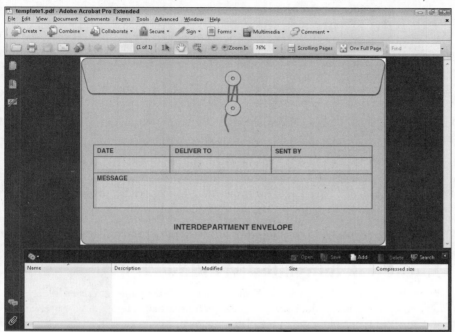

CROSS-REF For more information on creating Security Envelopes, see Chapter 26. For more information on adding Document Titles to PDF files, see Chapter 6.

Adding folder level JavaScripts

Whereas Adobe didn't intend to have you interact with the coversheet document or DocTemplates folders, the JavaScripts folder is one that you are encouraged to use when folder level scripts are needed. This is most evident on the Mac because you don't need to drill down through the application supporting folders to find the JavaScripts folder.

- On Windows, open the Acrobat folder and you'll find the JavaScripts folder.
- On the Mac, open your user logon folder and follow the path `Library/Acrobat User Data/9.0_x86/JavaScripts`.

You can add folder level JavaScripts to this folder that are executed at the time Acrobat is launched.

CROSS-REF For some examples for using folder level JavaScripts, look over Chapter 36 (on the CD-ROM).

Adding custom stamps

Some more resources available to you include the many different stamps images you can add to the Stamp tool in all Acrobat viewers. Buy default only a few of the files are loaded as stamp libraries.

- On Windows you'll find the libraries at `Acrobat/plug_ins/Annotations/Stamps/ENU`.

- On the Mac you'll find stamps at `Contents/Plug-ins/Comments.acroplugin/Stamps/ENU`.

Before you arrive at the ENU folder inside the Stamps folder you'll find a file called Words.pdf. This file has eight different images you can use as Stamp icons. When you open the ENU folder you'll find `Faces.pdf` and `Pointers.pdf`, each containing 11 icons each. Any one of these files can be added as new stamps using the Manage Custom Stamps wizard in all Acrobat viewers.

CROSS-REF For information related to creating and managing custom Stamps, see Chapter 20.

Using QuickBook templates (Windows only)

Another folder you find in the Acrobat folder on Windows is the QuickBooksTemplates folder. Open this folder and open the ENU folder and you find seven preinstalled templates for use with QuickBooks. In Figure 3.11, one of the seven templates is shown.

NEW FEATURE In Acrobat 9 you can interact with QuickBooks. From the Forms menu chose QuickBooks and choose a command from the submenu. You can export data to templates and populate a template with QuickBooks data.

All the template files you use with QuickBooks are forms created in Adobe LiveCycle Designer. You can create new templates and copy the templates to the QuickBooks/ENU folder.

CROSS-REF For more information on working with QuickBooks templates, see Chapter 35.

Using LiveCycle Designer resource files

Inside the Designer 8.2 folder which resides inside the Acrobat folder you find the EN folder. Open this folder and you find two folders with some resource files. The Templates folder contains a number of templates you can use to start a form in LiveCycle Designer. If you create some custom forms and want to use them as templates, copy your template files to this folder.

The Samples folder inside the EN folder is where you'll find some excellent examples of forms created with LiveCycle Designer. If you're new to Designer, be sure to look over the many samples you find here.

FIGURE 3.11

New in Acrobat 9 Pro and Pro Extended on Windows are templates for use with the QuickBooks account-ing software.

CROSS-REF For more information on using LiveCycle Designer, see Chapter 33.

Summary

- All Acrobat viewers have a help document you access via a menu command in the Help menu.
- Many online help resources are found via URL links from the Help menu commands.
- A number of resource files can be added to folders inside the Acrobat and LiveCycle Designer folders to customize templates.

Chapter 4

Getting Familiar with Adobe Reader

As a PDF author you need to be aware of the capabilities and the limitations of the Adobe Reader software. In some situations you can distribute PDF documents to users of the free Adobe Reader software for active participation in your workflow without all your clients and colleagues needing to purchase the full version of Acrobat Standard, Acrobat Pro, or Acrobat Pro Extended. In other situations where the Adobe Reader software does not contain tools or commands to properly edit a file for a given workflow, you may need to recommend to others which commercial viewer they need to purchase. Regardless of where you are with PDF creation and editing, at one time or another you'll be called upon to explain some of the differences between Adobe Reader and the other viewers.

Adobe Reader has evolved and each new upgrade offers users much more functionality than previous versions. Features that users have long requested such as the ability to save form data and add digital signatures were added in Adobe Reader 8. Two more features requested by many users involved having a method for converting application documents to PDF and a no-nonsense easy method for sharing files. Adobe Reader 9, combined with the new online Acrobat.com service, addresses these user requests.

IN THIS CHAPTER

Setting some important preferences

Understanding Adobe Reader tools and menus

Creating and sharing files

Working with enabled PDF files

Getting help in Adobe Reader

Getting more Adobe Reader solutions from Adobe Systems

Setting Some Critical Preferences

Like the Acrobat viewers, Adobe Reader has an enormous number of different preference options designed to add more functionality to the program and to help you tailor your workspace and tools to suit personal workflows.

Preferences settings are detailed throughout this book in chapters that specifically relate to tools and commands. A few preference options you want to start with in Reader include some settings to help you prepare for some of the features described in other chapters.

Setting up an Acrobat.com account

Open Preferences by pressing Ctrl/⌘+K. In the left pane, click Acrobat.com. Preference options you have for adding account information for Acrobat.com are shown in Figure 4.1.

NEW FEATURE Acrobat.com is a separate service provided free from Adobe. For a number of different tasks you perform in Acrobat including shared reviews, form distribution and collection, and sharing files online, you'll want to take advantage of this service.

FIGURE 4.1

Press Ctrl/⌘+K to open the Preferences dialog box and click Acrobat.com in the left pane.

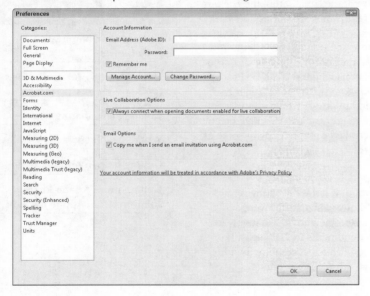

To use Acrobat.com, you need to sign up with an Adobe ID and password. Once you've set up an account, add your email address (from your Adobe ID account) and your password if you want to log on automatically each time you use the service. If you want to connect to Acrobat.com automatically when collaborating on documents set up for collaboration on Acrobat.com, check the Live Collaboration check box. Another check box is an option for copying email messages to your mail client each time you send an invitation for other users to engage in a comment and review session. Check this box if you want to copy messages to your email account.

For information on setting up an account and signing on to Acrobat.com, see Chapter 29. For information on collaboration in shared reviews, see Chapter 21.

Setting general preferences

Open the Preferences dialog box (Ctrl/⌘+K) and click General in the left pane. Check Use single-key accelerators to access tools at the top of the right pane. When this check box is checked, you can access tools by pressing a key on your keyboard. For example, when another tool is selected, you can access the Hand tool by pressing the H key.

Setting identity preferences

You'll also want to edit identity preferences. When you engage in comment reviews and add comments in review sessions, you're prompted to edit your identity preferences. To prepare your work environment, take time now to add your identity information. Press Ctrl/⌘+K to open the Preferences dialog box and click Identity in the left pane. In the right pane, fill in the text boxes with your personal identity information as shown in Figure 4.2.

FIGURE 4.2

Click Identity in the left pane and fill in the text boxes in the right pane to set up your identity preferences.

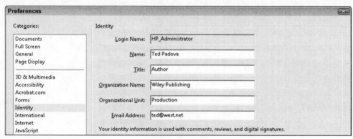

There are many more preferences you can adjust, but these few changes will get the Adobe Reader going for a good many viewing and editing sessions. After you make your edits in the Preferences dialog box, you're ready to go. Reader writes the preferences immediately so there's no need to quit the program and reopen to use the new preference choices.

Using Adobe Reader Tools and Menus

What distinguishes Adobe Reader and other viewers are, in part, the tools and menu commands. Knowing what the user can do with the Reader tools and what tools are not available in Reader is helpful if you intend to distribute documents to Reader users.

All tools available in Adobe Reader have counterparts in Acrobat Standard (Windows), Acrobat Pro, and Acrobat Pro Extended (Windows). The Reader tools are the same in the other viewers; however, some of the Adobe Reader tools offer more limited features than the same tools used in the other viewers.

Loading tools and toolbars

Before you take a look at the individual tools you have available in Reader, you should know how you go about loading tools and toolbars. A toolbar contains one or more tools that can be added or temporarily removed from a toolbar. You have one of two ways to access a window where toolbars are loaded and tools respective to a toolbar are added and removed.

Select Tools ➪ Customize Toolbars or open a context menu on a toolbar in the Toolbar Well (right-click on Windows or Ctrl+click on the Mac) and select More Tools, as shown in Figure 4.3. Accessing either Tools ➪ Customize Toolbars or the More Tools menu command opens the More Tools window shown in Figure 4.4.

FIGURE 4.3

Open a context menu on a toolbar in the Toolbar Well and select More Tools at the bottom of the menu to open the More Tools window.

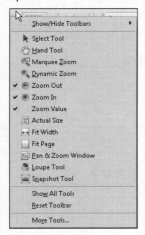

The More Tools window shown in Figure 4.4 is a scrollable window listing the various toolbars available to Adobe Reader. Toolbars appear in the list as a parent item. Indented below each toolbar are the tools you can display in the respective toolbar. For example, the first toolbar is the Analysis toolbar. Below the toolbar you see three tools (each denoted as a tool) indented below the parent toolbar. When you click the check box for Analysis Toolbar, the toolbar opens in the Acrobat window.

FIGURE 4.4

Check the tools and toolbars you want shown in the Reader workspace.

Click the check mark adjacent to a toolbar name and the toolbar opens as a floating toolbar in the Document pane. All tools marked with a check mark appear loaded in the toolbar. To hide tools from a given toolbar, uncheck the tools you want to remain hidden.

Once a toolbar is opened in Reader, you can dock the toolbar(s) by opening a context menu from the Toolbar Well and selecting Dock Toolbars. The toolbars are then organized within the Toolbar Well.

TIP   **Once you have a toolbar open in the Acrobat window, you can load and remove tools from the toolbar without returning to the More Tools window. Open a context menu on a toolbar — either a floating toolbar or one docked in the Toolbar Well. All tools assigned to the toolbar are displayed in the menu. You check or uncheck individual tools to open/close them.**

At the bottom of the More Tools window, you see a note indicating that the tools are only available when document rights are enabled. Note that the Measuring tool in the Analysis toolbar and all the Comment & Markup tools shown in Figure 4.4 appear with an asterisk (*). These tools are only available in Adobe Reader when you open a document that has been enabled with Adobe Reader usage rights.

CROSS-REF For more information on PDFs with usage rights, see "Enabling Adobe Reader Usage Rights" later in this chapter.

Getting familiar with the Reader tools

The first thing to understand about tools in Adobe Reader is you have two different tool sets dependent on the kind of PDF file you open. In addition, you have a few different menu commands depending on the kind of PDF file you open.

If you open a PDF document with no special usage rights, you have fewer accessible tools and menu commands than when you open PDFs having extended features. Notice that when you open the More Tools window, the second toolbar you see is the Comment & Markup toolbar. If you open a PDF file that isn't enabled for commenting, you can't open the Comment & Markup toolbar. If you open a file that has extended features for Adobe Reader for commenting, then you can open the Comment & Markup tools.

Default tools

To start off a discussion on Adobe Reader tools, let's first take a look at the tools you have available when opening a PDF document with no special features. In this section, I refer to these tools as the default tools. Later, I'll talk about the additional tools you have available when opening files having special features.

CROSS-REF For more on PDFs with special features, see "Enabling Adobe Reader Usage Rights" later in this chapter. For enabling features with Acrobat, see Chapter 19.

The Adobe Reader tools available to you when working on PDFs without special usage rights include the following:

■ **Analysis toolbar.** By default the Analysis toolbar displays two tools when you load the toolbar. The Object Data toolbar, explained in Chapter 1, is used to select objects (text, images, or vector art) on a document page. When you select an object with this tool, the Object Data dialog box opens and displays information about an object that was originally supplied in an authoring program. The Object Data tool works only with objects where certain metadata were originally supplied in another program such as AutoCAD or Microsoft Visio. The Geospatial tool reports geospatial data such as longitude and latitude on files where the data have been added. If a file is enabled with Adobe Reader usage rights, the Measuring tool is added to the toolbar.

CROSS-REF For more information on using the measuring tools, see Chapter 24.

- **Edit toolbar.** The Edit tools include Spell Check, Undo, Redo, and Copy.

- **File toolbar.** The File tools include the familiar tools from earlier Acrobat viewers Open, Print, Save a Copy, Search, and Email. New in Acrobat 9 are the Share tool and the Create Adobe PDF Online tool. The Share tool is similar to a Task button with a pull-down menu where commands offer you options for sharing files on Acrobat.com. Create Adobe PDF Online is a revised online service for Reader users who can now create PDFs in real time by sending them to Acrobat.com without a service fee for the first files you convert to PDF. After using the service to convert five files, you can continue using a subscription service.

NOTE Using the free service to convert up to five files to PDF is a lifetime free service. Once you've converted five files to PDF, you must use a paid subscription to convert additional files.

CROSS-REF For information related to using the Email tool, see Chapter 5. For information related to using the Print tool, see Chapter 31. For information related to using the Search tool, see Chapter 6. For more information on sharing files on Acrobat.com and creating PDFs online, see "Working with Acrobat.com" later in this chapter. Also look over Chapter 29 for more information on using Acrobat.com.

- **Find toolbar.** The Find tool enables you to perform a text search in the open PDF document.

CROSS-REF For information related to using the Find toolbar, see Chapter 6.

- **Page Display.** The tools all relate to the document display in the Reader workspace. You can view pages as single page layouts, continuous, facing, and so on. The Full Screen tool takes you into Full Screen mode. Tools for rotating pages and viewing line weights at 1-pixel widths are also included in this toolbar.

CROSS-REF For more information on page layout views, see Chapter 5. For more on Full Screen mode, see Chapter 28. For more on rotating pages, see Chapter 16.

- **Page Navigation toolbar.** This toolbar contains the First Page, Previous Page, Next Page, Last Page, Previous View, and Next View tools. Additionally, you can type a number in the text box to jump to a page.

CROSS-REF For information related to navigating PDF documents, see Chapter 5.

- **Select & Zoom toolbar.** The tools include Select, Hand, Marquee Zoom, Dynamic Zoom, Zoom Out, Zoom In, Actual Size, Fit Width, Fit Page, Pan and Zoom Window, Loupe, and Snapshot. The Select tool is used for selecting text and images, the zoom tools are used for page zooms, and the page layout tools are used for fitting the page to different sizes.

CROSS-REF For information related to using the Zoom, Loupe, and Pan and Zoom Window tools, see Chapter 5. For information related to using the Select tool, see Chapters 13 and 15. For more on page layout tools, see Chapter 5.

Tools available with enabled PDF documents

- **Comment & Markup toolbar.** All the tools in this toolbar are used for commenting on PDF documents with extended features.

CROSS-REF For a comprehensive view of using all the Comment & Markup tools, see Chapter 20.

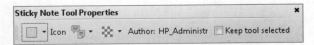

- **Properties Bar.** Even though Adobe Reader does have a Properties Bar that you can open on PDFs that are not enabled with usage rights, none of the default tools have options that appear in the Properties Bar. The Properties Bar is used in PDF documents carrying usage rights for commenting. When used in conjunction with the Comment & Markup tools, you see comment properties appearing in the toolbar — such as the Sticky Note Tool properties shown here.

CROSS-REF For more information on using the Properties toolbar, see Chapter 20.

- **Tasks toolbar.** The Tasks toolbar includes Comment tasks. Click the down-pointing arrow to see menu commands offering options for working in comment and review sessions.

CROSS-REF For more on using the Comment tools, see Chapter 20. For more information on shared reviews, see Chapter 21.

- **Typewriter toolbar.** The Typewriter tool is used to type text on forms where no form fields are available.

CROSS-REF For more information on using the Typewriter tool, see Chapter 34.

Using menu commands

In addition to tools, Adobe Reader 9 contains some important menu commands that you'll want to understand.

NEW FEATURE Under the File menu you find some new Acrobat 9 menu commands. The File ▻ Create Adobe PDF Using Acrobat.com menu command is used to submit files to Acrobat.com for conversion to PDF. This feature was available in earlier versions of Acrobat, but now rests with the Acrobat.com service, where you can convert up to five files free. After converting five files, the service is available as a paid subscription. The File ▻ Collaborate menu command has a submenu that includes the following commands:

- **Upload Documents to Acrobat.com.** Select this command to upload documents to Acrobat.com.

- **Share Documents on Acrobat.com.** Use this command to share files with other users on Acrobat.com.

■ **Create Buzzword Document (English only version).** Buzzword is a Web-based real-time Adobe word-processing application with an Adobe Flash interface. When you choose this command you are presented with a logon screen in your default Web browser. Either log on with your Adobe ID or sign up for a new account. After signing in, the Buzzword Web page opens as shown in Figure 4.5. Using Buzzword you can edit documents together in a group with other users to make text edits, add comments, make revisions, and publish documents in real time.

FIGURE 4.5

Choose File ➪ Collaborate ➪ Create Buzzword Document and log on to Adobe's Buzzword Web site.

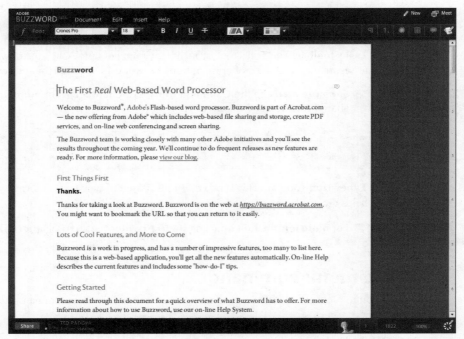

■ **Share My Screen.** Acrobat Connect, introduced with the release of Acrobat and Adobe Reader 8, offered you a meeting room to conduct online meetings. You needed a Connect account and you had to pay an annual fee for the service. Now in Acrobat 9 you can host meetings using the free Adobe Reader software for up to three participants without a service fee using Acrobat ConnectNow.

CROSS-REF   **For more information regarding online meetings, see Chapter 29.**

■ **Go to Acrobat.com.** Use this command to log on to Acrobat.com.

Using Navigation panels

Navigation panels that are open by default are docked in the Navigation pane. Depending on the content of a PDF file, you may see different panels open when viewing different documents. For example, if a document containing a digital signature opens in Reader, the Signatures panel is docked in the Navigation pane. If a document contains Adobe PDF layers, the Layers panel is docked in the Navigation pane.

You can open panels in any document by choosing a menu command. To view all the Navigation panels, select View ⇨ Navigation Panels. A submenu contains all the Navigation panels you can access in Reader, as shown in Figure 4.6. When you open a panel, it opens as a floating window. Click the panel tab and drag it to the Navigation pane, where you can dock it together with the default panels.

CROSS-REF   For more information on using Navigation panels, see Chapter 1.

FIGURE 4.6

Select View ⇨ Navigation Panels to see the Navigation panels available in Reader. When documents with special usage rights are open, the Document Extensions and Signatures panels are accessible.

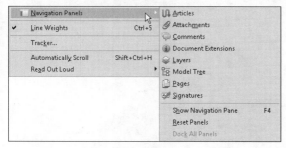

Working with Signatures

Open the Document menu and you find the Sign, Security, and Security Settings commands. If you want Adobe Reader users to digitally sign a document, they must create a digital signature. These commands are used to create signatures, manage signatures, and sign documents.

CROSS-REF   For more information on digital signatures, see Chapter 26.

Working with PDF Portfolios

Adobe Reader 9 has two different interfaces you use to view different types of PDF files.

NEW FEATURE Adobe Reader, like the other Acrobat viewers, displays a separate interface when viewing PDF Portfolios. In the PDF Portfolio interface you find additional tools and menu commands. The view you see in Adobe Reader (see Figure 4.7) is very similar to the view displayed in Acrobat viewers. The one view you don't have displays the Edit Portfolio panel used for editing PDF Portfolios or modifying the Portfolio.

FIGURE 4.7

Additional tools and menu commands are used when viewing PDF Portfolios.

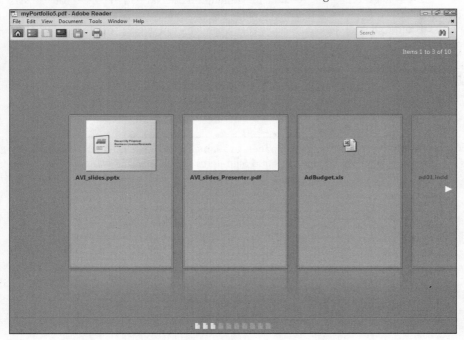

CROSS-REF PDF Portfolios are a new feature in Acrobat/Adobe Reader 9. For a complete description of creating PDF Portfolios and using tools and menu commands, see Chapter 12.

Working with Acrobat.com

Adobe Reader users can create PDFs online and explore a wide range of sharing options.

NEW FEATURE If a little voice popped up as you turn pages in this book, you'd hear me frequently exclaim that Acrobat.com and all the related features you have for working with documents using Acrobat.com are, in my opinion, the best single new feature introduced in any Adobe program over the past two decades. I believe Acrobat.com is perhaps the single greatest reason you should encourage all Adobe Reader users to upgrade to Adobe Reader 9.

All of what you can do with Acrobat.com and your documents is covered in Chapter 29. In terms of Adobe Reader users, there are a few distinctions you have related to the available services. For starters, Adobe Reader users cannot enable a PDF for commenting and cannot initiate a comment and review session. Therefore, Reader users cannot submit files for review in the same regard as the Acrobat users can.

Reader users, however, can share files on Acrobat.com, and other users of the Acrobat software can add comments. Reader users can also initiate and participate in online meetings for up to three people without purchasing an Acrobat Connect account. Furthermore, Reader users can submit native authoring application documents for PDF creation without any service fees — again only five files free as a lifetime service then offered on a subscription fee basis.

Creating PDF files using Acrobat.com

If your clients or colleagues don't have Acrobat Standard or one of the Acrobat Pro products and they need to create an occasional PDF file, they can download the free Adobe Reader 9 software and choose File ➪ Create Adobe PDF Using Acrobat.com. The Adobe Share dialog box opens as shown in Figure 4.8. A user needs to have an account to sign on or click Create an Adobe ID to Sign Up for the service.

FIGURE 4.8

Choose File ➪ Create Adobe PDF Using Acrobat.com and sign on to submit files for conversion to PDF.

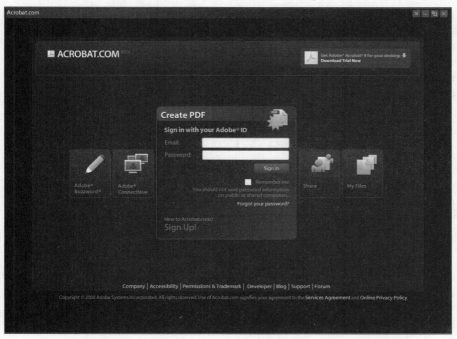

You are then taken to Acrobat.com. In the Acrobat.com interface, click the Create PDF button. Click Browse as you see in Figure 4.9. A Browse dialog box opens where you can select the file to upload. Select one or more files and click Open.

FIGURE 4.9

Click Create PDF in Acrobat.com, select a file, and click Upload to upload a native file for PDF conversion.

The wonderful thing about using the new Create PDF feature in Acrobat 9 and Acrobat.com is that your work is performed in real time. The server displays a progress bar as your file(s) is converted. When finished with the conversion, you open a drop-down menu ad. Choose Download to download the file. There's no waiting for an email and a link to locate a file. Everything is performed in real time, and your files are added to your Acrobat.com workspace for downloading any time or place you choose.

Create PDF supports many different file formats. The native document formats are as follows:

- **Microsoft Office.** All Microsoft Office files for Mac and Windows.
- **Other Microsoft formats.** Microsoft Publisher is supported.
- **Adobe formats.** Those programs not supporting direct export to PDF, such as earlier versions of PageMaker without the PDF plug-in, are supported. All Creative Suite programs now support export to PDF, and using a service to create PDF files is not necessary.

- **Adobe Flash files.** Adobe Flash .flv and .swf file formats can be converted.

- **AutoDesk AutoCAD.** AutoCAD is supported.

- **CAD File formats.** A huge range of different CAD formats can be converted.

- **Corel WordPerfect Office formats.** Corel WordPerfect files can be converted to PDF.

- **Adobe PostScript formats.** Any program you use that's capable of printing can be printed to disk as a PostScript file. You can submit the PostScript file for conversion to PDF.

- **Text formats.** All ASCII (American Code for Information Interchange) and Rich Text Format (RTF) files can be converted to PDF.

- **Image formats.** Most of the common image formats such as Windows bitmap (.bmp), GIF (.gif), JPEG (.jpg/.jpeg), PCX (.pcx), PICT (Macintosh) (.pct/.pict), PNG (.png), RLE (.rle), and TIFF (.tif) can be converted to PDF.

CROSS-REF For information on converting native application documents to PDF, see Chapters 7 through 9. For information on printing PostScript files and converting PostScript files to PDF, see Chapter 10.

Sharing files on Acrobat.com

Adobe Reader users can share files on Acrobat.com and invite selected users to download the shared documents. Open the File menu and choose Collaborate ⇨ Upload Documents to Acrobat.com. Any original authoring document can be uploaded for sharing.

Like other Acrobat.com services, you need to have an Adobe ID and log on with your account information. After logging on, your default Web browser takes you to the Acrobat.com Web site where you can initiate an upload.

When you arrive at Acrobat.com you have some options for who will see your shared file(s), an email address field for your recipient(s), a subject field for the email, and a message box as shown in Figure 4.10. Browse your hard drive to select the file you want to upload and fill in the fields for the email. Click the Share button and your default email client opens with a new message window that includes the To, Subject, and Message content you completed in Acrobat.com. Click the Send button and the email is sent to your recipient(s) with a file hypertext link for where the recipient(s) can download the file.

CROSS-REF There's much more to the Acrobat.com services than I've covered here. For a complete overview of all Acrobat.com services, see Chapter 29.

FIGURE 4.10

Upload a file to Acrobat.com fill in the email fields to share a file with other users.

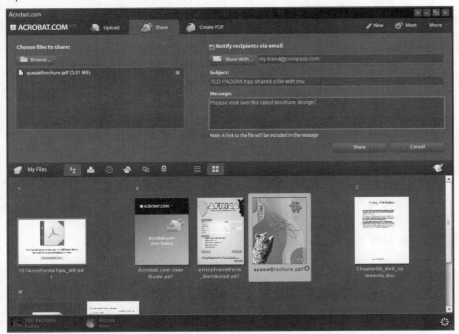

Enabling Adobe Reader Usage Rights

To create a Reader-enabled document for certain usage rights, you need Acrobat Standard, Pro, Pro Extended, or Adobe LiveCycle Reader Extensions ES. In Acrobat Standard, Pro, and Pro Extended you can add usage rights that enable an Adobe Reader user to comment on a PDF file, save the comments, invite Reader users to participate in an email–based review or shared review, save form data, and add digital signatures.

CROSS-REF **For a complete description of using comment tools, starting an email review, or starting a shared review, see Chapter 20. For more on saving form data from within Reader, see Chapter 34.**

All the comment and forms usage rights are enabled in one of the other Acrobat viewers. When you want to distribute a document for Reader users to mark up and comment, choose Comments ➪ Enable for Commenting and Analysis in Adobe Reader. When you want to distribute forms you use the Advanced ➪ The Enable Usage Rights in Adobe Reader command to open the dialog box shown in Figure 4.11. Click the Save Now button and the PDF is enabled for commenting, saving form data, and adding digital signatures.

For more on enabling PDFs with Reader usage rights, see Chapter 19.

FIGURE 4.11

With a simple menu command in Acrobat Pro or Pro Extended, you can enable PDFs for Adobe Reader users for commenting, saving data on forms, and adding digital signatures.

Commenting in Adobe Reader

Remember that you need to grant a PDF document usage rights in, Standard, Pro, or Pro Extended by choosing Comments ➪ Enable for Commenting and Analysis in Adobe Reader before a Reader user can make comments. When the file is enabled with usage rights, the Comment & Markup tools are accessible. If an Adobe Reader user opens a PDF document without usage rights enabled, the comment tools are not accessible.

NOTE   Some other actions, such as starting a shared review or distributing a form, automatically enable PDFs for Reader users when you step through the wizards used to initiate the sharing.

Notice that Adobe Reader users have access to all comment and markup tools, as well as the ability to create and use custom stamps. When an Adobe Reader user marks up a document with the commenting tools, the file can be saved and the comments preserved. Documents enabled with usage rights also include a File ➪ Save command. By default, Adobe Reader permits saving an unedited copy of a PDF document only if usage rights are not enabled.

CROSS-REF   For information on using the Comment & Markup tools and creating custom stamps, see Chapter 20.

Using file attachments

A file attachment is an external file that can be a PDF document or any other document saved from any program. The PDF acts as a wrapper container for the file attachment. File attachments can be extracted and saved to disk outside the PDF or opened in the native application in which the original document was created. In order to view a document in a native application, the original authoring program must be installed on your computer.

CROSS-REF For information on attaching and extracting files, see Chapter 20.

Another feature available in Adobe Reader is the ability to extract file attachments. Files can be attached to a PDF by a Reader user when a PDF document is enabled with usage rights for Adobe Reader users. When an Acrobat user attaches a file to a PDF, Adobe Reader users can extract the file attachments. A separate tab in the Navigation pane enables the Reader user to open, save, and search file attachments. Click the Attachments tab to open a panel where you can access tools to manage the attachments.

One great feature in all Acrobat viewers is the ability to attach any file type to a PDF document and secure the PDF with password protection. After a PDF has been encrypted with password security, the end user needs the access password in order to either open the PDF document or extract the attachment. With the process accessible to Adobe Reader users, business professionals in all industries will find much greater use for Adobe Reader 9.

CROSS-REF For information on adding permissions rights with Acrobat security, see Chapter 26.

Working with forms in Adobe Reader

The other half of enabling PDF documents for Adobe Reader users involves adding usage rights for saving PDF forms and adding digital signatures.

When you select Advanced ⇨ Extend Features in Adobe Reader in one of the other Acrobat viewers and click the Save Now button, your files are enabled for commenting, saving form data, and using digital signatures in Adobe Reader. As soon as you open a PDF with usage rights, you'll notice the Save command available in the File menu. The Reader user can then save any form data you add to form fields. In addition to saving form data, you can also create and use digital signatures on documents enabled with usage rights as well as add comments.

When you enable files for Reader users to save form data, some restrictions apply. You need to be aware of the stipulations in the End User License Agreement (EULA) and the limitations detailed in this agreement.

CROSS-REF For more information on limitations related to PDF forms and special usage rights for Reader users, see Chapter 19.

Getting Help

The Help menu provides a number of different options for help information and keeping the Reader product fine-tuned and updated. Click the Help menu and the menu options shown in Figure 4.12 appear.

The items in the Help menu are as follows:

- **Adobe Reader 9 Help.** Select this menu item and the complete online Help document opens. For just about any kind of help you need in working with Reader, this document provides you with detailed information on all Reader features.

- **About Adobe Reader 9.** This menu item opens a screen showing you the current version of Reader installed on your computer. This command is particularly helpful when you want to know the current maintenance upgrade you have installed on your computer.

- **About Adobe Plug-ins.** If you have any plug-ins installed, the plug-ins are displayed along with the Adobe default plug-ins. You can find plug-in descriptions and release dates in the About Adobe Plug-ins window.

Put Repair Back...

- **Improve Product Improvement.** Select this menu option and the Adobe Product Improvement Program dialog box opens. If you want to participate in the design of future revisions of Adobe Reader, click the Yes radio button and register for the program.

- **Purchase Adobe Acrobat.** When Reader users are ready to upgrade to Acrobat, they can click the menu command and order one of the Acrobat products online from Adobe Systems

- **Online Support.** Click this command and a submenu opens for accessing several online support areas.

- **Check for Updates.** If you suspect your version of Reader is not current, select this menu command to check for an update. If a newer version exists, you are prompted to install the newer version.

FIGURE 4.12

Click Help to open the Help menu, where additional help information and other services are accessed.

Check out Chapter 3 for more information regarding accessing help in Adobe Reader and Acrobat.

Adding More Functionality to Adobe Reader

You may look over the new Adobe Reader 9 and wish for more features or wonder why Adobe Systems didn't add more to the newest release. If the thought occurs to you, keep in mind that Adobe Systems offers the Reader software free of charge. Adobe Reader is certainly one of the most feature-rich applications that can be acquired without purchase.

If you want more from Adobe Reader, you do have other purchase options available to you from Adobe Systems. From PDF creation to saving form data for enterprise solutions, Adobe does make these features available to you in the form of online services and server-side applications.

For users of earlier versions of Acrobat, Reader Extensions enabled users of Adobe Reader versions below 7.0 to perform comment and markup, save forms, and digital signatures functions. Adobe LiveCycle Reader Extensions ES is an enterprise solution intended for large companies that have the technology and resources to offer cost-effective solutions for many users, or those who want to automate processes like adding these enabling rights to PDFs.

The addition of enabling documents for Reader users in Acrobat Standard, Pro, or Pro Extended to save form data and Pro/Pro Extended to add digital signatures carries limitations in the End User License Agreement. For enterprise solutions where the needs exceed the licensing limitations, Adobe LiveCycle Reader Extensions ES offers unlimited use of PDF files enabled with usage rights.

For information about Adobe LiveCycle Reader Extensions ES, log on to Adobe's Web site at www.adobe.com/products/readerextensions/. You'll find more information about the server-side software and how to acquire it for your company.

Summary

- Acrobat.com is a separate service offered by Adobe Systems and has nothing to do with the Acrobat 9.0 release. But Acrobat 9 viewers have many menu commands that can access the service for creating PDF files, sharing documents, and engaging in online meetings.

- Acrobat.com services are offered free everyone in the world.

- Adobe Reader usage rights are enabled in Acrobat Standard (Windows), Pro, and Pro Extended (Windows). When a PDF has been enabled with commenting, form data saving, and digital signatures usage rights, Reader users can comment and mark up a document, participate in an email–based review, save comment updates, save data on PDF forms, and add digital signatures.

- File attachments can be extracted from within Adobe Reader. When usage rights have been enabled in a PDF document, Adobe Reader users can attach files to PDFs.

- Help and product performance options are available from menu commands in the Help menu.

- Adobe Systems provides an online service for converting files saved in a number of different formats to PDF. You can easily access Acrobat.com where files can be submitted for conversion to PDF via menu commands in Reader.

- Adobe LiveCycle Reader Extensions ES is a J2EE-based server-side solution intended for automating the addition of user rights as well as meeting the needs for large-scale enablement requirements. With the Reader Extensions Server you can enable PDFs for using web services, spawning templates, decoding 2D barcodes, saving form data, and digitally signing PDFs from within Adobe Reader.

Chapter 5

Viewing and Navigating PDF Files

Acrobat viewers provide you with many different kinds of tools to view pages and move around PDF documents. As a visitor to PDFs created by other PDF authors, you can use many tools within the program to browse pages and find information quickly. As a PDF author you can create viewing options and links to views you know will help the end user explore your files. In this chapter, I cover all viewing tools, pages, documents, and the different kinds of viewing options you have available in Acrobat viewers. I leave the authoring items and how-to methods to other chapters. For now, just realize this chapter is an abbreviated form of looking at a huge list of possibilities for viewing and navigation. The amplified explanations follow in several other chapters.

If you're familiar with Acrobat 8 viewers, you'll find little change with viewing options in Acrobat 9, with the exception of viewing documents in the new Acrobat 9 PDF Portfolio feature. Most of the tools in Acrobat 9 are very similar to viewing tools you used in Acrobat 8.

Setting Up the Work Environment

At the beginning of all subsequent chapters, I begin the chapter by offering suggestions for setting up your work environment. As you can see in Chapter 1, all the Acrobat viewers contain many tools and panels, and most of these tools and panels are hidden when you first launch the program. Because Acrobat can do so many things for so many different working professionals, Adobe Systems didn't intend for you to use all the tools and panels in each editing session. Therefore, you have the opportunity to open and hide different tools and panels depending on the kind of edits you want to make. As you begin each chapter, look over the section related to setting up the work environment for suggestions on what tools and panels should be loaded to follow along as you read a chapter.

Open a context menu (right-click Windows or Control+click Mac) on the Toolbar Well and click More Tools. Scroll to the Page Navigation Toolbar and check all tools.

Scroll down to the File Toolbar and select the Organizer tool. Scroll to the Page Display Toolbar and check all tools. Scroll further down to the Select & Zoom Toolbar and check all tools. Click OK in the More Tools window.

Open a context menu on the Toolbar Well and select Dock Toolbars. Return to the context menu and select Button Labels ⇨ All Labels. This view shows the names of tools within toolbars to help you become more familiar with tool names.

After loading toolbars and making choices in the context menu opened from the Toolbar Well, your Toolbar Well should look like Figure 5.1.

FIGURE 5.1

The Viewing and Page Display toolbars loaded in the Toolbar Well

As is explained in this chapter, several tools and menu commands provide a means for navigating pages and documents. When you're familiar with alternative methods, you can leave the Navigation toolbar hidden, especially if you're using other toolbars that occupy a lot of room in the Toolbar Well. If you're new to Acrobat, keep the Navigation toolbar open as you work through this chapter.

Arranging Toolbars in the Acrobat Window

As you first start working with Acrobat, you'll want to make some adjustments to Preferences and setting up your work environment. Follow these steps to configure the program for most of the work you intend to do for any editing session:

STEPS: Organizing the Acrobat workplace

1. **Set Preferences.** A couple of Preference items will get you to a more familiar look when using Acrobat 8. Open the Preferences dialog box by pressing Ctrl/⌘+K. Alternately, on Windows choose Edit ⇨ Preferences and on the Mac choose Acrobat ⇨ Preferences. The preference items to change include the following:

- **Enable single key accelerators. Click General in the left pane to open the General preferences.** This option has always appeared off by default in Acrobat viewers since the preference was added to the General preferences. Check the box for Use single-key accelerators to access tools. Doing so means that when you're working on a document and you want to easily access the Zoom tool, you press the Z key. Pressing H gets you the Hand tool, and so on.

  There are many more preferences that apply to specific editing tasks and they are covered when we come to specific features in Acrobat 9 in forthcoming chapters. For now, these preferences in Acrobat can help shape your editing environment for viewing and navigating PDF files. Remember though, these are all personal preferences and you can feel free to change items to suit your workflow.

- **Always show document page size. Click Page Display in the left pane to open the Page Display preferences.** In earlier versions of Acrobat, a document's page size was reported in the document window. This is a critical bit of information for engineers, creative pros, and others who work with files other than standard letter sizes. By default, the information is not displayed. In the Page Display preferences check the box for Always show document page size.

NOTE If you don't have the Always show document page size preference enabled, you can see document page sizes by moving the cursor to the lower left corner of a page. A pop-up display opens when the cursor is positioned in the lower left corner, reporting page sizes in the current established units of measure.

- **Rendering.** Another Page Display preference you'll want to adjust is the Smoothed Text setting. If you use a laptop or LCD monitor, open the Smooth Text pull-down menu and choose For Laptop/LCD Monitors.

- **Set Identity Preferences.** Click Identity in the left pane of the Preferences dialog box. The information in the field boxes on the right is used with certain tools such as comment and markup, creating security envelopes, and with form workflows.

2. **Quit Acrobat.** After you customize your toolbars and preference settings, quit Acrobat. Acrobat remembers the last settings you made to the toolbars arrangement. Just in case you start moving toolbars around for temporary views, you can return to your initial default by first quitting Acrobat, then restating the program.

3. **Relaunch Acrobat.** Open Acrobat and your settings will appear as you left them before quitting.

Navigating PDF Documents

You can navigate pages in an Acrobat viewer via several means. You can scroll pages with tools, menus, and keystrokes; click hypertext links; and use dialog boxes to move through multiple documents and individual pages. Depending on how a PDF file is created and edited, you can also follow Web links and articles through different sections of a document or through multiple documents. All Acrobat viewers have many navigation controls and several ways to go about viewing and navigating PDF pages.

Navigation toolbar

The tools for navigation in Acrobat Pro Extended and other Acrobat viewers shown in Figure 5.2 with All Labels viewed are as follows:

- **First Page.** In the current active document, the First Page tool returns you to the first page in the document.

- **Previous Page.** The Previous Page tool moves you back one page at a time. Note that the icon for the Previous Page tool has changed in Acrobat 9 to an up arrow.

- **Next Page.** The Next Page tool scrolls forward through pages one page at a time. Note that the icon for the Previous Page tool has changed in Acrobat 9 to a down arrow.

- **Last Page.** The Last Page tool moves you to the last page in the document.

- **Go to Previous View.** The Go to Previous View tool returns you to the last view displayed on your screen. Whereas the four preceding tools are limited to navigation through a single open document, the Go to Previous View tool returns you to the previous view even if the last view was another file.

- **Go to Next View.** The Go to Next View tool behaves the same as the Go to Previous View tool except it moves in a forward direction. Use of the Go to Previous View and Go to Next View tools can be especially helpful when navigating links that open and close documents. The Next Page and Last Page tools confine you to the active document; whereas the Go to Previous View and Go to Next View tools retrace your navigation steps regardless of how many files you have viewed.

Clicking one of the tools in the toolbar invokes the action associated with the tool. If you want to move through pages left or right, click the left or right arrows. If you want to go to the first or last page in the file, click the respective tools described earlier.

FIGURE 5.2

The Page Navigation toolbar shows the icon and name for each tool when the Button Labels ➪ All Labels menu selection is made from a context menu command opened from the Toolbar Well.

Context menus

Acrobat viewers make use of context menu commands for page navigation. To use a context menu for moving forward and back in PDF pages and documents, select the Hand tool and click the right mouse button (Windows and two-button Macs) or Control+click (Macintosh) to open the context menu as shown in Figure 5.3.

FIGURE 5.3

Context menus opened on a document page using the Hand tool offer navigation commands to move forward and backward one page at a time and to previous and next views.

Navigation menu commands

The View menu contains all the page navigation commands contained in the Navigation toolbar. Notice that the View menu clearly describes viewing operations, and new users should be easily able to find menu commands associated with views.

Inasmuch as the View menu enables you to select menu commands that perform the same operations as those performed with the Navigation toolbar, you might opt for using the toolbar or keyboard shortcuts to navigate pages because other methods for page navigation are much easier than returning to menu commands. The real value in the View menu is all the other viewing commands you have accessible. The View menu contains many commands for viewing not only pages, but also toolbars and task buttons. When you choose View ⇨ Go To, the page navigation commands appear in a submenu, as shown in Figure 5.4.

Those viewing commands, apart from the same options you have for navigation with the Navigation toolbar, include commands for viewing tools, for various page views, and alternatives to viewing such as the Reading mode, Read Out Loud, and scrolling pages automatically. Following is a list of what you can find in the View menu.

FIGURE 5.4

The View menu contains many different commands for viewing pages, toolbars, and task buttons.

Go To

The commands that are equal to the actions you perform with the Navigation tools are contained in the Go To submenu. You can choose any of the Navigation commands in this menu and the results are the same as using tools and keyboard shortcuts. You'll probably avoid using the Navigation commands because using any one of the other methods to scroll through pages is so much easier. The exception is the Go To⇨ Page command. When you select Go To⇨ Page or press Shift+Ctrl/⌘+N, the Go To Page dialog box opens. Type a number in the text box and click OK and you jump to that page number.

 You can quickly jump to a page by typing a page number in the text box adjacent to the Last Page tool in the Page Navigation toolbar.

Zoom

A submenu provides menu options for zooming to different views. For more information on using the Zoom options, see "Zooming" later in this chapter. In addition to zooming in and out with tools and commands, the View⇨ Zoom submenu has a command for reflowing documents.

- **Reflow.** Document reflow enables users to view PDF documents on adaptive devices for the visually impaired and it is used when copying PDF files to handheld devices and tablets. When you reflow text onscreen or when using other devices, the text in the PDF wraps according to the zoom level of the page or the device viewing area. Therefore, when you zoom in on a paragraph of text and the text moves off the viewing area of your screen, you can use the Reflow command to make the text automatically scroll to your window size.

Reflow only works with tagged PDF documents in Acrobat viewers earlier than version 7. Acrobat 7 through 9 viewers can reflow any PDF document whether it is a tagged file or not. When you copy PDF documents to handheld devices such as Palm Pilots, Adobe Reader for Palm software wraps text to fit the width of the screen for untagged as well as tagged documents.

 For information about tagging PDF documents, see Chapters 10 and 25.

Page Display

The Page Display view can be any one of four different layout types. Choices for page layout are contained in the View ➪ Page Display submenu and also the Page Display toolbar. Depending on the way a PDF file has been saved and depending on what preference choices are made for the Initial View, a PDF layout may appear different on different computers according to each individual user's preference settings. Regardless of how you set your preferences, you can change the Page Display view at any time.

 For more information on setting Initial View preferences, see "Setting Initial View Attributes" later in this chapter.

- **Single Page.** This layout places an entire page in view when the zoom level is set to Fit Page. When you press the Page Down key or the down-arrow key to scroll pages, the next page snaps into view.

- **Single Page Continuous.** Formerly labeled Continuous in Acrobat 7 and earlier viewers. This page layout view show pages in a linear fashion, where you might see the bottom of one page and the top of another page in the Document pane as you scroll down. The difference between this view and Single Page views is that the pages don't snap to a full page when viewed as Single Page Continuous.

- **Two-Up.** Formerly labeled Facing in Acrobat 7 and earlier viewers. This view shows two pages — like looking at an open book. When the zoom level is set to Fit Page or lower, only two pages are in view in the Document pane.

- **Two-Up Continuous.** Formerly Continuous–Facing in Acrobat 7 and earlier viewers. This page layout view displays a combination of the preceding two options. When the zoom level is zoomed out, the view displays as many pages in the Document pane as can be accommodated by the zoom level.

- **Show Gaps Between Pages.** When you select View ➪ Page Display ➪ Show Gaps Between Pages, the page views for Single Page, Two-Up, and Two-Up Continuous are displayed as you see on the left side of Figure 5.5. Remove the check mark by the menu command and the display shown on the right appears.

FIGURE 5.5

Show Gaps Between Pages is turned on in the left side and off in the right side of the figure.

- **Show Cover Page During Two-Up.** When you view a document in a Two-Up page layout, page 1 and 2 are first shown in the Document pane. Click the Next Page tool and the Document pane shows you pages 3 and 4. If you want to show pages 2 and 3 together, select View ⇨ Page Display ⇨ Show Cover Page During Two-Up. If a document has more than two pages, the Two Columns and Two Pages views display the first page alone on the right side of the Document pane to ensure proper display of two-page spreads.

Rotate View

If your PDF opens in Acrobat with a rotated view, you can rotate pages clockwise or counterclockwise from two submenu commands. The same rotations are also available in the Page Display tools. Rotate View commands and tools rotate all pages in your PDF document and come in handy if the PDF pages are rotated on the initial view or if you want to view PDFs on eBook readers, tablets, or laptop computers. However, changes made with the Rotate View tools or the View menu commands are temporary and any saves you make do not record the rotated views. Another set of rotation commands is available in the Document menu. When you select Document ⇨ Rotate Pages, a dialog box opens where you can choose Counterclockwise 90 degrees, Clockwise 90 degrees, or 180 degrees. When using the Document menu and the Rotate pages dialog box, the rotation views can be saved with the file.

Reading mode

When you open a PDF document you can choose to view the file in one of two modes where the Acrobat menu remains visible. The two views include the default editing mode and Reading mode. Another mode available to you is Full Screen mode; however, in this mode the menu bar is hidden.

CROSS-REF For more information on Full Screen mode, see Chapter 28.

The Reading mode command changes the view of PDF files in the Acrobat window. To switch to Reading mode, select View ⇨ Reading mode or press Alt+H (Windows) or Control +⌘+H (Mac). The screen view immediately changes to a different view. All toolbars are temporarily hidden and the Navigation panel likewise disappears. If you have floating toolbars open, the toolbars are hidden when you enter Reading mode. Floating navigation panels remain in view when in Reading mode.

Reading mode provides you with more space dedicated to your document without the interference of the Toolbar Well and Navigation panel. This mode makes it especially easier to devote your attention to reading document pages on laptop and tablet computers.

To understand some of the advantages for using Reading mode, follow these steps:

STEPS: Changing a view to Reading mode

1. **Open a document in Acrobat.** Use a file you are most likely to read such as a manual, a book, or essay.
2. **Change the view to a Two Page layout.** Click the Two-Up tool in the Page Display toolbar in the Toolbar Well. Note that the tool should be visible if you loaded the tools mentioned in the section "Setting Up the Work Environment" at the beginning of this chapter.

CROSS-REF For more information on Page Layout views, see the "Changing Page Views" section later in this chapter.

3. **Open the Comment & Markup toolbar.** If you review a file or read an eBook, you might want to make some notes on the file. However, you can't stay in Reading mode if a toolbar is opened. Selecting a toolbar (View ⇨ Toolbars ⇨ Comment & Markup, for example) switches back to the standard edit mode as you see in Figure 5.6.

CROSS-REF For more information on using Comment & Markup tools, see Chapter 20.

4. **Change the view to Reading mode.** After making edits with tools such as the Comment & Markup tools, you can return to Reading mode by pressing Alt+H (Windows) or Ctrl/⌘+H (Mac).

FIGURE 5.6

When you load toolbars in Reading mode, the view changes to a normal Viewer mode.

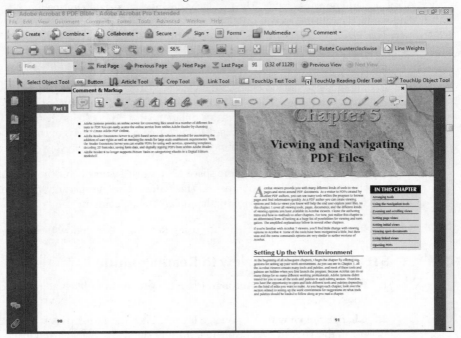

5. **Scroll through the document pages.** Navigating pages in Reading mode is not a problem without having the Navigation tools available. Move the cursor to the elevator bar on the right side of the Document pane and click the mouse button. As you move the bar up or down, you see a thumbnail view of pages as you scroll, as shown in Figure 5.7.

6. **Exit Reading mode.** Press Alt+H (Windows) or Ctrl/⌘+H (Mac) and you return to the default editing mode.

TIP   You can also scroll pages forward using the Right or Down Arrow key or the Page Down key. To scroll to previous pages use the Left or Up Arrow key or the Page Up Key. To jump to the first page in a document press the Home key. To jump to the last page in a document, press the End key.

FIGURE 5.7

Click the elevator bar on the right side of the document pane and you'll see page thumbnails as you scroll pages.

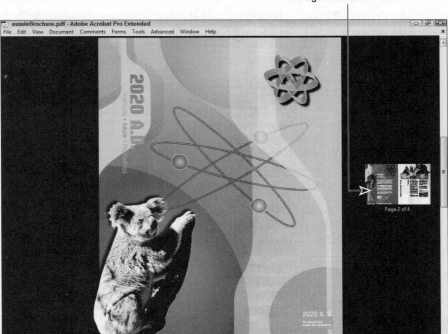

Page thumbnail view

Full Screen mode

Full Screen mode displays your documents without toolbars, menu bar, and Navigation panel. Many options exist for using Full Screen mode. See Chapter 28 for more information.

Menu Bar

Select View ➪ Menu Bar or press F9 (Windows) and the menu bar is temporarily hidden. To bring back the menu bar, press F9 (Windows).

If you're a Mac user working on OS X Leopard, the F9 function key used by Acrobat for hiding menu bars is occupied by OS X's default system shortcuts for Spaces and Exposé. If you want to make use of Acrobat's Function key shortcuts, you need to open the Mac OS X Preferences and reassign the default keys.

Toolbars

Open the View ⇨ Toolbars menu command and a submenu displays all the toolbars and menu options you have when opening a context menu on the Toolbar Well. This menu is just an identical repeat for the same items contained in the context menu. To access the complete set of tools and options for loading and unloading tools from toolbars, select More Tools at the bottom of either menu. Additionally you have options for selecting toolbars from the Tools menu. At the bottom of the Tools menu you find the Customize Toolbars command. Selecting this command is the same as selecting More Tools in either the View ⇨ Toolbars submenu or a context menu opened on the Toolbar Well. Any one of the three menu selections opens the More Tools window.

Navigation Tabs

Choose View ⇨ Navigation Panels and a submenu displays all the palettes that can be opened as floating palettes or docked in the Navigation panel.

CROSS-REF   **For a description of all the Navigation panels, see Chapter 1.**

Grid

If you need to examine drawings, a grid may help in your analysis. In Acrobat Professional, you can choose to view your file displaying a grid. Grids can be useful when you're authoring PDF files, particularly documents for engineers, architects, and PDF forms. For viewing purposes they can be useful where relationships to objects require some careful examination. To show a grid, choose View ⇨ Grid. By default, the grid displays in the Document pane with blue lines at fixed major and minor gridlines, as shown in Figure 5.8.

FIGURE 5.8

Choose View ⇨ Grid or press the Ctrl⌘+U to access the grid. You can change the grid lines for major and minor divisions in the Preferences dialog box.

If you want to change the distances for the major gridlines and the number of divisions for the minor gridlines, open the Preferences dialog box and select Units & Guides in the left pane. The preference settings enable you to change the units of measure and attributes for the grid layout, as shown in Figure 5.9.

FIGURE 5.9

Preference choices for Units & Guides offer you options for changing the units of measure and the grid layout.

The Units & Guides preference settings are also used for changing attributes for the grid layout and rulers. The attribute choices include the following:

- **Page & Ruler Units.** Five choices are available from the pull-down menu. You can choose Points, Picas, Millimeters, Centimeters, or Inches. Whatever you choose here is reflected in the rulers when you display the rulers (View ⇨ Rulers or press Ctrl/⌘+R). Choices here also affect the units of measure found in the Info palette discussed in Chapter 1.

- **Width between lines.** The horizontal distance between the major gridlines is determined in the field box for this setting. You can click on the arrows, enter a number between 0.028 and 138.888 in the field (when inches are selected for the unit of measurement), or press the Up or Down Arrow keys to change the values.

NOTE **The limit of 138.888 relates to inches. If you change the units of measure, the limits are roughly the same as the 138.888-inch limit. In points, the range measures between 2 and 10,000.**

- **Height between lines.** You can change the major gridlines appearing vertically with this field. Use the same methods of changing the values here as for the lines for the Width option.

- **Grid offset from left edge.** Each grid has x and y coordinates indicating where the grid begins on a page. You set the x-axis in this field.

- **Grid offset from top edge.** Use this field to set the starting point of the y-axis.

- **Subdivisions.** The number of gridlines appearing between the major gridlines is determined in this field. The acceptable values range between 0 and 10,000 (when units are set to points).

- **Grid line color.** By default, the color for the gridlines is blue. You can change the grid color by clicking the color swatch. When you click the blue swatch for Grid line color, a pop-up color palette opens, as shown in Figure 5.10. Select a color from the preset color choices in the palette or click Other Color. If you click Other Color, the system color palette opens, in which you can make custom color choices. The Windows and Macintosh system color palettes vary slightly, as shown in Figure 5.11.

FIGURE 5.10

Click the color swatch for the Grid line color to choose from a selection of preset colors, or select Other Color to open the system color palette.

FIGURE 5.11

When you select Other Color, the Windows system color palette opens (left) or the Macintosh system color palette opens (right).

■ **Guide color.** Guides are created from ruler wells, and you can manually position them in the Document pane. If you have ruler guides and a grid, you'll want to change one color to easily distinguish the guides from the grid. Both default to the same blue. To change the guide color, click the Guide Color swatch and follow the same steps as described for Grid line color.

Snap to Grid

When you choose View ⇨ Snap to Grid, objects you draw snap to the major and minor gridlines. This feature can be particularly helpful with form designs and engineering drawings.

 For more information on Snap to Grid, see Chapter 34.

Rulers

Acrobat supports viewing rulers, and you can turn them on via the View menu or using the keyboard shortcut Ctrl/⌘+R. When you choose View ⇨ Ruler or use the keyboard shortcut, rulers appear on the top and left side of the Document pane. Inside the top and left ruler is an inexhaustible supply of guidelines. To add a guideline on the document page, place the cursor within the top or left ruler, press the mouse button, and drag away from the ruler in the Document pane. Continue adding as many guidelines as you want by returning to the ruler wells and dragging out more guidelines.

TIP **You can also add guidelines by double-clicking a ruler. If you want guides positioned at 1-inch increments, as an example, move the mouse cursor to a ruler and double-click the mouse button on each 1-inch increment. Guidelines appear on the page in the Document pane with each double-click of the mouse button. If you attempt to double-click the ruler outside the page area, Acrobat sounds a warning beep and a guideline won't appear outside the document page. If you do want a guideline outside the page area, add a guideline within the page bounding box and drag the guide outside the page area.**

If you want to move a guideline after it has been placed in the Document pane, select the Hand tool and place the cursor directly over the guideline to be moved. The cursor changes from a hand to a selection arrow. Press the mouse button and drag the line to the desired position.

TIP **If you have multiple guidelines to draw on a page at equal distances, use the Units & Guides preferences and set the major guides to the distance you want between the guides. Set the subdivision guidelines to zero. For example, if you want guidelines two inches apart, set the major Height and Width guides to 2 inches and enter 0 (zero) in the subdivisions. Click OK and you save some time dragging guidelines from ruler wells.**

To delete a guideline, click the line and press the Delete key on your keyboard. You can also click and drag a guideline off the document page and back to the ruler well to delete it. If you want to delete all guides on a page, open a context menu (see Figure 5.12) on a ruler and select Clear Guides on Page. If you select Clear All Guides, all guides drawn throughout your document are deleted.

FIGURE 5.12

To clear guides on a page or throughout all pages, open a context menu on a ruler and select Clear All Guides.

The context menu for rulers also enables you to hide the rulers; you can also use the shortcut keys Ctrl/⌘+R or revisit the View menu. Hidden rulers don't affect the view of the guides that remain visible. Notice that the context menu also contains choices for units of measure, which makes changing units here much handier than returning to the preference settings mentioned earlier. The context menu also offers the option to show and hide guides.

Guides

When you draw guidelines the View ➪ Guides menu command is turned on. You can toggle the view of guidelines on and off by selecting View ➪ Guides.

Line Weights

Formerly labeled Wireframe in Acrobat 7, this item appears in both the View menu and the Page Display toolbar. When you zoom in and out of a drawing, the line weights zoom according to the zoom level. For example, a 1-point line zoomed in 400 percent produces a line weight view at 4 points. Zooming out reduces the line weight sizes to where lines can appear almost invisible. When you click the Line Weights tool or select View ➪ Line Weights, all lines appear at a 1-point size regardless of the zoom level.

Automatically Scroll

Automatic scrolling scrolls pages in the open file at a user-defined speed in all Acrobat viewers. When you select the command, Acrobat automatically switches the Single Page layout view to Single Page Continuous view and Two-Up views to Two-Up Continuous views. The pages in the document scroll up, permitting you to read the text without using any keys or the mouse. Attribute changes for automatic scrolling include the following:

- **Changing scrolling speed.** To change the scrolling speed, press a number key from 0 (being the slowest) to 9 (being the fastest) on your keyboard or press the Up or Down Arrow keys to speed up or down in increments.

- **Reverse scrolling direction.** Press the hyphen or minus key.

- **To jump to the next or previous page and continue scrolling.** Press the right or left arrow, respectively.

- **Stopping.** To stop the scrolling, press the Esc key.

CROSS-REF For information related to page layout views, see the "Setting Initial View Attributes" section later in this chapter.

Read Out Loud

This command is a marvelous accessibility tool in all Acrobat viewers. You can have Acrobat PDF documents read aloud to you without having to purchase additional equipment/software such as screen readers. If you want to turn your back on the computer while doing some other activity, you can have Acrobat read aloud any open document. For entertainment purposes, you can gather the family around the computer and have an eBook read to you.

CROSS-REF For information on screen readers, see the sidebar "About Screen Readers" later in this chapter.

When you choose View ➪ Read Out Loud, a submenu opens with four menu commands. The menu commands all have keyboard shortcuts associated with them, but before you can use the commands you must first select Activate Read Out Loud in the submenu. The menu commands then become active as you see in Figure 5.13. For pausing and stopping the reading, you may want to remember these keyboard shortcuts. The commands include:

- **Activate/Deactivate Read Out Loud** (Shift+Ctrl/⌘+Y). Select Activate Read Out Loud when you start a Read Out Loud session. The menu name then changes to Deactivate Read Out Loud. Make this choice to stop reading out loud.

- **Read This Page Only** (Shift+Ctrl/⌘+V). The current active page in the Document pane is read aloud. Reading stops at the end of the target page.

- **Read To End of Document** (Shift+Ctrl/⌘+B). The reading starts on the active page and continues to the end of the document. If you want to start at the beginning of your file, click the First Page tool before selecting this menu command.

- **Pause/Resume** (Shift+Ctrl/⌘+C). After the reading begins, you see the Pause command active in the submenu. Select Pause or press the keyboard shortcut keys and Resume appears in the menu. Use the same menu command or shortcut to toggle Pause and Resume.

- **Stop** (Shift+Ctrl/⌘+E). To stop the reading aloud, select the command or use the keyboard shortcut.

FIGURE 5.13

The Read Out Loud submenu commands provide options for audio output.

Deactivate Read Out Loud	Shift+Ctrl+Y
Read This Page Only	Shift+Ctrl+V
Read To End of Document	Shift+Ctrl+B
Pause	Shift+Ctrl+C
Stop	Shift+Ctrl+E

You change attribute settings for reading aloud in the Preferences dialog box, which you open by choosing Edit ➪ Preferences in Windows, Acrobat ➪ Preferences in Mac OS X, or use the keyboard shortcut (Ctrl/⌘+K). In the left pane shown in Figure 5.14, Reading is selected. The Reading preferences are displayed in the right pane (See Figure 5.14). Preference settings include the following:

- **Reading Order.** Three choices are available from the Reading Order pull-down menu. When in doubt, use the default setting to Infer reading order from document (recommended).

  - **Infer reading order from document (recommended).** With this choice Acrobat makes some guesses about the order for what items are read on the page. If you have multiple columns and the layout is not clearly set up as a page with no layout attributes, the reading order may need some finessing. Acrobat will do its best to deliver the reading in an order compliant to the page layout.

  - **Left-to-right, top-to-bottom reading order.** Reading order delivers the reading, ignoring any columns or heads that may be divided across a page. This choice might be best used for a book designed as text only in a single column.

  - **Use reading order in raw print stream.** Delivers words in the document in the order recorded in the print stream.

- **Override the reading order in tagged documents.** Tagged PDF documents contain structural information, and they are designed to be accessible with reading devices so the proper reading order conforms to the way one would visually read a file. Tagged PDF documents have a designated reading order based on the tree structure. If the PDF document is a tagged PDF with a reading structure defined and you want to ignore the order, deselect the check box. You might make this choice if the tagged PDF does not accurately support the proper reading order and the delivery is more problematic than reading an untagged file.

- **Page vs. Document.** Choices include Only read the current visible pages, Read the entire document, or For large documents, only read the currently visible pages. The difference between the first and last command is when the last item is selected (For large documents, only read the currently visible pages), the field box below the pull-down menu becomes active where you can specify the number of pages to be read.

- **Confirm before tagging documents.** If a document is tagged before reading aloud, a confirmation dialog box opens confirming the file is a tagged document. When the option is checked you can confirm the options that will be used before Acrobat prepares an untagged document for reading. Tagging can be a time-consuming procedure, especially for larger documents. This preference corresponds to the Confirm Before Tagging Documents option in the Accessibility Setup Assistant.

- **Volume.** You adjust volume settings in the Volume pull-down menu. Choose from 1 to 10 to lower or raise the volume.

- **Use default voice.** By default, the Use default voice check box is enabled. If you want to change the voice, deselect the check box and open the pull-down menu adjacent to Voice. The voice availability depends on voices installed with your operating system.

Your text-to-speech default voice installed with your operating system is used. By default you may only have a single voice available. If you want additional voices, consult your operating system manual. If no additional voices are installed, you won't be able to change the voice. If you have multiple voices installed, select a voice from the pull-down menu.

■ **Use default speech attributes.** The speech attributes are settings for the pitch and the speed the voice reads your file. If you want to change the pitch and/or reading rate, deselect the check box. Pitch can be changed to a value between 1 and 10. To completely understand what's going on with the pitch settings, experiment a little and listen to the various pitch changes with the voice you select from the Voice pull-down menu. Words Per Minute enables you to slow down or speed up the reading. The default is 190 wpm. If you want to make a change, type a new value in the field box.

■ **Read form fields.** This setting is designed for use with Acrobat PDF forms. Check the box to have form field default values read aloud. If default text is added to a field, the text is read aloud. If the default text (or any text added to a text field) is replaced, the content of the form fields are read aloud.

CROSS-REF For more information about setting form field default values, see Chapters 34 and 35.

FIGURE 5.14

To open Reading preferences, choose the Preferences command or press Ctrl/⌘+K. Click the Reading item in the list at the left side of the Preferences dialog box.

About Screen Readers

The term *screen reader* as used in this book refers to specialized software and/or hardware devices that enable the reading aloud of computer files. Software such as JAWS and Kurzwiel, and a host of other specialized software programs are sold to people with vision and motion challenges for the purpose of voice synthesizing and audio output. Many of these devices deliver audio output from proprietary formatted files or a select group of software applications. Some screen readers read raster image files saved in formats such as TIFF by performing an optical character recognition (OCR) on-the-fly and reading aloud text as it is interpreted from the image files. This method makes scanning pages of books and papers and having the scanned images interpreted by the readers easy.

Because Acrobat has implemented many tools and features for working with accessible files for the vision and motion challenged, screen reader developers have been supporting PDF format for some time. When a PDF is delivered to a reader and you select Read the entire document, the entire PDF file is sent to the reader before the first page is read. If you have long documents, you can choose to send a certain number of pages to the screen reader to break up the file into smaller chunks. When you select For long documents, read only the currently visible pages and the default of 10 pages is selected, ten pages are sent to the screen reader and the reading commences. After the pages are read, another ten pages are sent to the screen reader and read aloud, and so on.

CROSS-REF For more information on screen readers, tagged PDF files, and accessibility, see Chapter 25.

Scrolling

Anyone familiar with window environments is no stranger to scrolling. Fortunately, scroll bars behave in a standard fashion among computer platforms and various computer programs. Page scrolling works the same in an Acrobat viewer as it does in Microsoft Word (or any other Microsoft product for that matter), or any illustration, layout, or host of other applications that you may be familiar with. Drag the scroll bar up and down or left to right to move the document within the active window. Click between the scroll bar at the top or bottom of the scrolling column to jump a page segment or full page. The arrow icons at the top, bottom, left, and right sides allow you to move in smaller segments in the respective directions.

Acrobat 8 and 9 add a little flair to scrolling. When you drag the elevator bar up and down, you get not only the page number and total pages in the file but a thumbnail preview of each page as you scroll the pages. Note that the thumbnails only show up when in Single Page or Two-Up mode.

When you drag the scroll bar up or down in a multiple-page PDF file, a small thumbnail appears as well as a page number associated with the scroll bar position and the total number of pages in the document. (See Figure 5.15.) The readout is in the form of "*n* of *n* pages." The first number dynamically changes as you move the scroll bar between pages. This behavior works in all as long as you are in Single Page or Two-Up Mode.

CROSS-REF For information on auto scrolling, see the "Automatically Scroll" section earlier in this chapter.

FIGURE 5.15

When you click and drag an elevator bar used for page scrolling, a page thumbnail and a readout shows you page numbers and total pages.

Page thumbnail preview

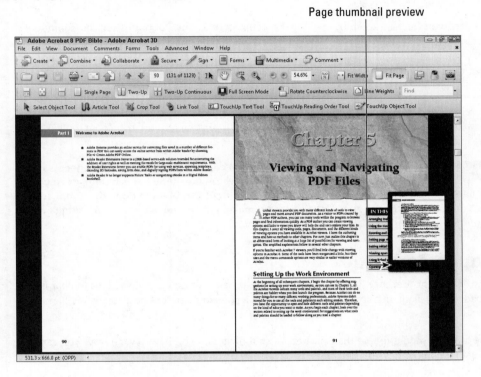

Zooming

Zooming in and out of document pages is a fact of life with many different programs. Even when you type text in a word processor, you often need to zoom in on text that is set in a style suited for printing, but looks horrible at a 100% view on your computer monitor. The same holds true for spreadsheets, all imaging and layout programs, and any kind of program where page sizes grow beyond a standard letter-size page.

Because Acrobat accommodates a page size of up to 200 × 200 inches, PDF documents sporting large page sizes need some industrial-strength zoom tools. Acrobat Professional contains a few more tools than other Acrobat viewers; however, all viewers enable you to zoom in and out of document pages using many tools consistent across all the viewers. The Zoom In and Zoom Out tools used in all viewers permit views from .33 percent to 6,400 percent of a document page.

Several tools are available for zooming. By default the Marquee Zoom and the Dynamic Zoom tools appear in the Select & Zoom toolbar docked in the Toolbar Well. If you load all the zoom tools in the Select & Zoom toolbar you can select from one of six zoom tools in Acrobat Professional. Four of the six tools are available in all Acrobat 9 viewers.

In all viewers, you can also zoom by clicking the Zoom In or Zoom Out buttons in the Zoom toolbar (represented by a + and – symbol) or editing the zoom percentage field in the toolbar — just type a new value in the field box and press the Enter/Return key to zoom. When you click the down-pointing arrow, the preset pull-down menu opens.

The View menu also has a Zoom To command. Select it and the Zoom To dialog box opens where you can select fixed zoom levels from a pull-down menu or type in a value from 0.5 to 6,400 percent. However, this menu command is redundant because you can also use the Zoom toolbar in the same manner.

TIP At first glance you may think that the menu command is useless and unnecessary. However, when viewing PDF documents where the menu bar is hidden or viewing files in Full Screen mode, you can use the keyboard shortcut Ctrl/⌘+M to open the Zoom To dialog box. You can then change zoom levels without making the menu bar visible or exiting Full Screen mode.

Marquee Zoom tool

🔍 Marquee Zoom By default the Marquee Zoom tool appears in the Select & Zoom toolbar. This toolbar is loaded by default and appears when you open a context menu on the Toolbar Well and select Reset Toolbars.

Click the Marquee Zoom tool in the Select & Zoom toolbar and you have several ways you can use the tool using modifier keys that include:

- **Click and drag.** Drag the tool to create a marquee to zoom in to an area.
- **Alt/Option+click and drag.** Press the Alt/Option key to marquee an area and you zoom the page out.
- **Click.** Click the Marquee Zoom tool and the zoom jumps a fixed percentage.
- **Alt/Option+click.** Press the Alt/Option key and click and you zoom out at fixed percentages.

Zoom In tool

⊕ Zoom In The Zoom In tool is restricted to its fixed position in the Zoom toolbar. Click the Zoom tool in the Zoom toolbar and you zoom in to the same fixed preset zooms as when using the Marquee Zoom tool.

Zoom Out tool

Zoom Out — The Zoom Out tool works in exactly the same way as the Zoom In tool, only it zooms out rather than in. It also has the same options associated with it as are associated with the Marquee Zoom tool when you press Alt/Option.

Dynamic Zoom tool

Dynamic Zoom — When you first use the Dynamic Zoom tool, you may feel like you're watching a George Lucas sci-fi movie. It's downright mesmerizing. This tool is available in all Acrobat viewers and is much handier than drawing marquees with the Marquee Zoom tool.

To use dynamic zooming, select the tool from the Select & Zoom toolbar. Click and drag up to zoom in and down to zoom out. Stop at the desired zoom level by releasing the mouse button. Acrobat displays a proxy view while zooming in and out and only refreshes the screen when you release the mouse button. Using this tool, therefore, is much faster because each zoom increment does not require a new screen refresh.

> **TIP** You can easily toggle between the Marquee Zoom tool and the Dynamic Zoom tool using a modifier key. When the Marquee Zoom tool is selected, press the Shift key and the tool changes to the Dynamic Zoom tool. Release the Shift key and you return back to the Marquee Zoom tool.

Loupe tool

Loupe — If you use other Adobe programs, such as Adobe Photoshop, Adobe Illustrator, or Adobe InDesign, you know about the Navigator palette. The Loupe tool, available in all Acrobat 9 viewers, works similarly to the Navigator palette found in other Adobe programs but with a little twist. Instead of viewing a complete page in the Loupe Tool window, you see just the zoom level of your selection while the page zoom remains static. This tool can be a great benefit by saving you time to refresh your monitor when you change screen views.

To use the Loupe tool, click in the Select & Zoom toolbar or press Z on your keyboard and then Shift+Z to toggle the Marquee Zoom tool, the Dynamic Zoom tool, and the Loupe tool. Move the cursor to an area on a page you want to zoom to and click the mouse button. The Loupe tool window opens and displays the zoomed area you selected, as shown in Figure 5.16.

> **CROSS-REF** When using keyboard shortcuts for accessing tools you need to enable the *Use single-key accelerators to access tools* preference setting. For more information on setting preferences for using keyboard shortcuts, see Chapter 1.

You can increase or decrease the magnification of the zoom area by adjusting the slider bar in the Loupe window or clicking the minus or plus symbols in the window. Clicking these symbols offers you smaller incremental changes than when using the same symbols in the Select & Zoom toolbar. If you want the Loupe tool to show a larger portion, you can resize the Loupe Tool dialog box by grabbing a corner of the box and dragging.

FIGURE 5.16

Click an area in the Document pane with the Loupe tool, and the target area is viewed at a zoom level in the Loupe window.

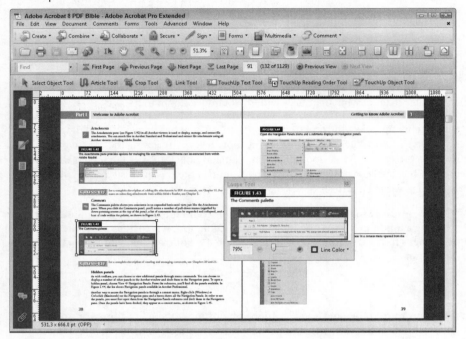

When you click in the Document pane with the Loupe tool, a rectangle appears around the area zoomed into the Loupe window (see Figure 5.16). You can place the cursor inside this rectangle and move it around the Document pane to view different areas at the same zoom level. As you zoom in, the rectangle reduces in size. At some point it would be impractical to select the rectangle on the page. If you can't find it, zoom out a little in the Loupe tool window until you see the rectangle on the page. Click and drag it to a new position and you can adjust your zoom.

Notice also in Figure 5.16 the four handles (squares) on the corners of the rectangle marking the Loupe tool zoom area. You can drag the handles in or out to zoom in or out, respectively.

If you have oversized documents that take a long time to refresh, using the Loupe tool helps speed up your PDF viewing. You can keep the document page in the Document pane at a reduced view while using the Loupe tool to examine areas in detail, which won't necessitate screen refreshes.

TIP The Loupe window displays the zoom level on an open document and remains fixed to that document until you target a new area. When you have multiple documents open, you can zoom in on one document and switch views in the Document pane to another document; the zoom display in the Loupe tool window remains fixed to the original document view. What you wind up with appears as if it's a picture-in-picture view such as you might see on a television set.

Pan & Zoom Window

Pan & Zoom Window

Whereas the Loupe tool displays the zoom view in its own window and the page in the Document pane remains static, the Pan & Zoom Window works in the opposite manner. The zoom level changes on the page in the Document pane while the original page view remains static in the Pan & Zoom Window. The zoom area is highlighted with a red rectangle in the Pan & Zoom Window. You can change the default red color of the zoom rectangle by opening the Line Color pull-down menu in the window and choosing from preset colors or choosing a custom color.

NOTE If you don't see a red square in the Pan & Zoom Window in the lower-right corner, you need to size the window larger to reveal the pull-down menu.

To use the Pan & Zoom Window, select the tool from the Zoom toolbar. The window displays a full page with the red rectangle showing the zoom area. If you open the Pan & Zoom Window when your PDF page is in Fit Page view, the page and the red rectangle are the same size.

To zoom a view in the Pan & Zoom Window, select one of the four handles on a corner of the rectangle and resize the rectangle by dragging in or out to zoom in or out, respectively. The page thumbnail view in the Pan & Zoom Window remains the same size while the rectangle is sized, as shown in Figure 5.17.

FIGURE 5.17

The Pan & Zoom Window displays a thumbnail view of the entire document page. The rectangle in the window shows the zoom level corresponding to the page zoom view.

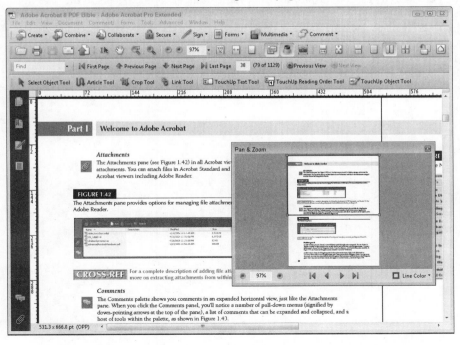

Also contained in the Pan & Zoom Window are navigation buttons. You can establish a zoom view and then scroll pages in your document with the page tools in the window. As you do so, the page views in the Document pane hold the same zoom level you set in the Pan & Zoom Window.

Zoom tool behaviors

A few specific differences exist between the Loupe tool and the Pan & Zoom tool that you should know. The Loupe tool targets an area on an open document and the zoom is fixed to that document while it remains open or until you target a new area. Regardless of the number of files you open, the Loupe tool window displaying your target view stays intact even if another document is brought to the front of the Document pane. If you close a file where the Loupe tool was set to view a zoom, the Loupe tool window clears and displays no view.

The Pan & Zoom tool always shows a target view of the active document brought forward in the Document pane. If you have multiple documents open, open the Pan & Zoom tool, then close a file, the page in view in the next file appears in the Pan & Zoom Window. If you close all files, the Pan & Zoom Window clears.

If you close a file during an Acrobat session, both the Loupe tool and the Pan & Zoom tool return you to the same views. The Pan & Zoom tool displays the opening page at the same zoom level as was last established in the window. The Loupe tool displays the same view last created with the tool. For example, if you zoom to 200% on page 25 of a file, close the file, and then reopen it, the Loupe tool window displays page 25 at 200% while the Document pane displays the opening page.

You can use both tools together to display different views in different documents. If the page in view in the Loupe window is not the current active document brought forward in the Document pane, you can still manage zooming on the hidden page. Use the slider between the minus/plus symbols to change zoom levels. In Figure 5.18, you can see the Loupe tool and the Pan & Zoom tool used together in different documents. The Loupe tool shows a zoom view on one page in a document while the Pan & Zoom tool shows a zoom view on a page in another document.

FIGURE 5.18

The Loupe tool and the Pan & Zoom tools show different zoom levels on different pages in different documents.

Changing Page Views

The page views for Actual Size, Fit Width, and Fit Page are static views that you want to access frequently when navigating through a PDF document. Acrobat viewers provide several ways to change a page view. Three tools appear in the Select & Zoom toolbar for toggling different page views. The different views include:

- **Actual Size.** Displays the PDF page at actual size (a 100 % view).

- **Fit Width.** The data on a PDF page are displayed horizontally without clipping. If the page is large and data appear only in the center of the page, the page zooms to fit the data. The white space at the page edges is ignored.

- **Fit Page.** Displays the page at the maximum size that fits within the viewer Document pane. If the Acrobat viewer window is sized up or down, the Fit Page view conforms to the size of the Document pane.

One of the keyboard shortcuts you'll want to remember is Ctrl/⌘+0 (zero). This enables you to view a page in a Fit Page view. As you browse pages in a PDF document, the page views are specific to the individual pages and not the document. Therefore, scrolling PDF files with different page sizes may require you to frequently change views if you want to see the full page in the Document pane. By using the keyboard shortcuts, you can reset page views much faster.

Page views can be established for the opening page according to user-specified zoom views. Setting these attributes was referred to as Open Options in earlier versions of Acrobat. In Acrobat 6 and later, they are referred to as Initial View. These and other kinds of page views available in Acrobat are covered in the following section.

Setting Initial View Attributes

Initial View is the page view you see when you first open a PDF document. You can set several different attributes for an opening view and you can save your settings with the document. These views are document specific so they only relate to a document where you save the settings. When no settings have been saved with a file, the file is saved with a default view.

CROSS-REF To understand more about default views, see "Understanding Initial View preferences" later in this chapter.

Coincidentally, even though previous versions of Acrobat provided you with options to save an initial view, most PDF authors rarely use them. You can find thousands of PDF files on the Internet and most of them have no settings enabled for an opening view other than the program defaults. I hope that by the time you finish this section, you can see some advantages for saving a particular initial view for the PDF documents you create and edit.

To set the attributes for the opening view, choose File ➪ Properties or use the keyboard shortcut Ctrl/⌘+D. The Document Properties dialog box opens, displaying a row of tabs at the top. Click the Initial View tab as shown in Figure 5.19.

NOTE Initial View settings are not available nor can they be changed in Adobe Reader even when usage rights have been added to the PDF. When Initial Views are saved from Acrobat Standard, Pro, or Pro Extended, PDFs open with the saved views in all Acrobat viewers.

FIGURE 5.19

To set the attributes for the opening view, choose File ⇨ Properties and click the Initial View tab when the Document Properties dialog box opens.

Acrobat provides you with many different choices for controlling the initial view of a PDF opened in any Acrobat viewer. Settings you make on the Initial View tab can be saved with your document. When you establish settings other than defaults, the settings saved with the file override the user's default preference settings. The options on this tab are as follows:

■ **Layout and Magnification.** The default opening page is the first page of a PDF document. You can change the opening page to another page and you can control the page layout views and magnification by selecting choices from the Layout and Magnification section. The choices include:

NOTE One reason you might want to open a PDF document on a page other than the first page is when you have a cover page or a title page that doesn't include content of interest to the reader. In such cases, you might want to open the PDF document on page two where a contents page or the first page of a section or chapter appears.

■ **Navigation tab.** Five choices are available from the Navigation tab pull-down menu. Select Page Only to open the page with the Navigation panel collapsed. Use the Bookmarks Panel and Page option to open the Bookmarks panel when the file opens. Use the Pages Panel and Page option to open the Pages panel where the thumbnails of pages are viewed. Use Attachments Panel and Page to open the Attachments panel when the file opens, and use Layers Panel and Page to open the Layers panel when the file opens.

■ **Page Layout.** The default for Page Layout is noted in the pull-down menu as Default. When you save a PDF file with the Default selection, the PDF opens according to the default value a user has set for page viewing on the user's computer. To override the user's default, you can set a page layout in the opening view from one of six choices. Your options include:

   ■ **Single Page.** This option opens a single page view that appears the same as when you click the Single Page layout tool.

   ■ **Single Page Continuous.** The same as the Continuous page layout view in earlier versions of Acrobat. This view appears the same as when you click the Single Page Continuous tool.

   ■ **Two-Up (Facing).** The Two-Up (Facing) view shows the first two pages in a file beside each other in a two-page layout. When you scroll, subsequent pages snap to a page view. This view is the same as clicking the Two-Up tool.

   ■ **Two-Up Continuous (Facing).** The view appears very similar to Two-Up (Facing) but when you scroll pages, partial pages can be viewed in the Document pane. For example, the bottom of the previous page and the top of the next page may appear. In other words, this view doesn't snap pages to fit in the Document pane.

   ■ **Two-Up (Cover Page).** The initial view shows one page as in the Single Page view. When you scroll pages, however, the subsequent pages are displayed in a Two-Up (facing pages) view.

   ■ **Two-Up Continuous (Cover Page).** The initial page opens on the right side of the Document pane in a Single Page view. When you scroll pages, the scrolling is similar to the Two-Up Continuous view where facing pages are shown.

   ■ **Magnification.** Choose from preset magnification views in the pull-down menu. If you want the PDF document to open in a fit-in-window view, select Fit Page. Choose from other magnification options or edit the text box for a custom-zoom level. If Default is selected, the document opens according to user preference magnification settings.

   ■ **Open to page.** You can change the opening page to another page by entering a number in the Page number text box. This setting might be used if you want a user to see a contents page on page 2 in a document instead of a title page that appears on page 1.

■ **Window Options.** The default window for Acrobat is a full screen where the viewing area is maximized to occupy your monitor surface area. You can change the window view to size down the window to the initial page size, center a smaller window onscreen, and open a file in Full Screen mode. If you enable all three check boxes, the Full Screen mode prevails.

■ **Show.** From the pull-down menu choose either File Name or Document Title. If you select File Name, the title bar at the top of the Acrobat window shows the filename. If Document Title is used, the information you supply in the Document Properties dialog box for Document Title is shown in the title bar.

CROSS-REF Document titles are very important when you're archiving volumes of PDFs and creating search indexes. For information on creating document titles and how they are used, see Chapter 6.

- **User Interface Options.** The Interface Options in the Initial View Document Properties dialog box have to do with user interface items in Acrobat viewers, such as menu bars, toolbars, and scroll bars. You can elect to hide these items when the PDF document opens in any Acrobat viewer. In Acrobat 9, you can hide only two of the three options for the User Interface Controls shown in Figure 5.19. You can choose to hide the menu bar and the window controls as shown in Figure 5.20, the menu bar and the toolbars, or ay one of the single items. Acrobat 9 doesn't permit you to hide all three options

    The window controls you see in Figure 5.21 include the scroll bars, the status bar, and the Navigation panel. If you hide the toolbars and menu bar but elect to leave the window controls visible, users can access tools for page navigation.

CAUTION If you elect to eliminate the toolbars and menu bar from view and later want to go back and edit your file, you need to use shortcut keys to get the menu bars and toolbars back. Be certain to remember the F9 key — F9 shows and hides the menu bar and the F8 key that shows/hides toolbars.

FIGURE 5.20

When toolbars and the menu bar are hidden, navigating pages requires keyboard shortcuts or navigational buttons on the pages.

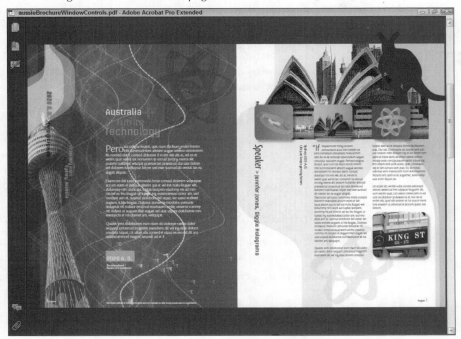

FIGURE 5.21

If window controls are visible, users can access tools for page navigation.

> **TIP** If you open a PDF document with Window Controls hidden, you can open the Navigation pane by opening a context menu on the far left side of the Document pane and choosing Show Navigation Panel Buttons.

Setting custom zoom levels

The Initial View options for the page zoom are at fixed magnification levels. If you want a PDF document to open at a zoom level of 69%, for example, you don't have the choice for this custom zoom option in the Initial View settings. To set a custom zoom level, you need to use a JavaScript. To add a JavaScript to open a PDF document at a custom zoom level, do the following:

Steps: Setting Custom Zoom Magnification with JavaScript

1. **Open a document and choose Advanced ⇨ Document Processing ⇨ Document JavaScripts.** The JavaScript Functions dialog box opens.

2. **Type a name for the script in the Script Name text box.** In my example, I'll name my script: *zoom*.

3. **Click Add to open the JavaScript Editor.**

4. Delete the default text in the JavaScript Editor window and type the following code:
   ```
   this.zoom=69;
   ```

5. Click OK in the JavaScript Editor to return to the JavaScript Functions dialog box as shown in Figure 5.22.

6. Close in the JavaScript Functions dialog box.

7. Save the file.

FIGURE 5.22

The JavaScript Functions dialog box showing a script to force a zoom magnification of 69%.

The above code forces the PDF document to open at 69%. If you want to use another magnification, just change 69 to another numeric value in the script.

CROSS-REF For more information on writing JavaScripts, see Chapter 36 (on the CD-ROM).

Understanding Initial View preferences

If you don't assign Initial View attributes in the Document Properties dialog box and save the file to update it, initial views are determined from individual user preferences. Because each user can set preferences differently, the same PDF may appear with a different page layout mode and a different zoom level on different computers. Depending on the design of your documents and how you want them viewed by end users, potential inconsistency in document views might make viewing difficult for those who view your files.

Users set initial view preferences in the Preferences dialog box. Open the Preferences dialog box by pressing Ctrl/⌘+K, and then click Page Display in the left pane. At the top of the right pane, a pull-down menu appears for Default page layout; at the bottom of the right pane another menu appears for Default zoom. You can select different page layout and default zoom views from the menus. In Figure 5.23, the Default page layout view is set to Single Page and the Default zoom is set to Fit Page. When you click OK to accept these changes, all PDF documents that have initial views set to Default will open on your computer with the views derived from your preference choices. Other users may choose different options from the pull-down menus, thereby displaying PDF documents with default views according to the choices they make in the Page Display preferences.

Be aware that the initial views you set in a PDF file from the Document Properties override the user preferences in the Page Display preferences pane. Therefore, you can control the initial views for all the PDFs you create. Doing so means your documents are viewed consistently across all computers regardless of the differences between individual user preference choices.

FIGURE 5.23

Changing the Default page layout to Single Page and the Default zoom to Fit Page opens all PDFs saved with default initial views with your new preference settings.

Saving the Initial View

When you decide what view attributes you want assigned to your document, you can choose one of two save options. The first option updates the file. Click the Save tool in the Acrobat File toolbar or choose File ⇨ Save. Any edits you make in the Initial View properties activates the Save command. The Save command is inactive and grayed out by default until you make any changes to your file or reset any kind of preferences that can be saved with the document. The other option is to use Save As. When you select File ⇨ Save As, you completely rewrite the file when you click the Save button in the Save As dialog box.

CROSS-REF   **You have different choices for saving files using either Save, Save As, or Save a Version a version. For a more complete understanding of saving, updating, and saving versions of PDFs, see Chapter 11.**

Viewing Files with the Window Menu

If you open a PDF file and then open a second PDF, the second file hides the first document. If several PDFs are opened, the last opened document hides all the others. Fortunately, the Acrobat viewers have made it easy for you to choose a given document from a nest of open files.

When you load an Acrobat viewer with several open files, you can use tools to help you manage them. If you need to visually compare documents, several different viewing options are available.

The Window menu contains options for helping you manage document views, and in particular, multiple documents. The options you find in the Window menu won't be found with tools or in the status bar, so you'll find yourself visiting this menu frequently if you work with multiple open files in Acrobat or if you need to create more than one view in the same document.

Minimize and zoom views

By default, when you open PDF files, the Acrobat window appears minimized. In other words, the application window doesn't zoom to the full screen size. This behavior can be a blessing for those with large monitors who want to work in Acrobat and another application alongside the Acrobat window, or a curse for those who want to take advantage of a full screen size when working in Acrobat alone.

 If you leave the preferences at the default, you can zoom the Acrobat application window by clicking the features button on the application window. Click the Maximize button represented by an X in the top-right corner (Windows) and the window zooms to a maximized view.

 On the Macintosh, click the plus icon in the top-left corner of the application window and the application window zooms to a maximized view.

New Window

New Window was a new feature in Acrobat 7 Professional. When you open a document and select New Window, a duplicate view of your existing document is opened in the Document pane. You can change views and pages in one window while viewing different page views in another window. This feature is handy for viewing a table of contents in one window while viewing content on other pages in the same file.

When you select New Window, Acrobat adds an extension to the filename in the title bar. If you have a document open in Acrobat with a filename like Employee Application and then select New Window, the title bar displays Employee Application:1 on one view and Employee Application:2 on the second view.

New Window can be particularly helpful when viewing PDF Portfolios. You can create a PDF Portfolio and view two or more files within the package in new windows and tiled views.

CROSS-REF For more information on PDF Portfolios and viewing options you have with these files, see Chapter 12. For more on tiling views, see "Tile" later in this chapter.

Cascade

If you have several files open and choose Window ➪ Cascade, the open files appear in a cascading view with the title bars visible much like you might view cascading Web pages. You can see the name of each file and easily select from any one shown in the Document pane. Click a title bar to bring a document forward.

After bringing a file forward, if you want to see the title bars in a cascading view again, choose Window ➪ Cascade again. The document currently selected in the foreground will appear first when you use this command.

The Window menu also lists the open files by filename at the bottom of the window. When you have multiple files open, the files are numbered according to the order in which they were opened, with the filename appearing in the list, as shown in Figure 5.24. Select any filename from the list in the Window menu to bring the file forward in the Document pane.

FIGURE 5.24

Acrobat lists all open files in the Window menu. To bring a document forward in the Document pane, choose the name of the file you want to view from the Window menu.

Tile

You can also choose to have your documents tiled horizontally or vertically via the Tile submenu in the Window menu. When you choose Window ➪ Tile ➪ Horizontally or Vertically, the PDF files appear in individual windows arranged to fit within the Acrobat window in either a horizontal or vertical view. If you have more than three documents open at one time, the display for Tile Horizontally and Tile Vertically appear identical. With any number of documents displayed in tiled views, the Navigation panel is accessible for each document. Also, when you choose Window ➪ New Window and open a second view of the same document, and then tile the views, each window appears in the tiled documents. In Figure 5.25, two documents appear in a vertical tiled view.

FIGURE 5.25

Tiling views neatly displays all open documents adjacent to each other within the Acrobat window.

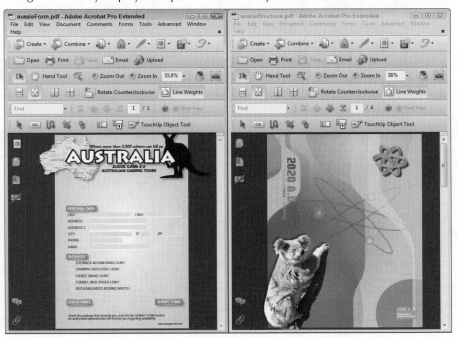

Tiling documents can be helpful when you need to edit documents and exchange pages between two or more PDF files or when you need to compare changes among documents.

CROSS-REF For information related to editing files, see the Chapters in Part III. For more information on comparing documents, see Chapter 20.

Split

Choose Window ⇨ Split and the Document pane splits into two horizontal views of the active document, similar to the way you might see a split view in a word processing or spreadsheet program. The two views are independent of each other and offer you much flexibility. You can view the same page in two different zoom views or you can view two different pages at the same zoom level or different zoom views. You can view one pane in a Single page layout and the other pane in one of the other page layout options. You can also combine the Split and Tile option to view two or more documents, each with split views tiled horizontally or vertically. You can adjust the window division by moving the horizontal bar up or down, thereby showing a larger view in one pane and a smaller view in the other pane.

Spreadsheet Split

Spreadsheet Split is the same concept as using a Split view except you now have four panes. Just choose Window ➪ Spreadsheet Split. Click inside the pane whose view you want to change and then zoom in and out and navigate pages as needed. Move the divider bars horizontally and vertically to size the panes to accommodate your viewing needs. Position the cursor at the intersection of the separator bars and you can move the bars vertically and horizontally together.

To remove the Spreadsheet Split view, return to the Window menu and select Spreadsheet Split again. The Document pane returns to the default view.

> **TIP** You can exit the Spreadsheet view by double-clicking the intersection of the cross-bars. If you want a split view vertically or horizontally, double-click the vertical (or horizontal) crossbar.

Full Screen Mode

Another viewing option found in the Window menu is the Full Screen Mode. Full Screen Mode displays your PDF document like a slide show and temporarily hides the menus, toolbars, and window controls. You can set up the Full Screen Mode for automatic page scrolling and then walk away from the computer — you'll have a self-running kiosk. You can give a presentation and automatically scroll pages or set preferences for pausing between slides.

> **CROSS-REF** There's a lot to Full Screen viewing. To learn more about working with Full Screen views, see Chapter 28.

Viewing Links

For the purpose of discussion, links in Acrobat are *hot spots* where you click somewhere in the Acrobat window and some action takes place. With regard to viewing PDF documents, clicking the mouse button on a link takes you to another view, opens a document or Web page, or executes some sort of action. Links can be any one of a number of items, including elements on a PDF page such as buttons, articles, fields, and so on, or they can be part of the user interface such as thumbnails and links you create from options in palettes. In this chapter, I stick to link behavior in Acrobat as it relates to page viewing and locating links.

> **CROSS-REF** For information on creating links and buttons that execute a variety of different actions, see Chapter 22.

Navigation pane

The Navigation pane contains the default panels discussed in Chapter 1. Most of these panels are connected to certain capabilities for linking to views and other kinds of actions that can be invoked with the click of a mouse button. In some cases, a single click takes you to another view and in other cases a double-click takes you to another view. The panels that contain some form of linking to views include:

CROSS-REF To learn more about the Navigation panels, see Chapter 1 and Chapter 3.

- **Pages.** To view thumbnails of each page, click the Pages panel in the Navigation pane. The page thumbnails are links to the respective pages. A single mouse click on a page thumbnail displays the respective page in the Document pane.

CROSS-REF For information on working with the Pages panel, see Chapter 22.

- **Bookmarks.** All Bookmarks in a PDF file are displayed in a list beside the Bookmarks panel. With a single click of the mouse button, a Bookmark may take you to another page or view, or invoke an action.

CROSS-REF For information on creating Bookmarks and setting link actions to them, see Chapter 22.

- **Signatures.** The Signatures panel contains a list of all digital signatures in a PDF document. You can open the Signatures panel and navigate to pages where signatures have been added to the file.

CROSS-REF For information on creating digital signatures, see Chapter 26.

- **Attachments.** The Attachments panel contains a list of all file attachments. Double-clicking an attachment, however, does not navigate to the page where the attachment is placed. Use the Attachments panel to search for the page where the attachment appears because double-clicking an attachment opens the attached file.

CROSS-REF For information on working with file attachments, see Chapter 12.

- **Comments.** The Comments panel contains any annotations added to the open file. You can navigate to any page where a comment has been added by double-clicking on a comment in the Comments panel.

CROSS-REF For information on working with comments, see Chapter 20.

Navigation panels

The additional panels you can access from the View ➪ Navigation Panels submenu described in Chapter 1 contain links to the content you create from various panel options. The panels not yet discussed that appear in the Navigation Panels submenu are as follows:

■ **Accessibility Report.** When you choose Advanced Editing ⇨ Accessibility ⇨ Full Check you are prompted to save an Accessibility Report file. Once the file is saved, the report appears in the Navigation pane in the Accessibility Report panel. Here you can analyze the document for compliance with document accessibility.

CROSS-REF For information on accessibility, see Chapter 25.

■ **Articles.** Article threads are like link buttons. You can create article threads in a PDF file and the threads are listed in the Articles panel. Use the panel to open an article thread and click the mouse button inside the article to follow the thread.

CROSS-REF For information on creating articles, see Chapter 22.

■ **Compare.** When you compare two documents to search for changes made between document versions, the Compare panel opens. From the Options menu you have a number of menu choices for displaying compared documents and analyzing the comparison as shown in Figure 5.26.

FIGURE 5.26

Choose Document ⇨ Compare Documents and the Compare Documents panel opens in the Navigation pane.

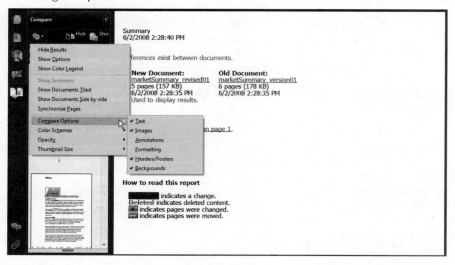

■ **Content.** Document content can be displayed in the Content panel. When you open the panel and select individual items, you can highlight the respective content item on the document page. In essence, the Content panel is linked to the content appearing on the PDF pages according to the natural reading order of the PDF file.

CROSS-REF For information on using the Content panel, see Chapter 25.

■ **Destinations.** Destinations are similar to Bookmarks and are linked to a specific location in an open PDF document or to secondary PDF documents. When you click a destination, the view associated with the destination opens in the Document pane.

CROSS-REF For information on destinations, see Chapter 22.

■ **Examine Document.** When you choose Document ⇨ Examine Document, the Examine Document panel opens in the Navigation pane. You have a number of options to analyze a document including examining metadata, file attachments, bookmarks, and form fields.

CROSS-REF For information on examining documents, see Chapter 14.

■ **Fields.** In Acrobat 9 you won't find the Fields panel located in the Navigation Panels submenu. The Fields panel has been moved to another interface where form field editing is performed. To see the Fields panel you need to choose Forms ⇨ Add or Edit Fields which takes you to Form Editing Mode. By default the Fields panel opens when you switch to Form Editing Mode. The Fields panel lists all form fields created in the open document. Click a field name in the panel and the field becomes highlighted in the Form Editing window.

CROSS-REF For information on creating form fields, see Chapters 33 and 34.

NOTE Having the document page size appear by default without having to move the cursor in the lower left corner of the Acrobat window is a matter of personal choice. I find it helpful having the page size reported when I'm opening PDF documents. As a matter of consistency in viewing the screen shots in this book, I have this preference option turned on for all the figures in the remaining chapters of this book.

■ **Layers.** The Layers panel shows all Adobe PDF layers contained in a document by layer names. If the panel is empty, no layers are contained in the file. You use the Layers panel to show and hide layers, set layer properties, and manage layers.

CROSS-REF For more information on using Adobe PDF Layers, see Chapter 24.

■ **Model Tree.** Model Tree is used with 3D graphics within a PDF. You can examine content, change views, shading, and many different aspects of 3D models. The Model Tree is also opened when you use the Object Data tool.

■ **Order.** When you open the Order panel, the reading order of your pages is displayed in the panel and on the document pages. You can easily change the reading order by moving the references in the Order panel around much like you would reorganize Bookmarks.

CROSS-REF For information on using use the Order panel, see Chapter 26.

- **Security Settings.** In Acrobat 9 you have a new Security Settings panel that appears in the Navigation pane when a file has security applied to the document. Click Permission Details in the Security Settings panel and the Document Properties Security tab opens displaying the permissions assigned to the document.

- **Standards.** When you create PDF files meeting standards such as PDF/A, PDF/X, PDF/E etc. the Standards panel opens in the Navigation pane. Among other things, you can verify compliance to a given standard and click a link to the Preflight tool where you can analyze a document for meeting conditions for a given standard.

CROSS-REF   **For information on using PDF standards, see Chapter 10. For more information on using the Preflight tool, see Chapter 32.**

- **Tags.** Tags list all the structural content in a PDF document. You can highlight an element from within the Tags panel to locate a tagged element. Whereas the Contents panel identifies all the page content in any PDF file, the Tags panel only shows the structure and elements of tagged PDF files. Together with the Order panel, Tags are used with accessible documents.

CROSS-REF   **For information on using the Tags panel and making documents accessible, see Chapter 25.**

Hypertext links

In an Acrobat viewer, hypertext references enable you to move around the PDF or many PDFs, much like surfing the Net. You've probably become so accustomed to clicking buttons on your desktop computer that link navigation is commonplace and needs little instruction. While invoking the action is nothing more than a click with the mouse, what it can do in Acrobat is simply remarkable. To help you gain an understanding of how Acrobat has employed hyperlinks, the following sections describe all the link actions as they can be created in Acrobat and executed in any viewer.

Hypertext references, or *buttons,* are easily identified in a PDF document. As you move the mouse cursor around the document window, a Hand icon with the forefinger pointing appears when you position the cursor over a button or a link. You click, and presto! — the link action is executed!

Link actions can be assigned to any one of several items in Acrobat. You can set a link action to links, fields, Bookmarks, and Page Actions. The action types available in Acrobat include:

NEW FEATURE   **All the Link Action types are available with all Acrobat products (Std, Pro, Pro Extended). Form fields can be created with all versions in version 9. Earlier versions of Acrobat Standard did support creating form fields.**

- **Execute a menu command.** This action links to commands found in the Acrobat menus. Unfortunately, many of the Execute a menu command options were removed in Acrobat 8. If you used some Execute menu items that are no longer available in Acrobat 8 and 9, you now have to turn to JavaScript programming and completely rework your files.

- **Go to a 3D/Multimedia view.** For PDF documents supporting 3D views, you can set an action to a specific 3D view.

■ **Go to a page view.** The Go to a page view action opens another view on the existing page, a view to another page in the same document, a view to a named destination, or a view in another document.

■ **Import form data.** This action imports data exported from other forms into the active document where form field names match those from where the data were exported.

■ **Open a file.** The Open a file link opens any kind of document. PDFs open in Acrobat. Other file types require having the authoring program installed on your computer. For example, if the link is to a Microsoft Word document, you need Word installed on your computer to open the link.

■ **Open a web link.** Opens a URL in your default Web browser.

■ **Play a sound.** Plays a sound imported into the active PDF.

■ **Play Media (Acrobat 5 Compatible).** Plays a movie file saved in formats compatible with Acrobat 5 and lower viewers. Note: Acrobat 5 compatible media cannot be embedded in a PDF document.

■ **Play Media (Acrobat 6 and Later Compatible).** Plays movie files saved in newer formats compatible with Acrobat 6 through Acrobat 9, and movie clips can be embedded in PDFs using this compatibility. This choice uses legacy methodology and requires the user to have a media player installed on their computer.

■ **Read an article.** This action navigates to the specified article in the open PDF document or another PDF document.

■ **Reset a form.** All the fields or user-specified fields on a form are cleared of data.

■ **Run a JavaScript.** Executes JavaScripts written in Acrobat.

■ **Set layer visibility.** This action can be set to either hide or show a layer.

■ **Show/hide a field.** With form fields, fields are hidden or made visible on a page.

■ **Submit a form.** This action is used for submitting data in user-prescribed formats to a specified URL.

The preceding list is a brief description of action types that can be associated with tools that support link actions.

 For more detail on how to create link actions and a host of attributes you can assign to them, see Part IV, "PDF Interactivity" and Part VI, "Acrobat PDF Forms."

Opening PDF Files

As with most computer programs you already use on either Windows or the Macintosh, you know that files are generally opened via the File ➪ Open command. In many programs, the keyboard shortcut used to open files is Ctrl/⌘+O. Acrobat uses the same menu and keyboard shortcuts to access the Open dialog box where you browse your hard drive, open folders, and ultimately select a file to open. When you double-click a filename or click the Open button when a file is selected, the file opens in Acrobat.

 All Acrobat viewers also offer you a tool to open files. Click the Open tool in the File toolbar and the Open dialog box appears just as if you had used the Open menu command or keyboard shortcut. Any one of these methods opens a PDF document or a document of one of many different file types that can be converted to PDF on-the-fly while you work in Acrobat.

CROSS-REF For information related to opening files that are converted to PDF with the Open command, see Chapter 7.

Opening recently viewed files

When you launch Acrobat and view and/or edit PDF documents, Acrobat keeps track of the most recently opened files. By default, Acrobat keeps track of the last five files you opened. In the Startup preferences you can change the value to as many as ten recently viewed files. The files are accessible at the bottom of the File menu (Windows) or the File ⇨ Open Recent File submenu on the Macintosh. In Figure 5.27, you can see five filenames at the bottom of the File menu from Acrobat running under Windows.

FIGURE 5.27

The most recently viewed files appear in the File menu (Windows) or File ⇨ Open Recent File submenu (Macintosh).

You have another option for viewing files that were previously opened in an Acrobat session. As shown in Figure 5.27, the History menu command appearing over the recent file list offers you submenus for viewing files from a history as long as the previous 12 months. Until you clear the History by selecting the Clear History menu command, all the files you viewed over the last 12 months are displayed in a scrollable list. You can break down the history according to the files viewed Today, Yesterday, the Last 7 Days, the Last 14 Days, and the Last 30 Days, as well as the Last 12 Months.

Macintosh users can find the History submenu command appearing at the top of the list of files when you choose File ⇨ Open Recent File.

Using the Organizer

The Organizer is a tool similar in some respects to Adobe Bridge, available in CS3 (or something). Although not all features within Adobe Bridge are available in Acrobat's Organizer, it has many impressive tools and commands that help you manage and access documents from within Acrobat. To open the Organizer, choose File ⇨ Organizer ⇨ Open Organizer, click the Organizer tool in the File toolbar, or press Shift+Ctrl/⌘+1. (You can also choose File ⇨ History ⇨ Open Organizer or press Shift+Ctrl/⌘+1.) When you select any of the options, the Organizer, shown in Figure 5.28, opens.

FIGURE 5.28

Click the Organizer tool or select Open Organizer from a menu command to open the Organizer window in Acrobat.

The Organizer window contains three panes, a number of tools, and menu commands that you select from context menus. When you first open the Organizer, you find three panes in the Organizer window divided by two separator bars. On the left side of the window is the Categories pane. In the center, you find the Files pane and the right side holds the Pages pane. You can adjust the size of the panes by clicking a separator bar and dragging it to the left or right. As one pane is sized down, the adjacent pane is sized up. You can adjust the size of the Organizer window by dragging the lower-right corner of the window.

Using the Categories pane

The Categories pane in the Organizer contains three types of categories. At the top of the pane is History followed by My Computer (Windows) or Macintosh HD (Macintosh) and at the bottom you find Collections. The History category offers you the same choices for viewing history as you find in the File menu in Windows as described in the earlier section "Opening recently viewed files." As you click one of the History options, the files listed in the Files pane reflect the history period you choose.

The My Computer/Macintosh HD category shows you a view of your hard drive and all servers and drives connected to your computer, similar to a Windows Explorer view or a Macintosh Finder view. You can select a folder, and all PDFs within that folder are listed in the Files pane regardless of whether they appear in the view history. Below your accessible hard drives and servers you find Favorite Places. If you keep documents within folders you frequently access, right-click (Windows) or Control+click (Macintosh) to open a context menu over Favorite Places or click the *Add Favorite Place* button at the bottom of the Categories pane. (See Figure 5.29.)

The Browse For Folder dialog box opens (Windows) or the Select a folder to add to your favorite places dialog box opens on the Macintosh after clicking the Add to favorite place button. Adding Favorites in this fashion is similar to adding Favorites in your Web browser.

After you select a folder and click OK, the folder you selected appears at the bottom of the Favorite Places list.

FIGURE 5.29

Click the Add a favorite place button to add to the Favorite Places.

The Collections category works similarly to Favorite Places, except that instead of adding folders to a list, you can select individual files and add them to a collection. You can add files to collections from different folders on your hard drive. By default, Acrobat offers you three collections — Collection 1, Collection 2, and Collection 3.

You manage collections through the use of a context menu. Open a context menu from any collection name in the Collections category and the menu options appear as shown in Figure 5.30.

FIGURE 5.30

To manage collections, open a context menu on any collection name.

Create a New Collection
Rename Collection
Delete Collection
Add Files...

The menu selections should be self-explanatory. Click Create a New Collection to add another collection to the list. Click Rename Collection to rename a collection. Click Delete Collection to remove the collection. Click Add Files to add documents to your collection. After you add documents to a collection and click the collection name, all files added to the collection appear in the Files pane.

TIP After installing Acrobat you may want to rename the default collection names to more descriptive names used in your workflow. Open a context menu on each collection name and select Rename Collection. The collection name is highlighted and ready for you to type a new name.

Using the Files pane

The Files pane contains a list of all files derived from the choice you made in the Categories pane. For example, click a History category, and all files viewed within the selected history timeframe appear in a list sorted by metadata that you select from the Sort by pull-down menu. In addition to the file list you have tools at the top of the pane and context menu commands when opening a context menu on a file in the list.

Beginning with the tools at the top of the pane, you find the following:

- **Open.** By default, the first file in the pane is selected. Click the Open tool to open the selected file. If no file is selected in the pane, the Open tool, as well as all other tools, is grayed out. A condition where you might not have a file selected is when you click a collection that contains no file in the collection folder or when viewing a folder that contains no PDF documents. Otherwise, the first file, by default, is always selected when files are shown in the list.

- **Print.** Click a file in the list and click the Print tool to print the file. When you click Print, the PDF document opens and the Print dialog box opens in the foreground. Make your print attribute choices in the Print dialog box and click Print to print the file.

- **Email.** Select a file in the list and click the Email tool, and your default email application opens with the selected file attached to a new email message.

- **Combine Files.** Click this tool to open the Combine files wizard. In the wizard window you can select PDF documents to combine into a single file or select a variety of different file formats that can be converted to a PDF. The tool works the same as selecting the Create PDF Portfolio tool in the Tasks toolbar.

CROSS-REF To learn how to convert files to PDF with the Combine files wizard, see Chapter 12.

- **Send for Review.** Select a file in the list and choose from the pull-down menu options to Send for Shared Review or Attach for Email Review.

CROSS-REF To learn how to send files for reviews and approval, see Chapter 20.

Below the tools is a pull-down menu used for sorting files. Files can be sorted on metadata contained within the file. From the pull-down menu you have several choices for sorting files.

Sorting by Filename is the default and lists files in an alphabetical ascending order. The Title, Subject, Author, and Keywords items are part of the Document Properties Description that you supply at the time of PDF creation from some authoring programs or that you later add in Acrobat. Creator and Producer are part of the Document Description supplied by Acrobat and relate to the original authoring program and the application producing the PDF file. Number of Pages, File Size, and Modified Date are data that Acrobat adds to the Document Properties derived from the structure of the file. The Last Opened Date sorts the files according to the last time you viewed them in Acrobat with the most recent file listed first and in descending order.

CROSS-REF To learn more about Document Descriptions and Document Properties, see Chapter 6.

You can also manage files from a context menu opened on a file in the list. This menu has commands to perform the same tasks handled by the tools at the top of the pane. In Figure 5.31 you can see the top portion of the menu, duplicating the tools' functions, such as Open, Print, Email, Combine Files, and Send for Review.

FIGURE 5.31

Open a context menu on a file listed in the Files pane and the menu options offer additional commands for managing files.

The Add to Collection menu item contains a submenu that lists all the collections in the Categories pane. As you add new collections to the Categories, they dynamically appear in the Add to Collection submenu. After you add a file to a collection, the context menu changes and displays a few more menu commands. Figure 5.31 shows the Move to Collection and Remove from 'Collection name' commands. The item within the single quotes denotes the collection name where a file has been added.

Select Move to Collection and the submenu displays all your collection names. Select a collection and the file is moved to the collection you choose in the submenu. Select Remove from '*n*' (where *n* represents the name of a collection) and a dialog box opens prompting you to confirm the deletion. When you delete a file from a collection, the file is deleted from the collection list but is not deleted from your hard drive.

The last menu item, Show in Explorer (Windows) or Show in Finder (Macintosh), takes you to Windows Explorer (Windows) or switches to Finder view (Macintosh) and opens the folder where the file is located.

Using the Pages pane

One of the great features of the Organizer is that it shows multiple pages in the Pages pane for all files containing more than one page. When you select a multipage document, all pages are displayed in thumbnail view in the Pages pane before you open the file. At the bottom of the pane is a zoom slider. Drag the slider left to display smaller thumbnails and to the right to make the thumbnail views larger. The minus and plus buttons display thumbnails smaller and larger, respectively, in zoom increments.

As you view multipage documents in the Pages pane, you can double-click any page thumbnail to open the respective page in Acrobat. Select a page thumbnail and open a context menu, and a single menu command appears, enabling you to open that page.

Another nice feature in the Pages pane is the display of a Document Status icon that appears when you save files that have a special status or special feature. Such features might include a document saved with layers, a file in a commenting review, or a certified document. In addition to the Document Status icon, some files may display a security key representing files that have been password secured.

Bookmarking Web-hosted PDFs

As I explain in Chapter 27, Acrobat is well integrated with many different Web services and support. The Organizer is no exception when it comes to supporting Web-related services. You can add anything you can view in Acrobat as a PDF document to your Organizer. When you add a document to a collection from a Web-hosted PDF, the link is made to where the file is hosted. In this particular case, it's a link to a URL that you can create as easily as adding files from your hard drive to your collections.

The first step is to view a PDF document as an inline view in a Web browser. Both Apple Safari and Microsoft Internet Explorer are supported. When you view a PDF in a Web browser, many Acrobat tools appear below your browser's tools. In Figure 5.32, you can see the Organizer tool in the top-left corner of the Acrobat window inside Apple's Safari Web browser. When you click the Organizer tool, the Add to Favorites dialog box opens. Click a collection and click OK to add the link to your collection.

CROSS-REF For more information on inline viewing in Web browsers, see Chapter 22.

FIGURE 5.32

Click the Organizer tool inside a Web browser to add the URL link to a collection.

When you return to Acrobat, you can view the URL link in the respective collection. Open the Organizer and click the collection name where you added the link. In the Files pane you see all documents added to the collection. Those files added from Web URLs appear with a different icon than standard PDF documents and the content of the page is not shown for these links, as you can see in Figure 5.33. You can add files from PDFs on your hard drive and view them from within a Web browser (something you might do when working with browser-based reviews), or from URL addresses on the Web. In the Files pane adjacent to the document icon, you see the URL address from where the document was retrieved.

CROSS-REF For more information related to shared reviews, see Chapter 21.

FIGURE 5.33

PDFs linked to URLs appear with a different document icon and a page preview is not available.

🗋 fw4.pdf

Organizer cannot show page thumbnails for files opened from web browsers. You can open this file by double-clicking it or by choosing Open in the Organizer toolbar.

Double-click any Web-linked file, and your default Web browser opens, takes you to the URL, and loads the PDF in the browser window.

Summary

This chapter offers you a brief overview of how to go about moving around PDF documents, using viewing tools, panels, and pages, as well as opening and managing files. As you can see, the list is long and there's quite a bit to understand in regard to viewing, navigating, opening, and managing files. Some of the more important points include the following:

- Page navigation tools are available in a toolbar not visible by default. You can place the toolbar in view and dock it to the left, right, top, or below the Document pane for easy access to navigation tools.

- The Reading mode feature optimizes your views for page content. You can easily scroll pages back and forth with simple mouse clicks.

- PDFs can be read aloud and pages can be autoscrolled without the need for any special equipment.

- PDF pages can be viewed in several different layout modes, with grids, guides, and rulers.

- Acrobat contains six tools used for zooming views. The Marquee Zoom tool is a new tool in Acrobat permitting you to zoom in and out by drawing marquee selections. In addition to the Marquee Zoom, Zoom In, Zoom Out, Dynamic Zoom, the Loupe tool, and the Pan & Zoom are available in all Acrobat viewers.

- Initial Views of PDF documents can be displayed with pages and palettes, at different zoom levels, with or without menus, tools, and window controls. These settings are document specific and can be saved with different options for different documents. The settings are established in the Initial View document properties dialog box.

- Links are built into many different Acrobat tools and they can be assigned to items created in Acrobat. Different action types can be assigned to many tools and object elements.

- Acrobat 8 and 9 do not support most of the Execute a menu item commands found in all earlier versions of Acrobat.

- Links can be made to Web pages and URLs.

- PDF files are opened through menu commands or by using the Open tool. The most recently opened files are listed in the File menu (Windows) or the File ⇨ Open Recent File submenu (Macintosh).

- The Organizer introduced in Acrobat 7 helps you manage files and access a file history of documents opened in Acrobat up to the previous 12 months. The Organizer enables you to view page thumbnails of PDF document pages before you open files and can be sorted on metadata, added to collections, and added to a Favorite Places list.

- You can add PDFs hosted on Web sites to collections in the Organizer.

Chapter 6

Searching PDF Files

Acrobat 9 continues with the search options you had available with Acrobat 8. You'll notice the Find tool and the Search pane are both present in this release.

You can find information contained in PDF documents with the Find tool for open documents. The Search window is available when a document is open in the Document pane or when no document is open. The Search window enables you to search PDFs scattered around your hard drive without the assistance of a search index. However, creating index files with Acrobat Catalog and searching the resultant index files is available to you for more feature-rich and faster searches. In this chapter, I cover all the tools and features available in Acrobat viewers for searching through PDF files and creating and searching index files.

All four Acrobat viewers (Adobe Reader, Adobe Acrobat Standard, Adobe Acrobat Pro, and Adobe Acrobat Pro Extended) support the exact same features for searching PDF content.

Setting Up the Work Environment

The Find toolbar is loaded by default when you open Acrobat. There's no real need to open the toolbar in the More Tools window if the toolbar is not present in the Toolbar Well. The toolbar automatically opens when you select a menu command or keyboard shortcut to use the Find feature. The Search window opens from a menu command; therefore, no special tool arrangement is needed when searching PDF documents.

For searching PDF documents you may want to load the Search tool. By default the tool is not loaded in the File toolbar. Open a context menu on the Toolbar Well and select More Tools. In the More Tools window, scroll down the File toolbar and check the box adjacent to the Search tool. Click OK and the Search tool is loaded in the File toolbar.

If you intend to engage in editing sessions, comment and review, printing files, and so on, your tool arrangement should reflect your editing ambitions. For this chapter, I load the Edit toolbar and leave the other tools at the default.

Using the Find Toolbar

In order to use the Find toolbar, you must have a document open in the Document pane. If you have more than one document open, you can search only the active document appearing in the foreground.

Finding words in an open document can be handled in the Find toolbar. If the toolbar is not loaded in the Toolbar Well, select Edit ⇨ Find or press Ctrl/⌘+F. The toolbar then opens as a floating toolbar.

Type a word in the field box in the Find toolbar and press the Enter/Return key. Acrobat searches the current active document and highlights the first occurrence of the found word. When a word is found, the Previous and Next buttons in the toolbar become active, as shown in Figure 6.1.

FIGURE 6.1

Enter the word(s) to be searched in the Find toolbar and press Enter/Return. The Previous and Next buttons appear in the toolbar.

Click the Next button in the toolbar, and Acrobat searches for the next occurrence and stops on the page where the word is highlighted again. Clicking Previous takes you to the last found word in the open document (if you click the button after the first search). When you click Next, and then click the Previous button, the search takes you to the previous found word. For example, if you search for a word in a 100-page document and the word appears on pages 5, 6, and 99, the first time you execute the Find, you stop at page 5. Clicking the Previous button takes you to page 99. However, if you click Next while on page 5, the next found word appears on page 6. Clicking Previous on page 6 takes you back to page 5.

The Find toolbar also includes a pull-down menu, as shown in Figure 6.2, containing several menu commands to assist you in narrowing your search.

FIGURE 6.2

Open the pull-down menu in the Find toolbar for more search options.

Click the down-pointing arrow to see the following menu commands:

- **Find Next in Current PDF.** The menu command finds the next occurrence of the found word just as it does when clicking the Find Next tool.

- **Open Full Acrobat Search.** Opens the Search window. This command performs the same function as clicking the Search tool or pressing the Ctrl/⌘+Shift+F keys.

- **Whole words only.** Returns words that match whole words only. For example, if you search for a word like *cat*, this command avoids returning words such as *catalog*, *catastrophe*, *category*, and so on.

- **Case-Sensitive.** Finds words that match the letter case of the word typed in the Find toolbar.

- **Include Bookmarks.** Finds words in bookmark descriptions.

- **Include Comments.** Finds words in comment notes.

You can choose one or any combination of the first four options to perform your search. For example, you can select Whole words only, Case-Sensitive, Include Bookmarks, and Include Comments, and Acrobat returns the first occurrence of only whole words matching the letter case in the search criteria whether it be in a bookmark, comment note, or on a document page.

Using the Find toolbar also makes active two other menu commands. After invoking a find, the Next Result and Previous Result commands appear active in the Edit ⇨ Search Results submenu. These commands are the same as using the buttons in the Find toolbar. They also are accompanied by keyboard shortcuts (Ctrl/⌘+G for Next Result and Ctrl/⌘+Shift+G for Previous Result. Note that the other two options in the submenu (Next Document and Previous Document) are grayed out when you use the Find toolbar. These commands are active only when you use the Search window.

Using the Search Window

You perform searches by accessing a menu command, clicking the Search tool, or by using shortcut keys. To search from the menu, choose Edit ⇨ Search, or open a context menu with the Hand tool and select Search. Click the Search tool in the File toolbar and the Search window opens. To use the keyboard shortcut, press Ctrl/⌘+Shift+F and likewise the Search window opens as shown in Figure 6.3. These all allow you to search for a word in an open document, in a collection of PDF files stored on your hard drive, or any type of external media. When you invoke a search, the Search window opens as a floating window. The window can be sized by dragging the lower-right corner out or in to size the width and height.

FIGURE 6.3

When you use the Search menu command or the Ctrl/⌘+Shift+F keyboard shortcut, the Search window opens as a floating window.

Basic search options

When the Search window is in view, you type a word or words to be searched for in the field box that appears at the top of the window. You are limited to the actual word(s) you want to find when you perform a simple search. You cannot use Boolean (AND, OR, and NOT) operators or any kind of search expressions if performing a simple search.

CROSS-REF For more sophisticated searches where you can use Boolean operators, see "Performing advanced searches in Acrobat/Reader" later in this chapter.

NOTE The area where you type words and phrases to be searched is in the field box following the text "What word or phrase would you like to search for?" in the Search window. Rather than describe this field box by name, the term "first field box" or "search field box" is used throughout this chapter. When you see such a reference, realize it refers to the area where you type words and phrases to be searched.

If you type more than one word in the search field box, the results are reported for the exact phrase. For example, if you search for "Adobe Acrobat Pro," all the occurrences of "Adobe Acrobat Pro" are reported in the results list. Individual occurrences of Adobe, Acrobat, and Pro are not reported. In other words, you don't need to place phrases within any quotes or special characters to find the results.

In the Search PDF window, you choose where you want to search and the options to narrow the search from the list following the first field box. The following sections describe several choices that are available.

Where to search

The question presented to you is "Where would you like to search?" Two radio buttons appear where you choose whether to search the current open file or search locally on your hard drive, a network server, or a media storage device attached to your computer such as removable media or CD-ROMs. If you select the second radio button for "All PDF Documents in," you can narrow the search to a directory, drive, or media device by opening the pull-down menu and choosing from the hierarchy of drives and folders appearing in the menu options.

Acrobat also permits you to search through bookmarks and comments as the Find toolbar does. Check boxes appear below the pull-down menu for these items. If bookmarks and comments are to be part of your search, check the respective item(s). After you choose the options you want, click the Search button.

The results appear in the Search window, as shown in Figure 6.4. The total number of found instances for your search is noted at the top of the window, and hot links appear in the scrollable list for the words found in the documents according to the search options you selected. Click any text and the respective document page opens in the Document pane with the first occurrence of the searched word highlighted.

Navigating search results

Menu commands are also available for navigating through search results. Choose Edit ⇨ Search Results to open a submenu where you find four menu commands used with searches. The Next Result and Previous Result items are discussed in the section "Using the Find Toolbar" earlier in this chapter. The other two items are as follows:

- **Next Document** (Alt/Option+Shift+Right Arrow): Click Next Document to bypass all found instances in the currently viewed file and open the next file listed in the Search results list.

- **Previous Document** (Alt/Option+Shift+Left Arrow): This command offers the opposite response as Next Document — it moves backward through previously viewed documents.

NOTE Next Result and Next Document are not available until you first invoke a search. Next Document becomes active only when a search result exists in two or more documents. Previous Result and Previous Document become active only after you have visited a result in a document more than once so as to retrace your steps backward to see previously viewed results.

FIGURE 6.4

The total number of occurrences in a single PDF or all occurrences in all documents searched is noted at the top of the window (1) and search results are reported in a scrollable list (2). Click any text in the Results list window to open a page (3) where Search found words matching your criteria.

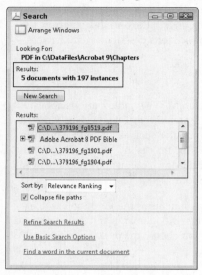

If you search an open document and the search results are reported in the Search window, you're better off clicking results in the window than using menu commands. When you select any menu command, the Search window disappears (on Windows) when viewing documents in Acrobat in a maximized view. This is most annoying when you want to keep the Search window open. On the Mac you don't have to worry about using menu commands or opening files. The Search window remains in view at all times until you close it.

Stopping a search

When you start a new search, a button appears in the Search window so you can stop the search. Click Stop and the results found prior to stopping are listed in the scrollable list. If you click Stop, you need to search again starting at the beginning of the search to continue. Click the New Search button and the search starts over from the beginning of the file.

Displaying results

The results list is neatly organized for you in the Search window. If you search the open document, the search results report found words beginning at the front of the document and list occurrences as they are found on following pages. If you search multiple documents, the occurrences are listed in groups according to the individual documents where the words are found. The hierarchy is similar to that of bookmarks. A plus symbol in Windows or a right-pointing arrow in Macintosh is shown for each document where results have been found. Click the icon, and the list expands the same way bookmarks and comments expand. The icon changes to a minus symbol in Windows or a down-pointing arrow in Macintosh when a list is expanded. Click the icon again to collapse the list.

NOTE You can use Search or the Find toolbar to find words in the open document. Search offers more search criteria options and shows a list of results. As a general rule, using Search is much more efficient than using the Find toolbar.

CROSS-REF For information on displaying bookmarks, see Chapters 16 and 22. For information on displaying comments, see Chapter 20.

Searching files and folders

If you search through a large collection of PDF files, Search works away loading up the results window. Clicking a link to open a page where results have been found won't interrupt your search. You can browse files while results continue to be reported. To search a hard disk, a media storage device, a network drive, or a folder in any of these locations, open the pull-down menu below All PDF Documents in and select a folder location. The moment you select a folder, the All PDF Documents in radio button is activated.

The pull-down menu lists the drives and servers active on your system. If you want to search a particular folder, select the item denoted as Browse for Location (Windows or Macintosh) at the bottom of the pull-down menu. The Browse For Folder (Windows) or Choose a folder to search (Macintosh) dialog box opens as shown in Figure 6.5. Navigate your hard drive as you would when searching for files to open. When you find the folder to be searched, click the folder name and click OK.

FIGURE 6.5

Select the folder to be searched in the Browse For Folder (Windows) or Browse for Location (Macintosh) dialog box. Select the folder name and click OK (Windows) or Choose (Macintosh) to return to the Search window.

> **TIP**   When you click a file in the Results window, the Search window becomes hidden by default. If you want to show the Search window after clicking a file in the Results window, click the Arrange Windows button at the top of the Search panel.

After you click OK in the Browse For Folder/Choose a Folder dialog box, the Search window returns. The search does not begin until you click the Search button. Before clicking Search, you can examine the name listed as the target folder. The selected folder is displayed in the Search window by folder name. If all looks as you expect, click Search.

Searching PDFs on the Internet

In Acrobat 6 we had Search the Internet using Google in the Search window and as a separate tool. In Acrobat 7 we had Search the Internet using Yahoo! in the Search window and as a separate tool. In Acrobat 8 we had nothing, and nothing in regard to searching the Internet using these search engines appears in Acrobat 9. The ability to search files on the Internet from a click in the Search window was removed in all Acrobat 8 viewers.

At first glance you may get a bit annoyed that you lost this feature in Acrobat and Reader. I can't give you a precise reason for the feature disappearing in Acrobat, but my hunch is that the problem lies more with the Web browser developers than it does with Adobe. It may be that Adobe just can't keep up with changes made by other developers when revisions are made to the browsers. Doing so may be cost prohibitive, and the functionality can easily be lost during an Acrobat version life cycle when developers upgrade their products.

For whatever reason we lost the ability to click a link in the Search window to search for PDFs on the Internet, you can still perform this kind of search. Using a search engine such as Google, just type your search word or phrase in the Search text box in the Google search engine, add a space, and then type **filetype:PDF.** For example if you want to search for Acrobat 8 and have only PDFs reported in your search results, type "**Acrobat**" **filetype:PDF.** The Google search results report only PDF documents containing your search phrase.

Not all search engines support the extension for searching for PDFs. If you use Yahoo! or Ask.com, for example, you can't use the extension. However, Yahoo! provides you with Advanced Search options. In Yahoo! click the Options pull-down menu and choose Advanced Search. The next page that opens provides you with options for choosing a file type such as PDF.

In some cases, advanced search options in search engines can help you narrow a search to report PDFs with the found results. Check your favorite search engine for advanced options to see if searching PDFs is supported.

Performing advanced searches in Acrobat/Reader

In all Acrobat viewers, you can search PDF documents with selected criteria without the assistance of a search index. To take advantage of searching with advanced options, click the Use Advanced Search Options link at the bottom of the Search window. When you click the link, a series of advanced options appears in the Search window, as shown in Figure 6.6.

FIGURE 6.6

Click Use Advanced Search Options to take advantage of more search options. When you select a folder of PDF files to search, the options in this figure are available.

NOTE When you click the link to show the advanced search options, the link at the bottom of the Search window changes to Use Basic Search Options. Click this link to return to searching with the basic options.

Depending on whether you search an open PDF document or a collection of PDFs stored on drives and external devices, the Advanced Search Options change, offering you different options.

CROSS-REF Advanced search offers you options for searching index files as well as PDF files. For information on searching index files, see the section "Searching an index" later in this chapter.

Searching the open PDF file with Advanced Search Options

When you select the Current PDF Document from the Look In pull-down menu, the search options shown in Figure 6.6 are available to you. These options are as follows:

- **Whole words only.** When checked, the search results return whole words. If you search for *forgiven*, the search ignores words like *for* and *give* that make up part of the whole word. If the check box is disabled, various stems and parts of a whole word are included with the search results.

- **Case-Sensitive.** Letter case is ignored if the check box is disabled. If enabled, then the search results return only words matching the precise letter case of the searched word.

- **Proximity.** Proximity is a powerful tool when performing searches. If you want to search for two independent words that may appear together in a given context — for example, *Acrobat* and *PostScript* — the Proximity option finds the two words when they appear within a range specified in the Search preferences. The default is 900 words. You can change the proximity range by opening the Preferences dialog box (Ctrl/⌘+K), clicking Search in the left pane, and editing the Range of words for Proximity searches text box.

- **Stemming.** If you want to search for all words stemming from a given word, enable this option. Words such as *header* and *heading* stem from the word *head* in the English language. If you type *head* in the first field box and select the Stemming option, all PDFs containing the search criteria from the word *head* are listed.

- **Include Bookmarks.** When Bookmarks are checked, the search results report the found instances in the bookmarks and the document pages.

- **Include Comments.** Text in comment notes and text on document pages are returned when this option is checked.

- **Include Attachments.** All document file attachments are searchable including file types other than PDF. Select the Include Attachments check box and found results are reported in the Results list for all occurrences of the searched word. Clicking a search result opens the attached file in the Document pane.

If you open a PDF Portfolio, the Search window changes to accommodate searching all files in the package. Select from the Look In pull-down menu and choose In the entire PDF Portfolio and Search will search all files in the package.

You can search PDF Portfolios using either the Basic search options or the Advanced search options. When searching package contents using Basic search options select the radio button for In the entire PDF Portfolio, as shown in Figure 6.7. When using the Advanced options, select In the entire PDF Portfolio from the Look In pull-down menu. Note that both these items are accessible only when you open a PDF Portfolio.

CROSS-REF   For more information on working with PDF Portfolios, see Chapter 12.

When all the search criteria have been established, click the Search button. The results are reported in the Search window like the searches performed with the Basic Search Options.

FIGURE 6.7

Select In the entire PDF Portfolio to search all files in the package.

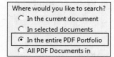

Searching multiple PDFs with Advanced Search Options

When you change the search parameters to search through a collection of PDF documents, the Advanced Search Options change, offering you more options to help narrow down your search, as shown in Figure 6.8.

FIGURE 6.8

Advanced Search Options offer you additional criteria when searching through multiple PDF documents.

These options are as follows:

- **Return results containing.** Four return result options are available from this pull-down menu:

  - **Match Exact word or phrase.** If you search for something like *Human Resource Forms*, only these three words together in a PDF document are returned as results. The results report the precise order of the words.

  - **Match Any of the words.** Using the same example, words such as *Human*, *Resource*, *Forms*, *Human Resource*, *Resource Forms*, *Human Forms*, and *Human Resource Forms* would be reported in the results. Any one of the words or any combination of words in a phrase is reported.

  - **Match All of the words.** In this case, all the words need to be contained in the document, but not necessarily in the order described previously. You might see returns such as Forms Human Resource returned from the search.

■ **Boolean query.** You can search PDF collections using Boolean expressions (AND, OR, NOT) without the assistance of a search index created with Acrobat Catalog. Note that Boolean queries are not available when you search an open document. You need to use the Advanced Search Options to search through a drive, external media, or a folder.

CROSS-REF For more detail on using Boolean queries, see the "Boolean queries" section later in this chapter. For more information on Acrobat Catalog, see the section "Creating Search Indexes (Acrobat Professional/Extended Only)" later in this chapter.

■ **Use these additional criteria.** Up to three check boxes offer you one or a combination of several different options to help you refine your search. The number of check boxes you have available depends on the vertical size of the Search window. If you reduce the size, you may see only a single check box, as shown in Figure 6.8.

From the first pull-down menu you select the primary category. The second pull-down menu to the right of each primary category helps refine that particular category. The options for each of the three check box pull-down menus are the same. You might, for example, choose Date Created from the first check box option and define the date from the options contained in the adjacent pull-down menu. You then might add another criterion and ask for the Keywords option. Adjacent to Keywords, you might specify that the file does not contain certain words. In the field box, you type any descriptions for the menu choices you make.

NOTE All the preceding items require that you supply at least one character in "What word or phrase would you like to search for?" The options that follow enable you to search for specific content related to the option of choice, and you do not need to supply a word in the first field box in order to execute a search. When you move around adjusting criteria, the Search button appears active or grayed out. If it is grayed out, you can't perform a search on the options you chose. In some cases, the missing option is a word or phrase that needs to be added to the first field box.

From the criteria selection pull-down menu, the choices available to you are as follows:

■ **Date Created.** If you look for PDF documents that you know were created before or after a certain date, use the Date Created menu option. You have four choices for options associated with this category available in the second pull-down menu adjacent to the first menu choice. These options are: Is exactly, Is before, Is after, and Is not. These four options are self-explanatory. When you make the choices from the two pull-down menus, your next step is to type the date criteria in the field box appearing below the pull-down menus. If, for example, you select Date Created and Is not, you then add the date you want to exclude from the search. As an additional aid to you, Acrobat offers a calendar when you select the pull-down menu from the field box, as shown in Figure 6.9 (Windows only). Make a date selection from the calendar and move to the option you want to change or click the Search button. If you click the month, a pop-up menu showing all months in a year opens. (Note that the calendar is not available on the Mac.)

FIGURE 6.9

After setting the date criteria from the pull-down menus, open the pull-down menu from the field box to open a calendar to help you find the date parameters to be searched. Click the month name and a pop-up menu opens showing all months in a year.

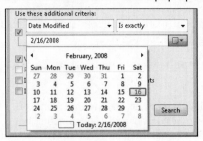

- **Date Modified.** The modified date searches for the date the PDF file was last modified. If you create a file on January 1, 2004 and then save some edits on July 1, 2004, the modified date is July 1, 2004. The manner in which you specify a date is the same as searching for the creation date.

- **Author.** The information is derived from the Document Properties in the Description tab. Any data typed in the Author field are searched. This choice and the remaining options offer two menu options in the second pull-down menu. You can select from Contains or Does not contain. In essence, your search includes or excludes the data you supply in the field box immediately following the pull-down menu choices.

CROSS-REF For information related to document descriptions, see the "Document Descriptions" section later in this chapter.

- **Title.** Same as the Author search except the Title field is used in the document description.

- **Subject.** Same as the Author search except the Subject field is used in the document description.

- **Filename.** The name you provide for the PDF document is searched.

- **Keywords.** Same as the Author search except the Keywords field is used in the document description.

- **Bookmarks.** When you select this option, Acrobat searches for the words in both the PDF document and in bookmarks. The results list includes the found words in both bookmarks and pages.

- **Comments.** Same as Bookmarks, but the comment notes are searched. The results report the found words appearing in comment notes.

- **JPEG Images.** Narrows the search for files meeting the search text criteria and where JPEG images are contained within the PDF.

■ **XMP Metadata.** Searches for words or phrases contained in the document metadata.

■ **Object Data.** Certain images contain metadata created from an original authoring application, such as MS Visio, Microsoft Project, and AutoDesk AutoCAD. Select an object with the Object Data tool and click. The metadata information displayed in the Object Data dialog box is searchable as well as the data contained in the Object Data dialog box. If you know certain attributes for images contained in a file, you can narrow your search by searching the object metadata.

CROSS-REF For more information on XMP and object metadata, see "Searching metadata" later in this chapter.

Below the Use these additional criteria pull-down menus are additional options. These options are the same as those used for the advanced searches on open PDF documents. Jump several pages back in this book to review the descriptions for the items listed at the bottom of the Search window.

Searching dates

To help you target the precise date with the field box and the calendar, Acrobat offers you several options. To change the year, you can edit the field box and type the year for the date to be searched. In the field box you can change dates by clicking the day, month, and year, and then use the up or down arrow keys to scroll dates. The dates revolve like an odometer. Select a day, and then click the month to highlight the value and press the arrow keys again until you find the correct month. Move to the year and follow the same steps to select the correct year. You can also select any one of the three values and type new values you want to search for when the text is selected. The text you type replaces all selected text. Acrobat accepts only a legitimate value, so if you type a value not permitted for a date search — for example, entering 33 in the day field — Acrobat will not accept it.

To change dates with the calendar, click the down arrow in the pull-down menu adjacent to the date in the field box to open the calendar. For a month change, left-click on the month name in the title bar of the calendar. For example, if July appears listed in the title bar, click July. Be careful not to left-click the mouse below the title bar because doing so selects a day and closes the calendar. When you left-click on the month name in the title bar, a pop-up menu displays the months of the year. Move the cursor to the desired month and left-click again.

NOTE You can also change months by scrolling the calendar backward or forward. Click the left arrow in the title bar to scroll backward or the right arrow to scroll forward. As you reach a year beginning or end, the next month in date order is opened. For example, scrolling backward from January 1996 opens December 1995.

When you click to select the desired month, Acrobat leaves the calendar view open so you can still make the year and day selections. To change the year in the calendar, left-click on the year in the title bar. The year becomes visible as editable text. You can edit the field or click the up or down arrows.

After you select the month and year, left-click on the desired day from the calendar displayed below the title bar. Acrobat supplies the new date in the field box, as shown in Figure 6.10, and closes the calendar.

FIGURE 6.10

Change the date for the calendar and the new date is shown while the current date is reported at the bottom of the calendar.

Searching metadata

The ability to search a document's metadata is a powerful tool in Acrobat. In order to use the tool, you need to know just a little bit about what *metadata* is.

Adobe Acrobat 5.0 and later contains metadata in XML (eXtensible Markup Language) format. In Acrobat 7 through 9 object metadata are accessible. The metadata of a file or an image is information related to the document structure, origination, content, interchange, and processing. Metadata might include, for example, the document author's name, the creation date, modified date, the PDF producer, copyright information on images, color space on images, and more. When you click Search, the search results report all files where the searched words are contained in a document's metadata.

XMP (eXtensible Metadata Platform) is an XML framework that provides all Adobe programs a common language for communicating standards related to document creation and processing throughout publishing workflows. XMP is a format, and document metadata viewed in XML source code can be exported to XMP format. Once in XMP, it can be exchanged between documents.

To take a look at the XML source code of the XMP metadata for a document, choose File ➪ Properties and click the Description tab. In the Description tab click on Additional Metadata to open the dialog box shown in Figure 6.11. Click Advanced and expand the listed items by clicking the symbol adjacent to each listed item.

At the bottom of the dialog box are buttons used for replacing, appending, saving, and deleting data. Click Save to export the XMP data that can be shared in workflows across many different file types. For the purposes of searching information, any of the text you see in the source code in the Advanced list can be searched.

Searching layers

The search criteria discussed on the preceding pages works for documents containing layers. When you invoke a search in documents containing layers, Search automatically searches through all layers for the criteria you specify in the Search window. The results list contains items on any hidden layers as well as all visible layers. When you click a result associated with a hidden layer, Acrobat prompts you in a dialog box, as shown in Figure 6.12, asking whether you want to make the layer visible.

FIGURE 6.11

To see document metadata click the Additional Metadata button in the Description Properties dialog box.

FIGURE 6.12

If searched words are found on hidden layers, Acrobat asks whether you want to make the hidden layer visible.

If you click Yes in the dialog box, the layer is made visible and the search stops at the found word. If you select No, the layer remains hidden and you are taken to the next search result.

Boolean queries

The Return results containing pull-down menu in the Search PDF window contains a Boolean query menu option for searching with Boolean expressions. Boolean expressions include AND, OR, and NOT. Acrobat recognizes these Boolean operators when you invoke a search. You can use all the previously listed criteria when you want to use the Boolean expressions option.

To search with Boolean expressions you need to search an index file. Boolean operators are not recognized when searching the current open document or when browsing folders.

CROSS-REF For more on searching indexes, see the section "Creating Search Indexes (Acrobat Pro/Extended Only)" later in this chapter.

- **AND operator.** Use AND between two words to find documents that contain both terms, in any order. For example, type Paris AND France to identify documents that contain both Paris and France. Searches with AND and no other Boolean operators produce the same results as selecting the All Of The Words option.

NOTE When using Boolean operators, the text is not case-sensitive. Uppercase letters for the Boolean expressions are used here to denote a Boolean operator as opposed to text. You can use lowercase letters and the results are reported the same, as long as the Boolean query pull-down menu item is selected.

- **OR operator.** Use to search for all instances of either term. For example, type email OR email to find all documents with occurrences of either spelling. Searches with OR and no other Boolean operators produce the same results as selecting the Any Of The Words option.

- **^ (exclusive OR).** Use to search for all instances that have either term but not both. For example, type **cat ^ dog** to find all documents with occurrences of either cat or dog but not both cat and dog.

- **().** Use parentheses to specify the order of evaluation of terms. For example, type **white AND (whale OR Ahab)** to find all documents that contain either white and whale or white and Ahab. (The query processor performs an OR query on whale and Ahab and then performs an AND query on those results with white.

- **NOT operator.** Use before a search term to exclude any documents that contain that term. For example, type **NOT Kentucky** to find all documents that don't contain the word Kentucky. Or, type **Paris NOT Kentucky** to find all documents that contain the word Paris but not the word Kentucky.

- **Multiple words.** Words appearing together such as "Acrobat PDF" can be included in quotes. You would supply "Acrobat PDF" in the field box (include the quotes) and all instances where these two words appear together are reported in the search results. If the words are not contained within quotes, the words *Acrobat*, *PDF*, and *Acrobat PDF* would all be returned in the search results. This behavior is similar to how you perform searches in Web browsers.

- **Searching and, or, not.** If you want to search for a term where these three words are part of the term, you can by distinguishing between words you search for and using operators. To search for something like *Ben and Jerry's* as a term, you would type **"Ben and Jerry's"** within quote marks. If you want to search for two terms and a Boolean operator you might use **"Ben and Jerry's" AND "Ice Cream" NOT yogurt.** The results report back to you the documents where the words *Ben and Jerry's* and *ice cream* are contained in the files and the words *Ben and Jerry's yogurt* are not reported in the search results.

To learn more about searching with Boolean operators, search the Internet using Boolean searches as your search criteria in any search engine.

Search preferences

To open preference settings for Search, choose Edit ⇨ Preferences (Windows) or Acrobat Preferences (Macintosh). In the left pane, select Search. The preference options available to you are shown in Figure 6.13.

FIGURE 6.13

Choose Edit ⇨ Preferences to open the Preferences dialog box. Click Search in the list at the left to display preference settings for using Search.

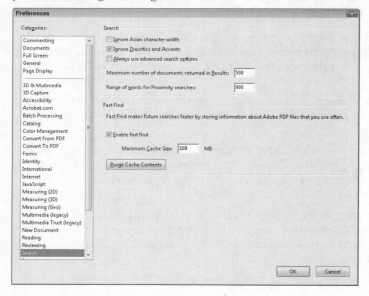

The preference choices listed on the right side of the dialog box are as follows:

- **Ignore Asian character width.** This setting ignores Asian character width and finds both half-width and full-width instances of Asian language characters.

- **Ignore Diacritics and Accents.** A diacritic is an accent mark like you might use on a word such as *resumé* or the cedilla on a word such as *façade* to indicate a special phonetic value. These and other accents are ignored during a search unless you check the box; so for example, if you have it checked Acrobat will find both *resume* and *resumé*. If it is unchecked, Search looks for *resumé* only.

- **Always use advanced search options.** Sets the Advanced Search Options as the default. When the check box is enabled you don't need to keep clicking the Use Advanced Search Options button in the Search window. Enable this setting if you find yourself always using the Advanced Search Options.

- **Maximum number of documents returned in Results.** The acceptable range is between 1 and 10,000. Enter a value and the results are limited to this number.

- **Range of words for proximity searches.** When using Boolean operators, you might want to search for two words within a defined range of words. You can enter a value between 1 and 10,000. Both words need to be within the range when you use a Boolean expression such as AND.

- **Enable fast find.** Searches are logged by Acrobat in a memory cache. If you perform a search and later in another session perform a search on the same information, Acrobat returns to the cache for the information, thus speeding up the search. You can edit the cache size by editing the field box for the number of megabytes on your hard drive you want to allocate to the cache. Be certain you have ample hard drive space when enabling the cache and raising the cache size.

- **Purge Cache Contents.** The cache occupies as much memory as is available on your hard drive. If you want to clear the cache, click the button to erase all the contents.

After changing any settings in the Preferences dialog box, click OK. The changes you make are dynamically reflected in Acrobat and take effect the next time you perform a search.

Document Descriptions

Document descriptions are user-supplied data fields used to help you identify PDF files according to title, subject, author, and keywords. At the time you create a PDF document, you may have options for supplying a document description. In other cases, you may add descriptions in Acrobat either individually or with Acrobat's batch processing features.

CROSS-REF To learn how to create batch sequences, see Chapter 18.

After you add descriptions and save your files, the data added to these fields are searchable via advanced searches and index file searches. Developing an organized workflow with specific guidelines for users to follow regarding document descriptions significantly helps all your colleagues search PDFs much more efficiently.

To add a document description, choose File ➪ Properties. When the Document Properties dialog box opens, click the Description tab, as shown in Figure 6.14.

FIGURE 6.14

You add document descriptions to the Descriptions tab in the Document Properties dialog box.

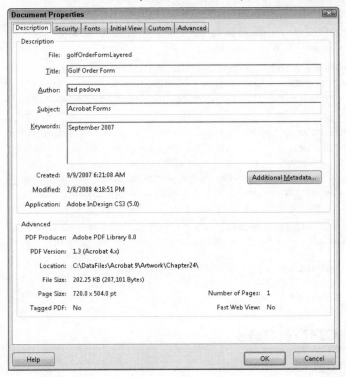

The four fields for document descriptions are as follows:

- **Title.** The Title field in this example contains a description of a form. Other forms in a company using a similar schema might use titles such as W-2 Form, Travel Expense, Employee Leave, and so on in the Title field.

- **Author.** In the example, the Author field contains the department authoring the form. Notice that an employee name is not used for the Author field. Rather than use employee names, use departments instead. Using departments is a much better choice because a company typically turns over employees more often than it renames departments.

- **Subject.** In the example, the Subject field contains Form. The Subject here might be used to distinguish a Form from a Policy, Procedure, Memo, Directive, and so on.

- **Keywords.** The first entry in the Keywords field is the form number used by the company to identify the form. Other words in the Keywords field are descriptors related to the form contents. If you want to add an employee author name, add it to the Keywords field.

TIP Notice the Location item in the Document Properties. The text reports the location on your hard drive where the file is located. This text is a link. Click the text and your file is opened on the Desktop (Finder on Mac) showing you the folder location.

The reason the field information is important for any organization using a PDF workflow is that document description information can be used when someone searches a collection of PDF files. Each field is searchable by the summary title and the words contained in the fields. Therefore, a user can search for all PDF files where the Title field contains the word *Purchase* and the Subject field contains the word *Form*. The search results display all PDF documents where the Title and Subject fields have these words contained in the document description.

As a comparison, imagine searching for the words *Purchase Order*. The search would return all PDFs where these words appear in either the document summary or the text in the PDF files. *Purchase Order* might be used in memos, policies, procedures, and forms. The user might have to search through many PDFs in order to find the Purchase Order form, thus spending much more time trying to locate the right document.

Searching document descriptions

To search for document descriptions, you need to use either the advanced search or an index file search. Press Ctrl/⌘+Shift+F to open the Search window in an Acrobat viewer and click Use Advanced Search Options. Select a folder to search from the Look In pull-down menu.

CROSS-REF For searching index files, see the section "Searching an index" later in this chapter.

Under Use these additional criteria, select one of the description items from the first pull-down menu (Title, Author, Subject, or Keywords). Select either Contains or Does not contain from the pull-down menu adjacent to the first menu. Type the words to be searched in the field box below the pull-down menus. Continue adding additional description fields as desired. In Figure 6.15, two description fields are marked for the search.

FIGURE 6.15

Two description fields are identified. When you click the Search button, Acrobat searches the document descriptions for matches.

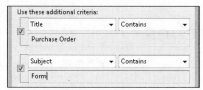

Note that no criteria need to be supplied in the first field box for specific words to be searched in the document. If you click Search in the Search window with the descriptions shown in Figure 6.15, all PDF files in the designated folder with the words *Purchase Order* in the Title field and *Forms* in the Subject field are returned in the results list for files matching the criteria.

Document descriptions and Boolean queries

You can add Boolean queries when searching document descriptions. You might know some content in PDF files as well as information contained in the document descriptions. In this case you address the additional criteria items in the same manner and add the Boolean query as discussed earlier in this chapter. In Figure 6.16, document descriptions are added to a Boolean query.

FIGURE 6.16

You can add Boolean queries to searches with additional criteria selections such as document descriptions.

When you click the Search button, the number of results returned in the Search window is significantly reduced compared to searching for individual words — especially when common words are contained in many PDF documents. What the document descriptions offer you is a method for targeting the exact file you're looking for as fast as possible. If you have 100 PDF documents in the search results list, looking through the list and finding the file you want will take some time. Compare that to two or three files listed. Obviously, the document descriptions offer significant time savings as you search PDFs from among very large collections.

Full-Text Versus Index Searches

This section represents a pivotal point in this chapter. What has been covered so far is information about finding content in PDF documents with a very elaborate *find* feature in Acrobat. The name used in Acrobat to refer to what has been discussed so far is "Search." Users of earlier versions of Acrobat may take this to mean using Acrobat Search as it was used in Acrobat viewers earlier than version 6.0. What has been covered thus far, however, is a Search of data files that was greatly improved in Acrobat version 6 and became more powerful in returning results in Acrobat version 8. To understand the difference between the preceding pages and what follows requires a little explanation.

In addition to full-text searches for documents, you can also create a separate index file and search one or more indexes at a time. Index files provide some benefit in that they are quite faster than full-text searches, can be automatically assigned to PDF documents in the Advanced tab in the Document Properties, and can be automatically loaded from a CD-ROM, and multiple indexes can be searched, so files can be scattered on your hard drive in different folders.

Search Index Procedures

I explain the details for working with search indexes in the remaining pages in this chapter. To provide you with an overall summary for how index file creation and management is dealt with in Acrobat, I give you a short summary of the procedures here.

Using index files to perform searches begins with using a current index file or creating a new one. Users who have been working with index files need to make sure that all their previous indexes are updated for compatibility with Acrobat 9.0 viewers.

Index files are created and updated with Acrobat Catalog with Acrobat Pro and Pro Extended only. Catalog is available from a menu selection in the Advanced menu. Select Advanced ➪ Document Processing ➪ Full Text Index with Catalog. You open Catalog and make a decision for creating a new index or opening an existing index file for rebuilding or editing in the Catalog window.

After an index file is created or updated, you load the index file into the Search window. Multiple index files can be loaded and searched. When you search index files, the results are reported in the Search window like all the searches discussed earlier in this chapter.

Earlier releases of Acrobat offered you options for various menu selections related to managing indexes and loading new index files. Earlier releases of Acrobat also offered you dialog boxes where results were reported and information about an index file could be obtained. In Acrobat 6.0 and above viewers, you handle all your index file management in the Search window. Menu commands are limited to viewing search results as described earlier in this chapter.

If you edit PDF documents, delete them, or add new documents to folders that have been indexed, you need to rebuild index files periodically. You can purge old data and re-index files in Acrobat Catalog. Index files can be copied to different hard drive locations, across servers, and to external media. When copying files, you need to copy all files and folders associated with the index file. Failure to copy all the files renders the index inoperable.

Creating Search Indexes (Acrobat Pro/Extended Only)

In order to search an index file, you must have one present on your computer, network server, some media storage device, or embedded in a PDF. When you install an Acrobat viewer, a help index file is included during your installation. You can use this file to search for words contained in any of the help documents. If you want to search your own files, you need to create an index. To create an index file, you use Acrobat Catalog.

> **NOTE** Acrobat Catalog is available only in Acrobat Pro and Acrobat Pro Extended. Search indexes can be used by all Acrobat viewers including Adobe Reader.

To launch Acrobat Catalog from within Acrobat Pro choose Advanced ⇨ Document Processing ⇨ Full Text Index with Catalog. Catalog is robust and provides many options for creating and modifying indexes. After a search index is created, any user can access the search index in all Acrobat viewers to find words using the Search window. However, before you begin to work with Acrobat Catalog, you need to take some preliminary steps to be certain all your files are properly prepared and ready to be indexed.

Preparing PDFs for indexing

Preparation involves creating PDFs with all the necessary information to facilitate searches. All searchable document description information needs to be supplied in the PDF documents at the time of PDF creation or by modifying PDFs in Acrobat before you begin working with Catalog. For workgroups and multiple user access to search indexes, this information needs to be clear and consistent. Other factors, such as naming conventions, location of files, and optimizing performance should all be thought out and planned prior to creating an index file.

> **NOTE** Adding document descriptions is not a requirement for creating search indexes. You can index files without any information in the document description fields. Adding document descriptions merely adds more relevant information to your PDF documents and aids users in finding search results faster.

Document descriptions

Document description information should be supplied in all PDF files to be searched. As discussed earlier in this chapter, all document description data are searchable. Spending time creating document descriptions and defining the field types for consistent organization will facilitate searches performed by multiple users.

The first of the planning steps is to develop a flow chart or outline of company information and the documents to be categorized. This organization may or may not be implemented where you intend to develop a PDF workflow. If your information flow is already in place, you may need to make some modifications to coordinate nomenclature and document identity with the document summary items in Acrobat.

Document descriptions contained in the Title, Subject, Author, and Keywords fields should be consistent and intuitive. They should also follow a hierarchy consistent with the company's organizational structure and workflow. The document summary items should be mapped out and defined. When preparing files for indexing, consider the following:

- **Title.** Title information might be thought of as the root of an outline — the parent statement, if you will. Descriptive titles should be used to help users narrow searches within specific categories. The Title field can also be used to display the title name at the top of the Acrobat window when you select viewing titles in the Initial View properties.

CROSS-REF For information on how to set document title attributes in the Initial View dialog box, see Chapter 5.

- **Author.** Avoid using proper names for the Author field. Personnel change in companies and roles among employees change. Identify the author of PDF documents according to departments, work groups, facilities, and so on.

- **Subject.** If the Title field is the parent item in an outline format, the Subject would be a child item nested directly below the title. Subjects might be considered subsets of titles. When creating document summaries, be consistent. Don't use subject and title or subject and keyword information back and forth with different documents. If an item, such as employee grievances, is listed as a Subject in some PDFs and then listed as a Title in other documents, the end users will become confused with the order and searches will become unnecessarily complicated.

- **Keywords.** If you have a forms identification system in place, be certain to use form numbers and identity as part of the Keywords field. You might start the Keywords field with a form number and then add additional keywords to help narrow searches. Be consistent and always start the Keywords field with forms or document numbers. If you need to have PDF author names, add them here in the Keywords fields. If employees change roles or leave the company, the Author fields still provide the information relative to a department.

To illustrate some examples, take a look at Table 6.1.

TIP Legacy PDF files used in an organization may have been created without a document description, or you may reorganize PDFs and want to change document summaries. To quickly (or efficiently) update these documents, you can create a batch sequence to change multiple PDF files and then run the sequence. Place your PDFs in a folder where the document summaries are to be edited. In the Edit Sequence dialog box, select the items to change and edit each document summary item. Run the sequence to update an entire folder of PDFs.

CROSS-REF For more information on creating batch sequences, see Chapter 18.

TABLE 6.1

Document Summary Examples

Title	Author	Subject	Keywords
Descriptive Titles Titles may be considered specific to workgroup tasks.	Department Names Don't use employee names in organizations; employees change, departments usually remain.	Subsection of Title Subjects may be thought of as child outline items nested below the parent Title items — a subset of the Titles.	Document numbers and random identifiers You can supply Forms ID numbers, internal filing numbers, and so on in the Keyword fields. If employee names a re a *must* for your company, add employee names in the Keywords field box. List any related words to help find the topic.
Employee Policies	Human Resources	Vacation Leave	D-101, HR32A, H. Jones, policy, employee regulations
FDA Compliance	Quality Assurance	Software Validation	SOP-114, QA-182, J. Wilson, regulations, citations, eye implant device
Curriculum	English Department	American Literature	Plan 2010, Martha Evans, senior English, Emerson High, 11th grade
Receivables	Accounting	Collection Policy	F-8102, M-5433, Finance, collections, payments
eCommerce	Marketing	Products	M-1051, e-117A, golf clubs, sports, leisure

Managing Multiple PDF Documents

Books, reports, and manuals can be broken up into separate files and structured in a way that it still appears to the end user as a single document. Assuming a user reads through a file in a linear fashion, you can create links to open and close pages without user intervention. Create navigational buttons to move forward and back through document pages. On the last page of each chapter, use the navigation button to open the next chapter. Also on the last page of each chapter, create a Page action that closes the current document when the page is closed. (See Chapter 22 for creating links and Page actions.) If the end user disables "Open cross-document links in same window" in the Documents category in the Preferences dialog box, the open file still closes after the last page is closed. All the chapters can be linked from a table of contents where any chapter can be opened. If you give your design some thought, browsing the contents of books will appear to the end user no different than reading a book in the analog world.

File structure

The content, filenames, and location of PDFs to be cataloged contribute to file structure items. All the issues related to file structure must be thought out and appropriately designed for the audience that you intend to support. The important considerations are as follows:

- **File naming conventions.** Names provided for the PDF files are critical for distributing documents among users. If filenames get truncated, then either Acrobat Search or the end user will have difficulty finding a document when performing a search. This is of special concern to Macintosh users who want to distribute documents across platforms. The best precaution is to always use standard DOS file-naming conventions. The standard eight-character maximum filename, with no more than three-character file extensions (`filename.ext`), will always work regardless of platform.

- **Folder names.** Folder names should follow the same conventions as filenames. Macintosh users who want to keep filenames longer than standard DOS names must limit folder names to eight characters and no more than a three-character file extension for cross-platform compliance.

- **File and folder name identity.** In previous versions of Acrobat and Acrobat Catalog you had to avoid using ASCII characters from 133 to 159 for any filename or folder name. Acrobat Catalog in earlier versions did not support some extended characters in this range, and you could experience problems when using files across platforms. (Figure 6.17 lists the characters we used to have to avoid.) In Acrobat 8 and 9, with more support for non-English languages and full Unicode characters, you don't need to be worried about file and folder identity that use special characters.

FIGURE 6.17

Extended characters from ASCII 133 to ASCII 159 used to be a problem when using Acrobat Catalog. In Acrobat 8 and 9 you'll find support for creating index files and searching files and folders containing these characters.

133	à	139	ï	144	É	149	ò	154	Ü
134	å	140	î	145	æ	150	û	156	£
135	ç	141	ì	146	Æ	151	ù	157	¥
136	ê	142	Ä	147	ô	152	_	158	_
137	ë	143	Å	148	ö	153	Ö	159	ƒ
138	è								

- **Folder organization.** Folders to be cataloged should have a logical hierarchy. Copy all files to be cataloged to a single folder or a single folder with nested folders in the same path. When nesting folders, be certain to keep the number of nested folders to a minimum. Deeply nested folders slow down searches, and path names longer than 256 characters create problems.

- **Folder locations.** Windows users must keep the location of folders on a local hard drive or a network server volume. Although Macintosh users can catalog information across computer workstations, creating separate indexes for files contained on separate drives would be advisable. Any files moved to different locations make searches inoperable.

- **PDF structure.** File and folder naming should be handled before creating links and attaching files. If filenames are changed after the PDF structure has been developed, many links become inoperable. Be certain to complete all editing in the PDF documents before cataloging files.

Optimizing performance

Searches can be performed very fast if you take a little time in creating the proper structure and organization. If you don't avoid some pitfalls with the way that you organize files, then searches perform much slower. A few considerations to be made include the following:

- **Optimize PDF files.** Optimization should be performed on all PDF files as one of the last steps in your workflow. Use the Save As optimizes for Fast Web View found in the General category in the Preferences dialog box and run the PDF Optimizer located in the Advanced menu (Acrobat Pro and Acrobat Pro Extended only). Optimization is especially important for searches to be performed from CD-ROM files.

CROSS-REF For information on PDF Optimizer, see Chapter 18.

- **Break up long PDF files.** Books, reports, essays, and other documents that contain many pages should be broken up into multiple PDF files. If you have books to be cataloged, break up the books into separate chapters. Acrobat Search runs much faster when finding information from several small files. It slows down when searching through long documents.

TIP If you have a single document such as a book you want to distribute on CD-ROM, you can embed an index file in the PDF. (See "Working with Embedded Index Files" later in this chapter).

Creating search help

You can have multiple indexes for various uses and different workgroups. Personnel may use one index for department matters, another for company-wide information, and perhaps another for a research library. In a search, all relevant keywords will appear from indexes loaded in the Index Selection dialog box. When using multiple indexes, employees may forget the structure of document summaries and what index is needed for a given search.

You can create README files and index help files to store key information about what search words can be used to find document summaries. You can create a single PDF file, text files, or multiple files that serve as help. Figure 6.18 shows an example of a PDF help file that might be used to find documents related to a company's personnel policies, procedures, and forms.

FIGURE 6.18

A PDF help file can assist users in knowing what keywords they need to use for the Title, Subject, Author, and Keywords fields.

Title	Subject	Author	Keywords
Policy	PTO	HR	HR 501
Policy	Maternity	HR	HR 521
Procedure	Maternity	HR	HR 520
Form	Payroll	Accounting	FM 261
Policy	Bonus	Accounting	AC 245
Policy	Manual	Admin	AD 109
Procedure	Grievance	HR	HR 546
Policy	EAP	HR	HR 593
Policy	Hiring	HR	HR 506
Form	ID	HR	FM 505
Chart	HR	Admin	AD 117
Form	Leave	HR	FM 531
Procedure	Pay deduction	Accounting	AC 228
Policy	Benefits	Table	Table
Procedure	Extended Leave	HR	HR 564
Policy	Education Leave	HR	HR 568
Form	Insurance	HR	FM 533
Form	Dental	HR	FM 512
Policy	401K	HR	HR 555

Widget Company
Human Resources Index Description

Title: HR
Subject: Table
Author: Table
Keywords: Table

In the top-right corner of Figure 6.18, the document summary for the help file is listed. The Title fields for this company are broken into categories for policies, procedures, forms, and charts. The Subject fields break down the title categories into specific personnel items, and the Author fields contain the department that authored the documents. Form numbers appear for all Keywords fields.

TIP   When creating help files that guide a user for searching document information, use a common identifier in the Subject, Author, and Keywords fields reserved for finding only help files. In Figure 6.18, the identifier is "Table." Whenever a user searches for the word *table* in the Author field, the only returns in the Search Results dialog box will be help files. When using the Title and Author field together, a user can find a specific help file for a given department. In the previous example, the Title is HR and the Author is Table. When these words are searched for the document information, the help file for the HR department is returned in the Search Results. If you reserve keywords for the document Summary fields, any employee can easily find information by remembering only a few keywords.

Creating a new index file

After your files are optimized and saved in final form, it's time to create the search index. Choose Advanced ➪ Document Processing ➪ Full Text Index with Catalog to open the Catalog dialog box, as shown in Figure 6.19. In the dialog box, you make choices for creating a new index file or opening an existing index file. Click the New Index button to create a new index file.

FIGURE 6.19

Click the New Index button in the Catalog dialog box to create an index file.

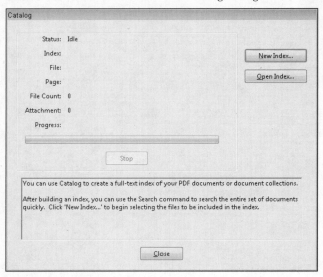

The New Index Definition dialog box shown in Figure 6.20 opens, in which you set specific attributes for your index and determine what folder(s) are to be indexed.

Index title

The title that you place in this field is a title for the index but not necessarily the name of the file you ultimately save. The name you enter here does not need to conform to any naming conventions because in most cases it won't be the saved filename. When you open an index file, you search your hard drive, server, or external media for a filename that ends with a .pdx extension. When you visit the Search window and select Look In ⇨ Select Index, the Index Selection dialog box opens, as shown in Figure 6.21. What appears in the Index Selection dialog box is a list of indexes appearing according to the Index Title names. These names are derived from what you type in the Index Title field in Acrobat Catalog.

NOTE   When you get ready to build a file, Acrobat prompts you for the index filename. By default the text you type in the Index Title field is listed in the File name field in the Save Index File dialog box. This dialog box opens when you click the Build button in the Catalog dialog box (see the section "Building the index" later in this chapter). In most cases where you supply a name as a description in the Index Title, you'll want to change the filename to a name consistent with standard DOS conventions (that is, eight-character maximum with a three-character maximum extension). Make this change when you are prompted to save the file.

FIGURE 6.20

You set attributes for your new index file in the New Index Definition dialog box.

FIGURE 6.21

Choosing Select Index from the Look In pull-down menu in the Search window opens the Index selection dialog box. All loaded indexes are listed according to the index title supplied in Acrobat Catalog at the time the index was created.

CAUTION If you see an index name grayed out, the index is not available to your Acrobat viewer. You may have moved the index file to another location on your hard drive, deleted the file, or tried to search an index on a CD-ROM that is not mounted. In order to bring back the index and make it available to your viewer, you need to delete the grayed out index name by clicking the Remove button and then add the file or rebuild and Add the file in the Index selection dialog box.

Index description

You can supply as many as 256 characters in the Index Description field. Descriptive names and keywords should be provided so that the end user knows what each index contains. Index descriptions should be thought of as adding more information to the items mentioned earlier in this chapter regarding document descriptions. Index descriptions can help users find the index file that addresses their needs.

When an index is loaded, the index title appears in the Select Indexes dialog box. To get more information about an index file, click the Info button shown in Figure 6.21. The Index information dialog box opens as shown in Figure 6.22. The Index information dialog box shows you the title from the Index Title field and the description added in Acrobat Catalog in the Index Description field.

FIGURE 6.22

The Index Description is contained in the Index information dialog box. Users can click on the Info button in the Index selection dialog box to see the description added in the Index Description field box in Acrobat Catalog.

Include these directories

If you add nothing to the Include these directories field, Catalog won't build an index because it won't know where to look for the PDF files to be included in the index. Adding the directory path(s) is essential before you begin to build the index. Notice the first Add button on the right side of the dialog box in Figure 6.20. After you click Add, a navigation dialog box opens, enabling you to identify the directory where the PDFs to be indexed are located. You can add many directories to the Include these directories list. These directories can be in different locations on your hard drive. When a given directory is selected, all subfolders will also be indexed for all directory locations unless you choose to exclude certain folders. When the directories have been identified, the directory path and folder name will appear in the Include these directories field.

Exclude these subdirectories

If you have files in a subdirectory within the directory you are indexing and want to exclude the subdirectory, you can do so in the Exclude these subdirectories field. The folder names and directory paths of excluded directories appear in the Exclude these subdirectories field, as shown in Figure 6.20.

Remove

If you decide to remove a directory from either the Include these directories or Exclude these subdirectories lists, select an item in the list and click the Remove button. You can add or delete directories in either list prior to building an index or when modifying an index.

Saving index definitions

Two buttons appear at the top right corner of the Catalog dialog box for saving a definition. If you begin to develop an index file and supply the index title and a description and want to come back to Catalog later, you can save what you type in the Index Definition dialog box using the Save As button. The Save button does not appear active until you have saved a file with the Save As option or you're working on a file that has been built. Saving the file only saves the definition for the index. It does not create an index file. The Save As option enables you to prepare files for indexing and interrupt your session if you need to return later. For example, suppose you add an index title and you write an index description. If you need to quit Acrobat at this point, click Save As and save the definition to disk. You can then return later and resume creating the index by adding the directories to be cataloged and building the index.

After you have saved a file, you can update the file with the Save button. After a definition is saved, when you return to Acrobat Catalog, you can click the Open button in the Catalog dialog box and resume editing the definition file. When all the options for your search index have been determined, you click the Build button to actually create the index file.

Using Save As or Save is not required to create an index file. If you set all your attributes for the index and click the Build button, Acrobat Catalog prompts you in the Save Index File dialog box to supply a name for the index and save the definition. Essentially, Catalog is invoking the Save As command for you.

If at any time you click the Cancel button in the lower-right corner of the Index Definition dialog box, all edits are lost for the current session. If you add definition items without saving you'll need to start over when you open the Index Definition dialog box again. If you start to work on a saved file and click Cancel without saving new edits, your file reverts to the last saved version.

Setting options

To the right of the Index Description field is a button labeled Options. Click this button and the Options dialog box appears, allowing you to choose from a number of different attributes for your index file, as shown in Figure 6.23. Some of these options are similar to the Preference settings for Acrobat Catalog you made in the Preferences dialog box. Any edits you make here supersede Preference settings.

CROSS-REF For information on setting Catalog preferences, see "Setting Catalog preferences" later in this chapter.

FIGURE 6.23

Clicking the Options button adjacent to the Index Description field opens the Options dialog box. Here you can assign further attributes to the index file.

Do not include numbers

The first item in the Options dialog box is a check box for excluding numbers. By selecting the Do not include numbers option, you can reduce the file size, especially if data containing many numbers are part of the PDF file(s) to be indexed. Keep in mind, however, that if numbers are excluded, Search won't find numeric values.

Add IDs to Adobe v1.0 files

Because Acrobat is now in version 9, finding old PDF 1.0 files that need to be updated with IDs may rarely happen. If you do have legacy files saved as PDF 1.0 format, it would be best to batch process the older PDFs by saving them out of Acrobat 9.0. As software changes, many previous formats may not be supported with recent updates. For better performance, update older documents to newer file formats.

CROSS-REF For more information on batch processing, see Chapter 18.

If you have legacy files that haven't been updated and you want to include them in your search index, check the box. If you're not certain whether the PDFs were created with Acrobat 1.0 compatibility, check it anyway just to be safe.

Do not warn for changed documents when searching

If you create an index file, and then return to the index in Acrobat Catalog and perform some maintenance functions, save the index, and start searching the index, Acrobat notifies you in a dialog box that changes have been made and asks whether you want to proceed. To sidestep the opening of the warning dialog box, check the Do not warn for changed documents when searching option.

Custom properties

The Custom Properties button opens the Custom Properties dialog box, as shown in Figure 6.24. Custom Properties are used when customizing Acrobat with the Acrobat Software Development Kit (SDK). This item is intended for programmers who want to add special features to Acrobat. To add a Custom Property to be indexed, you should have knowledge in programming and the PDF format.

You add Custom Properties to the field box and select the type of property to be indexed from the pull-down menu. You type the property values in the field box, identify the type, and click the Add button. The property is then listed in the window below the Custom Property field box.

FIGURE 6.24

You can add custom data fields to Acrobat with the Acrobat Software Development Kit.

The types available from the pull-down menu are as follows:

- **String.** This is any text string. If numbers are included with this option they are treated as text.

- **Integer.** The integer field can accept values between 0 and 65,535.

- **Date.** This is a date value.

Support for programmers writing extensions and plug-ins, and working with the SDK is provided by Adobe Systems. Developers who want to use the support program need to become a member of the Adobe Solutions Network (ASN) Developer Program. For more information about ASN and SDK, log on to the Adobe Web site at `http://adobe.com/go/acrobat_developer`.

XMP Fields

Click XMP Fields and another dialog box opens in which you add to a list of XMP fields. The dialog box is virtually identical to the Stop Words dialog box shown in Figure 6.25. Type a name in the field box and click the Add button. All new XMP fields are added to the list window.

Stop Words

To optimize an index file to produce faster search results, you can add stop words. You may have words, such as *the*, *a*, *an*, *of*, and so on that would typically not be used in a search. You can choose to exclude such words by typing the word in the Word field box and clicking the Add button in the Stop Words dialog box. Click Stop Words in the Options dialog box to open the Stop Words dialog box shown in Figure 6.25. To eliminate a word after it has been added, select the word and click the Remove button. Keep in mind that every time you *add* a word, you are actually adding it to a list of words to be excluded.

FIGURE 6.25

You can eliminate words from an index file by adding words in the Stop Words dialog box. Adding a word to the list excludes it from the index file.

TIP You can create an elaborate list of stop words and may want to apply the list to several index files, but Acrobat (as of this writing) does not include an ability to import or swap a list of words to be excluded from an index file. For a workaround, you can open any existing Index Definition field and change all attributes except the stop words. Add a new index title, a new index description, and select a new directory for indexing. Save the definition to a new filename and click the Build button. A new index is built using the stop words created in another index. In workgroups you can save an index definition file without adding directories and use it as a template so all index files have consistent settings for the stop words.

Structure tags

If you have a tagged PDF you can search document tags when the tags are included in the search index. Click Structure Tags in the Options dialog box to open the Tags dialog box shown in Figure 6.26. Tagged PDFs with a tagged root and elements can have any item in the tagged logical tree marked for searching. To observe the tags in a PDF file, open the Tags palette and expand the tree. All the tags nest like a Bookmark list. When you want to mark tags for searching, type the tag name in the Tags dialog box and click the Add button. You remove tags from the list window by selecting a tag and clicking the Remove button.

CROSS-REF For more information on tagged PDF documents and using the Tags palette, see Chapter 25.

FIGURE 6.26

You can mark tags for searches in index files by adding tag names in the Tags dialog box.

Building the index

After you've set all the attributes for the index definition, the index file is ready to be created. Clicking the Build button in the New Index Definition dialog box creates indexes. When you click this button, Acrobat Catalog opens the Save Index File dialog box where you supply a filename and target a destination on your hard drive. The default file extension is .pdx. Do not modify the file extension name. Acrobat recognizes these files when loading search indexes.

The location where you instruct Catalog to save your index file can be any location on your hard drive regardless of where the files being indexed reside. You can choose to save the index file inside or outside the folder that Catalog created during the indexing. Therefore, you have an index file and a folder containing index resources. The relationship between the index file and resource folder locations is critical to the usability of the index. If you move the index file to a different location without moving the supporting folder, the index is rendered unusable. To avoid problems, try to create a folder either when you are in the Save Index File dialog box or before you open Catalog and save your index file to your new folder. Make the name descriptive and keep the index file together in this folder. When you want to move the index to another directory, another computer, or to an external media cartridge or CD-ROM, copy the folder containing the index and supporting files.

Click the Save button in the Save Index File dialog box, and Catalog closes the Index Definition dialog box, returns you to the Catalog dialog box, and begins to process all the files in the target folder(s). Depending on how many files are indexed, the time to complete the build may be considerable. Don't interrupt the processing if you want to complete the index generation. When Catalog finishes, the progress bar stops and the last line of text in the Catalog dialog box reads "Index build successful." If for some reason the build is not successful, you can scroll the window in the Catalog dialog box and view errors reported in the list.

Stopping builds

If you want to interrupt a build, you can click the Stop button while a build is in progress. When building an index, Catalog opens a file where all the words and markers to the PDF pages are written. When you click the Stop button, Catalog saves the open file to disk and closes it with the indexed items up to the point you stopped the build. Therefore, the index is usable after stopping a build and you can search for words in the partial index. When you want to resume, you can open the file in Catalog and click the Rebuild button.

Building existing indexes

When files are deleted from indexed folders and new files are added to the indexed folders, you'll want to maintain the index file and update it to reflect any changes. You can open an index file and click Build for a quick update. New files are scanned and added to the index, but the deleted files are marked for deletion without actually deleting the data. To delete invalid data, you need to use the Purge button. Purging can take a considerable amount of time even on small index files. Therefore, your routine maintenance might be to consistently build a file, and only periodically purge data.

Building legacy index files

When you open an index file created with an Acrobat Catalog version earlier than 6.0, a dialog box opens, informing you the index is not compatible with the current version of Acrobat. In the dialog box you have three options: Create copy, Overwrite old index, and Cancel. Click the Create copy button to make a copy of the index file. A new index file is created leaving the original index file undisturbed. You can click the Overwrite old index button and the file rewrites, replacing the old index. If you choose this option your new index file won't be compatible with Acrobat viewers earlier than version 6.0. Clicking Cancel in this dialog box returns you to the Index Selection dialog box, leaving the index file undisturbed.

If you create a search index using Acrobat Catalog version 9, the index file is backward-compatible to Acrobat 6. All Acrobat viewers can use index files suited to the appropriate version.

If you know some users won't be working with the new Acrobat viewers, then be certain to make copies of your index files. Until all users have upgraded to a viewer 6.0 or higher, you may need to organize your indexes according to viewer versions.

The Structure of Index Files

Users who have created index files in all earlier versions of Acrobat are no doubt familiar with the end product of creating a search index. As you may recall, the index file with a .pdx extension and nine subfolders containing all associated files were produced by Acrobat Catalog for every new index. The relationship between the index file and subfolders in terms of directory paths needed to be preserved in order for the index to work properly. When you copied an index file to another directory or source, you needed to copy all the files together and keep the same relative path between the files.

When you produce an index file in Acrobat Pro, you won't find the same nine folders created during the index build with Acrobat version 5 and earlier. Acrobat Catalog 6.0 through 9creates a single folder where files with an .idx extension reside. The relative directory path is still a factor in relocating files, but in Acrobat 6.0 through 9 you need only copy an index file and a single folder to relocate your index and keep it functional.

The PDX file you load as your search index file is a small file that creates the information in the IDX and .info files. The IDX files contain the actual index entries the end user accesses during a search. When you build an index, rebuild an index, or purge data from an index, the maintenance operation may or may not affect the PDX file and/or IDX files depending on which option you choose. For specific information related to how these files are affected during index creation and maintenance, see the following pages for building, rebuilding, and purging index files.

Building index files from secure documents

In Acrobat versions lower than 6.0 you could not create index files from secure PDFs encrypted with either Acrobat Standard Security or Acrobat Self-Sign Security. Version 6.0 of Acrobat afforded complete access to secure files with Acrobat Catalog if the right permissions were applied. When applying Password Security in Acrobat 6 through Acrobat 9 you need to enable text access for screen reader devices in order to index a secure file. Creating an index does not compromise your security and doesn't affect all other permissions you set forth when the files are saved.

If you have legacy files that have been secured, you can index them like other files saved in earlier PDF format compatibilities. These files, and any other files you create with Acrobat Pro or Acrobat Pro Extended, can be used only by Acrobat viewers 6.0 and later.

 For more information on encryption and security, see Chapter 26.

Rebuilding an index

Rebuilding index files completely recreates a new index. You can open an Acrobat 9 compatible index file and click Rebuild. The file rewrites the file you opened much like you would use a Save As menu command to rewrite a PDF document. If a substantial number of PDF documents have been deleted and new files added to the indexed folders, rebuilding the index could take less time than purging data.

Purging data

As indexes are maintained and rebuilt, you will need to perform periodic maintenance and purge old data. A purge does not delete the index file, nor does it completely rewrite the file; it simply recovers the space used in the index for outdated information. Purging is particularly useful when you remove PDF files from a folder and the search items are no longer needed. If you have built a file several times, each build marks words for deletion. A purge eliminates the marked data and reduces the file size. With a significant number of words marked for deletion, a purge will improve the speed when using Search. This operation might be scheduled routinely in environments where many changes occur within the indexed folders.

> **TIP** When changing options for eliminating words and numbers from indexes or adding tags and custom properties in the Options dialog box, first open the index.pdx file in Catalog and purge the data. Set your new criteria in the Options dialog box and rebuild the index. Any items deleted will now be added to the index, or any items you want to eliminate will subsequently be eliminated from the index.

Setting Catalog preferences

Catalog preference settings are contained in the Preferences dialog box. Choose Edit ➪ Preferences and click the Catalog item in the left pane as shown in Figure 6.27. Notice that the Index Defaults items use the same settings as found in the Options dialog box from the New Index Selection dialog box. The top three options under Indexing in Catalog preferences are obtained only here in these preference settings.

FIGURE 6.27

Open the Preferences dialog box and click Catalog in the left pane to see the options settings for Acrobat Catalog.

Indexing

The four options found in the Indexing section of the Catalog preferences are as follows:

- **Allow indexing on separate drives.** When creating index files where you want to include folders on network servers and/or computers on your network, select this item in the Catalog preferences. The indexing option includes indexing files only on local networks. Unfortunately, you can't index files on Web servers and use indexes from within Web browsers.

- **Force ISO 9660 compatibility on folders.** This setting is a flag that tells Catalog to look for any folders that are not compliant with standard DOS conventions (eight-character maximum with three-character maximum extensions) for folder/directory names. If Catalog encounters a folder name that is not acceptable, the processing stops and an error is reported in the Catalog dialog box. Folder names and directory paths are listed for all incompatible names. You can review the list and manually rename folders. After changing folder names, try to create the index again.

- **Enable logging.** A log file is created during an index build that describes the processing for each file indexed. The file is ASCII text and can be opened in any text editor or word processor. Any errors occurring during the build are noted in the log file. All documents and directory paths are also contained in the log file. If you don't want to have a log file created at the time of indexing, clear the check box to disable the logging. When you disable logging, you are prevented from analyzing problems when you close the Catalog dialog box.

- **Allow Catalog batch files (.bpdx) to be run.** Permits batch processing of index files.

Index defaults

The options listed in the Index Defaults area of the Catalog preferences are identical to the options you have available in the New Index Description Options dialog box described earlier in this chapter. These default/options settings exist in two locations for different reasons.

When you set the options in the Preferences dialog box, the options are used for all index files you create. When you elect to use the options from the New Index Selection Options dialog box, the settings are specific to the index file you create. When you create a new index file, the options return to defaults.

If you set a preference in the Catalog preferences and disable the option in the New Index Selection Options dialog box, the latter supersedes the former. That is to say, the New Index Selection Options dialog box settings always prevail.

Using Index Files

As I stated earlier, one reason you create index files is for speed. When you search hundreds or thousands of pages, the amount of time to return found instances for searched words in index files is a matter of seconds compared to searching folders in the Search window.

Loading index files

To search using an index file, you need to first load the index in the Search window. From the Look In pull-down menu, choose the Select Index menu option, as shown in Figure 6.28.

The Index Selection dialog box opens after you make the menu selection. Click the Add button and the Open Index File dialog box opens. In this dialog box navigate your hard drive to find the folder where your index file is located. Click the index filename and click the Open button.

After selecting the index to load, you are returned to the Index Selection dialog box. A list of all loaded indexes appears in the dialog box. To the left of each filename is a check box. When a check mark is in view, the index file is active and can be searched. Those check boxes that are disabled have the index file loaded, but the file remains inactive. Search will not return results from the inactive index files. If an index file is grayed out as shown in Figure 6.21, the file path has been disrupted and Acrobat can't find the index file or the support files associated with the index. If you see a filename grayed out, select the file in the list and click the Remove button. Click the Add button and relocate the index. If the support files are not found, an error is reported in a dialog box indicating the index file could not be opened.

Your first step in using indexes is to load the index file(s) by choosing the Select Index menu option from the Look In menu in the Search window.

If you can't open a file, you need to return to the Catalog dialog box and click the Open button. Find the index file that you want to make active and rebuild the index. After rebuilding, you need to return to the Index selection dialog box and reload the index.

NOTE If you attempt to load an index file from a CD-ROM and the CD is not inserted into your CD-ROM drive, the index filename is grayed out in the Index Selection dialog box. After inserting the CD-ROM containing the index, the index filename becomes active. If you know index files are loaded from CDs, don't delete them from the Index Selection dialog box. Doing so requires you to reload the index file each time you insert a CD.

Attaching an index file to a document

You can associate an index file with a particular document. Open the Document Properties dialog box (Ctrl/⌘+D) and click the Advanced tab. Adjacent to the Search Index item is a Browse button. Click Browse and the Open dialog box appears. Navigate your hard drive to locate the index file created from a folder containing your document, select it, and click Open. When you save your file and reopen it, you can select Currently Selected Indexes in the Look In pull-down menu and your associated index file is automatically loaded for you.

Disabling indexes

If an index is to be eliminated from searches, you can deactivate the index by disabling its check box. In a later Acrobat session, you can go back and enable indexes listed in the Index Selection dialog box. You should always use this method rather than deleting an index if you intend to use it again in a later Acrobat session. However, at times you may want to delete an index file. If the index will no longer be used, or you relocate your index to another drive or server, you may want to completely remove the old index. If this is the case, select the index file to be deleted and click the Remove button. Indexes may be enabled or disabled before you select Remove. In either case, the index file is removed without warning.

If you inadvertently delete an index, you can always reload the index by clicking the Add button. Placing index files in a directory where you can easily access them is a good idea. To avoid confusion, try to keep indexes in a common directory or a directory together with the indexed PDF files. Acrobat doesn't care where the index file is located on your hard drive or server — it just needs to know where the file is located and the file needs to keep the relative path with the support files. If you move the index file to a different directory, be certain to reestablish the connection in the Index Selection dialog box.

Finding index information

When a number of index files are installed on a computer or server, the names for the files may not be descriptive enough to determine which index you want to search. If more detailed information is desired, the information provided by the Index Information dialog box may help identify the index needed for a given search.

PDF WORKFLOW Index information may be particularly helpful in office environments where several people in different departments create PDFs and indexes are all placed on a common server. What may be intuitive to the author of an index file in terms of index name may not be as intuitive to other users. Index information offers the capability for adding more descriptive information that can be understood by many users.

Fortunately, you can explore more descriptive information about an index file by clicking the Info button in the Index Selection dialog box. When you click the Info button, the Index information dialog box opens, displaying information about the index file, as shown earlier in Figure 6.22. Some of the information displayed requires user entry at the time the index is built. Acrobat Catalog automatically creates other information in the dialog box when the index is built. The Index information dialog box provides a description of the following:

- **Title.** The user supplies title information at the time the index is created. Titles usually consist of several words describing the index contents. Titles can be searched, as detailed earlier in this chapter, so the title keywords should reflect the index content.

- **Description.** Description can be a few words or several sentences containing information about the index. (In Figure 6.22, the description was supplied in Acrobat Catalog when the index was created.)

- **Filename.** The directory path for the index file's location on a drive or server is displayed with the last item appearing as the index filename.

- **Last built.** If the index file is updated, the date of the last build is supplied here. If no updates have occurred, the date will be the same as the created date.

- **Created.** This date reflects the time and date the index file was originally created, and is therefore a fixed date.

- **Documents.** Indexes are created from one or more PDF documents. The total number of PDF files from which the index file was created appears here.

- **Status.** If the index file has been identified and added to the list in the Index Selection dialog box, it will be Available. Unavailable indexes appear grayed out in the list and are described as Unavailable.

Searching an index

After your index file(s) is prepared and loaded in the Index selection dialog box, it is ready for use. You search index files in the Advanced Search window just as you search multiple files as explained earlier in this chapter. From the Look In pull-down menu, select Currently Selected Indexes.

All the options discussed earlier for advanced searches are available to you. Select from the Return results containing pull-down menu, enter your search criteria, and select the options you want. Click the Search button and you'll find the search results reported much faster than using other search methods.

Index files can be created from PDF collections contained on external media where the index file can remain on your computer without the need for copying the PDF documents to your hard drive. When you insert a media disk such as a CD-ROM, your search index is ready to use to search the media.

Practice searching your new index file using different options and search criteria. To compare the difference between using a search index file and using the advanced search options, you can choose the Browse for Location menu item and search the CD-ROM for the same criteria. Go back and forth to see the differences between searching folders and searching an index file.

Searching external devices

A computer network server, another computer on your network, a CD-ROM, DVD-ROM, external hard drive, and a removable media cartridge are considered external to your local computer hard drive(s). Any of these devices can be indexed and the index file can be located on any of the devices you index. If you want to save an index file on a device different from where the PDF collection is stored, you need to be certain to open the Preferences dialog box for the Catalog preferences and enable the check box for Allow indexing on separate drives. This preference setting enables you to index across media devices.

NOTE When you want to write index files to read only media such as CD-ROMs and DVDs, you need to create the index file from PDFs stored on your hard drive. After the index file is created, copy the index file, the supporting files, and the PDFs to your media and burn the disc.

When you want to search an index, you can activate the index in the Index selection dialog box and invoke a search whether your external media is mounted and accessible or not. The search index returns results from the index .pdx file and the .idx files without looking at the PDFs that were indexed. You can examine the results of the search in the Search window and find the files where the search criteria match the PDF documents in the index collection.

If you want to open the link to the PDF document where a result is reported, you need to have the media mounted and accessible. If a network server or other computer contains the related files, the server/computer must be shared with appropriate permissions and visible on your desktop. If you use external media storage devices, the media must be mounted and visible on your desktop in order to view the PDFs linked to the search results. If you attempt to view a document when the device is not mounted, Acrobat opens an error dialog box.

If you see an error dialog box, click OK in the dialog box and insert your media, connect an external hard drive, or access a computer or network server. You don't need to quit Acrobat to make your device accessible. Wait until the media is mounted and then click a search result. Acrobat opens the linked page and you're ready to continue your search.

A search index file created on one computer can be moved or copied to another computer. To copy an index file to another computer, be certain you copy the index file (.pdx) and all supporting files in the folder created by Catalog. Be certain you maintain the same relative directory path for the index file and the supporting files. If an index file appears in a root folder and the supporting files appear in a nested folder, copy the root folder to other media. If you place the index file in the same folder as the supporting files, copy the single folder containing all files to your media.

You can load the index file and external media on another computer and perform the same searches as were performed where the index file was created. When distributing CD-ROMs and DVDs you can copy these index files to your media and all users can access the index files. If you access an index file on a network server and the PDF collection is stored on an external device such as a CD-ROM, you cannot open files from another computer unless the CD-ROM is mounted. You may see your network server, but the associated devices with the server need to be individually mounted in order to open PDF files remotely.

Working with Embedded Index Files

Index files can be scattered all over your hard drive and, at times, it can be a chore to load them in the Index selection dialog box. In addition, when sharing PDFs where indexes have been created requires you to either attach an index file to a PDF or send along your index to recipients of your PDFs. Again, the steps involved can be aggravating if you have to spend time finding the index files on your hard drive.

Acrobat 8 simplified the steps for loading index files and sharing them. In Acrobat 8 and 9 you can embed an index file in PDFs. Embedding an index file is limited to a single PDF document or a PDF Portfolio and not a collection of PDFs. You won't gain any better performance embedding indexes in one-page PDFs or files containing few pages.

When you embed an index file you bypass all the steps for creating an index using Acrobat Catalog. Indexes are automatically created and embedded by Acrobat Pro and Acrobat Pro Extended through a simple button click in a dialog box.

To understand more about creating an index file and embedding it in a PDF document, follow these steps.

STEPS: Creating and embedding index files

1. **Open a PDF document in Acrobat Pro.** Try to find a PDF having 500 or more pages or a PDF Portfolio. Longer documents make index embedding more practical when using this feature. In this example I use a file containing 803 pages.

2. **Open the Manage Embedded Index dialog box.** Select Advanced ➪ Document Processing ➪ Manage Embedded Index. The Manage Embedded Index dialog box opens, as shown in Figure 6.29.

3. **Embed the Index.** Click the Embed Index button in the Manage Embedded Index dialog box.

4. **Click OK.** Click OK after Acrobat completes the index creation and your new index file is now embedded in your PDF. (See Figure 6.30.)

FIGURE 6.29

Select Advanced ➪ Document Processing ➪ Manage Embedded Index.

FIGURE 6.30

Click OK and your index is embedded in the PDF.

5. **Compare a search using the embedded index.** Open the original PDF without an index embedded in the document and press Ctrl/⌘+Shift+F to open the Search window. Select The Current PDF in the Look In pull-down menu and search for a work in the document. Notice the amount of time it takes to search all pages in the file.

    Bring the file with the embedded index forward in the Document pane or open the file if you closed it. Perform a search using the Current Document option in the Look In pull-down menu. Add the same search criteria in the Search window and search the document. You should see a noticeable difference in the speed for the returned results.

Summary

- Acrobat 9 viewers include a Find toolbar used for searching the current active document.

- Searching PDF files occurs in the Search window. When a search is requested, the Search window opens as a floating window.

- The Search window enables basic and advanced searches.

- Basic searches are used to search open PDF files but provide more options than the Find command.

- Advanced searches enable searching multiple PDFs locally, on external media, and across networks with the use of a search index file.

- Acrobat viewers 6.0 and greater support searching content of bookmarks and comments through advanced searches and index file searches. Acrobat 7.0 through 9 supports searching file attachments.

- Searches for PDFs on the Internet are no longer built into Acrobat. If you want to search for PDFs on the Internet, you need to use a Web search engine that supports searching for PDFs.

- Searches can be made with a variety of options, including Boolean queries, without the use of an index file.

- Search index files are created in Acrobat Catalog in Acrobat Pro or Acrobat Pro Extended only. Searching index files returns results for large collections of PDFs much faster than basic and advanced searches.

- Document descriptions can be searched with advanced searches and via index file searches.

- Index files can be built, rebuilt, and purged with Acrobat Catalog. Old index files created with PDF formats earlier than version 6.0 need to be rebuilt with Acrobat Catalog. Acrobat Catalog 9 index files are backward-compatible with Acrobat 6.0.

- Tags, XMP data, and object data can be searched with advanced searches and from index searches.

- Index files can be copied to other computers, network servers, and external media storage units. When copying search indexes, you need to duplicate all supporting files and the relative directory path(s) on the destination units.

- Index files can be embedded on a PDF-by-PDF basis in Acrobat 8 and 9. A single menu command creates and embeds an index in a PDF opened in the Document pane.

Part II

Converting Documents to PDF

This section deals with converting documents from authoring programs to PDF files that can be opened, viewed, and edited in Acrobat Standard (Windows), Acrobat Professional (Windows and Macintosh), and Acrobat Professional Extended (Windows). In Chapter 7 you find all the options available for converting files to PDF from within Acrobat. Chapter 8 is dedicated to using the PDFMaker installed with your Acrobat installation for converting Microsoft Office files. In Chapter 9 I talk about using many Adobe programs that support direct export to PDF, and in Chapter 10 you find everything you need to know about using Adobe Acrobat Distiller to convert PostScript files to PDF.

Chapter 7

Converting Files to PDF

Unlike almost every other computer program, Acrobat was never designed to support creating new files and editing pages to add content. Where Acrobat begins is with file conversion to the PDF format. Users start with a document authored in another program and the resulting document is converted to PDF using either tools from within Acrobat or tools or commands within programs that support PDF conversion from native documents.

With Acrobat Standard and Acrobat Pro, and Acrobat Pro Extended, the number of methods you can employ for converting documents to PDF is enormous. Any program file can be converted to PDF through a number of different methods offered by Acrobat, operating systems, and many different authoring applications. The method you use to convert a document to PDF and the purpose for which the PDF is intended require you to become familiar with a number of different options at your disposal for PDF file creation. This chapter begins a new part of the book entirely devoted to PDF creation. In this chapter you learn basic PDF conversion methods available in Acrobat Pro and Acrobat Standard. The following chapters in this part cover more advanced PDF creation methods.

For easier reading in this chapter, I'll refer to Acrobat Pro (Windows and Macintosh) and Acrobat Pro Extended (Windows only) simply as Acrobat Pro. Where a different feature is exclusive to Acrobat Pro Extended, I'll so state that the feature is exclusive to Acrobat Pro Extended.

IN THIS CHAPTER

Understanding the PDF creation process

Converting application documents to PDF

Creating new blank PDF pages

Converting to PDF from within Acrobat

Converting scans to PDF

Converting Web pages to PDF

Converting Flash animations to PDF

Converting to PDF from templates

Setting Up the PDF Creation Environment

You create PDF documents from within Acrobat with default tools and with menu commands. In addition to the default tools, this chapter makes use of the Snapshot tool, the Edit toolbar, and the Create PDF From Web Page tool in the File toolbar. To regain the default toolbars, open a context menu on the Toolbar Well and select Reset Toolbars from the menu commands or press Alt/Option+F8.

Open the More Tools menu from a context menu on the Toolbar Well. Scroll down to the Advanced Editing toolbar and check the box adjacent to the toolbar name. Scroll down the window to the Select & Zoom toolbar. Check the box for the Snapshot tool.

NEW FEATURE I'll talk about converting Flash files in this chapter, which is a new feature in Acrobat 9. In addition to menu commands, Acrobat 9 has introduced some new tools for handling Flash imports. Open a context menu on the Acrobat Toolbar Well and choose Multimedia. The Multimedia toolbar contains the new Flash tool.

If you intend to edit documents after PDF creation, you need to open toolbars specific to your editing session. Depending on the type of edits you anticipate, open toolbars as needed after you finish converting files to PDF. For this chapter, click OK in the More Tools window and select Dock Toolbars from a context menu opened on the Toolbar Well.

Understanding How PDFs Are Created

You can use Acrobat to open various file formats in the viewer; the files are immediately converted to PDF. You can also print a file to the Adobe PDF printer, installed with your viewer, from just about any authoring program, and the native document is converted to PDF. It all sounds like simple stuff, but two very important distinctions exist between these methods of conversion for certain file types that you need to understand before you start converting files to PDF. Quite simply, opening some files in Acrobat Pro or Acrobat Standard does not involve any intervention from companion programs. On the other hand, using some file formats and using the Adobe PDF printer requires some help from the Acrobat Distiller software. To understand the fundamentals of document conversion you need to know a little bit about Acrobat Distiller.

CROSS-REF Acrobat Distiller is thoroughly covered in Chapter 10, where you'll find information on setting all the options Distiller offers you.

Acrobat Distiller accepts either a PostScript file or an Encapsulated PostScript (EPS) file that it processes to produce a PDF document. Through the processing mechanism, Distiller applies different options during conversion. These options can include image sampling, font handling, color control, PDF format compatibility assignment, document encryption, hypertext linking, and a host of other settings. Each of the settings is designed to produce PDF files for different purposes. Because so many different options can be applied to PDF conversion via the Distiller software, Distiller provides you the capability to save an assortment of specific settings to individual Adobe PDF Settings files. When you save the files to a specific location on your hard drive, you can access them from a pull-down menu in Acrobat Distiller or from within authoring programs where Adobe PDF Settings are used.

NOTE Adobe PDF Settings were referred to as Job Options prior to Acrobat 6.

In addition to custom settings, you can save to Adobe PDF Settings files. Acrobat Distiller, when installed with Acrobat Pro or Acrobat Pro Extended, has nine settings, and Acrobat Standard has five settings. When you create a PDF file that calls upon Distiller to produce the PDF document, the Adobe PDF Settings last used by Distiller control the options for your resulting PDF document. The danger here is that if you intend to have a file created for printing, for example, and the settings are optimized for screen viewing, you wind up with a PDF document that won't be suitable for printing. Therefore, it is imperative that you know what settings are applied to PDFs created with the Acrobat Distiller software.

Prior to the conversion process you'll have an opportunity to make a choice for the Adobe PDF Settings that are applied during distillation. These choices may or may not be available depending on the type of files you convert to PDF. If the Adobe PDF Settings are not made available when you convert to PDF, the default settings in Acrobat Distiller are used. You need to be certain you open Acrobat Distiller and change the defaults when conversion of a particular file type does not open Acrobat Distiller. Regardless of where you access the settings choices, the same options are always available. If you haven't saved any custom settings, the defaults appear as shown in Figure 7.1.

FIGURE 7.1

The default Adobe PDF Settings are selectable from a pull-down menu in the Acrobat Distiller window in Acrobat Pro and Pro Extended. Acrobat Standard does not have PDF/X and PDF/A options.

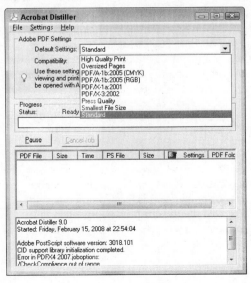

CROSS-REF For a complete description of the Adobe PDF Settings, see Chapter 10.

In this chapter, we'll look at using the High Quality, Press Quality, Smallest File Size, and Standard settings. Without an elaborate definition of these settings, for the purposes of this chapter, think of High Quality for business office printing, Press Quality as suited for commercial printing, Smallest File Size as suited for Web hosting and screen viewing, and the Standard settings as suited for everything else.

Converting Native Documents to PDF

Many authoring programs offer you methods for converting to PDF, such as exporting or saving to PDF directly, or using a utility installed with Acrobat that supports certain authoring programs. However, when these methods are not available you can use the Print command in your authoring program to produce a PDF document. Virtually any document created in an authoring program that allows printing can be converted to PDF through the use of the Adobe PDF printer (Windows and Mac OS X 10.2 and above).

You access the Adobe PDF printer in the application Print dialog box. Rather than print a file to a printer, you print your file to disk. During this process, the file is temporarily saved as a PostScript file and the PostScript file is distilled in Acrobat Distiller. The Adobe PDF Settings assigned to Distiller control the attributes of the resulting PDF file. The process is relatively the same on both Windows and Macintosh platforms, but initial printer selection and dialog box selections vary a little.

Adobe PDF printer (Windows)

When you install Acrobat, the Adobe PDF printer is installed in your Printers folder. As a printer driver, the file is accessible from any program capable of printing, including your computer accessories and utilities. Like any other printer you install on Windows 2000 with Service Pack 4, Windows XP Professional, Windows XP Home Edition, or Tablet PC with Service Pack 2, you can set the Adobe PDF printer as the default printer. Once you have set the default printer, you don't need to make a printer selection each time you want to create a PDF document.

NOTE You may also have the Acrobat Distiller printer installed in your Printer's folder. The features associated with the Adobe PDF printer and the Acrobat Distiller printer are identical.

To convert any application document to PDF, choose File ➪ Print or access the Print dialog box with the menu command in your authoring program. Some dedicated vertical market programs, such as accounting and other office programs, may have print commands located in menus other than the File menu. When you arrive at the Print dialog box, the various printer drivers installed on your computer are shown. Select the Adobe PDF printer in the Print dialog box, as shown in Figure 7.2.

FIGURE 7.2

From any authoring program, select the Print command, select the Adobe PDF printer, and click OK to convert the open document to a PDF file.

Before printing to the Adobe PDF printer, check your output options by clicking the Preferences button. In Windows 2000 and earlier, you will see Properties appear in the Print dialog box. If you see Properties, click the Properties button. The Adobe PDF Document Properties dialog box opens, as shown in Figure 7.3. In this dialog box you choose options for the resulting PDF document. Click the Adobe PDF Settings tab to choose the PDF options.

FIGURE 7.3

Set your PDF options in the Adobe PDF Printing Preferences dialog box in the Adobe PDF Settings pane.

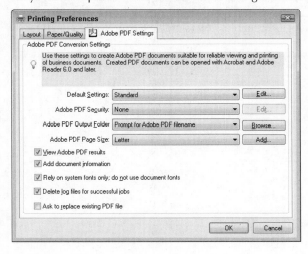

Choices you can make about the PDF file and handling the PDF conversion are contained in the Adobe PDF Settings window. Items you'll want to control include the following:

- **Default Settings.** This item relates to the discussion in the previous section concerning the Acrobat Distiller Adobe PDF Settings. The choices you have from the pull-down menu are the same nine preset choices (Acrobat Pro and Pro extended) or four choices (Acrobat Standard) provided with your Acrobat installation and any custom settings, if you've created them. It's important to make the proper choice for the options you want. When you print to the Adobe PDF printer, Acrobat Distiller is used in the background and applies the settings you specify in this dialog box.

CROSS-REF For a better understanding of Adobe PDF Settings, see Chapter 10.

- **Adobe PDF Security.** If you want to password-protect your document, you can apply security settings at the time the PDF is created. Choose the security options from the choices in the pull-down menu. The default choice for None results in PDF documents created without any password protection.

CROSS-REF To learn how to apply password protection to PDF documents, see Chapter 26.

- **Adobe PDF Output Folder.** Choose to save PDF files to a fixed folder and directory path or be prompted for a filename and directory path for the saved file.
- **Adobe PDF Page Size.** A pull-down menu offers an extensive list of page sizes derived from the printer driver and not the PPD (PostScript Printer Description file) for your printer. If you don't have a custom size that matches your document page, click the Add button adjacent to the Adobe PDF Page Size pull-down menu. The Add Custom Paper Size dialog box opens where you make choices for the custom page size and add the new page option in the pull-down menu, as shown in Figure 7.4.

FIGURE 7.4

The Add Custom Paper Size dialog box enables you to create a page size up to 200 × 200 inches.

Acrobat accepts sizes up to 200 × 200 inches (5,080 × 5,080 millimeters/14,400 × 14,400 points). Enter your new custom page size in the units of measure desired and click the Add/Modify button. Your new page size is added to the Adobe PDF Page Size pull-down menu and selected for you after you click the Add/Modify button. If you want to delete a page after it has been created, click Add in the Printing Preferences dialog box and select the page you want to delete from the Add Custom Paper Size dialog box. Click the Delete button and the page is deleted from both pull-down menus. Clicking Cancel (or pressing the Esc key) in the dialog box returns you to the Adobe PDF Document Properties dialog box without affecting any changes.

CROSS-REF Setting custom pages for the Adobe PDF Printer makes the custom page sizes accessible for this printer driver only. If using other methods for PDF creation such as using the PDFMaker tools in Office programs, you'll want to create custom page sizes in another preferences dialog box. For more information on creating custom page sizes and Microsoft Office programs, see Chapter 8.

- **View Adobe PDF results.** When the check box is enabled, the resulting PDF document opens in the Acrobat Document pane. If Acrobat is not open, the program launches after the PDF is created.

- **Add document information.** This item is a little misleading. You are not prompted in a dialog box to add document information. However, when using applications that support certain kinds of document information such as document title and author, the information from the native document is added to the Document Properties Description fields. The document properties in your native document are not translated precisely, though. You may have a Word file with custom properties set up in the Word Document Properties dialog box like a Title, Subject, Author, Keywords, and so on. When the Word file is converted to PDF, you'll find your Title information in Acrobat to be the name of the saved Word file and the Author is your computer log-on name. Regardless of the custom properties you add to the Document Properties text boxes in Word, the results in Acrobat default to descriptions you can't control. If you remove the check box for this setting, all the Document Properties Descriptions in the PDF file are blank.

CROSS-REF For more information on document descriptions, see Chapter 6.

- **Rely on system fonts only; do not use document fonts.** What this check box does is control whether fonts are put into the PostScript stream that are sent to the Adobe PDF printer. Since 99.9% of the time those fonts are resident on your system, there is no value in having them also embedded in the PostScript stream; it just makes the process of printing to Adobe PDF slower. By default, the check box is ON — it's faster. Leave this setting at the default.

CROSS-REF For more information on font management and font embedding, see Chapter 10.

- **Delete log files for successful jobs.** During PDF creation, the processing information is written to a log file in the form of ASCII text. You can open the log file in any text editor and review the steps used to produce the PDF. Each time a PDF is successfully created, the log file is deleted. In the event you want to review the PDF creation process logged in the text file, disable the check box and open the log file in a text editor.

- **Ask to replace existing PDF file.** If you elect to not have Acrobat prompt you for a file-name, the PDF file is created using the authoring document filename. If you make changes in the document and want to create a new PDF document, the second creation overwrites the first file if the check box is disabled. If you're creating different versions of PDF files and want to have them all saved to disk, be certain to enable the check box.

After you review all the options in the Adobe PDF Printing Preferences dialog box, click OK. You are returned to the Print dialog box and are ready to create the PDF document. Click Print in the dialog box and the PDF is produced with the options you chose in the Adobe PDF Settings dialog box. If the check box was enabled for View Adobe PDF results, the PDF opens in Acrobat.

Because this method of PDF creation uses a printer driver, you can create a PDF document from virtually any application program. The only requirement is that the program is capable of printing. If you use programs such as Microsoft Office, other Adobe programs, certain CAD drawing programs, high-end imaging programs, or a host of other applications, you may have other methods for creating PDF documents depending on the level of PDF support for the program. It is important to understand when to use the Adobe PDF printer and other methods available to you from different applications. Before you integrate using the Adobe PDF printer into your workflow, be certain to review the next two chapters because they discuss other options for creating PDF documents.

CROSS-REF For more information on creating PDFs from Microsoft programs, see Chapter 8. For more information on exporting to PDF from Adobe programs, see Chapter 9.

Adobe PDF (Macintosh OS X)

Mac OS X and Adobe PDF are married at the operating system level and you can find several ways to convert your authoring files to the PDF format. The Acrobat-supported method uses the same type of printer driver you find on Windows. From any authoring program, select the Print command (most commonly accessed by choosing File ⇨ Print). When the Print dialog box opens, select Adobe PDF 9.0 from the Printer pull-down menu. From the default selection for Copies and Pages, open the pull-down menu and select PDF Options, as shown in Figure 7.5.

The dialog box changes so that you can access Adobe PDF Settings from a pull-down menu. The default selection is Use Default. If you leave this option active, the most recent settings selected in the Distiller application are used to produce the PDF file. The remaining options are the same as those discussed for Windows users. When you add new custom settings, they appear in the Adobe PDF Settings pull-down menus from the Print dialog boxes on Windows and Macintosh operating systems.

FIGURE 7.5

PDF Options settings are available after you select the PDF Options pull-down menu command.

Another setting for viewing the PDF file appears in the pull-down menu: After PDF Creation. You can choose to view your PDF in the default Acrobat viewer or leave the default at Launch Nothing, which allows you to go about your work and view the PDFs later. After you choose the settings, click the Print button to convert the file to PDF using the Adobe PDF Settings you selected from the menu choices.

If you open the PDF pull-down menu at the bottom of the dialog box and select Save as PDF (see Figure 7.6), you create a PDF using the PDF engine built into Mac OS X. Checking this option also creates a PDF file, but the PDF creation is not an Adobe-based PDF creation method. This menu choice appears in a generic installation of Mac OS X (Jaguar through Leopard), and creating a PDF this way is supported by the operating system without the use of Acrobat Distiller. When you use Save As PDF, the PDF is created using the native Mac OS X PDF creation tools, which provides adequate PDF creation of non-prepress documents. The PDF documents created using this method will work fine for office uses; however, they will be significantly larger than those created by Adobe Acrobat.

CROSS-REF For more information on PostScript and creating PostScript files, see Chapter 10.

Save As PDF was designed by Apple to provide users with a PDF version of a document to send to people across the Internet for screen viewing and desktop printing. As a matter of practice, using the Adobe PDF printer is your best choice for creating PDFs suited for purposes other than screen displays.

FIGURE 7.6

Selecting the PDF pull-down menu and choosing Save as PDF creates a PDF file using Apple's OS X PDF creation tools.

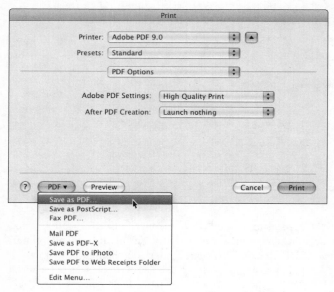

CAUTION A number of different clone printer drivers and clone PDF creators are distributed from developers and enthusiasts. Using a clone product can often produce unreliable PDF documents. If you purchased Adobe Acrobat, be sure to use the tools Adobe has provided you for PDF creation. Adobe and many Adobe partners that have licensed Adobe technology offer you the best results for reliable PDF creation.

When to Use the Adobe PDF Printer driver

On Windows you use the Adobe PDF Printer for authoring applications that don't support exports to PDF. Programs such as the Microsoft Office applications, Autodesk AutoCAD, Lotus Notes, and so on offer you better options for converting directly to PDF via tools installed with your Acrobat installation. Simple text editor documents, vertical market application programs such as accounting programs, shareware programs, and other types of application documents not normally used for professional design purposes are likely candidates for using the Adobe PDF Printer driver. If a program such as a Microsoft Office application supports direct exports to PDF, you're always best served by using the export tools Adobe provides you when you install Acrobat.

Macintosh users will find a much more liberal use for the Adobe PDF Printer. Inasmuch as there are some export options for programs like Microsoft Office programs, they generally don't work as well as using the Print dialog box and printing to a PDF document. Additionally programs like

Safari, Firefox, and Apple Mail don't have the same support for PDF creation as you find on Windows with Microsoft Internet Explorer and Microsoft Outlook. Unless you're using the Adobe Creative Suite applications, almost all other application documents on the Mac are best converted to PDF using the Print dialog box.

Viewing PDFs on the Mac

Apple's OS X also supports an Apple-developed PDF viewer called Preview. By default, double-clicking a PDF file opens the PDF in the Preview application. If you want to change the default viewer from Preview to Acrobat, select a PDF document and press ⌘+I to open the Document Info dialog box, as shown in the following figure.

From the Open with menu, select Adobe Acrobat Pro (or the viewer you want to establish as the default PDF viewer). Click the Change All button and all your PDF documents will open by default in Acrobat.

continued

continued

If you're using Mac OS X Leopard, you have another method for viewing PDF documents with Apple's QuickLook feature. Click a PDF document on the desktop or within a folder and press the Spacebar. The PDF document pops up on the desktop with the first page in view. You can scroll all pages in a PDF file using QuickLook by dragging the slider on the right side of the window up or down.

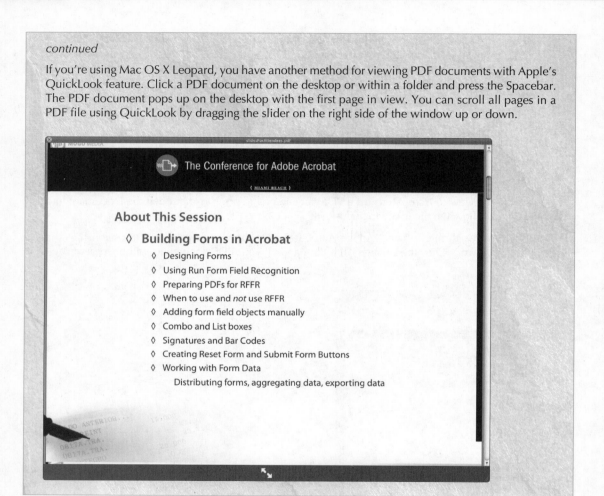

Creating Blank New Pages

Sometimes features added to programs are hidden in a menu command and may be undocumented. When Acrobat 7 was introduced, a menu command was added to create a new PDF document from within Acrobat. I missed this addition in Acrobat 7 because it was so obscure and it never occurred to me that the command existed.

To create a blank new page in Acrobat 7, press the Shift key on your keyboard and select File ➪ Create PDF ➪ From Blank Page.

In Acrobat 8 a menu command was introduced to create a blank new page via the File ➪ Create PDF submenu. In Acrobat 9 you find the same File ➪ Create PDF ➪ From Blank Page command to create a new blank page.

Note that you must select the File ⇨ Create PDF menu command for From Blank Page to appear as shown in Figure 7.7. Using the Create task button menu won't get you the option to create a new document. When you select the command, a single-page PDF is created. The page appears as a portrait standard letter-size page by default.

FIGURE 7.7

Select File ⇨ Create PDF ⇨ From Blank New Page and a blank page with a default text box and special toolbar opens in the Document pane.

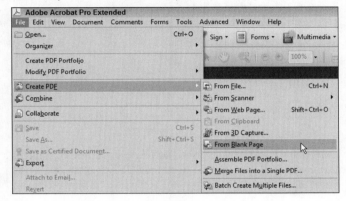

The blank page created appears with a default text box and a special toolbar used for setting type attributes for the text added to the text box. In addition, you have some preference options for selecting different page sizes, page orientation, and margins that define the size of the text box in the New Document preferences.

CROSS-REF Use of the type tools on blank new pages and setting preference options are all covered in Chapter 13.

Creating PDFs from Files

Adobe Acrobat offers you a number of options for converting application documents to PDF. For PDF creation supported by Acrobat, you don't need to leave the program to produce PDF files from a number of different file formats.

The Create task button pull-down menu offers a few different options for PDF creation, as shown in Figure 7.8 (left). If you choose File ⇨ Create PDF you find many more options for converting documents to PDF as shown in Figure 7.8 (right).

FIGURE 7.8

The Create task button (left) offers a few options for PDF file creation. Choose File ➪ Create PDF (right) and you find many more options for PDF file creation from within Acrobat.

You use Create PDF ➪ From File to convert any file format supported by Acrobat to a PDF document. You can also use File ➪ Open to convert to PDF. If using the Open dialog box, be certain to choose All Files (*.*) from the Files of Type pull-down menu (Windows) or Show pull-down menu (Mac).

 TIP   You can also convert any file compatible with the Create PDF ➪ From File menu command by dragging a document on top of the Acrobat window.

Supported file formats

To convert files to PDF from within Acrobat, you first need to understand all the supported formats. You can try to convert any file format to PDF with the Create PDF tool. If the file format is supported, the document is converted to PDF and opens in Acrobat. If the format is not supported, a dialog box opens informing you the format is not supported. It won't hurt to try, but knowing ahead of time what formats are supported is better.

Many file formats that are acceptable to Acrobat can also have conversion settings defined by you. Options for the conversion settings are the same as you have available with the Adobe PDF printer, as discussed earlier in this chapter, and they're accessible in the Preferences dialog box. Before you begin converting files to PDF with the Create PDF tool, be certain to choose Edit ➪ Preferences (Windows) or Acrobat ➪ Preferences (Macintosh) or use (Ctrl/⌘+K) and click the Convert To PDF item in the left pane. On the right side of the Preferences dialog box, you'll see a list of supported file formats, as shown in Figure 7.9 for Windows and Figure 7.10 for the Macintosh. As you can see at a quick glance, the Macintosh doesn't support as many file format conversions as Windows.

NOTE   Figure 7.9 shows file formats supported in Acrobat Pro Extended (Windows only). CAD formats such as 3D Studio Mesh, 3DXML, ACIS, CADDS, CATIA, CGR, Collada, I-DEAS, and so on are not supported in Acrobat Pro.

FIGURE 7.9

When using the Create PDF tool, you assign PDF Settings to different file formats in the Convert To PDF preferences. The Preferences dialog box lists all supported file formats in the Convert To PDF preferences.

FIGURE 7.10

Fewer file formats are supported on the Macintosh.

The file formats that are supported by Acrobat Pro (excluding those CAD formats supported by Acrobat Pro Extended) include the following:

- **Autodesk AutoCAD (Windows only).** Autodesk's AutoCAD files can be opened in Acrobat directly. Layered files are preserved and opened with data on different layers when layer data are created in the AutoCAD file. AutoCAD is also supported with the PDFMaker utility, which installs Acrobat tools and menu options in the authoring application at the time you install Acrobat.

- **BMP.** Bitmap is a file format that can be saved from many image-editing programs. Bitmap is also commonly referred to as a color mode in Photoshop. As a color mode, the file can be saved in other file formats. For example, a 1-bit bitmap image can be saved as a TIFF-formatted file. In regard to Acrobat, the bitmap file format that is capable of rendering images in 1-bit, 4-bit, 8-bit, and 24-bit color depths can be opened as PDF. Furthermore, a bitmap color mode saved as any of the compatible formats listed here can also be opened as a PDF.

- **CompuServe GIF.** CompuServe's Graphic Interchange Format (GIF) was developed years ago to port image files to and from mainframes and microcomputers. It remains a popular format for Web graphics, and the later version of GIF89a supports interlacing. If using Photoshop, you can either save in the CompuServe GIF87 format or use Photoshop's Save for Web command and choose the GIF89a format. Regardless of what format is used, Acrobat can import either as a PDF.

- **Flash.** Flash FLV and SWF (Windows and Macintosh) formats are supported in Acrobat 9.

- **HTML.** Hypertext Markup Language files are documents written in HTML for Web pages. You can open any HTML file and the file and file links convert to PDF. Clicking an HTML link in a converted file in Acrobat appends the linked file to the open document.

- **InDesign.** Adobe InDesign .indd files are supported. Click the Edit Settings button and you can choose from all the Adobe PDF Settings used by Acrobat Distiller. Note that exporting hyperlinks, interactive features, and layers require exporting from within Adobe InDesign.

- **JDF Job Definition.** You find JDF files in prepress workflows. The resultant PDF produces a standardized XML-based job ticket with information about the file for commercial printing uses, such as page size, crop and bleed areas, trapping, colorspace, and so on.

- **JPEG.** Joint Photographic Experts Group (JPEG) images are also used for Web graphics and file exchanges on the Internet. JPEG compression is a lossy compression scheme that can degrade images rapidly when they are compressed at high levels. These files are already compressed. Adding further compression with the PDF conversion options won't compress files smaller than the original compression. Inasmuch as the Settings button is active in the Open dialog box, you can't actually get more compression out of the file when converting to PDF.

- **JPEG2000.** JPEG2000 is a newer compression scheme that also offers a lossless option for compressing images. You can use JPEG2000 with lossless compression for the most discriminating quality required in high-end printing.

- **Microsoft Office (Windows only).** Microsoft Office files are from the office programs of Excel, PowerPoint, Project, Visio, Word, and Publisher. Each of the Office programs is listed separately because you can edit different settings that apply to each respective program. On the Mac, Office applications are not supported for conversion within Acrobat.

CROSS-REF For information related to settings adjustments with Microsoft Office programs, see Chapter 8.

■ **PCX.** PCX files are native to the PC and were commonly used as an extension for PC Paintbrush. Adobe Photoshop can export in PCX format, but today it is rarely used for any kind of image representation. The advantage you have in opening PCX files in Acrobat is when converting legacy files saved in this format. Rather than your having to do a two-step operation of opening a PCX file in an image editor and saving in a more common format for file conversions, Acrobat can import the files directly.

■ **PICT (Macintosh only).** The native Apple Macintosh equivalent to PCX (preceding bullet) is PICT (Picture). Photoshop supports PICT file exchanges in both opening and saving. However, Acrobat supports the format for conversion to PDF only via the From File or From Multiple Files commands.

■ **PNG.** Portable Network Graphics (PNG — pronounced *ping*) is a format enabling you to save 24-bit color images without compression. The format was designed for Web use and is becoming more popular among Web designers. Older Web browsers need a special plug-in in order to view the images, which have slowed its wide acceptance. Interestingly enough, PNG images are saved from image editors without compression, yet Acrobat can apply image compression when converting to PDF. You can use all the compression options in the Adobe PDF Settings dialog box with PNG images to reduce file sizes.

■ **PostScript/EPS.** PostScript and EPS files were formerly converted only with Acrobat Distiller. In Acrobat 8 you can open the files in Acrobat using the Create PDF tool and Distiller works in the background, handling the conversion to PDF.

■ **Text.** Text listed in the Convert to PDF preferences relates to plain text files. Unformatted text from word processors, text editors, and any file saved in a text-only format can be opened in Acrobat.

■ **TIFF.** Tagged Image File Format (TIFF) is by far the most popular format among the print people regardless of platform. TIFF files originate from image editors and scans. When scanning text you can save it as a TIFF, import the file in Acrobat, and then convert the image file to rich text with Acrobat's Text Recognition feature.

CROSS-REF For more information on Scan to PDF and Text Recognition, see Chapter 17.

■ **XPS.** XPS (XML Paper Specification) is a paginated representation of an electronic paper in an XML-based format. XPS documents can be converted to PDF from within Acrobat in Acrobat 8 and 9. The Settings adjustments let you choose from any of the Adobe PDF Settings, except the Standards formats such as PDF/A and PDF/X.

CROSS-REF For more on PDF Standards formats, see Chapters 10 and 32.

Applying settings

Many of the file formats supported by Acrobat can have PDF Options or other settings applied during conversion. These settings are available to all formats except CompuServe GIF, HTML, JDF Job Definition, JPEG2000, and Text. Depending on the file type to be created, you can edit the settings and apply some different options. You edit settings by selecting a file type from those listed in the Preferences dialog box shown in Figure 7.8 and clicking the Edit Settings button. If the settings cannot be adjusted, the Edit Settings button is grayed out.

Settings options for the different file formats include the following:

■ **Autodesk AutoCAD.** AutoCAD files can be converted with bookmarks and links, with layers, embedded data, and support for the new Engineering (PDF/E-1) standard as shown in Figure 7.11. The Adobe PDF Settings and Security options are also available with AutoCAD .dxf conversions. Click the Edit Settings button after selecting a file type to open the Adobe PDF Settings dialog box shown in Figure 7.11.

FIGURE 7.11

The Adobe PDF Settings for Autodesk AutoCAD documents dialog box offers an elaborate set of options for converting AutoCAD files.

In the Adobe PDF Settings for Autodesk AutoCAD documents dialog box, you find a Configuration Preferences button. Click the button and the Adobe PDFMaker dialog box opens where you can choose folders for AutoCAD resource directories. Choosing folders containing resource information instructs Acrobat to search the selected folders for embedding data when files are converted to PDF.

- **BMP/JPEG/PCX/PNG/PICT (Macintosh only)/TIFF.** These file formats all use identical settings. Whereas many other file formats use the Acrobat Distiller application in the background and have Adobe PDF Settings applied during file conversion, these image file formats don't use Distiller and no Adobe PDF Settings are applied during file conversion. Different conversion settings can be applied from the same options lists to each of the file types individually. Therefore, a BMP file, for example, can be converted with one level of image compression and a TIFF file can be converted with another level of compression.

All of these file formats are image formats and the types of settings you apply to them relate to image options, such as file compression and color management. The same set of options available from pull-down menus exists for all the different color modes listed in the Adobe PDF Settings dialog box shown in Figure 7.12.

FIGURE 7.12

Adobe PDF Settings for image files are available for file compression and color management.

NOTE   Inasmuch as the Adobe PDF Settings dialog box appears the same for all image formats, some options may be grayed out depending on the type of file to be converted. For example, TIFF images can have compression applied during PDF conversion, whereas JPEG images cannot. Therefore, the compression options for JPEG images are grayed out.

The top of the Adobe PDF Settings dialog box offers you options for file compression for monochrome (black-and-white line art), grayscale, and color images. The compression options you can select for each of these color modes include the following:

- **CCITT G4.** CCITT Group 4 compression is available only for monochrome images. This compression scheme, similar to the compression used by fax machines, works best for black-and-white images and results in smaller file sizes without data loss.

■ **JPEG (Quality: Low/Medium/High/Maximum).** For grayscale and color images you can select from several compression options to specify the acceptable amount of data loss. Medium is sufficient for almost any kind of desktop printing and low-end output. High and Maximum are more suited for high-end printing and digital prepress. Use JPEG for files that need to be exchanged with users of Acrobat versions below 6.0.

■ **JBIG2000 (Quality: Minimum/Low/Medium/High/Maximum).** JBIG2000 is a newer compression scheme that offers much better compression and image quality than JPEG. For the amount of compression to be applied, select from the Quality settings for Minimum, Low, Medium, High, and Maximum. High and Maximum settings result in very little data loss that can be visibly seen in printed documents and high magnification levels onscreen. Medium is sufficient for any kind of desktop printing, and the minimum and low compression levels are more suited to screen displays. Use JBIG2000 compression when exchanging files with users of Acrobat 6.0 and later.

■ **JPEG2000 (Quality: Lossless).** JBIG2000 lossless offers the most compression without data loss for grayscale and color images.

■ **ZIP.** ZIP compression is a lossless compression scheme. It works best where you have large areas of a common color — for example, a background with one color and a few foreground images with different colors.

The lower section of the Adobe PDF Settings dialog box handles Color Management. You have choices for applying settings to the three common color modes: RGB, CMYK, and Grayscale. The Other option at the bottom of the dialog box handles special color considerations such as spot colors you might find in duotones, tritones, and quadtones.

CROSS-REF For more information on color management and understanding different color modes, see Chapter 31.

The color management policies you can apply to each color mode are identical and they all include options from one of three choices:

■ **Preserve embedded profiles.** If you work with images that have been assigned a color profile, choosing this option preserves the profile embedded in the document. Theoretically, no color changes occur when porting the files across platforms and devices.

■ **Off.** If a color profile is embedded in an image, the profile is discarded.

■ **Ask when opening.** If you select this option, Acrobat prompts you in a dialog box to use the embedded profile or discard it. You can make individual selections as you open files.

CROSS-REF For more detail on color management and working with color profiles, see Chapter 31.

■ **Microsoft Office/PostScript/EPS.** The Microsoft Office and PostScript/EPS options include choices for Adobe PDF Settings and Adobe PDF Security. In addition, you have options for enabling accessibility, adding bookmarks from style sheets, converting an Excel workbook, and similar settings unique to each Microsoft program. With Microsoft

Publisher and PostScript/EPS files you have identical support for choosing Adobe PDF Settings and Security options. In Figure 7.13 the options are shown for Microsoft Word.

FIGURE 7.13

Settings for Microsoft Office applications include options for enabling accessibility and converting heads and styles to bookmarks.

CROSS-REF **Specific uses for enabling accessibility and adding bookmarks and links to PDFs from Microsoft Office applications a re covered in Chapter 8 and Chapter 25.**

After making choices for the options you want to use for file conversions, click the OK button in the Preferences dialog box. All the settings are set as new defaults until you change them. These settings are applied to documents you import from a file, from multiple files, and when you use the Open command in Acrobat.

Converting multiple files to PDF

The menu command you had available in Acrobat 7 for converting multiple files to PDF was Create PDF ⇨ From Multiple Files. This command disappeared from the Create PDF task button in Acrobat 8, and a new task button (Combine Files) was added in Acrobat 8 that has been rebranded as Combine in Acrobat 9. You can still use the Create task button in Acrobat 9 and choose Merge Files into a single PDF or use the Combine task button and choose the same menu command.

In Acrobat 9 you can convert multiple files to PDF or combine multiple PDF documents together in either a PDF file or a PDF Portfolio. Acrobat 8 supported PDF Packages that are gone in Acrobat 9 in favor of the new PDF Portfolios feature. Because there are so many options available when working with the Combine task button and menu commands, I added a chapter to cover all you need to know about working with both Combine and PDF Portfolios.

CROSS-REF **For more information on combining files into a single PDF document and creating PDF Portfolios, see Chapter 12.**

Converting Clipboard images

Suppose you have a map contained as part of a layout and you want to clip out the map and send it off to a friend for directions to an event, or perhaps you want to take a screenshot of an FTP client application to show log-on instructions, or maybe you want to clarify the use of a dialog box in Acrobat or another application. All of these examples and many more are excellent candidates for screen captures.

To capture a screenshot of the entire monitor screen in Windows, press the Shift+PrtScrn (Print Screen) or PrtSc keys. The keystrokes copy the current view of your monitor to the Clipboard. You can launch Acrobat or maximize it and select From Clipboard from the Create task button pull-down menu. The Clipboard data opens as a PDF document in the Acrobat Document pane. If you have a menu or dialog box open, the screen capture includes the foreground items in the capture like the screenshots shown throughout this book. Screens captured on Windows through these methods create 96-ppi (pixels per inch) images; captures on the Mac are 72 ppi.

If you want to capture a dialog box without the background on Windows, use Alt+PrtScrn (or PrtSc). The dialog box screenshots in this book were all taken by using these key modifiers.

NOTE Copying a screenshot to the Clipboard works with any program or at the operating system level when capturing desktop or folder views, accessories, or virtually any view you see on your computer monitor. Once data are on the Clipboard, you can open Acrobat and convert the Clipboard data to a PDF document.

Converting Clipboard images (Macintosh)

Converting Clipboard data on the Macintosh is handled exactly the same as when converting Clipboard data on Windows. However, if you want to first take a screenshot on the Mac, you use Acrobat instead of keystrokes.

NEW FEATURE On the Mac version of Acrobat you have additional commands for capturing screenshots. These commands are not necessary on Windows where your keyboard can easily capture screenshots; but on the Mac, no keystrokes exist for capturing a screen and saving the captured data to the Clipboard. All Mac keystrokes used for capturing screenshots record the data in a file saved to the Desktop as a .png file.

To capture a screen to the Clipboard, select File ⇨ Create PDF ⇨ and choose one of the three screen capture items you see listed in the menu as shown in Figure 7.14:

- **From Screen Capture.** Selecting this option is the same as using ⌘+Shift+3. The entire monitor window is captured and converted to PDF.

- **From Window Capture.** Using this option is like pressing ⌘+Shift+4 and then pressing the Spacebar. A camera icon appears as the cursor. Move the icon on top of a window and click to capture just that window.

- **From Selection Capture.** Using this option is like pressing ⌘+Shift+4, but without following with pressing the Spacebar. A crosshair appears as a new cursor. Click and drag the area to capture and release the mouse button. The selected area is converted to PDF.

When you select one of the options for capturing a screen, the screen capture is made and the capture is converted to PDF and opened in Acrobat.

FIGURE 7.14

Select File ⇨ Create PDF and select one of the three screen captures to convert a screen, window, or selection to PDF.

Taking snapshots

In the Select & Zoom toolbar, select the Snapshot tool and click on a PDF page. The entire page is copied to the Clipboard. You can then create a PDF file From Clipboard Image as described in the previous section. The page you create, however, is a raster image when you convert it to PDF. You lose all text attributes when copying a page in this manner. A better solution for converting an entire page is to use the Extract Pages command.

CROSS-REF For information on extracting pages, see Chapter 16.

The advantage of using the Snapshot tool is when taking a snapshot of a partial page in Acrobat. You can select the Snapshot tool and drag a marquee in an area you want to copy. When you release the mouse button, the selected area is copied to the Clipboard. Choose PDF from Clipboard from the Create task button to convert the selection to PDF. Again, you lose all type attributes, but you can use this method if retaining text is not an issue or if you want to crop an image. Using the Crop tool doesn't reduce the page size or file size of a PDF document. Using the Snapshot tool results in smaller file sizes when copying smaller sections of a PDF page.

Snapshots cannot be taken in password-protected files. If a file is encrypted, you need to eliminate the file encryption before using the Snapshot tool.

CROSS-REF For additional information on creating snapshots and setting resolution for snapshot captures, see Chapter 15. For information on using the Crop tool, see Chapter 16. For linking to snapshots, see Chapter 22. For information on file encryption, see Chapter 26.

Scanning to PDF

Click the Create task button and select PDF from Scanner. This option enables you to scan a document on your desktop scanner and convert to PDF. Acrobat 9 introduces some nice new features for scanning files into Acrobat that are covered in Chapter 17. Select Document ➪ Scan to PDF and the same dialog box opens as when using the Create > PDF from Scanner command.

CROSS-REF There's a lot to scanning from within Acrobat and converting scanned documents to recognizable text. Look over Chapter 17, where scanning and OCR conversion are covered.

Converting Web Pages to PDF

You use the Create PDF from Web Page menu command to convert Web pages to PDF. You can also use Create PDF task button and choose PDF From Web Page to convert Web pages hosted on Web sites or HTML files stored locally on your computer or networked servers.

Web Capture provides a complex set of preferences and tools with different options for converting Web pages, a Web site, Web links, HTML form fields, animations, or multiple sites to PDF. A captured Web site converts HTML, text files, and images to PDF, and each Web page is appended to the converted document. Conversion to PDF from Web sites can provide many opportunities for archiving information, analyzing data, creating search indexes, and many more uses where information needs to reside locally on computers.

Web pages containing animation such as Flash animation can be converted to PDF in Acrobat 6 and later. When animated pages are captured, the animation effects are viewed in the PDF file in any Acrobat viewer.

CROSS-REF For more information on converting Flash files to PDF, see "Converting Flash Files to PDF" later in this chapter.

Understanding Web site structure

To understand how to capture a Web site and convert the documents to PDF, you need a fundamental understanding of a Web page and the structure of a site. A Web page is a file created with the Hypertext Markup Language (HTML). There is nothing specific to the length of a Web page. A page may be a screen the size of 640 × 480 pixels or a length equivalent to several hundred letter-sized pages. Size, in terms of linear length, is usually determined by the page content and amount of space needed to display the page. PDF files, on the other hand, have fixed lengths up to 200 × 200 inches. You can determine the fixed size of the PDF page prior to converting the Web site from HTML to PDF. After the PDF page size is determined, any Web pages captured adhere to the fixed size. If a Web page is larger than the established PDF page, the overflow automatically creates additional PDF pages. Hence, a single converted Web page may result in several PDF pages.

Web site design typically follows a hierarchical order. The home page rests at the topmost level where direct links from this page occupy a second level. Subsequently, links from the second level refer to pages at a third level and so on.

When pages are captured with Acrobat, the user can specify the number of levels to convert. Be forewarned, however, that even two levels of a Web site can occupy many Web pages. The number of pages and the speed of your Internet connection determine the amount of time needed to capture a site.

Understanding captured pages structure

One or more levels can be captured from a Web site. You decide the number of levels to convert in the Create PDF from Web Page dialog box. PDF pages are converted and placed in a new PDF file or appended to an existing PDF file. One nice feature with Create PDF from Web Page is that it can seek out and append only new pages that have not yet been downloaded.

After pages are converted to PDF they can be viewed in Acrobat. Any URL links on the converted Web page are preserved in the resultant PDF and can be used to append files to the PDF or open the link destinations in your Web browser. The file types that can be converted to PDF include the following:

- **Adobe PDF format.** Although not converted to PDF because they already appear in the format, PDF pages can be downloaded with Create PDF from Web Page.

NOTE   XML forms created in Adobe LiveCycle Designer are not converted (nor do they appear in the Acrobat Document pane) when using the Create ⇨ PDF From Web Page command. Designer forms are added to blank pages converted to PDF as file attachments.

- **FDF.** Form Data Format files can be captured and converted to PDF. An FDF file might be form data exported from a PDF form.
- **GIF Image Format (Graphics Interchange Format).** GIF images, as well as the last image in an animated GIF, can be captured when you convert a Web site to PDF. GIFs, like JPEGs within the HTML file, can also appear on separate PDF pages.
- **HTML documents.** HTML files can be converted to PDF. The hypertext links from the original HTML file are active in the PDF document as long as the destination documents and URLs have also been converted.
- **JPEG (Joint Photographic Experts Group) image format.** Images used in the HTML documents are also captured and converted to PDF. JPEGs may be part of the converted HTML page. When captured, they can be part of a captured HTML page and can also appear individually on PDF pages.
- **Multimedia Content.** Multimedia content including Flash animation can be embedded in Web pages converted to PDF.
- **Plain text.** Any text-only documents contained on a Web site, such as an ASCII text document, can be converted to PDF. When capturing text-only files, you have the opportunity to control many text attributes and page formats.

- **PNG image format.** Portable Network Graphics (PNG) contained in Web pages can be converted to PDF just like GIF and JPEG images.

- **XDP.** Forms created with Adobe LiveCycle Designer can be saved in XDP (XML Data Package) that can be understood by an XFA plug-in.

- **XFDF.** XML-based FDF files typically exported from PDF forms can be converted to PDF.

- **Image maps.** Image maps created in HTML are converted to PDF. The links associated with the map are active in the PDF as long as the link destinations are also converted.

- **Password-secure areas.** A password-secure area of a Web site can also be converted to PDF. In order to access a secure site, however, you need the password(s).

Accepted file types and links

If a Web page link to another Web page or URL exists, it is preserved in the converted PDF document. Links to pages, sites, and various actions work similarly to the way they do directly on the Web site. However, if a PDF document contains a link to another PDF document, the converted file doesn't preserve the link. When the site is converted, the captured pages reside in a single PDF document. In order to maintain PDF links that open other PDF documents, the destination documents need to be captured as individual pages or extracted and saved from the converted pages.

Links to other levels are also inactive if they have not been converted during the capture. You can append individual linked pages to the converted PDF document by clicking Web links. Selections for converting individual links can be made available in a dialog box that opens after clicking a Web link. You can then append one or more links to the converted document. You can find the specifics on how to accomplish this task in "Appending pages" a little later in this chapter.

For executed animation, such as an animation from a GIF file or other programming application, the download contains only the last image in the sequence. A mouseover effect that changes an image is preserved in the converted PDF document as long as you download both the original image and the image associated with the mouseover. Additionally, you can capture sounds contained in documents.

You can also convert form fields to PDF, and field types such as radio buttons, check boxes, list boxes, and combo boxes often convert with the data intact. You might want to convert a form that has a list of countries and use the form field in your own PDF forms. The Acrobat implementation of JavaScript varies considerably from JavaScript written for Web pages, and therefore many JavaScripts do not work in converted Web pages.

CROSS-REF For more information on form field types, see Chapters 33 and 34.

For Web pages that contain non-English characters, you need to have the appropriate resources loaded in order to download and convert the files. Japanese characters, for example, require installation of the Far East language files and additional system files. Using non-English characters requires you to make additional settings choices for Language Scripts. The options are available in the HTML Conversion Settings dialog box in the Fonts and Encoding tab. For making adjustments in the HTML Conversion Settings dialog box, see the section "Conversion Settings" later in this chapter.

Bookmarks in converted pages

After you convert a Web site to PDF, you can edit the document in Acrobat as you would any other PDF. Links to pages become editable links — that is, you can modify their properties. When a site has been converted to PDF, all the PDF pages contain bookmarks linked to the respective pages, as shown in Figure 7.15. The first bookmark is a regular (unstructured) bookmark that contains the domain name from which the site was captured. All bookmarks appearing below the server name are structured bookmarks linked to the converted pages. With the exception of specific Web applications, you can edit these bookmarks like any other bookmarks created in Acrobat. Additionally, you can use structured bookmarks for page editing by moving and deleting the bookmarks and associated pages.

CROSS-REF For more information on bookmarks, see Chapter 22.

FIGURE 7.15

A captured Web site converted to PDF displays the domain name server as a normal bookmark and several structured bookmarks.

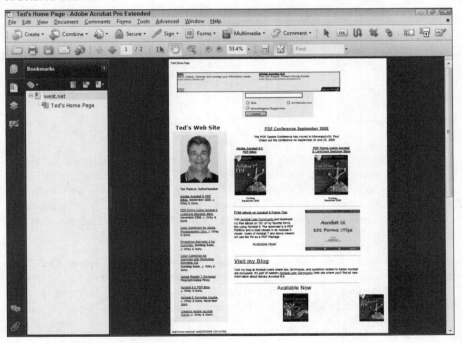

Capturing Web pages

To begin capturing Web pages, choose File ⇨ Create PDF ⇨ From Web Page. The Create PDF from Web Page dialog box opens, as shown in Figure 7.16.

NOTE Acrobat 9 doesn't have a Convert Web Page tool as was found in earlier versions of Acrobat. You can use the Fiule menu or click the Create task button and choose PDF from Web Page or choose Advanced ⇨ Web Capture ⇨ Create PDF From/Append Web Page.

FIGURE 7.16

When you select the From Web Page command, the Create PDF from Web Page dialog box opens.

In the Create PDF from Web Page dialog box, various settings determine many different attributes for how a Web page is converted to PDF and how it appears in the Acrobat Document pane. The first level of controls is handled in the Create PDF from Web Page dialog box. Additional buttons in this dialog box open other dialog boxes where you apply many more settings. If this is your first attempt at capturing a Web page, open the Create PDF from Web Page dialog box. Type a URL in the URL text box.

The default view shows you an abbreviated list of options as shown in the top of Figure 7.16. Click the Capture Multiple Levels button in the dialog box to expand the options as shown at the bottom of Figure 7.16. When the options are expanded, you can enter the number of levels in the Get only text box. Type 1 for the levels and click the Create button.

CAUTION Be certain the Levels text box is set to 1 on your first attempt. Entering any other value may keep you waiting for some time depending on how many pages download from additional levels.

Depending on the site, the number of different links from the site to other URLs, and the structure of the HTML pages, you often need to wade through the maze of dialog boxes that control settings for the PDF conversion from the HTML files. You don't need to memorize all of these settings; just use the following section as a reference when you capture Web pages.

Adjusting settings in the Create PDF from Web Page dialog box

The controls available to you in the Create PDF from Web Page dialog box begin with the URL you type in the URL text box. This URL determines the site where the pages, which are converted, are hosted. After you enter the URL, the remaining selections you need to set include:

■ **Get only *x* levels.** First, you need to click the Capture Multiple Pages button to expand the dialog box as shown in Figure 7.16. Appended pages can contain more than one level. The URL link may go to another site hosted on another server or stay on the same server. Select the levels to be downloaded by clicking the up or down arrows or entering a numeric value in the Get only text box.

CAUTION A Web site can have two levels of extraordinary size. If the Home page is on the first level and many links are contained on the Home page, all the associated links are at the second level. If you're downloading with a slow connection, the time needed to capture the site can be quite long.

■ **Get Entire Site.** When you select this radio button, all levels on the Web site are downloaded.

■ **Stay on same path.** When this option is enabled, all documents are confined to the directory path under the selected URL.

■ **Stay on same serve.** Links made to other servers are not downloaded when this option is enabled.

■ **Create.** When you're ready to convert Web pages from the site identified in the URL field box, click the Create button.

■ **Browse.** Selecting this button enables you to capture a Web site residing on your computer or network server. Click Browse to open a navigation dialog box where you can find the directory where HTML pages are stored and capture the pages.

■ **Settings.** Click this button to make choices for the conversion options. See "Conversion settings" later in this chapter.

TIP An alternative to using the Create from Web Page dialog box for a single Web page stored locally on your computer is to use drag and drop. Select the HTML document to convert to PDF and drag it to the top of the Acrobat window or program icon. If you have multiple HTML files to convert, you can also use the Create From Multiple Files menu command.

Although it may not be entirely practical, Web designers who are more comfortable with WYSIWYG (What You See Is What You Get) HTML editors than layout applications may find that creating layout assemblies in their favorite editor is beneficial. You can't get control over image sampling, but you can achieve a layout for screen display. Create the layout in a program such as Adobe Dreamweaver. When you're finished with the pages, launch Acrobat and select Create task button > PDF from Web Page. Click the Browse button in the Create PDF from Web Page dialog box and navigate to your HTML files. Click the Create button to convert your pages to PDF. You can send these pages as an email attachment to a colleague or print them to your desktop printer. One advantage for using this method is your client or co-worker can add comments with the Comment & Markup tools to mark corrections and/or revisions when reviewing Web page designs.

CAUTION Even though you may browse to a folder on your hard drive and convert a local Web site to PDF, any external links launch your Internet connection and capture pages on another site. If you want only local pages converted, be certain to click the Stay on same server button in the Create PDF from Web Page dialog box.

CROSS-REF You can create Web pages from tools installed by Acrobat in Microsoft Internet Explorer in Windows only. For information related to converting Web pages to PDF from within Microsoft Internet Explorer, see Chapter 27. For more information on using Comment & Markup tools, see Chapter 20.

Conversion settings

Clicking the Settings button in the Create PDF from Web Page dialog box opens the Web Page Conversion Settings dialog box, which has two tabs on which you supply file conversion attributes and page layout settings. The General tab deals with the file attribute settings, as shown in Figure 7.17.

FIGURE 7.17

The Web Page Conversion Settings dialog box offers controls for file types and how they will be converted to PDF.

Acrobat 9 limits your choices for file type conversion to HTML and plain Text. Earlier versions of Acrobat offered separate options for converting various image formats. Choose from the File Type menu either HTML or Text, and settings adjustments for these file types are further selected from another dialog box that opens when you click the Settings button.

At the bottom of the dialog box are three PDF Settings check boxes:

- **Create bookmarks.** When you enable this option, pages converted to PDF have structured bookmarks created for each page captured. The page's title is used as the bookmark name. If the page has no title, Acrobat supplies the URL as the bookmark name.

- **Place headers & footers on new page.** A header and footer are placed on all converted pages if this option is enabled. A header in the HTML file consists of the page title appearing with the <HEAD> tag. The footer retrieves the page's URL, the page name, and a date stamp for the date and time the page was downloaded.

- **Create PDF tags.** The structure of the converted PDF matches that of the original HTML file. Items such as list elements, table cells, and similar HTML tags are preserved. The PDF document contains structured bookmarks for each of the structured items. A tagged bookmark then links to a table, list, or other HTML element.

When you select HTML in the File Type menu and click the Settings button, a dialog box opens for HTML Conversion Settings, as shown in Figure 7.18.

FIGURE 7.18

When you select HTML in the File Description list and click the Settings button, the HTML Conversion Settings dialog box opens.

The two tabs in the HTML Conversion Settings dialog box are the General tab and the Fonts and Encoding tab. The first group of settings handles the general attributes assigned to the page layout:

- **Input Encoding.** Sets the Web page text encoding for body text, heads, and preformatted text. The default is consistent with the language you install. Other supported languages include Chinese, Japanese, Korean, and Unicode characters.

- **Language Specific Font Settings.** The items appearing under the Language Specific Font Settings section contain choices for font attributes and language choices. Choose from the menu options to select the Language, Body Text, and Base Font Size.

- **Default Colors.** Use this option to assign new default colors for Text, Background color, Links, and Alt Text. You can choose a color from a set of preset colors, or choose the option for custom colors, from a palette that opens after you click the swatch.

- **Force These Settings for All Pages.** HTML pages may or may not have assigned color values. When no color is assigned for one of these items, this setting defines the unassigned elements with the colors set in the Default Colors section. If this check box is enabled, all colors, including HTML-assigned colors, are changed to the Default Colors.

- **Multimedia.** Enables you to set options for handling multimedia clips. From the pull-down menu, you can choose from three options:

  - **Disable multimedia capture.** Movie and sound clips are ignored. Only the Web pages are converted to PDF and no links to the media are included in the capture.

  - **Embed multimedia content when possible.** Acrobat viewers 6 and above enable you to embed multimedia clips in the PDF document. Selecting this option captures the Web page and embeds any multimedia files that meet the compatibility requirements of Acrobat. Be aware that embedded multimedia files are available only to Acrobat viewers 6.0 or later.

  - **Reference multimedia content by URL.** The captured Web page contains a link to the URL where the multimedia files are hosted.

CROSS-REF   For more about the new features for handling multimedia in PDF documents, see Chapter 23.

- **Retain page background.** These include settings for the background colors used on the Web page, tiled image backgrounds, and table cells. When these check boxes are enabled, the original design is preserved in the PDF document.

TIP   If you find table cells, background colors, and tiled background images distracting when you're reading Web pages either in a browser or converted to PDF, disable the Background Options check boxes before converting to PDF. The original design is changed, but the files are easily legible for both screen reading and when printed.

- **Convert Images.** If checked, graphics are converted. If unchecked, the graphics are not converted.

To produce faster downloads, disable the Convert Images check box. The number of pages to be converted is significantly reduced, thereby reducing the amount of time to capture a Web site.

- **Underline Links.** Displays the text used in an <A HREF...> tag with an underline. This option can be helpful if the text for a link is not a different color than the body copy.

After making choices in the HTML Conversion Settings dialog box, click OK and you return to the Web page Conversions dialog box shown earlier in Figure 7.17. Choose Text from the File Type menu and click the Settings button to open options for handling text conversions as shown in Figure 7.19.

FIGURE 7.19

Choose Text from the File Type menu and click Settings to open the Text Conversion Settings dialog box.

Options for text conversions include many similar choices you have for HTML conversions with regard to Input Encoding, Language Specific Font Settings, and font color choices. One additional option appears for Wrap Lines at Margin that controls word wrap in unformatted text.

Page Layout conversion settings

All the settings discussed on the previous few pages were related to the General tab. In the Web Page Conversion Settings dialog box, another option is available. Page layout offers you options for describing the physical size and orientation of converted pages. Click the Page Layout tab and the Web Page Conversion Settings dialog box opens, as shown in Figure 7.20.

FIGURE 7.20

The Page Layout options are available from the Web Page Conversion Settings dialog box when you select the Page Layout tab.

Page layout attributes enable you to force long HTML pages into more standard page sizes for viewing or printing. If an HTML page spans several letter-sized pages, you can determine where the page breaks occur and the orientation of the converted pages. Many options are available in the Page Layout tab of the Web Page Conversion Settings dialog box:

- **Page Size.** This pull-down menu provides a variety of default page sizes. Acrobat supports page sizes from 1-inch square to 200-inches square. You can supply any value between the minimum and maximum page sizes in the Width and Height field boxes below the pull-down menu to override the fixed sizes available from the pull-down menu. To make changes in the field boxes, edit the text, click the up and down arrows in the dialog box, or click in a field box and press the up and down arrow keys on your keyboard. Press Tab and Shift+Tab to toggle between the field boxes.

- **Margins.** In the four Margins field boxes, you can set the amount of space on all four sides of the PDF page before any data appear. You make the changes for the margin sizes via the same methods described in the preceding bullet.

- **Orientation.** You choose portrait or landscape orientation from the radio button options. If a site's Web pages all conform to screen sizes such as 640 × 480, you might want to change the orientation to landscape.

- **Scale Wide Contents to fit page.** Once again, because HTML documents don't follow standard page sizes, images and text can be easily clipped when these documents are converted to a standard size. When this option is enabled, the page contents are reduced in size to fit within the page margins.

- **Switch to landscape if scaled smaller than.** The percentage value is user definable. When the page contents appear on a portrait page within the limit specified in the field box, the PDF document is automatically converted to a landscape orientation. The default is 70 percent. If the default value is used, any vertical page scaled lower than 70 percent is auto-switched to landscape as long as the orientation is selected for Portrait.

PDF WORKFLOW If your workflow is dependent on capturing Web pages routinely, then you'll want to use the same conversion settings for all your Web captures. Educational facilities, government agencies, research institutes, and large corporate offices may have frequent needs for archiving research information found on the Web.

Unfortunately, Acrobat makes no provision for saving and loading Web Capture settings established in the dialog boxes discussed in the preceding pages. To develop a workflow suited to organizations or workgroups, your alternative may be setting up a single computer dedicated to the task of capturing data from the Web. The computer needs to be licensed for Acrobat, but using a single computer ensures all Web captures are performed with the same conversion settings. Users with any Acrobat viewer can retrieve the PDF files that are captured across a network or intranet.

Determining download status

After you choose all settings and options in all the dialog boxes pertaining to converting Web sites to PDF, you can revisit the Create PDF from Web Page command from any one of the three methods discussed earlier. As pages are downloaded and converted to PDF, the Download Status dialog box opens displaying, appropriately, the download status. After the first page downloads, this dialog box, shown in Figure 7.21, moves to the background behind the converted Web pages.

CAUTION Web Capture places the converted PDF in memory and uses your hard drive space as an extension of RAM. The PDF is not saved to disk until you perform a Save or Save As operation. If your computer crashes or you quit without saving, the file is lost and you'll need to capture the site again.

The dialog box actually remains open, but hides behind the PDF pages being converted as the download continues. If you want to bring the Download Status dialog box to the foreground, choose Advanced ⇨ Web Capture ⇨ Bring Status Dialogs to Foreground. The dialog box opens in the foreground while Acrobat continues to convert pages.

FIGURE 7.21

The Download Status dialog box appears momentarily and then disappears as Acrobat continues to download pages and convert them to PDF.

Appending pages

When a PDF file is open in the Document pane, you can append pages from URL links by choosing Advanced ⇨ Web Capture and then selecting the appropriate choice from the submenu commands. The submenu options from the Advanced ⇨ Web Capture menu shown in Figure 7.22 relate to Web Capture features.

FIGURE 7.22

When you choose Advanced ⇨ Web Capture, the submenu displays options for treatment of Web captures.

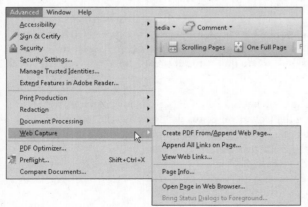

To append pages to the open PDF, make choices from the following selections in the Web Capture submenu:

- **Create PDF From/Append Web Page.** Selecting this option opens the Add to PDF from Web Page dialog box where you make attribute choices. The dialog box offers the same choices as originally displayed in the Create PDF from Web Page dialog box. When appending pages, you can change the attribute choices for all conversion options such as the URL, number of levels to be downloaded, and so on.

- **Append All Links on Page.** When you select this submenu option, no dialog box opens before the download commences. All Web links to other HTML pages are converted and appended to the PDF. Conversion settings are used from the last choices you made in the Create PDF from Web Page dialog box. If you need to change the conversion settings for links to other pages, you can use the View Web Links dialog box.

- **View Web Links.** The Select Page Links to Download dialog box opens when you select this menu command. This dialog box lists all Web links according to URL.

  The list contains an icon displayed at the far left of the URL list informing you that a link to the URL exists. You can select each of the items in the list. After you select a link, the Properties button on the right side of the dialog box becomes active. Click the Properties button and another dialog box opens. You'll notice in the next dialog box the options for conversion settings appear within three tabs. These options are the same as those you use with the Create PDF From Web Page command.

- **Page Info.** This option opens a dialog box displaying information about the current page viewed in the PDF file. As you scroll through pages, the page info changes according to the page viewed. The information supplied in the dialog box includes the original URL, title of the page, creation date, a description of the content, and the preferred zoom level for viewing.

- **Open Page in Web Browser.** Choose this option to open the linked page in your default Web browser. With new features in Acrobat 9 and Microsoft Internet Explorer you can capture a portion of a Web page if you only want partial data on the page converted to PDF.

CROSS-REF For more information on using the PDFMaker with Microsoft Internet Explorer, see Chapter 27.

- **Bring Status Dialogs to Foreground.** When capturing pages you may see the Download Status dialog box disappear behind the captured Web pages. While a capture is in progress, choose this menu command to bring the Download Status dialog box forward.

TIP You can also append Web pages by Control/Option+clicking a link on the PDF page. If the link destination is not contained in the PDF, the URL is contacted and the page is appended to the PDF. When you position the cursor over a link, the cursor displays a hand icon and index finger pointing upward. If a link has not yet been converted, the icon displays a W character inside the hand and a tooltip shows the URL where you can find the link. If the link has been converted to PDF, no plus (+) symbol and no URL are shown. If you want to open a link in your Web browser, click the link.

Locating Web addresses

Acrobat 7 through 9 are intelligent viewers when it comes to detecting URLs in text on PDF pages. You don't need a link or button to click URL text and launch your default Web browser. Acrobat 7 through 9 do that automatically for you.

In order for Acrobat viewers to recognize URLs in text, you need to be certain a Preference option is enabled in the General Preferences. Open the Preferences dialog box (Control/⌘+K) and click General in the left pane. Check Create links from URLs in the right pane as shown in Figure 7.23.

FIGURE 7.23

Open Preferences and check Create links from URLs from General.

If you prepare PDF files for users of earlier versions of Acrobat viewers, then you need to create links to URLs in text if you want users to click text to launch a Web page. You can easily create links from URLs in text using a simple menu command. But don't do this if you know your entire audience uses a 7.0 viewer or above. The more links or buttons you add to a PDF, the larger your file size will be.

The text must have a URL listing beginning with http://, https:, or www. In addition any email address such as designer@company.com will be recognized as a mailto: link that will open your default mail client. After the Web links are converted, you can also click the link and append pages by using Web Capture. PDF authors may also create Web links for end users when distributing files to others.

To create Web links on pages containing URLs, choose Advanced ➪ Document Processing ➪ Create Links from URLs. A dialog box opens, as shown in Figure 7.24.

In the Create Web Links dialog box, you specify page ranges for where Acrobat should create the links. Acrobat performs this task quickly and creates all links where the proper syntax has been used to describe the URL. If you want to delete links from a PDF document, open the Remove Web Links dialog box by choosing Advanced ➪ Document Processing ➪ Remove All Links. The Remove Web Links dialog box opens and you can supply page ranges for eliminating Web links.

FIGURE 7.24

FIGURE 7.24

The Create Web Links dialog box enables you to create Web links from text for user-defined page ranges in the open PDF file.

Converting Flash Files to PDF

It's been a few years since Adobe's acquisition of Macromedia. The engineers have been hard at work trying to integrate the Adobe programs with the newly acquired Macromedia programs. With the introduction of Acrobat 9, we begin to see the fruits of Adobe's labor — particularly with the integration of Adobe Flash and PDF.

NEW FEATURE 🖉 **Acrobat 9 has been introduced with a host of new features supporting Adobe Flash. In regard to converting file formats, you can convert Flash FLV and SWF files by using the Create > PDF from File command. In Addition, you'll find the new Flash tool in the new Multimedia toolbar for inserting Flash files into PDF.**

In Chapter 23 I talk about importing Flash video in PDF files and cover all the options choices you have when adding Flash files to PDF documents. For now, just know that you can convert a Flash FLV or SWF file to a PDF document by clicking the Create task button and choosing PDF from File. In the Open dialog box, select the file you want to convert and click Open. The Insert Flash dialog box opens as shown in Figure 7.25.

The Insert Flash dialog box provides many options choices for playing a Flash video, video frame appearance settings, launch attributes, and display quality. The initial pane in the Insert Flash dialog box offers a few choices for selecting some preset options from a pull-down menu. For customizing options click the Advanced button where the pane changes to display many more options for customizing the imports. For your first Flash import, leave the settings at the default and click OK. The Flash file opens in the Document pane as a new PDF, and the page size is determined by the size of the video file. In Figure 7.26 I imported an SWF file that was created with Adobe Flex.

CROSS-REF **For more information on all the settings available with Flash file imports, see Chapter 23.**

FIGURE 7.25

Open a Flash SWF file and the Insert Flash dialog box opens.

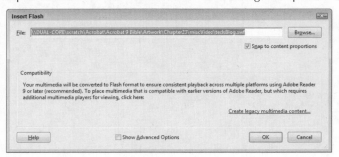

FIGURE 7.26

A Flash file converted to PDF

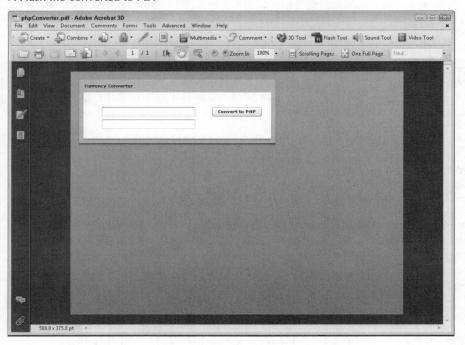

Creating PDFs from Templates

One thing I've wanted for a long time as a feature in Acrobat has been the ability to create a PDF document from a template. Many different authoring applications support creating new files from templates, but not Acrobat — at least not the way I want to create a new PDF. You might want to reuse a purchase order form, an invoice form, a vacation leave slip, or some other such document you work with on an ongoing basis.

The nice thing about using templates is that they prevent you from inadvertently overwriting the original. Every time you open a template it's a fresh original; and when you click the Save tool, you're prompted to type a new name. This feature, as well as having your templates always stored in the same location, helps save time and aggravation.

Why hasn't Adobe added a command like Create PDF ⇨ From Template? The primary reason is that not enough users have asked for this feature. I've asked Adobe for it for several years, but as a user of one, you can see how excited Adobe is to devote some engineering hours to the task.

But I'll bet many others have wanted such a feature in Acrobat, so I'm going to walk you through some steps so that you can actually create a workflow to create PDFs from template files. It might appear a little convoluted at first, but if you're like me, in the end it will save time over the hours you spend searching folders for files. The Adobe engineers didn't design this method to be used this way, but Acrobat is flexible enough that you can add some of your own personality in your workflow. If creating PDFs from templates is of interest to you, look over the following steps.

STEPS: Creating PDFs from templates

1. **Create a PDF document for use as a template.** You can use any kind of PDF document you like. In my example I use a form created in Adobe Designer.

CROSS-REF For more information on creating forms in Adobe Designer, see Chapter 35.

2. **Add a document title.** If using an Acrobat PDF form, open the Document Properties (Ctrl/⌘+D) and click Description. If using a LiveCycle Designer form, you can't edit the Document title. Skip this step when using Designer forms. In the Title field, type a descriptive title name to help identify your template.

CROSS-REF For more information on working with document properties and adding document titles, see Chapter 6.

3. **Save the PDF.** Select File ⇨ Save As and save the file to a location where you can find it easily — such as the Desktop. For the filename, use any name that easily describes the document. In my example I used `tedsInvoice.pdf` for the file name. Quit Acrobat.

4. **Copy the document to a templates folder.** On Windows, open the DocTemplates folder. The path is `C:/Program Files/Adobe/Acrobat 9.0/Acrobat/DocTemplates/[language]ENU`. Copy your template to the [language]ENU folder.

On the Macintosh open the `Macintosh/Applications/Adobe Acrobat 9.0 Pro` folder. Click the Adobe Acrobat Pro program icon once to select it. Open a context menu on the program icon (Ctrl+click) and select Show Package Contents. The folder that opens has two subfolders. Double-click the Contents folder to open it. Find the Resources folder and open it. Locate the en.lproj folder and open it. Inside this folder you find the DocTemplates folder. Open that folder and copy your template to this folder.

5. **Store the backup copy.** Copy your original file to a folder on your hard drive where you can easily return to it. If you upgrade your version of Acrobat, you can lose your DocTemplates folder. Try to keep some backup files in a folder location you can easily return to when upgrading the product.

6. **Launch Acrobat.** When Acrobat opens, click the Secure task button to open the pull-down menu and select Create Security Envelope, as shown in Figure 7.27. Creating a Secure Envelope was not designed for creating PDF files from custom templates, but we're going to fudge things a bit to create a workaround for not having a Create PDF⇨ From Template command.

FIGURE 7.27

Select Secure ⇨ Create Security Envelope to access your template.

CROSS-REF   For securing PDFs with Create Secure Envelope, see Chapter 26.

7. **Add a file attachment.** The Create Security Envelope Wizard opens, as shown in Figure 7.28. The first pane requires you to add a file attachment. You can't progress in the wizard unless you identify a file to be attached to the envelope. Don't worry — you delete the file attachment later. Click the Add File to Send button and attach any PDF document in the Choose files to enclose dialog box.

8. **Select your new template file.** Click Next and the second pane in the wizard opens. Here you'll find a list of default templates listed as `template1.pdf`, `template2.pdf`, and `template3.pdf`. Your new template should appear with a name you provided for your file name. If you added a document title to your file, the Document Title column lists your document title information. In my example, I used a form created in Adobe LiveCycle Designer. The Designer document title isn't reported in this wizard window, as you can see in Figure 7.29.

FIGURE 7.28

Click the Add File to Send button and select any PDF file to add as a file attachment.

FIGURE 7.29

Select your template file.

9. **Choose the delivery method.** Click Next and you arrive at the Delivery Method pane in the wizard. Click the first radio button on the right side of the pane for Send the envelope later.

10. **Choose a security policy.** Click Next and the Choose a security policy pane opens in the wizard. For a custom template used in this example, no security is applied to the document. Just click Next and a warning dialog box opens. Click Yes in the warning dialog box and you arrive at the final pane in the wizard.

11. **Finish the template creation.** Click Finish in the last pane and your document opens in Acrobat.

12. **Delete the file attachment.** Click the Attachments pane (the paper clip icon) and open a context menu on the file attachment listed in the Attachments pane, as shown in Figure 7.30. Select Delete to delete the attachment. Remember, you had to add a file attachment in order to proceed through the wizard window.

CROSS-REF For more information on working with file attachments, see Chapter 12.

FIGURE 7.30

Delete the file attachment and your template is ready for use.

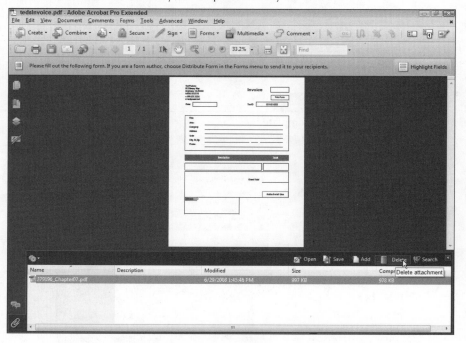

Your template is now ready for use. Make any changes you want on the file. When you click File ⇨ Save, a Save As dialog box opens prompting you to supply a filename. Your original file remains in the DocTemplates folder (until you upgrade Acrobat) and you can't inadvertently overwrite the file.

At first glance, working through these steps may seem a bit elaborate. However, once you create some template files and use them routinely, you can quickly find a template and work with it.

Note that you can always store a number of files in the Organizer, but using the Organizer files doesn't give you the same features as using template files where you are prevented from overwriting the file. You can also set file properties to Read Only to prevent overwriting, so the Organizer comes a little closer to being a good tool for this kind of workflow. However, if you work in an enterprise environment where many people use the same templates, copying custom DocTemplates folders to all users' computers is much easier than configuring individual Organizer file links.

 For more information on using the Organizer, see Chapter 5.

Summary

- You can create PDF documents with the Adobe PDF printer. You can use the Adobe PDF printer to apply a variety of Adobe PDF Settings to the PDF conversion. Adobe PDF Settings are used by Acrobat Distiller and the Adobe PDF Printer.

- You can use Acrobat to convert a variety of different native file formats to PDF using the Create PDF From File command. Multiple files can be converted to PDF and concatenated into a single document.

- You can use Acrobat to download Web pages and convert them to PDF. Web pages residing locally on hard drives can be converted to PDF. All Web page conversions preserve page and URL links.

- You can convert data copied to the system Clipboard to PDF on both Windows and Macintosh. Acrobat 9 provides new commands for Macintosh users to capture screen-shots and convert to PDF.

- A new feature in Acrobat 9 supports converting Flash video files via the Create PDF ⇨ From File command.

- Custom templates can be created using the Create Security Envelope features.

Chapter 8

Using Acrobat PDFMaker with Microsoft Programs

The last chapter covered PDF file creation from various programs and certain file types. Some of the PDF creation options you have from within Acrobat are also available directly from the authoring programs. Such is the case with the most popular Microsoft applications.

Adobe has devoted much development time to creating tools that easily convert most of the Microsoft applications to PDF along with certain other programs such as Autodesk AutoCAD discussed in Chapter 7 and Lotus Notes. With a one-button click in almost every Microsoft program you can convert your documents to PDF.

The common tool used in these programs is Acrobat PDFMaker created by Adobe Systems and automatically installed in every program supporting the tool when you install Acrobat.

In this chapter you learn how to use the PDFMaker tool in the most popular Microsoft programs.

Setting Up the Environment

This chapter is concerned with creating PDFs; therefore, no toolbars need to be loaded in the Toolbar Well as far as PDF creation is concerned. Later in this chapter, in the section "Working with comments in Microsoft Word" I talk about converting Word comments to PDF, but we'll load the Comment & Review tools when we come to that section. For now, don't be concerned about loading any toolbars. You'll load them when needed in the sections ahead.

Using Acrobat with Microsoft Word

Of all the Office applications, Microsoft Word gives you the best support for PDF file creation. Microsoft Word is the only word-processing application that provides access to the structural data of the document. The structural data of the Word document such as titles, heads, tables, paragraphs, figure captions, and so on can be converted to tagged bookmarks. Tagged bookmarks give you much more control over the PDF content. You can navigate to the element structures, and move, copy, extract, and delete pages through menu commands in the Bookmarks tab.

> **NOTE** Depending on the Acrobat viewer you use, the PDFMaker options are different. In Acrobat Pro Extended (Windows only), you have an Embed Video tool. This tool is not available in Acrobat Standard and Acrobat Pro.

With Word and all Microsoft Office programs you have several choices for PDF conversion. You can use the Create PDF From File command, use the Combine Task or command, drag and drop Microsoft Office files on the Acrobat Document pane, print to PostScript and convert the PostScript in Acrobat Distiller, and use a tool developed by Adobe called the Acrobat PDFMaker. This tool is installed in all Office programs and several other Microsoft programs.

> **CROSS-REF** For more information on Create PDF From File, see Chapter 7. For more on using Combine Task, see Chapter 12. For more on converting PostScript to PDF, see Chapter 10.

Of all the tools available to you, using PDFMaker is your best choice. Why? Because PDFMaker provides you with more options settings to control the attributes in the converted file. If, for example, you want to set up a hierarchy order for bookmarks to appear in the converted PDF, you need to use PDFMaker. If you want to convert PowerPoint files with transitions and media effects, you need to use PDFMaker. If you want to create layered PDFs from Microsoft Visio, again, you need PDFMaker. Other PDF conversion options don't provide you with support for many of these attributes.

PDFMaker offers several tools to control PDF file creation from within Microsoft Word and all other Microsoft programs that use the PDFMaker tools. After you install Acrobat and later open Word (or other Office programs), two Acrobat icons appear on the far left side of the toolbar and a menu command in MS Office 2003 products and you have a separate tab in the Office 2007 Ribbon.

> **NOTE** You have similar conversion options for using PDFMaker in Microsoft Office 2003 and Microsoft Office 2007. The user interface is obviously different between the different versions of Microsoft Office. This chapter covers using Office 2007, and all the screen shots appearing here were taken using Microsoft's newest Office release. If you're an Office 2003 user, you can find similar conversion settings using the Acrobat menu commands that are installed with PDFMaker.

Each of the Office 2007 programs display an Acrobat tab in the Ribbon after you install Acrobat on Windows. Click the Acrobat tab and you find several tools, shown in Figure 8.1, used for handling Adobe PDF files.

FIGURE 8.1

Click the Acrobat tab in the Ribbon to display all the tools installed with PDFMaker.

PDFMaker and the Macintosh

PDFMaker has vanished from the Macintosh in Acrobat 9. Earlier versions of Acrobat included the PDFMaker in the MS Office applications, but they weren't has robust as you had on Windows.

The alternative that consistently produces good PDF documents from MS Office programs is to use the File ⇨ Print command and print to a PDF document.

In any MS Office program choose File ⇨ Print. When the Print dialog box opens, choose Adobe PDF 9.0 from the printer pull-down menu. Open the PDF menu and choose Save as PDF. The Save dialog box opens. Name your file and locate a target folder and click Save.

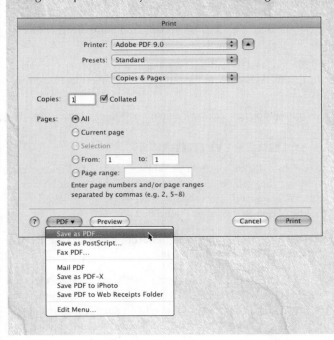

When you click the Acrobat tab in the Ribbon, you find the following tools.

- **Create PDF.** Click this button to open the Save Adobe PDF File As dialog box. Name the file and click Save to convert the Word document to a PDF.

- **Preferences.** Formerly called Conversion Settings in earlier versions of MS Office and PDFMaker, the Preferences button opens the Acrobat PDFMaker dialog box where you make choices for conversion options.

- **Create and Attach to Email.** Clicking this button performs two tasks. The Word document is converted to a PDF and the resultant PDF is attached to a new email message in your default email client.

- **Mail Merge.** A mail merge template is merged with a data file and the template and data are converted to PDF pages.

- **Create and Send For Review.** The Word file is converted to a PDF and opens in Acrobat with the Send for Shared Review dialog box open and ready for you to make a choice for starting a shared review on Acrobat.com or an internal server.

> **CROSS-REF**   For more information on Shared Reviews see Chapter 21. For additional information on using Acrobat.com, see Chapter 29.

- **Acrobat Comments.** Click Acrobat Comments and a pull-down menu opens with commands for Importing Comments from Acrobat, Continue Integration Process, Accept All Changes in a Document, Delete All Comments in a Document, and Show Instructions — a help information dialog box.

- **Embed 3D.** Click the Embed 3D tool and the Add 3D Data dialog box opens. You can choose a 3D file for embedding in the Word document and assign JavaScripts for setting different views and rotations.

- **Embed Video.** Click this button to embed an Adobe Flash animation or multimedia file.

Changing conversion settings (Windows)

PDFMaker uses the PDF Library to convert Office documents to PDF. When you click the Preferences button in the Ribbon, the Acrobat PDFMaker dialog box opens. In the dialog box, five tabs offer attribute choices for how the PDF is ultimately created. The tabs are Settings, Security, Word, Bookmarks, and new in Acrobat 9 you find Video as shown in Figure 8. 2.

> **CROSS-REF**   Acrobat Distiller is covered in Chapter 10. All subsequent references to Distiller in this chapter are explained in more detail in Chapter 10.

Different programs support many different features. For example, Microsoft Visio and Autodesk AutoCAD both support layers. Programs such as Word, Excel, and PowerPoint do not support layers. Excel supports workbooks, Word supports style sheets, and PowerPoint supports media and transitions. When you open PDFMaker in any program supporting the tool, you'll find different conversion settings options. Be aware that the dialog box you see in Figure 8.2 changes when opened in other programs. In Figure 8.2, the conversion settings options are specific only to Microsoft Word.

Click Preferences in the Ribbon and the Acrobat PDFMaker dialog box opens.

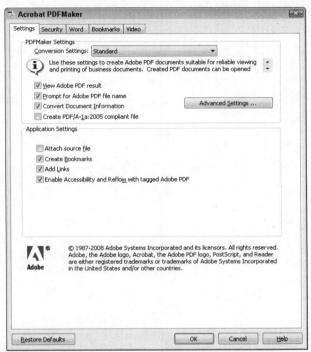

Settings

The Settings panel is the first of the four panels where you select options. At the top of the Settings panel is a pull-down menu for Conversion Settings. From this menu, you choose the same settings as are used by Acrobat Distiller to convert the file to a PDF. If you want to edit the settings or create a new Adobe PDF Setting, click the Advanced Settings button to open the Adobe PDF Settings Adobe PDF Settings shown in Figure 8.3 enable you to make choices for attributes used to convert the document to a PDF.

FIGURE 8.3

The Settings panel offers you choices for selecting the Adobe PDF Settings used to convert the file.

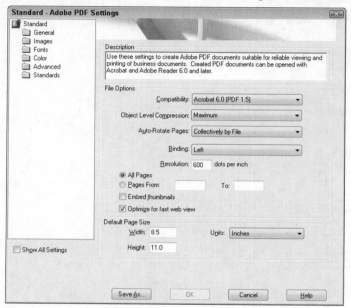

Options in the Settings panel are as follows:

- **View Adobe PDF result.** When the PDF is created, the document opens in Acrobat if this check box is enabled. If it's disabled, the PDF is created and the Word file remains in view.

- **Prompt for Adobe PDF filename.** If this check box is enabled, you won't inadvertently overwrite a file with the same name. Leaving this check box enabled is a good idea.

- **Convert Document Information.** This option ensures document information created in Word is added to the PDF Document Properties.

- **Create PDF/A-1a:2005 Compatible file.** Clicking this option automatically changes the Conversion Settings to the PDF/A-1a:2005(RGB) Adobe PDF Setting. The files are made compliant with PDF/A. Note that using PDF/A produces a PDF with Acrobat 5 compatibility; therefore, any features specific to PDF version 1.5 (Acrobat 6 and greater compatible) files are lost in PDF/A-compliant files.

- **Attach source file.** If you want to attach the Word file from which the PDF was created, enable this check box and the Word file is added as a file attachment.

- **Create Bookmarks.** Bookmarks are created from Word style sheets. Select this check box to convert styles and headings to Bookmarks. Make selections for what styles and headings to convert to bookmarks in the Bookmarks panel.

- **Add Links.** This option ensures that hyperlinks created in Word are converted to links in the PDF document.

- **Enable Accessibility and Reflow with tagged Adobe PDF.** This option creates document structure tags. Accessibility for the visually challenged and developmentally disabled that is contained in the Word document is preserved in the PDF. Reflowing text enables the Acrobat user to use the Reflow view. As a matter of default, leave this check box enabled. Tagged PDF documents also help you export the PDF text back out to a word processor with more data integrity than when exporting files without tags.

NOTE If you enable accessibility and reflow, the file sizes of your PDF documents are larger compared to files exported to PDF without accessibility and tags. If you need to produce the smallest file sizes for specific purposes where you know accessibility and preserving structure are not needed, disable the check box.

Security

Click the Security panel to open options for security settings. Security options for permissions are available only for High-Bit encryption (128-bit RC4). If you choose to add security from the Word options, the PDF document is compatible with Acrobat 5.0 viewers and greater. If you need additional security controls available in Acrobat 6, Acrobat 7, and Acrobat 9 compatibility options, apply the security in Acrobat.

CROSS-REF For specific definitions of the security options, see Chapter 26.

Word

Click the Word panel to choose options for Word content, as shown in Figure 8.4.

FIGURE 8.4

The Word panel contains items specific to some of the content in Word that can be converted in the resulting PDF document.

Options on the Word panel are as follows:

- **Convert displayed comments to notes in Adobe PDF.** Notes can be converted to annotation comments that will appear in a text note in the PDF file.

- **Convert footnote and endnote links.** Bookmark links are added for all footnotes and endnotes.

- **Enable advanced tagging.** The tagging features available in Word that export to PDF have been split for accessibility with the Enable Accessibility and Reflow with tagged Adobe PDF files you see in Figure 8.4. This option adds settings *over and above* document accessibility. Checking this box adds document structure for character styles such as underlines, superscript, subscript, outline, strikeouts, and so on that can be useful when exporting PDF files back to text such as exporting to Word or RTF formats. The downside for selecting this check box is that the PDF conversion will take longer and the file sizes will grow. Unless you anticipate a need for adding this kind of document structure in your converted files, leave the check box unchecked.

- **Comments.** The lower window lists all comments by author in the file. If you check the box in the Include column, the comments are converted to Acrobat comments. The Notes open column enables you to set the default for note comments with open note pop-up windows.

> **TIP** If you have a document with comments added by several individuals and you want each person's comments appearing with different note colors, click the icon in the Color column to change color. Keep clicking the icon to continue changing color. Word scrolls through eight different colors as you keep clicking the mouse.

Bookmarks

In the Bookmarks panel, there are three items that can determine what bookmarks will be created in the PDF file:

- **Convert Word Headings to Bookmarks.** Word headings can be converted to bookmarks. In the box below the check boxes, a list of all headings and styles contained in the Word document appears. Click the box under the Bookmark column to determine what heads to convert to bookmarks.

- **Convert Word Styles to Bookmarks.** You can select user-defined styles for conversion to bookmarks. Scroll the list of elements and place a check mark for the styles you want to convert.

- **Convert Word Bookmarks.** Converts all bookmarks created in Word to PDF bookmarks.

Click the number appearing in the Levels column and a pop-up menu becomes visible. Click the down-pointing arrow to open the menu and select the level of nesting for the bookmarks as shown in Figure 8.5. The nesting order you determine here in the Acrobat PDFMaker settings dialog box determines the order of parent/child relationships in the Acrobat Bookmarks panel when the file is converted to PDF. (See Figure 8.6.)

FIGURE 8.5

The Bookmarks panel offers three choices for determining what bookmarks are created in the PDF file. Clicking a number in the Levels column permits you to determine parent/child relationships for bookmarks.

FIGURE 8.6

Bookmarks from subheads are nested as child bookmarks below the top-level heads according to the Level order specified in Acrobat PDFMaker.

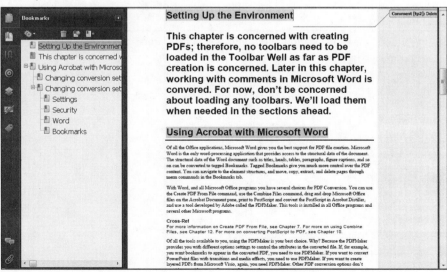

CAUTION If you select the Convert Word Styles to Bookmarks check box and you have a number of style sheets in your Word document, you end up with a huge list of bookmarks. At some point the bookmarks will appear overwhelming and difficult to manage. Unless you have a definite need for converting styles in some Word documents, stick with the Convert Word Headings to Bookmarks option and convert the heads to bookmarks.

After you select the options in the Acrobat PDFMaker dialog box, click the Convert to PDF tool or select the menu option to convert the file. In Figure 8.6, I converted a file having three levels of heads. Notice that when the Bookmarks panel is open, you see the bookmarks nested into parent/child relationships.

CROSS-REF For more information on Adobe PDF bookmarks and nesting bookmarks into parent/child relationships, see Chapter 22.

Video

The Video panel in Acrobat PDFMaker offers some choices for importing video files in a Word document. Click the Video tab and the options shown in Figure 8.7 include:

- **Location.** The video can be stored in the same folder as the Word document or a folder you choose by clicking the Browse button.
- **Quality.** From the Video Quality pull-down menu choose a quality setting for the video playback. If the video file is interlaced, an option to deinterlace the file is included below the menu.
- **Encode Audio.** Choose from options in the pull-down menu for audio quality.

FIGURE 8.7

Choose from options in the Video panel for location and quality settings for imported video files.

Working with comments (Windows)

Move to the right on the Ribbon and in the Review and Comment area you find Acrobat Comments. Clicking this button opens a pull-down menu as shown in Figure 8.8. The commands in the menu address merging your PDF comments back into the original Microsoft Word document. The menu items are as follows:

Click Acrobat Comments to open the pull-down menu for managing comments.

- **Import Comments from Acrobat.** This is a *round trip* process — that is, you need to start with a Microsoft Word document, send it out to be reviewed, and then merge the received comments back into the Word file. In addition, when you created the PDF file in the first place, you must use PDFMaker. When you select the menu item, the Import Comments from Adobe Acrobat help window opens. Read the helpful tips on how to import comments and click OK to proceed. The next dialog box that opens is Import Comments from Adobe Acrobat, as shown in Figure 8.9. In the dialog box, you make choices for what files to select, what comments to import, and whether you want to filter the comments.

The Import Comments from Adobe Acrobat dialog box offers choices for file selection and the comment types to import into the Word document.

■ **Continue Integration Process.** This continues the integration of PDF comments in the Word document for text edits such as inserts and deletions. If review tracking is on, you can merge tracked changes.

■ **Accept All Changes in Document.** After the comment integration, select this menu command to accept the comments. Comments such as text marked for deletion are deleted; text marked with insertion adds the inserted comments; and so on.

■ **Delete All Comments in Document.** All comments imported from the PDF document are deleted from the Word file.

■ **Show Instructions.** The dialog box that opens when you choose the Import Comments from Acrobat command (see the first bullet in this list) also opens when you choose the Show Instructions menu command.

To make the process for importing comments from Acrobat easier (or Exporting comments from Acrobat to Word), take a look at the steps that follow, which describe a workflow for exchanging comments in Word and PDF documents.

STEPS: Integrating Acrobat comments in Word documents (Acrobat Pro and Pro Extended — Windows Only)

1. **Convert a Word document to PDF using the PDFMaker Create PDF Tool.** Be certain to use PDFMaker to convert your Word file to PDF.

CAUTION You must be certain to check Enable Accessibility and Reflow with tagged Adobe PDF in the Settings panel in order to export/import comments between Acrobat PDF and Word files.

2. **Mark up the PDF file in Acrobat using the Comment & Markup tools.** Be certain to use the Text Edits tools in the Comment & Markup toolbar to comment on the PDF file. Text Edit comments get merged directly into the Microsoft Word document stream, whereas other comments are just applied as note comments in Word.

CROSS-REF For more information on commenting and using the Text Edits tools, see Chapter 20.

3. **Initiate an export of comments to Word.** You can export comments from Acrobat to Word or Import comments in Word from a PDF file. In Acrobat you use the Comments ⇨ Export Comments to Word menu command. In Word you use the Acrobat Comments ⇨ Import Comments from Acrobat menu command. Either menu selection opens the Import Comments from Adobe Acrobat dialog box. If you start in Acrobat, Microsoft Word is launched and the Import Comments from Adobe Acrobat Wizard is handled from within Word. The first dialog box describes the process for integrating your PDF comments back to a Word document. Click OK after reading the help information.

4. **Choose files and comment types.** The second dialog box is the Import Comments from Adobe Acrobat Wizard shown earlier in Figure 8.9. Choose the Word file you want to use for exporting comments and click OK.

5. **Import the comments.** Your comments are imported into the Word document in a seamless operation. After all the comments are imported you should see the Successful Import dialog box open, as shown in Figure 8.10.

FIGURE 8.10

If your comments are successfully imported, the Successful Import dialog box opens.

6. **Integrate Text Edits.** Open the Acrobat Comments pull-down menu in the Ribbon and choose Continue Integration Process. Another dialog box opens as shown in Figure 8.11 where you can selectively choose comments to integrate or click the Apply All Remaining button to integrate all Text Edits. After the comments are integrated another dialog box opens and reports the results. Click Done and your integration is complete.

FIGURE 8.11

Click Apply to apply each comment as you review it in the New Text window, or click Apply All Remaining to import all Text Edits comments.

Working with custom page sizes

The most common page size and output for Word files is standard letter or A4 page sizes that are printed to desktop printers. On occasion, documents are created for output to commercial printing equipment. Manuals, reports, books, and more are sometimes designed for printing on commercial printing machines for offset press or on-demand printing.

PDF WORKFLOW Whereas Microsoft Word is a superb word processor, the program was never designed to be a page layout application to prepare files for commercial printing equipment. Word does not support roll-fed machines, adding printer's marks, managing color, separating color images, halftone frequencies, and so on, that are all part of the tools you find in professional layout applications such as Adobe InDesign. When choosing a program where files need to be delivered to commercial print shops, use a program like Adobe InDesign or Microsoft Publisher.

A few problems arise when Word files are created for this kind of output. The first problem is outputting documents using nonstandard page sizes. If you set up a document for a 7-x-9-inch page size for example, Word doesn't have a matching page size available in the print dialog box. As a result, you need to create a custom page size to format the document and print the custom-formatted page size.

Second, files need to be printed with crop marks so the print shop knows where to cut the paper when it comes off press. As a word processor, Word is not designed for use as a page layout program. Professional layout programs such as Adobe InDesign have all the tools and features you need to print documents with crop marks and other attributes designed for output on commercial printing equipment.

One solution is to take the Word document and import it into a program such as Adobe InDesign. But doing so requires a lot of work on your part. You have to reformat the document for a custom page size before you can print it. Fortunately, there's a much easier way. You can format the document in Word with a custom page size, export to PDF using PDFMaker, and use Acrobat to create the necessary crop marks and make the file print-ready.

The steps for setting up custom page sizes differ a little between Windows and the Macintosh. Let's first take a look at creating custom pages on Windows, and then I'll move on to creating custom page sizes on the Mac.

Creating custom page sizes on Windows

On Windows you have two different ways to configure Word for formatting and printing custom page sizes. You can use the Page Setup dialog box in Word to create a custom page size, or you can add a custom page size to your printer driver. Adding a custom page size to the printer driver makes that page size available to all applications using the driver. Creating the custom page size in Word limits the page size to Word files.

For a more flexible use, create a custom page size in the Adobe PDF printer driver and you'll have the page size available for use with all applications. Here's how to do it.

STEPS: Creating custom page sizes in the print driver

1. **Open the Adobe PDF Properties.** From the Start menu select Settings ➪ Printers and Faxes. You should see icons for all printing devices installed on your computer when the Printers and Faxes window opens. Among the printer drivers, you'll find the Adobe PDF printer driver. Select this driver and either select File ➪ Properties in the Printers and Faxes window, or right-click the Adobe PDF driver to open a context menu and select Properties as shown in Figure 8.12.

FIGURE 8.12

Open a context menu on the Adobe PDF Printer and select Properties.

2. The Adobe PDF Properties dialog box opens as shown in Figure 8.13. Note that the default tab selected in the Adobe PDF Properties dialog box is the General tab.

3. **Open the Printing Preferences.** In the Adobe PDF Properties dialog box, shown in Figure 8.13, click the Printing Preferences button. The Adobe Printing Preferences dialog box opens. In this dialog box, click Adobe PDF Settings, as shown in Figure 8.14.

FIGURE 8.13

The Adobe PDF Properties dialog box default view is the General tab.

FIGURE 8.14

Click the Adobe PDF Settings tab in the Adobe PDF Printing Preferences dialog box.

4. **Add a new custom page size.** Click the Add button and the Add Custom Paper Size dialog box opens as shown in Figure 8.15.

FIGURE 8.15

Click Add to open the Add Custom Paper Size dialog box.

5. **Edit the Custom Page Size.** Type the width and height values in the Width and Height text boxes and select the unit of measure from the three choices in the Unit section of the dialog box. Type a name for the custom paper size in the Paper Name text box. Use a name that defines the page size as you see in Figure 8.15.

6. **Save the new custom page size.** Click the Add/Modify button in the Add Custom Paper Size dialog box and you return to the Adobe PDF Printing Preferences dialog box. Click OK and your new custom page size is available each time you use the Adobe PDF printer driver.

7. **Set up a Word document with a custom page size.** Open Microsoft Word and open a file or create a new document.

   By default Word 2007 doesn't have a Microsoft Menu ⇨ Page Setup command. You may need to open the Microsoft menu and choose Word Options. In the Word Options window click Customize and select Page Setup in the left column. Click the Add button to move the Page Setup command to the Quick Access toolbar. Click OK and click the Page Setup button in the Quick Access toolbar. In the Page Setup dialog box, choose the custom page size you want from the Page Size pull-down menu as shown in Figure 8.16.

8. **Convert to Adobe PDF.** Click the Create PDF tool in the Acrobat Ribbon. If you enabled View Adobe PDF result in the Acrobat PDFMaker Settings tab, the resulting PDF opens in Acrobat.

NOTE Creating custom page sizes is particularly important for programs such as Microsoft Visio, Microsoft Project, and AutoCAD where nonstandard sizes are commonly used. Acrobat supports a page size of up to 200 inches square. Make certain you have the proper page size defined for the Adobe PDF printer before attempting to Create PDF.

FIGURE 8.16

In Microsoft Word, open the Page Setup dialog box and choose the new paper size in the Paper size pull-down menu.

Creating custom page sizes on the Macintosh

The process for creating custom page sizes on the Mac is much the same as on Windows, but the dialog boxes are a little different. For custom page size creation on the Mac, follow these steps:

STEPS: Creating custom page sizes on the Macintosh

1. **Open Microsoft Word.** You can create a custom page size on the Mac from within any program. Because we're talking about Word here, I'll use Word as my starting point with a document open in the Word window that I want to reformat for a custom page size.

2. **Open the Page Setup dialog box.** Select File ➪ Page Setup to open the Page Setup dialog box. In the Page Setup dialog box select Adobe PDF 9.0 from the Format for pull-down menu. Open the Paper Size pull-down menu and select Manage Custom Sizes, as shown in Figure 8.17. Making the menu selection for Manage Custom Sizes automatically opens the Custom Page Sizes dialog box.

3. **Create a new custom page size.** Click the plus (+) symbol in the lower left corner of the dialog box. Your new paper size is listed as Untitled. Double-click Untitled in the list to select the name, and type a descriptive name for your new page size. My preference is to use the paper sizes for names, as shown in Figure 8.18. Type the Width and Height values in the text boxes up in the top-right corner of the Custom Page Size dialog box.

FIGURE 8.17

Format the page size for the Adobe PDF 9.0 printer driver and select Manage Custom Sizes from the Paper Size pull-down menu.

FIGURE 8.18

Click the plus (+) symbol, type a name, and edit the Width and Height text boxes.

4. **Use a custom page size.** Click OK in the Custom Page Sizes dialog box and you return to the Page Setup dialog box. Select the Adobe PDF 8.0 printer and your new page size in the Paper Size pull-down menu. Your document is then reformatted for the custom page size.

5. **Export to PDF.** Click the Convert to Adobe PDF tool and your Word file is converted to PDF using the new custom page size.

CAUTION If you begin with a document created on a standard letter or other page size and reformat the document to fit on another page size, you should review all document pages. As the document is reformatted you may find page breaks, headers and footers, tables, and other document elements needing some adjustments before converting to PDF.

Adding crop marks to PDFs

Regardless of whether your files are formatted for custom page sizes or standard page sizes, you need to add crop marks if your files are going to be printed on offset press or many on-demand printing devices. For some on-demand equipment such as Xerox DocuTechs and other devices that print on single-sheet standard page sizes, you won't need to add crop marks.

When crop marks are needed for printing your files, follow these steps to add crop marks in Acrobat.

STEPS: Adding crop marks to PDF documents (Acrobat Pro and Pro Extended only)

1. **Open a document in Acrobat Pro. Or Pro Extended** For these steps you need Acrobat Pro or Acrobat Pro Extended (Windows). Acrobat Standard (Windows) does not have a Print Production toolbar.

2. **Open the Print Production toolbar.** Open a context menu on the Acrobat Toolbar Well and select Print Production to open the Print Production toolbar. The Printer's Marks tool and the Crop tool shown in Figure 8.19 are needed to add printer's marks to your document.

FIGURE 8.19

Open the Print Production toolbar from a context menu opened on the Toolbar Well.

---

3. **Add Printer's Marks.** Click the Add Printer Marks tool in the Print Production toolbar and the Add Printer Marks dialog box opens. You can selectively add the type of marks you want to appear on your document by checking the various marks check boxes. In this example, I click the All Marks check box and all printer's marks are added to the file. For the Page Range, leave the default All selection checked if you want all pages to appear with the printer's marks as shown in Figure 8.20.

FIGURE 8.20

Check the boxes for the marks you want to appear on the PDF document and select the page range.

4. **Crop the pages.** When you click OK in the Add Printer Marks dialog box, you won't see any changes in your document — that's because the printer marks exist outside the page dimensions. You need to enlarge the pages so the crop marks are visible. To make the document pages appear larger, click the Crop Pages tool in the Print Production toolbar and the Crop Pages dialog box opens, as shown in Figure 8.21.

Click the Custom radio button and type a width and height larger than the page sizes. As a standard page size to accommodate crop marks, add 1 inch to the page width and height. In my example, my document is 7 × 9 inches. Therefore I added 8 inches for the width and 10 inches for the height. Over in the Page Range area of the Crop Pages dialog box, click All to apply your marks to all pages.

FIGURE 8.21

Click Custom and type the new dimensions for width and height. Click All to apply marks to all pages.

5. **Preview the PDF document.** Click OK in the Crop Pages dialog box and the printer's marks appear on all pages in the document. In Figure 8.22, the printer's marks are shown on the first page in my document.

CROSS-REF For more information on using the Print Production tools, see Chapter 32.

TIP When you add printer's marks to a document, the order in which you use the Print Production tools is critical. You must first use the Add Printer's Marks tool followed by using the Crop tool. This order may seem counterintuitive and confusing. To help you keep the order straight, just remember to use the tools in the same order they're displayed in the Print Production toolbar. The Add Printer's Marks tool appears first, followed by the Crop tool.

FIGURE 8.22

Click OK in the Crop Pages dialog box and the printer's marks appear on pages in your PDF.

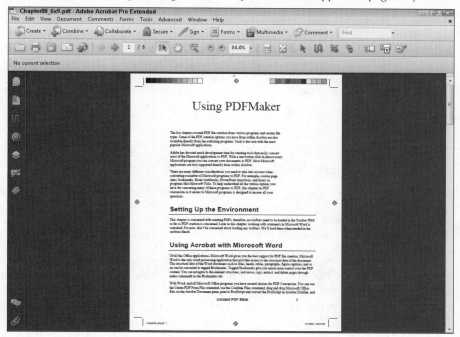

Using graphics in Word

Microsoft Word is first and foremost a word processing program. Inasmuch as many features have been added to the program to take it well beyond simple word processing, the program is not designed to be a layout program. Word lacks support for many features you find with layout programs such as supporting color management, printing color separations, controlling halftone frequency, and more.

CROSS-REF For more information on terms used in commercial printing such as color profiling, color separations, and halftoning, see Chapter 32.

As a matter of practice, you should avoid creating files for press, in particular for color separations, in Word. If it's an absolute must that you need to use Word for commercial printing, then you need to be aware of some things to avoid. These items include the following:

- **Use RGB images.** Be certain to not use Indexed color images in your Word files. Make certain all your images are edited and saved in an RGB color space and let the RGB to CMYK conversion take place at the time the files are printed.

- **Use TIFF format for raster images.** Avoid using GIF, JPG, PNG, PCX, PICT, BMP, and other file formats. Use only TIFF as the format to import photos and raster images.

- **Use EPS for vector objects.** Again avoid using any other formats for vector objects and use only EPS for these graphics. Do not use the clip art you can import in Word. Create vector objects in a program such as Adobe Illustrator and save as EPS.

- **Do not paste images in Word.** Pasting images in Word converts files to Windows Metafile (Window) or PICT (Macintosh). These file formats won't print properly on commercial printing equipment.

Again, I would caution you against using Word for printing files with graphics on commercial printing equipment. When you have no other alternative, make sure to follow the preceding tips.

CROSS-REF   **For more information on graphic file formats and commercial printing, see Chapters 7 and 32.**

Converting Snippets to PDF

You may have a passage of text, a graphic image, a table, a footnote or some other portion of data on a page in MS Word and want just a selected area converted to a PDF document. If this is your task, just select the data you want to convert in your Word document and click the Create PDF button in the Ribbon. The Acrobat PDFMaker dialog box opens. Select Options.

The default for the Page Range is All, which of course means that all pages in the Word document are converted to PDF when you click OK. Notice the Selection radio button in Figure 8.23. When you select any data in a Word file, the Selection radio button becomes active. Click this button and your selected data are converted to PDF.

FIGURE 8.23

Select data in a Word document and click Create PDF in the Ribbon. Select Options. Click Selection in the Acrobat PDFMaker dialog box to convert the selection to a PDF file.

Converting Microsoft Excel Files to PDF

When converting Microsoft Excel files, as with any other program using the PDFMaker, you'll want to open the Acrobat Ribbon. As is the case with Word, the tools are installed in Excel after you install Acrobat. When you open the Acrobat Ribbon and compare the tool choices with the same Ribbon opened in Word, you see a few differences between the Ribbon tools shown for Word in Figure 8.1 and the Ribbon tools for Excel shown in Figure 8.24.

FIGURE 8.24

The Acrobat menu as shown in Microsoft Excel

Notice the Mail Merge and Acrobat Comments tools are unique to Word and don't appear in the Excel menu. The remaining tools are the same as you find in Word; however, when converting to PDF, you have some different options to choose from for creating PDF files from Excel.

Open the Acrobat PDFMaker dialog box by selecting Preferences. The Acrobat PDFMaker dialog box opens, as shown in Figure 8.25.

Compare Figure 8.25 with the Acrobat PDFMaker dialog box opened in Word in Figure 8.2. All the settings are identical in the Excel Acrobat PDFMaker dialog box as the same dialog box opened from Word with the exception of the last three items:

- **Convert Comments.** Check this box when you want Excel comments converted to comment notes in the resultant PDF file.
- **Fit Worksheet to a single page.** Check this box to avoid tiling individual worksheet pages.
- **Fit to paper width.** Check this box to fit the spreadsheet to the width of the document page.
- **Prompt for selecting Excel Sheets.** Check this box to individually select worksheets in a workbook you want converted to PDF. If you create workbooks with multiple worksheets, be sure to keep this box checked as a default.

FIGURE 8.25

Select Preferences to open the Acrobat PDFMaker dialog box.

To understand a little more about converting Excel workbooks to PDF, follow these steps.

STEPS: Converting an Excel workbook to PDF

1. **Open an Excel workbook.** Try to use an Excel file having several worksheets in a workbook.

2. **Change conversion settings.** Click the Acrobat tab in the Ribbon and click the Preferences button.. In the Change Acrobat PDFMaker dialog box select the check boxes for Create Bookmarks and Prompt for selecting Excel Sheets. You can additionally make other choices such as Fit Worksheet to a single page if you like. Click OK to return to the Ribbon options.

3. **Convert to PDF.** Click the Create PDF tool in the Ribbon.

4. **Select worksheets.** As soon as you make a choice to convert to PDF, a second Acrobat PDFMaker dialog box opens. Because you selected Prompt for selecting Excel Sheets in the first Acrobat PDFMaker dialog box, Acrobat prompts you to select the worksheets you want to convert to PDF.

   Click the Entire Workbook radio button if you want all sheets converted to PDF, or individually select the sheets you want to convert and click the Add button. In my example I want to convert the first 5M sheet, the second 5M sheet, and the fourth 5M sheet you see listed in Figure 8.26. After making your selection(s), click the Convert to PDF button and your worksheet(s) is converted to PDF.

5. **View the PDF.** If you elected to view the PDF after conversion by selecting the View Adobe PDF result check box in the Acrobat PDFMaker dialog box, your file opens automatically in Acrobat. If you didn't check the box, open Acrobat and click the Open tool to locate and open your converted document. Click the Bookmarks panel and you should see bookmarks added for each worksheet in the converted workbook, as shown in Figure 8.27.

FIGURE 8.26

Select the sheets you want to convert and click the Add Sheets button.

Click the Bookmarks panel and you'll find bookmarks associated with each worksheet in the converted workbook.

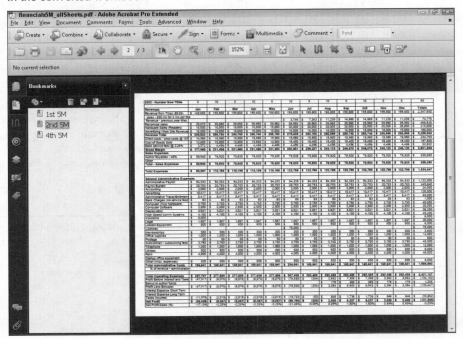

Converting Microsoft PowerPoint Files to PDF

PowerPoint Conversion Settings offer a few more options than you find with either Word or Excel. To open the Acrobat PDFMaker dialog box, click the Acrobat tab in the Ribbon and click Preferences. When the Acrobat PDFMaker dialog box opens you see four new items in the Applications settings that don't appear in the Word or Excel Acrobat PDFMaker dialog box.

The items shown in Figure 8.28 include the following:

- **Convert Multimedia.** Imported media such as sound and video in PowerPoint files can be converted to PDF media.

- **Preserve Slide Transitions.** Slide transitions can be saved in the PDF file and viewed when you view the PDF in Full Screen mode in an Acrobat viewer.

- **Convert hidden slides to PDF pages.** Check this box if you have hidden slides in PowerPoint and you want the hidden slides to appear as pages in the resultant PDF.

- **Convert Speaker Notes.** Speaker notes are converted to PDF when you check this box.

There are a number of options and reasons why you might want to convert PowerPoint slides to a PDF slide presentation. In addition, Acrobat Pro Extended 9 users can use Adobe Presenter for adding more effects to PDF files converted from PowerPoint. All you want to know about converting PowerPoint slides to PDF and using Adobe Presenter is covered in a separate chapter later in the book where I talk about PDFs and presentations.

CROSS-REF For more on PowerPoint conversions to PDF and using Adobe Presenter, see Chapter 28.

FIGURE 8.28

Click Preferences in the Ribbon in PowerPoint to open the Acrobat PDFMaker dialog box.

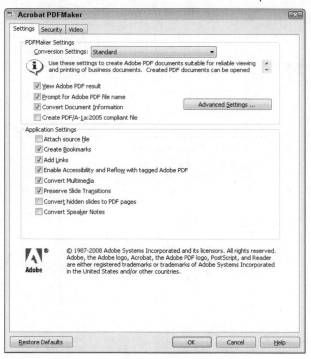

Converting Microsoft Publisher Files

Microsoft Publisher is Microsoft's effort at developing a more commercial and professional program designed for prepress and printing. Print shops and service bureaus shied away from Publisher in earlier versions for lack of essential tools such as adding printer's marks, color separation tools, and changing halftone frequency. However, Microsoft continued development of the product, and the latest version of Publisher includes all the features needed for prepress and commercial printing.

Unlike Word, Excel, and PowerPoint, Publisher doesn't have a separate Ribbon bar. From the top of the Ribbon, click Adobe PDF and a pull-down menu opens as shown in Figure 8.29. To open the Preferences similar to the Preferences button chosen in the other Office applications, choose Change Conversion Settings and the Acrobat PDFMaker dialog box opens as shown in Figure 8.30.

FIGURE 8.29

The Adobe PDF menu pull-down menu in Microsoft Publisher.

FIGURE 8.30

Acrobat PDFMaker preferences opened from Microsoft Publisher

When it comes to exports to PDF, Adobe supports some of the much needed file attributes required to print files on press. When you open the Acrobat PDFMaker from the Adobe PDF menu in Microsoft Publisher, the Acrobat PDFMaker dialog box displays some settings choices not found in any of the other Acrobat PDFMaker dialog boxes.

NOTE **When you first launch Microsoft Publisher after installing Acrobat, you are prompted in a dialog box for enabling macros. Because the Acrobat PDFMaker is a macro, you need to grant permissions for using the macro or you won't see the Adobe PDF menu or the Acrobat conversion tools.**

As shown in Figure 8.30 you have some unique settings that apply only to Microsoft Publisher. These settings include the following:

- **Conversion Settings.** The default Adobe PDF Setting is Press Quality. Like the other Acrobat PDFMaker dialog boxes, you can change the setting by clicking the Advanced Settings button.

- **Preserve Spot Color in Adobe PDF.** If spot colors are used in the Publisher file, you need to check this box to preserve the spot colors. If you fail to do so, spot colors are converted to CMYK.

- **Print Crop Marks.** As you can see by comparing this Acrobat PDFMaker dialog box with the others shown for Word, Excel, and PowerPoint, you see the first option for adding crop marks when a file is converted to PDF. This setting is very important if you have bleeds on pages in the Publisher document.

- **Allow Bleeds.** If bleeds are contained in the PowerPoint file, you must check the box to allow bleeds. When the box is checked, you have another setting to print separate bleed marks.

- **Preserve Transparency in Adobe PDF.** You can check the box to preserve transparency and let Acrobat flatten the transparency at print time.

The features added to the PowerPoint Acrobat PDFMaker are all related to commercial printing.

CROSS-REF **For more information on commercial printing and transparency flattening, see Chapter 32.**

Microsoft Visio and PDF Creation

Engineers, technical professionals, and architects are among the many users of programs such as Microsoft Project, Microsoft Visio, and Autodesk AutoCAD. Each of these programs has an Acrobat PDFMaker to produce PDF documents. Inasmuch as you can either print PostScript or save as EPS from one or the other and distill the files in Acrobat Distiller, using PDFMaker is a much better choice.

AutoCAD and Visio offer options for converting the AutoCAD and Visio layers to PDF layers. It is critical to be certain that the Acrobat PDF settings are enabled for converting layers with either program.

Converting Visio files to PDF

Like all the other Microsoft programs, Microsoft Visio has an Acrobat PDFMaker set of tools and menu commands. When you open the Adobe PDF menu, you see a single addition for Visio appearing as Convert all Pages in Drawing. Selecting this menu command converts all pages in the Visio file to PDF.

Additionally you have a Change Conversion Settings option in Visio like Microsoft Publisher. Select Adobe PDF ➪ Change Conversion Settings and the Acrobat PDFMaker dialog box shown in Figure 8.31 opens.

Acrobat PDFMaker preferences (or conversion settings) opened in Microsoft Visio

The settings unique to Visio are as follows:

■ **Include Visio custom properties as object data in the Adobe PDF.** Programs such as Visio and AutoCAD support adding asset information on all the objects added to drawings. The metadata are hidden from view in the drawing itself. When the PDF is produced, the object data are not visible in Acrobat in the document pane. However, a special tool known as the Object Data tool in Acrobat and the free Adobe Reader lets you view, search, count, select, and copy metadata. In Acrobat you can also export the metadata as XML. Check this box if you want to use the Object Data tool in Acrobat to work with the metadata.

CROSS-REF   For more on using the Object Data tool, see "Working with Object Data" later in this chapter.

- **Convert Comments to Adobe PDF Comments.** Comments added to a Visio file can be converted to Adobe PDF Comments.

- **Always flatten layers in Adobe PDF.** Microsoft Visio supports layers. If you want to retain layers in the resultant PDF, be certain to keep this check box unselected. You can keep the check box unselected as a default and when the need arises to flatten layers, you can handle layer flattening in Acrobat.

CROSS-REF   For more on working with Adobe PDF layers, see Chapter 24.

- **Open Layers Pane when viewed in Acrobat.** If layers are created in the PDF, checking this box sets the Initial View in Acrobat to view the Layers panel and Page, where the Layers panel is opened when the PDF is opened in Acrobat.

CROSS-REF   For more on setting Initial Views, see Chapter 5.

Notice that the default Conversion Settings in Figure 8.31 use the Standard Adobe PDF setting. This setting is Acrobat6–compatible. In earlier versions of Acrobat you had to edit the conversion settings in the Acrobat PDFMaker dialog box and be certain you selected Acrobat 6 or greater compatibility. Failure to do so flattened layers in the resultant PDF. In Acrobat 9, you don't have to worry about changing your Adobe PDF Settings to Acrobat 6 or greater compatibility. When you click select Adobe PDF ⇨ Convert to Adobe PDF, you are presented first with a dialog box asking you if you want to Include Custom Properties. Click Continue and you proceed to an advanced Acrobat PDFMaker dialog box. Click the Retain all layers radio button and the file is created with the Visio layers converted to Adobe PDF layers.

After converting a Visio document to PDF with layers, the file opens with the Layers panel in view, as you see in Figure 8.32.

Working with object data

Engineering and scientific programs often enable you to describe objects in drawings that result in object data that can be added to the metadata in a PDF document. When using Acrobat PDFMaker you can view certain metadata in the resultant PDF file.

Object Data Tool   To view the data, open a context menu on the Toolbar Well and select the Analysis toolbar. When the Analysis tools open, click the Object Data tool. Move to an object and click. The navigation pane opens to show the Model Tree, as shown in Figure 8.33. From the Options menu, you have a number of menu commands related to working with Object data.

FIGURE 8.32

A Visio file converted to PDF with Adobe PDF layers

FIGURE 8.33

Click an object and the Navigation pane opens showing assets identified in a drawing.

Objects in Visio are assigned custom properties for associating costs and comments with each milestone in a project. These data elements are added to the individual objects' metadata. As shown in the Options menu you have a number of commands available for copying data, selecting items, zooming views, counting objects, selecting similar objects, and so on.

Converting Web Pages from Internet Explorer to PDF (Windows Only)

In Chapter 7, I talked about PDF conversion using the Create PDF From Web Page command. In Chapter 27 I talk about PDFs and the Web. But because this chapter is focused on using the Acrobat PDFMaker tool, I thought it best to talk about the Acrobat PDFMaker and Microsoft Internet Explorer here in Chapter 8.

If you're working in an Acrobat session and you want to convert one or more pages to PDF, it makes sense to use the Create PDF From Web Page command. You don't need to launch a Web browser and open a page you want to convert to PDF. You can do all that within Acrobat.

So why does Adobe supply yet another tool for Web page conversion to PDF? Because sometimes you browse the Internet and find a page you want to convert to PDF. Because you're already in a Web browser, it makes sense to convert a Web page from the browser versus launching Acrobat and typing a URL in the Create PDF From Web Page dialog box.

As an example, let me share with you one Web page conversion I use routinely. When I book my airline tickets online, the ticket provider displays an itinerary showing my flight number, travel times, and travel dates. Of course the provider displays a print-ready Web page that I can send off to my printer, but I'm prone to losing things and printing paper is a surefire target for a lost item in my travel bag.

As an alternative to printing Web pages, I just do a quick conversion to PDF and copy my PDF to the laptop I carry to conferences and as a backup to a flash drive. When I'm in a hotel, I just open the PDF to check on my departure when I finish up my travels.

You may find many other uses for converting Web pages to PDF. Perhaps a map to a location, a latest recipe you saw on Emeril's show, some research information you're collecting, a new product description you want to study, or many other similar uses. Personally, I find it much easier to locate a PDF file on my computer than that last piece of paper I printed to my desktop printer.

Converting a Web page to PDF using PDFMaker

If you use Microsoft Internet Explorer on Windows, then you have the Acrobat PDFMaker installed in Explorer. In Internet Explorer you can click the pull-down menu adjacent to the Convert tool in the Internet Explorer toolbar to open the Adobe PDF menu and view the menu options, as shown in Figure 8.34. Notice in the menu you have a command for Preferences. Click Preferences in the menu and you find conversion options similar to those you use when creating a PDF from a Web page.

FIGURE 8.34

Open the Convert pull-down menu to view the options for converting Web pages to PDF.

CROSS-REF To learn more about conversion settings for Web page conversion to PDF, see Chapter 7.

To convert a Web page to PDF, open a Web page in Internet Explorer and click the Convert tool to open a pull-down menu. Choose Convert Web Page to PDF. Acrobat begins the conversion process and you'll see a progress bar similar to the one shown in Figure 8.35.

FIGURE 8.35

A progress bar reports the conversion of a Web page to PDF.

After conversion, the Web page opens in Acrobat. Notice that pages converted with Internet Explorer also include structured bookmarks like pages converted with the Create PDF From Web Page tool. If you open a context menu on a structured bookmark, you'll see the same menu options as you find with Web pages converted with the Create PDF From Web Page tool. Pages converted to PDF from Internet Explorer can also have additional pages appended to the converted file by selecting Append Next Level in a context menu, as shown in Figure 8.36.

CROSS-REF For more information on structured bookmarks and options for appending Web pages, see Chapter 7.

FIGURE 8.36

Creating PDFs from Acrobat PDFMaker in Internet Explorer produces structured bookmarks and menu options the same as when using the Create PDF From Web Page tool.

TIP Macintosh users may feel a little left out when converting Web pages to PDF from within programs such as Apple's Safari. No PDFMaker exists on the Mac for Safari or Microsoft Internet Explorer. However, the Mac user can still create PDF documents from any Web browser. Just open a Web page and select File ➪ Print. In the Print dialog box click the PDF button to open a pull-down menu and select Save as PDF. Your Web page is converted to PDF when you save the file. You don't have an option for appending Web pages as the Windows users have when using PDFMaker, but you can always use either the Create PDF From Web Page tool or navigate to other Web pages and print them to PDF.

Converting Web Page selections to PDF

At times you may want to use a portion of a Web page and convert it to PDF. You might find an airline schedule from your town to other cities and want just the information for departures from your town. You don't need a long table of flight schedules departing from other areas in the country. You may find a list of recent DVD releases and only want to select a few from a long list on a huge Web page, or you might want to capture a table without all the text preceding and following the table. These circumstances are ideal candidates for converting partial data on a Web page to a PDF document, and Acrobat 9 supports your every desire when using Microsoft IE and Acrobat.

To convert a selection on a Web page to a PDF file, follow these steps.

Steps: Converting Web Page selections to PDF (Windows only)

1. **Open a Web page in Microsoft Internet Explorer.** Note that these steps pertain only to Microsoft Internet Explorer on Windows.

2. **Drag through the content you want to convert to a PDF file.** You can drag through text and images, tables, and form fields on a Web page to select the data you want to convert to PDF.

3. **Open a context menu on the selection.** Right-click the mouse button to open a context menu on the selection as shown in Figure 8.37.

FIGURE 8.37

Create a selection and open a context menu.

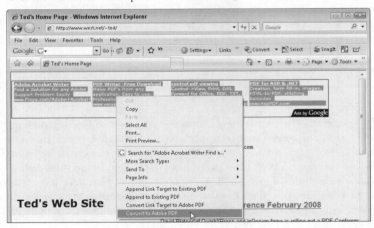

4. **Convert to PDF.** From the context menu options, choose Convert to Adobe PDF.

5. **View the resultant PDF in Acrobat.** PDFMaker converts the selection to a PDF file and opens in your Acrobat viewer as shown in Figure 8.38.

FIGURE 8.38

Only the selected data is converted to a PDF file.

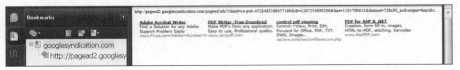

Notice in Figure 8.37 you see a Select button adjacent to the Convert button in Internet Explorer. Click this button and you can select sections on a Web page to convert to PDF. While the Select button is active, click an area on a Web page. Move to another area and click again. When you click the Convert to PDF button or choose Convert to PDF from a context menu, all the items you selected are converted to PDF.

If you want to deselect items, click the Select button again and the PDFMaker deselects all selected items. You can then click the Select button again and start over selecting items for conversion to PDF.

Converting Microsoft Outlook Emails to PDF (Windows Only)

Acrobat PDFMaker is also installed with Microsoft Outlook. When you open Outlook, you'll find two tools in the toolbar installed by Acrobat.

The first tool is the Create Adobe PDF from selected messages, and the second tool is Create Adobe PDF from folders. To convert mail messages listed in the Outlook Inbox or other mailbox, select messages you want to convert to PDF. You might have a mail thread related to a specific topic where you want to archive all mail related to the given topic. Use the Shift key or Control key to select messages in the mailbox you want to archive. After selecting the messages, click the Create Adobe PDF from selected messages tool. The Save Adobe PDF File As dialog box opens as shown in Figure 8.39.

FIGURE 8.39

Click Create PDF from selected messages to open the Save Adobe PDF File As dialog box.

Click the Save button after identifying a target folder for the saved file and PDFMaker converts your selected messages to PDF. The final result is a PDF Portfolio as shown in Figure 8.40. In the PDF Portfolio you'll find each message converted to a PDF file. You can search the content of the portfolio and find results based on text searches. The PDF Portfolio provides you with many options for viewing, modifying, and managing your converted messages.

FIGURE 8.40

The converted messages open as a PDF Portfolio.

CROSS-REF There's so much to working with PDF Portfolios that I've dedicated a chapter exclusively to combining files and working with PDF Portfolios. See Chapter 12 for more information.

The second button you find in Outlook is the Create PDF from folder tool. Click this tool and you can convert an entire mailbox of messages to PDF.

Summary

- Microsoft Office applications such as Word, Excel, and PowerPoint export directly to PDF with the assistance of PDFMaker. Office applications retain document structure and convert structured elements to bookmarks and links in exported PDFs when Acrobat PDFMaker is used.

- Custom page sizes can be added to the Adobe PDF printer driver on both Windows and Macintosh.

- The Print Production tools can add printer marks and crop marks to PDF files.

- Acrobat PDFMaker for Microsoft Publisher supports many features used for commercial printing.

- Microsoft Visio files can be exported with Adobe PDF layers using PDFMaker in Visio.

- Object Data contained in programs supporting the inclusion of certain metadata can be viewed using the Object Data tool in the Analysis toolbar.

- Microsoft Internet Explorer supports PDF-creating with PDFMaker very similar to PDFs produced with Create PDF From Web Page.

- New in Acrobat 9 you find an option for converting selected portions of a Web page to PDF using a context menu command.

- Microsoft Outlook files can be converted to PDF and assembled in PDF Portfolios using PDFMaker in Outlook.

Chapter 9

Exporting to PDF from Authoring Applications

C hapter 7 covered PDF creation from all the supported file formats contained in the Convert to PDF preferences. In Chapter 8 you learned about using the PDFMaker with Microsoft programs. Other PDF creation tools exist with programs such as QuarkXPress, CorelDraw, and Lotus Notes, and the list of programs supporting PDF creation continues to grow.

Where PDF exports from host applications are best is with Adobe's own Creative Suite applications. Many of the Adobe CS programs were created from the ground up using core PDF technology.

This chapter deals with PDF exports from the Creative Suite programs. Some options you find with exports to PDF in Adobe Programs are supported in other applications, but none have as comprehensive a set of PDF export choices as do the Adobe programs. If you're a user of any one of the Creative Suite applications, then this chapter is for you.

IN THIS CHAPTER

Working with Adobe Creative Suite

Exporting direct to PDF from design applications

Using Acrobat with non-Adobe programs

Setting Up the Environment

This chapter is concerned with creating PDFs; therefore, no toolbars need to be loaded in the Toolbar Well. You can leave your toolbars in Acrobat set to the default view to follow what's covered in this chapter.

Working with Acrobat and the Adobe Creative Suite

The Adobe Creative Suite (CS4) comes in several flavors. The Creative Suite Design Standard edition includes Adobe Illustrator CS, Adobe InDesign CS, Adobe Photoshop CS, Adobe Bride CS, Adobe Device Central CS, Adobe Acrobat Pro, and Adobe Version Cue CS. The Adobe Creative Suite Design Premium edition includes all these programs but replaces Adobe Photoshop CS with Adobe Photoshop CS Extended and adds Adobe Flash and Adobe Dreamweaver and Fireworks . Additional Creative Suite bundles are the Web Premium, the Web Standard, the Production Premium, and the top end Adobe Master Collection that includes every program in all the other bundles. Most of the CS applications support PDF documents with direct exports and imports. For the remainder of this chapter I'll refer to the CS4 and applications simply as the Creative Suite or CS programs. As of this writing, the current version is Adobe Creative Suite 4.

Acrobat and Adobe Photoshop

Adobe Photoshop CS supports creating and importing PDFs. When you create a PDF, you use the Save As command and save, and like all CS applications in the CS versions, the exports use Adobe PDF Settings to convert to PDF. When you import PDF documents that were not originally created in Photoshop, the files are rasterized. The process of rasterizing files converts all objects, such as type and vector objects, to raster images (pixels).

Saving to PDF from Photoshop

Creating a PDF file from Photoshop is nothing more than choosing the Photoshop PDF format from the Save dialog box. Photoshop supports many different file formats for opening and saving documents. In versions prior to Photoshop 6.0, you had to flatten all layers before you could save a document as a PDF file. In versions 6.0 and later, you can preserve layers and vector art. When you save a layered file from Photoshop CS as a Photoshop PDF and open it again in Photoshop, all layers are retained; however, a layered Photoshop file saved as PDF opens in Acrobat as a single-layer document. Type and vector art work the same way. You can create type without rasterizing it and save the file as a PDF. Later, if you want to edit the file, you can reopen it back in Photoshop and edit the type. What's more, you can search the text in Acrobat when you save the file as PDF from Photoshop.

 Flattening layers in Photoshop *always* rasterizes vector art and type. If you want to preserve vector art and type, you need to save the layered file as a Photoshop PDF document.

To save a multilayered Photoshop image, Photoshop document, or flattened image, you use the Save As command. In Photoshop CS, choose File ⇨ Save As. The Save As PDF dialog box opens. This dialog box is the same when saving from all other CS applications. If you're familiar with Acrobat Distiller, the Save Adobe PDF dialog box and the various panes contained within appear similar to the tabs in Acrobat Distiller. However, while the CS applications use a similar UI for consistency, they do NOT use Acrobat Distiller to create the PDF.

When saving as Photoshop PDF, the first pane in the Save Adobe PDF dialog box is the General settings, as shown in Figure 9.1. Options choices you make in the Save Adobe PDF dialog box include:

- **Adobe PDF Preset.** All the presets you create in Distiller are available from the pull-down menu. Any new presets created in Distiller are immediately made available to all CS programs.

- **Standard.** From the Standard pull-down menu you can select from the PDF/X subsets.

- **Compatibility.** Acrobat compatibility choices are available from the Compatibility pull-down menu. You find compatibility choices dating back to Acrobat 4 compatibility with all subsequent compatibility choices up to the current version when Acrobat was last upgraded. Because Acrobat's development cycle usually is ahead of the CS programs, you find the most recent Acrobat compatibility choice for Acrobat not available until you see the next upgrade of the Creative Suite that follows the most recent upgrade to Acrobat.

- **Description.** This area in the General pane is a text description of the compatibility option you choose.

- **Preserve Photoshop Editing Capabilities.** If you choose to uncheck the Preserve Photoshop Editing Capabilities and later open the PDF in Photoshop, the file is rasterized and all layers are flattened. Preserving Photoshop Editing Capabilities preserves layers and type. The type can be searched in Acrobat. If you don't need to preserve type and vector objects, remove the check mark and flatten the file. Flattened images result in smaller file sizes.

CROSS-REF For more on opening and rasterizing files in Photoshop, see the section "Acquiring PDF files in Photoshop" later in this chapter.

- **Embed Page Thumbnails.** As a general rule, be certain to leave this option off. This option was used for legacy formats and Acrobat no longer looks at embedded thumbnails. If for some reason you need to create page thumbnails, do it in Acrobat.

- **Optimize for Fast Web Preview.** Keep this option checked to optimize files. When downloading from the Web, files are downloaded much faster.

- **View PDF After Saving.** Checking this option launches your default Acrobat viewer and opens the file in Acrobat.

FIGURE 9.1

To export directly to PDF, use the Save or Save As dialog box in Photoshop. As with all other CS applications, the Save Adobe PDF dialog box opens.

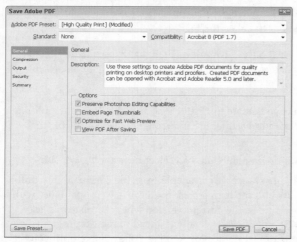

Click Compression in the left pane to open the compression choices. The options shown in Figure 9.2 include:

- **Compression.** In the Options area, leave Bicubic Downsampling To at the default. This option is likely to be the best choice for just about all your images. The two text boxes enable you to downsample images. For Photoshop files you're best off changing resolution before you come to the save options. Leave these two text boxes at the defaults and use the Image ➪ Image Size command in Photoshop to make resolution changes.

  Your choices include None, JPEG, JPEG2000, and ZIP. None adds no compression to the file. JPEG is a lossy compression scheme offering various levels of compression that you choose from the Image Quality pull-down menu. JPEG2000 requires Acrobat 6 compatibility or greater. Compression is greater with JPEG2000 than with JPEG. This compression scheme works with transparent layers and alpha channels. ZIP compression is lossless. Files are not compressed as much as with JPEG, but the data integrity is optimal. ZIP compression is usually preferred for images with large amounts of a single color.

  Convert 16 Bits/Channel Image to 8 Bits/Channel. Sixteen-bit images, such as those created with 16-bit or more scanners or digital cameras supporting Camera Raw and 16-bit, cannot be converted to PDF using the Create PDF ➪ From File command. 16-bit images, however, can be saved from Photoshop as Photoshop PDFs and opened in Acrobat. To preserve 16-bit images, save with Acrobat 6 compatibility or later.

- **Tile Size.** You're not likely to use Tile Size, because Acrobat supports large document sizes when printing to large format printers. Use this option to print tiled pages on desktop printers when you want to piece pages together for proofs.

FIGURE 9.2

Click Compression to advance to the next pane in the Save Adobe PDF dialog box.

Click Output in the left pane and your choices appear, as shown in Figure 9.3.

FIGURE 9.3

Output options offer choices for color profiling and color conversion.

You can handle color conversion and intent profiles here in the Save Adobe PDF dialog box, but you're most likely to handle these choices in your printer driver or layout program. The bottom half of the pane is only accessible if you select one of the PDF/X options in the Standards pull-down menu.

CROSS-REF **For more on color handling and profile conversion, see Chapter 31. For more on PDF/X, see Chapters 10 and 32.**

Click Security and the Security options are displayed. If you want security, click the check boxes and make choices for the security permissions you want to restrict.

The last pane displays a summary of the settings you chose to use to export to PDF. Click Save PDF and the file is saved as a Photoshop PDF file.

Working with Photoshop color modes

Photoshop provides a number of choices for the color mode used to express your image. You can open files from different color modes, convert color modes in Photoshop, and save among different formats available for a given color mode. File formats are dependent on color modes, and some format options are not available if the image data are defined in a mode not acceptable to the format.

TIP **See Table 9.1, later in this section, for Photoshop PDF exports supported by the Photoshop color modes and relative uses for each mode.**

Color mode choices in Photoshop include the following:

- **Bitmap.** The image is expressed in two colors: black and white. In Photoshop terms, images in the bitmap mode are referred to as line art. In Acrobat terms, this color mode is called monochrome bitmap. Bitmap images are usually about one-eighth the size of a grayscale file. The bitmap format can be used with Acrobat's OCR functionality for converting the image data to rich text.

- **Grayscale.** This is your anchor mode in Photoshop. Grayscale is like a black-and-white photo, a halftone, or a Charlie Chaplin movie. You see grayscale images everywhere, including the pages in this book. I refer to this as an anchor mode because you can convert to any of the other modes from grayscale. RGB files cannot be converted directly to bitmaps or duotones. You first need to convert RGB to grayscale, and then to either a bitmap or duotone. From grayscale, although the color is not regained, you can also convert back to any of the other color modes. Grayscale images significantly reduce file sizes — they're approximately one-third the size of an RGB file, but larger than the bitmaps.

- **RGB.** For screen views, multimedia, and Web graphics, RGB is the most commonly used mode. It has a color gamut much larger than CMYK and is best suited for display on computer monitors. A few printing devices can take advantage of RGB, such as film recorders, large inkjet printers, and some desktop color printers. In most cases, however, this mode is not used for printing files to commercial output devices, especially when color-separating and using high-end digital prepress.

- **CMYK.** The process colors of Cyan, Magenta, Yellow, and Black are used in offset printing and most commercial output devices. The color gamut is much narrower than RGB; and when you convert an image from RGB to CMYK using Photoshop's mode conversion command, you usually see some noticeable dilution of color appearing on your monitor. When exporting files to PDF directly from Photoshop or when opening files in other applications and then distilling them, you should always make your color conversions first in Photoshop.

- **Lab.** Lab color, in theory, encompasses all the color from both the RGB and CMYK color spaces. This color mode is based on a mathematical model to describe all perceptible color within the human universe. In practicality, its color space is limited to approximately 6 million colors, about 10+ million less than RGB color. Lab color is device-independent color, which theoretically means the color is true regardless of the device on which your image is edited and printed. Lab mode is commonly preferred by high-end color editing professionals when printing color separations on PostScript Level 2 and PostScript 3 devices. Earlier versions of PDFs saved from Lab color images had problems printing four-color separations. With Acrobat, you can print Lab images to process separations.

CROSS-REF For more information on printing color separations, see Chapter 32.

- **Multichannel.** If you convert any of the other color modes to Multichannel mode, all the individual channels used to define the image color are converted to grayscale. The resulting document is a grayscale image with multiple channels. With regard to exporting to PDF, you likely won't use this mode.

- **Duotone.** The Duotone mode can actually support one of four individual color modes. Monotone is selectable from the Duotone mode, which holds a single color value in the image, like a tint. Duotone defines the image in two color values, Tritone in three, and Quadtone in four. When you export to PDF from Photoshop, all of these modes are supported.

- **Indexed Color.** Whereas the other color modes such as RGB, Lab, and CMYK define an image with a wide color gamut (up to millions of colors), the Indexed Color mode limits the total colors to a maximum of 256. Color reduction in images is ideal for Web graphics where the fewer colors significantly reduce the file sizes. You can export indexed color images directly to PDF format from Photoshop.

TABLE 9.1

Photoshop Color Modes

Color Mode	Export to PDF	Screen View	Print Composite	Print Separations
Bitmap	Yes	Yes	Yes	No
Grayscale	Yes	Yes	Yes	No
RGB Color	Yes	Yes	Yes*	Yes
CMYK Color	Yes	No	Yes	Yes
Lab Color	Yes	Yes	Yes	Yes
Multichannel	Yes	No	No	No
Duotone	Yes	Yes	No	Yes
Indexed Color	Yes	Yes	No	Yes
16-bit	Yes	No	No	Yes

* When working with high-end commercial devices, CMYK is preferred.

Acquiring PDF files in Photoshop

PDF documents may be composed of many different elements depending on the design of the original file. If you design a page in a layout program for which you create text, import Photoshop images, and also import EPS illustrations, the different elements retain their characteristics when converted to PDF. Text, for example, remains as text, raster images such as Photoshop files remain as raster images, and EPS illustrations remain as EPS vector objects. Although the images, text, and line art may be compressed when a PDF file/document is created, all the text and line art remain as vector elements. In Photoshop, if you open an illustration or text created in any program other than Photoshop, the document elements are rasterized and lose their vector-based attributes. Photoshop rasterizes PDF documents much as it does with any EPS file.

In Photoshop, you have several methods of handling PDF imports. PDF documents opened in Photoshop are handled with the File ⇨ Open command, File ⇨ Place command, File ⇨ Import command, and through a File ⇨ Automate command. Each of the methods offers different options, so let's take the methods individually.

Opening PDF files in Photoshop

When you choose File ⇨ Open, select a PDF file, and click Open, the Import PDF dialog box appears. If your PDF document has multiple pages you can select one, all, or any number of pages to open. Press Ctrl/⌘ and click individual page thumbnails in the Import PDF dialog box shown in Figure 9.4 to select pages in a noncontiguous order. Click the first page, press the Shift key, and click the last page to select all pages.

FIGURE 9.4

The Import PDF dialog box enables you to pick the page number in a multi-page file to place in Photoshop.

Options choices in the Import PDF dialog box include the following:

- **Crop To.** There are six choices you can make from the pull-down menu. For Photoshop files, the choices typically show no difference. Files are imported the same size no matter which option you select. The options are more significant when using Adobe InDesign.

- **Resolution.** The default resolution regardless of the size is 72 ppi. You can choose to supply a user-defined resolution in this dialog box. If the original raster images were at a resolution different from the amount supplied in this dialog box, the images are resampled. Text and line art will be rasterized according to the amount you define in the dialog box without interpolation.

NOTE Image resampling is a method for tossing away pixels (downsampling) or manufacturing new pixels (upsampling). Either way the process is referred to as *interpolation* where Photoshop makes some guesses as to which pixels to toss or which pixels to create.

- **Mode.** Choose a color mode — Grayscale, RGB, CMYK, or Lab color — from the pull-down menu.

- **Bit Depth.** Choose either 8- or 16-bit for the bit depth. If the PDF contains photos, changing an 8-bit depth file to 16-bit won't add more data to the file. Any tone adjustments using Photoshop's Levels and Curves result in the same data loss on 16-bit as you find with 8-bit images, if the original image file(s) was 8-bit.

TIP For much better tone separation, working with true 16-bit images results in less data loss and smoother tonal transitions. You can convert 8-bit images to 16-bit in Photoshop. Open a PDF using the 8-bit option. Once opened in Photoshop select Image ⇨ Mode ⇨ 16-bit. Next, select Image ⇨ Image Size and downsample the image 50 percent. Select 71 percent for either the Width or Height and check the Resample check box. Use Bicubic for the method, click OK, and the image resolution is downsampled 50 percent. The pixels are compressed in a tighter relationship, resulting in a true 16-bit image. The file now contains enough data to prevent data loss when making tone corrections with Levels and Curves.

- **Anti-aliased.** Use this option to smooth edges of text, line art, and images that are interpolated through resampling. If you disable this option, text appears with jagged edges. Text in PDF files rasterized in Photoshop looks best when anti-aliased and when the display is more consistent with the original font used when the PDF was created.

- **Suppress Warnings.** Check this box to open the files without your having to respond to any warning dialog boxes that might report problems with the pages.

One problem you may encounter when rasterizing PDF documents in Photoshop is maintaining font integrity. Photoshop displays a warning dialog box when it encounters a font that is not installed on your system, which presents problems when you attempt to rasterize the font. If such a problem exists, the font can be eliminated from the document or changed after you open the file in Photoshop and edit the type layer.

When files are password-protected, users are prevented from opening a PDF file in Photoshop or any other application without a password to open the file. If you attempt to open a secure document, an alert dialog box opens prompting you for a password.

CROSS-REF For information about Acrobat security, see Chapter 26.

PDF WORKFLOW If you want to convert catalogs and lengthy documents to HTML-supported files, the PDF to PSD conversion can be useful. You can set up Actions in Photoshop to downsample images, convert color modes, and save copies of the converted files in HTML-supported formats.

Placing PDF files in Photoshop

Instead of opening a PDF file through the File ⇨ Open command, you can use File ⇨ Place to add a PDF to an open Photoshop document. Placing PDFs in all versions of Photoshop prior to CS2 rasterized the placed file. In Photoshop CS, placed PDF files retain all vector attributes. When you select Place, the Place PDF dialog box opens, as shown in Figure 9.5.

FIGURE 9.5

The Place PDF dialog box lets you pick the page number in a multi-page file to place in Photoshop.

The file appears within a bounding box containing handles in each corner, as shown in Figure 9.6. Click and drag a handle to resize the placed image. You can size the image up or down in the Photoshop document window. When finished scaling, press the Enter (Windows) or Return (Macintosh) key. Pressing the key after sizing rasterizes the file. All vector attributes are lost and when you save the file as Photoshop PDF, you won't be able to select text.

FIGURE 9.6

Placed PDF files retain all vector attributes.

Using comments in Photoshop

Photoshop supports the use of Comment tools. You can create a note or sound attachment in Photoshop much like you do in Acrobat. The comment is an object and won't be rasterized with any other Photoshop data. You can delete the annotation at any time by selecting the Note icon or Attach Sound icon and pressing the Backspace (Windows) or Delete (Macintosh) key.

You can also import comments from PDF files into Photoshop. You must use the Comment Note tool because Photoshop does not support the other comment types available in Acrobat. If a Note is contained in a PDF document and you want to import the Note into Photoshop, choose File ➪ Import ➪ Annotations. Photoshop can import an annotation only from PDF files.

CROSS-REF For more information about comment notes and sound attachments, see Chapter 20.

Creating PDF presentations

All the features for Photoshop discussed thus far are derived from the top-level menu commands directly in Photoshop. You can also use Adobe Bridge to convert image files to PDF. Among options you find in Adobe Bridge is a command for converting image files to a PDF presentation. In the Bridge window you can select files to choose in your presentation, invoke a menu command, and Photoshop does the work to create a presentation complete with slide transitions and user-defined time intervals. If you have Photoshop you also have Adobe Bridge. Open Adobe Bridge and follow the steps below to create a presentation.

STEPS: Saving a PDF presentation

1. **Select image files to include in a PDF presentation.** Open Adobe Bridge and open the folder containing images you want to include in a presentation. You can add files from other folders, but your task is a little easier if you first copy all the files you want to include in the presentation to a common folder.

2. **Select Tools ➪ Photoshop ➪ PDF Presentation.** With the files selected in the Bridge window, open the menu command, as shown in Figure 9.7.

FIGURE 9.7

Choose Tools ➪ Photoshop ➪ PDF Presentation in the Adobe Bridge window.

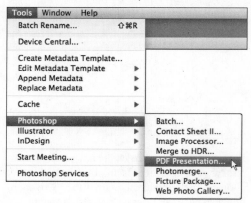

3. **Set the Presentation attributes.** The PDF Presentation dialog box opens, as shown in Figure 9.8. Click Presentation for the Output Options and make a choice for the time interval for advancing slides by editing the Advance Every text box. If you want the presentation to run in a continuous loop, check Loop after Last Page. If you want transitions, select a transition effect from the Transition pull-down menu. Note that you can also click the Browse button if you want to add more files to your presentation than those viewed in the Bridge window.

4. **Save the Presentation.** Click Save and the Save Adobe PDF dialog box, shown in Figure 9.1 at the beginning of this chapter, opens. Adjust settings as you like in the various panes in the dialog box. You might want to use some image downsampling in the Compression pane if you build a presentation from images taken with a digital camera. If you shot Camera Raw files with a camera of five or more megapixels, use the Compression options for lowering image resolution.

FIGURE 9.8

Click Presentation and make choices for advancing slides and transition effects.

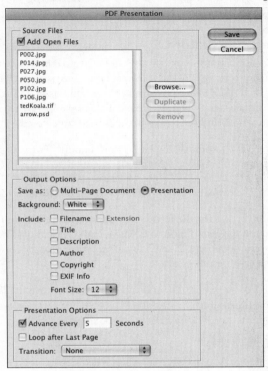

5. **View the presentation.** Click Save and Photoshop opens each image, samples the image, and converts to PDF. When the save is completed, open the file in Acrobat. Your presentation appears in Full Screen mode and slides change according to the interval specified in Step 3.

CROSS-REF For information on creating PDF presentations, see Chapter 28.

Adobe Illustrator CS

Adobe Illustrator, as with other Adobe programs, is built on core PDF technology. In fact, the native Adobe Illustrator file format is PDF, and as such it is one of the best applications supporting direct export to PDF.

Illustrator has evolved to a sophisticated integration with PDF and supports the following: transparency, editing capability, layers, blending modes, text, and filters. Further integration with the program in non-PDF workflows embraces exports for Web design, where its current iteration supports one-step optimization for formats such as GIF, JPEG, PNG, SWF, and SVG.

Saving PDFs from Adobe Illustrator CS

To export PDF files from Adobe Illustrator, you use the File ⇨ Save command. The format options available to you include the native Adobe Illustrator format (.AI), Adobe PDF (*.PDF), Illustrator EPS (*EPS), Illustrator Template (*AIT), SVG (*SVG), and SVG Compressed (*SVGZ). In Illustrator, choose File ⇨ Save from a new document window. A Save dialog box opens that enables you to name the file, choose the destination, and select one of the formats just noted.

Additional file formats appear in the Export dialog box (File ⇨ Export). Formats supported in this dialog box include AutoCAD Drawing (*DWG), AutoCAD Interchange File (*DXF), BMP (*BMP), Enhanced Metafile (*EMF), Flash (*SWF), JPEG (*JPG), Macintosh PICT (*PCT), Photoshop (*PSD), PNG (*PNG), Targa (*TGA), Text Format (*TXT), TIFF (*TIF), and Windows Metafile (wmf).

If you choose Adobe Illustrator (.AI) as the file format and click Save, the Illustrator Options dialog box opens. In this dialog box you have an option to Create a PDF Compatible File. Check the box and click OK and your Illustrator document is saved in native format that can be opened directly in Acrobat. No other PDF conversion is necessary.

If you want to convert to PDF from a layered Illustrator document and have the layers appear in Acrobat, you need to save your Illustrator file as Adobe PDF. (*.PDF) When you select Acrobat PDF and click the Save button, the Save Adobe PDF dialog box opens with many similar settings found when saving Photoshop files.

A few differences appear in the Save Adobe PDF dialog box when you compare the options to Photoshop. These options are as follows:

- **General.** In the General tab you find two additional settings, as shown in Figure 9.9. The Create Acrobat Layers from Top-Level Layers check box is active for Acrobat 6 compatible files and later. Check the box when you want an Illustrator file exported to PDF with Adobe PDF Layers.

FIGURE 9.9

Two additional options appear in the Illustrator Save Adobe PDF General settings when comparing the options to those found in Photoshop.

☑ Create Acrobat Layers from Top-Level Layers
☑ Create Multi-page PDF from Page Tiles

The Create Multi-page PDF from Page Tiles is used for creating multiple pages in Illustrator (see "Creating multi-page PDFs" later in this chapter).

- **Compression.** The appearance of the Compression pane is different than Photoshop, but you have all the options for downsampling files and the same compression options as found in Photoshop.

- **Marks and Bleeds.** Click Marks and Bleeds in the left pane and the options in the right pane change to settings you can apply for setting printer's marks. Options are similar to those you find when setting marks in the Acrobat Print dialog box.

CROSS-REF For information on setting printer's marks in the Print dialog box, see Chapter 32.

- **Output.** The same color conversion and support for PDF/X compliance options are available to Illustrator as found in Photoshop. One option is added in Illustrator to mark the file if the source document uses trapping.

CROSS-REF For more information on trapping, see Chapter 32.

- **Advanced.** Illustrator has an Advanced pane where Font subsetting, overprint assignments, and transparency flattening options appear, as shown in Figure 9.10.

FIGURE 9.10

Advanced settings offer options for font embedding, overprinting, and transparency flattening.

CROSS-REF For more on font subsetting and transparency flattening, see Chapter 10. For more on overprinting, see Chapter 32.

Saving layered files to PDF

You can save layered Illustrator CS files to PDF with Adobe PDF Layers. Creating layered PDF documents from Illustrator is supported in Illustrator CS version 1 and above. To create PDF layers you need an authoring program capable of creating layers and capable of saving or exporting to PDF 1.5 format (Acrobat 6 compatibility) and above — Illustrator CS does both.

When saving files with layers to PDF, create the default layer view you want to appear in Acrobat. As shown in Figure 9.11, one layer in an Illustrator file is hidden and four layers are visible. The layer visibility you see in Illustrator is the same visibility you'll see in Acrobat when saving as PDF.

In Illustrator, choose File ➪ Save or Save As and select PDF as the format. In the Adobe PDF Options dialog box select Acrobat 6 or greater compatibility and check the box for Create Acrobat Layers from Top-Level Layers. If the box is not checked, you won't see layers in the resultant PDF document.

When you open the PDF in Acrobat, you see the same layer view as when the file was saved from Illustrator, as shown in Figure 9.12.

CROSS-REF For more information on working with layered files in Acrobat, see Chapter 24.

FIGURE 9.11

When saving to PDF with layers, create the layer view in the authoring program that you want to appear as the default view in Acrobat.

FIGURE 9.12

The default layer view in Acrobat appears the same as the view from Illustrator when the file was saved.

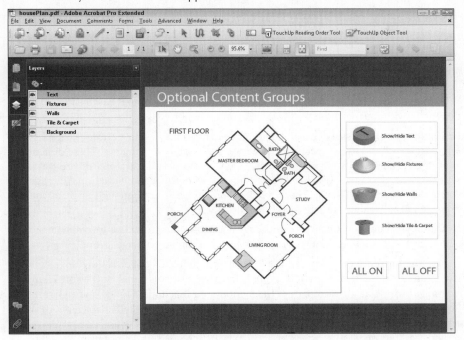

Creating multi-page PDFs

Quite often, with just about any application, users find ways to work with a program in a manner that was not intended by a developer. This is most apparent when looking at the way designers use Adobe Illustrator. Illustrator was created for artists who needed an electronic artboard to create illustrations and drawings. But when the program got to the hands of the graphic artists, it was frequently used as a page layout program. For years graphic artists pleaded with Adobe to offer support for multiple pages. No matter how many rich features were added to Adobe InDesign (which was created as a page layout program), the die-hard Illustrator users never abandoned their favorite tool. Today, great numbers of designers still first grab Illustrator to create page layouts.

It wasn't until Illustrator CS2 was released that Adobe responded. Perhaps not completely the way designers wanted to work with multiple pages, but in part, Illustrator now supports multiple pages. The only way you can create a multi-page document in Illustrator is when exporting to Adobe PDF.

Illustrator's approach to multiple page documents is quite different from that of any other application. If creating multi-page documents in Illustrator is your interest, follow the steps below:

STEPS: Creating multi-page PDFs from Adobe Illustrator

1. **Set up the page size.** For this demonstration I want to create four buttons to use in Acrobat as navigation buttons to move back and forth in a PDF document. Two buttons are needed for default appearances and two buttons will appear as rollovers so when the cursor appears over a button, the button color or shape changes — much like you find in Web page designs. Rather than create four separate files, I want to create a single PDF document with four separate pages.

   For buttons, my page size needs to be just large enough for all four buttons. When I select File ⇨ New in Illustrator, I specify my page size for 2 inches by 2 inches. These dimensions are sufficient to create four pages each at 1 inch square. The Illustrator artboard can be set up as a single page only. The page will be tiled to produce individual smaller pages when you create the PDF file. Therefore, 2 square inches is large enough to create four separate pages each at 1 square inch.

   Note that you could create an artboard large enough to accommodate several letter- or tabloid-size pages if you want to use Illustrator for a traditional page layout.

2. **Create the button icons.** You can use font characters from Symbols, Wingdings, or other stylized fonts, draw shapes, or add symbols from the Symbols panel, and so on. In my example, I use some characters from the Symbol font that appear as left and right arrows. I copied the two characters and changed the color on the duplicated characters. All this is arbitrary. Feel free to use any design of your choice. The point is you need four images centered in four quadrants, as shown in Figure 9.13. Notice guidelines were drawn to help position the characters in each quadrant.

3. **Set Print Attributes.** Chose File ⇨ Print and select Adobe PDF for the Printer and Adobe PDF 9.0 for the PPD at the top of the Print dialog box. Under the Media area, choose Custom and type 1 for the Width and Height. The Print dialog box General settings should appear, as shown in Figure 9.14.

4. **Set the Tile attributes.** Click Setup in the left pane of the Print dialog box and select Tile Imageable Areas from the Tiling pull-down menu. The tiled pages should appear with dashed lines in the page thumbnail preview, as shown in Figure 9.15. If you don't see dashed lines, the file won't export as multiple pages.

FIGURE 9.13

Create four shapes to be used as navigation buttons and position the shapes in the center of each quadrant on the 2-x-2-inch page.

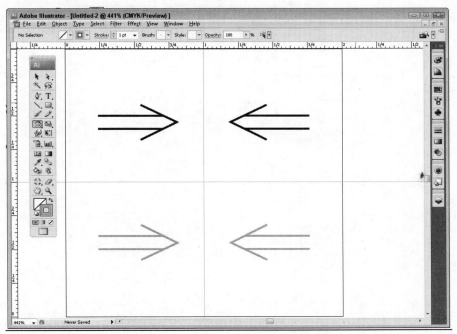

FIGURE 9.14

Set print attributes for Printer, PPD, and Size.

FIGURE 9.15

Select Tile Imageable Areas and observe the preview to be certain the pages are defined with dashed lines.

5. **Click Done.** Be certain to click Done and not Cancel or Print to preserve the settings.

6. **Save as Adobe PDF.** You must use the Adobe PDF (*.PDF) file format. A Native Illustrator .ai format won't produce multiple pages. Select File ⇨ Save As and choose Adobe PDF (*.PDF) for the Type (Windows) or Format (Macintosh). Click Save and the Save Adobe PDF dialog box opens.

7. **Check Create Multiple-page PDF from Page Tiles in the General settings.** (See Figure 9.9 earlier in this chapter.) Click Save PDF and the file is saved.

8. **Open the PDF in Acrobat.** When the file opens, click the Pages pane. You should see four separate pages, as shown in Figure 9.16.

TIP   You can bypass the step to open the Save As dialog box by clicking Print in Step 5 and simply print to a PDF document. Clicking Done sets up the pages for exporting to PDF and permits you to continue editing if needed.

FIGURE 9.16

Open the file in Acrobat and click the Pages tab to view thumbnails of the pages in the document.

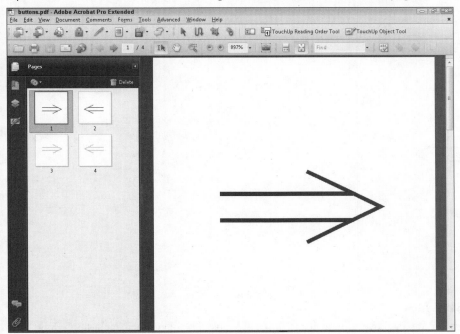

A file like the one created in these steps can be used as button faces with button form fields. Rather than have four separate files, you can choose any image in a multi-page document to add as a button face in Acrobat. In the Appearance settings in Button properties the Select Icon dialog box lists all pages in a PDF document. You can scroll the elevator bar on the right side of the dialog box to view different pages, as shown in Figure 9.17.

CROSS-REF For more information on creating button faces, see Chapters 22 and 34.

FIGURE 9.17

When assigning appearances in Button properties, you can choose any page in a multi-page document for a button appearance.

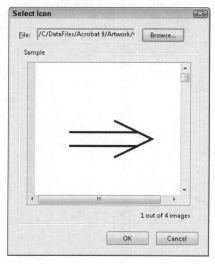

Saving SWF files

Acrobat versions 6 and above support many different kinds of media formats including Adobe Flash SWF. Using Illustrator CS you can create vector objects as animated sequences to embellish PDFs such as forms, diagrams, electronic brochures, and similar documents where you want to add animation to amplify your messages. To understand a little more about saving SWF files from Illustrator and importing them in Acrobat, follow these steps:

STEPS: Exporting SWF files to Acrobat

1. **Create a sequence in Illustrator.** Either draw vector shapes in Illustrator or drag a symbol from the Symbols palette to the document page. The shape you create is on a layer. Duplicate the shape and paste it to a second layer. Continue adding new layers and shapes to complete a sequence. You can change size, rotations, or shape designs for each shape on a different layer. In my example shown in Figure 9.18, I created a shape on one layer and sized the objects up 25 percent on each new layer.

> **TIP** To easily create a sequence for motion objects, drag a symbol from Illustrator's Symbols palette to the document page. Press the Control/Option key and click+ drag to duplicate the shape. Press Control/⌘+D several times to repeat the duplication. Select all the objects and open the Layers palette flyout menu. Select Release to Layers (Sequence) from the palette menu commands. All your objects are distributed to separate layers.

FIGURE 9.18

Add a shape to separate layers.

Export to SWF. Choose File ⇨ Export. In the Export dialog box, select Flash (swf) from the Format pull-down menu. Add a filename, select a target folder, and click the Export button. The SWF Options dialog box opens.

Choose the Export option. Choose All Layers to SWF Frames from the Export As pull-down menu. Click the Advanced button to display the Advanced settings.

4. **Set the SWF file format options.** In the SWF Options dialog box shown in Figure 9.19 are choices for the frame rate, exporting HTML-compatible files, and various appearance options. Be certain to check the box where you see Export Static Layers and make other choices as desired. Click OK to continue the export to SWF.

5. **Save the Illustrator file.** When you export to a file format from Illustrator, your file is not yet saved. If you want to return to the document to make additional edits, save the file. Choose File ⇨ Save and save the file as an .ai file with Create PDF Compatible File checked.

6. **Import the SWF file in Acrobat (Acrobat Pro/ Pro Extended only).** Open the Multimedia toolbar and select the Flash tool. Drag a rectangle on the document page where you want to import the SWF file (or just double click the get the default size of the SWF file. Click the Browse button in the Insert Flash dialog box, locate your SWF file, and import it. When you import the SWF file, the first frame in the sequence appears within the movie rectangle, as shown in Figure 9.20.

FIGURE 9.19

Set options in the SWF Options dialog box Advanced settings.

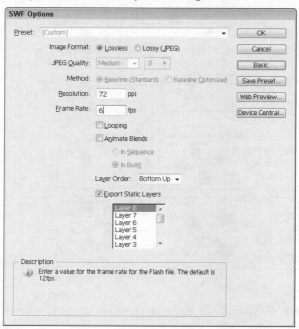

FIGURE 9.20

Select the Flash tool from the Multimedia toolbar and drag open a rectangle to import a Flash SWF file.

7. **Play the movie clip.** Select the Hand tool and click the movie frame. Figure 9.21 displays the last frame in a sequence. The effect is that the message box appears to explode in view as the sequence is played.

FIGURE 9.21

Select the Hand tool and click the movie box to play the sequence.

Whether you create SWF files from Illustrator or Adobe Flash, the SWF file imports in Acrobat are the same. Use the Flash tool in the Multimedia toolbar and locate an SWF file on your hard drive. Open the file and choose Acrobat 6 compatibility. You can add play buttons in Acrobat to play, stop, pause, and resume, and add JavaScripts for a variety of different play options. You can also convert Web pages containing SWF files to PDF. When Web pages are captured using Acrobat, the SWF files play as movies in the converted PDF.

CROSS-REF To learn more about importing SWF, movie files, and adding play buttons and Acrobat 5 and 6 compatibility, see Chapter 23. For more on capturing Web pages, see Chapter 7.

Opening Illustrator files in Acrobat

Illustrator native files do not need conversion to PDF to be viewed in Acrobat. Acrobat supports opening native Illustrator .ai documents. When you click the Open tool, choose File ➪ Open, or select Create PDF From File and select a native Illustrator .ai file, the file opens in Acrobat without conversion to PDF. All this is possible if the original Illustrator document was saved with an option for Create PDF Compatible File. When you save Illustrator files as native documents and click the Save button in the Save or Save As dialog box, the Illustrator Options dialog box opens, as shown in Figure 9.22. Under the Options, select the Create PDF Compatible File check box. You can then open the file in Acrobat without converting it to PDF.

FIGURE 9.22

Saving with PDF compatibility results in file types that can be opened in Acrobat without conversion to PDF.

Acrobat and Adobe InDesign

When it comes to original authoring programs to create designs for just about any use that ultimately end up as a PDF document, my personal choice is Adobe InDesign. Whether it be a slide presentation, an Acrobat PDF form, a form that you use a PDF template for in Adobe LiveCycle Designer, a brochure, a pamphlet, or any other kind of document outside a simple office memo, InDesign is the premier tool of choice.

With Adobe InDesign you can create layered files, expand your design horizons to new levels, create bookmarks and hyperlinks, export movie and Flash files, and a number of different features you just don't have available in any other application. With InDesign's style sheets for cells and tables, and tools for creating forms and dynamic linking to Excel spreadsheets, this program puts a of control in your hands for superb PDF creation.

To export to PDF from InDesign, choose File ➪ Export. In the Export dialog box, select Adobe PDF from the Format pull-down menu and click Save. The Export Adobe PDF dialog box then appears, as shown in Figure 9.23. Options here provide some similar settings as you find with Adobe Illustrator and Adobe Photoshop as well as a number of additional attribute choices for handling files designed for print, Web hosting, and screen viewing. You can export Bookmarks that appear in the resultant PDF file, export interactivity with buttons and actions, export HTML and hyperlinks, and create PDF documents designed for commercial printing.

FIGURE 9.23

InDesign can export documents with options settings to accommodate files designed for print, Web hosting, and interactive screen viewing.

Exporting PDFs for print

The Preset pull-down menu offers you choices for several Adobe PDF Settings that determine how your PDF is created. Among those options are selections for PDF/X files. PDF/X is a format specifically designed for printing and commercial prepress. When you export to PDF/X, you resolve colorspace problems, transparency problems, and other potential problems faced when printing documents on commercial devices.

CROSS-REF For a detailed explanation of PDF/X and Adobe PDF Settings, see Chapter 10.

Exporting Adobe PDF layers

Just as when exporting layers from Illustrator, you set the default layer view in InDesign that you want to appear in Acrobat as a default view. You can add interactive buttons in InDesign and export your interactive links that are also recognized by Acrobat. In the Export Adobe PDF dialog box shown in Figure 9.23, be certain to check the boxes for Create Acrobat Layers and the Include items such as Bookmarks, Hyperlinks, and Interactive Elements. Click the Export button to export your document to PDF. In Figure 9.24, a layered InDesign CS file with interactive buttons and imported video is prepared for export to PDF.

FIGURE 9.24

A layout is prepared in Adobe InDesign with imported video, interactive buttons, and multiple layers.

When you open the file in Acrobat, a modification of the button attributes sets a different layer visibility and plays the imported video, as shown in Figure 9.25. These kinds of design opportunities provide artists with tools to create effective presentations and electronic brochures that users who download the free Adobe Reader software can view.

FIGURE 9.25

A slight modification to the button attributes changes layer visibility and plays the imported video.

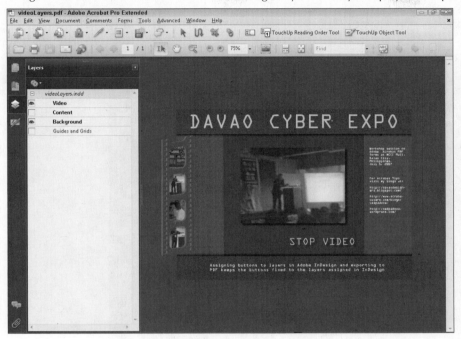

Expanding your design horizon

Something InDesign provides you that isn't available in any other program is a way to create a look where objects fall off the page when viewed in Acrobat viewers. As Brian Tamayo, a Dallas, Texas–based designer who first discovered this InDesign anomaly, says, "Think outside the page." Figure 9.26 shows you an example of an object breaking a page border.

FIGURE 9.26

Adobe InDesign is the only program that permits you to create objects that fall off a page when viewed in Adobe InDesign.

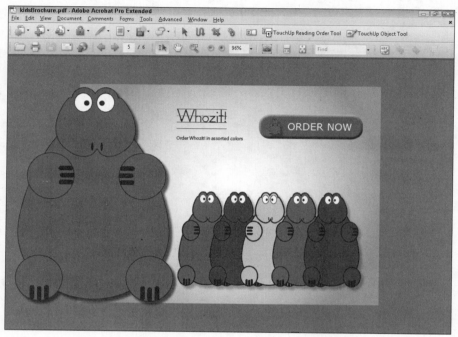

If you want to create a PDF document with a similar design, you need to use Adobe InDesign and follow these steps.

STEPS: Breaking page borders using Adobe InDesign

1. **Open a Master Page.** Open a Master Page in an Adobe InDesign document. This technique requires you to place the object you want to use for breaking a page border in a PDF file to place the image on a Master Page.

2. **Place a graphic.** Use File ➪ Place in Adobe InDesign to import a vector object or photo and place it on a Master Page.

3. **Position the graphic.** When you place a graphic and select it, a bounding box is shown with a midpoint square. The midpoint of the graphic must be inside a page border. Move the graphic so the midpoint falls within the page border.

4. **Convert the graphic to a button.** Choose Object ➪ Interactive ➪ Convert to Button. The object must be converted to a button to be shown in the resultant PDF file.

5. **Save the file.** Complete your design and assign the Master Page to one or all pages in your InDesign document and choose File ⇨ Save.

6. **Export to PDF.** Choose File ⇨ Export and select Adobe PDF from the Save as type (Windows) or Format (Macintosh) pull-down menu. Type a name for your file and click Save.

7. **Enable Interactive Elements.** In the Export Adobe PDF dialog box shown in Figure 9.23, be certain to check the box for Interactive Elements. Click Export and view the PDF document.

 If you want an object pushed outside the page border farther than the midpoint on a selected graphic, add a 1-pixel Photoshop file to your Master Page. Click the graphic and the 1-pixel image and group them. The midpoint will change. You can move a graphic well beyond a page if so desired by spacing the graphic and 1-pixel image apart from each other.

Using Acrobat with Non-Adobe Programs

A number of different application programs support PDF creation from file exports similar to the way Adobe handles exporting to PDF. Programs such as QuarkXPress, CorelDraw, and several others all have their own options for exporting native files to PDF. Many attribute choices featured in the CS programs are also available in those non-Adobe programs that export to PDF. You may need to poke around in the export dialog boxes to find various settings adjustments.

If you use a program that doesn't support direct exports to PDF, you should use the Adobe PDF print driver to create the PDF file.

CROSS-REF **For more information on using the Adobe PDF print driver, see Chapter 7. For more on using Acrobat Distiller, see Chapter 10.**

Summary

- Adobe Creative Suite is a sophisticated solution for file interoperability. All the CS applications export directly to PDF.

- Adobe Photoshop can export directly to PDF as separate files and presentations. Photoshop can open single and multiple PDF documents created by any producer and preserve text and vector art when exporting to PDF.

- Adobe Illustrator exports Flash and SWF () files that can be imported in PDF documents as movie files.

- Adobe Illustrator CS and Adobe InDesign CS export to PDF with layers intact.

- Adobe InDesign CS exports links, Bookmarks, and embedded media to PDF.

- Some non-Adobe programs offer export-to-PDF features similar to the CS applications. For those programs not supporting exports to PDF, you should use the Adobe PDF printer driver.

Chapter 10

Using Acrobat Distiller

Because PDF file creation has been much simplified in Acrobat 9, you may bypass thoughts of learning what Acrobat Distiller does and how PDF documents are converted with the Distiller application. If you remember the PDF conversion steps discussed in the previous three chapters, the Adobe PDF settings were mentioned many times. These settings apply to Acrobat Distiller, and also the conversion of documents for many options from within Acrobat and via exports from authoring programs. They all use the Adobe PDF settings.

In order to successfully produce quality PDF documents when using Distiller, you need to have a basic understanding of how Acrobat Distiller works and what the settings control in regard to converting files to PDF. In some cases Distiller works in the background using Adobe PDF settings you assign to the creation process. Therefore, it is essential that you know how to change settings and understand what options are available to you. In this chapter I cover some advantages of using Acrobat Distiller and discuss how to change the Adobe PDF settings.

IN THIS CHAPTER

Understanding the basics of PostScript

Understanding Distiller preferences

Controlling Adobe PDF settings

Saving and deleting settings files

Monitoring font folders

Creating Watched folders

Using non-Roman character sets

Distilling PostScript

Setting Up the Work Environment

You can access Acrobat Distiller in several ways. You can open Distiller from the Advanced menu command in Acrobat Standard, Acrobat Pro, and Acrobat Pro Extended, you can launch Distiller from the desktop, or you can drag and drop files to the Distiller program application. None of these methods require loading special tools.

CROSS-REF For a detailed description of the various ways to access Acrobat Distiller, see the section "Accessing Distiller" at the end of this chapter.

When you convert files to PDF you can create a PostScript file in other applications and convert the PostScript to PDF using Distiller or Print to the PDF Printer. Therefore, the default view of the toolbars is all you need to follow the instructions throughout this chapter.

Understanding PostScript

Adobe PostScript is a *page description language* — that is, it describes the text and images on your monitor screen in a language. A raster image processor (RIP) interprets this language. Whereas PostScript is the language, the RIP behaves like a compiler. The RIP interprets the file and converts the text and images you see on your monitor to a bitmap image in dots that are plotted on a printing device. In the office environment, you won't see a RIP independent of a PostScript laser printer you use — but it exists. It's built into the printer. With high-end devices such as imagesetters, platesetters, large-format inkjet printers, on-demand printing systems, high-end composite color devices, and film recorders, the RIP is often a separate component that may be either a hardware device or software operating on a dedicated computer.

One of the reasons PostScript has grown to its present popularity is its resolution independence. When you draw a Bézier curve, rectangle, oval, or other geometric object in a vector art authoring application, the resolution displayed by your monitor is 72 pixels per inch (ppi). This image can be printed to a 300 dots per inch (dpi) laser printer or a 3,600 dpi imagesetter. Through the resolution independence of PostScript, essentially the computer "says" to the printer, "Give me all you can." The printer responds by imaging the page at the resolution it is capable of handling. When the file is ripped, the laser printer RIP creates a 300-dpi bitmap, whereas the imagesetter RIP creates a 3,600-dpi bitmap.

With all its popularity and dominance in the market, PostScript does have problems. It comes in many different dialects and is known as a *streamed* language. If you have a QuarkXPress file, for example, and import an Adobe Illustrator EPS file and a CorelDraw EPS file, you'll wind up with three different flavors of PostScript — each according to the way the individual developer handles its coding. If the same font is used by each of the three components, the font description resides in three separate areas of the PostScript file when printed to disk. PostScript is notorious for redundancy, especially with fonts.

As a streamed language, PostScript requires the entire code to be processed by the interpreter before the image bitmap is created. Ever wonder why you need to wait while the RIP is churning for an endless amount of time only to eventually end up with a PostScript error or RIP crash? PostScript can't begin plotting the bitmap image until the entire PostScript stream has been interpreted.

About Imaging Devices

Imagesetters are high-end devices ranging from $10,000 to over $100,000 and are usually found in computer service bureaus and commercial print shops. Imagesetters use laser beams to plot the raster image on either sheet-fed or roll-fed paper or film. The paper is resin coated, and both paper and film require chemical processing through a developer, fix, and wash much like a photographic print. The material is used by a commercial printer to make plates that are wrapped around cylinders on a printing press. These prepress materials are an integral part of offset printing, and much of the printing performed today is handled from a form of digital output to material that is used to create plates for presses.

Direct-to-plate and direct-to-press systems bypass the prepress materials and expose images on plates that are used on print cylinders or directly to the press blankets where the impression receives the ink.

On-demand printing is a term describing machines that bypass the prepress process by taking the digital file from a computer directly to the press. Depending on the engineering of the output device, the consumable materials may consist of toner (as used in copy machines) or ink (as used on printing presses).

PDF, on the other hand, is like a database file — it has a database structure. PDF eliminates redundancy with file resources. Fonts, for example, appear only once, no matter how many occurrences are actually used. In addition, PDF takes all the dialectical differences of PostScript and converts them to a single dialect. Whereas a PostScript file containing many pages requires the entire file to be downloaded to the RIP and ultimately printed, a PDF file is page independent in that each individual page is imaged before proceeding to the next page. In short, PDF is much more efficient than PostScript for printing purposes.

Creating PostScript files

In some ways a PostScript file is very similar to a PDF file. If, for example, you create a layout in Adobe InDesign, Adobe FrameMaker, or QuarkXPress with images and type fonts, the document page can be printed to disk as a PostScript file. In doing so, you can embed all graphic images and fonts in the file. If you take your file to a service center, the file can be downloaded to a printing device. Assuming you created the PostScript file properly, the file prints with complete integrity.

On desktop printers, printing to a PostScript file is just like printing to a device. On printers in commercial imaging centers, there are additional requirements and considerations, including the following:

CROSS-REF The following items address PDF creation for the purpose of printing files on commercial printing equipment. For more information on commercial printing, see Chapter 32.

- **PPD device selection.** PostScript Printer Description files are used with specific devices, and you should always use a device PPD when printing the PostScript devices having PPDs. Distiller PPDs are used only with Acrobat Distiller.

- **Page size.** With desktop printers, you often have only a few page sizes. With printers that have multiple trays or interchangeable trays, you select the appropriate page size for the tray used. With imaging equipment, you need to be certain the page size is properly selected to include all image data and printer's marks. Assume for a moment a document is created in the standard page size for a letter (8.5 × 11 inches). However, to accommodate printer's marks (registration and color bars), it turns out that the page area needs to be defined larger than a letter page. In the Paper Size area of the dialog box shown in Figure 10.1, the word "Custom" appears, indicating the page is a custom size. The thumbnail in Figure 10.1 shows how the page fits within the defined size. In this example, all data and printer's marks print within the defined page. If your page is too small, some clipping of the data occurs when printed or when a PDF file is generated.

- **Font inclusion.** You may need to specifically tell the host application to include fonts in the PostScript file. If the file is printed at a service center, you definitely need to include the fonts in the file you submit for output. If you distill the file in Acrobat Distiller, the fonts need to be loaded on your system in order for you to embed the fonts in the PDF file. When you have options in Print dialog boxes for font inclusion, always choose to embed the fonts.

- **Screening.** Halftone frequencies, or *line screens,* can be printed at different settings. With desktop printers the maximum line screen available for the device is often the default. 600-dpi laser printers, for example, most commonly use a maximum line screen of 85 lines per inch (lpi). With imaging equipment, you need to first know the requirements of the commercial printer and take his/her advice depending on the paper, press, and pre-press material. Therefore, if your file is ultimately printed at 133 lpi, you must enter this value in the Print dialog box of the application creating the PostScript file.

  Setting the halftone frequency is an important issue only if the PostScript file is down-loaded to an imaging device where the default screens are not overridden by a technician. For files printed from Acrobat directly to printing devices, the technician who prints the file also sets the frequency in the Acrobat Advanced Printing dialog box.

  Screening can also be a particular type relative to the printing device and RIP. Stochastic screening, Crystal Raster, AGFA Balanced Screens, and others are available from a PPD selection for a particular device. For these settings you need to contact your service center for the precise screening options needed and use a device PPD.

- **Color.** If separations are to be printed, you must make certain all identified colors are properly named in the host document. There is often an option in a Print dialog box to select separations. As you view a color list of potential separations, it is imperative to verify all colors appearing are those you specified in the document. If a spot color is in the current document, the color doesn't print unless it is an identified color in the Print dialog box. Fortunately, in Acrobat 9 a method is available for previewing separations. Before sending files off to a service center, make a habit of previewing files for printing in Acrobat.

CROSS-REF   For information regarding separation previews and soft-proofing color, see Chapter 32.

FIGURE 10.1

The page size was defined as a custom size to include the printer's marks and page information.

Encoding

Encoding comes in two flavors: Binary and ASCII. Binary encoding results in smaller files and prints faster on PostScript Level 2 and PostScript 3 devices. As a default you'll want to use binary encoding if you see options in the Print dialog box to choose between ASCII and Binary. If no option is available for choosing between ASCII and Binary when you print a PostScript file, the file encoding defaults to Binary.

PostScript levels

PostScript originated sometime in 1976, and later it was updated to a version called Interpress at the Xerox Palo Alto Research Center (PARC). Interpress was designed for output to early laser printers. Xerox abandoned the project, and two of the staff at Xerox PARC decided to take it forth and develop it. In 1981, John Warnock and Chuck Geschke formed Adobe Systems Incorporated, and Adobe PostScript was their first product.

On March 21, 1985, the digital print revolution was founded when Apple Computer, Aldus Corporation, Adobe Systems, and Linotype collaborated on an open architecture system for electronic typesetting. Later that year Apple Computer introduced the LaserWriter printer that came with a whopping 13 fonts fried into the printer's ROM chips and a price tag of $6,500. If you were outputting to a PostScript device in 1987, when Adobe Illustrator first appeared, you may still be waiting for that 12K Illustrator file to spit out of your laser printer. PostScript Level 1 was a major technological advance, but by today's standards it was painfully slow. Many in the imaging world remember all too well still waiting at 3:00 a.m. for the final file to print after ripping over eight hours.

In 1990, Adobe Systems introduced PostScript Level 2, which was a more robust version of PostScript and a screamer compared to the first release. In addition to speed, PostScript Level 2 provided these features:

- **Color separation.** In earlier days, color was preseparated on Level 1 devices. PostScript Level 2 enabled imaging specialists to separate a composite color file into the four process colors, Cyan, Magenta, Yellow, and Black. Also, there was support for spot color in PostScript Level 2.

- **Improved font handling.** In the early days of PostScript imaging, there were more font nightmares than you can imagine. Font encoding for PostScript fonts handled a maximum of only 256 characters. Other font sets such as Japanese have thousands of individual characters. PostScript Level 2 introduced a composite font technology that handled many different foreign character sets.

- **Compression.** Getting the large files across a 10 Base-T network was also a burden in the Level 1 days. PostScript Level 2 introduced data compression and supported such compression schemes as JPEG, LZW, and RLE. The files are transmitted compressed, which means they get to the RIP faster, and then decompressed at the RIP. In a large imaging center, the compression greatly improved network traffic and workflows.

In 1996, Adobe introduced PostScript 3 (note that "Level" was dropped from the name). Perhaps one of the more remarkable and technologically advanced features of PostScript 3 is the inclusion of Web publishing with direct support for HTML, PDF, and Web content. PostScript 3 also provides the ability to create In-RIP separations. When you send a PDF file to an imaging center using PostScript 3 RIPs you can deliver composite color files that are sent directly to the RIP where they are separated at the imaging device.

Using Acrobat Distiller Preferences

Acrobat Distiller is launched from within Acrobat. As a separate executable application, Acrobat Distiller can also be launched from a desktop shortcut or alias or by double-clicking the program icon (acrodist) contained in the Acrobat folder.

NOTE   **Acrobat Distiller is accessible from the Advanced ⇨ Print Production ⇨ Acrobat Distiller menu command. The menu to open Distiller is nested in a submenu in the Advanced menu. In versions 7.0 and earlier of Acrobat, Distiller was accessed from within Acrobat via the Advanced ⇨ Acrobat Distiller menu command.**

When you first launch Acrobat Distiller, it looks like a fairly simple application. Examining the menus immediately tells you there's not much to do in the File menu. This menu is limited to opening a file, addressing preferences, and quitting the program. Distiller's real power is contained in the second menu item — the Settings menu. The commands listed in this menu offer all the control for determining how PostScript files are converted to PDF.

Before making choices in the Settings menu, look over the options in the Preferences menu. When you choose File ⇨ Preferences on the Distiller Window (Windows) or the top-level Distiller ⇨ Preferences (Macintosh), a dialog box opens. The options available are listed among three groups that include Startup Alerts, Output Options, and Log Files, as shown in Figure 10.2 for Windows and in Figure 10.3 for Macintosh.

FIGURE 10.2

Access Acrobat Distiller Preferences by choosing File ⇨ Preferences. Preferences enable you to customize startup and output options.

FIGURE 10.3

On the Macintosh, you select Preferences from the Distiller top-level menu.

Startup Alerts

The two items listed in the Startup Alerts section of the Distiller Preferences dialog box have to do with your initial startup upon launching the Distiller application:

- **Notify when Watched Folders are unavailable.** This command enables Distiller to monitor a folder or directory on your computer or network server to automatically distill PostScript files placed in watched folders. In an office environment, you can have different users create PostScript files and send them to a server for automatic distillation.

CROSS-REF For more information on working with watched folders, see the "Creating watched folders" section later in this chapter.

- **Notify when Windows TEMP folder is nearly full (Windows only).** Distiller needs temporary disk space to convert the PostScript files to PDF documents. If the available hard disk space on your startup volume becomes less than 1 megabyte, Distiller prompts you with a warning dialog box. Leaving this preference setting enabled is always a good idea. The amount of temporary space required by Distiller is approximately twice the size of the PostScript file being distilled.

Output Options

Output Options relate to what you intend to do with the PDF both in terms of where it is saved and what to do after conversion:

- **Ask for PDF file destination.** When enabled, this option prompts you for the location of the saved file.

- **Ask to replace existing PDF file.** Selecting this option warns you if a PDF of the same name exists in the folder where the new PDF is saved. If you want to use different Adobe PDF settings and create two PDF files, you may forget that you have a PDF with a filename the same as the new one you are creating. With this option, you are warned if Distiller attempts to overwrite your existing file.

- **View PDF when using Distiller.** After the PDF has been created, the default Acrobat viewer launches and the PDF opens in the Document pane.

TIP If you are running Adobe Reader and Acrobat on the same computer, open the viewer you want to designate as the default viewer. When prompted to set the viewer as the default, click Yes in the dialog box. All subsequent PDF files are opened in the default viewer.

Log Files

A log file describes the sequence of steps used to produce the PDF file. The Log Files section offers an option for what to do with the log file: the Delete Log Files for successful jobs option. A log file is an ASCII text file detailing the distillation process. If an error is produced during distillation, the log file records the error even though the PDF is not created. Viewing the log file can be helpful in debugging problems with files not successfully being converted to PDF. If the PDF is successfully created, there would be no need to keep the log file on your computer. By default, you'll want to enable this check box to eliminate the clutter.

Editing Adobe PDF Settings

Distiller can be assigned some custom settings and you can also choose from some preinstalled Adobe PDF settings. All settings are selectable from a pull-down menu. If you need to create some custom settings you open the Settings menu and select Edit Adobe PDF Settings.

Using the Default Adobe PDF settings

If your work can be satisfied using one of the preset settings, open the Default Settings pull-down menu, as shown in Figure 10.4. Select a setting you want to use and Distiller uses your selected setting as a new default. If you distill files from within Acrobat, the new default settings are used. Each time you open Distiller, you see the new default you last selected in Distiller. Open a PostScript or EPS file and the file is converted to PDF using the settings appearing in the Distiller window as Default Settings.

The Default choices for Adobe PDF settings when you install Acrobat are as follows:

- **High Quality Print.** The preset settings associated with this option are established for the highest-quality images for high-end digital prepress and printing. The lowest levels of compression and downsampling are used to preserve image quality.

- **Oversized Pages.** This option is designed specifically for PDFs of oversized pages that you might see from engineering drawings.

- **PDF/A-1b:2005(CMYK).** PDF/A is an ISO standard for archival purposes. Acrobat Distiller does a check to assure PDF/A compliance; hence you have PDF/A as an option choice. The CMYK version of the PDF/A standard is used with CMYK files.

- **PDF/A-1b:2005(RGB).** The same as the first PDF/A standard mentioned in the last bullet, this standard is used with RGB files.

- **PDF/X-1a:2001.** For prepress and printing, PDF/X files are streamlined for print output. PDF/X is an ISO standard. PDF/X files result in PDF documents that eliminate data not essential for printing. It does not mean the file sizes are necessarily smaller, but they are optimized for printing and produce fewer problems than non-PDF/X files. The PDF/X-1a format supports process (CMYK) and spot color.

- **PDF/X-3:2002.** Like PDF/X-1a, the file format is a subset of the PDF format. PDF/X-3 files support ICC profile embedding. If working in a color-managed workflow, use this flavor of PDF/X.

- **Press Quality.** These settings are virtually identical to the settings for High Quality (see first bullet). The difference between the two is that when you use the High Quality settings, any fonts not available for embedding during distillation are noted in the log file but the PDF is produced without the embedded fonts. When you use Press Quality, the job cancels at the first encounter of a font not available for embedding and the PDF is not produced.

- **Smallest File Size.** The intent for this option is to produce files for Web hosting, emailing, and screen views. The name implies that the file sizes are very small, but in reality, you can create smaller file sizes by editing the downsampling of the images. The sampling resolution only downsamples files above 150 pixels per inch (ppi) to 100 ppi. You can create a new set for smaller file sizes and downsample all images to 72 ppi for Web hosting when the images don't need to be displayed above a 100% view.

- **Standard.** The general-purpose setting and quite often the default when accessing settings the first time in Acrobat is the Standard choice. For office desktop color printers, laser printers, photocopiers, and general-purpose printing, the settings create PDF files with no lower than 150 ppi resolutions and embed fonts when necessary.

If one of these preset conditions comes close to producing the type of PDF you want to create, but it doesn't exactly meet your needs, go ahead and select that preset option and then choose Settings ➪ Edit Adobe PDF Settings to open a dialog box where you can make changes. When you finish editing the settings to your satisfaction, you have an opportunity to save your own custom preset file that you can access at a later time. There are six panes for which you can choose to change the settings — General, Images, Fonts, Color, Advanced, and Standards.

FIGURE 10.4

Open the Default Settings pull-down menu and select the Adobe PDF setting you want to use to convert a PostScript or EPS file to PDF.

Each setting in the list of default settings has different attributes for PDF conversion assigned to the setting. You can modify the default settings or create new settings. The settings choices you have available are all accessed in the Adobe PDF Settings dialog box.

Changing Adobe PDF settings

Select Settings ➪ Edit Adobe PDF Settings in the Distiller window (Windows) or from the top-level menu bar (Macintosh). The Adobe PDF Settings dialog box opens, as shown in Figure 10.5. You have six categories from which to choose different settings options. The default is General, as shown in Figure 10.5, followed by Images, Fonts, Color, Advanced, and Standards. With the exception of the PDF/A Standard in the Standards tab, all settings are identical to the same settings in Acrobat 7.

FIGURE 10.5

The default Adobe PDF settings for Press Quality

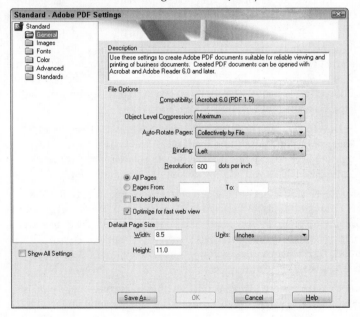

General settings

General settings are found under the General option in the Adobe PDF Settings dialog box (see Figure 10.5) and include the following options:

- **Description.** A field box at the top of the General pane is editable and enables you to add a message description about the new settings you create. Place the cursor in the field box, highlight any existing text, and delete it. Type your new description in the field box. When you save the new setting, the description is saved along with your chosen options.

- **Compatibility.** You have choices for Acrobat 4.0, 5.0, 6.0, 7.0, and 8.0 compatibilities. Using earlier compatibility versions may affect the visibility of PDFs with earlier viewers. If you work in an enterprise where a large installed user base is using a particular version of Acrobat, create files for the compatibility version consistent with the site license of the Acrobat version. If you're creating files for mass distribution, think about forgetting Acrobat 3 and 4 compatibilities and focus on versions 5 through 8. Be aware that if you create Acrobat 6 through 8 compatible files, users of earlier versions won't be able to view your files. Excluding older versions is always a trade-off, and you need to clearly think about whom you want to target when distributing content.

- **Object Level Compression.** Compressed objects are consolidated into streams for more efficient compression. You have choices for applying no compression (Off) or using Tags Only. You can reduce file sizes by selecting Maximum for Object Level Compression.

- **Auto-Rotate Pages.** You can have pages automatically or individually rotated during distillation. Choices from the pull-down menu include turning Off, rotating Collectively by File, and rotating Individually. When you select Collectively by File, Acrobat analyzes the text in the file and rotates pages based on the orientation of the majority of the text in the entire file. When you choose Individually, Acrobat rotates each page based on the majority of text on a given page. Selecting Off results in no page rotation.

- **Binding.** This setting relates to viewing pages in an Acrobat viewer with Two-Up and Two-Up Continuous page layouts and with thumbnails when viewed aside each other. In addition, the binding can affect other items like the direction of scrolling text across the screen and certain animated effects you add. By default, the binding is left-sided.

- **Resolution.** Settings for Resolution affect only vector objects and type in EPS files. The settings range between 72 and 4000 dpi. A handy Tool Tip appears when you click in the field box that shows the upper and lower limits of acceptable values. Lower resolution settings may create banding with gradients when files are printed. In practicality, you'll notice no visual difference if you change the resolution to the default of 600. Setting the resolution to 2400 adds less than 3K to your file size.

- **All Pages/Pages From.** You can choose to create a PDF within a specified range of pages from a PostScript file that has been printed to disk from a document containing many pages. If one page is having trouble converting to PDF, you can eliminate it from distillation by choosing a specified page range. The default, All Pages, distills all pages in the PostScript file.

- **Embed thumbnails.** Acrobat and Reader 9 no longer use embedded thumbnails even if they are present. This is a legacy feature for older viewers. There is never a good reason to embed thumbnails.

- **Optimize for fast web view.** An optimized PDF file may be smaller than one created without optimization. All files intended to be used for screen views, CD-ROM replication, and Web usage should all be optimized. Optimized files are primarily designed for byte-serving on Web servers for page-at-a-time downloads. Generally, almost any printing device also accepts optimized files. As a default, keep this option On. Acrobat optimizes files by eliminating repeating elements and supplying pointers to where the first occurrence of an object is found in the file. Optimization also prepares files for page-at-a-time downloading from Web servers. If byte-serving capability exists on a server, the optimized files download pages as they are viewed.

- **Default Page Size.** Setting page sizes in these field boxes only applies to distillation of EPS and PostScript files where page boundaries are not specified. Whatever you enter in the field boxes when distilling PostScript files is ignored if the page boundary is included in the file. If you want to trim a page size or create a larger page size for an EPS file, you can establish the dimensions in the field boxes for width and height. The Units pull-down menu enables you to choose from four different units of measure.

Images

Image settings are located under the second tab of the Adobe PDF Settings dialog box, as shown in Figure 10.6.

FIGURE 10.6

The second tab is Images.

Color images

The first category handles color images used in your original file. You have choices for the sampling method and the amount of compression you want to apply. These include:

- **Downsample.** The Downsample pull-down menu offers choices for no sampling or three different sampling methods that include:

    - **Off.** This turns off all compression for color images.

    - **Bicubic Downsampling to.** A pull-down menu and two field boxes appear as your first choices in the Color Image section. Bicubic Downsampling is the default setting for all preset Adobe PDF settings. Bicubic downsampling uses a weighted average to determine the resampled pixel color. The algorithm is much more mathematically intensive and, as a result, this method takes the longest time to complete distillation when files are downsampled. The upside is it produces the best image quality for continuous tone images. With this method as well as the other two choices for resampling images there are two field boxes where the amount of sampling is user defined. The values range between 9 and 2400 ppi. The "for images above" field box enables you to choose when an image is resampled.

    - **Average Downsampling to.** From the pull-down menu, the item following the Off selection is Average Downsampling to. When you resample an image by downsampling, the average pixel value of a sample area is replaced with a pixel of the averaged color. The field boxes to the right of the sampling method are for user-determined sampling amounts, used in the same way as the preceding Bicubic method.

    - **Subsampling to.** When Subsampling is specified, a pixel within the center of the sample area is chosen as the value applied to the sample area. Thus, downsampling noted previously, replaces pixels from averaged color values, whereas subsampling replaces pixels from a given color value. Of the two methods, subsampling significantly reduces the amount of time to resample the image. Because all that averaging is taking place with downsampling, the calculations are more extensive, thereby increasing the distillation time. Subsampling, however, may result in more problems in the printed PDF file. Unless you have a large single-color background, you are better off choosing Bicubic downsampling when printing to hard copy.

- **Compression.** The pull-down menu enables you to select from Automatic (JPEG), JPEG, ZIP, or Off, depending on the compatibility setting you use. When you select Automatic, Distiller examines each image and automatically determines which compression to use (that is, either ZIP or JPEG). If an image has large amounts of a common color value, ZIP compression is used. If an image consists of smooth transitions of color, such as a continuous tone photograph, JPEG compression is used. If you want to apply the same compression to all images, you can select either the JPEG or ZIP options. Doing so eliminates any decision making by Distiller about the type of compression to be applied. When you select Off, no compression is applied. Although you may want to downsample images as noted earlier with one of the downsampling options, you may not want to apply compression to the images.

- **Image Quality.** After you select the compression type, you have one of five choices (also depending on compatibility) for the amount of compression applied. Maximum relates to less compression, whereas Minimum relates to high compression. For high-end prepress, use the Maximum or High choice from the pull-down menu. For desktop color printers, use Medium quality; and for Web, screen, or CD-ROM replication, use Low quality. The Minimum setting might be used in some cases with screen or Web graphics, but continuous tone photographs often appear visibly degraded. You might use this setting to transfer files quickly across the Internet for client approvals and then later use a higher setting for the final production documents.

Grayscale

All the choices you have for color images are identical for grayscale images. You can use different settings for color and grayscale images by toggling through all the options. When the final PDF is produced, the sampling and compression for your images are respectively applied from choices made for each image type.

Monochrome images

Monochrome images include only two color values — black and white. Photoshop line art is a monochrome image. This is not to be confused with line art as we define it with vector art applications. The sampling methods available to you for monochrome images are identical to those described for color images. Compression settings, however, are much different. In addition to Off for applying no compression, the options include the following:

- **CCITT Group 3.** The International Coordinating Committee for Telephony and Telegraphy (CCITT) Group 3 compression is used by fax machines. The images are compressed in horizontal rows, one row at a time.

- **CCITT Group 4.** CCITT Group 4 is a general-purpose compression method that produces good compression for most types of bitmap images. This compression method is the default and typically the best method for bitmap images.

- **ZIP.** ZIP compression is more efficient than earlier versions of Acrobat that used LZW compression. ZIP achieves approximately 20 percent more compression. It should be used when large areas of a single color appear in an image.

- **Run Length.** The Run Length format is a lossless compression scheme particularly favorable to bitmap monochrome images. You can run tests yourself for the compression method that works best for you. Typically, CCITT Group 4 handles most of your needs when compressing these images.

- **Anti-Alias to gray.** Bitmap images may appear pixelated onscreen or, in some cases, when printed. By using anti-aliasing, images are rendered with a smoother appearance. You can choose the amount of anti-aliasing from the pull-down menu. Choices are for 2, 4, and 8 bits that produce 4, 16, and 256 levels of gray, respectively. If you use anti-aliasing with scanned type, small point sizes may appear blurry, especially with higher gray levels.

■ **Policy.** Click the Policy button and the Adobe PDF – Image Policy dialog box opens as shown in Figure 10.7. The options in the dialog box enable you to control a job determined from decisions you make about image resolution. From the pull-down menus below each resolution item you can select from Ignore, Warn and Continue, and Cancel Job. If a given image is below a resolution value you add to one of the three field boxes for a given image type, you can instruct Acrobat to honor the choice(s) you make from the menu selections. Ignore is the default and no result occurs if images fall below a certain resolution. Warn and Continue opens a warning dialog box, informs you that Distiller found an image below the resolution you specify in one of the field boxes, and continues producing the PDF. Cancel Job stops all distillation if an image is found below the resolution setting(s).

FIGURE 10.7

The Adobe PDF – Image Policy dialog box enables you to set options for a job determined on decisions you make for image resolution.

Guidelines for sampling images

Acrobat handles sampling appropriate for your output needs as long as the image sampling is equal to or greater than the requirements for the output. If image resolution is lower than the output needs, then Distiller isn't able to upsample images to provide the necessary resolution. Even though Distiller can effectively downsample images, you should observe a few rules.

First, you should sample the resolution for all images in a layout or design at the highest output requirement. For example, if you intend to use prepress and commercial printing, the image sample needs a resolution to support commercial printing. In this regard, you want to sample images in Photoshop at the required resolution. Don't rely on Distiller to downsample images during distillation for all your professional print jobs. The time you save can add up if you're converting many files with high-resolution images. When you open the Adobe PDF settings and select the Images pane, select Off for the sampling items.

You use the second rule when repurposing images. If you have a PostScript file that has been printed for a higher order of output, like the commercial printing discussed earlier in this chapter, then you don't need to create a second PostScript file for another output destination. Use the same PostScript file and select the sampling options appropriate for the output. Using this same example, if you now want to create a PDF for screen views, select Bicubic Downsampling to and set the resolution to 72 dpi.

PDF WORKFLOW The "Guidelines for sampling images" apply to workflows where you create PostScript files and can easily distill PostScript files using different Adobe PDF settings. If you have a collection of PDF files that were prepared for a given output such as commercial printing, and you want to repurpose the files for another output source such as Web hosting or screen viewing, use the PDF Optimizer in Acrobat Professional or Acrobat Pro Extended.

CROSS-REF For more information on repurposing PDF files and using the PDF Optimizer, see Chapter 18.

Fonts

The distinctive advantage of using the Portable Document Format is that it maintains file integrity across computers and across platforms. One of the greatest problems with file integrity is the handling of fonts. Fortunately, Distiller provides the ability to embed fonts within the PDF so the end user won't need font installations to view and print PDF files. The Fonts pane, shown in Figure 10.8, offers options for setting font-embedding attributes during distillation.

FIGURE 10.8

The Fonts item in the Adobe PDF settings displays the control over font embedding available to you during distillation.

Options in the Fonts pane include the following:

- **Embed all fonts.** Unless you have a specific reason not to embed fonts, this option should always be enabled for file exchanges and printing. You might choose not to embed fonts when you want to reduce files to the smallest possible size for Web hosting or if your documents will be exclusively in your organization and everyone has the fonts used.

CAUTION   **Many different font developers exist, and the permissions for use of fonts from these developers vary considerably. To legally include font embedding in a PDF file, you need to know whether the developer provides the permission for font embedding. Adobe original fonts that are owned by Linotype-Hell, International Typeface Corporation, AGFA, AlphaOmega, Bigelow & Holmes, Fundicion Typografica Neufville, and Monotype Typography, Ltd., as well as those in the Adobe library, can be used for font embedding without written releases. Fonts with licensing restrictions often appear with an explanation of the limitations of use. If in doubt, you'll need to check with the developer or distributor to inquire as to whether you can legally distribute PDF files that include certain fonts. Failure to do so may result in a copyright violation.**

- **Embed OpenType fonts.** The box is active only when using Acrobat 7 or greater compatibility. This option is not recommended for normal workflows. If you have a special need to embed the entire OpenType font, check this box.

- **Subset embedded fonts when percent of characters used is less than [ ].** Some PDF producers provide you an opportunity to subset PostScript, OpenType, and TrueType fonts. The difference between the subsetting in Distiller as opposed to other producers is your ability to determine when a font is subset. With Distiller, you can specify when you want subsetting to occur. The subsetting percentage has to do with the percentage of *glyphs* (special renderings) in the font. If 100% is selected, Distiller always subsets the embedded font. Lower percentages determine what characters among the set are embedded. Type 3, TrueType, and CID fonts are always embedded and subsetted regardless of what value is supplied. (For font format descriptions, see Table 10.1 later in this chapter.)

    When two or more PostScript files are converted to PDF with Acrobat Distiller using font subsetting, Distiller gives the resulting PDF only one font subset. The result is a more efficient PDF document and produces smaller file sizes, especially when combining several PostScript files to produce a single PDF.

- **When embedding fails.** This pull-down menu offers three choices. Choose Ignore to ignore a failed font being embedded, in which case distillation continues. The Warn and Continue option displays a warning and then continues distillation. Choose Cancel to cancel the distillation if a font embedding error occurs. When sending files off to service centers for imaging or when font substitution is not desired, use this latter option as your default. If the PDF is not produced, you won't inadvertently forget there was a problem with font embedding.

- **Embedding.** The left side of the dialog box lists all fonts available for embedding. From the pull-down menu, you select from the different folders Distiller monitors for fonts. Distiller can monitor font locations on your computer. If you want to view the font list from another monitored folder, click the pull-down menu and select the folder.

Regardless of what is listed in the Embedding list, Distiller can also embed fonts that were included in the PostScript file or all the folders listed for monitoring. The fonts to be embedded must be present in either the PostScript file or a monitored folder.

NOTE **Fonts that have license restrictions are shown in the Font Source list with a padlock icon. If you select the font, the restriction attributes are displayed in the Fonts pane. You cannot move locked fonts to the Always Embed list.**

■ **Always Embed.** A list of fonts for always embedding appears to the right of the Embedding list. You add fonts to this list by selecting them from the Embedding list and clicking the right-pointing chevron (double arrows). You can select multiple fonts by pressing the Ctrl (Windows) key or ⌘ (Macintosh) key and clicking all the fonts to be included. If the fonts are listed in a contiguous display, press Shift+click. After selecting the font(s), click the right-pointing chevron. A good use for the Always Embed list might be for a font that appears in your company logo. Regardless of the type of document you create, you may want to always include your corporate font set in all your documents to avoid any font substitution.

NOTE **The design of TrueType and OpenType fonts enables the type designer the ability to prevent font embedding. These fonts can be moved to the Always Embed list, but if they are designed without embedding permissions, they fail to embed in PDFs. Font embedding errors are reported in the log file, which you can view in a text editor. If a PDF is produced, you can choose File ⇨ Properties ⇨ Fonts to determine whether the font was embedded.**

■ **Never Embed.** This list operates the same way as the Always Embed list. You select fonts to be eliminated from the set of monitored fonts or fonts contained in a PostScript file. One use for this list might be to eliminate Courier, Times, Helvetica, and Symbol (the Base 14 fonts). Because they are usually burned into ROM chips on most PostScript devices, you rarely have a problem either viewing them or printing documents containing these fonts.

■ **Add Name.** You can add fonts to the Always Embed list or the Never Embed list by entering the font name in a separate dialog box. To add a font name, you must type the name in the dialog box precisely as the font is identified. When you click the Add Name button in the Fonts pane, the Add Font Name dialog box opens where you enter the name in the field box. Two radio buttons exist for determining where the font is added. Select either the Always Embed list or Never Embed list as needed. Click Done, and the font appears in the appropriate list.

■ **Remove.** If you add a font name to either the Always Embed list or the Never Embed list, and you want to delete that name, select the font name to be deleted and click Remove. You can't remove fonts from the Embedding list. The only time Remove is enabled is when you select a font name in either the Always Embed list or Never Embed list.

NOTE **The priority used by Distiller to decide whether to embed a font in the PDF follows an order to resolve ambiguity. The Never Embed list is viewed by Distiller as having the highest order of priority. If you place a font in the Never Embed list, it is not embedded even though you may add the same font to the Always Embed list.**

Font types

Any PDF author will tell you the continuing problem with file displays and printing, as well as producing PDFs, relates to font handling. People swear at times that they have enabled all the appropriate controls for font embedding and PDF file creation, yet the resulting PDF either displays or prints with font substitution. Gathering as much knowledge as you can with regard to font evolution, design, engineering, and proper use helps you understand how to overcome problems and provide solutions for your workflow. To gain a little more understanding, look at the font types, formats, and their characteristics:

- **Type 0.** Type 0 (zero) is a high-level composite font format that references multiple font descendents. Type 0 fonts use an OCF (Original Composite Font) format that was Adobe's first effort in attempting to implement a format for handling fonts with large character sets. A good example of a font using a large character set is Asian Language font types. Today, the OCF format is not supported.

- **Type 1.** Type 1 fonts used to be the most popular PostScript font; however, today the OpenType fonts have surpassed Type 1 in popularity. Type 1 fonts are single-byte fonts handled well by font managers and all PostScript printers. Type 1 fonts use a specialized subset of the PostScript language, which is optimized for performance.

NOTE The one problem with Type 1 fonts is there isn't a means for flagging the font for *don't embed*. As a result, the end user can't determine font permissions for embedding Type 1 fonts. As of this writing Adobe has converted all its Type 1 fonts to OpenType fonts. OpenType fonts always have an extra bit to determine embedding rights. For more information on OpenType fonts, see "OpenType Font Format" later in this section.

- **Type 2.** Type 2 fonts offer compact character description procedures for outline fonts. They were designed to be used with the Compact Font Format (CFF). The CFF format is designed for font embedding and substitution with Acrobat PDFs.

- **Type 3.** Type 3 fonts are special fonts that only exist in PostScript and PDF — you will never see them installed on your Mac or Windows computer. They were used in the early days of PostScript for the transition of bitmapped fonts to outline fonts and are rarely seen in modern typesetting solutions.

- **OpenType Font Format.** OpenType is a joint effort by Adobe Systems, Apple Computer, and Microsoft to provide a new generation of type font technology. OpenType makes no distinction between Type 1 and TrueType fonts. It acts as a *container* for both Type 1 and TrueType. OpenType doesn't care whether the font is Type 1 or TrueType; it uses the font inside the OpenType container accordingly. Font developers have a much easier way of porting font designs to a single format in production and mastering as well as across platforms. The OpenType format is supported with font embedding and distillation. Fonts eventually produced with this technology are as reliable as you find with Type 1 and TrueType fonts. In addition, OpenType offers a means for flagging the fonts for embedding permissions.

- **Compact Font Format.** CFF is similar to the Type 1 format but offers much more compact encoding and optimization. It was designed to support Type 2 fonts but can be used with other types. CFF can be embedded in PDFs with the PDF version 1.2 format and Acrobat 3.0 compatibility. Fonts supporting this format are converted by Distiller during distillation to CFF/Type 2 fonts and embedded in the PDF.

- **CID-keyed Fonts.** This format was developed to take advantage of large character sets, particularly the Asian CJK (Chinese, Japanese, and Korean) fonts. The format is an extension of the Type 1 format and supports ATM and PostScript printing. Kerning and spacing for these character sets are better handled in the OpenType format.

When distilling PostScript with Acrobat Distiller, font embedding and substitution are allowed as described in Table 10.1.

TABLE 10.1

Distiller Handling of Font Embedding and Subsetting According to Type Format

Font	Never Embed	Always Embed	Subset
Type 1	Yes	Yes	Yes
TrueType	Yes	Yes	Always subsetted
OpenType*	Yes	Yes	Always subsetted

*OpenType is supported only with Distiller 5.0 and greater.

Color

Adobe has been working on developing standard color viewing and file tagging for color spaces for some time. Releases of the latest software products continue to support sophisticated color-handling methods. Latest releases of products such as Adobe Illustrator and Adobe Photoshop have color control options consistent with the new color-handling features initially introduced in Acrobat 5. When making choices for color handling, your first decision is whether to convert color. After your conversion choice, you move on to working spaces and profile assumptions. If you tag a file for conversion, what profiles do you want to embed in the document? Under the Color Management Policies settings, you choose control for many conditions for prepress operations as well as onscreen viewing. As you view the Color pane in the Adobe PDF settings, examine each of the controls available for color handling, as shown in Figure 10.9.

TIP A thorough coverage of color management is a complex subject and beyond the scope of this book. If you are confused about many issues discussed in this chapter or you want to work on developing a color-managed workflow, open any Acrobat viewer. Select the Search tool and click Search PDFs on the Internet. Add color management for the search criteria and select Match Exact word or phrase from the pull-down menu. Click the Search the Internet button. Many PDF documents are available on the Internet that define color management and discuss how to set up color-managed workflows. You can build a library of articles and essays on the subject and keep them readily available on your local computer.

FIGURE 10.9

Manage color profiles in the Color pane.

Adobe Color settings

Working with a color management system requires you to make some decisions about how the color is viewed on your computer monitor and on the final output medium. In some cases the monitor view and output medium view are the same, such as Acrobat viewer files onscreen and Web files. You make the first of your color decisions from among the choices in the pull-down menu for Settings File.

When you select None from the pull-down menu, you can custom edit the Color Management Policies and Working Spaces choices. If you choose an option other than None, the Color Management Policies and Working Spaces options are grayed out. Other choices for settings include prepress defaults, Photoshop emulation, defaults for Web graphics, and turning off color management. When color management and profile embedding is controlled by other programs such as Photoshop, leave the setting to None and turn off all color management for the choices discussed next.

Color Management Policies

If you select None from the Settings pull-down menu, the options for Color Management Policies and Intent are active. If you make any other choice from the menu, these items are grayed out. Choices for the Color Management Policies are different depending on what compatibility choice you select in the General pane of the Adobe PDF Settings dialog box. Acrobat 4.0 compatibility offers different options than the 5.0, 6.0, 7.0, and 8.0 compatibilities. As you look at the following policy choices, keep in mind that the settings change according to the compatibility selection you made:

- **Leave Color Unchanged.** Enable this menu item if you presume all color handling in the PostScript file is defined for your specific needs. No color conversion occurs and device-independent colors remain unchanged. When you send files to color-calibrated devices, you should use this option. The presumption is the device specifies all color handling and the file is not to be tagged for color management.

- **Tag Everything for Color Management.** When you choose Acrobat 4.0 compatibility or above, a color profile selected in the Working Spaces section is used to Tag Everything for Color Management, which embeds an ICC profile for the images, artwork, and text. The printed (and viewed) PDF file maintains the integrity of any documents containing embedded profiles.

- **Tag Only Images for Color Management.** The same holds true as noted in the preceding entry except only raster images are tagged for color management according to the same compatibility options selected in the General pane. Text and vector objects remain unaffected.

- **Convert All Colors to sRGB.** Selecting this option converts all colors to sRGB. Converting colors to sRGB is best used for screen and Web images. The file sizes are smaller and screen redraws appear faster. Grayscale images are unaffected by choices made for color tagging and conversion.

- **Convert All Colors to CMYK.** This option provides RGB and spot color conversion to CMYK. If your job is to be printed as process color, select this menu item.

Below the Color Management Policies pull-down menu is the Document Rendering Intent pull-down menu, which you use for the Intent for how color will be mapped between color spaces. Choices for Intent include the following:

- **Preserve.** The first of the Intent choices is Preserve. Preserve involves no color compensation.

- **Perceptual.** Perceptual (Images) has to do with the mapping of pixels from one gamut to another. When you select this item, the image is mapped from the original pixels to the color gamut of the printer profile. All the out-of-gamut colors are remapped.

- **Saturation.** Saturation (Graphics) maintains relative saturation values. If a pixel is saturated and out of the color gamut of the printer, it is remapped preserving saturation but mapped to the closest color within the printer's gamut.

- **Absolute Colormetric.** This disables the white point matching when colors are converted. With no white point reference, you will notice a change in brightness values of all the remapped colors.

- **Relative Colormetric.** This preserves all color values within the printer's gamut. Out-of-gamut colors are converted to the same lightness values of colors within the printable gamut.

Working Spaces

Profile management for working spaces involves your decisions for embedding profiles for the color space while viewing your images onscreen. If a color space is defined for a given image and viewed on one monitor, theoretically it can be viewed the same on other monitors if the color profile is embedded in the image. Either of the two tagging options, Tag Everything for Color Management or Tag Only Images for Color Management, must be selected in order for a working space to be defined:

- **Gray.** Selecting None from this menu prevents grayscale images from being converted. The Dot Gain choices affect the overall brightness of grayscale images. Lower values lighten the image whereas values above 20 percent display grayscale images darker. Gray Gamma choices might be used for images viewed between computer platforms. A Gray Gamma of 1.8 is suited for Macintosh viewing whereas the higher 2.2 Gamma is better suited for Windows.

- **RGB.** If you use a color calibration system or monitor profile, you can select the respective profile from this pull-down menu. Choices available to you depend on profiles installed on your computer. If you have created custom profiles from Adobe Photoshop and saved them, they are listed as menu options. Default RGB profiles from Photoshop appear here after Photoshop is installed on your computer. The default option is sRGB IEC61966-2.1. If in doubt, use this option. It is becoming an industry standard and generally good for matching color between display and color output devices.

- **CMYK.** CMYK profiles also appear according to those stored in the respective folder according to platform as mentioned in the preceding bullet. Profile tagging is uniquely applied to images according to the color mode of the image. Thus, the Gray options apply only to grayscale images. RGB choices are applied to only RGB images whereas the CMYK choices tag only CMYK images. When using CMYK output for prepress you may have a profile embedded in the CMYK images. You can select None for this setting while changing the Gray and RGB working spaces, which preserves the color for output, enabling you to tag the other color modes for screen views. It would be unlikely that you would use RGB and CMYK images together for prepress, but you could set up the Adobe PDF settings for consistent display of files regardless of the color mode used.

CMYK color spaces

A single check box — Preserve CMYK values for calibrated CMYK color spaces — appears for this item. Unless you select Convert All Colors to CMYK in the Color Management Policies, the item is grayed out. Check the box when it's active and the CMYK color space is preserved when profile embedding has been applied.

Device-Dependent Data

All options available under the Device Dependent Data section are applied to images intended for prepress and printing. Whatever choices you make here have no effect on screen views:

- **Preserve under color removal and black generation.** If you made changes to undercolor removal or black generation settings in Photoshop, these changes are preserved when the file is distilled. Disabling the check box eliminates any settings made in Photoshop.

- **When transfer functions are found.** If you embed transfer functions in Adobe Photoshop, you can preserve them by selecting Apply from the pull-down menu. If transfer functions have not been saved with your Photoshop file, it won't matter if Apply is used. Use Apply when you intentionally set them up in a Photoshop image and you have the settings confirmed by your printer. If you select Preserve, the transfer functions are preserved without applying them. You can eliminate transfer functions set in a file by selecting Remove from the pull-down menu. As a matter of default, if you don't use transfer functions or know what they are, select Remove from the pull-down menu. If you inadvertently save a Photoshop file as EPS and embed transfer functions, they are removed when the file gets distilled.

- **Preserve halftone information.** Preserving the halftone information does not disturb halftone frequencies embedded in documents, as well as custom angles, spot shapes, and functions specified. Depending on the service center you use, they may want to have you set halftone information in the PostScript file and preserve it in the PDF. For PostScript 3 devices, PDFs can be sent straight to the imagesetter and printed at the halftone frequency preserved in the file. Service centers using PostScript Level 2 RIPs won't care if the halftone frequency is preserved or not. They'll have to manually print the PDFs using the Print and Advanced Print Setup dialog boxes.

Advanced

Advanced settings contain a variety of options for job ticketing, document structure, and other items not found in the previous panes, as shown in Figure 10.10.

FIGURE 10.10

The Advanced Adobe PDF Settings dialog box offers a group of miscellaneous settings often not available with other PDF producers.

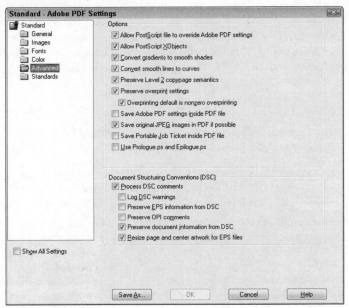

These options include:

- **Allow PostScript file to override Adobe PDF settings.** If you are certain the PostScript file you printed to disk has all the settings handled properly for output, enabling this option allows the PostScript file to supersede any changes you make in Adobe PDF settings. Disabling the check box allows all Options specifications settings to take precedence.

- **Allow PostScript XObjects.** A PostScript XObject stores common information in a document, such as backgrounds, headers, footers, and so on. When PostScript XObjects are used, printing is faster, but requires more memory. If you disable the check box, XObjects won't be used and the memory burden is reduced.

- **Convert gradients to smooth shades.** Gradients are converted to smooth shades and appear much smoother when rendered on PostScript 3 devices. The appearance of the gradients is improved when viewed onscreen and has noticeable differences when printing some files with more gray levels.

- **Convert smooth lines to curves.** Checking this box helps reduce file sizes significantly when creating PDFs from CAD drawing programs. Checking the box reduces the amount of control points used to build curves in CAD programs, resulting in much smaller file sizes and much faster displays on your monitor. You can experience similar results on files where the Auto Trace tool was used in Adobe Illustrator.

■ **Preserve Level 2 copypage semantics.** This setting has to do with semantic differences between PostScript Level 2 and PostScript 3. If you are imaging to PostScript Level 2 devices, enable this option. If you're printing to PostScript 3 devices, disable this option. If you are sending files to an imaging center, ask the technicians which level of PostScript is used on their devices.

■ **Preserve overprint settings.** Overprints manually applied in applications, such as illustration and layout programs, are preserved when you enable this option. Overprinting has an effect only when your files are color separated or possibly when you print composite color to proofing machines that display trapping problems from files printed as separations. If your workflow is consistent and you don't deviate between creating overprints and relying on a service center to perform them, you could leave this item as a default for your high-end output needs. Enabling the check box has no effect on images where overprints are not present.

■ **Overprinting default is nonzero overprinting.** When enabled, this option prevents objects with no color values specified as CMYK from knocking out other CMYK colors.

■ **Save Adobe PDF settings inside PDF file.** This option embeds the Adobe PDF settings used to produce the PDF inside the PDF document as a file attachment. Print shops can review the settings to diagnose problems that may have been produced during distillation. Open the Attachments pane to see the embedded file.

■ **Save original JPEG images in PDF if possible.** Distiller decompresses JPEG files during distillation. If you select this option, the decompressed JPEG files are not recompressed by Distiller.

■ **Save Portable Job Ticket inside PDF file.** Job tickets contain information about the original PostScript file and not the content of the PDF file. Information related to page sizes, page orientation, resolution, halftone frequencies, trapping information, and so on, is some of what is contained in job tickets.

■ **Use Prologue.ps and Epilogue.ps.** There are two files, named prologue.ps and epilogue. ps, available on the Acrobat Pro/Pro Extended 9 CD-ROM installer.

In order to use the files, you must move them to the same folder as the Acrobat Distiller application, and both files must reside together in this location. The files contain PostScript code appended to a PDF file when it is created with Distiller. By default the files do not contain any data that affect distillation. They serve more as templates where you can write code to append data to the PDF. You use the prologue.ps file to append information to the PDF such as a note, cover page, or job ticket information. You use the epilogue.ps file to resolve PostScript procedure problems.

NOTE You can edit both of these files; however, you need to be familiar with the PostScript language to effectively change the files. When relocating the files, be certain to place a copy in the Distiller folder and leave the original in the Data folder, especially if you decide to edit either file. You can also use the files with watched folders, as explained a little later in this chapter. When using watched folders, place the prologue.ps and epilogue.ps files at the same directory level as the In and Out folders.

- **Process DSC comments.** Document structuring comments (DSC) contain information about EPS files. Items such as originating application, creation date, modification date, page orientation, and so on, are all document-structuring comments. To maintain the DSC, enable this option. Because some important information such as page orientation and beginning and ending statements for the prologue.ps file are part of the document structure, you'll want to keep this item enabled as a default.

- **Log DSC warnings.** During distillation, if the processing of the document-structuring comments encounters an error, the error is noted in a log file. When you enable this check box, a log file is created. You can open the log file in a word processor or text editor to determine where the error occurred. Enable this option whenever document-structuring comments are processed.

- **Preserve EPS information from DSC.** This item is similar to the Process DSC comments option. If your file is an EPS file, enabling this check box preserves document-structuring comments.

- **Preserve OPI comments.** Open PrePress Interface (OPI) is a management tool used by many high-end imaging centers to control production. An OPI comment might include the replacement of high-resolution images for low-resolution FPO (for position only) files used in a layout program. OPI comments can include many different issues related to digital prepress such as image position on a page, crop area, sampling resolution, color bit depth, colors (in other words, CMYK, spot, and so on), overprint instructions, and more. If you're outputting to high-end imaging devices at service centers using OPI management, enable this option.

- **Preserve document information from DSC.** Document information items, discussed later in this book, include such things as title, subject, author, and keywords. Enabling this option preserves document information.

- **Resize page and center artwork for EPS files.** In earlier versions of Acrobat, distillation of a single-page EPS file, created from programs such as Adobe Illustrator, Macromedia FreeHand, or CorelDraw, used the EPS bounding box for the final page size. Many problems occurred when distilling EPS files directly as opposed to printed PostScript files. At times, a user would experience clipping and lose part of an image. With this option you have a choice between creating a PDF with the page dimensions equal to the artwork and having the artwork appear on the size of the original page you defined in your host application. When the check box is enabled, the page size is reduced to the size of the artwork, and the artwork is centered on the page. When the check box is disabled, the entire page appears consistent with the page size used in the host application.

Standards (Acrobat Pro/Pro Extended only)

The Standards pane provides options for creating subsets of the PDF file in the form of PDF/X and PDF/A documents designed for printing and archiving, respectively. Click the Standards folder and select a Compliance Standard from the pull-down menu options. Although there are several options from which to choose, the categories are centered on PDF/X and PDF/A.

PDF/X

As explained earlier, PDF/X is a subset of the PDF format developed by an ISO (International Organization for Standardization) standards committee outside Adobe Systems. Adobe is a participant on the committee and supports the development and advances in PDF/X standards.

PDF/X has gained much acceptance among commercial printing companies for the purposes of creating files suitable for printing. PDF is a reliable format for any kind of electronic file exchanges. However, files developed for viewing in Acrobat viewers, Acrobat PDF forms, Web-hosted documents, and so on, carry a lot of overhead not necessary for printing on commercial printing devices. The PDF/X compliance standard was developed to streamline documents by eliminating unnecessary data and optimizing files for print. The process of tailoring a PDF document for print by creating a PDF/X-compliant file does not necessarily reduce file size. In many cases, file sizes may grow from a standard PDF to a PDF/X file.

The PDF/X options available to you in Acrobat Distiller produce either a PDF/X-1a:2002, PDF/X-1a:2003, PDF/X-1a:2003, or PDF/X-3 compliant file. These file types are different versions of the PDF/X format. PDF/X-1a is designed to work well with both process and spot color, but no support is provided for color management or profile embedding. PDF/X-3 supports process and spot color and also supports color-managed workflows and ICC (International Color Consortium) profile embedding.

 The PDF/X pane appears only in Acrobat Pro and Pro Extended and is not available to Acrobat Standard users.

When you use PDF/X during distillation you are checking the file for PDF/X compliance. If the file does not meet the PDF/X standard you select (that is, PDF/X-1a or PDF/X-3), you can halt the distillation process much like halting distillation when fonts don't embed properly. If a file meets PDF/X compliance, you have much greater assurance that your PDF document will print on almost any kind of commercial printing device.

You create PDF/X-compliant files with Acrobat Distiller or an authoring program that specifically addresses PDF/X compliance when exporting to PDF. InDesign is one application that supports PDF creation with delivery of a PDF/X-compliant file. Other PDF producers such as PDFMaker used with Microsoft Office applications can also create PDF/X-compliant files.

The options you have in the Standards pane in Acrobat Pro, shown in Figure 10.11, include the following:

- **Compliance Standard.** The pull-down menu contains options for all the PDF/X compliance versions, a setting for PDF/A compliance, and an option for None.

- **When not compliant.** Two menu choices are available from this pull-down menu. Select Continue to create the PDF file if the file does not meet PDF/X compliance. The PDF file is created and a log file is generated reporting problems. If you select Cancel Job, the PDF is not created and assures you of only producing files that meet the PDF/X standards.

- **Report as error.** Enabling this radio button reports the file noncompliant if a trim box or media box is missing on any page in the document.

- **Set TrimBox to MediaBox with offset (Inches).** When the radio button is enabled, the trim box is calculated against the media box for offset distances if neither is specified in the PostScript file. The trim box is always equal to or smaller than the media box. Edit the field boxes for determining the offset amounts that are analyzed.

- **Set BleedBox to MediaBox.** Uses the media box values for the bleed box if no bleeds are specified in the PostScript file. In many layout authoring programs, you have options for specifying bleed areas. If no bleeds are defined in the print dialog boxes, the media box values are used.

- **Set BleedBox to TrimBox with offsets (Inches).** If the bleed box is not defined, the values specified in the field boxes are computed against the trim box.

- **Output Intent Profile Name.** If the file does not specify an output intent, such as SWOP for example, Distiller uses the intent you select from the pull-down menu. The field box is editable and you can type an output intent in the field box. When the file is distilled and no intent was used when the PostScript file was printed, selecting None forces the job to fail compliance.

- **Output Condition Identifier.** This item is a reference name specified by the Output Intent Profile Name's registry. The name is automatically supplied for known Output Intent Profile Names. If a conditional identifier is used, then the parameter must be manually added.

- **Output Condition.** This field box is where you supply the intended output condition. The field value is not assessed for compliance. It is used by the service center for information purposes. If you leave the field blank, it has no effect on whether the job meets compliance.

- **Registry Name (URL).** This item is also informational. For certain profiles selected in the Output Intent Profile Name pull-down menu, you'll see a URL where more information is hosted on a Web site related to the profile.

- **Trapped.** Three options are available from the pull-down menu. PDF/X compliance requires that the trapped state be either True or False. If you select Undefined it does not specify a trapping state the file fails PDF/X compliance. Insert True sets True as the trapped state. Insert False sets the state to no trapping.

- **Help.** The five icons to the right of the items in the Default Values if Not Specified in the Document area of the PDF/X pane offer help information. Click one of the icons and a pop-up menu opens with a definition for the respective option. In addition the Help button at the bottom of the dialog box opens the Complete Help document to the page where PDF/X information is found.

- **Save As.** The Save As button captures all the settings you make for the Adobe PDF settings and opens a dialog box that defaults to the Settings folder. If you change any item in one of the preset options and click OK in the Adobe PDF Settings dialog box, the Save As dialog box opens automatically to prompt you to save the new settings to a new file. Provide a filename and click the Save button to create a new settings file.

FIGURE 10.11

Click the Standards folder (Acrobat Pro/Pro Extended only) to open the Standards pane.

PDF/A

Adobe Systems has been working with international standards committees toward a goal of ensuring you that the documents of today can be electronically read 10, 20, even 100 years from now. One of the fruitions of these labors is the PDF/A-1b ISO standard developed for archiving purposes.

PDF/A files contain essentials in terms of document structure. The necessary essentials include raster images, fonts (embedded), and vector objects. Code used in documents such as JavaScript is deemed a nonessential ingredient as well as any form of security. Therefore, you cannot create PDF/A files containing any scripts or encryption. In general, you'll find PDF/A files are much leaner than other file standards such as PDF/X.

To select PDF/A-1b from the Compliance Standard pull-down menu you need to select Acrobat 5 or earlier compatibility in the General pane. When you select PDF/A-1b from the Compliance Standard pull-down menu the options in the PDF/A-1b pane appear as shown in Figure 10.12.

FIGURE 10.12

Select Acrobat 5 or earlier compatibility and select PDF/A-1b from the Compliance Standard pull-down menu.

The few options you have include the same options for file handling when a file is not compliant as you have with PDF/X files. Under the Output Intent Profile Name pull-down menu are options for choosing the output intent like you see available in the Color pane. The Output Condition is a field box for user-supplied data.

Managing Adobe PDF settings

You can manage Adobe PDF settings via commands in the Settings menu, as shown in Figure 10.13. From the same Settings menu in Distiller (Windows) or top-level menu bar (Macintosh), click Settings to open the Settings menu.

FIGURE 10.13

Adobe PDF settings are managed using commands in the Settings menu.

The Add Adobe PDF Settings dialog box opens where you can load a settings file created by other users in your workflow or a settings file sent to you by a service provider. You can load settings files from any folder on your computer. When you add the file using the Add Adobe PDF Settings dialog box, the file is moved to a folder where Distiller retrieves the settings and lists them in the Default Settings pull-down menu.

Choose Settings ⇨ Remove Adobe PDF Settings to open the Remove Adobe PDF Settings dialog box. The only settings you see displayed in the dialog box are custom settings files you added after your Acrobat installation. Select a file to remove and click Remove. When you click Remove, the file is discarded and doesn't appear in the Default Settings list in the Distiller window.

All additions and deletions for settings files can be accomplished through the menu commands. If you want to locate the folder where the settings files are located, look in C:\Program Files\Adobe\ Acrobat 9.0\Acrobat \Settings folder (Windows) or Library\Application Support\Adobe PDF \ Settings folder (Macintosh).

Identifying Font Locations

Font embedding occurs when Adobe PDF settings are enabled for font embedding and a font is contained in the PostScript file or loaded in the system with a font utility or the system folder where fonts are accessed. If fonts reside neither in the PostScript file nor are loaded in your system, Distiller offers another method for locating fonts. Choose Settings ⇨ Font Locations. The Acrobat Distiller – Font Locations dialog box opens, as shown in Figure 10.14.

In this dialog box, you add folders of fonts that Distiller looks in when a font is neither contained in the PostScript file nor loaded in the system memory. Monitored font folders are listed in the window shown in Figure 10.14. To add a new folder, click the Add button. To remove a folder, select it in the list and click the Remove button.

A check box at the bottom of the dialog box enables you to resolve some problems that may occur when a TrueType font has the same name as a PostScript font. To eliminate embedding TrueType fonts with the same names as PostScript fonts, check the box at the bottom of the dialog box.

FIGURE 10.14

Distiller monitors fonts installed on your hard drive when the fonts appear in a list in the Acrobat Distiller – Font Locations dialog box.

Using Watched Folders

Watched folders enable you to automate distillation of PostScript files in a business or production environment. When Distiller encounters a new PostScript file, the file is distilled in the background while foreground applications are running. The resulting PDF files are automatically moved to another folder or directory, and the PostScript files are either preserved or deleted automatically.

Licensing restrictions

Before moving on to working with watched folders, please look over this section carefully and try to understand the proper use and authorization of working with watched folders on networks. Adobe Systems grants you license for working on a single computer when installing Acrobat. When you create PDFs on your computer you can distribute them to anyone who uses an Acrobat viewer. Therefore, the PDFs you create can legitimately be distributed to anyone who acquires the free Adobe Reader software.

Creating PDFs, whether locally or on a network, assumes you have complied with the proper licensing agreements for use of the Acrobat Distiller application. Ambiguity arises when using the Distiller application on networks with watched folders. If you set up a watched folder on a network where multiple users access the watched folders, you need a site license to use the Acrobat Distiller application, you need to have a licensed copy of Acrobat Standard or Pro/Pro Extended for each user, or you can purchase Adobe LiveCycle PDF Generator. Because Distiller is used by multiple users in this example, site licensing or individual purchases of the product is required.

Therefore, the licensing policies in this regard are related not to distribution, but rather, how the PDFs are created. As I move through the discussion on watched folders, keep in mind that when I make mention of using watched folders on networks, I'm assuming you are compliant with the proper licensing agreements.

Creating watched folders (Acrobat Pro/ Pro Extended only)

Watched folders can be individual folders, hard drive partitions, or dedicated hard drives. When you choose Settings⇨Watched Folders, the Watched Folders dialog box opens, enabling you to establish preferences for the watched folders and distillation attributes.

The options available in the Watched Folders dialog box are as follows:

- **Path.** The list window displays all folders identified as watched folders. The name of the watched folder appears in the list as well as the directory path. In Figure 10.15, notice the directory path is shown.
- **Check watched folders every [ ] seconds.** This user-definable field accepts values between 1 and 9999 seconds. When Distiller monitors a watched folder, the folder is monitored according to the value entered in this field box.

FIGURE 10.15

Watched folder preferences are established in the Acrobat Distiller – Watched Folders dialog box. When you open this dialog box, a reminder for the licensing restrictions appears at the bottom.

- **PostScript file is.** Distiller automatically treats the PostScript file according to the options available in this pull-down menu. You can select the Deleted menu item, which deletes the PostScript file after distillation, or select Moved to "Out" folder, which moves the PostScript file to a folder entitled *Out*. If you intend to repurpose files for different uses, be certain to keep the PostScript file.

- **Delete output files older than [ ] days.** If you elect to keep the PostScript files in the Out folder, they can be deleted after the time interval specified in this field box. The acceptable range is between 1 and 999 days.

- **Add Folder.** To create a watched folder or add to the current list of watched folders, click the Add Folder button. A navigation dialog box opens. To add a folder to the watched folders list, the folder must first be created before you click the Add Folder button. Once you add a folder, Distiller automatically creates an In and Out folder inside your selected folder. Folders as well as partitions and drives can be added to your list. On a network, remote folders, partitions, and drives can also be added to the list. If you want to select a folder, browse your hard drive and select the folder name after clicking the Add Folder button. If you want to have the entire hard drive watched, select the drive designation (C:\, D:\, E:\, and so on in Windows or Macintosh HD, Hard Drive, and so on with a Macintosh) and click OK in the Browse For Folder dialog box.

- **Remove Folder.** To delete watched folders, select the folder name in the watched folders list and click the Remove Folder button. If a folder is moved or deleted from your hard drive, the next time you launch Distiller, a warning dialog box opens notifying you that Distiller cannot find the watched folder(s). Removal of watched folders must occur in the Acrobat Distiller – Watched Folder dialog box. If you inadvertently deleted a watched folder on the desktop, you need to delete the folder name in the watched folders list. Return to your desktop and create a new folder; then return to the dialog box and add the new folder to the list.

- **Edit Security.** You can apply security to PDF files during distillation. Adding security during distillation is handy for multiple files created in PDF workflow environments. Security used on a watched folder is inherited from the Job Options settings. For example, if you select Acrobat 5.0 compatibility in the General pane, the security settings available to you here are compatible with 128-bit RSA. However, if you select Acrobat 7.0 and higher for your compatibility, the security is set to 128-bit AES.

CROSS-REF For more information on applying security to PDF documents, see Chapter 26.

- **Clear Security.** Select any one or all of the watched folders in the list and click Clear Security. The security is removed from the folders.

- **Edit Settings.** The Edit Settings button becomes active when you select a watched folder name in the watched folders list. With a folder name selected in the list, click the Edit Settings button to open the Adobe PDF Settings dialog box. You can apply different settings to different watched folders. If, for example, you print PostScript files to disk and have them distilled for high-end output and Web page design, you will want compression and color modes distinctive for the output sources. You can set up two watched folders and have the same PostScript file distilled with the different settings. Editing settings here overrides Distiller's defaults and applies new options to the specific watched folder where the attributes are established.

- **Load Settings.** All the settings contained in the Settings folder are available for loading and applying to watched folders listed in the window. Click Load Settings to open the Settings folder.

- **Clear Settings.** This option removes any settings applied to a watched folder. If you leave the watched folder listed with no specific settings assigned to the watched folder, the current default Adobe PDF settings are used.

PDF WORKFLOW Watched folders greatly help your PDF workflow and assist you in automating the smallest office environment to large offices with multiple networks and servers. When you install a site-licensed copy of Acrobat Distiller on a server, the burden of PDF creation is dedicated to the server and relieves individual workstations.

In identifying watched folders, you need only have the directory or folder created on a hard drive. After you identify the watched folder, Distiller automatically creates the other folders needed to execute distillation from watched folder files. The In folder created by Distiller is monitored. When a PostScript file is placed or written to the In folder, the distillation commences according to the interval you establish in the Watched Folder settings dialog box. Files can be placed into the In folder, or you can print to PostScript directly to the In folder from within an application.

Watched folders work well in cross-platform environments, too. In order to use a watched folder from one platform and have the distillation performed on another platform, you need to have the computers networked and have software installed that enables you to communicate between two or more computers on your network.

Working with Non-Roman Text

Acrobat provides great support for text created from character sets foreign to U.S. English and other Roman text alphabets. Eastern languages such as Russian, Ukrainian, and similar languages based on forms of Cyrillic characters require proper configuration for font access and keyboard layouts. After configuring and using the fonts in a layout application, be certain to embed the fonts in the PostScript file or have Distiller monitor the font's folder of the character set used. As is the case with any font embedded in the PDF, the document is displayed without font substitution. In Figure 10.16, I used a Cyrillic font in Microsoft Word. The file was printed to disk as PostScript and font embedding was used in Distiller's Adobe PDF settings.

FIGURE 10.16

When fonts are properly configured from character sets foreign to Roman characters, the fonts can be embedded and viewed without font substitution.

Здравствуйте
Меня зовут Тед

Eastern language support is provided by Acrobat but requires much more in regard to configuration and proper installation of the Asian Language Support option (Windows) or the Asian Language Kit (Macintosh). As long as the language support respective to your platform is installed with the Acrobat installer, files can be printed as PostScript and embedded in the PDFs. PDFs with embedded Asian language options such as Traditional Chinese, Simplified Chinese, Japanese, and Korean (CJK) are displayed without font substitution.

When installing Acrobat for use with these languages, you need to use the custom installation and include the language support with the other Acrobat components. After the support is installed, font problems need to be resolved when you print to PostScript. PostScript fonts have fewer problems being embedded. TrueType fonts require special handling depending on the platform and type of fonts used. Special documentation for managing PostScript and TrueType fonts is included in the Acrobat documentation. For specific handling of Eastern Language support and TrueType fonts, review the documentation thoroughly before attempting to convert PostScript files to PDF.

Accessing Distiller

After all the controls have been established in the Adobe PDF settings dialog boxes, you're ready to use the Distiller application. Files used with Distiller need to be PostScript files printed to disk or EPS files. You can access the Distiller application several ways:

- **Open from Distiller.** Find the Distiller application on your hard drive and double-click the application icon to launch Distiller. When the Distiller application window opens, choose File ➪ Open. Navigate to the file you want to convert to PDF and select it in the Acrobat Distiller – Open PostScript File dialog box. Select multiple files by using the Shift key to select a contiguous group of files or Ctrl/⌘ to select a non-contiguous group. If the Preferences have been set up to ask for a filename or ask to replace a PDF, a navigation dialog box opens where you supply filename and destination.

- **Drag and drop to the application icon.** Either the application icon or a shortcut (alias in the Dock on Macintosh OS X) of the application can be used for drag-and-drop distillation. In this regard you can drag multiple PostScript files, EPS files, or a combination of both to either icon. Release the mouse button when the files are over the icon and Distiller launches and subsequently converts the file(s) to PDF.

- **Drag to the application window.** You can drag and drop a single file or multiple files on the Distiller application window. Launch Distiller to open the application window. Select a single file or multiple files and release the mouse button. All files are converted as individual PDFs.

- **Launch Distiller from within Acrobat.** To open Distiller from within Acrobat choose Advanced ➪ Print Production ➪ Acrobat Distiller. The Distiller application launches and opens in the foreground in front of the Acrobat window. Choose File ➪ Open or use the drag-and-drop method to open the file.

- **Print to Adobe PDF printer.** From any authoring program, open the Print dialog box and select Adobe PDF. Execute the Print command and the file is distilled with the current default Adobe PDF settings.

- **Use the Run command (Windows).** You can create PDFs with Distiller by accessing the Run command from the Windows status bar. Select Run and supply the directory path first for Distiller; then supply the path for the files to be converted. Syntax must be exact. Pathnames need to be contained within quotation marks and a space needs to separate the pathname for Distiller and the pathname for the file(s) to be converted. Filenames having spaces need to be contained within quotation marks. To distill multiple files enter the pathname and filename, and separate each file with commas. Inasmuch as Acrobat offers you this capability, you'll often find drag-and-drop methods much easier.

- **Exporting to PDF.** From many application programs, such as Microsoft Office, and illustration and layout programs as discussed in Chapters 7 through 9, Distiller is used to produce PDFs. When distillation is complete, the user is returned to the application document window.

- **Watched folders.** As described earlier in this chapter, copying a PostScript or EPS file to the In folder inside a watched folder prompts distillation at the interval specified in the Acrobat Distiller – Watched Folders dialog box. Distiller must be launched before distillation of files from watched folders occurs.

When Distiller is used in all the preceding circumstances other than the use of watched folders, the current Adobe PDF settings selected in Distiller are used to produce the PDF. That is to say, if Distiller is launched and the Standard settings appear in the pull-down menu, the Standard settings are used to create the PDF. When using watched folders, the settings associated with the watched folder are used to produce the PDF. If no settings are assigned to the watched folder, the current default settings are used.

Summary

- PostScript is a streamed language that can contain many different dialects and is often redundant in describing page elements for imaging. PDF is a much more efficient file format because it is structured like a database that offers logical order and eliminates redundancy.

- When creating PostScript files, the preferred PPD to use is the Acrobat Distiller PPD, or print to the Adobe PDF printer.

- Distiller preferences enable you to establish settings for filenaming and overwriting.

- Acrobat Distiller has many Adobe PDF settings enabling you to control font compression, image compression, color, high-end digital prepress output, PDF/X compliance, and PDF/A compliance. All Adobe PDF settings are available to Acrobat Standard users except PDF/X and PDF/A compliance.

- Additional font monitoring is established in the Distiller Settings menu for identifying different font locations on your computer.

- Watched folders enable you to create PDF workflows that automate the PDF creation process. Watched folders can be contained on local or remote storage systems in network environments. Use of watched folders with multiple-user access on a network requires strict compliance with Adobe's licensing agreements.

- Acrobat enables you to supply security passwords at the time of distillation. Security levels are applied consistent with PDF compatibility.

- Eastern language character sets and Asian text are supported font-embedding features as long as font formats and font management are properly configured.

- Access to Acrobat Distiller is supported from within Acrobat 9.0, by using shortcuts or aliases, printer drivers, and through a variety of drag-and-drop procedures.

Part III

Editing PDFs

art III covers the many different editing opportunities you have available with Acrobat. Beginning in Chapter 11 you find many ways to export PDF content for editing in original authoring programs. In Chapter 12 you find a wealth of information dedicated to combining documents and using the new Acrobat 9 PDF Portfolio features. Chapter 13 deals with text editing, followed by Chapter 14 where I cover redacting PDF files for those who need to remove sensitive information from PDFs.

In Chapter 15 I talk about editing images and objects, and in Chapter 16 you find many ways for editing PDF pages in Acrobat. In Chapter 17 you find some of the new improvements for scanning paper documents that ultimately are converted to PDF and the Optical Character Recognition (OCR) features you find in Acrobat.

In Chapter 18 you'll learn how to repurpose PDF files for screen viewing and Web hosting, as well as how to automate many tasks in Acrobat using batch sequences. This section on editing PDF files concludes with Chapter 19 where I talk about adding special features for Adobe Reader users for saving PDF forms and participating in comment reviews.

Chapter 11

Exporting PDF Content

To begin this section on editing PDF documents I'll start with saving files and exporting data. As you find in this chapter, Acrobat has Save tools and commands and supports exporting your PDF data in a variety of file formats. As you learned in Part II, files are not originally authored in Acrobat, but rather, they are converted to the PDF format. If you need to perform some major editing, it's always best to try to return to the original authoring application, make your edits, and then convert to PDF. In some cases, however, you may not have an original authoring application document. In such circumstances, you may need to get the PDF data in a format that you can manipulate and edit in another program. Fortunately, Acrobat supports exporting to many different file formats that can be imported in other programs.

IN THIS CHAPTER

Using the Save commands

Saving data in different formats

Setting Up the Work Environment

The only tool used in this chapter is the Save tool, which appears in the default File toolbar. To return to default tools, open a context menu on the Toolbar Well and select Reset Toolbars or press Alt/Option+F8. The remaining tools used with this chapter are derived from menu commands.

Saving PDF Files

When you open a PDF document in any viewer, the Save tool in the File toolbar and the File ➪ Save menu command are both grayed out. When you open the File menu and look at Save As, you notice the menu command is active.

Save

After you edit a file through the use of tools or menu commands, the Save tool and Save menu command become active.

You can use the File ➪ Save As command at any time. As you edit PDF documents, they tend to become bulky and contain unnecessary information. To optimize a file and make it the smallest file size, choose File ➪ Save As and select the default PDF format for the file type. If you save to the same folder location with the same filename, Acrobat rewrites the file as you use Save As. You should plan on using Save As and rewriting your file after your last edits. Doing so assures you of creating a smaller, more optimized file.

Another factor affecting optimized files is ensuring the default preferences are set to file optimization when using the Save As command. Open the Preferences dialog box (Ctrl/⌘+K) and click Documents in the left pane. In the Documents preferences pane, be certain the check box is enabled for Save As optimizes for Fast Web View. Enabling this option ensures that your files are always optimized when you use Save As.

Exporting Data

By default, when you use either Save or Save As, the file type is a PDF document. Using Save offers you no other option for changing the file type; but when you select Save As, you can choose to export your PDF document in one of a number of different file formats. If you need to update a file or export data from PDF files, choose File ➪ Save As and choose a file format from the Save as type (Format on Macintosh) pull-down menu, as shown in Figure 11.1.

FIGURE 11.1

Choose File ➪ Save As and choose the file format to be saved from the Save as type pull-down menu.

Users of Acrobat 8 may remember the Export Task button that provided a pull-down menu for choosing various export formats. The Export Task button has been removed from the Tasks tool-bar and now appears as a menu command. Choose File ➪ Export, and from the Export submenu shown in Figure 11.2 you can choose a number of different export formats.

FIGURE 11.2

Choose File ➪ Export and choose the file format to export PDF content from a number of different export formats.

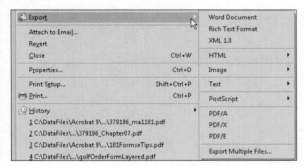

Use the menu command and you find file formats exactly the same as those supported in the Save As dialog box. (Exceptions in the Export submenu are the Adobe PDF Files (*.pdf) and Adobe PDF Files, Optimized (*.pdf) that are only found in the Save As dialog box). Using either the Save As dialog box or the Export menu commands results in file exports with options choices that are identical. You can use either command set to export in the following formats.

NEW FEATURE One item you find in the menu command that isn't available in the Save As dialog box is the Export Multiple Files command. Choose this item and you can batch process exporting PDF data to a given file format from a selection of multiple files (or folders) on your hard drive.

CROSS-REF For more on batch processing files, see Chapter 18.

Selecting all but the Adobe PDF Files (*.pdf), Tables in Excel Spreadsheet, and Text (Accessible) (*.txt) formats provides user-definable options in the Settings dialog box for the respective file type. When you select any of the formats other than the preceding two, the Settings button becomes active. Click Settings and the Save As Settings dialog box opens. The various options change according to the file format selected from the Save as type pull-down menu (Windows) or Format (Mac) in the Save As dialog box.

Adobe PDF files (*.pdf)

By default the Acrobat PDF Files (*.pdf) format is selected in the Save as type (Windows) or Format (Macintosh) pull-down menu. Saving as PDF without changing the filename updates the existing PDF by overwriting it.

Adobe PDF Files, Optimized (*.pdf)

Select this option and your file is optimized using the PDF Optimizer and saved in one step.

The Optimized PDF option in the Save As dialog box was introduced in Acrobat 8. Click the Settings button in the Save As dialog box and the PDF Optimizer dialog box opens. You can choose a preset or make custom adjustments in the PDF Optimizer, and then click OK and click Save in the Save As dialog box. Your file is first optimized and then saved to disk.

CROSS-REF   **For more information on using the PDF Optimizer, see Chapter 18.**

Encapsulated PostScript (*.eps) and PostScript (*.ps)

EPS files are saved as single page files. When multiple-page PDFs are saved to EPS, each page is saved as a new EPS document. PostScript files save the PDF to disk like you would print a file to disk as PostScript. PostScript files can then be redistilled in Acrobat Distiller to convert back to PDF. You can also download PostScript files to PostScript printers through a downloading utility or a hot folder, which is used for sending files directly to the printer.

Many of the options for creating either an EPS file or a PostScript file are identical. You'll notice some differences as you travel through the many options found in the Save As Settings dialog box. Select either Encapsulated PostScript (*.eps) or PostScript (*.ps) from the Files of type (Format on Macintosh) pull-down menu and click the Settings button. The options appear in the Save As Settings dialog box. Shown in Figure 11.3 is the EPS Save As Settings dialog box.

FIGURE 11.3

Select Encapsulated PostScript (*.eps) or PostScript (*.ps) from the Save as type (Format on Macintosh) pull-down menu. Click the Settings button to open the Save As Settings dialog box. In this figure, Save as Encapsulated PostScript (*.eps) was selected.

General settings

On the left side of the Save As Settings dialog box are several categories for choices you make on the right side of the dialog box. The first of the categories is the General settings where you set some general attributes for the way an EPS or PostScript file is saved. These settings are as follows:

- **Defaults.** The Defaults button at the top of the dialog box returns all settings to the original defaults. You can access this button at any time as you travel through the various option categories in the list at the left side of the dialog box.

- **ASCII.** PostScript files are encoded as ASCII (American Standard Code for Information Interchange). ASCII files are larger than binary files, which is the second option for encoding selections.

CROSS-REF For information on color separating EPS files and Acrobat PDF, see Chapter 32.

- **Binary.** Binary files are much smaller than ASCII files. Use binary encoding when the PostScript language level is 2 or 3.

- **PostScript.** Select the language levels from the pull-down menu choices. For ASCII encoding use Language Level 1 from the menu. For exporting EPS files to Adobe InDesign, you can use Language Level 2. If you're using Language Level 2 or 3, select binary encoding. Use PostScript 3 only when the output devices use PostScript 3 RIPs.

- **Font Inclusion.** You have three choices for font inclusion. Choose None to not embed fonts. Choose Embedded Fonts to keep the same fonts embedded in the PDF in the exported EPS file. Choose Embedded and Referenced Fonts to keep the PDF embedded fonts and fonts referenced from fonts loaded in your system. If you're using a font that is not embedded in the PDF document but is loaded as a system font, the font is embedded in the resulting PDF.

CROSS-REF For more information about font embedding and limitations of font embedding, see Chapter 10.

- **Include Comments.** When the check box is enabled, any comment notes are included in the resulting EPS or PostScript document. When the PostScript document is distilled in Acrobat Distiller, the comment notes are retained in the resulting PDF document.

- **Convert TrueType to Type 1.** Check the box to convert TrueType fonts to Type 1 fonts.

CROSS-REF For more information on TrueType and Type 1 fonts, see Chapter 10.

- **Include Preview (EPS file exports only).** The preview is a screen view of the EPS file. If this check box is not enabled, the EPS file appears as a gray box when you place the file in another program. The data are all there, but you won't be able to see the EPS image. When this check box is enabled, a preview is embedded in the EPS file. Preview image formats are TIFF on Windows and PICT on the Macintosh.

- **Page Range.** You can export all pages by selecting the All radio button or entering the page numbers for a range of pages to be exported. EPS files are exported as individual files for each page and automatically numbered by Acrobat.

Output

Click the Output item in the list on the left side of the Save As Settings dialog box and the options change, as shown in Figure 11.4.

FIGURE 11.4

Select Output and the options change to attribute settings designed for printing and prepress.

Output options enable you to control prepress output attributes, including the following:

- **Color.** The four choices for handling color in resulting EPS and PostScript file(s) are as follows:

    - **Composite.** Use this option to export the file as a composite image. If the file is a four-color image, you can still import an EPS file in a separating program and print separations. The intent for Composite is for use with composite color printing and printing separations to non-Adobe PostScript devices. For PostScript files, composites can be downloaded directly to PostScript 2 and 3 devices for In-RIP separating.

    - **Composite Gray.** If the files are grayscale, use Composite Gray.

    - **Separations.** This option creates a DCS (Desktop Color Separation) file, and each color as well as a composite is exported as separate files. If pre-separating the EPS file(s), be certain you use a program such as Adobe InDesign that supports DCS files, or you can directly download each plate to your RIP. For PostScript files, the file is separated. When you download the PostScript file, all colors print on separate plates.

CROSS-REF For more information about DCS files, color separations, and RIPs, see Chapter 32.

■ **In-RIP Separations.** This option works only on Adobe PostScript 3 RIPs. A composite color image is printed to the RIP and the RIP color separates the composite file.

 Separations and In-RIP Separations are only active when you have your page setup set to a PostScript printer.

■ **Screening.** You make choices for screening from this pull-down menu. Unless you have some special need for embedding half-tone frequencies in the EPS file, leave the Screening set to Default Screen and handle all your frequency control at the RIP. For PostScript files, set the screening as desired before downloading the file.

■ **Trapping.** You can apply trapping and choose trap presets.

■ **Apply Output Preview Settings.** Select this option to simulate the output of one device on another. This option simulates the output condition defined in the Output Preview dialog box on the current output device.

■ **Transparency Flattener Preset.** Choose from High Medium and Low resolutions for transparency flattening. Transparency is flattened according to your choice in the resultant EPS file.

■ **Simulate Overprinting.** Overprints and knockouts can be soft-proofed onscreen for color-separated devices. The check box is grayed out unless you choose one of the separation items in the Color pull-down menu.

■ **Use Maximum Available JPEG2000 Image Resolution.** For any raster images contained in the EPS file export, the file compression uses JPEG2000 at the maximum setting when this check box is enabled. If disabled, the original compression level at the time the PDF was created is used.

■ **Ink Manager.** Clearing the box on the far left of each color plate eliminates the plate for separated files. Scroll the box to see any spot colors and you can select spot colors for conversion to CMYK color.

CROSS-REF   **For more information about separations, overprinting, transparency, trapping, and managing inks, see Chapter 32.**

Marks and Bleeds

Select the Marks and Bleeds item in the list at the left of the Save As Settings dialog box and the options for adding printer's marks appear, as shown in Figure 11.5.

FIGURE 11.5

Select Marks and Bleeds to add printer's marks to the EPS/PS export.

The options are as follows:

- **All Marks/Marks.** You can check the box for All Marks and all the check boxes below the Style menu are checked. You can toggle on or off all check marks to create just the marks you want to appear in the resultant file.

- **Style.** You have choices for compatibility with authoring and illustration programs. Choose from different versions of InDesign, Illustrator, or QuarkXPress.

- **Line Weight.** From the pull-down menu, select line weights for the printer's marks from $^1/_8$-, $^1/_4$-, and $^1/_2$-inch choices.

PostScript Options

Click the last item in the list for EPS/PS exports and the options shown in Figure 11.6 appear. The PostScript options offer you settings for embedded PostScript attributes in the EPS/PS file.

The PostScript options include the following:

- **Font and Resource Policy.** You determine how fonts download to a printer's RIP via three choices in the pull-down menu:

  - **Send at Start.** The entire font sets for all pages are downloaded to the printer's RIP. The file prints faster than any of the other methods, but puts a memory burden on the printing device to hold all the font matrices in memory during printing.

  - **Send by Range.** Fonts are downloaded from the first page where the fonts are used and stays in memory until the job is printed. The font downloading occurs as each font is found on a page that uses them. The job prints a little slower than when using the Send at Start option, but uses less memory initially as the job is printed.

  - **Send for Each Page.** Fonts encountered on a page are downloaded to the RIP, and then flushed as the next page is printed. The second page's fonts are then downloaded and flushed after printing, and so on. This method requires the least memory. Files print slower than when using either of the other two methods.

FIGURE 11.6

Select PostScript Options to add various PostScript printing attributes to the EPS/ PostScript file(s).

- **Emit CIDFontType2 as CIDFontType2 (PS Version 2015 and greater).** Use this option to preserve hinting in the original font when printing. The option is available only for Language Level 3 output.

- **Emit Undercolor Removal/Black Generation.** GCR/UCR removal is necessary only if the original document contained assignments in the PostScript file converted to PDF. If you want to remove any embedded settings for handling the amount of black or compensating for black generation with different inks, check this box. If you don't know what any of this means, checking the box or not won't have an effect on your own personal documents.

- **Emit Halftones.** If a halftone frequency was embedded in the original file, you can eliminate it in the exported document. Unless you want to use embedded frequencies, leave the box checked in case you accidentally preserved a frequency in the original file for EPS files. When printing PostScript files to high-end devices, you'll want to assign frequencies at the time the PostScript file is created.

- **Emit Transfer Functions.** The same criteria as the preceding bullet apply to transfer functions. If you intend to use embedded transfer functions, leave the check box disabled. Otherwise, keep it checked as a default.

- **Emit Flatness.** Flatness settings applied in Photoshop, Illustrator, or other illustration programs are generally applied to clipping paths in images and on vector objects to ease the burden of printing complex objects. When checked, the flatness settings applied in the original authoring program are honored.

- **Emit PS Form Objects.** This option relates to PS Form XObjects. XObjects are used to create a description of multiple smaller objects repeated several times such as patterns, brushes, backgrounds, and so on. Emitting the XObjects reduces the size of the print job; however, more memory is needed to RIP the file(s).

Color Management

Color management has been removed from the Output options in Acrobat 8 to a new category for Color Management in Acrobat 9. Click Color Management in the left pane and the right pane changes to the view you see in Figure 11.7.

FIGURE 11.7

Click Color Management in the left pane to display choices for managing color and choosing color profiles.

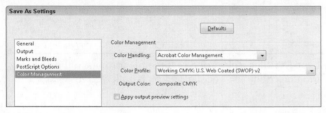

The Color Management options include:

- **Color Handling.** Make a choice from the pull-down menu for whether you want Acrobat or your printer driver to manage color or whether you want to use no color management.

- **Color Profile.** Choose a color profile from the pull-down menu.

CAUTION If you choose to let Acrobat manage color and you also choose a printer profile, you'll end up double profiling your output. The relationship between these two options is critical to understand. For a detailed explanation for how to manage color on your output, see Chapter 31.

- **Apply output preview settings.** Check this box to simulate an output on a specific printing device.

Click OK in the Save As Settings dialog box and click Save in the Save As dialog box. The PDF is exported in EPS or PostScript format, containing all the attributes you described for all the options listed earlier.

Because printing in Acrobat Pro takes care of all the print controls you need, exporting EPS files for printing is a task you won't need to perform unless there's some strange problem that needs to be resolved in a file that won't print. A more practical use for exporting EPS files from Acrobat is if you need to import a PDF file in another program that does not support PDF, but does support EPS. In such cases you'll find it helpful to understand all the options you have available for EPS exports.

You have many advantages in creating PostScript files from Acrobat. Files can be redistilled in Acrobat Distiller with PDF/X formats for printing and prepress, sometimes as a workaround for repurposing documents, and for downloading directly to PostScript devices — particularly for print shops using imposition software that only supports PostScript and not PDF.

CROSS-REF For more information about PDF/X files, see Chapters 10 and 32.

HTML 3.2 (*.htm), HTML 4.01 with CSS 1.0 (*.htm), XML 1.0 (*.xml), and Text (Plain) (*.txt)

Options available for exporting PDFs to HTML files, HTML files with Cascading Style Sheets, Plain Text, and XML files all use the same attribute settings. Text is exported according to the encoding method you select, and images are exported according to the format option you select. These settings are available when you select any one of the three file formats from the Save as type (Format on Macintosh) pull-down menu. Select a format and click the Settings button. The Save As *XXX* Settings dialog box opens, as shown in Figure 11.8.

FIGURE 11.8

To set attributes for file exports for HTML, XML, or TXT files, select one of three file formats in the Save as type (Format on Macintosh) pull-down menu and click Settings. The dialog box is called Save As *XXX* Settings, where *XXX* is the format you selected.

The attribute settings are as follows:

- **Encoding.** Choose the encoding method from options for Unicode settings (UTF-8, UTF-16, or UCS-4), ISO-Latin-1, HTML/ASCII, or the default setting of Use mapping table default.

- **Generate bookmarks.** Generates bookmark links to content for HTML or XML documents. Links are placed at the beginning of the resulting HTML or XML document.

- **Generate tags for untagged files.** Tags are temporarily created for file conversion for untagged documents. You need to select the check box for legacy untagged files or with files created with Acrobat 4 in order to complete the conversion. The tags are temporary for the conversion to work and are not added to the PDF. If you do not select this for legacy PDFs, you will not get the conversion.

- **Generate images.** Enable this check box for images to be exported as separate files.

- **Use sub-folder.** Images are saved to a subfolder below the directory where the HTML files are created. The default name for the folder is "images." In the field box you can change the folder name by editing the line of text.

- **Use prefix.** This option adds prefixes to image filenames. Check the box and supply the prefix text in the field box.

- **Output format.** Three options buttons enable you to determine the file format for the saved images. Choose from TIFF, JPG, or PNG.

- **Downsample to.** Images are downsampled to the setting selected from the pull-down menu. The settings are fixed with choices for 72, 96, 150, and 300 pixels per inch (ppi).

CROSS-REF Exporting to HTML does not preserve page geometry and layout in the HTML file. For more information on exporting HTML from Acrobat, see Chapter 27.

JPEG (*.jpg, .jpeg, .jpe), JPEG2000 (.jpf, *.ipx, *.jp2, *.j2k, *.j2c, .jpc), PNG (.png), and TIFF (*.tif, *.tiff)

You can export the PDF document as any one of the preceding image file formats. Each entire page, including text and images, is exported as a single image file. From the Settings dialog box, you choose options for image compression and color management. The options settings for exporting image file formats are the same as the options used when importing images in Acrobat with the Create PDF From File or From Multiple Files commands discussed in Chapter 7.

CAUTION When exporting PDF documents containing images, you cannot achieve a better resolution than the resolution in the source file. If you have, for example, a PDF document with a TIFF image where the image was originally sampled at 72 ppi, you cannot gain any resolution by saving the file from Acrobat as a TIFF file with 300-ppi resolution. The file is saved with the resolution you specify in the Save As *XXX* Settings dialog box, but image resolutions higher than source files are upsized with image interpolation. The results are often unusable and produce poor-quality images. If you need image resolutions higher than the source images, you need to return to your scanner and scan images at higher resolutions. Re-create the original document and convert to PDF.

CROSS-REF For a better understanding of image resolutions required for printing, see Chapters 10 and 32.

Microsoft Word Document (*.doc) and Rich Text Format (*.rtf)

For several generations of Acrobat, the Adobe development engineers have continually worked hard on preserving layout and appearance in documents exported to Microsoft Word and RTF formats. You'll find in Acrobat 9 more improvement in these areas, and to date, the best exporting features when you want to edit a file in Microsoft Word.

You can export PDF files to either Microsoft Word format or Rich Text Format files (RTF). The conversion settings include choices for image handling and sampling as well as a new feature for handling the document layout. Unlike HTML and XML files, exports to Word and RTF embed the images in the exported text files when you choose to export images. Acrobat does not offer an option for exporting images apart from the text data.

Be aware that although you can export PDF documents directly to Microsoft Word format, the integrity of your file depends on how well you created the PDF. If the PDF was created without tags and through less desirable PDF-creation methods, the ultimate file you produce in Word or RTF format may not be suitable for editing and converting back to PDF. Inasmuch as tags are added during conversion to PDF, the tagged structure is not retained in the resulting file.

CROSS-REF For more information on programs supporting exports to PDF as structured and tagged files, see Chapters 7, 8, and 25.

Notwithstanding tagging issues, the exports to Microsoft Word from Acrobat 9 are the best I've seen with any version of Acrobat. Clicking the Settings button in the Save As dialog box for exports to Microsoft Word or RTF opens the Save As Settings dialog box. The settings are the same for RTF as for Word-formatted file exports (shown in Figure 11.9).

FIGURE 11.9

Select either Microsoft Word or RTF for the file export and click the Settings button. The options in both dialog boxes are identical.

Settings for exporting to Microsoft Word or RTF formats include the following:

- **Layout Settings.** This is the marvelous new addition to Acrobat 9. You can choose to retain the document layout by clicking the Retain Page Layout radio button and the exported data appear in Microsoft Word almost exactly as you see the file laid out in Acrobat. Choose the Retain Flowing Text option to preserve text reflow.

- **Tag quality settings.** Select the check box to regenerate tags in the exported document.

- **Include Comments.** Like EPS and PostScript files discussed earlier, Comment notes can be exported to Word or with RTF files. Select the box for Include Comments and the Comment notes are exported.

- **Include Images.** You can extract image files from the PDF and embed them in the .doc or .rtf file in either of two formats. Select JPG or PNG for the image file format.

- **Use Colorspace.** You have choices for colorspaces from a pull-down menu. Choose from Determine Automatically, in which case Acrobat determines using either grayscale or color, or select Grayscale or Color from the menu options.

- **Change Resolution.** Downsampling and resolution issues are the same as those noted when exporting PDF documents to image formats.

CROSS-REF For more information on resolutions and sampling, see Chapter 18. To learn about tagging PDF files, see Chapter 25.

PDF/A, PDF/E, PDF/X (*.pdf)

Acrobat supports various standards for different uses and different markets. The PDF/A specification is used for archiving PDF documents so that files you create today can be viewed by users many years in the future. The PDF/E specification is a standard for engineers creating documents such as CAD drawings. The PDF/X specification is used by the print industry for insuring proper output on commercial printing devices. Each of the choices you have in the Save As/Export menus offer settings respective to the standard.

CROSS-REF For more information on adjusting settings for PDF standards, see Chapter 10.

Tables in Excel Spreadsheets (*.xml)

You can export tables to XML files that can be read by Microsoft Excel. In order to successfully export a table, the original file needs to have been created as a table in a program like Microsoft Word or Excel. If you try to export columns and rows that were not created as a table in an authoring program, no data are exported from the PDF file.

In handling table data exports, if the Save As ⇨ Tables in Excel Spreadsheets command doesn't work, you have other options for exporting table data using the Select tool to select a table and choosing either Save As Table or Open Table in Spreadsheet from a context menu opened on the selected data.

CROSS-REF For more information on exporting table data, see Chapter 13.

Text (Accessible) (*.txt)

Files are saved as text. For tagged PDF documents made accessible, all alternative text used to describe items like images and form fields that are contained in the document tags are converted to text. The alternate tags can be viewed in the Tags palette in Acrobat but won't necessarily appear in the document page. When you export PDFs as Accessible Text, the text is generated in the body of the document.

CROSS-REF For more information on document tags, see Chapter 25.

Summary

- Using the Save As command and overwriting a PDF document optimizes it and can sometimes result in much smaller file sizes.

- Acrobat can save PDFs in a variety of different formats. Many formats have an elaborate number of options settings to set attributes for the saved files.

Chapter 12

Combining, Packaging, and Attaching PDFs

I n Acrobat versions 6 and 7, we had a menu command for creating a single PDF from multiple files of different file formats. In Acrobat 8 we saw some improvements to combining files into a single PDF document, and we were introduced to PDF Packages. Acrobat 9 has not only built on features for combining and packaging files, the new improvements in the latest release are no less than spectacular.

Now in Acrobat 9 we can view content created in any application and convert pages, selections, and other user-defined content to PDF. PDF Packages have given way to the new PDF Portfolios, where you can combine multiple documents in a portfolio displayed in a new user interface, with many options you can choose to display your content such as adding Flash animation, animated views for scrolling documents, and creating custom cover pages.

In addition to using the Combine Files options and creating PDF Portfolios, I tossed in adding file attachments to PDF documents and cover the various options you have with adding attachments to PDFs and PDF Portfolios.

Read on to explore new Acrobat 9 features for merging files into single PDF documents and assembling files into PDF Portfolios, and learn some of the methods Acrobat provides you for attaching files to your documents.

Setting Up the Work Environment

Creating merged documents and PDF Portfolios requires no special tools loaded other than the default toolbars. However, later in this chapter I talk about adding file attachments that in some ways appear similar to files added in a PDF Portfolio. Therefore, you'll want to load some commenting tools.

When you get to the section related to working with file attachments, open a context menu on the Toolbar Well and select More Tools. Scroll down to the Comment & Markup toolbar and check the box adjacent to Attach a File as a Comment and check the box adjacent to Record Audio Comment. Check the box adjacent to the Comment & Markup toolbar and click OK.

Open a context menu on the Toolbar Well and select Dock Toolbars.

Note that if you want to work exclusively with combining files and creating PDF Portfolios, you don't need to bother using the Comment & Markup toolbar. In this chapter, the Comment & Markup toolbar is loaded in the "Working with File Attachments" section at the end of the chapter.

Merging Files into a Single PDF document

The Adobe Acrobat development team has spent considerable time over the last few versions of Acrobat to improve and deliver methods for us to combine multiple files into PDF documents. Adobe claims their research has found most knowledge workers today want to communicate messages based on the delivery of different files created in different authoring programs.

You might have a spreadsheet created in Excel, a presentation created in PowerPoint, an advertisement created in Adobe InDesign, and a media file created in Adobe Flash that collectively deliver the message you want to communicate or a file you want to share for comment and review.

In Acrobat 8 we had the Combine Files menu command that was used to combine multiple files of different types into a single PDF document. The Acrobat 9 command for combining files is Merge Files into a Single PDF. Although the nomenclature has changed, the results are the same. The Merge Files into a Single PDF command is used to combine native authoring application files such as a PowerPoint file, a Word File, a PDF file, and any other file formats compatible with the Create PDF From File command and merge them into a single PDF document.

CROSS-REF For more information on the file formats Acrobat supports for conversion to PDF, see Chapter 7.

The Merge Files into a Single PDF command enables you to combine files of any type and neatly organize the order of your files in the Combine Files wizard before creating the composite document.

Combining files is handled from the Create task button in the Tasks toolbar or from a menu command (File ⇨ Combine ⇨ Merge Files into a Single PDF) or the menu File ⇨ Create PDF ⇨ Merge Files into a Single PDF. In Figure 12.1, you can see the pull-down menu and the menu choices you have in the Combine Files task button. The Merge Files into Single PDF command is used to merge files from a number of different formats including PDF into a single document. The Assemble Files into a Portfolio command creates a package of documents assembled into a single PDF Portfolio file.

CROSS-REF For more information on PDF Portfolios, see "Creating PDF a Portfolio" later in this chapter.

FIGURE 12.1

The Create task button provides two commands used for merging files and creating a PDF Portfolio.

Combining files and folders on Windows

When you want to combine files into a single PDF document you can click the Create task button and select Merge Files into a Single PDF. Likewise you can choose File ➪ Combine ➪ Merge Files into a Single PDF or the menu File ➪ Create PDF ➪ Merge Files into a Single PDF. Either action opens the Combine Files dialog box. Before you use the command, there are a few restrictions you have with regard to the types of files you can combine. These restrictions include:

- **PDFs with security.** PDFs with security cannot be combined using this command.
- **Adobe LiveCycle Designer XML Forms.** Any form created in Adobe LiveCycle Designer cannot be added using this command.

CROSS-REF For more information on Adobe LiveCycle Designer XML forms, see Chapter 35.

- **Digital signatures.** You can use this command to add files that have digital signatures, but the signatures are removed when you combine the files.
- **Form fields.** Adding a form is no problem using the Merge Files into a Single PDF command, but if you have different files using the same field names, the fields are merged into one field. For example, if you merge a form populated with data and another identical form with the fields left blank, the data are merged together. The order of the files to be merged is important. If you have two identical forms and merge them with the blank fields file listed in the first position, both forms are merged and the second form (populated with field data) now appears with empty fields. Conversely, if the populated fields file is in the topmost position in the list along with a file with blank fields, both documents appear with the same data when you combine them. In other words, forms with identical field names inherit data from the first form in a list of files you merge.

Before I go on to explain all the features available to you when merging files into a single PDF document, launch Acrobat and follow along to see how easy it is to merge files using the revised Combine Files wizard.

STEPS: Using the Combine Files command (Windows)

1. **Click the Combine task button.** From the pull-down menu, select Merge Files into a Single PDF.

2. **Select files to merge.** When you select Merge Files into a Single PDF, the Combine Files wizard opens. Click the Add Files button and a pull-down menu opens. From the menu options choose Add Files. The Add Files dialog box opens, where you can browse your hard drive and select individual files to merge into a single PDF document. Select files you want to add to the file list and click the Add Files button. You can click a file and add it to the file list and click Add Files again and locate files in different folders. If you have a folder containing all the files you want to combine, you can choose the Add Folder item from the Add Files pull-down menu. All files within a folder are then added to the list.

    In Figure 12.2, I added several documents to my list: a Flash SWF file, three InDesign files, a Word file, an Excel file, and two PowerPoint files. Note that all files are in native file format.

FIGURE 12.2

Click the Add Files button to add files to a list.

> **TIP**   **Multiple files within the same folder can be added to your list. Click a file and Shift+click to select a group of files listed in a contiguous order. Click and press Ctrl/⌘+click to select files in a noncontiguous order.**

3. **Arrange the files in the order you want them to appear in the merged PDF document.** Click a file in the list and use the Move Up and Move Down buttons to arrange the files in the order you want them to appear in the resultant PDF document.

4. **Choose Pages.** Click a file in the list and the Choose Pages button becomes active (see Figure 12.3). Note that if you select an Excel document, the Choose Pages button changes to Choose Sheets, and selecting a PowerPoint file changes the button name to Choose Slides. In my example, I selected an Excel Workbook (.xls file).

FIGURE 12.3

Select a file and click Choose Pages (or Sheets or Slides).

5. **Select Pages (or Sheets or Slides).** A preview of your document is displayed in a separate window. You can scroll pages, worksheets, slides, and so on to preview the pages. At the top of the window you can make choices for the pages you want to add to the single PDF file. Make your choices and click OK.

6. **Create the merged PDF document.** Click Combine Files in the wizard window. Any files you added to your list that need conversion to PDF are converted on the fly. The original authoring program opens and files are converted to PDF. Wait for Acrobat to complete the conversion and concatenation and you'll be prompted to save your composite document.

7. **Save the composite file.** When prompted to save the file, click Save. A Save As dialog box opens. Type a name for your file, navigate to the folder you want to use for your saved file, and click Save again.

8. **Review the resultant PDF file.** The composite file opens in the Acrobat Document pane. Click the Bookmarks tab in the Navigation pane. Notice that any bookmarks in your

original PDFs containing bookmarks are preserved. Additional bookmarks are added to the file linking the first page of each separate document to a bookmark. In Figure 12.4, you see my composite document with the Bookmarks pane open.

CROSS-REF For more information on bookmarks, see Chapter 22.

FIGURE 12.4

Preview the composite file in the Document pane.

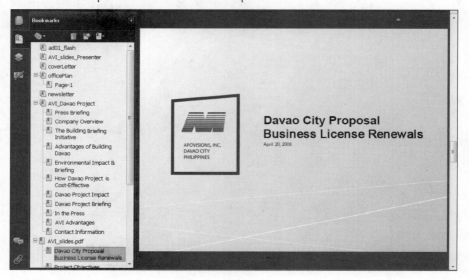

Combining files and folders on the Macintosh

As I mentioned in Chapter 8 when I covered converting Microsoft Office files to PDF, the preferred way to convert the files is to use the PDF Printer. Since the PDFMaker is not available on the Mac, you won't find native file format support for Merge Files into a Single PDF using MS Office applications.

You can use other file formats on the Mac such as Adobe InDesign .indd files, Adobe Illustrator .ai files, Adobe Flash .swf and .fla, image file formats such as gif, jpg, etc., and HTML files. Mac users can also use the Choose Pages button for MS Office files after you convert them to PDF. The nice thing about the Merge Files command is that you can also add PDF documents to the merged file.

CAUTION If you import video, sound, or Flash media in an Adobe InDesign file, you must use the Export command in InDesign to Export to Adobe PDF. In the Export Adobe PDF dialog box be certain to use compatibility above Acrobat 5 and check the Interactive Elements check box. This box must be checked for the media to show up in the resultant PDF document. Unfortunately, Adobe InDesign won't hold the last preset you chose in the program, so there's no way to use the Merge Files into a Single PDF command that will include the interactive elements when converting to PDF using the merge files command.

Using the Combine Files wizard

In Acrobat 8, the Combine Files wizard had two panes where you could choose attributes for your combined files or PDF Packages. In Acrobat 9, the Merge Files into a Single PDF document uses a single pane in the wizard, and the new PDF Portfolios are created in a separate interface. A few of the options you can choose in the Combine Files wizard in Acrobat 9 include:

As a first order of business, let's take a look at adding files to the wizard window when you first open the Combine Files dialog box. At the top of the wizard is a pull-down menu used to add files for combining into a single PDF document, as shown in Figure 12.5.

FIGURE 12.5

The Add Files pull-down menu displays four menu commands used to add files to the wizard list of files.

Your choices are as follows:

- **Add Files.** Use this menu command to open the Add Files dialog box. This dialog box behaves similar to an Open dialog box where you can navigate your hard drive and locate files to add to the list in the first pane.

  If you select a secure PDF or a file created in Adobe LiveCycle Designer, a warning message appears in the Combine Files dialog box as shown in Figure 12.6. As stated in the message, you cannot combine the selected file and must use the PDF Portfolio option if you want to merge the file with other documents.

- **Add Folders.** Use this command to add a folder of files.

FIGURE 12.6

A warning appears for all files that are not supported in the Combine Files wizard.

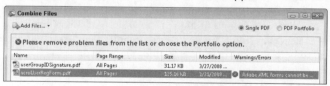

- **Reuse Files.** Choose this menu command and the Reuse Files dialog box shown in Figure 12.7 opens. Once you've created a PDF by combining files, you can open the Reuse Files dialog box and use one or any number of files combined together in a previous file.

  On the left side of the dialog box you see a list of files used in a previous session that were combined to create a single PDF document. On the right you see files made available for reuse. Click a file in the right pane and click Add Files to reuse it. The file is then added to the list in the Combine Files wizard.

FIGURE 12.7

Reuse Files enables you to select files used in a previous Combine Files session in a new session.

- **Add Open Files.** You can choose the Merge Files into a Single PDF command without having a file open in the Document pane. If you have a file open when you open the wizard window, you can choose to add your open file to other files you add to the list.

TIP From the desktop you can select files in a folder, open a context menu, and choose Combine supported files in Acrobat. When you release the mouse button, the files are added to the Combine Files wizard, where you can choose pages and merge the files into a single PDF document. If you want to convert the files to separate PDFs, choose the Convert to PDF command in the same context menu.

Organizing files

As you move below the file list in the wizard window, a series of buttons appear for organizing pages in the file you ultimately create, as shown in Figure 12.8.

FIGURE 12.8

Buttons below the file list are used to organize pages.

Your options include:

- **Move Up.** Click a file and click the Move Up button and the file is reordered in the list. If the file you select is at the top of the list, the Move Up button is grayed out and unusable.

- **Move Down.** This button behaves the opposite of the Move Up button. Clicking the button moves a selected or several selected files down. When you select a file at the bottom of the list, the button is grayed out and unusable.

- **Remove.** As you might suspect, clicking this button removes any selected file(s) from the list.

- **Choose Pages/Sheets/Slides/Layouts/Sheet Selection.** This option is available only for multiple page documents and documents of certain file types. Most MS Office files are compatible with the Choose (*button text*) option. Click this button and the Preview Selected *button text* dialog box opens. The *button text* varies according to the file type you choose to add in the Combine Files dialog box. For MS Word files the button text is Choose Pages. With MS Excel the button text is Choose Sheets. AutoCAD files appear with Choose Layout. Microsoft Visio files appear with Sheet Selection. If you select a PowerPoint file, the button name changes to Choose Slides. Clicking any option opens a Preview dialog box like the one shown when I select Choose Slides with a PowerPoint file selected as shown in Figure 12.9.

TIP If you want to open the Preview and Select Pages/Slides dialog box, you can also double-click on a file in the list window.

NOTE For simplicity, I'll refer to the item appearing in the Choose button as simply Choose or Choose Pages button when describing options for choosing pages/sheets/layouts and so on in the sections ahead.

FIGURE 12.9

Click Choose Pages to open a dialog box where pages in a file can be previewed.

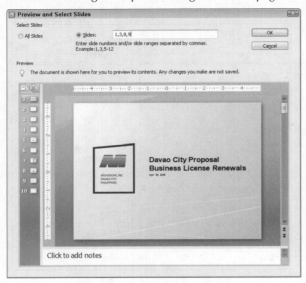

Previewing files

Files of several different file types — primarily those of the Microsoft Office flavor and PDF documents — permit you to create a PDF preview and choose pages within the document to add to your resultant file, and also offer many different editing features. However, what you do in the Preview window cannot be saved. If you want to alter content you need to return to the original authoring program and make your edits, then export back to PDF.

CROSS-REF For more information regarding exporting to PDF, see Chapter 7. For information related to Microsoft Office and PDF creation, see Chapter 8.

Once again, I can't cover all the options available to you when previewing files, but here are a few examples available with some Office applications:

- **Microsoft Word.** Click a multipage Word document in the file list and click Choose Pages, or simply double-click the Word document and the document opens in the Preview and Select Page Range dialog box. You can select specific pages you want added to the combined file by typing values in the Pages text box at the top of the dialog box. Noncontiguous pages are separated by commas and contiguous pages are separated by dashes. For example, 1,3,7-9 denotes using pages 1, 3, and 5 through 7 for adding to the combined file.

In long documents, it would be helpful to see a view of the document pages so you know what pages you want to include in your combined file. The Preview and Select Page Range dialog box offers you just that. In addition, you can make a number of temporary edits through commands from a context menu, as shown in Figure 12.10. For example, if you want to see a preview of your document with a larger font size, you can use the Font options to change font attributes.

FIGURE 12.10

Right-click (Windows) or Ctrl+click (Macintosh) to open a context menu where some editing commands appear.

Be aware that any edits you make won't be applied to the combined file. What you see available are commands designed to help you view files using temporary changes you can make to the document. If you need to make the changes permanent and reflected in the resultant PDF document, you must return to the original authoring program, make the changes, and save the file.

You can browse documents by tables, graphics, sections, comments, and much more. Just click the circle between the Previous and Next Page buttons represented by double arrowheads in the lower-right corner of the dialog box. A pop-up menu, shown in Figure 12.11, appears where you can choose to browse your file according to any one of 12 different options. All of the options are used for navigational purposes only. You can, for example, jump to different comments in a file, browse a file by section number, browse by table, and so on.

FIGURE 12.11

Click the small circle between the Previous and Next Page arrows to open a pop-up menu used for browsing different content.

- **Microsoft Excel.** Double-click an Excel Workbook file in the wizard window or click and select Choose Sheets. The Preview and Select Sheets dialog box opens, as shown earlier in Figure 12.3. As with MS Word, you also have context menu commands. An entire workbook can be displayed and you can scroll the pages selecting only the pages you want to appear in your combined file.

- **Microsoft PowerPoint.** You can choose a Slide Sorter view and an Outline view in PowerPoint which you open in much the same way as when opening Word and Excel files. In Figure 12.9, slides are shown in the Slide Sorter view.

  PowerPoint files can also be viewed with content changes, but like other files, the changes are only temporary while in the Preview dialog box. From a context menu you have choices for deleting slides, changing the slide design, changing layout, and changing the background.

Other similar options are available with Microsoft Visio files, Microsoft Project and Publisher files, and a number of different file formats including AutoCAD DWG and DWF files. Your clue as to whether you have an option to open files in the Preview dialog box is whether you see an active Choose button in the Combine Files wizard. If the button is grayed out, you don't have the option to preview pages.

Conversion options

On the right side of the bottom of the Combine Files dialog box you have three icons. These icons offer options for file optimization. Click Smaller File Size and images are downsampled to 150 ppi and compressed with a low-quality JPEG compression scheme. The file size will typically be smaller than your original file unless you used lower resolution images and low-quality JPEG compression. Click Default File Size (middle icon) to preserve the original file resolutions and the image size attributes are the same setting identified in the Edit ➪ Preferences ➪ Convert to PDF Settings. Click Larger File Size to create a file with optimum results. You may not see much difference in file sizes between Default and Larger file sizes if you used high-resolution images and high-quality JPEG compression.

> **NOTE**   Using Larger File Size does not upsample images. The image resolution won't be greater than the default resolution used when an image was saved. The primary change you experience with this option is when JPEG compression is set to Maximum Quality. If you saved your images with Medium Quality, the quality setting is changed.

These buttons affect files that need to be converted to PDF, and PDF documents. When PDF documents are included and you make a choice for the file size, the PDF Optimizer is used to resample images.

CAUTION   Creating Smaller File Sizes can result in much longer times to create a combined file. This option downsamples each image above 150 ppi and requires more time to produce the resultant PDF than the other two options.

At the very bottom of the wizard window the Help, Combine Files, and Cancel buttons should be self-explanatory. Additionally, you have an Options button. Click the Options button and the Options dialog box opens, as shown in Figure 12.12.

FIGURE 12.12

Click the Options button at the bottom of the first pane in the wizard to open the Options for Conversion Settings dialog box.

The four options you have are

- **Always enable accessibility and reflow.** This item makes your PDF conversions accessible.

CROSS-REF   For more information on accessibility, see Chapter 25.

- **Always add bookmarks to Adobe PDF.** By default, the check box is enabled. If you don't want bookmarks added to the resultant file, remove the check mark.

- **Continue combining if an error occurs.** If a file cannot be combined for one reason or another, you can halt the process by removing the check mark. If the check box is enabled, Acrobat skips over corrupt files and files that cannot be added to the merged document.

- **Convert all files to PDF when creating a Portfolio.** This choice relates to PDF Portfolios where you can package documents in a PDF wrapper and either convert to PDF or keep the files in their native file format. Remove the check mark if you don't want the files converted to PDF in a PDF Portfolio.

Working with PDF Portfolios

Acrobat 8 provided a way to package PDF documents together in the form of a PDF Package. The primary thinking behind the PDF Package in Acrobat 8 was to permit you to do all the things you couldn't do when combining PDFs such as:

- **Secure files.** PDF Packages enabled you to add secure files. In order to add a secure file to a package, you need the password(s).

- **Adobe Designer XML forms.** PDF Packages enabled you to combine files that were created in Adobe Designer.

- **PDF forms.** Actually this can be both PDF forms and XML forms. When you combine forms having identical field names, the data fields remain undisturbed.

- **Preserve original document format.** When you use Merge Files into a Single PDF, any document other than PDF is converted to PDF as long as the file format is compatible with the Create PDF From File command. When creating a PDF Package, files appear with a PDF preview but they retain original file format attributes and can be exported from the package back to the original file format.

In addition to the reasons stated in the above bullet points, PDF Packages were used for aggregating data from PDF forms and exporting form data to spreadsheets.

NEW FEATURE What you had available in Acrobat 8 in terms of creating PDF Packages was a new, impressive Acrobat feature. All the advantages for having PDF Packages have been implemented in Acrobat 9, but Adobe introduces a new method for packaging PDF content in the form of PDF Portfolios.

PDF Portfolios should be thought of more as a revelation in Acrobat functionality rather than an enhancement on packaging files. You have all the advantages you had available with PDF Packages, but PDF Portfolios are much more. In short, the focus of PDF Portfolios is on presentation, and it's presentation in a big way. The Adobe engineers have given you a new interface and new methods for displaying content in very exciting ways.

CROSS-REF PDF Portfolios can also be created from Microsoft Outlook e-mails and when compiling returned forms. To learn how PDF Portfolios are used with Microsoft Outlook, see Chapter 8. To learn more about compiling form data, see Chapter 35.

When you create a PDF Portfolio, you create a much different result than when merging files into one PDF document. PDF Portfolios are PDF documents and/or native application documents assembled together in a package (or collection) similar to adding file attachments to a PDF. The documents appear in a new interface introduced in Acrobat 9. During the assembly of a PDF Portfolio you have many different choices for how you want to display your portfolio and the documents contained therein.

PDF Portfolios opened in Acrobat 8 appear as PDF Packages. The coversheet for the PDF Package is a default coversheet created by Adobe and installed with your Acrobat installation. As you can see in Figure 12.13, a PDF Portfolio opened in Acrobat 8 informs the user that to see all features in a PDF Portfolio, the user needs to upgrade to Acrobat or Adobe Reader 9.

FIGURE 12.13

The coversheet of a PDF Portfolio opened in Acrobat 8

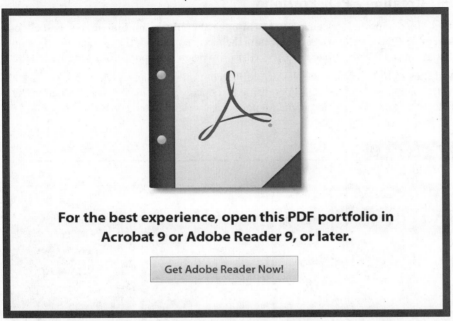

For the best experience, open this PDF portfolio in
Acrobat 9 or Adobe Reader 9, or later.

Get Adobe Reader Now!

If you open a PDF Portfolio in Acrobat 7, the file appears very similar to PDF Packages opened in Acrobat 8 viewers. In Acrobat 7 you see the coversheet and the files appear as file attachments.

CROSS-REF For more on file attachments see "Working with File Attachments" later in this chapter.

Creating a PDF Portfolio

To understand a little more about PDF Portfolios, let's first start by following some steps to create a portfolio and then look at some of the attributes for working in the new Acrobat 9 PDF Portfolio interface. You start a PDF Portfolio assembly by using one of several commands. You can choose File ⇨ Create PDF Portfolio, File ⇨ Combine ⇨ Assemble PDF Portfolio, open the Create task button and choose Assemble PDF Portfolio, open the Combine task button and select Assemble PDF Portfolio, or if you are already in the Combine Files wizard you can click the PDF Portfolio radio button. Regardless of which menu command you use, the Acrobat user interface changes to the PDF Portfolio interface where you add files, edit display appearances, specify document details, choose from among different publish options, and more.

To create a PDF Portfolio, follow these steps.

STEPS: Creating a PDF Portfolio

1. **Click the Combine Files task button (or open the File ⇨ Combine menu) and choose Assemble PDF Portfolio).** After selecting the menu command, the Acrobat interface changes to the PDF Portfolio interface where you begin your portfolio assembly.

2. **Add files to the portfolio.** Click the Add Files button in the lower left corner of the PDF Portfolio interface and the Add Files dialog box opens. Select files and click Open in the dialog box. Your files are shown in the portfolio, similar to what you see in Figure 12.14.

FIGURE 12.14

Files added to a portfolio

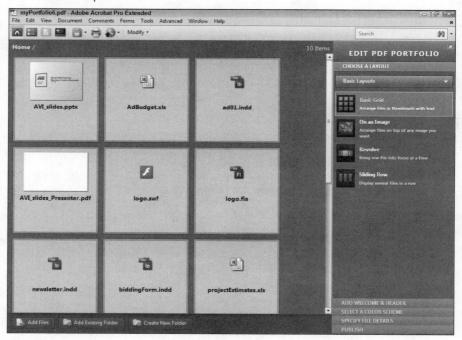

3. **Choose a layout.** The right panel contains many different categories for customizing the portfolio Welcome Page and options for changing color schemes, adding file details, and publishing your portfolio. At the top of the panel click Choose a Layout. Below the Choose a Layout text you find a pull-down menu. Open the menu and choose Revolve from the list. The display of the files changes to an appearance similar to Apple Computer's Cover Flow interface shown in Figure 12.15. In Adobe terms the design is called Revolve.

FIGURE 12.15

Select Revolve from the Choose a Layout panel and the document display changes to a Cover Flow–type layout called Revolve.

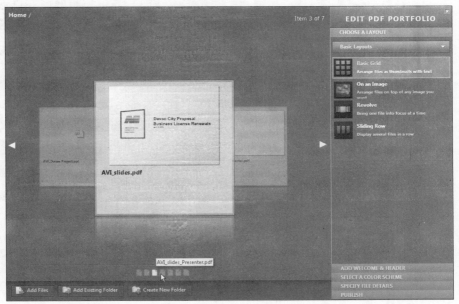

4. **Add a Welcome & Header.** Click the Add Welcome & Header button in the right panel and choose an option for the display of the Welcome page and a custom header. In my example I chose Logo & Text in the right panel as shown in Figure 12.16. Click the Add an Image item in the header to add a logo or photo. Type the text you want in the Add a title field and the header information is complete.

FIGURE 12.16

Add a Welcome & Header to the portfolio.

5. **Save the portfolio.** By default, Acrobat saves your portfolio as Portfolio1, Portfolio2, Portfolio3, and so on (in a single editing session) if you don't modify the file name. To save the portfolio with a name of your choosing, select File ⇨ Save Portfolio As. In the Save As dialog box locate a target folder and type a name for your portfolio. Click the Save button and the file is saved.

6. **Review the portfolio.** Close and reopen the file. Browse the files contained in the portfolio by clicking the navigation buttons or icons in the portfolio. For my example where I used the Revolve look and added a Welcome & Header, the appearance is shown in Figure 12.17.

FIGURE 12.17

Review the PDF Portfolio in Acrobat.

The steps outlined here are but a fraction of the choices you have for customizing the view and adding options for PDF Portfolios. Much more is available to you, including Flash animations you can add to the Home view of your portfolios.

Examining the portfolio interface

Many options are available to you in creating and setting up the display of PDF Portfolios. Some of the options you have relate to how you set up a portfolio for users to view your work, and other options relate to your editing tasks in creating the portfolios. When you choose a menu command such as File ⇨ Create PDF Portfolio, the interface shown in Figure 12.18 opens. The various tools and menu choices you have include:

FIGURE 12.18

The default appearance when you begin creating a PDF Portfolio

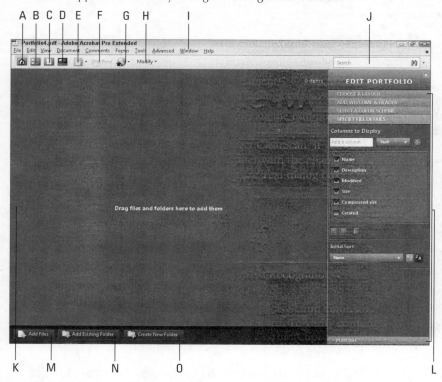

A. **Home.** Click this button and you return to the Home view. By default, the Home view is shown when you open a PDF Portfolio.

B. **List View.** Click this button and the files you add to the portfolio are shown in a list view. Choices you make in the Specify Details panel (shown in Figure 12.18) in the Edit Portfolio panel are displayed in columns in the list view.

C. **Preview.** Click this button and you change to a Preview mode where you see a selected file in a Preview interface.

D. **Open Welcome Page.** Click this button and the Welcome page opens. This button is handy when you use an Adobe Flash file for the welcome page and when previewing text and images added to the design of the Welcome page.

E. **Save.** The Save pull-down menu offers three options. You can click Save Portfolio from the menu choices and the file is updated as you make new edits. Click Save Portfolio As and save the portfolio under a new file name. Click Save Files from Portfolio and a Browse for Folder dialog box opens. You can create a new folder or locate an existing folder on your hard drive and save selected files from within the portfolio as separate files to a folder. Note that you do not create a new portfolio, and you must select individual files for the menu command to be active.

F.   **Print.** Only PDF files can be printed using this tool. If you have other file types added to a portfolio, you must open the native authoring program and print the file from that program. When the Print dialog box opens you can choose to Print All PDF Files and you can Preview all PDFs and all pages within the PDFs.

G.   **Share.** The Share pull-down menu offers two menu choices. Choose Share Portfolio on Acrobat.com to share the file with other users, or choose Email to add the portfolio as an attachment to a new message in your default e-mail client.

H.   **Modify.** The Modify pull-down menu offers several choices as shown in Figure 12.19.

FIGURE 12.19

Open the Modify pull-down menu to view more editing options.

- **Close Edit Portfolio.** Choose the first menu command to close editing mode and enter Viewer mode. If you change to the Viewer mode and choose the Modify ➪ Edit Portfolio command you return to Edit Portfolio mode.

- **Add Files, Add Existing Folder, Create New Folder.** See items M, N, and O later in this section.

- **Delete.** Click a file in the portfolio and choose Delete to remove the file from the portfolio.

- **Convert to PDF.** Select a native file format and click Convert to PDF to convert the file to a PDF document.

- **Convert to Flash Movie.** For supported file formats, choose this option to convert to an Adobe Flash SWF movie file.

- **Reduce File Size.** For PDF documents, select a PDF and choose this option to reduce file size. This command is the same as using the Document ➪ Reduce File Size menu command.

- **Secure Portfolio.** Choose this command to add security to the portfolio.

I. **Menu bar.** The Menu bar offers menu options the same as when in Viewer mode in Acrobat. Some menu choices are grayed out if they don't work while in a portfolio view.

J. **Search.** Type search criteria in the text box and click the search icon (represented by a pair of binoculars) or press the Enter key on your keyboard and Acrobat searches all files in the portfolio. Results are reported in a Results panel as shown in Figure 12.20.

FIGURE 12.20

Type search criteria in the Search text box and press Enter. The results are shown in a Results panel.

When you click an item in the Results panel, the document where the found word(s) exists opens in the foreground in your Layout view. For example, if you set up your portfolio using the Revolve design, clicking a result in the Search panel rotates the files to open the file containing the results in the foreground. Double-clicking a result opens the found word in the respective document in Viewer mode. Positioning the cursor over a found word listed in the Results panel displays the page number where the result was found.

CROSS-REF For more information on searching PDFs, see Chapter 6. For more information on searching PDF Portfolios, see the section "Using the Attachments panel" later in this chapter.

K. **Document pane.** The portfolio Document pane is where you see files added to a portfolio. You can add files to a portfolio by dragging files from your desktop to the Document pane or using the Add Files tools. Double-click any file in the Document pane and the file opens in Preview mode. In Preview mode you'll find an Open button. Click this button and the file opens in Viewer mode in Acrobat for PDF files, where you can navigate pages and edit the PDF. When opening other file types, the files open in the original authoring application.

L. **Edit Portfolio panel.** You have several choices in this panel for creating displays of the files and the portfolio. The items include:

- **Choose a Layout.** From the pull-down menu choose from Animated, Basic Layouts, or Organized. As you choose a menu item, the Document pane reflects your choice, enabling you to view files in different layouts.

- **Add Welcome & Header.** Click Add Welcome & Header and you are offered two choices. One choice is for adding a Welcome page and the other choice is for adding a Header. The Welcome page is shown when in the Home view (when clicking the Open the Welcome Page tool) and the Header is shown when viewing both the Welcome page and all files in the portfolio.

- **Select a Color Scheme.** You can change the interface color by choosing a color scheme from a list of preset colors, or click Customize Color Scheme and choose from an RGB color palette as shown in Figure 12.21. Colors can be represented in RGB and Web Safe color values. Web Safe color values can be edited by selecting colors in the color spectrum or by typing hexadecimal values in the text boxes adjacent to the items listed for primary and secondary colors.

FIGURE 12.21

Click Customize Color Scheme to display the custom color spectrum where Web Safe colors can be specified.

■ **Specify File Details.** File details appear when you view the portfolio in a List view. The items shown in columns in the List view are determined from the choices you make in the Specify File Details panel as shown in Figure 12.22. Acrobat has a set of predefined detail items appearing in the panel. Click the check boxes for all items you want displayed in the List view. Additionally, you can add custom descriptions by typing a column title in the Add a column text box and clicking the Plus icon. The custom detail items are then editable in the List view.

FIGURE 12.22

Click Specify Details and check the boxes for the items you want displayed when viewing files in List view.

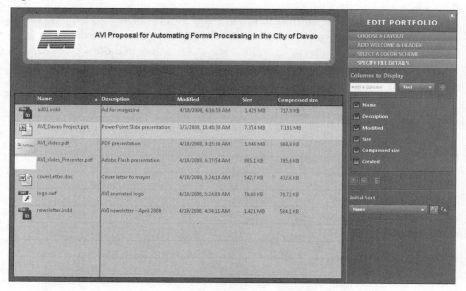

■ **Publish.** The Publish choices you have are similar to the Save and Publish pull-down menu choices. For the Save item, you have only one option for saving the portfolio. The other two options for sharing on Acrobat.com and Emailing the portfolio are identical to the Share pull-down menu choices.

M. Add Files. Click Add Files and the Add Files dialog box opens. You select individual files using this option.

N. Add Existing Folder. Assume you work on a project and save files to a common folder. You might have an advertisement created in Adobe InDesign, a cover letter created in MS Word, a PowerPoint presentation that was converted with Adobe Presenter as an Adobe Flash file, a spreadsheet created in MS Excel, and a few PDF documents related to the same project. If these files are all saved to the same folder, click Add Existing Folder. The Browse for Folder dialog box opens where you can select the folder in question, click OK, and all the files in the folder are added to the portfolio.

O. **Create New Folder.** This choice is used to create a new folder inside the portfolio. Click the button and the New Folder dialog box opens. Type a name for the folder and click OK. The new folder then appears in the portfolio. Double-click the folder and then click Add Files to add files to the folder. When you view files inside the folder, Acrobat displays text above the folder to show the directory path for nested folders. The first item is Home. This is a hot link that takes you back to the Home view. Click Home as you see in Figure 12.23 and you return to the Home view.

FIGURE 12.23

Click Home to return to the Home view.

379196_fg1204.tif

Working with context menus in portfolios

When you add files to a portfolio, you have access to the interface controls described in the section "Examining the portfolio interface." Some of the options you have from the interface tools and menus are also available in a context menu when you right-click (Control+click on Macintosh) on a file. Additionally, there are a few context menu commands that you don't find in other areas in the portfolio interface.

Open a context menu on a file in a portfolio and you see the menu options as shown in Figure 12.24. A few options not yet discussed include:

Three items exist in the context menu that you don't find from the tools in the portfolio interface. The Select All and Deselect All commands enable you to select or deselect files in the portfolio. You might use Select All (also available by pressing Ctrl/⌘+A) and then choose Convert to PDF for files that were added from native file formats.

The Properties menu choice opens a File Properties dialog box. Here you can type a description as shown in Figure 12.25. The description you add to the File Properties dialog box is dynamically displayed when you view files in the List View mode and check the Description check box in the Specify File Details panel.

FIGURE 12.24

Open a context menu (right-click in Windows or Ctrl+click in Macintosh) on a file in a portfolio.

FIGURE 12.25

Open a context menu (right-click in Windows or Ctrl+click in Macintosh) on a file in a portfolio.

If you open a context menu on an area outside a file, the menu commands display an abbreviated list that includes the commands shown in Figure 12.26.

FIGURE 12.26

A context menu opened without selecting a file

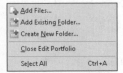

Editing PDF Portfolios

Earlier in this chapter, in the section "Examining the portfolio interface," I covered a brief description of the options you have in the Edit Portfolio panel. The introduction gives you a general idea of the kind of editing choices you can make in the individual panels.

There still remains much more in terms of detail that can be discussed related to several panels. In this section, I'll cover the more finite details for adding some polish to your portfolio presentations.

Choosing layouts

Click Choose a Layout in the Edit PDF Portfolio panel and you find four choices for the portfolio layout under the Basic Layout category. In Figure 12.15, shown earlier in this chapter, you can see the Revolve layout. Your other choices include Basic Grid, On an Image and Sliding Row.

Using the Basic Grid Layout

Click Basic Grid in the Basic Layouts menu. The Basic Grid choice displays a thumbnail image of the first page in PDF documents and an icon for native files along with the filename (see Figure 12.14). In addition, you see the description of the file that is provided when you address the File Properties and type a description. Regardless of whether the Description check box is checked in the Specify File Details panel, the description always appears in this view.

Using the On an Image Layout

Click On an Image and the left pane changes to display a button. Click the Pick an Image button and you can import an image for a background appearance. After you import an image, you drag the file names from the bottom of the PDF Portfolio window and arrange them on top of the image as shown in Figure 12.27.

FIGURE 12.27

Drag files on top of the imported image

Place files and folders by dragging onto the image

AVI_slides.pptx   AdBudget.xls   ad01.indd   AVI_slides_Presenter.pdf   logo.swf   lo

Working with Image Files

When importing images in the On an Image mode, try to use images that have been ghosted or contain transparency. A ghosted image is one that appears with more white than black so the image appears faded. You can easily ghost an image in Adobe Photoshop by using the Edit ⇨ Fill command. In the Fill dialog box choose White for the color, and choose an opacity value of 70% or more. When you add files on top of the image, you'll see more contrast between the file names and icons and the background image.

If you have a logo or irregular-shaped image you want to use for the Organized Layout, you may want to have the graphic appear with transparency on the edges — something like a circular object where you want the area outside the circle to remain transparent. You can easily handle the task of adding transparency by opening an image in Adobe Photoshop and placing the object on a layer. Note that if you create a logo in a program like Adobe Illustrator, you can open the file in Photoshop and the object appears on a layer with transparency.

To preserve transparency, use the File ⇨ Save for Web & Devices command. In the Save for Web & Devices dialog box, choose GIF for the format and check the transparency check box. A preview is displayed to show you all the transparency that will be preserved in the resultant file. The GIF image can then be imported into the PDF Portfolio with transparency preserved.

Ideally, you'll want to use a ghosted image for the background so the files appear clearly on top of the image as shown in Figure 12.27.

One disadvantage in using the On an Image layout is that there is no way to align the files when you drag them to the image. You have no grid and no alignment commands. You have to visually drag the files around the pane and eyeball them to fit in an organized view. Notice in Figure 12.28 getting a precise alignment is near impossible.

FIGURE 12.28

Files manually aligned on top of an image

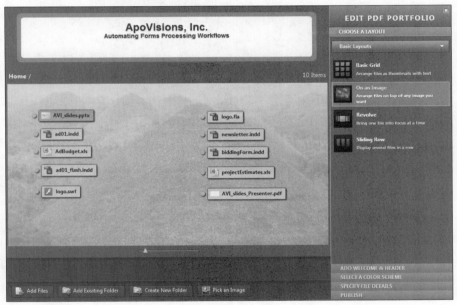

Using the Sliding Row Layout

The last choice you have for a Basic Layout is the SlidingRow view. Click SlidingRow and you f ind a view similar to the Revolve view available in the Animate panels. However, the SlidingRow appearance is a bit different. You see a thumbnail similar to the Basic Grid option along with the filename and description appearing in vertical images as shown in Figure 12.29. To the left and right sides of the Document pane are arrows used to navigate the files in the portfolio. Click these arrows to move back and forth to scroll through the files in the portfolio. Also notice at the bottom of the Document pane you see page icons. Place the cursor over a page icon and the filename appears as a tooltip. Clicking a page icon scrolls the view to the selected place in the Document pane foreground. To open a file in Preview mode, double-click the file in the Document pane. To return to the SlidingRow view from Preview mode, click the Home button.

FIGURE 12.29

Files appearing in the SlidingRow view

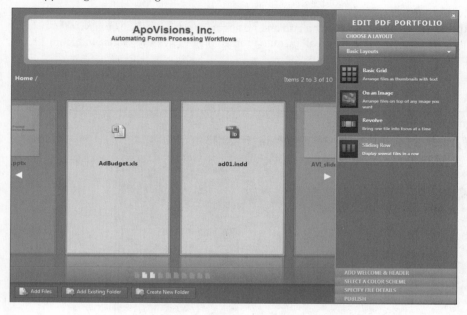

Adding a Welcome Page

The layout you choose in the Choose a Layout panel displays your documents in a view you chose from the layout options. The Welcome page is much different than the layout view. The Welcome Page is shown first when the PDF Portfolio is opened in an Acrobat 9 viewer. This page has a similar behavior as the coversheet we used with Acrobat 8 and should not be confused with either the layout or the Headers & Footers designs. The Welcome Page is new to Acrobat 9 and appears when you first open a file like the coversheet opens in Acrobat 8 when using PDF Packages. Acrobat 9 does have a coversheet separate from the Welcome Page that can be viewed via a menu command or when opening a portfolio in Acrobat 7 and 8 viewers.

To add a Welcome Page, click Add Welcome & Header in the Edit Portfolio panel. You'll see two options when the panel changes. The Welcome Page choice and the Header choice are both listed in this panel. Click Welcome Page and the Welcome Page options are displayed in the panel as shown in Figure 12.30.

FIGURE 12.30

Click Add Welcome & Header and click Welcome Page and the panel changes to display several options for different Welcome Page design styles.

As shown in Figure 12.30, you have several choices for the design of a Welcome Page.

No Welcome Page

Selecting No Welcome Page in the Welcome Page panel does as you might expect — it adds nothing for a Welcome page. The end user jumps right into the view you decide to use for the layout. If a Welcome page is added to a PDF Portfolio, the user needs to click a button to view the contents of the PDF. If you want the users to first see the layout view, use this option for the Welcome page.

Text Only

As the name implies, you can add a block of text to display a message for your Welcome page as shown in Figure 12.31. Formatting the text for the text block is handled in a pop-up toolbar you see at the bottom of Figure 12.31.

FIGURE 12.31

Click Text Only in the Welcome Page panel to display a text box where you type a message that appears as a Welcome page.

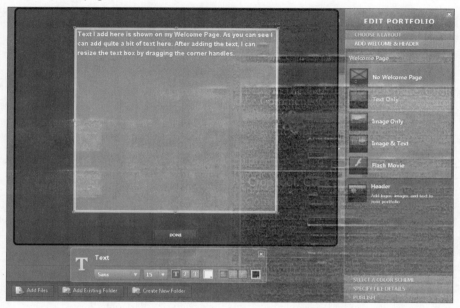

The text box can be resized by dragging the corner handles to reshape the text box. You can change text attributes easily using the pop-up Text toolbar. The same toolbar is used for all other choices you have for adding a Welcome page where text is part of the design. The individual choices you have by using the tools shown in Figure 12.32 include:

FIGURE 12.32

The pop-up Text toolbar is used to change text attributes.

A. **Font Family.** Limited choices appear in the pull-down menu. You have only three choices here. Choose from Sans (sans serif font), Serif, and Typewriter. The Typewriter option uses the Courier font.

B. **Font Size.** Choose from preset font sizes from the pull-down menu ranging from 8 point to 72 point. You don't have an option to use a custom size not offered among the presets.

C. **Bold.** By default, Bold type is turned on. Click this tool and the text is changed to Roman or normal.

D. **Italic.** Italicizes the text.

E. **Underline.** Underlines the text.

F. **Text Color.** Click this swatch and a color palette opens where you can specify a color for the text.

G. **Align Left.** Aligns text to left justified.

H. **Align Center.** Aligns text to center justified.

I. **Align Right.** Aligns text to right justified.

J. **Background Color.** Click the swatch and the pop-up color palette opens. Color changes you make are applied to the background color of the text box.

Note that when making changes to text, you can combine several styles in the same text box. Acrobat applies changes you make to only the selected text. Therefore, you could have a paragraph of text with the first word selected and apply a Bold style to the word. Select a sentence within the paragraph and you can apply an underline style to the selected text. The same applies to adding color values to text; only the selection is affected. In regard to justification, alignment is applied to all text within a paragraph. However, you can justify different paragraphs with different alignment options in the same text box.

Image Only

Use this option to add an image to your Welcome page. When you choose Image Only, a rectangle is shown with the text Add an image inside the rectangle. Click anywhere on the rectangle and the Browse for Image dialog box opens. Select a JPEG, GIF, or PNG image and click Open. The image is shown in the Document pane as you see in Figure 12.33.

FIGURE 12.33

The Image Only welcome page design enables you to import an image.

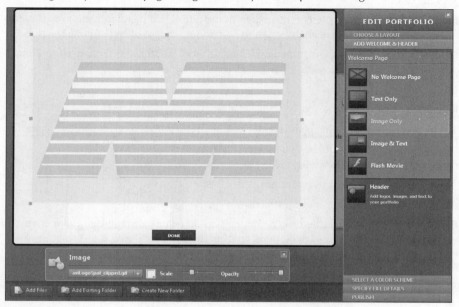

Below the imported image you find the Image pop-up toolbar as shown in Figure 12.34. The tools in this toolbar include:

FIGURE 12.34

The pop-up Image toolbar is used to change image attributes.

A. **Choose an image.** By default, the name of the file you imported for the image appears listed in the menu. Open the menu and select Choose. The Browse for Image dialog box opens where you can choose another image to replace the one currently in use.

B. **Background Color.** Click the swatch and select a color for the background surrounding your image. The color choice fills the rectangle placeholder for the image. If you change opacity the color begins to show through the image file.

C. **Scale**. Move the slider to scale the image. Adjustments are made in 2.50-percent increments.

   Opacity. Move this slider to change transparency in the image. The Opacity adjustments are made in 5.00-percent increments.

Image & Text

This option is a combination of the Text Only and the Image Only welcome page designs. You can add both text and an image and resize the placeholders to position the two objects in any relationship you want. In Figure 12.35 I placed the text block above the image.

FIGURE 12.35

Text & Image combines the two welcome page options of Text Only and Image Only.

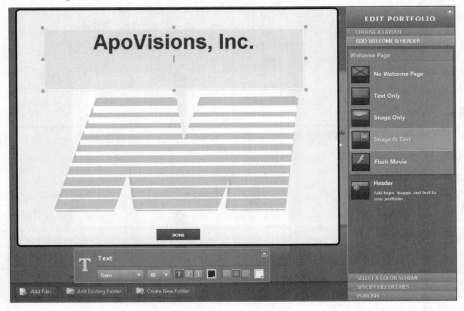

Flash Movie

The Flash Movie option provides you an opportunity to import Flash movies that are shown on the welcome page. Use this option to import an SWF Adobe Flash movie file. For more specific information on using Adobe Flash files with PDF Portfolios, see the section "Using Adobe Flash with PDF Portfolios" later in this chapter.

Finishing up the welcome page

 After you create a welcome page, click the Done button and you end up in the Layout view. If you want to view the welcome page while in Layout view or List view, click the Open the Welcome Page tool in the portfolio toolbar.

To return to the Layout view, click the Done button again on the welcome page. When a user opens a PDF Portfolio, the button appearing on the welcome page is shown as Get Started. Clicking the Get Started button takes the user to the Layout view.

When viewing PDF Portfolios, users can dismiss the welcome page by clicking the Don't show Welcome Page again check box. If you have essential information that you want a user to see when a portfolio is opened, place the information in a Header instead of the welcome page. Because users can dismiss the Welcome Page view, you'll want to add nonessential information to this page.

Adding headers

Headers appear when you view PDF Portfolios on the opening welcome page and when viewing the individual files in one of the layout views. In other words, the header is always shown when viewing a portfolio.

To open the Header panel, click Add Welcome & Header in the Edit Portfolio panel. Again you'll see two options — one for adding a welcome page and another for adding a header. Click Header and the panel changes to reflect the options you have for creating a header design as shown in Figure 12.36.

FIGURE 12.36

Click Header in the Add Welcome & Header panel to display options for creating a header design.

No Header

The first choice is No Header. Click this option and you can eliminate a header from the portfolio.

Simple Text

The Simple Text option provides a text box where you can add text to a Header field. Adding text to any of the options where text is part of the header design opens the Text pop-up toolbar. The options you have for setting font styles and attributes are the same as when adding text to welcome pages. See the section "Adding a welcome page" earlier in this chapter.

When you add any one of the header designs to a portfolio, you perform edits in either the Welcome Page view or the Layout View. You can toggle this view by choosing the layout you use and view the PDFs in your file along with the new header. In Figure 12.37 my header is edited in the SlidingRow layout view.

FIGURE 12.37

The Simple Text header provides a text box where you type text for the header design.

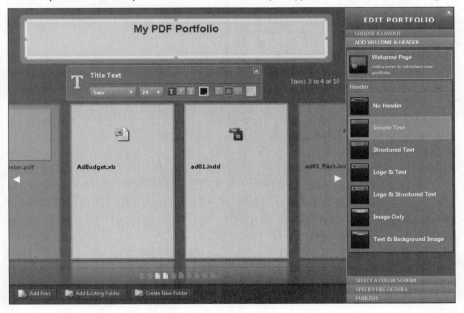

Structured Text

The Structured Text design adds some fields to the Simple Text options. You have the addition of Contact Info Text, Email Address Text, and the URL Text fields. Fill in these fields and you see a view similar to Figure 12.38.

FIGURE 12.38

Click Structured Text in the Header panel to add information related to contact info, e-mail address, and URL text.

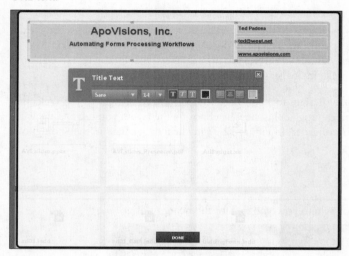

The Email Address Text field and the URL Text field are both hot links in the PDF Portfolio. A user who views your portfolio can click the links to open a new message in the user's default e-mail client, or click the URL text to open the user's default Web browser that links to the URL address specified in this field.

Logo & Text

Logo & Text is a design where you can import an image adjacent to a text field. In Figure 12.39 I added a logo to the Logo & Text design. Notice that the image controls you have are identical to those controls you have when adding images to a welcome pages (see "Adding a welcome page" earlier in this chapter).

Logo & Structured Text

This option is a combination of using a logo with the Structured Text design. In Figure 12.40 you can see an example of a header using the Logo & Structured Text design.

Image Only

This option is the same as using Image Only in welcome pages. The difference is the default size of the image placeholder. The default size is the same as you see in Figure 12.40. However, you can size the placeholder to the same size as the welcome page Image Only placeholder.

Text & Background Image

The Text & Background Image design enables you to place an image behind the text as shown in Figure 12.41. After placing an image, you can reduce the opacity to enable the text to be more prominent in the header.

FIGURE 12.39

The Logo & Text Header design enables you to import an image alongside a text box.

FIGURE 12.40

A header using the Logo & Structured Text design

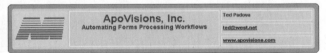

FIGURE 12.41

Text & Background Image enables you to import an image behind the header text.

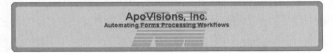

Working with File Details

The Specify File Details panel gives you feedback on your portfolio content and can help you organize files in the List View mode. To view details about files in a portfolio, click Specify File Details to open the panel as shown in Figure 12.42.

FIGURE 12.42

Click Specify File Details to open the Specify File Details panel.

The default list of columns you see in a List view include:

- **Name.** The first column in List view displays the file name of the files contained in the portfolio.

- **Description.** Descriptions are added in List view, or by selecting properties from a context menu and adding a description for the file properties as I described earlier in the section "Working with context menus in portfolios."

- **Modified.** Reports the date a file was last modified.

- **Size.** Reports the original file size.

- **Compressed size.** Reports the compressed file size.

- **Created.** Reports the creation date.

Adding a new column

Under the Columns to Display text you find a text box (Add a column) as shown in Figure 12.43. Typing a name in the text box and clicking the plus icon enables you to add a new column that appears in List View when you check the check box adjacent to the column name in the panel. You might want to add a column of numbers to sort your files in an order that you want to have the files seen in Layout view by those who review your portfolio.

FIGURE 12.43

New columns are created by first typing a name in the Add a column text box.

To add a new column and sort using that column, follow these steps:

Steps: Adding new columns to display

1. **Open a PDF Portfolio.**
2. **Select Modify ⇨ Edit Portfolio.** Selecting this command takes you into Edit mode.
3. **Open Specify File Details panel.** Click Specify File Details in the Edit Portfolio panel; the Specify File Details panel opens.
4. **Type a name for a new column.** In my example, I want to sort files according to an order I want to see in the Layout view that is different from the default order displayed when I open the portfolio. The name I use for my new column is Order. Type the name in the text box.

NOTE When you add files to a PDF Portfolio, the List view and Layout view displays files in an alphabetical ascending order.

5. **Assign a definition for the new column.** Adjacent to the text box where you type a name for the new column, a pull-down menu offers three options. The options include Text, Number, and Date. In my example I want to use number. Select one of the three options from the menu.
6. **Add the Column.** Click the plus symbol adjacent to the pull-down menu to add the item as a new column.
7. **Edit the column properties.** Again, in my example, I want to sort my files in an order I define using my new Order column. In the List view I type numbers for the order in which I want my files sorted.
8. **Sort the column.** Open the Initial Sort pull-down menu and choose the new column you added. The result of my new order is shown in Figure 12.44.

FIGURE 12.44

A new column is added, the properties are edited, and the column is sorted in ascending order.

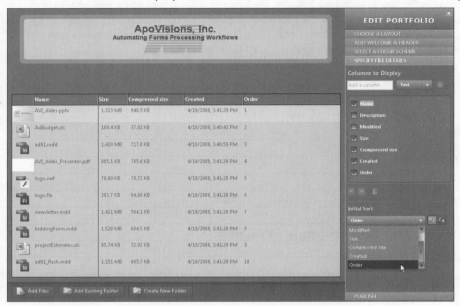

After a new column is added, you can change the column name by double-clicking the item in the list. After double-clicking, type a new name and press Enter. Note that the default items for Name, Description, Modified, Size, Compressed Size, and Created cannot be modified.

Managing details

 At the bottom of the list of detail items you find three icons. The Up and Down arrows are used to reorder the list. Changes you make in the list are reflected in the List view. For example, by default the Modified item follows the Description item, and the Created item appears last in the default display. If you want to move Created above Modified, click Created in the list in the panel and click the Up arrow. Keep clicking until the item is moved to the desired location. When you view the List view, you see the changes appearing in the column headings (that is, the Created column appears before the Modified column).

 The Trash icon is used to delete items. However, the default items shown in Figure 12.43 cannot be deleted. You use the Trash icon to delete new columns you add to the panel. For example, if I want to delete the Order column created in the preceding steps, I would click Order in the panel and click the Trash icon to delete the item. In this example, if I delete the column, the sort order is unaffected.

Managing the List view

Items are displayed in List view in columns according to the items checked in the panel. You can remove or add check marks to all items in the panel list. If you remove all check marks, the List view displays an icon representing the page thumbnail of a PDF page or an application icon for non-PDF file types.

You can resize the columns in List view much like you would resize cells in a spreadsheet application. Move the cursor to the top row where you see the column header names and click the vertical separator bar. Drag the cursor left or right to resize the columns.

A file in List view can be opened by double-clicking the image icon in the first column. If the file is a PDF document, the file opens in the Preview mode. If the file is a non-PDF document, the Preview mode displays an application icon for the file. You can click the Open button to open the file in the original authoring application.

Using Adobe Flash with PDF Portfolios

Adobe Flash Player runtime is embedded in Acrobat and Adobe Reader 9. It stands to reason then that you should have several different options for handling Flash files in PDF Portfolios — and you do. Adobe Flash is to PDF Portfolios like hot links are to Web browsing. Although not completely essential, adding Flash to a portfolio makes your presentations much more dynamic.

 For more information on using Adobe Flash files with PDFs, see Chapters 23 and 28.

Adding Flash files to the welcome page

Adobe Flash files are good candidates for welcome pages. Much like you might visit a Web site, you open the Home page and view a Flash movie that might be a short clip about your company. This information is nonessential relative to the contents of the portfolio. Like Web page designs, the user has the option to skip the intro each time the portfolio is opened by clicking the Don't show Welcome Page again check box that automatically appears on all welcome pages.

To add a welcome page to a PDF Portfolio you should create the Adobe Flash FLV file and save as an SWF Flash file. Once you have the SWF animation you follow steps like the following:

Steps: Using a Flash movie for a welcome page

1. **Create a new PDF Portfolio.** Choose File ➪ Create PDF Portfolio or use one of the other menu choices you have for creating a new PDF Portfolio.

2. **Click Add Welcome & Header in the Edit Portfolio panel.** Choose Welcome Page from the two options listed in the Edit Portfolio panel.

3. **Click Flash Movie.** In the Welcome Page list of options, click Flash Movie; the Document pane changes to display a hot link for importing a Flash file. The text reads as Add a Flash file.

4. **Import an Adobe Flash .swf file.** Click the text Add a Flash file; the Browse For Flash file dialog box opens. Notice that the Files of type option is limited to SWFs (*.swf). Locate the SWF file on your hard drive, click it, and click Open.

5. **Edit the Flash File attributes.** After importing the file, the Flash File toolbar opens in the PDF Portfolio interface as shown in Figure 12.45. Click the Background Color swatch to change the background color of the welcome page if desired. Move the Scale slider to scale the movie file to the desired size. If you want to add transparency, move the Opacity slider.

6. **Click Done.** Click Done and the Flash application (or file) is set to play when the portfolio is opened. From here you can click the Add Files or Add Existing Folder tools to import documents into your portfolio.

FIGURE 12.45

Use the Flash File toolbar to change display attributes.

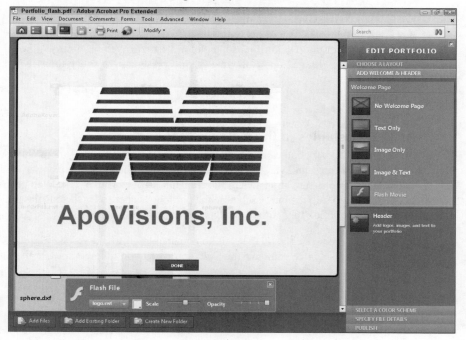

Importing Adobe Flash in a portfolio

You can import both Flash FLA native files and SWF movie files. Click Add Files and browse your hard drive to locate either file type. Select the file(s) and click Open. When a user views your portfolio, the SWF files play in the portfolio. The Flash FLA files require the user to have Adobe Flash installed on their computer.

Converting Flash files to PDF

Adobe Flash FLV (Flash Video Files) can be converted directly to PDF. When you convert a Flash FLV file to PDF, the file page size is equal to the movie page size. You can use the Create ⇨ PDF From File command prior to assembling your portfolio. You can also convert a Flash file to PDF after importing the file in a portfolio.

If you import a Flash file in a portfolio and want to convert to PDF, first select the file in the portfolio in Edit mode. Open the Modify pull-down menu and choose Convert to PDF. Acrobat opens the Convert to PDF dialog box and a progress bar reports the status of the conversion as shown in Figure 12.46.

A progress bar reports the status of converting an Adobe Flash FLV file to PDF.

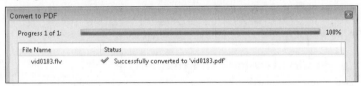

The file is converted to a PDF document and added to the portfolio. The original FLV document remains in the portfolio and the new flash PDF document is added to the portfolio as shown in Figure 12.47. If you want to delete the original FLV file after conversion, select the file and open a context menu, or open the Modify pull-down menu and choose Delete from either menu.

If you use Flash SWF files you can import them directly in Acrobat without a need for converting the file.

FIGURE 12.47

The converted FLV file is added to the portfolio.

Converting Flash files to Flash movies

You may import an Adobe Flash FLA native Flash file and want to convert the file to a Flash movie SWF file. In order to do so, you need to have Adobe Flash and export the file as FLV or SWF. Acrobat cannot convert FLA files to PDF.

 A number of options choices are available to you for converting Flash videos. For more information related to Adobe Flash and importing movie files, see Chapter 23.

Adding 3D content to a portfolio (Acrobat Pro Extended)

Although not Flash content, I tossed in 3D animation in this section. If you have Adobe Acrobat Pro Extended, you can convert a variety of native 3D application files to PDF from within a portfolio.

Any Acrobat Pro user can add a native file to a portfolio. However, the native documents require all users viewing your portfolio to have available the original authoring program in order to see the file. If you send 3D files to users who may have the original authoring application and some users who don't have it, you may want to add two files to your portfolio.

You can convert a 3D file format supported by Acrobat Pro Extended from within a portfolio. Add the original file to a portfolio and select the file in Edit mode. From a context menu or the Modify menu choose Convert to PDF. The Acrobat 3D Conversion dialog box shown in Figure 12.48 opens.

Set the file conversion attributes and click OK. A progress bar is shown similar to the one shown in Figure 12.46. After the conversion is completed, the new PDF document is added to the portfolio. Again, the original file remains in the portfolio while the new PDF document is added. In Figure 12.49 I converted an AutoDesk 3d-studio .3ds file to PDF. The new PDF document appears adjacent to the original file.

CROSS-REF **For more information on converting 3D files to PDF, see Chapter 23.**

FIGURE 12.48

Select a 3D native file in Acrobat Pro Extended and choose Convert to PDF from a context menu or the Modify menu.

FIGURE 12.49

When converting 3D files to PDF from within a portfolio, the original file remains in the portfolio while the converted file is added to the portfolios.

Adding selected pages to portfolios

If you add PDF documents to a portfolio and later decide to eliminate some pages, you can open the PDF documents in Preview mode by double-clicking a PDF or clicking the Preview tool in the portfolio toolbar. Open the Document menu and choose Delete Pages to open the Delete Pages dialog box, where you can select a page range for deletion. A better choice is to open the Pages panel and select pages in the panel. From a context menu or the Options pull-down menu, choose Delete Pages.

CROSS-REF For more information about inserting and deleting pages, see Chapter 16.

If you know ahead of time what pages you want to include in a PDF Portfolio from not only PDF documents, but also many native files, you have some alternatives available to you.

Using the Combine Files wizard

Earlier in this chapter in the section "Using the Combine Files wizard" I talked about combining files into a single PDF document. Because the Combine Files and PDF Portfolio commands are segregated and appear very distinct, you might think that these commands are limited exclusively to either combining files into a single PDF or creating a PDF Portfolio.

Using commands for creating a PDF Portfolio are indeed restricted to creating portfolios. However, the Combine Files wizard is not restricted to combining files into a single PDF. You can also use the wizard to create a PDF Portfolio.

When you use the Add Files tool, you don't have an option to select individual pages to add to your portfolio. However, if you use the Combine Files wizard, you can selectively choose pages from all files that offer options for choosing pages in the wizard. After choosing pages, you can select the PDF Portfolio radio button and create a PDF Portfolio containing documents with just the pages you want to add to the portfolio.

To selectively choose pages in documents that are added to a PDF Portfolio, follow these steps:

Steps: Choosing pages in files added to a PDF Portfolio

1. **Select File ⇨ Combine ⇨ Merge Files into a single PDF.** Notice this command doesn't provide a clue that you're about to create a PDF Portfolio.

2. **Add Files.** The Combine Files dialog box opens. Open the Add Files pull-down menu and choose Add Files. The Add Files dialog box opens. Select files and click Add Files to add files to the Combine Files list.

3. **Select Pages.** Select a file in the list and click the Choose Pages (or Sheets, Slides, and so on, for the file type). In the Preview and Select Page Range dialog box, select the pages you want to use in the portfolio and click OK (see Figure 12.50).

4. **Convert files to PDF.** Click the Options button to open the Options dialog box shown earlier in Figure 12.12. Check the Convert all files to PDF when creating a portfolio check box and click OK.

5. **Choose PDF Portfolio in the Combine Files dialog box.** By default the Single PDF radio button is enabled. Click PDF Portfolio as shown in Figure 12.51.

FIGURE 12.50

Select the pages you want to appear in the portfolio.

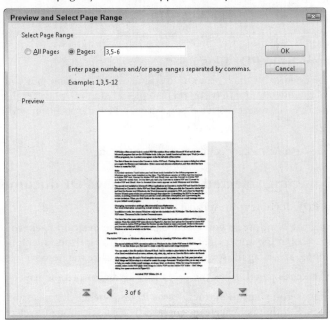

FIGURE 12.51

Click PDF Portfolio and click Combine Files.

6. **Click Combine.** Acrobat converts the files to PDF and processes the file. When conversion and assembly are complete, a Save As dialog box opens prompting you to save the portfolio.

7. **Save the file.** Click the Save button in the Save As dialog box. The files are assembled in a PDF Portfolio with the pages you chose in the Preview and Select Page Range dialog box.

Extracting pages from PDF files

You may have PDF documents that you want to add to a PDF Portfolio, but you only want selected pages to be part of the PDF Portfolio. If you prepare files ahead of time rather than use the Combine Files wizard, you can easily extract selected pages from a PDF file and later add the new PDF to a portfolio.

To add selected files to a new PDF document, follow these steps:

Steps: Extracting selected pages to a new PDF document

1. **Open a PDF document in Acrobat.**

2. **Minimize the window so you can see part of the desktop background.** Click the Minimize tool in the upper right corner of the Acrobat window (middle tool shown in Figure 12.52). Drag the lower-right corner to resize the Acrobat window.

3. **Open the Pages panel.** Click the Pages panel icon to open the panel.

4. **Select pages you want to extract.** In the Pages panel click a page and press the Ctrl/⌘ key and click additional pages for a noncontiguous selection. To select a range of pages, click a page, press Shift, and click the last page in the range.

5. **Drag the pages to the desktop.** If you have a folder open, you can also drag the selection to a folder. The pages are combined together to create a new PDF document. The default name of the document is Untitled Extract Pages as shown in Figure 12.52.

6. **Rename the file.** Click the file, open a context menu, and choose Rename. Type a name for the file and copy the file to a folder where you want to add files to a PDF Portfolio.

 For more information on editing pages in PDF documents, see Chapter 16.

 To extract files from a PDF Portfolio, open a portfolio and view the file in a Layout view. Click a document (PDF or any other file type) and drag the file to the desktop.

FIGURE 12.52

Select files in the Pages panel and drag the pages to the desktop to create a new PDF document comprised of the selected pages.

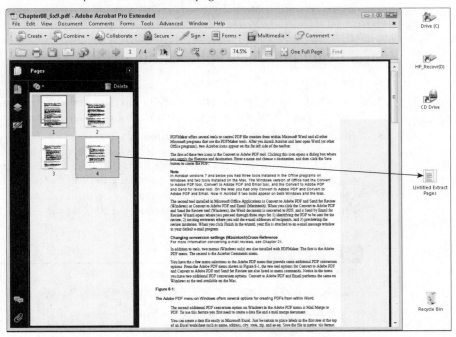

Publishing PDF Portfolios

Adobe's focus for Acrobat 9 is to make Acrobat and PDF file sharing more engaging for end users. Acrobat 9 is the pinnacle of Adobe's longtime pursuit to help users in this regard. In Acrobat 7, Adobe offered tools and methods to help people share files for commenting and review. In Acrobat 8 Adobe provided more simplified sharing methods for comment and review and introduced Acrobat Connect for hosting and participating in online meetings. In Acrobat 9, Adobe brings to Acrobat users a newer, easier, and free sharing service.

NEW FEATURE One of the best new features you'll find in Acrobat 9 is the support for the new Acrobat.com service. Acrobat.com is a separate service provided by Adobe and Acrobat 9 makes it easy to use the resources you have available on Acrobat.com. Acrobat.com is a free service that permits users to share files, engage in review sessions, manage form data, and track files.

CROSS-REF For more information on working in review sessions, see Chapter 21. For more information on using Acrobat.com, see Chapter 29.

Sharing files on Acrobat.com

Although I cover using Acrobat.com in much more detail in Chapter 29, I'll offer a brief introduction in this chapter for using Acrobat.com when working with PDF Portfolios. For a simple overview, follow these steps to send a portfolio to Acrobat.com and invite your colleagues to review the document.

Steps: Publishing PDF Portfolios on Acrobat.com

1. **Open a PDF Portfolio in Acrobat.**

2. **Open the Share tool in the PDF Portfolio interface and choose Share Portfolio on Acrobat.com.** The Share Documents on Acrobat.com dialog box opens.

3. **Fill in your Adobe ID log-on information.** If you have an Adobe ID, type your e-mail address and password in the Share Documents on Acrobat.com dialog box shown in Figure 12.53. If you don't have an Adobe ID, click Create Adobe ID. An e-mail is sent back to you asking you to click a link to complete the process for creating an Adobe ID. When you receive your ID confirmation, type your e-mail address and password in the Share Documents on Acrobat.com dialog box and click Sign In.

FIGURE 12.53

Fill in your log-on information and click Sign In.

4. **Click Next in the Share Documents on Acrobat.com.** After you log on to Acrobat.com, the Share Documents on Acrobat.com wizard opens. The default file selected for uploading is the PDF Portfolio in view in Acrobat. You can change the file in the wizard to another file or add additional files. To submit the current file, click the Next button and an Email wizard opens as shown in Figure 12.54.

FIGURE 12.54

Fill in the To text box with e-mail addresses of the people you want to share your portfolio with.

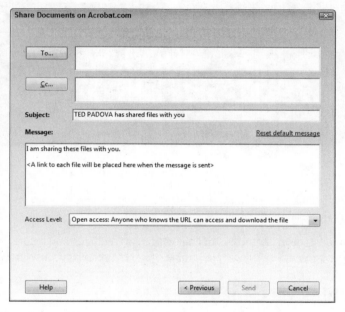

5. **Fill in the text boxes in the Email wizard.** Fill in the To field with email addresses for your recipients. A default subject and message appear in the wizard window. For the Access Level choose either Open Access or Limited Access. If you choose Open Access anyone visiting your Acrobat.com library can download the file. Limited Access limits the access to only those you invite to view the document.

6. **Click Send.** The file begins an upload and a progress bar appears showing you the upload progress. Wait for the upload to complete and a dialog box confirms the upload.

7. **Click View your document now.** Click the text link in the confirmation dialog box and you arrive at Acrobat.com.

8. **Log on to Acrobat.com.** When you arrive at Acrobat.com you need to log on again. Type your Adobe ID and password to log on as shown in Figure 12.55.

FIGURE 12.55

9. **Click My Files.** Click the My Files button after logging on to Acrobat.com to open your Acroabt.com library as shown in Figure 12.56. From here you can invite additional viewers as we explain in Chapter 29.

There's much more to using Acrobat.com than what's covered here. For a more detailed description of the options you have available on Acrobat.com, be sure to read Chapter 29.

Sharing files via e-mail

E-mailing a PDF Portfolio might be an option for you. It's best to use Acrobat.com for file exchanges especially when you have large files you want to share with other users. However, there may be times when you want to fire off a quick e-mail to a recipient when working with a smaller file.

To share a PDF Portfolio with other users, open the portfolio and open the Share pull-down menu. Choose Email from the menu options. A new message window opens in your default e-mail client as shown in Figure 12.57. Note that the new message automatically contains a file attachment. Fill in the To, Subject, and Message fields and click Send to send the mail.

FIGURE 12.56

Click the My Files button when you log on to Acrobat.com and you arrive at your Acrobat.com library.

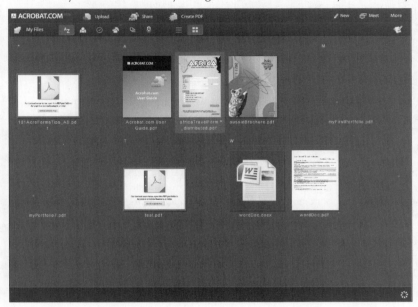

FIGURE 12.57

Fill in the To, Subject, and Message fields and click Send to send a PDF Portfolio attachment to another user.

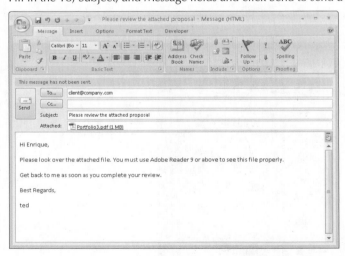

Navigating PDF Portfolios

What I've covered up to this point is creating and editing PDF Portfolios. As a recipient of a portfolio or to help guide others in viewing your portfolio content, you'll need to become familiar with PDF Portfolio navigation and viewing.

Using the Layout view

When you open a PDF Portfolio, the first page you see is the welcome page if the PDF author added one to the portfolio. If no welcome page exists in the Portfolio, you see the default Layout view the PDF author assigned to the portfolio. In Figure 12.58 the Layout view is the Revolve design. There's also a header in this file as you can see in Figure 12.58.

Scrolling pages in this view and other Layout view designs is a matter of clicking navigational buttons and document previews. In the Revolve design, click the arrow icons on either side of the window to scroll through the different documents in the portfolio. Additionally, you can click the page icons at the bottom of the window. Use these icons to jump to different files in a noncontiguous order.

Although the different Layout views appear with varying design elements, navigation is very intuitive when viewing portfolios in the Layout views. The best way to become familiar with navigating different layouts is to poke around and explore different designs.

FIGURE 12.58

A PDF Portfolio shown in Layout view with the Revolve design.

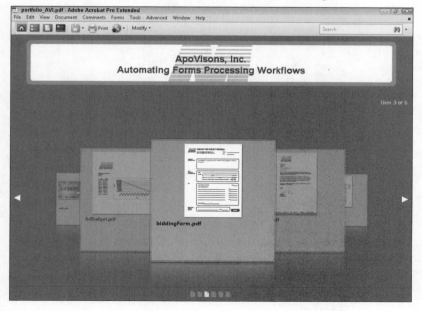

Previewing files

Each file contained within a portfolio can be shown in a separate preview window. If you have PDF files as part of your portfolio, you can open them in Acrobat and view the files just like you view other PDF documents. If the files are native authoring application documents, the Preview displays an Open button to use to open the file in the native application.

 You open a file in Preview mode in several ways. You can double-click the file in the Layout view, or you can click the Preview tool in the PDF Portfolio toolbar. Another method you can use is to select a menu command that I discuss later in the section "Using portfolio menu commands."

Click the Preview tool to see the selected document in Preview mode as shown in Figure 12.59. This view is still the view within the PDF Portfolio. From this view you can open a PDF document from Preview mode by clicking the Open button appearing in the top right corner of the window. If you want to edit a PDF document, you might click the Open button and open the PDF in the Normal viewer mode, where you have access to all the Acrobat tools and all the menu commands.

FIGURE 12.59

A PDF document shown in the PDF Portfolio Preview mode

If you want to simply browse a PDF document, you can stay in the PDF Portfolio Preview mode. Notice in Figure 12.59 you have access to Navigation panel buttons. You can view bookmarks, digital signatures, comments, and file attachments, and you can access other navigation panels by opening a context menu on the Navigation panel and choosing a panel you want to open.

 For more information on using Navigation panels, see Chapter 5.

You also have navigational tools to view other documents in the Preview mode. I cover these options later in the section "Navigating documents in Preview mode."

Open the Tools menu while in Preview mode to access some of Acrobat's tools. From the Tools menu you can open the Comment & Markup toolbar, the Analysis toolbar, and the Multimedia toolbar. Not all toolbars are accessible, but you can open the More Tools window by selecting Tools⇨ Customize Toolbars and load the tools that are supported in this viewer mode.

Note that inasmuch as the Advanced toolbar is not accessible in Preview mode, you can use a keyboard shortcut to access the Select Object tool by pressing the R key on your keyboard. Individual tools are available using keyboard shortcuts as long as the Use single-key accelerators to access tools check box is enabled in the General Preferences.

 Preferences are accessible in any view in PDF Portfolios. Press Ctrl/⌘+K to open the Preferences dialog box.

Returning to default views

One thing that's critically important to know is how to return to the default view when you open a PDF Portfolio. By default you start with the welcome page and then enter the Layout view. As you become familiar with navigating files in portfolios, this view will be commonplace to you, and you'll frequently want to return to the view when you branch out and explore other views such as the Preview mode or Normal viewer mode in Acrobat.

Just remember to always click the Home tool in the PDF Portfolio toolbar. Clicking this tool opens the last view you had in the Layout view. Also, remember that the Home view doesn't show you the welcome page. It only takes you to the Layout view.

If you want to open the welcome page, you can click the Open Welcome Page tool in the PDF Portfolio toolbar.

Using the List view

I covered using the List view earlier in this chapter in the section "Working with File Details." Review that section to learn more about the List view.

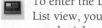 To enter the List view, click the List View tool in the PDF Portfolio toolbar. When you enter the List view, you can double-click a file icon in the far left column to enter Preview mode. Note that you don't have context menu commands for navigation or any other operation while in the List view.

CROSS-REF For more information on using List view, see the section "Working with File Details" earlier in this chapter.

Navigating documents in Preview mode

When you enter Preview mode, the PDF Portfolio tools change to offer you navigation options while remaining in Preview mode. You can open files in the PDF Portfolio without exiting the Preview mode.

Tools you find in the Preview mode toolbar shown in Figure 12.60 include:

FIGURE 12.60

Navigation tools available in Preview mode

A. **Preview the previous file.** Opens the previous file in the Preview mode. When in Layout view, the order you see the files listed is the same order you navigate in the Preview mode. Clicking this button is the same as clicking the left arrow in the Layout views but the file remains in Preview mode.

B. **Preview the next file.** Opposite of item A above. This tool takes you to the next file in the list order.

C. **Previous Page.** This tool is confined to the document in view. If viewing a PDF file, click the tool to open the previous page in the PDF in Preview mode.

D. **Next Page.** Opens the next page in the PDF file in view.

E. **Page number.** Displays the current page number for the file in view.

F. **Decrease magnification.** Click to zoom out on the page in view.

G. **Increase magnification.** Click to zoom in on the page in view.

H. **Current zoom level.** Displays the current zoom percentage of the page in view.

I. **Zoom Presets.** Open the pull-down menu and choose from preset percentages of zoom views. Additionally you have options for Actual Size, Fit Page, Fit Width, and Fit Visible.

J. **Fill Window/Continuous page view.** Opens with a Fit Width zoom and a continuous page view.

K. **Show one page at a time.** Changes from continuous view to single page view.

CROSS-REF For more detail on page navigation and zoom views, see Chapter 5.

Using Portfolio menu commands

Another method available to you for navigating PDF Portfolios is found in the View menu. When you open a portfolio in an Acrobat viewer, a new menu command with a submenu is added to the View menu. Choose View ➪ Portfolio and the submenu commands appear as shown in Figure 12.61.

When you open a PDF Portfolio in an Acrobat viewer, the Portfolio menu item is added to the View menu.

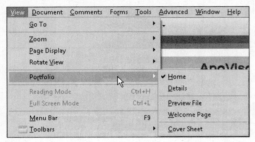

The first four items (Home, Details, Preview File, and Welcome Page) all have counterparts with the PDF Portfolio tools discussed throughout this chapter. The last command in the submenu shows you a cover sheet. Choose View ➪ Portfolio ➪ Cover Sheet and the cover sheet appears as shown in Figure 12.62.

If you share your files with users of Acrobat 9, they won't see the embedded cover sheet that is present in all PDF Portfolios. The cover sheet shows up when users of Acrobat prior to version 9 open your portfolios. The cover sheet also appears as a thumbnail image when uploading files to Acrobat.com.

You can change the cover sheet by creating your own design and saving to the appropriate folder inside your Acrobat folder. However, I don't recommend you mess with this page. In Acrobat 8 we used cover sheets to display the first page in an Acrobat PDF Package, and customizing the default Adobe cover sheet was a handy option for you. You could create your own custom designs and have the pages appear as the default view in a PDF Package.

However, in Acrobat 9, you upload files to Acrobat.com and users immediately notice the familiar cover sheet icon and realize immediately that you have a PDF Portfolio up for review. If you change the cover sheet image, you take away the immediate recognition by other users that the file is a PDF Portfolio. Furthermore, Acrobat 9 PDF Portfolios offer you many impressive options for creating a welcome page. You have control over the opening view of your portfolios and won't need to bother with a document that is rarely seen by users of Acrobat 9 viewers.

FIGURE 12.62

Choose View ⇨ Portfolio ⇨ Cover Sheet to open the cover sheet page.

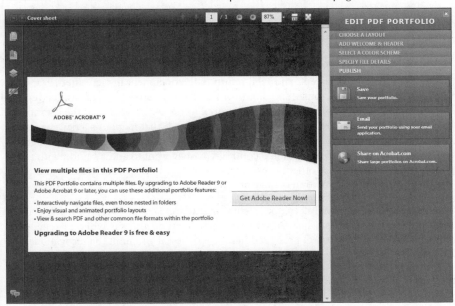

In the File menu you'll find some more menu commands related to PDF Portfolios. In the File menu the commands you find other than the PDF Portfolio creation commands include:

- **Save Portfolio.** Use this command to update a portfolio while you make edits. This command is the same as pressing Ctrl/⌘+S.

- **Save Portfolio As.** This command is the same as using a Save As command but the save is made for the entire portfolio. Use this command to overwrite a PDF Portfolio and optimize it.

- **Save File From Portfolio.** When you view a document in Preview mode and choose this command, you save the currently viewed file. The file can be any file type.

- **Attach Portfolio to Email.** Use this command to attach the portfolio in view to a new e-mail message in your default e-mail client.

- **Portfolio Properties.** Choose this command to open the Document Properties dialog box. You can add a Document Description and Security, edit the Initial View, and add Custom property metadata to the file. Note that each PDF document contained in a portfolio can contain its own individual document properties. When you use this command, it applies to the portfolio.

Adding navigation buttons to PDFs in a portfolio

As a general rule, PDF Portfolios have an impressive interface and intuitive design for navigating the contents of a portfolio. If you plan your work with user navigation and easy viewing in mind, you shouldn't have much need for navigational buttons. However, as is the case in all aspects of document viewing in the computer world, there are exceptions.

You might have a well-organized portfolio but an occasional need for a user to branch out to a page in another document to follow a concept, and then return to the document in view after reviewing supplemental information. Perhaps something on the order of a point stressed in an annual report with a link to a financial statement would be one example of a case where you want the user to easily link to another view. Another example might be a cover letter that mentions a newspaper article interview where you want the viewer to jump to the article, look it over, and return to the cover letter. If you want this type of navigational control, you may want to add a button with an action assigned to the button to open other pages in other PDF files to help your viewers branch out and review supporting documentation on a given concept.

Keep in mind that although you can link to documents other than PDF, the end user needs original authoring programs and there is a delay in viewing supplement documents while a program launches. The type of navigation control presented here works best if you limit the navigational links to PDF files.

To understand more clearly the task of creating navigation buttons in PDF Portfolios, follow these steps:

Steps: Creating navigation links in PDF Portfolios

1. **Open a PDF Portfolio containing several PDF files and at least one file having more than one page.**

2. **Open the page you want to link from in Preview mode.** Select a page in the Layout view and double-click the page or click the Preview tool in the PDF Portfolio toolbar.

3. **Select the Link tool.** Select Tools ⇨ Advanced Editing ⇨ Link Tool. The cursor loads the Link tool.

4. **Add a Link to the document page.** Move the cursor to the location you want to add a link and open a rectangle on the page for the Link.

5. **Set the Link Properties.** Choose either Visible Rectangle or Invisible Rectangle from the Link Type pull-down menu. Chose options for Line Style, Highlight Style, and Line Thickness if you want the rectangle visible as shown in Figure 12.63.

6. **Add the Action.** Leave the default Link Action at the Go to a page view radio button choice and click Next. The Create Go to View dialog box opens as shown in Figure 12.64.

FIGURE 12.63

Set the link properties in the Create Link dialog box.

FIGURE 12.64

Click Next to open the Create Go to View dialog box.

7. **Navigate to the target view.** Be certain to keep the Create Go to View dialog box open. You have full navigation control in the PDF Portfolio while this dialog box remains open. Click the Preview the previous file or Preview the next file arrows in the Portfolio toolbar to navigate documents until you locate the target document. When the document is in view, open the page you want to link to as shown in Figure 12.65.

FIGURE 12.65

Click Set Link when the target view is shown in the Document pane.

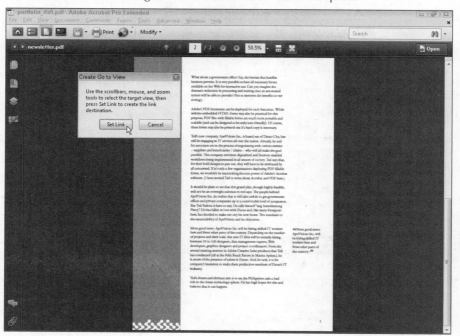

8. **Set the link.** Click Set Link in the Create Go to View dialog box. Once you set the link, you are returned to the document where the navigation link resides. At this point you can follow the same steps to create another link on the target page to return to the page with the original link.

CROSS-REF For more information on creating navigational links, see Chapter 22.

Working with File Attachments

File attachments enable you to attach any document file on your hard drive, a recorded sound, or a pasted image to an open PDF file. When you attach files, the file is embedded in the PDF document. Embedding a file provides other users the capability to view attachments on other computers and across platforms. At first it may appear as though the attachment is a link. However, if you transport the PDF document to another computer and open the attachment, the embedded file opens in the host application.

Users on other computers need the original authoring application to view the embedded file just like files added to PDF Portfolios. You can add file attachments in Acrobat Standard, Pro, or Pro Extended.. You can also add file attachments in Adobe Reader when PDFs have been created by using Adobe LiveCycle Reader Extensions ES. If you open the Attachments panel (click the paper clip icon in the Navigation panel) in Adobe Reader, you cannot add file attachments if the file has not been enabled with Adobe LiveCycle Reader Extensions ES. An alternative for those without the LiveCycle Reader Extensions ES is to enable PDFs for Commenting in Adobe Reader using Acrobat Pro or Pro Extended. Reader users can then add file attachments as comments.

CROSS-REF Enabling commenting in Adobe Reader is available in Acrobat, Pro, and Pro Extended in Acrobat 9. For more information on enabling files with Adobe Reader extensions, see Chapter 19.

There are two methods available to you when attaching files. You can use the Commenting toolbar and attach a file as a comment, or use the Attach a File menu command from the Document menu or Attachments panel. When files are attached using Attach a File as a Comment, the PDF needs to be enabled with usage rights for Adobe Reader users to extract the file. Additionally, when Attach a File as a Comment is used, the file attachments show up in any comment summary you create in Acrobat. Additionally, you can add file attachments to PDF Portfolios as well as PDF documents.

CROSS-REF The commenting tools used for file attachments are discussed in this chapter. However, commenting is a huge topic and you'll find Chapter 20 devoted to all the other features all Acrobat viewers offer you for commenting.

When using the Attach a File menu command, any Adobe Reader user in version 7.0 and later can extract the file attachment without the file enabled with usage rights. Unlike using commenting tools, files attached using the menu command do not show up in comment summaries.

CROSS-REF For more information on adding usage rights to PDFs for Adobe Reader, see Chapter 19.

Regardless of what attachment you add to a document, the attachments appear in the Attachments panel in the Navigation pane. If you add a file attachment to a PDF in a PDF Portfolio, the portfolio attachments are shown in the Attachments panel when you open the Navigation pane.

Using the Attach tools

 To attach a file to a PDF document, select Document ➪ Attach a File. The Add Attachment dialog box opens where you can navigate your hard drive, locate a file to attach, select the file, and click Open. The file is attached to the open document, and all users of all Acrobat viewers version 7.0 and later can extract the attachment.

To use the Attach a File as a Comment tool, select the tool and click in the Document pane. The Add Attachment dialog box opens, in which you navigate to a file and select it for the attachment. Any file on your computer can be used as a file attachment. Select a file and click Select. The File Attachment Properties dialog box opens with the Appearance tab in view as shown in Figure 12.66.

FIGURE 12.66

Select a file to attach and the File Attachment Properties dialog box opens.

NOTE To use the Attach a File as a Comment feature, it's handy if you load the Comment & Markup toolbar. See "Setting Up the Work Environment" at the beginning of this chapter for loading the tools necessary to follow along in this section.

The Appearance properties for file attachments offer you choices for icon appearances to represent file attachments. Choose from one of the four icon choices shown in Figure 12.66. By default the Paperclip icon is used.

The General tab shown in Figure 12.67 has editable fields used for Author name, Subject, and a Description. By default, the Author name is supplied by your Identity preferences.

FIGURE 12.67

The General properties offer choices for author name, subject, and a description of the attached file.

CROSS-REF For information on editing Identity preferences, see Chapter 20.

The Review History tab shown in Figure 12.68 is used for review sessions where information related to the review history and migration history are viewed.

CROSS-REF For information on review and migration history, see Chapter 21.

FIGURE 12.68

The Review History tab documents review and migration history.

If you position the cursor over a file attachment icon, a tooltip displays the author name, file name, and the description information.

Attach a File as a Comment does not support an associated pop-up note. Double-clicking an attachment icon opens the file attachment.

NOTE You must have the original authoring application to open file attachments when the attachments are other than PDF.

You can use PDF documents like a security wrapper for any file you want to exchange with colleagues and co-workers. Use the Attach a File as a Comment tool and attach one or more files to a PDF document. Secure the PDF with Password Security and use the E-mail tool to send the file to members of your workgroup. You can protect the document with password security and prevent unauthorized users from opening your PDF or extracting attached files. In this regard you can use Acrobat to secure any document you create in any authoring program. Of course, you can also secure PDF Portfolios and use files within a portfolio very similar to using file attachments.

CROSS-REF For more information on using password security, see Chapter 26. For more information about using the Email tool, see Chapter s 5 and 8.

File attachments are embedded in PDFs, and double-clicking the Attach a File as a Comment icon provides you access to the file. If you want to save an embedded file to disk without opening the file, open a context menu and select Save Attachment. Acrobat opens a dialog box where you can navigate your hard drive and designate a location for the file to be saved to. Neither opening a file nor saving the attachment file to disk removes the file attachment. If you want to delete a file attachment, open a context menu on the attachment icon and select Delete Attachment or select the icon and press Delete or the Del key.

Record Audio Comment tool

Sound comments are recorded from within the PDF document or from prerecorded sounds saved in WAV or AIFF format on both Windows and Macintosh. For recording a sound, you must have a microphone connected to your computer. The resulting sound file is embedded in the PDF when you use the Record Audio Comment tool.

Attaching prerecorded sounds

Select the Record Audio Comment tool and click on a PDF page. The Sound Recorder (Windows shown in Figure 12.69) or Record Sound (Macintosh shown in Figure 12.70) dialog box opens. Click Browse (Windows) or Choose (Macintosh).

FIGURE 12.69

To select a sound file to attach to the PDF (Windows), click the Browse button.

FIGURE 12.70

To select a sound file to attach to the PDF (Macintosh), click the Choose button.

The Select Sound File dialog box opens after you click Browse (Windows) or Choose (Macintosh). Navigate your hard drive and find a sound file to attach to the document. Select the sound file and click the Select button. Acrobat returns you to the Sound Recorder (Windows) or Record Sound (Macintosh) dialog box. At this point you can play the sound or click OK to embed the sound in the PDF. Click the right-pointing arrow (Windows) or Play (Macintosh) and you can verify the sound before importing it. After you click OK, the Sound Attachment Properties dialog box opens.

After the sound file has been embedded in the PDF document, you can play the sound by opening a context menu on the Record Audio Comment icon and selecting Play File.

Recording sounds

Click the mouse button with the Record Audio Comment tool to open the Sound Recorder (Windows) or Record Sound (Macintosh) dialog box. Click the record button and speak into the microphone connected to your computer. When you finish recording the sound, click OK (Windows) or Stop (Macintosh). The Sound Attachment Properties dialog box opens immediately after you stop the recording. The General properties are shown in Figure 12.71.

FIGURE 12.71

After you stop a recording, the Sound Attachment Properties dialog box opens (Windows).

When you close the Sound Attachment Properties dialog box, the sound can be played like imported sounds. Open a context menu and select Play File (or double-click the Record Audio Comment icon). Because the sound becomes part of the PDF document, you can transport the PDF across platforms without having to include a sound file link. All sound files are audible on either platform once imported into PDFs.

CROSS-REF For more information on importing sound files, see Chapters 23 and 28.

Attachments and PDF Portfolios

You might first think that file attachments are unnecessary when you create PDF Portfolios. After all, you can add any file to a PDF Portfolio, so why use a file attachment to add files to your document? Perhaps the primary reason for adding file attachments is when you want to share files with Adobe reader 7 or 8 users.

> **TIP** As an alternative to using file attachments you can create a new folder in a PDF Portfolio and store all your original authoring application documents in a folder. This method is preferred if you share files with users of Acrobat 9 viewers.

Creative pros and engineers might make use of PDF Portfolios and file attachments. You might have several brochures or similar documents created in Adobe InDesign that you want to share with your workgroup. You can create a package from InDesign that saves your InDesign document, fonts, and images to a package file. You can then use the Attach a File command to attach the InDesign package files to the PDF versions of the documents. Similar kinds of workflows might be used with engineers creating technical drawings or mechanical engineers creating 3D images.

> **TIP** Because of potential virus problems ZIP and EXE files are not recommended for use as file attachments. You can, however, attach Stuffit archives that can be extracted on both Windows and the Macintosh.

Another instance where a file attachment in a PDF Portfolio might be helpful is when adding audio comments. PDF Portfolios don't support audio comments quite like using the Record Audio Comment tool. If you prefer adding notes in audio form to PDF documents, using a recorded audio attachment might just be your solution.

If you ever find a need for adding file attachments to PDF Portfolios, there are a few things you should know about the structure of a PDF Package and attachments:

- Attachments, as well as comments, are attached to each file independently. In order to see an attachment either on a document page or in the Attachments panel, you need to place the respective PDF in view in the portfolio Preview mode. Attachments made to files not in view are not shown in the Attachments panel. It's like having a separate Attachments panel for each PDF in a package.

- File attachments can be searched in a PDF Portfolio. If you have attachments made to different PDFs, you can search all attachment files, as well as all PDFs in a portfolio. When you use the Search panel in a PDF Portfolio, you must click Search Entire Portfolio to search file attachments.

- Comment summaries are made specific to each PDF document. You cannot combine file attachments as comments made on different PDFs in a portfolio to a single summary.

> **CROSS-REF** For more information on creating comment summaries, see Chapters 20 and 31.

- PDF Portfolios and file attachments are viewed in separate panes. When you double-click a file attachment, the file opens in Normal viewer mode, not within the portfolio interface.

Using the Attachments panel

The Attachments panel docked in the Navigation pane appears by default. If you don't see the Attachments panel in a PDF Portfolio, open a context menu on the Navigation pane and choose Reset Panels. When you click the Attachments panel, the panel opens horizontally like the

Comments tab. The Attachments panel includes a list of file attachments contained in a document that were attached with either the Attach a File command or the Attach a File as a Comment tool.

File attachments can be added to PDF documents and PDF Portfolios. In Figure 12.72, a single file attachment was added to a PDF in a PDF Portfolio. The Attachments panel is opened and a file attachment on a page in the current document in the PDF Package is in view.

FIGURE 12.72

Click the Attachments icon to open the Attachments panel where a list of all file attachments appear when added with either the Attach a File as a Comment tool or the Attach a File menu command.

At the top of the Attachments panel, you find tools for the following:

- **Open.** Click an attachment listed in the panel and click Open. The attachment opens in the program that created the document.

- **Save.** Select an attachment and click Save to save the file to disk. Attachments are contained within PDF files and not accessible to authoring programs unless you open the file by using the Open tool or double-click an attachment icon. Clicking the Save tool extracts the attachment and saves the extracted file to disk. (Note: Extraction does not delete the file attachment from the PDF.)

- **Add.** Add is the only tool accessible when an attachment is not selected in the panel. Click Add to open the Add Attachment dialog box where you can attach additional files. As new files are added as attachments, they are listed dynamically in the Attachment panel.

- **Delete.** Click an attachment and click the Delete tool to remove the attachment from the host document.

TIP If you inadvertently delete an attachment, you can choose Edit ⇨ Undo and bring the attachment back. If you delete several attachments, you can select Undo several times and bring back each deleted attachment.

- **Search.** Clicking the Search tool opens the Acrobat Search panel as shown in Figure 12.73 — when viewing a PDF document. When searching attachments in PDF Portfolios, use the Search tool in the PDF Portfolio toolbar. If you view a file in a New Window view, you have access to the Search tool in the Attachments panel.

FIGURE 12.73

Click Search in the Attachments panel and the Acrobat Search panel opens as a separate window.

You enter search criteria in the Search panel (or PDF Portfolio toolbar) and click the Search Attachments button (or click the binoculars icon). Your Acrobat viewer searches all attached PDF files attached to files in the PDF Portfolio.

If you choose Edit ⇨ Search Entire Portfolio or press Ctrl/⌘+Shift+F, the search panel in the Portfolio opens as shown in Figure 12.74. Notice in Figure 12.74 you have options for searching for Whole Words, Case Sensitive, and Search Entire Portfolio. What doesn't appear in the list is searching bookmarks and comments like you have available with Acrobat Search.

CROSS-REF For more information on using Acrobat Search, see Chapter 6.

FIGURE 12.74

Choose Edit ⇨ Search or press Ctrl/⌘+Shift+F and a Search panel opens on the PDF Portfolio Toolbar Well with a pull-down menu to make choices to narrow the search.

 ■ **Options.** From the Options pull-down menu in the panel or from a context menu opened on a selected attachment, you have additional choices from menu selections. Click the down-pointing arrow adjacent to Options or open a context menu and the menu appears, as shown in Figure 12.75.

FIGURE 12.75

The Options menu and context menu opened from selected attachments offer the same menu commands.

The menu commands for Open Attachment, Save File From Portfolio, Add Attachment, Delete Attachment, and Search Attachments perform the same functions as their tool counterparts. The remaining two menu commands include Edit Description and Show attachments by default. Select Edit Description to open a dialog box where you change the description as you would edit a description in the File Attachment Properties dialog box.

Select Show attachments by default and the Attachments panel opens each time you open the current document. Selecting this option is document specific and you need to save the file after making the menu choice. This menu item is the same as selecting the Attachments Panel and Page option in the Show pull-down menu in the Initial View pane for the Document Properties.

CROSS-REF For more information on setting initial views, see Chapter 5.

Summary

- Separate files can be merged together in a single PDF file using the Combine Files task button.

- A PDF Portfolio is created with either several different menu commands or by using the same Combine Files wizard.

- PDF Portfolios open in a separate user interface much different than the Normal viewer mode in Acrobat 9 and above viewers.

- PDF Portfolios can contain secure files and Adobe Designer XML forms. Creating a single PDF from multiple files does not support secure files or Designer forms.

- PDF Portfolios use a number of different user-selectable templates for the display the Home page and the Layout view.

- Headers added to a PDF Portfolio appear on all pages including the Home page.

- The PDF Portfolio toolbar contains tools to help you easily navigate the portfolio.

- Files can be sorted in the List view according to default document characteristics or through custom properties added as new columns.

- Adobe Flash files can be used for welcome pages in PDF Portfolios.

- Navigating PDF Portfolios can be handled in the Layout view, the Preview view, and in the List view.

- PDF Portfolios can be published on Acrobat.com.

- Navigation links (if you are in preview mode) can be added to a document in a PDF Portfolio to open pages in other documents in the same portfolio.

- File attachments can be added to PDFs and to files within PDF Portfolios.

- Attachments can be made as file attachment comments or using a menu command.

- If files are attached you can extract the attachments in Adobe Reader.

- If you attach files other than PDF, you need the original application program that created the document installed on your computer in order to open the attached file.

- File attachments are viewed according to the PDF file in the Attachments panel. When viewing file attachments made on PDFs in a PDF Portfolio, only the attachments on the current file in view can be seen in the Attachments panel.

Chapter 13

Editing Text

I deally you should always return to an original document when you want to make changes on PDF pages that were converted from an authoring application. With all of Acrobat's impressive features, it is not designed to be used as a page layout program. The options you have in Acrobat for text editing are limited to tweaks and minor corrections. Inasmuch as Acrobat 9 greatly improved text editing on PDFs, returning to your authoring program, editing the pages, and converting them back to PDF is a preferred method.

For minor edits and for purposes of editing PDF files where original documents have been lost or are unavailable, Acrobat does provide you tools and means for text editing. As you look through this chapter, realize that the pages ahead are intended to describe methods for minor corrections and text editing when you don't have an option for returning to an original document.

Setting Up the Text Editing Environment

For text editing, there are several toolbars that you'll want to make visible and dock in the Toolbar Well or float in the Document window, depending on what is handier for you. Toolbars you need for text editing include:

- **Reset Toolbars.** Open a context menu on the Toolbar Well and select Reset Toolbars to return the tools and toolbars to defaults.
- **Access the tools.** Open a context menu on the Toolbar Well and select More Tools.

IN THIS CHAPTER

Editing text with the TouchUp Text tool

Adjusting text editing preferences

Using the Select tool

Looking up definitions

Setting text attributes in new blank pages

- **Advanced Editing.** Select the check box for the Advanced Editing Toolbar. Uncheck all tools except the Select Object tool, the Crop tool, the TouchUp Text tool, and the TouchUp Object tool.

- **File Toolbar.** Add the Organizer and Search tools to the File Toolbar.

- **Edit Toolbar.** Check the box for the Edit Toolbar and all tools are added by default.

- **Select & Zoom Toolbar.** For zooming in and out of the Document pane, use the Loupe tool. Add the Actual Size, Fit Width, and Fit Page tools.

Click OK in the More Tools window. Open a context menu on the Toolbar Well and select Dock Toolbars. After loading the toolbars, your Toolbar Well should look like Figure 13.1.

FIGURE 13.1

Load all editing tools in the Toolbar Well before beginning your text editing session.

Using the TouchUp Text Tool

🔲 TouchUp Text Tool   For minor text edits, the TouchUp Text tool on the Advanced Editing toolbar enables you to edit text along single lines of copy and edit bodies of text. Before you attempt to change text passages on a PDF page, you need to keep a few things in mind. Some of the considerations include:

- **Font embedding.** If you attempt to edit an embedded font, Acrobat prompts you in a dialog box to unembed the font. Text editing is only possible after a font is unembedded. Depending on the permissions granted by the font developer, some fonts can't be unembedded. If Acrobat informs you that font editing cannot occur, you need to make your changes in the original authoring document.

CROSS-REF   **For more information on font embedding, see Chapter 10.**

- **Tagged and untagged PDF documents.** Selecting text with the TouchUp Text tool was problematic with earlier versions of Acrobat. Blocks of text in untagged files were interpreted as separate passages and could not be selected in a contiguous area. Acrobat now has a more intelligent interpretation of text on a page, and tagged as well as untagged files display no difference when selecting text. In Figure 13.2, a page of text is selected with the TouchUp Text tool in an untagged document.

FIGURE 13.2

The TouchUp Text tool in Acrobat 9 can select multiple blocks of text in untagged PDF files.

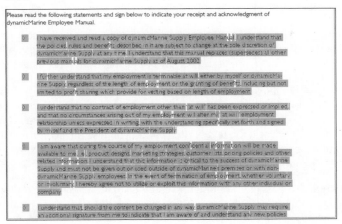

The ability to select lines of text, a paragraph, or multiple paragraphs with the TouchUp Text tool is not dependent on whether a PDF is tagged or untagged; but rather, it's dependent on the structure and content of a PDF. In some documents, you can't select more than single lines of text like the file shown in Figure 13.3.

FIGURE 13.3

The TouchUp Text tool can select only single lines of text on a page in some PDF documents.

CROSS-REF For more information on tagged and structured PDF documents, see Chapter 25. For information on creating tagged PDF files, see Chapters 9 and 10.

- **Property changes.** You can apply property changes for fonts, such as color, size, and other attributes, to text without unembedding the font.

Fortunately, Acrobat alerts you ahead of time if you attempt to edit a PDF document with embedded fonts and those fonts aren't installed on your computer. To edit fonts on a page, select the TouchUp Text tool, and click and drag over a body of text to be changed. Acrobat pauses momentarily as it surveys your installed fonts and the font embedded in the PDF document. Enter your changes and the selected text is replaced with the new text you typed.

You'll be able to see onscreen whether your text editing results in an acceptable appearance and the edits are properly applied. If the text scrambles and you lose total control over the document page, you need to either find the original authoring document or export text from Acrobat into a word processor or layout program to make the changes.

PREPRESS Editing text passages are fine for screen displays when the text flows in an acceptable manner. For high-end printing and prepress you might be able to successfully make changes and minor edits without experiencing printing problems. However, for any kind of paragraph editing you are best off returning to the authoring application. You might get away with some edits in Acrobat, but eventually they will catch up with you. If you do make a spelling error change or other minor text edit, be certain to re-embed the font (see "Changing text attributes" later in this chapter).

In addition to selecting the Properties menu command, a context menu opened from a TouchUp Text tool selection offers menu commands for insertion of special characters. Four choices are available to you when you open a context menu and select the Insert menu command. From the submenu you can choose:

- **Line Break.** This choice adds a line break from the cursor insertion. This command is handy when creating new text on a page or when pasting text. Text lines may extend beyond the page width when creating new text or pasting text. You can create line breaks to keep text within a specific area of the page.

- **Soft Hyphen.** This choice adds a soft hyphen for text scrolling to a new line.

- **Non-Breaking Space.** To add spaces without line breaks, choose non-breaking space.

- **Em Dash.** To add an em dash (—) at the cursor insertion, choose em dash.

When text is selected and you insert a special character, the selected text is deleted and the new character is added. If you use special characters in some files, the results may be less than desirable. Line breaks can flow text into following paragraphs and the text can overlap, making the page unreadable. If you encounter such problems and the edits are necessary to make your files more readable, you must return the file to the authoring program, make the edits, and re-create the PDF document.

Changing text attributes

You can make many text attribute changes without unembedding fonts. You can change colors, point sizes in lines of text, character and word spacing, and other similar text attributes, as well as make changes related to the document structure. You make all of these changes in the TouchUp Properties dialog box.

To edit text properties, select the characters, words, or paragraph(s) you want to change. Be certain the text is highlighted and open a context menu, as shown in Figure 13.4. From the menu options, select Properties.

FIGURE 13.4

To change text properties, select the text to be changed with the TouchUp Text tool and select Properties from the menu options.

CROSS-REF Two tools enable text selection — the TouchUp Text tool and the Select tool. Always use the TouchUp Text tool context menu when opening the TouchUp Properties dialog box. The Select tool context menu does not provide access to the TouchUp Properties dialog box. For information related to using the Select tool, see "Using the Select Tool" later in this chapter.

After you select Properties from the context menu, the TouchUp Properties dialog box opens, as shown in Figure 13.5. The first two tabs relate to changing tags and document structure. Leave these alone for the moment and look at the third tab labeled Text. The properties contained on it relate to changing font attributes for the selected text.

FIGURE 13.5

Select the Text tab in the TouchUp Properties dialog box to make changes to font attributes.

CROSS-REF For information on using the Content and Tag tabs, see Chapter 25.

Items contained in the Text tab include:

- **Font.** This pull-down menu contains a list of fonts for all the fonts loaded in your system and fonts embedded in the document. Keep in mind that just because a font is listed in the pull-down menu doesn't mean you can select the font. If the font is an embedded/subsetted font and you don't have a compatible font loaded in your system, Acrobat won't let you use that font. Fonts loaded in your system can be selected to replace fonts that are both embedded and not embedded.

NOTE The font list in the pull-down menu shows a line dividing the list at the top of the menu. All fonts appearing above the line are embedded fonts in the document. All fonts below the line are loaded in your system.

- **Font Size.** You select a preset font size from this pull-down menu. If the desired size is not listed among the menu choices, select the font size in the field box and type a new value to change the size.

- **Character Spacing.** You can move characters in a line of text closer together or farther apart. The values shown in the pull-down menu are measured in em spaces. Choose from the menu choices or type a value in the field box. Using negative (–) values moves the characters together.

- **Word Spacing.** This option controls the space between whole words. You make choices for distance the same way you do for the preceding Character Spacing option.

- **Horizontal Scaling.** Sizing of individual characters (narrower or wider) is set according to the percentage of the original size. Values above 100% scale characters larger than the original font. Values below 100% result in smaller characters.

- **Embed.** Check the box to embed the selected font.

- **Subset.** Check the box to subset the font.

CROSS-REF For information on font embedding and subsetting, see Chapter 10.

CAUTION In order to legally embed a font, you must own a copy of the font to be embedded and comply with the licensing restrictions of the font manufacturer. Be certain to review the licensing agreement that came with your fonts to verify embedding the font(s) is permitted. Some developers do not license fonts for embedding.

- **Fill.** The color swatch shows the default color of the selected font. Clicking the color swatch opens a pop-up menu, as shown in Figure 13.6. You select preset colors from the palette. When you click Other Color the system color palette opens. You can create custom colors from the system color palette and apply them to the text fill.

FIGURE 13.6

Click the color swatch in the TouchUp Properties dialog box to open the pop-up menu used for making color selections.

PREPRESS If you intend to print your PDFs for color separations, don't make color changes in Acrobat. Acrobat only supports RGB colors with no support for CMYK or spot colors using the TouchUp Properties dialog box. If color changes to text are needed, you would be best off returning to the original authoring application and making the color changes, and then recreating the PDF file. For more information on RGB, Spot, and Process color, see Chapter 32.

- **Stroke Width.** You change the weight (in points) of stroke outlines (if a font has a stroke) by making choices in the pull-down menu or by typing values in the field box.

TIP   If you want to create outline text, select No color from the Fill Color pop-up menu and add a stroke color and width. When stroke fills are set to No color, the fills appear transparent and show the background color.

■ **Baseline Offset.** You can raise or lower text above the baseline or below it. To move text up, enter positive values in the field box. To move text below the baseline, use negative values.

After making choices in the TouchUp Properties dialog box, click the Close button. The changes you make in the dialog box are reflected only on text you selected with the TouchUp Text tool.

Editing text on layers

You can edit text on layered PDF documents. When layer data are visible, you can use the TouchUp Text tool to select text and edit the properties as described in the section "Changing text attributes." If you have difficulty selecting text, you can hide layers and select just the text on visible layers.

TIP   If selecting text or images is difficult because images interfere with text selections or vice versa, you can send the text and images to new layers. New in Acrobat 9 you find the Create PDF Layers options. Open the Print Production toolbar and click the Examine Document tool. In the Preflight dialog box, expand the Create PDF Layers group and choose Create separate layers for vector objects, text, and images. After editing the document you can flatten the layers by opening the Layers panel and choosing Flatten Layers from the Layers panel Option menu. (See Chapter 24 for more on working with layers.)

You can also select and edit text appearing on all visible layers. If text appears on all layers, the edits are applied to all layers. If text appears on a single layer, the text edits reflect changes only on the respective layer.

NOTE   Engineers working in AutoCAD and Microsoft Visio can export drawings as layered files. When the PDF is opened in Acrobat, the layers created contain separate layer data. If you anticipate changing text, try to keep all the text on a single layer for a given drawing if it's practical. You can then hide layers and select all the text on the text layer. Make your edits and the changes are reflected only on the layer(s) that was edited.

 CROSS-REF   For more information on managing layers, see Chapter 24.

Adding new text to a document

You can also use the TouchUp Text tool to add a new line of text in a document. Select the TouchUp Text tool, press the Ctrl/Option key, and then click the mouse button in the area you want to add new text. The New Text Font dialog box opens as shown in Figure 13.7.

From the Font pull-down menu, you can select any font loaded in your system. You're safe when choosing a font from the Font pull-down menu in the New Text Font dialog box since all fonts appearing in the menu are only those fonts loaded in your system.

FIGURE 13.7

Ctrl/Option+click on a document page when you have the TouchUp Text tool selected and the New Text Font dialog box opens. Select a font from the Font pull-down menu and select text alignment — Horizontal or Vertical — from the Mode pull-down menu.

From the Mode pull-down menu, you can select between Horizontal or Vertical alignment. Click OK in the dialog box and the cursor blinks at the location where you clicked the mouse button. The words "New Text" appear in a text field box. Type the text you want to add and open the TouchUp Properties dialog box by choosing Properties from a context menu. Select the check boxes for embedding and subsetting to embed the new text font in the document.

> **TIP** Acrobat does not permit any edits on text where a font has been embedded and the font is not installed on your system. To resolve the problem, you can select the text, open the TouchUp Properties dialog box, and select a system font from the Font pull-down menu. After you change a font to one available to your system, you can make text edits. Note that this workaround can only be used with fonts that don't carry licensing restrictions.

Copying text with the TouchUp Text tool

The TouchUp Text tool is probably the last tool you want to use for copying text and pasting the text into other programs. I mention it here so you know what limitations you have in Acrobat for copying text with this tool. Inasmuch as the TouchUp Text tool enables you to copy multiple lines of text, you are limited to single paragraphs or short blocks of text.

To copy text with the TouchUp Text tool, click and drag the tool through the text block(s) you want to copy. The text is selected as you drag the mouse cursor. After making a selection, open a context menu and select Copy, as shown in Figure 13.8. Alternately, you can press Ctrl/⌘+C.

To paste text in a word processor or other application where pasting text is permitted, open the application and select the Paste command. Typically, you find Paste under the Edit menu. The text formatting of the pasted text can sometimes be better preserved if you copy text from tagged PDF documents.

FIGURE 13.8

Open a context menu on selected text and choose Copy.

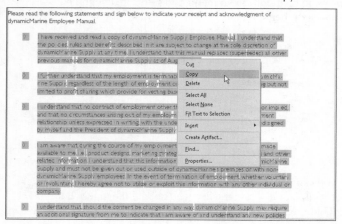

Setting Text Editing Preferences

You have some options for preference choices when using tools for text editing. Using the TouchUp Text tool doesn't require you to make any preference changes. However, when using the Select tool you have some options in the General preferences settings. To open the Preferences dialog box, press Ctrl/⌘+K. When the Preferences dialog box opens, click General in the left pane. At the top of the right pane under the Basic Tools category are options that affect selecting text, as shown in Figure 13.9.

FIGURE 13.9

Open the Preferences dialog box and click General in the left pane. Under the Basic Tools category are options for handling text selections.

Commenting	☑ Use single-key accelerators to access tools
Documents	☑ Create links from URLs
Full Screen	☐ Make Hand tool select text & images
General	☑ Make Hand tool read articles
Page Display	☐ Make Hand tool use mouse-wheel zooming
3D & Multimedia	☐ Make Select tool select images before text
3D Capture	

Selecting the order of objects

The Basic Tools options shown in Figure 13.9 reflect the order that objects are selected (consider a text block as an object as you review this section). When you check the box for *Make Select tool select images before text*, images are selected first when images and text occupy the same space on a page. You use the Select tool to click in an area and the selection is made according to the preference choice made in the Selection section of the General preferences. Selecting the *Make hand tool select text&images* check box and removing the *Make Select tool select images before text* reverses the order and, hence, text is selected before images when they both occupy the same space.

When I refer to occupying the same space, I'm talking about an image that may have a bounding box larger than the displayed image and text appears over the bounding box area, or when text is superimposed over an image.

Using the Hand tool for text selections

 If you're editing text on a page, you can choose to make text selections with the Hand tool instead of the Select tool or the TouchUp Text tool. The preference setting for using the Hand tool to select text is located in the General preferences as shown in Figure 13.9. Unfortunately, there is no context menu option for switching the Hand tool between selecting text and using the hand tool for moving the document page. You can see the menu options in Figure 13.10 when opening a context menu with the Hand tool selected.

FIGURE 13.10

A context menu opened from the Hand tool provides no option for switching the tool behavior between text selections and moving a document page around the Document pane.

With the Hand tool, you can move a page around in the Document pane or scroll pages when viewing pages in views other than Single Page view. If you move the cursor above any text, quickly drag the page around the Document pane to move the page. If you wait a moment, the cursor changes and any dragging you do selects text. If you accidentally select text when you wanted to move the page, deselect the text by clicking outside a text block. This can be frustrating because if you don't click and drag fast enough, the Hand tool will select text when the respective preference option is selected. To disengage the text selection with the Hand tool, press the Spacebar on your keyboard. While the Spacebar is held down, the Hand tool returns to normal behavior and you can move the document page around the Document pane.

CAUTION   If you enable text selection with the Hand tool and it's not working, you need to make an adjustment in the Accessibility preferences. Open the Preferences dialog box and click Accessibility in the left pane. Remove the check mark for *Always display keyboard selection cursor*. If this item is checked, the Hand tool preference options cannot be changed.

Using the Select Tool

Users of earlier versions of Acrobat prior to version 7 will immediately notice the absence of the Select Text tool, the Select Table tool, and the Select Image tool. All three of these tools, performing all three functions, were combined in Acrobat 7 in the form of the Select tool.

 The Select tool is a much better choice than the TouchUp Text tool for selecting text to be copied from a PDF document and pasted in an editor, especially if you have multiple text blocks to copy. With this tool you can select multiple blocks of text and text in columns. However, you cannot make text edits with the tool like you do with the TouchUp Text tool.

To select text with the Select tool, click and drag the tool through the text on a page you want to copy. If a single column appears on the page, click just before the first character to be selected and drag down to the last character. Alternately, you can press the Alt/Option key and drag through a column of text to select it. Generally using the Alt/Option key enables you to create a more precise selection when columns are positioned close together. Acrobat won't copy the text in the adjacent column as long as you stay within the boundaries of the column you are selecting. Figure 13.11 shows text selected with the Select tool where only one column in a multiple-column layout is selected.

In conjunction with the Select tool, shortcut keys and mouse clicks provide several ways to make various text selections, including the following:

- **Select a word.** Double-click on a word, space, or character.
- **Select a line of text.** Triple-click anywhere on a line of text.
- **Select all text on a page.** Click four times (rapid successive clicks) to select all text on a page.
- **Select a column of text.** Click outside the text area and drag through the column or press the Alt/Option key as you drag the Select tool through a column of text.
- **Select a contiguous block of text.** Click and drag through the block of text or click the cursor at the beginning of the text to be selected, press Shift, and click at the end of the text block.
- **Deselect text.** Click outside of the text selection or press Ctrl/⌘+Shift+A.

Depending on choices you make for copying text, text pasted in other programs can retain certain formatting attributes. Your options for what you copy are derived from menu choices when you select text with the Select tool and open a context menu. When you select text, open a context menu as shown in Figure 13.12.

FIGURE 13.11

To select a column of text, use the Select tool and drag down the column length.

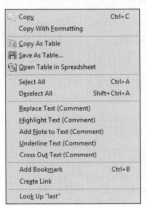

Widget Company
Human Resources Index Description

Title: HR
Subject: Table
Author: Table
Keywords: Table

Title	Subject	Author	Keywords
Policy	PTO	HR	HR 501
Policy	Maternity	HR	HR 521
Procedure	Maternity	HR	HR 520
Form	Payroll	Accounting	FM 261
Policy	Bonus	Accounting	AC 245
Policy	Manual	Admin	AD 109
Procedure	Grievance	HR	HR 546
Policy	EAP	HR	HR 593
Policy	Hiring	HR	HR 506
Form	ID	HR	FM 505
Chart	HR	Admin	AD 117
Form	Leave	HR	FM 531
Procedure	Pay deduction	Accounting	AC 228
Policy	Benefits	Table	Table
Procedure	Extended Leave	HR	HR 564
Policy	Education Leave	HR	HR 568
Form	Insurance	HR	FM 533
Form	Dental	HR	FM 512
Policy	401K	HR	HR 555

FIGURE 13.12

Select text with the Select tool and open a context menu.

Copy	Ctrl+C
Copy With Formatting	
Copy As Table	
Save As Table...	
Open Table in Spreadsheet	
Select All	Ctrl+A
Deselect All	Shift+Ctrl+A
Replace Text (Comment)	
Highlight Text (Comment)	
Add Note to Text (Comment)	
Underline Text (Comment)	
Cross Out Text (Comment)	
Add Bookmark	Ctrl+B
Create Link	
Look Up "last"	

The options shown in the context menu provides choices for marking text with a Highlight, Cross Out, Underline, Replace, and adding a note. These items are used for commenting on PDF files. Additionally, adding a Bookmark and creating a link appear in the context menu. The remaining options in the menu are used for copying and exporting text.

Copying text

Most often you'll find a difference when pasting text copied from tagged and untagged documents. In Figure 13.13, text was copied from an untagged file in Acrobat and pasted into a Microsoft Word document. Much of the text and paragraph formatting was lost when the data was pasted.

FIGURE 13.13

Text pasted from an untagged file loses much of the text and paragraph formatting.

Copying text from tagged PDF documents typically provides much better results, as shown in Figure 13.14.

CROSS-REF For information related to tagging PDF documents, see Chapter 25.

Copying multiple pages of text

If you view PDF files in a Single Page view, you can drag through the text on the page in view to select it. However, if you want to copy text on multiple pages, you need to change the view in a Scrolling mode. Zoom out of the document so you can see several pages in the Document pane and drag through the text you want to copy. If you need to copy more pages than those in view, drag the cursor to the bottom of the Acrobat window. The document pages scroll to place more pages in view. Keep the mouse button pressed as the pages appear in view, and release the mouse button on the last page you want to copy. In Figure 13.15, you can see a document in a Scrolling view and text selected on multiple pages.

To copy the text, select one of the Copy commands at the top of the context menu or choose Edit ⇨ Copy.

FIGURE 13.14

Text pasted from a tagged file retains much of the text and paragraph formatting.

This Employee Manual is an important document intended to help you become acquainted with dynamicMarine Supply. This manual will serve as a guide; it is not the final word in all cases. Individual circumstances may call for individual attention. Because the general business atmosphere of dynamicMarine Supply and economic conditions are always changing, the contents of this manual may be changed at any time at the discretion of dynamicMarine. No changes in any benefit, policy or rule will be made without due consideration of the mutual advantages, disadvantages, benefits and responsibilities such changes will have on you as an employee and on dynamicMarine.
Please read the following statements and sign below to indicate your receipt and acknowledgment of dynamicMarine Employee Manual.

•   I have received and read a copy of dynamicMarine Supply Employee Manual. I understand that the policies, rules and benefits described in it are subject to change at the sole discretion of dynamicMarine Supply at any time. I understand that this manual replaces (supersedes) all other previous manu als for dynamicMarine Supply as of August 2002.
•   I further understand that my employment is terminable at will, either by myself or dynamicMarine Supply, regardless of the length of em ploy ment or the granting of benefits, including but not limited to profit sharing which provide for vesting based on length of employment.
•   I understand that no contract of employment other than "at will" has been expressed or implied, and that no circumstances arising out of my em ploy ment will alter my "at will" employment relationship unless expressed in writing, with the understanding specifically set forth and signed by myself and the President of dynamicMarine Supply.
•   I am aware that during the course of my employment confi dential in forma tion will be made available to me, i.e., product designs, marketing strategies, customer lists, pricing policies and other related in forma tion. I understand that this information is critical to the success of dynamicMarine Supply and must not be given out or used outside of dynamicMarine's premises or with non dynamicMarine Supply employees. In the event of termination of em ploy ment, whether voluntary or involuntary, I hereby agree not to utilize or exploit this information with any other individual or company.
•   I understand that, should the content be changed in any way, dynamicMarine Supply may require an additional signature from me to indicate that I am aware of and understand any new policies.

FIGURE 13.15

Click Scrolling Pages in the Page Display Toolbar and drag the Select tool through multiple pages to select the text.

Using the Select All command

If you have a need to select all the text on a page or throughout a PDF document, you can use the Select All menu command. Depending on the tool you use and the page view mode, text selections behave differently. You must first determine whether you want to select all the text on a page or all text in the document. When selecting text on a PDF page, be certain the page layout view is set to a One Full Page layout. Click the Select tool and choose Edit ➪ Select All or press Ctrl/⌘+A. All the text on a single page is selected. To copy the text you just selected, open a pop-up or context menu and select Copy. All the text is copied to the Clipboard and ready to paste into an editor.

If you want to select all text in a PDF document, change the page view to Scrolling Pages mode. Click the Select tool and choose Edit ➪ Select All or press Ctrl/⌘+A.

TIP In earlier versions of Acrobat you had to click the Select tool and click the tool in a block of text, then use the Select All command. In Acrobat 8 and 9, just click the tool and then press Ctrl/⌘+A to select all text. If you want to select all document content (text and graphics), click the TouchUp Object tool and press Ctrl/⌘+A. For more on selecting images and graphics, see Chapter 15.

This method only works when you use the Select tool. If you select all text using the TouchUp Text tool, the selected text is confined to a bounding box and you must first click in a bounding box area in order to use the Select All command. On any given page there can be one or more bounding boxes, and using Select All selects all text only within a single bounding box. Regardless of which page layout view you choose, the TouchUp Text tool doesn't permit text selections across multiple pages.

Copying a file to the Clipboard (Windows only)

Clicking the Select tool and choosing the Select All command selects all text in a document. You can also accomplish the same task by choosing Edit ➪ Copy File to Clipboard. Open your word processor and you can paste the text into a new document.

If you don't see the menu command, you don't have OLE-compliant applications installed on your computer. Microsoft's OLE (Object Linking and Embedding) is installed by default with Office applications on Windows. If the menu command does not appear, use the Select All menu command to achieve the same results.

Copying and pasting text in word processors is best achieved by exporting PDFs using the File ➪ Save As command or by using File ➪ Export. You can export files as Microsoft Word and RTF (Rich Text Format) by selecting menu options from the task button pull-down menu. Much improved retention of formatting and page layout has been added to Acrobat 9, and you'll find these methods much better than using copy/paste commands.

CROSS-REF For more on exporting PDF data, see Chapter 11.

TIP If you have some major text editing needed on one or two pages in a document, you can use the Extract Pages command from the Document menu to create a new PDF of just the pages you need to edit. Choose File ➪ Save As or File ➪ Export and save to Microsoft Word format. Edit the pages in Word and export to PDF. Open the original document and use the Document ➪ Replace pages command to replace the pages in your file with the new PDF document. (For more on page editing, see Chapter 16.)

Working with table data

You can copy and paste formatted text in columns and rows with the Select tool. If you want to paste data as tables or spreadsheets, Acrobat provides you options for copying table data and opening selected table data in a spreadsheet program.

Copying and pasting table data

Select a table using the Select tool and choose Copy As Table from a pop-up or context menu. Once copied to the Clipboard, the data can be pasted in a word processing or spreadsheet program. When you paste the data in Microsoft Word, it appears as a table. Pasting in Microsoft Excel pastes the data in a spreadsheet document. If you use the Copy command, all data are pasted into a single cell in MS Excel. When selecting the Copy As Table command, the data are distributed into columns and rows in Excel.

Opening selected data in a spreadsheet document

To export a table directly to Microsoft Excel, select columns and rows of text. From a pop-up menu or a context menu, select Open Table in Spreadsheet. By default, Acrobat launches Microsoft Excel and the selected data appear in a new spreadsheet, as shown in Figure 13.16.

FIGURE 13.16

Select a table and choose Open in Spreadsheet from a pop-up menu or context menu and the data appear in a new spreadsheet in Microsoft Excel.

Saving data to a spreadsheet file

Another option you have for getting PDF data to a spreadsheet is to select the table with the Select tool and choose Save As Table from the Select tool pop-up or context menu. When you choose this command, the Acrobat Save As dialog box opens and offers you choices for saving your data in a variety of file formats. From the Save as Type (Windows) or Format (Macintosh) pull-down menu, select from the following:

- **Comma Separated Values (*.csv).** CSV-compliant applications can open files saved in this format. Microsoft Excel and Microsoft Access recognize CSV data, and you can open the files directly in Excel. If you use other applications recognizing the format, use CSV.

- **HTML 4.01 with CSS 1.0 (*.htm).** If you need to get table data to a Web page, you can save the data to HTML format.

- **Rich Text Format (*.rtf).** If you want to import data into programs such as word processing, accounting, and other applications that support RTF, save the file as RTF. If you want columns and rows of data without a table defined in the word processor, use the RTF format.

- **Text (Tab Delimited) (*.txt).** When you need to import data into a database management system (DBMS), export the data as tab delimited. Tab delimited tables import into programs such as FileMaker Pro with data in separate fields and records.

- **Unicode Text (Tab Delimited) (*.txt).** If you use some foreign language kits, Unicode might be a better choice for your file exports. Select Unicode and import the data into applications supporting Unicode text data.

- **XML 1.0 (*.xml).** Acrobat supports exporting tables in XML format. XML data can be exchanged between many programs. If your workflow uses XML, save in this format.

- **XML Spreadsheet (*.xml).** This is an XML format defined by Microsoft and used in Office 2007. Use XML Spreadsheet when using XML data with spreadsheet applications such as Microsoft Excel 2007

Click the Save button and the data are saved in the file format you select from the pull-down menu in the Save As dialog box.

Overcoming problems with recognizing table data

If you select text in a table and you don't see the Copy as Table, Save As Table, or Open Table in Spreadsheet command in a pop-up menu, Acrobat can't recognize the data as a table. This is typically due to a file not having tags and structure. If you want to copy the data as a table or send the data to a spreadsheet application, you need to add tags to the document. To add tags, follow these steps:

Steps: Adding Tags to a PDF Document

1. **Open the untagged file in Acrobat.**

2. **Add tags to the PDF.** Choose Advanced ⇨ Accessibility ⇨ Add Tags to Document. Wait while Acrobat processes the document and adds the tags.

3. **Close the Tags panel.** After Acrobat adds tags, a report is shown in the Tags panel.

4. **Select the table.** Use the Select tool and select the table to be exported to a spreadsheet.

5. **Open the pop-up menu.** You should now see the menu items in the pop-up menu for copying/exporting the data to a spreadsheet.

 For more on tagging files, see Chapter 25.

Looking Up Definitions

Whether you're editing a PDF file or browsing documents, you can find the spelling and word definition for any text in an open document. This very nice little feature in Acrobat saves you time when looking up a definition. To employ the Look Up command from one of two context menus, use either the Hand tool or the Select tool and open a context menu. Text does not need to be selected, but the tool you use must be positioned over the word you want to look up. If using the Select tool, open the traditional context menu by right-clicking the mouse button (Windows) or Ctrl+clicking (Macintosh). From the menu choices, select Lookup "...", placing your selected word inside the quotation marks. In Figure 13.17, you can see the context menu opened when the word *Encapsulated* was targeted for a lookup.

FIGURE 13.17

Click a word with the Select tool or Hand tool. Open a context menu (right-click or Ctrl+click) and select Look Up "..." at the bottom of the menu.

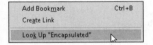

After you make your selection, Acrobat launches the default Web browser and the browser takes you to the Dictionary.com Web site. The Web page opens on the word selected in the PDF document. You can check for spelling errors, word definitions, pronunciation, and browse through a thesaurus. If you have an account for the Web site, you can click on the audio button to hear an audio pronunciation through your computer speaker(s).

Currently, Acrobat only supports U.S. English as a language. Regardless of whether you have a foreign language kit installed, Acrobat launches the Dictionary.com Web site.

Working with Text in New Blank Pages

Additional text tools and text editing features are available to you when creating a blank new page in Acrobat. A separate set of preferences and tools appear when you create a new blank page.

Acrobat is not intended to be an original document authoring program. The text editing feature in Acrobat is designed to offer a simple solution for creating documents when you want to write a memo, create a cover page for a PDF Portfolio, or add some text to a page and send your document as a PDF to other users.

Setting text attributes

To create a blank new page in Acrobat, select File ➪ Create PDF ➪ From Blank Page. A new blank page opens in the document pane with a text box and a toolbar that loads automatically when the new page is created. The New Document Toolbar shown in Figure 13.18 opens when a new page is created, or you can access the toolbar in the More Tools window. However, the tools in this toolbar can only be used in documents created from the New Blank Page command.

FIGURE 13.18

The New Document Toolbar tools are only available in documents created as blank new pages.

Tools you have available for formatting text only in the text box created on a new blank page include:

- **Text color.** The first tool in the New Document Toolbar contains a pull-down menu where a color palette opens. The choices you have for text colors are the same as you have available using the TouchUp Text Properties dialog box shown in Figure 13.6 earlier in this chapter.

- **Paragraph formatting.** The Left, Center, Right, and Justified tools are used to format text alignment.

- **Fonts.** The pull-down menu displays all the fonts loaded in your system. Select a font and the font name is displayed in the text box. Adjacent to the pull-down menu is the Size pull-down menu. Make a choice from fixed font sizes or type a font size in the text box. The sizes you can type in the Size text box range from 4 points to 300 points.

- **Text Style.** Text styles are from left to right in the New Document Toolbar: Bold, Italic, Underline, Strike-through, Superscript, and Subscript.

- **Indents.** The last two text tools in the New Document Toolbar are used for paragraph indenting. The Left Indent and Right Indent tools appear just before the Page Setup tool.

- **Page Setup.** Click the Page Setup tool and the Page Setup dialog box opens as shown in Figure 13.19. In the Page Setup dialog box, you can select from a number of fixed page sizes by choosing an option in the Size pull-down menu. Additionally, you can choose an option for Portrait or Landscape pages in the Page area of the dialog box. Margins are set in the four text boxes at the top of the dialog box. Click the Always use these settings check box and your settings are applied as a new default each time you create a new blank page.

NOTE You cannot resize the text box added to a blank new page using any tool in Acrobat. All text box sizes are determined by the margin settings in the Page Setup dialog box or the New Document preferences.

FIGURE 13.19

Click the Page Setup tool and the Page Setup dialog box opens where page size and margins attributes are selected.

Setting preferences

Preferences can be set for the page attributes by selecting New Document preferences in the Preferences dialog box. Open the Preferences dialog box by pressing Ctrl/⌘+K and click New Document in the left pane. The options for page setup shown in Figure 13.20 are the same as when clicking the Page Setup tool in the New Document Toolbar.

Using the PDF Editor

When you create a blank new page, Acrobat shifts the normal editing mode to a unique editor called the PDF Editor that is available only with blank new pages. By default a text box is created for you according to the preference options you made for page size and margins. Working in the PDF Editor differs from using other editing tools and commands in Acrobat when working in a normal edit mode.

Open Preferences and click New Document in the left pane to display the preference choices for creating new blank pages.

Keyboard shortcuts in the PDF Editor

At first you may think there are anomalies when trying to use keyboard shortcuts when the Page Editor is active. Using Ctrl/⌘++ (plus sign) and Ctrl/⌘+- (minus sign) won't zoom a page. Ctrl/⌘+0 (zero) is consistent with using the standard edit mode for fitting a page in the Document pane. Using keyboard shortcuts for sizing text and changing font styles are all different in the PDF Editor than you have available in standard edit mode. The keyboard shortcuts that are used with the PDF Editor include:

- **Bold text.** Ctrl/⌘+B.
- **Italicize text.** Ctrl/⌘+I.
- **Underline text.** Ctrl/⌘+U.
- **Increase text size.** Ctrl/⌘+] (right bracket).
- **Decrease text size.** Ctrl/⌘+[(left bracket).
- **Superscript text.** Ctrl/⌘+Shift++ (plus sign).

- **Subscript text.** Ctrl/⌘++ (plus sign).
- **Left Justify.** Ctrl/⌘+L.
- **Right Justify.** Ctrl/⌘+R.
- **Justified.** Ctrl/⌘+J.

Tools and commands in the PDF Editor

When you create a blank new page, the text box added to the page is not something you can delete. The Select Object tool is not functional while in PDF Editor mode. However, you can use the TouchUp Object tool to temporarily convert a text selection to an object. With an object you can perform various editing tasks you don't have available with the text tools such as rotating, clipping, scaling, and cropping objects.

You might use something like rotation to create a document you want to use as a watermark. In Figure 13.21, I created text with the text tools in the New Document toolbar. I clicked the text with the TouchUp Object tool and from a context menu I chose Rotate Selection.

- **Resume Editing.** If you click a tool like the Hand tool or the Select Object tool, you loose the text box on the new blank page. It's there, but appears invisible and you exit the PDF Editor. To switch back to the PDF Editor you can select Document ⇨ Resume Editing. Click in the text box and you can type or edit text. You can also reenter the PDF Editor mode by clicking the Select tool and click inside the text box or click any one of the text tools in the New Document Toolbar. If you save a file created as a blank new page and reopen the file in another Acrobat editing session, select Document ⇨ Resume Editing and you again gain access to the PDF Editor where text cane be added or edited in the default text box.

- **Prevent Further Edits.** You can lock the text you add to a text box by selecting Document ⇨ Prevent Further Edits. The Prevent Further Edits dialog box opens as shown in Figure 13.23. Click Prevent Further Edits and the text box is locked and remains not editable. Be aware that when you click the Prevent Further Edits button in the Prevent Further Edits dialog box that you cannot regain an editing status, nor can you use the Edit ⇨ Undo command. Selecting Document ⇨ Resume Editing won't bring the text box back to the PDF Editor where any text editing can be performed.

The conversion of text to an object is temporary. You can edit the text after converting to an object by clicking the Select tool in the text block. Doing so, however, removes all edits you made with the TouchUp Object tool.

CROSS-REF For more information on working with the TouchUp Object tool and objects, see Chapter 15.

FIGURE 13.21

Click text in the new blank page with the TouchUp Object tool to temporarily convert the text to an object.

PDF Editor behavior

A few things you'll notice when using the PDF Editor as you add other content to the page such as comments, form fields, and copied and pasted text include:

- **Comments.** You can add comments to the text block on a blank new page. However, the comments are static and remain fixed to the coordinates when you first added a comment. For example, using a Text Edit tool or a markup comment tool to highlight text or mark text on the page stays in position where you added the comment. If you type text in the text box, the text flows but the comments remain in the original position.

- **Form Fields.** Form fields can be added to the page and appear aside or over a text box. When you engage the PDF Editor to add or edit text in the text box, the form fields, as well as comment notes, are temporarily hidden.

- **Pasting text.** You can copy text from another PDF page or from a word processor or text editor and paste the text into the blank new page text box. To paste text in the text box, select Edit ⇨ Paste or press Ctrl/⌘+V. Text pasted in the text box retains formatting from the copied text. If the text overflows the text box, you can't resize the box and text after the last visible line of text at the bottom of the box flows to a new page.

- **Copying text.** When you select text in the text box on a blank new page, you don't have access to commands when copying text like you do when copying text using the Select Text tool. To copy text, use Edit ⇨ Copy or press Ctrl/⌘+C.

- **Adding new text.** Text on a blank new page can be added to the text box automatically added to the blank new page. You can use Ctrl/⌘ and click with the TouchUp Text tool only outside the text box to create new text. Pasted text that extends beyond the text placeholder automatically flows to create new pages.

Working around the PDF Editor

Unfortunately, Acrobat doesn't provide you a preference option to create a new blank document without the default text block. You might want to create a blank document you use to temporarily paste form fields or simply add images to a blank new document. The default text block can get in the way and make your editing task a little awkward.

To create a blank new document without the text block, use the File ➪ Create PDF ➪ From Blank Page command to create the new blank document. Next, choose Document ➪ Prevent Further Edits. The Prevent Further Edits dialog box opens as shown in Figure 13.22.

Click the Prevent Further Edits button and a Save As dialog box opens. Click Cancel in the Save As dialog box and you no longer have the txt frame on the blank page.

FIGURE 13.22

Choose Document ➪ Prevent Further Edits to open the Prevent Further Edits dialog box.

Alternate methods for creating blank pages

You can create a File ➪ New menu command using JavaScript that provides you options for creating predefined page sizes different than the From Blank Page command, and you can create custom pages that are user defined. In Figure 13.23 you can see such a command that was created with JavaScript added to the File menu.

FIGURE 13.23

Using JavaScript you can add new menu items to Acrobat such as this one for creating new blank pages.

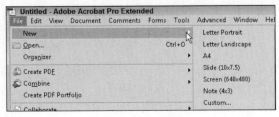

The script is a bit elaborate so I added the file containing the script to the CD-ROM accompanying this book. To add the menu item you need to copy the text file (newPage.js) containing the JavaScript to your JavaScript folder. Quit Acrobat and copy the file to:

On Windows, copy the file to `C:\Program Files\Adobe\Acrobat 9.0\Acrobat\ JavaScripts`.

On the Mac, copy the file to Macintosh HD: `Users: User name:Library: Acrobat User Data:9.0_x86:JavaScripts`.

Launch Acrobat and you'll find the File ⇨ New menu command with the same options shown in Figure 13.23.

Summary

- You use the TouchUp Text tool to make minor edits on PDF pages. You can use the tool to change font attributes, add new lines of text, and access a Properties dialog box where you can select fonts to embed and subset.

- The TouchUp Text tool is not well suited for copying and pasting text data into other programs. Text selections are limited and text formatting is lost when pasting text into other programs.

- Use the Select tool to select text on a page, across multiple pages, and all text in a document.

- When pasting text copied from a Select tool selection in a tagged file, the text data retains much integrity and can be edited with minimum character and paragraph reformatting.

- Text can be edited on visible layers. You can't select text on hidden layers with the Select All command. Edits made to text appearing on all layers result in changes on all layers. Edits made to text on a single layer result in changes on a single layer.

- You also use the Select tool to select table data. You can copy and paste tables in other applications and save the data to a number of different file formats.

- The File ⇨ Create PDF ⇨ From Blank Page menu command creates new pages with a text box and text tools that only appear when creating blank new pages.

- You can use JavaScript to add a menu command for creating blank new pages.

Chapter 14

Redacting PDFs

A marvelous feature introduced in Acrobat 8 was the Redaction tools, which are used for removing data from PDF documents. In Acrobat 9, Adobe has expanded the tool options that provide you more sophisticated options for searching and redacting content in PDF files.

The Redaction tools appear in Acrobat Professional on the Mac and Acrobat Pro and Acrobat Pro Extended on Windows. You won't find Redaction features in Acrobat Standard on Windows.

In this chapter you learn about redaction, why and when it is necessary, the new Acrobat 9 features, and how to use all the Redaction tools.

IN THIS CHAPTER

Understanding redaction

Using the redaction tools

Redacting documents

Setting Up the Work Environment

Load the Redaction and Advanced Editing tools for applying redactions to documents. You'll find Redaction tools in a separate toolbar and accessible from a context menu opened from the Toolbar Well, or select Tools ➪ Customize Toolbars to open the More Tools window. Alternately, you can select More Tools from the context menu. When the More Tools window opens, check the Advanced Editing Toolbar and scroll the list to the Redaction Toolbar and check the box adjacent to the toolbar name. You can selectively toggle individual tools within the toolbar in the More Tools window by checking and unchecking the tool names in the toolbar list. In this chapter, you look at all tools, so be certain check marks appear adjacent to all the tool names in the Redaction toolbar.

What Is Redaction?

Quite simply, *redaction* is the removal of visual information from a document. You might want to use redaction to remove sensitive information for security purposes, to protect rights and privacy information, to eliminate classified information, to delete names of minors in legal documents, or to delete any other information you don't want viewed by others.

Redaction is much different than blotting out or hiding text, graphics, handwriting, or any other kind of marks. If you use tools like some of the comment tools to create markups that blot out some text and graphics in a document, the items are not permanently deleted. It appears fine onscreen where you can't see items marked for deletion on a document page, but the PDF document still contains the original items. If the file is distributed, other users can access marked text and other data.

To understand why redaction tools are needed to permanently delete content from a PDF document, see the following steps.

STEPS: Understanding the need for redaction

1. **Open a PDF document in Acrobat.**

2. **Open the Comment & Markup tools.** Open a context menu on the Toolbar Well and select Comment and Markup. The Comment & Markup tools open in a floating toolbar.

3. **Mark out some text.** Select the Rectangle tool in the Comment & Markup toolbar. Draw a rectangle around some text. Alternately, you can use the Highlight tool so select text and hide it with a dark highlight color.

4. **Open the rectangle comment properties.** Right-click (Windows) or Control+click (Macintosh) to open a context menu on the rectangle. Select Properties from the context menu.

5. **Edit the properties.** Click the Color swatch for both Color and Fill Color. From the color choices select Black, as shown in Figure 14.1. Click the Make Properties Default check box. The next time you draw a rectangle the rectangle will have the same style and fill color.

6. **Draw additional rectangles.** Using the rectangle comment tool, draw some additional rectangles to block out more text. In Figure 14.2, I have a text document with several markings where I don't want the text to be seen. Onscreen this is fine, but the text is not deleted and can be extracted by other users.

7. **Copy the text.** Click the Select tool and drag through the text to select it. Select Edit ➪ Copy to copy the text, as shown in Figure 14.3. Note that you can also use the Search pane and search for text that you marked. You'll notice that the search results report all the hidden text.

FIGURE 14.1

Set the Rectangle comment properties to black color and black fill.

FIGURE 14.2

Text onscreen is blocked out, but the text can still be extracted.

1. The alleged intruder, ████████████ entered the victim's residence forcibly by
2. breaking a window pane on the patio door. ████████ proceeded to enter the
3. victim's (████████████████████) den and placed an assortment of the
4. victim's personal belongings in a sack. ████████ was witnessed by ██████
5. ████████ a minor and son of ████████████████, from his position hiding under
6. an office desk in the den.

FIGURE 14.3

Drag through all the text with the Select tool and choose Edit ➪ Copy.

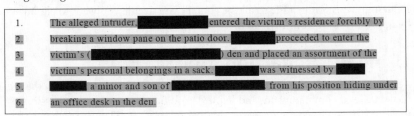

8. **Paste the text in a word processor.** In my example I open Microsoft Word and select Edit ⇨ Paste. As you can see in Figure 14.4, I was able to copy the text beneath all my comment markups.

When you paste all the text in a Word processor, the marked out text appears in the new document window.

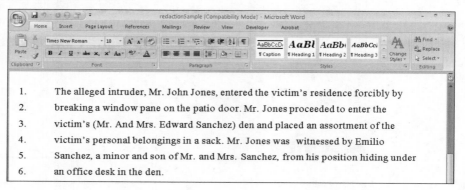

As shown in Figure 14.4, this form of redacting a document doesn't delete the marked text. You need another method to mark and eliminate data from PDFs. This is where the Redaction tools in Acrobat come into play.

Getting a Grip on the Redaction Tools

Redaction is permanently deleting text, graphics, signatures, handwriting, and any other data you want to remove from a document. In addition to marking and deleting text and other data that you can see, a good redaction tool also provides you a means for deleting certain metadata and hidden information in a file so all the content you decide you want to eliminate cannot be retrieved by anyone viewing your PDF files.

Using the Redaction tools

Acrobat 9 offers a few solutions for marking content for deletion, applying the redactions, eliminating metadata, and eliminating any hidden text. You first start a redaction session using the Redaction tools. When you open the Redaction toolbar by selecting View ⇨ Toolbars ⇨ Redaction, choosing Advanced ⇨ Redaction ⇨ Show Redaction Toolbar, or selecting the toolbar in the More Tools window, the tools contained in the toolbar appear as you see in Figure 14.5.

FIGURE 14.5

The Redaction toolbar contains four tools.

The tools on the Redaction toolbar are as follows:

- **Mark for Redaction.** Use this tool to mark text and other data that you want to delete from a document. Marking the content does not yet delete it from the file.
- **Apply Redactions.** When you are ready to permanently delete content that you marked for deletion, click the Apply Redactions tool.
- **Redaction Properties.** Use this tool to set the redaction-marking properties. You can mark content using the Mark for Redaction tool and the markings can be adjusted for color and other attributes in the Redaction Tool Properties dialog box. Click the tool and the Redaction Tool Properties dialog box shown in Figure 14.6 opens.

FIGURE 14.6

Click the Redaction Properties tool and the Redaction Tool Properties dialog box opens.

As you can see in the Redaction Tool Properties dialog box, you can select a color for your redaction marks, use text as an overlay, specify the font for the overlay text, set a number of different font attributes for the overlay text, and select from some redaction code standards. When you change the properties in this dialog box, the properties remain in effect for all redaction marks you make on a document until you again make settings adjustments in the Redaction Tool Properties dialog box.

■ **Search and Redact.** This tool is a powerful addition to the Redaction tools. Click the Search and Redact tool and the Search window opens as shown in Figure 14.7. Type a word or phrase in the first field text box and choose a location. Your options include searching the open document or a folder location on your hard drive or network server. You can mark content for redaction in a collection of PDF documents contained in a common folder. Select the All PDF Documents in radio button. From the pull-down menu below the radio button select Browse for Location. The Browse For Folder dialog box opens where you select a folder containing files you want to redact.

FIGURE 14.7

Click the Search and Redact button and the Search window opens. Type a word or phrase and select either the open document or a folder of PDFs you want to mark for redaction.

Click the Search and Redact button in the Search window and the Search window reports results of your search, as shown in Figure 14.8. As yet, no items have been marked for redaction. In the results list you see the reported results appearing next to check marks.

If you want all items in the list to be redacted, click the Check All button. If you want to individually mark the results items, scroll the list checking all boxes adjacent to the items you want to redact.

CROSS-REF For more information on using the Search window, see Chapter 6.

FIGURE 14.8

Click Check All or individually check the items you want to redact in the open PDF or from a collection of PDF files.

Searching Multiple Words and Phrases

You may want to develop a word list, import the word list into the Search and Redact window, and apply redactions from the word list. Using a word list where you can copy and paste names helps prevent spelling errors and can often make your redaction process much easier.

NEW FEATURE New in Acrobat 9 is the Select Words button in the Search pane. Click the Search and Redact button in the Redaction toolbar to open the Search window and you find the Select Words button. Click the button and the Words and Phrases to Search and Redact window opens as you see in Figure 14.9.

FIGURE 14.9

Click Select Words in the Search window to open the Words and Phrases to Search and Redact window.

To add words to the list, type a word or words in the New word or phrase text box and click the Add button. The word(s) is moved to the Word and phrase list. You can continue adding words by typing the word name and clicking the Add button to add more words to the list.

A nice addition to the Words and Phrases to Search and Redact window is the Import button. You can import a list of words from a text file. Click the button and select the file you want to import.

As a workflow solution you can open a PDF document, copy text on a page containing several words and phrases you want to redact, and paste the copied text in a word processor or text editor. Delete the text you don't want to redact and you're left with just those words you want to eliminate from the PDF file. Save the file as a text document and import the word list in the Search window. Using this method helps keep the spelling errors to a minimum and easily helps you form your word list.

The export button enables you to export a word list to a text file. This option can be handy when you have several documents you want to redact at different times. Perhaps, during a court case you may receive documents at different intervals, but the sensitive information remains the same on all documents. As new documents come in, you can import the text file you originally exported from the Search window.

Searching patterns

A pattern or mask is a formatted body of text — something like a social security number or phone number. Say you want to delete all social security numbers from a document but there are many unique numbers and without searching a pattern you would have to mark each individual number for redaction.

NEW FEATURE Acrobat 9 takes the redundant task of marking each individual pattern such as a social security number, a zip code, an email address, a phone number, credit card numbers, and dates away by providing you a method for searching patterns.

To search a pattern, click the Search and Redact tool in the Redaction toolbar. In the Search window, click the Patterns radio button and make a choice from the pull-down menu as shown in Figure 14.10. Click the Search and Redact button and Acrobat searches the open document or a folder of documents for the pattern and identifies it for marking for redaction in the Search window.

FIGURE 14.10

Click Select Words in the Search window to open the Words and Phrases to Search and Redact window.

NOTE When you use the Multiple words or phrase option, Acrobat identifies the words that need to be marked for redaction. When you click OK in the Words and Phrases to Search and Redact window, the words are marked for redaction in the document. You then need to click the Apply Redactions tool to delete the marked words. When searching for patterns, you click the Check All button after performing a search, then click the Mark Checked Results for Redaction to mark all found instances for redaction. You then need to click the Apply Redactions tool to permanently delete the marked items.

Redacting PDF Files

The tool set and options for redaction are very straightforward and intuitive. In the first section of this chapter, you looked at marking files to hide content that didn't remove the items you marked. Let's compare that first effort with a true redaction that Acrobat 8 provides you by following some steps.

STEPS: Redacting a PDF document

1. **Open a file you want to eliminate some content from by using the Redaction tools.**

2. **Click the Mark for Redaction tool.**

   When you first click the Mark for Redaction tool, the Using Redaction Tools help dialog box opens, as shown in Figure 14.11. This dialog box provides you some instructions on redacting documents. If you don't want the dialog box to open in future redaction sessions, click the Don't show again check box.

When you first click the Mark for Redaction tool, the Using Redaction Tools help dialog box opens.

3. **Mark a graphic for redaction.** If you have a graphic in the file either as a vector object or an image file, you can remove it just like removing text. In my example I have a logotype that is a graphic object. Clicking the Mark for Redaction tool changes your cursor to a crosshair when positioned over a graphic or an I-beam cursor when positioned over text. Draw a marquee around the object, as shown in Figure 14.12, or drag the I-beam cursor through text you want to redact.

TIP If you want to quickly mark a graphic object for redaction, select the Mark for Redaction tool and double-click on the graphic.

FIGURE 14.12

Draw a marquee around a graphic or select text to mark for redaction.

INVESTIGATIONS

1. The alleged intruder, Mr. John Jones, entered the victim's residence forcibly by
2. breaking a window pane on the patio door. Mr. Jones proceeded to enter the
3. victim's (Mr. And Mrs. Edward Sanchez) den and placed an assortment of the
4. victim's personal belongings in a sack. Mr. Jones was witnessed by Emilio
5. Sanchez, a minor and son of Mr. and Mrs. Sanchez, from his position hiding under
6. an office desk in the den.
7.
8. Approximately 15 minutes after placing a number of the victim's belongings
9. estimated at $2,500, in his sack, Mr. Jones discovered, Emilio Sanchez hiding
10. under the desk. Mr. Jones fled the crime scene carrying the sack containing
11. contents belonging to the victims.

4. **Mark text for redaction.** Drag the I-beam cursor through the first occurrence of text you want to redact. In my example I drag through a name I want to remove from the file.

5. **Click the Search and Redact tool.** The Search window opens. Type any other occurrence of the text you want to redact. In my example, I type the same name as the first text marked for redaction. Click the Search and Redact button and the first occurrence of the word to be redacted is highlighted.

6. **Check all occurrences for redaction.** In the Search window, click the Check All button and all occurrences of the search results are now marked for redaction.

7. **Mark the search results for redaction.** After clicking the Check All button, the Marked Checked Results button appears in the Search window. Click this button and all occurrences of the search results are now marked for redaction, as you see in Figure 14.13.

8. **Continue marking all the content you want to eliminate in your document.** If you have other text or graphics you want to redact, follow the same steps outlined in Steps 3 to 7.

9. **Apply Redactions.** Click the Apply Redactions tool. A warning dialog box opens. Click Yes and the redactions are applied.

FIGURE 14.13

After clicking Check All or individually checking the items you want to redact in the open PDF or from a collection of PDF files, click the Mark Checked Results for Redaction button.

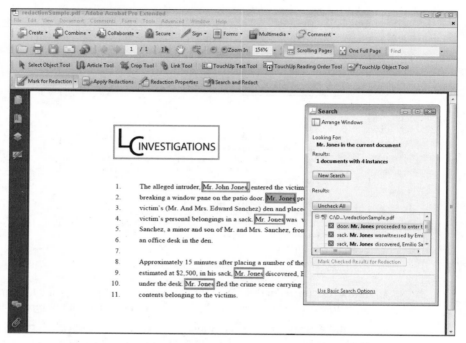

10. **Redact additional content.** After Acrobat redacts the items you marked, a dialog box opens confirming your action and prompts you to examine the document for additional content. Additional content might be in the form of metadata such as Document Properties information, hidden text, and a variety of other sources you don't see when viewing a PDF file in the Document pane. Click Yes in the dialog box shown in Figure 14.14.

11. **Examine the document.** When you click Yes in the confirmation dialog box, the Examine Document panel opens. A number of different items can appear in your file that don't appear on the document pages. You might have metadata, hidden text, file attachments, hidden layers, bookmarks, and other items that use the same text you want to delete. To be certain all information is deleted from the document, the Examine Document dialog box provides a list of found items matching the items you deleted. Click the Remove button in the panel shown in Figure 14.15 and all the selected items are removed.

FIGURE 14.14

Click Yes to open the Examine Document dialog box.

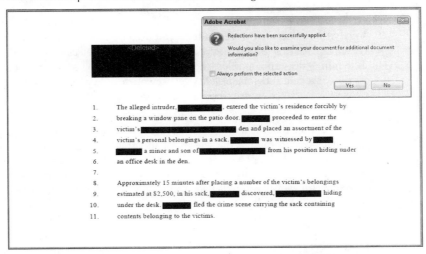

FIGURE 14.15

Click the Remove button in the Examine Document panel to eliminate any other occurrences of the text and graphics you want to delete.

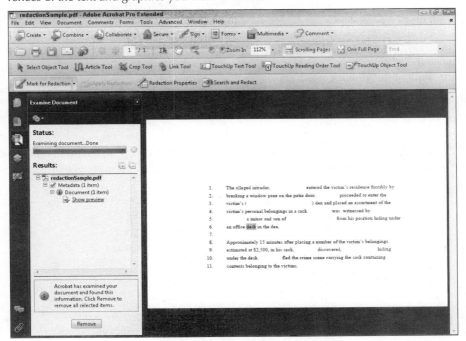

NEW FEATURE In Acrobat 8, a separate dialog box opened to inform you of the kind of document information that exists in your file and options via radio buttons for deleting the additional information. New in Acrobat 9 you find the Examine Document information hosted in a navigation panel and docked in the Navigation pane.

12. **Verify the redactions were made.** If you used objects with fills to redact the document, these objects are selectable and you can delete them. Select Tools ⇨ Advanced Editing ⇨ Touchup Object Tool to select the Touchup Object tool. Move the tool to one of your marks and click. Press the Delete (Del) key on your keyboard and the redaction frame is deleted. You can easily see that the redaction process did indeed remove the underlying content.

    You should see that the text beneath the redaction frames has truly been deleted from your document. When you use the select tool and drag through the text, you'll notice that no selection appears where you redacted text (and/or objects) as shown in Figure 14.16. Alternately, you can verify redactions by opening the Search window and invoking a search for the words you redacted. You should see no results reported for all text that was redacted.

FIGURE 14.16

After removing redaction marks and selecting all the text, the redacted file shows you all the text/objects have been successfully deleted from the file.

CROSS-REF Examine Document can also be helpful when you want to reduce file sizes. For more information on using the Examine Document panel, see Chapter 18.

Summary

- Redaction involves permanently removing data from a file.

- Acrobat 9 Pro (Windows and Mac) and Acrobat Pro Extended (Windows) contains tools for redacting content, searching and redacting, applying redactions, and examining documents for content not visible on pages. Redaction options are not available in Acrobat Standard (Windows).

- Using tools other than the Redaction tools won't delete data from PDF files.

- Redaction marks can be modified for color changes, the use of text, and formatted text used to replace deleted data.

- After redacting a document you can choose to Examine Document information for additional content that may appear as metadata or hidden text. The Examine Document information has been moved from a dialog box in Acrobat 8 to a navigation panel in Acrobat 9.

Chapter 15

Editing Images and Objects

IN THIS CHAPTER

Using image selection tools

Editing images and objects in external editors

Creating snapshots

Exporting images to files

Images and objects, such as raster images from programs like Adobe Photoshop, vector images like those created in Adobe Illustrator, and text, can be edited in external editors and dynamically updated in a PDF document. The process involves launching the external editor from within Acrobat, making changes in the external editor, and saving the file. The file is treated like a link to the PDF where the edits are updated. Acrobat itself doesn't have any image editing tools, but you can use the external editors provided through companion programs to help out when you need to make modifications to objects in a PDF file.

Like editing text discussed in Chapter 13, image editing with Acrobat is intended to be a minor task for last-minute small changes. For major editing tasks, you should return to the original authoring program. In circumstances where you do not have an original document, you may need to extend the editing a little further by updating documents or exporting them for new layouts. In this chapter, you learn how to handle images and objects for editing and exporting purposes.

Setting Up the Editing Environment

Tools used for image editing are the same as those used in Chapter 13 for text editing. Refer to Chapter 13 to load the necessary tools and toolbars to follow along in this chapter. Your Toolbar Well should look similar to Figure 15.1.

FIGURE 15.1

Tools loaded for an image editing session

Selecting Images

Two tools in Acrobat enable you to copy images and objects. You can use the Select tool discussed in Chapter 13 to select images as well as text, and you also use the TouchUp Object tool to select images and objects. Objects can be vector-based artwork created in programs such as Adobe Illustrator and blocks of text that Acrobat interprets as objects. Only the TouchUp Object tool can be used to select objects; therefore, you cannot use the Select tool unless the item is an image such as a Photoshop file contained in the PDF document.

The distinction between text as text and text as an object can easily be understood in what you see selected in the Document pane. If you drag the Select tool through text, the text becomes highlighted. When you see the text highlighted, realize that the text is selected as text. When you click a text block with the TouchUp Object tool, you'll see a bounding box (border) around the text block but the text itself is not highlighted. When you see this view, you can be assured the text is selected as an object. In Figure 15.2, text is selected as text by dragging through it with the Select tool, and in Figure 15.3, multiple text blocks are selected as objects when dragging through text with the TouchUp Object tool.

FIGURE 15.2

Text selected with the Select tool is selected as text and highlighted.

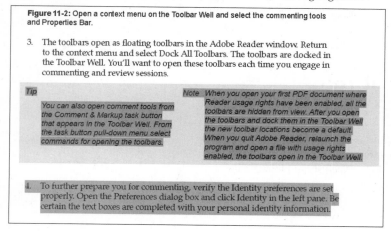

FIGURE 15.3

Text selected with the TouchUp Object tool is selected as an object and appears with a bounding box (border).

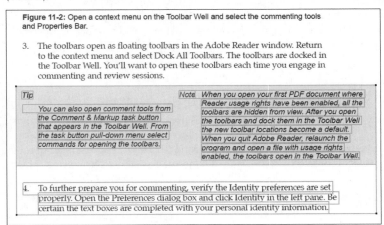

Figure 11-2: Open a context menu on the Toolbar Well and select the commenting tools and Properties Bar.

3. The toolbars open as floating toolbars in the Adobe Reader window. Return to the context menu and select Dock All Toolbars. The toolbars are docked in the Toolbar Well. You'll want to open these toolbars each time you engage in commenting and review sessions.

Tip

You can also open comment tools from the Comment & Markup task button that appears in the Toolbar Well. From the task button pull-down menu select commands for opening the toolbars.

Note When you open your first PDF document where Reader usage rights have been enabled, all the toolbars are hidden from view. After you open the toolbars and dock them in the Toolbar Well the new toolbar locations become a default. When you quit Adobe Reader, relaunch the program and open a file with usage rights enabled, the toolbars open in the Toolbar Well.

4. To further prepare you for commenting, verify the Identity preferences are set properly. Open the Preferences dialog box and click Identity in the left pane. Be certain the text boxes are completed with your personal identity information.

Each tool has different options and editing features associated with it. You use the Select tool, for example, when you want to select a photo image, copy it in Acrobat, and paste it in another program. Once copied to the Clipboard, you can also paste the image back into a PDF document, but the image is pasted as a Stamp comment. Double-click the image and an associated pop-up note appears like other comments, as shown in Figure 15.4.

The Select tool permits you to save an image as a separate file. Additionally, you can edit metadata for image files using this tool.

FIGURE 15.4

When pasting images copied with the Select tool, the pasted image appears as a Stamp comment.

The TouchUp Object tool permits you to copy an image in a PDF document and paste it back to the same document or another PDF document as an image. All the paste operations remain inside Acrobat, as you cannot copy with the TouchUp Object tool and paste an image or object into another program. Furthermore, you cannot save an image file using the TouchUp Object tool as you can with the Select tool, but you can launch an external editor to edit either an image or object. When you want to edit images in Acrobat, the TouchUp Object tool provides you a number of different editing options — more so than the Select tool.

Using the Select tool

 In Chapter 13, you used the Select tool to select text and tables. You can also select images with this tool. As was covered in Chapter 13, you have some preference choices for handling selections when using the Select tool. If your last visit to the General preferences was to select text before images, you need to return to the General preferences by pressing Ctrl/⌘+K, click General in the left pane, and select Make Select tool select images before text in the Basic Tool Options, as shown in Figure 15.5.

FIGURE 15.5

Open the General preferences and select the check box for Make Select tool select images before text.

```
┌─ Basic Tools ──────────────────────────────────────────────┐
│                                                             │
│   ☐ Use single-key accelerators to access tools             │
│                                                             │
│   ☑ Create links from URLs                                  │
│                                                             │
│   ☐ Make Hand tool select text & images                     │
│                                                             │
│   ☑ Make Hand tool read articles                            │
│                                                             │
│   ☐ Make Hand tool use mouse-wheel zooming                  │
│                                                             │
│   ☑ Make Select tool select images before text              │
│                                                             │
└─────────────────────────────────────────────────────────────┘
```

Click an image and select Copy Image from a context menu as shown in Figure 15.6.

Interactivity

From the context menu, you can add a Bookmark or link to the selected image. Click Bookmark from the context menu and the default view of the page is bookmarked. Click Create Link and the Create Link dialog box opens.

CROSS-REF   For more information on creating bookmarks and links, see Chapter 22.

FIGURE 15.6

FIGURE 15.6

Open a context menu with the Select Object tool and choose Copy from the menu commands.

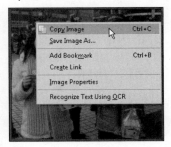

Pasting images

As I said earlier in this section, images copied with the Select tool are pasted back into PDF documents as Stamp comments. The appearance onscreen looks like an image pasted into a document, but it remains a comment. If you want to print images pasted from content copied with the Select tool, you need to print using the Document and Stamps option in the Print dialog box.

CROSS-REF For more information on printing documents and stamps, see Chapter 31.

Use the Select tool to paste images into other programs. Pasted images in Acrobat appear as Stamp comments, but in other programs pasting is handled as you would expect when copying and pasting between other programs. The complete image is pasted into documents such as Microsoft Office files and other application documents.

CAUTION If you use professional layout and illustration programs designed for commercial printing, don't paste files in these applications. A preferred method is to save an image file from Acrobat and place or import the image in your design application.

Transforming pasted images

When you paste an image as a Stamp comment, you can size and rotate the image. From the four corners on a Stamp comment you see corner handles and in the top center you see another handle. Click and drag any corner handle to size the image up or down. No modifier key is required to proportionally resize a Stamp comment. All the sizing is kept to proportions without pressing the Shift key.

To rotate a Stamp comment, place the cursor over the middle top handle. When the cursor appears over this handle, the cursor changes to a semicircle with an arrowhead, as shown in Figure 15.7. Click and drag when you see this cursor to rotate the Stamp.

Place the cursor over the top-center handle and click and drag to rotate the Stamp comment.

Saving image files

From a context menu opened by right-clicking (Windows) or Control+clicking (Macintosh) you can save an image file when using the Select tool. Select Save Image As (shown in Figure 15.7) and the Save Image As dialog box opens. From the Save as type (Windows) shown in Figure 15.8 or Format (Macintosh) pull-down menu you have options for saving in one of three file formats. Choose the default Bitmap Image Files (*.bmp), JPEG Image Files (.jpg), or TIFF Image Files (*.tif) format.

Choose Save As from a context menu and choose the file type from the Save as type pull-down menu.

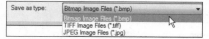

Saving as a bitmap file saves the file without compression and data loss. However, bitmap files may not retain all the data in the image. If you have images with clipping paths or drop shadows, for example, the saved image can appear significantly degraded, as shown in Figure 15.9.

NOTE A clipping path is a mask like a cookie cutter that cuts out all the image data outside the path. Without the clipping path and drop shadow the image in Figure 15.9 would have a white background around the image instead of transparent space.

JPEG files retain all data integrity; however, the downside to saving as JPEG is that the files are compressed and you end up with data loss. Use the TIFF format when you can and you'll save your files without data loss. As you can see in Figure 15.9, an image with a clipping path saved as a bitmap on the left is degraded compared to the correct detail shown in the TIFF export on the right.

TIP If you're not certain whether a BMP file will be saved, thus preserving all data integrity, you can select the image with the Select tool, copy the file to the Clipboard, and from the Create PDF Task Button pull-down menu, select Create File From Clipboard Image. Acrobat creates a separate PDF document and the image you see appears exactly as when saving as a BMP file. If the file looks good, save the PDF or return to the image and select Save Image As from a context menu.

FIGURE 15.9

Saving files with clipping paths in bitmap format can present problems with image quality. Saving the same file as a TIFF (right) preserves data integrity.

Image Properties

Select Image Properties from a context menu and document metadata are reported for the image. If you shot an image with a digital camera, the data recorded by the camera is reported in the Image Information dialog box shown in Figure 15.10.

CROSS-REF For more information related to working with document metadata, see Chapter 17.

Recognize Text Using OCR

You may not see the Recognize Text Using OCR menu command when selecting images with the select tool. Images imported in a layout program won't give you the option for converting image data to recognizable text. If you have a scanned document and open the image in Acrobat, you might see this command. Use it for converting images to recognizable text.

CROSS-REF For more information on scanning and converting image data to recognizable text, see Chapter 17.

FIGURE 15.10

Select Properties from a context menu using the Select tool, and the Image Information dialog box opens.

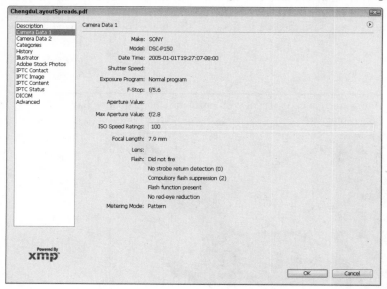

Using the TouchUp Object tool

You use the TouchUp Object tool for selecting objects on a page. You select photo images, drawings and illustrations, and blocks of text with the tool.

The TouchUp Object tool copies images and objects and pastes them back into a PDF or other PDF documents you open in Acrobat. You can click an image or object or marquee several images and/or objects to select multiple items. Acrobat interprets any text you click on with the TouchUp Object tool as an object. Hence, you can edit the object in an external editor or move the object(s).

CROSS-REF   For information on external editing, see the section "Image and Object External Editing" later in this chapter.

You can also use the TouchUp Object tool to move or nudge objects. Click on a single object or marquee a group of objects on a page, and then click and drag the selection to a new location. You are limited to moving objects on a single page. You can't select an object on one page and drag it to another PDF page. For moving objects to different pages you need to cut the selection, move to another page, and choose Edit ➪ Paste. If you want to nudge objects, create a selection with the TouchUp Object tool and press the arrow keys on your keyboard to move the object right, left, up, or down.

If two or more images or objects are spaced apart and each object is selectable, you can click to select an object and Shift+click to select additional images/objects. If you have objects such as vector graphics where many paths are contained within the object or you have multiple overlapping objects, marquee the objects to be certain you select all you want to copy.

To copy and paste objects, including photo images, illustrations and vector objects, and text blocks, you use the TouchUp Object tool. To select a single object, click the object with the TouchUp Object tool. A keyline border shows the bounding box for the selected item. Open a context menu and you find menu options different from those available with the Select tool, as shown in Figure 15.11.

The menu offers several commands related to handling images and objects. Select Copy to copy the image to the Clipboard and select Cut to cut the image from the page and place it on the Clipboard. From either choice you can then paste the data on another PDF page or into another PDF document.

Pasting images and objects

After copying with the TouchUp Object tool, choose Edit ⇨ Paste or use a context menu opened with the tool and select Paste. When pasting data, the new image or object is pasted in the foreground. If you need to keep a stacking order intact, you need to carefully plan out copying and pasting images and objects. In more complex documents, it makes sense to return to the original authoring program because you do not have commands in Acrobat to paste in front, paste in back, and paste in place. These kinds of commands are found in design programs where you can easily control the stacking order of images and objects.

FIGURE 15.11

Select an image with the TouchUp Object tool and open a context menu. Select Copy from the menu choices to copy the selection.

```
Cut
Copy
Paste
Delete

Select All
Select None

Place Image...
Delete Clip
Set Clip

Flip Horizontal
Flip Vertical
Rotate Clockwise
Rotate Counterclockwise
Rotate Selection

Create Artifact...

Find...

Edit Image...
Show Metadata...
Properties...
```

If you want to replace text, images, or objects on a page with a pasted block of text, an image, or an object, select the items you want to replace after copying the item you want to paste. Choose Edit ➪ Paste or use Paste from a context menu, and the pasted item replaces the selected items.

Place Image

Placing images is like using a Place command in a layout program. When you select the command, a dialog box opens where you can select an image on your hard drive and import the image in your layout.

Acrobat 9 supports placing images much like layout programs. Click the TouchUp Object tool and open a context menu on a document page. The Place Image command appears when opening a context menu on a page or when selecting an image and opening a context menu. The Open dialog box appears where you can navigate your hard drive and locate the file you want to import in your PDF file. File formats supported using this command include Bitmap, BMP (*.bmp, *.rle, *.dlb), CompuServe GIF (*.gif), JPEG (*.jpg, *.jpeg, .jpe), JPEG2000 (.jpf, *.ipx, *.jp2, .j2k, .j2c, jpc), PCX (.pcx), PNG (.png), and TIFF (.tif, *.tiff). When one of these file formats is imported into a PDF document, Acrobat converts to PDF and imports the image.

CROSS-REF For more information on file formats, see Chapters 11 and 12.

TIP If you select an image on a PDF page with the TouchUp Object tool and select Place Image from a context menu, the selected image is replaced with the new image you select in the Open dialog box.

CAUTION Be certain to not select any objects on a page with the TouchUp Object tool when you use Place Image. Placing image data while an object is selected will replace the selected object. This is handy if you intentionally want to replace an object, but can be troublesome if you don't want a selected object replaced.

Delete Clip

The context menu opened with the TouchUp Object tool contains the Delete Clip menu command. You can delete a clipping path from an image or object that had the path applied in an image editor like Photoshop or an illustration program such as Adobe Illustrator. Deleting a path shows data outside the defined path. In Figure 15.12 you can see an image where a clipping path was created in Photoshop to hide edge artifacts on the left and after removing the clipping path on the right side of the figure where the artifacts are visible.

Delete Clip also performs another function. You can set a clip on an image with or without a clipping path using the TouchUp Object tool context menu. Once a clip has been set, use the Delete Clip command to remove the clip. To completely understand the results, see the section "Set Clip" next.

FIGURE 15.12

Selecting Delete Clip from a context menu removes clipping paths assigned to objects and images.

Set Clip

Select the TouchUp Object tool, click an image on a PDF page, and from a context menu select Set Clip.

The Set Clip command enables you to clip (actually Crop) images. When using Set Clip, you'll find that three tools appear as you move the cursor around an image. The tools are shown in Figure 15.13.

FIGURE 15.13

The Scissors, Crop, and Move tools are used when setting a clip.

To crop an image, select the Set Clip command from a context menu opened from the TouchUp Object tool. The cursor immediately appears as the Scissors tool shown in Figure 15.14. This tool merely informs you that you are in Set Clip mode.

Move the cursor to one of the four handles you see on the four corners of the selected image. Place the cursor directly over one of the four handles. You may need to move the cursor around a bit or zoom into the document before you see the Crop tool shown in Figure 15.15. When you see the Crop tool, drag the corner in to crop the image. You can continue using the Crop tool as long as you don't click when the cursor changes from the Crop tool to another tool.

FIGURE 15.14

Select Set Clip from a context menu and the cursor changes to a scissors icon.

FIGURE 15.15

Move the cursor over a corner point to see the Crop tool. Click and drag to crop the image.

When your crop appears as desired, just click the mouse button and the cursor changes from the Crop tool to the Move tool, as shown in Figure 15.16. You can click and drag the cropped image anywhere on the page.

FIGURE 15.16

Click the mouse button and the cursor changes to the Move tool.

Now, let's return to the Delete Clip command. After you have cropped an image, you can return to the full-size image before the cropping. Just open a context menu again with the TouchUp Object tool and select Delete Clip. The image appears as you first opened your PDF document.

Rotations

Images can be rotated in many ways by using the context menu commands from the TouchUp Object tool. Open a context menu and five separate commands appear for rotating images.

You can rotate images Horizontally and Vertically (180°), rotate Clockwise and Counterclockwise (90°), and rotate images using arbitrary rotations. The first four rotation options in the context menu should be self-evident. The more complicated rotation, Rotate Selection, requires a little explanation.

When you click an image with the TouchUp Object tool and choose Rotate Selection from the context menu, you won't see any change appear in the Acrobat window. Invoking the command changes modes from a scaling mode to a transformation mode. After selecting the command, move the cursor to one of the four corner handles. You need to wait for the cursor to change appearance to a line with two opposing arrowheads, as you see in Figure 15.17.

FIGURE 15.17

Select Rotate Selection and move the cursor to a corner handle.

Click and drag the cursor to rotate the image and you can make an arbitrary rotation as shown in Figure 15.18. When you rotate the image as you want it, click on the image and the rotation mode is disengaged.

FIGURE 15.18

Click and drag to rotate the image.

Scaling images

You won't find a menu command for scaling images in a context menu, but scaling images is available to you.

In Acrobat 9 you can easily scale images. Just select the TouchUp Object tool and click on an image. Move the cursor to a corner handle and drag the handle in or out to size an image down or up respectively. You can constrain proportions by pressing the Shift key and dragging a corner handle.

Create/Remove Artifact

This menu command is used when working with tagged PDF documents and accessibility. Selecting the command opens the Create Artifact dialog box. Or, if an artifact has been created, you can remove an artifact by selecting Remove Artifact.

 For more on using the Create Artifact options, see Chapter 25.

Find

A number of search options are available that pertain to images. Select Find from a context menu and the Find Element dialog box opens, as shown in Figure 15.19. A number of options appear that relate to working with accessible files. You also have options for searching annotations and OCR Suspects.

CROSS-REF **For more information on accessibility, see Chapter 25. For more on annotations, see Chapter 20. For more on OCR Suspects, see Chapter 17.**

FIGURE 15.19

Select Find and the Find Element dialog box opens.

Show Metadata

Select this item and the same dialog box opens when you use the Select tool to select Image Properties.

Properties

Select an image with the TouchUp Object tool and select Properties from a context menu, and you arrive at the TouchUp Properties dialog box. When the TouchUp Properties dialog box opens, click the Color tab, as shown in Figure 15.20.

A number of tabs in the TouchUp Properties dialog box relate to accessibility and text editing, which are explained in Chapters 25 and 13, respectively. The one item in the Properties dialog box relating to image editing is contained in the Color tab.

FIGURE 15.20

Click Color in the TouchUp Properties dialog box.

The Color TouchUp Properties window provides you choices for converting color profiles. The current working color space is reported at the top of the dialog box. From choices in the Convert To pull-down menu, you can choose to convert color to a working space color or an output profile. Ideally, you should stick to the working space profiles, and most often your choices will be either sRGB or Adobe RGB (1998). Output profile selections can be made in the Advanced Print Options dialog box.

CROSS-REF For more information on working with color workspaces and color output profiles, see Chapter 31.

If you want to change a color profile, make the choice for the new profile in the Convert To pull-down menu, select a Rendering Intent, and click Convert Colors. If you want the profile embedded in the image, click the Embed Profile check box before clicking Convert Colors.

CAUTION Be aware that if you embed a profile you need to make proper selections for printing files in both the Acrobat Print dialog box and switches in your printer driver. Be certain to carefully read Chapter 31 before converting color on your images.

As a matter of default, you'll want to keep the Rendering Intent at Relative Colorimetric. This choice is the best choice for raster image files. If you have vector images, you may want to use another rendering intent. For a comprehensive source on color management, see *Color Correction For Digital Photographers Only* (Wiley, 2006).

The item yet to be discussed in the context menu opened with the TouchUp Object tool is Edit Image. Selecting this command launches an external image-editing program, which is covered in the next section.

Image and Object External Editing

As demonstrated in the first part of this chapter, Acrobat offers you methods for copying and pasting images, moving them around the page, and exporting them to files. However, changing the physical attributes of images and shapes, other than transformations and scaling, is not something you can do in Acrobat. To modify certain appearances or attributes of raster and vector objects, you need to use an external editor. When you launch an editor from a menu command in Acrobat, you can make changes to images, text, and shapes and save your edits in the external editor. These saves are then dynamically updated in the PDF document. Acrobat treats external editing like many programs that support file links. When you edit linked files, the links are updated in the program where they are imported.

To access an external editor, you need to use the TouchUp Object tool. You cannot access external editors with any of the other selection tools.

TouchUp preferences

By default, Acrobat's external editors are Adobe Photoshop for image editing and Adobe Illustrator for object editing if you have these programs installed on your computer. When you install Acrobat, the installer locates these editors on your hard drive, if they are installed, and designates them as the default editors. If you install Photoshop and/or Illustrator after Acrobat, you need to instruct Acrobat where to look for the application files to use as your image/object editors.

Choose Edit ⇨ Preferences to open the Preferences dialog box. Click the TouchUp item on the left pane of the Preferences dialog box. In the right pane are two buttons, as shown in Figure 15.21. Click Choose Image Editor to open the Choose Image Editor dialog box. The dialog box enables you to navigate your hard drive and locate Adobe Photoshop. Select the Photoshop application icon and click Open.

For page and object editing, Adobe Illustrator is the default tool if installed. If you need to locate Illustrator, click the Choose Page/Object Editor button. Find the Illustrator application on your hard drive and select it in the Choose Page/Object Editor dialog box. Click Open and Adobe Illustrator is enabled as your page/object editor. If you happen to use another object editor such as CorelDraw, you need to browse your hard drive and designate CorelDraw for your object editor. The same holds true for any other type of object editor.

FIGURE 15.21

Select TouchUp in the preferences list and the Choose buttons appear on the right side of the dialog box. Click one of the buttons to navigate your hard drive and select the respective editor.

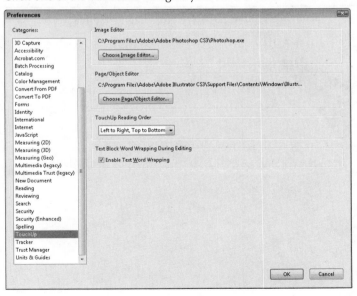

After identifying your editors, click OK in the Preferences dialog box. The choices you made are immediately available. If Acrobat loses contact with either program, you are prompted in a dialog box that external editing cannot be done. If you see warning dialog boxes open as you attempt to use an external editor, return to the Preferences and reestablish the connection to your editors.

Editing images in Adobe Photoshop

You launch Photoshop from Acrobat by selecting an image with the TouchUp Object tool and opening a context menu. From the menu commands, select Edit Image or press Control (Windows) or Option (Macintosh) and double-click. Depending on the speed of your computer and the amount of memory you have, Photoshop may take a few moments to launch. When the program opens, the image you selected is placed in a Photoshop document window.

You can change color modes and resolution, edit images for brightness and contrast, add effects, and just about anything else you can do in Photoshop to a single layer file. If you add type, add layers, or create transparency, you need to flatten all layers before saving the file. Layers added to a Photoshop file require you to use the Save As command to update the file. When you use Save As, the file is not updated in the PDF document. Flattening layers enables you to use the Save command that updates the PDF document when the file is saved. In Figure 15.22, a file in Photoshop was edited for color changes. Note that the file contains transparency and appears as a single-layer image. Because the file opened from Acrobat was a file on a single layer with transparency, all edits you make without creating additional layers enable you to still use the Save command.

FIGURE 15.22

You edit files in your image editor and dynamically update the PDF from which they originated.

Photoshop updates the PDF document dynamically according to the edits you make with the Save command. If you add a layer to the file, you are prompted by Photoshop to Save As a new filename. Selecting Save As and writing to a new file disrupts the link. If you save in this manner, your PDF document won't update. If the file is saved without writing a new file, the updates are dynamically recorded in the PDF when you return to Acrobat.

Editing objects in Adobe Illustrator

Objects, for the purposes of discussing external object editing, can be vector objects such as illustrations created in Illustrator, CorelDraw, or Adobe Freehand. Objects can also be text. Both vector objects and text are edited in Adobe Illustrator when you select Edit Object(s) from a context menu with the TouchUp Object tool.

To edit a single object, select the object with the TouchUp Object tool and open a context menu. The Edit Image command changes to Edit Object in the context menu. Select Edit Object and Adobe Illustrator launches. Changes you make to the object are dynamically updated when you save the file just as the file saves discussed with image editing are updated. If selecting a single object on the PDF page is difficult, you can marquee a group of objects and select Edit Objects.

If no object is selected and you open a context menu with the TouchUp Object tool, the menu command changes to Edit Page. To easily access the Edit Page command, you can also open a context menu outside the page boundary. When you click outside the page area, the Edit Page command appears in the context menu. Select Edit Page and all objects are opened in Adobe Illustrator.

Be certain to not use the Save As command when editing objects. The procedures for saving files with object editing follow the same principles as described with image editing. Regardless of whether you edit a single object, multiple objects, or the entire page, the edits you make in Illustrator are updated in the PDF document only when you choose File ⇨ Save.

Editing text in Adobe Illustrator

In some circumstances you may find editing text in an external editor to prove more satisfactory than editing text with the TouchUp Text tool. Editing text in Illustrator requires you to have embedded fonts loaded on your computer. Keep in mind that returning to an authoring application to apply major edits to documents is more advantageous than using the TouchUp Text tool. But, for those jobs where you don't have a document available and using the TouchUp Text tool just doesn't do the job, here's a little workaround you can try. I offer a disclaimer and tell you up front that these methods may not always work, but I've found more often than not that you can successfully edit text in Illustrator for some minor edit jobs.

One problem you can face when editing text in Illustrator is the text blocks are likely to be broken up and lose their paragraph formatting attributes. You need to select the text, cut it from the page, and paste it back, keeping the general size and position close to the original. You can then edit the text and choose File ⇨ Save to update the PDF document.

Using Edit Page in Adobe Illustrator

If you want to edit an entire page in Illustrator, click the TouchUp Object tool on a document page without selecting an image. Open a context menu and select Edit Page. The entire page then opens in Adobe Illustrator.

NOTE If you choose Edit Objects to open text in an object editor and the PDF file was created as a tagged PDF, a dialog box opens, informing you that the tags will be removed from the document if you proceed. Click Yes in the dialog box and the tags are removed from the document and the selected objects open in your object editor.

You can also click the TouchUp Object tool and choose Edit ⇨ Select All or press Ctrl/⌘+A. All objects and their respective bounding boxes are shown as selected. Open a context menu and choose Edit Objects. All the selected objects are then opened in Adobe Illustrator.

If you edit a page or all objects on a page in Illustrator, selecting File ⇨ Save (Ctrl/⌘+S) updates the PDF document. If working on a single PDF page, you can just as easily select File ⇨ Save As in Illustrator and save to a PDF file.

If you need to completely rework a PDF document, you can also open a PDF in Adobe Illustrator. Opening a file in Illustrator is the same as selecting Edit Page. All changes you make are dynamically updated in the PDF document after saving in Illustrator.

CROSS-REF For more information on editing PDF pages, see Chapters 9 and 16.

TIP If you want to edit a page in Adobe Illustrator, you can alternately open the page in Acrobat and choose Document ⇨ Extract Pages. Extract the page to edit and save as a new file name. The PDF can be opened in Adobe Illustrator, edited, and saved. When you return to Acrobat, choose Document ⇨ Replace Pages and replace the page you extracted with the page you edited in Adobe Illustrator.

Using the Snapshot Tool

 You use the Snapshot tool to create a marquee around any area on the document page. You can select text and graphics with the Snapshot tool. Select the tool from the Select & Zoom toolbar and click and drag a marquee around the area to be selected. When you release the mouse button, Acrobat takes a snapshot of the area within the marquee and copies it to the Clipboard. A dialog box opens to inform you the data has been copied to the Clipboard.

After you click OK in the Alert dialog box, the marquee is still active on the document page. You can open a context menu where you have options for copying the data or printing the selection. In addition, you can create a link to the snapshot by selecting Create Link in the context menu. These menu commands are the same as those shown in Figure 15.7 earlier in this chapter.

CROSS-REF For more information on creating links from snapshots, see Chapter 22.

Taking a snapshot of a page containing images and text or just text creates only a bitmap of the selected area. All text is converted to a raster image. If you intend to preserve text and edit it later, don't use the Snapshot tool. The text is not editable from snapshot images.

The Snapshot tool provides paste functions equal to both the Select tool and the TouchUp Object tool. Once you take a snapshot you can paste the data back to the PDF document or to another application document. By default, the Snapshot tool places a copy of the snapshot on the Clipboard and makes the Clipboard data available to Acrobat. When you open a context menu on the snapshot and select Copy Selected Graphic, you can paste the data to other application documents.

Changing snapshot resolutions

By default, snapshot resolutions are 72 ppi (pixels per inch), which is sufficient for screen views at 100 percent. If you want to print files or zoom in to a document view above 100 percent, 72 ppi is not sufficient for rendering images that appear without obvious image degradation.

To understand how image resolutions affect image quality, try the following steps.

STEPS: Changing snapshot image resolutions

1. **Change Preferences.** Open the Preferences dialog box by pressing Ctrl/⌘+K. Click General in the left pane and check the box for Use system setting. The system setting has a fixed resolution of 96 ppi, as shown in Figure 15.23.

FIGURE 15.23

Set the resolution for snapshots to 72 ppi.

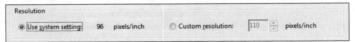

2. **Take a snapshot.** Open a file in Acrobat — preferably one with images and image resolutions above 200 ppi.

   Click the Snapshot tool. Drag a rectangle around the area you want to copy. When you release the mouse button, the data is copied to the Clipboard.

3. **Paste the data in an image editor.** Open an image editor such as Adobe Photoshop CS or Adobe Photoshop Elements. Paste the data in a new document window.

For information on pasting data in an image editor, see the next section, "Pasting snapshot data."

4. **Zoom in on the document.** Zoom to at least a 200 percent view and notice the quality of the image. You should see poor image quality especially if you copy any text. In Figure 15.24, the pasted data includes both image and text.

FIGURE 15.24

Zoom to a 200 percent view after pasting the data in an image editor.

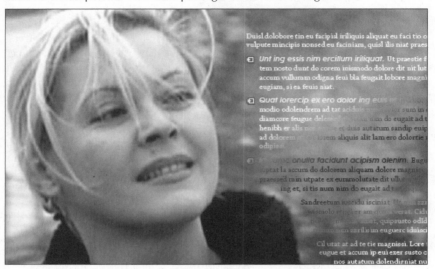

5. **Change preferences.** Return to the Acrobat Preferences dialog box as described in Step 1. Change the image resolution to 300 ppi.

6. **Take a Snapshot.** Try to take a snapshot as described in Step 2 in the same area of the PDF document as you took the first snapshot.

7. **Paste the data.** Paste the new Clipboard data in your image editor and zoom to the approximate same view as the first image you pasted in your image editor. Because the image resolution is much higher, the zoom will be much lower than a 200 percent view.

8. **Compare the two images.** Examine the second image you pasted at 300 ppi. You should see a noticeable difference in image quality. In Figure 15.24, compare the text with the text shown in Figure 15.25.

Note that boosting image resolution in the Preferences won't help create better-looking images than a value higher than the original image resolution. For example, if you convert to PDF using images at 72 ppi and try to take a snapshot at 300 ppi, you can't produce a better-looking image. The image file is interpolated as you size it up just like sizing up images in image editing programs.

FIGURE 15.25

Paste the image copied at 300 ppi and compare the document with the first image pasted at 72 ppi.

Pasting snapshot data

When you take a snapshot and paste the data in Acrobat, the pasted data becomes a Stamp comment just like using the Select tool. If you want to take a snapshot and paste as you can paste data using the TouchUp Object tool, you need to perform two operations.

First use the Snapshot tool to copy the area you want on a PDF page. When the data are copied, choose the Create PDF From Clipboard command. A new PDF document is created from your snapshot.

If you now want to copy and paste the data, you can use the TouchUp Object tool, click the page, and copy the data. The copied data can then be pasted into any PDF file.

You can also paste snapshot data into other programs. If you use the Select tool to copy an image, the image is pasted at 72 ppi in another application. If using the Snapshot tool, you can adjust resolution and paste into another application document. Again, you need to have sufficient resolution in the original image to make this method worthwhile.

Exporting Images

If you need to completely overhaul a document and want to lay it out in an authoring program, you might want to copy and paste text into a word processor, format your text, save the file, and then import the text into a program best suited for layout design, such as Adobe InDesign CS. If your PDF document contains photo images, you need to export the images and add them to your layout. Having to individually export images with the Select Image tool would be tedious for a large layout project containing many images. Fortunately, Acrobat offers you a feature for exporting all images in a PDF with a single menu command.

Choose Advanced ➪ Document Processing ➪ Export All Images. The Export All Images As dialog box opens where you can make selections for filename, destination, and the format you want to use for the exported images. In the Export All Images As dialog box, open the pull-down menu for Save as type (Windows) or Format (Macintosh). Four format options are available from the menu choices — JPEG, PNG, TIFF, or JPEG2000. Select one of the format options and click the Settings button to assign file attributes to the exported images.

CROSS-REF   **For more information on image file format definitions, see Chapter 10.**

When you select JPEG for the file type and click the Settings button, the Export All Images As JPEG Settings dialog box opens, as shown in Figure 15.26. The settings change according to the file type you select. Therefore, if you choose TIFF as a format, for example, you'll see changes for compression choices. The options for File Settings and Color Management are the same as those options discussed in Chapters 10 and 11. In addition to these settings, the Extraction item at the bottom of the dialog box enables you to eliminate certain files when the sizes are smaller than the size you choose from the pull-down menu.

From the pull-down menu, you choose a preset option for an image's physical size. You might have icons or logos appearing on all pages constructed at .75-inch sizes. You can elect to exclude these images by selecting the 1.00 inches item in the pull-down menu. When you click OK in the Extract All Images As dialog box, all files above the size selected from the pull-down menu choice are saved as separate files in the specified format. If you want every image extracted, choose the No Limit item from the pull-down menu.

CROSS-REF   **For information on saving PDF files in other formats, see Chapter 11.**

FIGURE 15.26

Make a choice for file format in the Export All Images As dialog box and click the Settings button. You choose options in the Export All Images As *(file format)* Settings dialog box for File Settings, Color Management, and Colorspace Conversion, and for eliminating image extractions falling below user-defined values.

Summary

- You use the Select tool to select individual photo images on PDF pages. You can select only a single image with the tool. Selected images can be copied to the Clipboard.

- You can convert images copied with the Select tool to PDF with the Create PDF tool, and you can paste them into authoring programs.

- To select objects use the TouchUp Object tool. Objects include photo images, illustrative artwork, and text. Dragging a marquee enables you to select multiple objects. Pressing the Shift key and clicking an object toggles between adding and eliminating an object from a selection.

■ You can paste objects and images copied with the TouchUp Object tool on PDF pages. You cannot paste them into authoring application documents.

■ External editing is handled by selecting an image or an object and opening a context menu. From the menu options, select Edit Image/Object.

■ If CS3 is installed, the default image editor is Adobe Photoshop and the default object editor is Adobe Illustrator. Select editors in the Preferences dialog box by clicking the TouchUp item in the left list and clicking the Change button on the right side of the dialog box.

■ You use the Snapshot tool to marquee an area on a page and select text, objects, and images within the selection marquee. Releasing the mouse button after you create a selection marquee copies the data within the marquee to the Clipboard.

■ Image resolutions for snapshots can be changed in the General preferences dialog box.

■ All images in a PDF can be exported as separate files with a single menu command. Choose Advanced ➪ Document Processing ➪ Export Images to open the Export All Images dialog box.

Chapter 16

Editing Pages

Chapters 13 and 15 covered editing content on PDF pages. Minor edits for text passages and images may be completed with the tools discussed in the earlier chapters. If you want to modify larger portions of a PDF document, then you'll want to know something about the tools Acrobat offers you for page editing. If you return to an authoring application and edit text, graphics, and layouts, you may want to update your PDF document according to the page edits made in other applications. Rather than re-create the entire PDF file, Acrobat enables you to selectively append, replace, delete, and extract pages in a PDF document.

In addition to the number of different page-editing tools found in earlier versions of Acrobat, the new version of Acrobat Pro and Pro Extended offers some impressive features in the new revised Add Headers and Footers dialog box and the ability to add backgrounds and watermarks. This chapter covers the page-editing tools in Acrobat and many new features that can help you modify documents.

Setting Up the Page-Editing Environment

For page-editing tasks, you need to use some viewing tools, advanced tools, and page-editing tools. Move the cursor to the Toolbar Well and open a context menu. From the menu options, select Reset Toolbars.

Open the More Tools window by selecting More Tools from a context menu opened on the Acrobat Toolbar Well. Click the check box for the Advanced Editing toolbar. Scroll down the window and click the check box for the Edit toolbar. Select the Organizer and Search tool in the File toolbar. Scroll to the Page Navigation toolbar and check all tools and the Page Navigation Toolbar check box. Scroll down to the Select & Zoom toolbar and check all but the Pan & Zoom Window tool. Click OK and return to a context menu on the Toolbar Well and select Dock Toolbars. Your toolbar assortment should look something like Figure 16.1.

FIGURE 16.1

A toolbar arrangement that works well when editing PDF pages

Working with Page Thumbnails

Thumbnails are mini-views of PDF pages that can be displayed in various zoom sizes. To see the thumbnail view of pages in an open document, click the Pages panel to open the pane, as shown in Figure 16.2. Thumbnail views are created on-the-fly when the pane is opened. Users of Acrobat 5 and below will remember the pane was referred to as Thumbnails. In Acrobat 6.0 viewers, the name was changed to the Pages panel and remains the same in Acrobat 7 through 9.

Navigating pages

The Pages panel can be used to navigate pages. Clicking a thumbnail takes you to the page associated with the thumbnail. The page opens in the Document pane at the currently established zoom view. You can zoom in or out of pages in the Pages panel by dragging the lower right handle on the rectangle appearing inside the page thumbnail. The changing zoom levels are reflected in the zoom view in the Document pane. In Figure 16.3, a rectangle shows the current page view in the Document pane. Click on the handle in the lower right corner and drag it into the center of the rectangle to zoom in on the page. Click and drag out to zoom out of the page.

The Pages panel and the Document pane are two separate compartments in the open PDF document. Clicking in the Pages panel activates the pane. Conversely, clicking in the Document pane activates the area where you view pages. Unfortunately, Acrobat does not highlight any part of either pane to inform you when a pane is active. So you just have to remember to click first in the area you want to be active.

FIGURE 16.2

Click the Pages tab to open the Pages panel where thumbnail views of the pages are created on-the-fly.

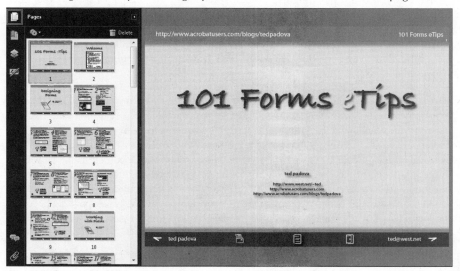

FIGURE 16.3

Thumbnails in the Pages panel are linked to the pages in the Document pane. Click a thumbnail to navigate to the page link. Drag the red rectangle to zoom in or out of the page displayed in the Document pane.

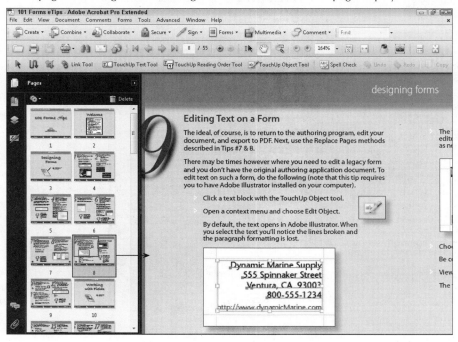

If you press the Page Down key or Down Arrow key while the Document pane is active, the pages in the Document pane scroll. As each page is scrolled, the Pages panel likewise scrolls pages and the respective page thumbnails are highlighted. When you click in the Pages panel, you experience a different behavior. Pressing the Page Down key scrolls several pages down only in the Pages panel. The respective pages in the Document pane are not scrolled. As you scroll through page thumbnails in the Pages panel, the Document pane remains fixed at its current view because as you scroll in the Pages panel, thumbnails are not actually selected. Instead, the selected thumbnail is linked to the view in the Document pane.

With reference to thumbnails, the term "selection" needs a little definition. When you click a page thumbnail, the number appearing below the page icon is shown selected (highlighted), and the thumbnail is further highlighted with a keyline border around the icon. Likewise, the respective page is placed in view in the Document pane. In essence, Acrobat communicates two selection messages to you. If you press the Down Arrow key on your keyboard, the page remains open in the Document pane. However, the page number highlight and keyline border move to the next page down, indicating the current thumbnail selection in the Pages panel. In Figure 16.4, page 9 in a PDF document is selected and page 9 is open in the Document pane. When the Down Arrow key is pressed twice, page 11 becomes selected in the Pages panel, while page 9 remains as the page viewed in the Document pane.

FIGURE 16.4

Click the cursor in the Pages panel to activate the pane, and then press the Down Arrow key. The keyline border shows the page selection in the Pages panel, while the highlighted page number on the previous page shows which page is in view in the Document pane.

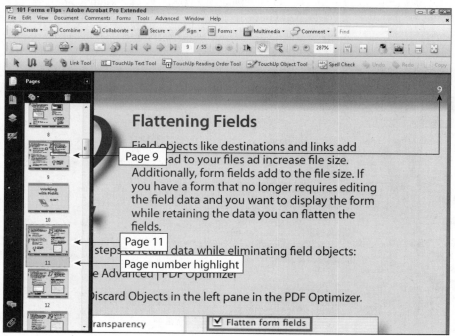

Moving Around Pages and Page Thumbnails

Anice new feature added in Acrobat 9 for quick thumbnail and page navigation is provided via a new context menu. If you position the mouse cursor between the scrollbar arrows in the Pages panel or on the far right scrollbar in the Document pane, a context menu opens offering you several options for navigating thumbnails/pages. Click Scroll Here to move a thumbnail/page and the thumbnail/page at the cursor position jumps into view. For example, if you open the Pages panel and position the cursor in the middle of a 500-page document, the thumbnail/page jumps to page 250 (or approximately the midpoint in the document).

Other nice features in the menu include Top and Bottom. If you want to jump to the beginning of the document, choose Top. If you want to jump to the end of the document, choose Bottom. The context menus operate independently so you can use the Bottom command in the Pages panel while the Document pane displays the first page in your document. The Pages panel jumps to the end of the document while the Document pane continues to display the first page.

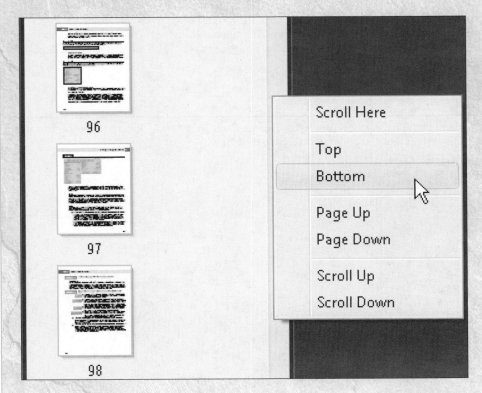

Changing thumbnail sizes

In Acrobat 6 and later, you can reduce the size of pages to a mini-thumbnail view and enlarge the size up to a maximum thumbnail view of about 300 percent. The support for increased thumbnail views in the Pages panel enables you to quickly find a page in a PDF document.

You reduce or enlarge page thumbnail sizes through menu commands. A context menu opened in the Pages panel or the pane pull-down menu includes the Enlarge Page Thumbnails and Reduce Page Thumbnails commands. Before using these commands, you should understand opening context menus.

If you click in the Pages panel on a page thumbnail and open a context menu, the Enlarge Page Thumbnails and Reduce Page Thumbnails commands are available as options in a menu that contains many different commands for page editing. Likewise, the pull-down menu adjacent to the top left of the Pages panel offers the same commands. Regardless of which menu you use, you can enlarge or reduce page thumbnail views.

To enlarge the size of the page thumbnails, click the mouse button anywhere inside the Pages panel and open a context menu. Select Enlarge Page Thumbnails from the menu options, as shown in Figure 16.5. Return to the menu and select the same menu command to enlarge again. Repeat the steps to zoom in to the desired view.

FIGURE 16.5

Open a context menu in the Pages panel and select Enlarge Page Thumbnails. Return to the context menu and repeat the steps several times to zoom in on a page thumbnail.

You'll notice that Acrobat makes no provision for selecting from among a number of preset zoom sizes. You need to return to the context menu or pull-down menu to successively increase or decrease page thumbnail views. If the zoom view in the Pages panel is larger than the panel width, click anywhere on the vertical bar on the right side of the pane and drag it to the right. The panel resizes horizontally to show more of the Pages panel while the Document pane is reduced in size. In Figure 16.6, I enlarged the thumbnail view, using repeated steps for enlarging the thumbnails, and I widened the panel so several large thumbnails could be viewed. The tiny thumbnail on the right side of Figure 16.6 shows the selected page in the Document pane.

FIGURE 16.6

To size the Pages panel, click on the vertical bar on the right side of the pane and drag it to the right.

Embedding and unembedding thumbnails

Page thumbnails are created on-the-fly each time you open the Pages panel. In long documents, you may find your computer slowing down each time the Pages panel is opened and the thumbnails are recreated. If this proves to be a burden, you can choose to embed thumbnails when working with the Pages panel and avoid the delay caused by creating them.

Thumbnails add some overhead to your file. Each page thumbnail adds about 1K to the file size. Unless your files are to be viewed by users of earlier Acrobat viewers that don't support creating thumbnails on-the-fly, delete them as one of the final steps in your editing session.

To embed thumbnails, select the Embed All Page Thumbnails command from the pane Options menu or a context-sensitive menu. Thumbnails can also be created by batch-processing PDF files using a Batch Sequence or at the time of distillation when using Acrobat Distiller.

PDF WORKFLOW You can delete thumbnails from PDF documents either individually in Acrobat or by using the Advanced ➪ Document Processing ➪ Batch Processing command in Acrobat Professional. If your work environment is such that you do a lot of editing in Acrobat and often use thumbnails, you may want to create them during distillation. When thumbnails are embedded, screen refreshes for multiple edits in long documents are faster. After you finish editing jobs and want to post PDF files on the Web or create CD-ROMs, you can batch-process the files for optimization and delete the thumbnails. Run the Edit Batch Sequences command to optimize multiple files and remove thumbnails.

CROSS-REF For information on creating and running batch sequences, see Chapter 18.

To unembed thumbnails, open a context menu on a page thumbnail and select Remove Embedded Page Thumbnails. All embedded page thumbnails are removed from the document. This step can be particularly helpful when working with Adobe Illustrator files, including the most current version of Adobe Illustrator CS and Acrobat 7 or less. When Illustrator embeds thumbnails, a bitmap representation of the page is created as a thumbnail and the thumbnail appearance is a poorly degraded image, as you can see on the left side of Figure 16.7. After the thumbnail is removed in Acrobat, the page thumbnail appears as you see it on the right side of Figure 16.7. Whenever you see thumbnail images with a degraded view, always check to see whether the thumbnail is embedded.

NEW FEATURE In Acrobat 9, the rendering of vector art embedded thumbnails has been improved. If you open the file shown in Figure 16.7 in Acrobat 9 and view the thumbnails, you see the thumbnail image on the right without having a need to unembed the thumbnails.

FIGURE 16.7

Adobe Illustrator exports thumbnails with a degraded bitmap view. Removing the thumbnail (shown right) improves the image quality when using Acrobat viewers 7 or less.

Embedded Thumbnails   Unembedded Thumbnails

Organizing Pages

The Pages panel offers you a wealth of opportunity for sorting pages and reorganizing them. You can move pages around, copy and paste pages when you want to duplicate them, delete pages, print selected pages within a document, and a host of other options specific to page management.

Reordering pages

Acrobat provides you with a marvelous slide sorter where you can shuffle pages and reorder them in a page sequence suited to your needs. Now with an opportunity to view page thumbnails in much larger views, you can easily see the content of text-only pages when no visible icons or graphics are present to distinguish differences in page content. Reorganizing pages in earlier versions of Acrobat was a little more difficult because of having to view text pages in small thumbnail views; however, now you can manage page order more easily by zooming in on pages to clearly view the content.

To rearrange pages in a PDF document, open the Pages panel to the full width of your monitor by dragging the right side of the pane to the far right of the Document pane. Open a context menu in the Pages panel and select Enlarge Page Thumbnails. Repeat the steps to enlarge the thumbnail views to a size that enables you to read text comfortably on the pages.

Click on a page and drag the page to a spot between the pages where you want to relocate the selected page. When you move a page around the Pages panel, a vertical bar appears where the page will be located. If the highlight bar is positioned in the area where you want to relocate a page, release the mouse button. Figure 16.8 shows page 7 selected. The page is moved to the area after page 3. Notice the vertical highlight bar appearing to the right side of page 3.

> **TIP** If you want to move pages between pages not in view in the Pages tab, click and drag a selected page up or down in the Pages panel and the screen automatically scrolls to reveal hidden pages when the cursor is at the top or bottom of the panel. Keep the mouse button depressed until you find the location where you want to move a page.

To select multiple pages, click a page to select it. Hold down the Control/⌘ key and click another page. If you want to select a block of contiguous pages, click the first page to be selected, hold down the Shift key, and click the last page within the group. All pages between the two selected pages are included in the selection. After you make your selection, click one of the selected pages and drag to a new location to reorder the pages.

> **TIP** For a super slide sorter, open the Pages panel and view thumbnails in a large size. Place the mouse cursor over the vertical bar to the right of the Pages panel and drag to the right of your monitor screen. Press the F8 and F9 keys to hide the menu bar and toolbars. Resize the viewing window to fit the screen size. You'll get as much real estate on your monitor as possible. Shuffling pages is much easier in Acrobat than in almost any other program.

FIGURE 16.8

To move a page in a PDF document, click a thumbnail and drag it to the area where you want to relocate the page. When you see a vertical highlight bar appear in the desired location, release the mouse button.

Copying pages

You can copy and paste pages within a PDF document or from one open PDF document to another. To copy a page with thumbnails, hold down the Ctrl/Option key as you drag a page to a new location in the same PDF file. Release the mouse button when you see the vertical highlight bar appear at the desired location. To copy a page from one PDF to another, open both PDF files and view them tiled either vertically or horizontally. The Pages panel must be in view on both PDF documents. Click and drag the thumbnail from one file to the Pages panel in the other document. The vertical highlight bar appears and the cursor changes, as shown in Figure 16.9. After the vertical bar is positioned at the desired location, release the mouse button, and the page drops into position.

CROSS-REF To learn how to tile PDF documents, see Chapter 5.

Removing pages

The previous example behaves like a copy-and-paste sequence. You can also create a cut-and-paste action whereby the page is deleted from one PDF document and copied to another. To remove a page and place it in another PDF file, hold the down Ctrl/Option key and then click-and-drag the page to another Pages panel in another file. The page is deleted from the original file and copied to the second file.

CAUTION Be certain not to confuse the shortcut keys. If Control/Option is used in the page thumbnails on one document with click and drag, the page is copied. If using the same keys between two documents, the page is deleted from the file of origin and copied to the destination file.

FIGURE 16.9

Dragging a thumbnail to a new location or copying between documents displays a vertical highlight bar where the page is placed.

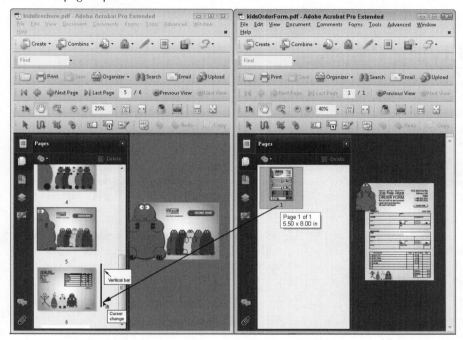

To delete a page with the Pages panel, use a context-sensitive menu or the panel Options pull-down menu. Select a single thumbnail or Shift+click to select multiple thumbnails in a contiguous order (Ctrl/⌘+click for a noncontiguous order), and select Delete Pages from the context menu. This command opens the Delete Pages dialog box, as shown in Figure 16.10.

FIGURE 16.10

When you select Delete Pages from the Pages context menu, the Delete Pages dialog box opens. Click OK to delete the selected pages.

In the Delete Pages dialog box, by default the selected page is marked for deletion. You can make a change in the dialog box by selecting the From button and entering a contiguous page number range in the field box. The Selected radio button deletes all pages selected in the Pages panel. You can click and select pages in a contiguous or noncontiguous group. After you select the pages you want to delete, click OK. The selected pages are deleted from the document.

Modifying Pages

In this context, *modifying pages* refers to the PDF page in its entirety and not individual page elements. Rather than look at changing single items on a page, such as text and graphics, this section examines some of the features for structuring pages as an extension of the commands found in the Pages panel. Page editing discussed here relates to the insertion, extraction, and replacement of PDF pages.

NOTE   **Most of the page-editing commands you have available in a context menu opened on a page thumbnail also appear in the Document menu. The commands for Insert Pages, Extract Pages, Replace Pages, Delete Pages, Crop Pages, and Rotate Pages appear in both menus.**

Before you go about creating a huge PDF document with links and buttons, understanding how Acrobat structures a page and related links is imperative. Bookmarks and other links are often created within a PDF document as user-defined navigation. Acrobat handles thumbnails and the link to the respective pages without user intervention. You have no control over the links from a thumbnail to respective pages.

CROSS-REF   **For information on creating bookmarks and links, see Chapter 22.**

With regard to links and bookmarks, think of Acrobat as having a background and an overlay — the navigation items are placed on the overlay and page content is placed on the background (or layers in a PDF having Adobe PDF Layers). In regard to a single-layer PDF document, links appear as if on an overlay over the background. When viewing a PDF file, you don't see the navigation items independent of page content. This said, when you delete a page, all the links to the page are lost. Acrobat makes no provision to go to the page that follows a deleted page when links are deleted. Therefore, if you set up a bookmark to page 4 and later delete page 4, the bookmark has no place to go. Such links are commonly referred to as *dead links*.

When editing pages in Acrobat, you can choose to insert a page, delete a page, extract a page, and replace a page. If you understand the page structure, you'll know which option is right for your situation. Choices described in the Pages panel Options menu permit access to each of the following choices by enabling you to select commands from the Document menu, or by providing a context-sensitive menu (refer to Figure 16.7) while clicking a thumbnail in the Pages panel.

CAUTION   **The menu commands for page editing are available only when you work with PDF documents that are not password protected, which prohibits page editing. If you attempt to edit pages in a secure PDF document, Acrobat prompts you for a password if the file is password protected. This behavior applies to all the options listed here.**

The page-editing options available either in a context menu opened on a page thumbnail, from the Pages panel Options menu, or from the Document menu commands include the following:

- **Insert Pages From File.** When you select this option, the Select File to Insert dialog box opens. Select a file to insert, and click the Select button in the dialog box. The Insert Pages dialog box opens next, enabling you to choose the location for the insertion regardless of the current page viewed (see Figure 16.11). You can choose to insert a page either before or after the page in view, within a page range, or before or after the first or last page. Inserted pages do not affect any links in your document. All the pages shift left or right, depending on whether you select the Before or After option.

FIGURE 16.11

The Insert Pages dialog box enables you to locate the page that precedes or follows another page for the target location.

TIP You can also insert pages via drag-and-drop actions. Select a file from the Desktop or a folder and drag the file to the Pages panel at the location where you want to insert a page. You can use any file type that Acrobat can convert to PDF. For example, drag a Microsoft Word or PowerPoint file to the Pages panel and the file is converted to PDF and inserted as new pages in the existing document.

- **Insert Pages From Clipboard.** When you copy data using a screen shot (Windows), the Snapshot tool, or data from other applications, the data is stored on the Clipboard. In Acrobat, you can convert the Clipboard data to a PDF document using the PDF from Clipboard command in the Create task button pull-down menu or by choosing File ➪ Create PDF ➪ From Clipboard.

NEW FEATURE In Acrobat 9 you can choose Insert Pages from a context menu, from the Pages panel Options menu, or from the Document menu; a submenu opens providing you two choices. The first choice opens the dialog box shown in Figure 16.11 where you can insert a page from a file. The second choice is to insert a page From Clipboard.

Choosing the From Clipboard option opens the same dialog box shown in Figure 16.11. The Clipboard content is inserted at the location you specify in the Insert Pages dialog box.

■ **Delete Pages.** When you delete a page, you delete not only its contents but also its links. If a link or bookmark is linked to a view in the deleted page, all links to the page become inoperable. When creating a presentation in Acrobat with multiple pages, you must exercise care when deleting pages to be certain links aren't broken.

Select a single thumbnail or multiple thumbnails in the Pages panel. Pages can be selected in a contiguous or noncontiguous selection. Open a context menu, the Options pull-down menu, or the Document menu and select the Delete Pages command. The Delete Pages dialog box opens where you can delete the selected pages by leaving the default Selected radio button active or by selecting a page range and clicking OK.

Acrobat opens a warning dialog box to confirm your choice. If you change your mind and want to keep the pages, click the Cancel button. To continue with the page deletion, click OK.

TIP   If you begin an editing session and work on files where you insert and delete pages frequently, you may find the confirmation dialog box annoying. To eliminate the dialog box opening every time you delete a page, open the Preferences dialog box (Ctrl/⌘+K). Click General in the left pane and select the box for Do not show edit warnings in the right pane. When you return to the Document pane, all subsequent page deletions are performed without the warning dialog box opening. Be certain to exercise care when targeting pages for deletion if you are not using the edit warnings. When you want to bring back the edit warnings, open the General preferences and click Reset All Warnings.

■ **Extract Pages.** Extracting a page is like pulling out single or multiple pages and creating a new PDF file with them. Extracting pages has no effect on bookmarks or links for the destination pages in the original document unless you delete pages when extracting them. All links are operable for pages among the extracted pages. For example, if you extract ten pages with bookmarks to each page, all the bookmarks within the extracted pages are functional in the new file. If you have a bookmark to a page not part of the extraction, the link is not operational.

When you select the Extract Pages command, the Extract Pages dialog box opens, as shown in Figure 16.12. You supply the page range in the From/To field boxes, and check boxes exist for Delete Pages After Extracting and Extract Pages As Separate Files. You can select these two options individually or together when extracting pages.

Pages are extracted and deleted from the original file when you select Extract Pages and you check the box for Delete Pages After Extracting. The new pages open in the foreground as a single PDF document and remain unsaved until you use the Save or Save As command.

The other option you have in the Extract Pages dialog box is Extract Pages As Separate Files. Check this box to extract pages and save them to your hard drive instead of having them open in the Document pane. When you select the page range and click OK after checking the box to create separate files, a Browse For Folder dialog box opens, enabling you to select a target folder for the saved files. Check the box for Delete Pages After Extracting and pages are deleted from the original file after the new files are saved. Each page you select for extraction is saved as a separate file.

FIGURE 16.12

If you want to delete the pages extracted from the original file, check the box for Delete Pages After Extracting. Checking the box for Extract Pages As Separate Files saves each page as a separate PDF to your hard drive.

- **Replace Pages.** This option affects only the contents of a PDF page — the overlay is unaffected. If you have links going to or from the replaced page, all links or interactive content is preserved. When editing PDF documents where page contents need to be changed, redistilled, and inserted in the final document, always use the Replace Pages command.

  Replace Pages is particularly helpful when recreating Acrobat PDF forms. If you create a form in an authoring program and add all the form fields in Acrobat, and then later decide you want to edit the form design, replacing the old design with a new design preserves the form fields.

  You can click a single page thumbnail or select multiple pages in a contiguous order and open a context menu. Select Replace Pages to open the Select File With New Pages dialog box. Navigate to the file containing pages that are to replace pages in the open file, and click Select.

  The Replace Pages dialog box opens. In the Original area of the dialog box shown in Figure 16.13, you select the page range in the open document for the target pages to be replaced. In the Replacement section of the Replace Pages dialog box, you select the first page number of the document selected in the Select Pages to Replace dialog box. The readout to the right of the field box automatically displays the range of pages that are targeted for replacement. At the bottom of each section, notice the filename listed for the open document and the selected document.

  If you disabled the edit warnings, the pages are replaced according to the selection made in the Replace Pages dialog box. If the edit warnings are not disabled (in this case, the check box isn't selected in the General preferences dialog box), a confirmation dialog box opens. Click OK to replace the pages.

TIP You can replace pages through drag-and-drop operations when viewing two documents in tiled views and when the Pages panel is opened for both documents. When you drag a page or a number of selected pages, hold down Ctrl+Alt (Windows) or ⌘+Option (Macintosh) and move the cursor in the target document on top of the page thumbnail for the first page to be replaced. Rather than place the cursor between pages where the highlight bar is shown, be certain to drop the selection on top of the page number. The target page is highlighted in black when the cursor appears directly over the page number. Release the mouse button and the pages are replaced.

Specify the page range for the pages to be replaced in the first two field boxes. Enter the page number for the first page in the target file.

Appending Pages to PDF Documents

If you want to create a PDF document by combining multiple files that may have been created from multiple authors and multiple authoring programs, you can choose some alternatives in Acrobat that permit you to concatenate files to form a single PDF document.

When you use the Insert Pages command, the Select File to Insert dialog box enables you to select multiple files stored in a single folder. You can select multiple files by holding down the Shift key and clicking on the target files in a listed order from within a folder, or pressing the Ctrl/⌘ key to select files in a noncontiguous order.

However, when you use the Insert Pages command, the order of the files is appended to the open PDF file, which does not follow the same file order you viewed in the list in the Select File to Insert dialog box. You have no control over rearranging the order or selecting additional files from within separate folders. Additionally, you can't add PDFs having security, forms created in Adobe Designer, or digital signatures. You can't retain form field data in multiple PDF forms having identical form data field attributes.

A much better alternative to use when appending pages is the Combine Files task button, and in some cases the new Assemble Files into a Portfolio option. Combining files permits you to establish the page order for the files you combine into one PDF document. It also enables you to choose specific pages within each PDF to add to a single PDF document. The Assemble Files into a Portfolio option permits you to assemble files into one document when you need to add PDFs having security or digital signatures, PDF forms created in Adobe LiveCycle Designer, or when aggregating forms among files having identical field names.

To review a thorough coverage on combining files using the Combine Files task button and the new Acrobat 9 features for creating PDF Portfolios, see Chapter 12. For a complete description on merging multiple emails together in a Portfolio, see Chapter 8.

You can approach page editing in Acrobat in many ways. Using the Pages panel helps you access menu commands quickly. You can also access the commands just discussed with the Pages panel collapsed by choosing the commands from the Document menu. In addition, you can open multiple documents, view them with horizontal or vertical tiling, and drag-and-drop pages to accomplish the same results. To help in understanding how page editing with tiled views is accomplished, try following these steps for a little practice.

STEPS: Editing pages with thumbnails

1. **Open two PDF documents where pages need to be arranged in a third document.** As an example for page editing, assume you have two files that need selected pages merged in a new, third file. Some of the pages need only to be copied to the new file and some pages need to be copied and deleted from the source document.

2. **Create a new blank page.** Select File ➪ Create PDF ➪ From Blank Page.

3. **Tile the page views.** Choose Window ➪ Tile ➪ Vertically (or Ctrl/⌘+Shift+L). Click the Pages panel in each file to open the panes. The two files you opened and the new file you created should appear similar to Figure 16.14.

4. **Replace a page.** The new document you created contains a blank page. One of the cover pages in the opened files is used as the cover in the new document. Select a page from one of the open document's Pages panel and press Ctrl+Alt (Windows) or ⌘+Option (Macintosh) and drag the page to the top of the page thumbnail in the new document. When the page is targeted for replacement, the entire page is highlighted in black, as shown in Figure 16.14.

FIGURE 16.14

The two opened files and the new file appear with the Pages panels open. Drag a thumbnail image to the target file and place the cursor on top of the page number. Release the mouse button when the page turns black.

5. **Insert pages.** Select a page in one of the open documents. Press the Ctrl/⌘ key and click on pages in a noncontiguous order. Release the modifier key and drag one of the selected pages below the title page in the new document. Wait until you see a highlight bar appearing below the page before releasing the mouse button.

6. **Extract pages with deletion.** Move to the second open file. In this document you copy pages to the new document while deleting them from the source document. Click on a contiguous or noncontiguous group of pages to select them. Press the Ctrl/Option key and drag the pages to the new document's Pages panel. Pages are inserted in the new file and deleted from the source document.

7. **Close the original source documents.** Click the close button or choose File ⇨ Close to close the documents. If you want to save the file where you extracted and deleted pages, save the document and close the file.

8. **Sort the pages.** Open the Pages panel by dragging the right side of the pane to the right side of the Acrobat window. Open a context menu and select Enlarge Page Thumbnails. Repeat the steps to enlarge pages until you have a comfortable view of the page content. Click and drag pages around the Pages panel to reorder the pages, as shown in Figure 16.15.

9. **Save the file.** Choose File ⇨ Save As. Supply a filename and select a destination in the Save As dialog box. Click the Save button.

FIGURE 16.15

Open the Pages panel and move the pages to the desired order.

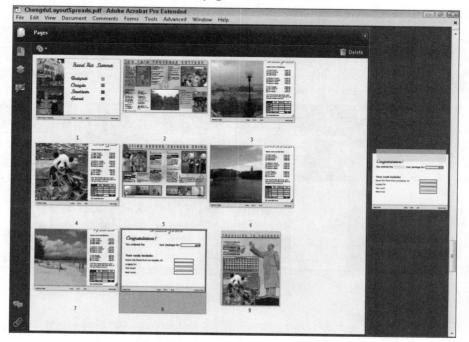

Save your work periodically if you have a major editing job. When you create a new file with the Create PDF ⇨ From Blank Page command, Acrobat creates a new Untitled document, but the file is not actually saved to disk until you save the file. Save the file after a few edits; then repeat the Save command as you work on the file. When you finish the job, choose File ⇨ Save As and rewrite the file. Page editing can add a lot of unnecessary data to a file during an editing job. When you rewrite the file, much of the redundancy is eliminated and the file size is reduced.

CROSS-REF For information on rewriting files with the Save As command, see Chapter 11.

Splitting Documents

In the "Extract Pages" section of this chapter I talked about pulling out pages in a PDF document that you can save as new PDF files. The Extract Pages command works fine for documents where you need to save a few pages here and there as new PDF files. But what if you have a book — a lengthy book — and you want to divide the book into individual chapters all saved as individual PDF documents? Using the Extract Pages command is going to take you a bit of time if you're working on a book with 20 or more chapters. There must be a better way.

NEW FEATURE Fortunately, Acrobat 9 makes the task of splitting up a document and saving the split parts into individual PDF files a simple feat. New in Acrobat 9 you find the Document ⇨ Split Document menu command.

To split a document choose Split Document from the Document menu and the Split Document dialog box opens as shown in Figure 16.16. The Split Document dialog box offers you three options for choosing how to split a PDF document into several files.

FIGURE 16.16

Choose Document ⇨ Split Document to open the Split Document dialog box.

- **Number of pages.** Type a value in the text box to split a document according to the number of pages you want for the maximum page count for each file.

- **File size.** Type a value for the maximum file size for each of the split files.

- **Top-level bookmarks.** This option enables you to split a file according to the parent bookmarks in a PDF. Nested bookmarks having a child order are not recognized for splitting the document.

CROSS-REF For more information on bookmarks, bookmark hierarchy, and nesting bookmarks, see Chapter 22.

Regardless of the choice you make for how to split a document, be sure to visit the Output Options by clicking the Output Options button in the Split Document dialog box. The Output Options dialog box, shown in Figure 16.17, offers settings to control file naming, location, and labeling.

FIGURE 16.17

Click Output Options in the Split Document dialog box to open the Output Options dialog box.

Some choices you'll want to make for saving split documents include:

- **Target Folder.** Choose to use the Same folder as originals, or click the Specific Folder radio button and then the Browse button to locate a folder where you want to save the new files.

- **File name.** Three radio button options are available to you. Choose to use the bookmark names for the file names, add a label and number before a file name such as *Part* and Acrobat automatically adds a number after the label beginning with 1, or add the label and number after the original name.

- **Use Label.** If you choose to add a label before or after the original file name, type the label in the text box here.

- **Use separator between original name and label.** Type a separator character in the text box such as an underscore if you want a separator to appear between the original file name and the label.

- **Do not overwrite existing files.** Use this option if you choose to save files to the same folder as the original files and you want to prevent overwriting the existing files.

All the options for splitting files can be applied to a single document, or you can either use the Apply to Multiple button in the Split Document dialog box or a batch sequence to split a folder of files.

 For more information on using batch sequences, see Chapter 18.

Cropping Pages

 In the Advanced Editing toolbar, you find the Crop tool. Cropping pages in Acrobat is performed with the Crop tool, Document ➪ Crop Pages, the Crop tool on the Print Production toolbar, or by selecting a menu command from the Pages panel. In Chapter 32 I talk about using the Crop tool from the Print Production toolbar. In this chapter I'll stick to using the Crop tool in the Advanced Editing toolbar.

Using the Crop tool

You can select the Crop tool and draw a marquee in the document window to define the crop region, double-click on the Crop tool in the Advanced Editing toolbar, or select the Crop Pages command from a context menu or panel menu in the Pages panel. Regardless of which manner you select to crop pages, the Crop Pages dialog box opens, as shown in Figure 16.18.

TIP To quickly access the Crop Pages dialog box, double-click the Crop tool.

FIGURE 16.18

The Crop Pages dialog box displays a thumbnail image of the document page and offers options for crop margins and page ranges.

Crop area

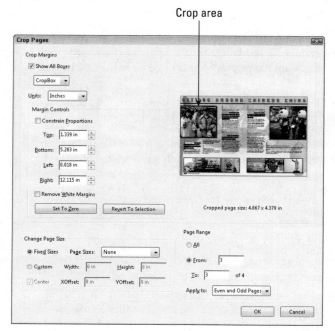

When you use the Crop tool from the Advanced Editing toolbar, the Crop Pages dialog box opens with a crop zone specified. You can edit the margins numerically where a keyline border displays the crop area dynamically as you change the margins. When you use the Crop tool, open a rectangle marquee and move the mouse cursor inside the rectangle. The cursor changes to a selection arrow, indicating that you can double-click the mouse button to open the Crop Pages dialog box. The Crop Pages dialog box enables you to refine the page cropping. You can select from the following options:

- **Crop Margins.** Four radio button options are available. When you choose one of the options, the keyline border displaying the crop region changes color according to the option selected. The four options are as follows:

  - **CropBox.** This is the default selection. It is shown with a black keyline for the cropped page when displayed or printed.

  - **ArtBox.** The Art box is shown with a red rectangle. The Art box size includes the entire bounding box for the page size.

- ▪ **TrimBox.** The Trim box is shown with a green rectangle. Trim areas are usually determined by the printer's marks indicating the finished paper size. The paper trim is made inside the bleed box.

- ▪ **BleedBox.** When you select the Bleed option, the keyline showing the crop area is blue. Bleeds allow colors to extend off the finished page size to account for paper trimming sizes.

- ■ **Show All Boxes.** Displays the Crop, Trim, Bleed, and Art boxes.

- ■ **Units.** From the pull-down menu select a unit of measure. The options include Points, Picas, Millimeters, Centimeters, and Inches.

- ■ **Margin Controls.** Choices for margins are available for each side of the page. In the field boxes for each side, you can use the up or down arrows and watch a preview in the thumbnail at the top of the dialog box. As you press the up or down arrow, the margin line is displayed in the thumbnail. If you want to supply numeric values, enter them in the field boxes.

- ■ **Constrain Proportions.** Check the box to keep proportions constrained. As you edit one text box in the Margin Controls, Acrobat supplies the same value in the remaining text boxes. For example, if you add one inch in the Top text box, Acrobat adds 1 inch to the Bottom, Left, and Right text boxes.

TIP To quickly adjust margins you can click in any field box and press the up and down arrow keys on your keyboard. The margins jump in increments according to the units selected from the Units pull-down menu. Press the Shift key and arrow keys and the margins jump to the next whole unit. For example, when inches are used for the units of measure, pressing Shift plus an arrow changes the amount in whole inches.

- ■ **Remove White Margins.** Acrobat makes an effort to eliminate white space on the page outside any visible data. Acrobat's interpretation is confined to true white space. If a slight bit of gray appears as a border, it is not cropped.

- ■ **Set to Zero.** This choice resets the crop margins to zero. If you change the dimensions with either of the preceding settings and want to regain the original dimensions of the crop boundary, click the Set to Zero button. From here you can redefine the margins. This button behaves much like a Reset button in other image editing programs.

- ■ **Revert To Selection.** If you open a crop range and open the dialog box, and then change the margins or click the Set to Zero button, the crop rectangle is restored to the size it was when the dialog box was opened. That is, it's restored to the original crop area. The view displays the crop area within the current page. In other words, the thumbnail preview displays the entire page with the crop area indicated by a red rectangle.

- ■ **Change Page Size.** You can change page sizes to standard fixed sizes by selecting options from the Page Sizes pull-down menu. You can also click the Custom radio button and the field boxes for Height and Width become active. Change values in the field boxes to create custom page sizes. When you add printer's marks to a page or document, you can crop the page(s) larger than the page size to accommodate adding printer's marks.

CROSS-REF The Crop tool in the Advanced Editing toolbar and the Crop Pages tool in the Print Production toolbar offer you different options. The Crop Pages tool doesn't permit you to crop a page down in size. For more information on adding printer's marks and cropping pages, see Chapters 8 and 32.

TIP If you want to see a larger view of what's happening on your PDF document while making adjustments in the Crop Pages dialog box such as changing the page sizes, move the dialog box aside, and the background display in the Document pane dynamically updates to reflect many changes made in the Crop Pages dialog box.

- **Page Range.** Pages identified for cropping can be handled in the Page Range options. If All is selected, all pages in the PDF file are cropped according to the sizes you specify in the dialog box. You can target specific pages for cropping by entering values in the From and To field boxes. You select choices for Even and Odd Pages, Even Pages Only, and Odd Pages Only from the Apply to pull-down menu. The Selected option is available when you select page thumbnails in the Pages palette. If you select pages in the Pages palette, use the Document ⇨ Crop Pages menu command. Using the Crop tool can deselect page thumbnails, and the Selected option appears grayed out when the Crop Pages dialog box opens.

TIP When creating PDFs for slide presentations or screen views, you may occasionally have an unwanted white border around the pages. This appearance may result from creating pages in layout or illustration programs when the image data doesn't precisely match the page size. To polish up the pages and eliminate any white lines, double-click the Crop tool or select the tool and double-click on the page. In the Crop Pages dialog box, select Remove White Margins and then select All for the page range. When the pages are cropped, the excess white lines are removed.

Cropping pages via context menu commands

Another choice you have for cropping pages is through the use of a context menu.

NEW FEATURE A new feature in Acrobat 9 provides you several choices from a context menu opened when using the Crop tool. Drag open a rectangle with the Crop tool from the Advanced Editing toolbar and right click (Windows or with a two button mouse on the Macintosh) or Control + click on the Macintosh to open a context menu as shown in Figure 16.19.

Notice in Figure 16.19 you have choices to set the ArtBox, TrimBox, BleedBox, and CropBox. The choices are the same as those explained in the last section.

If you open a PDF document and you don't see some or all the choices available in the context menu, it's because the PDF file already has the margins embedded in the file. If you export to PDF from a program like Adobe InDesign and the file contains a bleed you won't see all the menu commands appear in the context menu.

FIGURE 16.19

Drag open a rectangle with the Crop tool from the Advanced Editing toolbar and open a context menu.

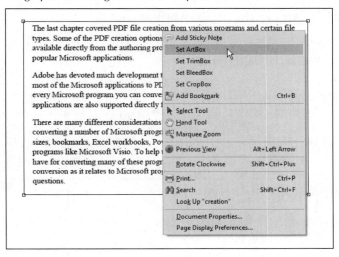

Eliminating cropped data

When you save a file after setting the crop margins, the data still remains in the PDF document. You can open a file that was cropped using the Crop tool or a menu command and open the Crop Pages dialog box. When you set the margins back to zero, the cropped region appears in the Document pane. In essence, you don't reduce a file size when using the Crop tool, because no data are eliminated from the file.

In previous versions of Acrobat you had to crop a page and save the file in an image format such as TIF to eliminate the data outside the crop margins. Doing so eliminated the data and produced a smaller file size. If you opened the file in Acrobat and used the Crop tool, you couldn't regain the cropped data.

NEW FEATURE In Acrobat 9 you can now crop a page and eliminate the area outside the crop region without having to export the PDF file to an image format. To eliminate data outside the crop margins, you need to use the Crop tool and the Preflight dialog box.

CROSS-REF For more information on using Preflight, see Chapter 32.

To crop a PDF page and eliminate the data outside the crop margin in the saved file, follow these steps:

Steps: Eliminating Data Outside the Crop Margins

1. **Open a file in Acrobat.** Open a file you want to crop in Acrobat Pro or Pro Extended.

2. **Click the Crop tool in the Advanced Editing toolbar.**

3. **Crop the page.** Drag a rectangle in the area you want to crop the page. After defining the crop area with a rectangle, press the Enter or Return key. The Crop Pages dialog box opens. Click OK to crop the page. In my example I have a two page spread and want to eliminate the right page shown in Figure 16.20.

FIGURE 16.20

Define the crop region using the Crop tool and press Enter/Return to open the Crop Pages dialog box.

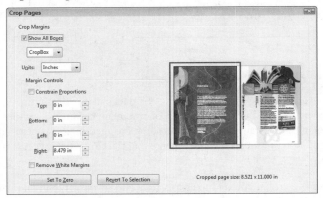

TIP After creating a rectangle with the Crop tool, open a context menu. If you see Set CropBox from the menu commands, select this command and the page is cropped without opening the Crop Pages dialog box.

4. **Open the Preflight dialog box.** Choose Advanced ➪ Preflight.

5. **Create a new profile.** Open the Options pull-down menu in the Preflight dialog box and select Create New Preflight Profile as shown in Figure 16.21.

6. **Name the profile.** Type a name in the Name text box. In my example I named my new profile *CropToMedia* as shown in Figure 16.22. The name is added to the list of profiles on the left side of the Preflight: Edit Profile dialog box.

FIGURE 16.21

Open the Options menu and select Create New Preflight Profile.

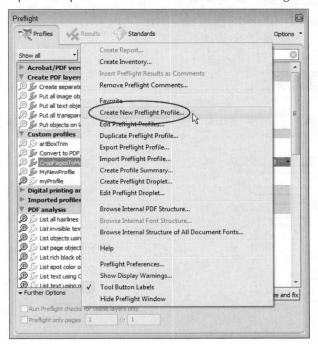

FIGURE 16.22

Type a name for the new profile in the Name text box.

7. **Choose a preflight group.** Below the new profile name on the left side of the dialog box you see a list of items. For this new profile we'll select the Fixups group. Scroll the list and click Fixups in the left panel.

8. **Choose New Fixup in the right panel.** On the right side of the dialog box, scroll the list and click New Fixup as shown in Figure 16.23.

FIGURE 16.23

Click Fixups in the left list and New Fixup in the right list.

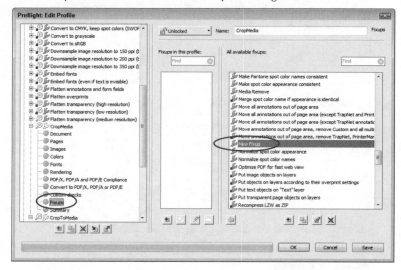

9. **Add the Fixup to the new profile.** Click the + (plus) icon in the center column to add the New Fixup to the column. The Preflight: Create Fixup dialog box opens.

10. **Set the attributes for cropping data outside the Crop box.** Choose Pages from the Fixup category list and scroll the Type of Fixup to Remove objects outside page area. Select this item and choose Crop box from the Completely outside pull-down menu as shown in Figure 16.24. Click OK after making the choices and click OK in the Preflight: Edit Profiles dialog box.

11. **Run the new profile.** After clicking OK in the Prelight: Edit Profile dialog box you return to the Preflight dialog box and find your new profile listed in the PDF Fixups group as shown in Figure 16.25. Click the Analyze and Fix button to run the profile.

FIGRUE 16.24

Click Pages and Remove objects outside page area. Choose Crop box from the Completely outside pull-down menu.

FIGURE 16.25

Select the new profile and click Analyze and Fix.

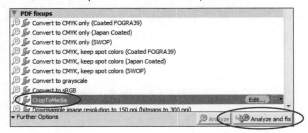

12. **Examine the document.** Click the Crop tool in the Advanced Editing toolbar and double click the document page. The Crop Pages dialog box opens and you should see the Margin Controls values set to zero and the thumbnail preview showing the cropped page as shown in Figure 16.26.

FIGURE 16.26

Open the Crop Pages dialog box to verify the area outside the crop box has been deleted.

Rotating Pages

PDF documents can contain many pages with different page sizes. You can have a business card, a letter-sized page, a tabloid page, and a huge poster all contained in the same file. Depending on the authoring program of an original document and the way a PDF is created, you may experience problems with pages appearing rotated or inverted. Acrobat offers you tools to rotate pages for viewing and printing solutions to correct such appearance problems.

You rotate pages with the Document ➪ Rotate Pages menu command or in the Pages panel via context or Options menus. When you select Rotate Pages through any of these methods, the Rotate Pages dialog box opens. You choose the direction of rotation from a pull-down menu that enables you to rotate the page three different ways, as shown in Figure 16.27. Options in the Rotate Pages dialog box include the following:

- **Direction.** Three choices appear from the Direction pull-down menu. Select from rotating pages clockwise 90 degrees, counterclockwise 90 degrees, or 180 degrees. Selecting clockwise or counterclockwise repeatedly rotates the page in 90-degree rotations.

- **Page Range.** Select All to rotate all pages in the PDF document.

- **Selection.** If you select page thumbnails in the Pages tab and select Rotate Pages from a context menu or by selecting Document ➪ Rotate Pages, the Rotate Pages dialog box offers you an option for rotating selected pages.

- **Pages.** Enter the page range you want to rotate in the From and To field boxes.
- **Rotate.** The pull-down menu for Rotate offers selections for Even and Odd Pages, Even Pages Only, or Odd Pages Only. The last pull-down menu offers choices for Portrait Pages, Landscape Pages, or Pages of Any Orientation.

NOTE Rotate Pages is a menu command found in the menus discussed previously. When you rotate pages with a menu command, the pages are rotated and you can save the PDF with the new rotated appearances. You also have tools in the Page Display toolbar used for rotating views. When you use these tools to rotate a view, the page rotation is a temporary view and cannot be saved.

FIGURE 16.27

The Rotate Pages dialog box offers options for rotating pages in a range or by selecting even or odd pages. The Even/Odd choices can be helpful when printing to devices requiring page rotations for duplexing.

Rotating PDF elements

When you rotate a page, all page content is rotated. If you have any layers, visible or hidden, they are rotated. Acrobat provides no means for rotating individual layers.

If you create comments on a page and later rotate the page, the comment notes rotate at the point of origin, but the note displays are not rotated. For example, if you create a comment note in the top-left corner of a page and rotate the page 90 degrees counterclockwise, the note icon on the page is rotated, eventually ending up in the lower left corner of the page. However, the open note is viewed at the default view with the note text in its original orientation.

Form fields behave differently than notes. If you create a form field containing text, the field and contents are rotated with the page.

Minimizing rotation problems

Among the major problems with PDF page rotation involves creating PDFs from layout programs. Layout programs such as Adobe InDesign or QuarkXPress enable you to transverse pages in the Print dialog box. This control is implemented for digital prepress and printing to high-end printing devices. In addition, many PostScript Printer Description files (PPDs) used with high-end devices include transverse page options for page size selections.

CROSS-REF   For more information on commercial printing and PPDs, see Chapter 32.

As an example, a portrait page that prints transversed is rotated 90 degrees to conserve media on roll-fed devices. If you print files to disk as PostScript and distill the files in Acrobat Distiller, don't transverse the pages. When transversed pages are opened in Acrobat, even though the auto rotate feature is enabled during distillation, Acrobat interprets the page coordinates with a 90-degree rotation. The end result is a zero point (0,0) located in the lower-right corner of the page. This interpretation can lead to problems when you're trying to define x,y coordinates for JavaScripts, replacing pages, and copying and pasting data between documents.

If you set up a landscape page in a layout program, print the file as a portrait page with the horizontal width described in field boxes for custom page sizes. Print the file to disk and distill in Acrobat Distiller. The end product is a PDF that winds up with the proper page orientation and is interpreted by Acrobat with the zero point (0,0) located in the default lower left corner.

PREPRESS   Design and print professionals who seek to print files from PDFs can create the PDFs without transversing pages. When printing the PDFs for prepress, use the Acrobat Print dialog box to control printing, and select device PPDs from within Acrobat. If you need to repurpose documents for Web or screen presentations, you can use the same file created for prepress without having to reprint and redistill the authoring document.

CROSS-REF   For more information on printing PostScript and using Acrobat Distiller, see Chapter 10.

Creating Headers and Footers

Headers and Footers can be used for adding page numbers, dates, and any custom data you want to add to a header and footer appearing on all or a range of pages.

When you select Document ➪ Header & Footer ➪ Add, the Add Header and Footer dialog box opens, as shown in Figure 16.28. You'll notice the Add Header and Footer dialog box is the same dialog box you use when adding Bates numbers (see "Using Bates numbering" later in this chapter).

NEW FEATURE   The Add Header and Footer dialog box in Acrobat 9 offers you the option for batch processing files. Click the Apply to Multiple button in the Add Header and Footer dialog box and you can load files in a wizard to apply settings to multiple files.

FIGURE 16.28

Select Document ⇨ Add Header & Footer to open the Add Header and Footer dialog box.

You create page headers and footers in this dialog box. Options exist for adding a date stamp, a page number, and a custom text description. In Figure 16.28, I added a page number as a header and a Web address as a footer to apply to all pages in my open document. Both headers and footers can be added in the same dialog box. Among your choices in the Add Headers and Footers dialog box are the following:

- **Saved Settings.** You can select options from the pull-down menu. By default no settings are listed in the menu. Make your settings adjustments in the dialog box and click Save Settings. Name your settings and they are added to the Saved Settings menu. If you want to delete a saved setting, select the setting and click the Delete button.

- **Font (Name).** All the system fonts available to you from your operating system are displayed in a pull-down menu. Click the down-pointing arrow and make your font choice. You can assign a different font to each line of text in the listed items in the six boxes below the menu.

- **Font (Size).** Font sizes can be assigned individually to each line of text. If you want custom text to appear larger than a date or page number, select the item after clicking an Insert button and choose a font size from the pull-down menu. You select a font from preset point sizes. You cannot edit the field box to add a point size other than the preset sizes.

- **Margins.** The four Margins field boxes are editable. You can physically position a header or footer at any location on a page. If you add a header, the options relate to the top, left, and right field boxes. Footers relate to all but the top field box. Entering values in the lower field box has no effect on the position where the text is added when adding headers. If you use top = 5 inches, left = 3 inches, and select the left alignment radio button, the text is added 5 inches from the top and 3 inches from the left side.

  Although a header or footer extending beyond the space shown in the Preview area (denoted by dashed lines) disappears from the preview, you can move data outside the guidelines by adding values in the Margins text box and clicking OK. When you view the PDF file, the data appear at the coordinates you described in the Margins text boxes.

- **Appearance Options.** Six boxes are shown for adding data. The top row of three boxes is used for adding headers. The second row of three boxes across is used for adding footers. You can type custom text in any one of the six boxes.

- **Insert Page Number.** Click the box in the Appearance Options where you want a date to appear and type the code used for a date format. The same five date formats you have available with page numbering are also available in the Add Headers and Footers dialog box. To select a date format, you can click the Page Number and Date Format link to the right of the Insert Date button (see Page Number and Date Format).

- **Insert Date.** Follow the same steps as when adding a page number. First click in the box where you want the data to appear, then choose a date format and insert it.

- **Page Number and Date Format.** The blue text is like a button. Clicking the text opens the Page Number and Date Format dialog box, as shown in Figure 16.29. From pull-down menus you select formats for Date, Page number, and a page to start adding the header and/or footer.

FIGURE 16.29

Click Page Number and Date format to open the Page Number and Date Format dialog box.

- **Page Range Options.** By default, all pages are used when you add a page header and/or footer. You can control page ranges by clicking the Page Range Options blue text. Clicking the text opens the Page Range Options dialog box shown in Figure 16.30. Select Pages from and type values in the text boxes. From the subset pull-down menu, you have All Pages, Even Pages Only, or Odd Pages Only.

FIGURE 16.30

Click Page Range Options to open the Page Range Options dialog box.

- **Preview.** The Preview Page text box and up/down arrows permit you to scroll through the document. Below this item are the preview boxes for headers and footers. You cannot type in either of the boxes. They are used only for previewing data added in the top six boxes.

Click OK after adding data to a header and/or footer and the data are applied to your selected page range.

TIP If the layout of your design elements on each page make it difficult to find a space to add a header or footer, you can use the Crop tool to add a little more space to the top, bottom, or both top and bottom of the pages. In the Crop Pages dialog box, uncheck Center and set the YOffset to add space to the top or bottom of the pages. A 0.5 YOffset adds one-half inch to the bottom of the page, and a –0.5 adds one-half inch to the top of the page. After cropping the pages, use the Document ➪ Header and Footer ➪ Add command to add a header or footer to the new space added to your pages.

Updating headers and footers

If you add or delete pages, the headers and footers are not dynamic and do not change when adding or deleting pages. You need to reedit the headers and footers to renumber pages deleted from a document or add header/footer data to pages inserted in your document. From the Document ➪ Header & Footer menu, select Update. The Update Header and Footer dialog box opens. Options in this dialog box are identical to the Add Header and Footer dialog box.

The Update Header and Footer dialog box displays the exact same settings you used when you first added a header and/or footer. Just click OK if you want the update to be exactly the same as your original assignment of headers and footers, and the file is updated.

Removing headers and footers

In earlier versions of Acrobat prior to version 8, the only way you could remove a background was to open the Add Header and Footer dialog box and return all settings to defaults, and then click OK. Acrobat essentially replaced your headers and footers with nothing. In Acrobat 8 and 9 you have a menu command specifically used for removing headers and footers. Select Document ⇨ Header & Footer ⇨ Remove. A dialog box opens prompting you to confirm the action. Click OK and your headers and footers are removed.

Numbering Pages

In Acrobat, page numbers appear in the Page Navigation toolbar at the top of the Acrobat window and in the Pages panel. When you open the Go To Page dialog box (View ⇨ Go To ⇨ Page or Ctrl/ ⌘+Alt/Option+N) and enter a value in the status bar and press Enter/Return, you may find that the destination page does not correspond with the page number you supplied in the dialog box. This is because certain documents may be numbered in sections where front matter, such as a table of contents, foreword, preface, and other such items precede the page numbering in a document. This is particularly true of books, pamphlets, essays, journals, and similar documents using numbering schemes other than integers for the front matter.

Numbering individual PDF documents

Pages in a PDF file can be renumbered using the Page Numbering dialog box that you access with a simple menu command. Open the Pages panel and open a context menu on a page thumbnail. From the menu options, select Number Pages. The Page Numbering dialog box opens, as shown in Figure 16.31.

FIGURE 16.31

The Page Numbering dialog box offers options for numbering pages.

The Page Numbering dialog box offers options for selecting a range of pages and renumbering them in sections or throughout the entire document. The choices available to you include:

- **Pages.** This area of the dialog box asks you to specify the page range. If you want to renumber all pages with the same numbering scheme, select the All radio button. You might use this option when numbering pages with integers.

  If you enable the radio button for Selected, only the pages selected in the Pages panel are affected. By default the Selected radio button is enabled if you click on a page or a page's thumbnail in the Pages panel and open the dialog box. If no page thumbnail is selected, the default radio button selection is From.

  Enable the From radio button and supply a page range in the field boxes to select a page range numerically according to page position in the document. That is to say, pages 1 to 10 are interpreted as the first ten pages in the file regardless of the page numbering scheme used before you open the dialog box. Perhaps you want to create a separate scheme for a document's front matter. Specifying the scheme in the Numbering section of the dialog box renumbers the selection. Click OK to accept the changes. If you want to renumber another section, return to the dialog box and select a new section and new scheme. Repeat the process for all changes in page numbering according to different sections.

- **Numbering.** This portion of the dialog box offers you options for determining the page-numbering scheme you want to use. From the Style pull-down menu select a number style (refer to Figure 16.24 for your choices).

  - **Style.** If None is selected, no page number is assigned to the page. The readout in the status bar would appear similar to this: (10 of 100). The numbers within the parentheses represent the original page number order preceded by a blank space where no number (None) is specified. If you want to add a prefix, you could add alphanumeric data to the Prefix field box and supply a prefix with no number. Using the same example, the readout would appear something like this: A000 (10 of 100), where A000 is the prefix and no number follows.

    The remaining options in the Style pull-down menu are specific choices for styles of page numbers. If you have front matter where you want to use Roman numerals, you can choose between the two styles shown in Figure 16.32. Alpha characters offer you options for uppercase or lowercase letters, and integers are also available. You can combine these options with special characters by typing data in the Prefix field box.

FIGURE 16.32

Select number styles from the Style pull-down menu.

      ■   **Prefix.** Type any character, number, or combination of numbers and characters in the field box for a prefix value. The prefix precedes the numbering scheme defined in the Style pull-down menu.

      ■   **Start.** The Start item is used to indicate the number a new section starts with. Typically you use 1 to start a new section, but you can begin sections with any number you want to type in the field box. Upon occasion you may have a document where page insertions might be added later. You can number pages in a section leaving room for new additions to be made later in another editing session.

■   **Extend numbering used in preceding section to selected pages.** For this option you need to select a range of page thumbnails in the Pages panel, and then open the Page Numbering dialog box. Selecting the radio button and clicking OK removes the currently assigned numbers and extends the previous section. For example, you may have Appendix A numbered A-1 through A-10. You later decide to combine Appendix B with Appendix A. Appendix B might be numbered B-1 through B-10. To extend the previous B numbered pages, you select the page thumbnails in the Pages panel, open the dialog box, and select this radio button. When you click OK, pages formerly numbered B-1 through B-10 are changed to A-11 through A-20.

> **TIP**   If you have multiple files you want to renumber, use a batch sequence to renumber a folder of PDF files. For more information on batch sequences, see Chapter 18. Note that using a batch sequence for renumbering pages is limited to renumbering each document individually. You cannot consecutively number multiple files using a batch sequence for page numbering.

Using Bates numbering

Bates numbering is a method to keep multiple documents in a recognizable order. The legal industry uses Bates numbering when identifying legal documents in court cases. During the discovery phase of a case in litigation, there might be an enormous number of documents submitted as evidence. A Bates numbering system is used to provide an arbitrary unique identifier for each document. The numbers are typically numeric, but they can also be alphanumeric. There is no standardized algorithm used for a Bates numbering schema in a court case for assigning numbers to documents; however, the numbers are generally eight or more characters in length. An example of a schema that might be used to disclose documents in the legal environment is shown in Figure 16.33.

Rather than open a PDF document in Acrobat and number each file individually, the Bates numbering feature lets you batch process multiple files and add unique numbers in a numeric order to multiple files without opening them.

FIGURE 16.33

An example of Bates numbers that might be used in a court case

Company	Sequence	Length <char>	Example	Multi-page divider	Example Muli-page divider
Universal Gas & Electric	numeric	10	2005684511	slash /	1001453289/5049
Small Town USA	numeric	8	15678907	slash /	10296733/002194
ACE Construction	alphanumeric	11	ACE45876302	space dash	ACE04876932 -1189
Edwards Trust	alphanumeric	9	ETU45632	space asterisk	ETU94560 *1022
ATC	numeric	8	08145633	not applicable	Start Bates: 45350001 End Bates: 45350871
Ewings & Sons	numeric	10	0258942356	not applicable	Start Bates: 0250000001 End Bates: 0250009657
GC Equipment Corporation	numeric	7	2034537	dash	5635891-56890

To see how the new Bates numbering feature works in Acrobat, follow these steps.

STEPS: Adding Bates numbers to multiple PDFs

1. **Open the Bates Numbering dialog box.** Select Advanced ⇨ Document Processing ⇨ Bates Numbering ⇨ Add. The Bates Numbering dialog box shown in Figure 16.34 opens.

2. **Select files to number.** Open the Add pull-down menu and choose Add Files. The Add Files dialog box opens where you select files you want to add to the Bates Numbering dialog box. Select files from a folder or multiple folders and click the Add Files button, and the files appear in the Bates Numbering dialog box as shown in Figure 16.34.

FIGURE 16.34

Click the Browse button to locate and add files you want to number.

3. **Order the documents.** Click a document and click the Up or Down buttons to organize the files in the order you want them to appear. Because the Bates numbering system uses no standardized algorithm and the numbers are arbitrary, you don't need to worry about organizing files according to dates, topics, and so on. Simply make some order arrangement that you want based on whatever criteria you elect to use.

4. **Click OK.**

5. **Add the number schema for the select documents.** When you click OK, a lightly modified version of the Add Header and Footer dialog box opens as shown in Figure 16.35. You can align the numbers left, center, or right by clicking in the Left, Center, or Right Header or Footer text box and then click the Insert Bates Number button.

   When you click Insert Bates Number, the Bates Numbering System dialog box opens. Add the total digits (including alpha characters if you use alpha characters for a number schema) in the Number of Digits text box. You have an option to type the start number, a prefix, and a suffix. Click OK and the Bates number is shown in the field box respective to your selection. In Figure 16.35, I added a three-character prefix and six numbers for my numbering schema.

FIGURE 16.35

Click inside the text box where you want your Bates numbers to appear and click Insert Bates Number. Add the numbering schema in the Bates Numbering System dialog box and click OK. Your Bates Numbering schema then appears in the text box.

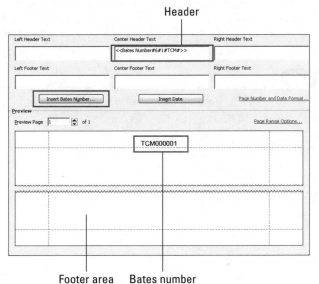

6. **Add the numbers to your selected documents.** Click OK in the Add Header and Footer dialog box and the numbers are added to all the selected PDFs. In Figure 16.36, you see one of several files where I added a Bates number. Each number in all documents is a unique number following the schema I identified in the Add Header and Footer dialog box.

FIGURE 16.36

A file where the Bates number was added as a footer

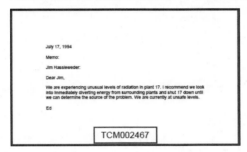

Removing Bates numbers

Removing Bates numbers is handled differently depending on whether a document is open in the Document pane and whether Bates numbers are actually included in the files where you want to eliminate the numbers. The various behaviors include the following:

■ **No documents open in Document pane.** Choosing Document ➪ Header & Footer ➪ Remove opens the Header & Footer dialog box shown in Figure 16.37. You can remove Bates numbers using this dialog box.

■ **Document open with no Bates number.** If you have a document open but the document contains no Bates number an alert dialog box opens informing you that no Bates numbers are detected.

■ **Document open with Bates number.** If you open a document that does contain Bates numbers, no dialog box opens. The numbers are removed by Acrobat.

PDF Portfolios with Bates numbers

If you want to group documents according to a certain Bates numbering schema, first use the Bates Numbering dialog box and add Bates numbers to all your PDF documents. Next, use the Assemble Files into a Portfolio option in the Combine Files task button menu. Create a PDF Portfolio and all your files are assembled in one PDF collection with Bates numbers. In Figure 16.38, you can see an example of a PDF Portfolio with Bates numbers.

CROSS-REF For information on how to create PDF Portfolios, see Chapter 12.

FIGURE 16.37

When no documents are open in the Document pane, you can remove Bates numbers from multiple files using the Header & Footer dialog box.

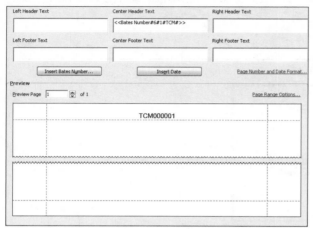

FIGURE 16.38

Bates numbers as they appear in a PDF Portfolio

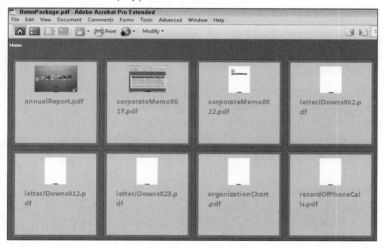

Adding Watermarks and Backgrounds

You add watermarks and backgrounds in different dialog boxes, but the attributes for both items are almost identical. A few options are different in the Add Watermark dialog box where you can add custom data in addition to importing files. You can also add a watermark in front of or behind page data. Backgrounds are only added behind page data.

Adding backgrounds

To add a background to a PDF document, choose Document ⇨ Background ⇨ Add/Replace. The Add Background dialog box opens, as shown in Figure 16.39.

Choose Document ⇨ Background ⇨ Add/Replace to open the Add Background dialog box.

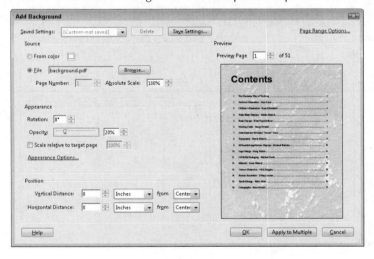

Choices you have for adding backgrounds include the following:

- **Saved Settings.** The options here are the same as when adding headers and footers. See the section "Creating headers and footers" earlier in this chapter.

- **Page Range Options.** Click the text and the Page Range Options dialog box opens. The same dialog box with the same options is opened as when adding headers and footers. See the section "Creating headers and footers" earlier in this chapter.

- **Source.** Choose From color or File to add a background color or import a file. To change the background color, click the From color radio button and a color palette opens where you make a color choice to apply as a background color.

To add a file for a background, click File and click the Browse button. The Browse dialog box opens where you select a file to import. File types supported include PDF documents, BMP, and JPEG. Note that choices for adding text along with a background are not available. Because the Add Watermark feature appears in a different dialog box, all text options are available only in the Add Watermark dialog box.

- **Appearance.** Several different options are listed in the Appearance settings. These include:

  - **Rotation.** You can rotate backgrounds in 1-degree increments by typing values in the Rotation text box or clicking the up and down arrows.

  - **Opacity.** Opacity adjustments are made by moving the slider, typing values in the text box, or clicking the up and down arrows. In Figure 16.40, objects were rotated in two separate documents. The object on the left was rotated +45 degrees. The object on the right was rotated +135 degrees with an opacity of 20%.

  - **Scale relative to target page.** By default, the scaling is set to 100%. Type a value in the text box for scaling up or down to the desired value.

  - **Appearance Options.** Click the Appearance Options blue text and the Appearance Options dialog box opens, as shown in Figure 16.41. In the dialog box you can toggle on and off showing backgrounds when printing and when displayed on your monitor.

FIGURE 16.40

Rotations of 45 and 135 degrees. The figure on the right is adjusted for a 20% opacity.

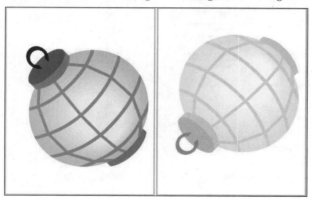

FIGURE 16.41

Click the Appearance Options blue text to open the Appearance Options dialog box. Check the boxes to show or hide a background when printing and when displaying on screen.

■ **Position.** Set options for the position of the background by typing values in the text boxes for Vertical Distance and Horizontal Distance. From the first set of pull-down menus, select a unit of measure. The second set of pull-down menus lets you position the vertical and horizontal placement from Top, Center, and Bottom. In Figure 16.42, the position of an object with the Vertical Distance menu options is shown first and the Horizontal Distance menu options is shown second. It also shows how the objects fall on a page when making the menu choices.

FIGURE 16.42

Nine different positions are available from the pull-down menu choices for Vertical and Horizontal placements.

Top: Left	Top: Center	Top: Right
Center: Left	Center: Center	Center: Right
Bottom: Left	Bottom: Center	Bottom: Right

■ **Preview Page.** In the preview area, you see a page preview of an imported background (or background color if you click the From color radio button). The Preview Page text box is used to type a page number, and the respective page appears in the Preview window. You can toggle through all pages and view the page previews before applying a background. Click OK in the Add Background dialog box and the background is added to pages in the selected page range.

Replacing backgrounds

From the Document ⇨ Background menu, the item for adding backgrounds and replacing backgrounds opens the same dialog box. Select Document ⇨ Background ⇨ Add/Replace and follow the same steps used for adding a background. If a file contains a background, the new background you select from either a color or a file replaces the old background.

Updating backgrounds

If you add a background to a PDF file from an image file, and then edit the image file and select Document ⇨ Background ⇨ Update, Acrobat won't update the edited background. A dynamic link is not made from Acrobat to the image file. If you want to update a background imported from an image file, you need to click again on the Browse button and identify your edited image file. Add it as you add a new background and the PDF background is updated.

Removing backgrounds

As with the menu command for removing headers and footers, you also have a new command in Acrobat 8 for removing backgrounds. To remove the current background, select Document ⇨ Background ⇨ Remove and a dialog box opens. Click OK and the background is removed.

Adding watermarks

Select Document ⇨ Watermark ⇨ Add to add a watermark to a PDF. Watermarks generally appear on top of page data, but in Acrobat 8 and 9 you can chose to have a watermark appear on top of or behind the page data. The Add Watermark dialog box that opens, as shown in Figure 16.43, is similar to the Add Background dialog box.

The Add Watermark dialog box contains a few different options than the Add Background dialog box. The first noticeable difference is the Source area in the Add Watermark dialog box. The first item and the default selection is Text. You have a text box where text is typed in the Add Watermark dialog box. Below the text box are some options for changing text attributes.

As yet, however, you don't have an option for creating outline text that would be helpful when creating watermarks. The only way to create outline text is to first create it in an illustration program such as Adobe Illustrator and import the text as a graphic in the Add Watermark dialog box.

In the appearance area of the Add Watermark dialog box, you find options for fixed rotations as well as arbitrary rotations. The Location options enable you to place your watermark behind or in front of the page data. The remaining choices are the same as those found in the Add Background dialog box.

FIGURE 16.43

Select Document ➪ Watermark ➪ Add to open the Add Watermark dialog box.

> **TIP** Graphics placed behind page data only appear in transparent areas on the page. To quickly check what areas are transparent (as opposed to opaque), open the Preferences dialog box (Ctrl/⌘+K) and click Page Display in the left pane. Click the Show transparency grid check box in the right pane and click OK. All the areas appearing with transparency are shown in the Document pane.

To create a watermark on a PDF document, follow these steps.

STEPS: Adding a watermark to a PDF document

1. **Open a file in Acrobat.** Use any PDF document that you want to appear with a watermark.

2. **Open the Add Watermark dialog box.** Choose Document ➪ Watermark ➪ Add. The Add Watermark dialog box opens.

3. **Type text in the Text box.** In my example, I typed Draft in the text box I'll use for watermarking draft documents.

4. **Set Font attributes.** Select a font from the Font pull-down menu, select a font size, and click the color swatch and choose a color. Note that if you select a particular hue in the color palette and you want that hue to appear lighter, you can reduce opacity with the Opacity slider. For example, to make a light gray, select the default black color and set the opacity to 20 to 30 percent.

5. **Edit appearance settings.** In my example, I wanted the text rotated, so I clicked the 45° radio button. I reduced the opacity of my black color selection to 30% and then I clicked the Scale relative to target page check box. This action scaled my text to fit the page size. Note that if you scale text to fit a page, any font size you select in the Source area of the dialog box works.

6. **Edit the location.** Determine whether you want your watermark on top of the page content or behind it. In my example, I wanted the watermark to appear behind my page data so I clicked the Appear behind page radio button.

7. **Preview pages.** Click the Preview Page arrows or type values in the text box to scroll through the pages to which you want to apply your watermark.

8. **Set Appearance Options.** Click the Appearance Options blue text to open the Appearance Options dialog box. Check the boxes to either show or not show the watermark when printing and screen viewing. Another check box is available to keep the watermark position and size constant on different page sizes. Check this box if you're working with files that have different page sizes and click OK.

   ■ **Set the Page Range.** Click the Page Range Options blue text in the top right corner of the dialog box to open the Page Range Options dialog box. If you want all pages to appear with a watermark, you don't need to open this dialog box. If you want a page range less than all pages, type the page numbers in the from and to text boxes and click OK.

   ■ **Save the settings.** If this is a watermark you intend to reuse with other documents, you can save the settings and use them whenever you want to apply the same watermark. Click the Save Settings button at the top of the dialog box and the Save Settings dialog box opens. Type a name for your new setting and click OK. The new setting now appears under the Saved Settings pull-down. In Figure 16.44, I added my new Draft settings to the menu.

FIGURE 16.44

The Settings menu after I saved my Draft custom setting

   ■ **Click OK.** The watermark is applied to the page range you chose in the Page Range Options dialog box.

CROSS-REF If you don't want anyone to tamper with watermarks added to your PDF files such as changing or deleting them, you can secure your file against editing pages using Acrobat Security. For more information on how to secure PDFs, see Chapter 26.

Removing and updating watermarks

The options for removing and updating watermarks are the same as removing and updating backgrounds. Select Document ➪ Watermarks and the submenu commands appear for Add, Update, and Remove. If you want to modify a saved setting, choose Document ➪ Watermark ➪ Update. Edit your settings and click OK. Acrobat updates all pages containing watermarks. Clicking Remove in the Watermark submenu opens the same dialog box as when removing backgrounds. Click OK and all watermarks are removed.

Note that if you want to remove backgrounds or watermarks from selected pages in a file while keeping backgrounds/watermarks on some pages, clicking the Remove menu item removes all watermarks/backgrounds from your document. You then need to add the watermarks/backgrounds to pages where you want them to appear.

When adding watermarks and backgrounds, you can't select pages in the Pages panel and apply watermarks/backgrounds to selected pages in the panel. You must use the Page Range dialog box to apply watermarks/backgrounds to a page range. Acrobat makes no provision for adding these items to noncontiguous pages. You have to individually apply watermarks/backgrounds to pages in a noncontiguous order.

TIP If you want to add a watermark or background on a form enabled with Adobe Reader usage rights, first apply the watermark or background to a PDF, and then enable the file with usage rights. If you attempt to add a watermark or background to an enabled file, you need to save a copy of the file, add the watermark or background, and then re-enable the file. (For more information on enabling files with Adobe Reader extensions, see Chapter 19.)

Summary

- You can enlarge or reduce page thumbnails through successive menu commands in the Pages panel.

- You can open the Pages panel to full-screen size where you can sort and reorder pages.

- Page thumbnails can be used to navigate pages and zoom in on pages.

- To copy pages in a PDF document and between PDF documents, you can use page thumbnails.

- Page thumbnails are created on-the-fly when you open the Pages panel. If you want to speed up the screen refreshes when opening the Pages panel, you can embed thumbnails from a menu option in the Pages panel and delete them after your editing sessions.

- Pages are inserted, deleted, extracted, and replaced through menu commands from the Pages panel context menu or the pane pull-down menu.

- New in Acrobat 9 is the Split Document command, enabling you to split files according to page count, file size, and top-level bookmarks.

- You crop PDF pages with the Crop tool. When you crop a page, the page view is reduced to the crop region, but all the original data in terms of page size is still contained in the file. You can return to the Crop Page dialog box and undo crops even after a file has been saved.

- You can eliminate data outside a crop box permanently using the Preflight tool.

- You can rotate PDF pages in 90- and 180-degree rotations via menu commands in the Rotate Pages dialog box.

- Enabling a preference setting for viewing logical pages helps you navigate to pages numbered with integers.

- Opening the Page Numbering dialog box from a context menu in the Pages panel enables you to renumber pages in a PDF file.

- To number multiple PDF documents with consecutive numbering, use the Bates Numbering dialog box. To add page numbers to a collection of PDFs without consecutive numbers, use the Batch Processing command.

- To add page numbers to a PDF document, use the Add Header and Footer dialog box.

- You can add different headers and footers to different pages in a PDF document. Each time the content for headers and footers changes, you open the Add Header and Footer dialog box, add the content, and specify the page range.

- To add a background to a document, use the Add Background dialog box. To add a watermark to a file, use the Add Watermark dialog box.

- Backgrounds and watermarks can be updated and removed

- After you save a PDF with a watermark and/or background, the data are embedded in the PDF document. In Acrobat 8 or 9, you can always return to a document and remove backgrounds and watermarks.

Chapter 17

Scanning and OCR Conversion

Welcome to the world of one-stop scanning and text recognition. Anyone who scanned documents in earlier versions of Acrobat will appreciate the one-step operation for scanning a text document and performing text recognition via Acrobat's Optical Character Recognition (OCR) engine and many new enhancements to Acrobat Scan. The one-stop scanning introduced in Acrobat 8 has been improved in Acrobat 9 through the implementation of a new scanning technology called ClearScan, the addition of presets that support custom settings you can configure for various source materials, creating multiple files from scanned documents, adding multiple scanned documents to a PDF Portfolio, and much more with the new Acrobat Scan features in Acrobat 9.

When performing a scan in Acrobat, you are not limited to scanning documents for text conversions. Acrobat enables you to scan photos and images that might have some other uses. Therefore, this chapter covers all the aspects of scanning from within Acrobat using the Scan to PDF command and the Text Recognition commands.

Setting Up the Scanning Work Environment

For scanning and text recognition tasks, you need access to the TouchUp Text tool. First, reset the tools from a context menu opened from the Toolbar Well and choose Tools ⇨ Advanced Editing ⇨ Show Advanced Editing Toolbar. When the toolbar opens, dock it in the Toolbar Well. Note that if you want to eliminate some tools from the Advanced Editing toolbar such as the Article tool and the Link tool, and other tools not likely to be used when scanning documents, you can open the More Tools window and choose the toolset you want in the Advanced Editing toolbar.

During text recognition, you may want to create several views that enable you to zoom in to see words requiring edits. Tools handy for displaying different views are found in the Page Display toolbar. Open the More Tools window and check the boxes for Single page continuous and One Full Page as well as the Page Display Toolbar check box and click OK. Dock the toolbars in the Toolbar Well by opening a context menu on the Toolbar Well and selecting Dock Toolbars.

Configuring Scanners

Before you can scan a page in Acrobat, you need to configure your scanner and be certain it functions properly. After you complete your installation of Acrobat, it should recognize your scanner immediately. If all the scanner hardware is in place and operational and Acrobat still does not recognize your scanner, the next step is to be certain Acrobat recognizes the scanner's software. If Acrobat doesn't see your scanner, you may need to relocate software to another location on your hard drive or acquire a software update from your scanner manufacturer.

You get access to your scanner in Acrobat through one of three methods: TWAIN drivers, Acquire plug-ins, or WIA-compliant drivers.

TWAIN software

TWAIN (Technology With An Important Name) software is manufacturer-supplied and should be available on the CD-ROM you receive with your scanner. In Windows, the TWAIN files are stored in the \Windows\twain_32 folder. When you install scanner software, the TWAIN driver should find the proper folder through the installer routine. On the Macintosh you'll find TWAIN resources in the System\Library\Image Capture\TWAIN Data Sources folder.

Many scanner manufacturers produce the equipment but use third-party developers to write the software. Adobe has certainly not tested the Scan plug-in with all scanner manufacturers and all software developers, but many of the popular brands have been thoroughly tested to work seamlessly with Acrobat. Theoretically, the TWAIN software should work in most cases. If you have problems accessing your scanner from within Acrobat, but can perform scans in other applications, then you most likely have a problem with the TWAIN driver. If this is the case, contact your scanner manufacturer and see whether it has an upgrade or whether you can get some technical support. In many cases, you can download upgrades for registered software on the Internet.

Adobe Photoshop plug-in software

Acrobat 9.0 supports Acquire plug-ins to use with Adobe Photoshop. More prevalent than TWAIN drivers, Photoshop plug-ins are available from just about every scanner manufacturer. If you use Adobe Photoshop or Adobe Photoshop Elements, you may need to copy your Photoshop Acquire plug-in to your Acrobat plug-ins folder. On Windows, copy the Photoshop Acquire plug-in and open the Acrobat\plug_ins\PaperCapture folder and paste your Acquire plug-in.

Mac OS X requires you to expand the Acrobat 9.0 Pro package in order to paste your Photoshop Acquire plug-in. To do so, follow these steps:

1. **Open your Applications/Adobe Acrobat 9.0 Pro folder and select (not double-click) Adobe Acrobat 9.0 Pro.**

2. **Ctrl+click to open a context menu, and select Show Package Contents.** The Contents folder appears in the Adobe Acrobat 9.0 Pro folder.

3. **Double-click the Contents folder and double-click the Plug-ins folder that comes into view.**

4. **Double-click the PaperCapture.acroplugin folder and drag your Photoshop Acquire plug-in into this folder.** (Option+click+drag to copy the plug-in to the target folder.) When you close the folders, the package is restored.

Configuring Windows Imaging Architecture (WIA) scan drivers (Windows only)

TWAIN drivers have been around for a long time and many developers are still supporting TWAIN drivers, buy many newer scanners are now supporting a more recent driver technology called Windows Imaging Architecture (WIA). WIA is a Microsoft-developed technology that provides developers a relatively easy way to write support for scanners. Developers such as Acer, Compaq, Epson, Fujitsu, HP, Kodak, Microtek, Ricoh, and UMAX have all embraced WIA in many of their newer models.

The good news from Adobe is that if you have a WIA-supported scanner you can configure your scanner's scan button with Acrobat. To do so, open the Start Menu and choose Control Panels/Scanners and cameras/<scanner name>. The Scanners and Cameras dialog box opens. Click your scanner name and click the Properties button to open the scanner properties.

Scanners and PDF

PDF is so popular that just about every developer in one market or another is supporting the Portable Document Format. Today, you find the support for PDF broadening with scanner developers. Many new scanner models support hardware buttons on the scanners for scanning to a PDF file. Additionally, you can find scanner proprietary software supporting scanning to PDF.

In some cases you can find scanners that do marvelous jobs of scanning to PDF files, but they don't support WIA architecture or TWAIN drivers — such is the case with the Fujitsu Scansnap 510 scanner. In these cases, you can use the scanner's button or the software to scan to PDF. Once the file is scanned to PDF it typically opens in Acrobat where you can recognize text and populate forms with form fields.

The WIA scanner properties dialog box opens as shown in Figure 17.1. Select your scanner's Scan, Copy, Photo, or other button you want to activate. When using scanners with a button to initiate a scan, choose the Scan button. Click the Start the Program radio button and choose Adobe Acrobat from the options in the pull-down menu. Click OK; the next time you hit your Scan button on your scanner, the scan is opened in Adobe Acrobat.

FIGURE 17.1

Choose an event and choose Adobe Acrobat from the pull-down menu.

Understanding Scanning Essentials

At this point you should have your scanner and Acrobat configured properly. Before I begin discussing how to use your scanner with Acrobat, take a moment to understand some of the essential issues to deal with in performing clean, accurate scans. A few items need to be discussed: the hardware and hardware-related issues; the types of scans to be produced; and understanding your scanner capabilities. A few moments here saves you much time in producing the best scans you can expect from your equipment.

The hardware issue to consider is your scanner. The single most important issue with scanner hardware is keeping the platen clean. If you have dust and dirt on the glass, these particles show up in your scans. Keep the platen clean, and use a lint-free cloth to clean the glass. If you use a solvent, always apply the solvent to the cloth and not the scanner glass.

Preparing a document

Just as your scans can benefit from careful attention to your scanner, exercising a little care with the source material can help produce clean scans. Bits of dust, improperly aligned pages, poor contrast, and degraded originals affect your ability to create scans that the text recognition software can read without many errors. A little preparation before scanning saves you much time in trying to clean up poorly scanned images.

Photocopying originals

Sometimes you can improve image and text contrast by photocopying original documents. Try some experiments to test your results. Placing photocopies made from large, bulky material on the scanner bed ultimately results in better scans than when using the original material.

Ensuring straight alignment

If you have documents with frayed edges or pages torn from a magazine, trim the edges and make them parallel to the text on the page. Precise placement of pages on the scanner bed facilitates clean scans. Even though Acrobat has a recognition capability within a 14-degree rotation, the straighter the page, the better the results. Acrobat 8 and 9 can actually rotates a scan 90 degrees and 180 degrees, and new text recognition improvements are spectacular with pages rotated 180 degrees. However, as a matter of practice, try to keep the source material rotated in the proper portrait view on the scanner platen.

CAUTION Be certain to observe copyright laws when scanning published material. If you scan text from books and magazines, you need to obtain permission from the publisher before using the material.

Try to remember the axiom "garbage in, garbage out" when you approach any kind of scanning. The better the source material, the better your scanned results. Exercise a little care in the beginning, and your Acrobat scanning sessions move along much faster.

Using Scan to PDF

As I mentioned in the beginning of this chapter, Acrobat offers you one-step scanning and OCR conversion. Before getting into all the options in dialog boxes and what they mean, let's look at scanning a document and recognizing text.

Scanning on Windows

Scanning on Windows and the Macintosh follows a similar path, but there are some differences in the options you have available on one platform versus the other. For Windows users, follow the steps below to scan a document and recognize the text.

STEPS: Scanning a text document (Windows)

1. **Place a document on the scanner platen.** Be certain your scanner is configured and operational.

2. **Select Document ⇨ Scan to PDF (or open the Create task button pull-down menu and select Create from Scanner) ⇨ Custom Scan.** The Custom Scan dialog box opens, as shown in Figure 17.2.

NEW FEATURE   Note that you have several submenu options on Windows to choose from for scanning to a PDF. If you haven't configured presets, try using the Custom Scan operation first. Later in this chapter in the section "Working with presets" you'll learn how to configure the presets.

3. **Select your scanner.** The first task is to be certain your scanner appears listed on the Scanner pull-down menu in the Custom Scan dialog box. If you don't see your scanner here, then you have a configuration problem. Assuming everything is working okay, select your scanner as shown in Figure 17.2.

FIGURE 17.2

The Custom Scan dialog box opens after you select Create PDF from Scanner.

4. **Select the resolution.** From the Resolution pull-down menu choose a resolution setting. Higher resolutions take longer but produce much better results. At a minimum you should use 300 dpi for the scan resolution.

5. **Paper size.** Choose a paper size for the artwork. If you use A4 paper, be sure to make the choice here for A4. Also, if using US Letter paper, make the choice accordingly.

6. **Select the output.** If you have a document open in the Document pane, you can append your document with the new scan. If you want to create a separate document, click New PDF Document in the Output section of the Custom Scan dialog box.

7. **Set document quality.** For a first-time effort, leave the slider at the default.

8. **Make searchable.** Check the box for Make Searchable (Run OCR). This check box informs Acrobat to use the OCR engine to convert the scanned image to recognizable text.

9. **Click Scan.** Leave the remaining items at the defaults and click the Scan button to commence scanning. Note that the resolution settings, paper size, and clicking the Scan button apply to WIA-compliant scanners. If your scanner is not WIA compliant, you may need to use a TWAIN driver that automatically opens your scanner interface. In your scanner's software, you need to make choices for the items you don't have available in Acrobat and click the Scan button.

10. **Check the document for recognizable text.** Click the Select tool in the Editing toolbar and drag through the document. You should see the text selected as you drag, as shown in Figure 17.3.

FIGURE 17.3

The scanned document appears in Acrobat with selectable text.

Scanning on the Macintosh

Some of the new features related to setting up scanning presets are not available to Macintosh users. In addition, you don't have WIA support on the Macintosh. All your scanning occurs using a TWAIN driver and making choices for scan attributes in your scanner's software. To create a scan in Acrobat on the Macintosh and recognize text, do the following:

STEPS: Scanning a text document (Macintosh)

1. **Place a document on the scanner platen.** Be certain your scanner is configured and operational.

2. **Select Document ⇨ Scan to PDF.** The Acrobat Scan dialog box opens as shown in Figure 17.4.

FIGURE 17.4

Choose Scan to PDF to open the Acrobat Scan dialog box.

3. **Choose your scanner.** Open the Scanner pull-down menu and choose your scanner.

4. **Leave the settings at the defaults and click Scan.** The default settings are set up to create a new PDF document and make your text searchable. Leave the settings at the defaults and click Scan to open your scanner's software via the TWAIN driver.

5. **Set the scan attributes.** Make choices for resolution, color mode, and page size in your scanner's interface. In Figure 17.5 you can see a scanner interface that was opened from Acrobat using a TWAIN driver.

6. **Click Scan.** Click the Scan button to commence scanning. The converted file opens in Acrobat with recognizable text.

FIGURE 17.5

Set scan attributes in your scanner software.

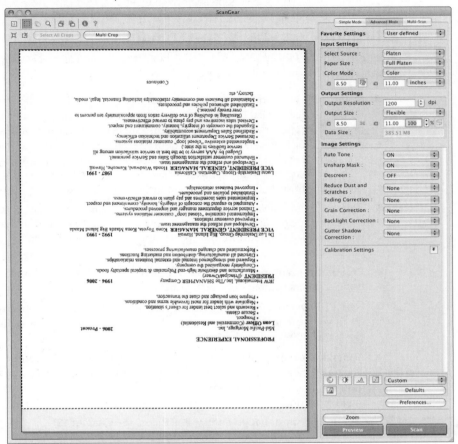

Using Acrobat Scan (Windows and Macintosh)

There are two different dialog boxes that open when you choose Document ➪ Scan to PDF. For WIA-compliant scanners on Windows only, you have a number of different options you can choose from within Acrobat. If you use a TWAIN driver that opens your scanner software to create a scan, the Acrobat Scan dialog box has much fewer options choices.

To differentiate the options, you have scanner settings in either the Custom Scan dialog box (like Figure 17.2) or when setting up scan presets using WIA-compliant scanners. If using a TWAIN driver, you open the Acrobat Scan dialog box (like Figure 17.4).

Setting options in Acrobat Scan

Beginning at the top of the Acrobat Scan dialog box, as shown in Figure 17.2, Input options you have available when using a TWAIN driver include:

- **Scanner.** The pull-down menu is used to select your scanner. When the scanner is online and recognized by Acrobat, you'll see the scanner plug-in software name appear in a pull-down menu. Some scanning software may not enable you to see other options such as Color Mode and Resolution in the Acrobat Scan dialog box. If these items are not available, you'll need to make the choices in the scanner plug-in. When you first select Acrobat Scan, a dialog box informs you that the Native Scanners Interface can't be hidden. In such a case, you need to make choices in your plug-in software.

- **Sides.** Choose from Single or Both sides. If your scanner is capable of scanning both sides of a paper document, the scan can be completed in one step. If your scanner doesn't support two-sided scanning, Acrobat pauses the scan and permits you to turn the paper over on the scanner platen.

- **Prompt for scanning more pages.** Check this box for multiple-pages scanning when using scanners without document feeders.

- **New PDF Document.** Click the radio button to create a scan that opens as a new PDF file. If you want to scan multiple pages and create separate new pages for each scan, check the Multiple files check box.

- **Append to existing file or portfolio.** You can append a scan to a file either open in the Document pane where you make choices from the pull-down menu, or one you choose from your hard drive by clicking the Browse button. You can also add a scan to an existing PDF Portfolio.

CROSS-REF For more information on PDF Portfolios, see Chapter 12.

- **Optimization.** The slider is used to adjust the quality of the scanned image. This quality setting has nothing to do with text recognition. Click the Options button to open the Optimization Options dialog box as shown in Figure 17.6. The default choice is Automatic. When you click Custom Settings, you can make choices for various optimization settings. Your choices include:

FIGURE 17.6

Click Options to open the Optimization Options dialog box.

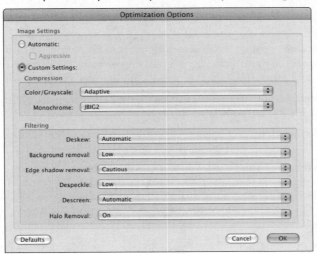

- **Compression.** For color/grayscale images, choose from Adaptive or JPEG for file compression. JPEG files result in smaller file sizes, but you experience data loss. In many cases the data loss may have no effect on appearance or Acrobat's ability to recognize text. If you do experience problems, try using Adaptive compression.

  Monochrome images are compressed with three different compression schemes depending on the choice made from the pull-down menu. JBIG2 is a JPEG compression scheme with little data loss. You can also use Adaptive like that used for color/grayscale images and CCITT Group 4, which is a common compression used by fax machines. When applying compression to images, try the defaults (Adaptive for color/grayscale and JBIG2 for monochrome) first. If your scans are presenting visual problems or Acrobat has difficulty in recognizing text, experiment with the other settings.

  You can adjust the quality slider for the amount of compression applied to the scans. As you move the slider left, the file size is smaller but the image quality is reduced. Move the slider toward Higher if you experience problems with text recognition.

- **Deskew.** Acrobat automatically straightens crooked scans when Deskew is set to automatic. To turn off the deskewing, select Off from the pull-down menu.

- **Background removal.** Removes background data. Use this option and choose from Low, Medium, High, or Off from menu choices. When text has drop shadows or original paper copies show dust and dirt, play with the amount settings to sharpen the text.

■ **Edge shadow removal.** If you want to scan in grayscale or color mode, Acrobat can eliminate levels of gray where shadows appear around type. For cleaner text scans, enable this option. Note that you need to have crisp, clean originals to see much of a difference between scanning with the option enabled versus disabled. Two settings are used for Cautious and Aggressive as well as Off. Use Aggressive for more removal.

■ **Despeckle.** This item and descreen are particularly helpful when scanning documents that have been printed and are subject to moiré patterns (a condition common when scanning printed documents) or when scanning documents with dust and dirt.

■ **Descreen.** Use Descreen like Despeckle mentioned previously when scanning printed documents and screened type.

■ **Halo Removal.** Artifacts creating halo effects around type can be cleaned up by setting this option to On.

■ **Make Searchable (Run OCR).** You can instruct Acrobat to recognize text using OCR at the time a document is scanned. If you disable this check box you can later use a menu command to run Acrobat's OCR engine. Clicking the Options button opens the Recognize Text – Settings dialog box shown in Figure 17.7. See "Text recognition options" later in this chapter.

■ **Make PDF/A Compliant.** Check this radio button to make a PDF/A-compliant file.

CROSS-REF For more information on PDF/compliance, see Chapters 10 and 32.

■ **Add Metadata.** If you check this box, the Document Properties Description dialog box opens after your scan is completed and the text recognized. You can add Title, Author, Subject, and Keywords to the Document Properties.

CROSS-REF For more information about editing Document Properties, see Chapter 6.

TIP The filtering options you have in Figure 17.6 are also available when choosing Document ⇨ Optimize Scanned PDF. Choosing this command opens the Optimize Scanned PDF dialog box. This menu command offers you an option to optimize scanned documents after scanning and after adding form fields when scanning forms.

Text recognition options

If scanning for OCR, check the box for Make Searchable (Run OCR). If you want to scan images, remove the check mark from this option. For searchable text, you have more choices when you click the Options button. Clicking this button opens the Recognize Text – Settings dialog box. As shown in Figure 17.7, you have three choices for PDF Output style, which determine how the text recognition is performed:

■ **Primary OCR Language.** By default, Acrobat installs 42 language dictionaries available for OCR. If you scan documents from any of the supported languages, select the appropriate language in the pull-down menu in the Recognize Text – Settings dialog box.

- **PDF Output Style.** From the pull-down menu shown in Figure 17.7, your options are as follows:

  - **ClearScan.** In earlier versions of Acrobat, this item was called Formatted Text & Graphics. When using the legacy format or the newer ClearScan technology, the bit-mapped image is discarded and replaced with searchable text and graphics. If there is an instance where the OCR engine does not have confidence, the original bitmap is left in place and the best guess is placed behind, mimicking the "Searchable Image" style.

    Formatted Text and Graphics had some problems related to color images. The newer ClearScan technology does a much better job of converting scanned images to text and file sizes are much smaller.

  - **Searchable Image.** Text is also placed behind the original image, preserving the integrity of the original documents. The image scan is compressed to reduce file size. Some of the quality of the original scan is lost.

  - **Searchable Image (Exact).** This option keeps the image scan in the foreground with text placed in the background. The appearance of the scanned image does not change. Text is added on a hidden layer that gives you the capability of creating indexes and performing searches. Use this option when you don't want to change a document's appearance, but you do want to be able to search the text of that document. Something on the order of a legal document or a certificate might be an example of such a document. This option produces the largest file sizes.

NOTE See the "Searchable Images Versus ClearScan" sidebar in this chapter for more detail on the differences among the PDF output styles.

- **Downsample Images.** This option enables you to downsample images or keep them at the original scanned resolution. If None is selected, no downsampling is applied to images. The remaining options offer downsampling values at 600 dots per inch (dpi), 300 dpi, 150 dpi, and 72 dpi.

FIGURE 17.7

Open the PDF Output Style pull-down menu and choose from one of three options for performing the OCR.

After you make choices in the Recognize Text – Settings dialog box and click OK, you return to the Acrobat Scan dialog box. When you click Scan or choose Document ⇨ OCR Text Recognition ⇨ Recognize Text Using OCR, the last settings you made in the Recognize Text – Settings dialog box are used by the OCR engine.

Searchable Image Versus ClearScan

When you search OCR pages with either Searchable Image (Exact) or Searchable Image, the pages are image files with searchable text. The original file is an image file produced from your scan designed to be viewed as an original, unaltered document. This option enables you to electronically archive documents for legal purposes or when unaltered originals need to be preserved.

When you convert a document with Recognize Text Using OCR, the OCR conversion places text behind the scan. The intent is for you to be able to archive files and search them either through using the Search panel to search files on your hard disk or by searching an index where these documents have been catalogued.

The text behind PDF Image is not editable with Acrobat. However, Adobe Acrobat Capture 3.0 does have tools to edit text in a PDF Image file. If Recognize Text Using OCR misinterprets a word, you cannot make corrections to the text. The text is selectable, and you can copy the text and paste it into a word processor or text editor. If you want to examine the OCR suspects, paste the text into a word processor and review the document. Or buy a copy of Adobe Acrobat Capture 3.0 to do the edits from within the PDF file.

To copy text from a PDF Image format, select the Select tool. Click the cursor anywhere in the text and choose Edit⇨Select All (Ctrl/⌘+A). Open a context menu and select Copy File to Clipboard. Open a word processor and choose Edit⇨Paste. You may find the number of suspects to be too many to be usable. If you want to improve the OCR conversion, return to the Create PDF from Scanner dialog box and rescan the file with a higher resolution or different scanning mode.

ClearScan files (previously referred to as PDF Formatted Text & Graphics in Acrobat 6 and later) are scanned documents converted to text. When you select ClearScan in the Recognize Text dialog box, the file conversion is made to a PDF with scalable text and graphics. Recognize Text reads the bitmap configuration of words and converts them to text. This text can be edited and altered on a page. When you make text corrections, you see the changes reflected on the document page.

When capturing pages, be certain to view the options and know the difference between capturing pages as PDF Scanned Image and ClearScan documents.

Using WIA Scan Drivers (Windows)

If you have a WIA-compliant scanner, your options for scanning from within Acrobat are much more plentiful than using the Acrobat Scan 5-button scan operation. Acrobat Scan has been greatly simplified in Acrobat 9 and the number of options you have are, although very simple, much fewer than using Scan to PDF on Windows.

Working with presets

Presets are settings you can configure and retain to perform scans with a set of options that you define or that Adobe creates as a series of defaults.

NEW FEATURE Acrobat 9 provides you with several presets used with black and white, grayscale, and color documents, and with color images. The settings for scanning each of these types of documents are preset for you. You can use them *out of the box,* or you can configure each preset for your own personal needs.

Adobe's intent is to help you simplify your scanning and OCR recognition by setting up some general options that apply for scanning a range of original document types. However, you may have some special needs. For example, you may be scanning a different paper size than the default choice for one of the scanning presets, or you may want to scan at a different resolution than the choice added to a given preset. If this is the case, you'll want to change a preset to suit your own personal scanning needs.

Take a quick look at some of the options you have available when you first start a scan. Choose Document ⇨ Scan to PDF and the submenu opens as shown in Figure 17.8. From the menu choices you have the four preset choices, a choice for Custom Scan, and a choice for Configure Presets. The Custom Scan choice is provided in case you have a scan where you want to deviate from all the presets and choose your options prior to a scan — more like a one-time use. The last item in the submenu is Configure Presets. Choose this option to configure any one of the first four presets listed in the menu.

FIGURE 17.8

Choose Document ⇨ Scan to PDF to open the submenu where the preset commands are listed.

To edit a preset, do the following:

STEPS: Editing a preset

1. **Choose Document ⇨ Scan to PDF ⇨ Configure Presets.** The Configure Presets dialog box opens as shown in Figure 17.9.

2. **Choose your scanner.** Open the Scanner pull-down menu and choose the scanner you want to use. If you have multiple scanners, all scanners configured properly appear in the menu.

3. **Choose the preset you want to edit.** From the Presets pull-down menu choose the preset you want to edit as shown in Figure 17.9.

FIGURE 17.9

Choose Document ⇨ Scan to PDF ⇨ Configure Presets to open the Configure Presets dialog box.

4. **Change the attributes.** From the options shown in the Configure Presets dialog box, use the menus and text boxes to make the changes you want for the preset. In my example I edited Resolution and changed my scanner's default A4 paper size to US Letter. For more detail on the options, see the section earlier in this chapter "Setting options in Acrobat Scan."

5. **Save the settings.** Click the Save button to apply your new settings to the preset. The next time you want to scan a document with the new preset, choose Document ⇨ Scan to PDF ⇨ <preset choice>.

NEW FEATURE You'll notice that when setting up the paper size you have an option choice from the Paper Size pull-down menu for Custom. Click Custom and edit the Width and Height text boxes to scan custom-size pages.

If you change a preset and you find that the settings have all been configured improperly and you want to start over, simply open the Configure Presets dialog box and choose your edited preset. Click the Defaults button to change the options back to the originally installed preset choices.

Creating a custom scan

For an occasional scan where options don't exist in one of your presets, you may want to use the Document ⇨ Scan to PDF ⇨ Custom Scan command. Choosing this option opens the Custom Scan dialog box shown earlier in Figure 17.2.

When you perform a scan using the Custom Scan dialog box, you need to address the choices in the dialog box before clicking the Scan button. If you find yourself scanning routinely using the Custom Scan dialog box, open the Configure Presets dialog box and edit a preset.

Setting scanner options

In both the Configure Preset and Custom Scan dialog box you find a button for Options adjacent to the Scanner pull-down menu. Click this button to open the Scanner Options dialog box (Figure 17.10) where you can make some choices for the transfer method and user interface.

Click the Options button adjacent to the Scanner pull-down menu to open the Scanner Options dialog box.

For the Transfer Method you can choose Native Mode or Memory Mode from the pull-down menu. Both modes prompt you to save your file in a Save dialog box. For faster scanning of multiple pages, choose the Memory Mode option.

For User Interface, choose between options in Acrobat or your scanner's interface. To use the options in the presets and the Custom Scan dialog box, you'll want to choose Hide Scanner's Native Interface. If the pull-down menu is grayed out, you are forced to use your scanner's interface.

The Invert Black and White Images check box is used for scanning white text on a black background. This option is a likely candidate for using the Custom Scan menu choice if you have an occasional piece of artwork designed with white text on a black background. You wouldn't want to change a preset if this type of artwork is used infrequently when scanning.

Appending scans to files and portfolios

You can open an existing PDF document or PDF Portfolio or choose a file stored on your hard drive and append scans to the document(s). In the Custom Scan dialog box (or when configuring a preset) or when using Acrobat Scan, click the Append to existing file or portfolio radio button.

If you have a document or portfolio open in the document pane, the Select path shows the open document's directory path by default. You can change the path and select another document by clicking the Browse button.

When you scan to a PDF Portfolio, Acrobat prompts you in a dialog box to name your file. Type a name to perform the scan. The file is saved using the filename you add to the Acrobat Scan dialog box shown in Figure 17.11 and appended to a PDF Portfolio. If you scan to a file, the new scan is appended to the selected document and there is no need to type a name for the new scan.

CROSS-REF For more information on PDF Portfolios, see Chapter 12.

FIGURE 17.11

When scanning to a PDF Portfolio, type a name for the new scan and click OK.

Creating Workflow Solutions

Scanning individual pages for limited use can easily be handled by the methods described in this chapter. As you scan documents, you need to attend to feeding papers under the scanner lid and manually clicking buttons to continue scanning. If you need to convert large numbers of pages to digital content, you may want to explore other solutions. Depending on how much money you want to spend, you may want to invest in a commercial-grade scanner with a document feeder.

Some scanners support automatic document feeders. If your workflow demands scanning volumes of papers, acquiring a good scanner with an automatic document feeder is a great advantage. When you scan in Acrobat, scanned pages are successively appended to a PDF. Therefore, you can leave a stack of papers in the scanner feeder and leave it unattended. Scanning can be performed automatically overnight. When you return to your computer, the PDF file is complete with recognized text and ready for saving to your hard disk.

TIP If you scan using a document feeder, open the Preferences and click Documents in the left pane. In the right pane, click Automatically save document changes to temporary file every [1]. Type 1 in the text box to save your updates every minute. If the scanning operation crashes, you may be able to rescue the file up to the last minute when pages were appended to the document.

A more expensive solution, but not out of the question for workflows needing automated means of capturing pages, is to purchase Adobe's stand-alone product, Adobe Acrobat Capture. Combined with a scanner and document feeder, the conversion of scanned images to text is handled in a single operation. You have other solutions from third-party vendors that support industrial-strength scanning and OCR conversion with the capability of converting the final file to PDF format.

PDF WORKFLOW Users in government and educational workflows seeking to scan volumes of text for document accessibility will find purchasing auto document feeding scanners and Adobe Acrobat Capture, or other software capable of batch scanning and OCR conversion, to be a much more effective means for converting publications and documents to accessible PDFs. Some hardware screen readers use proprietary software to read TIFF image files for document accessibility. Acrobat PDF is a much better solution over TIFF images and proprietary formats, because once converted to PDF, the document content is searchable and much smaller. If scanning textbooks and government papers is your task, PDF is a much better file format for document accessibility.

Using Text Recognition

You may have files scanned as image files and want to convert them to recognizable text, which is similar to performing OCR tasks in earlier versions of Acrobat. You handle scanning and OCR recognition in one of two ways in Acrobat. You can scan a document and run the OCR recognition in one step, or you can scan documents, save them as PDF files, and later use Acrobat to run the OCR recognition. The latter case might use other scanning programs such as a Photoshop plug-in or a dedicated scanning tool to perform the scans.

If you don't have a scanner or you're looking for a more efficient way to scan documents and recognize text, you can use a digital camera and a copy stand. A digital camera fires off images ten to one over a flatbed scanner, and you can import the images directly into Acrobat and run the Text Recognition command. If using a digital camera be certain to shoot JPEG images and not Camera Raw. Acrobat converts JPEGs to PDF via the Create PDF From File or the Merge Files into a Single PDF commands. Camera Raw conversion is not supported.

If you have scanned image files or digital camera files and you want to convert to searchable text, perform the following steps:

STEPS: Converting image files to searchable text

1. **Open files in Acrobat.** Use the File > Create PDF ➪ From File or the File > Create PDF ➪ Merge Files into a Single PDF menu command to convert image files to PDF.

CROSS-REF For more information on converting image files to PDF, see Chapter 7.

2. **Recognize text.** Select Document ➪ OCR Text Recognition ➪ Recognize Text Using OCR to open the Recognize Text dialog box shown in Figure 17.12.

3. **Set the PDF output style.** Click the Edit button in the Recognize Text dialog box to open the Recognize Text – Settings dialog box. (Refer to Figure 17.7.) From the PDF Output Style pull-down menu, select ClearScan. If you don't make this selection, you can't change misspelled words later with the changes visible on the document page(s). Click OK to return to the Recognize Text dialog box.

4. **Run the OCR engine.** Click OK to start the OCR engine converting the image file to recognizable text.

FIGURE 17.12

Choose Document ➪ OCR Text Recognition ➪ Recognize Text Using OCR to open the Recognize Text dialog box.

5. **Check for suspect words.** After Acrobat completes the text recognition, select Document ⇨ OCR Text Recognition ⇨ Find First OCR Suspect. The Find Element dialog box opens as shown in Figure 17.13. Suspect words are reported in the Suspect text box. If the word is correct as it is reported in the Suspect text box, click Accept and Find to move to the next suspect. If the word is incorrect, type the correct spelling on the document page and click Accept and Find to change the spelling and move to the next suspect. Continue moving through the document until you correct all suspects.

6. **Save the PDF.** Select File ⇨ Save As to optimize the file and update your corrections.

FIGURE 17.13

Click Accept and Find if the correct word is displayed in the Find Element dialog box.

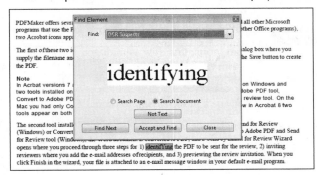

Recognizing text in multiple files

If you set up a workflow where you perform scans on multiple scanners and save files as PDFs or an image format compatible with the Create PDF From File command, you can recognize text in multiple files.

NEW FEATURE Acrobat 9 introduces a new submenu command in the Document ⇨ OCR Text Recognition submenu. Choose Recognize Text in Multiple Files Using OCR and you can perform text recognition in separate files. The files can be saved in any format compatible with the Create PDF From File menu command.

To recognize text in multiple files, follow these steps:

STEPS: Performing OCR on multiple files

1. **Choose Document ⇨ OCR Text Recognition ⇨ Recognize Text in Multiple Files Using OCR.** The Paper Capture Multiple Files dialog box opens.

2. **Add files.** Open the Add Files pull-down menu and choose from one of three menu commands. Add Files enables you to add individual files. Add Folders enables you to add a folder of scans. Add Open Files enables you to add all files open in the Document pane. You can combine choices in the Paper Capture Multiple Files dialog box. For example, you can add individual files, add a folder, and add some files open in Acrobat and list them in the Paper Capture Multiple Files dialog box shown in Figure 17.14.

FIGURE 17.14

Open the Add pull-down menu and choose files to add to a list for OCR conversion.

3. **Set the Output options.** Click OK in the Paper Capture Multiple Files dialog box to open the Output Options dialog box opens as shown in Figure 17.15. Make choices for the folder where you want to save the files, adding text to the file name, and an output format. You can also open the PDF Optimizer and choose optimization settings for the saved files.

4. **Click OK to start the OCR process and save the files.**

CROSS-REF For more information on optimizing files using the PDF Optimizer, see Chapter 18.

FIGURE 17.15

Make choices in the Output Options dialog box and click OK.

Understanding suspect words

A *suspect* word is one that the OCR engine interprets differently from the closest match found in the Primary OCR Language Dictionary. The word is suspect because it doesn't have a match in the Primary OCR Language Dictionary. You might have proper names, industry terminology, abbreviations, and so on that the OCR engine marks as suspects. Simply because the word(s) is marked as a suspect doesn't necessarily require changing the word. Therefore, when you review suspects, you have two choices: Either change the word to a correct spelling or inform Acrobat to leave it as is and move to the next suspect.

After the Recognize Text dialog box closes, the converted page(s) doesn't appear any different from before you began the OCR conversion. In order to see any words that may have been misinterpreted during the conversions, you need to access a menu command and tell Acrobat you want to view the suspect words. You have two choices in the OCR Text Recognition submenu.

NOTE In order to correct OCR suspects in Acrobat, you need to convert pages with the ClearScan output style.

If you choose Document ⇨ OCR Text Recognition ⇨ Find First OCR Suspect, Acrobat shows the first word that it interprets as a suspect, which means the interpretation of the OCR engine did not exactly match a word in its dictionary. The suspect word is highlighted in the document pane.

If you choose Document ⇨ OCR Text Recognition ⇨ Find All OCR Suspects, all the suspect words are highlighted with a red border across all pages converted. At a glance you can see the number of suspects that need to be reviewed.

TIP   When examining suspect words you should plan on zooming in to the suspects. If you prefer to view a page in a zoomed-out view, select the Loupe tool to zoom in on suspect words. You can keep the page view smaller while zooming in on suspects with the Loupe tool.

To leave a word unedited, you can choose either Find Next or Accept and Find. If the OCR engine recognized a graphic (such as a signature) as text, you can also select "Not Text" to return it to the original bitmap image. If you choose Find Next, the bitmap image of the text stays in place and the text behind the bitmap stays as is. When you click the Accept and Find button, the bitmap is thrown away and the word behind the bitmap is promoted to the text location. As you work with the text corrections, realize that you have two layers. The bitmap is the scanned image, and Recognize Text created the text below the scanned image. Therefore, as you edit the text corrections you can choose to throw away the bitmap image on top of the text layer or choose to preserve it. To make a correction, edit a suspect word and click Accept and Find. The new text you edited is promoted to the text layer while the bitmap is thrown away.

PDF WORKFLOW   If you want to develop a workflow in an office environment, you may want to have several machines perform the function of scanning documents and have other computers perform OCR functions. You can scan images in software such as Adobe Photoshop and save your files in either an image format or as Photoshop PDFs. The scans can be routed to other workstations used for the OCR conversion.

Reducing suspects

When you begin a new Acrobat session and want to scan many pages with OCR Text Recognition, scanning one or two pages representative of the pages you want to convert and examining the number of suspects in your sample scan is a good idea. If the suspects outnumber the number of correct interpretations, editing the suspect words could take you more time than typing the document in a word processor. At some point the ratio between the number of suspects to correct words can make capturing pages more of a burden than a solution.

If the number of suspect words is extraordinary, you may want to scan another few pages using different settings. For example, increase the image resolution or scan in a different color mode. Change the attributes in the Acrobat Scan dialog box or adjust settings in your Acquire plug-in to produce scans more suitable for capturing pages. Run Text Recognition and examine the suspects. When a scan results in fewer suspects, you can then go about scanning the remaining pages. In

Figure 17.16, I scanned a page at 200 ppi and converted the page with Recognize Text Using OCR. After viewing the number of suspects, I decided to scan the page again with a higher resolution. The results of my OCR suspects with a higher resolution (600 ppi) were significantly reduced, as you can see in Figure 17.17.

FIGURE 17.16

I scanned a page using Create PDF From Scanner and converted it with Recognize Text Using OCR. After I chose Document ➪ OCR Text Recognition ➪ Find All OCR Suspects, I determined that the number of suspects made this job too difficult to edit in Acrobat.

PDFMaker offers sevral tools to control PDF file creation from within Microsoft Word and all other Microsoft programs that use the PDFMakertools. After you install Acrobat and later open Word (or other Office programs), two Acrobat icons appar on the far left side of the toolbar.

The first of these two icons is the Convert to Adobe PDF tool. Clicking this icon opens a chalog box where you supply the filename and destnation. Enter a name and choose a destination, and then click the Save button to create the PDF.

Note
In Acrbat versions 7 and below you had three tools installed in the Office programs on Windows and two tools installed on the Mac. The Wndows version of Office had the Convert to Adobe PDF tool, Convert to Adobe PDF and Email tool, and the Convert to Adobe PDF and Send for review tool. On the Mac you had only Convert to Adobe PDF and Convert to Adobe PDF and Email. Now in Acrobat 8 two tools appear on both Windows and the Mac.

TIle second tool install led in Microsoft Ofice Applications is Convert to Adobe PDF and Send for Revie\w (Windows) or Convert to Adobe PDF and Fail (Macintosh). When you click the Convert to Adobe PDF and Send for Review tool (Windows), the Word doclment is converted to PDF, and a Send by Email for Review Wizard opens where you proceed through three steps for 1) identifying the PDF to he sent for the review 2) inviting reviewers where you add the e-mail addresses of recipients, and 3) previewing the revievi' invitation. When you click Finish in the wizard, your file is attached to an e-mail message window in your default e-mail program.

Changing conversion settings (Macintosh)Cross-Reference
For more information concerning e-mail reviews, see Chapter 21.

Tn addition to tools, tVi0 menus (Windows only) are also installed with PDFMaker The first is the Adobe PDF menu. The second is the Acrobat Comments menu.

You have the a few menu selections in the Adobe PDF menu tllmt provide some adchtional PDF conversion options. From the Adobe PDF menu shown in Figure 8-1, the two tool options for Convelt to Adobe PDF and Convelt to Adobe PDF and Send for Review are also listed as menu commands. Notice in the menu you have two additional PDF conversion options. Convert to Adbe PDF and Email pelfoTIns the same on Windows as the tool available on the Mac.

Figure 8-1:

The Adobe PDF menu on Windows offers several options for creating PDFs from within Word.

The second additiOlml PDF conversion option on Windows in tile Adobe PDF menu is Mail Merge to PDF To apply this feature you first need to create a data file and a mail merge document.

You can create a daLa hIe casly in .Microsoll Excel Just be cerLain to place labels in Lhe lisL row at the Lop of an Excel worksheel such as name, address city, state zip, and so on. Save the hIe in nativc .xls fonnaL.

After creating a data file and a Word template docmuent such as a letter, from the Task pane just select Mail Merge and follovi' steps in a wizard to create the merge doclmlent. Word provides you an easy vi'izard to help you create a letter, email message, envelope, lahel, or directory. When the merge document is created, select Adobe PDF @.@> Mail Merge to Adobe PDP and the Adobe PDF Maker - Mail Merge dialog hox opens as shovi'n in Figure 8-2.

FIGURE 17.17

I scanned the same page from Figure 17.16 at a higher resolution and converted it again. Fewer suspects were found and the job of correcting the suspects was more manageable.

PDFMaker offers sevral tools to control PDF file creation from within Microsoft Word and all other Microsoft programs that use the PDFMaker tools. After you install Acrobat and later open Word (or other Office programs), two Acrobat icons appar on the far left side of the toolbar.

The first of these two icons is the Convert to Adobe PDF tool. Clicking this icon opens a dialog box where you supply the filename and destnation. Enter a name and choose a destination, and then click the Save button to create the PDF.

Note
In Acrbat versions 7 and below you had three tools installed in the Office programs on Windows and two tools installed on the Mac. The Wndows version of Office had the Convert to Adobe PDF tool, Convert to Adobe PDF and Email tool, and the Convert to Adobe PDF and Send for review tool. On the Mac you had only Convert to Adobe PDF and Convert to Adobe PDF and Email. Now in Acrobat 8 two tools appear on both Windows and the Mac.

The second tool installed in Microsoft Ofice Applications is Convert to Adobe PDF and Send for Review (Windows) or Convert to Adobe PDF and Eail (Macintosh). When you click the Convert to Adobe PDF and Send for Review tool (Windows), the Word document is converted to PDF, and a Send by Email for Review Wizard opens where you proceed through three steps for 1) identifying the PDF to be sent for the review, 2) inviting reviewers where you add the e-mail addresses of recipients, and 3) previewing the review invitation. When you click Finish in the wizard, your file is attached to an e-mail message window in your default e-mail program.

Changing conversion settings (Macintosh)Cross-Reference
For more information concerning e-mail reviews, see Chapter 21.

In addition to tools, two menus (Windows only) are also installed with PDFMaker. The first is the Adobe PDF menu. The second is the Acrobat Comments menu.

You have the a few menu selections in the Adobe PDF menu that provide some additional PDF conversion options. From the Adobe PDF menu shown in Figure 8-1, the two tool options for Convert to Adobe PDF and Convert to Adobe PDF and Send for Review are also listed as menu commands. Notice in the menu you have two additional PDF conversion options. Convert to Adbe PDF and Email performs the same on Windows as the tool available on the Mac.

Figure 8-1:

The Adobe PDF menu on Windows offers several options for creating PDFs from within Word.

The second additional PDF conversion option on Windows in the Adobe PDF menu is Mail Merge to PDF. To use this feature you first need to create a data file and a mail merge document.

You can create a data file easily in Microsoft Excel. Just be certain to place labels in the first row at the top of an Excel worksheet such as name, address, city, state, zip, and so on. Save the file in native .xls format.

After creating a data file and a Word template document such as a letter, from the Task pane just select Mail Merge and follow steps in a wizard to create the merge document. Word provides you an easy wizard to help you create a letter, email message, envelope, label, or directory. When the merge document is created, select Adobe PDF @@> Mail Merge to Adobe PDF and the Adobe PDF Maker - Mail Merge dialog box opens as shown in Figure 8-2.

Exporting OCR text

If you want to take your scanned text to a word processor for editing and integration with other text documents, Acrobat provides an easy way to transfer data to word processors. After scanning a document with Scan to PDF with Make Searchable (Run OCR) or after running Text Recognition Using OCR on an image file, follow these steps to export your text to Microsoft Word.

STEPS: Exporting recognized text to Microsoft Word

1. **Export text.** After recognizing text, choose File ➪ Export ➪ Word Document. Note that you can also choose Rich Text Format (RTF) if you want to import the text in another application.

2. **Save the file.** A Save As dialog box opens. Choose a target location and type a file name in the Save As dialog box. Click Save to save the file in Microsoft Word format.

3. **Launch Microsoft Word.**

4. **Open the Word file.** Click the Microsoft Office button and choose Open. Locate the saved file and open it in Word. The text is shown with formatting as you see in Figure 17.18.

 CROSS-REF For more information on exporting PDF data, see Chapter 11. For more information on working with Acrobat and Microsoft Word, see Chapter 8.

FIGURE 17.18

Exported text is shown in Microsoft Word.

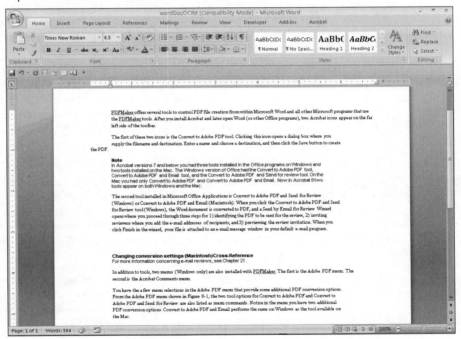

Scanning Paper Forms

If you scan paper forms that you want populated with form fields in Acrobat or Adobe LiveCycle Designer and you want to use auto field detection in Acrobat, you need to start with a form that has sufficient resolution for the form fields to be recognized by Acrobat. If the resolution and image contrast isn't sufficient for Acrobat to recognize form fields, your results will vary and you may often find very few fields created by Acrobat on low-resolution scans.

CROSS-REF For more information on auto field detection in Acrobat, see Chapter 34. For more information on creating forms in Adobe LiveCycle Designer, see Chapter 33.

Developing a workflow for scanning forms using your scanner and Acrobat requires some practice and testing. Scanners vary considerably with quality, options, and resolution choices. The first thing you need to do is run a series of tests to determine what settings are optimum for recognizing fields automatically in Acrobat. Some considerations include:

- **Resolution.** More is generally better when it comes to scanning forms. Almost all desktop scanners support two resolutions. Optical resolution is the true resolution of your scanner. You may have a 600-ppi (pixels per inch) scanner that supports an optical resolution of 600 ppi. Your scanner also supports an interpolated resolution. For the 600-ppi scanner, the interpolated resolution is likely to be 1200 ppi. A 1200-ppi optical resolution scanner often supports an interpolated resolution of 2400 ppi, and so on.

  Interpolated resolution is best suited for line art drawings. Because most office forms are black and white, your scan resolution for forms at the highest interpolated resolution (up to 1200 ppi) of your scanner usually produces the best results when it comes to recognizing form fields. In Figure 17.19 you can see three scans I created using Scan to PDF. The form on the left is a 150-ppi scan. In the middle is a 300-ppi scan and on the right is a 600-ppi scan. Although auto field detection isn't perfect, you can see that the 600-ppi scan produced more fields when the command was run in Acrobat.

NOTE The sample form used in these figures is a complex form having rows and columns of fields. Auto field detection provides you with a start in a complex form. You can expect to do some editing in Acrobat or Adobe LiveCycle Designer to polish up the fields and add fields where the auto recognition of form fields missed adding fields to the form. In much simpler forms, the auto field detection command does a superb job of automatically populating a form. See Chapter 34 for more on auto field detection.

- **Color Mode.** Black and white art is generally scanned in a line art (bitmap) color mode. However, when it comes to OCR Text Recognition and ultimately using auto field detection, the anti-aliasing of grayscale scans most often provides you with better results.

FIGURE 17.19

Three scans after selecting Forms ⇨ Add or Edit Fields and using auto field detection. On the left is a 150-ppi scan, in the middle is a 300-ppi scan, and on the right is a 600-ppi scan. The scans were performed on a scanner with an optical resolution of 600 ppi and an interpolated resolution of 1200 ppi.

- **Make Searchable (Run OCR).** When you use Scan to PDF for scanning forms on which you want to use the auto field detection, be certain to check the box for Make Searchable (Run OCR) in the Acrobat Scan dialog box. (See Figure 17.1 earlier in this chapter.) Using auto field detection produces no results if you attempt to run the command on a scan that hasn't been converted with the OCR engine.

> **TIP** Note that ClearScan works well for documents you intend to view in Acrobat. However, forms, and especially forms with check boxes, might be best scanned using Searchable Image. If ClearScan is picking up check boxes and converting the check boxes to fonts, change the PDF output style to Searchable Image.

- **Clean Up.** Ideally, you're best off using Scan to PDF and achieve optimum results using the controls in your scanner software for brightness, contrast, color mode choices, and scanning resolution. However, if your scanner software doesn't produce good results when recognizing form fields on your scans, you may be able to do a little image editing to adjust brightness and contrast. You'll need a program like Adobe Photoshop or Adobe Photoshop Elements to adjust Levels (Photoshop and Elements) and Curves (Photoshop only).

  If you do plan to do some image editing to adjust your scans' brightness and contrast, turn off Make Searchable (Run OCR) if using Scan to PDF. After editing a scan in Photoshop or Photoshop Elements, save as a Photoshop PDF file, open in Acrobat, and choose Document ⇨ OCR Text Recognition ⇨ Recognize Text Using OCR. After running the OCR engine, you can then choose Forms >> Add or Edit Fields.

If the quality of your original forms is poor and you can't adjust contrast in Photoshop or Elements sufficiently to convert text with the OCR Engine and ultimately recognize fields, you can use Photoshop or Photoshop Elements to improve image brightness. Duplicate the Background layer in the Layers palette in either program. For the layer's blending mode, change the default Normal to Multiply. Add more duplicate layers using the Multiply blending mode until you see enough brightness in areas such as text, lines, boxes, and so on. Flatten the layers and make your final adjustments in the Levels dialog box.

Plan to do a lot of testing if you need to scan many forms and populate them with form fields in Acrobat or Adobe LiveCycle Designer. Try scanning forms with different resolutions to pinpoint the resolution setting that works best for your forms. After you find the settings that work best, go about scanning the forms you need to prepare in Acrobat.

Converting a paper form to a fillable form

When scanning forms, you can use a one-button action to perform three steps in your paper form conversion to a PDF fillable form. By choosing Forms ➪ Start Form Wizard, the Create or Edit Form wizard provides a choice for creating a form from a paper form. When you make the choice, Acrobat Scan is used to scan the form, the scan is recognized using the OCR engine, and the form is automatically populated with form fields using Acrobat's ability to auto detect fields on a page.

NOTE The steps to convert a paper form can be completed in Acrobat Standard, Pro, and Pro Extended.

To convert a paper form to a fillable form, follow these steps

STEPS: Scanning a Form in Acrobat

1. **Choose Forms ➪ Start Form Wizard.** The Create or Edit Form Wizard opens as shown in Figure 17.20.

FIGURE 17.20

Select A paper form and click Next.

2. **Click A paper form.** From the radio button choices, click A paper form and click Next.

3. **Choose a preset or custom option (WIA-compliant scanners).** When you click Next in the Create or Edit Form Wizard, an Acrobat Scan dialog box opens as shown in Figure 17.21. If you have a preset already created for scanning forms, click the option (Black and White or Grayscale). If you want to adjust scan options, click Custom. In the Custom Scan dialog box make your choices for scan options.

FIGURE 17.21

Click a preset or click Custom.

If scanning using a TWAIN driver, your scanner software opens where you make your scan adjustments.

4. **Click Scan.** If you choose a preset, your scan commences and you don't need this step. If setting up a custom scan or using a TWAIN driver, click the scan button in the scanner's interface to start the scan.

5. **Edit the form.** The scan finishes and the OCR engine recognizes text. The document is then moved to Form Editing Mode where Acrobat automatically detects fields and populates the form. In many cases you may need to edit a form such as the form shown in Figure 17.22. In this form, Acrobat missed a few fields and the check box fields weren't recognized. The fields are added while you stay in Form Editing Mode.

6. **Save the form.** Preview the form by clicking the Preview button and test the fields. When all fields appear on the form, choose File ⇨ Save to save the form.

NOTE When you open a scan in Form Editing Mode, Acrobat prompts you in a dialog box to use Run Form Field Recognition. Click Yes in the Add or Edit Form Fields dialog box. Acrobat searches the document for the placement of field objects on the form.

CROSS-REF For more information on Form Editing Mode and adding fields to forms, see Chapter 34.

The scan moves to Form Editing Mode where auto field detection populates the form with field objects.

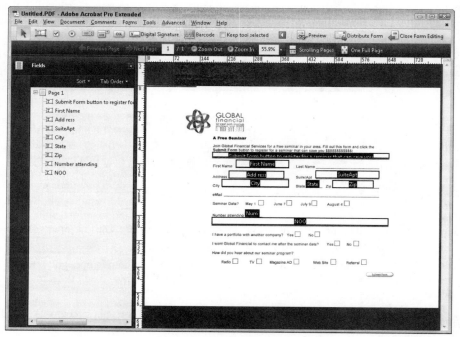

Scanning forms for Adobe LiveCycle Designer (Acrobat Pro and Pro Extended Windows only)

In earlier versions of Acrobat and LiveCycle Designer, the duties of scanning a form and auto detecting fields were the responsibility of LiveCycle Designer. In Acrobat 9, Acrobat takes control of the scanning, OCR recognition, and populating a form.

 Adobe LiveCycle Designer is available only in Acrobat Pro and Acrobat Pro Extended on Windows.

When you open the Create or Edit Form wizard the only option choice that takes you to LiveCycle Designer is No existing form. Click this radio button and click Next to open the New Form Assistant wizard shown in Figure 17.23. Notice that this wizard doesn't have a choice for scanning a paper form.

If you want to edit a form in LiveCycle Designer and use a form where you let Acrobat populate the form with fields using auto field detection, you need to scan from within Acrobat following the steps outlined earlier in the section "Scanning a form in Acrobat." Exit the Form Editing Mode after adding all the fields by clicking the Close Form Editing button shown in Figure 17.22. Save the form and choose Forms ⇨ Start Form Wizard.

In the Create or Edit Form Wizard, choose No existing form and click Next. This choice opens LiveCycle Designer and the New Form Assistant Wizard shown in Figure 17.23. Click Import a PDF Form and click Next. Add the Submit and Print buttons in the next pane and click Finish. The form with the fields added in Acrobat opens in LiveCycle Designer. From here, you can use Designer to add additional fields and modify the form.

CROSS-REF For more information on editing forms in Adobe LiveCycle Designer, see Chapter 33.

FIGURE 17.23

Click Import a PDF Document and click Next to proceed with editing a PDF form in LiveCycle Designer.

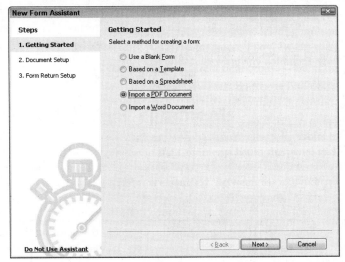

Using a digital camera in lieu of a scanner

If you have a number of forms you want to scan from paper and convert to either Acrobat PDF forms or Adobe LiveCycle Designer XML forms, you can use a good quality digital camera in lieu of a scanner. After properly setting up a camera, you can shoot a dozen paper documents or more in the same time as it takes to scan forms — and the ratio broadens when you need to scan forms at 1200 ppi or higher.

To use a digital camera, you need to consider some of the following:

- **Camera type.** You may find some point-and-shoot cameras providing you with satisfactory results, but the best results come from a DSLR (Digital Single Lens Reflex) camera and a good quality macro lens.

- **Copy stand.** For best results, either buy or create a makeshift copy stand. Outfit the stand with daylight lights and use cross lighting to avoid shadows.

- **Save as JPEG and Raw.** When running tests with your camera, save files to your camera's media card in JPEG and Camera Raw file formats. You can test the images to see if the JPEG files produce good results when running form field recognition. If you don't get the results with JPEG as you do when using Camera Raw images, you can set up some defaults in the Camera Raw converter in either Photoshop Elements or Adobe Photoshop to automate preparing Raw files for Acrobat.

- **Set up an action in Photoshop.** If you work with Adobe Photoshop, you can create an action to automate image correction and saving files to Photoshop PDF format. You can let an action run overnight if you have a huge number of files to convert to PDF forms.

- **Set up a nested batch sequence in Acrobat.** Two things need to be accomplished for preparing forms for editing in Acrobat or Adobe LiveCycle Designer. You need to Recognize Text Using OCR and Detect Form Fields. Open the Batch Sequences dialog box (Advanced ➪ Document Processing ➪ Batch Sequences) and create a new sequence. Select Recognize Text Using OCR and add it to the right pane in the Edit Sequence dialog box. Next, select Detect Form Fields in the Edit Sequence dialog box and click the Add button to add the item as a second sequence. (See Figure 17.24.)

  When you finish creating the sequence, the new sequence appears in the Batch Sequences dialog box as shown in Figure 17.25. Select the sequence and click Run Sequence. You can run the sequence on a folder of forms to convert the files with the OCR engine and add form fields to the documents. You can open the resultant files in either Acrobat or Adobe LiveCycle Designer for editing.

FIGURE 17.24

Create a batch sequence for Recognize Text Using OCR and Detect Form Fields on files you save from Photoshop or Photoshop Elements.

FIGURE 17.25

Select the sequence in the Batch Sequences dialog box and click Run Sequence.

NOTE You can use Document ➪ OCR Text Recognition ➪ Recognize Text in Multiple Files Using OCR to batch process the OCR function. However, using this command only gets you halfway. You still need to set up a batch sequence to use Detect Form Fields to populate the scanned forms.

CROSS-REF For more information on creating batch sequences, see Chapter 18.

If you have just a few forms, it makes no sense to go through the trouble of setting up a copy stand, shooting forms with a digital camera, editing the forms in Photoshop or Photoshop Elements, and creating a batch sequence. However, if you have 20, 50, or 100 or more forms to convert from paper to electronic forms, you'll find that using a digital camera can save you more time over scanning forms.

Summary

- Acrobat Scan provides choices for using presets and customizing presets with WIA-compliant scanners on Windows.

- Create PDF From Scanner on Macintosh and when using noncompliant WIA scanners uses TWAIN drivers or Adobe Photoshop Acquire plug-ins.

- Properly preparing the scanner and documents for scanning in Acrobat improves the quality of the scans. The scanner platen should be clean, the documents should be straight, and the contrast should be sharp.

- When scanning images in Acrobat, use the scanning software to establish resolution, image mode, and brightness controls before scanning. Test your results thoroughly to create a formula that works well for the type of documents you scan.

- Workflow automation can be greatly improved by purchasing Adobe's stand-alone product Adobe Acrobat Capture. When using Adobe Acrobat Capture with a scanner supporting a document feeder, the scanning and capturing can be performed with unattended operation.

- Acrobat Capture is a stand-alone application for optical character recognition used for converting scanned images into editable text.

- Acrobat 9 uses a new technology called ClearScan that replaces the Formatted Text & Graphics PDF output style used with earlier versions of Acrobat.

- Text can be converted and saved as a PDF ClearScan output style, where you can edit text and change the appearance of the original scan. Text can be converted with Optical Character Recognition and saved using the Searchable Image option, which preserves the original document appearance and adds a text layer behind the image.

- A new feature in Acrobat 9 enables you to perform OCR text recognition on multiple scanned documents saved in any format compatible with the Create PDF From File command.

- OCR suspects are marked when the OCR engine does not find an exact word match in its dictionary. Text editing is performed in the Find Element dialog box.

- To import text into Microsoft Word, use the File ⇨ Export ⇨ Word Document command in Acrobat to export to a Word file and open the exported file in Microsoft Word.

- Scanned paper forms can be populated with form fields when you enter Form Editing Mode. Acrobat automatically uses auto field detection to place field objects on a page when you enter Form Editing Mode.

- You can convert a paper form to a fillable PDF form using a single menu command in Acrobat.

- Digital cameras can be used in lieu of a scanner and can often speed up the scanning process.

Chapter 18

Repurposing and Batch Processing

PDF documents designed for one purpose, such as for commercial printing, might need to be repurposed for other output intent such as Web hosting or for copying to CD-ROMs. Rather than going back to the original authoring program and recreating PDFs for each purpose, you can use tools in Acrobat that enable you to downsample file sizes and strip unnecessary content. The resulting documents can then be more efficiently viewed on Web sites or exchanged via email.

You may have several files that need to be repurposed or edited in some other way using menu commands. Rather than open each file independently and apply menu commands, you can create batch sequences that apply commands to several files in one operation.

In this chapter, you learn how to repurpose PDF documents using some Acrobat tools and methods for downsizing file sizes and eliminating content unnecessary for other viewing purposes. In addition, you take a look at automating tasks by creating batch sequences.

Setting Up the Environment

To downsize files and optimize them for other output circumstances, you don't need to access any special tools. The menu commands offer all the means for repurposing files. Therefore, set up your Acrobat work environment by opening a context menu on the Toolbar Well and selecting Reset Toolbars from the menu options.

Reducing File Sizes

Reducing file sizes often occurs with downsampling images — that is to say, reducing the image resolution of all raster images or compressing images with higher compression options. In addition, you can reduce file sizes by eliminating redundant backgrounds; eliminating objects such as form fields, comments, Bookmarks, and destinations; unembedding fonts; and/or compressing the document structure. You can handle file-size reductions at the time of PDF creation when you control file compression, image sampling, and font embedding for PDFs designed for a specific output purpose. However, if you create PDFs for one purpose, such as commercial printing, and later want to host the same file on a Web site, you need to either create a new PDF document specifically for the new purpose, or use Acrobat tools to create smaller file sizes more suited for other output purposes. Fortunately, several means are available to you for squeezing file sizes down and optimizing PDFs for multiple purposes.

CROSS-REF For more information on understanding terms such as "downsampling" and "resampling," see Chapter 10.

Using the Reduce File Size command

All Products (Standard, Pro, Pro Extended) offer a menu command that enables you to reduce file sizes. Open a document and choose Document ⇨ Reduce File Size. The Reduce File Size dialog box opens, as shown in Figure 18.1.

FIGURE 18.1

Choose Document ⇨ Reduce File Size to open the Reduce File Size dialog box, where you select options for Acrobat version compatibility.

The Reduce File Size dialog box offers a pull-down menu with options for selecting Acrobat compatibility. The default is Retain existing, which means that the original PDF compatibility will not be changed when the file is reduced in size. If your PDF documents are to be viewed by Acrobat users of version 4 or later, choose the Acrobat 4 and later compatibility. If all users are using Acrobat 6 through 9 viewers, use Acrobat 6, 7, 8, or 9 compatibility, respectively. You might use Acrobat 4 compatibility for printing purposes because all the transparency will be flattened in Acrobat 4–compatible files.

CAUTION If you want to use many of the features available in Adobe Reader 8 and 9, such as commenting and markup and form field saving, you must use Acrobat 8 compatibility or greater. If you want to use the new features for viewing PDF Portfolios, you need to use Acrobat 9 compatibility. For more information on using Adobe Reader with usage rights enabled, see Chapter 19. For information on commenting, see Chapter 20. For more information on PDF Portfolios, see Chapter 12.

After you make the menu selection and click OK, the Save As dialog box opens. Provide a filename and save the file to disk. As a matter of practice it's a good idea to write a new file to disk in case the file reduction fails and you need to return to the original file to try another method of file reduction.

Examining documents

PDF files can contain artifacts and unnecessary elements that were either left behind from the original authoring program or that are not necessary for viewing content on the Web or screen viewing.

NEW FEATURE To determine if unnecessary elements are contained in a file, you can examine the document using the Examine Document panel. Although the Examine Document command is not new to Acrobat Pro or Pro Extended, the way the information is displayed has changed from a dialog box that was used in Acrobat 8 to a new panel in the Navigation pane in Acrobat 9 as you can see in Figure 18.2. To open the panel, choose Document ⇨ Examine Document.

FIGURE 18.2

Select Document ⇨ Examine Document to open the new Acrobat 9 Examine Document panel.

Eliminating some items can help reduce your file size. To see how items are eliminated from a PDF file, follow these steps.

STEPS: Eliminating items from a PDF file

1. **Open a PDF in Acrobat.** Try to use a file that was created with Acrobat 7 or greater compatibility and contains several high-resolution images. Check the file size by opening the Document Properties dialog box (Ctrl/⌘+D). Click the Description tab and note the file size.

2. **Examine the document.** Select Document ⇨ Examine Document to open the Examine Document panel shown in Figure 18.2.

3. **Preview the file.** Open the Options menu in the panel and choose Expand all. Items listed in the panel appear similar to bookmarks where you can expand individual items and collapse them by clicking the icon adjacent to an item name (+/- symbol on Windows or left/down-pointing arrows on the Mac).

4. **Search for hidden text.** Click Preview under the Hidden Text item to display any hidden text in your document. A dialog box opens, as shown in Figure 18.3, after clicking Show Preview. Click the Show Only Hidden Text radio button and scroll through the document by clicking on the arrow buttons. Reexamine the file by clicking Show Both Hidden and Visible Text and scroll through the pages. Showing both visible and hidden text gives you an idea for the location of any hidden text on pages.

FIGURE 18.3

Using the Preview, you can locate hidden text in a file.

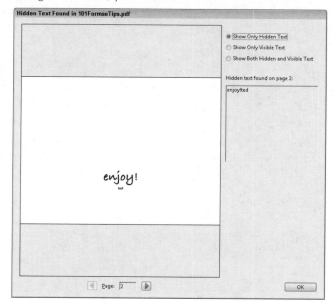

5. **Remove items.** Click OK in the Preview window and you return to the Examine Document dialog box. Click Remove to remove all the items checked in the Examine Document panel. You are prompted to confirm the action in a dialog box as shown in Figure 18.4. Click OK and the checked items are removed from the document.

FIGURE 18.4

A dialog box opens prompting you to confirm removing items.

6. **Save the file.** A progress bar is displayed as Acrobat removes the checked items. Wait until the progress finishes and choose File ➪ Save As and save the file under a new filename.

7. **Check the file size.** Press Ctrl/⌘+D to open the Document Properties dialog box. Click Description tab and check the file size. (See Figure 18.5.) You should notice a reduction in file size. The amount of the reduction depends on the elements contained in the original file and how much was eliminated. In some cases, your file size reduction may be very slight.

FIGURE 18.5

Check the file size in the Description properties.

Using PDF Optimizer (Acrobat Pro/Extended only)

Examining documents and eliminating items supported in the Examine Document dialog box might get you only a slight file reduction. A more aggressive tool is the PDF Optimizer that can significantly reduce file sizes — especially files with high-resolution images.

With PDF Optimizer you make the choices from a number of different settings in the PDF Optimizer dialog box for what data is affected during optimization. The PDF Optimizer also offers you an option for analyzing a file so you can see what part of the PDF document occupies higher percentages of memory.

For a fast look at how to use the PDF Optimizer, use the steps that follow. Later in this chapter, I'll point out the various options you have when using the PDF Optimizer.

STEPS: Using PDF Optimizer

1. **Open a PDF file in Acrobat.** Try to use the same file you used in the section "Examining documents" earlier in this chapter. If you followed the steps in that section, you should know the current file size of the document you saved in Step 7.

2. **Open the PDF Optimizer.** Select Advanced ⇨ PDF Optimizer to open the dialog box shown in Figure 18.6.

3. **Downsample images.** The PDF Optimizer has a number of different panes that offer settings for a number of different file attributes. The opening pane has options for downsampling files. Where you see Color Images and Grayscale Images you find text boxes where sampling amounts are edited. Type **72** and **108** for the sampling amounts for both sets of text boxes, as you see in Figure 18.6.

FIGURE 18.6

Downsample files to 72 ppi for all images above 108 ppi.

Click on the listed items on the left side of the dialog box, and you are offered a number of other choices for changing and removing data. For now, just use the defaults after changing the resolution amounts for color and grayscale images.

4. **Save the file.** Click OK and you are prompted to save your file. Type a new filename and click Save. The PDF Optimizer displays a progress bar as it optimizes the file.

5. **Examine the file size.** After the PDF Optimizer completes its task, open the Description properties. Press Ctrl/⌘+D and check the file size. You should see a substantial reduction in file size.

When you want to get the most out of reducing file sizes, you'll note that you can use both PDF Optimizer and Examine Document. Whether you first use one or the other method is unimportant. The final results are exactly the same file size.

> **TIP** You can also open the PDF Optimizer when saving files. Select File ⇨ Save As and choose Save as Optimized from the Save as type (Windows) or Format (Macintosh) pull-down menu when the Save As dialog box opens. Click the Settings button in the Save As dialog box and the PDF Optimizer window opens. You can choose a preset or make custom settings for the way you want to optimize your file. Click Save and the file is optimized and saved to disk. (For more on saving files, see Chapter 11.)

Auditing space usage

As a matter of practice, the first step you want to perform when optimizing files with the PDF Optimizer is to analyze a file so you can see what content occupies the larger amounts of memory. Analyzing a document and using the PDF Optimizer are handled in the PDF Optimizer dialog box, which opens when you choose Advanced ⇨ PDF Optimizer and is shown in Figure 18.6.

Click the button labeled Audit space usage. Depending on the size and complexity of the document, the analysis can take a little time. When the analysis completes, the dialog box shown in Figure 18.7 opens.

In the example shown in the preceding figure, notice that most of the document space is used for document overhead (69.95%) with Images occupying the second largest space at 23.62%. Document overhead might include items such as Named Destinations and links, while Images contains the space for image files. If the image resolution in this document is higher than images suited for screen viewing at 72 pixels per inch (ppi), then downsampling the images by reducing resolution would compact the file and make it significantly smaller. If you have documents designed for print and want to repurpose the documents for Web viewing, image downsampling is likely to be one of the things you'll want to adjust in the PDF Optimizer.

FIGURE 18.7

After the analysis is completed, the Audit Space Usage dialog box opens, where space usage according to different objects/elements is reported as a percentage of the total space.

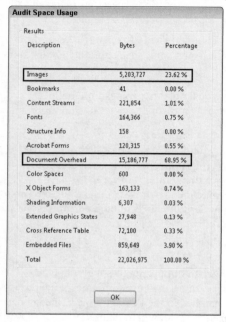

Optimizing files

Using the PDF Optimizer, you control a number of different attributes that contribute to a document's structure and content. By adjusting the number of different options found in the PDF Optimizer dialog box, you have the opportunity to produce documents much smaller than when using the Examine Document menu command. The options found in the PDF Optimizer include a Settings option, an option for changing PDF compatibility, and categories listed on the left side of the dialog box. Click on one of the items listed in the left pane and the right pane changes much like when using the Preferences dialog box. These categories include Images, Fonts, Transparency, Discard Objects, Discard User Data, and Clean Up.

Settings

This item appears first in the PDF Optimizer, but it's the last setting you address. When you open the PDF Optimizer, the default is Standard. Select Custom or make changes to any setting and the Save button becomes active. When you click Save, Acrobat prompts you to save your new settings as a preset. After saving, the name you define for the preset is added to the pull-down menu. When you return to the PDF Optimizer in another Acrobat session, you can select from the number of different presets and click OK to optimize files with the same settings defined for the respective preset.

If you want to clear a preset from the pull-down menu, select a preset in the menu and click the Delete button.

Make compatible with

From a pull-down menu you select Acrobat compatibility levels. You can make your optimized document compatible with Acrobat 4, 5, 6, 7, 8, and 9. The Retain existing menu command keeps the compatibility the same as the source file. When the need arises to serve users with earlier compatibility files, change the menu command to the desired compatibility level. By default, Retain Existing is selected in the menu. If you change from Acrobat 5 to Acrobat 6 or 7, some other attribute settings in the PDF Optimizer change to reflect choices supported by newer versions of Acrobat.

Images

To reduce file size with the PDF Optimizer, use the first set of options found in the left pane; the default Images pane appears, as shown in Figure 18.6. You can make choices for downsampling color, grayscale, and bitmap images by typing values in the field boxes for the sampling amounts desired. To the right of the downsampling amount, another field box is used to identify images that are downsampled. This box instructs Acrobat to look for any image above the setting defined in the field box and downsamples the file to the amount supplied in the first field box.

CROSS-REF The Images pane offers choices for the downsampling method. The default method is Bicubic Downsampling. Leave the choice for Bicubic Downsampling at the default selection. To learn more about the other methods and what they mean, see Chapter 10.

The Compression pull-down menu offers choices for Retain existing, JPEG, JPEG2000 (an additional setting available when Acrobat 6 through 9 compatibility is selected), and Zip compression. The Retain existing setting honors the original compression used when the PDF was created.

CROSS-REF For more information on the JPEG, JPEG2000, and Zip file formats, see Chapter 7.

For either form of JPEG compression you have additional choices for the amount of compression from the Quality pull-down menu. If you choose a JPEG compression and use Minimum for the Quality choice, your images may appear severely degraded. As a general rule, Medium quality results in satisfactory image quality for Web hosting. If you try one setting and the images look too degraded, you can return to the original file, apply a different Quality setting, and then examine the results.

Zip compression is a lossless compression scheme, which means that files are compressed without data loss. For Acrobat 4 and 5 compatibility, Zip offers a good choice when you want to maximize image quality. When using Acrobat 6 through 9 compatibility, you can select JPEG2000 for a better compression result and select Lossless from the Quality pull-down menu, which will save all the image data.

Fonts

Fonts won't always appear in a list in the Fonts pane when you click the word Fonts on the left side of the PDF Optimizer. Only fonts that are available for unembedding are listed on the left side of the Fonts pane. If no fonts appear in the list, you can move on to the Transparency settings. If fonts are listed in the box in the left side of the pane, select the fonts to unembed and click the Unembed button adjacent to the right chevron.

In the right box are fonts listed for unembedding. If you want to keep the font embedded, select it in the right box and click the Retain button adjacent to the left chevron. To select multiple fonts in either window, press Shift+click to select a list in a contiguous group, or press Ctrl/⌘+click to select fonts in a noncontiguous group.

NOTE   **By default, always choose to embed fonts in your documents unless you have some special reason for wanting to reduce the file size to a minimum and font appearances won't matter. One of the great things about PDF documents is that they retain the original design look, including font appearances, when files are exchanged among computer systems.**

Transparency

Transparent images and objects can be flattened in Acrobat 9 for all PDF documents created in Acrobat 5 and greater. If you select Acrobat 4 compatibility, transparency is automatically flattened because Acrobat 4 compatibility does not support transparency. When you select all other compatibility versions, you have options for flattening the transparency.

CROSS-REF   **For information on using transparency-flattening settings, see Chapter 32.**

Discard Objects

Discarding items such as comments, form actions, JavaScript actions, cross references, and thumbnails affects document functionality as you might suspect. If the respective items are eliminated, any PDF interactivity created with these items is also eliminated. If you know that one or any group of these items won't have an effect on the way the repurposed document is viewed or printed, enable the check boxes for the items you want to remove.

CROSS-REF   **Acrobat 8 and 9 provide a feature in the Discard Objects pane for flattening form fields. For more on using this option see "Redistilling Files" later in this chapter.**

Discard User Data

Comments, multimedia, file attachments, hidden layers, and more are listed in the Discard User Data pane. Like Discard Objects, if you choose to eliminate the items, the result can affect the way PDFs are viewed and remove some interactivity. Pick and choose these items wisely to retain the kind of interactive features you want in the resultant file.

Clean Up

Click on Clean Up in the left pane and you find a list of items checked by default that can be used safely without affecting the functionality of your document. Select the box for Remove unreferenced named destinations if the check box is not checked. Settings such as removing invalid Bookmarks, links, and destinations won't affect the document viewing, but removing the unnecessary items helps reduce file size. As a matter of practice, leave all the options in this pane checked.

After you make your preferred settings in the PDF Optimizer, click the Save button if you want to save the settings as a new preset or click OK to start the optimization process.

Redistilling Files

In each version of *Acrobat PDF Bible* dating back to version 4 of Acrobat, I've included some various reasons why you might want to export a PDF file back to PostScript and redistill the file. This is often referred to as *refrying* a PDF.

Before Acrobat 8, you might have used this method of document repurposing when you had a number of form fields for which you didn't need the field objects, but you wanted to retain the data within fields in a repurposed document. All previous versions of Acrobat couldn't perform this operation using the PDF Optimizer. In other cases, the PDF Optimizer was broken upon the first release of a new Acrobat version. In Acrobat 7, for example, I used the PDF Optimizer on a 10+MB file and the optimized file turned out a 295MB file. This wasn't fixed until the release of Acrobat 7.05. The only option I had to repurpose my document was to refry the PDF.

Acrobat 8 introduced an option in the PDF Optimizer to flatten form fields. (See Figure 18.8.) Doing so retains the form data but discards the field objects. On files with columns and rows of fields, you can produce a substantially lower file size after optimizing it and flattening the fields.

FIGURE 18.8

Acrobat 8 and 9 provide an option to flatten form fields in the PDF Optimizer.

☑ Images	Discard Objects Settings
☑ Fonts	☐ Discard all form submission, import and reset actions
☐ Transparency	☑ Flatten form fields
☑ Discard Objects	☐ Discard all JavaScript actions
☑ Discard User Data	☑ Discard all alternate images
☑ Clean Up	

I'm happy to report that the PDF Optimizer seems to be working very well in the first release of Acrobat 9. With the flatten form field option and the efficiency of the PDF Optimizer, there now appears to be very little reason to export a PDF document to PostScript and distill the PostScript in Acrobat Distiller.

 CROSS-REF **For information on creating PostScript files from PDF documents, using Acrobat Distiller, and making choices for Adobe PDF Settings, see Chapter 10.**

Obviously it's impossible to test PDF Optimizer on every kind of file. At times you may find an anomaly in a file where the PDF Optimizer just won't work. I haven't found it so far in Acrobat 9, but it is possible. Therefore, as a last-resort workaround, it may be worthwhile knowing a little about exporting to PostScript and using Acrobat Distiller to repurpose a PDF.

As a first effort in repurposing PDF files, users of Acrobat 9 Professional should try the PDF Optimizer. If the results don't satisfactorily downsize a file, you can select File ➪ Save As and choose PostScript (*.ps) for the file type. Launch Acrobat Distiller and select a PDF Setting; then open the PostScript file to distill it. Note that because Acrobat Standard doesn't offer the PDF Optimizer, this method of repurposing PDF files may be the only option you have.

TIP If you have interactive elements in a document such as Bookmarks, form fields, destinations, and so on and want to preserve the interactive elements when redistilling PDFs, realize that all such items are lost in the new file created with Acrobat Distiller. To regain Bookmarks, form fields, and so on, open the original file in Acrobat. Choose Document ➪ Replace Pages. Locate the new file created with Acrobat Distiller in the Select File With New Pages dialog box and replace all pages in the file. Choose File ➪ Save As to write a new optimized file to disk. The new file uses the optimized pages and the old file's interactive elements. You'll see a little increase in the file size because of the interactive elements, but the overall file size will be much smaller in your new file compared to the original file.

Batch Processing PDF Files

If you have multiple files that need to be refined for distribution on network servers, Web sites, or CD-ROM, then you'll want to create a batch sequence. *Batch sequences* are a defined series of commands in a specific order that can be run on multiple files. You create the batch sequence from a list of executable functions and determine the commands and order of the sequence.

Batch sequences help you automate tasks in Acrobat that might otherwise take considerable time, such as manually applying a common set of commands on many different files. After you develop one or more sequences, you can run the sequence(s) on selected PDF files, a folder of PDF files, or multiple folders of PDF files.

Tasks such as setting opening views of PDF documents, adding document descriptions, adding page numbers, or running the PDF Optimizer can be applied to multiple files you might want to distribute on CD-ROM or on Web sites. Before distributing files, you can run a batch sequence as a final step in your production workflow to be sure all files have common attributes.

Knowing Acrobat 9 changes in preset sequences

When you create a batch sequence, you use a predefined set of sequences or Run a JavaScript to add a custom sequence. For more information on creating a batch sequence using a predefined sequence, see the section "Creating a batch sequence" later in this chapter.

NEW FEATURE Acrobat 9 has added several new predefined sequences for batch processing, and you'll also find a few items that were eliminated from the Edit Sequence dialog box. The additions to the Edit Sequence dialog box in Acrobat 9 include:

- **Apply Redaction Marks.** If you mark multiple files for redaction, you can batch process applying the redactions to multiple files.

CROSS-REF For more information on redacting documents, see Chapter 14.

- **Examine Document.** You can choose individual items for removal when batch processing/examining a document. For example, you can check items such as removing hidden text, hidden layers, and file attachments while leaving other items unaffected in the Examine Document dialog box you open when defining the sequence.

CROSS-REF For more information on examining documents, see the section "Examining Documents" earlier in this chapter.

- **Import as Layer.** The new Acrobat 9 feature for importing layers can also be processed on multiple files. You may have a watermark or image that you want to import as a layer and add the same layer to multiple files.

CROSS-REF For more information on working with layers, see Chapter 24.

- **Optimize Scanned PDF.** You can choose from several options for optimizing scanned documents such as file sample size, edge shadow removal, and other items specific to scanned PDF files and apply the changes to multiple files.

CROSS-REF For more information on scanning to PDF, see Chapter 17.

- **Search and Redact.** If you want to search for data in documents that haven't been marked for redaction, use this batch sequence preset.
- **Split Document.** You can split a single PDF document into multiple documents according to top-level bookmarks, file size, or number of pages. You can apply the Split Document command to multiple files using this sequence.

CROSS-REF For more information on using Split Document, see Chapter 16.

In addition to using batch sequences for removal of Backgrounds, Headers & Footers, and Watermarks the Acrobat 9 user interface supports running batch processing for these options.

CROSS-REF For more information on batch processing the removal of Headers & Footers, Backgrounds, and Watermarks, see "Running UI batch sequences" later in this chapter.

Creating a batch sequence

To create a new sequence, choose Advanced ➪ Document Processing ➪ Batch Processing. The Batch Sequences dialog box opens, as shown in Figure 18.9. The dialog box lists several sequences that are predefined for you when you install Acrobat. From the list in the dialog box, you can run a sequence, edit one of the listed sequences, rename a sequence, or delete any one or more sequences from the list. The first button in the dialog box is used to create a new sequence where you choose what commands you want to run from a list in other dialog boxes.

FIGURE 18.9

Choose Advanced ➪ Document Processing ➪ Batch Processing to open the Batch Sequences dialog box.

Click New Sequence and the Name Sequence dialog box shown in Figure 18.10 opens. The first step in creating a batch sequence is to provide a name for the sequence. The name supplied in the dialog box ultimately is added to the list in the Batch Sequence window. When you want to run the sequence you can open the Batch Sequences dialog box, select any one of the sequences you added to the list, and click the Run Sequence button.

FIGURE 18.10

The first step in creating a new sequence is naming the sequence. You add the names of new sequences to the list in the Batch Sequences dialog box.

Type a name in the field box and click OK. The next dialog box that opens is the Edit Batch Sequence – Initial View dialog box shown in Figure 18.11. Three items are listed in the dialog box. The next step (the Batch Sequence dialog box actually lists this step as the first step in creating a sequence) is to click the Select Commands button. After you make choices for the commands added to the sequence, you are returned to this dialog box to make choices for items 2 and 3 where you identify the input location of files and the destination (output) location.

FIGURE 18.11

The Edit Batch Sequence – Initial View dialog box opens after you provide a name such as *Initial View* for a new sequence. Click the Select Commands button to choose the commands executed in the sequence.

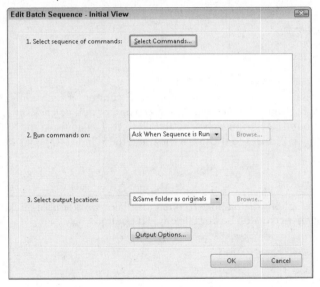

The Edit Sequence dialog box opens for you to make choices for the commands added to your new sequence. From the scrollable list on the left side of the dialog box, select a command and click the Add button to move the command to the right side of the dialog box. If you want more than one set of commands applied to your sequence, select a command and click the Add button; then select additional commands and click Add. In this example, I added a command for setting the Initial View by adding the Open Options item in the Document list. Click the icon adjacent to the sequence command and the options are displayed, as you see in Figure 18.12.

FIGURE 18.12

Select a command in the left window and click the Add button. Click the icon adjacent to the command name and a list expands displaying the options.

After the commands are added to the right window, you can make attribute choices for each command. From those commands in the right window, either select the command or double-click on the name to open dialog boxes where you make attribute choices. In Figure 18.13 I adjusted the Set Open Options dialog box where I made changes to the Initial View and the Window Options.

FIGURE 18.13

Initial View options are selected in the Set Open Options dialog box. To open the dialog box, double-click the command in the right window in the Edit Sequence dialog box or click the Edit button.

The settings applied for the Initial View are applied globally to files when you run the sequence. You can run the sequence on a folder of files if you want the files to share common attributes.

To finish creating your sequence, click OK and click OK again in the Edit Sequence dialog box. Your new sequence is added to the Batch Sequences dialog box that opened first when you selected Batch Sequences from the Advanced > Document Processing menu.

Setting output options

When you click the Output Options button in the Edit Batch Sequence dialog box, you'll find choices for file naming and output formats as well as file optimization. Select the Output Options check box when you create a new sequence in the Edit Batch Sequence dialog box and the Output Options dialog box opens, as shown in Figure 18.14.

You can add a suffix or prefix to filenames by clicking the Add To Original Base Name(s) button and editing the field boxes for Insert Before and Insert After. If you enter data in the Insert After field box the data is added before the filename extension. Select the box for Do not overwrite existing files to ensure that you won't inadvertently overwrite the original files.

FIGURE 18.14

Output Options offer you choices for naming the processed files as well as saving in different formats and optimizing files with the PDF Optimizer.

The Save File(s) As pull-down menu offers choices for the file formats to be exported. The default is Adobe PDF. If you want to save files in text formats (Word, RTF, XML, text only, and so on), you can make the choice for the text format from the pull-down menu options. Additionally, PostScript, EPS, image formats, HTML, and XML formats are available. One great feature introduced in Acrobat 8 and available in Acrobat 9 is the option for saving PDF documents compatible with specifications such as PDF/A, PDF/X, and PDF/E. Choose one of these formats and you can convert a collection of PDFs to a PDF/A, PDF/X, or PDF/E standard.

CROSS-REF For more information on the PDF/A, PDF/X, and PDF/E standards, see Chapter 10.

You'll note that the Save As options in the Output Format Save File(s) pull-down menu offers the same options as when you choose the File ➪ Save As command.

Running sequences

Presuming you created a sequence and added the new sequence, you can open the Batch Sequence dialog box by choosing Advanced ➪ Document Processing > Batch Processing and selecting the sequence you want to run. Click the Run Sequence button in the Batch Sequence dialog box and the Run Sequence Confirmation dialog box opens, as shown in Figure 18.15.

A list of commands appears in the dialog box where you can review the settings for each command by clicking the icon adjacent to the sequence commands to display the settings as discussed earlier in this chapter. If all the settings are appropriate for the sequence you want to run, click OK and the Select Files to Process dialog box opens. You can select a file or a contiguous or noncontiguous group of files by using Shift+click or Ctrl/⌘+Shift and click a folder or a group of folders for processing. Click the Select button, and the sequence runs. If you created a sequence to toggle open a dialog box for supplying unique data for each file, the dialog boxes open. Make changes in any dialog boxes, click the OK buttons, and the sequence continues. Files are saved according to the choices you made in the Output Options dialog box or the choice made from the Select output location pull-down menu in the Edit Batch Sequence dialog box.

After running a sequence, examine the files to ensure all files are created with the options you expect them to have. If there are any errors and you saved the new set of files without overwriting the original set, you can edit the sequence and run the edited version on the original files.

Running UI batch sequences

Running batch sequences in the Batch Sequence dialog box is something you might consider *outside* the user interface (UI) that runs via an Acrobat plug-in. You execute these sequences in a controlled environment where all the sequences and batch commands are nested into a single interface.

NEW FEATURE New in Acrobat 9 is an extension of batch sequences that are coded as part of the Acrobat user interface. They're hard coded and don't require you to set up options for executing batch operations from within the Batch Sequence dialog box.

FIGURE 18.15

Click Run Sequence in the Batch Sequences dialog box and the Run Sequence Confirmation dialog box opens. Click the icon adjacent to the command name to open a list of the settings.

At first glance you may not see the new batch operations in Acrobat 9. They may be a little obscure since they're included as new menu commands or appear when you click new buttons in dialog boxes. Following is a list of the new batch operations you find in Acrobat 9:

Recognize Text in Multiple documents. Choose Document ⇨ OCR Text Recognition ⇨ Recognize Text in Multiple Files Using OCR. Choosing the menu item opens the Paper Capture Multiple Files wizard. The wizard is similar in appearance to the Combine Files wizard where you choose files to add to a list by selecting options in the Add files pull-down menu. Choices you have for adding files to the list include Add Files where you select individual files in an Open dialog box, Add Folders for adding folders of files, and Add Open files for running Acrobat's OCR on files open in the Document pane.

After adding files to a list, click the OK button and the Output Options dialog box opens as shown in Figure 18.16. As you can see in Figure 18.16 a number of options are available for choosing target locations for saved files, file naming conventions, running the PDF Optimizer, and various output formats.

PDF Creation. Choose File ⇨ Create PDF ⇨ Batch Create Multiple Files to open the Batch Create Multiple Files wizard. You have choices for adding files or folders from the Add Files pull-down menu. This new command in Acrobat 9 differs from the Merge Files into a Single PDF. Instead of merging files into one PDF document, the Batch Create Multiple Files command converts documents to PDF as individual single files. After adding files to a list and clicking the OK button, the Output Options dialog box opens where you can make some choices for saving files to a target location and specify various file naming conventions. Note that the file export options are the same as those found in the File ⇨ Export submenu and the batch routine described in the next bullet point.

FIGURE 18.16

After adding files to a list, click OK to open the Output Options dialog box.

Export files. Choose File ⇨ Export Multiple Files. This command opens the Export Multiple Files dialog box. Add files to a list and click OK to open the Output Options dialog box. You have similar choices for target location and file naming as found in other batch operations. The file formats that are supported are the same as those found in the previous bullet point for PDF Creation.

Headers & Footers/Backgrounds/Watermarks. These processing are available in Batch Sequences Edit Sequence dialog box. They are now also included in the dialog boxes you use for adding Headers & Footers, Backgrounds, and Watermarks.

You can add page numbers (or add headers, footers, apply backgrounds, or watermarks) to multiple files of your choice. Choose one of the three Document menu commands (Header & Footer, Background, or Watermark) and the Add submenu command (for example Document ⇨ Header & Footer ⇨ Add) to open the Add Header & Footer (or Background or Watermark) dialog box. The new Apply to Multiple button in the lower right corner of the dialog boxes enables you to batch process multiple files with the respective task.

Split Documents. This feature is one I've asked of the Adobe development team for quite some time. With the selection of a single menu command you can divide a long document into smaller parts. Choose Document ➪ Split Document to open the Split Document dialog box. At the bottom of the dialog box you find the Apply to Multiple button where you can process a number of files.

CROSS-REF For more information on using the Split Document command, see Chapter 16.

Reduce File Size. Although using the PDF Optimizer is the better choice for repurposing files as I explain in this chapter, you can choose the Reduce File Size command and process multiple files when you need a quick reduction of file sizes for multiple files you intend to host on Web sites. Choose Document >> Reduce File Size and you find the Apply to Multiple button in the Reduce File Size dialog box.

CROSS-REF For more on Reduce File Size, see the section "Reducing File Sizes" earlier in this chapter.

Redaction. Redaction was a marvelous addition in Acrobat 8 for the legal and government industries and any other industry where eliminating sensitive information from documents was needed. In the Redaction toolbar click the Search and Redact button to open the Search pane. Similar to search options you have with Acrobat Search as I covered in Chapter 6, you can choose folders and drives to search and apply redactions to multiple files.

CROSS-REF For more information on Redaction and applying redactions to multiple files, see Chapter 14.

Editing sequences

If you create a sequence for one purpose and want to modify the sequence for another processing venture, you can edit the attributes of a command, add new commands, or delete commands from the original sequence. To edit a sequence, choose Advanced ➪ Document Processing ➪ Batch Processing. In the Batch Sequences dialog box, select the sequence you want to edit and click the Edit Sequence button. The Edit Batch Sequences dialog box opens.

In order to edit the commands, add new commands, or delete commands, you first need to click the Select Commands button. The Edit Sequence dialog box opens where you can add new commands or edit existing commands by following the information in the earlier section on creating sequences.

If you want to delete a sequence and all the commands associated with the sequence, click the Delete Sequence button in the Batch Sequences dialog box. This action removes the sequence from the list. If you delete commands in the Edit Sequence dialog box and keep a modified version of a sequence listed in the Batch Sequences dialog box, you may want to rename a sequence to more closely relate to the modified version. Click the Rename Sequence button in the Batch Sequence dialog box and edit the name in the Name Sequence dialog box.

Creating custom sequences

The batch sequences you create are chosen from the list of commands in the Edit Sequence dialog box. If you want to add a command that doesn't exist in the list in the Edit Sequence dialog box, you can create custom sequences from commands you add with JavaScript.

JavaScript offers you an infinite number of possibilities for automating commands and sequences applied to a group of PDF documents. As an example, suppose you want to add a Stamp comment to an assorted collection of PDFs designed to be documents in draft form. After the files have been stamped with a Draft icon from the Stamp comment, you disperse the documents, collect feedback, and use another batch sequence to delete all comments from the documents. The sequence for deleting comments is a preset installed with Acrobat. Adding Stamp comments, however, is something you need to do with a JavaScript. Use the steps that follow to add a JavaScript to a batch sequence, and in particular, to add a Stamp comment to a collection of PDF files.

STEPS: Creating a JavaScript batch sequence

1. **Create a new batch sequence.** Choose Advanced ➪ Document Processing ➪ Batch Processing. In the Batch Sequences dialog box, select New Sequence. When the Name Sequence dialog box opens, type a name for the sequence. In this example I use Add Stamp. Click OK.

2. **Select Execute JavaScript and add it to the list of sequences to be executed.** In the Edit Batch Sequence dialog box, click Select Commands to open the Edit Sequence dialog box. In the Edit Sequence dialog box, select Execute JavaScript from the list on the left and click the Add button to move the command to the right window.

3. **Add the JavaScript code to execute the action.** Select the command in the right pane and click the Edit button (or double-click on the command). The JavaScript Editor dialog box opens. In the JavaScript Editor, type the following code. (The same code is shown as it should appear in the JavaScript Editor in Figure 18.17.)

> **NOTE**   Line numbers in the code below are for reference only. Do not type the numbers in the JavaScript Editor.

```
1.  // adds a stamp to the first page //
2.  var annot = this.addAnnot ({
3.  page:0,
4.  type: "Stamp",
5.  name: "Draft",
6.  rect: [400, 700, 600, 790],
7.  popupOpen: false,
8.  author: "Ted",
9.  contents: "First Review",
10. });
```

FIGURE 18.17

Type the code in the JavaScript Editor dialog box.

```
JavaScript Editor

Create and Edit JavaScripts

// adds a stamp to the first page //
var annot = this.addAnnot ({
    page:0,
    type: "Stamp",
    name: "Draft",
    rect: [400, 700, 600, 790],
    popupOpen: false,
    author: "Ted",
    contents: "First Review",
});



                                        Ln 1, Col 33

        OK        Cancel        Go to...
```

NOTE　The coordinates for the position of the note are set for a standard US Letter size page (8.5 × 11 inches, portrait view). If you run the sequence on documents with different size pages or orientation, the results may not show the stamp on a page.

4. **Save the JavaScript.** Click OK in the JavaScript Editor dialog box. Click OK in the Edit Sequence dialog box to return to the Edit Batch Sequence dialog box. The script is saved when you exit the JavaScript Editor dialog box.

5. **Set the Output Options.** Leave Run commands on at the default for Ask When Sequence is Run. In the Select output location pull-down menu, select the option you want to use for the saved files location. If you want to be prompted at the time the sequence is run, select Ask When Sequence is Run. Click OK in the Edit Batch Sequence dialog box and the sequence is added to the list of Batch Sequences.

6. **Run the sequence.** Select the Add Stamp sequence in the Batch Sequences dialog box and click Run Sequence. (If you closed the Batch Sequences dialog box after the last step, choose Advanced ➪ Document Processing ➪ Batch Processing to reopen the dialog box.)

7. **Examine the results.** Select a single file to process when the Select Files to Process dialog box opens. You should see a Stamp comment in the top right corner of the document page. Double-click the Stamp icon to open the pop-up note window; the note contents are shown in Figure 18.18.

FIGURE 18.18

The Stamp comment is added to the first page of all documents processed with the Add Stamp routine created in the JavaScript Editor.

TIP To find coordinates to add to the script above, drag a rectangle with the Rectangle comment tool where you want your comment annotation to appear. Open the JavaScript Debugger (Ctrl/Cmd+J) and type the following code in the Debugger window:

```
this.getAnnots()[0].rect;
```

With the cursor placed on the line of code, press the Num Pad Enter key. The Debugger window reports the x,y coordinates at the four corners of the rectangle.

CROSS-REF For more information on creating stamps and using pop-up note windows, see Chapter 20.

The preceding steps create a Stamp comment (from the Stamp comment you last used in Acrobat) (Line 2) at the coordinates (Line 6) — note that the page size where the stamps are added is a standard US Letter 8.5 × 11 inches in portrait view. The note pop-up window is closed by default (Line 7), and the content of the note pop-up is *First Review* (Line 9). You can change the position of the note by editing the coordinates in Line 6, change the contents in Line 9, or change the stamp type in Line 4. The code can be easily modified or you can copy and paste the code in the JavaScript Editor if you want to create other similar sequences.

CROSS-REF For more information on writing JavaScripts, see Chapter 36.

Cropping Pages

Another method for reducing file sizes is using the Crop tool in Acrobat to trim page sizes when you need to have data outside crop boxes eliminated from PDF pages. You might have a spread with facing pages and want only the left or right page remain in a file or you might capture a Web page and want to retain only a small portion of the captured page in a final document.

CROSS-REF For more information on capturing Web pages, see Chapter 7.

In previous versions of Acrobat, cropping pages eliminated areas outside a crop box when viewing a cropped page in an Acrobat viewer, but the data outside the crop region remained with the file. You didn't experience any reduction in file size because the data was still there and you could easily re-crop the pages to regain the original data.

In Acrobat 9 we have methods for cropping pages in Acrobat and eliminating all data outside the crop area. I saved this section for last in this chapter because we need to use Examine Document as I covered earlier in the section "Examining Documents" and creating batch sequences as I covered earlier in the section "Batch Processing PDF Files."

Using the Crop tool

To crop a page in Acrobat, open the Advanced Editing toolbar and click the Crop tool. When the Crop tool is selected, you can click + drag to define a crop region or double-click the cursor to open the Crop Pages dialog box where you can define the crop box size.

In Figure 18.19 I dragged the Crop tool around the left page in a two-page spread.

FIGURE 18.19

Drag the Crop tool in the area you want to crop the page.

Once the crop box is defined on a page, double-click the cursor inside the crop box and the Crop Pages dialog box opens as shown in Figure 18.20. The preview in the Crop Pages dialog box shows you the entire layout however the Cropped page size text below the preview shows you the new page size that will result when you click OK in the Crop Pages dialog box.

FIGURE 18.20

Double-click the cursor inside the crop box and the Crop Pages dialog box opens.

Click OK in the Crop Pages dialog box and you return to the Document pane viewing the page cropped as you defined the crop region. However, at this point, you haven't permanently removed data from your document.

You can eliminate some data outside the crop area by using the Examine Document command. When you choose Document ➪ Examine Document and remove the selected items in the Examine Document panel, you remove content outside the crop area but the original page size does not change. In Figure 18.21, I chose Document ➪ Examine Document and the Examine Document panel reported information that could be removed from my file.

After clicking Remove in the Examine Document panel, you might think all data are removed outside the crop area. To see what data were removed outside the crop area, click the Crop tool in the Advanced Editing toolbar and double-click on the page. Again the Crop Pages dialog box opens and you can see what still remains in the file by looking over the thumbnail preview as shown in Figure 18.22.

To completely eliminate data outside the crop region, you need a little help from Acrobat's Preflight tool.

FIGURE 18.21

Choose Document⇨Examine Document to analyze the document for items that can be removed.

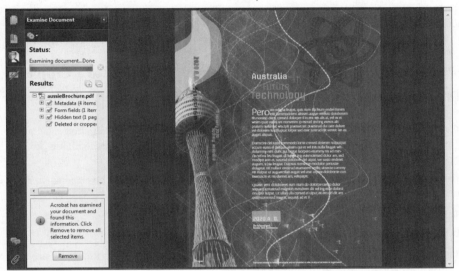

FIGURE 18.22

Click the Crop tool in the Advanced Editing toolbar and double-click the page. The Crop Pages thumbnail preview shows you the page size and data remaining in the document.

Creating a Preflight profile

Using the Preflight tool, you can permanently delete all data outside a crop region and trim the page to the crop area. If you plan to regularly crop pages, you'll want to create a custom profile that you can easily access to crop pages routinely.

In Acrobat terms, the crop area is known as the Crop Box and the page size is known as the Media Box. Our task at hand is to reduce the size of the Media Box (the page size) to the Crop Box (the area defined when using the Crop tool). To reduce the Media Box to the size of the Crop Box, do the following:

STEPS: Creating a Preflight profile to trim a Media Box to a Crop Box

1. **Open the Preflight window.** Choose Advanced ⇨ Preflight and the Preflight window opens.

2. **Create a new Preflight profile.** Click the Options pull-down menu and choose Create New Preflight Profile from the menu commands. The Preflight Edit Profile dialog box opens.

3. **Define the Profile attributes.** When the Preflight: Edit Profile dialog box opens, you need to make several options choices (see Figure 18.23):

   a. **Type a name for the profile.**

   b. **Choose Fixups from the hierarchical list in your new profile.**

   c. **Choose Remove page objects which are completely outside of trim area.** Scroll the list until you find this item and select it.

   d. **Add the fixup item to your profile.** With the fixup item selected in the right pane, click the left arrow to add the fixup to your profile.

   e. **Be certain the fixup is added to the profile.** You should see the item added to the middle column as shown in Figure 18.23. Leave the dialog box open to continue with the steps that follow.

FIGURE 18.23

Set the attributes for your new profile in the Preflight: Edit Profile dialog box.

4. **Edit the Fixup.** Double-click the fixup (item 5 in Figure 18.23) to open the Preflight: Edit Fixup dialog box shown in Figure 18.24. Several edits need to be made in this dialog box that include:

    a. **Choose Pages in the Fixup category.**

    b. **Choose Set page geometry boxes in the Type of fixup list.** Scroll the list and select this item.

    c. **Choose a Source.** Open the Source pull-down menu and choose MediaBox.

    d. **Choose a Destination.** Open the Destination pull-down menu and choose Relative to CropBox.

    e. **Click OK.**

FIGURE 18.24

Set the Edit Fixup attributes.

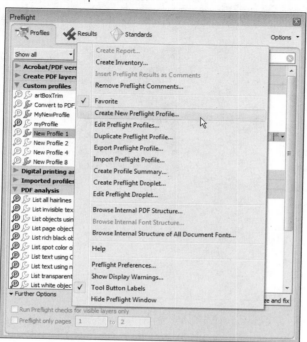

At this point your profile is available for use. To eliminate all data outside a crop box and to reduce the page size to the size of a crop box, you would open a document in Acrobat and crop a page(s). Use the Document ➪ Examine Document command and Remove all items listed in the Examine Document panel. Then choose Advanced ➪ Preflight to open the Preflight window. Click your profile and click Analyze and fix as shown in Figure 18.25.

Trimming media boxes with a batch sequence

You can automate the process for cropping pages and setting the media box size to the crop box size by using a batch sequence. To begin with, you might use the Crop tool to crop pages in a number of PDF documents and save the files.

FIGURE 18.25

After cropping and examining a page, choose Advanced ⇨ Preflight to open the Preflight window. Click your new preflight profile and click Analyze and fix.

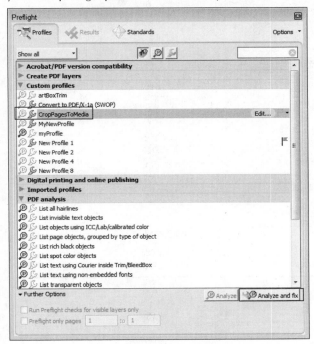

Open the Batch Sequences dialog box and create a new sequence as described earlier in this chapter in the section "Batch Processing PDF Files." In the Edit Sequence dialog box, add the Examine Document and Preflight items listed in the left pane to the right pane as shown in Figure 18.26.

Double-click the Preflight item in the right pane to open the Preflight: Batch Sequence Setup dialog box. Scroll the list to find the sequence you created to trim the media box and select it as shown in Figure 18.27. Click OK and save your sequence. When you run the sequence on files that have been cropped, the pages will be trimmed to the crop box sizes.

FIGURE 18.26

Add Examine Document and Preflight to a new sequence.

FIGURE 18.27

Select your profile and click OK.

Summary

- File sizes can be reduced with the Reduce File Size menu command. If you're cropping image files in Acrobat, save the cropped image to an image format, and then open the file in Acrobat to convert back to PDF.

- Examine Document offers some options for deleting content from files to help reduce file size.

- The PDF Optimizer (Acrobat Pro and Pro Extended only) is used to reduce file sizes and eliminate unnecessary data in PDF files. PDF Optimizer can often reduce file sizes more than when using the Reduce File Size command.

- Selecting options in the Discard Objects pane in the PDF Optimizer other than the default options can interfere with the PDF functionality. Care must be exercised in selecting options to prevent potential problems.

- The Flatten form fields option in the Discard Objects pane discards field objects while retaining data for optimizing forms when the fields are no longer needed.

- In some cases, saving a PDF file to disk and redistilling with Acrobat Distiller can reduce file sizes. Redistillation can be used with Acrobat Standard where no PDF Optimizer is available.

- Several new batch processing features have been added to menu commands in Acrobat 9, and new sequences have been added to the Edit Sequence dialog box.

- Batch sequences help you automate processing multiple PDF documents. From a standard set of sequence options you can create batch sequences for a limited number of actions. When custom options are needed, you can add JavaScripts for processing files with custom settings.

- You can eliminate data outside a crop box and reduce page sizes using the Preflight tool.

Chapter 19

Enabling Features for Adobe Reader

nabling features for Adobe Reader or adding special features for Reader users is a means whereby certain features not appearing in the default Adobe Reader program can be added to PDF documents. This enabling function can be handled by one of two applications. You can use a server product such as the Adobe LiveCycle Reader® Extensions ES or Adobe Acrobat 9 Standard, Pro, and Pro Extended.

In Acrobat 7, a single enabling feature was introduced that added these special features to permit Adobe Reader users participation in email–based reviews. When a PDF document was enabled for commenting and markup, all the comment tools appeared in Adobe Reader, they were usable, and the comments could be saved using Reader.

In Acrobat 8, Adobe introduced more enabling features such as those for saving form data and adding digital signatures. These options are not part of Adobe Reader. But when opening an enabled file in Reader, you can take advantage of the special features for saving form data and adding digital signatures.

In Acrobat 9, Adobe has broadened the enabling features to include the Acrobat Standard users (Windows only).

IN THIS CHAPTER

Using server products

Understanding licensing restrictions

Adding special features for Adobe Reader

Editing files enabled with usage rights

Setting Up the Enabling Work Environment

Enabling PDF files with Reader extensions is handled through menu commands. No special tool-bars need to be loaded to enable PDF files. Return to the default view by opening a context menu and selecting Reset Toolbars.

Adobe LiveCycle Reader® Extensions ES To get a grasp on enabling PDF files and to better understand what limitations you have for adding special features to PDFs, you should know a little something about Adobe's server product used for adding special features. The Adobe LiveCycle Reader® Extensions ES is a server product sold to enterprises and large organizations. The cost of the product is prohibitive for individual users and small companies not having industrial strength needs.

At first blush you might think the cost is extraordinary. But stop for a moment and think about an organization like the US Internal Revenue Service (IRS) that uses LCRE. The IRS processes millions of forms annually for income tax reporting. In an analog world where the IRS needs to print millions of tax forms and distribute them worldwide, the costs per form rise well above a more affordable solution such as the LiveCycle Reader Extensions Server.

You and I as individual users of Acrobat are not likely to purchase LCRE, but we may have an occasional need to work with forms that need to be enabled for Adobe Reader users. This being the case, Adobe recognized the gap between independent PDF authors and workers within small workgroups versus IT managers enabling forms for mass distribution. Hence, the enabling features have been enriched in Acrobat 9 Standard, Pro, and Pro Extended.

Restrictions for Enabling Features

As logic would have it, you're no doubt thinking there must be some restriction or limitation on enabling PDF files in Acrobat. After all, how could Adobe hope to sell one product that starts at $30,000 when a user could find the same thing purchasing a copy of Acrobat?

There are indeed limitations and they are all spelled out in the End User License Agreement (EULA) you agree to when installing Acrobat. Just in case you are confused about language in the agreement after reading it, let me paraphrase the licensing agreement and amplify some of the conditions. In addition to what is covered in this chapter, you should carefully read the agreement and understand the limitations of use.

Audience

Prior to Acrobat 8 there was no opportunity for users to enable features in PDF files that permit Adobe Reader users the ability to fill in form data, save the data, and digitally sign documents. Adobe recognized a clear distinction between users who have occasional and limited needs versus enterprises that distribute PDF forms to many thousands of people.

Small to medium businesses might have needs for people to fill out small batches of forms for travel expense claims, purchase orders, personal time off forms, and so on. Some of the data such as data compiled from expense forms might need to be exported to an Excel spreadsheet and integrated into an accounting program.

You might also have an annual charity golf tournament with a few hundred participants, a small annual conference with fewer than 300 registrants, or a similar need to distribute forms and collect data.

These kinds of examples fit within Adobe's EULA and target audience. On the other hand, if you have a commercial Web site and you're collecting PDF forms for point of sale purchases where the numbers of potential customers may be in the thousands, then this kind of use for your PDF-enabled forms is a clear violation of the licensing agreement.

Licensing restrictions

The language in the EULA suggests that you can enable PDF forms with forms saving for Adobe Reader users for up to 500 instances of a given document. The document usage can be one of two ways. You can distribute an unlimited number of enabled forms, but you can only aggregate up to 500 forms — something like hosting a form on your Web site where you might get less than 500 registrants for a conference. The other instance is distributing forms to 500 named individuals, and you can aggregate any number of those forms — something like expense accounts that people fill out and return monthly.

 For an up-to-date description of the Acrobat EULA or any other Adobe product, visit www.adobe.com/products/eulas. On the opening Web page you'll find links to Acrobat and other Adobe products specifying the conditions of the license agreements.

Enforcing the restrictions

Adobe uses no special coding or technology to ensure users are complying with the licensing agreement. Adobe believes that the enforcement for restricting users to the limitations is vested in the amount of work people need to perform. For limited use, the enabling features in Acrobat 9 serve a need for many PDF authors. However, the kind of use an LCRE user needs to process volumes of forms, such as parsing data and routing data to databases, is something to be found only in the server products from Adobe.

There remains a clear distinction between industrial strength use and limited use, not only in the licensing agreement but also in practicality. The enabling features do not diminish the need for the Adobe LiveCycle Reader® Extensions ES. Quite the contrary: Workgroups that begin to work more with enabling PDFs with Reader extensions are likely to experience needs for evolving to more sophisticated uses that can only be satisfied using LCRE.

Enabling PDF Documents with Reader Extensions

In Acrobat 9 Pro, and Pro Extended you can enable PDFs with special usage rights for adding comments and markups and save the comments once added in Adobe Reader. You can enable PDF forms using Standard, Pro, and Pro Extended, adding features for Adobe Reader users, permitting the Reader user to save form data and add digital signatures.

PDF files can be enabled for Comment & Markup, Digital Signatures, Digital Signature Tool (Acrobat 8 and higher) and Forms Fill/Save. How you go about enabling files from Acrobat is handled through menu commands. You choose from one of five menu commands for adding special features to PDF documents for Adobe Reader users.

Enabling PDFs for Commenting (Acrobat 9 Pro, Acrobat 9 Pro Extended)

The first of the five menu commands you can use to enable PDF files for Adobe Reader users is Comments ➪ Enable for Commenting and Analysis in Adobe Reader. The first time you select this command an application alert dialog box opens informing you that certain editing functions normally available to Acrobat users will be restricted. If you check the Don't show again check box as shown in Figure 19.1, the dialog box won't appear when enabling future documents.

FIGURE 19.1

The first time you enable a file for commenting in Adobe Reader an application alert dialog box opens.

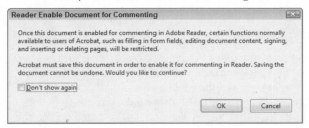

Click OK in the application alert dialog box and a Save As dialog box opens. Type a new name for your file to avoid overwriting the original and click the Save button. The PDF is now enabled with Adobe Reader usage rights for commenting and markup.

When an Adobe Reader user opens the enabled PDF document, the Comment & Markup tools are all accessible, as shown in Figure 19.2. You can add the same kind of comments as you can with either Acrobat Standard or Acrobat Pro, or Pro Extended. After adding comments, the Reader user also has access to a File ➪ Save command. This command is not available unless a file has been enabled. Selecting File ➪ Save permits the Reader user the opportunity to save all comments added to the PDF.

FIGURE 19.2

Adobe Reader users can add and save all comments and markups on PDF files enabled for commenting.

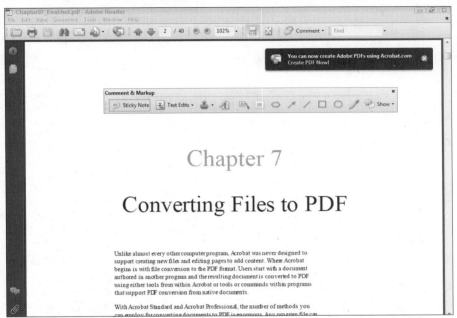

CROSS-REF For more information on limitations of Adobe Reader, see Chapter 4. For more information on comment and markup, see Chapter 20.

Enabling PDFs for Comment & Review

Enabling PDFs for Comment & Review provides essentially the same usage rights as when enabling for Commenting in Adobe Reader. You click the Comment tool in the Tasks Toolbar to open a pull-down menu. From the menu items, select Attach for Email Review. The Send by Email for Review wizard opens. Enabling the document is transparent to the user. In the Preview Invitation pane, you are shown a default message attached to a new email indicating that Adobe Reader users can participate in the review, as shown in Figure 19.3.

Although no options appear for enabling the document for Adobe Reader users, the process for sending a PDF document in an Email Review adds special rights to the file via the Send For Email Review wizard.

CROSS-REF For more information on comment reviews, see Chapter 21.

FIGURE 19.3

Click the Comment task button and choose Attach for Email Review to open the Send for Email Review wizard.

Enabling PDFs for form saves

The third of the five menu options provides you a complete set of enabling features for Adobe Reader users. In Acrobat Pro and Pro Extended select Advanced ⇨ Extend Features in Adobe Reader, and the Enable Usage Rights in Adobe Reader dialog box opens, as shown in Figure 19.4. In Acrobat Standard, choose Advanced ⇨ Extend Forms Fill-in & Save in Adobe Reader.

FIGURE 19.4

Select Document ⇨ Extend Features in Adobe Reader and a dialog box opens informing you of the features that you can enable.

Click Save Now and all the features listed in the dialog box are enabled in the PDF file for Adobe Reader users. This option provides a complete set of enabling features, including the following:

- **Save form data (for fillable PDF forms only).** Adobe Reader users can add data to PDF forms containing form fields and save the edited file.

- **Commenting and drawing mark-up tools.** The same comment and markup tools are available to Adobe Reader users as when enabling files for Comment & Markup and Review & Comment. All comments can be saved.

- **Sign an existing signature field.** Adobe Reader users can add a digital signature to a signature field on a form and save the edits.

- **Digitally sign the document on the page (supported in Adobe Reader 8 only).** As the text implies, this feature is available only to users of Adobe Reader 8 and above. It is also not available for XML forms created with LiveCycle Designer. A Reader 8 and above user can sign a document without the appearance of a signature file and save the edits.

When you click Save Now, the file is enabled with the usage rights.

CROSS-REF For more information on fillable form fields, see Chapters 33 and 34. For more information on using digital signatures, see Chapter 26.

Sending files for Shared Reviews

One of the most popular and requested features from users during the Acrobat 6 and 7 life cycles has been a means for sharing comments other than the options Adobe made available with Browser-Based Reviews. In local environments as well on Web servers, users wanted a way to comment on documents and have all the comments viewed by all participants in a review in a collaborative workflow.

Adobe responded to users' needs by introducing the Send for Shared Review command in Acrobat 8. From a menu command in the Comment task button, users could simplify the process for conducting shared reviews.

NEW FEATURE In Acrobat 9, shared reviews became much easier with the introduction of using Acrobat.com. Users can now use the Acrobat.com server on Adobe's Web site to conduct shared reviews. Choose Send for Shared Review from the Comment task button pull-down menu and the Send for Shared Review wizard opens. In the first pane of the wizard shown in Figure 19.5, you have an option for using Acrobat.com or your own server. Regardless of which choice you make, the file is enabled with Adobe Reader usage rights.

CROSS-REF For more information on using Acrobat.com, see Chapter 21.

FIGURE 19.5

The new Acrobat 9 Send for Shared Review wizard provides an option for sharing files on Acrobat.com.

Distributing Forms

The fourth of the five menu commands you can use to enable PDF documents is the Distribute Form command found when you enter Form Editing Mode (see Figure 19.6) or from the Forms menu in Viewer Mode.

Click the Distribute Form button or choose Forms ➪ Distribute Form to open the Distribute Form wizard shown in Figure 19.7. You'll notice this wizard is very similar to the Send for Shared Review wizard shown earlier in Figure 19.5.

NEW FEATURE You have the same options you found in Acrobat 8 for distributing a form as an email attachment or distribute to your own server location. However, in Acrobat 9 you have the additional option for distributing a form using Acrobat.com.

FIGURE 19.6

The new Form Editing Mode in Acrobat 9 provides a button to Distribute a form via the Distribute Form wizard.

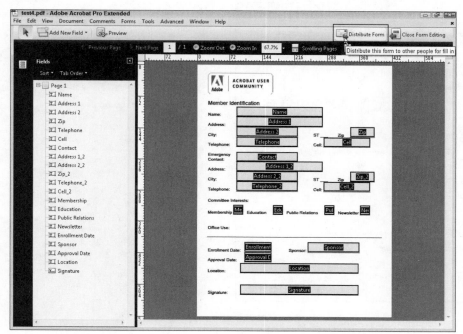

Your first step is to choose whether you want to email the form or save the form and email it later, send the form to your own local server, or send the form to Adobe.com. Regardless of the choice you make for where to send your form, the form is enabled with Adobe Reader usage rights and it is added to the Tracker History pane. You can easily find the form for later distribution by selecting Forms ➪ Track Forms and clicking the Forms item to expand a list, then clicking the Distributed item in the left pane.

CROSS-REF For more information on using the Distribute Form command, the Distribute Form wizard, and the Tracker, see Chapter 35.

FIGURE 19.7

The new Acrobat 9 Distribute Form wizard provides an option for distributing a form to Acrobat.com.

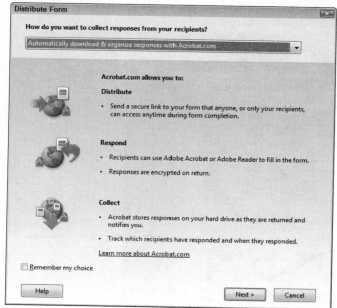

What about Adobe LiveCycle Designer Forms?

Anyone working with forms created in Adobe LiveCycle Designer knows you have limited editing possibilities when opening the forms in Adobe Acrobat. You cannot enable a form with Reader Extensions directly in Adobe LiveCycle Designer per se. You can select File ➪ Distribute Form in Adobe LiveCycle Designer, but doing so launches Acrobat and opens the Distribute Form wizard. All enabling features of Designer forms are handled within Acrobat Pro and Pro Extended.

You can open any form created in Designer in Acrobat 9 Pro or Pro Extended and use the same menu commands used for all enabling features as you do when enabling files for Comment & Markup, Comment & Review, and Enable Features in Adobe Reader (save form and digital signatures), and by using the Distribute Form command.

When you enable a form using the Comments ➪ Enable Commenting in Adobe Reader command, you don't have an option for enabling form saves and commenting in the same file. Likewise, you don't have an option to add a digital signature if a digital signature field is not contained on the form. When you use the Advanced menu for Extend Features in Adobe Reader or the Distribute Form command, both commenting and form saves and using digital signatures are enabled in the PDF for Reader users.

CROSS-REF　For more information on Adobe LiveCycle Designer, see Chapter 33.

Editing Enabled PDF Files

Upon occasion you may enable a PDF document using any one of the enabling options available in Acrobat 9 Pro or Pro Extended and then later decide you want to edit the file. When you enable a PDF document and try to edit it in Acrobat, an application alert dialog box opens as shown in Figure 19.8.

FIGURE 19.8

If you try to edit an enabled file in Acrobat, an alert dialog box opens informing you that you can't edit the file.

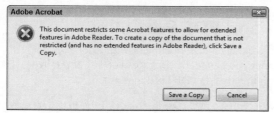

Modifying an enabled PDF file

To edit an enabled file in Acrobat you first need to save a copy of the document. When you open non-enabled PDF files, the File menu lists commands for Save and Save As. When you open an enabled file in Acrobat you find the commands Save, Save As, and Save a Copy. The addition of the Save a Copy command is unique to enabled PDF files and only this command will remove the restrictions applied when the PDF was enabled. The usage rights are removed when you save a copy, so after editing you need to re-enable the form.

Select File ➪ Save a Copy and the Save a Copy dialog box opens as you see in Figure 19.9. Click the Save a Copy button and a second Save a Copy dialog box opens where you can name the copy and select a folder where you want to save it. Once you save a copy, your copy file is not open in the Acrobat Document pane. It's merely saved to disk. Your original file remains open and it's not editable. Close the open file, then select File ➪ Open or click the Open tool in the Toolbar Well. When the Open dialog box appears, select the copy file and open it in Acrobat. You can edit this file and enable it after you complete your editing tasks.

FIGURE 19.9

Click the Save a Copy button to save an editable copy of the enabled PDF document.

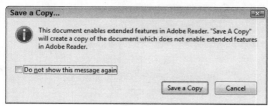

You'll find that most of the kinds of editing you typically perform on a PDF document aren't available with enabled documents. Items such as changing any of the Document Properties (Description, Security, Initial View, Custom and Advanced), adding headers and footers, changing backgrounds, adding comments, editing form fields, changing JavaScripts, and so on are all unavailable to you when working on an enabled PDF document. To edit any of these items, select File ➪ Save a Copy and open the copy file.

CROSS-REF For more information on changing Document Properties, see Chapter 6. For more information on adding headers and footers and changing backgrounds, see Chapter 16. For more information on adding comments, see Chapter 20. For more information on editing form fields, see Chapter 34. For more information on editing JavaScripts, see Chapter 36.

Working with enabled files and PDF Portfolios

When you create PDF Portfolios, you may want to enable a PDF document with Adobe Reader usage rights or edit an enabled PDF document after you create the package. The last of the five methods for enabling PDF documents is handled directly in a PDF Portfolio.

NEW FEATURE PDF Portfolios are a new feature in Acrobat 9 and take the place of the PDF Package that was introduced in Acrobat 8. In Acrobat 8 you worked within the Acrobat User Interface (UI) to edit and manage files within a PDF Package. In Acrobat 9, the UI changes and you lose access to most of Acrobat's tools and menus. Since you don't have access to the Comment or Advanced menus where you choose commands to enable a PDF document while working in the Home view, you need to change the portfolio view for a given file to Preview mode.

While in Preview mode, all the Comments and Advanced menu commands are available. Choose Advanced ➪ Enable Features in Adobe Reader as shown in Figure 19.10. The Enable Usage Rights in Adobe Reader dialog box shown earlier in Figure 19.4 opens. Click OK and the file is enabled with Reader usage rights.

If you need to edit a file in a PDF Portfolio, you have to select the file you want to edit and open a context menu and choose Open File. This command opens a PDF file in a new window where you have access to all the Acrobat tools and menu commands. Make your edits on the file and choose File ➪ Save. When you close the new window, you return to the PDF Portfolio and the file is dynamically updated.

FIGURE 19.10

You must view a PDF in Preview mode in a PDF Portfolio in order to enable a file with Reader usage rights.

Summary

- Adobe LiveCycle Reader® Extensions ES (LCRE) is a server product used for enterprise-enabling features for Adobe Reader users.

- The End User License Agreement (EULA) specifies the limitations you have for enabling PDFs with Reader extensions. When enabling forms for form saves for Reader users from within Acrobat, you are limited to 500 instances of use for unknown users. For known users, such as within a company of less than 500 employees, there is no limit to the number of uses of enabled forms.

- Acrobat Standard, Pro, and Pro Extended provide features for enabling PDF files for saving form data and digital signatures for Adobe Reader users.

- Forms created in Adobe LiveCycle Designer can be enabled for commenting, form data saving, and digital signatures.

- PDF files can be enabled from within PDF Portfolios.

Part IV

PDF Interactivity

Part IV deals with PDF interactivity, whether it be collaboration with others on sharing information or adding interactive features to PDF documents. In Chapter 20 we start with comment and markup where I cover using all the commenting features you have available in all Acrobat viewers. In Chapter 21, we move on to working in review sessions where you are introduced to the new Acrobat 9 features for sharing files on Acrobat.com and personal servers.

In Chapter 22 you find the many ways to make your PDF documents more interactive through adding bookmarks, links, and buttons. In Chapter 24 you find information on creating and working with Adobe PDF layers. This part finishes up with making PDF documents accessible for people using screen readers.

Chapter 20

Review and Markup

Adobe Acrobat is the perfect tool for workgroup collaboration. With sophisticated tool sets and a number of menu options, Acrobat provides you the ability to comment and mark up PDF documents and share your annotations with users dynamically on Web sites, through Acrobat.com, or through file exchanges on network servers or via email. For example, you can mark up documents, send your comments to a group of colleagues, ask for return comments, and track the review history. Where PDF documents may be too large to efficiently exchange files in emails, you can export comments to smaller data files or summarize them and create new PDF documents from comment summaries that can be sent to members of your workgroup. You can compare documents for changes, for comment status, and for errors and omissions, and, as with Acrobat 7 and 8 Pro, you can add usage rights in Acrobat 9 Pro to documents so Adobe Reader users can participate in reviews.

The review and comment tools and methods in Acrobat are extraordinary in number. Because Acrobat provides these great tools doesn't necessarily mean you'll use all of them in your daily work activities. The best way to decide what tools work best for you and your colleagues is to review this chapter thoroughly and pick and choose the tools you favor and the features in review and markup that work best in your environment. In this chapter, you learn how to use all the comment tools and compare documents for reviewing purposes.

PDF WORKFLOW All the tools and features discussed in this chapter are related to workflow environments. Regardless of what industry you work in, the many features related to review and comment and comparing documents can be applied to virtually all environments with two or more individuals collaborating on common projects.

Setting Up the Review and Comment Environment

You may be a user who adds comments infrequently with a few comment tools located in the Comment & Markup toolbar. However, to decide what tools work best in your workflow, you might want to add all the tools for review and markup to the Toolbar Well and look over all the tools available in your viewer.

To set up the review and comment work environment, open a context menu on the Toolbar Well and select Reset Toolbars to return to the default toolbar view. Return to the context menu and select More Tools to open the More Tools window (or select Tools ➪ Customize Toolbars). In the More Tools window, click the Advanced Editing toolbar and be sure to check the Select Object tool and the TouchUp tools. Check the Comment & Markup toolbar and add check marks to all the tools in this toolbar. Scroll down and pick and choose the Select & Zoom toolbar tools you want to use. Be certain to add the Snapshot tool.

Return to the context menu and select the Properties Bar. Again return to the context menu opened from the Toolbar Well and select Dock All Toolbars. After docking toolbars, your Toolbar Well should look similar to the one shown in Figure 20.1.

FIGURE 20.1

A view of toolbars set up for comment and review

Notice that the tools are grouped together in logical collections. In a real-world scenario, you might only use tools from a single group and not need to load all the tools in the Toolbar Well. If you work on a small monitor, you can see how expanding all the tools and the Comments panel can eat up a lot of screen real estate very quickly. If the view of your pages in the Document pane is too small to comfortably annotate files, close the less frequently used tools to open up more space in the Document pane.

CROSS-REF   Additional comment tools include the Measuring tools. These tools are often used with engineering and CAD drawings. For more information on using measuring tools consult the Acrobat Help document.

Setting Commenting Preferences

Acrobat provides an elaborate set of preference options that enable you to control comment views and behavior. As you draw comments on PDF pages you may see pop-up windows, connector lines across a page, changes in page views, and a host of other strange behaviors that might confuse you. Before you begin a commenting session, you should familiarize yourself with the commenting preferences and plan to return to the preference settings several times to completely understand how you control comment behavior in Acrobat.

Open the preference settings by pressing Ctrl/⌘+K or choosing Edit ➪ Preferences (Windows) or Acrobat ➪ Preferences (Macintosh). In the left pane, select Commenting. In the right pane, you'll see a long list of preference settings, as shown in Figure 20.2. Take a moment to review these settings before you begin a commenting session.

FIGURE 20.2

Open the Commenting Preferences by pressing Ctrl/⌘+K or choosing Edit ➪ Preferences. When the Preferences dialog box opens, select Commenting in the left pane.

- **Font (Windows only).** The comment tools are used to mark up text and create icons, symbols, and graphic objects on pages. Most of the comment tools have associated pop-up notes where you type remarks in a note window. By default, the font used for the note text is Tahoma. To change the font, select another font from the pull-down menu. All fonts loaded in your system are available from the menu choices. The fonts you use are not embedded in the file. If you exchange PDFs containing comment notes with other users, the fonts default to another user's preference settings.

Note that changing fonts and arbitrary font sizes is not available on the Mac. On the Mac the default Tahoma font is used and sizes are limited to Small, Medium, and Large.

- **Font Size.** Font point sizes range from 4 points to 144 points. You can type a number between these values in the field box or select one from the preset point sizes from the pull-down menu. Changing font size applies to note pop-up windows you see on your computer. If you change font size and share the file with other users, fonts appear in sizes set by individual user preferences.

- **Pop-up Opacity.** A pop-up note background color is white. At 100 percent opacity the note is opaque and hides underlying page data. You can change the opacity of pop-up notes for a transparent view so the background data can be seen when a pop-up note window is open. You adjust the level of transparency by typing a value in the field box or selecting one from the preset choices in the pull-down menu. The default is 85 percent.

- **Enable text indicators and tooltips.** Turns on or off tooltips when the Hand tool approaches a comment icon. The tooltip reports text contained in a comment note when the note is collapsed.

- **Print notes and pop-ups.** Enabling this check box prints the pop-up note contents for all pop-up note windows regardless of whether they are opened or collapsed.

- **Show lines connecting comment markups to their pop-ups on mouse rollover.** When you place the cursor over a comment markup, a line appears between the comment mark and the pop-up note, as shown in Figure 20.3.

- **Ensure that pop-ups are visible as the document is scrolled.** If a comment note extends beyond one page in a continuous page view, the note is visible when scrolling pages.

FIGURE 20.3

When the preference setting is enabled, connector lines are displayed on a mouseover between the comment and the associated note window.

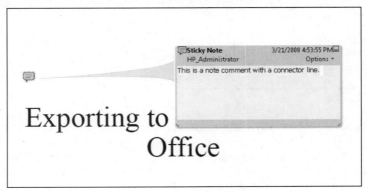

- **Automatically open comment pop-ups for comments other than notes.** As you create comments with drawing tools, the Text Box tool, or Pencil tool, the pop-up note windows are collapsed by default. If you want a pop-up note window opened and ready to accept type when creating comments, check the box.

- **Hide comment pop-ups when Comments List is opened.** The Comments List is contained in the Comments panel. When you open the Comments panel, the list shows expanded comment notes with the content displayed in the pane. To hide the pop-ups in the Document pane when the Comments panel is opened, enable the check box. If you set this item as a default, you can expand comments in the Comments panel by clicking icons to see the content of the pop-ups.

- **Automatically open pop-ups on mouse rollover.** Pop-up note windows can be opened or closed. Double-clicking a collapsed pop-up note window opens the window. If you want to have a pop-up note window open automatically as the cursor is placed over a comment icon, select this check box.

- **Always use Login Name for Author name.** Another set of preferences appears when you click on Identity in the left pane. The Login Name specified in the Identity preferences is used for the author name on all comments when this check box is enabled. If you are a single user on a workstation, setting the Identity preferences and enabling this check box saves you time creating comments when you want to add your name as the author name.

- **Create new pop-ups aligned to the edge of the document.** By default, the top-left corner of a pop-up note window is aligned to the top left corner of the comment icon. If you enable this check box, no matter where you create the note icon, the pop-up notes are aligned to the right edge of the document.

- **Copy encircled text into Drawing comment pop-ups.** When proofreading a document and using the Markup tools you mark text with the Rectangle tool, Circle tool, or Cloud tool. When this preference option is checked, the text you surround with one of these tools is placed in a comment note.

- **Copy selected text into Highlight, Cross-Out, and Underline comment pop-ups.** This enables the text selected with the Highlight Text, Cross Out Text, and Underline Text tools to automatically appear in the pop-up note window.

As you can see, there are many different preference settings. How you want to view comments and the methods used for review and comment is influenced by the options you set in the Commenting preferences. Take some time to play with these settings as you use the tools discussed in this chapter.

Looking at the Comment & Markup Toolbar

Users of Acrobat Pro Extended (Windows), Acrobat Pro, Acrobat Standard (Windows), and Adobe Reader (when a file is enabled with usage rights) can access the Comment & Markup tools.

Users of earlier versions of Acrobat will notice that all Comment & Markup tools are added to a single toolbar in Acrobat 8 and 9. In earlier versions of Acrobat, you had the Comment & Markup toolbar and the Drawing Markups toolbar. In Acrobat 8 and 9, all commenting tools with the exception of the Measuring tools are contained in a single toolbar.

The commenting and markup tools arranged in a single toolbar are shown in Figure 20.4.

FIGURE 20.4

All commenting and markup tools are nested together in a single toolbar.

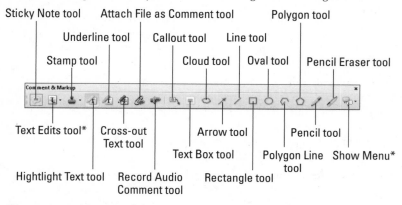

* Denotes more options in pull-down menu

The Comment & Markup toolbar essentially contains two tool subsets. The Commenting tools begin with the Sticky Note tool on the far left of the toolbar and move to the right to the Record Audio Comment tool. The Markup tools begin with the Callout tool in the middle of the toolbar and extend to the far right to the Pencil Eraser tool. While the Commenting tools are generally used for text documents, the Markup tools are used more with drawings and diagrams. All tools are accessible in any kind of PDF document you want to mark up with comments, and you can use any tool to mark up text and drawings.

Using the Comment & Markup Tools

The Comment & Markup tools are intended for use by anyone reviewing and marking up documents. Much like you might use a highlighter on paper documents, the commenting tools enable you to electronically comment and mark up PDF documents. A variety of tools with different icon symbols offer you an extensive library of tools that can help you facilitate a review process.

Most comment tools have a symbol or icon that appears where the comment is created. They also have a note pop-up window where you add text to clarify a meaning associated with the mark you add to a document. These pop-up note windows have identical attributes. How you manage note pop-ups and change the properties works the same regardless of the comment mark you create, with the exception of the Callout and Text Box tools. I explain how to use the Sticky Note tool in this section. All the features described for the Sticky Note tool are the same as when handling note pop-up windows for all the comment tools that accommodate note pop-ups.

Using the Sticky Note tool

 The Sticky Note tool is the most common commenting tool used in Acrobat and the oldest of the commenting tools dating back to Acrobat 2. To create a comment note, select the Sticky Note tool in the Comment & Markup toolbar and drag open a note window. When you release the mouse button, the note pop-up aligns to the top left corner of the note icon.

You can also select the Sticky Note tool and click the mouse button or open a context menu and select Add Sticky Note. Using either of these options adds a note comment on the right side of the document page away from the note icon if the Create new pop-ups aligned to the edge of the document preference option is checked in the Commenting preferences. If you disable the preference option, using either of these methods positions the note pop-up close to the right side of the note icon.

TIP You can also add notes to a page via menu commands. To add a note to a page, choose Comments ➪ Add Sticky Note. A comment note is added to the center of the page in view. For example, if the document is viewed in a Fit Page view, the note appears in the center of the page. If the document view is zoomed in to show only the top third of the page, the comment note appears in the center of the top third in view.

When you can click without dragging and release the mouse button, a pop-up note window is created at a fixed size according to your monitor resolution. The higher you set your monitor resolution the smaller the pop-up note window appears. On an 800×600 display, the window size defaults to 360×266 pixels. In Figure 20.5, I drew a comment note with the Sticky Note tool in the center of the page. On the left side of the page, I clicked the Sticky Note tool. Notice the center note is aligned with the note icon, whereas the icon on the left is linked to the note pop-up on the far right side of the page. Note also that because my cursor is not placed over either note, no connector lines appear between the Sticky Note icon and the pop-up note window.

To add text to the pop-up note, begin typing. Acrobat places an I-beam cursor inside the pop-up note window immediately after creating the note. For font selection and font sizing, you need to address the Commenting preference settings discussed earlier in this chapter.

When clicking and dragging the Sticky Note tool, the pop-up note aligns to the top left corner of the note icon. When clicking with the Sticky Note tool, a pop-up window is created at a fixed size away from the icon.

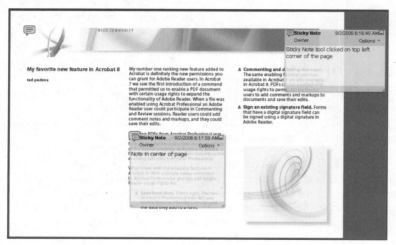

Managing notes

The color of a note pop-up and the note icon is yellow by default. At the top of the note pop-up the title bar is colored yellow and the area where you add the contents is white. The title bar contains information supplied by Acrobat that includes the subject of the note, the author, and the date and time the note is created. You can move a note pop-up independently of the note icon by clicking and dragging the title bar.

CROSS-REF The Subject of a note by default is titled *Sticky Note*. The default Author name is derived from either your computer logon name or your Identity depending on how your preferences are established. For information on how to change the Subject and Author in the title bar, see "Sticky Note tool properties" later in this chapter.

You delete note pop-up windows and Sticky Note icons either by selecting the note icon and pressing the Delete/Backspace or Del key on your keyboard, or through a context menu selection. If you use a keystroke to delete a note, you must be certain to select the icon; then press the Delete/Backspace or Del key. Selecting the title bar in a note pop-up and using the same keys won't delete the note.

To resize a note pop-up window, grab the lower-right corner of the window and drag in or out to resize smaller or larger, respectively. Note pop-ups containing more text that can be viewed in the current window size use scroll bars, so you can scroll the window much like you would when viewing pages in the Document pane. Only vertical scroll bars are shown in the pop-up windows. As you type text in the window, text wraps to the horizontal width, thereby eliminating a need for horizontal scroll bars. As you size a note pop-up window horizontally, the text rewraps to conform to the horizontal width.

Note Nomenclature

The tool you use to create notes is the Sticky Note tool. In earlier versions of Acrobat, this tool was called the Note tool. When referring to the tool throughout this chapter, I refer to it by its proper name in Acrobat 8 and 9 (Sticky Note tool). When you add comments from most of the other commenting tools, the tools have an associated note pop-up window. Throughout this chapter, I refer to this window as the pop-up note window or simply refer to it as a note or note window.

The official name for the toolbar where you select tools for comments and markups is called the Comment & Markup toolbar. For simplicity and ease of reading, I often refer to the tools in this toolbar as the commenting tools. When you see a reference to the commenting tools, realize that I'm talking about both comment and markup tools.

You open context menus from either the note icon or the note pop-up window. When opening a context menu from the note pop-up window, you have two choices: open the context menu from the title bar or open the context menu from inside the note window (below the title bar). Depending on where you open the context menu, the menu selections are different. Opening a context menu from the title bar or from the note icon shows identical menu options. You can also use the Options menu to open the same menu as when opening a context menu inside the note window. Click the right-pointing arrow adjacent to Options and the menu opens.

In Figure 20.6, I opened on the Options pull-down menu on a pop-up note window. The menu options are the same as if I had opened the context menu from the note icon. In Figure 20.7, I opened the context menu from inside the note pop-up window. Depending on edits you make in the note window and whether you have text selected, menu options change. In Figure 20.7, text was selected in the note window that adds the Cut, Copy, and Paste commands to the context menu. In both menus, you can select Delete to remove the note pop-up menu and the note icon.

FIGURE 20.6

This context menu is opened from the note pop-up window title bar. From the menu options, select Delete to remove the note icon and the note pop-up menu.

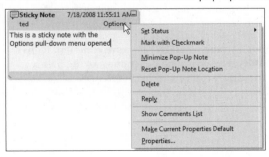

TIP   If you accidentally delete a note or several notes, you can select Edit ➪ Undo to bring back the note and Sticky Note icon. Successively select the Undo command and you can bring back several Sticky Note icons and note windows.

The context menus are similar, and most commands existing in the smaller menu are the same as those found in the larger menu. If two notes are selected, additional menu commands appear in a context menu.

FIGURE 20.7

When you open a context menu from the note pop-up window below the title bar, menu options change. If you select text in the note window, additional commands are added to the context menu.

Click the Select Object tool in the Advanced Editing toolbar and open a context menu on one of the note icons. You see different menu commands when two or more comment icons are selected as shown in Figure 20.8. The options you have in the context menu are the same as those you find when opening a context menu on two or more form fields.

CROSS-REF   Most of the context menu commands you see when two or more comment icons are selected should be self-explanatory. For a detailed description of the menu commands, I cover the same commands when managing form fields in Chapter 34.

FIGURE 20.8

Drag the Select Object tool through comment icons to select two or more. Open a context menu and new menu commands appear for organizing comments.

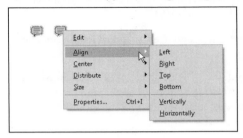

In Figure 20.7, you see a long list of menu commands. Let's take a look at these commands; the same commands found in the context menu shown in Figure 20.6 operate the same way.

- **Cut Text/Copy Text.** These items work as you might assume from using any text editor or word processor. The commands relate to typing text in the note pop-up window. You can also highlight text and use key modifiers (Ctrl/⌘+C for Copy; Ctrl/⌘+X for Cut; Ctrl/⌘+V for Paste).

- **Delete Text.** Select text and choose Delete Text. The selected text is deleted.

- **Check Spelling.** When you select Check Spelling in the note pop-up menu, the Check Spelling dialog box opens. When the dialog box opens, click the Start button and Acrobat checks the spelling for all the text typed in the note pop-up. When Acrobat finds a misspelled word, it is highlighted and a list of suggestions that closely match the spelling is shown in the lower window. Select a word with the correct spelling and click the Change button.

- **Remove "..." from Dictionary.** This menu item is active only when you have a word selected in the note pop-up window and that note is contained in your custom dictionary. It's a nifty little feature in Acrobat. Because Acrobat automatically spell-checks text you type in the comment note pop-up window by matching your words to those found in its dictionary, words not matched are underlined in red with a wavy line similar to those used in programs such as Microsoft Word. If you want Acrobat to alert you whenever you type a specific word, remove that word from the dictionary. Then Acrobat displays the word with a red underline each time you use it.

  When would you use this feature? Assume for a moment that you want to use a generic reference to users as opposed to a masculine or feminine reference. Highlight the word *he* or *she* and open a context menu from the note pop-up window. Select Remove "*he*" from Dictionary. Each time you type the word *he*, Acrobat underlines the word because it can't find a match in the dictionary. When you review your notes, you might substitute *s/he* for the word *he*.

- **Look Up "...".** The default menu command is Look Up Definition. When a word is selected, the menu command changes to Look Up *selected word*. For example, if you select a word like *reply*, the menu command changes to Look Up "reply." Select the menu command, which launches your Web browser, opening to the Dictionary.com Web site where the word is searched and a definition is displayed on the Web page.

CROSS-REF For more information on looking up a definition and the Dictionary.com Web site, see Chapter 13.

- **Text Style.** From a submenu, select from Bold, Italic, Underline, Superscript, Subscript, or Clear Formatting). Select any one of the formatting options to apply to selected text. You can combine format changes by selecting text and a format option, and then return to the context menu and select another option, and so on.

- **Mark with Checkmark.** Whereas the Set Status items are communicated to others, a check mark you add to a comment is for your own purposes. You can mark a comment as checked to denote any comments that need attention, or that are completed and require no further annotation. Check marks are visible in the Comments panel and can be toggled on or off in the pane as well as the context menu. Check marks can be added to comments with or without your participation in a review session. You can choose to have your comments sorted by those with check marks and those comments without check marks.

- **Minimize Pop-Up Note.** Selecting this command closes the note window. Click back on the Sticky Note icon and the note window opens again. The same close action is also available by clicking the minimize icon in the top right corner of the note pop-up window.

- **Reset Pop-Up Note Location.** If you move a note pop-up window, selecting this menu command returns the note pop up to the default position.

- **Delete.** Deletes the comment pop-up note and the note icon.

- **Reply.** When participating in a review, you select the Reply command to reply to comments made from other users. A new window opens in which you type a reply message. From the pop-up bar you can review a thread and click the Reply button to send your comments to others via email, using Acrobat.com, to a network folder, or to a Web-hosted server.

CROSS-REF For more information on comment reviews, see Chapter 21.

- **Show Comments List.** Selecting this item opens the Comments panel. Any comments in the open document are expanded in a list view in the Comments panel. When the Comments panel is open, this option toggles to Hide Comments List.

- **Make Current Properties Default.** Any attributes you changed in the Properties dialog box (see Properties below) such as changing the Author name or Subject can be set to new defaults. After making settings choices, select this menu item and all subsequent notes you add will use the same new defaults.

- **Properties.** Opens the Properties dialog box.

■ **Set Status.** Two submenu items are listed when you select Set Status. The Migration submenu command has three additional submenu options for migrating comments (comments can be migrated when you make document revisions and you want to migrate comments from an earlier PDF to a revised PDF). The Review submenu command enables you to choose from various status settings such as None, Accepted, Cancelled, Completed, and Rejected.

> **CROSS-REF** For more information on migration and reviews, see Chapter 21.

Sticky Note tool properties

Each comment created from any tool supporting a pop-up note has properties that you can change in a properties dialog box. Properties changes are generally applied to note pop-up windows and icon shapes for a particular tool. In addition, a variety of properties are specific to different tools that offer you many options for viewing and displaying comments and tracking the history of the comments made on a document.

With respect to note pop-ups and those properties assigned to the Sticky Note tool, you have choices for changing the default color, opacity, author name, and a few other options. Keep in mind that not all property changes are contained in the properties dialog box. Attributes such as font selection and point sizes are globally applied to note pop-ups in the Comment preferences.

Setting Up the Author Name for Comment Notes

If you add comment markups where associated note pop-ups are available, you may find the comment note author name to be the same as your computer log-on name. If you open a comment note Properties dialog box and change the name, and then open a context menu on the note icon and choose Make Current Properties Default, the author name doesn't honor the new default. It can be annoying to keep opening comment properties and changing the name on each individual comment note.

There is a reason for Acrobat not adhering to your wishes and it lies with the Commenting Preferences settings. If you want to change your author name from your computer log-on name, open the Preferences dialog box (Ctrl/⌘+K). Click Commenting in the left pane, and in the right pane where you find Making Comments, you find that a setting that enables you to use the author name. By default, Always use Log-on Name for Author name is checked. This check mark overrides the defaults you try to change using the comment note properties.

Remove the check mark and the next time you change the author name and set new defaults, all your comment author names are changed to your liking.

> Making Comments
> - ☑ Always use Log-in Name for Author name
> - ☑ Create new pop-ups aligned to the edge of the document
> - ☐ Copy encircled text into Drawing comment pop-ups
> - ☐ Copy selected text into Highlight, Cross-Out, and Underline comment pop-ups

CROSS-REF For information about Commenting preferences, see "Setting Commenting Preferences" at the beginning of this chapter.

Additionally, you have many options available to you in the Properties Bar. If you want certain attributes to be changed for a given comment type, first look at the Properties Bar after selecting a comment tool to see if a property you want to change exists in the toolbar.

In the Sticky Note tool you find attributes for changing pop-up note color, text color, icon shapes, and a variety of font styles. It is easier to change these attributes using the Properties Bar rather than the Properties dialog box. For other properties changes, such as comment author, subject, opacity settings, and editing the review history, you need to use the Properties dialog box.

You open the properties dialog box from a context menu. Be certain to place the cursor on a pop-up note title bar or the note icon before opening a context menu. Select Properties from the menu choices and the Sticky Note Properties dialog box opens, as shown in Figure 20.9.

NOTE When you create a comment with any of the Comment tools, the Hand tool is automatically selected upon releasing the mouse button. You can select a comment mark/icon or pop-up note with the Hand tool or the Select Object tool. Use either tool to open a context menu where the menu options enable you to select Properties. However, other menu items vary between the two context menus. For information regarding menu options from context menus opened with the Select Object tool, see the discussion on Drawing Markup tools later in this chapter.

TIP To keep a comment tool selected without returning to the Hand tool after creating a comment, check the box in the Properties Bar for Keep tool selected.

FIGURE 20.9

Select Properties from a context menu and the Sticky Note Properties dialog box opens.

The Sticky Note Properties dialog box contains three tabs. Select a tab and make choices for the items contained in the dialog box. For pop-up note properties, the items you can change include the following:

■ **Appearance.** Options in the Appearance tab relate to the note icon appearances and the pop-up note window appearance.

   ▓ **Icon.** From the scrollable list, select an item that changes the Note icon appearance. Selections you make in this list are dynamic and change the appearance of the icon in the Document pane as you click on a name in the list. If you move the Note Properties dialog box out of the view of the note icon, you can see the appearance changes as you make selections in the list. Fifteen different icons are available to choose from, as shown in Figure 20.10. The same options are also available in the Properties Bar. Click the Icon button in the Properties Bar and a pull-down menu opens where the same choices are listed.

FIGURE 20.10

You select icon shapes from the Icon list in the Appearance tab in the Note Properties dialog box or in the Icon pull-down menu in the Properties Bar. You can choose from 15 different shapes.

   ▓ **Color.** Click the color swatch to open the pop-up color palette shown in Figure 20.11. You select preset colors from the swatches in the palette. You add custom colors by selecting the Other Color item in the palette, which opens the system color palette. In the system color palette, make color choices and the new custom color is applied to the note.

FIGURE 20.11

Click the color swatch to select from preset colors or select Other Color to open the system color palette where you select custom colors.

Changing color in the Appearance properties affects both the color of the note icon and the pop-up note title bar. If you mark up and review documents in workgroups, different colors assigned to different participants can help you ascertain at a glance which participant made a given comment.

For a quick change in note colors, use the Properties Bar where you see the same color attributes found in the Properties dialog box in the Properties Bar Color pull-down menu.

■ **Opacity.** Global opacity settings are applied in the Commenting Preferences dialog box. You can override the default opacity setting in the Appearance properties for any given note pop-up window.

Additionally, opacity adjustments can be made in the Properties Bar by choosing fixed opacity percentages from the Opacity pull-down menu. One distinction between adjusting opacity in the Properties dialog box and making adjustments in the Properties Bar is that the Properties dialog box enables you to choose different opacities at 1% increments. The Properties Bar is limited to fixed opacity settings in 20% increments.

■ **Locked.** Select the Locked check box to lock a note. When notes are locked, the position of the note icon is fixed to the Document pane and cannot be moved when you leave the Note Properties dialog box. All other options in the Note Properties dialog box are grayed out, preventing you from making any further attribute changes. If you lock a note, you can move the pop-up window and resize it. The note contents, however, are locked and changes can't be made to the text in the pop-up note window. If you want to make changes to the properties or the pop-up note contents, return to the Note Properties dialog box and uncheck the Locked check box.

■ **General.** Click the General tab to make changes for items appearing in the note pop-up title bar. Two editable fields are available, as shown in Figure 20.12. The changes you make in the Author and Subject fields are dynamic and are reflected in the Document pane when you edit a field and tab to the next field. You can see the changes you make here before leaving the Note Properties dialog box.

■ **Author.** The Author name is supplied by default according to how you set your Commenting preferences. If you use the Identity preferences, the Author name is supplied from the information added in the Identity preferences (see "Setting Commenting Preferences" earlier in this chapter). If you don't use Identity for the Author title, the name is derived from your computer log-on name. You might see names like Owner, Administrator, or a specific name you used in setting up your operating system.

If you want to change the Author name and override the preferences, select the General tab and edit the Author name. The name edited in the General preferences is applied to the selected note. All other notes are left undisturbed. Note that you also need to change Identity preferences if you want to make a new default for the author name. (See the sidebar "Setting Up the Author Name for Comment Notes" earlier in this chapter.)

FIGURE 20.12

Make changes to the Author name and the pop-up note Subject in the General preferences.

- **Subject.** By default, the Subject of a note for the Sticky Note comment is titled *Sticky Note,* which appears in the top left corner of the pop-up note title bar. When you use other comment tools, the subject defines the tool used. For example, when using the Highlight tool, you'll see *Highlight* as the subject, using an Approved stamp comment places *Approved* in the Subject field, and so on.

  You can change the subject in the General properties by typing text in the Subject line. You can add long text descriptions for the Subject; however, the text remains on a single line in the pop-up note properties dialog box. (The total characters you can type for the Subject field is 255.) Text won't scroll to a second line. The amount of text shown for the Subject field relates to the horizontal width of the note window. As you expand the width, more text is visible in the title bar if you add a long Subject name. As you size down the width, text is clipped to accommodate the note size.

  Text added to both the Author and Subject text boxes is searchable using Acrobat Search when you check the box in the Search panel for Include Comments.

CROSS-REF For more information on using Acrobat Search, see Chapter 6.

- **Modified.** This item is informational and supplied automatically by Acrobat from your system clock. The field is not editable. The readout displays the date and time the note was modified.

- **Review History.** The Review History lists all comment and status changes in a scrollable list. The list is informational and not editable.

CROSS-REF For more information on review history, see Chapter 21.

After making changes in the Note Properties dialog box, click the OK button to apply the changes. Clicking on the close box or pressing the Esc key cancels any changes you make to note properties.

> **TIP** The Properties dialog boxes for all Comment tools are not dynamic in Acrobat 9. You need to exit the Properties dialog box before making any other edits in your document or accessing any tool or menu command.

Setting default properties

If you use the Make Current Properties Default menu command from a context menu opened on a comment tool or comment pop-up note, the new default is applied only in your current Acrobat session. Quit Acrobat and all the defaults are lost.

You can globally change defaults for comment and markup tools and retain the new defaults in subsequent Acrobat sessions. To set these defaults, open a context menu on a tool in the Comment & Markup toolbar and select Tool Default Properties — be certain to open the context menu on a tool in the Comment & Markup toolbar and not a space between the tools. A properties dialog box for the selected tool opens. Make any settings changes, click OK in the Properties dialog box, and your new defaults remain in effect until you change them again or select Reset Toolbar from the same context menu. (Note that the context menu opened on a tool in the Comment & Markup toolbar also displays commands for selecting each and every tool in the toolbar as well as opening the Customize Toolbars window.)

Using the Properties Bar

If you set up your work environment to view the Properties Bar while working in a review session, you can address several properties options from it. The attributes you can change for Sticky Notes have all been mentioned in the section "Sticky Note tool properties" earlier in this chapter.

One additional item you have in the Properties Bar, shown in Figure 20.13, is the More button. This button appears for all comment markups that support options in the Properties Bar. Click the More button after selecting a comment icon and the Properties dialog box opens.

You can change some properties options in the Properties Bar. To open the toolbar, open a context menu on the Toolbar Well and select Properties Bar.

> **TIP** If you're proofreading a document and you prefer another term or word, you can find word definitions or access a thesaurus by opening a context menu with the Hand tool and selecting Add Note. Type a word in the note pop-up window and highlight the word. Open a context menu from the highlighted word and select LookUp ". . . ". The Dictionary.com Web site opens in your Web browser with the word definition, access to a thesaurus, and an encyclopedia on the open Web page.

Working with the Text Edits tools

 The Text Edits tools can be acquired from several menu locations. When you load the Comment & Markup toolbar, the Text Edits tools are all located in a pull-down menu adjacent to the Sticky Note tool in the toolbar. The Text Edits tools are the only comment tools you won't find in the Comments➪Comment & Markup Tools submenu. The Text Edit tools can be used for any kind of review session; however, they were designed to be used for comments that you want to export to source documents that originated in programs such as Microsoft Word and Autodesk AutoCAD.

CROSS-REF For more information on exporting comments to Microsoft Word, see Chapter 8.

To use the tools, click the Select tool and click or select text in the Document pane. A blinking cursor or selected text needs to appear in a document before the Text Edits tools can be selected. When text is selected, you have access to all the tools in the Text Edits pull-down menu, as shown in Figure 20.14.

As you move to text you want to mark, drag the cursor to highlight text to be annotated. When text is selected, open the Text Edits pull-down menu and select the tool you want to use for your edit.

FIGURE 20.14

Use the Select tool to click on a body of text or select text where you want to add a comment. Open the Text Edits pull-down menu and select the tool respective to the type of edit you want to make.

The Text Edits tools include:

- **Text Edits Tool.** You'll notice the Text Edits tool looks like the Select tool. This tool is not used to make a comment in the document. Click the tool and a dialog box opens where you find help information on using all the other Text Edits tools.

NOTE All the tools below the Indicate Text Edit tool are grayed out unless you select the Select tool and click or click and drag in a text block. Selecting either option without a cursor insertion on the document page or without highlighting text does not enable any of the Text Edit tools.

- **Replace Selected Text.** Use this tool to mark text for replacement. The line appears similar to the Cross Out Text for Deletion mark, but the caret at the end of the mark distinguishes this tool from the aforementioned one. A note pop-up window opens where you can add comments. The note contents do not include the text marked for replacement.

- **Highlight Selected Text.** This tool works like the Highlight tool and similar to a yellow highlighter you might use on paper documents. Select the Highlight tool and drag across a block of text. The text is highlighted and a note pop-up window enables you to add comments.

- **Add Note to Selected Text.** Select a word, a paragraph, or a body of text. When you release the mouse button a note pop-up window opens in which you add a comment. Selecting the text does not include the selected text in the pop-up note.

- **Insert Text At Cursor.** Select the menu command and move the cursor to the document page. The cursor appearance changes to an I-beam, informing you that text can be selected. Rather than selecting text, clicking the cursor at a specific location is the method most often used with this tool. The intent is to suggest to a reviewer that text needs to be inserted at the cursor position. When you click on a document page, a caret is marked on the page at the insertion location and a note pop-up window opens. Type the text to be inserted in the note pop-up.

- **Underline Selected Text.** Use this tool to underline the selected text. A note pop-up window opens where you can add comments.

- **Cross Out Text for Deletion.** Select text and the text mark appears as a strikethrough. The symbol is used to mark text that needs to be deleted. A note pop-up window opens where you can add comments.

Working with the Highlight tools

 The three tools appearing after the Stamp tools are the Highlight tool, the Underline tool, and the Strikethrough tool. When you have comments that are to be exported to MS Word documents, don't use these tools because the comments made with the tools cannot be exported to MS Word. Use the Text Edits tools for highlighting, strikethrough, and underlining. Where these three tools are helpful is when you want the text you mark to be added to a comment note. Especially if you have long passages of text, you'll want to have the text added to a note where you can easily make some corrections/suggestions. The tools have their place, but if you don't need text added to the comment note pop-ups, then always opt for using the Text Edits tools for the same types of markups.

Attaching files as comments

The next tool in the Commenting toolbar lineup is the Attach File as Comment tool. You use this tool to attach files as comments. Users of Adobe Reader can open your attached files without any special usage rights added to the file for Adobe Reader users. The Attach File as Comment tool differs somewhat from another tool you have available for adding file attachments to PDFs. For detailed information related to using the Attach File as Comment tool and using the Attachments panel for adding file attachments to PDFs, see Chapter 12.

Recording audio comments

 Next on the Commenting toolbar you find the Record Audio Comment tool. This tool is used to add audio to a PDF document. You need to have a microphone properly set up on your computer, and you can use audio recordings in lieu of or in addition to other comments you add to a document. For more information on using the Record Audio Comment tool and adding rich media to PDF files, see Chapter 23.

Using the Stamp tool

 The Stamp tool is part of the Commenting tools, but it differs greatly from the other tools found in the Comment & Markup toolbar. Rather than mark data on a PDF page and add notes to the marks, Stamps enable you to apply icons of your own choosing to express statements about a document's status or add custom icons and symbols for communicating messages. Stamps offer a wide range of flexibility for marking documents similar to analog stamps you might use for stamping approvals, drafts, confidentiality, and so on. You can use one of a number of different icons supplied by Acrobat when you install the program, or you can create your own custom icons tailored to your workflow or company needs.

CROSS-REF All the features related to the Stamp tool, including creating your own custom stamps, are treated in Adobe Reader the same as Acrobat Standard, Acrobat Pro, and Acrobat Pro Extended when PDFs contain usage rights for Adobe Reader. To learn more about usage rights with Adobe Reader, see Chapters 4 and 19.

Whether you use a preset stamp provided with your Acrobat installation or create a custom stamp, each stamp has an associated note pop-up window where you add comments. You select stamps from menu options in the Stamp pull-down menu where stamps are organized by categories. Add a stamp to a page by clicking the Stamp tool after selecting a stamp from a category; or you can click and drag the Stamp tool to size the icon. After creating a stamp, you access Stamp properties by opening a context menu and selecting Properties.

Selecting stamps

Using a stamp begins with selecting from among many different stamp images found in submenus from the Stamp tool pull-down menu. Click the down-pointing arrow and the first three menu commands list categories for stamps installed with Acrobat. If you have at least one Custom stamp added to your stamps library, then the custom category you added appears in addition to the three default categories. Notice in Figure 20.15 I added a custom category called My Custom Stamps that appears at the top of the Stamps pull-down menu. Selecting one of the menu items opens a submenu where you select specific stamps from the respective category, as shown in Figure 20.15.

FIGURE 20.15

Select the pull-down menu from the Stamp tool and select a Stamp category. Select a subcategory and slide the mouse over to the Stamp name. Release the mouse button and the selection becomes the new default stamp.

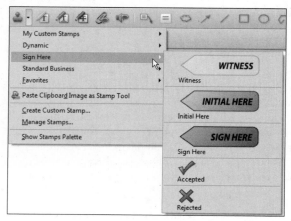

Adding a stamp to a page

The stamp name you select in the menu becomes the new default stamp. When you click the Stamp tool or click and drag open a rectangle with the Stamp tool, the default stamp is added to the document page. Stamps are created by default with the pop-up note window collapsed unless you enable the Commenting preferences for "Automatically open comment pop-ups for comments other than notes." To open the pop-up note window, click the mouse button on the stamp image. The pop-up note opens and appears the same as other pop-up note windows for other Comment tools.

If you want to resize a stamp after creating it on a page, select the Hand tool and click the stamp icon to select it. Move the cursor to a corner handle and the cursor changes shape to a diagonal line with two opposing arrowheads, as shown in the lower left handle in Figure 20.16. Drag the handle in or out to resize the stamp.

 Stamps are always proportionately sized when you drag any one of the corner handles. You don't need to drag handles with a modifier key to proportionately size the image.

Stamps can also be rotated. Click the top center handle and the cursor changes to a circle with an arrowhead, as shown in Figure 20.16. Drag left or right and the stamp icon rotates. You can rotate stamps in arbitrary 1-degree rotations or in constrained 45-degree rotations. To perform an arbitrary rotation, drag the center handle left or right. To constrain rotations to 45 degrees, press the Shift key and drag the center handle left or right. When you rotate a stamp, the note pop-up remains fixed in the same view as when you first open the note.

FIGURE 20.16

To resize a stamp, drag a corner handle using the Hand tool and drag in or out to size the icon. To rotate a stamp, drag the top center handle left or right to rotate counterclockwise or clockwise respectively. Pressing the Shift key constrains rotations to 45 degrees.

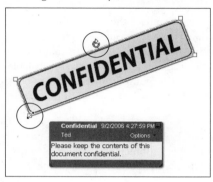

CROSS-REF **You can also size and rotate images and objects. For more information on scaling and rotating items in Acrobat, see Chapter 15.**

Acrobat offers you an assortment of stamps you can select from the category submenus in the Stamp tool pull-down menu. These stamps are created for general office uses, and you'll find many common stamp types among the sets. The three categories of stamps and their respective types and icons are shown in Figure 20.17.

FIGURE 20.17

Choose stamps from three categories. The stamps installed with Acrobat are general office stamps used in many traditional workflows.

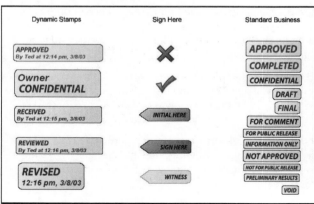

You should think of these stamps as a starter set and use them for some traditional office markups when the need arises. The real power of stamps, however, lies in creating custom stamps where you can use virtually any illustration or photo image.

Changing stamp properties

You change stamp properties in the Stamp Properties dialog box. You have the same options in the Stamp Properties as those found in the Note Properties dialog box, with one exception. In the Note Properties dialog box, you make choices for the icon appearance from a list in the dialog box. Because stamps have appearances determined before you create the stamp, no options are available for changing properties for the stamp image. The color options in the Stamp Properties dialog box apply to comment notes and not the stamp images. Opacity settings, however, can be applied to the stamp image.

If you want to change the appearance of a stamp, you need to delete the stamp and create a new stamp after selecting the category and stamp name from the category submenu. You delete stamps by opening a context menu and selecting Delete, or selecting the stamp icon and pressing the Backspace/Delete or Del key.

Resizing Stamps

The stamps you find installed by Acrobat are all vector art images created in Adobe Illustrator. When you resize vector art images, the display quality remains the same no matter how large you size the stamp.

When creating custom stamps you can use a program such as Adobe Illustrator and use vector art for your stamp design. You can also create custom stamps from Photoshop files. These files, however, are raster art. If you size raster artwork above a 100% actual view size, you can see distortion in your stamp image.

If you plan on using photographs or other artwork created in Adobe Photoshop, be certain to anticipate the largest size you might need to size up a stamp icon. When you view a Photoshop image created at 72 ppi (pixels per inch), the largest size you can see on your monitor without distortion is a 100% actual size view. If you size the stamp up 200% or more, you'll notice image degradation, and the image is likely to display jagged edges.

If you anticipate sizing stamps up to a 400% view, for example, create your stamps from Photoshop images at 288 ppi. This calculation is determined by taking 72 ppi and multiplying times 4 (72 × 4 = 288). Hence, when you size the stamp up to 400%, the actual size view is 72 ppi. As size increases, resolution decreases.

If you plan your work and anticipate the size you might use for custom stamps created from Photoshop files, you can avoid any display problems when viewing files in Acrobat. The sizing issues only have to do with physically sizing a stamp image containing raster artwork. If you use zoom tools in Acrobat, the stamps appear at the same size no matter what zoom level you view a document page.

Creating custom stamps

You might create custom stamps with a company logo or personal identification so users in your workgroup or recipients of your files can see at a quick glance that files received are coming from you. You might use a custom stamp for approving documents in a review session, for asking others to review one of your documents, or for other business uses such as marking documents for signatures, confidentiality, time stamping, or other similar tasks.

To understand how custom stamps are created, follow these steps:

STEPS: Creating a custom stamp

1. **Create the stamp icon image.** Using your favorite authoring program capable of exporting to one of the formats supported by creating a custom stamp, create an icon or image you want to use for your stamp. My tool of choice for creating custom stamps is Adobe Illustrator — but feel free to use the program you like to create your stamp image.

   File formats compatible with custom stamp creation are shown in Figure 20.18. (See the sidebar on file format compatibility later in this chapter.)

   FIGURE 20.18

   File formats compatible with creating custom stamps as available with Acrobat Pro Extended (Windows)

2. **Select an image to use as the new custom stamp.** Open Acrobat and select Create Custom Stamp from the Stamp tool pull-down menu. The Select Image for Custom Stamp dialog box opens. Click the Browse button in the dialog box and select your image file in the Open dialog box. Click Open and you return to the Select Image for Custom Stamp dialog box with a preview of your new stamp, as shown in Figure 20.19.

FIGURE 20.19

Select a file and an image preview is shown in the Select Image for Custom Stamp dialog box.

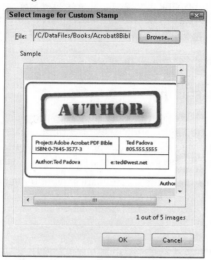

3. **Create a new stamp category.** Click OK in the Select Image for Custom Stamp dialog box and you arrive at the Create Custom Stamp dialog box. The Category text box appears with the default text: *<type here to name a new category>*. Select the text and type a new category name. (Note you can also select a category from the pull-down menu and add your new stamp to an existing category.) In my example, I typed MyStamps for a new category.

4. **Name your stamp.** Tab to the Name text box in the Create Custom Stamp dialog box and type a name for your stamp. I used the name Author Stamp for my stamp, as shown in Figure 20.20.

   If you want to downsample a large image file, check the Down sample stamp to reduce file size check box. If you want to change your design and not use the image shown in the preview, you can click the Select Image for Custom Stamp button and locate another image.

   When all the attributes are assigned for your new stamp, click OK.

FIGURE 20.20

Type a Category and Name for your new custom stamp.

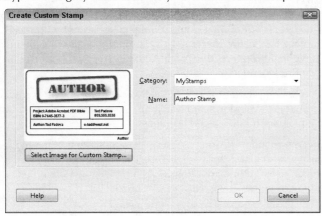

5. Use your new stamp. Open the Stamp pull-down menu and you should see your new stamp category. Select the category name and the new stamp appears in a submenu, as shown in Figure 20.21. Click the new stamp and click in a document to apply the stamp.

FIGURE 20.21

Select the stamp from the new category submenu and click in a document to add the stamp.

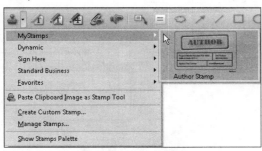

File Format Compatibility with Stamp Comments

Depending on what type of Acrobat product you use, the file formats you can import when creating custom stamps will vary. File format compatibility is consistent with the PDF conversion options you have available when using the File ➪ Create PDF ➪ From File menu command. In Acrobat Standard, you have fewer options than with Acrobat Pro. Acrobat Pro has fewer options than you find with Acrobat Pro Extended.

In addition to all the 3D drawing program applications available for conversion with Acrobat Pro Extended (Windows), Acrobat Pro (Windows and Macintosh) offers you conversion options for rich media files such as movie files, sound files, and Flash files.

When you use a multimedia format for creating a custom stamp, the first frame in the file is used as a poster view and graphic representation for your stamp. The media does not play within a stamp comment. You can however, use a multimedia frame when reviewing a document when you want to make comments regarding multimedia imports.

Appending stamps to a new category

After creating a custom stamp and adding a new category, the next time you open the Create Custom Stamp dialog box, you have a choice for adding a new category or appending a new stamp to your existing category. Here's how you append a stamp to an existing category:

STEPS: Appending stamps to an existing category

1. **Select Manage Stamps from the Stamp tool pull-down menu.** The Manage Stamps dialog box opens, as shown in Figure 20.22.

FIGURE 20.22

The Manage Custom Stamps dialog box shows all stamps appended to categories.

2. **Click Create.** Click the Create button and the Select Image for Custom Stamp dialog box opens.

3. **Add a new stamp.** Follow the same steps for adding a stamp as you do when creating a new stamp. When you arrive at the Create Custom Stamp dialog box, select the category you want to add your stamp from in the Category pull-down menu. Type a name for your stamp and you arrive at the Manage Custom Stamps dialog box, as shown in Figure 20.22. In Figure 20.22, I appended a stamp to the MyStamps category.

4. **Click OK.** Your new stamp appears listed in the category submenu.

In the Manage Custom Stamps dialog box, you have several tools for managing stamps. Click the Create button to append stamps to a category or create new categories. Select a stamp and click Edit to modify an appearance, category name, or stamp name. Select a stamp and click Delete to remove a stamp from a category, or select a category and click Delete to remove an entire category. Click a stamp and click the Down sample stamp to reduce file size option if you want to downsample images. Apply edits and click OK. When you return to the Stamp tool pull-down menu, the additions/deletions are shown when you open the menu.

Pasting a Clipboard image as a stamp

Yet another Stamp tool in Acrobat is the Paste Clipboard Image as Stamp tool. Any data you copy to the Clipboard can be pasted as a stamp. You might want to copy an image and text together in a document to make a comment about a layout design or the relationship between a drawing and image. In a comment pop-up note, you can add annotations describing your point.

To paste data back in a document as a stamp comment, you need to first copy data; then paste it as a stamp comment. Listed below are the steps to copy data and paste the Clipboard data as a stamp.

STEPS: Pasting image data as a stamp comment

1. **Open a document in Acrobat containing both images and text.** For this example, we'll look at copying an image and a text passage.

2. **Take a snapshot.** Select the Snapshot tool from the Select & Zoom toolbar. Marquee an area you want to capture for your stamp image. When you release the mouse button, the data are copied to the Clipboard.

3. **Open the Stamp tool pull-down menu and select Paste Clipboard Image as Stamp Tool.** The cursor changes to load the Stamp tool cursor.

4. **Add the stamp to a document page.** With the cursor gun loaded as a new stamp, click and drag open a rectangle where you want the stamp to appear.

> **TIP** You can also press Ctrl/⌘+V to paste any Clipboard data as a stamp. When files are enabled with Adobe Reader usage rights, this keyboard shortcut also works in Adobe Reader.

5. **Add a comment note.** Select the Hand tool and click the stamp icon and a pop-up note window opens. Type a message in the note window, as shown in Figure 20.23.

FIGURE 20.23

Click the stamp icon with the Hand tool and type a comment in the note pop-up window.

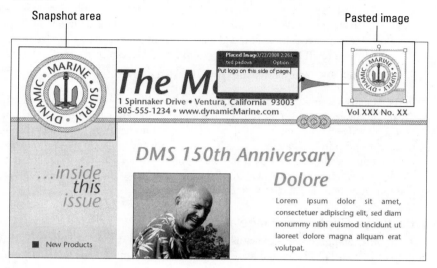

> **TIP** If the Paste Clipboard Image as Stamp command is grayed out, you don't have an image copied to the Clipboard. To verify content on the Clipboard, open the Create Task Button pull-down menu. If the PDF from Clipboard menu item is grayed out, no data exist on the Clipboard.

Attaching files

File attachments enable you to attach any document file, recorded sound, or pasted image on your hard drive to an open PDF file. When you attach files, the file is embedded in the PDF document. Embedding a file provides other users the capability to view attachments on other computers and across platforms. At first it may appear as though the attachment is a link. However, if you transport the PDF document to another computer and open the attachment, the embedded file opens in the host application. Users on other computers need the original authoring application to view the embedded file. You can add file attachments in Acrobat Standard, Acrobat Pro, and Acrobat Pro Extended. You can also add file attachments in Adobe Reader when PDFs have been created with usage rights for Adobe Reader.

> **CROSS-REF** For more information on using the File Attachments tools and the File Attachments panel, see Chapter 12.

Using the Markup Tools

As I mentioned earlier in this chapter when introducing the Comment & Markup tools, the tools in the Comment & Markup toolbar can be categorized into two subsets. All the previous pages in this chapter dealt with the comment tools from the Sticky Note tool through the Attachments tools. Beginning with the Callout tool and moving to the right in the Comment & Markup toolbar, you have tools that fit into the Markup tools category.

Markup tools offer you a range of different tools that can be used with technical drawings, manuals, brochures, design pieces, as well as routine office memos and other such documents. These tools deviate from the standard highlighter and Text Edits tools in that they tend to be used as graphic enhancements for communicating messages. If you're an engineer or technical writer, you may be inclined to use all the tools. If you're a business professional, you may pick and choose certain tools when reviewing and marking up documents. At the least, Acrobat provides a tool for just about any user in any environment when it comes to review and markup.

Callout tool

 The Callout tool is used to note attention to an object, block of text, image, or other element on a page where you want to focus comments about a specific item. Notice in Figure 20.24 the Callout in the upper right corner of the figure.

Cloud tool

 The Cloud tool is used similar to the Polygon Line tool where you click, release the mouse button, move the cursor, click, move the cursor again, and continue until you draw a polygon shape. Return to the point of origin and release the mouse button and Acrobat closes the path. The paths appear as a cloud shape. The shape can be filled and stroked. In Figure 20.24, a shape was drawn with the Cloud tool, and an opacity of 25 percent was applied so the underlying area could be viewed with transparency.

Line tools with inline text

 You use the Line tools with inline text like the Dimension tool was used in earlier versions of Acrobat to mark or comment about the distance between two points. The mark is drawn with two lines at right angles to the distance line, as shown in Figure 20.24. After you draw a line you can reshape it, changing the angle or the length of the two lines at right angles to the distance line.

Text Box tool

 You use the Text Box tool for creating large blocks of text. You have more control over fonts, text attributes, and flexibility with the Text Box tool than when using a Note comment. Notice in Figure 20.24 the text in the Text Box and the options available in the Properties Bar at the bottom of the Toolbar Well. As text is selected in the Text Box, you have an abundant number of font attribute choices in the Properties Bar.

FIGURE 20.24

Markups shown are the 1) Cloud tool, 2) Callout tool, 3) Line tool, and 4) Text Box tool.

In the Text Box Properties dialog box, you can change opacity for text boxes, background colors, and line styles for borders. The remaining options are similar to properties for other comment tools.

Drawing tools

The Line tools are used for creating straight lines. You might use Line tools with or without arrowheads to illustrate points of interest, point out where background elements need to be moved, point to an object, or similar kinds of notations. These tools include:

- **Arrow tool.** The Arrow tool can be used with arrowheads, although applying arrowheads is a matter of user preference. You can draw straight lines on a 360-degree axis.

- **Line tool.** The Line tool can have the same attributes assigned as the preceding Arrow tool, making them indistinguishable from each other. The intent is for the Arrow tool to provide you with a line for arrowheads, whereas the Line tool remains without arrowheads. When marking up a document and using both line tools, you don't need to keep addressing the Line Properties dialog box each time you want to toggle on or off arrowheads. It's a matter of user preference, though, as you can choose to add or eliminate arrowheads from either tool.

- **Rectangle tool.** Use this tool to draw rectangle or square shapes. To keep the object constrained to a square, hold down the Shift key as you click and drag.

- **Oval tool.** Using this tool involves the same process as the Rectangle tool for constraining objects to circles. Oval shapes are drawn without adding the Shift key.

- **Polygon Line tool.** The Polygon Line tool also creates straight lines, but the lines are connected as you click the cursor to move in another direction. When you finish drawing a shape or lines with angles, double-click the mouse button to complete the line.

- **Polygon tool.** Use the same sequence of clicking and moving as described earlier for the Cloud tool. When you release the mouse button back at the point of origin, the shape closes with flat edges instead of semicircles like the Cloud tool.

- **Pencil tool.** You use the Pencil tool to draw freeform lines. Whereas all the line tools draw straight lines, you use the Pencil tool for marking a page by drawing with a pencil, as you would with pencil and paper. The properties for pencil markings include choices for line weights, line colors, and line opacity settings.

  Pencil comments are one contiguous line. If you stop drawing by releasing the mouse button, click, and drag again, a new comment is added to the document.

- **Pencil Eraser tool.** The Pencil Eraser tool erases lines drawn with the Pencil tool. Lines drawn with other tools cannot be erased with this tool. When you draw a line with the Pencil tool and erase part of the line, the remaining portion of a Pencil comment is interpreted as a single comment. Broken lines where you may have several smaller lines remaining after erasing part of a Pencil comment are considered part of the same comment.

A note pop-up is associated with the entire group of Drawing tools. You can access tool properties by opening a context menu on a mark drawn with any tool. In the Properties dialog box for the respective tool, you can change stroke and fill colors and opacities. For strokes, you can change line weights. As with other comment tools, you also have available in the Properties dialog box General attributes options and Review History options.

Drawing tools and context menus

One addition to an open context menu on one of the drawing tools is the Flip Line command. If you have an arrowhead on one side of a line and you want the direction to be pointing in the opposite way, open a context menu and select Flip Line.

Line tool properties

Many of the same Sticky Note properties — color assignment, opacity, author, subject, and reviewing — are available for line tools. Additional line tool properties include line weights and end caps. More options are available for end caps in the Properties dialog box than in the Properties Bar. In Figure 20.25, the line attributes are compared between settings with the Properties Bar on the left and the Properties dialog box on the right.

FIGURE 20.25

Line settings available in the Properties Bar and the Properties dialog box

Line styles are the same in both the Properties Bar and the Properties dialog box, as shown in Figure 20.26.

FIGURE 20.26

Line Style properties are the same in the Properties Bar and the Properties dialog box.

The Default Font Attributes

During the initial days of the Acrobat 8 release, many users complained that they didn't know how to change the font color for Text Box comments from the default red text to black text. Perhaps more important to Text Box comments than any other commenting tool, you need to consistently be aware that there are two areas where you change properties for comment and markup tools.

When you open a context menu on a comment or markup tool and choose Properties, the Properties dialog box opens. You make choices as I've consistently addressed in this chapter for changing various properties. However, all properties for many tools are not included in the Properties dialog box — particularly the Text Box font attributes. To change text attributes for Text Box comments, you need to make those changes in the Properties Bar. The Text Box Text Properties open in the Properties Bar when the cursor is active inside a Text Box comment.

Once you change text properties in the Text Box Text Properties Bar, click outside the Text Box and then click the Text Box again and open a context menu. From the menu options choose Make Current Properties Default to change the default for the text attributes. Note that while you see an I-beam cursor, opening a context menu won't provide you an option to change the defaults, which is why you need to first click outside the Text Box comment area.

Managing line comments

To move drawing objects, align them, or reshape them, you need to select an object with the Hand tool. If you experience difficulty selecting a line, it may be because the Make Hand tool select text check box for the Hand tool preference option is selected. If selecting drawing tool objects is awkward, open the Preferences dialog box (Ctrl/⌘+K) and select General in the left pane. Disable the check box for Make Hand tool select text.

 If you want to keep the Hand tool preferences set to select text with the tool and you have difficulty selecting markups, open the Comments tab and click a comment to select it.

 For more information on using the Hand tool for text selections, see Chapter 13.

Click an object and handles appear either at the line ends or at each end of line segments around polygon objects. (See Figure 20.27.) You can drag any handle in or out to resize or reshape objects. To move an object, click on a line or a fill color and drag the shape.

FIGURE 20.27

To reshape objects, select the Hand tool, click on a handle (square shape on a line), and drag to change the shape.

Drawing tools comments can be copied, cut, pasted, deleted, aligned, distributed, and sized. Use the Select Object tool and open a context menu while one or more objects are selected. Choose a menu command for the operation desired.

> **TIP** When selecting objects with the Select Object tool, you can draw a marquee through objects to select them. You don't need to completely surround comments within a marquee to select them.

Adding Comments to Video Files

If you opened up this book and jumped right into Comment & Markup, you missed my earlier claims regarding the great new integration with Adobe Flash and multimedia in Acrobat 9. As I covered in Chapter 7, you can drag an Adobe Flash file or any of the supported media types to the Acrobat 9 document pane, and your file is embedded in a new PDF document created at the frame size of the multimedia clip.

> **NEW FEATURE** Once you convert to PDF, import a multimedia file in a PDF, or add a multimedia file to a PDF Portfolio, you can add comment markups to the media. All the comment tools you use for marking up PDF documents are available to you when commenting on media clips.

Adobe has added some special features to commenting on media. When you use any one of the Comment & Markup tools that support a note pop-up window and when using the Callout or Text Box tool, the time code for the video frame is reported in the first line of text in the note.

In Figure 20.28 I added comments to four video frames in a movie clip. Notice that the time code for each frame is reported in all the notes.

As is with any type of comments and markups, you can view the annotations in the Comments panel. When you click on a comment shown in the Comments panel, the video jumps to the frame where the comment was added.

> **CROSS-REF** For more information on using the Comments panel, see "Using the Comments Panel" later in this chapter.

All the Comment & Markup tools are supported when commenting on media clips. The first line of text in the notes reports the time code for the clip.

Using the Show Menu

 You can adjust several settings for comments and comment pop-up notes in the Show tool contained in the Comment & Markup toolbar. Options for the pull-down menu are also found in the Comments panel. Open the pull-down menu to see the menu commands shown in Figure 20.29.

The Show tool pull-down menu offers commands for working with comments and comment note pop-ups.

From the menu selections, you have the following choices:

- **Show Comments List.** Select this command to open the Comments panel. You can also open the Comments panel by clicking the Comments tab.

- **Hide All Comments.** Selecting the command opens a warning dialog box indicating that all replies in a review will be hidden. Click OK in the warning dialog box and all comments are hidden from view, but still attached to the document. Return to the menu and Show All Comments.

- **Show by Type.** You can selectively show comments by type. Choices from the submenu include All Types, Notes, Drawing Markups, Text Editing Markups, Stamps, and Attachments. You can select multiple types by returning to the submenu and making additional selections. For example, if you want to show Notes, Stamps, and Attachments while hiding Drawing Markups and Text Editing Markups, select Notes, return to the menu, and select Stamps. Notes remain selected when you make the second selection. Return again and select Attachments and all three types remain in view while the other types remain hidden from view.

- **Show by Reviewer.** You can choose to show comments by one or more reviewers for documents retrieved from a review session. The method of selecting multiple reviewers follows the same behavior as with Show by Type.

- **Show by Status.** Also used with review sessions, you can show comments by selected Review status and by Migration status.

CROSS-REF For information on status assignment, see "Using the Comments Panel" later in this chapter. For information on the migration options, see Chapter 21.

- **Show by Checked State.** You can check comments for your own personal use. Comments are either Checked or Unchecked in the Comments panel. From the submenu options, you can choose to show all checked comments, unchecked comments, or both.

- **Open All Pop-ups.** Opens all pop-up notes.

- **Minimize All Pop-ups.** Closes all pop-up notes.

- **Show Connector Lines.** When the mouse cursor appears over a comment, connector lines are shown from the comment to the comment note. If you don't want to show the connector lines, select this command. By default, connector lines are shown.

- **Align New Pop-ups by Default.** By default, comment notes are aligned to the right side of the document page. When this menu item is checked, the comment notes appear aligned together on top of each other. Removing the check mark from this option causes note pop-ups to align with the note icon.

Using the Comments Menu

A menu dedicated to comments appears at the top-level menu bar. Open the Commenting menu and you find several commands redundant with the Show pull-down menu and a single command not available in other menus.

Unique commands in the Comments menu include:

- **Commands for Comment Reviews.** A fw commands appear for comment reviews such as Attach for Email Review, Send for Shared Review, Migrate Comments, and Track Reviews. Note that Tracker is also accessed in the Comments panel.

CROSS-REF For information on all the commands related to reviews, see Chapter 21.

- **Enable for Commenting and Analysis in Adobe Reader.** When you chose this command and save the PDF file, the file is enabled only for commenting. No provision is made for saving form data or adding digital signatures.

CROSS-REF For information on enabling PDFs for commenting in Adobe Reader, see Chapter 19.

- **Summarize Comments.** You also have the same commands available in the Comments panel. See "Using the Comments Panel" later in this chapter.

- **Print with Comments Summary.** This command is also available in the Comments panel. See "Using the Comments Panel" later in this chapter.

- **Importing and exporting comments.** You have the same commands available in the Comments panel. See "Exporting and Importing Comments" later in this chapter.

CROSS-REF For more information on importing and exporting comments, see Chapter 8.

Using the Comments Panel

The Comments panel conveniently contains many tools and options for managing comments. By default, the Comments panel opens horizontally across the bottom of the Acrobat window like the Attachments panel and lists all the comments created in a PDF document. If you toggle views between several PDF files, the Comments panel dynamically updates the list of comments to reflect comments on the file active in the Document pane or in two document panes.

Depending on the size of your monitor, you'll find that viewing the panel occupies substantial space in the Acrobat window. If you're working on a small monitor, the amount of room left over for viewing pages, after loading toolbars in the Toolbar Well and expanding the Comments panel, can be very skimpy. Fortunately, you can view the panel docked in the Navigation pane and control the size by dragging the horizontal separator bar at the top of the panel down to reduce size, as shown in Figure 20.30.

FIGURE 20.30

Drag the separator bar up or down to resize the Comments panel.

Separator bar

You also have a choice for floating the panel by undocking it from the Navigation pane and resizing the panel. To undock the Comments panel, click on the tab and drag it to the Document pane. You can resize the panel by dragging the lower right corner in or out to reduce or expand the size.

Either way you choose to view the Comments panel, you'll find using it to be a great asset when reviewing documents and participating in review sessions. At first it may be a struggle to find the right size and location for the panel, but with a little practice you'll find the many tools contained in the panel much easier to access than using menu commands.

Viewing comments

The Comments panel lists all the comments contained in the active document. By default the comments are listed by page. In a multi-page document, you'll see Page 1, Page 2, Page 3, and so on displayed in the list on the left side of the panel.

You can view the list of comments expanded or collapsed. In Figure 20.30, you see the list expanded. Expanded lists show comments in a hierarchy as bookmarks are shown in the Bookmarks pane. You can expand individual pages that contain comments by clicking on the plus (+) symbol (Windows) or the right-pointing arrow (Macintosh). To expand all comments, click the Expand All button in the Comments panel toolbar shown in Figure 20.31. Conversely, you can collapse all comments by clicking the Collapse All button. Note that in Figure 20.31 the minus (–) symbol shows the Collapse All tool but the text is not shown because of a lower resolution monitor view.

Comments are listed in a hierarchical order. If you have several comments on a page and you click on the icon to the left of the comment to expand the page comments, you see the Comment icon, author, and content of a note pop-up. You can further expand each comment in the expanded list by clicking on the plus (+) symbol (Windows) or right-pointing arrow (Macintosh). When further expanded, the comment subject and the creation date are displayed in the pane.

FIGURE 20.31

Comments are ordered in a hierarchical list. By default, comments are viewed nested in a page order. The first three pages are expanded while the individual comments remain collapsed.

Sorting comments

You can change the default Page sorting to any of the following:

- **Type.** Comments are sorted together by the type of comment contained on pages. All Note comments appear together, all highlight comments appear together, all stamps appear together, and so on.

- **Page.** The default. Comments are listed together successively by page.

- **Author.** If a document has comments from several different authors, the comments are listed by author and sorted in an alphabetical order by author name.

- **Date.** The creation date is the sort order with the most recent date appearing first in the list.

- **Color.** Comments are sorted according to the color settings made in the comment Properties dialog boxes.

- **Checkmark Status.** You can check a comment for your own personal method of flagging a comment. Checking comments might be made for you to alert yourself to review comments, perhaps to mark them for deletion, or to spend more time in a later editing session reviewing the comments made by others. The choice for what the check mark signals is a personal choice. When you view comments according to Checkmark Status, all unchecked Comments (Unmarked) are listed first followed by comments marked with a check mark.

■ **Status by Person.** The menu option includes a submenu where you can select an author. Select an author name from the submenu and comments are sorted with the comments for the selected author appearing first. The unchecked comments are listed next by author name. You must have Status set on at least one comment to activate this command.

Navigating comments

 The up and down arrows in the Comments toolbar enable you to move back and forth between comments. Click the down-pointing arrow to move to the next comment in the list. Click the up-pointing arrow to navigate to a previous comment. The arrow tools are grayed out when comments are collapsed. In order to use the tools, you need to have one or more groups of comments expanded and have a comment selected.

Double-clicking a comment in the list takes you to the page where the comment appears. When you double-click the comment in the Comments panel, an associated pop-up note also opens. You must uncheck Hide comment pop-ups when Comments List is open for the note pop-ups to open from clicking the notes in the Comments panel.

Searching comments

 You can search the contents of comment pop-up notes. To find a word in a pop-up note, select the Search comments tool. Enter the search criteria and click Search Comments. You can also open the full or generic Search pane and select the Include Comments check box. The Search pane offers you the same search options used for searching open PDF documents. You can match case, search for whole words only, and other search criteria. The results of your search, however, return words found in the document as well as words found in comment pop-up notes.

When a word is found in a comment pop-up note, the page where the note appears opens and the pop-up note opens with the found word highlighted.

CROSS-REF For more information on using the Search pane, see Chapter 6.

Printing comments

The Print Comments tool does more than print the comments in a document to your printer. When you select the Print Comments tool, a pull-down menu opens where you can choose from two menu options. These menu commands include the following:

■ **Print Comments Summary.** Use this command to create a summary page as a new PDF file and print the summarized comments to your default printer. The comment summary is a temporary file that Acrobat creates while you print the summarized comments. After completing the print job, Acrobat deletes the summary.

- **Create PDF of Comments Summary.** Use this command to create a new PDF document that summarizes the comments in your document, rather than print a file to your printer. You can save this file and keep it around to review a summary of the comments.

From each of the menu commands, Acrobat defaults to "Document and comments with sequence numbers on separate pages." If you want to print pages with comments configured with different settings, select from one of four radio button options for the way you want to view a summary. The radio button options appear in the Summarize Options dialog box that opens when you select either menu command in the Print Comments menu.

CROSS-REF For details in regard to working with comment summaries, see the section "Creating Comment Summaries" later in this chapter.

Deleting comments

In addition to deleting comments from the context menus used when creating comments, you can delete comments from within the Comments panel. Select a comment in the pane and click on the Trash icon to delete the selected comment. After deleting a comment, you have one level of undo available to you. If you change your mind after deleting a comment, choose Edit ⇨ Undo. You can also undo selecting multiple comments and clicking on the Trash icon. Choose Edit ⇨ Undo successively if you change your mind after deleting multiple comments. In the event you lose the Undo command, you need to choose File ⇨ Revert to bring back the comment. Be certain to update your PDF file after reviewing any comment deletions. The Revert command reverts to the last saved version of the file.

Marking comments

The Checkmark tool is used to flag comments for a special purpose. You can select a comment in the Comments list in the panel and select the tool to checkmark the current selection. You can also apply check marks to comments by clicking in the open check mark box when a comment is expanded. Between the expand/collapse icon and the comment icon is a check box. Click the box to checkmark a comment. When viewing an expanded comments list, you do not need to select comments in order to mark the check boxes.

Setting comment status

Marking a comment with a check mark, described in the preceding section, is a method for you to keep track of comments for your own purposes. The Set Status tool is used to mark a comment's current status that is intended for use in comment reviews and when shared with other users. From the tool pull-down menu you have two subcategories for marking the status of a comment. Under Review you have five choices: None, Accepted, Cancelled, Completed, and Rejected. Under Migration you have three choices: None, Not Confirmed, and Confirmed. These options are the same as those you have in the Show tool pull-down menu.

CROSS-REF For more information on using the status marks in review sessions, see Chapter 21.

Editing comment pop-up notes

A very handy feature available to you when viewing comments in an expanded list is the ability to edit note pop-up text. Rather than navigating to each page containing a comment and opening the associated note pop-up window to make your edits, you can delete, change, or modify text listed in the Comments panel.

When you select the note pop-up text in the Comments panel, the note pop-up window opens in the Document pane. In order for the note pop-up window to open when you click a comment in the Comments panel, you need to make certain the Commenting preference option for Hide comment pop-ups when Comments List is open is unchecked. You don't need the comment pop-up note open to make edits in the Comments panel, but if you want to examine note pop-ups on the document pages, disable this preference option.

As you make changes in the Comments panel, changes are dynamically reflected in the pop-up note window. If you edit text in the pop-up note window, the text edits are reflected in the Comments panel.

Exporting and Importing Comments

If you ask a colleague to comment on a document, you can bypass the email, shared, and Acrobat. com reviews by having a reviewer export comments and email the exported file to you. When you export comments from a PDF document, the data are exported as an FDF or XFDF file. The data file results in much smaller file sizes than PDF documents and can easily be imported back into the original PDF or copy of the original PDF document.

To export comments from a PDF document, open the Comments menu. Three menu commands exist for exporting comments. Choose Comments ⇨ Export Comments to Word to export the comments directly to a Microsoft Word document. Choose Export Comments to AutoCAD to export comments directly to an AutoCAD .dwg file. The third option is Export Comments to a Data File. When you choose this option you can select either FDF or XFDF as your file format. Using these two formats, you can import the data file comments back into your PDF document. Choose Comments ⇨ Import Comments to import the data file comments into your PDF file.

CROSS-REF For information on exporting comments to AutoCAD files, see Chapter 7. For exporting to MS Word files, see Chapter 8.

Exporting/importing comments to and from a file

When you export comments to a file, the Export Comments dialog box opens. The dialog box behaves similarly to a Save As dialog box where you select a destination folder, provide a filename, and click a Save button. Acrobat provides a default name by using the PDF filename with a .fdf extension. You can use the default name or change the name in the File Name field box. From the Save as Type (Windows) or Format (Macintosh) pull-down menu, you can select between FDF formatted files and XFDF (XML-based FDF) files. The default is FDF.

Click Save in the Export Comments dialog box. The resulting file can be exported to a user who has the same PDF document from which the FDF file was created. If you receive an FDF file and want to load the comments, choose Comments ➪ Import Comments. The Import Comments dialog box opens. Navigate to the location where the data file is located and select it. Click the Select button and the comments are imported into the open PDF document.

NOTE You have three file format options — not only FDF and XFDF for export, but also PDF. If someone sends you a PDF with comments, you can import those comments directly to your version without having to export them from your reviewer's copy and then import into your copy.

When you import comments in a PDF document, all the comments are imported in the exact location where they were originally created. If you delete a page in a PDF file and import comments, Acrobat ignores comments where it can't find matching pages. Note pop-ups and icons are matched with the way they appear in the file from which the comments were exported.

Exporting selected comments

You can select comments and choose to export only the selected comments to an FDF or XFDF file. Open the Comments panel and select comments according to the sort order listed in the Comments panel. The default is by page. Select a page in the list and open the Options pull-down menu from the Comments panel toolbar. Select Export Selected Comments from the menu options.

The Export Comments dialog box opens. Navigate your hard drive to find the folder where you want to save the FDF or XFDF file, provide a name for the file, and click the Save button.

TIP When exporting all comments leave the filename for the FDF or XFDF exported file at the default provided by Acrobat. When exporting Selected Comments, be certain to edit the filename. By default, Acrobat uses the same name. If you elect to export all comments and then want to export selected comments, you might mistakenly overwrite files with the same filename. By getting into a habit of being consistent when naming files, you'll prevent potential mistakes.

Filtering Comments

You can further enhance the features available to you for review and markup, exporting and importing comments, and viewing comments in the Comments panel, by filtering comments in groups. Filtering comments temporarily hides comments you don't want to use at the moment. You can choose to display all comments by an author, a date, a reviewer, selected types of comments, and a range of other criteria. When comments are filtered, exporting comments or creating comment summaries (explained in the next section) is applied only to those comments currently viewed. Any hidden comments are excluded from the task at hand.

Show ▾   You manage the comment filter via the Show pull-down menu. The options in the Show pull-down menu in the Toolbar Well are identical to the menu options in the Show tool pull-down menu in the Comments panel.

CROSS-REF   To understand more about the Show menu options, see the section "Using the Show Menu" earlier in this chapter.

TIP   If you know ahead of time that you want to export edits back to Microsoft Word, you can mark only those comments received from reviewers that you intend to export to Word. When the review session is completed, choose Show ⇨ Hide All Comments. Open the menu again and choose Show by Type ⇨ Text Editing Markups. Return to the menu and choose Show by Checked State ⇨ Checked. Export the comments, and only the Text Edit comments with the items you checked during the review are exported to Word.

The remaining menu options include non-filtering menu choices such as opening/closing note pop-ups, showing connector lines, aligning icons and pop-up notes, and accessing the Comment preferences. You can also make these menu selections from other tools and menus as described earlier in this chapter.

Creating Comment Summaries

If you create an extensive review from many participants over a period of time, the number of comments may become too many to comfortably manage in the Comments panel or on the document pages. Or you may have a need to create a comment summary you want to distribute to users after filtering out comments that you don't want included in a summary. Furthermore, you may want to print a hard copy of comments that show the PDF pages with connector lines to a summary description. You can accomplish all these tasks and more when you create comment summaries.

To create a comment summary, you need to have a PDF document open in the Document pane and comments in view in the Comments panel. The pane can be open or collapsed. Comments can be filtered according to the sorts and filtering you want to apply, but at least one comment with the criteria must exist for a summary report to contain comment information.

If the Comments panel is collapsed, you create a comment summary by opening the Comment menu and selecting Summarize Comments. If the Comments panel is open, you can choose the menu command from the Options menu.

When you select Summarize Comments from either menu command, the Summarize Options dialog box opens, as shown in Figure 20.32.

The first four radio buttons in the dialog box offer you choices for the way the summary pages are created and the page layout view, which may contain single page views or Continuous – Facing Pages views. The resulting summaries are created as separate PDF documents.

FIGURE 20.32

Select Summarize Comments from the Comments menu or a context menu in the Comments panel to open the Summarize Options dialog box.

Choices for creating a comment summary in the Summarize Options dialog box include:

- **Document and comments with connector lines on separate pages.** This option creates a comment summary with each summary page aside the respective document page with connector lines from each comment on a page to the summarized item in a new summary. When the summary is created, Acrobat automatically switches to a Two-Up Continuous layout. If you don't want a continuous view and you want the pages to snap to fit in the Document pane, select View ⇨ Page Display ⇨ Two-Up. In Figure 20.33, you see a summary of a document and comments with connector lines on separate pages shown in a Two-Up view.

- **Document and comments with connector lines on single pages.** The summary is similar to the preceding option; however, the PDF document and the summary are created together on a single landscape page. The size of the paper is determined by the setting specified in the Paper size pull-down menu. One advantage for this summary view compared to the preceding summary is the comments, connector lines, and summary data require a little less room on your monitor to view the original file and the summary information. Furthermore, if you export summaries for other users, the summarized information and original file are assembled together in a single document.

FIGURE 20.33

A summary shown in a Two-Up view

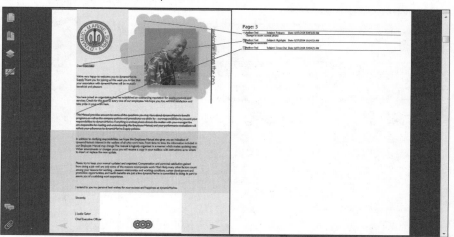

- **Comments only.** Only the summarized data are assembled together on single pages. The comment summaries are shown in a hierarchy according to the sort order you select in this dialog box. The page layout is a single page view.

- **Document and comments with sequence numbers on separate pages.** Summaries are created similarly to the method described in the preceding bullet, but with the addition of sequence numbers assigned to each comment according to the sort order and the order in which the comments were created. The page layout view is Two-Up Continuous, which shows the comments with sequence numbers and the resulting summary in the opposing page view.

- **Paper size.** From the pull-down menu, select a paper size according to the sizes available for your selected printer.

- **Sort comments by.** From the pull-down menu you can choose from four different options. The default is a sort according to Page. If you want another sort order, choose from Author, Type, or Date from the pull-down menu options. The sort order selected in the Summarize Options dialog box supersedes the sort order selected in the Comments panel.

- **Font Size.** Applies to the font used in the comment summary description on the newly created pages. Depending on the size selected, the summary pages may be fewer (Small) or more (Large). The point size for small is 5 points, for medium 6.75 points, and for large 9 points.

- **Include.** All comments summarizes all comments on the PDF pages regardless of whether the comments are in view or hidden. The Only the comments currently showing option creates a comment summary from the comments visible in the Comments panel.

- **Pages containing no comments.** Check the box if you want pages containing no comments included in the summary. Disable the check box and only pages with comments are included in the summary.

- **Pages.** Specify the page range for the summary in the text boxes.
- **Connector Line Color.** Click the color swatch and you can choose a color for connector lines from the pop-up color palette.
- **Opacity.** Applies an opacity setting for the connector lines.

Comment summaries are particularly useful when sending PDF documents to Adobe Reader users. Although Reader users can see comments you create in a PDF document, they cannot create comment summaries. You can create a summary for a Reader user and append the new document to the existing PDF file, and then send the file to other members in your workgroup.

Comparing Documents

If you set up a review for users to provide feedback on a document, you may incorporate recommended changes in a file. As you work on modifying files, you may end up with several documents in different development stages. If you aren't quite certain which document contains your finished edits, you may have a need to compare files to check for the most recent updates. Acrobat's Compare Documents feature (Acrobat Pro and Acrobat Pro Extended only) provides you a method for analyzing two files and reporting all differences between them.

To compare two documents choose Document ⇨ Compare Documents. The Compare Documents dialog box opens. You can open the dialog box without any file open in the Document pane, or open both files to compare and then select the menu command. In Figure 20.34, I have two files titled `Chapter08tn.pdf` and `Chapter08wd.pdf`. Because these two files are similar documents, I'm not certain which document contains revisions. Therefore, the documents are selected for comparison to check the differences.

FIGURE 20.34

Choose Document ⇨ Compare Documents to open the Compare Documents dialog box.

The Compare Documents dialog box contains the following options:

- **Compare (older document)/To (newer document).** The first two items are used to identify the documents for comparison. If no files are open in the Document pane, click the Choose button and select a file in the Open dialog box that appears. Click the second Choose button and open a second file. If you have the two documents to be compared open in the Document pane before opening the Compare Documents dialog box, the pull-down menus show you both open files. Select one file in the top pull-down menu and the second file in the next pull-down menu.

- **Document Description.** Three options are available from radio button choices at the bottom of the dialog box. Depending on which item you choose, the reports are more or less detailed and the speed in which the documents are compared relate to how much detail you want to analyze. Reports, spreadsheets, and magazine layouts perform textual searches and may take longer than the other choices.

- **Presentation decks, drawings or illustrations.** Use this option when comparing documents with vector art illustrations, PowerPoint presentations, and other documents that contain heavy illustration components.

- **Scanned documents.** Choose this option when comparing raster artwork scanned from paper documents such as forms (or two photographs).

The Compare Documents feature in Acrobat 9 is one of the major new improvements to Acrobat Pro and Acrobat Pro Extended. When you make your choices in the Compare Documents dialog box including selecting the files you want to compare and click OK, Acrobat reports results in the Compare panel shown in Figure 20.35. The summary shown in the Document pane immediately reports back to you if differences exist between the documents.

Acrobat makes it easy for you to begin your examination of the compared documents. Click the Get started: First change is on page *n* (where n reports the page where the first change is encountered). Also on the summary page you see a legend indicating markups you'll find in the compared documents. As shown in Figure 20.35 these include Highlight, Deleted, an up arrow, and two opposing arrows with definitions for what the symbols mean.

Click the text where you see Get started: First change is on page 1 and the page where the first change occurred is opened in the Document pane as shown in Figure 20.36. In the top right corer of the Document pane you find another legend reporting the types of changes found between the documents. Above the highlights on the page are comment notes that offer more detail on the specific differences found between the documents.

FIGURE 20.35

When you click OK in the Compare Documents dialog box the Compare panel opens reporting any differences between the compared documents.

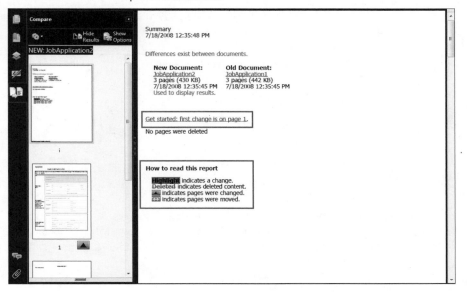

FIGURE 20.36

Click Get started: First change is on page 1 and the page containing the first change opens in the Document pane.

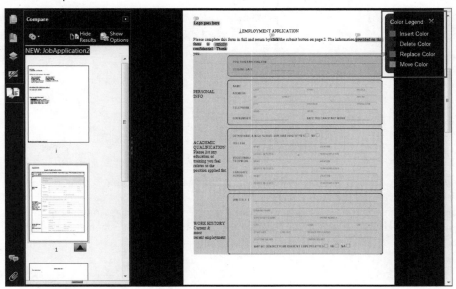

As you browse the report you can open the comment notes and view the detail information regarding a change found between the documents as shown in Figure 20.37. Acrobat makes it easy to detect where the change was found between the Old text and the New text as you can see in the comment note shown in Figure 20.38.

FIGURE 20.37

Comment notes report specific changes found between the compared documents.

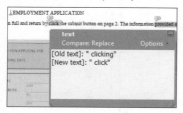

When comparing images Acrobat provides a nice quick view to detect changes. As you move the cursor over an image that has been changed in one of the documents, a popup window opens displaying both documents and the image comparison as shown in Figure 20.38.

FIGURE 20.38

Click in an area where an image has been changed in one document and a popup window displays both files where the image change occurred.

In the Compare panel you can scroll pages to examine additional comparison notations and you have some choices for viewing the found changes. Click Show Options in the Compare panel and the panel offers some options form viewing various changed items such as Annotations and Formatting. Below the check boxes, you find options for changing the Color Scheme in the legend as shown in Figure 20.39. If you use text or graphics colors that don't show enough contrast between the original text and the highlights for the changes found, you can change the color scheme to more clearly see the annotations.

FIGURE 20.39

The Compare panel offers options to include/exclude items in the comparison and choices for changing the color scheme for annotations and the legend.

Summary

- Acrobat provides an extensive set of Comment preferences. Before beginning any review session you should review the preference settings by choosing Edit ⇨ Preferences and clicking on Commenting in the left pane.

- A single toolbar in Acrobat 8 contains all the Comment & Markup tools.

- Most comments created in Acrobat have associated note pop-up windows where you can type comments.

- You access comment properties by opening context menus from a note icon or pop-up note title bar.

- You can create custom stamps in Acrobat from a variety of different file formats.

- Acrobat 9 enables you to add all the comment and markup types to video frames in movie clips and Flash video files.

- The Comments panel lists all comments in a PDF document. Additional tools are available in the Comments panel where you can mark status changes in comments, check comment status, and filter comments.

- You can enable usage rights for Adobe Reader users to participate in comment reviews from Acrobat Pro. And Acrobat Pro Extended.

- Comments can be filtered and sorted to isolate authors, types, dates, and other criteria. When exporting comments, only the sorted comments in view in the Comments panel are exported.

- Comments exported from a document can be imported into a matching PDF file, a Word file, and an AutoCAD file.

- When exporting comments from Acrobat as a file, the comments data are saved as FDF or XFDF and result in smaller file sizes.

- Comment summaries are displayed in one of four different report styles. When a summary is created it can be sorted upon creation and saved as a separate PDF file.

- The new Acrobat 9 Compare Documents feature enables you to locate differences between two PDF documents and analyze the comparison in the Compare panel. Reports are generated with comments describing found differences in detail.

Chapter 21

Working with Review Sessions

Throughout this book, I address the use of PDFs on the Web, and in several chapters, I've talked about Acrobat.com. As I discussed in Chapter 9, you can download selected Web pages or entire Web sites and have all the HTML pages converted to PDF. In Chapter 12 I talked about sharing PDF Portfolios on Acrobat.com.

Coming ahead in Chapter 29 I talk about Web conferencing and sharing files. In Chapter 30, I talk about eBooks and downloading eBooks; in Chapter 34 I talk about submitting form data to Acrobat.com; and in other chapters you find similar discussions on Acrobat PDFs hosted online and using the new sharing services provided via Acrobat.com. In short, the Web plays a major role with much of your Acrobat activity.

This chapter builds on information covered in Chapter 20 where I discussed using the commenting tools, menus, and Comments panel. In this chapter I cover commenting through Attach for Email Review and Send for Shared Review on Acrobat.com, which are, again, other uses for PDFs and the Internet.

Setting Up the Commenting for Reviews Environment

Commenting in review sessions requires use of the same tools discussed in Chapter 20. If you haven't read Chapter 20, take a moment to read how to load commenting tools and open the Comments panel. The tools you need to follow along in this chapter are the Comment & Markup tools and the Properties Bar. Load these tools as explained in Chapter 20.

Creating an Attach for Email Review

The abundant number of comment tools, properties, and menu commands are nothing more than overkill if all you want to do is add some note comments on PDF pages for your own use. Acrobat is designed with much more sophistication when it comes to commenting, and the tools provided to you are intended to help you share comments in workgroups.

Comment and review among workgroups is handled in two ways. You can set up an Attach for Email Review and exchange comments with your co-workers and colleagues where PDFs and data are exchanged through email, or you can set up a Send for Shared Review where participants upload and download comments to a shared folder on a network or Web server in the review process.

Adobe's Acrobat team wanted to make it almost seamless for any user to not only start a review session but participate in review sessions. With the ability to enable documents with usage rights for Adobe Reader users, anyone with the free Adobe Reader software can participate in an email or shared review.

CROSS-REF   For more information on adding usage rights to PDFs, see Chapters 19 and 20.

Initiating an Attach for Email Review

An Attach for Email Review is a method for you, the PDF author, to share a document that needs input from other members of a workgroup (in an email exchange), such as a proposal or draft document, and ask them to make comments for feedback. As comments are submitted, you can track comments from others and make decisions about how the comments are treated. Decisions such as accepting or rejecting comments are part of this process. The comment exchanges between you and your workgroup members are handled through email. When using this kind of review, the review initiator is the only person who sees comments from all the reviewers.

When you send a file for review, the PDF contains information about you, the author/initiator, who's invited to the review, and where the original is located on your system. When a recipient receives the email inviting him or her to review your document, the attachment to the email is a PDF the recipients use to make comments. The recipients open the PDF email attachment in Acrobat or Adobe Reader and make comments. When a reviewer finishes commenting, the reviewer sends the data back to the PDF author. The data sent from the reviewers can either be a Form Data File (FDF) or both the data and the PDF document (choices are made in Reviewing preferences discussed later in this chapter). If you start with a large PDF file, the comment exchanges using FDF data require much less data transfers because the comment data are typically much smaller than original PDF files.

When reviews are initiated, you *must* send the PDF file to all reviewers. You can then make a decision in the Reviewing preferences for whether the PDF or an FDF file is returned back to you. In the Preferences dialog box, click Reviewing and type a value in the Send comments as FDF for files greater than text box. The default is 5MB. Therefore, FDF data are returned for all files greater than 5MB. You can raise or lower the number by typing a new value in the text box. This setting is applied only to comments returned back to you. If you have a PDF greater than 5MB — or any file size for that matter — you must first send the PDF document to the recipients.

When comments are returned to you either in PDF or FDF form, double-click the file attachment in your email application. Double-clicking either file type appends comments from recipients to your original PDF you used when you invited recipients to participate in a review.

NOTE Before initiating a review, be certain to add your email address in the Identity preferences. If you don't add the Identity preferences, Acrobat prompts you in a dialog box and opens the Identity preferences for you. You can't proceed until you fill in the preference text boxes. Open the Preferences dialog box and select Identity. Add your personal identity information including your email address. The email address supplied in the Identity preferences is used when emailing PDFs from within Acrobat.

To understand how to start an email-based review, follow these steps.

STEPS: Initiating an email-based review

1. **Open a document in Acrobat Pro or Pro Extended.** Opening a document is optional because you can begin a review without a document open in the document pane. In this example, I start with a document open in Acrobat Pro. If using Acrobat Standard, you can initiate an email-based review, but you cannot enable the document with usage rights for Adobe Reader users for commenting. Enabling usage rights in Acrobat Standard is limited to enabling forms for form saves and digital signatures. If using Acrobat Pro or Pro Extended, you have an option for enabling the document for Reader users to participate in your review.

CROSS-REF For more information on enabling PDF documents using Acrobat products, see Chapter 19.

2. **Initiate the review.** If you want to make a comment on your document you can do so, but you need to be certain to save all your updates. After saving the file, select Attach for Email Review from the Comment task button pull-down menu. The first pane in the Getting Started wizard opens, as shown in Figure 21.1. This is the first of three panes appearing in the wizard when you initiate a review.

   By default, documents active in the document pane are specified in the field box in the first pane. If you change your mind or you start a review without a document open in Acrobat, click the Browse button and browse your hard drive to locate a file.

NOTE You can also access the same menu command by choosing Comments ➪ Attach for Email Review.

FIGURE 21.1

To start a review session, open the PDF to be used for the review and choose Attach for Email Review from the Comment task button pull-down menu or the Comments menu.

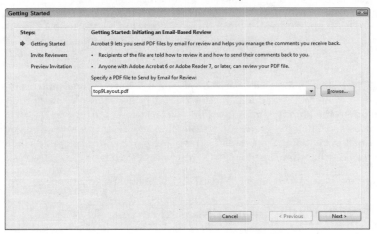

3. **Invite reviewers.** After identifying the file to send out for review, click the Next button to open the Invite Reviewers pane, as shown in Figure 21.2. The Address Book window will contain a list of recipients for your review. Type the email addresses for the people you want to participate in the review or click Address Book to launch your email address book to select reviewers to invite.

FIGURE 21.2

Add email addresses for the review participants.

4. **Preview the invitation.** Click Next to arrive at the Preview Invitation pane, as shown in Figure 21.3. This pane displays a preview of the email message you are about to send to reviewers. You can edit the Subject or Message by typing in the respective text boxes.

FIGURE 21.3

Preview the message to be sent to reviewers and click Send Invitation.

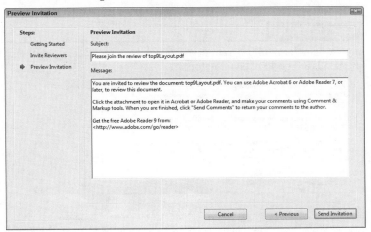

5. **Send the invitation.** Click Send Invitation in the third pane of the wizard. The Outgoing Message Notification dialog box opens as shown in Figure 21.4. This dialog box informs you that your document is attached to a new message in your default email client. You are also alerted to the fact that if you don't have your email application configured to send email automatically, you need to manually send the mail. Click OK to dismiss the dialog box.

FIGURE 21.4

Review the information in the Outgoing Message Notification dialog box and click OK.

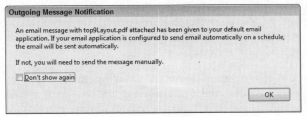

6. **Send the mail.** If your email program does not immediately send the invitation to reviewers, open your default email program and click the Send (or Send/Receive) button to commence the email initiation. In Figure 21.5, an invitation appears in Microsoft Outlook showing a recipient in the To field, the Subject of the email, and a file attachment. The message is derived from the Preview Invitation dialog box. Note that before initiating a send, you can still edit the message. Click the Send (or Send/Receive) button to send the email and attachment to the reviewers.

FIGURE 21.5

If your default email program does not send the message, open the program and click the Send (or Send/Receive) button.

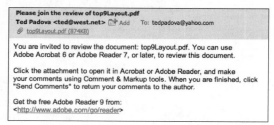

When you send your file for an email review by following the steps in the Attach for Email Review wizard, your file is enabled automatically with Adobe Reader usage rights. There's nothing special you have to do to enable the PDF document for Adobe Reader users to participate in the review. Be certain all your Reader users are working in Adobe Reader version 7 and above and all Acrobat users are working with Acrobat 6 and above.

Any kind of review you initiate appears in the Tracker where you can monitor reviews, invite new reviewers, set deadlines and end a review session. For more information on the Tracker, see the section "Using the Tracker" later in this chapter.

Participating in a review

Participants in a review include you — the PDF author and review initiator — and the people you select as reviewers. In your role, you field all comments from reviewers. If you use Attach for Email Review to send comments back to users, Acrobat does permit you to reply to users' comments. A review session is designed for a single set of responses; however, if you want, you can exchange comments back and forth with the reviewers.

Before you begin a review, be certain to save any edits made on the PDF. If you insert pages, delete pages, or perform a number of other edits without saving, the comments retrieved from others will appear out of place and make it difficult to understand where comments are made from the reviewers. Also, be certain to keep the original PDF in the same folder. If you decide to move the PDF to another folder, be certain to keep track of the location where the PDF resides. As you update comments, Acrobat needs to keep track of the directory path where the original PDF can be found. If Acrobat can't find the PDF, you are prompted to search for it.

> **TIP** If you want to relocate a PDF file in a review to another folder while maintaining the link in Acrobat to the file, use the Tracker and send the file to a new folder. For more on the Tracker, see "Using the Tracker" later in this chapter.

During a review period you and your recipients use tools in Acrobat designed for use with email reviews. When starting an email review, the first time you access the Attach for Email Review menu command, the PDF is sent to recipients. All subsequent comment exchanges between you and reviewers are handled with other tools. Be certain to not return to the Attach for Email Review command if you decide to respond to user comments. Doing so sends another PDF to a recipient.

Recipient participation

A recipient receiving your email with the PDF attachment can open the attachment directly within the email message. Double-clicking the email file attachment launches Acrobat and loads the PDF in the document pane.

Managing an Address Book for Review Sessions

When you open the Address Book from the Invite Reviewers section, shown earlier in this chapter in Figure 21.2, when using Microsoft Outlook as your default mail program, you can use names in your Address Book to invite reviewers. Just double-click the names you want to add to the email review; the names appear in the To text box at the bottom of the Address Book dialog box.

After entering email addresses in your Address Book and identifying the names you want to use for the review, click OK to add the addresses to the second pane in the Attach for Email Review wizard.

NOTE Reviewers make comments with any of the comment tools discussed earlier in this chapter and in Chapter 20. After a reviewer completes a review session, the reviewer clicks the Send Comments button in the Document Message bar, as shown in Figure 21.6.

FIGURE 21.6

When working on a PDF in review, the Send Comments button appears in the Document Message bar.

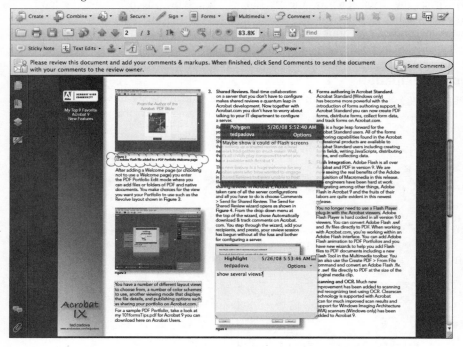

When the reviewer sends a response to the PDF author, the PDF author's email address is automatically supplied in the To field in the email program. The reviewer clicks Send and either a PDF or FDF is sent back to the PDF author. Again the file type is determined in the Reviewing preferences.

CROSS-REF Remember, as I discussed in Chapter 20, you can also comment on Adobe Flash files.

Author participation

When a reviewer sends a comment to you, you double-click the email attachment and Acrobat detects that the attachment is part of an email review. A dialog box opens as shown in Figure 21.7, prompting you to merge the comments with your original file that you sent for review.

FIGURE 21.7

Double-click an attachment with recipient comments and you are prompted to merge the comments in your original PDF that you submitted for an email review.

Click Yes and Acrobat opens with the Comment & Markup toolbar as a floating toolbar and the Comments panel expanded as shown in Figure 21.8. As comments are submitted from reviewers, you'll want to track reviews and decide to mark them for a status. If you want to reply to the recipients you can elect to send a reply to recipient comments; however, in some cases you'll want to make corrections and start a new review session. If you send a reply, each comment is treated as a separate thread in Acrobat. Instead of your having to select different tools to make responses scattered around a document page, Acrobat keeps each thread nestled together to make following a thread easier. Replies are contained in Note pop-up windows as shown in Figure 21.8. If you want to reply to a comment, open a context menu on the note pop-up and select Reply, or select Reply from the Options pull-down menu on a comment note. Additionally you can click the Reply tool in the Comments panel.

 For more on using Reply with note comments, see Chapter 20.

TIP You can open a context menu on a comment in the Comments panel and select Reply to reply to a comment.

FIGURE 21.8

Double click a file attachment and the Comment & Markup toolbar automatically opens in the Acrobat viewer.

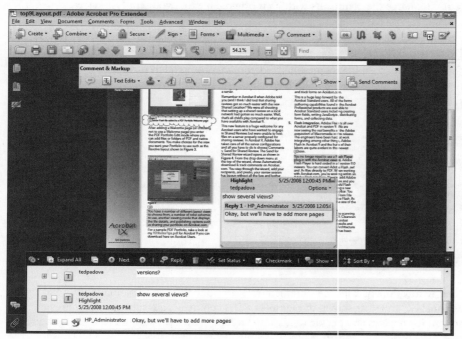

Updating comments

You send a file to recipients for review. The reviewers then send comments back to you. Your original document needs updating to reflect the new additions added by other reviewers. When you receive an email attachment, the comment data are submitted back to you. Only a single PDF resides on your computer. If you want to merge the data sent by other reviewers with your existing PDF document, double-click the file attachment sent back to you. Acrobat updates the original PDF document with the new comments.

Asking new reviewers to participate

You may begin a review and later decide you want to add new users to participate in the review. You can add new reviewers to a review at any time. To add a reviewer, choose Comments ➪ Invite Additional Reviewers or you can open the Tracker and invite additional reviewers directly in the Tracker (see the next section in this chapter). The same Attach for Email Review wizard opens as shown earlier in Figure 21.1. Walk through the steps to add new reviewers and the same PDF file is sent to additional reviewers via an email attachment. Note that you can also add new reviewers in the Tracker.

Using the Tracker

The Tracker is a separate window that opens on top of the Acrobat window where you find menu commands to help manage email-based, browser-based, and shared reviews. To open the Tracker, select Track Reviews from the Comment task button or choose Comments ➪ Track Reviews; or, from the Options pull-down menu in the Comments panel, select Track Reviews. Any one of the three menu items opens the Tracker shown in Figure 21.9.

FIGURE 21.9

The Tracker window provides information and tools for working with documents in review.

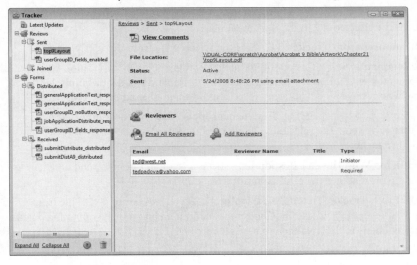

Viewing documents in the Tracker

The left pane in the Tracker lists all documents you have in review. From the list, select a filename and open a context menu. From the menu choices select Open. The respective file opens in the document pane.

Two categories appear in the left pane in Figure 21.9. All reviews I initiated are listed in the Sent list. Expand the list to see reviews by filename. The Joined list contains all reviews sent to me by another review initiator. Additional categories can appear in the Tracker depending on the work you perform for reviews and for distributing forms.

From a context menu opened on a document listed in the Reviews ➪ Sent list, shown in Figure 21.10, you have the following commands:

FIGURE 21.10

Open a context menu on a file in the left pane in the Tracker.

- **Open.** Opens the selected file in the document pane.

- **Remove Responses from Tracker.** Removes the selected file from the review.

- **Email All Recipients.** Select this option to open your default email application with the To field populated with all review participants. This command is a review reminder for participants who receive an email from you to remind them to send back comments.

- **Add Recipients.** Also launches your default email application with an automated message to invite other reviewers. The selected PDF file used for initiating the original review is added as a file attachment.

- **Email Recipients Who Haven't Responded.** This is a reminder item to send an email to all those recipients who haven't send comments to you.

- **Create PDF From Tracker Details.** New in Acrobat 9 you can create a PDF file from the details for a given review session. Choose the menu item and a PDF containing details about a review opens in the document pane as a new PDF file.

- **Create New Folder.** Choose Create New Folder to open the New Folder dialog box. Type a name for the new folder and the folder appears in the Reviews ➪ Sent list. You can add reviews and save the files together in the new folder.

- **Send To Folder.** From the submenu all the new folders you create are listed here. Rather than drag and drop files to new folders you create, open a context menu on a file and choose Send to Folder ➪ <new folder name> to neatly organize your reviews in individual folders.

On Windows a collapsed list is marked with a plus (+) symbol. On the Macintosh, a collapsed list is marked with a right-pointing arrowhead. Click this symbol to expand the list. If a list is already expanded, a minus symbol (Windows) or down arrow (Macintosh) appears. Click this symbol to collapse the list.

Tracking forms

The Tracker also lists all forms you have distributed. Clicking a form changes the Tracker options in the right pane. You have many new options in Acrobat 9 for tracking distributed forms. Rather than go into detail now about tracking forms, I explain more in Chapter 35.

Working with Shared Reviews

In Acrobat 8, Adobe made an effort to make shared reviews a little easier; however, the complicated process for configuring servers remained a mystery to many Acrobat users and didn't eliminate a necessary dependence on an IT department to help configure a server for online commenting. From the beginning when browser-based reviews where introduced in Acrobat 5, Adobe has been trying to simplify review sessions for people to comment on documents in real time where all participants can see each other's comments, or comment online where people can easily exchange comments in a review session. We've seen simplicity added in each release of Acrobat, but one aspect for developing a seamless environment for online commenting was still needed.

The bottleneck in the seamless operation of the shared review process has always been working with online servers. Unless you had a properly configured server, sharing comments online was impossible in Acrobat 8 and earlier viewers. What was required was technical assistance by a company's IT department to configure a server to support online commenting. For individual users and small businesses without sophisticated IT departments, online commenting just wasn't available in Acrobat 8 and earlier viewers.

 Now in Acrobat 9, Adobe has developed the last leg of the seamless operation for online comment and review. This final element of simplicity for engaging in shared reviews is handled through the Acrobat.com services available to users in the entire Acrobat 9 family of products.

CROSS-REF **For more information on Acrobat.com, see Chapter 29.**

Understanding shared review options

You have several choices to make when engaging in shared reviews. You can share reviews locally on your computer and on network servers, or you can share reviews on a Web server. In regard to Web servers, you have several types of Web servers from which to choose. Depending on the choice you make, the process can be very simple or quite complicated.

Among the choices you have for setting up a shared review are

- **Acrobat.com.** You can set up review sessions on Acrobat.com without having to worry about any special configurations of a server to collect comments and integrate the comments from multiple users.

- **Network Folder.** You can configure a network folder locally on your intranet to set up a shared review among a workgroup.

- **SharePoint Workspace.** For Windows SharePoint workspaces, users need to have read and write access to engage in reviews. This option requires some help from your IT department to configure the server and set up the permissions for the participants.

- **Web Server.** Again, this option requires some help from your IT department to configure a Web server with a shared folder and configure the participants for read/write services.

NEW FEATURE **One of the best new additions to Acrobat 9 is the introduction of Acrobat.com. This choice takes the configuration steps out of the process for initiating and engaging in shared reviews. For individuals and small companies without intranets and sophisticated IT departments, using Acrobat.com is something you'll learn to love.**

For the purposes of this chapter, I'll cover only two of the options you have for conducting shared reviews — setting up network folders and using Acrobat.com. If you work in an enterprise where you want to share reviews on Web servers, look to the Acrobat Help document and online information you can find at `www.adobe.com/devnet/acrobat/pdfs/online_collabora-tion.pdf` and `www.adobe.com/devnet/acrobat/online_review_admin.html`.

Using network folders

Setting up a network folder for shared reviews is intended for workgroups having internal local area networks. You begin setting up a network folder the same way as when using Acrobat.com for shared reviews. From a menu command, a wizard opens that walks you through the steps to configure a folder on a network server.

To see how easy it is to set up a network folder for shared reviews, do the following:

STEPS: Starting a shared review using a network folder

1. **Open the Comment task button pull-down menu and select Send For Shared Review.** The Send for Shared Review Wizard opens as shown in Figure 21.11.

2. **Choose a location for collecting reviewer's comments.** Open the pull-down menu at the top of the Send for Shared Review wizard and choose Automatically collect comments on my own internal server.

FIGURE 21.11

Open the pull-down menu at the top of the Send for Shared Review wizard and choose Automatically collect comments on my own internal server.

3. **Select a host.** Click Next in the Send for Shared Review wizard and the second pane in the wizard opens as shown in Figure 21.12. For setting up a network folder, click the first radio button for Network folder.

4. **Target a location to host your review.** Click the Browse button to open the Browse For Folder dialog box as shown in Figure 21.13. Choose a directory path, and if you need a new folder created, click the Make New Folder button. Name a new folder and click OK. Click OK in the Browse For Folder dialog box and you return to the second pane in the Send for Shared Review wizard.

FIGURE 21.12

Click the Network folder radio button and click the Browse button to identify a folder where the review data are collected.

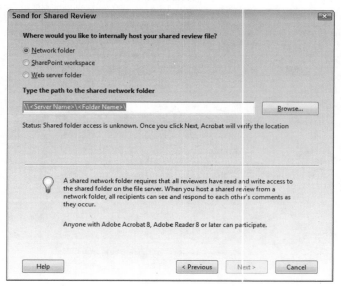

FIGURE 21.13

If you want to create a new folder, click the Make New Folder button. When the directory path is established, click OK to return to the Send for Shared Review wizard.

5. **Review the configuration summary.** Click Next and the third pane in the Send for Shared Review wizard opens. This pane summarizes your choice for the location where the comments will be collected as shown in Figure 21.14. Review the summary and click Next.

FIGURE 21.14

FIGURE 21.14

Review the summary and click Next to complete the network folder setup.

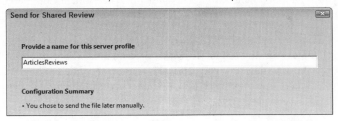

6. **Determine how you want to distribute the PDF document for review.** You basically have two choices when you arrive at the last pane in the Send for Review wizard. Choose either Adobe Acrobat or Save a local copy and manually send the file later to recipients. If you choose the second option, you have to manually send the document to reviewers. The space on the network server will collect comments from all the reviewers. When you finish the setup, the PDF document appears in the document pane with a message informing you that the file has been saved to your local hard drive and you can send the file at any time to recipients as shown in Figure 21.15.

FIGURE 21.15

When you finish the network folder setup, the PDF document appears in the document pane with a message informing you that you can send the file at any time to recipients.

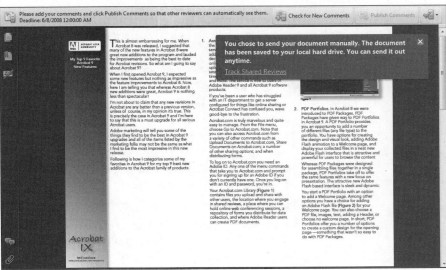

In the Document Message bar in Figure 21.15, you find some new options for commenting. The Check for New Comments button checks the network folder for new comments that recipients add and populates your PDF document with new comments. The Publish Comments button uploads any new comments you add to the PDF file as XML data collected at the network folder.

From the pull-down menu adjacent to the Publish Comments button, you have a few choices for opening the Tracker and working offline. If you work in an area where you don't have access to your server, choose Work Offline and you can make comments while on the road. When you return to your office and connect to the network folder, your offline comments can be published.

Setting up shared reviews on Acrobat.com

Perhaps the easiest way to initiate and participate in shared reviews is via Acrobat.com. As I've said before in this chapter, you don't have to worry about any configurations as long as you have set up your Adobe ID and can log on to Acrobat.com. This option provides you a seamless, hassle-free approach to engaging in shared reviews.

 For setting up an Adobe ID and logging on to Acrobat.com, see Chapter 29.

To learn how easy it is to initiate and participate in shared reviews on Acrobat.com, do the following:

STEPS: Starting a shared review using Acrobat.com

1. **Open the Comment task button pull-down menu and select Send For Shared Review.** The Send for Shared Review wizard opens the same as shown earlier in Figure 21.11.

2. **Choose Acrobat.com for your host.** When you open the Send for Shared Review wizard, choose Automatically download & track comments with Acrobat.com.

3. **Log on to Acrobat.com with your Adobe ID.** Click Next to open the Send for Shared Review Adobe ID log-on pane as shown in Figure 21.16. Type your ID and password and click Sign In to log on to Acrobat.com.

4. **Identify recipients.** The next item you see is an email message box in the Send for Shared Review wizard as shown in Figure 21.17. Type the names of recipients in the To text box. If you want to edit the subject and/or message you can edit the respective items in the wizard. Click Send and several things happen to your PDF document:

    ■ The file you send to Acrobat.com is enabled with Adobe Reader usage rights so Adobe Reader users can participate in the review.

    ■ The email message is sent to your list of recipients when you click the Send button.

    ■ The file is automatically uploaded to Acrobat.com. You don't need to bother with anything else other than identifying your recipients and clicking the send button. What could be easier?

FIGURE 21.16

Type your Adobe ID and password and click Sign In to log on to Acrobat.com.

FIGURE 21.17

Type recipient names in the To text box and click Send to initiate the review.

Amazingly, the list of the four preceding steps is all you have to do to initiate a shared review using Acrobat.com. Comments, publishing comments, and downloading comments is handled just like using network folders described in the section "Using Network Folders" earlier in this chapter.

Acrobat confirms your upload with a message box, as shown in Figure 21.18, when you click the Send button in the email message. As with network folder reviews, you have a Check for New Reviews button and a Publish Comments button to download recipient comments and upload your own comments.

FIGURE 21.18

The same buttons for checking for new comments and publishing comments available with network folders are identical when engaging in reviews on Acrobat.com.

When you check for comments on Acrobat.com by clicking the Check for New Comments button in the Document Message bar, new comments added in the review are reported in a message box as shown in Figure 21.19. To accept the comment, click the Click here to accept text link and the comments are downloaded and populate your PDF document on your computer.

FIGURE 21.19

When new comments are downloaded from Acrobat.com, a message box reports the number of comments added to your PDF file.

On Windows, you can easily monitor new comment additions on Acrobat.com in the Windows Status Bar as shown in Figure 21.20. A mouseover on the Tracker icon in the Status Bar reports any activity or no activity with shared reviews. Right-click the Tracker icon and choose Open Tracker from a context menu and the Tracker opens.

FIGURE 21.20

You can open the Tracker for reviews and when distributing forms from a context menu opened on the Tracker icon in the Windows Status Bar.

Additional items you have available in the Tracker when working with shared reviews include changing the deadline for a review and ending a review. In Figure 21.21 the text for these items open windows for informing recipients that a review deadline has been extended or the review has ended.

FIGURE 21.21

You can extend a review or end a review using the Tracker.

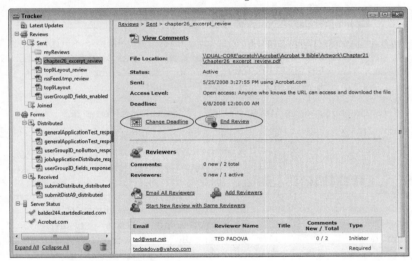

PROXY Reviewers

One of the coolest things that shared reviews can offer is PROXY. Imagine an Adobe (or any company) employee wants to invite you to participate in a review. The Adobe employee uses a shared folder to start a review. However, access to the Adobe Web server is limited to only Adobe employees.

An employee decides to add you to the review, but you don't have access to the shared folder on the Adobe network. You receive the PDF via email and try to *connect* to the shared folder and, of course, you can't. Using shared reviews still makes it possible for you to add your comments to the document.

Participating in such a review provides you new options on the status bar (see Figure 21.22) where you select Send Comments. Instead of accessing the secure network folder limited to Adobe employees, your comments are emailed to the review initiator who can then inject these comments to the review and (here's the cool part) they show up as "Reviewer name (Adobe employee) by your name," making it clear that the Adobe employee made the comment but you added it to the review cycle.

FIGURE 21.22

When participating as a PROXY reviewer, click Send Comments in the status bar to email your comments to the review initiator.

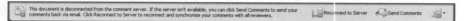

Commenting in Real-Time

An option for the hurried or impatient user is real-time commenting. Through the use of Acrobat. com and Web conferencing, you can host a meeting where you can share files. Without a commercial subscription to Acrobat Connect or Acrobat Connect Pro, your real-time commenting is limited to three people (you and two participants).

 Web conferencing and sharing files in real time is covered in Chapter 29.

Migrating Comments

You might have an edit you make on a document and want to populate the document with comments made in review sessions. Acrobat provides you a method to import new or unresolved comments to a PDF after the document has been revised using the Migrate Comments feature. This feature attempts to place comments in the correct location by searching specific word groupings and structural elements in a revised PDF.

 Results may be less reliable in untagged PDFs that lack the internal structure necessary to correctly place imported comments in a revised document.

In order to migrate comments from one file to another, you need both documents open in Acrobat. Bring the document you want to import comments into forward in the document pane. Select Comments ➪ Migrate Comments to open the Migrate Comments dialog box, as shown in Figure 21.23. Select the other file open in the document pane in the From pull-down menu and click OK. Your file gets populated with all the comments from the review file.

Select the file containing comments in the From pull-down menu and click OK to import the comments from the review file.

If you open the properties on a comment markup and check the Review history, you should see a list of the Migration history in the dialog box, as shown in Figure 21.24. All comment migration is listed in the Review History tab for assessing the dates and times you migrated comments.

The Review History in the comment properties shows a list of Migration history.

Sharing Comments in PDF Portfolios

The one item that we don't have available with shared reviews is sharing PDF Portfolios in review sessions. Adobe admits that there are case uses for engaging in shared reviews with PDF Portfolios, but unfortunately it's just not in the cards in this release of Acrobat.

With all the new tools you have available with Acrobat 9, you can create some workarounds. Here's a list of some of the more important issues related to commenting on files in PDF Portfolios:

- **Share files in review sessions before you assemble a PDF Portfolio.** You can share individual files using shared reviews on Acrobat.com, then assemble your PDF Portfolio after completing review sessions. This option could be the easiest workaround you have if there are many files in your portfolio.

- **Enable PDFs before sharing a portfolio.** If you decide to share a PDF Portfolio, you'll need to enable each PDF document in the portfolio if you intend to share the portfolio with Adobe Reader users.

 You can assemble a PDF Portfolio and enable PDFs within the portfolio after assembly.

- **Share a portfolio on Acrobat.com.** If you want to share a portfolio with other users for the purpose of commenting and review, choose File ⇨ Collaborate ⇨ Share Documents on Acrobat.com. You'll need to send an email invitation to the recipients and let them know they must download the shared file, make comments, and submit the comments to you.

- **Integrating comments.** You have two methods for adding comments from recipients to your files in a PDF Portfolio. You can use the Comments ⇨ Import Comments command or use Comments ⇨ Migrate Comments. In either case you need to open each PDF document individually by clicking the Preview button or double-click a file in the PDF Portfolio interface. When the file opens in Preview mode, you must click the Open button to open the file in a new window. You need to do this for both your master file and a PDF Portfolio that has been returned to you. When both files appear in a new window, you have access to all the Comments menu commands.

CROSS-REF For more information on PDF Portfolios, see Chapter 12. For more information on sharing files on Acrobat.com, see Chapter 29.

As you can see from the list of the things you need to do to merge comments from reviewers into a PDF Portfolio, the task of sending out files for individual reviews provides you the best solution for reviewing the content for each document. When using shared reviews, you have all the tools needed to migrate comments, track the comment reviews, and send reminder notices quite easily.

If you need an overall review of the look and feel of a PDF Portfolio, you can merge all edited files in a PDF Portfolio after completing individual review sessions and gather comments on the shared portfolio using several manual steps listed here.

Summary

- You can initiate email and shared reviews in Acrobat and participate in reviews in any Acrobat viewer. Following steps in a wizard automatically prepares a file with Adobe Reader usage rights so Adobe Reader users can participate in review sessions.

- The Tracker lists all documents initiated from Attach for Email Reviews and Send for Shared Review.

■ You can host shared reviews using network folders, SharePoint servers, Web servers, and Acrobat.com. When it comes to server configuration, Acrobat.com is the easiest method for sharing reviews on servers.

■ When files are enabled with Adobe Reader usage rights, the Adobe Reader users can participate in ad-hoc review workflows.

■ Migrating comments is used for moving comments from a review in progress to an updated version of the reviewed document that might have been modified during the review cycle.

■ PDF Portfolios cannot be handled in shared reviews. In order to comment and review on PDF Portfolios, you must follow several steps to create a workaround for distributing files and migrating comments.

Chapter 22

Creating Links and Actions

O ne of the truly great features Adobe Acrobat offers is the ability to create interactive documents containing hot links that invoke many different actions. Acrobat provides you with many tools and methods for making your PDFs come alive, and Acrobat helps you refine documents for user navigation and interactivity. Regardless of whether you post PDFs on Web servers, communicate via email, replicate CD-ROMs, or work with documents on local network servers, Acrobat offers tools and features that help you create dynamic documents.

In this chapter, you learn how to create links with a variety of Acrobat tools, and you learn some of the differences between several methods for linking views. With hypertext links originating from various elements such as bookmarks, page actions, links, and destinations, you have a number of action tools that provide you with an almost limitless opportunity for handling views and relationships between documents. This chapter covers creating hot links and all the different actions you can associate with links.

Setting Up the Links and Actions Environment

Reset the toolbars (open a context menu on the Toolbar Well and select Reset Toolbars). Open the More Tools dialog box (open a context menu on the Toolbar Well and select More Tools) and scroll down to the Advanced Editing Toolbar. Select all tools and select the Advanced Editing Toolbar check box. Move down to the File Toolbar and check the box for the Organizer. Scroll to the Page Display toolbar and select the tools you want to use for page displays. If you want the Navigation tools accessible, check the Page Navigation toolbar. Scroll to the Select & Zoom toolbar and select the Actual Size, Fit Width, and Fit Page tools.

Click OK to open the toolbars not loaded by default. Another toolbar that can be helpful when creating links and buttons is the Properties Bar. Open a context menu on the Toolbar Well and select Properties Bar. Return to the context menu and select Dock All Toolbars. When finished, your Acrobat application window should look like Figure 22.1.

FIGURE 22.1

Toolbars loaded for editing PDFs with interactive links and buttons

Working with Bookmarks

If you use programs that support exporting to PDF with structure, you can add bookmarks automatically at the time PDF files are created. Programs such as Microsoft Word, Microsoft Excel, Microsoft PowerPoint, Microsoft Visio, Autodesk AutoCAD, Adobe PageMaker, Adobe InDesign, Adobe FrameMaker, and QuarkXPress support bookmark creation from style sheets when you use export tools in the authoring programs. Ideally, in a workflow environment where these programs are used, it is advantageous to create bookmarks from authoring applications when permitted by the program and when the bookmark action relates to page views. In other programs, or when editing PDFs with bookmarks, you may need to reassign bookmark actions, order bookmarks in a hierarchy, or create additional bookmarks.

CROSS-REF For more information regarding bookmark exports from authoring programs, see Chapters 8 and 9.

The most common bookmark action in Acrobat is navigating page views. Whereas analog bookmarks mark pages, the electronic bookmarks in a PDF document enable you to navigate to different pages and different zoom views. You can capture various page views and zoom in on images, text, tables, and so on in Acrobat as bookmark destinations. In a broader sense, you can use bookmarks to invoke actions such as opening/closing files, opening secondary files, executing menu commands, submitting forms, playing sounds and movies, executing JavaScripts, and a host of other related actions.

Creating bookmarks

As long as you understand the sequence of steps, creating bookmarks is easy. Creating a bookmark is like capturing a snapshot. The process involves navigating to the page and view you want to capture and then creating the bookmark. Therefore, if you want to capture page 13 of a document in a Fit Page view, you navigate to page 13, click on the Fit Page tool, and then create the bookmark.

You create bookmarks from several options. When the page view is in place, open the Options menu in the Bookmarks panel and select New Bookmark. You can also open a context menu on a page and select Add Bookmark from the menu options. In Figure 22.2 the Bookmark panel Options menu is shown.

FIGURE 22.2

To create a bookmark, navigate to the desired page view and select New Bookmark from the Options pull-down menu in the Bookmarks panel (left).

By default, the items Paste under Selected Bookmark and Paste after Selected Bookmark are grayed out. You need to select Cut from the menu options to make the two Paste commands active.

Click on the Bookmarks panel to access the Options menu for bookmarks. Using a context menu, you can create a bookmark when the Navigation panel is collapsed. When you create a bookmark from a context menu while the panel is collapsed, the Navigation panel opens and the Bookmarks panel is placed in view.

If you open the Options menu in the Bookmarks panel, the menu options appear as shown in Figure 22.2. However, if you first select a bookmark and then open a context menu, the menu commands change to menu commands shown in Figure 22.3. As shown in Figure 22.3, you have fewer menu choices in the context menu than the Options menu.

FIGURE 22.3

If you select a bookmark in the Bookmarks panel, the context menu is as shown here.

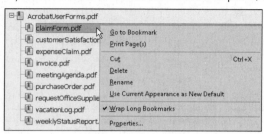

You can also use shortcut keys to create a bookmark when the Bookmarks panel is either opened or closed. Press Ctrl/⌘+B on your keyboard to create a bookmark. In all of these methods, a bookmark defaults to the name Untitled. Acrobat highlights the Untitled bookmark name after the bookmark is created. You type a name and press the Enter or Return key when you are finished typing.

On pages where text corresponds to names you want to use for bookmarks, Acrobat helps simplify the naming process. Click the Select tool and highlight the text you want to use as your bookmark name. From a context menu, select Add Bookmark. The bookmark is created and the highlighted text is used as the bookmark name. The stages of creating a bookmark in this manner are: 1) the page view is in place, 2) text is selected on the page and a context menu opened, 3) Add Bookmark is selected from the menu options (see Figure 22.4), and 4) the bookmark is created using the selected text for the bookmark name. You can also use the Options menu or modifier keys to create a bookmark while text is selected.

FIGURE 22.4

To automatically name a bookmark, select text with the Select tool and create the bookmark.

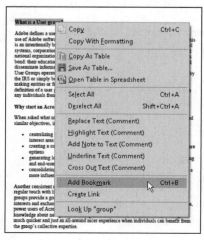

TIP If you want to add a new bookmark in a list following a specific bookmark name, click the bookmark preceding the one you want to add. Leave the bookmark selected and navigate to the page and view for your new bookmark using the Navigation tools. Press Ctrl/⌘+B and the new Untitled bookmark is added below the selected bookmark in the Bookmarks panel.

Managing bookmarks

Bookmarks created in a document appear in the Bookmarks panel in the order they are created, regardless of the page order. For example, if you create a bookmark on page 15, and then create another on page 12, the bookmarks are listed with page 15 before page 12 in the Bookmarks panel. At times you may want to have the Bookmarks list displayed according to page order. Additionally, bookmarks may appear more organized if they are nested in groups. If you have a category and a list of items to fit within that category, you may want to create a hierarchy that expands or collapses. Fortunately, Acrobat enables you to change the order of bookmarks without recreating them. Additionally, you can categorize the bookmarks into groups.

To reorder a bookmark, select either the page icon or bookmark name in the list and drag it up or down and left or right. A triangle with a dotted line appears when you drag a bookmark, as shown in Figure 22.5. To nest a child bookmark below a parent bookmark, drag straight up. The triangle and line show you the target area for the bookmark.

FIGURE 22.5

The triangle indicates where a bookmark is to be reordered.

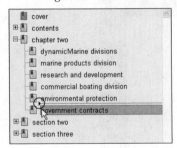

If you have a parent bookmark with several child bookmarks nested below it, you can move the parent to a new location. Drag the parent bookmark and all child bookmarks below it move with the parent. If you want to remove a child bookmark from a nest, click and drag the bookmark to the left and either down or up to the location desired.

In addition to moving bookmarks, you can cut and paste them. Select a parent or child bookmark, and from a context menu or the Bookmark panel Options menu, select Paste under Selected Bookmark or Paste after Selected Bookmark. When you choose Paste under Selected Bookmark the cut bookmark(s) is pasted as a child bookmark under the selected bookmark. Pasting after a selected bookmark pastes the cut bookmark(s) after the selected parent and all child bookmarks.

Copying and Pasting Bookmarks

With all the great new features that have been continually added to Acrobat since version 6, the age-old fundamentals of bookmark copying and pasting that could have been implemented in Acrobat 1 are still not available in Acrobat 9. Considering the many new wonderful features added to Acrobat 9, it's not much of a disadvantage for users to not have these features added in the newest release, but I know many users who frequently work with long documents and continually bookmark sections of PDF documents would like to see some options for copying and pasting bookmarks.

There are some third-party developers who do offer solutions for adding more functionality to managing bookmarks. If bookmarking documents is a routine task you perform in Acrobat, you may want to search for some third-party tools to help you out. If you're an occasional bookmarker, then perhaps a workaround just might be helpful.

Assume you have several documents and in each of your PDF files you want to create a bookmark action to open files. You have the same files to open and close from within each separate document. Do you need to manually create bookmarks in each file? Not necessarily.

To begin a workaround for not having a copying and pasting bookmarks feature in Acrobat, create all the bookmark actions you want for opening files in a master file. You might have a document used as a contents page that links to other files via bookmarks. All the necessary bookmark actions designed to open secondary files would be part of this document.

Verify all your bookmark actions work properly and save the file. Next, choose Document ⇨ Replace Pages and choose one of the linked files to replace all pages in your master file. If your secondary document has more pages, use the Document ⇨ Insert Pages command. You can always delete old pages without disturbing bookmarks assigned to open files.

After the pages are added to the master file, delete the bookmark link that opens the file you used to replace the pages. Choose File ⇨ Save As and save the master file under a new name. Repeat the same steps to use the same bookmarks with other files.

Multiple nesting is also available with bookmark organization. A bookmark can be subordinate to another bookmark that is itself nested under a parent bookmark. To subordinate a bookmark under a child bookmark, use the same method as described previously for creating the first order of children. As you drag right and up slightly, you can nest bookmarks at several levels.

You can also relocate multiple bookmarks at one time. To select several bookmarks, Shift+click each bookmark in a group. As you hold down the Shift key, you can add more bookmarks to the selection. If you click one bookmark at the top or bottom of a list and Shift+click, all bookmarks between are selected. For a noncontiguous selection, Ctrl/⌘+click. Once selected, drag the bookmarks to a new location in the list. Their order remains the same as it was before the move.

By default, new bookmarks appear at the end of a bookmark list. If you want to place a bookmark within a series of bookmarks, select the bookmark you want the new bookmark to follow. When you select New Bookmark from the Bookmarks Options menu, from a context menu, or press Ctrl/⌘+B, the new bookmark is created at the same level after the one you selected.

CROSS-REF For more information on replacing and inserting pages, see Chapter 16.

Renaming bookmarks

If you create a bookmark and want to change the bookmark name, select the bookmark to be edited from the Bookmarks panel. From the Options menu, select Rename. Acrobat highlights the name in the Bookmarks panel. Type a new name and press the Return or Enter key on your keyboard to finish editing the bookmark name. You can also click the cursor anywhere in the Document pane to finish editing the name.

You can rename bookmarks by clicking on a bookmark name and clicking again on the bookmark. You can also use a context menu, but be certain you first select the bookmark; then open a context menu to select the menu option for Rename. When you click on a bookmark, you go to the associated bookmark view. Clicking a second time informs Acrobat you want to edit the name. To select the text, click and drag across the part of the name you want to edit or press Ctrl/⌘+A to select all text. When you type a new name, the selected text is deleted and replaced with the new text you type.

Structured bookmarks

Structured bookmarks retain document structure in files generated from tagged PDF files. You can use structured bookmarks to navigate PDF pages, reorganize the pages, and delete pages. If you create PDFs without tags, you can add structure to a document by choosing Advanced ➪ Accessibility ➪ Add Tags to Document. After you have a structured document and you create bookmarks, more options are available to you. For example, you can delete and extract pages via structured bookmarks.

CROSS-REF For more information on creating tags and working with structured documents, see Chapter 25.

Depending on whether you have a bookmark or a structured bookmark, context menu commands and the Options menu commands appear differently. When you open a context menu from a standard bookmark, the menu commands appear as shown in Figure 22.3. When you open a context menu from a structured bookmark, the menu commands are as they appear in Figure 22.6. Notice the items that relate to Delete Pages and Extract pages that are available when you open a context menu from a structured bookmark.

When you create a bookmark, the destination for the bookmark is a link to a page view. In the context menu for standard bookmarks, you see the menu command for Set Destination. You can navigate to a new page and select this command to change the bookmark link to a new view. With structured bookmarks, you capture the page structure (a page view, a table, a head, and so on). In the context menu, be certain to select Delete and not Delete Page(s) if you want to delete a bookmark. The Delete command deletes just the bookmark. Delete Page(s) deletes the bookmark and the page associated with the bookmark.

FIGURE 22.6

These menu commands are available when you open a structured bookmark context menu.

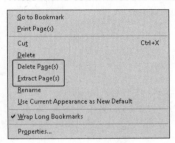

Bookmark appearances

Both bookmarks and structured bookmarks contain menu options for Use Current Appearance as New Default. This menu choice is like a bookmark style sheet where you first select the appearance of the bookmark in terms of font style and color; then you select this menu option to set the attributes as a new default. For example, change the bookmark to small text, italicized, in red; then open a context menu and select Use Current Appearance as New Default. All subsequent bookmarks you create use the same style until you change the default.

The Wrap Long Bookmarks option from either menu creates a word wrap for the bookmark name in the Bookmarks panel. By default Bookmarks are wrapped. If you want more Bookmarks to appear in the vertical list, you can unwrap them. An unwrapped Bookmark appears as you see in Figure 22.7. When the cursor is placed over a Bookmark, a tooltip displays the entire bookmark name. When the Bookmark is wrapped, it appears as you see in Figure 22.8.

FIGURE 22.7

When a Bookmark name is longer than the panel width, a tooltip shows the complete name extended beyond the panel width.

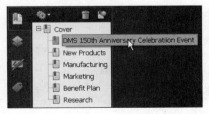

FIGURE 22.8

When Wrap Long Bookmarks is selected in a Bookmarks context menu, bookmark names are wrapped to the panel width and shown in multiple lines of text. This display appears by default.

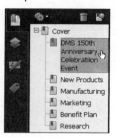

If you open the Options menu, you have more choices for how the bookmarks appear in the panel. In Figures 22.7 and 22.8, bookmarks are expanded. The minus (–) symbol (a down-pointing arrow on Macintosh) shows all nested child bookmarks below it. Click on the symbol and the bookmark collapses to hide all child bookmarks below the parent. If you want to show all top-level bookmarks expanded, select Expand Top-Level bookmarks from the Options pull-down menu. To collapse the bookmark list, select Collapse Top-Level bookmarks from the same menu. The latter menu command is dynamic and is accessible only in the menu if you have first expanded bookmarks.

Select Hide After Use from the Options menu if you want to hide the Bookmarks panel after you select a bookmark. To change text sizes, make selections from the Options pull-down menu. Select Size and choose from one of the three submenu items for Small, Medium, or Large point sizes.

Adding special characters to bookmark names

Acrobat doesn't offer much in terms of changing fonts and font attributes for bookmark names. However, you are not limited to the default font used for bookmarks; and, when you need some special characters or foreign language text for a bookmark name, you can garner a little help from your operating system.

On Windows, open the Character Map. This file is located by clicking the Start Menu and choosing Programs ⇨ Accessories ⇨ System Tools ⇨ Character Map. The Character Map program opens as shown in Figure 22.9.

From the Font pull-down menu, choose a font. Be certain to use fonts with Unicode character equivalents. Not all fonts and not all characters within a font will work. You need to look around for those fonts having a Unicode character set. For starters, try to pick some of the Adobe OpenType Pro fonts when you want to add special characters to your bookmark names.

Click a character in the scrollable window and click Select. The character is added to the Characters to copy text box. You can add several characters to the text box. When finished, click Copy and the character(s) is copied to the Clipboard. Open the Bookmarks panel and create a new bookmark, or edit a bookmark name and choose Edit ⇨ Paste. The character(s) is pasted into a bookmark name. In Figure 22.10 I created several bookmarks using nonstandard characters.

FIGURE 22.9

Choose Programs ⇨ Accessories ⇨ System Tools ⇨ Character Map.

FIGURE 22.10

Special characters copied from the Character Map and pasted into bookmark names

On the Macintosh, you'll find a menu command in the Edit menu used for a similar purpose. Open the Edit menu and choose Special Characters (Macintosh only). The Characters window opens as shown in Figure 22.11. To insert a special character on the Mac, place the cursor inside a bookmark name and double-click a character in the Characters window. Alternately, you can also click a character and click the Insert button in the Characters window.

FIGURE 22.11

Choose Edit ⇨ Special Characters on the Mac to open the Characters window.

Bookmark properties

The Options pull-down menu offers you choices for text sizes. For other text attribute changes you need to use the Bookmark Properties dialog box. Select Properties from a context menu and the Bookmark Properties dialog box shown in Figure 22.12 opens.

FIGURE 22.12

The Bookmark Properties dialog box opens when you open a context menu from either a standard bookmark or a structured bookmark.

You select type styles from the Style pull-down menu. Select from Plain, Bold, Italic, or Bold_Italic. Clicking the Color swatch opens the color pop-up window where you select preset colors or custom colors. You can capture changes from these style options when you select the Use Current Appearance as New Default menu command previously discussed.

The Actions tab enables you to change bookmark actions. By default, the bookmark action is set to open a view within the active PDF document. You can assign many other actions to bookmarks in the Actions properties.

 For assigning bookmark actions, see the section "Working with the Link Tool" later in this chapter.

Using the Properties Bar

The Properties Bar also offers options for appearance settings. (Remember, we loaded that toolbar when we set up our editing environment at the beginning of the chapter.) Using the Properties Bar is a trade-off. On the one hand, it's so much easier to make changes to bookmark appearances using the toolbar; but on the other hand, it takes up a row in the Toolbar Well. If your monitor is large enough and your viewing space adequate to comfortably see page content, then take a look at the options you have in the Properties Bar shown in Figure 22.13.

FIGURE 22.13

Select a bookmark and the Properties Bar reflects options for editing bookmark appearances.

When you select a bookmark, options in the Properties Bar include the following:

- **Color.** Click the Color down arrow and the color palette opens where you can assign a preset color or a custom color to a bookmark name.
- **Text.** Click Plain and a pull-down menu opens displaying font attribute choices.
- **More.** Click the More button and you get a quick launch of the Properties dialog box, as shown in Figure 22.12.

All in all, the Properties Bar is helpful when you need to make bookmark appearance and property changes. If the Toolbar Well isn't too crowded, keep this toolbar open when you make edits for bookmarks and other types of link options.

Setting bookmark opening views

If you create bookmarks in a document and want the document to open with the Bookmarks panel open, you can save the PDF document in a manner where the Bookmarks panel opens in the Navigation panel each time the PDF is opened.

Choose File ⇨ Properties or press Ctrl/⌘+D to open the Document Properties dialog box. Click the Initial View tab. From the Navigation panel pull-down menu, select Bookmarks Panel and Page, as shown in Figure 22.14. Save the file after making the properties change. The next time you open the document, the Bookmarks panel opens.

FIGURE 22.14

Choose Bookmarks Panel and Page from the Navigation panel pull-down menu.

CROSS-REF   For more information on setting Initial Views, see Chapter 5.

The width of the Bookmarks panel is a user default specific to Acrobat on the end user's computer and not the file you distribute. If you open the Bookmarks panel to a wider view than the default, each time you open a PDF with the bookmarks in view, the Bookmarks panel is opened at the width you last adjusted. If you save the file with the Initial View showing Bookmarks and pages, Acrobat does not take into consideration your Bookmarks panel width. Other users who open your files see the Bookmarks panel sized to their personal panel width default sizes. This default is made from the last time you adjusted the panel size.

Working with Articles

Acrobat offers a feature to link text blocks together for easy navigation through columns of text. User-specified ranges of text can be linked together, thereby forming an article. Articles help a user navigate through a PDF file, enabling the user to read logical sequences of paragraphs throughout a document. Working with articles is particularly helpful when you view PDF files on the World Wide Web. PDF files can be downloaded a page at a time in a Web browser. If you have a column or group of paragraphs of text that begins on page 1 and continues on page 54, an article thread can assist a reader in jumping from page 1 to page 54 without his or her having to download the remaining pages in the document.

Viewing and navigating articles

You need to know a few basics on navigating through an article in a PDF.

Article Tool To determine whether articles exist, choose View ⇨ Navigation Panels ⇨ Articles. A panel opens with tabs for Articles. You can dock the panel in the Navigation pane by dragging the Article tab to the pane as shown in Figure 22.15.

FIGURE 22.15

Drag the Articles tab to the Navigation pane to dock the panel.

The Articles panel displays any articles existing in the PDF file in the panel list. If you select the Article tool from the Advanced Editing toolbar, the article definition boundaries are shown. In Figure 22.16, the Article tool is selected. The defined article is contained within a rectangular box with an identifier at the top of the box. In this example, 1-1 indicates that this is article number 1 and box number 1. If the article is continued on another page, the subsequent boxes read 1-2, 1-3, 1-4, and so on, indicating they are continuations of the same article thread. If you create a second article, the article begins with numbers 2-1, indicating the second article in the document and the first box of the second article.

Article properties

The article properties are contained in a dialog box that opens immediately after you create an article or double-click an article with the Article tool. The Properties dialog box shown in Figure 22.17 is informational. When you view Article Properties, information supplied at the time the article was created is displayed for four data fields. The Title, Subject, Author, and Keywords fields are the same as those found in the Document Information dialog box. Inasmuch as the data for these fields are identical to that found in document information, Acrobat Search does not take advantage of the article properties information. Properties are designed to help you find information about an article before you jump to the page where the article is contained. All the fields are editable when you open the Article Properties dialog box.

Select the Article tool and the article boundaries are shown on pages.

The Article Properties dialog box displays user-supplied information for Title, Subject, Author, and Keywords fields. These fields are not searchable with Acrobat Search.

Viewing articles

Articles are viewed at the maximum view established in the Preferences dialog box. When you view an article, you select the Hand tool and click an article thread. The screen view jumps to the maximum view assigned in the Page Display Preferences. By default, the zoom is set to an 800% view or a view that accommodates the complete width of a column of text. In most situations this view is much larger than needed for comfortable viewing. In earlier versions of Acrobat you could choose Edit ⇨ Preferences and click General in the left panel. From the Max Fit Visible Zoom pull-down menu select a zoom view comfortable for reading on your monitor. However, this preference setting was removed in Acrobat 8 viewers and you no longer have control over zoom levels when reading articles.

In order to read articles you need to have a preference option enabled in the General preferences dialog box. Open Preferences (Ctrl/⌘+K) and click General in the left pane. Check Make Hand tool read articles in the right pane. If the check box is disabled, the Hand tool won't recognize articles.

Alternately, you can open the Articles panel by choosing View ⇨ Navigation Panels ⇨ Articles. The Articles panel can remain open as an individual panel, or you can drag it to the Navigation pane and dock it. The panel pull-down menu in the Articles panel offers only one option. If you select Hide After Use from the panel pull-down menu, the panel disappears when you view an article. If you want to have the panel remain open, but want more viewing area in the document, dock the Articles panel in the Navigation panel.

Double-click an article to jump to the first view in the thread. When you double-click an article in the Article panel, the article jumps in view in the document pane and the Article pane displays an arrow adjacent to the selected article in the Articles panel. In Figure 22.15 you see the arrow in view in the first article. The change in the icon appearance in the Articles pane keeps you informed of what article is currently being viewed.

Acrobat places the top-left corner where the article begins in view when you double-click an article name in the Articles pane or choose Read Article from the Articles pane Options menu. You immediately see a right-pointing arrow blink on the left side of the first line of text. Once an article is in view, select the Hand tool and position the cursor over the article (be certain the General preferences are set up to read articles with the Hand tool). The cursor changes to a Hand tool icon with an arrow pointing down. As you read articles, the cursor changes according to the direction Acrobat takes you when you're reading an article. For example, if you're viewing a column up instead of down, the cursor changes to inform you which direction you're going. The different cursor views are shown in Figure 22.18.

FIGURE 22.18

When you view articles, different cursors inform you ahead of time the direction you need to navigate.

A   B   C

You can use several keyboard shortcuts to help you navigate with the Article tool. The cursor changes according to the following modifier keys:

- **Click.** The first click zooms to a zoom level up to 800%. If you read columns of text, you may find the zoom level lower, such as 200%. Click the cursor again to continue reading down a column. Click at the end of an article box, and the view takes you to the beginning of the next column.

- **Shift+click.** Moves backward or up a column.

- **Ctrl+click or Option+click.** Moves to the beginning of the article.

- **Return or Enter.** Moves forward down the column or to the top of the next column.

- **Shift+Return or Shift+Enter.** Moves up or to the previous column.

Defining articles

You define articles by drawing rectangular boxes around the text you want to include as part of your article thread. While you're using the Article tool, the rectangular boxes are visible. When the tool is not active, the rectangular boxes are invisible.

Click and drag open a rectangle surrounding the column where you want to begin a new article. When you release the mouse button, the rectangular box displays on the page. At each corner and side of the article box are handles that you can grab and move to reshape the box. Notice that the lower-right corner of the article box contains a plus (+) symbol. When you finish your edits, deselect the Article tool to exit edit mode. You can return to edit mode and add more columns after reselecting the Article tool. Click the aforementioned plus symbol to let Acrobat know you want to extend the article thread (see the later section "Combining articles" for more on extended article threads).

TIP You can create article threads at the time the PDF file is either exported or distilled with Acrobat Distiller. Many layout applications support creating articles prior to exporting to PDF. In some cases, you may want to have a single article thread to help user navigation through your document. To practice, identify an article in one of the programs discussed in Chapter 7 and then export to PDF either through the program's export feature or by printing to PostScript and later distilling in Acrobat Distiller.

Ending an article thread

When you reach the end of the article, Acrobat needs to know you want to finish creating the thread. To end an article thread, press Return, Enter, or Esc. Acrobat prompts you with a dialog box in which you supply the Title, Subject, Author, and Keywords fields for the article properties. This dialog box appears immediately after you define an article. Supplying the information at the time the dialog box opens is a good idea because then you won't need to worry about returning to the Article Properties dialog box for last-minute cleanup.

Deleting articles

You might want to delete a portion of an article thread or an entire article. To delete either, select the Article tool and click an article box. Press the Backspace (Delete) key on your keyboard or open a context menu and select Delete from the menu options. A dialog box opens providing options for deleting the currently selected box or the entire article. To delete the entire article from within the Article panel, select the article and click the Trashcan icon, or open a context menu and select Delete.

If you select the Box button in the Article dialog box, the deletion eliminates the article box within the article thread you selected when you pressed the Backspace (Delete) key on the keyboard. Clicking the Article button deletes all boxes in the thread across all pages in the document.

Combining articles

At times you may want to join two articles to create a single article. To join two articles, you must first have them defined in the PDF document. Move to the last column of the first article and click the plus symbol in the last box. This click loads the Article tool. Next, move to the beginning of the article to be joined to the first article and Ctrl+click or Option+click inside the first box. While you press the shortcut keys, the cursor icon changes, as illustrated in Figure 22.19.

FIGURE 22.19

When you press the Ctrl or Option key while clicking the mouse button, the cursor changes to an icon, informing you that the selected articles are to be joined.

The numbering at the top of each box in the second article changes after the articles are joined. For example, if you have two articles, the first numbered 1-1, 1-2, 1-3, and the second article numbered 2-1, 2-2, the new numbering for the second article changes to 1-4 and 1-5. Article 2 takes on the attributes of article 1 and assumes the next order of the article boxes. In addition, the properties identified in the second article are lost. Because the continuation of the thread is from article 1, all attributes for article 1 supersede those of article 2. You can select multiple articles and join them all together in a single article by following the same steps.

TIP When combining two articles, always start with the article containing the attributes to be retained. For example, in the preceding case, to retain the attributes of article 2, select the plus symbol at the end of the last column in article 2 and click. Ctrl+click or Option+click in the first box for article 1. When the two articles are combined, the attributes of article 2 are retained.

Working with the Link Tool

Links are no mystery to any user who has browsed the Web. Buttons and text that open other Web pages and invoke various actions are something that's commonplace to any computer user. With Adobe Acrobat Standard, Pro, and Pro Extended, you have many tools to create hypertext links that ultimately appear very similar to the kinds of links you find on Web pages.

You use the Link tool to create links from a rectangle drawn with the tool to other pages, other documents, and a host of other link actions you can define in the Link Properties dialog box. The area within a link rectangle is the hot spot for invoking a link action. Links used with tools such as Bookmarks and Form Field buttons have the same attribute choices for the actions associated with the objects created with the respective tools.

> **TIP** You can also create a link without drawing a rectangle when you want a link to appear from text on a page. Use the Select tool and drag across some text to select it. From a context menu, select Create Link. A rectangle is automatically created for you around the selected text. You then target the link destination and the link action is created.

When creating links with the Link tool, you encounter two dialog boxes used to establish link actions. For link actions used in opening a view, opening a secondary document, or opening a Web page, the action choices are contained in the Create Link dialog box, which opens when you click and drag open a link rectangle and release the mouse button. If you want to assign different link actions, you create a custom link and make attribute choices in the Link Properties dialog box. The Create Link dialog box requires you to make all option choices in the dialog box before you can access any commands in the Document pane. The dialog box is static, which means you need to cancel out of the dialog box or click OK to use menus, shortcut keys, or select objects on a page in the Document pane. When you work with the Link Properties dialog box you can access tools and menu commands, and select items such as buttons and other links on pages while the dialog box remains open.

Creating links for page navigation

To help you understand how to use the Link tool, it might be helpful to walk through some steps first before you go on to read over all the attribute choices you have for links. To follow the steps that follow, you should have two documents. In one document you'll create a link to another file, and in the other document you'll create a link to a specific page in another file. To see how all this comes about, try following these steps.

STEPS: Creating links to page views

1. **Open a file in Acrobat.** For these steps you should have two documents. The first document should be a multiple-page file.

2. **Navigate to a page other than the opening page.** Use the Next Page tool or press the Page Down key on your keyboard to open a second page in the document. If you want to open another page, press Next Page or Page Down to scroll pages. Find a page other than the opening page. In my example, I start on page 2.

3. **Create a link.** Select the Link tool in the Advanced Editing toolbar and draw a rectangle with the tool in the area you want the link to appear. You should have text or an icon on the page that makes it intuitive for a user to know a link exists: a graphic, blue text, or some other indication that clicking in an area will invoke an action much like you might see on a Web page.

4. **Identify the link attributes.** When you click the link tool and draw a link rectangle, the Create Link dialog box opens. Click Open a file and click Next. The steps are shown in Figure 22.20.

5. **Select a file to open.** The Select File to Open dialog box appears after clicking Next in the Create Link dialog box. Navigate your hard drive and locate the file you want associated with the link. Click Select in the Select File to Open dialog box.

CAUTION You should copy all PDFs that are linked to the same folder. If you create links to files scattered on your hard drive and then relocate the files, Acrobat will lose the link destinations. When copying files to the same folder, you can relocate your folder on your hard drive, network server, or CD-ROM without disturbing the link destinations.

FIGURE 22.20

1) The Link tool is used to draw a link rectangle; 2) The Create Link dialog box opens after creating a link; 3) Link actions are shown in the Create Link Properties window; and 4) clicking Next opens the Open dialog box where a file to open from the link action is chosen.

6. **Set the Open Preferences.** After identifying a file to open, the Specify Open Preference dialog box (formerly known as Window Preferences in versions prior to Acrobat 8) appears. Click Existing Window, as shown in Figure 22.21. Making this choice opens your target link while the file containing the link closes.

FIGURE 22.21

Select Existing window to open a file. The current open document closes in the Document pane as the new file opens.

7. **Save the file.** Select File ⇨ Save or click the Save tool in the File toolbar to save your edits. Because this file will close when the new file opens, you need to be certain your edits are saved.

8. **Open the linked file.** Select the Hand tool and click the link. The target file should open in the Document pane.

9. **Create a second link.** Select the Link tool and draw a link rectangle. Select Go to a page view in the Create Link dialog box. Click Next to open the Create Go to View dialog box.

10. **Select the target page to open.** While the Create Go to View dialog box (shown in Figure 22.22) is open, you have complete access to all the tools and menu commands in Acrobat. Just leave the dialog box in view and click the Open tool or select File ⇨ Open. Locate the file you added a link to in Step 1 and open it. Navigate to the page containing your original link by clicking the Next Page tool or the Page Down key on your keyboard. When the page is in view at the zoom level you want, click Set Link.

FIGURE 22.22

Open the target page and click Set Link.

11. **Save your edits.** When you click Set Link, you are returned to the page from which the link originated (your second file in this example). Click the Save tool or select File ➪ Save to save your edits.

12. **Test the links.** Close all documents and open the file containing the first link. Click the link and the second file opens. Click the link on that page and the first file opens, but this time the page that opens should be a page other than the first page in your document.

Note that you created two different links in these steps. The first link used the Create Link dialog box and you opened a file. When the file was opened you arrived at the default view on the first page in the file. The second link opened a page other than the opening page (in my example it was page 2). To link to specific document pages in secondary files you need to use the Go to a page view option and set the link in the Create Go to View dialog box.

The steps outlined here are but a fraction of the many different attribute choices you have for creating links and choosing actions. A host of other actions are available to you when you create custom links. Read on to find out more about creating different kinds of links.

Linking to views

In the Create Link dialog box (opened when you draw a link rectangle with the Link tool) you make one of four radio button selections. The first three radio buttons enable you to specify link attributes in the Create Link dialog box shown back in Figure 22.20. If you select the fourth radio button and click OK, the Link Properties dialog box opens where you select different actions for the link behavior.

The first three radio button choices offer you options for selecting a page view or a file to open. Options shown in the Create Link dialog box include the following:

- **Go to a page view.** Use this option to link to a page in the open document or create a cross-document link that opens a page in another document. When you click the Next button, the Create Go to View dialog box opens as shown earlier in Figure 22.22. While the dialog box remains open, you have access to menu commands and tools. Navigate to a page in the open document or click the Open tool, open a second file, navigate to the desired page, and click Set Link.

- **Open a file.** Select this option if you want to open a PDF document or any file from another authoring program. When you click the Next button, the Select File to Open dialog box opens and allows you to select any file on your system. If you select a file other than files that can be opened in Acrobat, you (or your customer) must have the native authoring program installed in order to click on the link and open the file. If you select a PDF document, you link to the Initial View in the secondary document.

CROSS-REF Initial View is typically the first page in a PDF document, but it can be changed to another page in the Initial View properties. For more information on setting the Initial View, see Chapter 5.

■ **Open a web page.** When you select this radio button, the Edit URL field is enabled. You type a URL in the Edit URL field to link to a PDF hosted on a Web site. When you add a URL, be certain to supply the complete Web address, including http://www. After you add a URL, the address becomes a new default. Each time you create a new link, the last URL added to the Edit URL field box is inherited and appears in the field box.

■ **Custom Link.** Custom Link in and of itself contains no properties. You select this radio button if you want to set a different action for a link. If you select Custom Link and click OK, the Link Properties dialog box opens.

TIP URLs in text on PDF pages don't require links. Acrobat versions 7 and above are intelligent and they interpret URLs created in authoring programs from text with either http://www. or www. prefixes as URLs. When you place the Hand tool over URL text in a document, the Hand tool shows an icon with a Hand and a W inside the Hand indicating a live Web link. Click the link and your default Web browser opens the linked page. For earlier versions of Acrobat having URLs in text, you need to create URL links in the PDF files. Note that end users must have the option Create links from URLs enabled in the General preferences in order for Acrobat to recognize URLs from text.

CROSS-REF For more information on creating Web links, see Chapter 27.

Editing a link action

If you create a link using any one of the first three radio buttons in the Create Link dialog box and later want to edit the link, you are not returned to the Create Link dialog box. The Create Link dialog box opens only after you first use the Link tool to create a link.

To change a link action, use either the Link tool or the Select Object tool. Double-click the mouse button with either tool to open the Link Properties. If you select the Hand tool and click on a link, the link action is employed.

Link appearance properties

The link appearance applies to the rectangle drawn when you drag the Link tool on a page in the Document pane. Default appearances are established from the last appearance settings made for the link properties. To change properties, you have two choices. You can use the Properties Bar (described in "Setting Up the Links and Actions Environment" at the beginning of this chapter) or the Link Properties dialog box.

When using the Properties Bar, you make changes to link appearances for the items contained across the bar, as shown in Figure 22.23.

FIGURE 22.23

Select a link with the Link tool or the Select Object tool to enable the options in the Properties Bar.

The choices in the Properties Bar include the following:

- **Color.** The Color pop-up window opens when you click on the square at the far left side of the Properties Bar. Choices for color apply to strokes only and the options are the same as you find when changing colors in Note properties.

CROSS-REF For more information on changing Note properties, see Chapter 20.

- **Line Style.** You have choices from the pull-down menu for No Line, Solid, Dashed, and Underline. No lines might be used when you have a graphic image or text on a page and a link is apparent to a user. For example, if text appears blue and underlined, you might use No Line for the line style.

- **Line Thickness.** The default shown in Figure 22.23 is 1 pt. You have choices for Thin, Medium, or Thick that translate to 1 point, 2 points, or 3 points, respectively. The line weight you choose appears in the Properties Bar. If you select No Line in the Line Style menu, 0 pt is listed in the Properties Bar.

- **Highlight Style.** Use this option to display highlights when the mouse button is pressed. When you select the Hand tool and click on a link, the highlight is shown within the link rectangle while the mouse button is pressed. You can choose from No Highlight, Invert, Outline, and Inset.

- **More.** Clicking the More button opens the Link Properties dialog box just as a context menu command does.

Note that when you click the Link tool in the Advanced Editing toolbar and before you create or select a link, the Properties Bar becomes active. You can make choices for Color, Line Style, Line Thickness, and Highlight Style. But the More button is not active unless you select a link. When you click the Link tool before selecting a link and make appearance changes, the changes become a new default and will remain as a default until you change them again. If you quit Acrobat and relaunch the program, the default changes you made are still honored.

Link properties

To open the Link Properties dialog box, you can open a context menu and select Properties; double-click on a link with the Link tool or the Select Object tool; select a link and press the Enter or Return key; or, with a link selected, click the More button in the Properties Bar. A right-click in Windows or Ctrl+click on Macintosh opens a context menu where you can select Properties to open the Link Properties dialog box.

When the Link Properties dialog box opens, you have options nested in two tabs: the Appearance tab and the Actions tab. By default, the Appearance tab is placed in view, as shown in Figure 22.24.

Two tabs exist in the Link Properties dialog box where you select appearance and actions options.

The same options offered in the Properties Bar for appearance settings are available in the Appearance tab with the addition of the Link Type and a check box for Locked. Link Type is a choice you have in the Create a Link dialog box as well as here in the Link Properties. Choose from Visible Rectangle or Invisible Rectangle to make the link rectangle visible or hidden.

If you enable Locked, the link rectangle is locked to position on the document page and cannot be moved; however, when you select the Hand tool and click on a locked link, the action associated with the link still executes. Locking a link also disables all option choices in the Properties Bar and the Link Properties dialog box for that link. If you need to change properties for a locked link, open the Appearance tab and disable Locked.

Link actions properties

Click on the Actions tab to assign an action to a link. The default link action is Execute a menu item (the top item in the Actions list). Open the Select Action pull-down menu and you find a scrollable list of Action types, as shown in Figure 22.25. After you create a link with another action type, the new action becomes the default.

The Select Action pull-down menu offers a number of actions you can assign to a link. You can select an action and repeat a selection for a different action to nest action types that are executed in the order displayed in the Actions window. In Figure 22.26, three separate actions are associated with the same link. When you click the link with the Hand tool, a page opens, a Web link opens that launches your default Web browser, and a menu item is executed to quit Acrobat.

FIGURE 22.25

Click the Select Action pull-down menu to view all the Action types.

FIGURE 22.26

Action items can be nested in the Link Properties. The order of link execution is the same as the order listed in the Actions window.

From the pull-down menu, you can choose action types such as the following.

Go to a 3D View

If you have a PDF containing a 3D drawing, you can create links and buttons to open different views in the drawing such as wireframe, shading, and various other views. The Add this action option opens the Select a 3D View dialog box where the views are selected.

Go to a page view

You add the action and the Create Go to View dialog box opens. Navigate to a page in an open document or a secondary document and click Set Link.

You can also link to pages in secondary documents using the Go to a page view in the Link Properties dialog box.

Execute a menu item

All versions of Acrobat prior to Acrobat 8 provided options for executing almost all the menu commands you see from the top-level menus.

Now in Acrobat 9, instead of using pull-down menus in a Menu Item dialog box, the Menu Item dialog box opens where you select from a list organized by menus with more limited commands. A number of different menu commands were eliminated from the Execute a Menu Item action beginning with Acrobat 8, including several items that relate to changing PDF content such as adding bookmarks; creating page templates; adding headers, footers, watermarks, and backgrounds; adding comments and markups; and using Forms menu commands. The Advanced menu commands have also been eliminated.

Adobe's reasoning for this is that it's answering user demand for the capability to protect files against document changes that an end user may not be aware of. For example, if you create a button that creates a bookmark or comment, adds a form field, and so on, the end user may not be aware that the button action altered the document. You are now just limited to executing a selected set of menu commands, as shown in Figure 22.27.

Import form data

When you select the Import form data option and click Add, the Select File Containing Form Data dialog box opens. Select the file containing the form data you want to import and click the Select button. Imported form data is from files saved in FDF (Form Data File) or XML format that are exported from PDF documents. When you click the Select button, the data matching identical form fields is imported. Using Import form data limits you to importing data saved only in FDF format. If you use the Forms ⇨ Manage Form Data ⇨ Import Data menu command, data can be imported when saved as FDF, XFDF, XML, FormFlow99 Data Files(.xfd), and TXT. Note that you must have at least one form field on the page for this to work.

FIGURE 22.27

Select menu commands from the Menu Item dialog box when using the Execute a menu item action type.

Multimedia Operation (Acrobat 9 and later)

Following the Import form data action you find the Multimedia Operation (Acrobat 9 and later) action.

NEW FEATURE New in Acrobat 9 is an action that permits you to select various multimedia annotations and assign actions to video and sound clips. You can select from a variety of actions to play, stop, rewind, pause, mute, set volume, and add custom JavaScripts.

In order to use this action, you must have a multimedia file either converted to PDF or imported in a PDF document. When you add the action the Multimedia Operations dialog box opens as shown in Figure 22.28.

CROSS-REF For more information on converting multimedia files to PDF and importing media in PDF documents, see Chapter 23.

FIGURE 22.28

Choose Multimedia Operation (Acrobat 9 and later) and click Add to open the Multimedia Operations dialog box.

Open a file

You use Open a file to open any file on your computer. When you select the action type and click the Add button, the Open dialog box opens. Browse your hard drive and select the file you want to open. If the file is not a PDF file, you (or your customer) need to have the authoring application that created the file installed on your computer in order to execute the link action. Creating the link does not require you to have any external programs installed on your computer.

Open a web link

The Open a web link option enables you to associate a link action to a Web address. Web links can be contained in PDF documents locally on your computer or within a PDF page where the PDF is hosted on a Web server. If a Web link is contained locally in a PDF document, selecting the link launches the browser configured with Acrobat and establishes a URL connection. Acrobat remains open in the background while the Web browser appears in the foreground. Always use the complete URL to identify a Web address.

When you specify a URL in the Edit URL dialog box that opens after you click the Add button in the Link Properties, you can add custom viewing in the URL address for the way you want to open a PDF document. For example, if you want to view a page other than the opening page you can add to the URL a request for opening any page number. To open a specific page, enter:

```
http://www.mycompany.com/myDoc.pdf#page=3
```

In this example the file myDoc.pdf opens on page 3 in the Web browser. In addition to opening a specific page, you can add other viewing parameters such as zoom levels, page modes such as viewing layers or bookmarks, named destinations, and so on.

CROSS-REF For more information on setting viewing options with Web links, see Chapter 27.

Play a sound

You can create a link or button to play a sound in a PDF document. When you select the Play a sound action and click the Add button, the Select Sound File dialog box opens for you to locate a sound file on your hard drive and import the sound. Acrobat pauses a moment while the sound is converted to a format usable in Acrobat viewers. After it's imported in the PDF, the sound can be played across platforms. When the link button is selected, the sound plays. Sounds imported with the Play a sound action and those added with the Record Audio Comment tool support only Acrobat 5 media. If you use the Sound tool you can choose to import either Acrobat 5– or Acrobat 6–compatible sounds.

CROSS-REF For importing sounds with the Sound Attach tool, see Chapter 12. For information on using Acrobat 5– and Acrobat 6–compatible sound and media, see Chapter 23.

Notice the Multimedia task button pull-down menu contains a Sound Tool. You can use the Sound tool to import sounds. In addition, you can use the Record Audio Comment tool to import sound files. Playing sounds from any of these tools is identical. The Sound tool and the Record Audio Comment tool are limited to adding sounds on a page where a user needs to click or double-click a button to play the sound. The link action is more versatile as you can add sounds with nested link actions, page actions, and form fields. Sound files are supported from files saved as AIFF or WAV.

CROSS-REF For information on using the Sound tool, see Chapter 23, and for information on using the Attach Sound tool, see Chapter 12.

Play media (Acrobat 5 compatible) & Play media (Acrobat 6 and Later Compatible)

Acrobat 9 has an entirely new way to handle multimedia than previous versions of Acrobat. The Play Media (Acrobat 5 Compatible) and Play Media (Acrobat 6 and Later Compatible) actions are used with legacy files where play buttons were added in Acrobat 8 and earlier. These actions are not used in Acrobat 9 when importing media using the Multimedia tools. The alternative to creating play buttons in Acrobat 9 is to use the Multimedia Operation (Acrobat 9 and later) action.

If you have legacy files with media clips and play buttons earlier than Acrobat 9, you can edit the play actions by opening a link or button properties and edit the properties in the Play Media (Acrobat 5 or 6) compatible dialog boxes as shown in Figure 22.29.

FIGURE 22.29

Buttons created in earlier versions of Acrobat for playing media can be edited in Acrobat 9.

Read an article

When you select Read an article as the action type for a link, the Select Article dialog box opens when you click the Add button. If no articles are present in the PDF document, you receive a dialog box alerting you that there are no articles present and you can't use this link action. When articles are present, select the article you want to associate with the link from the listed articles in the Select Article dialog box. When you select the link in the navigation mode, Acrobat opens the page where the first box in the article appears. Additionally, the cursor changes to the Article icon that enables you to continue reading the selected article.

Reset a form

The Reset a form link action relates to PDF documents with form fields. When a form is filled out, you can reset the form to remove all data contained in the form fields. Acrobat provides an opportunity to clear the data from all fields or from selected fields you identify individually. A Reset a form dialog box opens, enabling you to select the fields to clear.

 For more information on resetting forms, see Chapter 34.

Run a JavaScript

JavaScript adds great opportunity for making PDF documents interactive and dynamic. You can add JavaScripts to link button actions as well as form fields. When you select Run a JavaScript and click the Add button, the JavaScript Editor dialog box opens. You type the code in the dialog box, or copy and paste code from a text editor to the JavaScript Editor. Click OK to commit the JavaScript.

CROSS-REF For more information on writing JavaScripts, see Chapter 36 (on the CD-ROM).

Set layer visibility

For PDF documents containing layers, you first create the layer view you want in the Layers panel.

 Open the Layers panel and show the layers you want displayed when a user clicks on the link. In Figure 22.30, four layers are hidden, as shown in the Layers panel. When you use the Set layer visibility action type, the layer view at the time you create the link is what is shown to the user when he or she clicks the link. This behavior works similarly to bookmarks in which you place in view in the Document panel your resultant view, and then create the bookmark. Layer visibility works the same. Set the visibility you want, and then set the link.

FIGURE 22.30

When using the Set layer visibility action type, you first show the layer view you want to display to assign it to the link action.

After setting your layer view for the display when the user clicks the link, create a link and click the Custom Link button. Select Set layer visibility from the Actions pull-down menu and a dialog box opens, informing you the current layer state has been captured.

 For more information on layer visibility, see Chapter 24.

Show/hide a field

The Show/hide a field action enables the user to allow selected form fields to be visible or hidden. Forms can be created to display and hide form fields for help menus and informational items, to protect data, and so on. You can make a hidden field visible by opening the Show/Hide Field dialog box and selecting the Hide radio button. Within this dialog box the options for both hiding and showing fields are enabled through radio buttons.

 For more information on working with Acrobat PDF forms, see Part VI.

Submit a form

Form and comment data contained in PDF documents can be transported on the World Wide Web. When a user completes a form, the data can be submitted to a URL as a Form Data File (FDF), HTML, or XML data. Additionally, the entire PDF can be submitted. The PDF author can then collect and process the data. Using form and comment data with Web servers has some requirements you need to work out with the ISP hosting your Web site. If you use forms on PDF Web pages, include a button that submits data after the user completes the form. Using the Submit a form action enables you to identify the URL where the data is submitted and determine which data type is exported from the PDF document. If comment data is to be submitted, a check box enabling comment delivery appears in the dialog box.

NEW FEATURE   New in Acrobat 9, you can submit form data without a button. Acrobat 9 provides users the option for submitting form data to Acrobat.com without the need to configure Web servers and without a need for creating submit buttons. To learn more about data handling with the new Acrobat 9 features, see Chapter 35.

Managing links

Acrobat provides many menu options for link management. You can copy/paste, align, and distribute links and more through the use of a context menu. If you need to apply these editing tasks to multiple links, select the Select Object tool and click and drag through the links you want to manage.

After selecting multiple links with either the Select Object tool or Link tool, open a context menu as shown in Figure 22.31. The context menu offers several menu categories with submenu items used for managing links.

FIGURE 22.31

Select multiple links with the Link tool or the Select Object tool and open a context menu. Select a menu category and select the command you want to use from the submenu items.

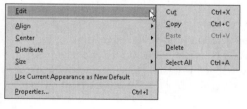

The menu items include the following:

- **Edit.** The Edit menu contains several items in a submenu for cut/copy/paste, accessible in the top-level Edit menu. You can delete a link or group of links by selecting Delete.

- **Select All.** Select All deserves some special comment. When you select a link with the Link tool or choose Edit ➪ Select All, all links are selected on a page. If you click on a link with the Select Object tool and choose Select All from the Edit submenu, all objects selectable with the Select Object tool are selected on the page. For example, if you have links and form fields, Select All selects all links and form fields on the target page. If you want to edit the links for deletion, alignment, copying, and so on, be certain to click on the Link tool and then use Edit ⇨ Select All.

- **Align.** You can align multiple links Left, Right, Top, Bottom, and along the vertical and horizontal centers. Choose the respective submenu command for the alignment option of your choice.

- **Distribute.** If you have a row or column of links and you want to position them equidistant from each other, choose the Distribute command and select from either Vertically or Horizontally. Vertically distributes a column and Horizontally distributes a row of link objects.

- **Size.** As you create link rectangles, you may draw the links at different sizes. To resize links on a given page to the same size, select one of the links with the Link tool. Using a context menu, click Select All, move the Link tool to the target size link rectangle, and open a context menu. (The target link rectangle is displayed with a red keyline and red handles while the other rectangles in the selected group are highlighted blue.) Select from the submenu Height, Width, or Both. The selected link rectangles are resized to the size of the target link.

- **Properties.** Use this option to open the Link Properties dialog box. If you select more than one link rectangle, the link actions shows Varies in the action list if the link actions are different among other selected links. You can apply common appearance settings to all selected links or you can edit actions if the actions are all the same among the selected links.

> **TIP** If you want to change appearances for multiple links or button fields, use the Select All menu command to select all the objects, or drag through a group of objects with the Select Object tool and edit the object attributes in the Properties Bar. You can change the color of borders (and fills on button fields), line thickness, and highlight style for multiple objects.

Working with Page Properties

A page action is like a link button that invokes an action when a page is opened or closed in the Document pane. You don't have to click on anything because the trigger for executing the action type is handled by Acrobat when the page opens or closes. All the action types available with links are the same actions that are associated with page actions.

To create a page action, open the Pages panel. Select a page with the Hand tool and open a context menu. From the menu options select Page Properties. The Page Properties dialog box opens with two sets of properties types available. The default page properties options are contained in the panel for Tab Order, but these settings don't have anything to do with setting a page action, so I'll skip them for the moment.

> **CROSS-REF** For information related to setting tab orders, see Chapter 34.

It is the second tab in the Page Properties dialog box that is used for setting page actions. Click on the Actions tab shown in Figure 22.32, and the options for defining actions to page behavior are displayed. Two areas are used for applying a page action to any page in a PDF document. You first select the trigger for either Page Open or Page Close and then select the action from the Select Action pull-down menu. The options in this menu are the same as you have available with link actions.

FIGURE 22.32

Open the Page Properties dialog box from a context menu on a page thumbnail. Click the Actions tab to open the page actions options settings.

Page actions help you make your PDF documents more automated. You might select a sound to play when a page opens, as shown in Figure 22.32. You may want to set layer visibility, play a movie, or execute a menu item. Of all the options available for action types, with page actions you have the addition of an infinite number of choices when running JavaScripts. You might want to run a script that analyzes the Acrobat viewer version when a user opens a PDF document and alerts the user that Acrobat 6 is needed to properly view your document if the user opens the file in a viewer version earlier than Acrobat 6. This example and many more options are available to you when running JavaScripts from page actions.

CROSS-REF   To see examples of JavaScripts that analyze Acrobat viewer versions and viewer types, see Chapter 36 (on the CD-ROM).

Creating Destinations

A destination is a specific location in a document. Whereas a bookmark and a link may link to page 5 in a file, a destination links to the location where page 5 resides. If you delete page 5, bookmarks and links have no place to go and the links are often referred to as *dead links*. If you delete page 5 where a destination has been created, the destination remains at the same location — that is, following page 4 and preceding page 6. Furthermore, if you insert a page after page 4, the bookmarks and links are linked to page 6. All pages shift to make room for a new page, but the links from bookmarks and links remain fixed on a specific page. With destinations, if you insert a page after page 4, the destination takes you to the new page 5.

You can also use destinations when you want to use JavaScripts for creating pop-up menus and smart forms, and for adding other interactive features.

It all sounds pretty nifty but there's a downside to using named destinations. Adding many destinations in a PDF document adds a lot of overhead to the file size. Destinations can make a PDF bulky and slow if they are used extensively. Destinations should not be thought of as a substitute for bookmarks and links, but rather, a complement for creating interactive documents when other methods don't support the same features.

Destination tools

You create, organize, and display destinations within the Destinations panel. To open the panel, choose View ➪ Navigation Panels ➪ Destinations. If you want to use the Destinations panel frequently in an Acrobat session, you can drag the panel into the Navigation pane. As a panel in the Navigation pane it is visible and easily accessible until you remove it by dragging it out of the pane.

The panel contains a few icons and a pull-down menu, as shown in Figure 22.33. In addition to the panel tools, context menus offer several menu options. You create, edit, and manage all destinations through this panel.

FIGURE 22.33

Open the Destinations panel by choosing View ➪ Navigation Panels ➪ Destinations. Several icons and a list of destinations appear in the panel.

The options are as follows:

- **New.** Click the New icon or a context menu option to create new destinations. You create a destination by first navigating to the page and view, and then creating the destination, much like you create bookmarks.

- **Delete.** You can use the Trashcan icon in the panel, as well as a menu command available when opening a context menu on a selected destination to delete the destination.

- **Sort by Name.** Open the Options pull-down menu and select Sort by Name. Destinations are sorted alphabetically by name. Alternately, you can click on Name or Page in the Destinations panel title bar and sort by Name or Page.

- **Sort by Page.** Open the Options pull-down menu and select Sort by Page. Destinations are sorted by page number.

- **Go to Destination.** Open a context menu on a destination and select Go to Destination. When you invoke the command, Acrobat opens the destination page.

- **Set Destination.** Also from a context menu opened in the Destinations panel, Set Destination can reassign a new target destination. First navigate to a new view, and then select Set Destination.

- **Rename.** From a context menu opened on a destination name, select Rename. The name becomes highlighted and ready for you to type text for a new name.

Creating a pop-up menu

You can use destinations to create a pop-up menu on a page that displays menu options for navigating to other pages and other files. To create a pop-up menu that links to other pages, you create destinations and then add some JavaScript to a link or button field. When a user selects a menu item, the page destination opens in the Document pane.

Follow these steps to experience how easy it is to create an application pop-up menu.

STEPS: Creating application pop-up menus

1. **Open the Destinations panel.** Open a PDF file with multiple pages. Select View ➪ Navigation Panels ➪ Destinations.

2. **Create destinations.** Navigate to each page and set the view using the Zoom tools. Click New in the Destinations panel for each page view you want to capture. As you create new destinations, type a name for each destination in the Destinations panel. In my example, I created five destinations, as you can see in Figure 22.34.

FIGURE 22.34

After you add destinations, the Destinations panel displays the names you used when creating each new destination. The destinations are sorted by name in the list. To sort the list by page number, select Sort by Page from the Options pull-down menu.

3. **Create the JavaScript.** After you have finished adding new destinations, you need to do a little programming. If you haven't used the JavaScript Editor, don't panic. These steps are no more complicated than following a few simple directions.

CROSS-REF For a better understanding of using JavaScript and the script created here, see Chapter 36 (on the CD-ROM).

Select the Link tool and click and drag open a link rectangle. Ideally, it's best to have some text or an icon on the page indicating that a button or link is present. If you don't use button faces and icons, you can also simply use a keyline border to show where the link appears on the page. In the Create Link dialog box, select Custom link and click OK. The Link Properties dialog box opens. Click Actions and from the Select Action pull-down menu, select Run a JavaScript.

Click Add and the JavaScript Editor opens. In the JavaScript Editor, type the following code:

```
1. var c = app.popUpMenu
2. (["Blogs", "Thom", "Ted"]
3. ["User Groups", "Chapters"],
4. ["Forms", "Claim Forms"]);
5. this.gotoNamedDest(c);
```

See the sidebar "Analyzing the Script" later in this chapter for a detailed explanation of the code. In my example, the code appears as you see in Figure 22.35.

FIGURE 22.35

JavaScript code to create an application pop-up menu

771

NOTE   The items category1, category 2, and so on, are used to describe a category you want to appear in your pop-up menu. Something like *Accounting*, *Human Resources*, *Manufacturing*, and so on. The items listed in the code (item1, item2, and so on) would be the destination names. You might use something like *Accounting Policies*, *Accounting Procedures*, *HR Polices, HR Procedures,* and so on, as the destination names.

4. **Exit the JavaScript Editor and Link Properties.** Click OK in the JavaScript Editor and click OK in the Link Properties dialog box.

5. **Test the pop-up menu. Select the Hand tool and click the link.** You should see a pop-up menu similar to Figure 22.36. In this example, I included two items in the first category to appear in a submenu. In Figure 22.36, User Groups and Forms are labels. The submenus open Chapters and ClaimForm items that are the destinations.

FIGURE 22.36

If the pop-up menu was created properly, you should see submenu items listed when selecting a category.

Analyzing the Script

In the script, the first line of code sets a variable c for a pop-up menu. Regardless of what your destinations are named or the contents of your PDF, copy this line of code into your JavaScript Editor exactly as you see it.

Lines 2 to 4 contain the categories and submenu commands that link to the destinations you created. Here's where you need to modify your code. Where you see "category x," replace the name with a category title of your choosing. You might want to use names such as Personnel, Administration, and Finance, or you can use category names such as Designs, Illustrations, and Photos, or any other combination of names that relate to the categories you want to use. Notice that line 2 begins with an open parenthesis, (, followed by a left bracket, [. These characters are important to include in your code.

In lines 2 through 4 are three item numbers contained in quotes and separated by commas. These names need to be the same as your destination names. Type the destination names exactly, including letter case, as you created them in your Destinations panel. The order in which you add the names is unimportant. Also notice that after the last destination name and quote mark, no comma is inserted. Lines 2 and 3 end with a comma and line 4 ends with a semicolon. It is also important to type these characters just as you see them in the sample code.

Line 5, the final line of code, is the instruction to take the user to the destination selected from the menu options. Type this line exactly as you see it into your JavaScript Editor.

NOTE To modify JavaScript code, select the Link tool and double-click the link. In the Link Properties dialog box select the item denoted as Run a JavaScript in the Actions list and click the Edit button. The JavaScript edit dialog box opens where you can make changes to the code.

In this example, destinations are used to navigate pages in a PDF document via a pop-up menu. If the design of your PDF documents better suits pop-up menus, you have many options when using JavaScripts. You can also create pop-up menus with JavaScripts that open other PDF documents or specific pages in other PDF documents and that execute many different menu commands.

CROSS-REF For an example of a pop-up menu that opens secondary PDF documents, see Chapter 36 (on the CD-ROM).

Working with Buttons

In the previous section you saw how to use the Link tool to navigate pages and open files. When links are created, you need some kind of icon or text that lets a user know that a link button exists. If you add links on a page in empty white space with no border keyline, users won't know where or when to click on a link button. If you want to use images or icons for button appearances, you can use another form of link tool with the Button tool that supports importing icons.

NEW FEATURE Prior to Acrobat 9, the button tool and other form field objects were limited to Acrobat Professional and Acrobat 3D. In version 9, you find the button tool and all other form tools available in Acrobat Standard (Windows), Acrobat Pro (Windows and Macintosh), and Acrobat ProExtended (Windows).

Creating a button field

Using form fields instead of links has some advantages. You can add image icons to button fields, use rollover effects, and copy and paste fields across multiple pages, and you have all the same action types accessible as those used with bookmarks, links, and page actions.

CROSS-REF The discussion of button fields in this chapter is limited to creating button fields with actions similar to those discussed in this chapter when creating link actions. For a more thorough discussion on using form fields in Acrobat, see Part VI.

NEW FEATURE Creating buttons in Acrobat 9 permits you to add form fields in Form Editing Mode or by using the Button tool in the Advanced Editing toolbar in Viewer mode.

Choose Forms ⇨ Add or Edit Fields to enter Form Edit mode or click the Button tool in the Advanced Editing toolbar in Viewer mode. From the Add New Field menu in Form Editing Mode choose Button and click the tool on a document page. An abbreviated Properties window opens where you can edit the default name for the field. Click Properties and the Button Properties dialog box opens showing the General tab.

If you don't change the name when you create a button, Acrobat automatically names the field for you beginning with Button1, then Button2 for the next button you create, then Button3, and so on. When you open the Properties dialog box you can additionally change the field name in the General tab. Highlight the default name and type a new name. In this example, I want to create some navigation buttons. The name of the button I'll use is goNext, as shown in Figure 22.37.

FIGURE 22.37

Type a name for the button field in the General tab.

Button faces are handled in the Options tab. Click the Options tab and select Icon Only from the Layout pull-down menu. Click the Choose Icon button and the Select Icon dialog box opens. From this dialog box you need to access yet another dialog box by clicking the Browse button. The Open dialog box opens to a view where you can navigate your hard drive and select a file to import as your button face. Any file format compatible with the Create PDF from File tool is acceptable. Select a filename in the Open dialog box and click Select. Acrobat returns you to the Select Icon dialog box where you can see a preview of the imported file, as shown in Figure 22.38.

If the preview looks like the file you want to use as a button face, click OK to return to the Button Properties dialog box. Click the Actions tab where you assign the action type associated with your button. In this dialog box you make a choice for the trigger action. The default is Mouse Up, which means when the mouse button is released the action executes. Leave the Select Trigger menu option at the default and open the Select Action pull-down menu.

Select Execute a menu item from the pull-down menu. Click the Add button and the Menu Item dialog box opens. Select View ⇨ Go To ⇨ Next Page, as shown in Figure 22.39.

FIGURE 22.38

The Select Icon dialog box displays a thumbnail preview of the imported file. Click OK to return to the Button Properties dialog box.

FIGURE 22.39

Add a menu item to navigate to the next page.

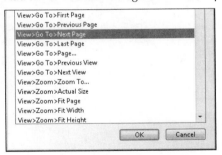

Now repeat the preceding steps to create a second navigation button for moving to previous pages and using a different icon to represent moving backward in the PDF file.

To move a button field, select either the Button tool or the Select Object tool. In the example here, two buttons are created to provide navigation back and forth between pages as shown in Figure 22.40. If you want to move the two buttons together, you need to use the Select Object tool. Drag the buttons to an area on the page where you can easily click the buttons to navigate pages.

FIGURE 22.40

Two buttons used to navigate forward and back through document pages

Duplicating buttons

At this point, the obvious advantage of using a button field over a link is when you want an image or icon appearance used with the button. Another advantage for using button fields over links is the ability to duplicate button fields across pages. The hard part is finished after you create the fields and add the button faces. The next step is to duplicate buttons so you don't have to copy/paste them on each page.

With the button fields in place, select the Select Object tool and click and drag through both fields. Be certain to click and drag outside the first field so as not to select it while dragging. When both fields are selected, open a context menu and select Duplicate, as shown in Figure 22.41.

FIGURE 22.41

Open a context menu on selected buttons and choose Duplicate.

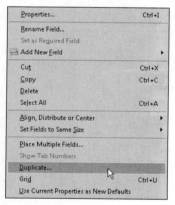

When you release the mouse button, the Duplicate field dialog box opens as shown in Figure 22.42. In the dialog box, select the page range for the duplicated fields. If you created fields on the first page, enter **2** in the first field box and enter the last page number in the second field box. Click OK and the fields with the same field properties are duplicated across the specified pages.

FIGURE 22.42

Enter the page range in the Duplicate Field dialog box and click OK. The fields are duplicated on the pages you specified.

Click the buttons to navigate pages. Notice that each button appears in the same relative position on each page.

The important thing to remember as you work with bookmarks, links, page actions, destinations, and fields is that each is designed for different purposes. Although you can create the same results with one method or another, at times you'll favor one method over the others for a particular editing assignment. Acrobat offers many tools and features for creating dynamic interactive documents, often limited only by your imagination. The more time you invest in learning all that Acrobat affords you, the more impressive results you'll produce.

Summary

- You can name, organize, and create bookmarks with different appearance properties. You can move, reassign, and delete standard bookmarks without affecting page content. When you delete structured bookmarks, the respective pages are deleted.

- Bookmarks support the same actions you can apply to links. Actions enable you to view pages, open documents, create Web links, and write JavaScripts and other types of commands that act as hypertext links.

- Article threads enable viewers to follow passages of text in a logical reading order.

- Links support many different actions from page navigation to running JavaScripts. Links can be copied and pasted and the link properties are retained in the pasted objects. Links cannot be duplicated across PDF pages, and links do not support content files with colors or images.

- Acrobat supports opening user-defined pages in external PDF documents via link actions.

- You select link properties in the Create Link dialog box, from a context menu command, or by double-clicking on a link. All link actions are changed in the Link Properties dialog box.

- You make links from text by selecting text with the Select tool and choosing Create Link from a context menu.

- All the actions assigned to links can also be assigned to page actions. Page actions are established in the Page Properties dialog box accessed by opening a context menu on a page thumbnail and selecting Properties.

- Page actions are invoked when a page opens or a page closes.

- Destinations are similar to bookmarks. Destinations do not support actions. Destinations tend to make file sizes larger than when using bookmarks and links.

- You can use destinations, together with a JavaScript, to create pop-up menus.

- You can assign form field buttons different button faces from external files.

- Form fields are supported in Acrobat Standard (Windows), Acrobat Pro (Windows and Macintosh), and Acrobat Pro Extended (Windows).

- Form fields can be duplicated across multiple pages. Duplicated fields are placed on all pages in the same relative position as from where they were duplicated.

Chapter 23

Working with Multimedia and PDFs

Acrobat offers a wide range of possibilities with animation, motion, and sound. You can import sound files in PDFs, import movie files, import and convert Flash files to PDF, convert Web pages with Flash animation, convert PowerPoint files with motion objects using Adobe Presenter, and create animation by writing JavaScript routines. With the exception of writing JavaScripts, you create animation and sound in other applications and import them in PDF documents or you can convert a media file directly to PDF.

Movie files added with the Video tool and sounds added with the Sound tool are available only in Acrobat Pro and Acrobat Pro Extended. Acrobat Standard does not have these tools and you have no way of adjusting properties for movie and sound files with Acrobat Standard. However, after you've added movie and sound files in Acrobat Pro or Pro Extended, all Acrobat viewers, including Adobe Reader, can play the movies and sounds.

In this chapter you learn how to import multimedia files into PDF documents, set a number of import options choices, import 3D files, adjust media properties, and convert media files directly to PDFs.

Setting Up the Multimedia Environment

You import sound and video files with the Video, Flash, or Sound tools and import 3D files with the 3D tool. All the tools are available from the new Acrobat 9 Multimedia toolbar. To open the toolbar, either select Tools ⇨ Multimedia ⇨ Show Multimedia Toolbar, open a context menu on the

Toolbar Well and select Multimedia, or use the More Tools window and check the Multimedia tool-bar. When the toolbar opens, right-click to open a context menu from the Toolbar Well and select Dock Toolbars. Additionally, you can select all tools from the Multimedia task button.

Working with Sound Files

You import sounds in Acrobat in one of two ways. You can use the Record Audio Comment tool and record or import a message in the form of a comment. Once recorded, the sound is embedded in Acrobat and not accessible for importing via an action. The other method of handling sound in PDF documents is to import sounds from files saved on your hard drive. By importing sounds you can invoke a sound with various action types — for example, using a page action to play a sound when the user opens or closes a page or clicks a button or link field.

CROSS-REF For information on using the Record Audio Comment tool and setting action types, see Chapter 20. For more information on action types, see Chapter 22.

You import sound files with the Sound tool found on the Multimedia toolbar or by selecting the Sound tool from the Multimedia task button. Be certain to understand the difference between creating an audio comment and importing a sound with the Sound tool. Using the Record Audio Comment tool enables you to record a sound or import a sound file from your hard drive. Using the Sound tool enables you to import a sound from a file saved in a format compatible for import-ing sounds, but does not offer you an option for recording a sound. Before you can use the Sound tool, you need to either acquire or edit sounds and save them to a file format Acrobat recognizes.

NOTE The Record Audio Comment tool is available in all Acrobat viewers including Adobe Reader when PDFs have been enabled with Adobe Reader usage rights. For more information on enabling PDFs with Adobe Reader usage rights, see Chapter 19.

Creating sound files

If you are so inclined you can purchase a commercial application for editing sound and saving recordings that Acrobat can recognize. If recording sounds is an infrequent task and does not war-rant the purchase of expensive commercial software, you can find sound-recording applications as shareware and in the public domain that can satisfy almost any need you have for using sounds on PDF documents.

Web sites change frequently, so you may need to do a search for public domain and shareware applications for your computer platform. As of this writing you can find sound-editing programs at www.freewarefiles.com (Windows) or www.macupdate.com (Macintosh). You can find applications that enable you to record sounds and save them in formats acceptable to the platform you use that can then be recognized by Acrobat. The most common of the file types Acrobat recog-nizes is WAV for Windows and AIFF for Macintosh.

NOTE You can import video and sound files that are compatible with Apple QuickTime, Flash Player, Windows Built-In Player, RealOne, and Windows Media Player. Windows media files need to be converted to QuickTime if you're importing a Windows Media file on a Mac. Windows needs a QuickTime installation in order to import QuickTime files on Windows. Sound files saved as WAV and AIFF can be imported in Acrobat running on either platform.

Be certain you have a microphone properly connected to your computer according to your computer's user manual. Launch the sound-editing application you downloaded from a Web site or use a commercial application if you have one available. Most programs offer you a record button similar in appearance to a tape recorder or VCR. Click the Record button and speak into the microphone. When finished recording, click the Stop button. Depending on the application, you may be prompted in a dialog box to save the file, or you may see a window where you can further edit the sound, as shown in Figure 23.1.

FIGURE 23.1

To record sounds and save the sound to a file available for importing in Acrobat, use a sound-editing program.

If a dialog box does not prompt you to save the recording, select Save or Save As from a menu option. Typically the commands are under the File menu, but these may vary depending on the program you use. When you save the file, be certain to save in a format acceptable to Acrobat. A WAV (Windows) or AIFF (Macintosh) file format can be imported in Acrobat, but be careful of any file compression applied to the file when saved. You may need to test various compression options in order to find a format that Acrobat can recognize. After choosing the format, supply a name for the file with the proper extension, as shown in Figure 23.2.

FIGURE 23.2

After editing a sound, save the file in either AIFF (Macintosh) or WAV (Windows) format.

Adding sounds to page actions

A sound might be added to a Page Open or a Page Close action to provide informational instructions to complete a form, play a music score, or other similar function. In order to add a sound to a page action, you must have the sound file saved to disk as described in the preceding section. To add a sound to a page action, follow these steps:

NOTE   Acrobat Standard does support importing sounds on page actions, bookmarks, and with links. Although you have no Sound tool in Acrobat Standard, you can use an action to import sounds.

STEPS: Adding sounds to page actions

1. **Open the Page Properties.** Be certain your sound file is available in a directory on your hard drive and click the Pages tab in the Navigation pane. From a context menu opened on the page where you want the sound to play, select Page Properties. The Page Properties dialog box opens.

2. **Set the action trigger.** Click the Actions tab and select either Page Open or Page Close from the Select Trigger pull-down menu.

3. **Set the action type.** Open the pull-down menu for Select Action and choose Play a sound from the menu options as shown in Figure 23.3.

NOTE   By default, the Play a sound menu item in the Select Action pull-down menu may not be in view. Scroll the menu down to show the command.

4. **Add the action to the page trigger.** Click the Add button in the Page Properties dialog box to add the sound to your PDF.

FIGURE 23.3

Choose Play a sound from the Select Action pull-down menu.

5. **Select the sound file.** The Select Sound File dialog box opens. Navigate your hard drive to find the sound to import, select it, and click the Select button. After importing the sound, click Close in the Page Properties dialog box.

NOTE Acrobat may pause momentarily. The sound file imported in Acrobat is converted during the import. When a sound is imported in a PDF file, the sound can then be played across platforms. Therefore, a WAV file can be played on a Macintosh computer and an AIFF file can be played on a Windows computer.

6. **Save the file.** Choose File ⇨ Save As and rewrite the file to disk. Close the file and reopen it to test the page action.

After you save the PDF file and reopen it, the sound is played. You can also test the sound by scrolling a page in the PDF file and returning to the page where the sound was imported. The action is dynamic and the sound plays before you save the PDF file.

Adding sounds to form field actions

Of the mouse behavior types, you may find that Mouse Enter, On Focus, or On Blur behaviors work equally as well as using a Mouse Up or Mouse Down trigger. As an example, you might have a descriptive message display when the user places the cursor over a button field and before he or she clicks the mouse. Or you may want to invoke a sound when the user tabs out of a field as a reminder to verify data entry in a PDF form. In these situations and similar uses, the sound is played from a mouse behavior related to a data or button field. To understand how to use sound actions with data fields, follow these steps:

STEPS: Adding sounds to form fields

1. **Open a PDF document with form fields.** In Figure 23.4, I use a form with several check boxes. I want to create a sound when the user places the cursor over one of the check boxes or tabs to the field.

FIGURE 23.4

Four check boxes are to be configured to play a sound on a Mouse Enter trigger.

2. **Open the field properties.** Choose the Select Object tool in the Editing toolbar and double-click the field you want to edit. If no fields exist in your document, you need to enter Form Editing mode and add all but button fields in the Form Editing mode. If a field exists on a form, you can use the Select Object tool in Viewer mode. The Field Type Properties dialog box opens when you double-click a field with the Select Object tool.

CROSS-REF For more information on creating form fields in Acrobat and using the Form Editing mode, see Chapter 34.

3. **Select the mouse trigger.** In the Check Box Properties dialog box, click the Actions tab and select Mouse Enter as the Select Trigger, as shown in Figure 23.5.

FIGURE 23.5

Choose Mouse Enter from the Select Trigger pull-down menu.

4. **Add a sound action to the field.** Open the Select Action pull-down menu and select Play a sound.

5. **Select the sound file.** Click the Add button to open the Select Sound File dialog box. Select the file to import and click the Select button.

6. **Close the Check Box Properties dialog box.** Check to be certain the mouse trigger is set to Mouse Enter (or another trigger you chose to use). Click Close in the Check Box Properties dialog box.

7. **Test the sound.** Select the Hand tool and place the mouse cursor over the check box where you added the sound. (Note: To play the sound by tabbing to the field, use the On Focus mouse trigger.)

When the mouse enters one of the check boxes, the respective sound plays. The sound plays completely even if the cursor leaves the field. Sounds added to forms either for page actions or field actions can be played from any Acrobat viewer.

TIP A sound continues to play to completion. If you want to stop the sound while editing a document, select the Select Object tool or press the R key on your keyboard to activate the Select Object tool. (Note: You need to enable Use single-key accelerators to access tools in the General Preferences to use key modifiers to select tools.)

Using the Sound tool

🔊 Sound Tool Importing sounds with page actions, form fields, links, bookmarks, and so on limits your import options to fewer file formats and limits the attributes you can assign to the imported file. In essence, you import the file and play the sound. Not much else is available when you use the Select Action command. Another method for importing sound files in PDF documents is with the Sound tool. When you use the Sound tool to import sounds, your options are much greater for the kinds of files you can import and attributes you can assign to the imported sounds.

To import a sound with the Sound tool, select the tool from the Multimedia toolbar and just double-click or drag open a rectangle on a document page. The area contained within the rectangle becomes a trigger to play the sound. When you release the mouse button, the Insert Sound dialog box opens, as shown in Figure 23.6.

TIP You can manage sound and movie links similarly to links and form fields where context menu options enable you to size, align, copy, paste, and distribute fields. You can access these menu commands when you select sound and movie links in a group together with links and form fields. For more information on managing links and form fields, see Chapters 22 and 34.

FIGURE 23.6

Double-click the Sound tool or click+drag on a document page to open the Insert Sound dialog box.

Click the Browse button and locate a file on your hard drive to import. Acrobat pauses a moment while the file is converted to a format that all Acrobat viewers recognize. If using Adobe Acrobat Pro Extended, the file is converted to Adobe Flash format.

You also have a link to open the Add Sound dialog box in the Insert Sound dialog box. Click the blue text where you see Create legacy multimedia content to open the Add Sound dialog box. The settings in this dialog box are the same as those you found in earlier Acrobat viewers. You have options for choosing Acrobat 6 (and Later) Compatible Media and Acrobat 5 (and Earlier) Compatible Media as shown in Figure 23.7.

If you use Acrobat Pro (Windows and Macintosh), you only have access to the legacy content settings unless you use H.264 (MPEG-4 Part 10) compression. If you have Acrobat Pro Extended, you can import sound in the Insert Sound dialog box or click the Create legacy multimedia content link and use the Add Sound dialog box. If you don't use the Add Sound dialog box and add sounds using the Insert Sound dialog box (only in Acrobat Pro Extended) shown in Figure 23.6, the sound is converted to Adobe Flash.

CROSS-REF See the sidebar later in this chapter on using H.264 compression.

FIGURE 23.7

The Add Sound dialog box opens in Acrobat Pro automatically or Acrobat Pro Extended when you click the Create legacy multimedia content link in the Insert Sound dialog box.

If using legacy files or preparing media for legacy viewers, you set the attributes for sound imports in the Add Sound dialog box. In the Add Sound dialog box, you have the following options:

NOTE Initial settings you apply to an imported sound are handled in the Add Sound dialog box for Acrobat Pro or Acrobat Pro Extended when you click the Create legacy multimedia content blue text. If you later want to edit the sound settings, the changes are made in either the Movie Properties (for Acrobat 5 or earlier compatible files) or the Multimedia Properties (for Acrobat 6 or later compatible files) dialog box. Either of these dialog boxes opens when you open a context menu on a sound rectangle using either the Sound tool or the Select Object tool and select the Properties command. The Multimedia Properties dialog box offers you many more settings options than the Add Sound dialog box. For more information on the Multimedia Properties options, see Acrobat 6 Multimedia Properties later in this chapter.

- **Select new content's compatibility.** From the radio button choices you decide whether the sound import is Acrobat 6 (and Later) Compatible Media or Acrobat 5 (and Earlier) Compatible Media. If you select Acrobat 5 (and Earlier) Compatible Media, the format options are limited to WAV and AIFF formats. If you use Acrobat 6 (and Later) Compatible Media, the sound may not play with earlier Acrobat viewers depending on the file types you import and attributes assigned to the sound.

- **Browse.** By default, you identify the media in the Insert Sound dialog box. If you want to change the source file, click the Browse button in the Add Sound dialog box to locate a different sound you want to import.

- **Content Type.** By default, the type of the file you import is listed automatically in the field box. By clicking the down arrow you can open a pull-down menu where all compatible file formats are listed. A total of 46 different file formats are supported. When you import files, let Acrobat interpret the file format and leave the format unchanged. If you select a sound for which Acrobat does not know the Content Type, Acrobat prompts you to click in a dialog box to select a content type.

- **Embed content in document.** Using Acrobat 5 compatibility automatically links a sound file to a PDF document. If you send your PDF to another user, you need to send the sound file along with the PDF document. Note that if you use an action to import a sound such as adding a sound to a bookmark action, the sound is always embedded in the PDF document. Furthermore, you don't have a choice for compatibility.

  If you use Acrobat 6 compatibility you can choose to link the sound file to the PDF or embed the sound in the PDF document. If you disable the check box for Embed content in document, you need to send the sound file as well as the PDF to a user in order for other users to play the sound.

- **Poster Settings.** If you select Acrobat 5 (and earlier), this option is not available. The rectangle you create appears similar to a button field. If you leave the default at Use no poster, then nothing appears inside the sound rectangle. If you select Create poster from file, you can fit a graphic to the rectangle — for example, something similar to using button faces for form field buttons. You click the Browse button to select the file you want to use for the poster. You can choose any file type that is compatible when using the Create PDF From File command. If the file type is other than PDF, Acrobat converts the file to PDF as it imports the image. If you're using a multi-page PDF document for the poster, the first page in the PDF document is used for the poster.

CROSS-REF For information on creating button faces, see Chapter 22.

Click OK after selecting options in the Add Sound dialog box. When you return to the document page, the rectangle is visible. You assign additional properties when you open the sound properties from a context menu. When the properties dialog box opens, the title of the dialog box is Multimedia Properties if Acrobat 6 (or Later) Compatible Media is selected and Movie Properties if Acrobat 5 (or Earlier) Compatible Media is used.

Using advanced settings

The Insert Sound dialog box in Figure 23.6 shows you an abbreviated list of options choices you have when importing sound files. You can expand the dialog box by clicking the Show Advanced Options check box. When the Insert sound dialog box is expanded you find a number of additional choices you can make for importing sounds as shown in Figure 23.8.

FIGURE 23.8

Click the Show Advanced Settings check box to expand the Insert Sound dialog box.

The choices you have available for the advanced settings include:

- **Enable When.** Earlier in this chapter in the section "Adding sounds to page actions" I talked about importing sounds on page actions using Page Open and Page Close triggers. If you use the Sound tool and open the advanced settings, you can trigger a sound to play on opening and closing pages. From the Enable When pull-down menu, choose the default to play a sound when the sound media box is clicked, or choose one of the other two triggers in the menu that include The page containing the content is opened or The page containing the content is closed. These last two menu choices are the same as when you use Page Action triggers to play a sound.

- **Disable When.** You have the same choices from this menu as you have with the Enable When menu. You can choose to stop a sound from playing when making a choice from a context menu, when a page opens, or when a page closes.

- **Playback Style.** Two choices are available from the pull-down menu. The default is to play the content on the page, in which case you won't see any visual changes on the page when the sound plays. The other choice is a floating window. A sound file does not actually appear in a floating window. A floating window is shown with a Flash file that acts like a placeholder. If you assign a poster to the sound object, the poster and sound object remain fixed on the page while a floating window like the one shown in Figure 23.9 opens.

FIGURE 23.9

A floating window assigned to a sound file

- **Width/Height.** These text boxes are used to set the width and height of the floating window.
- **Border Width.** Choose from No border, Thin, Medium, and Thick.
- **Transparent Background.** Assigns the background to transparency.
- **Poster Image.** Your choices are: Keep current poster, where no change in the poster occurs; Retrieve poster from file, which doesn't apply to sounds because sound files have no images in the file; and Create poster from file, where you can import any file consistent with the Create ⇨ PDF From File menu command. The Browse button opens a dialog box where you select the file you want to use for a poster.

Most of the options you have available in the Insert Sound Advanced Settings are accessible in the Properties dialog box. You can initially insert a sound using the abbreviated settings shown in Figure 23.6 and later adjust properties as needed.

Acrobat 5–compatible Video (Sound) Properties

After you've imported a sound or video using the legacy content, you may want to adjust the properties. To open sound or video properties, use the Select Object tool and open a context menu. From the menu choices choose Properties. When you open properties on Acrobat 5 Compatible Media, the Movie Properties dialog box opens as shown in Figure 23.10. The Movie Properties dialog box contains three tabs used for selecting more options than were available in the Add Sound dialog box.

FIGURE 23.10

When working with Acrobat 5 (and earlier) media, to open the Movie Properties dialog box, use the 3D tool, the Sound tool, the Flash tool, the Video tool, or the Select Object tool and select Properties from a context menu.

General properties

The default properties are the General Movie Properties. In this dialog box, you make the following selections:

- **Title.** By default, the title of the sound clip is the filename. Edit the title name in the field box to change the title.

- **Media location.** Local files are stored on your hard drive. You can change the sound to another file by clicking the Change Location button. Click the button to open the Select Multimedia File dialog box. Select another file and click the Select button to change the sound to another file. If you select URL, another dialog box opens asking you to specify a URL where a sound file is located. If importing sounds, you need to add the sound filename as part of the URL when using Acrobat 5 compatibility. When you deselect the option to embed the file with Acrobat 6 compatibility, the directory path is all you need to address in the line where the URL is specified.

Playback

The Playback tab offers options settings for playing sound clips and movies, as shown in Figure 23.11.

FIGURE 23.11

Click the Playback tab to set options for playing sounds.

- **Show player controls.** If this check box is enabled, a control palette opens when a sound is played. In the control palette you have a button to play/pause and a slider. Click and drag the slider to move forward or backward in the sound file. In Figure 23.12, the sound rectangle appears without a poster. The Show player controls check box was checked in the Movie Properties dialog box and the player controls are shown after you click once inside the rectangle. At the top of the rectangle is the player control. The sound is currently stopped. Clicking the right-pointing arrow with the Hand tool continues the play.

- **Use floating window.** With sounds, the sound file is fixed to a location. With video clips you can select the Use floating window option to float a video clip in a window centered in the Acrobat window. If you select floating window for a sound file, the player control opens in a floating toolbar. In Figure 23.13, player controls are very similar to those shown in Figure 23.12. When Use floating window is added in the Playback tab in the Movie Properties dialog box, the player control appears as a floating window.

FIGURE 23.12

Player controls appear when you check the Show player controls check box in the Movie Properties Playback tab.

FIGURE 23.13

When Use floating window is checked, the player controls open in a floating toolbar.

One reason you might use a floating window with a sound file is if you place the sound rectangle on a page where you don't want the rectangle visible to the end user — for example, something like a tiny rectangle in the top left corner of the page. If you add a page action to start the sound to play and you want the end user to stop or pause a sound, add the floating window. The window opens in the center of the page irrespective of where the sound rectangle is placed. The viewer of your PDF file can then pause, stop, and resume play.

- **Size.** For sound imports, the Size pull-down menu and field box are disabled. These options relate to sizing video clips, explained in the "Playback" section later in this chapter.

- **Play.** From the pull-down menu you can choose to play a sound Once; play a sound Once (keep player open); Loop, which loops through the sound and continues playing it over and over again; and play Forward and backward, which provides an interesting way of hearing your voice played backward. The latter option is best used for video clips without sound.

Appearance

Many of the options for appearance settings are the same as those found for link and form field appearances. Click the Appearance tab and make choices for the appearance of the rectangle border and the contents of the rectangle as shown in Figure 23.14.

- **Type.** From the Type pull-down menu select from Visible Rectangle or Invisible Rectangle. If Invisible Rectangle is selected, the following options for Width, Style, and Color are grayed out.

- **Width.** The same three choices for link and form field rectangle widths of Thin, Medium, and Thick are listed in the pull-down menu.

- **Style.** Two choices appear for either setting the rectangle to a solid line or a dashed line.

- **Color.** You can choose from the same color options you have available for links and form fields by clicking the color swatch and selecting either preset or custom colors.

- **Option.** The Option pull-down menu applies to video files. If you select Put in Document from the pull-down menu when using a sound file, the menu defaults back to Don't Show. With sound files you cannot show a poster image because the sound contains no graphic data.

- **Colors.** The Colors pull-down menu and field box are disabled for sound files.

- **Locked.** The Locked check box is accessible from all tabs. When you select the Locked check box the sound rectangle is locked to position on the document page and the attributes are locked. If you want to make any edits on the Movie Properties dialog box, you first need to uncheck the Locked item.

FIGURE 23.14

Click the Appearance tab to change border colors and the poster image.

Acrobat 6–compatible Multimedia (Sound) Properties

If you elect to use Acrobat 6 compatibility, the options in the Add Sound dialog box are the same as discussed in the "Using the Sound tool" section earlier in this chapter. After you create a sound and import and select Properties from a context menu, a different set of property options appear in the Multimedia Properties dialog box. In Figure 23.15, the Multimedia Properties dialog box used with legacy files shows the default Settings tab options.

Settings

The Settings tab offers options for labels and renditions. By default the Settings tab is placed in view when you open the Multimedia Properties. As you can see in Figure 23.15, the Appearance tab is consistent with the Movie Properties dialog box, but the other two tabs (Settings and Actions) offer options much different from those found with Acrobat 5–compatible sound files. In the Settings tab you have options for the following:

- **Annotation Title.** Add a title for the sound in this field. The title supplied here can be different from the filename.

- **Alternate Text.** When creating accessible files for vision- and motion-challenged users, you can add alternate text that can be read by screen-reading software.

- **Renditions.** A good number of options available when editing renditions apply to video clips. For information on setting rendition options for sound files, see the section "Adding a rendition" later in this chapter.

FIGURE 23.15

Select Properties from a context menu to open the Multimedia Properties dialog box for Acrobat 6–compatible legacy sounds.

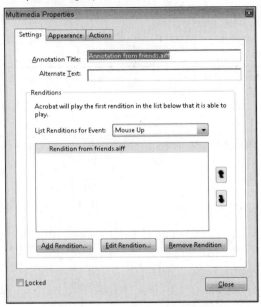

Appearance

The Appearance tab (shown in Figure 23.16) in the Multimedia Properties dialog box offers options similar to those found in the Movie Properties for defining the attributes of a rectangle border for Type, Width, Style, and Color. In addition to these settings, other options include:

- **Annotation is hidden from view.** The annotation added to the field box in the Settings tab is visible by default. To hide the annotation, enable this check box.

- **Change Poster Option.** Options for the poster image are similar to those used with Acrobat 5–compatible files. The settings appear in a dialog box, shown in Figure 23.17. When you click the button for Change Poster Option, you find the following three options:

  - **Use no poster.** This choice is the same as selecting Don't Show in the Movie Properties dialog box. No poster is shown in the sound field.

  - **Retrieve poster from movie.** Also a similar choice as you find in the Movie Properties dialog box. With sound files a dialog box opens informing you that no support for a poster is retrievable from sound files. For movie files the poster is retrieved from the first frame in the movie file.

  - **Create poster from file.** The Movie Properties dialog box used with Acrobat 5–compatible files offers you an option for Retrieve From Movie as the third choice in the pull-down menu. This choice is the same as the preceding option and pulls the first frame in the movie clip as the poster image. With Acrobat 6 compatibility, the Create poster from file option enables you to use a PDF or file compatible with the Create PDF From File command as the poster image. To add a poster from a file, click the Browse button and select the file you want to import.

FIGURE 23.16

The Appearance tab offers options for setting the field rectangle appearance and a button to access the Change Poster Options dialog box.

FIGURE 23.17

When you click the Change Poster Option button, a dialog box opens, offering three choices for poster displays.

Actions

The Actions tab offers you options for setting an action on mouse triggers much like you apply actions to links, bookmarks, page actions, and form fields. Options from the Select Trigger pull-down menu differ slightly from those you select for links, bookmarks, page actions, and form fields. The same triggers are available for video and sound files. Additionally, you have the same options for selecting an action, and you can manage actions such as changing the order, adding additional actions, deleting actions, and so on.

The options in the Actions tab include:

- **Select Trigger.** Open the pull-down menu to see the trigger actions like those shown in Figure 23.18.

FIGURE 23.18

Open the Select Trigger pull-down menu in the Actions tab to select a mouse trigger.

CROSS-REF For more information on selecting trigger options, see Chapter 22.

- **Mouse Up.** The behavior is identical to the same trigger used for other items such as page actions, links, and buttons where actions are applied.
- **Page Visible.** A current page active in the Document pane can be different than page visibility. When using Continuous page layout, Facing Pages, or Continuous – Facing Pages, you can have one page active while other pages are visible in the Document

pane. When this trigger is selected, the media clip plays dependent on page visibility and not necessarily the current page.

- **Page Invisible.** If a page is not visible in the Document pane, the media clip can be played on an action such as a button, link, or bookmark.

- **Page Enter.** This trigger is like setting a page action. When the page becomes the current page, the media plays.

- **Page Exit.** The opposite of the preceding option. When you scroll to another page, the media clips play.

- **Mouse Down.** When the mouse button is pressed down, the trigger is invoked.

- **Mouse Enter.** When the mouse cursor enters the focus rectangle, the media clips play.

- **Mouse Exit.** Opposite of the preceding option where the sound or video plays when the mouse cursor exits the focus rectangle.

- **On Receive Focus.** This trigger is similar to the On Focus mouse trigger used with form field buttons. Pressing the Tab key activates the focus rectangle and the media clip plays.

- **On Lose Focus.** The opposite of the preceding option and like the On Blur mouse trigger where a media clip plays when you tab out of the field.

- **Select Action.** From the Select Action pull-down menu, you can select any action type that is also available to links, fields, bookmarks, and page actions. You might nest different actions and use the Select Action menu to add additional actions. For example, you might play different media clips with a single mouse trigger, play a media clip and then open a URL to display a Web page in your Web browser, change a layer view, or any number of other actions.

CROSS-REF   For more information on Select Action options, see Chapter 22.

- **Add.** When you select an action, click the Add button to include the action in the Actions list window. New actions are added at the end of the action list in the Actions list window as shown in Figure 23.19.

FIGURE 23.19

Multiple actions can be added in the Actions tab.

- **Actions.** The Actions list window shows all the trigger options and actions assigned to the sound or video clip. You can add multiple actions with different triggers and view all the additions in the Actions list.

- **Up/Down.** The buttons at the bottom of the Actions tab enable you to reorder multiple actions. Select an item in the Actions list and click the Up or Down button to move the selected action before or after other items in the list. When the actions are invoked, the play order is shown in the Actions list.

- **Edit.** Select an item in the Actions list and click the Edit button to edit action item attributes. If you select a sound or video file in the Actions list and click the Edit button, the Play Media (Acrobat 6 and Later Compatible) dialog box opens as shown in Figure 23.20. From the pull-down menu, you make choices for changing the play options. Notice you also have an option for writing a custom JavaScript.

FIGURE 23.20

When you select Edit in the Actions tab for media files, the Play Media (Acrobat 6 and Later Compatible) dialog box opens. Make choices in the dialog box for play options you want to change.

- **Delete.** If you want to delete an item in the Actions list, select the item to be removed and click the Delete button.

- **Locked.** Check the Locked check box to lock the media rectangle to position on the document page. You can't move a media placeholder when the Locked check box is checked. To unlock the media placeholder, open the Multimedia Properties dialog box and uncheck the box for Locked.

Importing Video Files

As with sound files, video files require that you create video clips in other authoring programs. No tools or features are contained in Acrobat for editing movies. However, after you create video clips in authoring applications, you have the wealth of import options and play opportunities similar to those used with sound files.

NOTE One exception to editing movies in Acrobat is an option to clip a video that is available in Acrobat Pro Extended. See the section later in this chapter on "Importing video (Acrobat Pro Extended)."

NEW FEATURE Video files are not limited to movie files. You can also use the various attribute choices for importing and changing properties with Adobe Flash files. Both video and Flash files can be imported and managed in Acrobat similarly.

Video editing at the high end is handled by sophisticated software such as Final Cut Pro, Adobe Premiere, Adobe After Effects, and other similar professional programs designed to offer you limitless choices for editing video and audio channels. On the low end, you have some impressive features in programs that cost very little. For Windows, Adobe's marvelous consumer image editor, Adobe Photoshop Elements, is a low-cost editing program that offers you options for exporting to PDF slide shows, embedding sound files, and mixing slides and video clips. The great advantage of using Photoshop Elements for media creations is that the program exports direct to PDF along with side transitions and imported sounds that open directly in Acrobat in Full Screen mode. In addition to video editing, you can use Adobe Flash CS3 to create Flash FLV and SWF files that can be converted to PDF.

For Macintosh users, Apple's own iMovie is a free application shipping with System OS X that produces QuickTime movies. iMovie supports PDF imports as well as still photos and video clips. If you happen to be a cross-platform user, the combination of using Photoshop Elements 6 and iMovie offers you a sophisticated editing environment where you can produce PDF presentations and displays for just about any purpose.

CROSS-REF Discussion in this chapter is related to multimedia authoring and working with video, Flash, and sound in PDF documents. For additional information related to creating presentations and other application support for various kinds of animation, see Chapter 28.

There are other programs that enable you to create movie files. You can use Adobe Premiere Elements (Windows only), Microsoft Media Maker (Windows only), Final Cut Express HD (Macintosh only), and a number of different shareware programs that enable you to edit digital video clips. You can also use Adobe Illustrator to export Flash SWF files and Photoshop CS4 to edit movie clips. Regardless of the video editor you use, you can import video clips in PDF files from a huge range of supported video formats.

Importing video legacy content (Acrobat Pro and Pro Extended)

Video Tool   When you import video in Acrobat Pro on either Windows or the Macintosh, you must use the legacy content import options unless you import H.264 (MPEG-4 Part 10) compression on the video files. Legacy content has the same video import options you had available with Acrobat 8 and earlier viewers. When importing video you have choices to link a video file to a PDF or embed a video file in a PDF. If you use Acrobat Pro Extended (Windows), you can choose to import files using the legacy content methods or the new Acrobat 9 option for transcoding video to Adobe Flash.

Use the Video tool in the Multimedia toolbar to import video files in Acrobat Pro viewers. Select the Video tool from the Toolbar Well and double-click the mouse button or click and drag open a rectangle. When you release the mouse button, the Insert Video dialog box opens, as shown in Figure 23.21. When you use the Video tool to import video clips, the initial dialog box appears very similar to the Insert Sound dialog box.

FIGURE 23.21

The Insert Video dialog box offers you options similar to the Insert Sound dialog box.

TIP   When you double-click the mouse button, the movie frame defaults to the size to which the video was compressed. If you want to size the frame up or down, press Shift and drag one of the four handles with the Video tool or the Select Object tool to reshape the rectangle after a video has been imported. Know that if you size up the movie frame from the default size, the video looks distorted when played.

Be aware that if you have Acrobat Pro (Windows or Macintosh), you only have options for using the legacy content method for importing video if importing files not compressed with H.264 compression. This section relates exclusively to using Acrobat Pro on Windows and the Macintosh on files not compressed with H.264 compression. For more options with Acrobat Pro with H.264-compressed video and Acrobat Pro Extended, see the section "Importing Video (Acrobat Pro Extended)" later in this chapter.

When you click the Browse button, the Select a file dialog box opens. Select a file to import and click Open. If you're using Acrobat Pro an alert dialog box opens and informs you that the file is not supported for direct playback in Adobe Reader. (Actually, it's Adobe Reader 9 that has the Flash player hard coded in Reader 9). The message continues with: Acrobat Pro Extended is required to convert to a compatible format. To place this file for playback requiring an external system player click Continue.

What the dialog box means is that if you import the video using Acrobat Pro you're forced to use a legacy format and the Add Movie dialog box opens as shown in Figure 23.22. From here you can choose to import video using Acrobat 6 (and Later) Compatible Media and Acrobat 5 (and Earlier) Compatible Media. If you are using Acrobat Pro Extended you have other options for converting the video as I explain later in the section "Importing Video (Acrobat Pro Extended).

FIGURE 23.22

When importing video in Acrobat Pro, the Add Movie dialog box opens after you select a video file.

Travel back to Figure 23.21 for a moment and check out the blue text link that reads Create legacy multimedia content. Clicking this link opens the Add Movie dialog box. For Acrobat Pro Extended users, this link is essential if you want to create legacy content supported in Acrobat viewers earlier than version 9.

Triggering Players

If you travel the route of the legacy path using the Add Movie dialog box in either Acrobat Pro or Acrobat Pro Extended, the playback of your video uses an external player. The player may be the external Adobe Flash Player, Windows built-in player, RealOne Player, Windows Media Player, or Apple's QuickTime. This behavior is the same as all versions of Acrobat supporting media playback prior to Acrobat 9.0.

If you use the Insert Media dialog box and insert media without following the legacy path, your media is transcoded to Adobe Flash format and the built-in Flash player handles the playback. No external player including the external Adobe Flash Player is needed to play back the video using the new Acrobat 9–compatible media imports.

Acrobat 5–compatible media

In Acrobat Pro, double-click the Video tool on a page to open the Insert Video dialog box. If using Acrobat Pro, click the Browse button to locate a video file, select the file, and click Open. If using Acrobat Pro Extended, click the blue text link in the Insert Video dialog box to Create legacy multimedia content. In either case you end up at the Add Movie dialog box. Click Acrobat 5 (and Earlier) Compatible Media and the dialog box changes to what you see in Figure 23.23.

FIGURE 23.23

Click Acrobat 5 (and Earlier) Compatible Media to show options for importing video using Acrobat 5–compatible format.

Figure 23.23 shows the Add Movie dialog box options for Acrobat 5–compatible movies. You have options for selecting either Acrobat 5 or Acrobat 6 compatibility like you do with sound imports. When you select the Acrobat 5 (and Earlier) Compatible Media radio button, the dialog box reduces in size and displays only the options available when using Acrobat 5 or earlier compatibility.

Add Movie

You make choices in the Add Movie dialog box when you first create a movie field. After creating the field, you can make changes and select attributes in the Movie Properties dialog box that are similar to the Sound properties choices. In the Add Movie dialog box, you select from the following:

- **Content Settings.** Click on the compatibility for either Acrobat 5– or Acrobat 6–compatible media. If you select Acrobat 5 compatibility, the movie clips cannot be embedded in the PDF file — the files are *linked* to the PDF. Therefore, you need to send the PDF and the movie file to other users or host both on a Web site in order for users to view the movies. If you use Acrobat 6–compatible media, you have a choice to either embed the media in the PDF or link the media to the PDF. If using Acrobat 6–compatible media and embedding movie clips in a PDF, Acrobat users with viewers earlier than Acrobat 6 won't be able to see your movie files.

- **Location.** On local drives, the location of the movie file is added to the Location field box. When you first import a movie, identify the movie in the Add Movie dialog box and leave the Location at the default. After you create the movie rectangle, you can change the location to a URL for Web-hosted documents in the Movie Properties dialog box.

- **Browse.** Click this button to open the Select Movie File dialog box. If importing a movie from your hard drive, select the video and click Select to import the video. You may need to wait momentarily as Acrobat reports the import status.

> **NOTE** If you move a movie file on your hard drive to another location, the path to the file is broken and the movie won't play. To reset the directory path, click the Browse button, find the movie file, and click Select in the Select Movie File dialog box.

- **Snap to content proportions.** When enabled, the movie remains proportional as you drag open a rectangle, preventing distortion when the movie is played. The media file's original dimensions are preserved no matter how large you draw the rectangle.

- **Poster Settings.** Select the Use no poster option to show a blank video frame. Select the Retrieve poster from movie option to show the first movie frame in the movie rectangle when the movie is not playing.

Import a movie using the Acrobat 5 (and Earlier) Compatible Media choice.

Acrobat 5 Movie Properties

After you import a movie with Acrobat 5 compatibility, you can make further attribute choices in the Movie Properties dialog box. Select either the Movie tool or the Select Object tool and open a context menu. From the menu options, select Properties. The Movie Properties dialog box opens, as shown in Figure 23.24.

FIGURE 23.24

The General Movie Properties are identical to the Sound Properties.

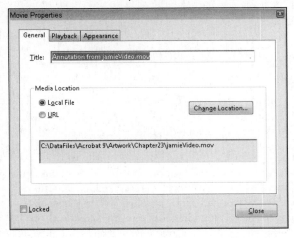

General

Notice that options in the General tab are identical to the Sound Properties. For further definition of the options refer to the section "Using the Sound tool" earlier in this chapter.

If you want to link the movie to a URL location, select the URL radio button. The Enter URL dialog box opens where you add the URL. Be certain to include the complete URL address, beginning with *http://*.

Playback

Playback options are also identical to the options found with Sound files with the exception of the pull-down menu for Size. This option is available only for video files. From the menu options, you make choices for the size of the video frames during playback, as shown in Figure 23.25. If you choose a size above the Default (1x) size, the video may be distorted when played.

FIGURE 23.25

Playback options are identical to the Sound properties with the exception of the Size options. Choose the playback size from the menu choices.

If you choose Full Screen from the menu choices, the video plays at the largest possible size on your monitor in a separate window. However, the video playback does not change the view to Full Screen mode.

Options for showing the player controls and using a floating window are handled a little differently than when enabling the same options for sound files. The player controls are fixed at the bottom of the video clip for viewing movies either with or without a floating window. When you choose Floating Window for a video file, the media opens in a floating window with the player controls fixed at the bottom of the floating window. In Figure 23.26 you can see the video frame playing with the player controls visible at the default size of the video. In Figure 23.27 the player controls are enabled as well as the floating window option.

Appearance

Appearance options are also the same as those discussed for Sound properties. In the Appearance options, you have access to showing the movie poster in the file when the movie is still and not playing. If you choose to Put the Poster in the Document, you can also make choices for the color display of 8-bit (256 colors) or 24-bit (millions of colors).

FIGURE 23.26

Player controls are enabled and the floating window option is disabled.

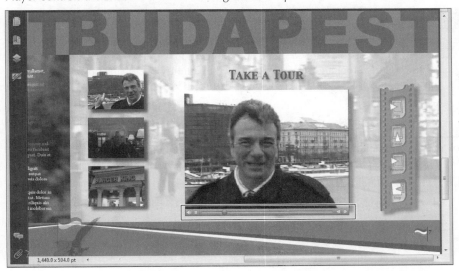

FIGURE 23.27

Player controls are enabled and the floating window option is enabled.

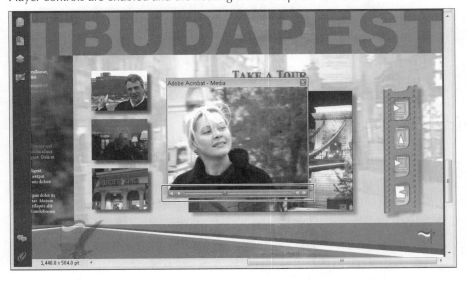

Acrobat 6–compatible movies

If you decide to use Acrobat 6 compatibility, you need to do it when you open the Add Movie dialog box shown in Figure 23.22. If you create a movie annotation and specify Acrobat 5 compatibility, and then change your mind and want to use Acrobat 6 compatibility, you need to delete the first movie annotation by clicking it with the Video tool or the Select Object tool. Press Backspace/ Delete on your keyboard or open a context menu and choose Edit ⇨ Delete. Double-click the mouse button with the Video tool and select Acrobat 6 compatibility; the dialog box changes to reflect the Acrobat 6–compatible options, as shown in Figure 23.28.

FIGURE 23.28

Select the Video tool and draw a rectangle or double-click in the Document pane. In the Add Movie dialog box, select Acrobat 6 (and Later) Compatible Media.

Add Movie

Select Acrobat 6 (and Later) Compatible Media and you'll notice the dialog box expands to offer more options than when you use Acrobat 5–compatible files. The settings are the same as those discussed in the section "Acrobat 6–Compatible Multimedia (Sound) Properties." When adding movies you have options for the poster view in a still frame while the movie is not playing. Select from Use no poster, Retrieve poster from movie, or Create poster from file. These options are the same for sounds with the exception of Retrieve poster from movie. Whereas sound files produce an error when you make this menu choice, movie files retrieve the first frame in the video for the poster image.

After making choices in the Add Movie dialog box, access more options in the Multimedia Properties dialog box. Click OK after selecting the Acrobat 6–compatible settings. Open a context menu with either the Movie tool or the Select Object tool and choose Properties from the menu options.

Acrobat 6 Multimedia Properties

The Multimedia Properties dialog box shown in Figure 23.29 contains the same options found when you open Acrobat 6–compatible sound files properties. The first stop is the Settings tab, where you see options for annotation text and alternate text. The items below the text fields contain options for renditions. Because I didn't cover renditions earlier in the sounds discussion, I address the options you have for adding renditions here.

FIGURE 23.29

Open a context menu and select Properties to open the Multimedia Properties dialog box.

Understanding renditions

When you import a sound or video, the rendition of the clip is assigned to a Mouse Up trigger and plays according to the properties you enable for the play options. By default, imported sounds and videos have a single default rendition. When using Acrobat 6–compatible media options, you have an opportunity to add different renditions to the same media clip or multiple media clips. For example, you may have a rendition that plays full screen from a large file, and you may want to add an alternate clip of a duplicate movie with a smaller file size. If hosting the media on a Web site, you can assign what media clip is downloaded to a user's computer based on the end user's connection speed. The movie field remains the same, but the attributes contain two different renditions for the same field.

You have options for editing existing renditions after importing a media clip, or you can add new renditions to an imported file. When you add new renditions, they are listed in the Settings tab in the Multimedia Properties dialog box.

Adding a rendition

By default, a rendition is listed in the lower window in the Settings properties. To add a rendition, click the Add Rendition button. A pull-down menu opens where you make choices for one of the following:

- **Using a File.** For local files select Using a File. The Select Multimedia File dialog box opens where you navigate your hard drive and select the file to use. This option might be used to select a duplicate file smaller or larger in size than the original rendition.

- **Using a URL.** If you want files downloaded from Web sites, select Using a URL. The Add a New Rendition Using a URL dialog box opens where you add the URL address for where the file is located. When you add the URL, a pull-down menu opens where you can select the content type for the media format.

- **By Copying an Existing Rendition.** If you want to use the same rendition as one listed in the Settings list window for the purpose of duplicating the rendition and providing alternate attributes, select By Copying an Existing Rendition. The Copy Rendition dialog box opens in which you select the rendition to copy from a pull-down menu. The new rendition is not actually *copied*, but instead points to another file and adds about 4K to your file size.

Select any one of the three options and click the Edit button to open the Rendition Settings dialog box.

Editing a rendition

You can choose to edit an existing rendition or edit the new rendition you added to the media file (see the preceding section). If you want to edit an existing rendition, click the Edit Rendition button from the Settings properties. If you've added a new rendition, it now appears in the list window, so you can select it and click the Edit button. In either case, the Rendition Settings dialog box opens, as shown in Figure 23.30.

FIGURE 23.30

Select a rendition and click the Edit button. The Rendition Settings dialog box opens.

A considerable number of options are available in the various tabs of the Rendition Settings dialog box. By default, the dialog box opens at the Media Settings tab. The various tabs and choices you have include:

- **Media Settings.** Make choices from the Media Settings tab for the rendition name, the media location and content type, and the rendition for alternate text, and choose from the Allow Temp File pull-down menu for various options related to accessibility. If the media is to be made accessible to JavaScript, be certain to check the box for enabling JavaScript.

- **Playback Settings.** Click the Playback Settings tab to make choices for the player window visibility, volume settings, showing player controls, continuous looping, or times played. In the list at the bottom of the Playback Settings tab, click the Add button to add the type of media players you want users to use for playing the media. You have an option for enabling all players and a setting for the preferred player.

- **Playback Location.** Make choices on this tab for where the media is played, such as in the document, floating window, or full screen. If you select floating window, you have many different choices for document size and position.

- **System Requirements.** From a pull-down menu you have choices for connection speeds. If you want a particular rendition to be downloaded for all users with 384K connections or greater, you can make the choice in this dialog box. In addition you have choices for screen displays, captions, subtitles, and language.

- **Playback Requirements.** Based on options you selected in the other settings tabs, a list is displayed in the last settings tab. Each item has a check box for enabling a required condition. Check all the boxes for those items you want to make a required function.

Click OK in the Rendition Settings dialog box when you're finished setting the options in the various settings tabs. If you need to add another rendition with some alternate options to the last rendition you edited, copy the rendition and make the necessary edits. You can list as many different renditions as you like to provide more flexibility for your viewer audience and the systems it uses.

 There are a considerable number of options in the Rendition Settings dialog box. For more information on editing renditions, refer to the Acrobat Help document.

Appearance

The Appearance tab in the Multimedia Properties dialog box offers the same options as those you find when editing Sound Properties. Options are available for poster display in the Change Poster Option dialog box when you click the Change Poster Option button shown in Figure 23.31. The poster options are the same as those discussed in the "Acrobat 6–Compatible Media (Sound) Properties" section earlier in this chapter.

FIGURE 23.31

Click the Change Poster Option button to change the poster image.

Actions

The Actions tab also offers the same choices as those available with sound files for adding an action to the media clip. You can choose an action from the Select Action pull-down menu the same as when using action types with Acrobat 5 media.

Importing video (Acrobat Pro Extended)

Notice you have the same option for choosing legacy multimedia content in the Insert Video dialog box. Click the blue text link to open the Add Movie dialog box as shown earlier in Figures 23.22 and 23.23. If you prepare files for Acrobat viewers earlier than version 9, use the settings you have available for either Acrobat 6 (and Later) Compatible Media or Acrobat 5 (and Earlier) Compatible Media. Options you find in the Properties dialog boxes for these media types are the same as those options described in the sections "Acrobat 5–compatible media" and "Acrobat 6–compatible media."

Acrobat Pro Extended users can import a video file without changing settings and exploring the many options you have for importing a video file. You can simply click a few buttons and your video is imported in a PDF and transcoded to an Adobe Flash file. The video can be played in all Acrobat viewers version 9 and above. If you intend to share PDFs with users of Acrobat viewers earlier than version 9, you need to use the legacy multimedia content options.

For a quick look at importing a video in Acrobat Pro Extended, follow these steps.

Steps: Importing a video with Acrobat 9 compatibility (Windows only)

1. **Open a PDF document in Acrobat Pro Extended.**

2. **Click the Video tool in the Multimedia toolbar or open the Multimedia task button and select the Video tool.**

3. **Double-click the Video tool on a document page.** When you double-click using the Video tool, the video is imported at the same size the video was originally compressed.

4. **Browse for the file location.** The Insert Video dialog box shown earlier in Figure 23.21 opens. Be certain to not click the link for Create legacy multimedia content. Click the Browse button to locate the file and leave all the other settings at the defaults.

5. **Import the video.** The Select a file dialog box opens. Select the file you want to import and click Open. Note that you may have to wait a few minutes for Acrobat to read the file.

6. **Set the attributes for importing the file.** After you click Open in the Select a file dialog box, the Insert Video dialog box changes as shown in Figure 23.32. Below the preview of the first video frame you see two sliders. You can move the left and right sliders to clip the movie and convert only the portion of the clip that you want to import. In Figure 23.32 I moved the left slider to about halfway along the path, resulting in clipping the first half of the video.

   Click the button Set Poster Image from Content Frame to capture the content frame as a poster and click OK.

FIGURE 23.32

Set the poster image and clip the video as desired in the Insert Video dialog box.

TIP You can capture any frame in your video clip to use as a poster image. Move the sliders to view the video in the Insert Video dialog box and stop at the frame you want to capture. Click the Set Poster Image from Current Frame button to capture the frame. Readjust the sliders to clip the video or return to the default positions. When the video is imported, the first frame you see is the captured frame.

7. **Wait for transcoding to complete.** Acrobat begins transcoding the video to an Adobe Flash file. A progress bar is displayed during the transcoding process as shown in Figure 23.33. Wait for the transcoding to complete. Acrobat returns you to the document pane where your imported video is shown with the poster image you chose in the Insert Video dialog box.

FIGURE 23.33

Wait for the progress bar to complete and the video is displayed with the selected poster frame on the document page.

For quick and easy video imports, you can follow the steps outlined here. However, Acrobat 9 offers you a number of options for importing video files and changing properties. Becoming familiar with the options helps you take advantage of Acrobat's impressive video viewing and playback opportunities. You can make option choices during the import steps or address properties after videos have been imported.

Using advanced settings

When you open the Insert Video dialog box you see an abbreviated set of options that are available for video imports. To expand the dialog box, click the Show Advanced Options check box to expand the dialog box to the view shown in Figure 23.34.

FIGURE 23.34

Click the Show Advanced Settings check box to expand the Insert Video dialog box.

Using H.264 (Part 10) Compressed Files

H.264 or MPEG-4 Part 10 is a newer compression format for video. It's an ISO standard for video compression that takes up less capacity when it is stored or transmitted. H.264 compression can be applied to a variety of video formats and also plays back directly in all Acrobat viewers including Adobe Reader 9. As the H.264 format is gaining in popularity, Adobe's expectation is that you'll be able to place video without importing in legacy formats.

If you use H.264-compressed video, you have access to the Advanced Settings in the Insert Video dialog box, and you can bypass the legacy multimedia content dialog boxes. You have options for choosing among all the Launch settings and playback skins in the Insert Video advanced settings.

Before you import a video in Acrobat Pro or Pro Extended, you have a number of settings choices in the Insert Video Advanced Options dialog box. Your choices include:

NOTE You only see the Quality tab if the video is not H264 encoded.

- **Launch Settings.** The first of four tabs appears as the default. In the Launch settings tab you make choices for launching the video.
  - **Enable When.** Earlier in this chapter in the section "Adding sounds to page actions," I talked about triggering a sound to play based on Page Open and Page Close actions. When using Acrobat 9–compatible media, you can choose to trigger a video to play on a page open or page close action from choices in this menu.
  - **Disable When.** You can stop play on the same choices you have for Enable When. If you want to stop the media from playing when you navigate to the next page, open this pull-down menu and choose The page containing the content is closed.
  - **Playback Style.** Your choices are to play the content on the page or play the content in a floating window.
  - **Width/Height.** You can edit the annotation frame for the size by typing values in the text boxes for floating windows only.
  - **Border.** Choose from Thin, Medium, or Thick to add a border to the annotation frame.
  - **Poster Image.** You make choices here for the poster image. If you click Create poster from file, click the Browse button to locate a file to use as a poster image. File formats that are supported are Adobe PDF, BMP, Compuserve GIF, JPEG, and PNG.
- **Quality.** Click the Quality tab to find settings for the display of the video quality as shown in Figure 23.35.
  - **Video Quality.** Choose from Very Low, Low, Medium, High, and Very High for the video quality.
  - **Deinterlace.** If the video was interlaced, check this box. By default you typically won't need to deinterlace videos for most of the content you import in PDF documents.

FIGURE 23.35

Click the Quality tab to display the Quality settings.

- **Resize Video.** Choose from Percent or Pixels and edit the Width and Height text boxes to resize the video.
- **Audio.** Choose from the pull-down menu options for Very Low to Superior audio quality.

■ **Controls.** This tab offers settings for player control displays as shown in Figure 23.36.

- **Skin.** The pull-down menu offers options for displaying Flash video skins that enable you to play, pause, and resume video playback. Choose the option you want from the Skin pull-down menu. For more information on skins, see the sidebar "Using Skins."
- **Color.** Click the color swatch to change the skin color.
- **Opacity.** Type a value in the text box to change the opacity of the skin.
- **Auto-Hide controls.** If you check this box, the skin is hidden as the cursor moves away from the media box.

FIGURE 23.36

Click the Controls tab to show settings for playback displays.

■ **Video.** The Video tab enables you to add chapter points and assign actions when the video plays to a chapter point. In order to assign chapter points, the video must have been created with chapter points.

Using Skins

Skins are Adobe Flash files that display player controls when you enable the player controls options in the Insert Video dialog box or Movie Properties. By default, Acrobat installs seven different skins you can use when playing video, with or without volume controls, muting sound, and showing captions.

You can add your own custom skins and have them appear in the Playback tab Skin pull-down menu. To add your own custom skins you'll need to use Adobe Flex and export the files as Flash movies. After you create a custom skin, you then need to add the file to the appropriate folder in Acrobat.

On Windows, open the Acrobat 9.0/Acrobat/Multimedia Skins folder and copy your custom skins to this folder.

On the Macintosh open the Applications/Adobe Acrobat 9 Pro folder and Control+click the Adobe Acrobat Pro icon. From the context menu options choose Show Package Contents. (Note that Multimedia Skins are not installed in the Acrobat User Data folder on the Macintosh). When the package contents are shown, open Contents/MacOS/Multimedia Skins. Copy your custom skins to this folder. For Macintosh users, the skins are available only when using H.264-compressed video or playing FLV videos.

Editing a video

When you adjust settings in the Insert Video dialog box in Acrobat Pro Extended, you apply all the properties settings you want to use for the imported video. If you import a video and open the properties, the Edit Video dialog box opens. Unlike legacy content, you have choices matching most of the settings you apply when you initially import the video using Advanced Settings in the Insert Video dialog box.

In the Edit Video dialog box, you find the same choices you have for Launch Settings, Controls, and Video. The options not accessible when you choose Properties from a context menu opened on an imported media are the Quality Controls. If you want to change the quality for video and/or sound, you must delete the video and import it again, making adjustments in the Advanced Settings in the Insert Video dialog box.

Importing Flash Video (Acrobat Pro and Pro Extended)

The file formats you can import related to Adobe Flash include Flash Video File (FLV) and Flash Movie File (SWF). An FLV file is a native file saved from Adobe Flash, and an SWF file is a movie file exported from Adobe Flash or another program supporting SWF exports.

If you use the Video tool, you can import both FLV and SWF files. However, the default file formats support only FLV files. If you want to use the Video tool to import an SWF file, you must change the Files of type menu choice to All Files (*.*); you'll see the SWF files accessible in the Select a file dialog box.

NEW FEATURE A better choice is to select the Flash tool from the Multimedia toolbar or from the Multimedia task button pull-down menu. When you use the Flash tool, all supported Adobe Flash formats appear in the Files of type pull-down menu.

Flash Tool Double-click the Flash tool to import a Flash FLV or SWF file. The Insert Flash dialog box opens. This dialog box is similar to the Insert Video dialog box. An abbreviated list of settings is shown similar to Figure 23.21. Clicking the Show Advanced Settings check box expands the Insert Flash dialog box to display similar settings you have when importing video.

Only three tabs are shown in the Insert Flash dialog box. The tabs include:

- **Launch Settings.** The Launch Settings include identical settings you have when importing a video file.
- **Flash.** The Flash tab offers you an option to pass Flash variables (ActionScript 2.0 and 3.0 FlashVars) to a URL string.
- **Resources.** The Resources tab enables you to bind a file, multiple files, or a directory of files to video.

Like the Insert Video dialog box you make choices for the settings and select a file to import. Click the OK button to import the Flash file in a PDF document.

Importing 3D Content

3D Tool The 3D tool in the Multimedia toolbar is used for importing 3D content in a PDF file. Select the tool from either the Multimedia toolbar or the Multimedia task button pull-down menu. Double-click the tool on a document page to open the Insert 3D dialog box.

Again this dialog box is similar to the Insert Video dialog box. When you click the Show Advanced Settings check box, the Insert 3D dialog box expands to show several tabs. The first tab choice is Launch Settings and offers the same choices you find in the Insert Video and Insert Flash dialog boxes. The third tab is Resources and offers the same choices you find in the Insert Flash Resources tab.

TIP You can also capture a view in your CAD drawing program and convert the capture to PDF. Click the Capture 3D button in the Insert 3D dialog box and open your drawing program. Navigate to the view you want to capture and make sure your screen is refreshed. Press the Print Screen key on your keyboard to open the capture automatically in Acrobat.

The 3D tab and Geospatial tabs are unique to the Insert 3D dialog box. The 3D tab shown in Figure 23.37 contains settings for the lighting, rendering, and animation style of the 3D model. You have navigation choices for viewing various isometric views and choosing to open the Model Tree panel in the Acrobat viewer opening the file. You can also add a JavaScript for custom viewing and displays.

FIGURE 23.37

The 3D tab offers unique settings for displaying 3D imports.

To the right of the 3D tab you find the Geospatial tab. Settings in this tab offer choices for displaying 3D mesh quality.

The number of options you have available in the Insert 3D dialog box Advanced Settings are extraordinary and beyond the scope of this book. For a complete listing of all options, refer to the Acrobat Pro Extended Help document.

After you import a 3D file, the default settings you choose in the Insert 3D dialog box can be changed by using the 3D toolbar. If you enable the Show Toolbar check box in the 3D tab, the toolbar is shown by default when the mouse cursor is placed over a 3D import. From the toolbar shown in Figure 23.38 you have a number of choices to change views, lighting, perspective, model rendering views, background color choices, cross section viewing, and adding comments.

The 3D toolbar offers many options to change views from the defaults you set up in the Insert 3D dialog box.

Converting Media to PDF

Another option you have with Acrobat 9 is direct conversion of media files to PDF. Rather than import a media file, you use the Create task button and choose the PDF from File command. When you choose a video file, an Adobe Flash file, or a 3D file, the file is converted to PDF and opens in Acrobat at the default size the file was originally created in the authoring program.

You can convert a file to PDF and use the Select Object tool to select the media box. Open a context menu and choose Edit ➪ Copy. Once copied to the Clipboard, you can paste the media in another PDF document.

 For more information on converting files to PDF, see Chapter 7.

Summary

- Sound files can be imported with either Acrobat 5 or Acrobat 6 compatibility. Acrobat 5–compatible sound imports can be used with earlier Acrobat viewers. Acrobat 6–compatible sounds are available only to Acrobat 6 or later viewers. Acrobat 6 compatibility offers more options for attribute settings and file format compatibility.

- You can add sounds to page actions, links, bookmarks, and form fields, or by using the Sound tool.

- Importing sounds on actions or with the Sound tool requires you to have access to a sound file. You create and save sound files from sound-editing programs. A number of sound-editing programs are available as freeware or shareware on the Internet.

- You can edit movie files in multimedia authoring programs. Among low-cost alternatives for creating movie files are Adobe Photoshop Elements and Apple Computer's iMovie. You can save Photoshop Elements files direct to PDF. You save iMovie files in QuickTime format and import them in PDFs with the Movie tool.

- Movie and sound legacy content can have several renditions. Renditions offer you many options for assigning attributes to sound and media clips, as well as providing end users with alternatives for downloading different versions of the same file.

- You can embed Acrobat 6–compatible media files in PDF documents. Acrobat 6–compatible media files offer much more support for importing different file formats than Acrobat 5–compatible media imports.

- A poster is a still image that appears inside a sound or movie field. Posters for movie fields can be retrieved from a movie. Posters for sound and movie fields can be created from files including all file formats supported by the Create PDF From File menu command.

- Importing video in Acrobat Pro requires you to use legacy content options.

- Importing video using Acrobat Pro Extended enables you to import video as legacy content or as Acrobat 9 video where the video is transcoded to Adobe Flash format.

- Importing video in Acrobat Pro Extended enables you to clip video files prior to import.

- The new Acrobat 9 Flash tool is used to import Adobe Flash FLV and SWF files.

- The 3D tool in Acrobat Pro Extended enables you to convert native CAD files to PDF. (what about the 3D tool in Pro)

- All media files can be converted to PDF. Use the Create task button pull-down menu and choose PDF from File. Select the file you want to convert and click Open. The media is converted to a PDF document at the default of the original file size.

Chapter 24

Working with Layers

L ayers are an integral part of many professional imaging applications and specialized technical programs, such as AutoCAD and Microsoft Visio. In Acrobat versions 6 through 9 you can view native layered documents and toggle on and off different layer views.

With the introduction of the Adobe Creative Suite, support for Adobe PDF layers has been integrated into Adobe Illustrator CS and Adobe InDesign CS. As we advance in time and software development, more applications are supporting exports to PDF with layer data.

Design and creative, scientific, and engineering professionals can find many uses for communicating ideas and concepts with layered documents. To help simplify the viewing of layered documents, you can add interactive buttons for guiding users through various layer views. In this chapter, you learn about what constitutes a PDF with layers, how to manage them, and how to create links to different layer views.

Setting Up the Work Environment

Viewing layers requires no special set of toolbars — the tools you need are dependent on what you intend to do with a PDF containing layers when you begin editing. If, for example, you intend to review and comment layered documents, you'll open the Comment and Markup toolbar.

If you work with engineering drawings, you'll want to open the Analysis toolbar and the Advanced Editing toolbar. For other layered documents, you won't need any special tools. If you open these toolbars, your Toolbar Well will look like Figure 24.1.

FIGURE 24.1

Open the Advanced Editing toolbar and the Analysis toolbar, and dock the toolbars in the Toolbar Well.

You may also need to load the Layers panel if not currently shown in the Navigation pane. Select View ➪ Navigation Panels ➪ Layers. Drag the Layers panel to the Navigation pane to dock it.

Understanding Layers

Acrobat supports the creation of layered documents from several authoring programs. Among the programs supporting the PDFMaker are Microsoft Visio, Microsoft Project, and Autodesk AutoCAD. In regard to exporting to PDF with Adobe PDF layers, you can use Adobe Illustrator CS and Adobe InDesign CS and some specialized programs such as ESRI's ArcGIS (`www.esri.com/software/arcgis/`). When layers are created in these programs, the document can be converted to PDF with Adobe PDF layers and viewed in all Acrobat viewers 6.0 and above with the layers intact. Other Creative Suite programs such as Adobe Dreamweaver and Adobe Photoshop CS do not support layered PDFs.

The creation of Adobe PDF layers requires Acrobat Pro or Acrobat Pro Extended; however, after the PDF creation, layers can be viewed in any Acrobat 6.0 or later viewer, including Adobe Reader.

There are two important points to understand when creating layered PDF files. First, you must begin with an authoring program that supports layers. Adobe Illustrator, Adobe PageMaker, Adobe InDesign, CorelDraw, Autodesk AutoCAD, and Microsoft Visio are some of the popular imaging programs that support layers. Second, the authoring application must export to the PDF 1.5 format or above (Acrobat 6 compatibility or later). Just because the authoring program supports layers is no guarantee that your resultant PDF will contain layers.

If you use a program that enables you to create and save layered documents and the program does not currently export to Acrobat 6 or later compatibility, log on to your software manufacturer's Web site and see whether a new version of the program is available and whether the latest release exports to PDF v1.5 or higher.

NOTE   Layers in Acrobat terms are referred to as Optional Content Groups (OCGs). When you see the term OCG, understand that the term refers to a PDF document with Adobe PDF layers.

Layer Visibility

When you open a layered document in Acrobat and the Layers panel is open in the Navigation pane, you see a list of all the layers contained in the document and an eye icon adjacent to each layer name when the respective layer is in view. A layer's visibility is either on or off, as shown in the Layers panel.

Initial visibility is determined from the visibility shown in the original authoring program when the PDF is created. In Figure 24.2 you see a layered document with three layers visible as indicated by the eye icons in the Layers panel. The remaining layers in the document are hidden and the hidden state is expressed in the Layers panel by the absence of an eye icon adjacent to the layer names.

FIGURE 24.2

The initial visibility of layers in this file shows three layers in view as indicated by the eye icons. Those layers where no eye icon appears are hidden.

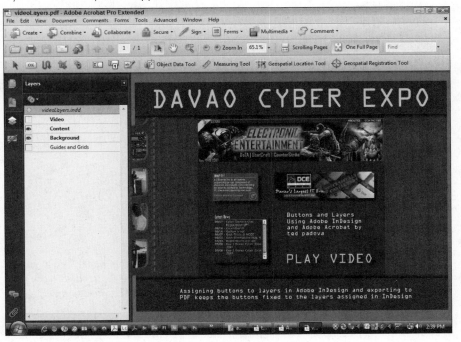

Setting initial visibility

The initial layer visibility is the default view of visible layers when you open a PDF document. The layers in view when you open a layered PDF document are determined from the visibility of the layers in view in the original authoring application. If layers are hidden in the authoring application, the Initial View in Acrobat viewers shows the same layers hidden as well. The Initial View or *state* is the same view displayed in the authoring application at the time of PDF creation. As you browse a file in an Acrobat viewer and turn on and off different layer views, you may want to return to the initial state. You return to the default view with the Reset to Initial Visibility menu command in the Options pull-down menu in the Layers panel, as shown in Figure 24.3. Select this command to return to the layer views you saw when you first opened the PDF document.

To return to the default layer visibility, open the Options pull-down menu in the Layers panel and select Reset to Initial Visibility.

Showing/hiding layers

You show and hide individual layers by clicking on the eye icons in the Layers panel. When an eye icon is hidden, the respective layer is hidden. If you want to display a hidden layer, click in the box adjacent to a layer name; the eye icon appears, and the layer is made visible in the Document pane.

At times, you may have pages in a PDF with different layers associated with different pages. If you want to display all layers on the page in view in the Document pane while hiding layers on other pages in your document, select List Layers for Visible Pages in the Options pull-down menu. All layers not contained on the pages in view in the Document pane are hidden. If the same layer spans more than one page and you select this menu command, the layer is made visible only when the layer is contained on the active page.

When you change layer visibility in the Layers panel and save the PDF document, the layer visibility is not recorded when you save the file. When you open a file after saving with a different layer view, you are still returned to the initial visibility from your first editing session. To create a new default Initial View, you need to change the Layer properties.

Initial Views

You can open the Layers panel when the PDF is opened in the Document pane by setting the Initial View in the Document Properties. Choose File ⇨ Properties and click the Initial View tab. From the Navigation tab pull-down menu, select Layers Panel and Page. Save the PDF document. When you reopen the file, the Layers panel is expanded to show the layers.

CROSS-REF For more information on Initial Views, see Chapter 5.

Layer Properties

Layer properties are specific to each layer. To open the Layer Properties dialog box, you must have a layer selected in the Layers panel. Click on a layer name and open a context menu (or choose Options ⇨ Layer Properties). The context menu contains two menu options — one for Show Layer and the other for Properties (unless it is a locked layer, in which case Properties is the only option). Select Properties to open the Layer Properties dialog box, as shown in Figure 24.4.

FIGURE 24.4

To open the Layer Properties dialog box, select a layer in the Layers panel, open a context menu, and select Properties from the menu options.

You adjust layer properties for individual layers only. Acrobat does not permit you to select multiple layers. If you need to make changes in visibility for several layers, you must open the Layer Properties dialog box independently for each layer or, alternately, return to the original authoring program and set the default layer visibility and convert to PDF.

When you open the Layer Properties dialog box, the layer name appears in the dialog box for the respective layer contained in the Layers panel. Two radio buttons exist for the Intent. By default you see View selected, which is normal viewing mode. Select View to allow the layer to be turned on or off. If you click Reference, the remaining items in the dialog box are disabled and the eye icon in the Layers panel disappears. All layer attribute choices are disabled and the behavior is similar to locking a layer. You use View to keep the layer on at all times, which permits editing layer properties. When a layer is set to the Reference Intent, the layer name appears in italics.

Changing the default state

The Default state pull-down menu contains menu options for either On or Off. The menu choice you make here determines the layer visibility when a file is opened. If you want to change the default state, select On or Off from the pull-down menu. When you click OK in the Layer Properties dialog box and save the PDF document, the default visibility changes according to the views you set in the Layer Properties.

Locking visibility

When you select the Locked check box, you lock the layer visibility (either on or off). A lock icon appears in the Layers tab and prevents you from turning the visibility on or off from the tab. You need to return to the Properties dialog box and disable the check box to return visibility control to the Layers panel. You might use Reference and Lock, and then secure a PDF file to prevent users from seeing information on a given layer.

CROSS-REF For more on securing PDF files, see Chapter 26.

Changing the initial state

Initial State settings include Layer Visibility, Print, and Export. The default state described previously enables you to determine whether a layer is visible or hidden when a PDF document opens. To apply the individual settings for layer states, you enable a preference setting. Open the Preferences dialog box and select Documents in the left pane. Check the box for Allow layer state to be set by user information, as shown in Figure 24.5.

FIGURE 24.5

Open Preferences and click Documents in the left pane. Check Allow layer state to be set by user information.

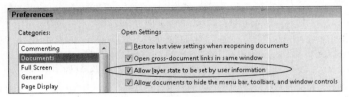

When this preference option is enabled, the layer state options chosen from the Initial State pull-down menus override the layer visibility set from the Default State pull-down menu. For example, if the default state is set to On and the preference item is deselected, the PDF opens with the layer visible. If you enable the preference settings and select Always Visible from the Visibility pull-down menu, the layer is always visible regardless of whether you have the default state On or Off.

The options for initial states include the following:

■ **Visibility.** Three choices are available from this pull-down menu. They include Visible When On, Never Visible, and Always Visible. The first option displays a layer according to whether you have the eye icon visible in the Layers panel. When toggled on, the layer is visible. When toggled off, the layer is hidden. Never Visible hides the layer data regardless of whether the default state is on or off. Always Visible always shows the layer.

■ **Print.** You may have a watermark or message that you want to eliminate or display on a printed page. The three choices, Prints When Visible, Never Prints, and Always Prints, are similar to the options for visibility. Printing a layer does not require the layer to be in view in the Document pane at the time you print the file if Always Prints is selected.

■ **Export.** This setting applies to exporting PDF documents back into authoring programs using a Save As command and selecting a file format compatible with your intended authoring program. Export provides you the same three options when exporting layer data as are available for printing. You can eliminate layers exported by selecting Never Exports, or hide or show a layer and choose Exports When Visible. Likewise, you can choose to always export a layer regardless of the visibility and print settings by selecting Always Exports.

CROSS-REF For information on exporting PDF data back to authoring programs, see Chapter 9.

The window at the bottom of the dialog box displays information according to the initial state(s) you select from the pull-down menu. When you open the Properties dialog box you can see, at a glance, the options for each initial state. At the bottom of the scrollable list is information related to the authoring document that was exported to PDF. By default when the initial state is set to Visible When On, you see no view information in the window at the bottom of the Properties dialog box.

Change the Visibility to Never Visible or Always Visible. Click OK and when you open the Layers Properties dialog box, a new category labeled "View" appears at the bottom of the window. Below the category name you see ViewState: ON or ViewState: OFF depending on the respective visibility choice you made after changing the initial state.

A good real-world condition for setting a layer state to be visible when printing is when you want to use a watermark or stamp on printed copies. If you want the watermark or stamp to be hidden when viewing the PDF in Acrobat, set the layer visibility for Print to Prints When Visible. If you distribute the document and want all users to print a watermark or some symbol, secure the document with Acrobat security and other users won't be able to avoid printing the file without the mark. In Figure 24.6 you see a PDF file as it prints. The watermark is not visible when viewed onscreen.

CROSS-REF   For more on creating and using watermarks, see Chapter 16.

Overriding defaults

In your original authoring program you can create PDF documents with layers that aren't visible in the Layers panel. You can also hide layers in the Default State or the Initial State pull-down menus. If you change defaults to hide layers in the Layers panel, you can change layer visibility in the Options menu. If the Options menu shows a menu item for overriding a layer state grayed out, the menu choice is not available. To change the options, you need to return to the Layer Properties dialog box.

Open the Options pull-down menu to see the following three options for overriding defaults:

- **Apply Print Overrides.** When selected, this option overrides any options you made for not printing layers. When you select this menu item in the Options panel, when you print the PDF all the layers are printed.

- **Apply Export Overrides.** When selected, this option overrides any options you made for exporting layer data. When you select this option, all layer data are exported.

- **Apply Layer Overrides.** Layer Overrides relates to the layer visibility. When this option is enabled, all layers are visible in the Document pane, but the individual layer visibility options are no longer available to you. You cannot click on an eye icon for hiding a layer when the override is enabled. To individually show or hide a layer, you need to deselect the Apply Layer Overrides menu option and use the Layers panel for showing/hiding layers.

Watermarks on separate layers can appear on a printed document but are not visible when a PDF is in view in the Document pane.

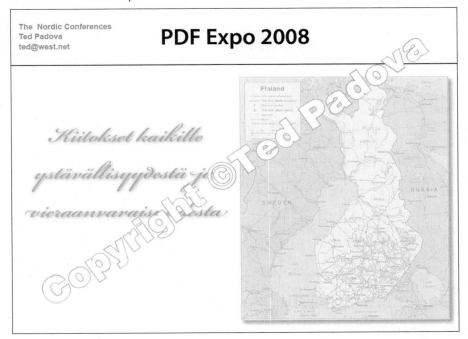

Managing layers

You can edit layers in that you can name, merge, and flatten them. However, you cannot rearrange layers in Acrobat. To rename a layer, select the layer in the Layers panel and click a second time on the layer name. The layer name is highlighted. Begin typing, and the text you type replaces the highlighted text. You can click and drag across a layer name and edit a portion of the text much like you might change names in Bookmarks. You can also edit layer names in the Layer Properties dialog box. If you are changing properties and decide you also want to change a layer name, select the name in the Layer Name field in the Layer Properties dialog box and edit the name.

Merging layers

You can merge layers whether they are visible or hidden. All layer merging takes place in the Merge Layers dialog box and is available only to users of Acrobat Pro and Acrobat Pro Extended. To open the dialog box, select Merge Layers from the Options pull-down menu in the Layers panel. The Merge Layers dialog box opens, as shown in Figure 24.7.

To merge layers, select Merge Layers from the Options pull-down menu. The Merge Layers dialog box opens where all layers (visible and hidden) are listed in the Layers to be merged column.

Regardless of whether a layer is visible or hidden, the list in the Layers to be merged column on the left side of the dialog box includes all layers in the document in a scrollable window. You can merge visible layers with hidden layers. To merge layers, select the layers to be merged into a single layer from the list on the left and click the Add button. You can select multiple layers by holding down the Shift key for a contiguous selection or by using the Ctrl key (Windows) or ⌘ key (Macintosh) to randomly select layer names in a noncontiguous group.

When the layers to be merged are visible in the center column, select the target layer in the Target layer to merge into column. The name you select here is the name listed in the Layers panel and contains all the data from the other layers. The properties associated with the target layer become the properties in the merged layer. After you merge layers, all previous layer names are removed from the Layers panel.

When adding layers to the list in the center of the dialog box (add list), you can move the target layer to the add list or elect to not move the target layer to the list. For example, if you have Text as a target layer where you want to merge Text02 and Text03 together with Text, you can add Text to the center window or not add Text to the list. When you select Text as the target layer and click OK, Text01 and Text 02 are added to Text regardless of whether Text was added to the center column.

> **TIP**   If you want to merge a group of layers to a new layer name, you can edit the name of one of the layers to be merged in the Layers panel. Click, and click again, on the layer name in the Layers panel to edit the layer name. Open the Merge Layers dialog box and merge the desired layers to the new target layer name.

Flattening layers

Users of Acrobat Pro and Acrobat Pro Extended can flatten a group of layers or all layers in a PDF document into a single layer. Neither the merging layers option discussed earlier nor the flattening layers option is available to Acrobat Standard users. You may want to flatten layers to simplify printing a document, exchange a PDF with users of an Acrobat viewer earlier than version 6, or reduce the file size. When layers are flattened, the layer visibility is taken into account. If you have four layers and two layers are visible, the flattened PDF document results as a combination of the visible layers only. Be certain about what layer data you want to remain visible before selecting the Options menu and choosing Flatten Layers, as you won't be able to undo the operation and regain the data that was discarded from the hidden layers.

TIP A good use for merging layers is when creating graphically rich Acrobat PDF forms. If you use the Add or Edit Fields command to populate a form in Acrobat, the fields most often won't be picked up when Acrobat auto detects fields on forms where the form design uses beveled field boxes, gradients, drop shadows, and other similar graphic elements. To optimize your chances for using auto field detection you can create a temporary layer (in a program like Adobe InDesign) for designing the field locations with simple field objects such as boxes and underlines that are easily picked up by Acrobat. After adding fields, hide the temporary layer and flatten the layers.

CROSS-REF For more information on auto detecting fields, see Chapter 34.

Creating New Layers in PDF Files

Acrobat 9 provides you some new features for handling layers in an area you just might not first notice when you start using the program. Open any flat PDF file — one without layers or even a layered file. Open a context menu on the Acrobat Toolbar Well and choose Print Production to open the Print Production toolbar shown in Figure 24.8.

FIGURE 24.8

Open a context menu on the Toolbar Well and choose Print Production to open the Print Production toolbar.

CROSS-REF For more information on using the Print Production tools and preflighting documents, see Chapter 32.

NEW FEATURE The third tool from the left side of the toolbar as shown in Figure 24.8 is the Preflight tool. Click this tool and the Preflight window opens. In the first profile listed, you will find the Create PDF layers category. Click the arrow adjacent to the category name and the Create PDF layers options expand similar to bookmark expansions. In Figure 24.9 you can see five different options for creating PDF layers.

FIGURE 24.9

Click the arrow adjacent to Create PDF layers and five options for creating layers appear in an expanded list.

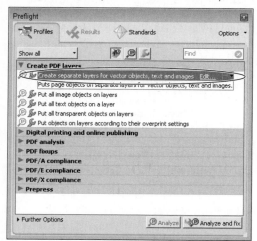

The options shown in the Preflight window should be self-explanatory. If you want to create a layered document with vector objects, text, and images appearing on their own layers, choose the first item in the list (Create separate layers for vector objects, text, and images) then click the Analyze and Fix button in the lower right corner of the Preflight window. In an instant, your PDF document is converted to a PDF with Adobe PDF Layers. Click the Layers panel button in the Navigation pane and you'll see layers with default names such as Images, Text, and Vector objects.

NEW FEATURE If you want to add content to a PDF document as a separate layer, you'll find a new command in Acrobat 9 in the Layers panel. From the Options menu in the Layers panel choose Import as Layer. The Import as Layer dialog box opens as shown in Figure 24.10. This dialog box works similar to adding watermarks when you choose Document ⇨ Watermark ⇨ Add.

CROSS-REF For more information on adding watermarks to PDF files, see Chapter 16.

Click the Browse button to search for a file you want to import as a new layer. You can choose any file type consistent with those file types you can convert to PDF from within Acrobat. If you import a file in a layered document, you have choices for importing the new data on an existing layer or as a new layer.

CROSS-REF For more information on converting to PDF from within Acrobat, see Chapter 11.

The new layer document can be sized by adjusting the Scale options, and the position of the imported layer is set using the Vertical and Horizontal text boxes as shown in Figure 24.10.

FIGURE 24.10

Choose Import as Layer from the Layers panel's Options menu to open the Import as Layer dialog box.

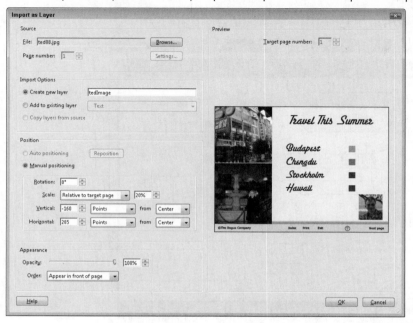

Creating Layer Visibility Buttons

You may have a document in which you want to create navigation buttons to help a user easily navigate through different layer views. Having some buttons that link to different layer views can help users understand the document structure and quickly navigate different views.

 Users of Acrobat Standard as well as Acrobat Pro and Acrobat Pro Extended can add buttons to PDF documents in Acrobat 9.

Changing layer visibility with buttons

Creating buttons for layer visibility is much like creating Bookmarks. You first establish the view you want as the destination view of a link action, and then you create the link button.

CROSS-REF **For more information on creating Button form fields, see Chapter 34.**

Adding field objects has changed quite a bit in Acrobat 9. When you want to add a field object such as a text field, you first need to choose Forms➪Add or Edit Fields. This action moves you into Form Editing Mode and the interface changes as you see in Figure 24.11.

FIGURE 24.11

The Form Editing Mode in Acrobat 9

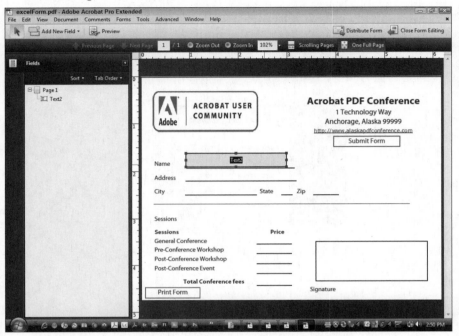

To add a field object to a page you can open the Add New Field menu (top-left corner), open a context menu, or choose Forms ➪ Form Tools and choose a tool from the submenu. Once the cursor is loaded, you can click the mouse button to drop a field object on the page or click and drag to set the field bounding box.

Adjusting properties can be handled in Form Edit Mode or the Acrobat view that you can return to by clicking Close Form Editing in the top-right corner of the window. In regard to changing layer visibility, it's a better choice to create the field object and do the rest of your editing back in the Acrobat Viewer mode. While in Form Edit Mode you don't have access to the Navigation panels, so changing layer visibility is not possible while in this mode.

The one form tool you do have access to in Viewer mode is the Button tool that appears on the Advanced Editing toolbar. You can stay in Viewer mode and add button fields that you can use to change layer visibility.

Create a button field in Viewer mode by clicking the Button tool in the Advanced Editing toolbar and click on the page where you want the field to appear. Click Show All Properties to open the Properties window. At this point you can change the layer view while the Properties dialog box is open. Choose the target view you want and click the Actions tab in the Field Properties. Choose Set Layer Visibility from the Select Action menu and click Add (see Figure 24.12). The button is now configured to display the view you see in the Layers panel.

CROSS-REF For more information on using the Form Editing Mode and adding field objects to a PDF, see Chapter 34.

TIP If you want more control for working with layers such as creating layers in existing PDF documents, you can find third-party plug-ins supporting more features for working with layers. Plug-ins such as ARTS PDF Stratify extend the editing of PDF documents with features not supported in Acrobat. Search the Internet for tools that work with PDF layers or visit www.artspdf.com/arts_pdf_stratify.asp for more on ARTS PDF Stratify.

FIGURE 24.12

Set the target view and choose Set layer visibility, then click Add in the Actions tab.

Changing layer visibility with JavaScripts

If you set a button action to change visibility in the Actions tab in the Button Properties dialog box, you must be able to see the button on the layer where you create the button and the layer for the target view. If you select a button to edit the properties and change the view to the target view for the button action, the button must still be visible to set the action.

Having buttons in view on all layers is not a problem when you add button fields to a PDF in Acrobat. All field objects and other types of annotation objects are visible on all layers regardless of the layer on which you create the object. However, there is one application that upsets the PDF applecart. Buttons created in Adobe InDesign are visible only on the layer where they were created. When you export to PDF, you'll see the InDesign buttons appear on a layer when it is visible. Hiding the layer also hides the button.

With Adobe InDesign buttons, the problem becomes setting an action to show the target layer. You cannot use the Set Layer Visibility action in the Button Properties dialog box to change layer visibility with buttons that were created in InDesign. If you select the button and change a layer view, the button hides and therefore no action can be assigned to the button.

To work around the problem, you need to use a JavaScript. Rather than use the Set Layer Visibility action in the Button Properties dialog box, choose Run a JavaScript and click the Add button to open the JavaScript Editor. In the JavaScript Editor ,you might use a script as follows to change the OCG (layer) state:

```
var docOCGs = this.getOCGs();
for (var i=0; i < docOCGs.length; i++)
{
   if(docOCGs[i].name == "Video")
   {
        docOCGs[i].state = !docOCGs[i].state;
   }
   if(docOCGs[i].name == "Content")
   {
        docOCGs[i].state = docOCGs[i].state.off;
   }
}
```

The above script changes OCG states between the "Video" and "Content" layers in the PDF document. To see a sample of this script in action and examine buttons that were originally created in Adobe InDesign, take a look at the file videoLayers.pdf on the CD-ROM accompanying this book. The Play button shown in Figure 24.13 contains the script described above.

CROSS-REF For more information on JavaScript, see Chapter 36 (on the CD-ROM).

FIGURE 24.13

A PDF document with a button created in Adobe InDesign and a JavaScript that changes OCG states

Some Practical Uses for Layered PDFs

I talked about using Adobe PDF Layers for multilingual documents earlier in this chapter as one good example for why you might want to use layers in PDFs. Other uses for working with PDFs are limited only by your imagination. You can vastly expand your imagination and use Adobe PDF layers in a number of ways.

On the CD-ROM accompanying this book you'll find a few files with Adobe PDF layers. The *video-Layers.pdf* document changes the layer state to open a layer where a video is played.

The AUC_regForm.pdf document is an Acrobat PDF form. Click the item denoted as LOCATION MAP shown in Figure 24.14 and the layer state changes to view a map of a convention site. Click the Show Stage button on the new layer view and a Flash animation explodes a seating chart. This kind of form is but one example of creating more dynamic interactive forms using Acrobat and Adobe PDF layers.

FIGURE 24.14

Click LOCATION MAP to change the OCG state.

The file `101FormseTips.pdf` is contained in the Chapter 24 folder on the CD-ROM. Open page two and you see a license agreement. If you click the Agree button all pages are made visible. The Agree button has a JavaScript that changes the OCG state to view the hidden layer. In this example you are shown how a license agreement can be added to a PDF where a user must agree to the terms of the agreement in order to see the PDF content.

The `101FormseTips.pdf` document is not secured to provide you access to the PDF content. In a real-world situation you might secure the file against any kind of editing so users won't be able to change layer visibility via the Layers panel, thereby bypassing the license agreement. Note that in the Layers Properties both layers are Locked, meaning a user can't change visibility by clicking on the eye icons in the Layers panel.

 For more information on Acrobat security, see Chapter 26.

Summary

- The PDF 1.5 and above formats support layers from authoring applications that are capable of creating layered files and exporting with Acrobat 6 or greater compatibility.

- You can view and hide individual layers in Acrobat. The initial visibility of the layers in view and what layers are hidden are determined at the time the PDF is created.

■ Saving files after showing and hiding layers does not change initial visibility. You change initial visibility in the Layer Properties dialog box, where you toggle layers on and off.

■ You change layer states for visibility, printing, and exporting data in the Layer properties. Layers can be printed or exported without visibility.

■ You merge and flatten layers using menu commands from the Options pull-down menu in the Layers panel.

■ You can create link buttons to display different layer visibility. To create a link action to a view, you first create the desired view in the Layers panel and then set the link action in the Link or Button Properties dialog box.

Chapter 25

Accessibility and Tagged PDF Files

A dobe Acrobat 9 is compliant with United States federal code regulating document accessibility for vision- and motion-challenged persons. This means that screen readers can intelligently interpret the PDFs you create; in other words, PDF files can be read aloud in a reading order as a sighted person would read a document. Through an extensive set of keyboard shortcuts available in Acrobat, almost anyone with vision or motion challenges can share your documents and read them.

In order for a document to be accessible, you must use authoring applications capable of delivering a document's structure to Acrobat. Hence, you need to know something about the internal structure of documents and what programs to use to create the structure required by Acrobat to make a document accessible. Not all the content in a document travels through the PDF creation process with information necessary to make a document completely accessible. Therefore, you need to perform some work in Acrobat to either add accessibility or to polish up a document for delivery to a screen reader in a form that makes sense to the user. In this chapter, I cover how to make documents accessible from authoring programs, as well as how to use Acrobat tools to make existing documents accessible.

IN THIS CHAPTER

Making documents accessible

Working with tags

Changing views for accessible documents

Setting Up the Work Environment

The essential tools for working with document accessibility include the Tags panel, Content panel, and Order panel. To view the panels, you need to have a document open in Acrobat. When you start working with accessibility in a document, select View ➪ Navigation Panels ➪ Tags. The Tags panel opens in a panel that also includes the Content, Order, and tabs. You can drag the tab for each panel to the Navigation pane to dock it among the other tabs in the "'free" or "open'" region below the Signatures panel and above the Comments tab. Click the Close box in the top-right corner of the palette to close the palette containing the

The TouchUp tools are important not only for editing text and objects, but the TouchUp Reading Order tool was specifically designed to work with reading order on accessible documents. Be certain to load the TouchUp tools. Select Tools ➪ Customize Toolbars or open a context menu on the Toolbar Well and select More tools. Check the check box in the Advanced Editing toolbar for TouchUp Reading Order Tool. Pick and choose other tools in this toolbar you expect to use, and click OK. To dock the toolbars, select Dock All Toolbars from a context menu opened from the Toolbar Well.

Creating Accessible Documents

The terms "document accessibility," "structure," and "tagged PDFs" may be a mystery to you. If the term "accessibility" is new, then you need to begin with an understanding of what accessible documents are before working with them. After you know more about document accessibility, you can move forward to look at how to create an accessible document, and then look at how you can edit accessible documents. Therefore, the three areas to work with are understanding accessibility, creating accessible documents from authoring programs, and finally, working with accessible documents in Acrobat.

Screen Readers

I use the term "screen reader" extensively in this chapter. When I use this term, I'm referring to tools created by third parties to read open documents aloud in Acrobat and other programs or from files in various formats saved to disk.

Screen readers range in price from $99 to over $1,000. The advantage of using third-party products with Acrobat PDF files is that they can read aloud single words as well as spell out words character by character. Through keyboard controls, users choose reading rates, audio output levels, voices, and navigation.

Screen readers are typically software programs installed on either Mac OS or Windows. More programs support Windows than Macintosh operating systems, but developers have been increasing their support for both platforms. The most popular screen reader used today is Freedom Scientific JAWS for Windows. Version 4.5 and later is also compatible with Flash Player 6 and later. In past years, PDF documents were not supported by many developers. Today, much more support exists for reading PDF documents with the Adobe Reader software.

For a complete list of screen readers that have been tested with Acrobat, log on to Adobe's Web site at www.adobe.com/accessibility. From Adobe's Web page you'll find URL links to vendor sites as well as general information about accessibility.

Understanding accessibility

Sighted people can view a document on the computer or read a printed page and easily discern the difference between titles, subtitles, columns, graphic images, graphic elements, and so on. With regard to Acrobat PDFs, you can easily see the difference between background designs, button links, bookmarks, animation, and form fields, and you typically see visual clues to know where buttons and fields exist.

With regard to screen-reading devices, which depend on software to generate audio output from an Acrobat PDF file, the software readers aren't intelligent enough to distinguish differences based on visual clues. For example, a screen reader may interpret a three-columned document as one continuous column and read the text from left to right across all three columns row by row. Obviously the output is useless to the end user working with a screen reader. Screen readers interpret headings, subheadings, and tables the same as body copy, and they offer no distinction in the structure unless the screen reader software has some clue that these items are different from the body text.

Some authoring programs provide you an opportunity when creating the PDF file to retain the underlying structure of a document in the resulting PDF file. With a series of tags and retention of the document structure, screen readers use alternate text to make distinctions in the document much like the visual user would interpret a page. The document flow, alternate text for graphic elements, distinctions between headings, and so on, can all be managed in Acrobat when the internal document structural tree is included in the PDF export. When files are not exported with the document structure, you can use Acrobat commands to add structure to PDFs. In order to make it possible for people with screen readers to navigate your PDF documents correctly, the underlying structure must be present.

PDF files fall into three categories when you are talking about a document's structure:

- **Unstructured PDF files.** Unstructured PDF documents could not be interpreted by screen readers with complete document integrity in earlier versions of Acrobat. For example, when you exported the PDF to other formats such as a Rich Text Format (RTF), the basic paragraph structure was preserved, but tables, lists, and some text formatting were lost. In Acrobat 8 and above, unstructured documents can be interpreted by screen readers with accuracy. What remains as an unstructured document when using Acrobat 8 and 9 are image files converted to PDF such as scanned documents. These files clearly are not structured.

- **Structured PDF files.** Structured PDF files can be read by screen readers, but the reliability is much less than the next category of tagged PDF documents. When you export structured PDF files to other formats, more structural content is preserved, but tables and lists can be lost. Additionally, structured documents, such as the unstructured documents discussed previously, do not support text reflows for different-sized devices.

- **Tagged PDF files.** Tagged PDFs contain both the document structure and a hierarchical structure tree where all the internal structure about the document's content is interpreted. Tagged PDFs have the highest reliability when you're repurposing files for screen reader output and saving files in other formats such as RTF, HTML, XHTML, and XML. In addition, tagged PDF files support text reflow for viewing on different-sized screens and devices and accommodate any zoom level on a monitor.

CROSS-REF For more information on exporting PDF content, see Chapter 9. For more on document structure, see "Understanding Structure" in this chapter.

NOTE Structured documents were introduced with Acrobat 4 (PDF 1.3) and tagged documents were introduced with Acrobat 5 (PDF 1.4). PDFs created prior to version 1.3 had no document structure, and PDFs created before version 1.4 could not be tagged. With later versions of Acrobat, document structure and tagging could be added to these PDFs from within Acrobat.

The goal for you when creating PDF documents for accessibility is to be certain you use PDF documents that are not only structured, but also tagged. After you create tagged PDFs, you can work with the structure tree and modify the contents for optimum use. In terms of making Acrobat PDFs accessible, you must consider several criteria to optimize files for effective handling by screen readers:

- **Assessing accessibility.** Fortunately, Acrobat provides tools for determining whether a PDF file is an accessible document. As a first order of business you should plan on assessing a file for accessibility. If you work with legacy files or files that are created from authoring programs that don't support the export of the document structure, be certain to make the document accessible before beginning an editing session.

CROSS-REF For adding accessibility to PDF files from within Acrobat, see the section "Making existing PDFs accessible" later in this chapter.

- **Logical reading order.** The text should follow a logical flow. You need to properly define column text in terms of the path that a screen reader follows (that is, down one column, then begin at the top of the second column, and so on). You should also mark headings and subheadings for distinction.

- **Alternative text descriptions for image and graphic elements.** Those familiar with HTML know that you can code an HTML document with alternate tags so users with text-only browsers can understand the structure of Web pages. The same principle for accessible documents applies. Alternate text needs to be inserted so the screen reader can interpret graphic elements.

- **Form field descriptions.** Form fields need to be described with text to inform a user with a screen reader that a form field is present.

- **Field tab order.** Setting the logical tab order for fields on a form is important for the visual user. With screen readers it is essential. The logical tab order for fields should be strictly followed.

- **Document security.** If documents are secured with Acrobat security, you must use 128-bit encryption compatible with Acrobat 5 and above. If you use compatibility less than Acrobat 5 or 40-bit encryption, the PDF is rendered inaccessible.

- **Links and interactivity.** Use form fields for link buttons with descriptions so the user knows that another destination or a link action is invoked if he or she selects the field.

- **Document language.** Screen readers typically deliver accessible documents in only one language. To protect your documents against inoperability with new releases, specify a document language when creating accessible PDFs. Document language specification is also important when using tools in Acrobat for checking accessibility.

CROSS-REF For more information on field tab order, see Chapter 34. For more information on document security, see Chapter 26. For more information on links and interactivity, see Chapter 22.

Adding accessibility in authoring applications

Not all authoring programs currently support accessibility. This phenomenon may change with new upgrades to software, so what is said today may change tomorrow. As of this writing the programs offering the best support for document accessibility include Microsoft Word version 2000 or higher, Adobe PageMaker 7.0 or higher, Adobe FrameMaker, Adobe LiveCycle Designer, and Adobe InDesign 2.0 or higher. If you use other authoring applications, you do have the option to make documents accessible with Acrobat Standard and Acrobat Pro, or Acrobat Pro Extended.

When converting Microsoft Word files to PDF, be certain to use the PDFMaker in the Word toolbar or from the Adobe PDF menu in Word. Set up the conversion settings for enabling accessibility and reflow with tagged PDF documents. This option is available in the Settings tab in the Acrobat PDFMaker dialog box. Select the "Enable Accessibility and Reflow with tagged Adobe PDF" check box.

CROSS-REF For more on creating PDF files with accessibility and tags from Microsoft Office applications, see Chapter 8.

When creating documents with text, images, charts, diagrams, and so on, using a professional layout program often works better than a word processor. Adobe InDesign CS is an ideal tool for creating layouts that you need to make accessible. When you design a document for accessibility, be precise about how you add elements on each page. The order in which you lay out documents can have an effect on the order of the exported structure. For example, adding a block of text, and then importing an image, may result in the text appearing first in the structure tree and the image following the text even if you move the elements so the image appears first on the page. The only way to observe the results of how the document structure ultimately converts to PDF is to practice and examine the tags structure tree in Acrobat versus your layouts. You can develop a workflow that minimizes the work in Acrobat to properly create the structure needed for optimum performance when read by a screen reader.

TIP If you arrange objects in an authoring program like Adobe InDesign and the reading order is not following the viewing order, you can cut either text or images and paste them back into the document. If, for example, an image should be first in the structure tree followed by text, but the order is reversed when you examine the tags in Acrobat, cut the text block and paste it back into the document in InDesign. Recreate the PDF and you'll find the order changed according to the order that the elements were last placed on the page. This method is not always a precise solution for reordering elements, but it can often be used to resolve problems.

Making existing PDFs accessible

If you have PDF documents either from legacy files or from files converted from authoring applications that do not support exports to PDF with tags, you can use Acrobat commands to add structure to the document and make the files accessible. The first step is checking a document for accessibility. If the document contains no tags, then you can add tags in Acrobat Standard or Acrobat Pro, or Pro Extended.

Performing a Quick Check

To determine whether a document is accessible, you can perform a Quick Check. In Acrobat Standard, Acrobat Pro, or Acrobat Pro Extended choose Advanced ➪ Accessibility ➪ Quick Check (or press Shift+Ctrl/⌘+6). In Adobe Reader, choose Document ➪ Accessibility Quick Check (or press Shift+Ctrl/⌘+6). This method of checking the PDF is a quick analysis to determine whether tags exist in the file. When the check is completed, a dialog box opens informing you of the accessibility status. If the document is not accessible, the dialog box message states that the document is not structured and reading problems may occur.

 Document accessibility can be checked in Adobe Reader. Making a document accessible, however, requires Acrobat Standard or Acrobat Pro, or Pro extended.

Performing a Full Check (Acrobat Pro and Pro Extended only)

Acrobat Pro and Pro Extended offer you a more sophisticated analysis, where more file attributes are checked and a report is created either in a file or by adding comments to the open PDF document, or both. To use the Full Check option, follow these steps.

STEPS: Checking accessibility in Acrobat Professional

1. **Choose Advanced ➪ Accessibility ➪ Full Check.** The Accessibility Full Check dialog box, shown in Figure 25.1, opens.

2. **Check the box for Create Accessibility Report and Create comments in document.** Checking these boxes creates a report and adds comment notes in the document pertaining to the results of the analysis. All errors found during the check are reported in comment notes.

3. **Select the Checking Options for the items you want to check.** Enable the check boxes in this section for items you want to check. In this example I selected all the check boxes.

4. **Click the Browse button.** Identify the location for the report file if you want a report saved to an HTML file, which you can view in the Accessibility Report panel (see Figure 25.2).

5. **When you set all the attributes, click Start Checking.** Acrobat opens a dialog box similar to Figure 25.2, reporting the findings.

FIGURE 25.1

When you run a Full Check in Acrobat Pro or Pro Extended, you can choose options for what content to check.

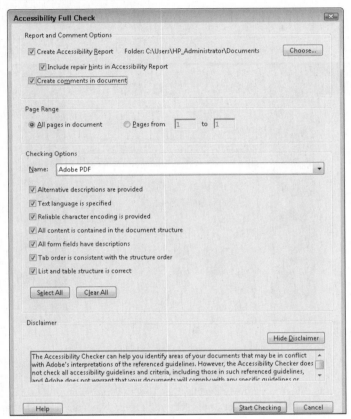

FIGURE 25.2

After running the Full Check, the findings are reported in a dialog box.

After completing the check, the Accessibility Report panel opens and displays a more detailed report as shown in Figure 25.3. If you selected Create comments in document, comment notes may appear, reporting problems in untagged documents.

The Accessibility Report panel shows you a detailed report of the full accessibility check findings.

An Accessibility report is also saved to your hard drive in HTML format. If you click the Browse button in the Accessibility Full Check dialog box, you can target a location for the saved report. By default, the report is saved to your My Documents folder (Windows) or your Documents folder (Macintosh). Open your Web browser and select File Open. Navigate to the folder where the report is found and open the file. The report is displayed in the browser window.

The links in the HTML document link directly to the PDF file and highlight the item associated with the link. Click a link in your Web browser and the PDF file opens in the foreground with the respective item highlighted, as shown in Figure 25.4. You can correct problems by clicking links in the Web browser and correcting the problems in the PDF document.

FIGURE 25.4

Click a link in the Web browser and the referenced item in the PDF is highlighted.

- 1 images(s) with no alternate text. (How to Add Alternate Text)
    1. No alternate text
- 1 element(s) that are not contained within the structure tree. (How to Add Tags)
    1. Inaccessible page content

Adding accessibility

Keep in mind you are always best served by adding accessibility at the time a PDF document is created from authoring programs supporting exports to PDF with accessibility and tags. If you have files for which either returning to the authoring program is impractical or the authoring program is incapable of exporting to PDF as tagged files, choose Advanced ⇨ Accessibility ⇨ Add Tags to Document. Or from the Tags panel in the Navigation pane, select Add Tags to Document from the Options pull-down menu. Immediately after you select the menu command from either Acrobat Standard or Acrobat Professional, a slider bar opens displaying Acrobat's progress in adding tags to the document. After completion, no confirmation dialog box opens to report the status. If problems were encountered while adding the tags, a dialog box opens, reporting the problems found.

After adding the tags, you can return to the Quick Check or Full Check menu command and check the document for accessibility.

If a file has tags and you choose Advanced ⇨ Accessibility ⇨ Add Tags to Document, Acrobat opens a dialog box informing you that the file already has tags. Adding tags is not permitted using the menu command. If you are unhappy with the current tagging, you can remove all tags from the document, and then reapply with this method. To remove all tags, open the Tags panel in the Navigation pane. Select the topmost tag (typically labeled "Tags") and select Delete Tag from the Options pull-down menu.

Understanding Structure

To understand more clearly the need for creating accessibility and adding tags to a document, look at Figure 25.5 as an example. This document contains several items that need attention to make the file accessible and comprehensible when read by a screen reader.

FIGURE 25.5

A document with images, illustrations, and text in multiple columns needs to have the structure modified for proper reading by a screen reader.

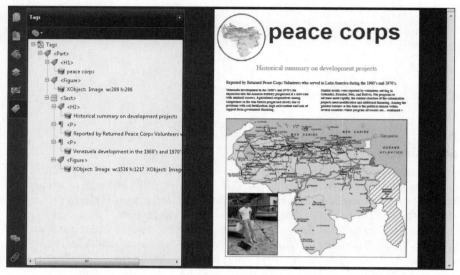

In Figure 25.5 the items of importance in terms of accessibility include the following:

- **The first element on the page is a logo.** A screen reader won't interpret the logo unless you add some alternate text to the document describing the object. Adjacent to the logo on the right side is text that a screen reader can read after you make the document accessible. If the text does not read properly, the two lines of text need to be modified for the proper interpretation by the screen reader.

- **The two lines of text are in a single column.** These lines should be read in logical order without any problems. They are shown here to illustrate the difference between the two lines and the two columns following.

- **The text is blocked in two columns.** Unless the structure is established for the screen reader to read down one column before moving to the second column, the screen reader defaults at a left-to-right reading order, reading across both columns.

- **Item four is a large map.** Alternate text for the illustration is needed for the screen reader to explain what graphic appears on the page.

■ **Item five is an inset photo.** The alternate text for the map can describe the photo, or the photo can have an alternate text description. Either way, you need to create the alternate text for the screen reader to fully interpret the graphics.

When you export to PDF from authoring programs with tags, the structure of the document for the blocks of text in logical reading orders is preserved. In the example in Figure 25.5, the single and double-column text is typically not a problem when the file is read by a screen reader. Images, however, need some form of manual editing. Even the best source exporting with tags wouldn't be able to describe the visual elements in the layout. These are subjective items that need a description.

If using a program such as Microsoft Word, you can add alternate text in Word before the file is exported to PDF. In other applications you need to create the alternate text in Acrobat.

Using the Tags panel

When you export a document from an authoring program with tags or use the Add Tags to Document menu command, a *structure tree* is created in the PDF file. The structure tree is a hierarchical order of the elements contained in the file. Elements may be in the form of heads, subheads, body text, figures, tables, annotations, and other items identified as separate individual structural elements. The hierarchy contains a nested order of the elements with parent/child relationships. A heading, for example, may have a subhead. The heading in this case is a parent element with the subheading a child element.

When a document contains tags, you view the tag elements and the structure tree in the Tags panel. Open the Tags panel and click on the top item. By default, you see an icon labeled Tags with a plus (+) (Windows) or right-pointing arrow (Macintosh) symbol adjacent to it. Click the symbol and you open the tree at one level. Other child elements are nested below.

The Tags panel may have an extensive list of elements depending on your document length and complexity. If you want to edit an element or find it in the document, you need some help from Acrobat to find out exactly what tag in the Tags panel is related to what element on a given page. The help comes in the form of a menu command in the Tags panel. Click the down-pointing arrow adjacent to Options in the Tags panel and select Highlight Content. The content is highlighted as shown earlier in Figure 25.5.

When you return to the structure tree, the items you select are highlighted on the respective elements on pages in the Document pane. Click an element and Acrobat navigates to the page where the content is located. The object is highlighted with a keyline border, as shown in Figure 25.5.

Adding alternate text

In the example in Figure 25.5, the logo appearing at the top of the page is an image file. When a screen reader reads the document, no specific instructions are contained in the document to interpret this image. As an option, you can create alternate text so a visually challenged person knows a graphic element exists on the page. To add alternate text in a tagged PDF document, follow these steps.

STEPS: Adding alternate text to tagged elements

1. **Open a tagged PDF file.** Or add tags to a document. Open the Tags panel in the Navigation pane. Note: If you didn't set up the working environment as described in the beginning of the chapter, choose View ⇨ Navigation Panels ⇨ Tags to open the Tags panel.

2. **Open the structure tree.** Click the Tags Root icon to the left of the text. On Windows a plus (+) symbol appears adjacent to the text. On the Macintosh, a right-pointing arrow appears next to the text. Clicking the icon opens the tags tree.

3. **Select Highlight Content.** If you haven't selected the menu command for highlighting content, open the Options palette in the Tags panel and select Highlight Content.

4. **Find the element for which the alternate text is to be added.** In this example, the figure below the second paragraph (<P>) was selected. When you click the Figure tag, the logo at the top left corner of the page is highlighted. Alternately, you can also select the TouchUp Object tool, click an object on the page, and select Find Tag from Selection from the Tags palette Options pull-down menu.

5. **Open the element's properties.** Select the TouchUp Object tool from the Advanced Editing toolbar you opened earlier. If you do not have this tool available, choose Tools ⇨ Advanced Editing ⇨ TouchUp Object Tool. Click the element and open a context menu. Select Properties from the menu options.

6. **Add alternate text.** Click the Tags panel. Add a title for the tag by typing a title in the Title field box. The title is not necessary for, nor read by, the screen reader. Add the text you want the screen reader to read out loud in the Alternate Text field. Select the pull-down menu for Language and select a language. The edits made in this example are shown in Figure 25.6.

7. **Close the TouchUp Properties dialog box.**

Fill in the fields for a title and alternate text, and select a language in the TouchUp Properties dialog box.

Using the Content tab

The Content tab contains a hierarchical list of the objects in the PDF file. Objects are listed in the order in which they appear on the page, similar to the logical structure tree in the Tags panel. Click the Content tab to open it in the Navigation pane and you see a view similar to Figure 25.7. Click an object and move it up or down to change the order of the objects.

The Content tab can be helpful when you want to navigate to and highlight a content item listed in the tab. Click an item such as a text item or figure and the page appears in the Document pane with the respective item selected.

In addition to physically reordering objects, a number of menu commands are available from the Options pull-down menu. Among the menu commands is an option to create a New Container. Notice in Figure 25.5 that all the tags are nested within containers. You can select a tag and select New Container to add alternate text to any area in the document.

FIGURE 25.7

Click objects and drag up or down to reorder the objects in the Content pane.

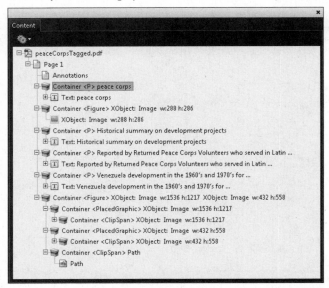

Using the Order tab

You use the Order tab to correct reading order problems. After you create a tagged PDF document, Acrobat infers the reading order from the document structure. You may need to change the order for text and images to create a more logical flow in the document.

You use the Order tab in conjunction with the TouchUp Reading Order tool. Select the tool and open the Order tab. Acrobat lists the reading order of the elements according to page as shown in Figure 25.8. To reorder the elements or regions, click and drag a tag up or down to change the reading order. Each tagged object is numbered on a page indicating the order the tags are read. From the Touchup Reading Order dialog box you can change the attributes of tags and renumber them to change the reading order. Figure 25.8 shows the tagged elements and the reading order defined by numbers adjacent to each tagged object.

FIGURE 25.8

To change reading order, click and drag tags up or down in the Order tab.

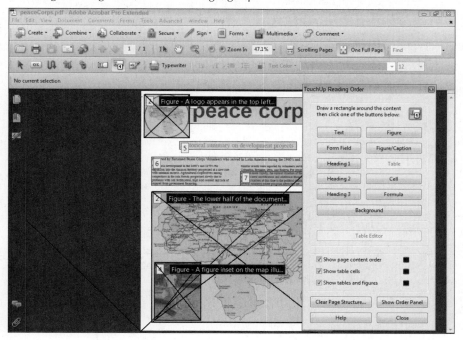

Checking accessible tags

You can check your work easily in Acrobat by having Acrobat read the document. Choose View ⇨ Read Out Loud ⇨ Activate Read Out Loud. Return to the same menu and choose Read This Page Only. The default text-to-speech voice installed on your computer reads the text as a screen reader would interpret it. If you prepare files for screen readers, you can use Acrobat's built-in reading engine to read aloud the text in the document and the alternate tags you add to the file.

Although the Read Out Loud menu command is not intended to replace screen readers, the feature in all Acrobat viewers offers you a good means for checking files that meet accessible standards.

TIP You can save PDF files as accessible text. Select File ⇨ Save As and select Text (Accessible).txt from the Save as Type (Windows) or Format (Macintosh) pull-down menu. The saved text is saved in the same reading order as when you read a document aloud.

CROSS-REF For more information on Read Out Loud and controlling voices and reading speeds, see Chapter 5.

In addition to using Acrobat's built-in function for reading documents aloud, you can acquire a low-cost plug-in from a third-party developer without purchasing a screen reader. PDFAloud, marketed by textHELP Systems (`www.texthelp.com`), is more robust than Acrobat's Read Out Loud command. With PDFAloud you can read text a word, sentence, or paragraph at a time. The plug-in also offers you synchronized colored highlighting while the text is read.

Viewing Accessible Documents

Some accessibility requirements extend beyond text-to-speech reading. Individuals with assistive devices for visual impairments can view documents when text is zoomed and when text color significantly contrasts with background colors. You can modify the display of documents on your screen by adjusting preferences for Accessibility in the Preferences dialog box, or you can customize viewing by choosing Advanced ➪ Accessibility ➪ Setup Assistant (in Adobe Reader, select Document ➪ Accessibility Setup Assistant), which opens the Accessibility Setup Assistant dialog box, shown in Figure 25.9.

FIGURE 25.9

The Accessibility Setup Assistant contains options for screen displays and reading orders.

You make attribute choices in a pane and click the Next button to advance through the Accessibility Setup Assistant. You can make choices for color displays, text smoothing, zoom displays, reading orders, and page delivery by moving through the panes. When you finish, these selections will be set in the Accessibility Preferences for you.

Summary

- Screen readers can interpret accessible PDF files and create audio output for people with vision and motion challenges.

- Adobe PDFMaker for Microsoft products version 2000 or higher, including Word, Excel, Visio, and so on; Adobe PageMaker 7 and higher; and Adobe FrameMaker, Adobe LiveCycle Designer, Adobe InDesign 2.0 and higher are capable of creating tagged and accessible PDF forms.

- You can add tags to PDF documents from a menu command within Acrobat Standard and Acrobat Pro, and Pro Extended.

- You check files for accessibility with the Quick Check command in Adobe Reader, Acrobat Standard, and Acrobat Pro and Pro Extended or with a Full Check in Acrobat Pro and Pro Extended.

- Tagged documents contain a structure tree. Elements in the tree locate respective elements in the document if you enable the Highlight Content menu command.

- You can add alternate text to elements in Acrobat by addressing the element's properties.

- You can make text and background color changes in the Accessibility Preferences dialog box or via the Accessibility Setup Assistant.

Part V

PDF Publishing

This part deals with publishing PDF files in various ways that include adding file security before deployment, hosting PDFs on the Web, creating presentations and hosting meetings, distributing eBooks, and printing files. In Chapter 26 you find information on securing PDF documents and adding digital signatures. Chapter 27 covers PDFs and the Web where you learn how to host PDFs on the Web, create Web links, and convert PDF content to HTML.

In Chapter 28 we move on to creating presentations using Acrobat, PDF, and Adobe Presenter. Chapter 29 follows with online meetings to share PDFs and PDF presentations with others via Acrobat Connect and Acrobat.com.

In Chapter 30 you'll find information related to creating and viewing PDF eBooks. This part ends with printing PDF documents when hard copy is needed. In Chapter 31 you find information related to printing PDFs to desktop printers, and Chapter 32 follows with printing PDFs at commercial print shops using the Print Production tools.

Chapter 26

Authentication and Security

A crobat PDF documents can be secured using a host of different security methods and encryption tools to prevent unauthorized users from opening files and changing documents. Acrobat Security combined with digital signatures enables you to protect data and secure files for just about any purpose. There's much to learn about using Acrobat Security and digital signatures, and it's important to know what levels of security are available to you and what kinds of security you can apply in many different circumstances. This chapter covers a broad description of security and digitally signing PDF documents and the methods you use to protect files against unauthorized viewing and editing.

Setting Up the Work Environment

You add security to a PDF document through menu commands and the Secure Task button that appears in the Tasks toolbar when you return to the default view. If all you want to do is add security to PDFs, you can open a context menu and select Reset Toolbars from the menu options.

If you want to add digital signature fields on a form where users can digitally sign documents, you need to use Form Edit mode or use a document created in Adobe LiveCycle Designer that contains signature fields. Documents can be signed without using signature fields, but when you want to add a field for signing the document, you'll want to work on a form created in Adobe Designer with signature fields or add signature fields in the Form Edit mode. Adding signature fields doesn't require loading any tools; however, the Select Object tool in the Advanced Editing toolbar can be helpful. From a context menu opened on the Toolbar Well, select the Advanced Editing toolbar. Dock the toolbar after loading it.

For information on creating signature fields in Form Edit mode, see Chapters 33 and 34.

Restricting the Opening and Editing of Files

Acrobat security comes in many different forms, allowing you to secure PDF files against user viewing and/or editing in many ways based on the level of security you assign to a PDF document. However, depending on what level of security you apply to a file, the document may or may not be able to be opened by users of earlier versions of Acrobat. Therefore, when you add security it is critical to know your audience and what versions of Acrobat they are using to view files.

Methods of security available in Acrobat include three types of restrictions. You can secure a file against opening and editing by using Password Security at different levels of encryption. You can also secure files using public key certificates, or if your organization is using Adobe LiveCycle Rights Management Server, you can apply security policies from there. You should think of the first method (Password Security) as security you might apply globally to PDFs when you want the public to have a password to open your PDFs or you want to restrict certain Acrobat features, such as content editing or printing. In this regard, you secure documents for what is referred to as *unknown* users. You can further delineate securing individual files into two categories. You can secure documents by applying security settings that you select via options in security windows, or you can create a security policy in which the same level of security and encryption attributes are applied to documents each time you secure files.

Think of the second method (Certificate Security) as restrictions you want to apply for a selected group of people, or what are referred to as *known* users. You might want to restrict opening documents or PDF editing to a group of co-workers, colleagues, or individuals with whom you have direct communication. This method requires the use of digital IDs and public key certificates. This form of security also uses a security policy you create from public key certificates derived from users' digital IDs.

The third method is securing files with the Adobe LiveCycle Rights Management Server. Adobe LiveCycle Rights Management as a product is not covered in this book; see the Acrobat Help Guide for more details or information. Adobe LiveCycle Rights Management Server enables you to apply server-based security policies to PDF documents. One of the great benefits for using a policy server is that you can encrypt documents for limited time use.

Keep in mind that Security Policies can be used with either Password Security or Certificate Security.

The discussion on Acrobat Security starts with the first method of applying security for a more global environment of unknown users. Later in this chapter, encryption using a security policy with public key certificates for known users is covered along with digital signatures.

Using password security

To secure an open document, choose File ⇨ Properties. Click the Security tab in the Document Properties dialog box. Notice the Security Method pull-down menu. Four options are listed in the menu for different security methods. The default selection is No Security. Open the pull-down menu and select Password Security. The Password Security – Settings dialog box shown in Figure 26.1 opens. Depending on which compatibility option you select from the Compatibility pull-down menu, the bottom of the dialog box activates additional options or removes options. In Figure 26.1, you can see that when choosing Acrobat 9 compatibility, all options are available in the dialog box. If you select an earlier version, such as Acrobat 3 compatibility, some options are grayed out, such as two of the options in the Select Document Components to Encrypt section.

FIGURE 26.1

Depending on what level of compatibility you choose, the options available for Password Security change.

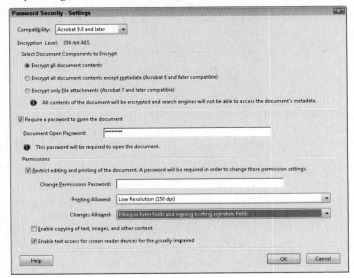

NEW FEATURE At first glance you may not see any difference in the options for Acrobat 9 security compared to Acrobat 7 security. All the radio buttons and menu choices are the same for Acrobat 7, 8, and 9. However, take a look at the Encryption Level in Figure 26.1. Acrobat 7 and 8 security used 128-bit encryption. Acrobat 9 provides you with 256-bit encryption.

Creating a Policy for Adding Security

If you've used earlier versions of Acrobat, accessing the Document Properties dialog box is something you are probably familiar with. It's a fast and easy way for adding document security, and it's okay when you have a single document you want to secure and never again want to secure additional documents with the same permissions and restrictions. Since Acrobat 7, Adobe Systems has made securing PDF documents much easier when you want to routinely secure PDF files using the same permissions settings. The preferred method for securing files in Acrobat 7 through 9 is to create a *security policy*.

To create a security policy you use the Secure Task button pull-down menu and select Manage Security Policies or Advanced ➪ Security ➪ Manage Security Policies. Either choice opens a dialog box where you create a new policy. You step through a New Security Policy Wizard where you make choices for the security method you want to use and make choices for the permissions you want to assign to a document.

Once you create the policy, you can easily apply the same policy when you want to secure additional documents without the need to select the different permissions options each time you apply security. For more detailed information on creating and using security policies, see "Using a security policy" later in this chapter.

You add Password Security via this dialog box any time you want to restrict users from opening a file and/or making changes to the content. Users must know the password you add in this dialog box in order to open a file and/or make changes. The options available to you include the following:

- **Compatibility.** The options from this pull-down menu include Acrobat 3.0, Acrobat 5.0, Acrobat 6.0, Acrobat 7.0, and Acrobat 9.0 compatibility. If you select Acrobat 9.0 compatibility and save the PDF document, users need an Acrobat 9 viewer or greater to open the file. The same holds true when saving with Acrobat 7 compatibility. Users need Acrobat 7 or greater to view PDFs created with Acrobat 7 compatibility.

- **Encryption level.** Below the Compatibility pull-down menu, Acrobat informs you what level of encryption is applied to the document based on the compatibility choice made in the pull-down menu. If you select Acrobat 3 from the Compatibility pull-down menu, the encryption level is 40-bit encryption. Acrobat 5 and Acrobat 6 compatibility are encrypted with 128-bit RC4 encryption. Acrobat 7 and 8 supports 128-bit AES. Acrobat 9.0 supports 256-bit AES. All the higher encryption levels offer you more options for restricting printing and editing.

  - **Encrypt all document contents.** This option applies encryption to all document contents.

  - **Encrypt all document contents except metadata (Acrobat 6 and later compatible).** Use this option to apply encryption to all document contents except document metadata. As the item name implies, this level of security is compatible with Acrobat 6 and later. This is a good selection if you want to have the metadata in your secure documents available for a search engine.

■ **Encrypt only file attachments (Acrobat 7 and later compatible).** Use this option to encrypt file attachments but not the PDF document. This option is compatible only with Acrobat 7 and above. You might use this when sending an eEnvelope or a PDF Portfolio where you want to encrypt the contents only.

> **TIP** Encrypting only file attachments is a nifty feature that was introduced in Acrobat 7. As an example for using this feature, you might have a document such as a memo you want to distribute to all employees. Attached to the memo you might have a financial report, draft company policy document, or some other file you want to have reviewed by management personnel only. All company personnel can see the memo, but only those who have a security password can open the file attachments. You can likewise secure files in a PDF Portfolio. The entire portfolio, or individual files within the portfolio, can be secured.

■ **Require a password to open the document.** Select this check box if you want a user to supply a password to open the PDF document. After selecting the check box, the field box for Document Open Password becomes active and you can add a password. Before you exit the dialog box, Acrobat prompts you in another dialog box to confirm the password. Note: if you select Encrypt only file attachments (Acrobat 7 and later compatible), you must enter a password to be able to open the attachment(s).

■ **Restrict editing and printing of the document. A password will be required in order to change these permission settings.** Select this check box if you want to restrict permissions from the items active in the Permissions area of the dialog box. You can use this with or without a Document Open Password.

■ **Change Permissions Password.** Fill in the field box with a password. If you also have a Document Open Password, the passwords must be different. Acrobat opens a dialog box and informs you to make different password choices if you attempt to use the same password for opening the file and setting permissions.

■ **Printing Allowed.** If you use Acrobat 3 compatibility, the options are available to either enable printing or disallow printing. The choices are None and High Resolution. Even though the choice reads High Resolution, the result simply enables users to print your file. With Acrobat 5 and above compatibility, you have a third choice for enabling printing at a lower resolution (150 dpi). If you select Low Resolution (150 dpi) from the menu options, users are restricted to printing the file at the lower resolution. This choice is typically something you might use for files intended for digital prepress and high-end printing, eBooks or eContent, or to protect your content from being printed and then rescanned.

■ **Changes Allowed.** From this pull-down menu you make choices for the kinds of changes you allow users to perform on the document. Acrobat 3 compatibility offers you four choices; Acrobat 5 and above compatibility offers you five choices. These options include the following:

  ■ **None.** This option prevents a user from any kind of editing and content extraction.

  ■ **Inserting, deleting, and rotating pages.** This option is not available when using Acrobat 3 compatibility. Users permitted to insert, delete, and rotate pages. If you create PDFs for eBooks, allowing users to rotate pages can be helpful when they view PDFs on tablets and portable devices.

■ **Page layout, filling in forms, and signing existing signature fields (Acrobat 3 only).** Select this option to enable users to extract pages, insert pages, and also perform actions on form fields.

■ **Filling in form fields and signing existing signature fields.** If you create Acrobat forms and want users to be able to fill in the form fields and digitally sign documents, enable this check box. Forms are useless to users without the ability to fill in the form fields.

■ **Commenting, filling in form fields, and signing existing signature fields.** You might use this option in a review process where you want to have users comment on a design but you don't want them to make changes to your file. You can secure the document against editing, but allow commenting and form field filling in and signing. When you enable form filling in with this option or the Filling in form fields and signing existing signature fields option, users are restricted against changing your form design and cannot make edits other than filling in the fields. A good example of using this option might be having your customers fill out a form and also add comments to describe their selections.

■ **Any except extracting pages.** With this option, all the permissions are available to users except extracting pages from the document and creating separate PDFs from selected pages.

■ **Enable copying of text, images, and other content and access for the visually impaired.** This option is available when selecting Acrobat 3.0 and later. If you restrict permissions for any of the previous pull-down menu options, users aren't allowed to copy data. You can add permission for content copying by enabling this check box. Enable copying of text, images, and other content: The setting above was replaced with two settings in Acrobat 5.0 and higher security. This setting restricts the user from copying information from your PDF.

■ **Enable text access for screen reader devices for the visually impaired.** This option is available for all versions except Acrobat 3 compatibility. As a matter of practice, checking this box is always a good idea. If you check this box, you can restrict all editing features while permitting users with screen reading devices the ability to read your files. If the check box is not enabled, screen readers and other devices designed for accessibility are not able to read the PDF document and all the options for using the View ➪ Read Out Loud menu command are grayed out. Furthermore, users can index your files with Acrobat Pro by using Acrobat Catalog when this check box is enabled, regardless of the other items you prevent users from accessing.

CROSS-REF For more information on screen readers and accessibility, see Chapter 25. For more information on creating index files, see Chapter 6.

After you make choices for the password permissions, click OK, click OK again in the Document Properties dialog box, and then save your file to apply the security. If you close the document without saving, the security settings are not applied.

Understanding Password Encryption

When you encrypt a file with password security, it's important to understand that tools exist that can decrypt files. Just about anything that can be encrypted using a password can be broken given enough time with the right tools. Software applications used for decryption run through cycles combining different characters to arrive at the right combination that accesses the encrypted file.

If you use a three-character password, the amount of time to break your password by a sophisticated decryption tool might be a matter of a few hours. As you add characters to the password, the decryption tool requires more time to explore all combinations of characters. If you add 10 to 12 characters to a password, the most sophisticated tools on the fastest computers can take decades of constant running to come up with the right combination of characters to break a password.

As a matter of practice when assigning permissions for sensitive material, always use no fewer than eight characters to secure a file. Adobe Systems has provided a sophisticated tool that enables you to protect your content if you observe a few simple rules.

In Acrobat versions prior to 9.0, only roman characters were permitted for passwords. Languages such as Middle Eastern, Hebrew, and Asian character sets were left out. When using the new Acrobat 9 encryption codes, you find full Unicode support and can encrypt PDF files using a number of non-Roman character sets.

Using a security policy

Security policies are settings you save that are later used when securing documents — similar to creating style sheets in word processors or layout programs. The three different options for creating a security policy are as follows:

- **Use passwords.** This option is the same as applying a password to a document via the Document Properties Security pane. The difference between applying password security in the Password Security – Settings dialog box shown in Figure 26.1 and adding a security policy is that the latter is more efficient when you're applying the same security settings repeatedly to multiple documents. If you use the Password Security – Settings dialog box you need to set options each time you secure a document by selecting check boxes and making choices from pull-down menus. When you use a security policy, the options you choose are captured and saved as part of the policy; you just use the policy each time you want to encrypt documents with the same settings.

- **Use public key certificates.** Use this option to share files with users who have a public certificate. These certificates include ones you've added to your Trusted Identities list, or by searching online certificate directories you have access to. You can create a policy that applies different permissions to different users. Using this policy ensures that every document is encrypted with the same settings for the recipients.

- **Use Adobe LiveCycle Rights Management.** If you have access to an Adobe LiveCycle Rights Management Server, you can create a security policy that is enforced by connecting to the Adobe LiveCycle Rights Management Server. PDF documents and attachments can be secured for a selected group of users or for a period of time you determine when creating the policy. When a policy changes or expires on the server, the documents tied to the policy respect these changes as well.

To make the process of creating a security policy a little more clear, try the following steps to create a policy using password security.

STEPS: Creating a password security policy

1. **Open the Managing Security Policies Wizard.** You open the Managing Security Policy Wizard by selecting Manage Security Policies from the Secure Task Button pull-down menu. You can access the wizard with or without a file open in the Document pane.

2. **Create a new policy.** In the Managing Security Policies Wizard, click the New button to open the New Security Policy Wizard pane, as shown in Figure 26.2. You have three options from which to choose. The default is Use passwords as shown in Figure 26.2. Leave the default settings as is and click Next. The Use the Adobe LiveCycle Rights Management Server is grayed out if you don't have access to an Adobe LiveCycle Rights Management Server or you have not subscribed to the hosted Protect PDF service from Adobe Systems.

3. **Add a name and description for the new policy.** Type a policy name and description in the respective field boxes in the General Settings panel of the New Security Policy Wizard as shown in Figure 26.3. Select the box for Save passwords with the policy. The name and description you add in the second pane appears when you access the Managing Security Policies dialog box. Try to add information in the field boxes that describes the settings you use when creating the policy.

 If you want to periodically change passwords, leave the check box unchecked. Each time you use the policy, Acrobat prompts you for a new password.

FIGURE 26.2

Click New in the Managing Security Policies Wizard to open the New Security Policy dialog box.

FIGURE 26.3

Name the policy and add a text description.

4. **Add the security settings.** Click Next. You arrive at the Document restrictions panel of the New Security Policy dialog box. This is the same dialog box you see in the Password Security – Settings dialog box shown earlier in Figure 26.1. Here you set the attributes for the security to be applied when using the policy. In my example, I selected Acrobat 7 compatibility; checked the box for "Restrict editing and printing of the document. A password will be required in order to change these permission settings"; added a password; selected None from the Print allowed pull-down menu; and checked the last check box in the dialog box.

5. **Review the policy.** Click Next. The last pane (Summary) appears with a Finish button as shown in Figure 26.4. Click Finish to create the policy. You are returned to the Managing Security Policies dialog box where your new policy is listed in the policy list window, as shown in Figure 26.5. Notice that the name and description you added when creating the policy now appear in the Name and Description headings. Additionally you see a description of the policy details and encryption components for the policy you created. If creating multiple policies, select a policy name in the top window to change the policy details and encryption components in the lower half of the dialog box to reflect attributes for the selected policy. Click the Finish button to save the policy.

6. **Secure a document.** By default the Managing Security Policies dialog box opens as shown in Figure 26.5. Your new policy is listed in this dialog box. If you have a document open in the Document pane, you can apply the policy to the open document.

   Select the policy you created and click the Apply to Document button. Acrobat opens a dialog box informing you that you need to save your file after applying the policy to complete the security. Click OK and save the file. Your file is now secure using the permissions you identified for the policy.

FIGURE 26.4

Review the policy in the Summary pane.

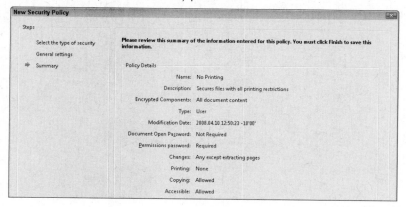

FIGURE 26.5

Select the policy you want to use for securing a document and click the Apply to Document button.

If you work with documents where you need to add different permissions depending on the document content and the users to whom you want to distribute your files, you'll want to add additional policies each designed with different permissions. As you add additional policies, you can choose what policy you want to use to secure a document in one of two areas. Open a document and open the Secure task button. The pull-down menu shows your policy added as a Favorite by default and appearing in the task button pull-down menu. Select the menu command and click Yes when prompted in a dialog box. Save your file to apply the policy to the document.

The second area you find your policy listed is in the Managing Security Policies dialog box shown earlier in Figure 26.5. You open this dialog box by selecting Manage Security Policies from the Secure task button pull-down menu; the Managing Security Policies dialog box opens. Select the policy and click Apply to Document. Click Yes when prompted in a dialog box and save the file.

Managing security policies

You can add several policies using different permissions settings. Each time you create a new policy, it appears in the Managing Security Policies dialog box. Each time you want to secure documents with the same settings, open the Managing Security Policies dialog box and select a policy from the list. Click the Apply to Document button to secure the open document with the settings created from the selected policy.

The Secure task button lists all your Favorites at the top of the pull-down menu. You add or delete Favorites in the Managing Security Policies dialog box. Select Manage Security Policies to open the Managing Security Policies dialog box. In the far left column you see a star icon adjacent to policy names. You also may not see a star icon adjacent to a policy name, as shown in Figure 26.6.

FIGURE 26.6

Select a policy and click the Favorite button. The policy is then listed in the Secure task button pull-down menu.

To make a policy a Favorite, select a policy where you see no star icon and click the Favorite button. When you add a Favorite the policy is added to the Secure task button pull-down menu. If you want to remove a Favorite from the menu, open the Managing Security Policies dialog box and select the policy you want to remove. If it's already a Favorite, the policy appears listed with a star icon adjacent to the policy name. Click the Favorite button to remove the policy from the Favorites list in the Secure task button pull-down menu.

Copying and editing policies

If you want to create a policy that's based on an existing policy, you can copy the policy in the Managing Security Policies dialog box and modify the policy attributes. Assume for a moment you want to add password protection to open a file and use all the same attributes of an existing policy that doesn't restrict the permissions to prompt for a password when a file is opened.

Select the policy you want to duplicate and click the Copy button. Acrobat opens the Creating a New Security Policy from an Existing Security Policy Wizard. This wizard offers the same options as shown earlier in the New Security Policy Wizard (see Figure 26.2 earlier in this chapter) for the General Settings, Document Restrictions, and Summary. In the General Settings pane, type a new name for the new policy and type a description. Click Next and set the permissions for the policy. Click Next to open the Summary pane. Review the permissions and click Finish. Your new policy is added to the Managing Security Policies dialog box.

Select a policy and click the Edit button to get the same wizard options as when copying files. You can modify a policy name and description and edit the permissions for an existing policy.

Viewing and deleting policies

Select a policy and click the View button. The Viewing a Security Policy Wizard opens where you can review settings for a given policy. In this wizard you can't make any changes to the policy. If you need to change settings, use the Edit button.

Select a policy and click the Delete button. Acrobat prompts you in a warning dialog box to confirm the action. Click Yes to delete the policy. Click No and the policy remains without changes.

Understanding Digital IDs

A digital ID is a file that you create in Acrobat or acquire from a third-party signature provider. Your ID, also known as a *credential* or *profile or certificate*, is password protected and used to electronically sign or certify documents. Before you can digitally sign a document you need to create or acquire your own personal ID.

Digital IDs have two components important to understand — your personal or private digital ID and your public certificate. When you create a digital ID with Acrobat you are creating your private ID and your public certificate. The public certificate is a file you share with other users so they can encrypt files that they send to you. In order to open such encrypted files you need to supply the password used when you created your personal profile.

As a matter of understanding the security involved when using digital signatures, realize that, every time you want to sign a document you need to supply your password. Therefore, anyone having access to your computer cannot sign or certify a document on your behalf unless the user has your password. When a file is encrypted using your public certificate, the file is opened only when you have the digital ID and supply your password. Again, anyone having access to your computer cannot open a document encrypted with your public certificate unless that user has access to your password. Private digital signature IDs are used to sign and decrypt documents. Public certificates are used to encrypt documents and validate signatures.

As mentioned earlier, each digital ID has two components — the private ID and the public certificate. The private ID can be used to either digitally sign a PDF or to decrypt documents encrypted with the public certificate, and conversely, the public certificate can be used to encrypt documents or to validate digital signatures.

Digital IDs can be created in Acrobat or acquired from other parties. They can then be accessed locally from your computer or from a remote server. For a quick look at the options available when working with digital IDs and public certificates, select Advanced ⇨ Security Settings to open the Security Settings dialog box shown in Figure 26.7. This dialog box is used to manage and create digital IDs. You also use this dialog box to configure servers, time stamp digital IDs, and use the Adobe LiveCycle Rights Management Servers.

Choose Advanced ➪ Security Settings to open the Security Settings dialog box as shown in Figure 26.7. Here you choose from an option listed in the left pane of the wizard.

As shown in the dialog box, the options you have for working with digital IDs and configuring server access include the following:

- **Digital IDs.** There are three types of IDs available that include:

  - **A file.** Available on Windows and Macintosh, this form of ID is similar to what you had available in earlier versions of Acrobat when using Acrobat Certificate Security. You can select Add ID (which opens the Add Digital ID dialog box to find an existing digital ID, create a new Acrobat Self-Sign, or get a third-party certificate).

  - **A roaming ID stored on a server.** This option permits you to host your ID on a Web site server. You can access your ID anywhere in the world by logging on to the server that contains your roaming ID and digitally sign documents using any one of your IDs available on the server. Roaming ID accounts are available to both Windows and Macintosh users.

  - **A device connected to this computer.** Use this option if you have a hardware device such as a token connected to your computer.

  - **A new digital ID I want to create now.** You use this option when you want to create your own personal ID that will be stored on your computer.

FIGURE 26.7

In the Security Settings dialog box you have four options for managing digital IDs and servers.

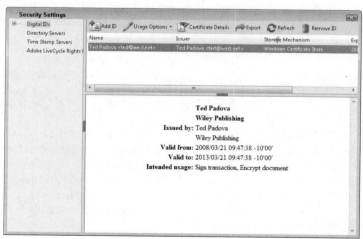

- **Directory servers.** This option is used to enable you to locate specific digital ID certificates from network servers for encrypting documents using Certificate Security. Directory servers can be added by importing a configuration supplied by a System Administrator, or by entering the parameters required to configure the server.

- Time Stamp Servers. This option is used if you need the additional security and authentication features of a time stamp as part of your signature. As with Directory Servers, Time Stamp Servers are added by importing a configuration from a system administrator or by adding parameters required to configure the server.

- **Adobe LiveCycle Rights Management Servers.** Adobe LiveCycle Rights Management Server (`www.adobe.com/products/server/policy/main.html`) is a server–based security solution from Adobe Systems that provides dynamic control over PDF documents. Policies created with Acrobat or Adobe LiveCycle Rights Management Server are stored on the server and can be refreshed from the server. Once you've configured an Adobe Rights Management Server, all polices maintained on this server are available to you. You must log into Adobe LiveCycle Rights Management Server to use these policies. This option also requires that you access a URL provided by a System Administrator and add the server to your list of Adobe LiveCycle Rights Management Servers.

Creating a personal digital ID

Digital IDs can be created with or without custom appearance settings. The appearance of your signature has no effect on the kind of security you add to a signature. If you want to create a custom signature appearance such as a scanned analog signature, it's usually best to first create the appearance, and then create the digital ID.

Using Third-Party Signature Handlers

Digital signature handlers, tokens, biometrics, hardware solutions, and other similar products are available from third-party providers and offer you many different options for securing PDF documents depending on the product and manufacturer. To find information on acquiring third-party products for signature handling, take a look at Adobe's Web site at `http://partners.adobe.com/security`. On the Adobe Security Partner Web pages you find links to digital signature and document control vendors worldwide.

If you use Acrobat for languages other than US English, go to your local Web page and log on to Adobe's Web site. You might use, for example, a URL such as `www.adobe.com.fr/security` for a French language document page. This page includes a link to security partners supporting the localized products.

When you create a digital ID in Acrobat by choosing Advanced ➪ Security Settings, the Security Settings dialog box opens. Select Directory Servers and click New. The Edit Directory Server dialog box opens where you identify a third-party server and provide log-on information and password.

Creating a custom appearance

Appearances for your digital IDs in Acrobat viewers earlier than version 9.0 required you to use the Security preferences dialog box. In Acrobat 9, you can create an appearance for a signature on-the-fly when you sign a document and need to create a signature. If you don't sign a document and start from scratch, you need to use the Security Preferences dialog box to add an appearance. What follows here assumes you are creating a new signature and not signing a form.

Open the Preferences dialog box (Ctrl/⌘+K) and click Security in the left pane. The right pane changes as shown in Figure 26.8.

FIGURE 26.8

Click Security in the left pane in the Preferences dialog box to change the right pane changes where you can add a new appearance for a digital ID.

Two preferences dialog boxes are used for creating an appearance and setting some attributes for your signatures. These include:

- **Security Preferences.** You use the Security Preferences to create digital ID appearances for your personal digital IDs. If you want to add a logo, analog signature, symbol, or some text to an ID, you can do so by clicking the New button and choosing from various settings in the Configure Security Appearance dialog box.

- **Advanced Preferences.** If you have an ID configured such as the one shown in Figure 26.8, the ID(s) appears in the Appearance list in the Security Preferences dialog box. Select an ID and click Advanced Preferences to open another dialog box where a number of options exist for verifying signatures, creating them, and, on Windows, options for settings for Windows Integration. A number of different options exist in three tabs (Windows) or two tabs (Macintosh). For a detailed description of each item, consult the Acrobat Help document.

 If you have not created a digital ID yet, you will not see anything listed in this box, but you still can create appearances that can later be used with a digital ID.

To understand how to create a custom appearance for a digital ID, follow these steps:

STEPS: Creating a custom digital ID appearance

1. **Open the Security preferences.** Press Ctrl/⌘+K. Click the Security item in the left pane.

2. **Click the New button in the right pane to open the Configure Signature Appearance dialog box.**

3. **Configure the appearance.** Type a title in the Title text box. This title will appear as the name for your appearance and one you'll select when configuring a digital ID. If you want to use a graphic, click the Imported graphic radio button and click File to open the Select Picture dialog box. Locate and select the graphic you want to use for the appearance. (Note that the file can be any file type supported by the Create PDF From File command.)

   Select the text items you want to display on your signature by checking boxes in the Configure Text area of the Configure Signature Appearance dialog box. In my example, I removed all check boxes, as shown in Figure 26.9.

4. **Click OK in the Configure Signature Appearance dialog box.** The signature is listed by Title in the Security preferences. Click OK in the Preference dialog box to configure your appearance for a signature.

FIGURE 26.9

Type a title in the Title text box, import a graphic, and check the boxes you want to use for text appearances.

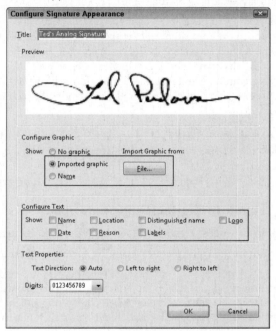

Creating a digital ID

The steps used to create a signature appearance are optional. You don't need to use a custom appearance when creating a digital ID. If you do create a signature appearance, you can use it when creating a new ID.

To understand how digital IDs are created, follow these steps.

STEPS: Creating a digital ID and appearance

1. **Open the Security Settings dialog box.** Click Advanced ➪ Security Settings. The Security Settings wizard, shown earlier in this chapter in Figure 26.7, opens. When the wizard opens, click Digital IDs in the left pane.

2. **Create a Self-Signed digital ID.** Click Add ID in the Security Settings dialog box. The Add Digital ID Wizard opens, as shown in Figure 26.10. Select A new digital ID I want to create now and click Next.

FIGURE 26.10

Click Add ID in the Security Settings dialog box to open the Add Digital ID dialog box.

3. **Select the area in which you want to store your ID.** The next pane has two options for where you can store your digital ID. Select the first radio button (New PKCS#12 digital ID file to create a password-protected ID on either Windows or the Mac. Select the second radio button (Windows Certificate Store) if you want your ID made available to Acrobat and Windows applications. Click Next to arrive at the new pane in the wizard.

4. **Add identity information.** The next pane opens with text boxes for you to supply identity information. If you added identity information in the Identity preferences, the information is transposed to the pane shown in Figure 26.11. If you want to use special characters, non-Roman languages, or non-ASCII, check the box for Enable Unicode Support.

NEW FEATURE Choose a key algorithm from the Key Algorithm pull-down menu. In earlier versions of Acrobat the highest encryption level you had was 128-bit encryption. New in Acrobat 9 you find an option for 256-bit encryption. If you choose 256-bit encryption, you can validate signatures in Acrobat viewers earlier than version 9.0.

5. **Choose where you want to store the ID and type a password.** Click Next in the wizard and click the Browse button to locate a folder where you want to save the ID (for New PKCS#12 digital ID files). Type a password in the Password text box and type the password again in the Confirm Password text box.

6. **Click Finish.** Click Finish in the Add Digital ID dialog box to return to the Security Settings dialog box. Your new digital ID is now ready to use.

Notice as yet, we have not selected an appearance for the digital ID. You can store multiple appearances in the Security preferences and each time you sign a document, you can choose which appearance you want to use for your signature. You might, for example, sign documents internally in your company using one appearance, and with the same ID sign documents coming from other sources outside your company with another appearance.

FIGURE 26.11

Add identity information if all fields are not completed in your Identity preferences.

Managing multiple IDs

If you create several IDs used for different purposes, you may have a need to remove old IDs and add new IDs. In the Security Settings you have options for assigning attributes to your IDs, adding new IDs, and removing IDs. Choose Advanced ⇨ Security Settings to open the wizard shown earlier in this chapter in Figure 26.7.

Click an ID in the Name column to select it and click the Remove ID button to delete an ID. You also have options in the Security Settings dialog box for Exporting Certificates, selecting Usage Options, and viewing certificate details.

Setting usage options

You can create several digital IDs and assign different usage options for each ID. After adding IDs to the Security Settings dialog box, select an ID and open the Usage Options pull-down menu. From the commands shown in Figure 26.12, you have a number of different usage options. Click one of the options shown to assign that option to the selected ID. Click another ID and assign another option. You can assign only one option to an ID. If an option is used with one ID and you apply that option to another ID, the option is removed from the first ID and assigned to your new selection. After assigning options, you'll notice the appearance of the options icons adjacent to the ID names.

FIGURE 26.12

Click an ID in the Security Settings dialog box and select a usage option.

Using signature fields

To sign a document containing a signature field, click the field with the Hand tool. The Sign Document dialog box opens, as shown in Figure 26.13. Choose an ID from the Digital ID pull-down menu. Type your password in the Password text box and select an appearance from the Appearance pull-down menu.

When you click Sign you are prompted to save your file. Locate the folder where you want to save the file and click Save. The document is signed using the Usage Options assigned to the signature.

FIGURE 26.13

Select an ID to sign a document from the Digital ID list, type the password for the ID, and choose an appearance setting.

Creating a signature field when signing a document

If no signature field appears on a document, you can sign a document by accessing Sign Document from the Sign task button pull-down menu. This method of signing prompts you to marquee an area on a page where you want to create a signature field on the document. Click OK in the dialog box informing you what to do and draw a rectangle. When you release the mouse button, the Sign Document dialog box opens. Follow the same steps outlined in the next section.

Certifying a document

You have two choices for certifying a document with a digital ID. You can choose to certify a file with or without a visible signature. From the Sign pull-down menu, select Certify with Visible Signature to have your signature shown on the document. Choose Certify without Visible Signature to add an invisible signature to the file. Using either option opens the Save as Certified Document dialog box shown in Figure 26.14.

FIGURE 26.14

Using either menu command in the Sign task button pull-down menu for certifying documents opens the Save as Certified Document dialog box.

You have choices for acquiring a digital ID you have set up with an Adobe partner, or click OK to open the Sign Document dialog box where you apply a signature using the same criteria as when signing with and without signature fields.

A second option exists in the File menu. Select File ➪ Save As Certified Document. The same dialog box opens prompting you to select an ID from an Adobe partner or click OK to open the Sign Document dialog box.

Working with PDF Portfolios

If you have multiple documents and you combine the files into a PDF Portfolio, all signatures on the documents that are added to the portfolio are retained. Furthermore, you can add signatures to PDFs after a PDF Portfolio has been assembled. In addition, you can secure individual documents before or after adding them to a PDF Portfolio. IN addition you can also sign and/or secure the portfolio.

Using signatures in PDF Portfolios

You might have a series of drawings that need to be signed by different engineers that is used for signing off on PDF documents within a Portfolio. The portfolio may be comprised of several drawings or a series of forms in a portfolio with multiple signatures.

In Figure 26.15, a PDF Portfolio is shown with four PDF documents containing signatures. In this example all documents were signed before the files were assembled in a PDF Portfolio.

CROSS-REF For more information on creating PDF Portfolios, see Chapter 12.

FIGURE 26.15

A document open in a PDF Portfolio containing multiple signatures

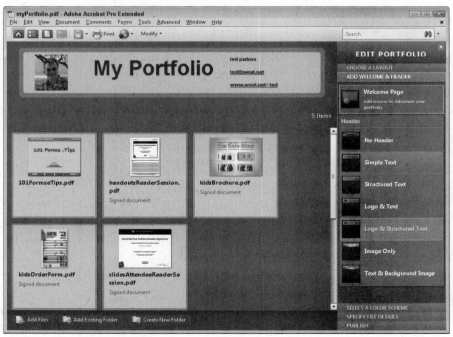

If a document in the portfolio is deleted or an edit is made to any one of the PDFs within the portfolio, signatures remain valid for the PDFs that remain unedited. Each individual signed page in the file remains with a valid signature (see Figure 26.16) and the only signature that is invalidated is the signature-edited pages.

After you assemble a PDF Portfolio you can use the Advanced ➪ Sign & Certify ➪ Sign Document command to add digital signatures to a document within a portfolio. You don't have access to the Form Edit mode while viewing a PDF Portfolio, but using this command enables you to add a signature field to any page on any file in a portfolio.

CROSS-REF For more information about adding digital signature fields to a document, see Chapter 34.

TIP If you want to use the Digital Signature tool or any form tool in a PDF Portfolio, you can load form tools using a keyboard shortcut. Press the F key on your keyboard and press Shift+F to toggle all the form tools. When you arrive at the right form tool, click to add the field to a PDF Portfolio document.

FIGURE 26.16

Editing any file within a PDF Portfolio or deleting a file from the portfolio does not disturb signatures on other files in the portfolio.

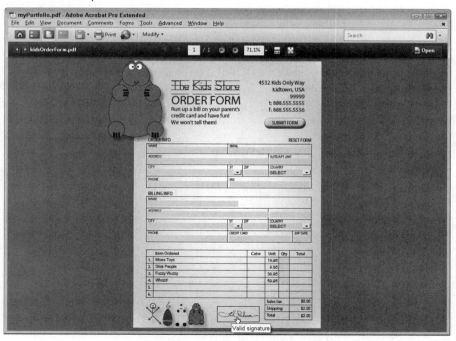

Adding security to PDF Portfolios

You can add security to individual files before assembling a PDF Portfolio. Acrobat permits you to add PDF documents to a PDF Portfolio without having to decrypt files. However, the viewer of the portfolio needs to decrypt files that have been password protected in order to see and/or edit the PDF content.

You can also secure an entire PDF Portfolio. Acrobat provides two ways to add security to PDF Portfolios. You can choose File ➪ Portfolio Properties and click the Security tab in the Document Properties dialog box. Security is added the same as I explained in the section "Using password security" earlier in this chapter.

Another method you can use to add password security to PDF Portfolios is the Modify ➪ Secure Portfolio menu command as shown in Figure 26.17. Select the command to open the Password Security – Settings dialog box as shown earlier in this chapter in Figure 26.1.

You can also add security policies to PDF Portfolios. Open the Advanced menu while viewing a portfolio and choose Security. At the top of the Security submenu you'll find a list of your Favorites for the security policies you added to the Favorites list. Choose a Favorite to apply the policy to the portfolio.

FIGURE 26.17

PDF Portfolios can be secured using the Modify ➪ Secure Portfolio command.

Using Trusted Identities and Certificate Security

Trusted identities are added to the Trusted Identities Manager dialog box. The list of trusted identities is like an address book where you can add contacts and set certificate properties. You can maintain a contact list of trusted identities from people you do business with or may do business with. Each user listed in Trusted Identities can be used to validate digital signatures and encrypt PDF documents for these users. The Trusted Identities Manager additionally permits you to set levels of trust from the users listed in your contact list.

Understanding Encryption, Validation, and the Trusted Identities Manager

In the Manage Trusted Identities dialog box (shown in Figure 26.19), a pull-down menu provides two choices: Contacts and Certificates. Items listed in the menus do not have to match. You can have certificates in the list that are not in the Contacts list. From the Display pull-down menu you can select either Contacts or Certificates and you can Add Contacts or Certificates respective to the menu item you select.

In order to encrypt documents you do *not* have to have a public certificate in your trusted identities. For example, a company may have a corporate-level security solution in which each employee is issued a certificate that is stored on a network server. You can search certificates on your company's LDAP (Lightweight Directory Access Protocol) server to find someone you want to encrypt for and just use their certificate without adding the certificate to your list of trusted identities.

To validate a signature, you do not have to have the public certificate in your trusted identities if you've already established a trust with a parent in the chain of trust. For example, you can create a Class 1 certificate for a security partner. So the chain might be Your Company, Inc. ⇨ Partner Class 1 ⇨ Your Name.

You can then *trust* Your Company, Inc. (the root) and therefore everybody under that chain is automatically trusted by you so you don't need any individual's certificate in your local trusted Identities for validation. However, if you want to give any user a different trust setting than the trust settings used by the parent, then you do need to add the individual's certificate to your trusted identities.

Does an individual need to send you a public certificate? The answer is no, not if the user sends you a file signed with his/her certificate. You can always get the public certificate from a file sent to you.

To acquire a public certificate from a signed document, open a context menu on the signature and select Properties. In the Signature Properties dialog box, click the Show Certificate button. The Certificate Viewer dialog box opens. Click the Export button; you are prompted to save the certificate as a file or email the certificate.

The entire range of possibilities regarding using digital IDs, signing documents, and authenticating signed or certified documents is a very complex subject. In an effort to break it down to a more simplified view, the detail in this chapter assumes you are working in an environment where you are not using a corporate-wide security solution and you're using the self-sign methods of security. If you want the highest levels of security and the most efficient means for securing documents, I encourage you to carefully review the Acrobat Help document and explore all the security information on Web pages hosted by Adobe Systems.

Using certificate encryption

Encryption using certificates is a means for you to add security for a selected group of users. The advantage of using certificates is you can control the permissions settings individually for each user in the same PDF document. In addition, since the user needs not only a password but the digital ID file, it becomes impossible for someone else to "crack." For example, you may want to allow one user to view your document, but restrict printing. For another user you may want to disallow editing, but enable printing. For a third user you may want to allow editing and printing. All these permissions can be set for each user in the same PDF document using the Certificate Security Settings dialog box.

To encrypt a file using certificates, you need access to the public certificate. You can either search for the public certificates, which may be located on a network server, or you can collect the public certificates for each user and load them into your Trusted Identities list. Keep in mind, the Trusted Identities Manager is like an address book and merely is a convenient location where you can store contact and certificate information for users you frequently work with. During encryption you can specify permissions settings individually for each user.

Exporting public certificates

Public certificates are used for validating signatures on documents received and encrypting files which you plan to share. For another user to validate your signature or encrypt a file unique to your profile, you need to export your public certificate and share it with other users. Your public certificate does not compromise your password settings or ability to secure your own files. Public certificates are generated from your profile, but do not send along your password to other users.

NOTE Companies using directory servers to host public certificates do not need to export certificates. For self-sign security you also don't need to acquire a certificate from another user. A user can sign a document and you can open the signature Properties dialog box and click the Export button to gain access to the certificate. The only thing you need to be concerned about is that the first signed file you receive from a given recipient has an authentic signature from the user you know has signed the document. If you trust the file, export the certificate. You can use that certificate for all subsequent documents from the user in question.

To export a public certificate you need to start with a digital ID you have already created. Choose Advanced ⇨ Security Settings. The Security Settings dialog box shown earlier in Figure 26.7 opens. If you have more than one ID listed in the dialog box, select the ID you want to use and click the Export button. The Data Exchange File – Export Options dialog box opens, as shown in Figure 26.18.

FIGURE 26.18

When exporting your certificate, you can choose to save the public certificate as a file or email the certificate to another user.

In this dialog box you make a choice for saving your public certificate to disk or emailing the certificate directly to another user. If you select Save the data to a file, you can later attach it to an email message and send it to users as needed. If you select the Email the data to someone radio button and click the Next button, the Compose Email dialog box opens where you add the recipient's email address. Enter an email address and click the Email button to attach the data file to a new email message. Acrobat supplies a default message in the email note for you providing instructions for the recipient, but you can edit if desired.

Requesting contacts

If you want to add a contact and/or certificate to your list of trusted identities, select Advanced ⇨ Manage Trusted Identities to open the Trusted Identities dialog box. Click the Request Contact button to open the Email a Request dialog box. You add your name, email address, and any contact information you want to supply in the text boxes in the Email a Request dialog box. Click the Next button to open the Compose Email dialog box. In this dialog box, you add the recipient email address. A default subject and message appear in the Compose Email dialog box informing the recipient you are requesting a copy of the individual's certificate. Click the Email button to email the request to the recipient. Note that you may need to open your default email program and click the Send or Send/Receive button to initiate a send.

When a copy of a certificate is emailed back to you, the file appears in a message window as a file attachment. Double-click the attachment to add the certificate is automatically to your list of trusted identities after you approve adding the ID or click OK.

Managing trusted identities

After you collect public certificates, you can load the certificates into your Trusted Identities list for easy management and quick access of the certificates. To load certificates, choose Advanced ⇨ Manage Trusted Identities. The dialog box shown in Figure 26.19 opens.

Emailing Certificates vs. Exporting from Signatures

Since a user who receives a signed document from you can open the signature Properties and acquire your signature by showing the certificate and clicking an Export button, you may feel that exporting a certificate and emailing your public certificate to a user is an unnecessary step. In some cases it is unnecessary.

Where you have an advantage for exporting a certificate and emailing to others is simply adding another level of security to your workflow. If a signed document is sent to a user, the user may not be certain that the document came from you. If you sign a document, send it to a user, then email your exported certificate to the same user in a separate email, the recipient receives two mails. This workflow simply adds one more level of assurance that the certificate came from you.

FIGURE 26.19

You use the Manage Trusted Identities dialog box to add identities from public certificates you collect from other users.

To add a recipient, click the Add Contacts button. The Choose Contacts to Import dialog box shown in Figure 26.20 opens where you can browse your hard drive or network server to locate certificates from other users. When adding identities collected by other users, click the Browse button. The Locate Certificate File dialog box opens where you navigate your hard drive and locate certificates to add to a recipient list. Click Open; the recipient's name appears in the top window of the Choose Contacts to Import dialog box. Select the name of the added contact and click the Import button to add the certificate to the identities list. You use the Search button to search through network servers configured in your Directory Servers.

Add the certificate and return to the Manage Trusted Identities dialog box and continue adding new certificates to your list of recipients.

FIGURE 26.20

Use the Choose Contacts to Import dialog box to add new recipient identities.

Setting certificate security permissions

One thing to keep in mind is that when you have circumstances that require you to repeat document security for the same set of users or when encrypting documents with the same set of permissions, you'll always want to set up a security policy. In those instances where you intend to secure a document using certificates one time only, you can set permissions without creating a policy. To help simplify the process, this section refers to setting up permissions using certificates for a one-time use.

To secure a document using Certificate Security, open the Document Properties dialog box (File ➪ Properties). Click the Security tab and select Certificate Security from the Security Method pull-down menu. The Certificate Security Settings Wizard opens. The General settings panel offers you the choice to save your settings as a policy or discard the settings after applying the security. In addition you have options for what you want to encrypt, such as the document only or the document and file attachments and the type of encryption you want to apply. In Figure 26.21, you can see the options in the General settings pane. Make a choice for saving your settings as a policy or discarding the settings after applying them. If you choose to create a policy, add a name and description. At the bottom of the General pane, make a choice for the type of encryption you want to apply and click Next.

FIGURE 26.21

Select Certificate Security from the Security Method pull-down menu in the Security tab from the Document Properties dialog box to open the Certificate Security Settings dialog box.

NOTE When working with PDF Portfolios, open the File menu and choose Portfolio Properties. You can use Certificate Security and apply the security settings to the entire portfolio.

The Select Recipients pane opens, as shown in Figure 26.22. Click Browse and locate the file(s) you want to add. You can add only one file at a time. Keep clicking Browse and add all the files you want to use for this particular Certificate Security. In Figure 26.23, I added three recipients to my list.

Select a recipient in the list and click the Permissions button. The Permissions Settings dialog box opens where you choose individual permissions for a selected recipient, as shown in Figure 26.23. Set permissions for the selected user and click OK. Select another recipient and set permissions for that user. Continue setting permissions for each user.

FIGURE 26.22

Several certificates are added to the Select recipients pane in the wizard.

FIGURE 26.23

Select the permissions you want to assign to the selected user and click OK.

The great strength for using Certificate Security is that all the recipients in your list can be assigned unique permissions. For example, you can prohibit printing for one user, and allow low-resolution printing for another user and high-resolution printing for a third user. In addition, you can protect against a number of different editing options. All of these permissions settings are applied to individual recipients in the same PDF document or PDF Portfolio. Each user needs to open the file using his or her own digital ID and password.

To complete the Certificate Security, click the Next button to open the Summary panel. A summary for your policy is listed in the panel. If you want to make any changes, click the Back button. To accept the settings you made, click Finish. Save the file and all the permissions assignments to your recipients are encrypted in the document.

Validating Signatures

Digital signatures would be of no value unless you could confirm that a document was signed by the individual claiming to have signed the document. For confirmation purposes you use menu commands and options to validate signatures. You have several options when validating signatures, and all depend on different circumstances, which include:

- If you have established trust with a parent, you don't need the certificate listed in your trusted identities. See the "Understanding Encryption, Validation, and the Trusted Identities Manager" sidebar earlier in this chapter. When you open a signed PDF from another person using a third-party security partner certificate, the signature appears as Unknown. Select Properties from a context menu you open on the signature. In the Signature Properties dialog box, click Verify Signature. The signature appears valid without adding to your trusted identities. If you want to change the level of trust, you can add the certificate to your trusted identities and set the trust in the Manage Trusted Identities dialog box. See the "Managing trusted identities" section earlier in this chapter.

- If you open a self-signed document and the user hasn't used a third-party security partner, and you know the document has been sent to you by the PDF author, you can retrieve the certificate from the document without needing the individual to send you the certificate. You might receive files from members of your workgroup where you are confident the document you receive comes from the individual who signed it. In this case, you can open the Signature panel, select the Signature, and select Validate Signature. Another Signature Validation dialog box opens. Click Signature Properties in this dialog box to open the Signature Properties dialog box. Open the Trust tab in the Signature Properties and click the Add to Trusted Identities button. The certificate is added to your trusted identities where you can set the level of trust and use the certificate to validate signatures.

■ If you open a document from an anonymous user or one where you question the document authenticity, you can request a certificate. You add the certificate you receive from a PDF author to your trusted identities, and you can choose to set the level of trust following the same steps outlined in the section "Managing trusted identities" earlier in this chapter.

To validate a signature, open the Security panel and choose Validate Signature. Choose Validate All Signatures from the same menu if you want to validate all signatures in a document where multiple signatures exist.

When you open a signed document and view signatures in the Signatures panel, an icon with a question mark may appear adjacent to the signature(s). In addition, you'll notice the text below the signature icon often states that the signature validity is unknown; or for valid signatures, the text reads: Signature is valid. You'll also find the validity of a signature reported in the Signature Message Bar as shown in Figure 26.24.

NOTE   Contained in the Security Preferences (Ctrl/⌘+K and click Security in the left pane) is a check box for Verify signatures when the document is opened. If the check box is enabled, the signatures in the document are validated when the document opens. In this case, you do not need to manually access a menu command to validate a signature. Acrobat 9 automatically validates signatures when a document is opened. You do, however, still need to have a trusted certificate from the individual who signed the document in order to validate upon opening the file. If using an external certificate authority, you need to have an active Internet connection to your service to verify signatures. If this box is unchecked, you must manually validate your signatures. Be aware that if your document has more than 10 pages, Acrobat may not validate signatures automatically upon opening the document. This behavior prevents a document from slowing down during open time. If you find documents not certifying signatures at open time, manually review the signatures in the Signatures panel and use the Validate Signature command in the Options pull-down menu.

When you validate a signature, Acrobat opens a dialog box reporting the validation status. If the public certificate is loaded and the validation is true, a dialog box opens reporting the certificate is valid.

If you get UNKNOWN, this certificate is not in your trusted identities. Select the Signature Properties menu command in the Signature panel Options menu or a context menu opened on a signature in the Signatures panel. From the Summary tab select Show Certificate. From the Trust tab, select your Trust Settings and select Add to Trusted Identities. The Import Contact Settings appear when you determine which Trust Settings you want. Select OK in the Certificate Viewer window. You are returned to Signature Properties. Select Validate Signature. This signature will now be Valid. Select Close to return to the Document pane.

You can view the signature properties in the Signature Properties dialog box, which reports all the properties of the certificate including the reason for signing, the email address of the person signing the document, and the certificate fingerprint. The Signatures panel reflects a valid signature, as shown in Figure 26.24.

FIGURE 26.24

After a signature is validated, the icon adjacent to the signature name changes to a pen and check mark, and the status is reported as valid.

Creating a Security Envelope

Another security option you have in Acrobat is creating a secure envelope adding any file you want to use as a file attachment. You can create eEnvelopes containing file attachments and secure the PDF and file attachment(s) against unauthorized access. Users of Acrobat or the free Adobe Reader software with access rights can open the PDFs and extract the file attachment(s).

To understand how files are attached in a Secure PDF Delivery workflow, follow these steps.

STEPS: Creating a secure eEnvelope

1. **Open the Create Security Envelope dialog box.** Open the Secure task button pull-down menu and select Create Security Envelope. Note that you do not need to have a document open in Acrobat to access this menu command.

2. **Choose files to include.** The Files to Enclose panel in the Create Security Envelope Wizard opens as shown in Figure 26.25. Click the Add File to Send button to open the Files to Enclose dialog box. Navigate your hard drive, select the file you want to include, and click Open. Note that any file of any type can be added to the security envelope. In my example, I use a Microsoft Word document.

FIGURE 26.25

Click Add File to Send and locate the file to add to your eEnvelope.

3. **Select a template.** Click Next to open the Envelope Template panel. You can select from preinstalled templates or click the Browse button to locate a PDF file you want to use for your template. Select a preinstalled template from the list shown in Figure 26.26 and click Next.

NOTE You have templates available for date stamping the envelope and signing the envelope. Choose from template2.pdf to date stamp an envelope and choose template3.pdf to open a template with a digital signature field. All templates have field boxes where you can add addressee information.

4. **Choose a delivery method.** The next panel that opens is the Delivery Method panel. You have two choices for delivering your eEnvelope. Choose from options for sending the envelope later or emailing it now from the two radio button options. Select Send the envelope now and click the Next button.

5. **Choose a security policy to apply.** The Security Policy pane opens, as shown in Figure 26.27. Click the Show all policies check box and select a policy in the list and click Next.

FIGURE 26.26

Select a template and click Next.

FIGURE 26.27

Select a security policy and click Next.

6. **Finish.** The last pane shows the directory path for the selected file. Review the summary and click Next. Click OK to attach the Security Envelope with the file attachment to a new email message, as shown in Figure 26.28. Edit the message text if you so choose and add a recipient to the To field. Click Send and your security envelope is on its way.

FIGURE 26.28

Click Finish and the security envelope is attached to a new email message.

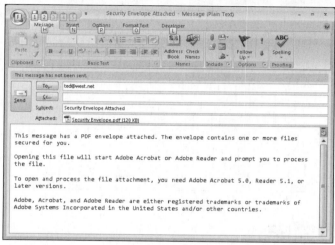

Summary

- PDF documents can be secured with built-in Acrobat Self-Signed Security and security handlers acquired from third-party developers. Files can be secured from users opening documents, editing documents, or both.

- Different levels of security can prevent users of Acrobat viewers earlier than version 6 from opening files. It is important to know your user audience and what version of Acrobat viewers they use before securing files.

- To digitally sign a document you need to create a digital ID. You create and manage digital IDs via several menu commands and menu options found in the Secure Task Button pull-down menu.

- You can apply appearance settings to your signatures in the form of scanned documents, icons, and symbols from files saved as PDF or other file formats compatible with the Create PDF From File command. You add signature appearances via the Security Preferences dialog box.

- You can digitally sign a document by using an existing signature field or by selecting a menu command where you are prompted to create a signature field.

- You can certify a document using your signature by selecting a menu command to certify the document.

- Security and certificate security can be applied to PDF Portfolios.

- Trusted identities are a list of digital ID certificates from people you share information with. You can export your public certificate to a file or attach your public certificate to an email message from within Acrobat. When other users have your public certificate, they can validate your signature or encrypt documents for your use.

- You can encrypt files for a group of users by using their public certificates stored as trusted identities. A single PDF document can be secured for different users and with different permissions for each user.

- In order to validate a signature, the public certificate for that digital ID needs to be loaded into your Trusted Identities list.

- Any file of any type can be added to a secure envelope. The only way for an end user to access the file attachment is to have the password to open the attached file.

Chapter 27

Working with PDFs
and the Web

IN THIS CHAPTER

Viewing Web-hosted PDFs

Working with Web links

Exporting PDFs to HTML

Throughout this book, I address using PDFs on the Web. As I discussed in Chapter 7, you can download selected Web pages or entire Web sites and have all the HTML pages converted to PDF. In Acrobat 6 and greater you can convert media, animation, and sound to PDFs with the animated pages appearing the same in Acrobat viewers as when you see them on Web sites. In Chapter 8 I talked about using the PDFMaker with Microsoft Internet Explorer and Microsoft Outlook.

In Chapter 20, I discussed comments and, in Chapter 21, I covered online reviews. Coming ahead in Chapter 30, I talk about eBooks and downloading books as Digital Editions. In Chapter 34, I talk about submitting form data. And in other chapters, you find similar discussions on Acrobat PDFs hosted online. In short, the Web plays a major role with much of your Acrobat activity. In this chapter, I cover more about using PDFs online for viewing in Web browsers and linking to PDF views on Web sites.

Setting Up the Environment

To accomplish the tasks in this chapter, you use other authoring applications and set preferences for Acrobat viewers to accommodate viewing PDFs in Web browsers. When creating links and form fields in PDFs designed for Web viewing, you need to open several toolbars.

Open the More Tools window by opening a context menu on the Acrobat Toolbar window and select More Tools or select Tools ➪ Customize Toolbars. In the More Tools window, check the toolbar check boxes for Advanced Editing Toolbar. When creating form buttons and links, the Properties Bar can be helpful. To open the Properties Bar, open a context menu on the Toolbar Well and select Properties Bar or press Ctrl/⌘+E.

When the toolbars are opened, open a context menu on the Toolbar Well and select Dock All Toolbars. If the space available in the Document pane is too small for comfortable editing, you can collapse toolbars by hiding toolbar labels. Right-click in the Toolbar Well and select Show Button Labels ⇨ No Labels. For clarity in this chapter, I keep the tool labels in view.

When viewing PDFs in Web browsers, you may need additional tools depending on what you do in Acrobat sessions related to viewing PDFs on the Web. As you need additional tools when viewing PDFs in a browser window, you can open toolbars through the same context menu opened from the Toolbar Well in the browser window. Rather than setting up the work environment ahead of time with these additional tools, leave the tools used for viewing PDFs online hidden until you need them during a Web-viewing session.

Viewing PDFs in Web Browsers

You open a PDF in a Web browser just as you open a file to view an HTML document. You specify a URL and filename to view the PDF directly in the browser or click on a Web link from within a PDF document to open a URL where a PDF is hosted. For example, logging on to `www.provider.com/file.pdf` results in the display of the PDF page inside the browser window. This type of viewing is referred to as *inline viewing*, an example of which appears in Figure 27.1.

FIGURE 27.1

Inline viewing of PDFs offers you access to many Acrobat tools, which are available from the Toolbar Well, just as when viewing PDFs in Acrobat.

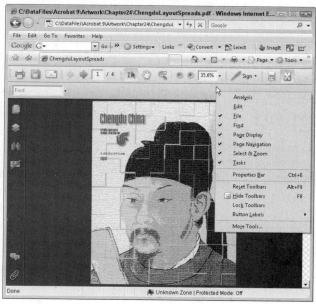

You can also open PDFs on your local hard drive by selecting File ⇨ Open (Windows) or File ⇨ Open File (Macintosh). In the Open dialog box, click Browse (Windows), navigate your hard drive, and select the file you want to open. On the Mac just navigate your hard drive in the Open dialog box and select the file you want to open. Click Open and the file opens in the Web browser window. On the Mac, Safari is supported the same as you have available with Microsoft Internet Explorer, as shown in Figure 27.2.

In Figures 27.1 and 27.2, toolbars are open and docked in the Toolbar Well. You have access to tools, commands, and preference settings while viewing PDFs online or locally from your hard drive directly in a browser window. You open toolbars in Web browsers the same way you open them in Acrobat: open a context menu opened from the Toolbar Well and select More Tools. In the More Tools window, check the boxes for the toolbars you want to appear in the browser window.

By default, all Web-hosted PDFs are opened inside your browser. From the browser application you can save a PDF document to your hard drive by choosing File ⇨ Save As.

FIGURE 27.2

PDF files can be opened locally on your hard drive in a browser application. On the Mac, you find Safari supporting inline PDF views just as Windows does.

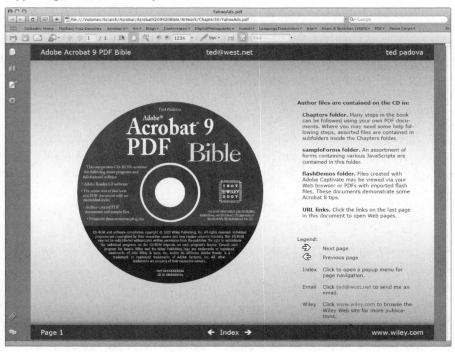

If you prefer to open Web-hosted PDFs in Acrobat, you need to adjust preferences in Acrobat. Preference options provide you choices for viewing PDFs inside your Web browser as an inline view or viewing Web-hosted PDFs inside Acrobat the same as you would view locally hosted PDF documents. To change preferences, choose Edit ➪ Preferences. In the Preferences dialog box, select Internet in the left pane. The viewing preferences appear in the right pane, as shown in Figure 27.3.

FIGURE 27.3

To change Web viewing preferences, open the Preferences dialog box and select Internet in the left pane.

Options for handling PDFs on Web sites with Acrobat viewers include the following:

- **Display PDF in browser.** The check box is enabled by default, and PDFs viewed on Web sites are displayed as inline views in browser applications. If you disable the check box as shown in Figure 27.3, PDFs are displayed in Acrobat viewers. The default Acrobat viewer installed on your computer opens if no viewer is currently open and the target document is shown in the Acrobat viewer Document pane.

- **Allow fast web view.** This option speeds up viewing PDFs on Web servers. When this option is enabled, a single page is downloaded to your computer and shown according to how you set your preferences — in the browser window or in an Acrobat viewer window. As you scroll pages in a PDF document, each new page downloads when the page is loaded in the Document pane. If you deselect the check box, the entire PDF document is downloaded to your computer before the first page appears in the browser window or the Acrobat Document pane. You must save the PDF with Fast Web View and the server must be capable of byte-serving for fast Web view to work.

- **Allow speculative downloading in the background.** If you select the preceding Allow fast web view option, and want to continue downloading multiple page PDF documents, check this box. As you view a page, the remaining pages continue to download until the complete PDF is downloaded from a Web site.

- **Connection Speed.** Select the speed of your Internet connection from the pull-down menu choices. This setting applies to viewing Web pages, but also influences the speed selection for viewing multimedia.

- **Internet Settings.** If you click the Internet Settings button, the Internet Properties dialog box opens. In the Internet Properties dialog box you can make choices for configuring your Internet connection, choosing default applications for email, making security settings choices, setting privacy attributes, and other such system-level configurations.

Working with Web links

Web links to PDFs hosted on Web sites occur from within HTML documents and from within PDF files. If using an HTML editor like Adobe Dreamweaver, or writing HTML code, you create Web links the same as you link to Web pages. A PDF Web link in HTML might look like `http://www.mycompany.com/brochure.pdf` — where the link is made to the PDF instead of a document that ends with an .htm or .html extension.

Web addresses contained in the text of a PDF document can be hot links to URLs where PDFs are hosted. In earlier versions of Acrobat you needed the complete URL address including http:// for a Web link to be recognized. In Acrobat 8 and 9, a URL like `www.adobe.com` is recognized as a Web link. Text in PDF documents with URL addresses can be converted to Web links via a menu command. If you distribute PDF files to users of Acrobat 6 or below, you need to add links to the PDF document for the users of these viewers to access Web pages from a PDF.

To create Web links from text in PDF documents, choose Advanced ➪ Document Processing ➪ Create Links from URLs. Acrobat opens the Create Web Links dialog box shown in Figure 27.4. In the dialog box you make decisions for the pages where the links are created. Select All to create Web links from all pages in the PDF. The From button enables you to supply page ranges in the two field boxes.

FIGURE 27.4

The Create Web Links dialog box enables you to target pages for creating Web links.

CAUTION   Be aware that you don't need to create links in PDF files distributed to Adobe Reader or Acrobat version 7 and above. However, the end user needs to have a preference option enabled in order for an Acrobat viewer to recognize text as a URL. Open the General preferences and look at the check box where you see Create links from URLs. By default the check box is checked. If this check box is not enabled, links aren't recognized from text.

Acrobat can also globally remove Web links from all pages or a specified page range. To remove Web links, choose Advanced ➪ Document Processing ➪ Remove All Links. The same options are available in the Remove Web Links dialog box as those found in the Create Web Links dialog box.

TIP   You can create Web links only from text that has been properly identified in the text of the PDF file (either www.Company.com or http://www.company.com). If you need to add a Web link, you can easily create the text in Acrobat without having to return to the authoring program. Select the TouchUp Text tool from the Advanced Editing toolbar. Hold down the Ctrl key (Option key on Macintosh) and click. The text cursor blinks where you click and is ready for you to add new type on the page. Type the URL for the Web link, deselect the text by selecting the Hand tool, and then click in the Document pane. Choose Advanced ➪ Document Processing ➪ Create Links from URLs. Acrobat creates the Web link from the URL you added to the document.

Web links in the Organizer

The Organizer behaves like a Web browser bookmark repository when you're creating links to URLs. You first view a PDF document as an inline view in your Web browser and access the Organizer tool in the Acrobat Toolbar Well within the browser window. The URL for the current viewed document in the Web browser is captured when you add the URL to a collection. After quitting your Web browser, you can access the URL from within Acrobat and the Organizer collections. Opening a document within a collection launches your Web browser and takes you to the URL where the PDF is located. The PDF is then opened inside the browser window, if your viewing preferences remain at the defaults.

 CROSS-REF   For more information on using the Organizer, see Chapter 5.

Adding Web links to multiple pages

You may have documents that need Web links created across multiple pages. An example might be a document that has been repurposed from an original design that was created for output to prepress, and then later downsampled and hosted on a Web site. In the original design, you might have a Web link on the cover page, but for the Web-hosted document you may want to create a Web link to an order form or your home page on each page in the brochure document. Where the same URL is specified on each page and the location of the Web link is the same on every page, you can create the Web links in Acrobat after the PDF has been sampled for Web display. The following steps outline a procedure for creating Web links on multiple pages for similar designs or legacy files that don't have Web addresses added in the original authoring application document before a PDF has been created:

CROSS-REF For information related to repurposing documents and downsampling, see Chapter 18.

STEPS: Creating Web links on multiple PDF pages

1. **Add a header/footer to a multi-page PDF document.** Open the file where the Web links are to be added and choose Document ➪ Header & Footer ➪ Add. In the Add Header and Footer dialog box, create a header or footer and set the type size, the alignment, the color, and the offset distance desired. In this example, I added a footer (center aligned), used Arial 8-point text, and left offsets at the defaults, as shown in Figure 27.5. (In this example, I used an incomplete URL but I started my URL address with *www*.)

2. **Click OK.**

3. **Save the file.**

4. **Open the Web link.** Move the Hand tool to a Web link and a tooltip reports the full URL address as shown in Figure 27.6. Click the link and the file opens in your Web browser.

FIGURE 27.5

Click on one of the Header or Footer alignment boxes (Left, Center, Right) and add the URL text. Select a font, font size, and offset distance, and then click the OK button.

FIGURE 27.6

When you select the Hand tool and place the cursor over a Web link, the URL appears in a tooltip.

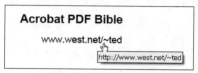

CROSS-REF For more information on creating headers and footers, see Chapter 16.

TIP If you want Web links to appear rotated along the left or right side of your PDF document, choose Document ➪ Rotate Pages. Add a header or footer as described in the preceding steps. Choose Document ➪ Rotate Pages and select the rotation option that turns the pages back to the original view. Save the document, and the Web links are positioned vertically on each page.

Controlling links view behavior

By default, when you click on a URL link to a PDF document, whether from within your Web browser or from within Acrobat, the resulting view takes you to the same view established in your Initial View properties. Therefore, if your Initial View properties are set to Page Only, Single Page, Fit Page, and Page number 1, the PDF document opens in the Web browser according to these settings just as you would view the file in Acrobat.

The links you create to open different documents and different pages in a PDF file are often unusable when you're viewing PDFs in Web browsers. A link, for example, that opens a secondary PDF won't work in a Web browser unless you modify the link properties and link to the URL where the destination document resides. The Web browser needs URL links to open secondary files. Inasmuch as you may have all links working well for CD-ROM distribution, the links need to have some adjustments made before you can host the PDF documents with usable links on Web servers.

As an example, suppose you want to open page 2 in a PDF file on a Web server. You create a link in one document, direct the link to the URL where the PDF is hosted, and instruct the Web browser or Acrobat viewer to open page 2. To create the link, use either the Link tool or a form field button and enter the following code in an Open Web Link action:

```
http://www.west.net/~ted/pdf/manual.pdf#page=2
```

In this example, the #page=2 text following the PDF filename is the trigger to open page 2. In addition to accessing user-specified pages, you can control viewing behavior for page layouts, page views, zooms, linking to destinations, and a host of other attributes you assign to the Open Web Link action. Some examples of the code to use following the PDF document name in URL links include the following:

- **Zoom changes:** #zoom=50, #zoom=125, #zoom=200
- **Fit Page view:** #view=Fit
- **Destinations:** #nameddest=Section1
- **Open Bookmarks palette:** #pagemode=bookmarks
- **Open Pages palette:** #pagemode=thumbs
- **Collapsing palettes:** #pagemode=none
- **Combining viewing options:** #page=3&pagemode=bookmarks&zoom=125

TIP More information related to file links on Web hosted documents can be found on Adobe's Web site. Log on to www.adobe.com/education/pdf and type Web linking in the Search box. A number of different articles discussing Web links in PDFs are reported in the search results. In addition, you can find several articles covering Web links in PDFs on the Acrobat User Community Web site. Log on to www.acrobatusers.com and visit the blogs and articles sections.

The preceding are some examples for controlling view options when opening PDFs in Web browsers. For each item be aware that you need to use the complete URL address and add one of these options following the location where the PDF document is hosted. Using the page mode example, the complete open action URL might look like http://www.mycompany.com/file.pdf#pagemode=bookmarks.

Opening Web links in new browser windows

If you have a PDF file viewed as an inline view in a browser window, you might want a link to a second PDF document that opens in a new browser window. Using the Open a web link action in the Button field properties always opens a Web link in the same browser window. To trigger a link action for opening a second browser window requires a JavaScript.

To set up a link to open a PDF in a second browser window, follow these steps.

Steps: Opening Web links in new browser windows

1. **Create a button link.** Open the Advanced Editing toolbar, click the Button tool, and create a button on a PDF page.
2. **Click Show All Properties in the abbreviated properties window to open the Button Properties dialog box.** Note that you can change the name of the button immediately after clicking the Button tool by typing a name in the Field Name text box.
3. **Click the Actions tab.** If you want to change appearance settings, first click Appearance and set the properties for the Button border and fill colors.
4. **Choose Run a JavaScript from the Select Action pull-down menu.**
5. **Click the Add button to open the JavaScript Editor.**
6. **Type the following code in the JavaScript Editor:**
   ```
   app.launchURL("http://www.company.com/myFile.pdf", true);
   ```
7. **Click OK in the JavaScript Editor and click Close in the Button Properties dialog box.**

The JavaScript in line 6 of the steps above opens a PDF named myFile.pdf hosted at company.com. The *true* flag instructs Acrobat to open the PDF in a second browser window.

CROSS-REF For more information on writing JavaScripts, see Chapter 36 (on the CD-ROM).

Adding URL links to text fields

Suppose you have a form and you want a user to supply a Web address in a field. After the form is completed by a form filler, a reviewer may want to visit the URL to view the Web page. You can copy the text from the field and paste the URL in the Location bar in your Web browser. However, you can simplify the process by adding a Web link to the field so the reviewer of a form just clicks the text field to launch the default Web browser and open the associated URL.

Follow these steps to add a URL Web link to a text field.

Steps: Opening Web links from text fields

1. Create a text field on a form or open a form with a text field.
2. Click the Select Object tool and double-click the text field to open the Text Field Properties dialog box.
3. Click the Actions tab.
4. Choose Run a JavaScript from the Select Action pull-down menu.
5. Click the Add button to open the JavaScript Editor.
6. Type the following code in the JavaScript Editor:

   ```
   if ( !/^\s*$/.test(event.target.value) ) app.launchURL(event.
       target.value);
   ```

7. Click OK in the JavaScript Editor and click Close in the Text Field Properties dialog box.

When the form filler clicks in the field the form field is ready to accept text. After adding text, tabbing out of the field, and clicking again in the field, the JavaScript is executed and the user's default Web browser opens the URL specified in the text field.

CROSS-REF For more information on working with form fields, see Chapter 34.

Converting PDF to HTML

In Chapter 9, I talked about exporting PDFs to a number of different file formats using the Save As command and the File ➪ Export menu command. In that chapter, you find a summary of the attributes for exporting documents from PDF including exports to HTML. In this chapter, I move forward a little and cover exporting to HTML in a little more depth.

At the onset, let me say that Adobe hasn't done much with the exports to HTML features in Acrobat. With the exception of adding an Export task button in Acrobat 8 and the File ⇨ Export menu in Acrobat 9, the options you have for exporting to HTML are identical to the options you had in Acrobat 6 and 7 Standard and Professional.

Using the export to HTML features in Acrobat can get your PDF content into HTML format, but page geometry and formatting is generally lost when you try to get PDF content to HTML. The best you can hope for is exporting text and images that permit you to use the assets in a program like Adobe Dreamweaver where you re-create the Web page using the tools and formatting capabilities of an HTML editor.

Setting export options

You can control option settings in the Preferences dialog box (Ctrl/⌘+K) by clicking on the Convert from PDF item in the left pane. The right pane displays a list of export formats including HTML 3.2 and HTML 4.01 with CSS 1.0 (Cascading Style Sheets). Click the Edit Settings button and you see a list of options you can edit. These same options are also available to you in the Save As dialog box when you use the Export command.

Open a PDF document and choose File ⇨ Export ⇨ HTML (either 3.2 or 4.01 format). After selecting the Format, click the Settings button and you see the settings options as shown in Figure 27.7. Again, these options are the same as you have available in the Preferences dialog box. In addition, the Settings options are the same for both HTML formats.

FIGURE 27.7

The Settings adjustments in either the Preferences dialog box or the Save As dialog box are identical.

The settings options include:

- **Encoding.** A number of encoding options appear from the pull-down menu. If you have special characters in text, use either UTF-8 or UTF-16. If you use an encoding method such as UCS-4, the special characters won't be recognized.

- **Generate bookmarks.** Links to sections in the HTML document are made from the PDF bookmarks.

- **Generate tags for untagged documents.** If a document is not tagged, check this box to add tagging for accessibility.

- **Generate images.** If your PDF document has images and you want them converted to a format recognized by HTML, be certain to check this box.

- **Use sub-folder.** All images can be saved to a subfolder nested below the HTML file. Check this box to copy the images to a separate folder. The default folder name is *images*. You can edit the name and provide a name of your choosing for the folder where the images are saved.

- **Use prefix.** If you want a prefix added to your images, check the box and type a prefix name in the text box.

- **Output format.** Choose from the options for the image format you want for the exported images. Use JPG if you have photo images.

- **Downsample to.** Check this box and select an amount to downsample images. The default is 150 ppi. Change this item to 72 ppi for Web viewing.

Converting text documents to HTML

One thing to keep in mind when you convert PDF files to HTML is that the entire PDF document is converted to a single HTML file. If you want separate HTML documents your best option is to first Select Document ➪ Extract Pages. Enter the page numbers you want to extract for one HTML file and click OK. Convert the pages to HTML using the Export ➪ HTML command. Then return to the original document and extract the pages you want for your second HTML file and convert to HTML, and so on.

CROSS-REF For more information on extracting pages in PDFs, see Chapter 16.

If you have a PDF with bookmarks, you can convert to HTML with the bookmarks appearing in the HTML document and linked to the sections of the document that are bookmarked in the original PDF file. To see how to convert a text file with bookmarks, follow these steps:

STEPS: Converting PDF text-only documents to HTML

1. **Open a file containing bookmarks in Acrobat.** In this example I open a file converted from Microsoft Word containing bookmarks.

2. **Open the Export to HTML dialog box.** Select File ➪ Export ➪ HTML and choose either HTML export option. The export dialog box is the Save As dialog box you get when you also select File ➪ Save As.

3. **Adjust Settings.** Click the Settings button in the Save As dialog box and make setting adjustments as described in the "Setting export options" section earlier in this chapter. In this example, I check the box for Generate bookmarks. Because there are no images in my file, I don't need to address any of the options for exporting images.

4. **Click OK.** Depending on the size of your file, you may see a progress bar report the export progress or you may just see a flash on your screen. The file is exported without any confirmation dialog box.

5. **View the exported HTML in a Web browser.** Open your Web browser and select File Open. Navigate your hard drive and select the exported file and open it. If you had Bookmarks in the file, they appear as links as shown in Figure 27.8.

FIGURE 27.8

The exported HTML file is opened in a Web browser with links appearing for the Bookmark items that were contained in the PDF file.

Bookmarks converted to links

Exporting PDF files with images to HTML

The process for exporting images is much the same as exporting text files. However, the one option you'll want to edit in the Settings dialog box is the image attributes. To see how PDFs with images are converted to HTML, follow these steps:

STEPS: Converting multi-page PDFs with images to HTML

1. **Open a PDF file with multiple pages and images.**

2. **Select File ⇨ Export ⇨ HTML and choose an HTML format.**

3. **Adjust Settings options.** Click Settings and select the Output format. In this example, I check the JPG radio button. Click Downsample to and select 72 from the dpi pull-down menu.

4. **Click OK.** The file may take a little time to export depending on the size of your PDF document. When the progress bar finishes, the file is ready to open in your Web browser or HTML editor.

5. **Open the file in your Web browser.** In Figure 27.9, you can see a partial view of my exported file. The original document had two letter and two tabloid pages with several images on each page. This document needs a lot of editing in an HTML editor to format text and graphics for a Web page design.

FIGURE 27.9

The HTML file needs a lot of work to polish up the design.

Figure 27.10 shows the portion of the original PDF document that was exported to HTML.

FIGURE 27.10

The original PDF document that was used to export to the HTML file shown in Figure 27.9

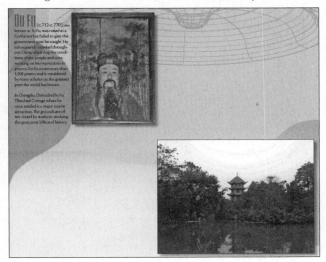

The best you can hope for with the PDF exports to HTML is a good starting place for editing the HTML in an HTML editor. Acrobat provides you some basic tools to get a PDF document to HTML format. From there, you can expect to do some editing in your favorite HTML editor.

One alternative you have available is to explore using a third-party plug-in designed for exporting PDFs to HTML. A number of different plug-in products are distributed by a number of developers. To find some of the latest plug-ins and obtain some demo copies you can test, visit the Adobe Plug-in finder Web site. Log on to www.adobe.com/special/acrobat/pluginfinder.html. A comprehensive list of third-party plug-ins is also listed at the PluginsWorld Web site. Log on to PluginsWorld.com to find third-party products supporting Acrobat.

Summary

- PDFs can be viewed inside Web browser windows. When viewed as inline views in Web browsers, Acrobat toolbars and menu options are contained within the browser window.

- You change preferences settings for Web viewing PDFs in Windows in the Acrobat viewer Preferences dialog box.

- To make links from text in PDFs for users of Acrobat 6 and earlier, choose Advanced ⇨ Document Processing ⇨ Create Links from URLs.

- To create multiple identical Web links across several pages, use the Add Header and Footer dialog box. Type a URL as a header or footer and save the file. Close and reopen the file and the links are active in Acrobat viewers 7 and above.

- By modifying code in the Open Web Link Action properties you can control opening views and override Initial View defaults. Add the code following the URL link to adjust page views, zooms, page modes, and so on.

- You can export PDF to HTML. In most cases you need to polish up the Web page design in an HTML editor after exporting to HTML.

Chapter 28

Creating PDF Presentations

Among the many uses for Acrobat PDF files are presentations. Acrobat does not provide the robust features for creating title slides, importing text and graphics in an open PDF document, or creating handouts such as those found in dedicated slide-authoring programs such as Microsoft PowerPoint and Apple's Keynote. However, if you're willing to put a little work in either designing a slide presentation in a layout program or converting a slide show from PowerPoint or Keynote to PDF, you can explore many other opportunities in Acrobat for making slide presentations dynamic and suitable for any kind of audience through the use of file linking, JavaScripts, and other interactive elements.

If you're an Acrobat Pro Extended user (Windows only), you have many more options for creating dynamic presentations with Adobe Presenter. Adobe Presenter is an add-on support for Microsoft PowerPoint where you can add animation, sound, and multimedia, and convert your presentations to Flash videos.

In this chapter, you learn some helpful methods for producing PDF documents suited for presentations and discover some of the power you have available for dynamic presentations created with Adobe Presenter.

Setting Up the Work Environment

Interactivity is one element you'll want to add to documents designed for presentations. To add interactive buttons and fields, open the More Tools window by selecting More Tools from a context menu and check the Advanced Editing toolbar. Deselect any tools you are not likely to use in this toolbar such as the Article tool and the TouchUp Reading Order tool. For access to all the navigation tools, scroll down to the Page Navigation toolbar and check all the boxes for the Navigation tools and check the Page Navigation toolbar. You may want to import media when creating presentations. Check the box for the Multimedia toolbar. Click OK to open the toolbars as floating toolbars.

When using the Advanced Editing tools or the Button tool, you'll find the Properties Bar a valuable asset. To open the toolbar, open a context menu from the Toolbar Well and select Properties Bar. After opening the toolbars, open a context menu on the Toolbar Well and select Dock Toolbars.

If you're familiar with the toolbar icons and don't need the tool labels, open a context menu on the Toolbar Well and select Button Labels ⇨ Default Labels. For the figures in this chapter, the toolbar labels are displayed (Button Labels ⇨ All Labels).

Creating Presentation Documents

The first step in creating presentations for viewing in Acrobat is to decide what authoring program you want to use. If you are familiar with either Microsoft PowerPoint or Apple's Keynote, you can create a slide presentation and convert the authoring application file to PDF. For PowerPoint, you'll want to determine whether the PDF conversion is worthwhile. If your slide presentation is about Adobe Acrobat, it makes sense to show the slides in Acrobat. If the presentation is about another topic, you need to determine if it is more beneficial to display the presentation in an Acrobat viewer or directly in PowerPoint. By converting to PDF, you make your presentation available to all Adobe Reader users. If you need to pass your presentation through a review committee, you can enable the presentation with Adobe Reader usage rights and provide Adobe Reader users the option for adding comments and notes to your presentation.

CROSS-REF For more information on enabling PDFs with usage rights for Adobe Reader users, see Chapter 19.

If you prefer other author applications to PowerPoint or another dedicated slide application program, conversion to PDF for showing slides in an Acrobat viewer is an ideal solution. Obviously, PDFs offer you more functionality when showing slide presentations than most original authoring applications. Ideally, the best authoring applications to create a slide presentation, if you don't use dedicated slide authoring programs, is a layout program such as Adobe PageMaker, Adobe InDesign, Adobe FrameMaker, or QuarkXPress. These programs offer you the ability to create documents with multiple pages and assign different backgrounds to pages via master pages. In addition, some programs offer you the ability to create text blocks on master pages so the text placement, font sizes, and paragraph properties are identical on each page.

Converting PowerPoint slides to PDF (Windows)

Microsoft PowerPoint files are converted to PDF in much the same way that you convert other Microsoft Office files. The Adobe PDFMaker tool is installed in PowerPoint just as you find with many other Microsoft programs.

CROSS-REF For more information on conversion to PDF with the PDFMaker tool and Microsoft Office applications, see Chapter 8.

From the PowerPoint Ribbon in PowerPoint 2007, click the Acrobat tab. Click Preferences in the Acrobat Ribbon to open the Acrobat PDFMaker dialog box shown in Figure 28.1. Select the Adobe PDF settings you want to use for your file conversion. For presentations without transitions and animations, the Standard Adobe PDF settings should work sufficiently for showing slides on screens and overheads as well as printing handouts for your audience. If you want to change the compatibility settings, click the Advanced Settings button to custom-design Distiller job options.

NOTE I focus primarily on Office 2007 applications in this book. If you're an Office 2003 user, you'll find the PDFMaker tools installed in Office applications (Windows only) as well as menus where you can edit conversion settings. Although the path for choosing options is different between the Office versions, the options available to you are very similar.

CROSS-REF For more information on changing Adobe PDF settings and using Acrobat Distiller, see Chapter 10. For a description of all the settings you can make in the Acrobat PDFMaker dialog box, see Chapter 8.

As with the other Office applications discussed in Chapter 8, you click the Create PDF tool in the Acrobat Ribbon to convert the slides to a PDF file. Conversion of a PowerPoint slide presentation without adding special features is a relatively easy operation.

FIGURE 28.1

Click Preferences in the Acrobat Ribbon to open the Adobe PDFMaker dialog box.

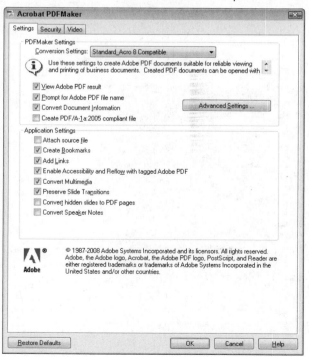

Converting PowerPoint notes to PDF notes (or annotations)

If you want to create notes for your audience, you convert notes to Adobe PDF comments that are created on a separate layer. The layer can be shown and hidden in Acrobat. The setup for printing notes is handled in the PowerPoint View tab in the Ribbon. Click Notes Page; the current default Notes Master displays the notes at the bottom of the document page. Notes you add to each slide are added as comments in Acrobat. To convert PowerPoint Notes to PDF comments, do the following:

STEPS: Converting notes to PDF

1. **Open a presentation in PowerPoint.**

2. **View the Notes page.** Click the View tab in the Ribbon and click Notes Page in the top-left corner of the View tab.

3. **Add notes to the slides.** The current slide is shown at the top of the page. Below the slide is a text box. Type your speaker notes in the text box. Scroll the slides and add notes to all slides where you want notes added to the respective slide.

4. **Convert to PDF.** Click the Acrobat tab in the Ribbon and click Create PDF. The Save Adobe PDF File As dialog box opens. Choose a target folder for your notes file and click Save. A dialog box opens and asks you if you want to convert the speaker notes to comments. Click Yes to add the notes as comments on a separate layer in the PDF file as shown in Figure 28.2.

FIGURE 28.2

Notes are added as comments in the PDF file on a separate layer.

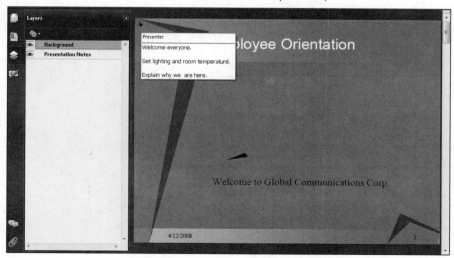

Converting handouts to PDF

In PowerPoint you can print handouts to your printer; however, you can't convert a handout page to a PDF document via the Create PDF tool in the Acrobat Ribbon. If you want to print handouts and carry the printed documents to your session, it's best to leave the task to PowerPoint. If you want to distribute handouts to session attendees and leave the task of printing to others, then you need to convert a handout page to a PDF document.

Here are the steps to accomplish the task:

Steps: Creating PDF handouts

1. **Set up the Notes pages in PowerPoint.** Rather than create a handouts page, use a note page in PowerPoint. Follow the steps outlined earlier in the section "Converting PowerPoint notes to PDF" to create note pages in PowerPoint, but don't convert to PDF.

2. **Open the Print dialog box.** Converting to PDF from the Create PDF tool in the Acrobat tab won't do the job. You need to use another method of PDF creation. In the Print dialog box choose Adobe PDF as your printer. Choose Notes Pages and Grayscale in the Print what section of the Print dialog box as shown in Figure 28.3. If you want a keyline border for your slides, check Frame Slides.

FIGURE 28.3

Open the Print dialog box and choose Notes Pages.

3. **Create the PDF document.** Click OK to open the Save PDF File As dialog box. Open a target folder for the saved file and click Save. The notes pages are converted to PDF.

4. **Create text boxes for the notes pages.** If you want users to interact with an electronic file, you can add form fields to the PDF. If you want users to print files and have lines added to the document, you might create a background comprised of lines for attendees to write notes and add the background to the pages in the PDF document. In this example I'll use form fields to prepare a file for electronically adding notes.

   In the open PDF document choose Forms ⇨ Add or Edit Fields. The interface changes to Form Editing Mode. Add a text box field to the first page using the Text Field tool.

CROSS-REF For more information on adding text fields to a PDF document, see Chapter 34.

5. **Change the Text Field Properties.** Type a name (any name) for the text field and click Properties in the mini properties window to open the Text Field Properties dialog box. Click the Appearance tab and set the appearance properties for border and fill color as desired. From the Font Size pull-down menu choose a font size. Be certain to not use Auto. Choosing Auto sizes text to the size of the field box. If you use different sizes for field boxes, the text sizes will appear different.

   Click the Options tab and choose Multi-line. Click Close after setting the properties.

6. **Duplicate the field.** Open a context menu on the text field and choose Duplicate. In the Duplicate Field dialog box, click the From radio button and type **2** in the first text box. Leave the default number in the second text box to duplicate fields from page 2 through the end of the document.

7. **Rename the fields.** The duplicated fields have the same name. You need to rename the fields in the Fields panel to provide a unique name for each field. Click the field names in the Fields panel and type a new name for each field. In my example I use n.1, n.2, n.3, and so on, as shown in Figure 28.4.

8. **Save the file.** Click Close Form Editing and review the slides. Test each slide by typing data in the field on each respective page to be certain unique data can be added to each page. Choose Forms ⇨ Clear Form to eliminate the data on each page. Use the File ⇨ Save As command and overwrite the last saved version to optimize the file.

FIGURE 28.4

Rename the duplicated fields in the Fields panel.

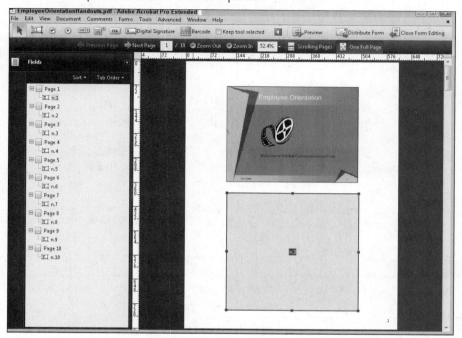

If you want a different design for your notes to appear under the slide images, you can create any kind of design in your favorite authoring program and convert to PDF. Use the design as a background and use the Document ➪ Background ➪ Add/Replace command to add the design to each page in the slide presentation.

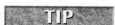 **CROSS-REF** For more information on using backgrounds, see Chapter 16.

TIP If you want to add page numbers to the notes pages, use the Document ➪ Header & Footer command and add a header or footer with page numbers.

Converting PowerPoint slides to PDF (Mac)

A long-standing problem we've had ever since the introduction of the PDFMakers is that they just don't work well with PowerPoint on the Mac. As a result, the PDFMakers are gone in Acrobat 9.

To create a PDF from an Office application, use the Print dialog box and print your presentation to PDF. Although you can create PDF files by printing to PDF, you'll struggle to get the right page size when converting PowerPoint slides to PDF. On Windows you get the exact page size you specify from the default slide page size. On the Mac you get something like a page shown in Figure 28.5.

What's your alternative? If you happen to have a dual-core Mac and you run a virtual desktop application with Windows XP or Vista, you might look into installing Acrobat on Windows running on your Mac. If you have a friend or colleague using Acrobat and PowerPoint on Windows, you could send your file to your colleague to convert to PDF. Doing so, of course, means that you should both be licensed users of Acrobat. The PowerPoint files are easily transferred between computer platforms as long as you use fonts available on both operating systems.

Finding a workaround will save you much time and aggravation. Do your best to get a little help in converting these files to PDF.

FIGURE 28.5

Creating PDF files from PowerPoint on the Mac is problematic when you want to create PDFs from slide presentations.

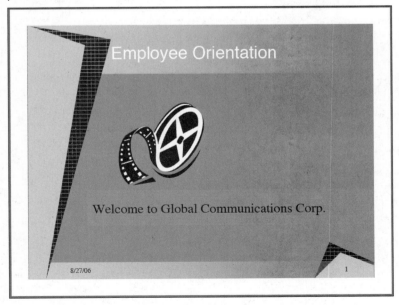

Converting Apple Keynote slides to PDF (Mac)

Another option Mac users have for converting PowerPoint slides to PDF is to open them in Apple's Keynote. Keynote is a dedicated slide presentation authoring application that offers a robust authoring environment providing simplicity and ease in creating slide shows. The charting features in Keynote are easy to use with intuitive palettes for editing chart types and data. Whether you use Keynote to convert PowerPoint slides or use it as your original authoring program, Keynote easily converts presentations to PDF.

Keynote supports file imports for many image formats, video, and sound, and PDF imports that can be sized and scaled. The templates installed with the program are attractive and well designed. After creating a slide show in Keynote, choose File ➪ Export. A dialog box drops down from the application menu bar where you are offered format options for exporting to QuickTime, PowerPoint, or PDF formats. To export directly to PDF format, select the PDF radio button and click Next. Locate the folder where you want the PDF file saved and click the Export button. You won't find Keynote giving you the same problems for matching page sizes between Keynote and PDF.

Converting authoring application documents to PDF

Many creative professionals use layout programs for a variety of purposes, including slide presentations. If you use QuarkXPress, Adobe InDesign, Adobe PageMaker, or Adobe FrameMaker for creating a slide presentation, you can export your documents to PDF via the same methods used for PDF exports when preparing files for print. For notes and handouts, you can create master pages in any one of the applications with the graphics, lines, and styles you want, and you can import the PDF document into the layout application. Each of the aforementioned programs supports PDF imports.

> **CROSS-REF** For more information on converting layout program documents to PDF, see Chapter 7.

Depending on the program you use, you can either set up master pages with graphic placeholders or place and size PDF pages individually. In a program such as Adobe InDesign CS, creating note pages is more work than using PowerPoint, but you can create some workarounds for adding notes to presentations. You begin by creating a master page with the design you want to use for the note handouts. On the master page, add graphic elements such as the lines, text, logo, or other data. Next, create a rectangle with the Rectangle Frame tool. In this example the slide pages need to be sized down to 75 percent; therefore, I created the rectangle and used the Transformation palette to size the rectangle to 75% to accommodate the PDF slide pages.

After creating the template, add pages to the document and assign the template to each page. When it comes time to import the slide file, select File ➪ Place. In the Place dialog box, be certain to select Show Import Options. When the check box is enabled, InDesign opens the Place PDF dialog box, shown in Figure 28.6, where you determine what page is placed.

FIGURE 28.6

To make choices for what page to place in the InDesign file, be certain to enable Show Import Options in the Place dialog box. After clicking OK in the Place dialog box, the Place PDF dialog box opens where you can scroll pages to place the page of choice.

In the Show Import Options dialog box, click the left- or right-pointing arrows to scroll pages. Select a page and click OK. Click the cursor in the area where the rectangle frame was drawn on the master page to place and size the PDF page to the exact fit, including scaling. When the page is placed, move to the next InDesign page and place the next PDF page.

After placing all pages and using a template master for the design layout, select File ➪ Export. Select Adobe PDF in the Export dialog box and export the file to PDF.

 For more on exporting to PDF from Adobe InDesign, see Chapter 9.

Using Adobe Presenter (Acrobat Pro Extended only)

Earlier attempts by Adobe for converting PowerPoint animations to PDF have been hit and miss. In a few earlier versions of Acrobat the PDFMaker successfully converted animation effects you added in PowerPoint and the animations were retained in PDF documents. In other versions of Acrobat, the PDFMaker couldn't convert PowerPoint animations.

If you create PowerPoint presentations with animations such as text in motion, exploding objects, fading elements, and so on, and you want to convert these effects to PDF, Adobe provides you a solution in the form of Adobe Presenter. Adobe Presenter is a separate installation you find on the Acrobat Pro Extended installer CD; Pro Extended is made available only to Windows users.

When you install Adobe Presenter, a new tab appears in the Ribbon in PowerPoint. Click the Adobe Presenter tab to change the Ribbon as you see in Figure 28.7. In Office 2007, you have a menu for Adobe Presenter vs. a tab.

FIGURE 28.7

Click the Adobe Presenter tab in the PowerPoint Ribbon to display the Adobe Presenter tools. Adobe Presenter is available only on Acrobat Pro Extended (Windows).

Looking at the Adobe Presenter tools

Adobe Presenter offers you a number of options for creating presentations with animation, sound, video; support for PowerPoint animations; and much more. The tools include:

- **Publish.** The Publish tool is used instead of the Acrobat Ribbon's Create PDF tool. In Presenter you have three publishing options. You can create an Adobe Flash SWF file, create a PDF you can host anywhere, or host a PDF on Acrobat.com.

- **Slide Manager.** The Slide Manager enables you to add navigational links, specify options for playing media, adding an author name, and locking slides.

- **Settings.** The Settings options provide you choices for changing the template design for the presentation. You have a number of different designs from which to choose, as well as the ability to add custom templates. Playback options are also included as well as control over audio quality, image quality, downloading options, and publishing locations. The settings also provide you options for adding file attachments that are accessible in Acrobat viewers after the presentation is converted to PDF.

- **Audio.** The Audio section includes 4 tools: Record tool enables you to overlay sound from audio you record via a microphone attached to your computer, import sound files, sync sound, and edit sound files.

- **Video. The Capture tool …. Capture.** You can capture video and attach the video to different slides or export the video as a separate file. Import Video, Edit Video…

- **Flash. Two tools: Insert Swf File and Manage Swf File Insert SWF.** This tool permits you to import Flash SWF video files.

- **Quiz includes 1) Manage, 2) Import and 3) Add New. Manage.** The Manage tool is used to add Quizzes to your presentation. You have options for adding questions, supplying answers, defining appearances, adding labels, and more.

- **Preferences.** The Preferences tool opens the Adobe Presenter – Preferences dialog box where you can add a photo, logo, and biography, identify servers for sharing your files, and determine audio sources.
- **Help.** The Help tool opens the Adobe Presenter Help guide where you can view help information to assist you in working in Adobe Presenter.

Publishing a presentation using Adobe Presenter

Each of the Adobe Presenter tools opens dialog boxes where options choices are made. In several cases you have multiple tabs to change panes where more options are found. It is beyond the scope of this book to thoroughly cover all options choices you can make in Adobe Presenter. What is offered here is a glimpse at converting files to PDF and a discussion on a few of the impressive features you have available with Adobe Presenter. To start off with, let's take a look at converting files to PDF using Adobe Presenter.

To convert a PowerPoint file to interactive or multimedia PDF, do the following:

Steps: Converting a PowerPoint file using Adobe Presenter

1. **Open a PowerPoint document.** You might use a PowerPoint document that contains animations such as Effects for text and objects.

2. **Change Settings.** Click the Settings tool in the Adobe Presenter tab in PowerPoint. The Adobe Presenter – Presentation Settings dialog box opens as shown in Figure 28.8.

   By default the Appearance tab is shown. The Summary text box is where you can add a document summary. Type the desired text in this box. From the Theme pull-down menu choose a theme. If you don't want to use the existing selection of various themes, click the Theme Editor to create custom themes.

   Click the Playback tab and make selections for advance intervals, looping the slide show, including slide numbers, and setting intervals for pausing the slide show after animations are played.

   Click the Quality tab to make choices for audio and image quality. You also make a choice for publishing the file for your computer, which provides you an HTML version of the slide animation, publish for Acrobat Connect Pro, and publishing a PDF. Choose the option you want from the Publish For pull-down menu.

   Click the Attachments tab to add file attachments to your published work. Click OK when finished making choices.

FIGURE 28.8

Click the Settings tool in the Adobe Presenter Ribbon to open the Adobe Presenter – Presentations Settings dialog box where you make a number of choices for exporting and viewing the published work.

3. Set the Publish attributes. Click the Publish tool in the Adobe Presenter Ribbon to open the Adobe Presenter – Publish Presentation dialog box. The first item to check is the left side of the dialog box shown in Figure 28.9. You have choices for publishing the work as SWF to your computer, to your Acrobat Connect Pro account, or as an Adobe PDF file. In my example I use Adobe PDF as my output source.

Click the Choose button to locate a folder where you want to save the export. If you select Acrobat Connect Pro, the Choose button changes to Edit Servers where you can edit the URL, logon, and password for your Acrobat Connect Pro account.

FIGURE 28.9

Click the Publish tool in the Adobe Presenter tab to open the Adobe Presenter – Publish Presentation dialog box.

4. **Open the Slide Manager.** The Slide Manager enables you to make some choices for the display and navigation of the published document. Click Slide Manager in the Adobe Presenter – Publish Presentation dialog box to arrive at the Adobe Presenter – Slide Manager dialog box shown in Figure 28.10.

   Click the Presented By item and choose a presenter from a pull-down menu. You can add multiple presenters and edit the Presenter information in the Adobe Presenter - Preferences dialog box you access by clicking the Preferences tool in the Adobe Presenter tab. This feature is handy when you have multiple presenters for a given session.

   Make other choices by clicking items in the Slide Manager. You might want to jump around the presentation. You can open a pull-down menu (shown in Figure 28.10) from the Go To menu and choose from the list of slides where you want to go next.

   Set all the options you want to use and click OK to return back to the Adobe Presenter – Publish Presentation dialog box.

5. **Publish the Presentation.** After making all your choices in the various dialog boxes, click the Publish button. Your presentation is exported to the location/format you chose in your settings.

FIGURE 28.10

Click the Publish tool in the Adobe Presenter tab to open the Adobe Presenter – Publish Presentation dialog box.

Examining the interface

I used Adobe PDF as my output source in the previous steps. When you open a PDF document exported from Adobe Presenter, such as the one I created (see Figure 28.11), one of the first things you notice about the file is that all the slides you published appear on one page. After a first glance you may be tempted to return to PowerPoint thinking that you missed identifying a page range for exporting the presentation.

FIGURE 28.11

Slides exported from Presenter as a SWF file show the entire presentation on one PDF page

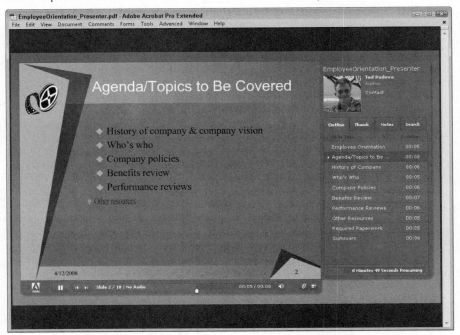

The reason your presentation appears on one page is because the end result is an Adobe Flash file that contains all the transitions, effects, and slides inside the Flash animation, embedded in a PDF document. As you can see in Figure 28.11, you end up with a beautiful design where you have many choices for displaying the animated file.

Some of the areas you'll want to become familiar with in the Flash interface include:

- **Animated effects.** In Figure 28.11, notice the last bullet point on the slide. The screen shot was captured while text was moving from the left side of the slide. All the effects you add in PowerPoint are retained in the PDF file.

- **Status bar.** The tools appearing at the bottom of the slide enable you to pause the presentation and move forward and backward in the presentation (these tools being represented by the arrows). A slide for setting the sound level is represented by the speaker icon on the right side of the status bar. The Attachments tool opens the Attachments pop-up panel where you can view file attachments. The last tool enables you to toggle views where you can display or hide the side panel on the right. When I click the tool shown in Figure 28.11, you see the display as it appears in Figure 28.12.

Click the last tool in the status bar to change views.

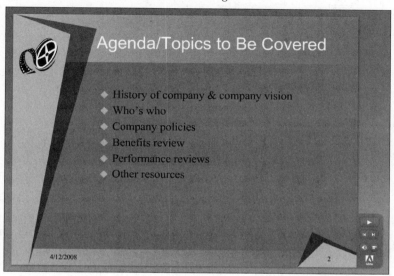

- **Outline.** The Outline tab in the side panel displays the speaker assigned to the current open slide. Below the Slide Title heading you see a list of all the slides in the presentation. Click any slide title and you can jump to that slide.

- **Thumb.** Click the Thumb tab to see a scrollable list of all slides showing a thumbnail image of the slides.

- **Notes.** Click Notes to see speaker notes attached to each slide.

- **Search.** Click the Search tab and type a search item in the text box. Press Enter/Return and the results are reported in the same tab as shown in Figure 28.13. Click a result and the result is hyperlinked to the slide where the found word(s) appears. As you click a result and jump to another slide, the results remain in view so you can navigate to several different slides where results are found without having to repeat your search.

- **Time readout.** At the bottom of the side panel you find a readout where the time remaining for the slide presentation is reported. This time is based on the interval you set up in Adobe Presenter before converting to PDF.

FIGURE 28.13

Type search criteria in the Search text box and press Enter/Return to display a list of found instances of the search criteria.

To play the slides click the Play tool in the status bar. In Figure 28.11 you see two parallel lines as the first tool. The presentation is currently in a pause mode. Clicking the tool changes the icon to a right-pointing arrow. Click the arrow to play the presentation. You can start and pause the Flash animation at any time by clicking the Play and Pause tools.

TIP You can enter Form Editing Mode on a file converted from Adobe Presenter and add form fields to the document. You might want to create a button and set the button action to open another file during a presentation. For example, you might want to display a financial summary document while addressing an annual shareholders meeting. Because Presenter slides all appear on one page, your button is shown as the Flash animation plays and changes slide views. If you have multiple buttons or other form fields that you want to add to a presentation, you can create separate PDF documents and use the Create PDF task button and choose Merge Files into a Single PDF to create one file as a single presentation. On each page you can then add button fields that execute different actions.

There's much more to Adobe Presenter than covered in this chapter. For information related to importing sound, rich media, Flash files, creating quizzes, and more features, consult the Adobe Presenter Help document.

Working with Page Transitions and Effects

Page transitions can be added in PowerPoint and converted to PDF when you use the PDFMaker in PowerPoint either from Acrobat Pro or Acrobat Pro Extended on Windows. You also have options for adding transitions directly in Acrobat viewers. Acrobat lacks the ability to provide you animations with text and images such as text flying in or out of a slide, text rotations, fades and dissolves, and so on.

PowerPoint also supports the import of video, sound, and page transitions; and these imports are also converted to PDF when using the PDFMaker. You can choose to add video, sound imports, and page transitions in PowerPoint that can be converted with Acrobat as well as when using Adobe Presenter; or you can use tools in Acrobat Pro or Pro Extended to import media and create page transitions in any Acrobat viewer including Adobe Reader.

 For more information on working with video and sound in PDFs, see Chapter 23.

Converting animations to PDF from PowerPoint

You can convert imported media to PDF from PowerPoint using Acrobat Pro or Acrobat Pro Extended. In PowerPoint you click the Insert tab and click the Movie tool. When you import a movie in PowerPoint and use the Create PDF tool, the movie is transcoded to a Flash file.

If you use Acrobat Pro Extended , click the Embed video tool in the Insert Ribbon. The Insert Video dialog box opens where you can Browse your hard drive and locate the media file you want to import. The media file is transcoded to Adobe Flash upon import. If you import media in a PowerPoint presentation in Acrobat Pro Extended, you can export the file to PDF using either the Create PDF tool (Acrobat tab) or the Adobe Presenter Publish tool (Adobe Presenter tab).

Adding page transitions in Acrobat viewers

Page transitions are available in Full Screen mode in Acrobat. You can set page transitions for all pages in a file or from selected pages in the Pages palette. You can batch-process files and apply transitions on a group of documents with a batch command.

 For more information on creating batch sequences, see Chapter 18.

To set transitions on all pages or a specified range of pages in a document while remaining in Edit mode (as opposed to Full Screen mode) do the following:

STEPS: Adding page transitions to a document

1. **Open a slide presentation in any Acrobat viewer.**

2. **Open the Pages panel by clicking the Pages icon.** Note that in Acrobat, you can add page transitions using a context menu or a menu command from the Options pull-down menu and selecting Page Transitions. You also have the option of selecting the Advanced ⇨ Document Processing ⇨ Page Transitions menu command.

   You might want to use the Pages panel to access the Set Transitions dialog box because you can easily select a range of pages or a group of noncontiguous pages, or you can make a choice to apply transitions to all pages from selections you make in the Pages panel and then easily access the Page Transitions command.

If you use Adobe Reader to set page transitions, you don't have access to menu commands from the top-level menu bar or a context menu in the Pages panel. You need to handle page transitions settings in the Full Screen Preferences.

3. **Select pages you want to appear with transitions.** If you want all pages to appear with transitions, skip this step and move to the next step. If you want only a selected range of pages to appear with transitions, click the page thumbnails you want to appear with page transitions. For a noncontiguous selection, press the Ctrl/⌘ key and click each page you want to use.

4. **Open the Set Transitions dialog box.** After selecting pages or when applying transitions to all pages, you can choose Page Transitions from a context menu, the Pages panel Options pull-down menu, or the Advanced ➪ Document Processing submenu. Any one of these choices opens the Set Transitions dialog box shown in Figure 28.14.

FIGURE 28.14

The Set Transitions dialog box offers you a wide range of choices for transition effects you can apply to pages while viewing documents in Edit mode.

5. **Set the transition attributes.** A number of choices are available for applying page transitions. Make some settings adjustments for the following:

   ■ **Transition.** From the Transition pull-down menu, you select the transition effect to be applied for the pages selected either in the dialog box or from the range of pages selected in the Pages panel. Acrobat offers you a total of 16 different choices. One choice is to set No Transition, with the remaining 15 choices representing different effects.

- **Direction.** Not all transitions use options in the Direction menu. When an option is available, open the pull-down menu and select a command for the direction you want the transition to move.

- **Speed.** Make a selection for Fast, Medium, or Slow in the Speed pull-down menu.

- **Auto Flip.** If you enable Auto Flip, pages are scrolled at an automatic interval according to the number of seconds you select from the pull-down menu below the Auto Flip check box. Choices for the interval are between −21474833648 and +21474833648.00 seconds. You can select fixed interval options or type a value within the acceptable range. If you want to manually scroll pages, leave the check box disabled.

- **Page Range.** If you don't select pages in the Pages tab, use the Set Transitions dialog box to apply transitions to All pages in document, or specify a page range in a contiguous order by clicking on the Pages range and typing in the page From and To field boxes. When you select pages in the Pages panel, the pages become active by default and the transitions are applied to the selected pages.

After setting the effects and page range, click OK to apply transitions to the pages when you scroll pages in Edit mode.

Although it isn't necessary with all the features in Acrobat 9, you can apply page transitions in authoring applications prior to PDF conversion. If you happen to have an old Acrobat 3 installer CD, you'll find a folder on the CD titled Transitions. The Transitions folder contains EPS files with PostScript code to create transitions when pages are scrolled in Edit mode. If you use a layout application to create your slide presentations, place one of the EPS transition effects on a master page in your layout program and convert to PDF. The transitions are applied to all the pages as you scroll through the document. If you elect to use this method, you don't have the flexibility for quickly changing transition effects. The one advantage is that any user of older versions of Acrobat can create PDF documents with transitions by using this method.

Using Full Screen Views

Full Screen mode offers you many different viewing options when you want to show a slide presentation. If your presentation requires a discussion of Acrobat and you want to access tools and menu commands, working in Edit mode is the most obvious choice. When you use Full Screen mode, the menu bar and tools are hidden from view, but the viewing options and alternatives for showing slides in Acrobat are much greater.

Setting Full Screen preferences

The first task in working with Full Screen mode is to set up the environment for showing slides by setting the Full Screen preferences. Choose Edit ➪ Preferences (Acrobat ➪ Preferences on the Macintosh) or press Ctrl/⌘+K. In the left pane, select Full Screen; the preference choices appear, as shown in Figure 28.15. Note that Full Screen viewing can be applied to any PDF document, including PDFs that were created using Adobe Presenter in PowerPoint.

FIGURE 28.15

To set up the Full Screen view, open the Preferences dialog box and click Full Screen in the left panel.

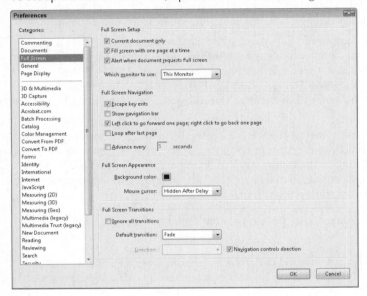

The preference choices include:

- **Current document only.** You can set up Full Screen viewing as a default for all files you view or apply it only to the current PDF document. When the check box is disabled, your settings are applied to any file. When the check box is checked, your settings are applied only to the file open in the Document pane.

- **Fill screen with one page at a time.** Sets the page view to the maximum screen coverage by a single page.

- **Alert when document requests full screen.** You may have noticed that if you click a link to open a file or use the Open tool to open a file where the Initial View is saved to open in Full Screen mode, a dialog box, as shown in Figure 28.16, asks if you want to open in Full Screen mode. This preference choice setting controls a dialog box that opens and prompts a user to choose whether to open in Full Screen mode or not. If the user clicks Yes, the file opens in Full Screen mode. If the user clicks no, the file opens, but it opens in Edit mode.

- **Which monitor to use.** From a pull-down menu, you have several choices for monitor viewing. Some of the menu choices are helpful when displaying presentations on projection systems. To find out what menu choice works best for you, change the viewing preference when you prepare a presentation by selecting different menu options before your presentation session and when viewing the presentation on a projection system. When viewing presentations on your own monitor, leave the default setting as This Monitor.

FIGURE 28.16

Check the Alert when document requests full screen check box to open a dialog box prompting a user to accept viewing in Full Screen mode.

- **Escape key exits.** Entering the Full Screen mode is handled by setting the Initial View options or by pressing Ctrl/⌘+L. If you want to exit Full Screen view, you can press the Esc key when this check box is enabled. Be certain to leave the check box at the default switch. If you disable the check box, you need to remember to use Ctrl/⌘+L to exit Full Screen view.

- **Show navigation bar.** When the check box is enabled, icons appear in the lower left corner of the screen, permitting you to go to the previous slide or next slide, or exit Full Screen mode (third icon). In Figure 28.17 the three arrow icons are visible when this preference choice is checked.

FIGURE 28.17

To display navigation buttons while in Full Screen mode, check the Full Screen preference choice for Show navigation bar.

- **Left-click to go forward one page; right-click to go back one page.** When this check box is enabled, you can navigate pages with mouse clicks. For both Windows and Macintosh users who use a two-button mouse, clicking the left or right button navigates pages in the respective direction.

- **Loop after last page.** Using this option and the next setting for auto advancing, you can set up a kiosk and have the slide presentation continue with auto repetition. After the last page is viewed, the presentation begins again, showing the first page and continuing in an infinite loop.

- **Advance every.** If you enable the check box, the slide presentation automatically scrolls pages at the interval specified in the field box adjacent to the check box. The values permitted for the interval are between 1 and 60 seconds.

- **Background color.** Click the color swatch to open the preset color palette, where you can make choices for the background color. The background color appears outside the slide pages on all pages that do not fit precisely within the monitor frame. If you want to use a custom color, click Other Color at the bottom of the palette and select a custom color from your system palette.

- **Mouse cursor.** You have three choices from the pull-down menu for the mouse cursor display while viewing slides in Full Screen mode. You can choose from Always Visible, Always Hidden, or Hidden After Delay. The Hidden After Delay menu choice shows the cursor position when you scroll pages, and then hides it after a short delay (usually a two- to three-second delay).

- **Ignore all transitions.** If you set transitions while in Edit mode and want to eliminate the transition effects while in Full Screen view, enable this check box.

- **Default transition.** From the pull-down menu you have choices for one of 16 different transition effects. If you apply a transition in the Full Screen preferences, all pages use the same transition. If you select Random from the menu choices, effects change randomly as you move through slide pages. If you want to use specific transitions that change for selected pages, set the transitions from the Advanced ⇨ Document Processing ⇨ Page Transitions menu command before opening the Preferences dialog box. Disable Ignore all transitions and the effects you choose for page transitions applied to selected pages in the Pages panel are used when you enter Full Screen mode.

- **Direction.** This is the same option you have when using the Set Page Transitions dialog box. See the section "Adding page transitions in Acrobat viewers" earlier in this chapter.

After setting the Preferences, you can enter Full Screen mode by pressing Ctrl/⌘+L or selecting View ⇨ Full Screen Mode.

Saving Initial View options for files opening in Full Screen mode

If you want your PDF document to always open in Full Screen view, you can control the Full Screen view in the Initial View Document Properties dialog box. Settings for initial views are made on a document-by-document basis, and the settings you make override an end user's viewing preferences.

To set Initial Views for Full Screen viewing, use the steps that follow.

STEPS: Setting the Initial View for Full Screen viewing

1. Open a presentation in Acrobat.

NOTE You can't change any Document Properties in Adobe Reader even when files are enabled with Reader usage rights.

2. Press Ctrl/⌘+D to open the Document Properties dialog box.

3. **Click the Initial View tab.**

4. **Check the Open in Full Screen mode check box.** Note that the choices for Navigation tab, Page layout, Magnification, and Window Options have no effect on files opening in Full Screen mode. If all of the check boxes are selected, as shown in Figure 28.18, the Full Screen view overrides all other Window Options.

5. **Save the file.** Before your new settings are applied to the file, you must save the document. Click OK in the Document Properties dialog box and select File ⇨ Save As to optimize the file. Click Save to rewrite your file with optimization and save the new Initial View options with the file. You must close and reopen the file to see the new Initial View options take effect.

CROSS-REF For more information on initial views, see Chapter 5. For more information on using Save As to optimize file sizes, see Chapter 11.

FIGURE 28.18

Full Screen mode overrides all other preference options selected in the Initial View settings.

Scrolling pages in Full Screen mode

To advance through slides when in Full Screen mode, you can use the preference setting to scroll pages with mouse clicks. If the preference choice for "Left click to go forward one page; right click to go back one page" is disabled, you can scroll pages with keystrokes. By default the mouse cursor changes regardless of what preference option you choose. Each time you click the mouse button, the pages scroll regardless of whether you have the "Left click to go forward one page; right click to go back one page" check box enabled.

> **TIP** You may have navigational links on the PDF document and not need users to click the mouse button or use the Navigation bar to scroll pages. If this is the case users who click outside a button may inadvertently move forward in the document. If you want to disable the advance click, you can do so with a simple JavaScript. Choose Advanced ➪ Document Processing ➪ Document JavaScripts. In the JavaScript Functions dialog box, type a name for the script and click Add. The JavaScript Editor opens. Type the following script in the JavaScript Editor:

```
app.fs.clickAdvances=false;
```

Click OK and click Close. Save the file. The next time you open the document the cursor advance is disabled.

Press the Page Down or Page Up keys to move forward and backward through slides. In addition, you can use the up or left arrow keys to move backward and the down or right arrow keys to move forward. Use the Home key to move to the first page and the End key to move to the last page. If you want to move to a specific page without leaving Full Screen mode, press Shift+Ctrl/⌘+N to open the Go to Page dialog box. Enter the page number to open in the field box and click OK.

Creating interactivity in Full Screen mode

You may have a slide presentation that does not require access to Acrobat menus and tools, but you want to show cross-document links. Perhaps you have a presentation about a company's financial status, economic growth, or projected growth and you want to show a financial spreadsheet, another PDF document, or a scanned image of a memo or report. The slide show created in PowerPoint with the motion objects and viewed in Full Screen mode is what you want, but you also want the flexibility for opening other files without leaving Full Screen mode.

Creating links and buttons for cross-document linking

If you want to open a secondary document while in Full Screen mode, you can create links or form field buttons to secondary files. When you click the link, the link action is invoked. If opening a secondary file, the file link opens in Full Screen mode. After viewing the file, press Ctrl/⌘+W to close the file and return to the last slide view, also in Full Screen mode.

To set up a file link, create a link or Button field and select Open a file in the Select Action pull-down menu. Click the Add button and select the file to open. When the Specify Open Preference dialog box opens, select New window, as shown in Figure 28.19. Click OK and click the Close button. When you view the file in Full Screen mode and click the button, the secondary file opens in Full Screen mode, leaving the slide presentation open in Acrobat.

The same behavior exists with other link actions. You can create a URL link to display a Web site while in Full Screen mode by using the Open a web link action. Click the link to open your Web browser at the specified URL. When you quit the Web browser, you are returned to the slide presentation in Full Screen mode. If you use PowerPoint effects and export to PDF using Adobe Presenter, the effects are not disturbed.

> **CROSS-REF** To learn more about setting link actions, see Chapter 22.

FIGURE 28.19

Select New window in the Specify Open Preference dialog box. When you click the link, the secondary file opens in Full Screen mode.

Using interactive devices

Another interactivity tool that you can use with Full Screen view is a remote control device. For about $50 to $75 US, you can purchase a handheld remote control. The control comes in two parts. The control device has two buttons used for moving forward and backward in the slide presentation. The companion unit is plugged into a USB port on your laptop or desktop computer. You open the slide presentation in Full Screen view and click the left or right button to navigate slides while you walk across a stage. Some devices also have a button for cursor control. You can remotely move the cursor on a slide and click a button that opens a secondary file, Web link, or other action associated with the button or link.

When using remote devices, be certain to set your Full Screen preferences to "Left click to go forward one page; right click to go back one page." The USB devices have two buttons enabling you to move backward and forward through your slide presentation. When the check boxes are enabled, the back and forward buttons on the handheld device are supported.

Conducting Presentations and Online Meetings

Dynamic and real-time delivery of presentations to workgroups, conference attendees, and expo participants is extended to online presentations. Adobe's answer to providing an online viewing environment is handled through either Acrobat Connect Pro or ConnectNow, a service of Acrobat.com.

The free service you have available is ConnectNow, a service of Acrobat.com. You can have up to three other individuals in a meeting room and share your presentation with them. For a more robust online meeting where you can make a presentation for up to 2,500 people with much dynamic interactivity, Acrobat Connect Pro supports your needs.

CROSS-REF For more information on hosting and participating in ConnectNow and Acrobat Connect Pro online meetings and a description of the differences between ConnectNow and Acrobat Connect Pro, see Chapter 29.

Summary

- You convert PowerPoint slides to PDF with the PDFMaker tool.

- To create note handouts from PowerPoint, use the Print dialog box and print the file to the Adobe PDF printer after making the attribute choices in the Print dialog box for the type of handouts you want to create.

- Apple Keynote slides can be exported to PDF and PowerPoint formats. Keynote offers Macintosh users a robust slide creation program with easy, intuitive palettes and tools.

- You can use layout programs to create slide presentations. For creating handout notes, set up a master page with objects and elements to be added to each page. Import the PDF slide presentation and convert to PDF to distribute handouts.

- Adobe Presenter is a program available free to Acrobat Pro Extended users (Windows). Presenter enables you to export animations created in PowerPoint and converts the slide presentation to an Adobe Flash file inside a PDF document.

- You apply page transitions to pages individually using the Advanced ➪ Document Processing ➪ Page Transitions command or using menu commands in the Pages panel. To apply different transitions to different pages, select pages in the Pages panel and adjust the transitions in the Set Transitions dialog box.

- When using Full Screen mode, open the Preferences dialog box and select Full Screen. Make choices for options used in Full Screen viewing and click OK.

- Full Screen views support file linking with link and button actions, Microsoft PowerPoint animation, and transitions applied to pages with either the Full Screen preferences or the Set Page Transitions command.

- Online presentations can be delivered using ConnectNow and Acrobat Connect Pro.

Chapter 29

Using Acrobat.com for Online Collaboration

A crobat Connect was a new program Adobe Systems provided in version 8 and made accessible from within all Acrobat viewers as well as Adobe Bridge CS3. In Acrobat 8 you had two versions of Acrobat Connect designed to satisfy remote meeting needs for large organizations and individual users. Acrobat Connect Professional is a powerful online collaboration program, and Acrobat Connect is a personal collaboration meeting room.

Together with the release of Acrobat 9, Adobe has introduced the separate Acrobat.com service. Among the features available with Acrobat.com, you have another online collaboration tool called ConnectNow.

Acrobat.com is a collection of online collaboration tools that provide you free services for sharing files, sharing reviews, distributing forms, using an online word processor and collaborating in online meetings — something similar to Web conferencing.

Acrobat Connect Pro is still with us in Acrobat version 9 as a paid service. Through the Connect workspace you can host a meeting complete with screen sharing on your computer and a host of industrial-strength tools for conducting online meetings. ConnectNow is a free service that provides some similar features available with the Acrobat Connect Pro service, but with several fewer features among which is the limitation of the number of people who can attend a meeting. With Connect Pro you can conduct meetings with 1,500 people. With ConnectNow you are limited to hosting meetings with three people — including yourself.

For more sophisticated online collaboration events you'll want to learn more about Acrobat Connect Pro. Log on to www.adobe.com/products/acrobatconnectpro/ to discover how this product can serve your

IN THIS CHAPTER

Setting up the Acrobat.com workspace

Getting familiar with Acrobat.com

Creating Web conferencing sessions

Getting to know the Acrobat. com interface

company's online collaboration needs. In this chapter, I'll stick primarily to discussing ConnectNow as it pertains to serving individual and small group online conferencing.

Setting Up the Work Environment

To follow along in this chapter, just open a context menu on the Toolbar Well and select Reset Toolbars. No special tools need to be loaded to access Acrobat.com.

Understanding Acrobat.com

If you read Chapters 4, 21, and 35 you should have some idea of what Acrobat.com is and how to log on to find all Acrobat.com services. I briefly discussed using Acrobat.com with Adobe Reader in Chapter 4 and conducting shared reviews in Chapter 21, and discuss hosting and tracking forms coming up ahead in Chapter 35.

Acrobat.com is your central online workspace for sharing files, collecting data, engaging in review sessions, and conducting online collaboration sessions. In regard to online meetings, you have three alternatives Adobe Systems offers. These meeting room alternatives include:

- **ConnectNow (free service).** Using Acrobat.com from any Acrobat 9 or greater viewer, you can conduct online meetings as a host and have a maximum of two other participants. This service is free from Adobe Systems.

- **Acrobat Connect (annual subscription fee).** In Acrobat 8, Adobe introduced Acrobat Connect. Acrobat Connect is a meeting room you use as a subscription service where you can host meetings for up to 15 people. This service is still offered by Adobe Systems.

- **Acrobat Connect Pro (annual subscription fee).** Acrobat Connect Pro is an industrial-strength application of Acrobat Connect. With Connect Pro you can host meetings of up to 1,500 people. Like Connect, this service is acquired through an annual subscription fee.

The content in this chapter is related to Acrobat.com and using the free online meeting room. If you need to host meetings with 15 or less people, or meetings with Acrobat Connect Pro that provides hosting meetings of up to 1,500 and a number of features such as VoIP, integrated audio, customizable layouts, multiple meeting rooms per user, and more, then log on to `www.adobe.com/products/acrobatconnect/`. The Adobe Acrobat Connect Web site contains information about the Connect products, free trial downloads, and online ordering and subscription services.

In addition to the meeting room service on Acrobat.com, you also have a place where you can upload files to share with other users, invite users to participate in online reviews, submit forms and have the forms uploaded to Acrobat.com for data collection and tracking, and more.

Using ConnectNow for Online Collaboration

I'll break this chapter up into two primary areas of discussion — Web conferencing and sharing files. To begin with, I'll cover the Acrobat.com services for Web conferencing. Look at the section later in this chapter "Using Acrobat.com for File Sharing" to learn more about sharing files on Acrobat.com.

Getting into real-time collaboration

Before I get into using Acrobat.com for Web conferencing, I want to point out one of the outstanding features you find with the design of the Acrobat.com services. In Acrobat 8 we had Acrobat Connect to allow users to host a meeting. You might have a PowerPoint presentation that you want to step through in an online meeting to describe some aspect of your business such as the introduction of a new product, a new marketing campaign, a sales meeting, or some similar type of discussion.

Using Acrobat 8 and the PDF documents you created, using Acrobat 8 worked well for an Acrobat Connect meeting. The only pauses you experienced was a momentary delay when a new slide came into view.

In Acrobat 9 we have a quantum leap in the delivery of PDF files. The PDF audience palette has changed over the past several years, and people are asking for more dynamic presentations such as those you create with Adobe Presenter as I discussed in Chapter 28, adding Adobe Flash to PDFs as I discussed in Chapter 23, and presenting documents in the form of PDF Portfolios as I covered in Chapter 12.

If you view the media-rich PDF files in a Web conferencing application like Acrobat Connect, as was introduced with Acrobat 8, the meeting participants have to wait for video, manipulation of 3D objects, and Adobe Flash animations. These files come across the Internet very choppy and sluggish and are painfully slow even with the fastest Internet connections.

In Acrobat 9 using Acrobat.com (and the new versions of ConnectNow) Adobe introduces real-time collaboration. When you choose File ➪ Collaborate ➪ Send & Collaborate Live, a recipient is invited to a real-time collaboration session. Instead of viewing your screen on a remote system and waiting for the video to play from the host machine, each participant downloads the same PDF file containing the video file. When the host triggers something like a play button, the play is sent to other users as an *event*. Instead of the video streaming to other users from the host's computer, only the events are passed to the participants. Each user then watches a video locally but the host controls the events. This is real-time collaboration and a huge development edge provided by Adobe.

Setting up an Adobe ID

All the work you do with Acrobat.com requires you to create an Adobe ID. Each time you start a session, you need to log on with your ID (email address) and password. For the remainder of this chapter, I'll assume you've created an Adobe ID and you can log on to Acrobat.com using your log-on ID and password.

If you don't have an Adobe ID, choose File ⇨ Collaborate ⇨ Go to Acrobat.com. Or you can simply open your Web browser and log on to www.acrobat.com. The initial screen opens as shown in Figure 29.1.

FIGURE 29.1

Choose File ⇨ Collaborate ⇨ Go to Acrobat.com to open the Acrobat.com log-on page.

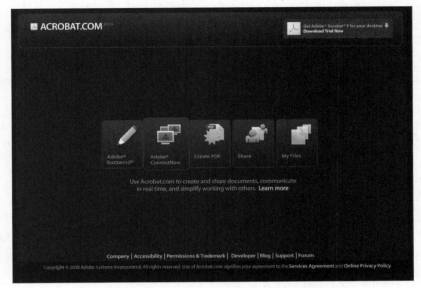

At the log-on Web page you have a choice for the type of activity you want to begin. For Web conferencing, click Adobe ConnectNow and the Adobe ConnectNow pop-up window opens as shown in Figure 29.2.

Click Begin and the log-on window opens as shown in Figure 29.3. Type your Email address and Password and click Enter Meeting. If you don't have an Adobe ID, click the Sign Up text at the lower-left corner of the pop-up window to create an Adobe ID.

If you want to bypass the log-on each time you access Acrobat.com, you can add your email address and password to your Acrobat viewer preferences.

FIGURE 29.2

Click Adobe ConnectNow and a pop-up window opens prompting you to begin a ConnectNow session.

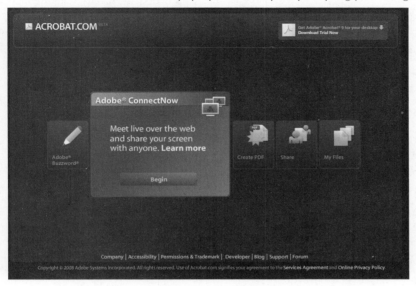

FIGURE 29.3

Type your email address and password to begin a ConnectNow session.

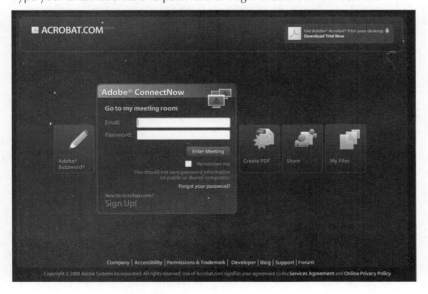

In any Acrobat viewer, open the Preferences dialog box (Ctrl/⌘+K) and click Acrobat.com in the left pane. Fill in the email address you used for your Adobe ID and type your password. Check the Remember me check box. Also check Always connect when opening documents enabled for live collaboration. Setting up the Acrobat.com preferences in this manner eliminates a need to type your ID and password each time you log on to Acrobat.com.

NOTE Setting the Acrobat.com preferences is optional. If you use your computer in a workgroup where others have access to your computer, you may want to avoid filling in the Acrobat.com preferences and use a manual logon each time you access the Acrobat.com Web site. If you are confident that no one can access your computer, go ahead and set up the preferences so you can use an automatic logon each time you visit Acrobat.com.

Before you read further in this chapter, be certain to have your Adobe ID confirmed and ready to go. Make sure you can log on to Acrobat.com by choosing File ➪ Collaborate ➪ Go to Acrobat.com.

Sharing your computer screen

There are some different options you have for online collaboration. You can choose to share your computer screen and control a meeting as a presenter, you can choose to share files for online comment and review, and you can choose to engage in real-time conferencing. To start with, let's take a look at sharing your computer screen in an online collaboration session.

Starting a share session

Acrobat and Adobe Reader 9 make it easy to share your computer screen. Once you enter your personal meeting room you have options for controlling a meeting as a presenter, promoting other users to a presenter level, taking control over another user's computer, and allowing another user to take control over your computer. Using ConnectNow you have one of two categories to experience — that of a host, and that of a participant.

To host a session, try following these steps:

Steps: Sharing your screen

1. **Log on to Acrobat.com.** In any Acrobat viewer 9 and above, including Adobe Reader, choose File ➪ Collaborate ➪ Share my Screen.

2. **Log on to Acrobat.com.** If you elected to not use an automatic logon by setting up your Acrobat.com preferences, log on with your Adobe ID and password. Click the Adobe ConnectNow button on the Acrobat.com opening page and click Begin when the pop-up window opens prompting you to begin a ConnectNow session. Fill in your email address and password to open your meeting room. You can also choose File ➪ Collaborate ➪ Share My Screen and you'll go directly to your meeting room log on.

3. **Share your screen.** The first page you see contains a pop-up window displaying the URL for your meeting room as shown in Figure 29.4. Click Close to dismiss the window and the Screen Sharing window is displayed as shown in Figure 29.5.

FIGURE 29.4

Click Close to dismiss the pop-up window.

FIGURE 29.5

Click Share My Computer Screen to begin your sharing session.

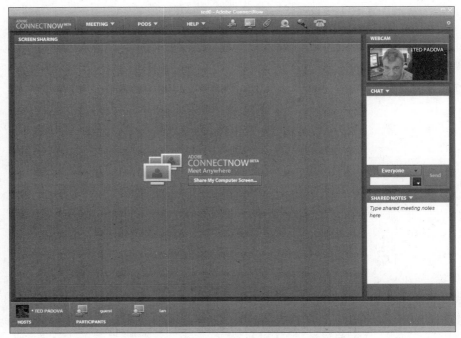

4. **Start screen sharing.** After clicking Close to dismiss the pop-up window, click Share My Computer Screen in the Screen Sharing window. Another pop-up window appears. Click Share to confirm sharing your computer screen.

The first time you start sharing your screen, you'll be prompted to install an add-in. Click OK and let the installation complete before proceeding.

5. **Review the introduction screen.** After you click Share in the pop-up confirmation window, an infor mation window opens as shown in Figure 29.6. Look over the help information if this is your first attempt at sharing your screen. You might want to review this information in future sessions. When you don't want this screen to appear, click the Do not show this message again check box.

6. **Click OK.** The screen changes again where the ConnectNow Screen Sharing panel opens (see Figure 29.7) on your desktop or application window. This panel remains in the foreground no matter what application you launch and is used to control your sharing session. In Figure 29.7 a PDF Portfolio is opened in Acrobat in a sharing session. The ConnectNow Sharing Panel appears in the foreground. You can minimize the panel by clicking the minus (-) icon in the top right corner.

FIGURE 29.6

Click Share and the Introduction to Screen Sharing window opens.

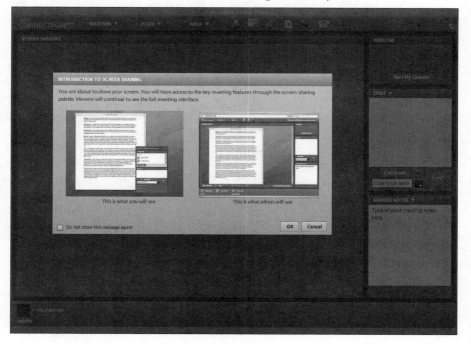

7. **Invite participants.** In the Screen Sharing panel click the Invite button shown in Figure 29.7.

8. **Send an email invitation to participants.** When you click the Invite Participants button in the Screen Sharing panel, your default email client opens with an automated message as shown in Figure 29.8. Type email addresses (for up to a maximum of two participants) and modify the Subject and Message fields as desired. However, don't change the URL link. When your participants receive your invitation, they only need to click the link to take them to your meeting room. Click Send to send the mail to your list of participants.

As participants log on to your meeting, you'll see buttons appear to Accept or Reject the person trying to attend your meeting. Click Accept as each individual you invited logs on; your list of participants is shown in the Screen Sharing panel.

FIGURE 29.7

After sharing your screen, the ConnectNow Sharing Panel opens in the foreground.

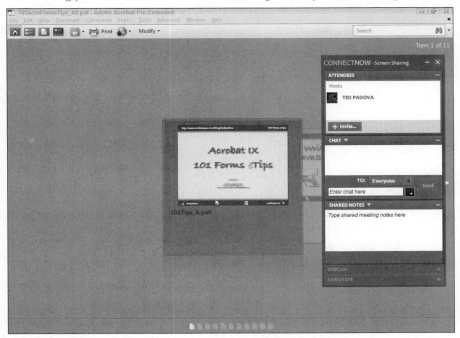

FIGURE 29.8

Fill in the To line with up to two participant email addresses and click Send.

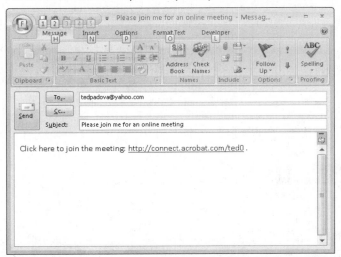

9. **Start your presentation.** When the Screen Sharing panel is open, the application document behind the window remains in view for the participants. You see the screen with the ConnectNow Screen Sharing panel open as shown in Figure 29.7, but the participants see your application window only inside a screen similar to Figure 29.7.

   With the Chat panel in view other users can text message questions to you. If you set up your session with a phone connection, other users can listen on the phone to your audio. If using an application like Yahoo! Messenger or Skype, you can have participants listen virtually anywhere in the world to your presentation.

Examining the sharing tools

While you're sharing your screen the Screen Sharing panel remains open and available to you for controlling your sharing session. In Figure 29.8 you see the Screen Sharing panel, which includes the following panels:

■ **Attendees.** The host and attendees are listed in this panel.

■ **Chat.** In Figure 29.8, the Chat History panel is open. You type messages in the text box at the bottom of the panel to chat with all attendees or selected attendees.

■ **Shared Notes.** Click the plus (+) icon to open the Shared Notes panel. You can type notes during your session in this panel and save the text as a text file.

 Open a context menu in the Chat History panel and you find menu options to Clear the History and Save the history file.

■ **WebCam.** Click the plus (+) icon to open the Webcam panel where you can view webcams from transmissions from attendees.

■ **Annotate.** Click Start to add annotations to your presentation. Doing so however, stops your screen sharing. After you add an annotation, click Start to resume screen sharing.

CROSS-REF For more information on the Annotation tools, see the section "Using the Annotation tools" later in this chapter.

Loading pods

When you log on to your meeting room before you start sharing your screen, you'll find several pull-down menus at the top of the meeting Screen Sharing window. Many of the menu commands are covered in the section "Participating in a sharing session" later in this chapter. A few items you don't find when logging on as a participant include the Pods menu and the Invite Participants tool Clicking the Invite Participants tool results in the same action as when inviting participants from the Screen Sharing panel.

The Pods menu has several menu commands as shown in Figure 29.10, and this menu is available only to those who host a meeting.

FIGURE 29.9

The Screen Sharing panel remains open during your screen sharing session.

FIGURE 29.10

Open the Pods menu to display the Pods menu commands.

By default, the Screen Sharing, Chat, Shared Notes, and Webcam pods are open. The Files pod displays all the files you add as attachments, and the Whiteboard opens the Tools panel discussed later in the section "Participating in a sharing session." The Whiteboard is used to mark up notes on a file shared in a session by the host. The recipients have access to drawing tools when a participant shares a screen and opens the Screen Sharing panel. Clicking the Pause and Annotate button opens the same Tools panel as the host has available with the Whiteboard.

Participating in a sharing session

If you receive an email invitation to participate in a sharing session, the only thing you need on your computer is a Web browser. Acrobat.com meeting rooms support all Web browsers on all platforms. Getting into a meeting is as simple as clicking a URL link in an email message and logging on. When you arrive at a meeting, your screen changes to the view shown in Figure 29.11. At this point a message is sent to the host who needs to accept you into the room.

After the host accepts you to enter the meeting room, you see the screen shared by the host as shown in Figure 29.12

The meeting room pull-down menus shown at the top of Figure 29.12 also apply to a host sharing a computer screen. If you're a host or participant, there are some settings you'll want to make when you log on to a meeting room.

NOTE One difference you'll see between the host's computer screen at log on time and a participant is that the host has an extra button in the menu used to invite participants. The participants cannot invite others to attend a meeting hosted by another individual.

Setting preferences

Open the Meeting pull-down menu when you log onto a meeting and choose Preferences from the menu options. The Preferences dialog box opens as shown in Figure 29.13. In this dialog box you can make some choices for handling your audio and video equipment, your chat default text size and color, and your connection speed.

FIGURE 29.11

Join a meeting as a participant and your screen displays a screen informing you the host has been notified of your arrival.

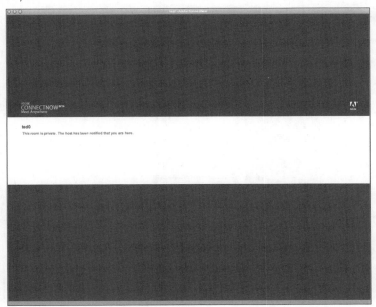

Getting help

The Help pull-down men u (accessed by clicking the Help button) provides some choices for help information. Click Troubleshooting to be taken to an Adobe Web page that provides information related to setting meetings. Click Flash Player Settings to open another Web page with information about the Adobe Flash Player.

Share My Computer Screen

Attendees can share their screens in a meeting. The host has control over what screen is shown in the meeting room; however, the host needs permission from each participant for screen sharing. Choose this menu item so your screen can be shared with others in a meeting.

Share My Microphone

Click the Share My Microphone icon in the menu bar to open the Adobe Flash Player Settings dialog box as shown in Figure 29.14. If you want to share your microphone, click Allow and click Remember in the Adobe Flash Player Settings dialog box. While you share your microphone, other members in the meeting need to turn their microphones off to avoid an echo sound in the audio. You can minimize the echo in the audio by clicking the Advanced button in the Adobe Flash Player and making some settings choices for handling the audio.

FIGURE 29.12

After a host accepts you, you see the screen shared by the host.

FIGURE 29.13

Open the Meeting pull-down menu and make choices in the Preferences dialog box.

Click the Share My Microphone button and make choices in the Adobe Flash Player Settings dialog box.

Using the Annotation tools

When a participant shares a screen and the host gives control over the sharing to a participant, the participant's screen changes to a view similar to the host where the Screen Sharing panel opens. If a participant clicks the Annotate button in the Screen Sharing panel, the Annotations toolbar opens. When you click a number of different tools in this toolbar, a pop-up toolbar opens as shown in Figure 29.15 where you can assign attributes to the annotations you add on a document.

Click any one of a number of different tools and a pop-up toolbar opens.

The different tools and the markup attributes you find in the Tools panel include:

A. **Selection Arrow tool.** This tool is used to select an annotation after you draw one on a document page. When you select the object, you can use the Selection Arrow tool to reshape the annotation and rotate it.

B. **Arrow tool.** Draw lines with arrowheads.

C. **Highlighter Pen tool.** Highlights text.

D. **Highlight Rectangle tool.** Used to create a rectangle to highlight text. Note text can be added to the text rectangle.

E. **Text tool.** Add a text annotation.

F. **Shapes tools.** Click the Shapes tools to open a pop-up toolbar as shown in Figure 29.16. You have a Line tool and several geometric shapes to choose from in the pop-up menu.

FIGURE 29.16

Click the Shapes tools to open the Shapes pop-up toolbar.

G. **Undo.** Undo the last action.

H. **Redo.** Redo the last action.

I. **Delete Selected Shapes tool.** Use the Selection Arrow tool to click an annotation and click this tool to delete the annotation.

J. **Save tool.** Click the Save tool and a screen capture is taken of the page and saved as a PNG file like the one shown in Figure 29.17.

K. **Color.** Click the color swatch to open a pop-up color panel where an annotation color can be changed.

L. **Point Size.** For use with the text tool and markups that support note text, use this pull-down menu to change the text point size.

M. **Opacity.** Change the opacity of the annotation in 25-percent increments from 25 percent to 100 percent.

FIGURE 29.17

Click the Save tool to take a screen capture of the annotations. A Save As dialog box opens where you can save the file as a PNG image file.

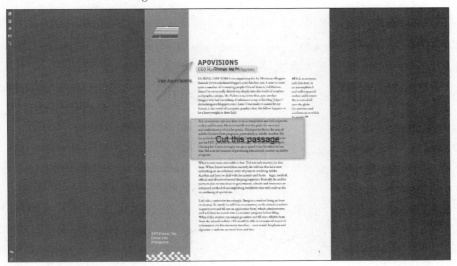

Using the Acrobat.com Interface

When you participate in a meeting, the meeting is held in a Flash-based interface. Although you need to have an active Internet connection and a Web browser, once you're in, there's no visual clue that you're working within a Web browser.

When you choose File ➪ Collaborate ➪ Go to Acrobat.com and log on, the Acrobat.com interface appears within a browser window using an Adobe Flash interface as you see in Figure 29.1 shown earlier in this chapter. You first make a choice for the activity you want to begin by clicking one of the buttons on the opening page of the Acrobat.com window.

Click My Files to open your Acrobat.com library where you can store 5 GB of data. The user interface changes as shown in Figure 29.18.

FIGURE 29.18

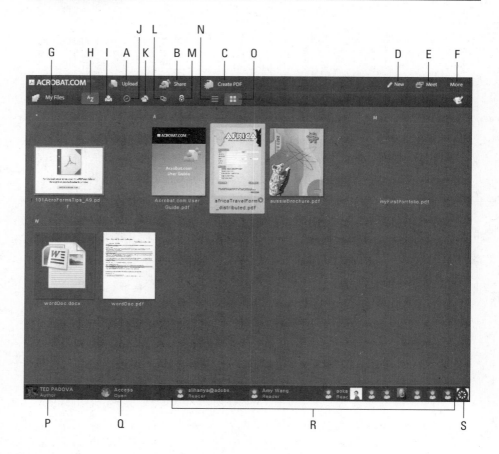

Exploring the Acrobat.com interface

Once in the Acrobat.com interface, you have a number of options to choose for viewing files, uploading files, exploring collections, adding contacts, printing files, and more. The tools, buttons, and panels you find in the default window include:

A. **Upload.** Click this button and the Share panel changes as shown in Figure 29.19. Click the Browse My Computer button and a Browse dialog box opens. Select a file or multiple files and click Open to add the file(s) to a list in the Share panel. Once you see the files listed for upload, you can remove a file by clicking the X to the right of the file name. You can also click the Browse My Computer button to add more files to the list. Click the Upload button below the list to upload the files to your Acrobat.com library. A progress bar reports the status of the upload.

FIGURE 29.19

Click Share and click the Browse My Computer button to add files to a list for uploading.

B. **Share.** Select a file thumbnail in the library and click the Share button and the interface changes as you see in Figure 29.20. Note that you can also click Share without selecting a file and browse your computer to locate a file on your hard drive for sharing by clicking the Browse My Computer button.

·FIGURE 29.20

Click Share to upload files for sharing with other users.

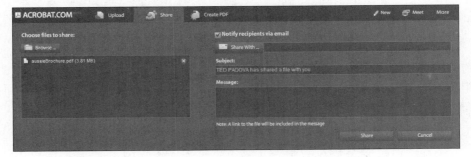

In the Share view you make several choices for sharing files that include:

■ **Share With (button).** Click the Share With button and your Contacts list opens in a pop-up menu. You can check boxes adjacent to contact names to add a list of recipients that are added to the Share With text box.

■ **Share With (text box).** Type email addresses in the Share With text box of those you want to share a given file with. If you click the Share With button to add contacts in your Contacts list, you can append names to the list by typing additional email addresses in this text box.

■ **Subject.** Acrobat.com automatically adds a subject line to a default email message. The text box is editable where you can add your own subject text.

■ **Message.** Type text in the message box that you want appearing in an email message. In addition to the text you type here, an automated message that includes the URL link where your file is hosted is automatically added by Acrobat.com. (Notice the Note below the Message box).

■ **Share.** Click the Share button below the Message box and your default email client opens with the To, Subject, and Message fields filled in according to what you typed in the Share interface. Click the Send button in your email client to send the message to your recipients.

CROSS-REF   For more information on sharing files, see Chapter 4.

C. **Create PDF.** Click the Create PDF button and the interface changes to the view shown in Figure 29.21. You can choose a library file shown in your Acrobat.com library, or click the From my computer radio button and click Browse to locate one or more files to convert to PDF. All files you select in both the From Acrobat.com and From my computer radio button options must be a file format that can be converted to PDF.

FIGURE 29.21

Click Create PDF to convert native files to PDF documents.

CROSS-REF   For more information on using Create PDF on Acrobat.com and file formats acceptable for conversion, see Chapter 4.

Create PDF is intended for Adobe Reader users because the free Adobe Reader software doesn't provide options for converting native documents to PDF. There are limitations for use. Adobe offers a free number of trial conversions (5). After the number of free conversions is exhausted, PDF conversion is offered on a subscription fee basis.

D. New. Click this button to create a new Adobe Buzzword document. Buzzword is an Adobe online word processing program where you can create documents online and store them for access anywhere you have an Internet connection.

E. Meet. Click this button to start an online meeting via ConnectNow.

F. More. Click More to open a pull-down menu containing commands to access help information, set preferences, and review licensing terms.

G. My Files. Click this button to list the files stored in your Acrobat.com library.

H. A/Z. Click this button to list files alphabetically.

I. List by author. Click this button to list files according to author.

J. List by when added or updated. Clicking this button displays files in a date order according to when added to your library and when last updated.

K. List by file type. Lists files according to file type.

L. List by size. Lists files according to file size.

M. List by shared status. Lists files according to Not Shared, Open Access, and Closed Access. When you share files you have a choice for sharing a file with Open Access where anyone who visits your Acrobat.com library can download the file or Closed Access where only those you invite to view the files can access them.

N. View as list. The List view displays the files in your Library in a list as shown in Figure 29.22. This view is similar to the List view you have available with PDF Portfolios. When you engage in shared reviews and collect PDF form data, the List view is something you'll use frequently.

In both List view and Thumbnail view, a down-pointing arrow adjacent to the file name opens a pop-up menu where you can choose from a number of options as shown in Figure 29.22.

FIGURE 29.22

Click the List View icon and the Library displays files in a list.

O. **View as thumbnails.** When in List view, click this button to return to Thumbnail view.

P. **Log-on name.** Displays your log-on name.

R. **Share recipients.** Click a file and a list across the bottom of the window displays all those with whom you've invited to share a file.

S. **Storage results.** Move the cursor over the icon on the far right lower-right portion of the window and a pop-up display shows you how much storage space you've used for your library and the storage space available to you as shown in Figure 29.23.

FIGURE 29.23

Move the cursor over the icon in the lower-right portion of the window to see how much storage space you have remaining in your library.

Viewing files

As files are uploaded to your Acrobat.com library, you find several different viewing options. By default, you'll see files appearing with thumbnail views as shown earlier in Figure 29.20. The files can be changed from the default Thumbnail view to List view by clicking the List View icon.

Viewing Detail information

When you view files in either Thumbnail view or List view and click the down pointing arrow adjacent to the file name, detail information is displayed in the menu as shown earlier in Figure 29.22.

Viewing source documents

If you use Create PDF, the resultant PDF document is added to your library and the original source document remains in the library. The two files appear as a stacked group. When you view a document that has been converted to PDF on Acrobat.com, you find two mini icons appearing in the top left corner of the Thumbnail view. If you want to share the PDF version of the document with another user, position the cursor over the icon representing the PDF and a tooltip displays the file type. Click the mouse button and the PDF document is brought forward in the stack. From this point you can click the Share button and share the PDF version with another user.

Viewing files

Double-click a thumbnail or a file in List view and you move out of the Library View mode into a File View mode as shown in Figure 29.24. In the File View mode you can view the contents of a document, scroll pages, zoom views, and more. The tools available to you in File View mode include:

FIGURE 29.24

Double-click a file thumbnail or a file name in List View mode and the document opens in a File
View mode.

A. **File name.** Displays the file name for the file in view.

B. **Go to previous page.** In multi-page documents, click this tool to open the previous page.

C. **Go to next page.** In multi-page documents, click this tool to open the next page.

NOTE Because you're viewing your files in an Adobe Flash interface, an animated effect appears as you scroll pages.

D. **Go to a particular page.** Type a value to jump to a corresponding page in the document.

E. **Zoom out.** Click to zoom out.

F. **Change zoom level.** Move the slider left to zoom out and right to zoom in.

G. **Zoom in.** Click to zoom in.

H. **Toggle display of mini navigator.** Click the tool and the mini navigation panel opens as
   shown in Figure 29.25. This panel behaves similar to the Pan and Zoom window in
   Acrobat where you drag a slider in the panel to change zoom views.

FIGURE 29.25

Click Show/hide mini navigator and the mini navigator opens.

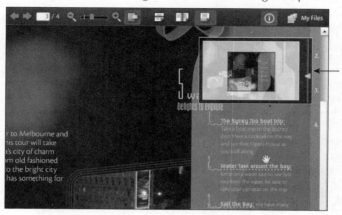

I. **Scroll pages continuously.** Changes the view to a continuous pager view.

J. **Show pages side by side.** Similar to a 2-Up view in Acrobat where pages are viewed side by side.

K. **Single page view.** Click the tool to display single pages.

L. **Hide info panel.** Click to hide the info panel on the right side of the window.

M. **Details.** The first panel at the top of the Info panel is the Details panel. File details are reported at the top of the panel.

N. **Copy URL.** Click this button for the URL of the file location. You can paste the copied text in an email message to invite additional viewers.

O. **Copy Embed Code.** Copies the URL location as HTML text that can be pasted into an HTML editor like Adobe Dreamweaver.

P. **Shared With panel.** If you shared the file with other users, a list of names appears of those you invited to view the file.

Q. **Add/Delete reviewers.** Click the plus (+) icon and the Share with more people panel opens as shown in Figure 29.26. You can add reviewers by typing in an email address, a message, and click the Add button.

R. **Access panel.** The access to the document is shown. In Figure 29.24, the document is an Open access file which means anyone visiting the site can download the file.

CROSS-REF   For more information on viewing PDF documents, see Chapter 5.

FIGURE 29.26

Add more reviewers to a review session by clicking the plus (+) icon to open the Share with more people panel.

Getting Acrobat.com for your desktop

When you first log on to Acrobat.com, you'll find a link to download an application for launching Acrobat.com from your desktop as shown in Figure 29.27.

If you happen to miss the link and want to download the application, open the More pull-down menu and choose Get Acrobat.com for My Desktop. A Web page opens in your default Web browser where you can click a Download button to download the application. Double clicking the downloaded file installs the application on your desktop. Click the shortcut Acrobat.com icon and you launch Acrobat.com.

FIGURE 29.27

When you first log on to Acrobat.com a link is displayed for downloading an application to launch Acrobat.com from your desktop.

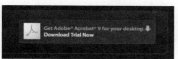

Using context menu commands

Context menus are scarce in Acrobat.com. Right-click (Windows) or Control+click (Macintosh) in any view to open a context menu and you find only three menu commands. The commands include Print, Settings, and About Adobe Flash Player as shown in Figure 29.28.

FIGURE 29.28

Open a context menu anywhere in the Acrobat.com interface and you find three menu commands.

Printing a file

The first of the menu commands you have available with a context menu is the Print command. Open a context menu on one or several selected files and choose Print. The Print dialog box opens as shown in Figure 29.29. When you choose Print from a context menu and click the Print button in the Print dialog box, your file is printed.

 For more information on printing, see Chapters 31 and 32.

FIGURE 29.29

Open a context menu and choose Print to open the Print dialog box.

Setting Flash preferences

Open a context menu in the Acrobat.com interface and choose Settings. The Adobe Flash Player Settings dialog box opens as shown in Figure 29.30. At the bottom of the dialog box you find five icons used to switch panes where you make some settings adjustments. The adjustments include:

FIGURE 29.30

Open a context menu and choose Settings to open the Adobe Flash Player Settings dialog box.

A B C D E   F

A. **Display.** Click the Display icon and the panel changes to the Display settings. You have a single item in this panel. Check the Enable hardware acceleration check box to take advantage of hardware acceleration if it's available on your computer.

B. **Privacy.** Check the Allow radio button to allow Acrobat.com to access your camera and microphone when you want to use a webcam and microphone in your share sessions. An Advanced button also appears in this panel. Click Advanced and a Web page opens in your default Web browser where you can find Flash Player help.

C. **Local Storage.** You can set the amount of local storage you want to dedicate to Acrobat. com. The default is 100K, which is sufficient for almost all uses. If you need to increase the amount of local storage space, move the slider to the right.

D. **Microphone.** Click Microphone and you find settings for your microphone driver, volume settings, and a check box to reduce echo noise. If you find an echo when using your microphone on Acrobat.com, be sure to test the settings to see if you can reduce the noise.

E. **Camera.** Click Camera and you can select your camera driver from a pull-down menu.

F. **Close.** Click Close and the settings you make in the Adobe Flash Player Settings are set as new defaults until you change them again.

About Adobe Flash Player 9

The last of the three context menu commands is Acrobat Adobe Flash Player 9. Choose this menu command and the Adobe Flash Player Web page opens in a new browser window. Here you'll find the latest information about using the Adobe Flash Player, upgrade information and downloads, system requirements, and a variety of information related to the Adobe Flash Player plug-in.

Summary

- Acrobat.com is a free online service available to users of Adobe Reader 9 and all other Acrobat 9 viewers.

- Using Acrobat.com you can host Web conferences free with up to three participants (including yourself) in each session.

- Acrobat Connect and Acrobat Connect Pro are Web conferencing tools available on a subscription fee basis.

- Using ConnectNow you can share your screen with other users and promote individual users to a level where others can share their screens.

- During an Acrobat.com session you can mark up documents as a host and as a participant with real-time annotations.

- The Acrobat.com interface permits you to share files, engage in review sessions, collect form data, and create PDFs online.

- You can upload files to Acrobat.com for limited access or open access. Limited access permits only those you have invited to share files with you or to view and download your files.

Chapter 30

Using PDFs and eBooks

The promise of eBooks has been a roller coaster ride for users, providers, and would-be authors in recent years. The fall of some important content providers, coupled with some not-so-impressive display mechanisms, has slowed down an industry that many thought had a lot of promise. Notwithstanding hardware-display mechanisms and user acceptability, the software used to secure eBooks and make them accessible to every potential consumer was not as robust as viewing documents in Acrobat viewers.

With the introduction of Acrobat 6, Adobe Systems waved good-bye to the Adobe eBook Reader software and offered users, content providers, and content authors a much more attractive means of creation, protection, and delivery of eBooks. In Acrobat 7, the eBook branding was changed to Digital Editions, but the development and delivery for eBooks remained the same in Acrobat 7 as was introduced in Acrobat 6.

In Acrobat 9, Adobe changed the user interface for acquiring and managing Adobe Digital Editions (notice the rebranding of Digital Editions, now referred to as *Adobe* Digital Editions). You'll find the new interface to be attractive and intuitive. Adobe Digital Editions are easy to read in the new interface, and acquiring new books has been made much easier.

The responsibility for restricting eBook viewing and file exchanging is all within the hands of the content provider using special software to guard and protect eBooks and any other type of PDF document against unauthorized viewing, printing, and file exchanging. In addition, end users can now use an Adobe online service to protect their PDFs without using content providers.

Not known as a company that stands on its laurels, Adobe has added something new to this notion of digital editions. Since the hosting and securing of

IN THIS CHAPTER

Creating eBooks

Acquiring eBooks

Reading eBooks

Adding ads to eBooks

documents by content providers has been a roller coaster ride, Adobe added a little something to PDFs that takes the need for security and relationships with content providers out of the equation. In Acrobat 9 you'll find a marvelous new feature called Ads for Adobe PDF Powered by Yahoo!.

Setting Up the eBook Work Environment

The Digital Editions menu commands were changed in Acrobat viewers in version 8 and 9. You'll find access to Adobe Digital Editions in Acrobat by selecting Help ➪ Digital Editions. In Adobe Reader 9, look at the File ➪ Digital Editions menu command. No special tools are required for acquiring or reading Adobe Digital Editions. The Adobe Digital Editions reading mode has its own set of tools used for navigating pages, returning to last viewed pages, and opening new books.

Creating eBooks

If you're an end user who purchases content in the form of eBooks and protected files, you really don't need to know much about how the files are created. If you're a content provider, then understanding the options available to you and the restrictions you can apply to eBooks and any other type of PDF file are important to you.

On the user end, you can acquire PDF documents with special encryption that restricts your viewing, exchanging, and terms of use without activating your Acrobat viewer. On the content provider end, you have a very impressive solution available from Adobe in the form of a server-side product that can handle all your Digital Rights Management (DRM) needs.

Adobe Content Server 3

At first view, content providers may feel that Adobe has been fickle in deciding how to handle DRM (Digital Rights Management) and restricted use of not only eBooks but also any PDF file. A few generations ago we had the Adobe eBook Reader that was a special software tool designed to view content that was protected against unauthorized distribution and viewing.

During the initial life cycle of Acrobat 7, we had the Adobe Content Server software that was used to restrict viewing and distribution through the use of Digital Editions. On November 30, 2004, Adobe discontinued the Adobe Content Server software and introduced the Adobe LiveCycle Rights Management ES. What has transpired is not a matter of fickle judgment, but rather, an evolution of a very sophisticated solution for any enterprise interested in restricting the viewing of PDF files.

Adobe LiveCycle Rights Management ES

Adobe LiveCycle Rights Management ES (formerly known as Adobe LiveCycle Policy Server in Acrobat 8 — www.adobe.com/products/livecycle/rightsmanagement/) is truly a marvelous product. With the Rights Management, an enterprise can track the viewing of any PDF file by any user, set time limits for use, update viewing restrictions, control the online and offline document usage, and revoke use at any time. The entire burden for activation and use is placed on the content provider, and the end user merely needs the same version of an Acrobat viewer for viewing any PDF file.

Acquiring Adobe Digital Editions

With just about every upgrade to Acrobat, you also find upgrades to many Adobe server products. With eBooks for example, the previous versions of Acrobat required a content provider to purchase the Adobe Policy Server to encrypt eBooks. With Acrobat 8, Adobe announced hosted Adobe Policy Services. With Acrobat 9 Adobe has introduced the Adobe LiveCycle Rights Management ES Server. (The ES is an acronym for Enterprise Suite).

Adobe's methods for working with eBooks became much easier in Acrobat 8. Rather than end users needing to configure their security settings in Adobe Reader or Acrobat, an FDF file is sent to a user. No configurations are needed to view the PDF in a protected environment. All security permissions are handled transparent to the end user.

With the use of Create Protected PDF Online, you can create a PDF document with the necessary security settings that will protect your content against unauthorized distribution without having to use a content provider or the Adobe LiveCycle Rights Management ES. You can send the FDF file to the end user complete with the restrictions applied via the Create Protected PDF Online service.

 For more information on Adobe Server products and the new Create Protected PDF Online service, select Help ⇨ Adobe Online Services.

Adobe introduced, in conjunction with Acrobat and Reader 8, a new consumer-optimized application for reading and managing eBooks and other digital publications. This new solution, called Adobe Digital Editions, replaced the eBook functionality that had been in Adobe Acrobat and Reader 6 and 7. It is a standalone application (based on Adobe Flash Player) that is a 2.5MB download.

Adobe Digital Editions is found on the Adobe Labs Web site. To install the Flash Player and activate Adobe Digital Editions, select Help ⇨ Digital Editions in Acrobat or File ⇨ Digital Editions in Adobe Reader. You can also log on to `www.adobe.com/products/digitaleditions/?source=acromenu` to open the Adobe Digital Editions home page shown in Figure 30.1. The home page provides information about Adobe Digital Editions and informs you that you need to install the Adobe Flash Player application. Click the Download and Install button and the installation proceeds. You arrive at a page that confirms your installation. If the installation was not successful, you see a message informing you that your computer doesn't have the system requirements to install the Flash Player application.

FIGURE 30.1

Choose Help ➪ Digital Editions to arrive at the Digital Editions home page.

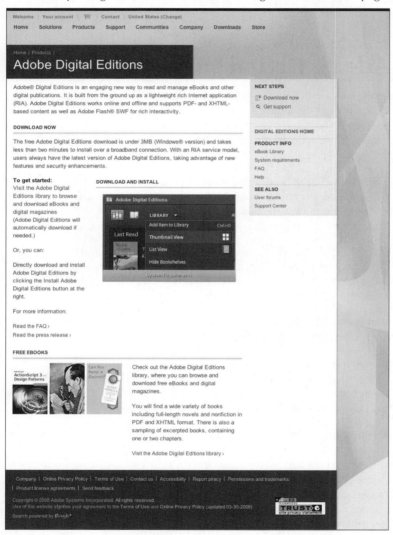

Exploring the Adobe eBook Library

A number of different eBook providers are listed on Adobe's Web site. You can find eBooks in several languages distributed by a number of different providers. To view Adobe's Web page, select

Help ⇨ Digital Editions (Acrobat) or File ⇨ Digital Editions (Adobe Reader). Your default Web browser opens the Adobe Digital Editions Web page. Click *Visit the Adobe Digital Editions library to browse and download eBooks and digital magazines* on the Adobe Digital Editions home page. A list of free downloads appears on the linked Web page. Click the Read button appearing adjacent to an eBook to download the file. When the file is downloaded to your computer it appears in your Adobe Digital Editions. In Figure 30.2 you can see the Adobe Digital Editions with several eBooks I downloaded to my computer.

FIGURE 30.2

Download eBooks from the sample library.

> **TIP** Among the free downloads you'll find an eBook titled *Inside the Publishing Revolution: The Adobe Story* by Pamela Pffifer. For an informative essay on how Adobe Systems evolved to become a major influence on how we use computers today and the relationships between the major computing developers, read this book. You'll find many interesting historical events documented and information to help you understand early strategies of the company and where Adobe is headed with the Acrobat family of products and other applications in its product line.

Reading eBooks

After installing the Adobe Digital Editions and downloading some eBooks, just click a publication you see in Figure 30.2 and your book is displayed in a reading mode within the Adobe Digital Edition interface as shown in Figure 30.3.

FIGURE 30.3

Click an eBook in the Adobe Digital Editions window and you can start reading the book.

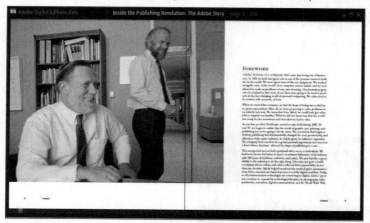

For books, manuals, and large documents, you might want to look at a preference setting that can help you bookmark pages in the files you read. This type of bookmark is like an analog bookmark you might use to mark the place in a book when you pause and come back later to continue reading from the place you left off.

Open the Preferences dialog box (Ctrl/⌘+K) and click Documents in the left pane. In the right pane, check Restore last view settings when reopening documents, as shown in Figure 30.4. You can choose to open all files on the page last viewed in your Acrobat viewer. For example, if you view a PDF document and quit Acrobat after viewing page 125, and then open Acrobat in another session, the PDF opens to page 125.

FIGURE 30.4

Check Restore last view settings when reopening documents to view the last page viewed in a document when you reopen Acrobat.

Preferences	
Categories:	Open Settings
Commenting Documents Full Screen General Page Display	☑ Restore last view settings when reopening documents ☑ Open cross-document links in same window ☑ Allow layer state to be set by user information ☑ Allow documents to hide the menu bar, toolbars, and window controls

You move around the Adobe Digital Editions window by clicking tools and opening menus. From the Reading menu you can see a list of commands to change the page display and navigate pages as shown in Figure 30.5. The Library menu offers commands to display your book list as with the default thumbnail view or a list view. You also have access to the Help command that opens an FAQ (Frequently Asked Questions) Web page on Adobe's Web site where you can find some help in downloading and viewing eBooks. Another comment in the Library menu enables you to add documents to your library. Select Library ➪ Add Item to Library and a dialog box opens where you can navigate your hard drive and select any PDF file stored locally on your hard drive and add it to your library.

FIGURE 30.5

Open a menu at the top of the Adobe Digital Editions window to select menu commands for viewing, navigation, searching, and accessing help with eBooks.

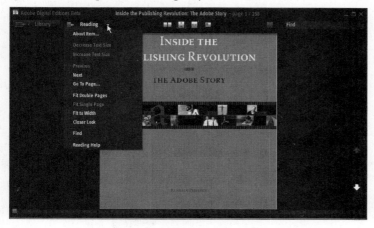

Keep in mind that the screen shots shown here are taken from the beta versions of the Adobe Digital Editions. When the product is out of beta and finally shipped, you may see different menus and menu commands.

Ads for Adobe PDF

Become your own publisher and give away your eBooks! That's right. Adobe has provided a way for you to bypass content providers, a need for securing documents, and paying royalties to third-party vendors. It's all handled through a program that, as of this writing, is in public beta.

Ads for Adobe PDF is a means for you to monetize your documents through a free service provided by Adobe. You don't need to worry about protecting files because you'll want to encourage wide distribution. As a matter of fact, the more people who view your files, the more chance you have in earning more money.

How it works

Ads for Adobe PDF is a free service available from Adobe. To use the service do the following:

- You need to apply to the program by submitting the application form found on the Adobe Labs web site.

- If you are accepted into the program, you'll receive an email containing instructions on how to create your account.

- Submit your PDF documents to Adobe. Log on to Adobe Labs at `http://labs.adobe.com/technologies/adsforpdf/`.

- Set up an account on the Adobe Labs Web site by following the Getting Started steps. In addition you'll find a list of FAQs, information on earning money, and general help information.

- Upload your file(s) to the Adobe service via the service web site URL.

- The Adobe service analyzes your files to enable Yahoo! ads to be matched and displayed in the PDF document as shown in Figure 30.6.

- Download the ad-enabled PDF document and distribute it on your Web site or via email.

Each time a reader of your eBook clicks on an ad, you earn money.

FIGURE 30.6

Yahoo! ads appear to the right of the PDF document.

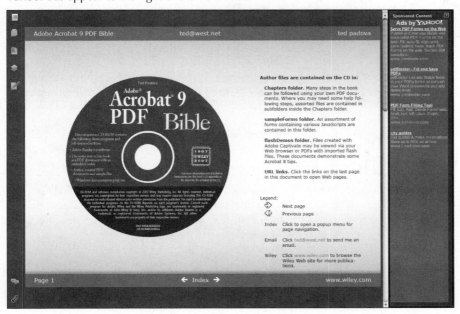

Currently, there is one set of ads that show up for an entire PDF and appearing on all pages. However, by the time you have this book in your hands, Adobe will have upgraded the service to provide you with options for displaying page-specific ads.

What makes this next upgrade attractive is that ads are added to each page in your document relative to the content on the respective page. For example, if you have an eBook about how to lower your golf handicap and you talk about golf courses on page one, the ads on page one might show a list of golf clubs and golf resorts. Turn to page two where you talk about the golf grip and you might find ads related to golf gloves. Move on to page three where you talk about driving long distances and you might find ads related to drivers and long-distance golf balls. In short, each page displays ads according to the content displayed on the page.

Adobe also built in a way for you to be selective about the kind of ads you want shown in your eBooks. If you're Toyota, you won't want ads popping up from competitors such as Ford and Chevrolet. You have choices for blocking out competitor ads and selecting the kinds of ads you want to include in your files. All the questions you may have about Ads for Adobe PDF are answered on the Adobe Labs Web site.

Editing PDF documents with ads

When Adobe creates the sidebar that supports the Yahoo! ads, the ad metadata are digitally signed to prevent tampering. This prevents another user from cracking the metadata and redirecting revenue elsewhere.

Any content changes are viewed as tampering and the signature is corrupted. Therefore, if you need to edit a file such as changing anything on the document pages, inserting new pages, deleting pages, or replacing pages, the ads are invalidated. You need to resubmit an edited file to the Adobe service to have the document re-enabled with ads.

When you prepare PDF files for distribution, be aware that you need to make all edits on your files before submitting them to Adobe for enabling the files with Yahoo! ads. If you want to distribute files on CD-ROM or the Web and you want links to open and close files or use URL links, you must add these link actions before the files are edited by Adobe. Adding link actions on files with ads disturbs the metadata signature and breaks the ad links.

If you have eBooks of substantial size you may need to break up the eBooks into chapters and use a contents page to link to the various chapters. As of this writing PDFs with Yahoo! ads are limited to files of 10MB or less.

Summary

- Any PDF file can be restricted for use with the Adobe LiveCycle Rights Management ES.

- PDF authors can use the Create Protected PDF Online service to protect eBooks when not using a content provider.

- In order to download and view eBooks you must install the Adobe Flash Player application.

- Adobe LiveCycle Rights Management ES is a server-side product made available to content providers.

- eBooks and other PDF documents can be opened on the last viewed page when you reopen your Acrobat viewer.

- The Adobe Digital Editions library window provides tools and menu commands for viewing and navigating eBooks.

- Ads for Adobe PDF is a free service provided by Adobe Systems that permits you to monetize your PDF content via Yahoo! ads.

- A limit of 5MB is imposed on all files that are empowered with Yahoo! ads.

Chapter 31

Printing to Desktop Color Printers

O ne of the primary problems many Acrobat users experience is printing files with proper color. Notwithstanding any problems with printing fonts and getting a print out, the most problematic issues with printing PDFs that contain graphic images is accurate reproduction of color. Whether you are a creative professional or a novice to graphic design, some basic issues need to be understood when printing any kind of document containing images or other graphics to a desktop color printer.

This chapter is concerned with printing to local printers of the desktop variety from Acrobat viewers, and remarks made in this chapter are not intended for commercial printing. For professional printing and prepress, take a look at Chapter 32.

Setting Up the Work Environment

No special editing tools are required for desktop color printing. There is a special toolbar for Print Production, but you won't need any of the Print Production tools to print to your desktop printer. To maximize your space in Acrobat, reset the toolbars to their default positions. Open a context menu on the Toolbar Well and select Reset Toolbars.

IN THIS CHAPTER

Understanding color management

Understanding color profiles

General printing considerations

Understanding how color is managed at print time

Printing to desktop color printers

Printing comments and form field data

Understanding Color Management

Quite a bit can be said about color management, and certainly more attention can be devoted to it than I have room for in this book. Quite simply, there are three basic areas you need to address in creating a color-managed workflow:

- **Monitor calibration.** There are software tools on both Windows and the Mac that can help you calibrate your monitor to eliminate color casts and color tints and set the *gamma* (neutral midtone grays) of your monitor. I won't talk about them because most are useless on LCD-type monitors, and many people are using LCDs these days. Ideally you would use a calibration device. For low-end color calibration of monitors you can purchase the Pantone Huey (www.pantone.com/products/products.asp? idArea=2&idProduct=103) or ColorVision Syper2express (http://spyder. datacolor.com/product-mc-s2e.php) calibrator for as low as $69 US. More sophisticated calibrators such as Gretag Macbeth EyeOne 2 calibrators are above $250 US. I'll leave it up to you as to how far you want to go with calibrating your monitor, but I strongly recommend that if color output is important to you that you at least purchase one of the low-end color calibration devices.

- **Color workspace.** Whether you work in Acrobat or in an imaging program like Adobe Photoshop you need to set up your color workspace. Selections for color workspaces vary with programs. The two primary workspaces are Adobe RGB (1998) or sRGB. Choices vary according to the files you prepare and the printing equipment you use.

- **Output color profile.** Each printer and every paper you print on should have a defined color profile. Color profiles are often installed with your printer. You can also acquire or create custom color profiles to print to a specific paper on your printer.

> **NOTE** Creating custom printer profiles requires more expensive color calibration equipment. For a source of calibration equipment, take a look at the Gretag MacBeth Web site at www.xrite.com/.

Don't be concerned yet about which profile to use. More important, try to understand how these three items interact with each other and what they do. First off, your monitor color profile created with a hardware device adjusts the overall brightness of your monitor. When you print a file, you want to be sure that the print outputs are not darker or lighter than the images you see on your monitor. A balance needs to be made between monitor and output so you can safely judge what a print looks like when you print to your printer.

Color workspace affects how you view color on your monitor. You want to try to get as close to seeing all the colors that can be reproduced on your printer. This happens when you choose the proper color workspace. You then select a color output profile when it comes time to print your file. Your color is converted from your workspace color to your printer's colorspace so that all the colors fit within the output space as closely as possible. Quite simply, if you see a bright red color on your computer monitor and the overall brightness matches your output, you want to be certain that same color red gets printed on your printer. This happens when the color is converted from your monitor workspace to your printer's colorspace.

Assuming you can set up your color environment to handle monitor color, workspace color, and output color, the next thing to understand is how color is managed at print time. You have some choices here. You can choose to manage color at print time through your printer, by selecting a printer profile, or by printing a converted color file that requires no color management. This is the one item that is most confusing for people to grasp — when to manage color at print time and when not to manage color. For the answer and examples, I'll cover that when we look at printing to specific printers later in this chapter.

Selecting a Color Workspace

Your first step after calibrating your monitor in creating a color managed workflow is to choose your color workspace. In Acrobat open the Preferences dialog box by pressing Ctrl/⌘+K. In the left pane, click Color Management and the right pane changes to the view shown in Figure 31.1.

FIGURE 31.1

Click Color Management in the Preferences dialog box to access the Color Management options.

In the Working Spaces section, open the RGB pull-down menu and choose your RGB color workspace. Here you have one of two choices:

- **sRGB.** The name is much longer, as you see in Figure 31.1, but I'll use the abbreviated label and simply call this by the common term — sRGB. Traditionally, this color workspace has been used when files are prepared for screen and Web viewing. This colorspace comes as close as you can get from all the choices available to represent color consistently across all monitors. Of course, there are many variables that prevent you from matching color exactly on all monitors. We'll assume the software engineers are telling us the truth when they say that the best monitor color matching is made by selecting the sRGB colorspace.

More important, you should be aware that many desktop color printers convert color from sRGB better than other workspaces. Some online photo services and photo service providers may ask you to keep your files in sRGB. For example, if you send photos to a Costco store to print on their Noritsu photo printers, they'd ask you to keep your files in sRGB. At the desktop printer level, you'll need to either run tests or take a look at your printer's user manual to find out if your printer supports sRGB better than other color workspaces.

- **Adobe RGB (1998).** The Adobe RGB colorspace has a wider color gamut than sRGB (meaning you can see a bit more colors in this workspace). If you prepare files for press and commercial printing, you're best off using Adobe RGB. Also, some desktop color printers can take advantage of the wider color gamut, so your printer might give you more accurate color matching when converting your files from Adobe RGB to your printer's color output profile. Again though, you need to run tests or turn to the user manual to see what the manufacturer recommends.

If all your work is designed for output to desktop color printers using an RGB colorspace, you don't need to be concerned about the CMYK choices in the Color Management preferences. If you prepare files for press and commercial printing, then CMYK will be a consideration. Make a choice for the color workspace recommended by your commercial printer. If using print shops in the United States, the U.S. Web Coated (SWOP) v2 profile is likely to be your best choice. But be sure to talk to your print shop technicians first.

On Windows, set the Grayscale option to Gray Gamma 2.2, and on the Mac, set the Grayscale to Gray Gamma 1.8. Clear the check box for Output Intent overrides working spaces if your PDF files do not contain embedded Output Intent profiles.

CROSS-REF For more information on output intent profiles, see Chapter 10.

For the Conversion options, select Adobe (ACE) for the conversion engine. On Windows, you'll have a choice for Adobe (ACE) or Microsoft ICM. On the Mac, you'll have choices for Adobe (ACE) or Apple Colorsync or Apple CMM. Use the Adobe (ACE) color engine for the best results.

Finally, check the box for Use black point compensation. Checking this option gets you closer to a rich black.

Click OK in the Preferences dialog box after you make all your choices and your color settings stay intact until you change them again.

Using Color Output Profiles

Color output profiles come in a number of different flavors. You can use color output profiles supplied by your printer manufacturer that are installed with your desktop printer, use color profiles created by paper manufacturers that are designed for use with specific printers, or create custom profiles for your printer and the papers you use.

NOTE There are several services available to you for creating custom color output profiles. If you're a creative professional, you might want to look at using a service to prepare a custom profile for your printer and the papers you use. Just go to the Internet and search for custom profiling services. Custom color profiles are offered as low as $25 US. The cost is minimal considering all the consumables you'd waste running tests to get color right on your equipment.

Because most users printing from Acrobat are likely to use printer profiles that were shipped with their desktop printer, I'll stick to talking about these profiles. If you're a creative professional who depends on accurate color proofing, take a look at *Color Correction For Digital Photographers Only* (Wiley Publishing, 2006) or *Color Correction For Digital Photographers For Dummies* (Wiley Publishing, 2007). There's much more to color profiling than can be described here, so a little research can help you get closer to producing accurate color.

When you print your PDF files to your color desktop printer, you make a choice for using a color profile at the time you print your file. You may see a list of color profiles in the Advanced Print Setup dialog box or you may only see the name of your printer. If you see just your printer's name, color profile selection is made automatically by the print driver. Choosing a paper in your print driver options tells the printer what profile to use, hence the color profile choice is automatic.

Regardless of how the color profile is selected, a color conversion takes place from your color workspace to the colorspace of your printer. In essence, the conversion is an attempt to fit all the color you see on your monitor into the printable colorspace on your printer with as close a match as possible.

Some Printing Basics in Acrobat

Before you start printing files to your printer, there are a few toggles and switches you need to verify. If you don't have some options enabled, you may have a more difficult time printing your documents. The essentials for setting up your printing environment and some toggles you should understand are as follows:

- **Turn Show page thumbnails in Print dialog ON.** A preference choice appears in the General preference settings that controls the print preview in the Print dialog box. A thumbnail preview helps you determine whether the page will print without clipping off edges. As a matter of default, you'll want the print preview enabled. Press Ctrl/⌘+K to open the Preferences dialog box and click General in the left pane. In the right pane, check the box where you see Show page thumbnails in Print dialog, as shown in Figure 31.2. Click OK to dismiss the Preferences dialog box.

FIGURE 31.2

Check Show page thumbnails in Print dialog in the General preferences.

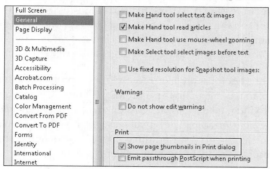

- **Set the print attributes.** Several settings in the Print dialog box shown in Figure 31.3 are globally set for all printing on desktop printers. These options are as follows:

  - **Printer selection.** From the Name pull-down menu, select the printer you want to output your file.

  - **Comments and Forms.** Above the Preview area, you see the section Comments and Forms. For printing composite prints without any comments or markups, select Document from the pull-down menu. For printing with these markups, see the section "Printing Comments, Forms, and Summaries" later in this chapter.

  - **Page Scaling.** Ideally, you should print files to papers large enough to accommodate your document page size. If your document fits on a standard page size, select None for Page Scaling. If you do need to shrink a document to fit a paper smaller than the document page size, select Shrink to Printable Area or Fit to Printable Area from the Page Scaling pull-down menu. If you need to tile pages, you can make selections for tiling in the same pull-down menu.

  - **Page Orientation.** On Windows, click the Properties button in the top right corner of the Print dialog box to select either Portrait or Landscape Orientation. Note that you can also select orientation and page size by selecting File ➪ Page Setup before you open the Print dialog box.

  - **Booklet Printing.** Open the page Scaling pull-down menu and select Booklet Printing to print spreads as shown in the Preview Composite in Figure 31.3. You can choose from three additional options for printing booklets. Print Both sides, Front side only, or Back side only. On desktop printers capable of printing two sides, you can print first on one side, turn the paper over, and print on the second side.

- **Tile large pages.** This option is a great benefit for those who send files to service centers for printing on large format inkjet printers. When you need a proof on your desktop printer for an oversized print, you can print multiple pages of tiled sections of the larger image. You have choices for displaying cut marks, overlap areas, and scaling.

- **Tile all pages.** Choose his option to tile all pages in a document.

- **Multiple pages per sheet.** You can reduce the number of pages printer to fit a given number of pages per sheet. You have options for customizing the number of pages per sheet and the page range per sheet.

FIGURE 31.3

Select your printer from the Name pull-down menu. Booklet printing can be chosen from the Page Scaling pull-down menu.

You have some other options in the print dialog box for page range, reversing pages, using auto rotations, choosing a paper source by page size, printing to a file, and so on. All these other options are very similar to printing from other programs and should be familiar to you.

Who's Going to Manage Color?

Acrobat offers you three different options for managing color. Your choices appear when you open the Print dialog box (Ctrl/Command+P) and click the Advanced button. In the Color Management pane open the Color Handling pull-down menu and find see the options shown in Figure 31.4. The three choices include:

FIGURE 31.4

Open the Print dialog box, click on Advanced, and click Color Management in the left pane. Open the Color Handling pull-down menu to find your options for managing color at print time.

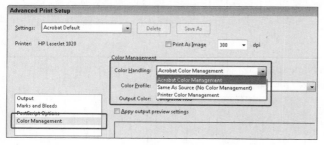

- **Acrobat Color Management.** This choice gives the control for managing color to Acrobat. If you make this choice, you need to turn off color management in your printer driver.

  If you don't turn color management off at the last stage (in the printer driver), you wind up with a double profiled print. This results in a severe color shift and color output very different than your monitor view. (See the sidebar in this chapter for more on printing with color shifts.)

NOTE See the section Printing to Desktop Printers later in this chapter to learn how to turn color management on and off in the printer driver).

- **Same As Source (No Color Management).** If you convert an image in a program like Photoshop to your color output profile, the color is ready for output and no further conversion is needed. Because the color is already converted to your printer's color, you need to turn color management off throughout the print process. Most likely you won't be working with files that have embedded color output profiles in the images; therefore, you won't need to worry about printing using this option. If, perchance, you do work with images that have color converted to a printer profile, you would make this choice.

- **Printer Color Management.** When you make this choice in your Advanced Print Setup dialog box, you enable the printer to choose the color profile; however, using this option only works with PostScript printing devices. If this choice is selected, you can manage the color in the advanced print settings in your color printer driver. Typically, you'll find this option to work only when using PostScript printers. As a general rule, for non-PostScript printers, you need to use the Acrobat Color Management and choose sRGB color as your color profile.

CROSS-REF For more information on selecting profiles in the Advanced Print Setup dialog box, see the next section, "Printing to Desktop Printers."

When printing from Acrobat you most often have one of two choices to make. Either enable your printer to determine color, or enable Acrobat to determine color. If you choose to enable your printer to manage the color, you turn color management on. If you enable Acrobat to manage the color, you turn color management off. However, where you turn color on and where you turn color off varies differently between color printers. To demonstrate how color is managed, we need to look at printing Acrobat files from a few different desktop color printers.

Printing to Desktop Printers

Print settings vary according to manufacturers, and I can't hope to cover all printers in this chapter. For a representative sample, I'll use three of the more popular color printers to show you how to print files from Acrobat. To demonstrate how color profiling is handled, I'll use Epson, HP, and Canon printers as examples. If you have a different color printer, you should be able to understand the process and apply similar choices when printing to your color printer.

When you install your printer driver, the installation utility may also install a number of color profiles. In some cases, individual profiles won't be installed — all depends on your printer and the printer driver. If individual color profiles are not installed, then your printer driver contains profile information and makes profile choices within the driver itself. For profiles installed with your printer, you can choose profiles in Acrobat's Advanced Print Setup dialog box and control all the printing using a profile provided by your printer manufacturer.

You have a choice for how these profiles are used. You can choose to select the profile in the Print dialog box, or you can choose an automatic method where the manufacturer created a no-nonsense process of automatic profile selection using your printer driver. The color profile is automatically selected when you choose the paper source.

Printing to Epson printers

For the first example I'll use Epson printers to demonstrate how to print a PDF file from Acrobat using the printer to manage color and using Acrobat to manage color. Because the dialog boxes differ so much between platforms, I'll include printing from Windows and from the Mac in separate descriptions.

Printer profile selection on Windows

In this first example, let's take a look at how to print to an Epson low-end color printer on Windows while allowing the *printer to manage the color*. Depending on the model of your printer, you may see some slight differences in menu names, but the process will follow the same steps.

To print to an Epson printer while enabling the printer to manage the color, follow these steps.

STEPS: Printing from Windows enabling Acrobat to manage color

1. **Open the Print dialog box.** Select File ⇨ Print or press Ctrl/⌘+P to open the Print dialog box shown in Figure 31.5.

   Make all the attribute choices for printing to your printer as was described in the section "Some Printing Basics in Acrobat" for page orientation, page scaling, and so on.

2. **Select your printer.** Open the Name pull-down menu and select your printer as shown earlier in Figure 31.3.

FIGURE 31.5

Select your printer from the Name menu in the Print dialog box.

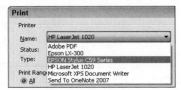

3. **Open the Advanced Print Setup dialog box.** Click Advanced in the Print dialog box.

4. **Select the color profile.** Click Color Management in the left pane of the Advanced Print Setup dialog box and open the Color Handling pull-down menu shown in Figure 31.4. From the menu options, choose Acrobat Color Management. This choice tells Acrobat to manage the color.

5. **Choose a color profile.** When using Acrobat to manage the color, you need to choose a color profile from the Color Profile pull-down menu. From the menu choices choose sRGB IEC61966-2.1. This choice is not an accurate profile for your printer and paper but it servers as a generic profile that works best for most low-end devices.

6. **Return to the Print dialog box.** Click OK in the Advanced Print Setup dialog box to return to the Print dialog box.

7. **Open the printer driver dialog box.** At this point we have made all our settings in the Acrobat workspace. Now, we need to make choices in the printer driver to decide how

the color is managed. Because we do not want the printer to manage the color, we'll verify settings to insure that indeed the printer does not manage the color.

Click Properties in the Print dialog box to open the Printer Properties dialog box. In this example, I use an Epson Stylus C59 printer. The Epson C59 is a very low-end printer that doesn't ship with custom color profiles. Therefore, the only choice I have for managing color is to let Acrobat manage the color and choose a generic color profile such as sRGB.

8. **Choose the paper source.** This first choice determines the amount of ink to be used for your print. If printing to a glossy paper, more ink is used. If printing to a plain bond paper, less ink is used. From the Type pull-down menu, make the paper choice for the paper you use. In this example, I use Premium Glossy Photo Paper as shown in Figure 31.6.

FIGURE 31.6

Select the paper source you use to print your files.

9. **Don't Color manage your output.** Now it's time to color manage your file, and this step is critical in your print production workflow. For the Epson printer without a color profile available for your paper choice, you need to click on the Advanced button shown in Figure 31.6 that opens a warning dialog box. Simply click Continue to open the advanced settings dialog box as you see in Figure 31.7.

FIGURE 31.7

Click Advanced, and then click Continue to access the advanced settings in the Epson print driver.

A few choices need to be made in this dialog box. The most important are as follows:

- **Select a paper type.** Choose the same paper here as you did back in Step 7.

- **Turn color management off.** Because we are enabling Acrobat to determine the color, we need to be certain the Color Controls radio button is disabled. This setting tells Acrobat to manage color using the color profile we selected in Step 5.

- If you frequently print files using the same settings, you can save your settings by clicking the Save Setting button.

10. **Print the PDF.** Click OK and OK again in the Print dialog box and your file is sent to your printer. The color is converted automatically from your source workspace of sRGB or Adobe RGB (1998) to the profile the Printer Driver automatically selects for you.

Printing from the Macintosh enabling Acrobat to determine color

On the Macintosh the Epson Printer Driver offers you some different settings although the process is quite similar. Again, we are going to use the automatic method for color conversion and allow the print driver to handle the conversion.

The Acrobat Print dialog box settings and the Advanced Print Setup dialog box settings are identical on the Mac as you find in Windows. You make choices for paper orientation, page scaling, and so on in the Print dialog box and choose Printer/ Color Management in the Advanced Print Setup dialog box just as Windows users. However, on the Mac you don't have a Properties button. All color management choices are made directly in the Acrobat Print dialog box.

To print to an Epson printer when enabling the Printer to manage color, do the following:

1. **Select Print Settings.** Select File ➪ Print and make the same choices as Windows users for print attributes and select Printer Color Management in the Advanced Print Setup dialog box.

2. **Select your printer.** At the top of the Acrobat Print dialog box you make a choice for your printer from the Printer pull-down menu, as shown in Figure 31.8.

FIGURE 31.8

Select your printer from the options listed in the Printer pull-down menu.

3. **Select the Media Type and Print Quality.** Where you see Copies & Pages, click to open a pull-down menu and select the option for Print Settings. In the Print Settings pane, you make selections for Media Type and Print Quality as shown in Figure 31.9. In this example, I use an Epson Stylus C62 printer and choose Premium Glossy Photo Paper and select Best Photo from the Print Quality pull-down menu.

4. **Choose how to manage the color.** Now it's time to select the color management method. From the pull-down menu where you now see Print Settings, click to open the menu and select Color Management, as shown in Figure 31.10.

FIGURE 31.9

Make choices for Printer, Media Type, and Print Quality in the Acrobat Print dialog box.

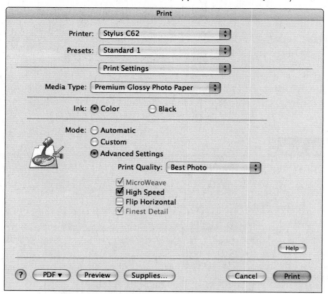

FIGURE 31.10

Click Print Settings to open the pull-down menu and select Color Management.

Click Off (No Color Management). Making this choice tells the print driver to not manage the color.

5. **Print the file.** Click Print and the file is printed to your printer with an automatic color conversion from your workspace color to the printer color profile.

Selecting a custom printer profile

Your second method for managing color when printing files is to select a printer profile installed with your printer driver or a custom profile you create using a color profiling system. You choose from the available list of color profiles in the Color Profile pull-down menu. Whereas the last section used a generic profile, this time we'll let Adobe Acrobat manage the color using a custom color profile. Again, the Windows options and Macintosh commands vary a little, so I'll discuss how to print by selecting a profile for each operating system.

Printing using a custom printer profile on Windows

The steps are the same as those described in printing files for automatic profile selection when setting up the page and selecting a printer. When you select File ➪ Print, you open the Acrobat Print dialog box as described in the previous section. Your steps now change when you enable Acrobat to handle the color conversion and you proceed through the Print dialog box as follows:

STEPS: Using custom color profiles on Windows

1. **Choose Acrobat Color Management.** Open the Print dialog box and click Advanced. Click Color Management in the left pane and choose Acrobat Color Management from the Color Handling pull-down menu.

2. **Select a color profile.** Note that the Color Profile pull-down menu becomes active when you choose Acrobat Color Management. From the Color Profile pull-down menu, select the color profile designed for use with the paper you have chosen to print your image. In this example, I use a fine art paper color profile as shown in Figure 31.11.

FIGURE 31.11

Choose a printer profile that matches the paper you use.

3. **Open the printer Properties.** Click Properties and the properties settings for your selected printer driver open. Check the radio button for Best Photo. From the Type pull-down menu, select the recommended paper choice. Note: If you use a custom color profile, the profile is usually shipped with guidelines for selecting proper paper.

4. **Manage the color.** Click Advanced and click Continue to arrive at the same dialog box shown earlier in Figure 31.7. The paper choice selection is automatically carried over from the previous properties dialog box (from Step 1). A different setting is in the Color Management section. This time click the ICM (Image Color Management) radio button and click Off (No Color Adjustment), as shown in Figure 31.12. Because you selected the color profile in Step 1, and you are enabling Acrobat to manage the color, you need to be sure that Color Management is OFF. If you don't turn color management off, you end up double profiling your print.

FIGURE 31.12

Click ICM and click Off (No Color Adjustment).

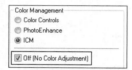

5. **Print the file.** Click OK and click Print to print the file.

Printing using a printer profile on the Macintosh

All the steps to print a file enabling Acrobat to manage color are the same as Windows until you get to the printer driver. On the Mac, do the following to print a PDF document enabling Acrobat to manage color.

STEPS: Enabling Acrobat to Manage Color on the Macintosh

1. **Set the print attributes.** Follow the same steps to make choices for the print attributes and your printer. Go to the Advanced Print Options and select a printer profile for your target paper.

2. **Set the Print Settings.** Use the same settings, as shown earlier in Figure 31.9, to select the Media Type and Print Quality.

3. **Make a choice for Color Management.** Click Print Settings and select Color Management from the pull-down menu in the Print dialog box. This time, because we chose a color output profile and Acrobat is determining the color, we turn color management off. In the Color Management pane, select No Color Adjustment, as you see in Figure 31.13.

4. **Print the file.** Click Print to print the file.

FIGURE 31.13

Select Color Management and click No Color Adjustment.

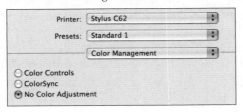

Printing to HP inkjet printers

Regardless of the printer you use, the process for printing follows the same logic. Unfortunately each manufacturer uses different dialog boxes and different menu command names that can leave you completely confused if you try to apply steps from printing to one printer to a different printer.

The two methods for managing color (enable the printer driver to determine color by selecting Printer Color Management, or enable Acrobat to determine color by selecting a specific color profile) are applied to all printers but the dialog boxes, buttons, and menu choices appear differently.

The critical steps you need to be concerned about when printing files is the profile selection, the paper selection, and when to turn color management on or off. If you own an HP printer you probably know where to make your paper selection and your best photo selection. The more obscure setting is likely to be the color management choice. Rather than discuss each detail step for printing to an HP low-end desktop printer, let's take a look at how to manage color.

Printing to HP printers on Windows

Again, you have two choices as follows:

- **Let your printer determine color.** For PostScript printers, you use this option. Select Printer Color Management in the Advanced Print Setup dialog box. Click Properties to open the printer driver properties. Click the Advanced tab when you arrive at the printer driver properties dialog box. Click Graphic and click Image Color Management. From the ICM Method pull-down menu, select ICM Handled by Printer, as shown in Figure 31.14.

- **Let Acrobat determine color.** Select a color profile in the Advanced Print Setup dialog box and select ICM Disabled in the Advanced tab in the HP printer driver properties.

Printing to HP printers on the Macintosh

HP has come a long way with printing to the Macintosh. The HP Next Generation Inkjet Print Products have a number of color management solutions for Macintosh users working with newer HP printers such as ColorSmart/sRGB shown in Figure 31.15. Rather than go into detail here, log on to: `http://h10025.www1.hp.com/ewfrf/wc/document?docname=c00284884&lc=en&cc=us&dlc=&product=3204765` where you'll find all the information you need to color manage print jobs using HP printers.

FIGURE 31.14

Open Graphic and select ICM Method. Choose ICM Handled by Printer from the pull-down menu.

FIGURE 31.15

Select an HP paper in the Paper Type/Quality dialog box.

Printing to Canon printers

Again we follow the same logic and choose to either enable or disable color management. With Canon color printers, the area in the print driver dialog box is even more hidden than you find in Epson and HP desktop printers.

Printing to Canon printers on Windows

Using the same two options you control color management as follows:

- **Let your printer determine color.** Select Printer Color Management in the Advanced Print Setup dialog box. Click Properties in the Acrobat Print dialog box and click Manual for Color/Intensity in the Main tab, as shown in Figure 31.16.

  Click the Set button to open the Manual Color Adjustment dialog box. Check the box for Enable ICM (Windows Color Management), as shown in Figure 31.17.

- **Let Acrobat determine color.** First select your printer profile in the Advanced Print Setup dialog box and follow the same steps as above. This time uncheck the Enable ICM (Windows Color Management) check box.

FIGURE 31.16

Click the Manual radio button for Color/Intensity.

FIGURE 31.17

Check Enable ICM (Windows Image Color Management).

Printing to Canon Printers on the Mac

You make the same choices on the Mac as you do on Windows for how you want to manage color on a Canon printer. Enable the printer to manage the color and make a paper choice in the Quality & Media dialog box, as shown in Figure 31.18.

FIGURE 31.18

Select Quality & Media and select the paper type in the Media Type pull-down menu.

From the pull-down menu below the Presets menu, select Color Options. Here you choose BJ Standard when permitting the printer driver to determine color and None when selecting a printer profile in the Advanced Print Setup dialog box. The options are shown in Figure 31.19.

FIGURE 31.19

Select BJ Standard for printer color management and None when you select a printer profile.

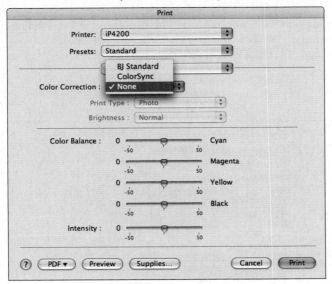

Printing Comments, Forms, and Summaries

You can print document markups as well as form field data from Acrobat viewers. The options are straightforward and easy to use. However, one limitation you should know about is that comment pop-up notes are not printed and you cannot print the content of a note.

TIP **To see exactly what you can print when using comment notes in Acrobat, open the Print dialog box. The thumbnail preview in the Print dialog box shows you the types of comments that Acrobat will print before actually printing the file.**

Printing comments

To print comments you need a file that contains some comment notes. To learn more about commenting, see Chapter 20.

To print a file with comments and markups, follow these steps.

STEPS: Printing document markups

1. **Open a document containing comments and markups.** You can use the Text Edits tools, Highlight tool, and other comment tools as well as any of the Markup tools such as the Rectangle tool, Cloud tool, Callout tool, and others.

2. **Open the Print dialog box.** Select File ➪ Print.

3. **Select Document and Markups in the Comments and Forms area of the Print dialog box.** When you make the selection for Document and Markups, the page preview in the Preview Composite area of the Print dialog box shows you exactly what elements print, as you see in Figure 31.20.

FIGURE 31.20

Select Document and Markups from the Comments and Forms pull-down menu.

4. **Click Print.** Your print appears with the comments and markups as was shown in the Preview Composite in the Print dialog box.

You have another choice for printing comments. You can choose to print a document with just Stamp comments. From the Comments and Forms pull-down menu, select Document and Stamps. A preview also appears when you choose to print stamp comments. Just make the selection for Document and Stamps and click Print.

Printing form field data

Another option you have is printing just form field data. You can print all form field data with just one exception. Button faces don't print. All the other fields including check boxes, radio buttons, and barcode data print.

To print just the data fields without the background content, select Form fields only in the Print dialog box in the Comments and Forms pull-down menu and print the file.

CROSS-REF For more information on form fields, see Chapter 34.

Printing comment summaries

Yet another option you have when printing PDF documents is creating a comment summary and printing it in one step. Click the Summarize Comments button at the bottom of the Print dialog box. The Summarize Options dialog box opens, as shown in Figure 31.21, where you can make a choice for the type of comment summary you want to print. Select an option and click Print Comment Summary. The file that's printed contains just the comments in one of the four summary formats available to you.

CROSS-REF For more information on creating comment summaries, see Chapter 20.

FIGURE 31.21

The Summarize Options dialog box offers choices for using one of four different templates for comment summaries.

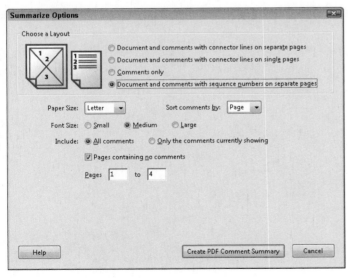

Summary

- A well-managed color workflow requires calibrating your monitor, using a proper workspace color, and printing using a color profile designed for your printer and paper source.

- The two most common methods for managing color with desktop color printers in Acrobat are to enable the printer to manage the color or enable Acrobat to manage the color.

- When you choose to let your printer manage color, you need to use a PostScript printer and you turn color management on in advanced settings in your printer driver.

- When you choose to select a color profile and enable Acrobat to manage color, you turn color management off in your printer driver advanced settings.

- Comment markups can be printed with your document. You choose to print comment markups in the Acrobat Print dialog box in the Comment and Forms pull-down menu.

- You can print form field data without the background PDF design. Choose Form fields only in the Comment and Forms pull-down menu.

- You can create and print comment summaries in one step in the Print dialog box by clicking the Summarize Comments button.

Chapter 32

Commercial Printing and Prepress

At some time or another, the files you output to your desktop printer may be candidates for offset printing. The tools and commands you use for desktop printers, as I explained in Chapter 31, are sufficient for printing to all the printers you have in your office and home. However, when printing PDF documents on commercial printing devices, you must address a number of issues.

For high-end digital prepress and commercial printing, Acrobat Pro and Acrobat Pro Extended include all the print controls that the commercial printing community desires. Combined with features for previewing color, preflighting jobs, and printing color separations, Acrobat Pro (henceforth meaning both Pro and Pro Extended) ranks as a strong competitor against any layout or other professional applications designed to serve creative professionals. In this chapter I cover printing from Acrobat Pro using many commercial printing tools.

Setting Up the Work Environment

In Acrobat Pro, you have a toolbar used specifically for print production. Open a context menu on the Toolbar Well and select Print Production. The Print Production toolbar opens as a floating toolbar, as shown in Figure 32.1. Select Dock Toolbars at the bottom of the context menu.

FIGURE 32.1

FIGURE 32.1

The Print Production toolbar

For printing large documents and when soft proofing files, the Loupe tool is often used. Open a context menu on the Select & Zoom toolbar that appears loaded in the Toolbar Well by default. From the context menu options click the Loupe Tool. The Loupe tool is loaded in the Select & Zoom toolbar.

 Adobe Reader 9 and Acrobat Standard 9 contain both the Loupe tool and the Pan and Zoom tool.

Soft Proofing Color

Soft proofing color refers to viewing color on your monitor with a screen preview of the way color will be printed to hard copy. Soft proofing is a digital process whereby you use your computer monitor screen to preview things such as proper color assignments, overprints, separations, transparency, and similar issues that might cause problems on printing devices, rather than print a test proof and consume paper and ink.

With the exception of previewing overprints, all soft proofing options are contained in the Acrobat Pro programs only. Most of the options you find for soft proofing apply to high-end commercial printing; however, some features can be useful when you're printing to desktop color printers.

Setting up your color management environment

As discussed in Chapter 31, color management is equally important when printing to commercial printing devices and prepress systems. You first begin with monitor calibration and set up your color management preferences. Whereas your workspace color choice is best using the sRGB color space for most desktop printers, the Adobe RGB (1998) color workspace is a better choice for most commercial printing equipment.

 Most of what you need for color management in Acrobat is covered in Chapter 31.

Output Preview

 Soft proofing color is handled in the Output Preview dialog box. This dialog box does not provide you options for altering the content. It is used as a viewing tool to diagnose any potential printing problems. From a Preview menu, you select one of three categories in which to preview your document — Separations, Color Warnings, or the new Acrobat 9 Object Inspector. To open the Output Preview dialog box, click the second tool (Output Preview) in the Print Production toolbar. The Output Preview dialog box opens.

Color Warnings

Click Color Warnings in the Output Preview dialog box. The Color Warnings pane opens, as shown in Figure 32.2.

Several settings in the Color Warnings pane are the same as those found in the Separations pane. The unique options in this pane are the Warnings items. You use this pane to preview any problems that are shown with keylines using the colors in the Warnings areas. If you need more contrast against the background colors, click one of the Warnings color swatches to open a color palette where another color can be selected to display the Warnings keyline borders.

Other areas in the Color Warnings dialog box include the following.

FIGURE 32.2

Open the Output Preview dialog box and click Color Warnings.

Simulation Profile

Simulation Profile enables you to select from a list of ICC (International Color Consortium) profiles. A number of preset profiles are available from which to choose, and you can also create your own custom profiles and add them to the list. You create custom profiles with hardware/software devices that are designed specifically for calibrating monitors and creating ICC profiles. As a profile is created, it is saved as a file to your hard drive. Graphic designers can also often acquire custom profiles from print shops and service centers.

In order for Acrobat to recognize the ICC profiles you create, you must be certain that the profiles are stored in the proper directory. By default, utilities and commercial devices used for calibrating color save profiles to a directory that makes them accessible to Acrobat. If you want to remove ICC profiles so fewer profiles show up in the Proof Colors dialog box or you have problems getting a profile to the right directory, open the folder where the profiles are stored. On Windows Vista, the path is `System32\Spool\Drivers\Color`. On Macintosh OS X, look in `MacintoshHD: Library:ColorSync:Profiles`. When new profiles are added to the appropriate folder on your computer, you can access the profiles in Acrobat after you quit the program and relaunch it if the profile was added while Acrobat was open.

To select a profile for color proofing, open the Simulation Profile pull-down menu and choose a profile to preview. Selecting the option does not change the color in the document, and you can select different profiles from the menu selections without permanently changing color in the file.

From the pull-down menu you'll see a number of different profiles appear in a long list. Select the output device profile you want to simulate. In order to do so, you need to acquire an output profile from your printer or service bureau or use a custom profile you created and added to your Profiles folder. For printing on an offset press on coated stock in the United States, use U.S. Web Coated (SWOP) v2 if your printer doesn't have a custom profile to provide you. When you select one of the presets for soft proofing prints, the two check boxes for simulating ink and paper become accessible. (Outside the U.S. you might want to use a Japan or European option available in the CMYK profiles from the CMYK pull-down menu.)

TIP To ensure your color proofing uses the same profile each time you view a file on-screen, open a document in Acrobat. Select the profile you want to use as a default from the Simulation Profile pull-down menu. Quit Acrobat and relaunch the program. The last choice you made becomes the new default. You don't need to quit the program to make the profile choice a new default, but if the program crashes during a session, you lose preferences applied in that session. Quitting after making a preference choice ensures that the preference is held in all subsequent Acrobat sessions.

Simulate Black Ink

When the Simulate Black Ink check box is enabled, the preview shows you the dynamic range of the document's profile. Dynamic range is measured in values usually between 0 and 4, although some scanner developers claim dynamic ranges of 4.1, 4.2, or higher. A dynamic range of something like 3.8 yields a wide range of grays between the white point and the black point in a scanned image. If the dynamic range is high, you see details in shadows and highlights. If the dynamic range is low, highlights can get blown out and shadows lose detail. When you enable the Simulate Black Ink check box, look for the distinct tonal differences in the preview and detail in shadows and highlights.

Simulate Paper Color

If the check box for Simulate Paper Color is enabled in the Output Preview dialog box, the preview shows you a particular shade of gray as simulated for the paper color by the profile you choose. You may find that the preview looks too gray or has too much black. This may not be the result of the profile used but rather the brightness adjustment on your monitor. If your monitor is calibrated properly and the profile accurately displays the paper color, the preview should show you an accurate representation of the document as it is printed on paper.

Warnings

Two different warnings dynamically display potential printing problems. As you select a check box, you can move the Output Preview aside and preview the results in the document pane. When you select a box and preview the results, the display appears only when the Output Preview dialog box is open. Closing the dialog box returns you to the default view of the document page before you opened the Output Preview.

By default, the options in the Warnings section show potential problems using default colors adjacent to the warning item. You can change the warning colors by clicking the color swatch and selecting from a preset palette or selecting a custom color from your operating system color palette.

Overprints are often used to *trap* colors when files are intended for printing separations. Trapping a color creates an overlap between colors, so any movement of the paper when printed on a printing press prevents printing colors without gaps between the colors. In other cases, overprints may be assigned to colors in illustrations intentionally when a designer wants to eliminate potential trapping problems. For example, you might assign an overprint to text to avoid any trapping problems where black text is printed on top of a background color. In some instances, a designer might unintentionally assign an overprint to a color during the creative process. As a measure of checking overprints for those colors that you properly assign and to review a document for potential problems, you can use Acrobat's Show Overprinting preview to display on your monitor all the overprints created in a file. To view overprints in a PDF document, select the Show Overprinting check box in the Output Preview dialog box.

NOTE Acrobat 9 now has an automatic overprint preview that displays CMYK files with overprint previews by default. Additionally, all files saved as PDF/X also show overprints as a default.

To understand what happens with overprints and knockouts, look at Figure 32.3. The composite image is created for printing two colors. These colors are printed on separate plates for two different inks. When the file is separated, the type is *knocked out* of the background, leaving holes in the background. Because the two colors butt up against each other, any slight movement of the paper creates a gap between where one ink color ends and the other begins. To prevent the problem, a slight bit of overprinting is added to the type. In an exaggerated view in Figure 32.3 you can see the stroke around the type character. The stroke is assigned an overprint so its color, which is the foreground color, prints on top of the background color without a knockout.

TIP To carefully examine overprints assigned to type characters, select the Loupe tool in the Zoom toolbar. Move the cursor around the document to preview overprints on small type.

FIGURE 32.3

If an overprint is assigned to the type, the overprint area of the type color prints on top of the background color. If the paper moves slightly, the overprint prevents any paper color showing through gaps created by the misregistration.

Rich black

When files are printed with rich black, all the black in the document prints with more density. This is often a common setting used when printing to inkjet printers and commercial oversized printing devices to eliminate any muddy appearance when files contain a substantial amount of black. Select the box to preview how the black will lay down on the printed output. If you see too much density in black, be certain to avoid using rich black when printing the file.

Separations

One of the great features for soft proofing color in Acrobat Pro is the ability to preview a color separation where colors can be viewed individually or in combinations — for example, previewing cyan and magenta instead of previewing all colors. To preview a separation, select Separations from the Preview menu in the Output Preview dialog box. The pane changes to the view shown in Figure 32.4.

If you intend to print a file in four-color process, the Separation Preview dialog box helps you identify any potential problems such as spot colors that may be contained in the file, as in the file used when I opened the Separations preview in Figure 32.4. Likewise, if a spot-color-only job contains colors not intended to be printed, they also show up.

FIGURE 32.4

The Separations window shows all colors contained in a file.

You can selectively view individual colors by disabling the check boxes adjacent to each color name, viewing selected colors only, and viewing spot colors converted to CMYK. When you click the X in a check box for a color, all images and objects containing a percentage of that color are hidden. Click again and the color is displayed.

You evaluate color values by moving the cursor around the document with the Output Preview dialog box open. Notice the percentage values on the far right side of Figure 32.4. These values represent the percent of ink at the cursor position.

Object Inspector

Open the Preview pull-down menu and choose Object Inspector as shown in Figure 32.5.

NEW FEATURE New in Acrobat 9 you find the Object Inspector. This marvelous new addition to Acrobat enables you to inspect objects in the PDF file. Objects can be text, images, and vector art. With the Object Inspector pane open in the Output Preview dialog box, move the cursor around the document. The area where you click the mouse is reported in the dialog box with feedback about the object properties.

You can review information on object properties such as color space, profile information, transparency, blending modes, image attributes such as size and resolution, and more.

FIGURE 32.5

The Object Inspector provides feedback on text, image, and object attributes.

Convert Colors

 The Convert Colors tool in the Print Production toolbar is truly great whether you soft proof files for commercial printing or you print your PDF documents on your local desktop color printer. Click this tool and the Convert Colors dialog box opens, as shown in Figure 32.6.

NEW FEATURE Perhaps one of the most dramatic changes in print production in Acrobat 9 is related to the Convert Colors options. You have an impressive set of controls that enable you to selectively convert and/or preserve colors according to object type. Radical changes have been made to the convert color settings shown in Figure 32.6 as compared to all earlier releases of Acrobat.

FIGURE 32.6

Click the Convert Colors tool in the Print Production toolbar to open the Convert Colors dialog box.

The choices you have in the Convert Colors dialog box include:

- **Conversion Commands.** Here's where you find a truly new impressive feature in Acrobat 9. Click the Add button and a new conversion item is listed in the Conversion Commands list. Select the item and you can choose the object type from the Object Type pull-down menu (see Object Type in this list) and the color type from the Color Type pull-down menu (See Color Type in this list). You can add another conversion command by clicking the Add button and define settings for a different object type. Under the Conversion attributes you can choose to preserve or convert color. The Move Up and Move Down buttons enable you to choose what commands are executed first.

- **Save/Load buttons.** You can define a series of commands and color conversion options and save the settings to a file. Click the Load button and you can load settings you create by clicking the Save button.

- **Matching Criteria.** You have choices for setting attributes according to Object Type and Color Type.

    - **Object Type.** There are four choices from the pull-down menu commands. Choose Any Object to apply the conversion settings to all objects. Choose Image, Text, or Line Art to apply conversions to one of these object types. Smooth Shade is the final choice, which enables you to apply conversions to gradients. Notice in Figure 32.6 I have three different object types with different conversion settings for each type.

- **Color Type.** From the Color Type pull-down menu you choose the colorspace for the object in question. You might choose Any RGB to convert RGB color to CMYK color. The choice you make here is the existing color of the object. You make a choice for the conversion target color in another menu.

- **Minimum Text Size.** Choose from preset point sizes or type a value in the text box. (Values range from 1 to 1 million). Conversion is applied to the minimum size defined in this menu. Sizes below the minimum are ignored.

- **Maximum Text Size.** Essentially this setting is the opposite of Minimum Text Size. Define a size for the maximum point size for text.

- **Convert Command.** From the pull-down menu choose Preserve, Convert to Profile, or Decalibrate. The Preserve choice preserves the color. Convert to Profile converts the color from the Color Type setting to the selected destination Profile. Decalibrate removes profiles from the identified object in the Object Type menu.

- **Conversion Profile.** Choose a profile from this menu for the destination of the conversion.

- **Rendering Intent.** Choose from Use Document Intent, Relative Colormetric, Absolute Colormetric, Perceptual, or Saturation. For more information on Rendering Intents, check out the Acrobat Help file.

- **Output Intent.** Check the check box for Convert to Output Intent and choose a profile from the Profile pull-down menu for the Output Intent if you want to convert all objects to a single output intent.

- **Convert Options.** Check the boxes for handling black and CMYK primary colors in the output.

- **Convert Pages.** Choose All or a page range for the pages to be converted.

CROSS-REF For more information on using output profiles in the Advanced Print Setup dialog box, see Chapter 31.

Ink Manager

The Ink Manager dialog box enables you to change ink values and convert colors. Changes you apply to the options aren't saved with the PDF file. If you convert spot colors to CMYK, for example, and save the document, the colors are unaffected when you reopen the file. The changes applied in the Ink Manager take effect only when you print a PDF document. To open the Ink Manager, click the Ink Manager tool in the Print Production toolbar; the Ink Manager dialog box shown in Figure 32.7 opens.

FIGURE 32.7

The Ink Manager enables you to change ink densities and convert color spaces.

NOTE **If you use the Ink Manager from inside the Color Convert dialog box, your choices can be made permanent.**

You change density values and the trapping sequence by editing the field box. To alias spot colors, select a spot color and map the color to the same angle and density as a process color. One of the great settings in this dialog box is the check box for Converting All Spots to Process. If you have one or more colors defined as spot colors, you can convert the spot color to process color by checking the box and clicking OK. Another advantage you have with the Ink Manager is when you need to remap one spot color value to another. If you have two colors that are supposed to be printed with the same spot values (such as Pantone 185 CVC and Pantone 185 CV), you can map the color so both color names are printed on the same plate.

TIP **You can interact with the Ink Manager directly from the Advanced Print Setup dialog box. If printing color separations from Acrobat, you can verify colors at the final stage of printing to be certain your colors are converted, remapped, or preserved by clicking the Ink Manager button in the Advanced Print Setup dialog box.**

Transparency Flattener Preview

Transparency creates problems when printing to various PostScript devices because the PostScript RIPs don't support transparency. For resolving printing problems with transparency, you need to flatten the transparency, which results in files that print successfully on any kind of PostScript device. When transparency is flattened in a file the transparent vector objects are converted to non-transparent objects or raster images. Through this conversion, the colors meld together to form a simulated view of transparency. The amount of blending that transparent colors need depends on the amount of transparency you apply to the objects. As you move the Raster/Vector Balance slider to the left to flatten transparency, all vector objects are rasterized. When you move the slider to the right, the transparency flattener maintains as many vector objects as needed in order to successfully print the file.

You can flatten transparency in degrees, and objects in a document are affected according to the degree of transparency flattening you apply. Determining how the other objects are affected is the purpose of the transparency flattener in Acrobat.

When you use the Transparency Flattening tool in the Print Production toolbar, the transparency changes that you make to the PDF are preserved when you save the file. To open the Flattener Preview dialog box, click the Flattener Preview tool in the Print Production toolbar; the options appear as shown in Figure 32.8.

FIGURE 32.8

When the Flattener Preview dialog box opens, click Refresh to see a preview of the document page.

Previews are displayed only for PostScript printing devices. Be certain you have a PostScript printer selected in your Print Setup dialog box before previewing transparency. Beginning with the Highlight pull-down menu you have options for the following:

- **Refresh/Highlight.** Click Refresh when you make attribute changes to see a preview of the results. The Highlight pull-down menu offers selections for areas in the PDF file you can preview.

- **Transparency Flattener Presets.** Select a preset from the pull-down menu. Your options are Low, Medium, and High Resolution. You can reset the preset, save a preset that is added to the menu, and delete a preset after you saved one to the menu.

- **Raster/Vector Balance.** Move the slider left to add more transparency flattening. Click the Refresh button each time you make readjustment of the amount of flattening to see a preview of the results.

- **Line Art and Text Resolution.** Use the text box to edit resolution for line art.

- **Gradient and Mesh resolution.** Change values in the field box to edit the resolution you want to apply to gradients and gradient meshes.

- **Convert All Text to Outlines.** If you intend to convert text to outlines, you can see a preview for how text objects are affected in complex regions. When printing a file, you'll want to avoid globally converting text to outlines because the files are more difficult to print, and small text on output devices that print at lower resolutions may appear unsatisfactory.

- **Convert All Strokes to Outlines.** Converts all strokes to outlines. Just as is the case with text converted to outlines, the files will take longer to print if you convert strokes to outlines.

- **Clip Complex Regions.** The boundaries between vector objects and raster objects change as you move the slider. Some objects remain in vector form according to the degree of rasterization you apply. This option ensures the boundaries between the vector and raster objects fall within clipping paths, preventing artifacts appearing outside the path boundaries. As with any illustration artwork, the more clipping paths used in a file, the more difficult the printing.

- **Preserve Overprint.** Preserves all overprints assigned in the document.

- **Color Space.** Click the Change button to change the transparency blending space to a profile you can choose from the Color Space drop-down menu in the Change Page-Level Transparency Blending Space dialog box.

- **Page Range.** Apply the settings to all pages or select a page range.

- **Apply to PDF.** After making your choices from the various options, click the Apply button. You can save the PDF document and all the transparency flattening is saved with the document.

Trapping Files

You can trap PDF files for commercial printing by applying trap presets from a selection installed as defaults or from custom trap presets you create in Acrobat. The Trap Presets dialog box provides you options for creating custom trap presets, editing a custom preset, assigning presets, and deleting custom presets. Although Acrobat provides you with trapping options, creative professionals should leave the trapping of your files to professional technicians at imaging centers. Unless you completely understand trapping, you can run into trouble by manually trapping your files. Imaging centers either use expensive custom trapping software or In-RIP trapping — both of which are much preferred over what Acrobat provides you with the trapping options.

> **TIP** If you have a file that uses Overprinting but not transparency, and you want to ensure that it always prints correctly regardless of the whether the output device is overprint aware, you can flatten the overprinting via the transparency flattener. Just make sure Preserve Overprints is off.

Fixing hairlines

 You may need to fix hairline rules. Click the Fix Hairlines tool in the Print Production toolbar to open the Fix Hairlines dialog box. You can thicken up any line that falls below a specified value to a new value you supply in a field box.

To fix hairlines, click the Fix Hairlines tool in the Print Production toolbar. The Fix Hairlines dialog box opens, as shown in Figure 32.9. In this dialog box, you specify the amounts for hairline fixes.

FIGURE 32.9

Click the Fix Hairlines tool in the Print Production toolbar to open the Fix Hairlines dialog box.

Creating trap presets

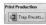
Make adjustments as needed in the Fix Hairlines dialog box, and then click the Trap Presets tool to open the Trap Presets dialog box shown in Figure 32.10.

FIGURE 32.10

Click the Trap Presets tool to open the Trap Presets dialog box.

The first dialog box that opens enables you to select an existing preset or create a new one. Click the Create button to open the New Trap Preset dialog box as shown in Figure 32.11. In order to make adjustments in the dialog box you should be familiar with trapping and the acceptable amounts to apply for trap widths, miter adjustments, and attributes assigned to images and thresholds. If you know how to trap a file, you'll know what settings to apply. If you don't know anything about trapping, it's best to leave the job to your commercial printer.

FIGURE 32.11

Set the attributes for the trap preset in the New Trap Preset dialog box.

Click OK after providing a name for the new preset and making the adjustments. You are then returned to the Trap Presets dialog box where your new preset is listed in the window. Click the Assign button to apply the trap values to the document.

Cropping Pages

Two tools appear in the Print Production toolbar for cropping pages in Acrobat. Ideally, you'll want to export to PDF from an authoring program with crop marks at the time you convert to PDF. Acrobat won't retain any bleeds in your document. If you don't have bleeds, these tools can help you set up the proper page size and add crop marks. A document such as a Microsoft Word file that needs to go to press is an ideal candidate for these tools because you won't find bleeds in Word files.

Adding printer marks

 When cropping pages, you'll typically add crop and other printer's marks to the cropped page so you'll know the correct trim size.

CROSS-REF For a description on using the Add Printer Marks tool, see Chapter 8.

Cropping pages

 When cropping pages, the thing to remember is to first use the Add Printer Marks tool, and then use the Crop Pages tool in the Print Production toolbar. When you click the Crop Pages tool, the Crop Pages dialog box opens where you set the page size, select the range of pages you want to crop, and view a preview before you exit the dialog box.

After adding crop marks, click OK; the printer marks appear on the page. The process for adding printer marks and using the Crop Pages dialog box is covered in Chapter 8.

PDF Optimizer

PDF Optimizer is a menu command available under the Advanced menu. You can choose Advanced ⇨ PDF Optimizer or open the Print Production toolbar and click the PDF Optimizer tool.

 When you click the PDF Optimizer tool in the Print Production toolbar, the PDF Optimizer dialog box opens. A number of options appear in several panes for deleting nonessential data from files, changing PDF compatibility, and optimizing the file for smaller file sizes. All the options you have in the PDF Optimizer are detailed in Chapter 18.

CROSS-REF For a description on using PDF Optimizer, see Chapter 18.

Working with Job Definition Files

You use a Job Definition File (JDF) in production workflows to include information necessary for a production process and information related to the PDF creation.

 You assign the information in a JDF file through a collection of dialog boxes that begins with your clicking on the JDF Job Definitions tool at the far right side of the Print Production toolbar. Clicking the tool opens the JDF Job Definitions dialog box, as shown in Figure 32.12.

FIGURE 32.12

Click the JDF Job Definitions tool to open the JDF Job Definitions dialog box.

Click the New button to open the Create New Job Definition dialog box. You make choices for creating a new definition, using the open document's structure, or applying a definition from another file saved to your hard drive. If you create a new definition, you need to supply a name in the Name field box and click OK; the Edit JDF Job Definition dialog box opens, as shown in Figure 32.13.

In the default General tab you can define some production information and binding settings, preflight information, PDF conversion settings, and Job ID information. Click the Customer Info tab to add contact and identifying information.

The entire process for creating and using JDF files is extensive and beyond the scope of this chapter. For more information about JDF, see the Help document installed with Acrobat.

FIGURE 32.13

Create a new JDF Definition and the Edit JDF Definition dialog box opens.

Preflighting PDF Files

Preflighting is a term creative professionals and service technicians use to refer to analyzing a file for suitability for printing. A preflight assessment might examine a file for the proper color mode of images, whether images are compressed, whether fonts are either embedded or accessible to the operating system, or any number of other conditions that might interfere with successfully printing a job.

NEW FEATURE The Preflight features have had quite a bit of overhaul in Acrobat 9. In addition to similar options you had with earlier Acrobat viewers for preflighting files, Preflight now offers some impressive new features such as the ability to create new Adobe PDF layers, additional presets for online publishing, and more PDF standards support.

CROSS-REF For more information on creating Adobe PDF layers using the Preflight tool, see Chapter 24.

I saved mentioning the Preflight tool in the Print Production toolbar to last because preflighting PDF files is a bit complicated and quite complex. In addition to clicking the Preflight tool, you can also open the Preflight dialog box by selecting Advanced ➪ Preflight or pressing Shift+Ctrl/⌘+X. Any one of these actions opens the Preflight dialog box shown in Figure 32.14.

FIGURE 32.14

Click the Preflight tool in the Print Production toolbar or select Advanced ➪ Preflight to open the Preflight dialog box.

The tools used to preflight files might be stand-alone applications or features built into programs used for printing to commercial printing equipment. Prior to Acrobat 6 you needed to preflight a file before converting to PDF with a stand-alone product that analyzed the original authoring application file prior to conversion to PDF, or a third-party plug-in for Acrobat that performed pre-flighting on PDF files. Preflighting PDFs from within Acrobat was introduced in Acrobat 6 and has been polished and greatly improved in Acrobat 9.

As a matter of fact, there's so much to Preflight and the various options you can use, covering all features would take about half the size of this book to thoroughly explain all features. I cover some of the more important and impressive features here in this chapter. For more information on Preflighting files and complete coverage of all the options available to you, consult the complete Acrobat Help file.

Preflighting a file

Acrobat requires you to have a file open in the document pane in order to run a preflight check unless you use a batch sequence or droplet. To preflight a document, be certain a file is open and click the Preflight tool in the Print Production toolbar. The Preflight dialog box shown previously in Figure 32.14 opens. In the scrollable and resizable window, you see a number of preinstalled profiles listed with a description for the kind of preflighting each profile performs. Use the scroll bar on the right side of the window to display additional profiles, and open & close the various disclosure triangles. If the number of items gets too many, try using the Show & search/filter options.

The Options menu contains a number of menu choices for editing profiles, importing and exporting profiles, and creating profile reports.

If a profile exists containing the conditions you want to check, select a profile and click the Analyze button. After analyzing a file, a summary report appears in the Results tab in the Preflight window as shown in Figure 32.15. Any errors in the file are reported in the summary. The summary report is listed in a hierarchy with subnotations listed under parent categories. Click the icon to the left of each category to expand the list.

FIGURE 32.15

After analyzing a file a summary report is shown in the Results tab in the Preflight window.

If you see errors reported after preflighting a file, you need to fix the problems either in Acrobat using Preflight's FixUps, the Print Production tools or back in the original authoring program, and recreate the PDF file.

Creating a new profile

If none of the preset profiles do the job of file checking for your workflow, you can create your own custom profiles. Acrobat offers you more than 400 different conditions that you can use in preflighting files. Click the Options down-pointing arrow in the Preflight window and you'll find a list of commands that relate to creating and editing profiles, as well as other commands for examining the internal structure of a PDF document as shown in Figure 32.16.

FIGURE 32.16

Open the Options menu and you find all the commands you need for creating, editing, and modifying profiles.

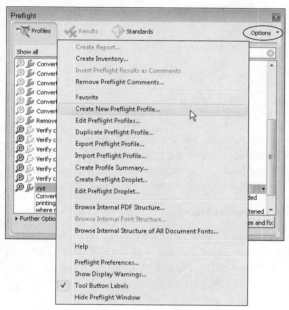

To create a new profile, choose Options ➪ Create New Profile. The Preflight: Edit Profile dialog box opens, as shown in Figure 32.17.

Along the left side of the dialog box you find the list of installed profiles. These profiles are listed in hierarchical order. To expand a category, click the Plus (+) symbol. To the top right of the list you find a pull-down menu. The default choice when creating a new profile is Unlocked as shown in Figure 32.17. If you attempt to edit an existing profile, the profile will be locked and you'll need to open the menu and choose Unlocked before you can make any edits.

FIGURE 32.17

Choose Options ⇨ Create New Profile to open the Preflight: Edit Profiles dialog box.

The Name text box is where you add a name for your profile. Below the Name text box you find the Purpose text box where a description can be added to define the profile's purpose. Following the Purpose description you find an Author field, Email field, and a menu for targeting a group location for saving the file. At the bottom of the list, several tools appear for creating and managing profiles.

  From left to right, the tools are as follows:

- **Create a new profile.** Click the icon to create a new profile. This tool might be used when reviewing another profile. When you open the Create New Profile menu command and arrive at the dialog box shown in Figure 32.17, clicking this tool does nothing. If you are on another pane and click the tool, the Preflight: Edit Profile dialog box opens as shown in Figure 32.17.

- **Duplicate the selected profile.** Click the icon to duplicate a selected profile. Once it's duplicated, you can edit the profile to change conditions.

- **Delete the selected profile.** Select a profile and click the icon to remove the profile from the list window. You cannot delete the profile if Locked is selected in the Preflight: Edit Profile pane.

- **Import.** Click the Import tool to import a profile created by a vendor or a user in your workgroup.

- **Export.** If you are responsible for creating profiles at a service center or in a company where you want to implement a set of standards, click the Export button. The profile selected when you click this button is exported to a file that you can send to other users who in turn import the profile.

To create a new custom profile, you should be at the screen shown in Figure 32.17 — that is, you should have chosen Options ⇨ Create New Profile. Type a name in the Name text box. From here, it's a matter of selecting items in the list on the left side of the dialog box and editing the changes appearing in the right pane. For example, I started a new profile by clicking Document in the left pane. I then opened the pull-down menu for the first choice and chose an icon to present a flag for the summary report. Below the icon choice (the X you see in Figure 32.18) I chose Acrobat 5 compatibility. My next choice was an icon for encryption followed by a choice for flagging the report when a PDF document is damaged. These choices are clearly shown in Figure 32.18.

FIGURE 32.18

Click an item in the left pane and the right pane changes to reflect options choices you can make for the selected item.

The rest of your new profile creation follows the same steps. You find the categories in the left pane, select a given category, and choose from menu items the options you want to include in the profile for preflighting the document.

After you create a new custom profile, click the Save button to save the new profile to your list of profiles.

Creating reports and comments

After you create a profile, open a PDF document and open the Preflight dialog box. Choose the profile from the list and click the Analyze button as I described earlier in the section "Preflighting a file." A summary report then appears directly in the Preflight dialog box. This summary is an initial description of any errors found or a list of checked items and a statement confirming the file meets the conditions specified by the profile.

For a more informative document, you can create a report that lists the text summary and highlights on all pages in the document where errors are found. Click the Create Report button in the Preflight dialog box after analyzing a document to create a new PDF file as a report summary. When you open the PDF, you'll see the first page listing the summarized comments for errors found, and on each subsequent page you'll find highlights marking each area where an error was found as shown in Figure 32.19.

FIGURE 32.19

Each page contains highlights of any errors found after preflighting a document and creating a summary report.

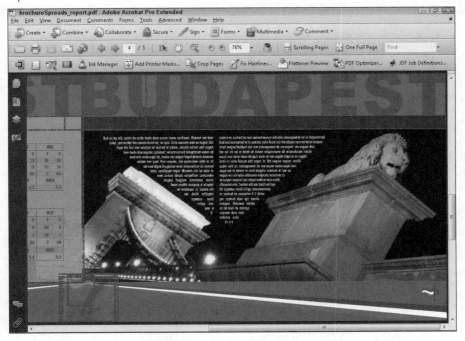

Creating droplets

A great new feature added in Acrobat 8 was the preflight droplets. A droplet is an executable file created from the Preflight options where you can drag and drop PDF documents to preflight them. To create a droplet, follow these steps.

STEPS: Creating a droplet

1. **Open the Preflight dialog box.** If you don't have a PDF document open in the document pane, you can open the Preflight dialog box by choosing Advanced ➪ Preflight. You can also use the same command when a document is open.

2. **Set up the droplet.** Choose the profile you created or select an existing profile and choose Options ➪ Create Profile Droplet. The Preflight: Droplet Setup dialog box opens as shown in Figure 32.20.

In the Preflight: Droplet Setup dialog box make choices for the location where you want the successful files saved, the files with errors saved, and the reports you want to create. You can toggle through this dialog box and get a good idea for how to identify locations and make choices for reports.

FIGURE 32.20

Make choices for saved file locations and report settings in the Preflight: Droplet Setup dialog box.

3. **Save the settings.** Click the Save button to open the Save droplet as dialog box. Locate a target folder and supply a name for your file. Click Save to save the droplet.

4. **Run a preflight.** Open the folder where you saved the preflight droplet and drag a PDF document or multiple PDF documents on top of the droplet icon. A Preflight dialog box opens and a progress bar shows the preflight progress.

5. **Examine the report.** After the preflight progress has completed, a preflight summary report opens as a PDF Portfolio. In my example I dropped four files on my preflight droplet. The files are shown in the PDF Portfolio interface in Figure 32.21. From here you can double-click a file to view the summary report.

FIGURE 32.21

The report(s) opens in a PDF Portfolio.

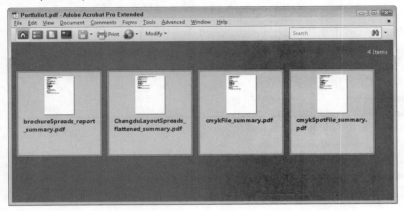

CROSS-REF **For more information on PDF Portfolios, see Chapter 12.**

Examining PDF structure

Another option you have available with the Preflight tool is examining PDF structure. You have a few choices in the Options menu in the Preflight dialog box. Open a file and open the Preflight dialog box (Advanced ➪ Preflight). From the Options menu, choose Browse Internal Structure of all Document Fonts. The Preflight: Browse Internal Structure of all Document Fonts dialog box opens as shown in Figure 32.22.

The report shows all document fonts and a detail of the font attributes. You can check this report for font embedding, subsetting, name, family, and a host of related font information.

Close the dialog box to return to the Preflight dialog box. Open the Options menu again and choose Browse Internal PDF Structure. A report is shown in the Preflight: Browse Internal PDF Structure dialog box as shown in Figure 32.23.

Here you'll find a report on the structure of the PDF in terms of page size, art, media, trim, and crop boundaries, rotations, and various content information.

FIGURE 32.22

Choose Options ⇨ Browse Internal Structure of all Document Fonts.

FIGURE 32.23

Choose Options ⇨ Browse Internal Structure to display a report on the PDF structure.

Creating an inventory

Another report you can generate using the Preflight tool is an inventory of PDF internal data and metadata. Quite simply you create the inventory report by opening a document and opening the Preflight dialog box. From the Options menu choose Create Inventory. Acrobat displays a progress bar as the report is generated. When finished, you see a report saved as a PDF file like the report shown in Figure 32.24.

FIGURE 32.24

Choose Options ⇨ Create Inventory to create a PDF report of document information and metadata.

Preflight Summary Report for: brochureSpreads_secure.pdf
Profile: Create inventory (Processed pages 4 to 4)
Processed by HP_Administrator, Date: 4/8/2008 9:17 PM

⊤ **Document information**
File name: "brochureSpreads_secure.pdf"
Path: "C:\DataFiles\Acrobat 9\Artwork\Chapter23"
PDF version number: "1.6"
File size (MB): 13.6
Title: "brochureLayers.indd"
Creator: "Adobe InDesign CS (3.0)"
Producer: "Adobe PDF Library 6.0"
Created: "2/5/2004 9:25 AM"
Modified: "4/8/2008 9:16 PM"
Trapping: "False"
Additional actions
   Page open action
     Type: Go to page in current document
Number of plates: 4
Names of plates: "(Cyan) (Magenta) (Yellow) (Black) "

▦ **Environment**
Preflight, 9.0.0 (042)
Acrobat version: 9.00
Operating system: Microsoft Windows Vista Home Edition (Build 6000)

The Create Inventory command can be applied to a PDF document that has been secured with Acrobat Security. Therefore, if you don't find access to all the metadata in a file, use this feature to create a summary report.

CROSS-REF **For more information about metadata, see Chapter 6.**

Checking and Fixing Up Files

One of the great new additions to Acrobat 9 is the work that's gone into checking files and fixing them up. You can use profiles you create for your own use and you can use profiles sent to you by service centers. But the tools you have available in Acrobat offer you an abundance of opportunity to analyze and repair files for various output sources.

In the Preflight dialog box you find settings under the Digital Printing and online publishing area. You also have PDF/X options in the Preflight dialog box to make PDF files compliant with PDF/X standards. For digital printing checks and fix-ups, look at Figure 32.25. Click this item and at the bottom of the Preflight dialog box and click the Analyze and Fix button.

FIGURE 32.25

For analyzing and fixing files to be printed on digital printing devices make the choice in the Preflight dialog box and click Analyze and Fix.

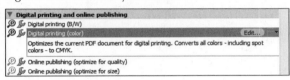

Acrobat opens another window in the Preflight dialog box that shows a progress bar as items are analyzed and it makes its best effort to fix the problems. Wait until the progress bar, shown in Figure 32.26, has finished before proceeding. As items are analyzed they are listed in the dialog box.

When Acrobat completes the analysis a report appears in the Preflight dialog box as shown in Figure 32.27. Items essential to printing the file that cannot be fixed need to be addressed back in the original authoring program. For non-essential errors and a complete fix of issues that might impair printing, Acrobat can make many files print ready.

Printing PDFs for Commercial Printing

Acrobat Pro contains all the print controls you need for printing files to commercial devices. To access the options, choose File ➪ Print or click the Print tool in the Toolbar Well. In the Print dialog box, click the Advanced button.

When you select Advanced in the Print dialog box in Acrobat Pro, the Advanced Print Setup dialog box shown in Figure 32.28 opens. There are four categories in the left pane. When you select a category, the right pane changes, just as the Preferences dialog box changes when you select a category.

NOTE You must have a PostScript printer selected in the Print dialog box in order to see all the options in the left pane. If the Adobe PDF Print Engine is detected, Acrobat will send the PDF directly to the printing device.

FIGURE 32.26

Wait for the progress bar to finish.

FIGURE 32.27

A report is created to show you any errors in the file.

FIGURE 32.28

Click the Advanced button in the Print dialog box to open the Advanced Print Setup dialog box.

Output

Output options enable you to set the color and frequency controls for the output. At the top of the dialog box a check box is available for printing the document as an image. For desktop printing when you have trouble printing the file, you can use the Print As Image option as a last resort. Print As Image rasterizes the PDF document, and type usually looks poor on the final output. Don't enable the check box for professional printing. This option is also available in the Advanced Print options for Adobe Reader and Acrobat Standard. The remaining items are used for commercial printing and they include the following:

- **Color.** Select from composite or separations. Users with PostScript 3 RIPs can choose either Separations or In-Rip Separations depending on how you set up your RIP defaults. For creative professionals printing separation proofs to desktop printers, select Separations. For composite color, select Composite from the pull-down menu. For printing RC Paper or composite images to film, select Composite Gray.

> **NOTE** If Separations is not available, you don't have a PostScript printer capable of printing separations selected for your printer. If you don't see separations active, cancel out of the dialog box, select the Adobe PDF printer in the Print dialog box, and then click Advanced to return to the Advanced Print Settings.

- **Color Profile.** Select from the pull-down menu items the color profile used in your workflow.

- **Flip.** For emulsion control, select horizontal from the Flip pull-down menu to print with emulsion down. You have options for flip vertical and flip vertical & horizontal.

NOTE Adobe's print controls in Acrobat Pro are *almost* perfect. However, one limitation still exists in Acrobat 9. There is no emulsion control for composite printing. Emulsion control is available only when printing separations. Therefore, service centers needing to print emulsion-down composites on LexJet, mylar, transwhite, and other substrates on large-format inkjet printers need to flip files prior to PDF creation or by using the rotation tools in Acrobat.

- **Screening.** If you're using the Adobe PDF printer as the printer driver, the screening options won't match the device where you print your job. If you're using a device printer, the screening options for the device are derived from the PPD (PostScript Printer Description). If the frequency is not available from the pull-down menu, you select custom screens and angles from the Ink Manager (discussed later in this list).

- **Trapping.** If trapping is assigned to the document, you can turn trapping on and load a trap preset.

- **Transparency Flattener Preset.** Default and custom presets appear in the pull-down menu. Select a preset if you want to flatten transparency at print time.

- **Simulate Overprinting.** This option, also available for composite, prints only the print results in a proof, showing the results of overprints assigned in the document. This feature emulates the overprinting previews of high-end color proofers, such as what was introduced with the Imation Rainbow printer.

- **Use Maximum Available JPEG2000 Image Resolution.** When the check box is enabled, the maximum usable resolution contained in JPEG2000 images is used.

- **Frequency/Angle.** To edit the frequency and angle for each plate, type the desired values in the text boxes. Click each color and edit the Frequency and Angle text boxes.

- **Ink Manager.** Click the Ink Manager button and the Ink Manager dialog box opens, providing options the same as those available when you click the Ink Manager tool in the Print Production toolbar. If spot colors are contained in the file, you can convert spot or RGB to CMYK color by selecting the Convert All Spots to Process check box. The spot color converts to CMYK when you check the box. (See "Ink Manager" earlier in this chapter).

Marks and Bleeds

Select Marks and Bleeds in the left pane of the Advanced Print Setup dialog box, and the right pane changes to show options for adding printer's marks. All marks added in the Advanced Print Setup dialog box apply only to the printed file. If you want to save a file with printer's marks, use the Add Printer Marks tool in the Print Production toolbar.

Select All to show all printer's marks. If you want individual marks, clear All Marks and select the check boxes individually below the Marks Style pull-down menu. From the pull-down menu options, you can choose Western Style or Eastern Style. Use Eastern Style for printing files in far-eastern countries.

Marks and bleeds are also available for composite proofs as well as separations.

PostScript Options

Click PostScript Options in the Advanced Print Setup dialog box, and the right pane changes to display options for PostScript attributes as shown in Figure 32.29.

FIGURE 32.29

Click PostScript and the right pane changes to reflect options for PostScript output options.

The options include the following:

- **Font and Resource Policy.** Three options are available from the pull-down menu. Select Send at Start to send all fonts to the printer as the print job starts. Select Send by Range to send fonts as they are encountered on the pages as new pages print; the fonts stay in memory until the job finishes printing. Select Send for Each page to conserve memory; the fonts are flushed after each page prints. The last selection takes more time to print but can overcome problems when you are experiencing difficulty in printing a job.

- **Print Method.** Choose from PostScript Level 2 or PostScript 3 depending on the level of PostScript used by the RIP.

- **Download Asian Fonts.** Check the box if Asian characters are in the document and not available at the RIP.

- **Convert TrueType to Type 1.** Converts TrueType to Type 1 fonts.

- **Emit CIDFontType2 as CIDFontType2 (PS version 2015 and greater).** Converts TrueType fonts to PostScript font equivalents.

- **Emit Undercolor Removal/Black Generation.** GCR/UCR removal is necessary only if the original file contained embedded settings. Clear the box to remove any embedded settings that might have been inadvertently added and saved in Photoshop. If you want to apply any embedded settings, selecting the box to Emit the settings applies them as if they were embedded in the authoring program.

- **Emit Halftones.** In the event that the PostScript file contained embedded halftones, you can preserve them here, and the frequency assigned in the Output options is used to print the file. Select the box to apply the frequency embedded in a file. You want to preserve halftones when you want an embedded halftone frequency in an image to print at a different frequency than the rest of the job.

- **Emit Transfer Functions.** Clear the box to eliminate any transfer functions that might have been embedded in Photoshop images. If you know you want images to print with embedded transfer functions you may have applied according to instructions provided from a publication house, select the box to preserve the transfer functions.

- **Emit Flatness.** If flatness was exported from files created in Adobe Photoshop with clipping paths, or if a vector art image has flatness applied, the flatness values are retained in the output.

- **Emit PS Form Objects.** PostScript XObject stores common information in a document, such as backgrounds, headers, footers, and so on. When PostScript XObjects are used, the printing is faster, but it requires more memory. To speed up the printing, select the box to emit PostScript XObjects.

CROSS-REF To understand more about XObjects, see Chapter 10.

- **Discolored background correction.** Corrects any problems with discoloring on backgrounds.

- **Always use host collation.** If collating is assigned in the Print dialog box, checking this box collates pages according to the settings used for the print engine.

Color Management

Click Color Management in the left pane and the right pane changes to display settings for managing color. For information on options for color management and setting up color management at print time, see Chapter 31.

You can capture and save the settings you select in the Advanced Print Setup dialog box as a printing profile. Click the Save As button to open the Save Print Settings dialog box. Provide a name and click OK. You select the profiles from the pull-down menu for Settings in the top left corner of the Advanced Print Setup dialog box.

If you create a setting and want to later delete it from the Settings pull-down menu, select the setting to delete and press the Delete button.

Summary

- You can change page sizes with the Crop Pages tool. You add trim marks with the Add Printer Marks tool in the Print Production toolbar in Acrobat Pro.

- Both Acrobat Pro products provide several tools for soft proofing color, overprints, separation previews, and transparency flattening. Acrobat Standard and Adobe Reader do not support tools used for commercial printing.

- Traps are defined with the Trap Presets tool in Acrobat Pro.

- JDF (Job Definition Files) are defined using the JDF Job Definitions tool in Acrobat Pro.

- Preflighting files is a manner of checking a document for potential errors in printing. Acrobat Pro offers you an extended set of conditions to check files before sending them to prepress centers and print shops.

- You save PDF/X-compliant files from the Preflight dialog box. Sending PDF/X files to service centers and print shops optimizes your chances for successful output when printing to commercial printing devices.

- A set of preset profiles is installed with Acrobat Pro for preflighting jobs. You can create custom profiles by adding preset conditions in the Preflight dialog box.

- You can import and export profiles. You can acquire profiles from service centers and add them to your profile list for preflighting files.

- Acrobat provides several preflight options for examining PDF structure and content. Use the Options menu in the Preflight dialog box and choose the Browse Internal Structure and Create Inventory commands.

- Preflight droplets are executable files you create to preflight one or more PDF documents. The result is a PDF Portfolio containing a summary report of all files preflighted via a drag-and-drop function.

- The Advanced Print Setup dialog box in Acrobat Pro offers you options for color separations, printer's marks, frequency control, emulsion control, and other print attributes associated with commercial printing.

Part VI

Acrobat PDF Forms

Part VI is all about forms. In Chapter 33 we first take a look at Adobe LiveCycle Designer (Windows only) for creating dynamic forms. More than 70 pages comprise this chapter that provides you a foundation and start for using LiveCycle Designer. In Chapter 34 we switch gears and look at creating Acrobat PDF forms using Acrobat Standard (Windows), Acrobat Professional (Windows and Macintosh), and Acrobat Professional Extended (Windows). You'll discover the new Form Edit mode in Acrobat 9 and learn how to quickly create fillable forms using any one of the commercial Acrobat products.

In Chapter 35 we look at managing form data through new features in Acrobat 9 for sharing data on Acrobat.com and tracking returned forms. To learn more about using Acrobat JavaScript for adding interactive and dynamic features to PDF forms, see Chapter 36 on the CD-ROM.

Chapter 33

Using Adobe LiveCycle Designer ES (Windows Only)

W hen it comes to Acrobat and forms, essentially two different types of forms can be created with tools from your Acrobat Pro or Acrobat Pro Extended installation in Windows only. Acrobat Pro lets you create Adobe PDF forms within Acrobat on either Windows or Macintosh. In Windows, you have another tool installed with Acrobat Pro called Adobe LiveCycle Designer ES that is a separate executable application. Forms created in Adobe LiveCycle Designer ES (or simply Designer, or LiveCycle Designer as I refer to it in this chapter) are an XML Forms Architecture (XML), which is an application of XML for electronic forms.

What's important to remember is that PDF forms created in Acrobat are very different than XML forms created in LiveCycle Designer. Among other things, you can't edit XML forms in Acrobat, and there are some limitations to what you can do with Acrobat PDF forms you edit in Designer.

As a forms development tool, LiveCycle Designer is one of the best applications you can find to create forms that can be filled out and submitted using any Acrobat viewer. However, Designer is not a panacea for all forms development. You do have many opportunities for impressive forms creation in Acrobat, as I explain in the remaining chapters of this book.

For now, we're concerned with Designer and how to use the application to create XML forms. As I stated at the beginning of this book, the *Adobe Acrobat 9 PDF Bible* is not a book on forms and not a book on LiveCycle Designer. There's much more to Designer than can be covered in this book. As a matter of fact, there's so much to creating PDF forms in Acrobat and LiveCycle Designer that I've written a comprehensive work — *PDF Forms Using Acrobat and LiveCycle Designer Bible* (Wiley Publishing 2009).

What I can hope to do in this chapter is provide a brief introduction to Adobe LiveCycle Designer and talk about some of the neat things you can do with the program. For a much more thorough description of the tools, commands, and features, be certain to look over the Help document provided with your Acrobat installation, and look for another source to help you learn more about creating dynamic XML forms using LiveCycle Designer.

Setting Up the Work Environment

Adobe LiveCycle Designer is a standalone program used to design XML forms. When you create forms in Designer, you cannot edit the form fields in Acrobat. Therefore, the work environment in Acrobat does not require any special tools to edit forms created in Designer. To view and fill out forms in Acrobat use the default toolbar setup. Open a context menu on the Toolbar Well and select Reset Toolbars.

In the LiveCycle Designer workplace are a number of different options for setting up your work environment. Designer makes extensive use of palettes with fewer tools, as in Acrobat; so setting up your workplace is primarily a matter of opening and closing palettes. In Figure 33.1 you can see a number of palettes loaded in palette wells for an editing session.

FIGURE 33.1

The LiveCycle Designer workplace with a number of palettes loaded in palette wells

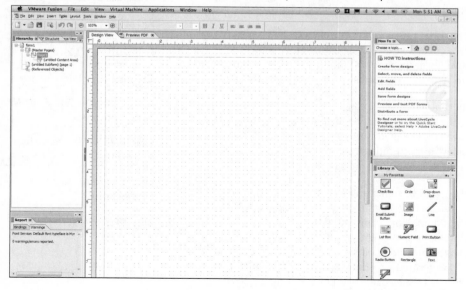

Running LiveCycle Designer on a Macintosh

If you're a Macintosh user, you may feel left out when it comes to forms development using Acrobat. You do have all the tools you need to create PDF forms in Acrobat, as I explain in Chapter 34. However, you don't have a Mac version of LiveCycle Designer shipped with your Mac Acrobat software.

There is one solution available to you if you want to use your Mac and you want to create forms with LiveCycle Designer. All you need is an application that permits you to install Windows on an Intel Mac. You can use Apple's Boot Camp (www.apple.com), Parallels Desktop for Mac (www.parallels.com), or VMware's Fusion (www.vmware.com).

Once you install one of the three virtual desktop applications, you then need to install Windows (XP or Vista). After you have the Windows operating system installed, you need to install Acrobat Pro or Acrobat Pro Extended — Windows version.

I've found VMware's Fusion software, shown in Figure 33.2, to work exceptionally well on a Macintosh. I can exchange files between OS X Leopard and Windows Vista. LiveCycle Designer works just the same on Windows for an Intel Mac as you find on a dedicated Windows machine.

FIGURE 33.2

LiveCycle Designer running on an Intel Mac

This solution requires Mac users to spend a little more money for a virtual desktop application, Acrobat Pro or Pro Extended for Windows, and the Windows operating system. However, if your work is primarily devoted to creating forms, you'll find the little expense you need to make to install LiveCycle Designer well worth it when you need to create dynamic forms.

Preparing the workspace

Unlike Acrobat in which you engage in very different editing tasks, Designer is all about creating forms. There are some palettes that you won't use in an editing session and others that may be used in some layouts. For example, you might use the Data Connection tools when you want to make a connection to a database file. When designing other forms you might not use the tools. In some forms you may add barcodes, while in other forms you won't need the barcode tools. This is the case for several palettes in Designer.

Regardless of what kind of form you create there are some common palettes needed in almost all form designs, and you'll want to set up your work environment with the essential tools first. These palettes are as follows:

- **Object.** The Object palette contains three tabs. The Field tab provides options for assigning appearance attributes to fields. The Value tab contains options for assigning attributes to field values. Among other attributes, the Value tab lets you change field types — something you can't do in Acrobat. The Binding tab lets you set up data connections to bind fields to a database.

- **Layout.** The Layout tab provides a number of attribute choices for field layouts such as size, margins, captions, and so on.

- **Border.** The Border tab provides extensive choices for creating field appearances. Acrobat offers a few choices for borders and fills. In Designer, you can format field appearances similar to the way you can format cells in a program such as Microsoft Excel.

- **Font/Paragraph.** By default, the Font and Paragraph tabs don't appear in the Designer workspace. If you want to change fonts and set font and paragraph attributes, select Window ➪ Font and both tabs open. Keep this palette open when designing a form. You'll use it often.

- **Object Library.** The Object Library is your repository containing the fields you add to a Designer form. In Acrobat, you choose a tool in Form Edit mode from the Add New Field pull-down menu. Acrobat supports eight different field types. Designer supports 25 different field types/objects in the Object Library Standard tab alone that you drag from the palette tab to the document page. Among other tabs in the Object Library palette you also have an option for adding your own custom designed fields that can be reused on many different forms.

- **How To.** Designer's How To tab is where help information is quickly accessible. When you first start using Designer, it's a good idea to keep this palette open. After you know your way around the Designer workspace, you can close the palette to make more room for other palettes.

- **Hierarchy.** On the left side of the Designer workspace, you see the Hierarchy palette. Keep this palette open for all your forms designs. The palette lists all the fields, subforms, master pages, and structure on your design in a hierarchical order. This palette is indispensable and you'll need to use it frequently when creating dynamic forms.

- **Data View.** The Data View tab is where you make database connections. You may or may not need this tab open depending on the kind of form you design.

- **Report/Warnings.** The Report tab provides you with information about the form design. The Warnings tab is loaded when you select Window ➪ Report (or Warnings). This tab can be very helpful when creating a new form. The Warnings tab dynamically lists errors and messages for potential problems in your form.

- **Script Editor.** In Designer 7 the Script Editor opened by default. The Script Editor takes up some precious room at the top of the Designer window, and hiding it in Designer 7 always required you to adjust the Script Editor to move it out of view. By default, the Script Editor is hidden in Designer 8 and 8.2. If you want to open the Script Editor so that you can write code in FormCalc or JavaScript, select Window ➪ Script Editor. You'll notice in the menu command that you now have a keyboard shortcut to open and close the Script Editor. Press Ctrl+Shift+F5 and the Script Editor opens and closes on the keyboard shortcut. By default, leave the Script Editor hidden to provide you with more room for editing a form, and press Ctrl+Shift+F5 when you need to write a script.

- **Design View/Preview PDF.** The two tabs at the top of the layout area in the Designer window enable you to see the layout (Design view), and a PDF Preview of the form. The Design View and PDF Preview tabs appear by default. To open the Master Pages tab, select View ➪ Master Pages. Additionally, you can add another tab for viewing XML source code. Select View ➪ XML Source to display the tab.

  When designing a form you need to view the form in PDF Preview in order to execute actions from fields and fill in data. Be sure to keep the two default tabs open for any design you create. If you lose a tab, look in the View menu to bring it back.

There are additional palettes and tabs you can load from the Window menu. The preceding list covers some of the most essential palettes you need for just about any form design. As you poke around the Window menu, a few other palettes that are self-descriptive can be added to your workspace. Be aware, however, that as you add more palettes to the workspace, you reduce the amount of work area you have to lay out your form design.

In addition to palettes, you also have options for displaying a number of hidden tools. By default, Designer opens with a limited tool set. You can add tools and load toolbars by selecting Tools ➪ Customize. The Customize dialog box opens where you can select additional tools and display several toolbars. In addition, you can create a custom toolbar by clicking the New button in the Customize dialog box and add the individual tools you want to use in a toolbar you design.

Understanding the Why for Adobe LiveCycle Designer ES

When you purchase Adobe Acrobat Pro or Adobe Acrobat Pro Extended, one of your first thoughts might be, "Why is Adobe providing me with a standalone program to design forms when I can do the job in Acrobat Pro?" This is an important question and you need to understand not only the purpose for using Designer, but also the advantages you have with using the program. As a matter of support, Adobe invests time equally between adding new features for AcroForms and LiveCycle Designer forms.

Adobe LiveCycle Designer is a client-based point-and-click graphical design application that simplifies the creation of forms. In Acrobat you need to create a form design in another application, convert to PDF, and add form fields in Acrobat. Designer includes the ability to create the form layout as well as the form fields that your form recipient will populate with data, or you may bind a data source to your form and flow the data spawning fields and pages as needed. Forms created with LiveCycle Designer are intended to be delivered either as PDF or HTML that supports user-defined data structures, like XML. In support of standards-based data formatting, such as XML, Adobe is de-emphasizing its proprietary FDF (Form Data Format) as a data exchange format and migrating to XML as an open standard. With tools that help you easily design forms through drag-and-drop methods for handling images and form data fields, LiveCycle Designer is a tool that simplifies data management and data exchanges.

It's data handling that takes Designer to a level well beyond the capabilities of Adobe Acrobat. Form designers using LiveCycle Designer can create simple data-capture solutions and use the Acrobat products to consolidate data received from clients. The ability to easily transport data to and from other applications via XDP and XML format makes Designer a much less complicated and efficient solution than what you have available using Adobe Acrobat.

As of this writing, Macintosh users are at a disadvantage because Designer is available on Windows only. However, you may expect to eventually see Designer supported on both platforms as development in technology applied to Designer is likely to increase, while Adobe still intends to completely support Acrobat PDF form technology. Considering the fact that Adobe is investing as much research and development into Designer as they are devoting to Acrobat, the more you know about Designer today, the better off you'll be when future Acrobat products are released. If you are a serious form designer, you will want to begin using Designer right away.

Getting Started with a New Form Design

LiveCycle Designer offers you several options for designing forms when you first choose a menu command to create a new form. By default, when you launch Designer by double-clicking the application icon (or use the Start Menu or an application icon alias) you arrive at the Welcome to Adobe LiveCycle Designer Welcome screen. You can choose to dismiss the screen when you launch Designer by removing the check mark in the lower left corner of the Welcome screen where you see Show this Dialog at Startup. If you click New Form in the Welcome screen or you select File ⇨ New, the New Form Assistant Wizard opens as shown in Figure 33.3. Starting a Designer work session when creating a new form usually begins by clicking New Form in the Welcome screen or selecting File ⇨ New. In both cases you start your project by first making a decision for a method to use from options in the New Form Assistant Wizard.

FIGURE 33.3

The New Form Assistant Wizard opens by default when you first launch LiveCycle Designer.

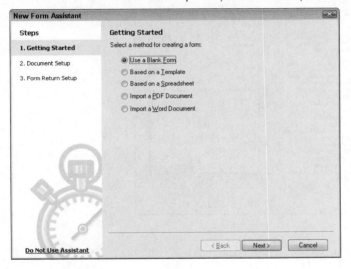

As shown in the New Form Assistant Wizard, you have five different options for creating a form in Designer. These options are as follows:

- **Use a Blank Form.** This option opens a blank page where you add all the design elements on your new form. Essentially you start with a blank page and create the design using tools in Designer for text, graphics, and form fields.

- **Based on a Template.** Unlike Acrobat, you have a number of different preinstalled template files that help you get started in creating a new form design. Click this option and the New Form Assistant changes panes to a view shown in Figure 33.4. From the scrollable list of different preinstalled form designs, select the design most similar to the kind of form you want to create and click Next.

- **Based on a Spreadsheet.** You have an option to create a form design from cells in a spreadsheet. You click through the Next buttons assigning different attributes to the form and on the last page in the New Form Assistant Wizard you're prompted to copy cells in a spreadsheet document. You can leave the wizard pane open, launch Microsoft Excel, and copy the cells you want to appear as form fields. Close the Excel worksheet and return to Designer. Once data is copied to the Clipboard, the Finish button is active. Click Finish and the copied cells are added as fields to a new form.

FIGURE 33.4

Select a template you want to start with for creating a new design.

■ **Import a PDF Document.** You can create a design in any authoring program and export to PDF. After PDF conversion, use the Import a PDF Document option and you can import the PDF into Designer. If you create a form design in Acrobat and import a PDF file containing fields, Designer recognizes the fields created in Acrobat.

When you choose Import a PDF Document and click Next in the New Form Assistant Wizard you identify a PDF document, click Next, and arrive at the Setup: Import Options pane shown in Figure 33.5.

Designer needs to know how you want to work with the PDF file. You have two options from the radio buttons in Figure 33.5.

Designer 8.2 supports a feature called PDF background artwork. When you select Create an Interactive Form with Fixed Pages, you are importing the PDF document as a background layer with the background appearing behind form fields (either from a PDF converted with form fields or a PDF with no fields and fields you ultimately add in Designer). PDF background artwork cannot be edited for any content on the background layer. It's important to note that you lose some of the benefits of creating original forms in Designer such as creating dynamic forms, using master pages, and using a grid. However, you have the advantage of maintaining the exact layout of the original PDF including color assignment and font embedding.

The Create an Interactive Form with a Flowable Layout option imports and converts the PDF into an XML template. In this case, you can edit the imported PDF content. If you choose this option you may find much of the original design such as graphics on the PDF layout not fully translated to the XML form.

- **Import a Word Document.** This option lets you import a Microsoft Word file as a new form design. Designer 8.2 (like Acrobat) has a run form field recognition function that is automatically run when you convert the Word file. All areas on the form design that clearly indicate form field positions such as lines, boxes, and so on are populated with form fields when the file opens in Designer.

FIGURE 33.5

In the Document Setup: Import Options pane, you make a decision for how the PDF will be imported.

Creating a Simple Form in Designer

You follow several steps to create a form in LiveCycle Designer whether it is a form from a template, starting with a blank new page, importing a PDF document, converting a Word file, or converting a spreadsheet file. You typically follow steps initially in the New Form Assistant where Designer helps you by providing some options to decide how your form will be deployed and offering other choices depending on the type of conversion you decide to use.

Creating a blank new page

All the form field attributes are assigned on any kind of form you create in Designer — whether you start from scratch or import a document. Let's start off by creating a simple form in a blank document so you can see how a form is created in Designer. The initial steps follow.

STEPS: Creating a form on a blank page

1. **Launch LiveCycle Designer.** You can launch LiveCycle Designer from Acrobat 9 (you need to select Start Form Wizard and select "No Form" which will launch Designer) and the New Form Assistant opens where you make choices for creating a new form using one of the options shown in Figure 33.3. You can also use the Start menu to open Designer or double-click the program icon. Either of these choices opens the Welcome screen where you have choices for creating a new form, creating a form from a template, or opening an existing form.

2. **Click New Form in the Welcome to Adobe LiveCycle Designer Welcome screen.** Click the New Form button. (Note that if you want to open Designer without the Welcome screen opening, select the check box where you see Show this Dialog as Startup and remove the check mark).

3. **Select Use a Blank Form in the New Form Assistant Wizard.** After clicking New Form in the Welcome screen, the New Form Assistant Wizard opens. Click Use a Blank Form and click the Next button to open the Document Setup pane in the wizard.

4. **Select a page size.** In the Document Setup pane, select a page size from the Page Size pull-down menu. Select an orientation by clicking either the Portrait or Landscape radio button and select the number of pages you want from the Number of Pages pull-down menu. (Note that the maximum number of pages you can add in the wizard is 10; however, there is no limit to the number of pages that can be dynamically created in Designer.)

5. **Click Next and select the return method.** The final pane in the New Form Assistant Wizard is the Form Return Setup: Adding Buttons. Here you select a return method. If you want the form emailed back to you, select Add an email button. If you want the end user to print the form, select Add a print button. Note that you can choose both options, as shown in Figure 33.6.

6. **Click Finish and your form opens in the Designer window.** In Figure 33.7, you can see the start of my new form where I selected a 6 3/4 Envelope with a Landscape orientation for my page size and added an email button and submit button. I hid the left palettes by selecting Window ⇨ Workspace ⇨ Left Palettes. I also hid the Script Editor for now by pressing Ctrl+Shift+F5.

FIGURE 33.6

Select both options if you want an email button and a print button to appear on the form.

FIGURE 33.7

The start of a new form in the Designer window

A Word About Page Sizes

Designer offers you a huge number of fixed page sizes, but another limitation and an obvious indication that Adobe didn't initially create this software product is that you have no option for creating a custom page size — something Adobe has always provided in programs to create freedom in the design environment. This probably won't matter much to the IT-type people, but it surely will drive the graphic design people crazy.

If you want to create a custom page size that doesn't fit within the sizes available in the Page Size pane in the New Form Assistant Wizard, you can create a custom page size in another program and import the file into Designer. Doing so, however, has some limitations.

If you create a blank page in Microsoft Word and import the page from a .doc file format, you can add text, images, and form fields to the document in Designer, but you won't be able to see the design grid.

If you create a blank page and convert it to PDF, you can't see the design grid; you can add form fields, but you cannot add any text or images to the design.

Your best option for creating a new form design is to try to find a page size in the New Form Assistant Wizard Page Size pull-down menu as near as you can to your desired page size. If you must create a custom page size, create your background in a design program with all the background elements and convert to PDF. Import the PDF file and you can add the form fields in Designer.

Save your file after you open the document in Designer. Be certain to periodically save the document as you work through additional steps. When you select File ➪ Save (or Save As) the Save dialog box opens. The Save as type pull-down menu offers several options, but for this series of steps, don't bother with all the options now. Select Adobe Static PDF Form (*.pdf).

If you are new to Designer and you're familiar with other Adobe software, your first efforts in Designer are likely to be very frustrating. Adobe is the master of the free-form graphic design applications where you can click and grab an object in programs such as Adobe InDesign, Adobe Illustrator, Adobe Photoshop, Adobe Dreamweaver, and even to some degree in Adobe Acrobat. Just click with a selection tool and you have complete freedom of movement without obstruction. This is not the case with LiveCycle Designer.

There are structured elements in a Designer form and you can't move objects around to the same degree as you can in other Adobe software. Before you add any content to the form, you should familiarize yourself a bit with some of the structural elements.

Click Master Pages in the Designer window and you see a rectangle appearing as a blue dashed rectangle. Select the rectangle and handles appear at the four corners and four midpoints on each side. This area determines the boundaries of your content. While in the Master Pages view you can click and drag handles to reshape the object. If you click the Design View tab, you see the same rectangle, but you can't resize it while in the Design View mode. Any resizing you do in the Master

Pages view restricts all the elements in the Design view to the boundaries of the rectangle on the Master Page. In Figure 33.8, I moved the top side of the Master Page rectangle down, and my two buttons were moved in the layout to stay within the rectangle.

FIGURE 33.8

Moving the rectangle on the Master Page moves all elements in the layout to keep them within the rectangle.

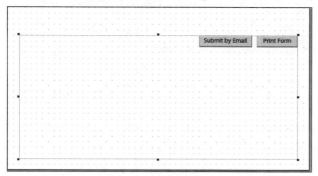

Working with master pages is not unfamiliar to people who create layouts in programs such as Adobe InDesign. Most layout programs offer you many options for creating master pages and placing elements on the master pages without having options to move the master elements on other pages. What's different about Designer is that elements are created for you. Therefore, you need to poke through a design to discover items that you did not create and how they affect the form. This is particularly true when you start working with subforms, as I explain later in the section "Creating Dynamic Forms."

Adding an image

Since you're creating a design from scratch, you'll import graphics as well as add graphic elements with tools in Designer. You can import a variety of different raster image formats including BMP, JPG, GIF, PNG, and TIF into your design.

In Designer 8.2 you now can also import EPS files. Like the image file formats, be certain your image color modes are all RGB. CMYK images won't display properly in Designer. If you have problems importing an EPS file in your design, open the EPS in an image editor such as Adobe Photoshop and rasterize the image. Save the raster image as a TIFF file and you should have no problems.

TIP If you create a Designer form that you will eventually output to press, use RGB images in your Designer form. Import the form in Adobe InDesign and let InDesign convert color from RGB to CMYK plus all the other print controls you need for prepress and commercial printing. Note that you lose many Print Production tools in Acrobat when you open forms created in Designer. As such, you'll find InDesign a much better tool to print files for commercial printing than Acrobat. For more information on prepress and printing, see Chapter 32.

To import images into a Designer form, follow these steps.

STEPS: Importing images into a Designer form

1. **Open the Object Library palette.** By default, the Object Library palette opens when you launch Designer.

2. **Drag the Image Object to your document.** The Object Library palette contains most of the objects you use in all Designer forms. You have field styles and objects for text and images. Locate the Image Object (not the Image Field Object) and drag it to the document page. When the object appears on the page, drag open the handles to accommodate a rough size for your imported image. The size doesn't have to be precise. You can make adjustments after importing an image.

3. **Select an image to import.** Open a context menu on the object and select Choose image (or simply double-click the object). When you release the mouse button the Browse for Image File dialog box opens. Locate the image to import, select it, and click the Open button. The image appears inside the Image Object, as shown in Figure 33.9.

4. **Size the object.** Drag the handles in or out to accommodate the size of the image without clipping it.

Using the Libraries

Designer provides you with several libraries containing the field objects and text objects you add to a form design. By default, you may see a single library open in the Libraries palette. Click the down-pointing arrow adjacent to the library name to collapse the palette and you'll find the list of other libraries available to you. When you collapse all palettes you'll see a right pointing arrow adjacent to each library name. Click any one of the right arrows to expand the respective library.

The installed libraries include My Favorites, Standard, Custom, and Barcodes. In these libraries you'll find all the form field and object tools necessary to create any kind of form in Designer. The My Favorites library is designed for you to drag field objects you commonly use to this palette.

In addition to the four libraries Designer provides you with a Fragment library. The Fragment library is designed for you to add subforms, scripts, and other fragments of forms that you may commonly use. Drag elements to this library to create a list of commonly used objects and scripts.

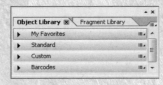

> **TIP** The default cursor in Designer is the selection arrow. If you select the Image Object or any other tool in any palette and you want to return to the selection arrow, press the Esc key on your keyboard.

FIGURE 33.9

Drag the Image Object from the Object Library palette and select Choose image from a context menu (or double-click the Image Object). After the image is imported, it appears inside the object.

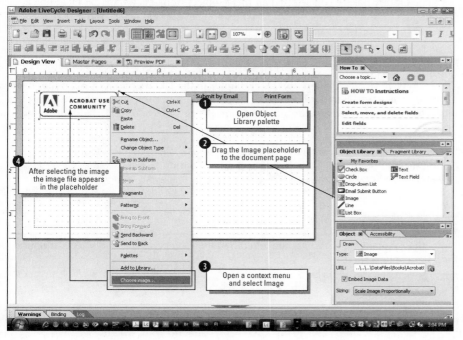

Working with text fields

In Acrobat you click the Text Field tool in Form Editing Mode or draw a text field rectangle to create a field where text (and numbers that are read as text) is added on a form. The Text Field Properties dialog box offers you a few choices for setting the field appearances such as border and fill colors, insets, embossing, dashes and underlines, and a few different line weights. Adding text fields in Acrobat presumes you have text descriptors in the form design for users to know what data to add to various fields. For example, you might have the text Name appearing in the background layout, and adjacent to the Name text you create a text field where a user types a name.

In Designer, you can add the text descriptors along with the field types (this applies not only to text fields but to most of the other field types you have available in the Library tabs). When it comes to appearances, Designer offers options similar to the way you can assign cell appearances in spreadsheet programs. You can control many more field appearances in Designer than you have available in Acrobat.

To learn how to format text fields in Designer, follow these steps.

STEPS: Adding text fields to a form

1. **Drag a Text field from the Standard (or Favorites) tab to the document page.** From the same Library palette you selected an Image object from, click the Text Field object and drag it to the document page. Notice that you have a Text object and a Text Field object in the Standard tab in the Library palette. The Text object is used to add text on the page. The Text Field object permits you to add both text and a field to the page. Be certain to drag the Text Field object to the page.

> **TIP** If you want to quickly find objects and fields in the Library palettes, open the Insert menu and select Standard. From the submenu you can see all the objects/fields in an alphabetical list. Select any item in the submenu and the respective object is added to your document page.

2. **Set the field appearance.** Open the Object palette and click the Field tab. From the Appearance pull-down menu, select an appearance option. For my example, I select Underlined from the Appearance menu, as shown in Figure 33.10.

FIGURE 33.10

Open the Appearance menu in the Field tab in the Object palette and select an option for a field appearance.

Note that you also have an option for selecting a Custom appearance in the pull-down menu. Click Custom and the Custom Appearance dialog box opens, as shown in Figure 33.11. From the Edges pull-down menu, you can select Edit Together or Edit Individually. The Edit Individually option lets you edit each of the four rectangle sides for border options. The Corners choices let you modify the corner appearances. The Style menu offers options for creating gradients and pattern fills.

FIGURE 33.11

A number of different appearance options can be selected in the Custom Appearance dialog box.

3. **Set the Value options.** In the Value tab, you have some options for specifying the user requirements for filling in the field. From the Type pull-down menu you can force a field to be filled in by selecting the User Entered – Required option from the menu, as shown in Figure 33.12. Other options shown in the figure include choices for optional, recommended, and calculations. Make a choice for the field value attributes and click the Binding tab.

FIGURE 33.12

Make a choice for user data entry attributes in the Value tab.

4. **Name the field.** Type a name in the Name text box in the Binding tab. If you want to bind the field to a data source, click the icon to the right of the Default Binding text to open a pop-up menu. For a form that you email or submit for printing, the Default Binding is set at Normal, as shown in Figure 33.13.

FIGURE 33.13

Type a name for the field in the Binding tab and leave the default binding at Normal.

> **NOTE** The name you provide in the Binding tab is the field name. Text you type on the form adjacent to the field is a design issue and is not related to the form data.

5. **Add the field caption.** Formatting the data attributes is complete. Now you need to set up the field as it appears on the form. The first item to deal with is typing the text you want to place as the field caption. Click in the default Text Field caption that appears when you first drag a text field to the document page and drag across the text. Type a new name for the text. In my example I used Name, as shown in Figure 33.14, to indicate the end user should type his or her name in the field.

FIGURE 33.14

Type text you want to appear on the form adjacent to the text field.

6. **Size the field.** The default text may be too long or too short in relationship to the field position. You can add more or delete some space between the text you type for the field caption and the field. Move the cursor to the separator bar between the text and the field and drag left or right to size the space occupied by the text. When you move the cursor over the separator bar, the cursor changes appearance, as shown in Figure 33.15.

FIGURE 33.15

Drag the separator bar left to expand the field area.

TIP As you work with fields, by default the field appearance has a highlight around the field border. If you want to view the fields without the highlight, select View ⇨ Object Boundaries (or press Ctrl+;). The fields will appear the same as when you open the form in an Acrobat viewer.

Formatting Text Fields

When you drag a text field (or other field types) to the document page, the field appears with a text caption, by default, on the left side of the actual field, as shown in the following figure.

• Text Field

If you're familiar with creating forms in Acrobat, the default appearance of many Designer fields is probably foreign to you. LiveCycle Designer includes a text caption bound to a field because, unlike Acrobat, Designer is intended to be a design tool as well as a form data creation tool. As such, you need methods for labeling fields in designs you create from blank new pages.

Designer does provide you with a text object tool that enables you to place text near a field to provide a field description or to use the bound text to describe the field. In many cases you'll want to adjust the placement of text relative to the field, or you may want to completely get rid of the text. Designer provides you with all the tools you need for modifying the text appearance or eliminating text and reformatting the field, but it may not be completely intuitive.

If you want to eliminate the default formatting and create a field with a rectangle box, you need to visit several palettes. All the options for changing the appearance are not included in a single palette.

If you delete the text caption bound to a field by selecting the text with the cursor and pressing the Delete key, you end up with a field where the field contents are about one half to two thirds the size of the entire object. You'll immediately notice a large empty space to the left of a field when the field is selected after deleting the text. Designer automatically reserves the space for you to add text. If you want to delete the reserve space, open the Layout palette and open the Position menu in the Caption area and select None. Note that selecting None when you have a text caption on a field object eliminates the caption and reserve space with one menu selection.

continued

continued

That's one palette down and two more to go. The next issue is the Sunken text appearance. If you want to eliminate that, you need to open the Object palette and click the Field tab. From the Appearance pull-down menu, select None to eliminate the embossed look on the field.

Your final step is to set the appearance to a solid border, underline, or whatever other type of appearance you want. Borders and fills are handled in the Border palette. Open the palette and select Solid from the pull-down menu below the Edges pull-down menu, as shown in the following figure.

You can minimize your palette selections a bit and set the margins to zero (0) in the Layout palette that substitutes for using the settings in the Object palette, but I find that for almost all designs you continually interact with these three palettes, so they should all be open and accessible when designing any form.

When you want text bound to a field you may want to relocate the text to a position other than the default at the left side of the field. In the bottom left corner of the Layout palette is a pull-down menu in which you can reassign the text position. Open the Position pull-down menu in the Caption area of the Layout tab and make a choice for Left, Right, Top, or Bottom. The None choice in this menu eliminates the text entirely.

If you do decide to use text with your field, you may want the vertical or horizontal position of the text to be different than the default position that appears as Align Left and Align Top. To change the position alignment, you need to visit yet another palette. Open the Paragraph palette and click the icon for Align Left, Align Center, Align Right, or Justify (the first four icons in the Paragraph palette) and click Align Top, Align Center, or Align Bottom (for vertical alignment from the last three icons in the palette). These icons are shown in the following figure.

Duplicating fields

When you create a form in Acrobat, you can duplicate fields by pressing the Ctrl key and dragging a field to duplicate it (yet another standard Adobe convention). In Designer you can duplicate a field by pressing Ctrl+Alt+click and drag a field. You also have the standard Cut/Copy/Paste commands in Designer, but if you create a number of different forms and you want field attributes to appear similar, you can store copies of fields in a custom library.

TIP   If you want to duplicate a field several times, press Ctrl+D. Designer duplicates a selected field. You can move the duplicate horizontally or vertically to a distance away from the original field — for example, 1/2 inch. Press Ctrl+D again and the next duplicate is created at the same distance — 1/2 inch in this case.

To add a custom library group to the Library palette, follow these steps.

STEPS: Creating a custom library group

1. **Add a New Group.** Notice the small icon at the top right corner of each Library tab. Go to the topmost icon in the Library palette and click the mouse button to open a menu. From the menu choices, select Add Group.

2. **Name the new group.** When you select Add Group, the Add Library Group dialog box opens, as shown in Figure 33.16. Type a name for your custom library group in the text box and click OK. The new group appears in the Library palette.

FIGURE 33.16

Type a name and click OK in the Add Library Group dialog box to create a custom library group.

3. **Drag the field you created on the form to the new group.** Drag the field to the group name you see in the Library palette. Watch for the cursor to change to an arrowhead with a plus symbol, as shown in Figure 33.17. You need to place the cursor over the group name and release the mouse button when you see the cursor change appearance. Click the right arrow to expand the palette and you should see the field within the custom group tab. When you release the mouse button, the Add Library Object dialog box opens.

4. **Type a name for your field in the Add Library Object dialog box.** This name is used to merely identify the field in your custom group. It has no value and is not a default text object when you add the field to a page.

   Type a description in the Description text box. Notice a pull-down menu at the bottom of the Add Library Object dialog box in Figure 33.18. You can add an object to any group by selecting a group from the menu. Click OK and your new field is added to your custom library.

FIGURE 33.17

Drag an object to the new custom library palette.

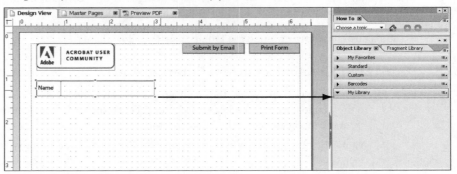

FIGURE 33.18

Type a name and description in the Add Library Object dialog box.

5. **Add a field to the document page.** Drag the field you added to your custom library to the document page. Position the field as you want it to appear in relation to the first field you created.

6. **Change field attributes.** Edit the text adjacent to the field and edit the name. You can change the name in the Binding tab or open a context menu on the object and select Rename Object. The Rename Object dialog box opens. Type a new name in the dialog box and click OK.

7. **Add additional fields.** Add more fields by dragging the field from your custom library group to the document page and format the fields.

8. **Add multiple fields to your custom library group.** Drag a marquee around the fields to select them and drag the selected fields to your library group. In the Add a Group dialog box, add a name and description. I named my group Identifying Information, as you can see in Figure 33.19.

> **TIP** You can alternately add objects to any library group by opening a context menu on a selected object and choosing the Add to Library menu command. The Add Library Object dialog box opens where you can add a name and description, and choose the library where you want the object to be stored.

FIGURE 33.19

Dragging multiple fields to the custom library group adds the fields as a grouped object.

> **TIP** If you don't see the selection arrow for your cursor, you may have a tool selected such as a field tool. To return to the selection arrow when another tool is selected, press the Esc key.

The beauty and the power of using LiveCycle Designer when it comes to field duplication are in adding multiple fields to a custom library group. When you create new forms, you can drag the grouped item in your custom library group to a document page, and all the fields in that group are added to the document.

Field Naming Conventions Used by LiveCycle Designer

When you drag a field from any library group to a document page, Designer automatically adds a field name to your new field. If you add a text field to a page, for example, Designer names the field in the Binding tab TextField1. The next time you drag a text field to the document page, Designer names the next field TextField2, and so on. This naming convention assures you that all fields have a unique field name.

Check boxes also follow the same conventions as other fields. However, radio buttons are named RadioButtonList and additional radio buttons you add to a page are named the same field name. When you open the form in Acrobat and click one radio button, it is turned on. Clicking another radio button in the same group turns the other radio buttons off.

Working with Tables

Obviously, when you want to create multiple fields in columns and rows, dragging individual fields from a Library tab will take you quite a bit of time. Fortunately, Designer 8.2 provides you a feature for creating and editing tables that helps you automate adding tables on your forms. Much like the options we have in Acrobat for duplicating fields, you duplicate columns and rows in Designer using menu commands in the Table menu. However, Designer offers you much more than is available in Acrobat.

To insert a table, you select Table⇨Insert Table. The Insert Table dialog box opens, as shown in the following figure, where you can define columns and rows and add a header and/or footer. Click OK and Designer creates a table automatically without your having to start out with any fields laid down on the page.

Much more power for designing a table is available in the Table Assistant Wizard, shown in this figure. Click the Create Table Using Assistant radio button in the Insert Table dialog box, click OK, and the Table Assistant Wizard opens.

Options available in the Table Assistant are similar to options for creating tables in Adobe InDesign or Microsoft Excel. You can add rows and columns, apply shading to alternating rows, add headers and footers, and divide the table into sections. After creating a table, you can apply edits using the Table menu for adding and deleting rows and columns, merge and split cells, and distribute and group sections.

Adding graphic objects to a form

In the Standard library group you have graphic objects in addition to field objects. The Line object and the Text object are used to draw lines and add text that's not part of a field identifier.

Click the Line object in the Standard library group and draw a line on the form. Attributes for a line object are shown in the Object palette. You can edit orientation, line color, and line styles such as solid, dashed, dotted, and dots with dashes. Draw a line on your form to separate the fields created in all previous steps from the bottom portion of the form.

The Text object is used to add text on a page. You might use text for a group identifier, a column heading, and so on, where the text is not bound in any way to a field. Drag the Text object to the document page and click the cursor inside the text. Select the default text and replace it with the text you want to add to the object. If you want to assign attributes to the font and style, open the Window menu and select Font to open the Font tab. In the form I've created thus far, I added the text Acrobat User Level.

Adding radio buttons to a form

Radio buttons are intended to be used for mutually exclusive choices. You might use radio buttons on a form for asking for a credit card type where only one response is acceptable. As a user clicks one radio button, all other radio buttons are off. Clicking a second radio button deactivates the first radio button, and so on.

By default, LiveCycle Designer expects you to add radio buttons in this manner. If you want to use radio buttons for multiple responses, you need to set up some custom field attributes. For the sake of staying with standards, let's look over how radio buttons are used with their default values.

STEPS: Adding radio buttons to a form

1. **Drag a radio button from the Standard library group to the Designer page.** Continue adding a few more radio buttons by dragging from the Standard library group to the document page. In my example, I added three buttons, as shown in Figure 33.20.

FIGURE 33.20

Drag three radio button fields from the Standard library group to the document page.

2. **Change the field names.** Click one radio button to select it and open the Binding tab in the Object palette. Type a new name in the Name text box. In my example I used userLevel for the field name, as shown in Figure 33.21. When you change the name of one field in a radio button group, Designer automatically changes all the objects in the same group to the same name. Note that alternately you can select an object and open a context menu. From the menu options, select Rename Object. Type a new name in the Rename Object dialog box and click OK. All radio button objects in the same group are renamed.

FIGURE 33.21

Click the Binding tab in the Object palette and change the radio button name. All radio buttons in the same group are renamed.

3. **Change the position of the radio button relative to the text.** By default, a radio button appears to the left of the default text identifier. To change the position, open the Layout palette. At the bottom of the palette, click the Position pull-down menu. Select the position you want for your radio button. In my example, I want the text to appear to the left of the radio button; therefore, I select Left in the menu as shown in Figure 33.22.

FIGURE 33.22

Open the Position pull-down menu and select a position for the caption relative to the field.

4. **Edit the text.** In my example I edited the text for the radio buttons and added Beginning, Intermediate, and Advanced for the three buttons, as shown in Figure 33.23.

Edit the text for each button to identify the button selection.

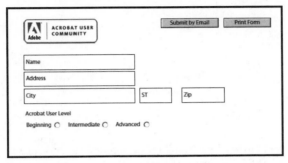

Adding a Drop-down list to a form

A drop-down list in Designer is the same as a combo box in Acrobat terms. The names are different but the attribute assignments are very much the same. Drop-down lists, like combo boxes, can be assigned permissions for custom text entry as well as custom options from a list appearing as a pull-down menu. You add list items in the Field tab in the Object palette, and Designer, like Acrobat, offers a choice for sorting the list names.

To learn how to add a drop-down list in Designer, follow these steps.

STEPS: Adding a drop-down list to a form

1. **Drag the Drop-down List object from the Standard library tab to the document page.**

2. **Name the field.** Open the Binding tab and type a field name or open a context menu and select Rename Object. In my example, I use the name jobRole.

3. **Add a text caption.** Type the name you want to appear on the form adjacent to the drop-down list.

4. **Set the list attributes.** Open the Field tab in the Object palette and click the + symbol in the List Items area. Type a name for your list and press the Return key. Continue adding list names and press the Num Pad Enter key when finished or press the Esc key.

5. **Sort names.** After you create a list, look it over and see if you want to reorder some of the items. If you want an alpha list and some items are out of order, select an item you want to move and click the up or down arrows to reorder the list, as shown in Figure 33.24.

FIGURE 33.24

Add items to a list and select names in the list, and click the up and down arrows to reorder items.

6. **Enable custom text entry.** If you want a user to be able to add custom text, select the box where you see Allow Custom Text Entry.

Using the Object Editor

The Object Editor (formerly called the Field Editor in Designer 8.0) is accessed by selecting View ⇨ Object Editor. When the Object Editor is on, selected field objects appear with a blue border and pop-up menus. At the top of a field object when the Object Editor is turned on, you can edit field names by clicking in the field box (1). At the bottom of the field object, a menu lists all field object types where you can convert a field object of one type to another (2). On the lower-right corner you can open a pop-up menu (3) where field object attributes can be changed and some commands available in the Edit menu appear.

Other field types available in Designer such as the List Box, the Check Box, and the barcode are also available in Acrobat. Use of the remaining fields follow similar steps: You rename fields in the Binding tab and assign various attributes in the Field and Value tabs.

CROSS-REF For more information on creating some additional field types, see Chapter 34.

Finishing up a form

I really don't like the default appearances on the Submit by Email and Print Form buttons. As an optional task, open the Border tab and remove the fill from the buttons. Note that you can select both buttons and change the fill in one step.

For the last steps, select File ➪ Form Properties to open the Form Properties dialog box. Add document title information in the Info properties. In my example, I added the document information you see in Figure 33.25.

FIGURE 33.25

Fill in the document info fields and click OK.

Click OK and save your file one more time. Click the Preview PDF tab in the Designer window and the file displays as a PDF. Test the form by filling in the fields as shown in Figure 33.26. Be certain to observe the layout and design as much as you assess the field contents. In my example, I need to return to Design View and put a little more space between some of the fields and the text. To return to Design View click the Design View tab and make the necessary edits to the form. Click Preview PDF and again preview the form as it will appear in an Acrobat viewer.

FIGURE 33.26

Fill in the form fields to check the layout by clicking the Preview PDF tab.

Importing a PDF Document

When you design a form in an authoring program and export to PDF, you make some design decisions for the field appearances. You have essentially two choices. You can design field appearances in your authoring program for field design attributes such as borders, fills, type fonts, and so on, or you can leave the design decisions to LiveCycle Designer.

There are pros and cons to designing layouts in either program. If you design field appearances in an authoring program and convert to PDF, after adding fields in Designer, you may need to go back to the authoring program to touch up the appearances. This requires you to go back and forth to polish your design because it can be difficult to anticipate the final look of your form while preparing it in the authoring program.

TIP If you find yourself going back and forth between a layout in Designer and a layout in an authoring program to polish up your design, save the Designer form as a temporary file. After you convert the final layout from an authoring program, you can open the temporary file and copy the fields. Open the final layout in Designer and paste the fields. This saves you time because you don't have to re-create fields each time you update a layout.

If you leave assigning field appearances up to Designer, then you may have problems trying to align fields because Designer doesn't support using grids and snapping fields to a grid when working with PDF backgrounds.

I find adding the field appearances in Designer to be the best option for me. However, it's a personal choice and you should determine the workflow that best suits your personal preferences. To see how to create a Designer form from a PDF document, let's walk through a series of steps.

Converting a PDF document to a Designer form

Create a layout in your favorite authoring program. I typically use Adobe InDesign or Adobe Illustrator to create form designs, but I'll deviate for this example and create a design in Microsoft Excel. Rather than import the Excel worksheet in Designer, I'll use PDFMaker and convert to PDF. Excel worksheets can be converted to Designer forms, but when creating more than just numeric cells, the Designer conversion leaves much to be desired. Not all graphic objects get translated properly, and your design can appear as a mess if you copy and paste the cells from Excel to Designer.

Figure 33.27 is the layout created in Microsoft Excel that I want to use for my Designer form. On this form I have some numeric fields, a calculation field, and a signature field in addition to some text fields. As yet, no field appearances such as underlines, borders, or fills appear where the fields will fall on the page. I'll add these items in LiveCycle Designer.

FIGURE 33.27

I start with a form originally created in Microsoft Excel and converted to PDF using PDFMaker.

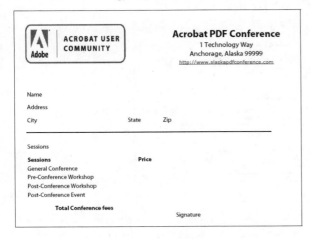

CROSS-REF For more information on converting Microsoft Excel files to PDF using PDFMaker, see Chapter 8.

To begin the creation, you first need to open the form in Designer. The following steps show you how.

STEPS: Open a PDF document in LiveCycle Designer

1. **Create a new document in Designer.** If you launch Designer, the Welcome screen opens. Click the New Form button in the Welcome screen. If you already have Designer open, select File ⇨ New or press Ctrl+N. By default, the New Form Assistant Wizard opens. If you have a PDF document open in Acrobat, select Forms ⇨ Edit Form in Designer and click OK in the alert dialog box.

2. **Select Import a PDF Document in the Getting Started pane.** Click the radio button in the first pane in the New Form Assistant Wizard.

3. **Select the PDF file to import.** Click the Next button in the wizard and you arrive at the Document Setup pane. Click the Browse button and locate your file to import. Select the file and click the Open button.

4. **Choose how you want to work with the PDF file.** Click Next and you arrive at the Document Setup: Import Options pane. Click the first radio button choice in this pane, as shown in Figure 33.28.

FIGURE 33.28

Select Create an Interactive Form with Fixed Pages.

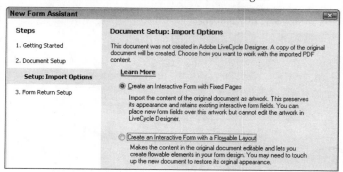

5. **Add an email and print button.** Click Next and you arrive at the last pane in the wizard. By default, the check boxes are selected for adding an email button and a print button. Leave the check box selections at the default choice and type your email address in the Return email address text box.

6. **Open the form in Designer.** Click Finish and a new form is created with a PDF background artwork.

7. **Save the file.** Before adding any fields, save the file and routinely press Ctrl+S to update your file as you add new fields.

Add text fields

My example form has the same identifying fields as the form I created earlier in this chapter in the section "Working with text fields." In that section I added the identifying fields as a group to my custom library group. Unfortunately, you can't add a group of fields when using a PDF background. The single text field I copied to my custom group, however, can be used.

I drag my single text field from the custom group to the document page, and all the attributes previously assigned to the field are copied with the field to the document page. Adding the identifying information is simply a matter of dragging a field from the custom palette, resizing the fields to fit the design, and continuing the steps to populate all the identifying information fields.

The Submit by Email button and the Print Form button may need some appearance alterations and placement on your form. Drag the fields to the desired position and open the Object palette. Open the Appearance pull-down menu and select Custom. In the Custom Appearance dialog box, choose the appearance options you want for borders and fills. (Refer to Figure 33.11.)

After adding the identifying fields and modifying button appearances, click the Save tool or press Ctrl+S to update the document.

Adding numeric fields

When you create a form in Acrobat, you use text fields for both text and numeric values. In Designer, you have two different field types — a text field and a numeric field. Because Designer has so many more attributes that you can assign to fields, having two separate field types makes it much easier to work through the different tabs in the Object palette.

 You can type numeric values in text fields, but the data is read as text and not numbers. In order to calculate values, you need to use numeric fields.

To add and configure numeric fields in Designer, follow these steps.

STEPS: Assigning attributes to numeric fields

1. **Open the Standard tab in the Library palette and drag a Numeric Field from the palette to the document page.**
2. **Set the field appearance attributes.** Click the Field tab in the Object palette and select an appearance option from the Appearance pull-down menu shown in Figure 33.29.

FIGURE 33.29

Select an appearance and display pattern.

3. **Click the Patterns button to open the Patterns — Numeric Field dialog box, as shown in figure 33.30.** Display patterns are used to format numeric values. A pattern such as $z,zz9.99 results in a figure like $5,432.66. If your total value exceeds the pattern, the result loses the pattern attributes. For example, using the same pattern with a number like 10,345 results in 10345 in the field box. Both the currency symbol and the comma are lost. When you format fields, be certain to anticipate the largest value that might be added to a numeric field box and create a pattern to accommodate the largest size.

FIGURE 33.30

Click a display pattern and click OK.

4. **Name the field.** Click the Binding tab, use the Object Editor, or open a context menu and select Rename Object to change the field name. The default name appears as

NumericField1. When we come to calculating fields, this name is a little long to type in the Script Editor. To simplify the job, I name my field "price."

5. **Size and position the field.** Drag the handles to size the field and drag the field to position on the form.

6. **Format the text.** If the text is too large, you can reduce the point size in the Font tab. Click the Paragraph tab and click the Right Justify icon shown in Figure 33.31.

FIGURE 33.31

Click the Right Justify icon in the Paragraph tab.

7. **Add the formatted field to your custom library group.** Drag the field to the custom library group.

8. **Add more numeric fields to the document page.** Drag the numeric field from the custom library group to the document page and populate all the remaining fields that will be summed in a calculation. Don't worry about aligning fields now; you'll take care of that in the next steps.

NOTE In my example, I use just four fields. If I use a larger number of fields in a column or row, I would insert a table to create my fields. (See the sidebar "Working with Tables" earlier in this chapter).

Managing fields

Because you can't use a grid view or snap fields to a grid when working with PDF background artwork, you need some way to organize your fields in aligned positions, sizes, and distributions. Acrobat provides a number of context menu commands for sizing, aligning, and distributing fields. Fortunately, you have the same options in LiveCycle Designer through menu commands.

Follow these steps to organize your fields in a precise order.

STEPS: Organizing fields

1. **Select the numeric fields on a form.** Using my example I created four fields that will be used to enter data, and the result will be computed in another field. I drag a marquee through the fields and select Layout ⇨ Align.

2. **Align the fields. From the Align submenu select an alignment option.** As shown in Figure 33.32, you have several alignment options. In my example, I chose Layout ⇨ Align ⇨ Left. (Note that all the alignment options in Designer have keyboard shortcuts assigned to the menu commands.)

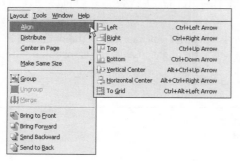

FIGURE 33.32

Select an alignment option from the Layout ⇨ Align submenu.

3. **Distribute fields.** The top field in a column should already be in the correct position on the form. If it is not, drag the fields together, placing the top field in the proper position. Drag the bottom field to position the field at the bottom of the column. Select Layout ⇨ Distribute ⇨ Down. This command neatly positions the fields equidistant from each other.

4. **Realign the fields.** One very common use of a modifier in almost all programs is using the Shift key to constrain movement. Unfortunately, Designer doesn't support constraining movement by using a modifier key. If you moved the bottom field down to position the field, you more than likely disturbed the left alignment in step 2. Realign the fields by selecting Layout ⇨ Align ⇨ Left.

Calculating fields

Designer supports two different scripting languages — FormCalc and JavaScript. FormCalc is a simple scripting language that follows syntax similar to spreadsheets. JavaScript is similar to the JavaScript you find in Acrobat, but some objects supported in Acrobat are not available in Designer. For example, the `docTemplate` object is not something you have access to in Designer.

Acrobat supports two scripting languages, too — Simplified Field Notation and JavaScript. Simplified Field Notation is also modeled after a spreadsheet language, and JavaScript is similar to Designer JavaScript.

You need to use one of the scripting languages in Designer to calculate data. Because Designer supports two languages, you have to tell Designer which language you want to use to create your calculations. To see how you go about calculating field data in Designer, follow these steps.

STEPS: Calculating field data

1. **Identify the language you want to use for calculations.** You can dynamically switch between the two scripting languages in the Script Editor and make a choice for the language

you want to use when you decide to write a script. However, it's always a good idea to set up some form properties when you begin to design a form. Among the properties you can assign to a new design is the default scripting language.

2. **Select File ⇨ Form Properties.** The language you identify as your default scripting language is handled in the Defaults tab in the Form Properties dialog box. When the Form Properties dialog box opens, click the Defaults tab. From the Default Language pull-down menu, select FormCalc as shown in Figure 33.33. For forms returned to you via email, be certain the Default Run At pull-down menu selection is Client.

FIGURE 33.33

Select FormCalc for the scripting language.

3. **Click OK in the Form Properties dialog box.**

4. **Format the target field.** On my example form I have a field titled total. This field is the target for my calculation. Open the Object palette and click the target field and select Calculated – Read Only in the Value tab from the Type pull-down menu.

5. **Open the Script Editor.** Press Ctrl+Shift+F5 to open the Script Editor window. To reveal more space in the Script Editor, you can open the window by dragging down on the separator bar appearing between the page layout and the Script Editor. (See Figure 33.34.)

6. **Type the calculation script in the Script Editor.** Select calculate from the Show pull-down menu and type the following formula in the Script Editor:

```
Sum (price[*])
```

This simple formula takes all the price number fields and sums them. In Figure 33.34 you can see the steps taken to produce the calculation.

FIGURE 33.34

Steps taken to produce a calculation for summing a group of fields

Adding a signature field

To complete the form, I'll add a signature field that locks the field data after the form is signed. Follow these steps to complete the form.

STEPS: Adding a signature field

1. **Add a digital signature field.** Open the Standard library tab and drag a Signature Field to the document page.

2. **Format the appearance attributes.** Open the Object tab and add appearance settings in the Field tab. In my example I added a border to my signature field.

3. **Set the Signature properties.** Click the Signature tab and click Lock Fields After Signing. This option renders all fields as Read Only, and the fields can't be edited after signing the document.

4. **Set the Signature Handler.** If you don't assign a signature handler, the end users can sign the form with any technology they have. Skip this step if you want to provide the option for using any signature handler. If you want to force a signature type, click Settings in the Signature palette to open the Signature Settings dialog box. In the Signature Handler pane shown in Figure 33.35, select Adobe.PPKLite (for example) from the Name pull-down menu and click OK. Note that this action forces a signature type on the form.

FIGURE 33.35

Select Adobe.PPKLite in the Document Signature Settings.

CROSS-REF For more information on Signature Handlers, see Chapter 26.

5. **Test the form.** Save the form to update it and click the Preview PDF tab in the Designer window. Fill in the form fields to be certain the appearances and calculations work. (See Figure 33.36.)

FIGURE 33.36

Preview the final form in Acrobat and fill in the form fields to be certain the scripts work and the fields are properly aligned.

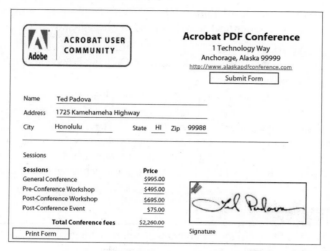

Creating Dynamic Forms

All of what's been covered up to this point falls into the category the Adobe LiveCycle Designer people at Adobe Systems call *static forms*. The steps in all preceding pages of this chapter could be accomplished in Adobe Acrobat as well as with LiveCycle Designer. The real power of Designer, however, is producing what Adobe calls *dynamic forms*.

CROSS-REF For information on creating forms in Acrobat, see Chapter 34.

What exactly is a dynamic form? In Adobe LiveCycle Designer terms, a dynamic form is one that, among other things, can adjust itself to accommodate the data a user supplies or when flowing data in a form from a database file. This is to say that the form fields can grow in size and spawn new fields as dictated by user/database needs on a form. The options for adding more content to a dynamic form are in your hands. The choice to use them rests with the end user or the amount of data merged with the form. The magic in this dynamic atmosphere is that the end user can work with any Acrobat viewer to populate a dynamic form — even the Adobe Reader users. Furthermore, no special features need to be added to a PDF document for a Reader user to fill out a dynamic form.

For an example of a dynamic form, take a look at Figures 33.37 and 33.38. In Figure 33.37 I start in Adobe Reader filling in two data fields on a form that was created in LiveCycle Designer.

FIGURE 33.37

Two data fields are filled in using Adobe Reader

Ted Padova
555 Binary Way
Anytown, CA 95555
t:800.555.5555
c: 800.555.5556
e: ted@west.net

Invoice

Date:

Tax ID   555-55-5555

To:

Attn:

Company

Address

Suite

City, St, Zip

Phone

Description	Total
Consultation with Project Leader to develop plan. 2 hours	$200.00

Grand Total $200.00

Add a Detail Line

Notice the Add a Detail Line button at the bottom of the form in Figure 33.37. When I click this button, the form spawns two new fields, and all the elements below the two fields are moved down to accommodate the added space on the form. In Figure 33.38, you can see that the Description field grows in size to accommodate my need for adding several lines of text by expanding the field as I type. The Grand Total line sums data added to the Total fields.

FIGURE 33.38

Fields are spawned and expanded according to the user needs.

Description	Total
Consultation with Project Leader to develop plan. 2 hours	$200.00
Plan development session with staff Project leader Marketing Engineering 10 hours	$2,000.00

Data summed from Total fields

Grand Total $2,200.00

Field dynamically expands
to accommadate
user unput needs

Click the button and
fields are added to the form

Add a Detail Line

Keep in mind that this form is completed in Adobe Reader, and no special usage rights for Reader users have been added to the form. These kinds of dynamic forms can be created for use with printing forms or when managing forms on a server where data streams populate form fields.

ON the CD-ROM You can find a copy of the form shown in Figures 33.37 and 33.38 on the book's CD-ROM in the Chapter 33 folder.

The anatomy of a dynamic form

When you work in Acrobat to create forms, you're working in a static two-dimensional environment. Inasmuch as form fields simulate a layer-type behavior, you lay down the form fields on a flat page. In Designer, you work in a more three-dimensional environment. The distinguishing features in a dynamic-form-creation environment include the separate areas of the form you have to work with. In Acrobat, you add form fields to a page in a single content area. Anywhere on the page is open territory for your form fields. Designer offers two primary areas where fields and content are added. These two areas include the Content area and Subforms. The various components of a dynamic form are shown in Figure 33.39.

FIGURE 33.39

A dynamic form has several different components.

Before you can create a dynamic form, you need to clearly understand these components and how they relate to each other. Whereas you can start tossing fields on a page in Acrobat or when creating a static form in Designer, creating a dynamic form requires precision and planning. You need to know a little bit about what fields are going to be added and what kind of subform treatment the fields require *before* you start editing a form.

The various components of a dynamic form include the following:

- **Boilerplate.** Boilerplate objects are like headers and footers on PDF documents. If you want to add a page number or some text to your form pages, you use options for creating boilerplate type data.

- **Fields.** Fields are added to a content area, and they are confined to an area defined as the content area. By default, when you create a new document or use one of the other methods to create a PDF form as I explained earlier in the section "Creating a Simple Form in Designer," Designer defines the content area at the full-page size. This content area can be modified. If you inadvertently change the content boundaries and you don't know why you can't get fields to move to an area on your page, it can be very frustrating.

- **Subforms.** Subforms are the heart of the dynamic form in Designer. A subform is a defined area within the content area where you can add fields and objects. Subforms, among other attributes, can be defined to flow content. Flowing the content is what makes the form shown in Figure 33.38 a dynamic form. The area where you see the Description, Total, and GrandTotal fields was included in a subform in my original design. Without a subform, I wouldn't be able to make the data flow.

  It's critical that you completely understand working with and using subforms if you want to create dynamic forms. As I said at the beginning of this chapter, LiveCycle Designer wasn't developed from the ground up by Adobe Systems. The kind of elements Adobe surely would have included in Designer if Adobe first developed the program would have been layers and modifier keys to easily select nested objects on a page. These tools are simply not in Designer, and Designer has its own way of selecting and modifying objects that may be intuitive to the IT people, but surely it will drive the graphic design people crazy.

  In Figure 33.40, the body page appears with two areas defined as subforms for this particular design. The dashed lines show the boundaries of the separate subforms.

- **Body pages.** Body pages are where you lay out your design, integrating components of a master page and content you add to the body page. You can have one or more body pages and one or more master pages in a Designer form. A form doesn't require any content on a master page, but you do need at least one layout on a body page to create a form.

- **Content areas.** Content areas are where you place fields and objects on body pages. Content areas have defined boundaries, and you can place fields and objects only within the boundaries. You can have one or more different content areas on a body page.

- **Master pages.** Master pages in Designer are like master pages in layout programs. You have a separate tab in Designer to open a master page and add content. You might put some text and fields on a master page such as your identifying information, a purchase order or invoice number, and a date. When you click the Body page tab, the master page data is not selectable, just as when working with a layout program such as Adobe InDesign. You can have more than one master page on a form, and you can choose which master page to apply to a body page. In Figure 33.41 you can see the master page content in the Master Page view and the defined content area. When you open a body page, no content can be added to the area outside the dashed line.

FIGURE 33.40

Two subforms are used in this dynamic form.

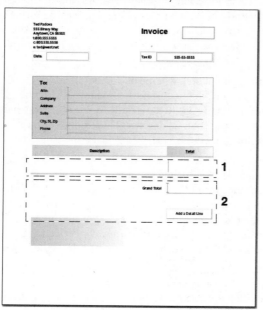

- **Header and footer rows.** If you are creating a dynamic area (something like a purchase order form) on a form template, you might typically create a table with a header (and optionally a footer) row. If you don't use tables, you create a positioned subform with a header and trailer. The headers and trailers can be dynamic and will appear at the top (and bottom) of each new page that's added to a form to accommodate additional data when imported from a database or filling out a form.

Setting up the form properties

When you create a blank new form or open a document you want to use as a form, your very first step is to set up the form properties. You'll want to address properties before you start working with the object and field tools in Designer.

To open the Form Properties dialog box, choose File ⇨ Form Properties. The default tab in the Form Properties dialog box is the Info tab, as shown in Figure 33.42. Fill in the Title, Description, Author, and Contact fields in this pane.

FIGURE 33.41

A master page showing objects and fields added to the master page; the dashed line represents the content area.

FIGURE 33.42

Add document title information in the Form Properties dialog box.

Click the Preview tab and you arrive at the Preview pane. If you have a data file you use with your form for importing XML data, click the icon on the far right of the Data File text box and import your data file (more on that later in the section "Creating Data Connections"). Choose Dynamic XML Form from the pull-down menu where you see Preview Adobe XML Form As and click Generate Preview Data as shown in Figure 33.43.

CROSS-REF For more on Acrobat compatibilities, see Chapter 10.

FIGURE 33.43

Choose Interactive Form, import an XML file (optional), and select a preview option in the Preview tab.

Working with subforms

Perhaps the most difficult part of learning LiveCycle Designer is understanding subforms and the scripting languages. To create dynamic forms, you need some comprehension of both. Subforms are used to make your forms dynamic so you can flow data and populate your forms with new content on demand.

When you first begin to prepare a form for dynamic content, you need a mini paradigm for your workflow to understand the direction in which you want to proceed to create a dynamic form. In a simplified outline here's the order of how you approach creating a dynamic print form.

1. **Set the form properties.** As I've explained already in this chapter, set up the form properties in the Form Properties dialog box.

2. **Create the Master Page (per UI) layout.** Add all the objects and fields you want to appear on your master page and set the Content area below/above the master page objects.

3. **Create the layout with objects and fields.** For a first effort in Designer, try to lay out the document as you want it to appear when distributed. Notice that you first create the layout here before you start creating subforms.

4. **Add the subforms for your design.** Subforms can be added to your layout as you design a form or after the initial design has been created. If you add subforms while designing a layout, you can easily get confused, and it's much more difficult to rearrange elements when you have several subforms on the page.

5. **Add scripts to field objects.** You need all the field objects and the subforms on the page in order to add scripts that invoke actions. This would be the last step in your design process before you preview the form.

When you graduate to binding fields to data, you'll have a good idea for how forms are created in LiveCycle Designer, and you can choose to bind data and when to add subforms to suit your own personal needs. For an introduction to LiveCycle Designer, try to follow the steps outlined here and practice creating enough dynamic forms so you completely understand all the elements and how to arrange and modify them. Try to get a handle on working with subforms before you begin to delve into binding data to fields and forms.

Adding subforms to a document

There are three locations from which you can add subforms to a document. The most common method is using the Hierarchy palette. (See "Using the Hierarchy palette" later in this chapter.)

Another method is to use the Insert ➪ Standard menu, and from the submenu select Subform. This menu command adds a subform to the center of the open document page. Subforms can be added to both Master Pages and Body Pages (Design View).

The other way you can add a subform to a document is to open the Standard library palette and drag the Subform tool to the document page, as shown in Figure 33.44.

FIGURE 33.44

Click the Subform tool and drag a subform to the document page.

If you start with a subform on a page, you can drag objects and fields within the subform rectangle to bind them to the subform. You can also cut or copy objects and fields, add a subform to the page, resize it by dragging the handles on a selected subform, and then paste. When you paste Clipboard data on the page containing a selected subform, the data is pasted into the subform, which also results in binding the data to the subform, as shown in Figure 33.45.

FIGURE 33.45

Two data fields are contained within a subform.

If you add a subform to a page after creating fields and the subform appears on top of the fields, you haven't bound the fields to the subform. Any effort to flow data or work with subform properties respective to the data fields won't be possible.

Using the Hierarchy palette

If there's any gold in LiveCycle Designer, it's in the Hierarchy palette. This palette dynamically lists all the assets included in your Designer form. Data connections and XML file links are handled in other palettes, but the objects, fields, and subforms you add to a form are all here in the Hierarchy palette.

When you create a new document and open the Hierarchy palette on the left side of the Designer workplace, you see the items Designer automatically added to the new blank page. In the Hierarchy palette you see an untitled Subform. If you have more than one page, you'll see an untitled Subform for each page, and the subforms are denoted according to page number so they can be easily distinguished from one another.

Click on the "(untitled Subform) (page 1)" item in the Hierarchy list and you see the content area selected on the blank page, as shown in Figure 33.46. Every Designer document including static forms has at least one *root* subform and a defined content area. If you attempt to delete the subform shown with handles in Figure 33.46, Designer won't let you do it. This is a must when working with Designer.

FIGURE 33.46

Click (untitled Subform) (page 1) in the Hierarchy palette and the default Content area is selected.

NOTE   If you use a PDF background artwork, you can't use subforms. Subforms require XML templates, which are negated by importing a PDF as background artwork. All forms using PDF background artwork are static forms.

If you reduce the size of the Content area, all the objects, fields, and additional subforms will be confined to your new Content area size. If you find you can't move an object to the edge of your form, go back and check the Content area. Chances are you sized the rectangle to a smaller size than you thought.

Using the Hierarchy palette you can precisely define the sizes of your subforms and bind the elements on your page to the subforms you create. To see how you approach designing a dynamic form with subforms, follow these steps.

STEPS: Designing a dynamic form

1. **Create a new blank document.** Create a new blank document and set up the Form Properties as mentioned in the section "Setting up the form properties" earlier in this chapter.

2. **Create your layout.** Add fields and objects to a master page and to the body page shown in the Design View using tools covered in the section "Creating a Simple Form in Designer" earlier in this chapter. Lay out your form page as precisely as you can. Size fields and objects and place them in the position that you want them to appear in your final layout.

3. **Organize the objects.** Open the Hierarchy palette and move the objects around in an order that will make it easy to group objects together in subforms. The logic should look the same as the final design you want to create.

The Hierarchy palette works very similar to the Bookmarks panel in Acrobat. You can click and drag items in the list up or down to reorder them. Items can also be nested in parent/child relationships like Acrobat's bookmarks. The Hierarchy palette for my example form is shown in Figure 33.47.

FIGURE 33.47

The Hierarchy palette is used to organize the content on the form.

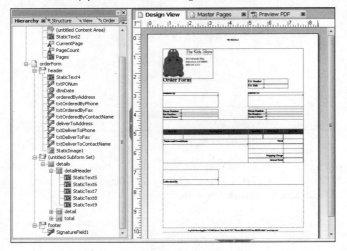

CROSS-REF   For more information on working with bookmarks in Acrobat, see Chapter 22.

CAUTION   Be absolutely certain to order the objects together that need to be grouped in a common subform, and double-check your layout to be certain the design appears as you want before creating a single subform. If you create one or more subforms and then try to move objects around the Hierarchy palette, you'll have a nightmare of a time trying to get the order correct by moving objects on either the document page or in the Hierarchy palette.

4. **Add a subform.** Start at the top of the Hierarchy palette and select items that belong to one subform group. Open a context menu from the selected fields in the Hierarchy palette and choose Wrap in Subform from the menu choices. Your new subform is created with an untitled label. To rename the subform, open a context menu on the new untitled subform and select Rename Object. Type a new name for the subform and press the Enter key on your keyboard.

You can also rename subforms in the Binding tab in the Objects palette.

In my example, I renamed the default root subform rootSubform, and I added a new subform for the header data and named the subform HeaderData, as shown in Figure 33.48. My new subform will be added as a child item below the root subform (rootSubform) in the Hierarchy palette.

FIGURE 33.48

I created a new subform for the header data on my form and named it HeaderData.

5. **Insert a subform.** I have several content areas that need to flow on my example form. I'll go ahead and create a parent subform without binding any data to the new subform. To do this, I find an empty spot in the Hierarchy palette below all the items in the list, and without any object selected I open a context menu and select Insert Subform. This new subform is a child to the root rootSubform. (See Figure 33.49.)

 To clear all items in the Hierarchy palette, click the cursor in an open area on the document page.

6. **Move a subform in the Hierarchy palette.** You reorder subforms in the Hierarchy palette just as you reorder bookmarks in Acrobat, and the way bookmarks are ordered in Acrobat is precisely the way Designer handles moving the subforms around the palette. To nest a subform as a child subform, click and drag up to the subform you want as the parent. When the parent subform is highlighted, release the mouse button and the new subform is nested below the parent as a child subform. To move objects in and out of subforms, you drag around the palette and move horizontally to nest objects below other

children in other subforms. At times it can feel a little awkward, but a little practice gets you up to speed fast.

On my example form, I moved my new inserted subform below the HeaderData subform but not as a child to the HeaderData. This new subform is a child to the root subform in my document. The position of the new item is shown in Figure 33.49. After moving the new subform, I renamed it "detail."

CROSS-REF For more information on organizing bookmarks in Acrobat, see Chapter 22.

FIGURE 33.49

Create a new subform and nest it under the root subform.

7. **Nest additional subforms under the inserted subform (now named detail).** On my example form, I have four different groups I want to flow in my document. Later, I'll target the new inserted subform as a Floating subform and the remaining subforms as Content subforms (see "Subform types" coming up next in this chapter). All subforms nested below a Flowed subform will flow the content.

   To create the new subforms, I select the objects I want to group in a subform, and from a Context menu I select Wrap in Subform. I create four new subforms and name them GroupLeaderSubform, item, GroupTrailer, and GroupTotal. In Figure 33.50 I collapsed the HeaderData subform, and my four new subforms according to parent/child relationships are shown with the content grouped for each item.

8. **Save the document.** If you find that things get scrambled a little, save your file under a new filename so you can return to a previous file before you encountered any problems. When your design looks like things are working out as expected, save your edits regularly. If you created a similar type of document as the example shown here, save the file now.

FIGURE 33.50

Create new subforms by selecting data and choosing Wrap in Subform from a context menu.

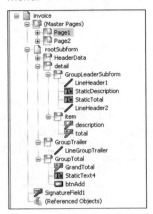

Subform types

Designer provides you two options for setting subform attributes. You can define a subform that flows content or a positioned subform where the content remains static. As you might imagine when you format a subform to flow content, the form takes on dynamic attributes that enable you to create a form that spawns new fields and accommodates sizing fields according to the amount of user data added to a given field. A subform formatted for positioned content doesn't flow on a page within its own subform, but may flow according to attributes of the parent subform. If the field attributes are defined to Allow Multiple lines for positioned content, the text exceeding the field borders is set up to be viewed in a scrollable window. In other words, the field doesn't grow to accommodate the text.

When you select a subform in the Hierarchy palette and open the Object palette, your options are very different than those you have with other objects and form fields. Using my example file, I click on the detail subform and take a look at the Object palette. This subform is the one I want to format for a data flow. From the Object palette, open the Content pull-down menu; you see two choices. For my detail subform I want the Flowed option you see in Figure 33.51. The other four fields appearing as children under my detail subform are formatted as Positioned subforms.

FIGURE 33.51

Open the Object palette and click the Subform tab. Select Flowed from the Content pull-down menu.

Below the Content pull-down menu is another pull-down menu for selecting the direction of the flow. The Flow Direction pull-down menu options are available only when formatting the subform to flow text. The first menu item is Top to Bottom. As the name suggests, data is flowed from the top of the page toward the bottom. The second menu choice is Western Text. This option flows data from left to right beginning at the top of the subform and continuing across to the right. The next flow of data is in the second row left to right, and so on. On my example form, I chose the Top to Bottom option for this design.

One more item in the Subform tab in the Object palette is the check box for Allow Page Breaks within Content. Select this box if you want the data to flow across multiple pages.

In the Object palette, you also have another tab that relates specifically to subforms. Click the Pagination tab and you have options for flowing content and handling data overflows. The options you have in this tab are generally applied to flowing data into XML forms from external data sources. In my example file, I left the options at the defaults, as shown in Figure 33.52.

FIGURE 33.52

Leave the Pagination tab at the default settings.

Calculating data

Another book the size of *Adobe Acrobat 9 PDF Bible* could be written on just the JavaScript and FormCalc scripting languages supported by LiveCycle Designer. In Chapter 36 (on the CD-ROM), I talk about JavaScript and all the code listings in that chapter. With the exception of using the docTemplates object, the JavaScript in Chapter 36 (on the CD-ROM) is equally applicable to Designer. To learn more about Acrobat and Designer JavaScript, download the Acrobat JavaScript Scripting Guide at www.adobe.com/devenet/acrobat/javascript.

For more information on FormCalc, a manual is available on Adobe's Web site at www.adobe.com/devenet/. Both the JavaScript and FormCalc manuals should be stored locally on your hard drive when creating forms in either Designer or Acrobat.

CROSS-REF For more information on using JavaScript, see Chapter 36 (on the CD-ROM).

In terms of the example form I've used in this section, the form requires only a single short script to complete the design. If you could create the same design in Adobe Acrobat it would take pages of JavaScript to produce the same results. In Designer, you need to add only a few lines of code to complete the design.

The actions for spawning fields and expanding field sizes in Designer are automatic and don't require any special scripting code. If you set up your subforms correctly, Designer handles all you need for managing the data fields on my example form. What you do need, however, is a script to tell your Acrobat viewer to calculate the total data and when you want to spawn new fields. These two scripts belong to the GrandTotal field for summing the data and the btnAdd field on the Add a Detail button.

Here's what to do to add scripts that will sum data and spawn new fields.

STEPS: Add a script to a Designer form

1. **Select the field to sum a total.** Open the Hierarchy palette and click the field where the data sum is calculated. In my example form, I click the GrandTotal field.

2. **Open the FormCalc Script Editor.** Press Ctrl+Shift+F5 to open the script window at the top of the Designer window and select FormCalc from the Language pull-down menu.

3. **Type the code to calculate a sum.** Select calculate from the Show menu and type the following code in the Script Editor window, as shown in Figure 33.53.

   ```
   Sum($form.invoice.#subform[0].detail.item[*].total)
   ```

FIGURE 33.53

Select FormCalc from the Language pull-down menu, select calculate from the Show pull-down menu, and type the code in the Script Editor.

4. **Select the btnAdd button in the Hierarchy palette.**

5. Type the following script in the FormCalc Editor:

```
detail.item.instanceManager.addInstance();
GroupTotal.GrandTotal.execCalculate();
```

The first line of code adds the instance for spawning new fields and flowing the fields on the form. The second line of code executes the `GrandTotal` field calculation.

6. **Set the button properties to hide the button when printing.** One last item to deal with before your form is complete is to change the button properties. On my example form, I want the Add a Detail item for the `btnAdd` field to be invisible when the form is printed. The Add a Detail text and the button field are one item. The field has a caption assigned to it for the Add a Detail text. Click the `btnAdd` field in the Hierarchy palette and open the Field tab in the Object palette. Select Visible (Screen Only) from the Presence pull-down menu, as shown in Figure 33.54.

FIGURE 33.54

Select Visible (Screen Only) to hide the button when the file is printed.

7. **Save your form and test it in Acrobat by clicking the Preview PDF button in Designer.**

Distributing forms

Distributing forms from LiveCycle Designer is handled the same as you distribute forms from Acrobat. In Acrobat 9 you have more options for distributing forms and collecting data. Check out Chapter 35 to learn more.

Run-time events

When you browse the Designer menus, you'll notice that the Insert menu lists a number of different commands that always seem to be inaccessible. You may wonder what these commands do and how to make them active. The commands require a little different treatment than the fields and objects you add to pages from other areas in the Insert menu or the Library palette. The items you see grayed out in Figure 33.55 are special properties that are assigned to a few objects and used for run-time events.

FIGURE 33.55

The first eight commands in the Insert menu are used for run-time events.

Run-time is when an application or server retrieves a form design and, among other things, might merge data with the form. In a very simple way, something like executing a mail merge from a word processing program is a run-time event. When you merge the data from a letter, for example, the data is introduced into the letter template merging a data form and a data file with a design producing new pages. A run-time event is also when you open the form in Acrobat. You might want the current date reported on a form when a user opens the form in an Acrobat viewer. Reporting the date when the file opens is also a run-time event.

Designer provides you tools to display certain types of information at run-time. Where and how you insert run-time properties is limited to a few objects. These objects are as follows:

- **Text.** A text object can be used to insert a run-time property.
- **Text Fields.** Text fields can be used to insert a run-time property.
- **Numeric Fields.** Numeric fields can be used to insert run-time properties.

To format a text object with a run-time property, you insert the cursor in the text object and then open the Insert menu. When the cursor appears inside the text, the grayed out items in Figure 33.56 are all made active. When you want to format a run-time property for a text field or a numeric field, select the field and open the Object palette. From the Type menu you have only one choice to format the field for a run-time property. Select Calculated – Read Only from the menu options. Below the menu, click the Runtime Property radio button and open the pull-down menu to select a run-time event, as shown in Figure 33.56.

FIGURE 33.56

Text fields and numeric fields are formatted for run-time events in the Object palette.

All run-time properties are available to Static Text objects. Text fields can use all properties except the Current Date/Time. Numeric fields can use only properties that report data in numbers such as the Current Page Number, Number of Pages, Current Sheet Number, and Number of Sheets. All other properties are not allowed with this field type.

The options you have for formatting include the following:

- **Current Page Number.** Places the current page number respective to the page where the field properties are assigned.

- **Number of Pages.** You might use this property to report the total pages in a dynamic form that flows data, adding new pages until the data is exhausted.

- **Current Date/Time.** Reports the current date and time.

- **Viewer Locale.** This property is used to report the locale for the application that is processing the form. For example, you might design a form in the United States and the form may be processed in India. The field result would report India for the locale.

- **Viewer Name.** Reports the Acrobat viewer name. If the form is run in Adobe Reader, for example, Adobe Reader is reported in the field.

- **Viewer Version.** Reports the Acrobat viewer version (such as 8).

- **Current Sheet Number.** Reports the sheet number. If the form produces 10 sheets of paper and the field is on sheet 10, the number reported is 10.

- **Number of Sheets.** Reports total sheets produced.

To understand more about inserting properties for run-time events, follow these steps to report a current date.

STEPS: Assigning run-time properties to a text object

1. Open a form or create a blank new form.

2. **Add a static text object to the page.** Select Insert ➪ Standard ➪ Text or drag the text object from the Standard library palette. Be certain to use the Text object and not the Text Field object.

3. **Drag across the default text and type the text you want to appear on the form.** In my example I use "This form is completed on:". I'll insert a date that will calculate at run-time.

4. **Insert a date.** While the cursor appears in the text box, select Insert ➪ Current Date/Time (alternately open a context menu and select Current Date/Time). You'll see the text following the text you type appear as {current date/time} as shown in Figure 33.57.

FIGURE 33.57

With the cursor in the static text field, select Insert ➪ Current Date/Time.

> This form is completed on: {current date/time}

5. **Preview the file in Acrobat.** Click Preview PDF and the file opens in Acrobat. The date is reported as you see in Figure 33.58.

FIGURE 33.58

When opened in Acrobat, the date is reported in date, hours, and minutes.

> This form is completed on: 2006-09-14 16:48:44

6. **Save the file from Designer.**

7. **Open the file in Acrobat, save it, and close the file.**

8. **Reopen the document in Acrobat.** Wait a few minutes until you're certain the time has changed significantly since you last viewed the file in Acrobat. You'll notice that the date remains fixed to the date stamp when you first opened the file. The field data was created at run-time in Acrobat when you first opened the file. After saving in Acrobat, the field data is static and won't run again.

Enabling Forms with Reader Extensions

Adobe LiveCycle Designer has no direct command for enabling PDFs with Adobe Reader extensions. If you select the File ➪ Distribute Form command in Designer, the Form Distribution Options Wizard opens in Acrobat. When you distribute a form, the form is automatically enabled with usage rights for Adobe Reader users. Reader users can fill out the form and save the form data before submitting the form back to you.

Whereas many editing features for static and dynamic Designer forms are lost in Acrobat, the enabling commands are accessible for any kind of Designer form. You can choose to enable a Designer form for Commenting in Adobe Reader using the Comments ⇨ Enable for Commenting and Analysis in Adobe Reader command, and you can enable the form for saving field data, commenting, and digital signatures using the Advanced ⇨ Extended Features in Adobe Reader command.

CROSS-REF **For more information on enabling documents with usage rights for Adobe Reader, see Chapters 19, 34, and 35.**

Creating Data Connections

Binding fields in a form design to a data source is one of the true great features in LiveCycle Designer. If using Acrobat to bind to data sources, you need to have a sophisticated level of JavaScript programming background and a lot of finesse to create the resources that successfully bind data to other sources. With Designer, the process is greatly simplified and the program does much of the mind-wrenching work for you.

When binding fields on a form design to a data source, you create an association between the form and some data source that lets you capture, process, output, and print information from the data entries on a form. Designer enables you to bind data either as client-side, where you might bind data locally on a hard drive to a backend database file, or as server-side binding. Client-side binding enables you to make changes immediately to the data, while server-side binding requires you to submit data to a server where changes are made.

You create a new connection to a data source by opening the Data View palette and clicking the icon in the top right corner of the palette to open the palette menu. Choose New Data Connection from the menu and the New Data Connection Wizard opens as shown in Figure 33.59.

FIGURE 33.59

Choose New Data Connection from the Data View palette menu and the New Data Connection Wizard opens.

In the New Data Connection Wizard, you make a choice for the type of data connection you want.

XML schema and XML data sources

You can import an XML schema definition into a form design and then bind objects in the form to elements in the XML schema. If you have an XML file and not an XML schema, you can bind objects to the XML data form. The process for binding both a schema and a file are similar. The option that differs between the two is selecting which source you want in the New Data Connection Wizard.

To create an XML schema connection, select File ➪ New Data Connection or click the icon in the Data View palette to open the New Data Connection Wizard. In the New Data Connection Wizard, select XML Schema or Sample XML Data. Click Next and click the icon you see with an *i* appearing over a folder on the far-right side of the Select XML Schema File text box. Browse your hard drive and select the XML schema file. Click OK and the file is added to the Select XML Schema File text box, as shown in Figure 33.60. For connecting to a Sample XML Data File you have the same options for selecting the file in a similar wizard pane.

FIGURE 33.60

Click the icon to the right of the text box to select the XML Schema file.

Connecting to OLEDB data sources

OLE Databases (OLEDB) are sets of Component Object Model (COM) interfaces that provide applications with uniform access stored in diverse information sources. In short, these interfaces support DBMS (Database Management Systems) functionality appropriate to the data source that enables it to share data. You might have databases such as Microsoft Access files, Excel spreadsheet files, or other database types you want to share data with PDF forms. You might have a situation in which you use a single identifying field a user types into a form, such as an employee ID or Social Security number. Using this one piece of data, you can connect to a database to retrieve additional information (or records) associated with this information.

To dynamically edit data in your database file, you make a connection to the database and then bind fields on the form to the corresponding columns in the database.

Designer supports a number of OLEDB drivers. Click the OLEDB radio button in the New Data Connection Wizard and click the Next button. The second pane in the wizard prompts you for the Connection string. Click the Build button and the Data Link Properties dialog box opens, as shown in Figure 33.61. The list in the figure shows you the supported drivers.

You need to name your connection and set up your database connection string. Setting up a database connection string may require you to research your database user manual. From the Provider tab you select the OLEDB provider, and then click the Connection tab to specify the source of the data. A number of different options appear in the Connection, Advanced, and All tabs. In order to make an effective connection, you need to thoroughly understand your database file and the many options you have to specify the properties for the connection.

FIGURE 33.61

Click Build in the New Data Connection Wizard and the Data Link Properties dialog box opens. Select a data connection you want to make from the list of providers.

WSDL file

Web Services are applications that run remote over the Web. For example, your form might include a field where the current mortgage rate needs to be calculated. You can connect to a Web Service that determines the daily mortgage rate based on your address. A Web Service Description Language (WSDL) is an XML document (or file) that describes the Web Service and the services and operations (or methods) offered by the service. The connection supports a number of operations. The WSDL file defines the request and response requirements (or syntax) for each operation.

Input messages are sent to a server. The server can then reply with an output message. Using Designer you can create and bind fields in a form design to one of many different Web Services.

Aside from connecting to a WSDL via the New Data Connections Wizard, you can:

- Bind one or more operations within one or more Web Services.
- Attach fields, subforms, and exclusion groups to the execution of a Web Service operation using a button click event.
- Execute a Web Service operation from any event by way of a script.
- Enable script access to all returned elements of a Web Service regardless of whether those elements are bound to fields.
- Use Simple Object Access Protocol (SOAP) 1.1 style communication.
- Exchange data with a Web Service by using doc/literal exchange format SOAP can be either Doc/literal or RPC/encoded. Doc/literal supports drag and drop for automatic population of Data View.
- Write client-side scripts by using the Acrobat SOAP JavaScript Object, which supports RPC/encoded. If you use RPC/encoded, you have to do all the connections by hand using JavaScript.

To connect to a WSDL service you need to find it on the Internet. You can find lists of WSDL services by visiting `www.webservicex.net` and `www.xmethods.net`. Both these sites post links to WSDL services. To make a connection to a WSDL service and design a form utilizing WSDL data, follow these steps.

STEPS: Binding data to a WSDL service

1. **Create a form design in LiveCycle Designer.** If you want to test a WSDL connection, you can use a blank new page; otherwise, create a form where you want to introduce the WSDL connection data. Open your form or create a blank new page.

2. **Open a WSDL service in your Web browser.** Use one of the services listing WSDL Web sites (`www.webservicex.net` or `www.xmethods.net`) and click a link to a service you want to use. In my example, I use a currency exchange service located at `www.webservicex.net/CurrencyConvertor.asmx?WSDL`.

3. **Copy the Web URL from the location bar in your Web browser.**

4. **Open the New Data Connection Wizard.** Switch to LiveCycle Designer. You can leave your Web browser open and use the Windows status bar to open your form in Designer.

   Select File ➪ New Data Connection or open the Data View palette and click the icon in the palette to open a pull-down menu and select New Data Connection. In the New Data Connection Wizard, select WDSL as shown in Figure 33.62.

5. **Paste the copied URL in the New Data Connection Wizard.** Click the Next button and paste the copied URL in the text box, as shown in Figure 33.63.

FIGURE 33.62

Open the New Data Connection Wizard and select WSDL File for the connection type.

FIGURE 33.63

Paste the copied text in the WSDL File text box.

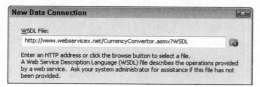

6. **Select an operation.** Click the Next box and Designer connects to the WSDL service. In the last wizard pane you'll see a list of operations. Select the first item in the list and click the Finish button, as shown in Figure 33.64. Note that you may have a variety of operations from which to choose. Many services list duplicated names in the list, while others may have unique names for a number of different services. Browse the list box and select the item that suits you needs. Some will have the word "Next" grayed out– these do not support Doc/literal which is the supported format for LC Designer.

7. **Drag the Data Connection to the form page.** When you click Finish, you'll see a parent item in the Data View palette as the data connection. Below the parent name shown in Figure 33.65 are several child items representing fields and buttons. To add all the items to your form, select the Data Connection parent item and drag it to the form page.

What you see in the Data View is a set of fields for the Request. This is what you need to send to the Web service. You also see a set of fields for the Response. These fields will contain what is returned from the Web service. You also see a button field object that contains the information to connect to the Web service.

FIGURE 33.64

Select an operation and click Finish.

FIGURE 33.65

Drag the Data Connection item from the Data View palette to the form page to easily include all elements on your form.

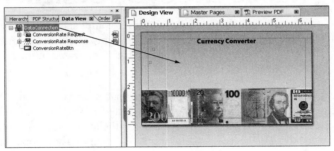

8. **Format the fields.** Move the fields to position and edit any appearance items you want using the Object and Layout tabs.

9. **Save the file.** Select File ⇨ Save As and save the file to disk.

10. **Test the form.** Open the form in Acrobat. Add data to the fields for the service you decided to use and click the button to invoke the action. Acrobat makes a data connection to the WSDL server and reports the results back in your form. In my example I used a currency converter. From the From Currency pull-down menu I select EUR for Euros, and in the To Currency pull-down menu I selected USD for US Dollars. After clicking the Conversion Rate Btn, the conversion rate was reported in my form by retrieving the most up-to-date conversion rate from the WSDL server. (See Figure 33.66.)

FIGURE 33.66

My final form reported the results from the WSDL server after I clicked the Conversion Rate Btn.

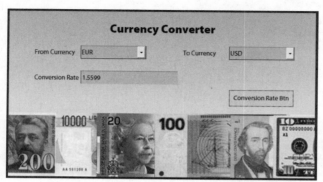

Learning Adobe LiveCycle Designer

If you followed all the steps in this chapter and read it over completely, you know that there's quite a bit to Adobe LiveCycle Designer. I haven't been able to go into all the detail for everything you can do with Designer, so there's quite a bit more than what was covered in the previous pages in this chapter.

If you have a background in programming and database logic, then you may find much of the program to be intuitive and easy to learn. If you don't have skills in programming and understanding database management, then you are likely to have much difficulty getting up to speed in the program. Some people say that Designer is easy and intuitive. I define easy as something a child or elderly grandparent can learn in 30 minutes time. This program doesn't fall into that category. If someone tells you it's easy to learn, don't believe it! LiveCycle Designer is complex and tough to learn — especially if you're trying to learn the program from the online guide. You won't become a Designer expert by reading a single chapter in a book on Acrobat. For a good many users, what is needed is some sort of formal training.

If you intend to spend a good part of your workday designing interactive dynamic forms, then you might want to look at a framework for learning the program in detail. Here are some of my recommendations for getting the most out of LiveCycle Designer:

- **Practice with the program.** Nothing beats practice with a software program than to dive in and start using it. But before you attempt to create some sophisticated forms, try to design static forms. Don't jump into adding subforms and try to create dynamic forms, and don't worry about database connections. The more you can become familiar with the different field types and setting field properties, the better off you'll be when it comes time to design more complex forms. Be sure you understand the Library palette, the Object palette and its Value tab, and the Border palette thoroughly. Practice so that it becomes very intuitive and you know exactly where you want to go to change properties for objects and fields. Like any other kind of learning, starting with the basics helps you trim some time off the learning curve.

■ **Attend a class.** Some type of formal training is always best when working with a program as complex as LiveCycle Designer. Search out your local community colleges, universities, and private training centers that offer classes on Designer. But be certain to carefully review the class content before you enroll in a class. If you see classes advertised as "Creating PDF Forms" or "Learning Adobe LiveCycle Designer," make sure that the class instructor and the contents of the class cover creating dynamic forms. An overview of working with fields and creating static PDF forms isn't going to do much more for you than what you can learn by yourself.

Some private training centers may boast about their credentialed instructors, claiming them to be Adobe Certified Experts in Photoshop, Illustrator, InDesign, GoLive, Acrobat, Flash, and a few other programs. My guess is you won't find anyone claiming to have all these certificates to know Designer in depth, at least to the level you need. Look for people who live in the program and do some sort of professional forms design work or are celebrated speakers frequently talking at conferences and expos.

Adobe has a full-blown certification program in Designer. You can find special certified trainers by logging on to `http://partners.adobe.com` and select Training Providers from the "Find products and services" list on the home page.

■ **Get a video.** This book is written in the early days of Acrobat 8, and we have yet to see if after-market books and videos will appear for Designer. Check regularly on the Internet to see if a video or DVD is released as an instructional tutorial. Videos and DVDs can cover much more territory in less time than reading the online guide.

■ **Attend a conference.** One of the best ways to learn features, tips, and workarounds about a program is to attend a conference. There are some extra special benefits to attending a conference. You can attend sessions and sometimes find pre- or post-conference workshops that offer full-day courses on Designer. The added benefit is that you can gather some email addresses for Adobe employees, speakers, and other conference participants. There's probably not a more valuable asset than having someone to call when you really get stuck on a problem.

■ **Visit `www.acrobatusers.com`.** The Acrobat Users Web site hosts many tutorials and articles with up-to-date information about LiveCycle Designer and Adobe Acrobat.

■ **Be patient.** Learning Designer for the average person is like learning a foreign language. You have to start with basics, add continual reinforcement, and keep practicing. Don't try to create complex forms too quickly. Take your time and learn a little each day. Try to devote some time to concepts and practice many times over so the steps in a process become intuitive and second nature. When you get frustrated, move away from the program and come back the next day. Sometimes a good night's rest can help you solve a problem in a matter of a few minutes that was an all-day burden the day before.

Summary

- You can access Designer from within Acrobat or by opening the program icon.

- Adobe LiveCycle Designer is a Windows-only program that ships free with Acrobat Pro and Acrobat Pro Extended. Macintosh users can use LiveCycle Designer on Intel Macs after installing a virtual desktop program, Windows XP or Windows Vista, and an Acrobat Pro product for Windows.

- LiveCycle Designer is a point-and-click graphical design application that simplifies creation of form templates intended to be delivered as PDF or HTML.

- LiveCycle Designer represents a new direction in form design from Adobe Systems. Designer provides Windows users a more sophisticated form designer environment than adding form fields to a PDF document in Adobe Acrobat.

- LiveCycle Designer supports the use of many different tools, commands, and an extensive number of palettes used to create form elements and bind data to external sources.

- You can create new form designs by starting with blank document pages, using PDF background artwork, converting Microsoft Word files, copying spreadsheet data, or using one of many preinstalled templates.

- Form elements are added to a layout from objects in the Library palette or from the Insert menu.

- You can create custom objects and add them to custom libraries complete with scripts and attribute assignments.

- Fields can be grouped in collections and added to custom libraries where they can be reused in subsequent forms.

- Subforms are added to a design to flow data and make the form dynamic, where fields and content can be assigned to flow according to user input.

- Field calculations and actions assignments are added in a Script Editor window using either the FormCalc or JavaScript language.

- Designer offers easy access to database connections for fields and forms.

- Designer forms can be enabled with Adobe Reader extensions in Acrobat.

- You can save designer forms as templates, PDF files, and Adobe XML form files.

Chapter 34

Understanding Acrobat Form Tools

In the last chapter, I covered creating forms using Adobe LiveCycle Designer. Unfortunately, Adobe Designer is one of the only features covered in this book that isn't available to Mac people. If you're a Mac person, you may have felt left out while reading Chapter 33. But don't despair. There are plenty of forms features still available for both Macintosh and Windows users in Acrobat 9.

Adobe PDF forms can be created in Acrobat Standard (Windows), Acrobat Pro, and Acrobat Pro Extended (Windows) using the form tools and many commands for creating a different kind of form. XML forms are created in Adobe Designer and Acrobat PDF forms are created in Acrobat (Standard, Pro, and Pro Extended). In some cases, an Acrobat PDF form might be preferred over an XML form. These two form types are distinctive in both the creation process and the intended use.

Before you delve into this chapter, realize that creating both Acrobat forms and Adobe LiveCycle Designer forms covers as much territory as the complete *Adobe Acrobat 9 PDF Bible*. As a matter of fact, I've written a book titled *PDF Forms Using Adobe Acrobat and LiveCycle Designer Bible* (Wiley Publishing 2008). That book equals the size of the *Adobe Acrobat 9 PDF Bible*. Therefore, all I can hope to do in this chapter is give you a brief introduction to creating PDF forms. If your primary work is creating forms, look

IN THIS CHAPTER

Defining PDF forms

Filling-in PDF forms

Understanding forms editing

Setting field properties

Managing fields

Creating PDF forms

Working with the Fields panel

to other sources for a comprehensive coverage of creating forms in both Acrobat and LiveCycle Designer.

In this chapter, you learn how to use the new Acrobat 9 Form Editing Mode and create PDF forms in one of the Acrobat viewers, and find an introduction to using the different form tools. The good news is you can create PDF forms in Acrobat on either Windows or the Macintosh.

Setting Up the Environment

Working with PDF forms requires the use of the form tools. However, there is no form toolbar in Acrobat 9. Form tools are accessed when you change views from the Viewer mode to the Form Editing Mode. You won't need to set up your work environment for adding form tools to the Acrobat Toolbar Well.

Tools such as the Select tool are used when working on forms. In addition, you have a tool for adding text to fill in a form without form fields called the Typewriter tool. Add the Advanced Editing toolbar and the Typewriter tool to the Acrobat Toolbar Well. Open a context menu on the Acrobat Toolbar Well and choose More Tools. Check the check boxes for Advanced Editing Toolbar and Typewriter Toolbar and click OK. Alternately, you can open the Tools menu and open the Advanced Editing Toolbar and Typewriter Toolbar from menu choices.

As a last item, return to the context menu on the Toolbar Well and select Properties Bar. When all toolbars are visible in the Document pane, select Dock All Toolbars from a context menu opened from the Toolbar Well.

After loading toolbars, your Toolbar Well should look similar to Figure 34.1.

NOTE In Acrobat 9 you can create PDF forms in Acrobat Standard (Windows), Acrobat Pro (Windows and Macintosh), and Acrobat Pro Extended (Windows). Throughout this chapter I refer to these viewers simply as Acrobat. When you see a reference to Acrobat in this chapter, realize I am talking about all three viewers.

FIGURE 34.1

Tools loaded for a PDF form-editing session

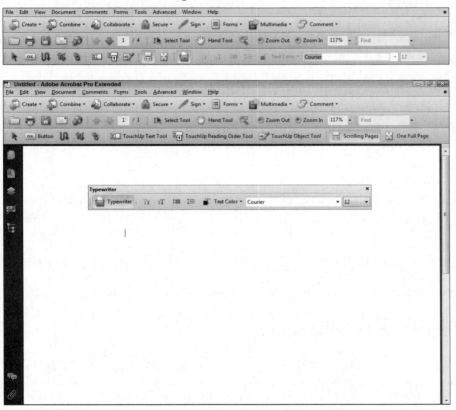

What Are Acrobat Forms?

Forms in Acrobat are PDF files with data fields that appear as placeholders for user-supplied data. In Acrobat, you can use text string fields, numeric fields, check boxes, radio buttons, date fields, calculation fields, signature fields, and a variety of custom fields created with JavaScripts. The advantage of using forms in Acrobat is that doing so enables you to maintain design integrity for the appearance of a form while providing powerful control over data management. Rather than using a database manager, which may limit your ability to control fonts and graphics, Acrobat PDFs preserve all the design attributes of a document while behaving like a data manager.

PDF WORKFLOW   Forms are created in Acrobat or Adobe Designer. Form field data can be saved with Acrobat and also with Adobe Reader when the PDF form has been enabled with usage rights for Adobe Reader. When opening PDFs in Adobe Reader that have not been enabled with Reader Extensions, you cannot save, import, or export data. In developing PDF workflows for a company or organization, all users expected to design forms in Acrobat need to use one of the Acrobat software applications. Corporations and enterprises seeking an affordable solution for extending Adobe Reader to support forms features beyond the licensing limitations of Acrobat should look at acquiring the Adobe LiveCycle Reader Extensions ES (). For more information about LRES, log on to `www.adobe.com/products/livecycle/readerextensions/`.

CROSS-REF   See Chapter 19 for more information on enabling PDFs for filling in and saving forms in Adobe Reader, and also for information on licensing restrictions applied to the use of enabling features in Acrobat.

The non-PDF form

The one thing to keep in mind regarding Acrobat and forms is that a form in the context of PDF is not a paper form scanned as an image and saved as PDF. Tons of these so-called forms are around offices and on the Internet. These documents may have originated as forms, but by the time you understand all of Acrobat's form creation features, you'll see that these scanned documents can hardly be called forms. Simply put, they're scanned images saved to PDF. The power of Acrobat gives you the tools to create *smart forms*. These forms can be dynamic, intuitive, and interactive, and save both you and the recipient much time in providing and gathering information.

Development of a PDF form

In Chapter 33, you learned that forms could be created in Adobe LiveCycle Designer from scratch. Adobe Designer has all the tools you need to create a form design starting with a blank page. Inasmuch as you can create a Blank New Page in Acrobat, PDF forms created in Acrobat usually start out as a document converted to PDF from an authoring program. Programs like Microsoft Office, Adobe InDesign, Adobe Illustrator, or one of your favorite design programs creates the layout and background for a PDF form. After the design is created in an authoring program and converted to PDF, you use tools in Acrobat to add form field objects and form field attributes.

CROSS-REF   For information related to PDF creation from authoring programs, see the chapters in Part II.

TIP   If you create a design and then add form fields in Acrobat, and then even later decide to change your design, you can edit the design back in your original authoring application. Simply save the design and open the form you created in Acrobat. Select Document ⇨ Replace Pages and select the modified PDF document. Replace the page and your modified design appears without disturbing any added form fields on the original design.

Filling In PDF Forms

When you receive or download a PDF form you will encounter one of two types of forms. The so-called PDF form that was created from a scanned document or a PDF document containing no form fields is one type of form. The other type of form is the PDF document containing form fields. In all Acrobat viewers you can populate form data in either type of form.

Using the new improved Typewriter tool

The Typewriter tool is used to fill in a form containing no form fields. You use the Typewriter tool like a text tool is used in other authoring programs.

 To use the Typewriter tool, open a document in an Acrobat viewer and click the Typewriter tool. Click on the page where you want to type text and an I-beam cursor appears. Type the text on a line. This tool was a little clumsy in performance and took a little time to get used to in Acrobat 7, but the performance of the tool was much improved in Acrobat 8, and now in Acrobat 9 you find much more control over type.

NEW FEATURE By default, the Typewriter tool uses the Courier font. In versions of Acrobat prior to Acrobat and Adobe Reader 9, you could choose fonts only within the Courier family. Now in Acrobat 9, you can choose any font among your installed system fonts.

The tools in the Typewriter toolbar from left to right, as shown in Figure 34.2, include the Typewriter tool, the Text Smaller tool, the Text Larger tool, Decrease Line Spacing tool, Increase Line Spacing tool, Text Color, a pull-down menu listing all your installed system fonts, and a choice for font sizes. If you want to move a text block after typing, use the Select Object tool.

You have a number of options from a context menu you open using the Select Object tool on type added with the Typewriter tool. Text blocks can be aligned, centered, distributed, and sized the same as the options you find when managing field objects.

CROSS-REF For more information on using the context menu commands, see "Managing fields" later in this chapter.

Using the Comments panel

The Typewriter tool adds annotations to your document. The text you type with the tool is not text applied to the document the same as when using other options available to you for adding text. Each line of type you add with the Typewriter tool adds the type as an annotation, and the annotations can be viewed and selected in the Comments panel. Type a few lines of text with the Typewriter tool and click the Comments Navigation panel button to expand the Comments panel, and you see a view like the one shown in Figure 34.3.

FIGURE 34.2

Click the Typewriter tool and click on a page to type text. New in Acrobat 9 you can change fonts and font colors.

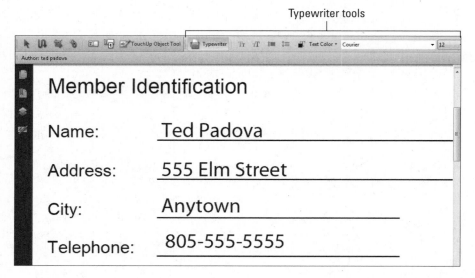

FIGURE 34.3

Click the Comments Navigation panel button to open the Comments panel and you see a list of the entire Typewriter text added to your file.

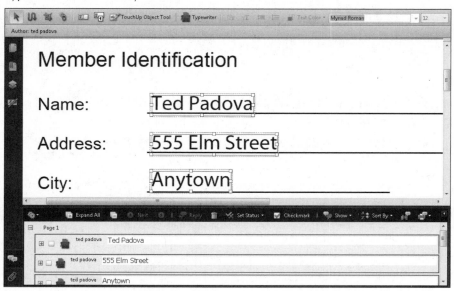

The Comments panel list of the Typewriter additions can be very handy when editing a document. If you want to delete a line of type, click the line in the Comments panel and click the Trash icon or press the Del key on your keyboard. You can also edit the type directly in the Comments panel and the changes are applied to the document page.

CROSS-REF For more information on annotations and using the Comments panel, see Chapter 20.

Filling in forms containing form fields

As you view the form shown in Figure 34.4, notice it contains several text fields, a few combo boxes, a list box, radio buttons, check boxes, and a signature field. To fill out a text field, you need to select the Hand tool, place the cursor over the field, and click the mouse button. When you click, a blinking I-beam cursor appears, indicating that you can add text by typing on your keyboard.

FIGURE 34.4

A form containing many different field types: A) text fields, B) radio buttons, C) check boxes, D) combo box, E) list box, and F) signature field.

TIP To begin filling in a form, press the Tab key on your keyboard. When the Hand tool is selected and the cursor is not active in any field, pressing the Tab key places the cursor in the first field on the form.

To navigate to the next field for more text entry, you can make one of two choices: Click in the next field or press the Tab key on your keyboard. When you press the Tab key, the cursor jumps to the next field, according to an order the PDF author specified in Acrobat when the form was designed. Be certain the Hand tool is selected and a cursor appears in a field box when you press the Tab key. If you have any other tool selected, you can tab through the fields and type data in the field boxes; however, if you click with the mouse when another tool is selected, you make edits according to the active tool.

When selecting from choices in radio button or check box fields, click in the radio button or check box. The display changes to show a small solid circle or check mark within a box or other kind of user-defined symbol from options you select for button/check box styles. When using a combo box, click the down-pointing arrow in the field and select from one of several pull-down menu choices. List boxes are scrollable fields. Scroll to the choice you want to make using the up and down arrows.

Form field navigation keystrokes

As mentioned in the preceding section, to move to the next field, you need to either click in the field or press the Tab key. Following is a list of other keystrokes that can help you move through forms to complete them:

- **Shift+Tab.** Moves to the previous field.
- **Esc.** Ends text entry.
- **Return.** Ends text entry for single line entries or adds a carriage return for multi-line fields.
- **Double-click a word in a field.** Selects the word.
- **Ctrl/⌘+A.** Selects all the text in a field.
- **Left/Right Arrow keys.** Moves the cursor one character at a time left or right.
- **Up Arrow.** Selecting options in the combo and list boxes moves up the list.
- **Down Arrow.** Selecting options in the combo and list boxes moves down the list.
- **Up/Down Arrow with combo and list boxes selected.** Moves up and down the list. When the list is collapsed, pressing the Down Arrow key opens the list.
- **Ctrl/⌘+Tab.** Accepts new entry and exits all fields. The next tab places the cursor in the first field.

Viewing fields

You may open a form in Acrobat where the fields are not clearly visible. Creating form fields on white backgrounds for fields with no border or fill color makes a field invisible when opened in an Acrobat viewer.

If you start to fill in a form and can't see the form fields, click the Highlight Fields button on the Document message bar. All fields are highlighted with a color specified in the Forms Preferences. In Figure 34.5, the fields are white. When I click the Highlight Fields button in the top-right corner of the Document message bar, the fields are highlighted, making it easy to see where each field appears in the form.

FIGURE 34.5

Click Highlight Fields in the Document message bar to display fields with highlights.

Document
Message Bar

Highlight
Fields

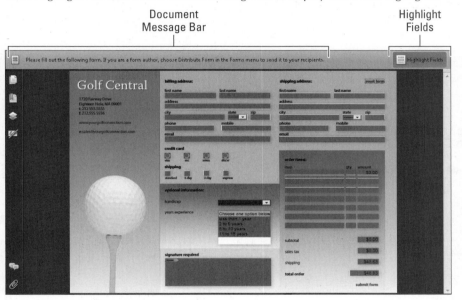

If you don't see the Document message bar, you need to adjust a preference setting. Press Ctrl/⌘+K to open the Preferences dialog box. Click Forms in the left pane and remove the check mark where you see Always hide forms document message bar. Remove the Always hide forms document message bar check box as shown in Figure 34.6 to display the message mar in the Document pane.

FIGURE 34.6

Remove the Always hide forms document message bar check box to display the message bar in the Document pane.

Using Auto-Complete features

While filling in a form, you can enable Acrobat to record common responses you supply in form fields. After recording responses, each time you return to similar fields, the fields are automatically filled in or a list is offered to you for selecting an option for auto-completing fields.

To turn the recording mechanism on, you need to address the Forms preference settings. Open the Preferences dialog box by pressing Ctrl/⌘+K and select Forms in the left pane. In the right-hand pane, open the pull-down menu under the Auto-Complete section of the Forms preferences. You can make menu choices from Off, Basic, and Advanced, as shown in Figure 34.7. Selecting Off turns the Auto-Complete feature off. Selecting Basic stores information entered in fields and uses the entries to make relevant suggestions. Select Advanced from the pull-down menu to receive suggestions from the stored list as you tab into a field. If a probability matches the list, using the Advanced option automatically fills in the field when you tab into it.

FIGURE 34.7

Click on Forms in the Preferences dialog box and select Basic or Advanced from the Auto-Complete pull-down menu to use the auto-completion feature.

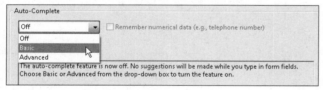

By default, numeric data are eliminated from the data stored for the suggestions. If you want to include numeric data for telephone numbers, addresses, and the like, check the Remember numerical data check box.

The list grows as you complete forms when either the Basic or Advanced choice is enabled in the pull-down menu. You can examine the list of stored entries by clicking the Edit Entry List button; the Auto-Complete Entry List dialog box opens as shown in Figure 34.8. To remove an item from the list, select it and click the Remove button. To remove all entries, click the Remove All button.

In order to record entries, you need to first make the selection for using either the Basic or Advanced Auto-Complete feature. To have suggestions for entries submitted as you type in fields, one of the two menu options needs to be enabled. When you select Off in the pull-down menu, both recording entered data and offering suggestions is turned off.

After selecting either Basic or Advanced in the Forms preferences and editing entries, fill out a form. If you recorded data after filling out one form, the next time you fill out another form you'll see suggestions, as shown in Figure 34.9. The cursor appears just below City and the suggestion (Fairways) is derived from recorded data supplied on another form.

FIGURE 34.8

To remove entries from your suggestion list, click the Edit Entry List button in the Forms preferences. Select items in the Auto-Complete Entry List and click the Remove button.

FIGURE 34.9

Enter a field and a data suggestion(s) appears in a pull-down menu.

How good is the Auto-Compete feature in Acrobat? When the feature was first introduced several generations ago, it was pretty clumsy. There wasn't much sophistication in controlling what data were recorded and what data were suggested when filling in a form. After several Acrobat revisions, there remain no changes in the Auto-Fill feature. It's still quite clumsy, and you'll find sometimes it may work well for you and in other cases, you'll find turning off the Auto-Fill option less distractive when completing a form.

Working in the Form Editing Environment

Up to this point I've covered filling in PDF forms as you might do in Adobe Reader or Adobe Acrobat. Let's shift gears now and take a look at how we create a PDF form in Acrobat — remember, the options listed here are available to you in all the Acrobat commercial products including Acrobat Standard (Windows), Acrobat Pro (Windows and Macintosh), and Acrobat Pro Extended (Windows).

If you're an Acrobat Standard user, there are no limitations you find when authoring forms in Standard. All the tools and features are identical in Acrobat Standard as they are in the Acrobat Pro products.

NEW FEATURE   **In Acrobat 8 and versions dating back to Acrobat 3, you used form tools in the Viewer mode to populate a form. Beginning in Acrobat 8, you were able to use a menu command to automatically populate a form with field objects. You still have the Form Field Recognition command in Acrobat 9 that instructs Acrobat to search through a form and automatically add field objects, but authoring a form begins in the new user interface called Form Editing Mode.**

To enter Form Editing Mode, you begin by selecting Forms ⇨ Start Form Wizard. This menu command is available to you even when you don't have a document open in the Document pane. If a document is open in the Document pane, you can also choose Forms ⇨ Add or Edit Fields. Choosing either command opens a PDF file in Form Editing Mode.

Starting the Form Wizard

When you choose Forms ⇨ Start Form Wizard, the Create or Edit Form Wizard opens in Acrobat. Again, you can start the wizard with or without a file open in the Document pane. Figure 34.10 shows the wizard as it appears on Windows (left) and the Macintosh (right).

FIGURE 34.10

The Create or Edit Form Wizard provides different options for Windows and Mac users.

On Windows you find three options in the wizard for creating a PDF form. On the Macintosh, you find two options. Your options include:

- **An existing electronic document (Windows)/Start with a PDF document (Macintosh).** On Windows, you can begin with a native MS Office file, a PDF, or other file format that can be converted to PDF consistent with your viewer's support for converting documents to

PDF via the File ➪ Create PDF ➪ From File command. Acrobat performs three functions when you choose a file format other than PDF. Your native file is first converted to PDF, and Acrobat's auto field detection operation is invoked where Acrobat automatically recognizes fields on the form, and the form opens in Form Editing Mode.

On the Macintosh, you don't have options for converting MS Office applications and several other file formats. You do have a choice for converting InDesign files to PDF directly from within Acrobat. When you convert a PDF to a fillable form, Acrobat does two things. Acrobat runs auto field detection and automatically populates the form and the form opens in Form Editing Mode.

■ **A paper form (Windows/Macintosh).** Choosing this option performs several steps. Acrobat Scan is chosen where you can scan a paper document, the Recognize Text Using OCR command is invoked where the scan is converted to rich text, auto field detection is invoked, and the form opens in Form Editing Mode.

CROSS-REF For more information on using Acrobat Scan and the Recognize Text Using OCR command, see Chapter 17.

■ **No existing form (Windows only).** This choice opens Adobe LiveCycle Designer. Since Designer is available on Windows only, the choice is not available on the Macintosh.

CROSS-REF For more information on using Adobe LiveCycle Designer, see Chapter 33.

Adding or editing fields

Your second choice for entering Form Editing Mode is to use Forms ➪ Add or Edit Fields. This option is only available when you have a PDF file open in the Document pane. You can open a PDF file without any fields, choose the Add or Edit Fields command and Acrobat immediately assesses the document. If no form fields exist on the document, a dialog box opens asking you if you want Acrobat to detect form fields for you. If you click Yes in the dialog box, auto field detection populates the form. The form then opens in Form Editing Mode. If you click No in the dialog box, the form opens in Form Editing Mode where you can manually edit the form by drawing field objects on the page.

Changing modes

When you choose either the Start Form Wizard command or the Add or Edit Fields command from the Forms menu, you eventually end up in the Form Editing Mode. As you can see in Figure 34.11 this mode is a completely different view as you have in Acrobat in what I refer to as the Viewer mode. In this viewer interface you find several options via buttons and menus that include:

The Form Editing Mode displays a completely different interface than Acrobat's standard Viewer mode.

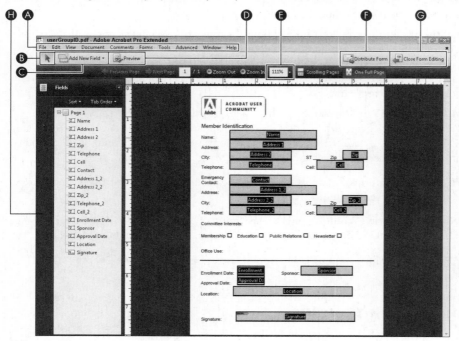

A. **Menu bar.** The same menu items are listed in the menu bar as you find in the Viewer mode. However, very few menu items can be selected when in Form Editing Mode.

B. **Select Object Tool.** The Select Object tool is the default tool used in the Form Editing Mode. Other than the tools you select from the Add New Field menu, there is no access to any other tool while you remain in Form Editing Mode.

C. **Add New Field.** The pull-down menu offers you all the form tools that were previously available in earlier Acrobat toolbars. There is no separate toolbar for form tools in Acrobat 9. The only way to manually add a field is to enter the Form Editing Mode and choose a tool from this menu or expand the toolbar in the Form Editing Mode Toolbar Well.

D. **Preview.** Click Preview and your form is shown as a recipient will see your form. In Preview you can add data to form fields, check tab order, calculations, and other items to verify the form field objects behave as you designed them. You still remain in Form Editing Mode when you choose this option, but the form changes from an editing view to a recipient view.

E. **Page View Tools.** Tools are available for changing zoom views and scrolling pages while you remain in Form Editing Mode. Note that keyboard shortcuts for zooming in and out of a page do not work while in Form Editing Mode.

F. **Distribute Form.** This button was positioned on the Form toolbar in Acrobat 8. You use this option for distributing a form to selected recipients.

G. **Close Form Editing.** Click this button to bail out of Form Editing Mode and return to Viewer mode. The only way to return to Form Editing Mode is to choose Forms ➪ Add or Edit Fields.

H. **Fields panel.** The Form Editing Mode is the only place you'll find the Fields panel. You cannot access the panel in Viewer mode by opening the View ➪ Navigation Panels menu command. The Fields panel doesn't appear as a choice in the submenu.

CAUTION Be aware that you toggle views between Form Editing Mode and Viewer mode by clicking buttons or accessing menu commands. If you need to return to the Form Editing Mode from the Viewer mode, you need to choose Forms ➪ Add or Edit Fields. Acrobat doesn't provide another menu command or a button to enter the mode from Viewer mode. When you want to return to the Viewer mode and access other menu commands or use other Acrobat tools, you must exit the Form Editing Mode by clicking the Close Form Editing button.

Editing according to mode

One thing to keep in mind is that Form Editing Mode is the place you want to use for applying fields. Most of the other kinds of editing you do with form fields can be handled in the Viewer mode. For example, if you create a button field and use the button for a navigational link, you would first enter Form Editing Mode and create your button. Once the button is created, you could exit Form Editing Mode and add the link options such as opening a page in another document, opening a file, linking to a view, and so on. Although some of these actions can be assigned while in Form Editing Mode, some are not. Therefore you'll frequently find adding actions and JavaScripts much easier while in the Viewer mode.

Table 34.1 shows a list of the kinds of edits you can make respective to Form Editing and Viewer modes.

TABLE 34.1

Form Editing According to Mode

Editing task	Viewer mode	Form Editing Mode
Access form tools		X
Copy/paste fields	X	X
Align/size/distribute/delete fields	X	X
Place multiple fields	X	X
Assign actions to fields	X	X
Distribute form	X	X

continued

TABLE 34.1   *(continued)*

Editing task	Viewer mode	Form Editing Mode
Compile form data	X	
Show tab numbers		X
Import/export form data	X	
Merge data into spreadsheets	X	
Track forms	X	X
Clear form data (menu command)	X	X
JavaScripts (Debugger, Edit All, Document, Set Document Actions)	X	X
Highlight fields	X	X
Page templates	X	

Creating a PDF Form

You have three means for creating an AcroForm — that is, a form created in Acrobat. You can start with a form design where fields are clearly identified with design elements such as lines and boxes, you can scan a paper form, and you can add form field objects from scratch using the form tools. For the first two options, you let Acrobat automatically add field objects through auto detecting fields that is invoked when you enter Form Editing Mode. Using the third option assumes Acrobat cannot detect any fields on a form design and you need to manually add all the field objects.

Using auto field detection

In Acrobat 8 you needed to open the Forms menu and choose the Run Form Field Recognition menu command to let Acrobat automatically populate a form. In Acrobat 9, the command is automatic when you enter the Form Editing Mode. You can choose to automatically run the command or bypass it if you want to manually add field objects.

You also have a choice for how you want to open your form design. If you have an original design in a program like MS Word on Windows, you can choose to open the original Word document in Acrobat. Acrobat will convert your Word document to a PDF file, open the Form Editing Mode, and use the Form Field Recognition action. It's all accomplished in one step, making conversion of files like MS Word, Adobe InDesign, and a host of other file formats to PDF forms a super-easy task.

Let's take a minute to see how easy it is to convert a Microsoft Office document to a PDF form by following these steps:

Steps: Converting a document to a PDF form

1. **Start the Form Wizard.** Choose Forms ⇨ Start Form Wizard to open the Create or Edit Form wizard shown earlier in Figure 34.10. Using this command presumes you have a form design saved from a Microsoft Office application or other file format compatible with creating a PDF from within Acrobat (Windows).

   If you're a Mac user, you need to begin with a PDF document. If you have an Office file, convert the file to PDF before using the Form Wizard.

2. **Select the file to convert.** In the Create or Edit Form wizard click the Next button and click Browse to locate a file. Locate a file and click Next. Acrobat will convert the file, open the document in Form Editing Mode, and use auto field detection.

   Mac users can select a PDF document in the Create or Edit Form wizard and the PDF document opens in Form Editing Mode and auto field detection is automatically invoked.

3. **Review the Welcome to Form Editing Mode welcome dialog box.** When you enter Form Editing Mode and Acrobat automatically detects field objects, a welcome dialog box opens as shown in Figure 34.12. This dialog box offers some information about creating form field objects in Form Editing Mode. Look over the information and click OK. After you become familiar with creating forms in Acrobat, you can click the Don't show again check box to prevent the dialog box from opening in future form-editing sessions.

FIGURE 34.12

Look over the information in the Welcome to Form Editing dialog box and click OK.

4. **Review the form.** After auto detecting fields on your form, you should always look over the form to be certain all fields were properly added. Although auto detection does a great job in adding fields to a form, it's not perfect and you can often find a little polish is needed to finalize the form. In my example, I have a few problems on my form.

Two extra fields were added to the form where form field objects shouldn't appear as shown in Figure 34.13. These fields need to be deleted. The first row of boxes is check box fields that should be radio buttons designed as mutually exclusive fields. As one button is checked, the others should remain unchecked. The second row of fields is radio buttons, but they are not designed as mutually exclusive fields.

FIGURE 34.13

Examine the form.

Radio buttons need reworking   Extra fields

5. **Delete unnecessary fields.** Locate any fields that were created and not needed on your form. Click a field and press the Del or Backspace key to remove a field object. If you intend to redesign radio buttons or check boxes, delete all the buttons/check boxes in a row by dragging through the objects and pressing the Del or Backspace key.

6. **Add radio button fields.** Open the Add New Field pull-down menu and select the Radio Button tool. Move the tool to the location on the form where you want to add a radio button and click the mouse to drop the field on the page.

7. **Name the field and set the button value.** A mini properties box opens when you add a field to a page. You can type a name for the field and set a button value when adding radio buttons to a form. In Figure 34.14 I name my new radio button field seminarDate and I set the button value to May 1.

FIGURE 34.14

Name the field and add a button value.

8. **Add a new field.** Click Add another button to group and the cursor changes to a crosshair. Click or click+drag to place another button field on the page. By default, your field name remains the same. Just type another Button Value for the field. By adding buttons (or check boxes) with the same name and changing the values, you create a mutually exclusive set of radio buttons (or check boxes).

9. **Preview the form.** Click Preview and add data to all your field objects. Be certain the fields are designed properly and the data you add to the form conforms properly to your form design.

10. **Save the form.** Choose File ➪ Save As and rewrite the file. If you save periodically, rewriting the file reduces the final file size.

TIP While working on a form you may need to zoom in and scroll the screen to display hidden areas of your form. While in Form Editing Mode you don't have a Hand tool to scroll the window. To gain temporary access to the Hand tool, press the Spacebar and drag the screen to display hidden areas.

TIP You may notice that Acrobat successfully creates check boxes and radio buttons on some forms you open in Form Editing Mode, and none of these kinds of fields are created on other forms. The reason is easily explained. If you use a text character in an authoring program such as a Wingding font to create a box, Acrobat interprets the character as text and won't create a radio button or check box. If you draw a rectangle or square using a drawing tool, Acrobat always creates a radio button or check box. Be certain to avoid using fonts where you want these field types to appear on a form.

Preparing Files for Auto Field Detection

Acrobat's auto field detection does a very good job of recognizing form fields on simple forms. However, when forms become more complex and when you create forms with graphics, gradients, and complex design elements, auto field detection falls apart and won't create fields on most graphically intense form designs. For example, take a look at the figure below. When I enter Form Editing Mode and Form Field Recognition is run, no fields are recognized on the form.

If you use programs like Adobe Illustrator or Adobe InDesign to create forms with complex graphic elements, you can prepare your files for using auto field detection by adding an extra layer that you use just for the detecting fields. Using programs like Illustrator or InDesign provide you the benefit for using layers in your design. You can easily create a background with all the graphic elements, a text layer containing all the text in the form, a layer for fields used in the final design, and a separate layer for temporary fields designed for auto detecting fields in Acrobat. An example of such a form I created in Adobe Illustrator is shown below.

If you create a similar form in a program like Adobe Illustrator or Adobe InDesign, save your file to PDF as a PDF version 1.5 or greater document (Acrobat 6 and above compatibility) and check options for creating Adobe PDF Layers. You must save the file that appears with Layers in Acrobat. (See Chapter 24 for more on PDFs and layers.) In Acrobat you can view just the Text and Temp Fields layers, all layers, or any combination of layers. Acrobat won't complain and the auto field detection creates form fields from the Temp Fields layer whether it is visible or not.

You may need to add a little polish on the form for sizing some field boxes, adding/deleting some fields, and adding the radio button and check box fields, but the little time it takes to create a temporary layer in an authoring application is a fraction of the time you would need to spend in Acrobat to manually create all the text fields. By using an authoring application supporting layers, you can easily create a PDF file that is Form Field Recognition–friendly. Planning ahead when designing forms in authoring programs can save you much time when using the auto field detection.

To finish up a form design in Acrobat, you can flatten the layers. Be certain to turn off all layers you want discarded, and when you select Flatten Layers from the Layers panel Options menu the hidden layers are discarded and the PDF is flattened. All field objects remain undisturbed regardless of what layer views you have on or off.

Scanning paper forms

Converting paper forms to electronic forms is performed by first using Acrobat Scan to scan a document into a PDF file. When you open the Create or Edit Form wizard and click the A paper form radio button and then click Next, the Acrobat Scan dialog box opens as shown in Figure 34.15.

FIGURE 34.15

Choose A paper form option in the Create or Edit Form wizard and the Acrobat Scan dialog box opens.

The first step in converting a paper document is to scan it using Acrobat Scan. The choices you have for scanning from within Acrobat via Acrobat Scan are all covered in Chapter 17. Look over that chapter if you want more information on scanning in Acrobat.

If you do use Acrobat Scan to convert a paper form to PDF, Acrobat automatically runs the internal OCR feature and converts the scan to rich text. From there, the file opens in Form Editing Mode and fields are automatically added via auto field detection.

You have the same issues to deal with converting a paper form to PDF as you do when converting a file to PDF in regard to the field objects. Look over the form while in Form Editing Mode and delete any unwanted fields. Be sure to double-check the form to see if all fields have been added, and check the radio buttons and check boxes for mutually exclusive fields. Like other forms you create in Acrobat, it's a good idea to check the fields in Preview mode to be certain all fields are formatted properly.

Manually creating field objects

Forms contain different types of data fields that hold data, act as buttons that invoke actions, and call scripts to execute a series of actions. Form fields can assume different appearances as well as possess the capability to include graphic icons and images to represent hot links that invoke actions. Acrobat forms are more than a static data filing system — they can be as vivid and dynamic as your imagination.

In Acrobat, the form data fields are created by making selections from the Add New Field pull-down menu in Form Editing Mode. Making a menu choice loads the cursor with a tool you use to either click on the form where a field is to be placed at a default size or click and drag the cursor to create a custom size.

For an overview of the field types, look over the following list:

- **Button.** A button is usually used to invoke an action or hyperlink. A button face can be text or a graphic element created in another program that you could apply as an appearance to the button. You can also use different appearance settings in the button properties for adding stroke and fill colors. Buttons are also used to import images.

- **Check Box.** Check boxes typically appear in groups to offer the user a selection of choices. Yes and no items or a group of check boxes might be created for multiple-choice selections.

- **Combo Box.** When you view an Acrobat form, you may see a down-pointing arrow similar to the arrows appearing in panel menus. Such an arrow in a PDF form indicates the presence of a combo box. When you click the arrow, a pull-down menu opens with a list of choices. Users are limited to selecting a single choice from combo boxes. Additionally, if designed as such, users can input their own choices.

- **List Box.** A list box displays a box with scroll bars, much like windows you see in application software documents. As you scroll through a list box, you make a choice of one or more of the alternatives available by selecting items in the list.

- **Radio Button.** Radio buttons perform the same function in PDF forms as radio buttons do in dialog boxes. Usually you have two or more choices for a category. Forms are usually designed with radio buttons offering mutually exclusive choices so that when one radio button in a group is turned on, the other buttons in the group are turned off.

- **Text Field.** Text fields are boxes in which the end user types text to fill out the form. Text fields can contain alphabetical characters, numbers, or a combination of both.

- **Digital Signature.** Digital signatures can be applied to fields, PDF pages, and PDF documents. A digital signature can be used to lock out fields on a form.

- **Barcode.** The Barcode tool is not a completely new feature in Acrobat 8. Acrobat 7 supported a plug-in to create 2D and 3D barcodes that was shipped long after the initial release of Acrobat 7.0. Now with Acrobat 8.0, you get the Barcode tool appearing in the Forms toolbar. This tool provides you options for adding barcodes to a PDF form.

All these form field types and tools are available to you in Form Editing Mode from the Add New Field pull-down menu. In almost all editing sessions you'll find a need to manually add a field to a form. If using Form Field Recognition, you may add only a few form objects. If you manually create fields on a form, you'll find frequent uses for all the form tools you select from the Add New Field menu.

Assigning Form Field Properties

Field Properties provide you a number of options for setting field attributes for all the form field types. There are a number of common properties that all fields share such as field names, appearances, and actions choices, and there are a number of properties that are unique among the various field types.

In Acrobat 9 you have two different properties environments. When in Form Editing Mode you add a new field to a document, an abbreviated properties wizard helps you identify essential properties for new fields added to a form. For all field types other than radio buttons, your properties choices are limited to typing a name for the new field. With radio buttons you have an additional choice for adding fields to a group.

When in Form Editing Mode or Viewer mode, you can open a context menu on a field and choose Properties. This choice provides you with a much more expanded version of properties choices. In the Properties dialog box, you choose options from several different panes. Depending on the field type you create, the panes in the Properties dialog box vary for different field types. Some field properties are common among several fields, while other properties are unique to each field type.

To open the Properties dialog box, click a field in Form Editing Mode or use the Select Object tool in Viewer mode and click a field. Open a context menu and choose Properties. If opening the Properties on a text field, the Text Field Properties dialog box opens, as shown in Figure 34.16.

TIP When creating fields in Form Editing Mode, click Show All Properties in the abbreviated properties window to open the expanded properties dialog box.

FIGURE 34.16

When you open the Properties dialog box on a text field, the General field properties appear as the default.

General properties

The General properties tab is the default tab where general properties are assigned. These properties are common to all field types. The properties include:

- **Name.** By default, Acrobat adds a name in the Name field. As a matter of practice you should type a descriptive name in the Name text box. Don't use names with spaces, and try to use parent/child names for fields in common groups. A parent/child name might appear as item.1, item.2, item.3 and so on; or you might have client.first, client.last, client.address, and so on.

- **Tooltip.** Type a name and when the cursor is placed over the field in Preview mode, the text appears as a tooltip below the Hand tool cursor.

- **Form Field.** From the pull-down menu, make choices for visibility and printing. By default, the field is visible and prints when the file is printed.

- **Orientation.** A field and a field's contents can be rotated in 90-degree rotations. By default, fields are at a 0 (zero)-degree rotation. Select from 90, 180, and 270 to rotate fields in fixed rotations.

- **Read Only.** When a field is marked as Read Only, the field is not editable. The user is locked out of the field. A Read Only field might be something you use to show fixed price costs where you don't want users changing a fixed purchase price on an order form. Another example is a value that is pre-populated from a database or with fields that show results of other calculated data.

- **Required.** If a field needs to be filled in before the data is submitted, select the Required box.

■ **Locked.** Locking a field prevents the field from being moved. You can still type data in the field or make a choice from options for other fields. This item is used to fix fields in position as you edit a form.

Appearance properties

The Appearance tab relates to form field appearances. The rectangles you draw can be assigned border colors and content fills. The text added to a field box or default text you use for a field can be assigned different fonts, font sizes, and font colors. These options exist in the Appearance properties for all field types except barcode fields (barcode fields don't have an Appearance tab). Figure 34.17 shows the Appearance properties for a selected text field.

FIGURE 34.17

Click the Appearance tab for any field properties and make choices for the appearance of fields and text.

The Appearance options include the following:

■ **Border Color.** The keyline created for a field is made visible with a rectangular border assigned by clicking the Border Color swatch and choosing a color.

■ **Background Color.** The field box can be assigned a background color. If you want the field box displayed in a color, enable this option, click the color swatch next to it, and choose a color the same way you do for the borders. When the check box is disabled, the background appears transparent.

■ **Line Thickness.** Options are the same as those available for link rectangles. Select the pull-down menu and choose from Thin, Medium, or Thick. The pull-down menu is grayed out unless you first select a Border Color.

- **Line Style.** You can choose from five style types from the pull-down menu. The Solid option shows the border as a keyline at the width specified in the Width setting. Dashed shows a dashed line; Beveled appears as a box with a beveled edge; Inset makes the field look recessed; and Underline eliminates the keyline and shows an underline for the text across the width of the field box. See Figure 34.18 for an example of these style types.

- **Font Size.** Depending on the size of the form fields you create, you may have a need to choose a different point size for the text. The default is Auto, which automatically adjusts point sizes according to the height of the field box. Choices are available for manually setting the point size for text ranges between 2 and 300 points.

FIGURE 34.18

Five choices for a border style are available in the Appearance tab when selecting from the Line Style pull-down menu.

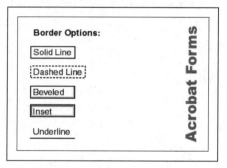

- **Text Color.** If you identify a color for text by selecting the swatch adjacent to Text Color, the field contents the end user supplies change to the selected color.

- **Font.** From the pull-down menu, select a font for the field data. All the fonts installed in your system are accessible from the pull-down menu. When designing forms for screen displays, try to use sans serif fonts for better screen views.

The Appearance settings are identical for all field types except Digital Signature fields, Radio Button fields, Check Box fields, and Barcode fields. The Radio Button and Check Box fields use fixed fonts for displaying characters in the field box. You choose what characters to use in the Options tab. When creating Radio Button and Check Box fields, you don't have a choice for Font in the Appearance properties. By default, the Adobe Pi font is used.

Options properties

The Options tab provides selections for specific attributes according to the type of fields you add to a page. Options are available for all fields except the Digital Signatures field. Options tab attributes for the other six field types include options for text, radio buttons, combo and list boxes, and buttons.

Text options

When you use the Text Field tool to create a field and you click on the Options tab, the Properties window appears, as shown in Figure 34.19.

FIGURE 34.19

FIGURE 34.19

The Options settings in the Text Field Properties dialog box

Each of the following attribute settings is optional when creating text fields:

- **Alignment.** The Alignment pull-down menu has two functions. First, any text entered in the Default field is aligned according to the option you specify from the pull-down menu choices. Alignment choices include Left, Center, and Right. Second, regardless of whether text is used in the Default field, when the end user fills out the form the cursor is positioned at the alignment selected from the pull-down menu choices. Therefore, if you select Center from the Alignment options, the text entered when filling out the form is centered within the field box.

- **Default Value.** The Default Value field can be left blank, or you can enter text that appears in the field when viewing the form. The Default item has nothing to do with the name of the field. This option is used to provide helpful information when the user fills out the form data. If no text is entered in the Default field, when you return to the form, the field appears empty. If you enter text in the Default field, the text you enter appears inside the field box and can be deleted, edited, or replaced.

■ **Multi-line.** If your text field contains more than one line of text, select the Multi-line option. When you press the Return key after entering a line of text, the cursor jumps to the second line where additional text is added to the same field. Multi-line text fields might be used, for example, as an address field to accommodate a second address line.

■ **Scrolling long text.** If Multi-line is selected and text entries exceed the height of the field, you may want to add scroll bars to the field. Enable the check box to permit users to scroll lines of text. If the check box is disabled, users won't be able to scroll, but as text is added, automatic scrolling accommodates the amount of text typed in the field.

■ **Allow Rich Text Formatting.** When you check this box, users can style text with bold, italic, and bold italic font styles. You may want to enable the check box if you want users to emphasize a field's contents.

■ **Limit of [ ] characters.** The box for this option provides for user character limits for a given field. If you want the user to add a state value of two characters, for example, check the box and type **2** in the field box. If the user attempts to go beyond the limit, a system warning beep alerts the user that no more text can be added to the field.

■ **Password.** When this option is enabled, all the text entered in the field appears as a series of asterisks when the user fills in the form. The field is not secure in the sense that you must have a given password to complete the form; it merely protects the data entry from being seen by an onlooker.

■ **Field is used for file selection.** This option permits you to specify a file path as part of the field's value. The file is submitted along with the form data. Be certain to enable the Scrolling long text option described earlier in this list to enable this option.

■ **Check spelling.** Spell checking is available for comments and form fields. When the check box is enabled, the field is included in a spell check. This can be helpful so the spell-checker doesn't get caught up with stopping at proper names, unique identifiers, and abbreviations that may be included in those fields.

■ **Comb of [ ] characters.** When you create a text field box and enable this check box, Acrobat automatically creates a text field box with preset spacing according to the value you supply in the Characters field box. For example, if you set the value of the characters to 7, the spacing between the characters when data is added to the form spaces the characters equidistant to fit seven characters for the field size. Setting a lower value adds more space between characters, and adding higher values reduces space between characters. In Figure 34.20 you can see a comb field designed for seven characters. Be certain to disable all other check boxes. You can set the alignment of the characters by making a choice from the alignment pull-down menu, but all other check boxes need to be disabled to access the Comb of check box.

NOTE   Comb fields are limited to single characters. If you need to create comb fields where two characters are contained in each subdivision, you need to create separate field boxes for each pair of characters.

TIP   When you create a new form and use auto field detection, Acrobat can pick up comb fields and format them properly. Be certain to carefully design comb fields with hatch marks spaced the same height and distance in your authoring program and you'll find Acrobat doing a good job in formatting the fields as comb fields. If hatch mark line widths, distances, or sizes vary, Acrobat won't recognize the fields as comb fields.

FIGURE 34.20

A comb field designed for seven characters

Check box and radio button options

Check boxes and radio buttons have similar Options attribute choices. When you select either field and click on the Options tab, the settings common to both field types include:

- **Button/Check Box Style.** If a radio button is selected, the title is Button Style as shown in Figure 34.21. If the field is a check box, the title is listed as Check Box Style. From the pull-down menu, you select the style you want to use for the check mark inside the radio button or check box field.

FIGURE 34.21

You can choose various options for radio buttons and check boxes, including those for the style of the check marks or radio buttons.

■ **Button/Export Value.** When creating either a check box or radio button, use the same field name for all fields in a common group where you want one radio button/check box enabled while all the other radio buttons/check boxes are disabled. To distinguish the fields from each other, add a Button Style (radio buttons) Export Value (check boxes) that differs in each field box. You can use export values such as Yes and No or other text, or number values such as 1, 2, 3, 4, and so on.

The creation of radio buttons and check boxes on Acrobat forms has been confusing to many users, and users often inappropriately create workarounds for check boxes and radio buttons to toggle them on and off. To help eliminate confusion, notice the Options properties in Figure 34.21 include a help message informing you to name fields the same name but use different export values.

■ **Button/Check box is checked by default.** If you want a default value to be applied for either field type (for example, Yes), enter the export value and select the box to make the value the default. One distinction appears in the Options dialog box between radio buttons and check boxes. The second check box in the radio button properties is unique to radio buttons.

■ **Buttons with the same name and value are selected in unison (applies to radio buttons only).** For data export purposes, you'll want to add a different button/export value for each radio button and check box. If you don't need to export data to a database with unique export values for each radio button, you can add radio buttons to a page with the same export values and, by default, when a user clicks one radio button all other radio buttons are disabled. If you want all radio buttons to be selected when clicking one button in a group having the same name and export value, check this check box.

The Button/Check Box Style selection from the pull-down menu in both field types provides identical appearances. The styles are shown in Figure 34.22.

FIGURE 34.22

Six icon options are available for check boxes and radio buttons.

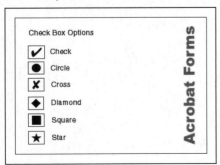

Combo box and list box options

Combo boxes enable you to create form fields with a list of selections appearing in a pull-down window. The user completing a form makes a selection from the menu items. If all items are not visible, the menu contains scroll bars made visible after selecting the down-pointing arrow to open the menu. A list box is designed as a scrollable window with an elevator bar and arrows as you see in authoring application documents, as shown in Figure 34.23.

FIGURE 34.23

View the combo box items by clicking the down arrow. After you open the menu, the scroll bars become visible. List boxes enable users to select multiple items in the scrollable window.

The two field types differ in several ways. First, combo boxes require less space for the form field. The combo box menu drops down from a narrow field height where the menu options are shown. List boxes require more height to make them functional to the point where at least two or three options are in view before the user attempts to scroll the window. Second, you can select only one menu option from a combo box. List boxes enable users to select multiple items. Finally, combo boxes can be designed for users to add text for a custom choice by editing any of the menu items. List boxes provide no option for users to type text in the field box, and the menu items are not editable.

The data exported with the file include the selected item from the combo boxes and all selected items for list boxes. The item choices and menu designs for the field types are created in the Options tab for the respective field type. Attributes for list boxes, shown in Figure 34.24, are also available for combo boxes.

FIGURE 34.24

The Options settings for list boxes have common properties also found in combo boxes.

The options include:

- **Item.** You enter the name of an entry you want to appear in the scrollable list in this field.

- **Export Value.** When the data are exported, the name you enter in this field box is the exported value. If the field is left blank, the exported value is the name used in the item description typed in the Item field. If you want different export values than the name descriptions, type a value in this field box. As an example, suppose you created a consumer satisfaction survey form. In that form, the user can choose from list items such as Very Satisfied, Satisfied, and Unsatisfied, and you've specified the export values for these items to be 1, 2, and 3, respectively. When the data are analyzed, the frequency of the three items would be tabulated and defined in a legend as 1=Very Satisfied, 2=Satisfied, and 3=Unsatisfied.

- **Add.** After you enter the Item and Export Values, click the Add button to place the item in the Item List. After adding an item, you can return to the Item field and type a new item in the field box and, in turn, a new export value.

- **Item List.** As you add items, the items appear in a scrollable list window. To edit a name in the list window, delete the item, type a new name in the Item text box, and then click the Add button to add the newly edited item back in the list.

- **Delete.** If an item has been added to the list and you want to delete it, first select the item in the list. Click the Delete button to remove it from the list.

- **Up/Down.** Items are placed in the list according to the order in which they are entered. The order displayed in the list is shown in the combo box or list box when you return to the document page. If you want to reorganize items, select the item in the list and click the Up or Down button to move one level up or down, respectively. To enable the Up and Down buttons, the Sort Items option must be disabled.

- **Sort items.** When checked, the list is alphabetically sorted in ascending order. As new items are added to the list, the new fields are dynamically sorted while the option is enabled.

- **Multiple selection (List box only).** Any number of options can be selected by using modifier keys and clicking on the list items. Use Shift+click for contiguous selections and Ctrl/⌘+click for noncontiguous selections. This option applies only to list boxes.

- **Commit selected value immediately.** The choice made in the field box is saved immediately. If the check box is disabled, the choice is saved after the user exits the field by tabbing out or clicking the mouse cursor on another field or outside the field.

With the exception of the multiple selection item, the preceding options are also available for combo boxes. In addition to these options, combo boxes offer two more items that include:

- **Allow user to enter custom text.** The items listed in the Options tab are fixed in the combo box on the Acrobat form by default. If this check box is enabled, the user can create a custom value. Acrobat makes no provision for some items to be edited, and others are locked out from editing.

- **Check spelling.** Spell-checking is performed when a user types in a custom value. As text is typed the spelling is checked.

Button options

Buttons differ from all other fields when it comes to appearance. You can create and use custom icons for button displays from PDF documents or file types compatible with Convert to PDF from File. Rather than entering data or toggling a data field, buttons typically execute an action. You might use a button to clear a form, export data, import data from a data file, or use buttons as navigation links. When you add a button to a page, the Options tab attributes change to those shown in Figure 34.25.

FIGURE 34.25

The Options tab for the Button field properties includes options for button face displays and several different mouse behaviors.

When you create a button, you make choices from the Options tab for the highlight view of the button, the behavior of the mouse cursor, and the text and icon views. The Options attributes for buttons are as follows:

- **Layout.** Several views are available for displaying a button with or without a label, which you add in the Label field described later in this list. The choices from the pull-down menu for Layout offer options for displaying a button icon with text appearing at the top, bottom, left, or right side of the icon, or over the icon. Figure 34.26 shows the different Layout options.

- **Behavior.** The Behavior options affect the appearance of the button when the button is clicked. The None option specifies no highlight when the button is clicked. Invert momentarily inverts the colors of the button when clicked. Outline displays a keyline border around the button, and Push makes the button appear to move in on Mouse Down and out on Mouse Up.

- **Icon and Label State.** Three choices are available in the list when you select Push in the Behavior pull-down menu. Up displays the highlight action when the mouse button is released. Down displays the highlight action when the mouse button is pressed. Rollover changes the icon when a second icon has been added to the rollover option. When the user moves the mouse cursor over the button without clicking, the image changes to the second icon you choose — much like a rollover effect you see on Web pages.

- **Label.** If you've selected a layout type that includes a label, type text in the field box for the label you want to use. Labels are shown when one of the options for the layout includes a label view with or without the icon.

FIGURE 34.26

The Layout options include Label only; Icon only; Icon top, label bottom; Label top, icon bottom; Icon left, label right; Label left, icon right; and Label over icon.

- **Choose Icon.** When you use an icon for a button display, click Choose Icon to open the Select Icon dialog box. In the Select Icon dialog box, use a Browse button to open a navigation dialog box where you locate a file to select for the button face. The file can be a PDF document or a file compatible with converting to PDF from within Acrobat. The size of the file can be as small as the actual icon size or a letter-size page or larger. Acrobat automatically scales the image to fit within the form field rectangle drawn with the Button tool. When you select an icon, it is displayed as a thumbnail in the Select Icon dialog box.

TIP An icon library can be easily created from drawings using a font such as Zapf Dingbats or Wingdings or patterns and drawings from an illustration program. Create or place images on several pages in a layout application. Distill the file to save out as a multiple-page PDF document. When you select an icon to use for a button face, the Select Icon dialog box enables you to scroll pages in the document. You view each icon in the Sample window as a thumbnail of the currently selected page. When the desired icon is in view, click OK. The respective page is used as the icon.

- **Clear.** You can eliminate a selected icon by clicking the Clear button. Clear eliminates the icon without affecting any text you added in the Layout field box.

- **Advanced.** Notice the Advanced button at the top of the Options tab. Clicking the Advanced button opens the Icon Placement dialog box where you select attributes related to scaling an icon. You can choose from icon scaling for Always, Never, Icon is Too Big, Icon is Too Small to fit in the form field. The Scale option offers choices between Proportional and Non-proportional scaling. Click Fit to bounds to ensure the icon placement fits to the bounds of the field rectangle. Sliders provide a visual scaling reference for positioning the icon within a field rectangle.

Barcode options

Barcode fields have unique options designed to work with barcode scanners. You have options from pull-down menus and pop-up dialog boxes opened from buttons, as shown in Figure 34.27. In order to make choices for the items in the Options pane in the Barcode Field Properties dialog box, you need to know what parameters are used by your barcode scanner, fax server, or document scanner. Setting the options requires reviewing the documentation supplied by the hardware used to scan barcodes.

FIGURE 34.27

The Options tab for barcodes requires setting options conforming to the tools you use to scan barcodes.

Barcodes need to calculate the data in the form in order to form the barcode. When you create barcode fields, the fields should be created with sample data on a form in order for the barcode to perform the necessary calculation to form the bar code image. You'll find at times that the barcode field isn't large enough to accommodate all data. If this occurs, you need to make the field larger or eliminate some data from the barcode.

CROSS-REF Managing the data is handled in the Value tab. See the section "Barcode properties" later in this chapter.

Actions properties

The Actions tab enables you to set an action for any one of the eight field types; the attribute choices are identical for all fields. The same action items available for links, bookmarks, and page actions are also available to form fields. Click the Actions tab and the pane changes, as shown in Figure 34.28.

CROSS-REF For more information on selecting action types, see Chapter 22.

From the Select Trigger pull-down menu, you make choices for different mouse behaviors that are assigned to invoke the action. From the menu options you have choices for:

- **Mouse Up.** When the user releases the mouse button, the action is invoked.
- **Mouse Down.** When the user presses the mouse button, the action is invoked.
- **Mouse Enter.** When the user moves the mouse cursor over the field, the action is invoked.
- **Mouse Exit.** When the user moves the mouse cursor away from the field, the action is invoked.
- **On Focus.** Specifies moving into the field boundaries through mouse movement or by tabbing to the field. As the cursor enters the field, the action is invoked.
- **On Blur.** Specifies moving away from the field boundaries through mouse movement or by tabbing to the field. As the cursor exits the field, the action is invoked.

Actions assigned to the cursor movements are similar to those in the context of creating links. You first select the trigger, and then select an action type from the Select Action pull-down menu. Click the Add button to add the action to the Actions list.

The action is assigned to the mouse cursor option when you click Add. The default is Mouse Up. When Mouse Up is selected, the action is invoked when the mouse button is released.

CAUTION Trigger choices other than Mouse Up may sometimes complicate filling in form fields for end users. Just about any program dealing with link buttons has adopted the Mouse Up response to invoke an action. Many users often click down, think about what they are doing, and then move the mouse away without releasing the button. This behavior enables the user to change his/her mind at the last minute. Deviating from the adopted standard might be annoying for a user.

When you click the Add button, a dialog box specific to the action type you are adding opens. The actions listed in this dialog box are the same as those in the Link Properties dialog box discussed in Chapter 22. Turn back to Chapter 22 for examples of how the following action types work. A few of the more important action types used with form fields include importing form data, resetting a form, submitting a form, and showing and hiding a field.

FIGURE 34.28

Actions are available for all field types.

Importing form data

You can export the raw data from a PDF file as a Form Data File (FDF), XFDF, XML, or TXT that can later be imported into other PDF forms. To import data, you use a menu command from the list of action types (Import Form Data) or create a JavaScript. Rather than retyping the data in each form, you can import the same field data into new forms where the field names match exactly. Therefore, if a form contains field names such as First, Last, Address, City, State, and so on, all common field names from the exported data can be imported into the current form. Acrobat ignores those field names without exact matches.

NOTE   In earlier versions of Acrobat, you also had an option to Execute a menu item that appears in the Select Action pull-down menu. From the menu items you could select Import (or Export) Data. In Acrobat 8 and 9, the Execute a menu item options have been greatly reduced and you can no longer manage data using this action type. For more information on the items available with the Execute a menu item action type, see Chapter 22.

PDF WORKFLOW   The Import Data command (Forms ⇨ Manage Form Data ⇨ Import Data) enables you to develop forms for an office environment or Web server where the same data can easily be included in several documents. When designing forms, using the same field names for all common data is essential. If you import data and some fields remain blank, recheck your field names. You can edit any part of a form design or action to correct errors.

Acrobat's Data Search

When a data file is identified for an import action, Acrobat looks to the location you specified when creating the action. Acrobat also searches other directories for the data. On the Macintosh, Acrobat looks to the Reader and Acrobat User Data directories for the data file. On Windows, Acrobat looks to the Acrobat directory, Reader directory, current directory, Windows directory, and Application Data directory. If Acrobat cannot find the data file, a dialog box opens containing a Browse button to prompt the user to locate the data file.

Resetting a form

This action is handy for forms that need to be cleared of data and resubmitted. When the Reset a form action is invoked, data fields specified for clearing data when the field was added are cleared. When you select Reset a form and click the Add button, the Reset a Form dialog box opens. You make choices in this dialog box for what fields you want to clear. Click the Select All button and all data fields are cleared when a user clicks on the button you assign with a Reset a form action. When you use this action, it's best to associate it with Mouse Up to prevent accidental cursor movements that might clear the data and require the user to begin over again. Reset a form can also be used with a Page Action command. If you want a form to be reset every time the file is opened, the latter may be a better choice than creating a button.

 When you design a form and view the form in either Form Editing or Viewer mode, select Forms ➪ Clear Form to reset a form. Using this command is handy if you have not yet added a Reset button to your form.

 For more information on using page actions, see Chapter 22.

Submitting a form

Acrobat allows Form data to be e-mailed, submitted to Acrobat.com, or submitted to Web servers. You can design forms so users of the Adobe Reader software can submit data via e-mail or to Web servers. When using the Submit a form action, you have access to options for the type of data format you want to submit.

 For more information on submitting form data, see Chapter 35.

Format properties

The General, Appearance, and Actions tabs are available for all field types. Option attributes are available for all field types except digital signatures. The options vary significantly depending on which field type is used. For a quick glance at the tab differences according to field type, take a look at Table 34.2.

TABLE 34.2

Tab Options for Field Types in the Field Properties Window

Field Type	Appearance	Options	Actions	Format	Validate	Calculate	Selection Change	Signed	Value
Button	X	X	X						
Check Box	X	X	X						
Combo Box	X	X	X	X	X	X			
List Box	X	X	X				X		
Radio Button	X	X	X						
Text	X	X	X	X	X	X			
Signature	X		X					X	
Barcode	X	X	X						X

As shown in Table 34.2, the Format, Validate, and Calculate tab options are available only for Combo box and Text field types. To access the Format tab, select either of these field types. The Format options are the same for both field types.

When you click the Format tab, you'll find a pull-down menu for selecting a format category. To define a format, open the Select format category and choose from the menu choices the format you want to assign to the Text or Combo Box field. As each item is selected, various options pertaining to the selected category appear directly below the pull-down menu. When you select Number from the menu choices, the Number Options appear as shown in Figure 34.29.

The Select format category menu options include:

- **None.** No options are available when None is selected. Select this item if no formatting is needed for the field. An example of where None applies would be a text field where you want text data such as name, address, and so on.

- **Number.** When you select Number, the Number Options choices appear below the Select format category pull-down menu. The options for displaying numeric fields include defining the number of decimal places, indicating how the digits are separated (for example, by commas or by decimal points), and specifying any currency symbols. The Negative Number Style check boxes enable you to display negative numbers with parentheses and/or red text.

- **Percentage.** The number of decimal places you want to display for percentages is available when you select Percentage from the pull-down menu. The options are listed for number of decimal places and the separator style.

- **Date.** The date choices offer different selections for month, day, year, and time formats.

FIGURE 34.29

When you choose either Combo Box or Text as the field type, you can select data format options from the Format tab.

- **Time.** If you want to eliminate the date and identify only time, the Time category enables you to do so, offering choices to express time in standard and 24-hour units and a custom setting where custom formats are user-prescribed in a field box.

- **Special.** The Special category offers formatting selections for Social Security number, Zip code, extended Zip codes, phone numbers, and an arbitrary mask. When you select Arbitrary Mask, a field box is added where you define the mask. The acceptable values for setting up an arbitrary mask include:

  - **A.** Add *A* to the Arbitrary Mask field box, and only the alphabetical characters A – Z and a – z are acceptable for user input.

  - **X.** When you add *X* to the Arbitrary Mask field box, most printable characters from an alphanumeric character set are acceptable. ANSI values between 32 – 166 and 128 – 255 are permitted. (To learn more about what ANSI character values 32 – 166 and 128 – 255 are translated to, search the Internet for ANSI character tables. You can capture Web pages and use the tables as reference guides.)

  - **O.** The letter *O* accepts all alphanumeric characters (A – Z, a – z, and 0 – 9).

■ **9.** If you want the user to be limited to filling in numbers only, enter 9 in the Arbitrary Mask field box.

■ **Custom.** Custom formatting is available by using a JavaScript. To edit the JavaScript code, click the Edit button and create a custom format script. The JavaScript Editor dialog box opens where you type the code. As an example of using a custom JavaScript, assume that you want to add leading zeros to field numbers. You might create a JavaScript with the following code:

```
event.value = "000" + event.value;
```

The preceding code adds three leading zeros to all values supplied by the end user who completes the form field. If you want to add different characters as a suffix or prefix, enter the values you want within the quotation marks. To add a suffix, use

```
event.value = event.value + "000";
```

Validate properties

Validate helps ensure proper information is added on the form. If a value must be within a certain minimum and maximum range, select the radio button for validating the data within the accepted values. (See Figure 34.30.) The field boxes are used to enter the minimum and maximum values. If the user attempts to enter a value outside the specified range, a warning dialog box opens, informing the user that the values entered on the form are unacceptable.

Selecting the Run custom validation script radio button and clicking the Edit button enables you to add a JavaScript. Scripts that you may want to include in this window would be those for validating comparative data fields. A password, for example, may need to be validated. If the response does not meet the condition, the user is denied access to supplying information in the field.

FIGURE 34.30

Validate is used with Combo Box and Text field types to ensure acceptable responses from user-supplied values.

Calculate properties

The Calculate tab (supported in Text and Combo fields) in the Field Properties window enables you to calculate two or more data fields. You can choose from preset calculation formulas or add a custom JavaScript for calculating fields, as shown in Figure 34.31.

The preset calculation formulas are limited to addition, multiplication, averaging, assessing the minimum in a range of fields, and assessing the maximum in a range of fields. For all other calculations you need to select the Simplified field notation or Custom calculation script radio button and click the Edit button. In the JavaScript Editor, you write JavaScripts to perform other calculations not available from the preset formulas. Simplified field notation is written in the JavaScript editor and follows syntax similar to writing formulas in spreadsheets. JavaScripts, also written in the JavaScript Editor, require you to know JavaScript as it is supported in Acrobat.

CROSS-REF For more information on calculating data, see Chapters 35 and 36 (on the CD-ROM).

FIGURE 34.31

The Calculate tab offers options for calculating fields for summing data, multiplying data, and finding the average, minimum, and maximum values for selected fields. In addition, you can add custom calculations by writing JavaScripts.

Selection Change properties

The Selection Change tab, shown in Figure 34.32, is available for List Box fields only. If a list box item is selected, and then a new item from the list is selected, JavaScript code can be programmed to execute an action when the change is made. As with the other dialog boxes, clicking the Edit button opens the JavaScript Editor dialog box where you create the JavaScript code.

A variety of uses exist for the Selection Change option. You might want to create a form for consumer responses for a given product — something such as an automobile. Depending on information preceding the list box selection, some options may not be available. For example, a user specifies "four-door automobile" as one of the form choices, and then from a list, that user selects "convertible." If the manufacturer does not offer a convertible for four-door automobiles, then through use of a JavaScript in the Selection Change tab, the user is informed that this selection cannot be made based on previous information supplied in the form. The displayed warning could include information on alternative selections that the user could make.

FIGURE 34.32

The Selection Change tab is available only for List Box fields. When using a Selection Change option, you'll need to program JavaScript code to reflect the action when a change in selection occurs.

Digital Signature fields properties

The Digital Signature tool enables you to create a field used for electronically signing a document with a digital signature. The Signed tab offers options for behavior with digital signatures as follows:

- **Nothing happens when signed.** As the item description suggests, the field is signed but no action takes place upon signing.

- **Mark as read-only.** When signed, the selected fields are changed to read-only fields, locking them against further edits. You can mark all fields by selecting the radio button and choosing All fields from the pull-down menu. Choose All fields except these to isolate a few fields not marked for read-only, or select Just these fields to mark a few fields for read-only.

■ **This script executes when the field is signed.** Select the radio button and click the Edit button to open the JavaScript Editor. Write a script in the JavaScript Editor that executes when the field is signed.

Digital signatures can be used to lock data fields. You can also use them to indicate approval from users or PDF authors, or you may want to display a message after a user signs a form. In Figure 34.33, a JavaScript was added to the Digital Signature Signed Properties.

The script in this example instructs a user to print the form and hand-deliver it to the accounting department. A dialog box opens after the user signs the form.

 For setting up digital signatures and finding out more information related to signing documents, see Chapter 26.

FIGURE 34.33

For custom actions when a user signs a form, use a JavaScript.

Digital Signature Properties

| General | Appearance | Actions | Signed |

○ Nothing happens when signed

The following option is compatible only with Acrobat 6.0 and later.

○ Mark as read-only: All fields ▾

Pick...

● This script executes when field is signed:

```
var msg = "Please print this form
and hand deliver to accounting
department.";

app.alert(msg);
```

Edit...

☐ Locked   Close

Barcode properties

The unique property settings in the Barcode field are located in the Value tab. Options in this tab are available only with barcode fields, as shown in Figure 34.34. You have options for Encoding from a pull-down menu offering a choice between XML and Tab Delimited data.

Click the Pick button and the Field Selection dialog box opens as shown in Figure 34.35. You use this dialog box to determine what field data are added to the barcode. Uncheck those items you don't want added, such as buttons that invoke actions, temporary calculation fields, and so on. The Include field names text box offers an option to include field names along with the data in the barcode.

FIGURE 34.34

The Value tab appears only in Barcode fields.

FIGURE 34.35

Click Pick and check the items you want to appear as data in the barcode.

An additional box appears for adding a Custom calculation script. Click the radio button and click Edit to open the JavaScript Editor.

Managing Fields

For purposes of explanation, I'll use the term *managing fields* to mean dealing with field duplication, deleting fields, and modifying field attributes. After you create a field on a PDF page, you may want to alter its size, position, or attributes. Editing form fields in Acrobat is made possible by using one of several menu commands or returning to the respective Field Properties window. This kind of editing can be performed in Form Editing Mode or Viewer mode.

Organizing fields

To edit a form field's properties, use the Select Object tool. If you work in Form Editing Mode, the Select Object tool is the tool selection by default. Unless you choose a tool from the Add New Field menu, the only tool available to you without using a key modifier is the Select Object tool. In Viewer mode, you need to click the Select Object tool to make it the active tool. In either mode, open a context menu and choose Properties to open a field's properties. Alternately, you can also double-click a field to open the properties dialog box.

When you select multiple fields and choose Properties from the context-sensitive menu, options in the General tab, the Appearance tab, and the Actions tab are available for editing. Specific options for each different field type require that you select only common field types. For example, you can edit the appearance settings for a group of fields where the field types are different. However, to edit something like radio button field options for check mark style, you need to select only radio button fields in order to gain access to the Options tab.

TIP If the fields you want to select are located next to each other or you want to select many fields, use the Select Object tool and drag a marquee through the fields to be selected. When you release the mouse button, the fields inside the marquee and any fields intersected by the marquee are selected. The marquee does not need to completely surround fields for selection — just include a part of the field box within the marquee.

Renaming fields

When you create a field in Form Editing Mode, an abbreviated properties window opens where you can name a field and set field attributes as a required field — meaning the field must be filled in before the data can be submitted. If you open a context menu in either Form Editing Mode or Viewer mode, the same properties window opens offering you the same options choices as shown in Figure 34.36.

NEW FEATURE Acrobat 9 provides you a fast and easy method for changing field names using the Rename Field menu command. To change the field name, type a new name in the Field Name text box.

FIGURE 34.36

Open a context menu and choose Rename Field to open the abbreviated properties where a field name can be changed.

Duplicating fields

You can duplicate a field by selecting it and holding down the Ctrl/Option key while clicking and dragging the field box. Fields can also be copied and pasted on a PDF page, between PDF pages, and between PDF documents. Select a field or multiple fields, and then choose Edit ➪ Copy. Move to another page or open another PDF document and choose Edit ➪ Paste. The field names and attributes are pasted together on a new page. Copying and pasting fields works well while in Form Editing or Viewer mode.

> **TIP**   **To ensure that field names are an exact match between forms, create one form with all the fields used on other forms. Copy the fields from the original form and paste the fields in other forms requiring the same fields. By pasting the fields, you ensure all field names are identical between forms and can easily swap data between them. If you have JavaScripts at the document level, use the Document ➪ Replace Pages command when you want to populate a form having a similar design to an original form.**

Moving fields

You can relocate fields on the PDF page by using the Select Object tool and clicking and dragging the field to a new location. To constrain the angle of movement, select a field with the Select Object tool, press the Shift key, and drag the field to a new location. For precise movement, use the arrow keys to move a field box left, right, up, or down. When using the arrow keys to move a field, be certain to not use the Shift key while pressing the arrow keys because doing so resizes field boxes as opposed to moving them.

Deleting fields

You delete fields from PDF documents in three ways. Select the field and press the Backspace key (Windows) or Delete key (Macintosh). You can also select the field and then choose Edit ➪ Delete, or open a context menu and choose Edit ➪ Delete. In all cases, Acrobat removes the field without warning. If you inadvertently delete a field, you can Undo the operation by choosing Edit ➪ Undo.

Aligning fields

Even when you view the grids on the PDF page, aligning fields can sometimes be challenging. Acrobat simplifies field alignment by offering menu commands for aligning the field rectangles at the left, right, top, and bottom sides, as well as for specifying horizontal and vertical alignment on the PDF page. To align fields, select two or more fields and then open a context menu and select Align ⇨ Distribute Center, as shown in Figure 34.37. The alignment options for Left, Right, Top, Bottom, Horizontally, and Vertically appear in a submenu.

FIGURE 34.37

Open a context menu using the Select Object tool on one field in a group of selected fields and choose Align from the menu.

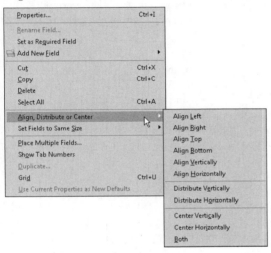

Acrobat aligns fields according to the first field selected (the anchor field appearing with a red highlight). In other words, the first field's vertical position is used to align all subsequently selected fields to the same vertical position. The same holds true for left, right, and top alignment positions. When you use the horizontal and vertical alignments, the first field selected determines the center alignment position for all subsequently selected fields. All fields are center aligned either vertically or horizontally to the anchor field.

TIP Fields are aligned to an anchor field when multiple fields are selected and you use the align, center, distribute, and size commands. The anchor field appears with a red border whereas the remaining selected field highlights are blue. If you want to change the anchor (the field to be used for alignment, sizing, and so on), click on any other field in the selected group. Unlike other multiple object selections, you don't need to use the Shift key when selecting different fields from among a group of selected fields. All fields remain selected until you click outside the field boundaries of any selected field.

You can distribute fields on a PDF page by selecting multiple fields and choosing Distribute (Vertically or Horizontally) from the same submenu. Select either Horizontally or Vertically for the distribution type. The first and last fields in the group determine the beginning and ending of the field distribution. All fields within the two extremes are distributed equidistant between the first and last fields.

 For an example of how to use the Distribute commands, see "Creating multiple copies of fields" later in this chapter.

Center alignment is another menu command available from a context menu. When you choose Center (Vertically or Horizontally) from the same submenu shown in Figure 34.37, the selected field aligns to the horizontal or vertical center of the page. Choose Both to align a field to the center of a page. If multiple fields are selected, the alignment options take into account the relative positions of the field boxes and center the selected fields as a group while preserving their relative positions.

Sizing fields

Field rectangles can be sized to a common physical size. Once again, the anchor field determines the size attributes for the remaining fields selected. To size fields, select multiple field boxes, and then open a context menu and choose Size Fields to Same Size and choose Width, Height, or Both from the submenu. To size field boxes individually in small increments, hold down the Ctrl/ Option key and move the arrow keys. The Left and Right Arrow keys size field boxes horizontally, whereas the Up and Down arrow keys size field boxes vertically.

Creating multiple copies of fields

To create a table array, select fields either in a single row or single column and open a context menu. From the menu options, select Place Multiple Fields. The Create Multiple Copies of Fields dialog box opens, as shown in Figure 34.38. In the Create Multiple Copies of Fields dialog box, enter a value in the field box for Copy selected fields down (for creating rows of fields) or Copy selected fields across (to create columns of fields). In Figure 34.38, I created three fields and wanted my duplicated fields to be added below the top row. Notice when you make selections in the Create Multiple Copies of Fields dialog box with the Preview check box enabled, you see a dynamic preview in the document for how the fields appear when duplicated.

NOTE **You can also create a table array by first creating a single field and then selecting options for both Copy Selected Fields down and Copy Selected Fields across.**

If you want to add both rows and columns, you can supply values in both field boxes for the desired number of columns and rows. The Change Width and Change Height field boxes enable you to adjust the field distance respective to each other — editing the values does not change the physical sizes of the fields. Click the Up/Down buttons for moving all fields vertically or the Left/ Right buttons to move fields horizontally. When the preview box is enabled, you'll see a preview of the duplicated rows and columns before you accept the attribute choices by clicking OK.

If, after you click OK, you need to polish the position of the new fields, you can move the top and bottom fields (for aligning single columns), then open a context menu and choose Align, Distribute, or Center ⇨ Vertically (or Horizontally) — depending on whether you're adjusting a row or column.

FIGURE 34.38

To create a table array, select a row or column of fields and open a context menu. Select Place Multiple Fields and make selections in the Create Multiple Copies of Fields dialog box for the number of rows or columns to be duplicated.

When using the Distribute command, you can distribute only single rows or columns. If you attempt to select all fields in a table and distribute several rows or columns at once, the results render an offset distribution that most likely creates an unusable alignment.

Duplicating fields

Using the Place Multiple Fields menu command from a context menu enables you to create table arrays or individual columns or rows only on a single page. If you want to duplicate fields either on a page or through a number of pages, another menu command exists for field duplication.

You can use the Duplicate command to duplicate fields; however, in most circumstances when you want to duplicate a field, press the Ctrl/Option key and click+drag a field. The field and the properties are duplicated. If you need to change the field name, open the properties dialog box and edit the Name in the General properties.

Setting attribute defaults

If you spend time formatting attributes for field appearances, options, and actions, you may want to assign a default attribute set for all subsequent fields created with the same form tool. After creating a field with the attributes you want, open a context menu and select Use Current Properties as New Defaults. The properties options used for the field selected, when you choose the menu command, become a new default for that field type. As you change form tools and create different fields, you can assign different defaults to different field types.

Setting field tab orders

You have two options for setting the tab order on a form. This is one item you should address before saving your final edited form. You should be able to press the Tab key to enter the first field on a page and tab through the remaining fields in a logical order to make it easy for the end user to fill in your form. Before deploying your form, be sure to check the tab order.

The first option you have for setting Tab order is in the Pages panel. Enter Viewer mode and open the Pages panel. Open a context menu on the page where you want to set tab order. Select Properties from the menu options and the Page Properties dialog box opens, as shown in Figure 34.39. By default the Tab Order pane opens with options for setting tab order by making radio button selections.

FIGURE 34.39

To set tab order, open the Pages panel and open a context menu on the page where you want to edit the tab order. Select Properties from the menu choices and click on Tab Order in the Page Properties dialog box.

The options for setting tab order include the following:

- **Use Row Order.** Tabs through rows from left to right. If you want to change the direction for tabbing through fields, choose File ⇨ Properties. Click on Advanced in the left pane and select Right Edge from the Binding pull-down menu. When you select Use Row Order and the document binding is set to Right Edge, the tab order moves from right to left.

- **Use Column Order.** Tabs through columns from left to right, or right to left if you change the binding as described in the preceding bullet.

- **Use Document Structure.** When selecting this option, you first need to use a PDF document with structure and tags. The tab order is determined by the structure tree created by the original authoring application when the file was exported to PDF.

- **Unspecified.** The default for all documents you created in earlier versions of Acrobat that you open in Acrobat 6 through 8 have the Unspecified option selected. Unless you physically change the tab order to one of the preceding options, the tab order remains true to the order set in Acrobat 5 or earlier.

The order in which you create fields and add them to a page is recorded. If you happen to create a row of fields, and then change your mind and want to add a new field in the middle of the row, Acrobat tabs to the last field in the row from the last field created. Changing the tab orders in the Page Properties won't help you fix the problem when the fields need to be reordered.

Fortunately, you do have more options for setting tab orders. The second method, and perhaps your best choice, is the Form Editing Mode for arranging fields in the proper tab order.

NEW FEATURE In Acrobat 9 you can drag and drop fields in the Fields panel to change the tab order. Click a field in the Fields panel in Form Editing Mode and drag the field up or down in the Fields panel to change the tab order.

If you want to see a visual order of your fields on a form, open a context menu on any field and choose Show Tab Numbers. Each field displays the tab order number in the top-left corner of the field box as shown in Figure 34.40.

FIGURE 34.40

Numbers on each field show you the current tab order.

Summary

- Acrobat forms are not scanned documents converted to PDF. They are dynamic and can include interactive elements, data fields, buttons, and JavaScripts.

- Automatic form fill-in is enabled in the Preferences dialog box. Form fields can be displayed on PDF pages with a highlight color to help identify field locations.

- Data fields are created from many different field types including text, buttons, combo boxes, list boxes, signatures, check boxes, radio buttons, and barcodes.

- You set all data field attributes in the Field Properties window. Properties can be described for fields by selecting the tabs labeled Appearance, Options, Actions, Calculations, or other tabs associated with specific field types.

- Acrobat 9 has a new Form Editing mode where you add field objects via a pull-down menu where the various form tools are selected.

- In Acrobat 9, you edit forms in Form Editing Mode and fill in or check form functionality in Preview mode.

- You can edit fields with a context-sensitive menu. Acrobat has several editing commands used for aligning fields, distributing fields, and centering fields on a PDF page.

- Field duplication is handled in a context menu. You can duplicate fields on a page to create tables with the Place Multiple Fields command, or duplicate fields across multiple pages with the Duplicate command.

- The Fields panel dynamically lists all fields created in a PDF file. The panel menus and options can be of much assistance in editing field names and locating fields. The panel is in view only in Form Editing Mode.

- A form's tab order can be easily reordered by dragging fields up and down in the Fields panel.

Chapter 35

Working with Form Data

After you get a handle on creating form fields, as covered in Chapter 34, you'll want to know some things about managing data to help economize your efforts when working with distributed forms and performing routine calculations on data fields. When forms are completed, you have the option of printing a form, compiling form data distributed via emails or your Acrobat.com account, or sending the data off to a form server product that processes the field data. In this chapter, I cover data management from calculating field data to importing, exporting, and submitting data, and compiling data using the new Acrobat.com features in Acrobat 9.

As is the case with most of the content in Chapter 33, this chapter is also targeted at users working with Adobe LiveCycle Designer as well as Acrobat. Most of what is covered in this chapter can be handled by Designer, however, if you're a Macintosh user or you want to do some editing in Acrobat, what follows is strictly related to working with data and form fields in Acrobat Standard, Acrobat Pro, and Acrobat Pro Extended. Furthermore, the content is restricted to using Acrobat tools and commands for data management. No discussion on using server products, other than a brief explanation about additional products you can acquire, is covered in this chapter.

For Windows users, if you need to with other data systems the best opportunity you have when working with form data is to create your form designs in Adobe LiveCycle Designer as explained in Chapter 33. Designer provides you with XDP, XML, and as export data format options and XDP, XML, and XFD as import format options. With Acrobat form data imports you get FDF, XFDF, XFD, TXT, and a version of XML; and export formats consisting of FDF, XFDF, XML, and TXT. Designer has much fewer import/export formats as compared to Acrobat.

Setting Up the Environment

As described in the previous chapter, creating form fields requires you to use the Form Editing Mode. The same toolbars used in Chapter 34 (Advanced Editing and the Properties Bar) are used to handle form field editing and field property changes. For setting up the Toolbar Well, refer to Chapter 34.

In addition to using form fields, having access to menu commands helps you manage data while working with forms. Nothing specific needs to be opened for menu access. As you move through this chapter, I'll cover the various menu options used for data management and the new options for using Acrobat.com introduced in Acrobat 9.

NOTE Just in case you jump to this chapter and haven't reviewed earlier chapters in this book, be aware that you have two working modes when creating/editing PDF forms. Form fields and a number of form editing tasks are handled in the new Acrobat 9 Form Editing Mode, and other edits are performed in normal Viewer mode. When I refer to Viewer mode in this chapter, be aware that this view is the standard Acrobat editing mode you're familiar with in all viewers prior to Acrobat 9.

CROSS-REF For more information on using Form Editing Mode, see Chapter 34.

Calculating Field Data

More often than not, you'll want to create forms that use some kind of calculation for data fields. Calculations might be used for summing data, calculating averages, adding complex formulas, assessing field responses, or many other conditions where results need to be placed in separate fields.

Acrobat offers you a few limited built-in functions for performing math operations. When your needs extend beyond these simple functions, you need to write JavaScripts. Some math operations, as simple as subtracting data or producing a dividend, require use of a JavaScript.

Even though I address JavaScript in some detail in the next chapter, you need to begin learning about JavaScript as it pertains to calculating data. Therefore, I'll start this chapter with some examples on using the built-in functions for calculations in Acrobat and move on, later in this section, to cover some JavaScript basics.

Formatting for calculations

Math operations can be performed on data fields without any formatting applied to either the fields to be calculated or the result field. Although doing so is not required, as a matter of practice applying formats to all fields where calculations are made and to those fields participating in the calculation result is a good idea. As you create a PDF form, you may need to use a particular format that eventually is required either in the formula or for the text appearance in the result field. Rather than going back to the fields and changing the format, you'll save time by supplying proper formats as you create fields.

When creating text fields, open the Format tab in the Text Field Properties window and select the format you want for the field. If Number is the desired format, select Number from the pull-down menu and make choices for the number of decimal places, the display for negative numbers if it applies, and the use of a currency symbol if it applies.

TIP You can open the field Properties dialog box either in Form Editing Mode or Viewer mode. In Viewer mode use the Select Object tool and double-click a field object to open the Properties dialog box.

CROSS-REF For more information on using the Text Field tool, see Chapter 34.

Many times, once you get a field formatted, you want to replicate the attributes on subsequent fields. When you set the attributes for one field, select the field with the Select Object tool and open a context menu in either Form Editing Mode or Viewer mode. Select Use Current Properties as New Defaults. As you create additional fields, the new defaults are applied to all subsequent text fields. If you create a field that needs a different format, you can change the format for the new field without affecting the defaults.

TIP Although you can't create new fields while in Viewer mode using a form tool, you can duplicate a field by clicking with the Select Object tool and pressing Ctrl/Option while dragging the field.

Using the preset calculation formulas

Preset math calculations include sum, product, average, minimum, and maximum. After formatting fields, select the field where you want the result to appear and click the Calculate tab in the Text Field Properties dialog box, as shown in Figure 35.1. For adding a column or row of data, select the *Value is the* radio button. The default is sum (+). Click the down-pointing arrow to open the pull-down menu to make formula choices from the list of other preset formulas.

NOTE Be certain numeric data is formatted using number format options in the Format tab of the Text Field Properties dialog box when creating form fields.

For summing data, leave the default as it appears and click the Pick button. The Field Selection dialog box opens, as shown in Figure 35.2. You can see the fields added to your form and grouped together. To sum a group of fields, select the check box to the left side of each field you want to add to the formula.

Click OK to leave the Field Selection dialog box and return to the Calculate properties. Click Close, and the calculation is ready. In this example, the sum of the data for the selected fields updates as the user enters data in the fields assigned to the calculation.

FIGURE 35.1

To add a preset calculation to a field, click the Calculate tab in the Text Field Properties dialog box. Select the calculation formula from the pull-down menu next to the "Value is the" radio button.

For performing other preset calculations, you follow the same steps. Select the formula you want to use from the pull-down menu options and select the check boxes for all fields you want to add to the calculation.

NOTE When using the Average formula, Acrobat averages all fields regardless of whether the fields used in the formula contain data. If you have three fields, but only two have values — for example, 3 and 3 — Acrobat returns a result of 2 ((3+3+0) ÷ 3=2). The preset formula doesn't take into consideration whether or not a field has data in it. To perform an average calculation where you want to average only fields containing a response, you need to write a JavaScript.

Summing data on hierarchical names

If you've read Chapter 34, you may remember that I mentioned advantages when using parent/child names for form fields. As you can see in Figure 35.2, all the fields in your form are listed in the Field Selection dialog box. If you want to sum data in large tables, clicking all the boxes in the Field Selection dialog box to select fields for columns or rows in a table can take some time. However, when you use hierarchical (or parent/child) names, the task is much easier.

In Figure 35.3, the Field Selection dialog box is open and a check mark appears next to the *item Total* field. Notice below this field you have a group of fields using the same parent name. The child names 0 through 6 are calculated with just the check box selection made on the parent name when summing the fields. If you write calculation scripts, your scripting is made much easier when using parent/child names.

FIGURE 35.2

Identify the fields used for the calculation in the Field Selection dialog box by selecting the check box for each field name.

FIGURE 35.3

If you select the Value is the Sum(+) of the following fields radio button and check a parent name in the Field Selection dialog box, all child field names are added in the calculation.

Imagine a table that contains 25 rows of data with a total field at the bottom of each column; it has 10 columns across the page. By using the parent name in the formula, you can easily create total fields at the bottom of the page by duplicating fields and editing the parent names in the Calculate properties as was described in Chapter 34.

Using hidden fields

Complex formulas can be written in the JavaScript Editor. However, if you aren't up to speed in JavaScript programming or you want to simplify the code you write, you may want to break down a series of calculations and place results in separate fields. For example, suppose you want to calculate the result of A - B * C. If you don't know the code to create the calculation to first subtract two values and multiply the result by another value, you can use separate fields to hold results. In this example, you need a field to hold the result of A – B. In another calculation, you take the result field containing A – B and multiply it by C.

On the PDF form, the result of A – B is not needed for user input — it's simply a container to use as part of the larger formula. To help avoid confusion, you can hide the field. When data are contained in hidden fields, the data can still be used for calculations.

To create such a field, add a text field anywhere on a page and add the calculation in the Calculate properties. In the General properties, select Hidden from the Form Field pull-down menu. If you need to edit a hidden text field, you can do so with either the Text Field tool or the Select Object tool.

When using hidden fields, you can create calculations and access the fields in the Field Selection dialog box or use parent names in the Calculate properties as described in the preceding section.

CROSS-REF For more information related to hiding fields, see Chapter 34.

Using Simplified Field Notation

In addition to performing simple calculations and writing JavaScripts, the Calculate pane also offers you an option for using simplified field notation. When you select the radio button for Simplified field notation and click Edit, the JavaScript Editor dialog box opens. In the dialog box you don't write JavaScript code. The code added here is based on principles used with spreadsheet formulas.

Simplified field notation can be used in lieu of writing JavaScripts for many different math operations. As an example, suppose you want to calculate a sales tax for a subtotal field. To calculate an 8 percent sales tax with a JavaScript you would open the JavaScript Editor and type the following code:

```
1. var f = this.getField("subtotal");
2. event.value = Math.round(f.value * 8) / 100;
```

As an alternative to using JavaScript, select the Simplified field notation radio button and click the Edit button. In the JavaScript Editor, you type the following code to produce the same sales tax calculation:

```
1. subtotal * .08
```

Notice in the JavaScript code you need to identify each field used in a calculation and assign a variable to the field name. Line 1 of the preceding JavaScript code assigns the variable f to the field subtotal. Notice that in the Simplified Field Notation script the field name does not get assigned to a variable. You simply use all field names as they appear on the form and introduce them in your formulas.

CAUTION You cannot use hierarchical names when using simplified field notation.

Using JavaScripts

You need to write JavaScripts for all calculations that cannot be made with either the preset formulas or the simplified field notation method. If you are a novice, you'll find writing simple JavaScripts to be a relatively easy task if you understand a few basic concepts in regard to performing simple calculations, as follows:

- **Variables.** Variables consist of using characters (alphabetical and numeric) to identify a field, a result, or other variable used in the formula. You can use something as simple as a character name or a long descriptive name. Variables might be f, amt, item0grandTotal, Price Amount, and so on.

- **Identifying fields.** You need to tell Acrobat in the JavaScript code that you want to assign a variable name to a field that exists on your form. The syntax for assigning a field to a variable name might look like

  ```
  var f = this.getField("item");
  ```

  In the preceding code the field name appears in quote marks and the quote marks are contained within parentheses. The variable f is assigned to the field name item on this (the current open) document.

- **Algebraic formulas.** After identifying the variables, you use standard algebraic notation. Therefore, to divide one value by another (something not available to you with the preset formulas), you might enter the code shown in Figure 35.4 in the JavaScript Editor as follows:

  ```
  1. var f = this.getField("amount");
  2. var g = this.getField("itemNumber");
  3. event.value = f.value / g.value;
  ```

  The first line assigns the variable f to the field amount. The second line of code assigns the variable g to the field itemNumber. The third line of code is the formula where f is divided by g. The result is placed in the field where you add this script in the JavaScript Editor. The trigger to put the result in the field where the calculation is coded is the event.value item.

FIGURE 35.4

Select Custom calculation script in the Calculation properties and enter the code to perform the calculation in the JavaScript Editor.

Without going into loops and more complex formulas, the beginning Acrobat forms author can do quite a bit by just following the preceding simple example. The code is all case sensitive and your field names need to be identical to the name of the field on the form as you code in the JavaScript Editor.

My good friend and colleague Thom Parker who hosts the JavaScript Corner on Acrobat Users (www.acrobatusers.com/go/javascript) fields questions almost daily from Acrobat users about JavaScript-related questions. The first question Thom asks people who contact him is, "Have you looked at the Acrobat JavaScript Scripting Reference?" This document is Thom's Bible, and even accomplished JavaScript programmers like Thom use it regularly as a reference. If you want to learn more about JavaScript, you can download the reference from www.adobe.com/devnet/acrobat/javascript.html. You can also find much help related to JavaScript on Adobe's Web site at www.adobe.com/devnet/acrobat/pdfs/js_api_reference.pdf.

Managing Form Data

Managing form data, whether it is Acrobat PDF form data or data in the Adobe LiveCycle Designer environment, essentially falls into two categories. One category is industrial-strength data management satisfying needs of business enterprises and organizations requiring sophisticated tools beyond Acrobat for collecting and routing data. The other category is local data management you handle using Acrobat and tools within the Acrobat environment for individual and small business needs.

In regard to enterprise data management solutions, you'll find a number of server products developed by Adobe Systems to satisfy the most demanding data management needs. Adobe markets products like Adobe LiveCycle Forms (formerly Adobe LiveCycle Form Server) and several other server products designed to satisfy just about any business need for managing documents and data. All of the Adobe Server products can be found at www.adobe.com/products/server or www.adobe.com/livecycle/.

Another avenue for enterprise solutions is the Adobe Partner community. Adobe works together with a great number of third-party developers to provide an array of solutions satisfying vertical market needs. You can learn more about Adobe partners and the solutions they offer at www.adobe.com/enterprise/partners. In addition to Adobe Systems and Adobe partners, several independent developers provide more server solutions and services to help you define needs and customize your data management requirements. You can find out more about some other developers by searching the Internet.

In short, when it comes to handling data for large-scale business transactions, you need to look outside Acrobat and find a provider that can deliver the solution that fits your specific needs. One thing to keep in mind is that you don't use Acrobat to take form data for invoices and sales receipts for companies such as Sprint, Boeing, Time-Warner, and similar large enterprises, and expect to write backend code to route data. You need Acrobat and some help from other products designed to work with PDF data.

As an example, take the US Internal Revenue Service. The US IRS certainly has more money and programming staff than one can imagine. However, the IRS has outsourced data routing since it began using online fillable PDF forms in the early 2000s — initially using the Adobe Form Server product and later using a third-party product. The IRS has never handled data routing for its huge number of forms with in-house programming staff.

In terms of local data management, and because this book is about Acrobat and what you can do with the product as it comes out of the box, you have many tools, commands, and Adobe services for managing form data. To begin understanding the handling of form data, let's start by looking at how to import and export PDF data in a local environment.

CROSS-REF What I can hope to do in this book is expose you to a limited view for handling data and working with PDF forms. For a more comprehensive view of creating PDF forms in Acrobat and LiveCycle Designer and managing form data, see the *PDF Forms Using Acrobat and LiveCycle Designer Bible* (Wiley Publishing, Padova/Okamoto).

Importing and exporting data

One of the great benefits of importing and exporting data is the ability to eliminate redundancy in re-creating common data used in different forms. Among the most common redundant data entries is your personal identifying information. Adding your name, address, phone number, and so on to forms is often a common practice. In an environment where you need to supply your personal identity information, you could keep an FDF (Form Data File) or XML file on your hard drive and load it into different PDF forms, thereby eliminating the need to re-key the data.

Understanding PDF Form Data Formats

FDF is a legacy format supported by earlier versions of Acrobat from 4.0 and above. This is a proprietary Adobe format and not a data file you can use with a lot of applications or that you can open for editing. XML is a newer format introduced in Acrobat 6 and available in Acrobat 7 through 9. You can open XML files in a text editor and edit the data. You can also view the data in a Web browser.

I make references to FDF/XML throughout this chapter for those who need to work with legacy files not supporting XML and for those Acrobat 6-or-greater-compatible files where XML can be used. If you have a choice when exporting or importing data in Acrobat 6–compatible files or greater, use XML as your default data file format. If you need to add JavaScript to handle the data you may want to stick with FDF as the export format.

In order to swap data between forms, you need to observe one precaution. All data fields used to import FDF/XML data must have identically matched names to the fields from which the data were exported, including case sensitivity. Therefore, the data from a field called *Name* in a PDF that exports to FDF/XML cannot be introduced in a PDF with a field called *name*. Setting up the fields is your first task, and then you can move on to data exports and imports. To clarify this concept further, I first show you how to design forms with common fields, and then export and import data.

Creating common fields

To be certain your field names match exactly between two forms, the easiest and most efficient way to duplicate the fields is to copy fields from one form and paste them into another form. In Figure 35.5, I have a form designed as an annual tournament schedule. Some of the data from my schedule card is identical to some data on a scorecard shown in Figure 35.6.

> **TIP**   You can copy/paste fields while in normal Viewer mode without having to enter Form Editing Mode. Just use the Select Object tool to select fields for copying.

After copying fields from the schedule card and pasting the matching fields into the scorecard, I know I have an exact field match, and the data exported from the populated form will find the matching fields in the form shown in Figure 35.6.

> **TIP**   If you need to copy all fields on the form, select the Select Object tool and press Ctrl+A (Windows) or ⌘+A (Macintosh) to select all fields — in either Form Editing Mode or Viewer mode. Press Ctrl+C (Windows) or ⌘+C (Macintosh) to copy all the selected fields to the Clipboard.

FIGURE 35.5

A tournament schedule card populated with data

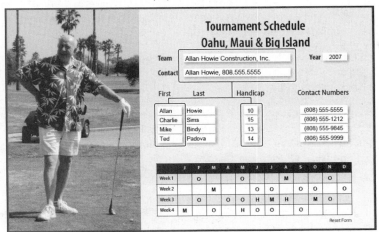

FIGURE 35.6

The scorecard form uses some of the exact same data as the schedule card.

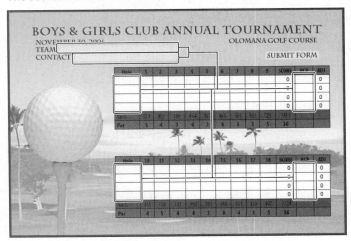

Exporting FDF/XML data

After the forms have been created with matching fields, complete a form and fill in all the data fields. If you have some fields on one form that have been excluded on a second form, Acrobat ignores any field data where it can't find a matching field name. Therefore, you need not worry about having the same number of fields on both documents.

Exporting data from a PDF file is handled with a menu command. If you want to export the data from a form, choose Forms ⇨ Manage Form Data ⇨ Export Data. A dialog box opens where you name the file and designate a destination for the FDF/XML data.

When you select the menu command, the Export Form Data As dialog box opens. By default, the name of your PDF file and a .fdf (or .xml) extension are supplied in the File name field box. This name is used as the FDF/XML filename. If you want to change the name, edit text in the File name field, but be certain to leave a .xml (or .fdf) extension after the filename. Click Save to save the file as an XML (or FDF) file.

The file you save as FDF/XML contains only the data from the form fields. Therefore, the file size is considerably smaller than the PDF that produced the data. The file can be stored on a local disk or network server, sent as an email attachment to another user, or uploaded to your Acrobat.com library. If another user has a PDF with the same field names, the data can be imported with one of the Acrobat products.

Exporting Form Data

The default export format when you choose Forms ⇨ Manage Form Data ⇨ Export Data is Acrobat FDF (*.fdf* extension files). In the Export Form Data As dialog box you can also choose to export data as Acrobat XFDF, XML, or Text formats. Depending on your uses for the data, be certain to check the export format shown in the Export Form Data As dialog box. The default choice is FDF. If you want to export and use XML data, choose XML Files (*.xml) from the Save as type (Windows) or Format (Macintosh) pull-down menu.

Something else to remember is that you can only export and import form data while in normal Viewer mode. You don't have access to these menu commands when in Form Editing Mode.

Importing FDF/XML data

As with form data exports, importing FDF/XML data in PDF forms is handled with menu commands. Choose Forms ⇨ Manage Form Data ⇨ Import Data (in Viewer mode). The Select File Containing Form Data dialog box opens where you can navigate your hard drive and find the FDF/XML file to import.

Select the FDF/XML file to be imported and click the Select button in the dialog box. When you import data from common field names, the fields are populated for all matching fields as shown in my new scorecard file after the data import in Figure 35.7. Acrobat ignores all data where no matching fields are found.

FIGURE 35.7

Only data with matching field names are imported. All other data is ignored.

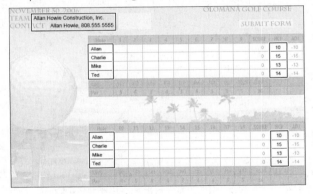

Creating spreadsheets from form data

Exporting data to spreadsheets can be handled in a few different ways. You can select from two different menu commands to export data that can be opened in a program such as Microsoft Excel, or you can aggregate form data from multiple forms into a single spreadsheet.

Exporting data to a spreadsheet

Two different menu commands enable you to export PDF data and open the exported data in a spreadsheet. You can open a PDF document and select Forms ⇨ Manage Form Data ⇨ Export Data. In the Export Form Data As dialog box, open the Save as type (Windows) pull-down menu or Format (Macintosh) pull-down menu and select Text as the file format. Click the Save button and the data can be opened in a spreadsheet program.

Using Import Buttons and Page Actions

Another method you have available for importing data is to create a button or page action and use the Import form data action type. Create a button or open the Pages panel and select Page Properties from a context menu. In the Page Properties dialog box, shown in the following figure, click the Actions tab and select the Page Open trigger (this menu choice opens by default). From the Select Action pull-down menu, choose Import form data and click Add.

The Select File Containing Form Data dialog box opens. Select the data file you want to import and click the Select button. Save your file, and when the document opens on the target page Acrobat automatically imports data from the data file. You might use this method when you prepare forms such as a purchase order form for a vendor where you want your identifying information and the vendor information imported when preparing the order form. If you use a text file containing several vendors, click the vendor you want to use to import the respective data.

You'll note that you have no option for exporting data using a button or page action. In earlier versions of Acrobat you could get around the absence of an action type for exporting data by using an Execute a menu item action type. In Acrobat 8 and 9, however, the Execute a menu item list is more limiting and you can't select a menu command from the list to export data using a button, bookmark, link, or page action.

Note that if you add the Import Form Data action to a button, link, bookmark, or page action, the only file format supported by the action type is FDF data. If you want to import other file formats such as TXT or XML, you need to write a JavaScript.

CROSS-REF   For more information on using page actions and learning more about limitations with the Execute a menu item command, see Chapter 22.

When you open the exported text data in MS Excel, the Text Import Wizard opens as shown in Figure 35.8. Step through the wizard and click Finish to open the data in a new Excel spreadsheet.

Acrobat also provides a means for aggregating data from multiple forms into an Excel spreadsheet. Select Forms ⇨ Manage Form Data ⇨ Merge Data Files into Spreadsheet. This command works when you want to export data from a single file, but the real power in using the command is when you export data from multiple files. If you have a single PDF document and you use this command, the result is similar to exporting data from the Export Data command. Using the Export Data command exports to a text file, and using the Merge Data Files into Spreadsheet command exports to a CSV comma-delimited file or XML file. The text file created from the Export command is also a delimited file. As a result, you see very little difference when either file is opened in a program such as Microsoft Excel. All the data fall into rows and columns.

FIGURE 35.8

The Text Import Wizard is launched in MS Excel when you open an exported text file from Acrobat.

Aggregating data from multiple files into a single spreadsheet

As I mentioned before, the real power in using the Merge Data Files into Spreadsheet command is when combining data from multiple PDFs into a spreadsheet. To see how this command works, follow these steps:

STEPS: Combining data from multiple PDFs into a spreadsheet file

1. **Collect some forms with different data fields.** To follow these steps, start with a form saved as different files having unique data. Save several forms to a common folder. In my example I used a simple form, as shown in Figure 35.9. Notice that the fields are highlighted so you can clearly see the form fields. I edited this form and changed the data for three additional forms and saved them all to the same folder.

 You can add files from different folders to merge the data into a spreadsheet.

FIGURE 35.9

Use the same form with different data, saving each file to a common folder.

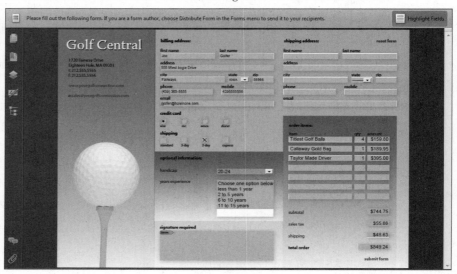

2. **Select Forms ➪ Manage Form Data ➪ Merge Data Files into Spreadsheet.** Note that you don't need a document open in the document pane. If a document is open, the merge command doesn't use the open file. The Export Data From Multiple Forms dialog box opens.

3. **Add Files.** Click Add Files and select the files you want to combine together in a single spreadsheet.

   The Select File Containing Form Data dialog box opens. Select the files you want to combine together and click Select. When you return to the Export Data From Multiple Forms dialog box, the files you selected are shown in a window as you can see in Figure 35.10.

4. **Click Export.**

5. **Name and save the file.** When you click the Export button in the Export Data From Multiple Forms dialog box, the Select Folder to Save File dialog box opens. In this dialog box you locate a target folder and type a name for your file. By default the name provided in the File name text box is *report*. Edit the name and type a descriptive name for the file you save.

6. **Click Export.**

7. **View the file.** In a very short time the Export Progress dialog box opens as shown in Figure 35.11. Click the View File Now button and Microsoft Excel is launched, displaying the merged data.

FIGURE 35.10

Selected files are shown in the Export Data From Multiple Forms dialog box.

FIGURE 35.11

Click View File Now to open the exported data in Microsoft Excel.

Aggregating FDF/XML data

When you create a Submit button, as I explain in the next section "Submitting and Receiving Form Data," Adobe Reader users can't submit a PDF document back to you unless the form is enabled with Reader usage rights. If a form is not enabled, Reader users can submit the FDF/XML data back to you (without the PDF document) and you can use the Import Data command to import the FDF/XML data into a PDF form residing on your computer.

If you send files for Reader users and the data are returned to you as FDF/XML, you can aggregate the data in a spreadsheet using the same menu commands as you do when aggregating form data derived from PDF documents. Using the Forms ⇨ Manage Form Data ⇨ Merge Data Files into Spreadsheet menu command, follow the same steps as when merging PDF forms data. When you click Add Files and open the Select File Containing Form Data dialog box, notice the formats supported in the Files of type (Windows) or Format (Macintosh) pull-down menu. You find FDF/XML included as a format as well as PDF and XFDF.

> **TIP** If you use a wizard to distribute forms, all wizards in Acrobat 9 automatically enable PDF forms with Adobe Reader usage rights. The only time you need to enable a PDF using the Advanced ⇨ Extend Features in Adobe Reader menu command is when you distribute a form manually as opposed to using a wizard.

Submitting and Receiving Form Data

We've come a long way with data exports, imports, submissions, and retrieval in Acrobat. Several generations ago, back in Acrobat 5, Adobe Reader users needed to view a PDF document inside a Web browser to submit form data. With the last few releases of Acrobat, Adobe Reader users could click a button designed for submitting data on PDF forms inside Acrobat without having to view the PDF in a Web browser. In Acrobat 8, we were introduced to form submissions from Reader users via email attachments where the Reader users could submit the entire PDF document with the form data back to the forms author. Inasmuch as the great developments in Acrobat 8 provided much easier forms distribution and data merging, we still had limitations with data retrieval on servers. Unless you are a programmer or have a friend in the IT department, setting up a server for data collection was out of the question.

> **CROSS-REF** For more information on viewing PDFs inside Web browsers as inline views, see Chapter 27.

> **NEW FEATURE** All this has changed in Acrobat 9. Now with the opportunity to manage forms on Acrobat.com many forms authors don't need to hassle with server configurations to collect and track distributed forms. You still have the option to share and collect forms via email attachments, but the great new features you find in Acrobat.com are likely to minimize the number of forms you distribute via email attachments.

> **CROSS-REF** Acrobat.com is a separate service provided by Adobe Systems. Together with Acrobat 9, you can use Acrobat.com services to submit forms and collect data that can be downloaded from recipient responses from your Acrobat.com account. To learn more about using Acrobat.com, see Chapter 29.

Creating a Submit Form button

In all Acrobat viewers 8 and below that supported PDF forms, a Submit button was added to a form when you wanted the form to be sent someplace — either back to you as an email attachment or to a server where you collected forms.

> **NEW FEATURE** In Acrobat 9 you have two different options for using a Submit Form button. The button can be constructed with a Submit Form action and appear on your form like it did with earlier Acrobat viewers, or a Submit Form button can appear in the Document Message Bar automatically when you distribute a form. If you have a form that you email to recipients, you can use a form containing a submit button you add to the form. If you use the Forms ⇨ Distribute Form command, Acrobat opens a wizard where you make choices for distributing a form and a submit form button is automatically added in the Document Message Bar.

Distributing forms can be handled in one of several ways. You can send a form via email to recipients, in which case you'll need to perform some manual tasks to prepare your form for distribution, or you can use the Distribute Form command in either normal Viewer mode or Form Editing Mode. When distributing a form, you can elect to use Acrobat.com, your own internal server, or send forms via email attachments.

If you choose to use the Distribute Form command, Acrobat takes care of some tasks automatically for you. You don't have to create a Submit Form button, and you don't have to manually enable a PDF form with Adobe Reader usage rights. Through an easy process of walking through some wizard steps, Acrobat takes care of these details for you.

You can also let Acrobat take care of automating tasks when you want forms emailed back to you. Again, you follow some steps via a wizard and submit your form via an email attachment. And again, Acrobat takes care of the Submit Form button and enabling tasks.

CROSS-REF For more information on enabling forms with Adobe Reader usage rights, see Chapter 19.

A third option is to avoid working with a wizard and manually send a form off to a recipient. You might have a form stored locally on your hard drive and occasionally send the form for a user to complete and send back to you. In this case, you're not interested in aggregating data from multiple users, but simply collecting some data related to some sort of specific instance.

If you decide to email a form without using a wizard, you need to manually address two things. First, your form needs a Submit Form button with your email address specified in the Submit Form action, and the form needs to be enabled with Adobe Reader usage rights when Adobe Reader users participate as form recipients.

When you want to distribute a form using a wizard, follow these steps:

STEPS: Distributing a Form

1. **Open a PDF form with form fields in Acrobat.** In these steps we'll set up a form for email distribution. Since we'll use a wizard to distribute the form, we don't need a button on the form to submit the form back to you.

2. **Distribute the form.** Choose Forms ➪ Distribute Form in either normal Viewer mode or Form Editing Mode. The Distribute Form wizard opens as show in Figure 35.12.

3. **Choose a collection method for acquiring the form data.** From the pull-down menu in the wizard choose the form collection method you want to use. For this example I use Manually collect responses in my email inbox as shown in Figure 35.12

4. **Click Next.** The second pane in the wizard opens as shown in Figure 35.13.

5. **Choose a method for distributing the form.** When you choose to collect data in your email inbox you have two options for distributing the form as shown in Figure 35.13. You can choose to send the form automatically to Acrobat.com (this requires you to have an MAPI compliant client email) or save a local copy and manually send the form as an email attachment later. In this example I choose Save a local copy and manually send it later.

FIGURE 35.12

Choose a collection method from the pull-down menu at the top of the Distribute Form wizard.

FIGURE 35.13

Choose a distribution method.

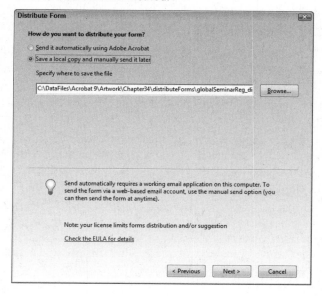

6. **Click Next.** You arrive at the last pane in the wizard. At the bottom of the wizard window a check box is checked by default as shown in Figure 35.14. If you keep the checkbox checked, email addresses of recipients are added to the Tracker to help you track the responses. If you don't want to collect the recipient email addresses uncheck the check box. Do so means the form recipient will be prompted to add your email address when the form is submitted back to you.

7. **Click Finish.** Click the Finish button in the last wizard pane and the Tracker opens in Acrobat.

FIGURE 35.14

Click Finish after completing all the steps to distribute the form.

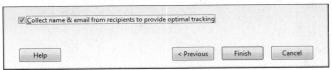

8. **Open the Original Form.** When the Tracker opens, click the blue text where you see Open Original Form as shown in Figure 35.15.

FIGURE 35.15

Click Open Original Form in the Tracker to review the form.

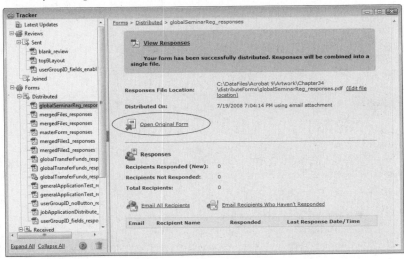

9. **Review the form.** Notice in the Document Message Bar you see the Submit Form button (see Figure 35.16) that was automatically added by Acrobat.

FIGURE 35.16

When you open the form, you find the Submit Form button in the Document Message Bar.

When the form is distributed via a wizard, the form is automatically enabled with Adobe Reader usage rights. Enabling forms via a wizard is available to users of Acrobat Standard as well as the Acrobat Pro and Pro Extended users.

CROSS-REF   For more information on enabling features and using digital signatures in Adobe Reader, see Chapters 19 and 34.

If you chose to add a submit button to a form and not use a wizard to distribute your form, you use a button action in the Actions tab for the Button Field Properties. From the Select Action pull-down menu you choose Submit a form and click the Add button. The Submit Form Selections dialog box opens where you find quite a few options for choosing what data are collected when a form is returned to you via email. Let's take a look at all the options choices you have in this dialog box.

■ **Enter a URL for this link.** If you have a data management system or a server product that routes data and manages a database, you can add a URL to the text box. This option requires you to have programming on your server that collects the data when it hits the URL specified in the text box. If you don't have server-side programming to manage the data, your only other option is to add an email address, as shown in Figure 35.13.

- **Export Format.** Along the left side of the dialog box you find several options for the type of export format users can send back to you.

  - **FDF Include.** The FDF data is sent to the server. The three options below the FDF Include item offer you choices for sending the Field data; Comments, which includes any comments created on a form; and Incremental changes to the PDF, which should be used when digital signatures have been used to save updates. Any one or all of the selections can be made for this data type.

  - **HTML.** The data is sent in HTML format as name/value pairs. Much as you might create a form on a Web page using HTML and JavaScript, the HTML option processes the same data type.

  - **XFDF Include.** The data are sent in XML format. Two options are available for sending the Field data or the Comments data or both. You cannot submit digital signatures via XFDF.

  - **PDF The complete document.** This option enables you to submit the PDF populated with the field data. This option is useful for Digital Signature workflows or for archiving the complete document. Additionally, if you use bar codes on forms, you'll want to have the complete PDF document sent back to you.

- **Field Selection.** On the right side of the dialog box are options for including all or selected field data in your submission. If fields are to be eliminated, select the Only these button and then click the Select fields button. The Field Selection dialog box opens where you select which fields to use for the data export.

- **Date Options.** Dates are converted from the format specified on the form to standard date formats when the Date Options check box is enabled.

When the user clicks a Submit button, the form data from the choices you made in the dialog box are sent to the specified URL/email address. Keep in mind that if you do not have the necessary server-side programming, nothing happens to the data and it won't be found on your server. You need intervention from the host to collect and route the data.

> **TIP** By default Acrobat doesn't submit the value of a button field, so if you have a form containing button fields and you want to export the buttons data as well as the text field data, select the Only these radio button in the Submit Form Selections dialog box. The Field Selection dialog box opens after you click the Select Fields button. In the Field Selection dialog box, select the check boxes for all fields you want to submit.

Distributing forms via email

Deploying PDF forms in Acrobat 7 and earlier was limited to emailing PDFs and using the Submit button for users to mail data back to you. You had to deal with the data on a file-by-file basis without any tools locally on your computer to merge data or display it in a single file source. What was left out of the loop was a method for aggregating data when users returned forms to you — that is, if you don't have a server to manage data.

Acrobat 8 helped bridge the gap for data collection with the introduction of PDF Packages. In Acrobat 8 you could distribute a form and collect forms that were appended to a PDF Package where the data could be exported to a CSV file and opened in Microsoft Excel. This development in Acrobat 8 was a huge step in helping forms authors collect data from forms fillers and analyze the data.

Inasmuch as we applauded Adobe for providing us with the new features in Acrobat 8, we still had one issue that remained a problem for forms authors who didn't have sophisticated IT departments to set up servers where data could be collected. All the data collection for individual users and small businesses was dependent on email exchanges.

NEW FEATURE In Acrobat 9, Adobe hasn't stepped forward in regard to data collection; rather, Adobe has leaped forward in huge bounds to help forms authors collect data. Without any need for complicated server configurations, you can now collect data on Acrobat.com, download your data for analysis, easily track forms, send reminders to users for filling out forms, and time limit your data collection.

The beauty of using a server to collect data is that you can have data collected and download the results when you have time to log on to your Acrobat.com workspace; you no longer have to depend on email collections piling up in your inbox. You can log on to Acrobat.com with a laptop while traveling, download recent responses, and keep up to date with a form collection process without having to log on to your email account.

Distributing forms in Acrobat 9 is handled in the Distribute Form wizard. When you distribute a form, you have three options in the wizard. You can collect form data on an internal server, manually collect data via email, and collect data via Acrobat.com. For data collection on your own internal server, I'll refer you to the Acrobat Help document and the Adobe Web site to browse information related to internal server configurations. For starters take a look at the Web pages found at www.adobe.com/devnet/acrobat/.

Emailing forms using Adobe Acrobat

Distributing a form using the Distribute Form wizard for manually collecting email responses in your mailbox is handled via a menu command. Choose Forms ➪ Distribute Form to open the Distribute Form dialog box shown earlier in Figure 35.12. From the pull-down menu at the top of the wizard you have a choice listed as Manually collect responses in my email inbox. I covered manually distributing forms using your email inbox to collect data earlier in this chapter in the section "Creating a Submit Form button."

You have two choices for distributing a form to manually collect data in your email inbox. You can save a file and distribute it later like I explained in the section "Creating a Submit Form button" or you can use Acrobat to send the form now. When you choose Send it automatically using Adobe Acrobat (see Figure 35.13) Acrobat opens a default email message window as shown in Figure 35.17.

FIGURE 35.17

Acrobat opens an email message window when you choose to have Acrobat email a form.

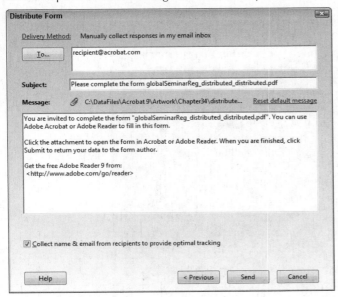

Fill in the To information and make any edits you want to make in the Subject field and the Message window. Click Send and Acrobat attaches the form to an email and sends the message and attachment.

Analyzing data

When you collect forms from recipients a special distributed responses PDF Portfolio document collects the data. For forms distributed via email attachments you double-click a file attachment and the form data are added to your response file. This file is created automatically when you distribute a form. In Acrobat you see a welcome page in the PDF Portfolio response file like the one shown in Figure 35.18.

The Welcome Page has a list of items with descriptions. When you open the response file, a special set of tools are added to the left side of the Document pane. The items tasks you can perform with data collected from forms are shown in Table 35.1.

FIGURE 35.18

As forms are collected in a PDF Portfolio response file the Welcome Page opens when you double-click a file attachment.

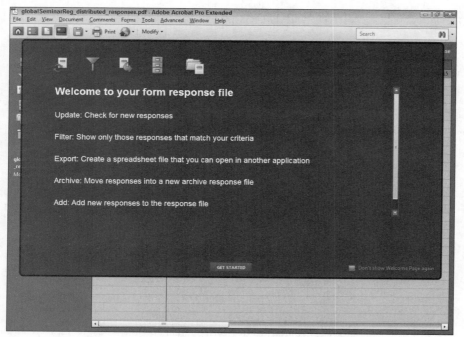

TABLE 35.1

Options Available for Data Collection and Management

Icon	Item	Description
	Update	Click Update and Acrobat checks for new updates to the response file.
	Filter	Choose Filter and a side panel opens where you can filter data on any field name on a form.
	Export	From a pull-down menu choose Sort All or Selected. If you choose Export all or Export selected, the data are exported as a CSV or XML file that can be opened in Microsoft Excel or a database.

Icon	Item	Description
	Archive	You can archive selected response data or all response data. The archive can overwrite the existing dataset file or create a new dataset file. Note: when you archive, the data is removed from your response file.
	Add	Click Add and you can add new responses to the response file.

Click the Get Started button on the Welcome Page and you see the files shown in a List View in the PDF Portfolio like you see in Figure 35.19. This view is the Home view with a special layout designed for the response file. You cannot edit the layout view in the PDF Portfolio.

FIGURE 35.19

Responses are collected in a PDF Portfolio file with a custom layout view.

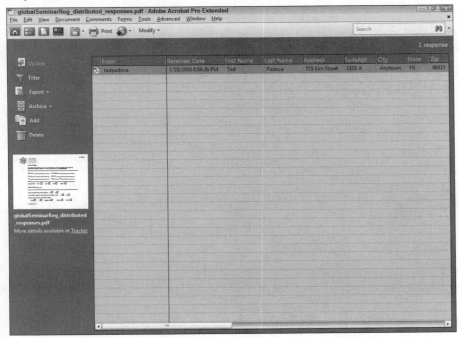

CROSS-REF For more information on PDF Portfolios and changing views, see Chapter 12.

> **TIP** When retrieving data that's added to your response file, you'll want to bypass the Welcome Page each time you open the file. On the Welcome Page, check Don't show Welcome Page again. The next time you open the response file you are taken directly to the view shown in Figure 35.19.

You also have a List View using the response file PDF Portfolio like you do with other PDF Portfolios. The List View provides you with a little more viewing area to examine the data because the tools from the left panel in Figure 35.18 are not shown in this view as you can see in Figure 35.20.

FIGURE 35.20

Click the List View tool to change to a List View.

In List view you also have a sort option. Click any column head and you'll find an up or down pointing arrow. Click again and the arrow changes direction. You can individually sort columns in either ascending or descending order.

While in the Home View you can sort data for any field contained on the form and reported in the response file. Click the Filter tool on the left side of the Home View and the Filter Settings open in the left panel as shown in Figure 35.21. The scrollable list contains all the field names on the form.

FIGURE 35.21

Click Filter to open the Filter panel.

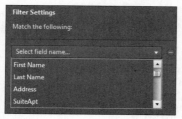

To filter data choose a field from the scrollable list. Something like State or City if such fields exist on your form. Below the item selection you have a number of choices such as *is, contains, starts with, is blank, is not blank, etc.* Choose an item to match the date that you want. If you want to sort multiple columns, click the + Add Filter button and a new set of menus is added to the panel as shown in Figure 35.22.

FIGURE 35.22

Click + Add Filter and you can add multiple match items in the Filter Settings panel.

 If you want to sort all data for a given field, use the *is not blank* choice in the Filter Settings. All the data in the response file are sorted for the field.

In the response file you can easily sort the data as you like. If you want to export the data to a database or spreadsheet, click Done when finished filtering the data and click the Export tool in the left panel. From the Export tool pull-down menu you can choose to export the data as all the filtered data or you can select rows in the data table and export selected data. The exported data is saved as a CSV file that can be opened in a spreadsheet program or various database programs.

If you receive a file that wasn't emailed back to you, for example a file that may be delivered on a flash drive or across a network, you can easily add files to the response file. Click the Add button and a dialog box opens where you can choose files to add to your document.

If you want to break down the data and create separate files based on some filtering of the data, click the Archive tool in the left panel. You can choose to archive filtered data or selected data. Choose an option from the pull-down menu and the Archive Data dialog box opens as shown in Figure 35.23. From this dialog box you can choose to create a new response file or merge data with an existing response file. Either action you take removes data from the existing file while adding the data to the target file.

FIGURE 35.23

Click the Archive tool and choose an option from the Archive pull-down menu and the Archive Data dialog box opens.

Distributing forms via Acrobat.com

We need to roll back momentarily to the Forms ➪ Distribute Form command that opens the Distribute Form wizard. When you open the wizard, instead of choosing the option for distributing forms manually, choose Automatically download & organize responses with Acrobat.com.

> **NOTE** As of this writing Acrobat.com is in public beta and may be continually changing before the service is out of beta and in final form. You may find some changes to Acrobat.com and some of the screen shots in this chapter differing from those found when Acrobat.com moves out of public beta. To stay up to date with any changes on Acrobat.com services or the appearances of the workspace, keep in touch with articles you'll find on www.acrobat.com and look for the errata page for the Acrobat 9 PDF Bible on the www.wiley.com web site.

When you choose Forms ➪ Distribute Form the Distribute Form wizard opens as shown in Figure 35.24. At first glance the Distribute Form wizard selections for using Acrobat.com appear identical as when choosing to distribute forms via email. Upon closer look, however, you see that the descriptions for handling distribution, responses, and data collection do vary some.

FIGURE 35.24

The Distribute Form wizard as it appears after choosing Automatically download & organize responses with Acrobat.com.

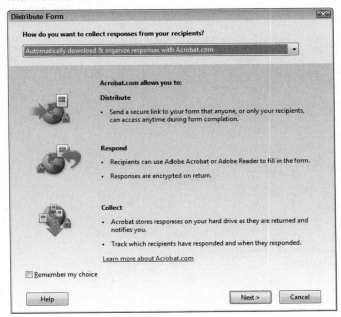

The differences between Acrobat.com and emailing forms include:

- **Distribute.** The message you send to recipients contains a secure link to your form that recipients can access. You have a choice for allowing anyone who visits your Acrobat.com library to download the form, or you can choose to restrict access to only those whom you've invited to complete the form.

- **Respond.** In addition to enabling the form the same as email distributions, responses are encrypted when returned to you.

- **Collect.** Acrobat stores responses on your hard drive as the forms are returned to you. All the forms processing actions can be monitored in the Tracker.

When you choose Automatically download & organize responses with Acrobat.com and click the Next button in the wizard the Distribute Form log on dialog box opens as shown in Figure 35.25. If you have an Adobe ID, use your log on information and click the Sign In button. If you don't have an Adobe ID, click the Create Adobe ID text you see in Figure 35.25.

FIGURE 35.25

Log on using your Adobe ID or click Create Adobe ID if you don't currently have an Adobe ID.

CROSS-REF For more information on creating an Adobe ID and setting up an account on Acrobat.com, see Chapter 29.

Once you log on to Acrobat.com the next screen you see is the Distribute Form email message window. Notice the difference in Figure 35.26 and the Distribute Form email message window shown earlier in Figure 35.17. In Figure 35.26 you see an option for Access Level. Since the file is going to be a hosted file, recipients need to download the file to fill in the form. When you submit the form you have an option to choose an Access Level. You can choose to permit anyone who visits your Acrobat.com library to download the form or limit the access to only those recipients who receive an email from you.

Fill in the To addresses for you form recipients, edit any changes you want made in the Subject and Message fields, choose an Access Level and click Send. At this point Acrobat serves as your email client. The email message and attachment don't ever see your email client. Everything is handled by Acrobat which is the reason why you had to log on in the beginning of the process. Acrobat needs a connection before the form can be sent.

NOTE If you make changes in the Message text box in the Distribute Form email message window, be certain to not disturb the URL link that appears in the message as a default. This link is needed for recipients to download your file.

FIGURE 35.26

Log on with your Adobe ID and the next screen you see is the Distribute Form email message window.

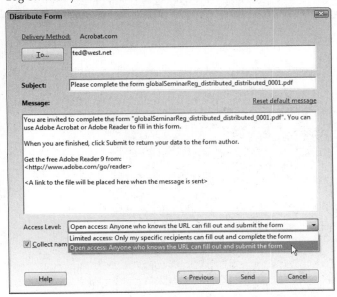

After Acrobat uploads the file, the Tracker opens as shown in Figure 35.27. Notice in the Tracker you see that you have similar information as shown in the Tracker in Figure 35.15. The Tracker shows you that the file was distributed to Acrobat.com and you see an additional item for Stop Collecting Data. When you click Stop Collecting data the form is closed so no additional data are uploaded to Acrobatc.com.

FIGURE 35.27

The Tracker opens in Acrobat immediately after a form is submitted to Acrobat.com.

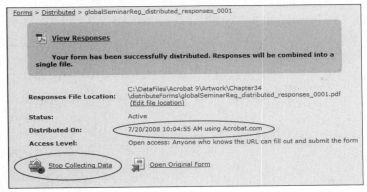

When a recipient receives an email sent by Acrobat to the recipient email address and clicks the file attachment the recipient is taken to Acrobat.com. All recipients do not need an Acrobat.com account to access your file. The Acrobat.com window opens as shown in Figure 35.38. A recipient can download the form by clicking the Download button, fill in, and submit the form.

FIGRUE 35.28

Recipients who arrive at your Acrobat.com workspace can click the Download button to download the form.

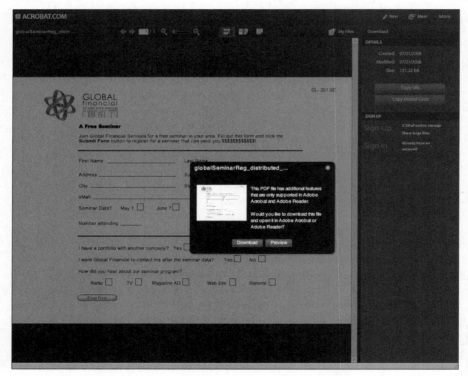

When forms are submitted to Acrobat.com you retrieve the form via the Tracker. Open the Tracker (Forms ⇨ Track Forms) and click View Responses and the data are downloaded from Acrobat.com and added to your response file. The process for analyzing the data is the same as I covered earlier in this chapter in the section "Analyzing data."

Using the Tracker

If you have several forms distributed and you're waiting on recipients to send back forms to you, things can quickly get a little disorganized and confusing. What you need is a management system to keep track of the forms currently being reviewed by recipients. In Acrobat 9 your management system is available in the Tracker that you can access in either Form Editing Mode or Viewer mode by choosing Forms ⇨ Track Forms. When you choose this command, the Tracker opens as was shown earlier in Figure 35.15.

In the Tracker, you see a list of forms you either distributed to be filled out or forms you were asked to fill out by another user as shown in Figure 35.29.

FIGURE 35.29

The left panel in the Tracker lists all forms you have distributed and received.

In the right pane you have several options for distributed forms and forms received from other PDF authors. At the top of the right pane you handle tasks related to distributed forms as shown in Figure 35.30.

FIGURE 35.30

The top right pane in the Tracker is where you manage distributed forms.

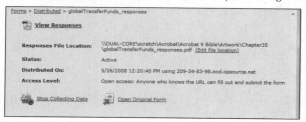

Your choices in this section of the Tracker include:

- **View Responses.** Click the blue text to open the response file where you can view and analyze the response data.

- **Edit file location.** Click the blue text to open the Choose a new response file location dialog box. The location shown in the dialog box is the folder where your dataset file is located. If you want to change the file where the data are collected, you can browse your hard drive and select a new file. You can also use this dialog box to re-establish a link to the dataset file if you happen to relocate it on your computer.

- **Stop Collecting Data.** Clicking the blue text opens a dialog box, as shown in Figure 35.31, asking you to confirm the fact that you want to terminate data collection for the form. Click Yes, and the data collection stops. Any user attempting to submit data for the form is prevented from doing so. If you want to extend the form collection period, you need to start over and redistribute the form again.

FIGURE 35.31

Click Yes to stop data collection on a form.

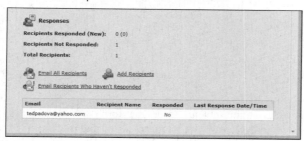

- **Open Original Form.** Clicking the blue text and the original form you distributed opens in the document pane.

The bottom right side of the Tracker handles responses for a distributed form as shown in Figure 35.32.

FIGURE 35.32

The bottom right pane in the Tracker is where you manage responses.

Items you have to choose from within this section of the Tracker include:

- **Email All Recipients.** Click the blue text to send an email to all recipients of the distributed form. You might have an issue that needs some explanation and want to send a mail to all the recipients to clarify a point. When you send the mail, Acrobat acts as your mail client and sends the message (and a copy of the form again).

- **Add Recipients.** Click Add Recipients to include additional recipients to fill in the distributed form.

- **Email Recipients Who Haven't Responded.** The Tracker maintains information on recipient responses and can filter those who haven't responded. When you click the blue text, an email is sent to only those recipients who have not returned the form back to you.

 To learn more about the, see Chapter 21.

Summary

- Acrobat offers a few preset calculation formulas used for calculating data. For more sophisticated calculations, you need to use Simplified Field Notation scripts and JavaScripts.

- When using hierarchical names, you can easily sum data by adding a parent name in the Calculate properties and selecting the sum (+) menu command.

- Form data can be exported from populated PDF forms in a variety of different file formats. The data can be introduced into any form having matching field names as from where the data were exported.

- To ensure that fields have the same exact names between different forms, copy fields from one document and paste the fields in all other documents.

- Button fields can be created to submit form data from any Acrobat viewer. For Adobe Reader users to submit a PDF with data back to the PDF author, the form needs to be enabled with Adobe Reader usage rights.

- Data can be exported from a PDF document directly to a spreadsheet program.

- Forms can be distributed manually via email or directly using Acrobat.com.

- Forms in progress can be managed and organized in the Tracker.

Appendix

What's on the CD-ROM

This appendix provides information on the contents and system requirements of the CD-ROM that accompanies this book.

IN THIS APPENDIX

System requirements

Installation instructions

CD-ROM contents

Troubleshooting

System Requirements

The CD is a cross-platform CD and can be read by both Macintosh and Windows computers. Macintosh users need System 10.2 or above. Windows users need Windows XP Service Pack 2 or above or Windows Vista.

Installation Instructions

To gain access to the CD-ROM contents, follow these steps:

1. **Insert the CD-ROM in your CD drive.** An autorun program automatically opens a window.

2. **Click the Install button and locate a folder on your hard drive where you want the files installed.**

3. **Click Install to install the files in your target folder.**

Contents

The CD contains the following four folders:

- Adobe Reader 9.0 software
- The entire text of this book as a PDF document with an embedded index
- Author-created PDF documents and sample files
- Author-created video files
- Author-created eBook on PDF forms tips
- Bonus Chapter on JavaScript

Adobe Reader 9.0

Double-click the Adobe Reader installer and install the Reader software from the book's CD. There are two different installers for Adobe Reader for the Mac, so be sure to choose the installer appropriate for your computer.

NOTE Before you install Adobe Reader 9 on your computer, check out Adobe's Web site at www.adobe.com/products/acrobat/readermain.html to see if there's a newer version of the Reader software than Adobe Reader 9.0, because you may have purchased this book after Adobe has updated the Reader software. If you find a version later than 9.0 on Adobe's Web site, download that version.

PDF version of the book

The entire text of the *Adobe Acrobat 9 PDF Bible* is available on the CD as a PDF document. Any Acrobat viewer 7.0 and above can open the PDF file and view the contents. Look inside the PDF eBook folder to view a PDF portfolio of the *Adobe Acrobat 9.0 PDF Bible*.

To search the embedded index, open the Search panel by pressing Ctrl/⌘+Shift+F. When the Search panel opens, type a word in the first text box. Acrobat will automatically use the embedded index to find searched words.

CROSS-REF For more options on searching PDF documents, see Chapter 6.

Author-created PDF documents

The Documents folder contains PDF documents and sample files to help you through some of the steps in the text of the book. The AuthorFiles folder contains four folders, which include:

- **Chapters.** When reviewing steps, open the chapter respective to the folder to see if a file exists to help you through the steps. For many steps in chapters, you can use any PDF document you want to follow the steps.

- **Forms Designs.** Several original forms designs are contained in this folder in Adobe InDesign format. You need Adobe InDesign CS3 or greater to open the files. The PDF document exported from InDesign is also included in the respective folders.

- **Forms Folder.** Several different PDF forms are contained in this folder complete with JavaScripts.

- **Video Files.** Several Flash video files are contained in this folder and some sample Flash FLA files. In order to open the FLA files, you need Adobe Flash CS3 or greater.

An electronic brochure courtesy of Robert Connolly of pdfPictures.com (www.pdfPictures.com) and Aruba Bonbini is placed in the Chapter 22 folder inside the AuthorFiles/Chapters folder. This file is available for you to explore how dynamic content and pop-up menus are used in PDF files.

PDF forms eBook

An author-created eBook on 101 forms tips is included in the AuthorFiles/Chapters/Chapter36 folder. Any Acrobat viewer version 7.0 and above can view the file. This file contains many JavaScripts and tips on using Acrobat and LiveCycle Designer for creating forms.

Bonus chapter

Chapter 36 — Understanding JavaScript is contained on the CD-ROM.

Author-created video files

Video files demonstrating many different features in Acrobat 9.0 are included in AuthorFiles/Video Folder. These files are PDF documents with Adobe Flash–embedded content. All you need is Acrobat or Adobe Reader 9.0 to view the files.

In addition to the video files, some sample Adobe Flash FLV files are contained in the AuthorFiles/Video Files/FLV folder. You need Adobe Flash CS3 or above to open these files. If you're not a Flash developer, these files show some simple Adobe Flash development. You can tear apart the files and see how they were constructed.

Troubleshooting

If you have difficulty installing or using any of the materials on the companion CD, try the following solutions:

- **Turn off any antivirus software that you may have running.** Installers sometimes mimic virus activity and can make your computer incorrectly believe that it is being infected by a virus. (Be sure to turn the antivirus software back on later.)

- **Close all running programs.** The more programs you're running, the less memory is available to other programs. Installers also typically update files and programs; if you keep other programs running, installation may not work properly.

- **Reference the ReadMe.** Refer to the ReadMe file located at the root of the CD-ROM for the latest product information at the time of publication.

If you have trouble with the CD-ROM, call the Wiley Product Technical Support phone number at (800) 762-2974. Outside the United States, call 1(317) 572-3994. You can also contact Wiley Product Technical Support at `http://support.wiley.com`. John Wiley & Sons will provide technical support only for installation and other general quality-control items. For technical support on the applications themselves, consult the program's vendor or author.

To place additional orders or to request information about other Wiley products, call (877) 762-2974.

Index

Symbols and Numerics

^ (exclusive OR) operator, 163
() parenthesis, 163
3D content, importing, 819–821
3D drawings, 760

A

About Adobe Plug-Ins dialog box, 53–54
accessibility
    adding
        in authoring programs, 847
        in existing PDFs, 848–851
    alternative text descriptions for image and graphic
        elements, 846, 854–855
    assessing, 846
    customizing viewing for, 858
    document structure relating to, 845, 851–856
    form field descriptions, 846
    form field tab order, 846
    Full Check for, 848–850
    language, specifying, 847
    links, requirements for, 846
    logical reading order for, 846
    overview, 844–847
    Quick Check for, 848
    reading document out loud, 857–858
    reading order for, 856–857
    security requirements, 846
    tools and toolbars for, 843–844
Accessibility Report panel, 134
Accessibility Resource Center, 65
Accessible Text files, exporting PDF files to, 374
Acrobat
    help
        accessing, 60
        Contents tab, 60–61
        navigating topics in, 61
        printing in, 61–62
        Search tab, 61
        zoom views, setting, 62

non-Adobe programs used with, 315
overview, 3–5
product line strategy, 52–53
version 5
    sound files, 790–794
    video files, 803–807
version 6
    sound files, 794–799
    video files, 808–813
Acrobat Catalog
    overview, 170
    search indexes
        building, 183–185
        Catalog preferences, setting, 186–187
        creating, 175–179
        custom properties, 181–182
        date created, 190
        definition for, saving, 179
        descriptions, 178, 190
        directory paths for, 178–179
        disabling, 189
        document, attaching to a, 189
        external devices, searching, 191–192
        file structure for, 173–174
        filename, 190
        help files for, 174–175
        information on, finding, 189–190
        loading, 188–189
        numbers, excluding, 180
        options for, setting, 180–183
        overview, 170
        PDFs for, preparing, 170–175
        performance, optimizing, 174
        purging data, 186
        rebuilding, 185
        saving, 179, 183
        searching, 190–191
        status, 190
        stop words for, 182
        structure of, 185
        structure tags for, 183

Wiley Publishing, Inc.
End-User License Agreement

READ THIS. You should carefully read these terms and conditions before opening the software packet(s) included with this book (*"Adobe Acrobat 9 PDF Bible"*). This is a license agreement ("Agreement") between you and Wiley Publishing, Inc. ("WPI"). By opening the accompanying software packet(s), you acknowledge that you have read and accept the following terms and conditions. If you do not agree and do not want to be bound by such terms and conditions, promptly return the Book and the unopened software packet(s) to the place you obtained them for a full refund.

1. **License Grant.** WPI grants to you (either an individual or entity) a nonexclusive license to use one copy of the enclosed software program(s) (collectively, the "Software") solely for your own personal or business purposes on a single computer (whether a standard computer or a workstation component of a multi-user network). The Software is in use on a computer when it is loaded into temporary memory (RAM) or installed into permanent memory (hard disk, CD-ROM, or other storage device). WPI reserves all rights not expressly granted herein.

2. **Ownership.** WPI is the owner of all right, title, and interest, including copyright, in and to the compilation of the Software recorded on the disk(s) or CD-ROM "Software Media." Copyright to the individual programs recorded on the Software Media is owned by the author or other authorized copyright owner of each program. Ownership of the Software and all proprietary rights relating thereto remain with WPI and its licensers.

3. **Restrictions on Use and Transfer.**

   (a) You may only (i) make one copy of the Software for backup or archival purposes, or (ii) transfer the Software to a single hard disk, provided that you keep the original for backup or archival purposes. You may not (i) rent or lease the Software, (ii) copy or reproduce the Software through a LAN or other network system or through any computer subscriber system or bulletin-board system, or (iii) modify, adapt, or create derivative works based on the Software.

   (b) You may not reverse engineer, decompile, or disassemble the Software. You may transfer the Software and user documentation on a permanent basis, provided that the transferee agrees to accept the terms and conditions of this Agreement and you retain no copies. If the Software is an update or has been updated, any transfer must include the most recent update and all prior versions.

4. **Restrictions on Use of Individual Programs.** You must follow the individual requirements and restrictions detailed for each individual program in the "What's on the CD-ROM" appendix of this Book. These limitations are also contained in the individual license agreements recorded on the Software Media. These limitations may include a requirement that after using the program for a specified period of time, the user must pay a registration fee or discontinue use. By opening the Software packet(s), you will be agreeing to abide by the licenses and restrictions for these individual programs that are detailed in the "What's on the CD-ROM" appendix and on the Software Media. None of the material on this Software Media or listed in this Book may ever be redistributed, in original or modified form, for commercial purposes.

5. **Limited Warranty.**

   (a) WPI warrants that the Software and Software Media are free from defects in materials and workmanship under normal use for a period of sixty (60) days from the date of purchase of this Book. If WPI receives notification within the warranty period of defects in materials or workmanship, WPI will replace the defective Software Media.

   (b) WPI AND THE AUTHOR(S) OF THE BOOK DISCLAIM ALL OTHER WARRANTIES, EXPRESS OR IMPLIED, INCLUDING WITHOUT LIMITATION IMPLIED WARRANTIES OF MERCHANTABILITY AND FITNESS FOR A PARTICULAR PURPOSE, WITH RESPECT TO THE SOFTWARE, THE PROGRAMS, THE SOURCE CODE CONTAINED THEREIN, AND/OR THE TECHNIQUES DESCRIBED IN THIS BOOK. WPI DOES NOT WARRANT THAT THE FUNCTIONS CONTAINED IN THE SOFTWARE WILL MEET YOUR REQUIREMENTS OR THAT THE OPERATION OF THE SOFTWARE WILL BE ERROR FREE.

   (c) This limited warranty gives you specific legal rights, and you may have other rights that vary from jurisdiction to jurisdiction.

6. **Remedies.**

   (a) WPI's entire liability and your exclusive remedy for defects in materials and workmanship shall be limited to replacement of the Software Media, which may be returned to WPI with a copy of your receipt at the following address: Software Media Fulfillment Department, Attn.: *Adobe Acrobat 9 PDF Bible*, Wiley Publishing, Inc., 10475 Crosspoint Blvd., Indianapolis, IN 46256, or call 1-800-762-2974. Please allow four to six weeks for delivery. This Limited Warranty is void if failure of the Software Media has resulted from accident, abuse, or misapplication. Any replacement Software Media will be warranted for the remainder of the original warranty period or thirty (30) days, whichever is longer.

   (b) In no event shall WPI or the author be liable for any damages whatsoever (including without limitation damages for loss of business profits, business interruption, loss of business information, or any other pecuniary loss) arising from the use of or inability to use the Book or the Software, even if WPI has been advised of the possibility of such damages.

   (c) Because some jurisdictions do not allow the exclusion or limitation of liability for consequential or incidental damages, the above limitation or exclusion may not apply to you.

7. **U.S. Government Restricted Rights.** Use, duplication, or disclosure of the Software for or on behalf of the United States of America, its agencies and/or instrumentalities "U.S. Government" is subject to restrictions as stated in paragraph (c)(1)(ii) of the Rights in Technical Data and Computer Software clause of DFARS 252.227-7013, or subparagraphs (c) (1) and (2) of the Commercial Computer Software - Restricted Rights clause at FAR 52.227-19, and in similar clauses in the NASA FAR supplement, as applicable.

8. **General.** This Agreement constitutes the entire understanding of the parties and revokes and supersedes all prior agreements, oral or written, between them and may not be modified or amended except in a writing signed by both parties hereto that specifically refers to this Agreement. This Agreement shall take precedence over any other documents that may be in conflict herewith. If any one or more provisions contained in this Agreement are held by any court or tribunal to be invalid, illegal, or otherwise unenforceable, each and every other provision shall remain in full force and effect.

The books you read to succeed.

Get the most out of the latest software and leading-edge technologies with a Wiley Bible—your one-stop reference.

0-471-78886-4
978-0-471-78886-7

0-470-04030-0
978-0-470-04030-0

0-7645-4256-7
978-0-7645-4256-5

0-470-10089-3
978-0-470-10089-9

WILEY
Now you know.
wiley.com

Office heaven.

Get the first and last word on Microsoft® Office 2007 with our comprehensive Bibles and expert authors. These are the books you need to succeed!

978-0-470-04691-3

978-0-470-04403-2

978-0-470-04689-0

978-0-470-04368-4

978-0-470-04702-6

978-0-470-04645-6

978-0-470-04673-9

978-0-470-00861-4

WILEY
Now you know.

Available wherever books are sold